Alessandro Del Sole

Visual Basic® 2012

UNLEASHED

 | 800 East 96th Street, Indianapolis, Indiana 46240 USA

Visual Basic® 2012 Unleashed

ISBN-10: 0-672-33631-6
ISBN-13: 978-0-672-33631-7

Library of Congress Cataloging-in-Publication Data is on file.

Printed in the United States of America

First Printing: January 2013

Trademarks

Warning and Disclaimer

Bulk Sales

Pearson offers excellent discounts on this book when ordered in quantity for bulk purchases or special sales. For more information, please contact:

U.S. Corporate and Government Sales
1-800-382-3419
corpsales@pearsontechgroup.com

For sales outside of the U.S., please contact:

International Sales
+1-317-581-3793
international@pearsontechgroup.com

Editor-in-Chief
Greg Wiegand

Executive Editor
Neil Rowe

Acquisitions Editor
Brook Farling

Development Editor
Mark Renfrow

Managing Editor
Kristy Hart

Project Editor
Anne Goebel

Copy Editor
Megan Wade

Indexer
WordWise Publishing Services

Proofreader
Debbie Williams

Technical Editor
Matt Kleinwaks

Publishing Coordinator
Cindy Teeters

Cover Designer
Anne Jones

Compositor
Nonie Ratcliff

Contents at a Glance

Table of Contents

Foreword

From his blog posts (in Italian and English) to his forum answers, from his online articles to his code snippets, from his technical speeches and user-groups to his books, the breadth of Alessandro's reach has been astounding.

Now is a particularly good time for Alessandro to write this book, because the current release of Visual Basic has so many new features. I'd like to tell the story behind the most important of them, "Asynchronous Programming," explained in Chapter 44. We introduced this feature because everyone wants their interactive applications to be fast and responsive, but the code to achieve this has traditionally been too convoluted. Now, thanks to asynchronous programming, the code has become straightforward. Although the code itself is straightforward, our small design group at Microsoft knew we were producing something unfamiliar as we sat down to design the feature in early 2010—something not taught in college courses, something whose success would depend on the ability of authors like Alessandro to explain it (which he does well).

As Language Designer of VB, I implemented the initial prototype of the feature within the VB and C# compilers. Our team first revealed it behind closed doors to MVPs ("Most Valued Professionals") such as Alessandro at a small gathering in New Orleans, hoping that the attendees would see its worth but daunted by the challenge of explaining something so unusual. The MVPs understood the feature's potential. They also asked us to integrate it better with other parts of Visual Studio such as debugging (Chapter 5) and unit-tests (Chapter 56), which we then did.

Indeed, there are many useful parts to Visual Studio and .NET, and Alessandro knows them all. In this book, he makes sure that you will know all the important ones, too, and he sets them in context by explaining when and why to use them. I myself was happy to learn how to do localization (Chapter 33) and deployment (Chapters 51 and 52) from this book—both topics that I was aware of but hadn't explored before.

Alessandro has found just the right blend of text, code, and screenshots to explain Visual Studio effectively. Beginners and experts alike will find much of value in this book.

—Lucian Wischik
Seattle, Washington
December 2012

About the Author

Alessandro Del Sole, a Microsoft Most Valuable Professional (MVP) for Visual Basic since 2008, is well known throughout the global VB community. He is a community leader on the Italian Visual Basic Tips and Tricks website (http://www.visual-basic.it) that serves more than 42,000 VB developers, as well as a frequent contributor to the MSDN Visual Basic Developer Center. He enjoys writing articles on .NET development, writing blog posts on both his Italian and English blogs, and producing instructional videos as well as apps for Windows 8 and Windows Phone. You can find him online in forums or newsgroups. Alessandro has been awarded MVP of the Year for Visual Basic in 2009, 2010, and 2011.

Dedication

To my parents, I'm learning from you how one should never give up even when life becomes the hardest possible. As usual, you taught me the most important lessons in life. The more time goes on, the more I understand what you have done for me. Thank you!

To my best friend Nadia, who always finds a way to make me smile when things become so difficult and is always able to find positive perspectives when I cannot. You have really been one of the most important people in my whole life for more than 10 years, and I will always be there for you.

Acknowledgments

First of all, I would like to thank Neil Rowe, Mark Renfrow, Anne Goebel, and all at Sams Publishing for trusting me enough to write the second edition of this book about Visual Basic. Writing books like this is hard work, not only for the author, but also for all the people involved in the reviews and in the production process. Working with these guys made the process much more pleasant. Thank you!

Very special thanks to Matthew Kleinwaks, who has been the technical editor for this book and who is a Microsoft Visual Basic MVP. Matthew did an incredible job, walking through every single word and line of code, engaging interesting technical discussions. His suggestions have been so important and made the content as accurate and interesting as possible. You can visit Matthew's blog at http://zerosandtheone.com/. Thank you so much, Matt!

Special thanks to all the Microsoft Visual Basic Team for doing a great job; particularly I would like to give my special thanks to Lucian Wischik, Lisa Feigenbaum, Beth Massi, and Anthony D. Green for providing opportunities of continuous interactions and technical discussions. They contribute and keep the passion for Visual Basic alive around the globe.

Great thanks also to the guys from the Italian subsidiary of Microsoft: Alessandro Teglia (my MVP lead), who has a great passion for his work and for the MVP community; he did a really great job when I had some important questions related to information required for this book, quickly pointing me in the right direction. Also, special thanks to the local Development and Platform Evangelism Division (Marco Agnoli, Francesca Longoni, Francesca Marinoni, Lorenzo Barbieri, Vito Lorusso, Pietro Brambati, Mario Fontana, Gabriele Castellani, and Irina Turcu) for their continuous support and encouragement for my activities.

Thanks to Alfonso Ghiraldini and Francesco Bosticco for their cordiality.

I would like to thank my everyday friends who are always ready to encourage me even if they are not developers and will never read my books. Most importantly, these people always support me when I need their help. So my deep thanks to Roberto Bianchi, Alessandro Ardovini, Michela Santini, Leonardo Amici, Francesca Bongiorni, Paolo Leoni, Nadir Mariotti, Blerina Spahiu, Karin Meier, and Sara Gerevini. You guys really rock!

I'm a community leader and vice president in the Italian Visual Basic Tips and Tricks community (www.visual-basic.it); therefore, I would like to thank all those guys who are the right stimulus for making things better every day; all those people who visited my blogs at least once or who read even one article of mine; and all those people who visit our website and follow us on forums, videos, articles, and blogs. Special thanks to my MVP colleagues Diego Cattaruzza, Antonio Catucci, Renato Marzaro, Massimo Bonanni, Matteo Pagani, and Raffaele Rialdi for their great support and valuable suggestions. Thanks to Marco Notari for his continuous support and encouragement.

We Want to Hear from You!

As the reader of this book, you are our most important critic and commentator. We value your opinion and want to know what we're doing right, what we could do better, what areas you'd like to see us publish in, and any other words of wisdom you're willing to pass our way.

As an executive editor for Sams Publishing, I welcome your comments. You can email or write me directly to let me know what you did or didn't like about this book—as well as what we can do to make our books better.

Please note that I cannot help you with technical problems related to the topic of this book. We do have a User Services group, however, where I will forward specific technical questions related to the book.

When you write, please be sure to include this book's title and author as well as your name, email address, and phone number. I will carefully review your comments and share them with the author and editors who worked on the book.

Email: feedback@samspublishing.com

Mail: Neil Rowe
         Associate Publisher
         Sams Publishing
         800 East 96th Street
         Indianapolis, IN 46240 USA

Reader Services

Visit our website and register this book at informit.com/register for convenient access to any updates, downloads, or errata that might be available for this book.

CHAPTER 1

Introducing the .NET Framework 4.5

As a Visual Basic 2012 developer, you need to understand the concepts and technology that empower your applications: the Microsoft .NET Framework. The .NET Framework (also simply known as .NET) is the technology that provides the infrastructure for building the next generation's applications that you will create for the Desktop, the Web, the Cloud, and over the most recent operating systems such as Windows 8. Although covering every aspect of the .NET Framework is not possible, in this chapter you learn the basis of the .NET Framework architecture, why it is not just a platform, and notions about the Base Class Library and tools. The chapter also introduces important concepts and terminology that will be of common use throughout the rest of the book.

SUPPORTED OPERATING SYSTEMS

Visual Studio 2012 and the .NET Framework 4.5 run on Windows 8, Windows 7, and Windows Vista with Service Pack 2. Applications built with the .NET Framework 4.5 cannot run on Windows Vista without SP 2 and, most importantly, on Windows XP.

What Is the .NET Framework?

Microsoft .NET Framework is a complex technology that provides the infrastructure for building, running, and managing next-generation applications. In a layered representation, the .NET Framework is a layer positioned between the Microsoft Windows operating system and your applications. .NET is a platform but also is defined as a *technology* because it is composed of several parts such as libraries, executable tools, relationships, and integrates with the operating system. Microsoft Visual Studio 2012 relies on the new version of the .NET Framework 4.5. Visual Basic 2012, C# 5.0, and F# 2012 are .NET languages that rely on and can build applications for the .NET Framework 4.5. The new version of this technology introduces important new features that will be described later. In this chapter you get an overview of the most important features of the .NET Framework so that you will know how applications built with Visual Basic 2012 can run and how they can be built.

Where Is the .NET Framework?

When you install Microsoft Visual Studio 2012, the setup process installs the .NET Framework 4.5. .NET is installed to a folder named %windir%\Microsoft.NET\Framework\ 4.0.30319 (see the paragraph titled "Differences Between .NET 4.0 and 4.5" later in this chapter for details about versioning). If you open this folder with Windows Explorer, you see a lot of subfolders, libraries, and executable tools. Most of the DLL libraries constitute the Base Class Library, whereas most of the executable tools are invoked by Visual Studio 2012 to perform different kinds of tasks, even if they can also be invoked from the command line. Later in this chapter we describe the Base Class Library and provide an overview of the tools; for now you need to notice the presence of a file named vbc. exe, which is the Visual Basic Compiler and a command-line tool. In most cases you do not need to manually invoke the Visual Basic Compiler because you will build your Visual Basic applications writing code inside Visual Studio 2012, and the IDE (Integrated Development Environment) invokes the compiler for you. But it is worth mentioning that you could create the most complex application using Windows' Notepad and then run Vbc. Finally, it is also worth mentioning that users can get the .NET Framework 4.5 from Microsoft for free. This means that the Visual Basic Compiler is also provided free with .NET, and this is the philosophy that has characterized the .NET development since the first version was released in 2002.

The .NET Framework Architecture

To better understand the structure of the .NET Framework, think about it as a layered architecture. Figure 1.1 shows a high-level representation of the .NET Framework 4.5 architecture.

The first level of the representation is the operating system; the .NET layer is located between the system and applications. The second level is the *Common Language Runtime (CLR)*, which provides the part of the .NET Framework doing the most work. We discuss the CLR later in this chapter. The next level is the *Base Class Library (BCL)*, which provides all .NET objects that can be used both in your code and by Visual Basic when creating applications. The BCL also provides the infrastructure of several .NET technologies that you use in building applications, such as WPF, Windows Forms, ASP.NET, WCF, and so on. The last level is represented by applications that rely on the previous layers.

FIGURE 1.1   The .NET Framework 4.5 layered architecture.

Although the various frameworks exposed by the BCL are discussed later in the book, in this chapter, now you get an overview of the library and can understand how it works and how you can use it.

Differences Between .NET 4.0 and .NET 4.5

The .NET Framework 4.5 is basically a replacement of the .NET Framework 4.0. In fact, they both have the same version number. In particular, the version number of an assembly of .NET 4.0 is 4.0.30319.261, whereas the version number of an assembly of .NET 4.5 is 4.0.30319.17626. From a practical perspective, you can consider .NET 4.5 as an update for 4.0. If you try to install the .NET Framework 4.5 on a machine where .NET 4.0 is already installed, this will be simply overwritten in the same directory and new assemblies and tools, specific to the new version, will be added. As a consequence, applications that you created with Visual Studio 2010 (including the Express editions) will still run with no problems, but will not take advantage the new version's features. As another consequence, migrating a project from Visual Studio 2010 to Visual Studio 2012 should be painless. Of course version 4.5 provides a lot of changes and improvements at the architecture level, so installing the new version will update existing assemblies of the .NET 4.0 (if any) with more recent files but will also update the architectural infrastructure of the Common Language Runtime. If you're a developer, you should be comfortable searching for .NET files and tools in the same location as the previous version; this will be good for both Visual Studio 2010 and 2012, avoiding confusion and saving some time.

The Common Language Runtime

As its name implies, the Common Language Runtime provides an infrastructure that is common to all .NET languages. This infrastructure is responsible for taking control of the application's execution and manages tasks such as memory management, access to system resources, security services, and so on. This kind of common infrastructure bridges the gap that exists between different Win32 programming languages because all .NET languages have the same possibilities. Moreover, the Common Language Runtime enables applications to run inside a managed environment. The word *managed* is fundamental in the .NET development, as explained in the next paragraph.

Writing Managed Code

When talking about Visual Basic 2012 development and, more generally, about .NET development, you often hear about writing *managed code*. Before the first version of .NET (or still with non-.NET development environments), the developer was the only responsible person for interacting with system resources and the operating system. For example, taking care of accessing parts of the operating system and managing memory allocation for objects were tasks that the developer had to consider. In other words, the applications could interact directly with the system, but as you can easily understand, this approach has some big limitations both because of security issues and because damages could be dangerous. The .NET Framework provides instead a managed environment. This means that the application communicates with the .NET Framework instead of with the operating system, and the .NET runtime is responsible for managing the application execution, including memory management, resources management, and access to system resources. For example, the Common Language Runtime could prevent an application from accessing particular system resources if it is not considered *full-trusted* according to the Security Zones of .NET.

SPEAKING WITH THE SYSTEM

You can still interact directly with the operating system, for example invoking Windows APIs (also known as Platform Invoke or P/Invoke for short). This technique is known as writing unmanaged code that should be used only when strictly required. This topic is discussed in Chapter 48, "Platform Invokes and Interoperability with the COM Architecture."

Writing managed code and the existence of the Common Language Runtime also affect how applications are produced by compilers.

.NET Assemblies

In classic Win32 development environments, such as Visual Basic 6 or Visual C++, your source code is parsed by compilers that produce binary executable files that can be immediately interpreted and run by the operating system. This affects both standalone applications and dynamic/type libraries. Actually Win32 applications, built with Visual Basic 6 and C++, used a runtime, but if you had applications developed with different programming languages, you also had to install the appropriate runtimes. In.NET development things are quite different. Whatever .NET language you create applications with, compilers generate an *assembly*, which is a file containing .NET executable code and is composed essentially by two kinds of elements: CIL code and metadata. CIL (formerly known as MSIL) stands for Common Intermediate Language and is a high-level assembly programming language that is also object-oriented, providing a set of instructions that are CPU-independent (rather than building executables that implement CPU-dependent sets of instructions). CIL is a common language in the sense that the same programming tasks written with different .NET languages produce the same IL code. Metadata is instead a set of information related to the types implemented in the code. Such information can contain signatures, functions and procedures, members in types, and members in externally referenced types. Basically metadata's purpose is describing the code to the .NET Framework. Obviously, although an assembly can have an .exe extension, due to the described structure, it cannot be directly executed by the operating system. In fact, when you run a .NET application the operating system can recognize it as a .NET assembly (because between .NET and Windows there is a strict cooperation) and invoke the Just-In-Time compiler.

The Execution Process and the Just-In-Time Compiler

.NET compilers produce assemblies that store IL code and metadata. When you launch an assembly for execution, the .NET Framework packages all the information and translates it into an executable that the operating system can understand and run. This task is the responsibility of the *Just-In-Time (JIT)* compiler. JIT compiles code on-the-fly just before its execution and keeps the compiled code ready for execution. It acts at the method level. This means that it first searches for the application's entry point (typically the Sub Main) and then compiles other procedures or functions (*methods* in .NET terminology) referenced and invoked by the entry point and so on, just before the code is executed. If you have some code defined inside external assemblies, just before the method is executed the JIT compiler loads the assembly in memory and then compiles the code. Of course, loading an external assembly in memory could require some time and affect performance, but it can be a good idea to place seldom-used methods inside external assemblies, the same way as it could be a good idea to place seldom-used code inside separated methods. The .NET Framework 4.5 introduces important improvements to performance by enabling the so-called *Parallel JIT Compilation*. This improvement takes advantage of multicore processor architectures and runs the JIT process on a background thread that works on a separate processor core. In this way, the JIT compilation is faster and, therefore, the application execution is also faster.

The Base Class Library

The .NET Framework *Base Class Library (BCL)* provides thousands of reusable *types* that you can use in your code and that cover all the .NET technologies, such as Windows Presentation Foundation, ASP.NET, LINQ, and so on. Types defined in the Base Class Library enable developers to do millions of things without the need of calling unmanaged code and Windows APIs and, often, without recurring to external components. A *type* is something that states what an object must represent. For example, String and Integer are types, and you might have a variable of type String (that is, a text message) or a variable of type Integer (a number). Saying Type is not the same as saying Class. In fact, types can be of two kinds: *reference types* and *value types*. This topic is the specific subject of Chapter 4, "Data Types and Expressions"—a class is just a reference type. Types in the BCL are organized within *namespaces*, which act like a kind of types' containers, and their name is strictly related to the technology they refer to. For example, the System.Windows.Controls namespace implements types for drawing controls in Windows Presentation Foundation applications, whereas System.Web implements types for working with web applications, and so on. You will get a more detailed introduction to namespaces in Chapter 3, "The Anatomy of a Visual Basic Project," and Chapter 9, "Organizing Types Within Namespaces." Basically each namespace name beginning with System is part of the BCL. There are also some namespaces whose names begin with Microsoft that are still part of the BCL. These namespaces are typically used by the Visual Studio development environment and by the Visual Basic compiler, although you can also use them in your code in some particular scenarios (such as code generation).

The BCL is composed of several assemblies. One of the most important is MsCorlib. dll (Microsoft Core Library) that is part of the .NET Framework and that will always be required in your projects. Other assemblies can often be related to specific technologies; for example, the System.ServiceModel.dll assembly integrates the BCL with the Windows Communication Foundation main infrastructure. Also, some namespaces don't provide the infrastructure for other technologies and are used only in particular scenarios; therefore, they are defined in assemblies external from MsCorlib (Microsoft Core Library). All these assemblies and namespaces will be described in the appropriate chapters.

Programming Languages Included in .NET 4.5

Microsoft offers several programming languages for the .NET Framework 4.5. With Visual Studio 2012, you can develop applications with the following integrated programming languages:

▶ Visual Basic 2012

▶ Visual C# 5.0

▶ Visual F# 2012

▶ Visual C++ 2012

You can also integrate native languages with Microsoft implementations of the Python and Ruby dynamic languages, respectively known as IronPython and IronRuby.

WHERE DO I FIND IRONPYTHON AND IRONRUBY?

IronPython and IronRuby are currently under development by Microsoft and are available as open source projects from the CodePlex community. You can download IronPython from http://ironpython.codeplex.com. You can find IronRuby at http://ironruby.codeplex.com.

There are also several third-party implementations of famous programming languages for .NET, such as Fortran, Forth, or Pascal, but discussing them is neither a purpose of this chapter nor of this book. It's instead important to know that all these languages can take advantage of the .NET Framework base class library and infrastructure the same as VB and C#. This is possible because of the Common Language Runtime that offers a common infrastructure for all .NET programming languages.

Additional Tools Shipping with the .NET Framework

The .NET Framework also provides several command-line tools needed when creating applications. Among the tools are the compilers for the .NET languages, such as Vbc.exe (Visual Basic compiler), Csc.exe (Visual C# compiler), and MSBuild.exe (the build engine for Visual Studio). All these tools are stored in the C:\Windows\Microsoft.NET\Framework\v4.0.30319 folder. In most scenarios you will not need to manually invoke the .NET Framework tools because you will work with the Microsoft Visual Studio 2012 IDE, which is responsible for invoking the appropriate tools when needed. Instead of listing all the tools now, because we have not talked about some topics yet, information on the .NET tools invoked by Visual Studio is provided when discussing a particular topic that involves the specific tools.

Windows Software Development Kit

When you install Visual Studio 2012, with the .NET Framework and the development environment, the setup process will also install the Windows SDK on your machine. This software development kit provides additional tools and libraries useful for developing applications for the .NET Framework. Microsoft released the Windows SDK that provides tools for building both managed and unmanaged applications. The Windows SDK is installed into the C:\Program Files (x86)\Microsoft SDKs\Windows\v8.0A folder for 32-bit systems or into the C:\Program Files\Microsoft SDKs\Windows\v8.0A folder for 64-bit systems. It includes several additional tools also used by Microsoft Visual Studio for tasks different from building assemblies, such as deployment and code analysis, or for generating proxy classes for Windows Communication Foundation projects. Also in this case you will not typically need to invoke these tools manually because Visual Studio will do the work for you. You can find information on the Windows SDK's tools in the appropriate chapters.

What's New in .NET Framework 4.5

Assuming you have some knowledge of .NET Framework 4.0 and previous versions, following are new additions introduced by .NET 4.5 for your convenience:

▶ .NET for Windows 8 Store Apps, a subset of the Framework that developers can use in conjunction with the Windows Runtime to build Windows 8 apps for Windows 8.

▶ Portable Class Libraries, which allow writing reusable code across multiple platforms like desktop, Silverlight, Windows Phone, and Xbox. They are discussed further in Chapter 17, "Creating Objects: Visual Tools and Portable Libraries."

- ▶ Support for HTML5, unobtrusive JavaScript, asynchronous HTTP requests, modules, and handlers in ASP.NET.

- ▶ Asynchronous input/output (I/O) operations against files (see Chapter 18, "Manipulating Files and Streams" and Chapter 44, "Asynchronous Programming").

- ▶ Support for ZIP archives (see Chapter 18).

- ▶ Architectural improvements that include support for arrays larger than 2 GB in 64-bit applications, better performance in the Garbage Collection process, faster application startup with background JIT, and better performance when retrieving resources.

- ▶ A new programming model for HTTP applications with the new `System.Net.Http` and `System.Net.Http.Headers` namespaces.

- ▶ Support for generic types, multiple scopes, and support for naming conventions in the Managed Extensibility Framework.

Additional new features and updates target specific technologies; these are discussed in the appropriate chapters.

How .NET Meets Windows 8 and the Windows Runtime

As you might know, Windows 8 is the new operating system from Microsoft that also provides the so-called Windows 8 Store Apps that you can build with Visual Studio 2012 and the .NET languages (in addition to HTML 5/JavaScript). Windows 8 Store Apps rely on a special framework called Windows Runtime (WinRT). WinRT is a framework based on the COM architecture and on unmanaged resources, and the possibility of building Windows 8 Store Apps for .NET developers is due to the presence of a subset of the .NET Framework, which is specific for WinRT and that wraps WinRT's objects into a managed fashion. This explanation is important to make you understand the focus of this book. This book is language-oriented and focuses on Visual Basic 2012 with the .NET Framework 4.5; most of the language-related concepts explained up to Chapter 20, "Advanced Language Features," (with the exclusion of the `My` namespace) will be also valid for Windows 8 development and WinRT, but the .NET Framework and WinRT are two completely different platforms exposing different libraries and types. Therefore, concepts explained about desktop and web development or strictly related to the .NET Framework will not also be valid for the Windows Runtime. Just to provide an example, in both .NET and WinRT (with the layer of the .NET subset) you use the `System.IO` namespace to manipulate files and directories, but the way you do it is different because the same namespace exposes different classes according to the runtime platform. This explanation can be disregarded if you plan to build only classic desktop or web apps for Windows 8 with the .NET Framework, as well as for Windows 7, Windows Vista with Service Pack 2, Windows Server 2008, and Windows Server 2012.

Summary

Understanding the .NET Framework is of primary importance in developing applications with Visual Basic 2012 because you will build applications for the .NET Framework. This chapter presented a high-level overview of the .NET Framework 4.5 and key concepts such as the Common Language Runtime and the Base Class Library. It also explained how an application is compiled and executed. You even got an overview of the most important command-line tools and the .NET languages.

1

Getting Started with the Visual Studio 2012 IDE

You develop Visual Basic applications using the Visual Studio 2012 Integrated Development Environment (IDE), which is the place where you will spend most of your developer life. Before diving deep into the Visual Basic language, you need to know what instruments you need to develop applications. Although the Visual Studio IDE is a complex environment, this chapter provides you with an overview of the most common tasks you will perform from within Visual Studio 2012 and the most important tools you will utilize so that you can feel at home within the IDE. You get an introduction to some of the new features introduced by the new version of the development environment, which can provide the basis for the rest of the book. You also learn about other advanced IDE features in the last part of the book.

What's New in Visual Studio 2012

The Visual Studio 2012 IDE retakes the infrastructure that was first introduced by its predecessor, which is written in managed code and in which several parts are based on the *Windows Presentation Foundation* framework, such as the code editor, menus, and floating windows. On the other hand, Visual Studio 2012 has a completely different look, which is now based on the Microsoft Design Style, with a simplified approach to commands and tools via a flattened user interface in which there are only a few colors.

WHAT IS THE MICROSOFT DESIGN STYLE?

The Microsoft Design Style is a design language for user interfaces that Microsoft started to introduce with the first version of Windows Phone; it is also one of the most important characteristics of Windows 8. This design language relies on the principles of abstraction, simplicity, and geometric shapes. Its goal is avoiding complex and overcolored user interfaces in favor of simple drawings. For example, it is common in the Microsoft Design Style to find monochromatic shapes rather than drawings with millions of colors that can be confusing. After its adoption in Windows Phone and Windows 8, Microsoft is bringing the new design style into a number of other programs. Visual Studio 2012 is an example of how the layout of a powerful and complex desktop application can be simplified by following some of the Microsoft Design Style principles. You can find a more detailed explanation of such principles at: http://goo.gl/uqA5V.

The goal is helping the developer focus on writing code or on designing the application, not on the development environment. So, the environment now has fewer colors than in the previous versions, but commands are still recognizable via familiar icons; parts of the IDE that you interact the most with (typically the code editor and designers) are still rich with helpful colorizations. Although this innovation is important, you will still feel at home with the new version. This is because the instrumentation is located and behaves the same as in the past. This chapter gives you an overview of the most common tools you need for developing your Visual Basic applications. (Deeper details on advanced IDE features are provided starting from Chapter 53, "Advanced IDE Features.")

Status Bar and Start Page

When you first run Visual Studio 2012, you notice a new layout and the Start Page, as shown in Figure 2.1.

You can immediately notice the new look of Visual Studio 2012 based on Microsoft Design Style. The colored status bar is new in Visual Studio 2012, and its color changes according to the particular task Visual Studio is running. Following is a list of possible colors for the status bar (see Figure 2.2 for a graphical representation):

▶ **Violet**—This is the color for the status bar when Visual Studio is ready (for example, at startup).

▶ **Light blue**—This is the color for the status bar at development time, which means coding, designing the user interface, or any other task you run before compiling the code and running the application.

▶ **Blue**—This is the color for the status bar when Visual Studio 2012 is building the solution and compiling the code.

▶ **Orange**—This is the color for the status bar when you are running the application in debugging mode (that is, by pressing F5).

FIGURE 2.1   The Start Page in Visual Studio 2012 and the new look.

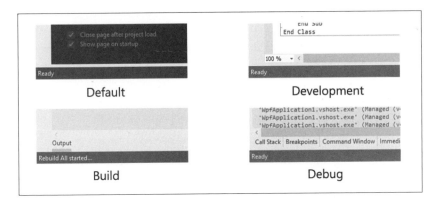

FIGURE 2.2   The status bar colors and related moments.

THEMES FOR VISUAL STUDIO 2012

Visual Studio 2012 ships with two themes, Light and Dark. Light is the default setting and is also the one that is used in this book. The Dark theme reproduces the look of Microsoft Expression Blend and is based on the black color and dark tones. You can change the theme by going to Tools, Options and then selecting a different theme in the Color Theme drop-down box in the Environment tab. At the time this chapter is being written, there are no additional themes, but you can download a nice extension called Visual Studio 2012 Color Theme Editor, available at: http://visualstudiogallery.msdn. microsoft.com/366ad100-0003-4c9a-81a8-337d4e7ace05. This extension provides a number of ready-to-use themes and allows creating custom ones.

The Start Page is a central point in the IDE. First, it offers a better organization of the most common tasks, based on *tabs*. Tabs are located on the right side of the screen and enable access to specific contents. On the left side of the screen you can instead find links for creating new projects and opening existing projects, as well as the list of recently opened projects. You can easily remove recent projects by right-clicking the project name and then selecting the deletion command. It is worth mentioning that the Start Page relies on the Windows Presentation Foundation *technology and is completely written in XAML code*. This means that it can be customized according to your needs. Customizing the Start Page is beyond the scope of this chapter, whereas a deeper discussion on the default settings is absolutely necessary. The two default tabs are Get Started and Latest News. The following paragraphs discuss them in detail.

Get Started Tab

The Get Started tab (refer to Figure 2.1) offers links to important resources, such as MSDN Walkthroughs (which are step-by-step tutorials on specific topics related to Visual Studio 2012); community and learning resources, and extensions for the IDE; such as custom add-ins or third-party components. (This topic is discussed later in the book.) This tab is divided into subcategories, each related to a specific development area such as Windows 8, Web, and Windows Azure. When you click each subcategory, you access a number of links to resources for learning about the selected area. The Get Started tab's purpose is to offer links to useful resources about the development environment and to new and existing .NET technologies.

The Latest News Tab

As in its predecessors, Visual Studio 2012 can also show a list of news based on RSS feeds so that you can stay up-to-date with your favorite news channels. Now the list appears in the Latest News tab, as shown in Figure 2.3.

By default, the news channel is an RSS feed pointing to the MSDN developer portal, but you can replace it with one of your favorites. To accomplish this, you have the following alternatives:

▶ Open the Latest News tab and replace the default link in the RSS feed field with a valid XML feed link (this is the easiest way).

▶ Open the Options window (for example, by clicking the Settings link in the Visual Studio tab), and then select the Startup item. In the text box named Start Page news channel (see Figure 2.4), you can insert your favorite link. Just be sure you are writing a valid XML feed link.

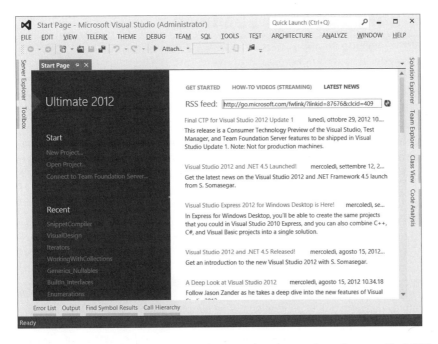

FIGURE 2.3   The Latest News tab shows updated news from the specified RSS channel.

FIGURE 2.4   The Options window enables customizing the RSS Feeds news channel.

If you want to stay up-to-date with Visual Basic news, consider replacing the default news channel with the Visual Basic page of the Visual Studio Developer Center, which is at the following: http://sxp.microsoft.com/feeds/3.0/msdntn/VB_featured_resources. After this brief overview of the Start Page, we can begin discussing the tooling that you use for creating Visual Basic projects within Visual Studio 2012.

Working with Projects and Solutions

Each time you want to develop an application, you create a *project*. A project is a collection of files, such as code files, resources, data, and every kind of file you need to build your final assembly. A Visual Basic project is represented by a .Vbproj file, which is an Extensible Markup Language (XML) file containing all the information required by Visual Studio to manage files that constitute your project. Projects are organized into solutions. A *solution* is basically a container for projects. In fact, solutions can contain infinite projects of different kinds, such as Visual Basic projects, projects produced with programming languages other than Visual Basic, class libraries, projects for Windows client applications, Windows Communication Foundation services, and so on. In other words, a solution can include each kind of project you can create with Visual Studio 2012. Solutions also can contain external files, such as documents or help files, and are represented by a .Sln file that has an XML structure and stores information required to manage all the projects contained in the solution. Visual Studio 2012 can also open solutions created with previous versions of the IDE.

PROJECT UPGRADES AND "ROUND-TRIPPING"

You can upgrade previous versions of your solutions by simply opening them in Visual Studio 2012. The new version of the IDE introduces the so-called project round-tripping, which means that solutions created with Visual Studio 2010 with Service Pack 1 can be opened in Visual Studio 2012 with no upgrades; then you can open the same solution back in Visual Studio 2010 with SP 1. For solutions created with other versions, the Upgrade Wizard can guide you through the upgrade process in a few steps. There are some exceptions to project round-tripping, which you can read in the specific MSDN page: http://msdn.microsoft.com/en-us/library/hh266747(v=vs.110).aspx.

Typically you manage your projects and solutions using the Solution Explorer window discussed later in this chapter. We now focus on the creation of Visual Basic 2012 projects.

Creating Visual Basic Projects

Creating a new Visual Basic project is a simple task. You can click either the **File, New Project** command or the **New Project** link from the Start Page. In both cases, Visual Studio shows the New Project window, which you can see in Figure 2.5.

As you can see, the look of the New Project window is quite different from previous versions of Visual Studio and still retakes the Windows 8 style. To understand what kind of Visual Basic applications you can create, you simply need to select the **Visual Basic** node on the left side of the window. After you click the node, you see a lot of different kinds of applications you can create with Visual Basic 2012, such as Windows applications, web applications, Office System customizations, Silverlight applications, Windows Communication Foundation Services, the new Windows 8 Store Apps for Windows 8, and so on.

FIGURE 2.5   The New Project window for Visual Basic.

NOTE ABOUT AVAILABLE PROJECT TEMPLATES

The list of installed project templates can vary depending on either the Visual Studio 2012 edition or additional items installed later (for example, from the Visual Studio Gallery).

Each kind of application is represented by a specific project template, which provides a skeleton of a project for that particular kind of application, including all the references or the basic code files required. For example, the WPF Application project template provides a skeleton of a project for creating a Windows application using the Windows Presentation Foundation technology, therefore including references to the WindowsBase. dll assembly, specific Imports directives, and WPF objects represented by the appropriate code files. Moreover, Visual Studio will automatically enable the WPF designer. Notice the detailed description for each template on the right side of the window every time you select a particular template.

NOTE

In the second part of this book you find several kinds of applications you can build with Visual Basic 2012. For this reason, a full description of each project template will be provided in the proper chapters. At the moment, the description provided by Visual Studio for project templates is sufficient. Also consider that in this first part of the book the Console Application project template is used because it is the most appropriate for learning purposes.

When you create a new project, Visual Studio usually creates a solution containing that project. If you plan to add other projects to the solution, it can be a good idea to create a directory for the solution. This allows for a better organization of your projects, because one directory can contain the solution file and this directory can then contain subdirectories, each of them related to a specific project. To accomplish this, ensure that the Create Directory for Solution check box is selected. The New Project window also offers some interesting features: the .NET Framework multi-targeting, the ability of searching through templates, the ability of managing templates, and finding samples on the Internet. We now discuss each of these features.

Multi-targeting

Like in Visual Studio 2010, in Visual Studio 2012 you can choose which version of the .NET Framework your application targets. This can be useful if you plan to develop applications with high compatibility levels and without new language features but still want to take advantage of the new features of the IDE. You can choose one of the following:

▶ .NET Framework 4.5 (proposed by default)

▶ .NET Framework 4.0

▶ .NET Framework 3.5

▶ .NET Framework 3.0

▶ .NET Framework 2.0

To accomplish this, just select the appropriate version from the combo box at the top of the window, as shown in Figure 2.6.

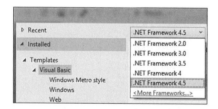

FIGURE 2.6   Choosing the .NET Framework version for your application.

NOTE

Remember that, depending on the version of the .NET Framework you choose, you might not be able to use some libraries or technologies. For example, if you choose .NET Framework 3.0 as the target version, you cannot use LINQ, which is instead exposed by .NET Framework 3.5 and higher. So keep in mind these limitations when developing your applications on previous Framework versions.

Accessing Recent and Online Templates

Visual Studio 2012 provides the capability to access the most recently used templates and install additional templates from the Internet. You can easily access the most recently used project templates by clicking the **Recent Templates** item on the left side of the New Project window. In this way, you get a list of the recently used project templates in case you still need them (see Figure 2.7). You can also find additional online templates and install them to the local system. To accomplish this, simply click the **Online Templates** item in the New Project window. Visual Studio checks for the availability of online templates and shows a list of all the available templates (see Figure 2.8).

As you can see, Visual Studio is listing all the online templates for both Visual Basic and Visual C#, showing a description of the template, information about the author, and a small picture with ratings when available. To download and install a template, simply double-click its name. After a few seconds you will be prompted to agree to the installation. You will be warned in the case that the new extension for Visual Studio does not contain a digital signature. If you trust the publisher and want to continue, click **Install**. After a few seconds, you will see the newly installed project templates available among the other ones.

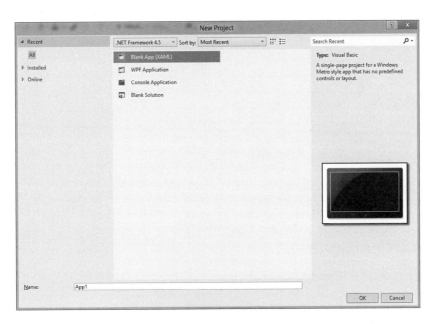

FIGURE 2.7   Accessing the most recently used projects templates.

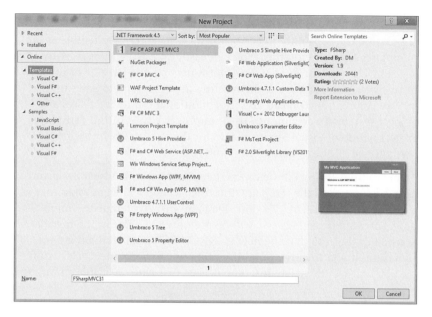

FIGURE 2.8   Additional online templates you can add to Visual Studio 2012.

As in the previous versions of Visual Studio, you can still export projects as reusable project templates. We discuss this feature later in Chapter 53, "Advanced IDE Features."

Searching for Installed Templates

Visual Studio 2012 provides lots of default project templates, and as you saw before, you have the ability of adding your own custom ones. Therefore, finding the necessary template at a certain moment can be difficult. Because of this, the New Project window provides a search box that is located in the upper-right corner of the window (see Figure 2.9). Just begin typing the name of the project template you are looking for, and the New Project window shows all the project templates that match your choice. Each time you type a character, the window updates showing the results matching your search string. As you can see in Figure 2.9, Visual Studio is showing all the project templates whose names match the *wor* search string.

> **NOTE**
>
> Remember that the search functionality can retrieve all project templates related to your search string. This means that the search result can contain not only Visual Basic projects but also every template name matching your criteria (for example, Visual C#, Visual F#, and so on).

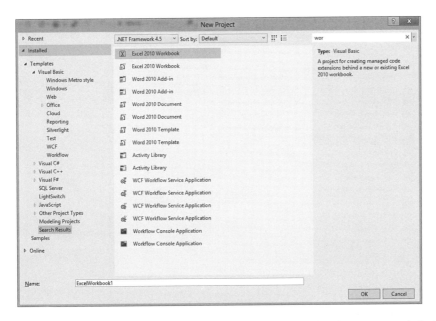

FIGURE 2.9 Searching for installed project templates using the new search feature.

Finding Code Samples on the Internet

One of the great new features of Visual Studio 2012 is the ability to search for sample code on the Internet directly from the New Project dialog box. Visual Studio performs this search inside the MSDN Code Gallery (http://code.msdn.microsoft.com), a website where developers can publish sample code they want to share with others. To find code samples, click the Samples item at the bottom of the list of templates in the New Project dialog box (see Figure 2.5). After you select this item, you will be able to browse the Code Gallery from within the dialog box. For example, if you search for a specified language, you will then be able to discover samples of each language based on technologies (such as Windows, Web, Cloud, Windows Phone, and so on). For each of these categories, you will find additional subcategories where samples are divided by framework; for instance, Windows development samples are divided into WPF, Windows Forms, Windows Runtime, and so on. Figure 2.10 shows how you can browse samples online from Visual Studio 2012.

You select a sample from the list and then click OK or simply double-click the sample. Visual Studio 2012 will download the sample to your hard disk and will ask you to accept the license agreement that the developer who published the code added to the sample. After it's downloaded, the sample is opened in Visual Studio 2012 under the form of a normal project. This is possible because, to upload a sample to the gallery, you must supply a full project (or an entire solution) to enable other developers to reuse your code with ease.

FIGURE 2.10   Browsing online code samples from Visual Studio 2012.

Creating Reusable Projects and Items Templates

As in the previous versions, in Visual Studio 2012 you can create your custom projects and items templates, exporting them to disk and making them available within the IDE. (This topic is discussed in Chapter 53.) Now that you have seen the main new features for project creation, you are ready to create your first Visual Basic project.

Creating Your First Visual Basic 2012 Project

This section shows how easily you can create a Visual Basic 2012 application. If you have experience with Visual Studio, you'll notice the differences in the development environments between the new version and the previous ones. You can create a new project for the Console by first opening the New Project window and then selecting the **Console Application** project template.

> **NOTE**
>
> Until Part IV, "Data Access with ADO.NET and LINQ," all code examples, listings, and code snippets are based on Console applications, so remember to create a Visual Basic project for the console when testing the code.

Name the new project **MyFirst2012Program** and then click **OK** (see Figure 2.11).

FIGURE 2.11   Creating your first VB 2012 application.

After a few seconds the new project is ready to be edited. Figure 2.12 shows the result of the project creation.

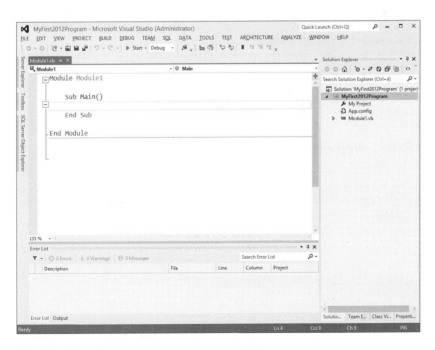

FIGURE 2.12   The creation of the first VB 2012 project.

As mentioned at the beginning of this chapter, the code editor and floating windows are based on Windows Presentation Foundation. You see the new Windows 8 look for the tooling, but this change does not modify your development experience. You should feel at home with the new version of the environment because you can still find tools as in the previous versions—maybe just with fewer colors. For example, you can access Solution Explorer, the Properties window, or the Error List exactly as you did before. An interesting feature in the code editor is that by pressing **Ctrl** and moving up and down the mouse wheel, you can zoom in and out with the code editor without the need to change the font settings each time the Visual Studio options changes. For our testing purposes, we could add a couple of lines of code to the `Main` method, which is the entry point for a Console application. Listing 2.1 shows the complete code for creating a VB 2012 application.

LISTING 2.1   Creating the First VB 2012 Application

```
Module Module1

    Sub Main()
        Console.WriteLine("Hello Visual Basic 2012!")
        Console.ReadLine()
    End Sub
End Module
```

WHAT IS A CONSOLE?

In a Console application, the `System.Console` class is the main object for working with the Windows console. Such a class provides methods for reading and writing from and to the Console and for performing operations against the Console itself.

The code simply shows a message in the Console window and waits for the user to press a key. This is obviously a basic application, but you need it as the base for understanding other topics in this chapter.

Finding Visual Basic Projects

As in the previous versions, Visual Studio 2012 stores by default its information in a user-level folder called **Visual Studio 2012** that resides inside the My Documents folder. Here you can find settings, add-ins, code snippets, and projects. For example, if you run Windows Vista, Windows 7, or Windows 8, your projects should be located in C:\Users\ UserName\Documents\Visual Studio 2012\Projects, in which UserName stands for the user logged in to Windows. Of course, you can change the default projects directory by opening the Options window (Tools, Options command), selecting the Projects and Solutions item on the left side, and replacing the value for the Projects location text box.

Working with the Code Editor

The code editor, together with designers, is the place where you spend most of your developer life in Visual Studio, so knowing how to get the best out of it is very important. This is what I explain throughout the whole book. In this chapter you see just a few of the code editor features because the other ones are related to specific topics discussed later. We now focus on the zoom functionality in the code editor and IntelliSense.

Zooming the Code

You can zoom the code editor in and out by simply pressing the **Ctrl** key and moving the mouse wheel up and down. This is a useful feature, particularly if you are a presenter of technical speeches because you can enlarge the code without modifying Visual Studio settings in the Options window. Figure 2.13 shows an example of this feature; notice how the font for the code is greater than the default settings and how the zoom percentage is visible at the bottom-left corner.

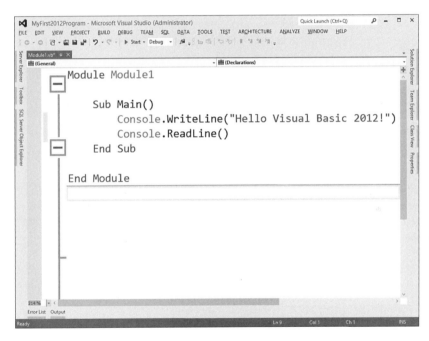

FIGURE 2.13   The code editor zoom feature enables real-time enlarging and reducing of the font size of the code without changing settings in Visual Studio.

If you already used this feature in Visual Studio 2010, you might remember how the scroll bar on the right also changed its size according to the zoom. This has been fixed in Visual Studio 2012; the bar size is always the same and independent from the zoom.

IntelliSense Technology

IntelliSense is one of the most important technologies in the coding experience with Visual Studio. IntelliSense is represented by a pop-up window that appears in the code editor each time you begin typing a keyword or an identifier and shows options for auto-completing words. Figure 2.14 shows IntelliSense in action when adding a new instruction in code.

FIGURE 2.14   IntelliSense in action.

To auto-complete your code typing, you have the following alternatives:

▶ **Tab**—Pressing this auto-completes your words and enables you to write other code.

▶ **Space**—Pressing this auto-completes your words, adding a blank space at the end of the added identifier and enabling you to write other code.

▶ **Enter**—Pressing this auto-completes your words, adding a couple of parentheses at the end of the completed identifier and positioning the cursor on a new line. Use this technique when you need to invoke a method that does not require arguments.

▶ **Left parenthesis**—Pressing this auto-completes your words, adding a left parenthesis at the end of the completed identifier and waiting for you to supply arguments.

▶ **Ctrl + Space**—Pressing this brings up the full IntelliSense listing.

IntelliSense has been improved since Visual Studio 2008. In fact, it is activated just when typing one character and is also active versus Visual Basic reserved words. Moreover, it remembers the last member you supplied to an object if you invoke that particular object more than once. For example, if you use IntelliSense to provide the `WriteLine` method to the `Console` object as follows:

```
Console.WriteLine()
```

and then try to invoke IntelliSense on the Console object again, it proposes as the first alternative of the WriteLine method you supplied the first time. IntelliSense is important because it lets you write code more quickly and provides suggestions on which member to add to your code.

Working with Tool Windows

As in the previous versions, lots of the Visual Studio tools are provided via *tool windows*. Tool windows are floating windows that can be docked to the IDE interface and are responsible for a particular task. As a general rule, in the View menu you can find the tool windows provided by Visual Studio 2012. Exceptions to this rule are the Test tool windows and the analysis tool windows that can be invoked from the Test and Analyze menus, respectively, and tool windows specific for debugging, available in the Debug menu (see Chapter 5, "Debugging Visual Basic 2012 Applications"). In this book we utilize several tool windows, and in this chapter you get an overview of the most frequently used ones. In particular, we now focus on Solution Explorer, Error List, Properties, and Output windows. This is because these are the tool windows you will use in each of your projects. Other tool windows will be analyzed when applied to specific topics. To dock a tool window to the desired position in the IDE, just move the window onto the most appropriate arrow in the graphical cross that you see on the IDE and then release. Figure 2.15 represents this situation.

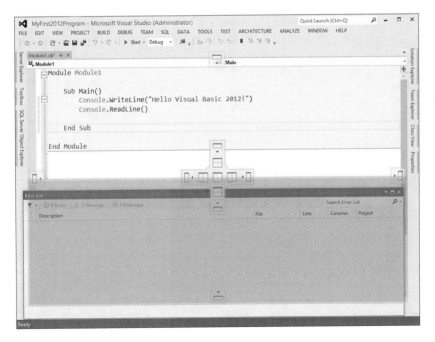

FIGURE 2.15   Docking a floating tool window to the IDE's interface.

Visual Studio 2012 automatically positions some tool windows in specific places of the IDE, but you can rearrange tool windows as much as you like. We now discuss the previously mentioned tool windows.

The Solution Explorer Window

Solution Explorer is a special tool window that enables managing solutions, projects, and files in the projects or solution. It provides a complete view of which files compose your projects and enables adding or removing files and organizing files into subfolders. Figure 2.16 shows how a WPF project is represented inside Solution Explorer.

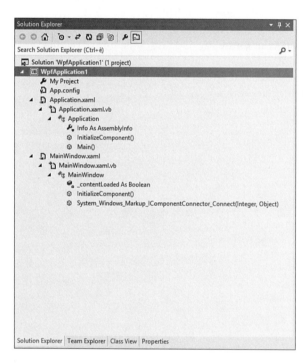

FIGURE 2.16   An example of the Solution Explorer tool window.

As you can see, at the root level there is the project. Nested are code files, subfolders containing pictures, data, and documents. You can also get a list of all the references in the project. You use Solution Explorer for adding and managing items in your projects as well as getting a representation of which files constitute the project itself. By default, Solution Explorer shows only the items that compose the project. If you need a complete view of references and auto-generated code files, you need to click the **Show All Files** button located on the upper-left portion of the window. Solution Explorer has been deeply revisited in Visual Studio 2012 and, if you had a chance of using the Power Tools extension for Visual Studio 2010, you might notice how it retakes most of the features of a tool window called Solution Navigator. Solution Explorer now shows the list of types and members that a code file defines, by expanding the name of a code file. For instance, you can see in Figure 2.16 how the MainWindow.xaml.vb code file defines a class called `MainWindow`, which exposes a field called `_contentLoaded` of type `Boolean`, and two methods, `InitializeComponent` and `System_Windows_Markup_IComponentConnector_Connect`. By double-clicking a member you will be automatically redirected to its definition in the code file. The window also shows arguments and their type. This is useful when you have hundreds of files and just need to know which types are defined within a file without searching inside all the others. Also, Solution Explorer has a useful search box in which you can type a search key and the IDE will search for all the items in the solution that contain the specified word(s). Another interesting feature of the new Solution Explorer is that you can discover the following behaviors for members defined in code:

- Calls that the member makes
- Members that are calling the selected member
- Members that are using the selected member

You can simply right-click a member defined inside a code file and then select the desired command. At that point, Solution Explorer will show the list of members that are invoked by, are calling, or are using the selected member. To go back to the full list you simply use the Back button in the toolbar (see Figure 2.16). The new Solution Explorer also provides interaction with Team Foundation Server and the possibility of generating visual representation of the object graph for the selected node. To manage your project's items, you just need to right-click the project name and select the most appropriate command from the pop-up menu that appears. Figure 2.17 shows this pop-up menu.

FIGURE 2.17   Solution items can be managed in Solution Explorer using the pop-up menu.

As you can see from Figure 2.17, the pop-up menu shows several tasks you can perform on your projects or solutions. You can easily add new items by selecting the **Add** command; you also can perform tasks against specific files if you right-click items in the solution instead of the project's name.

NOTE ABOUT ADDING ITEMS TO PROJECTS

In this book you will be asked lots of times to add new items to a project or to a solution, so you should keep in mind that this can be accomplished by right-clicking the project name in Solution Explorer and then clicking the Add, New Item command from the pop-up menu.

You can easily find Solution Explorer by pressing **Ctrl+Alt+L** if it is not available yet in the IDE. The enhancements that Visual Studio 2012 brings to Solution Explorer make this tool window a very important productivity tool, rather than a simple project browser.

The Error List Window

The Error List tool window can show a list of all messages, including warnings and information, which are generated by Visual Studio during the development of your applications. Figure 2.18 shows the Error List tool window.

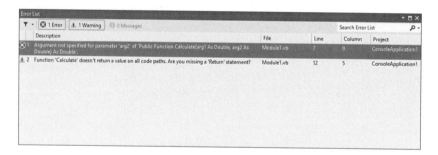

FIGURE 2.18   The Error List tool window.

Typically the Error List window can show three kinds of messages:

▶ Error messages

▶ Warning messages

▶ Information messages

Error messages are related to errors that prevent your application from running—for example, if your code cannot compile successfully. This can include any kind of problems that Visual Studio or the background compiler encounter during the development process, such as attempting to use an object that has not been declared, corrupted auto-generated Windows Presentation Foundation files that must be edited in the Visual Studio designer, or corrupted Visual Studio files in situations that throw error messages you can see in the Error List. Another kind of message is a warning. Warnings are related to situations that will not necessarily prevent your code from being successfully compiled or your application from running; in such cases warnings can be simply ignored. It's good practice to try to solve the problems that caused these messages to be shown. For example, running the Code Analysis tool will throw warnings on code that is not compliant with Microsoft guidelines for writing code. This means that the application will probably work, but something in your code should be improved. In both error and warning messages, you can be redirected to the code that caused the message by double-clicking the message itself. You can also get some help about the message by right-clicking it and then selecting the **Show Error Help** command from the pop-up menu, or simply by pressing F1. Information messages are just to inform you about something. Usually information messages can be ignored with regard to the code, although they could be useful for understanding what the IDE wants to tell us. By default, the **Error List** shows the three kinds of messages together, but you could also choose to view only some of them—for example, error messages excluded and so on. To filter the Error List results, click the tab related to the kind of message you do not want to be shown. For instance, click the **Messages** tab if you want information messages to be excluded by the errors list. To include back information messages, click the same tab again. The Errors List can also be easily invoked by pressing **Ctrl+\, Ctrl+E**.

The Properties Window

In the .NET development, everything has *properties*, which are the characteristics of a particular item. Classes can have properties; files can have properties; and so on. For example, the filename is a property of a file. You often need to set properties for your code, for .NET objects you use in your code, and for your files. To make things easier, Visual Studio provides a tool window named Properties window, which is a graphical tool for setting items' properties. Figure 2.19 represents the Properties window showing properties for a button in Windows Presentation Foundation.

We could define the Properties window's structure as a two-column table, in which the left column specifies the property and the right column gets or sets the value for the property. Although you often need to set properties in code, the Properties window provides a graphical way to perform this assignment and can be particularly useful when designing the user interface or when you need to specify how a file must be packaged into the executable assembly. The Properties window can be easily invoked by pressing **F4**.

The Output Window

Visual Studio often recurs to external tools for performing some actions. For example, when compiling your projects, Visual Studio invokes the Visual Basic command-line compiler, so the IDE captures the output of the tools it utilizes and redirects the output to the Output window. The Output window's purpose is to show results of actions that Visual Studio has to perform or that you require to be performed by Visual Studio. So, when you compile your projects, the Output window shows the results of the build process. Figure 2.20 shows the Output window containing the results of the build process of a Visual Basic project.

FIGURE 2.19   The Properties window.

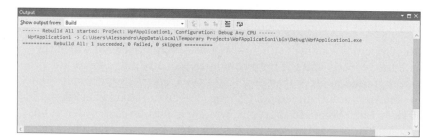

FIGURE 2.20   The Output window showing results of a build process.

The Output window is also interactive. To continue with the example of compiling a program, if the compiler throws any errors, these are shown in the Output window. You can click the **Go to Next Message** or **Go to Previous Message** button to navigate error messages. After you do this, the current error message is highlighted. Each time you move to another error message, you will be redirected to the code that caused the error. The Output window can capture the output not only of the compiler, but also of other tools

Visual Studio needs to use, such as the debugger. By the way, you can get a list of the available outputs by clicking the **Show Output From** combo box. After this first look to the main tool windows, we can begin examining another important feature of the Visual Studio IDE for Visual Basic: the My Project window.

My Project

My Project is a special tool that enables developers to set project properties. My Project is a window that can be invoked by double-clicking the **My Project** item in Solution Explorer or by clicking the **Project, Properties** command (the menu item text also includes the current project name). Figure 2.21 shows how My Project looks regarding the sample application we previously created.

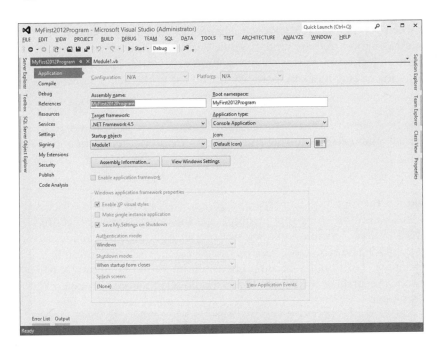

FIGURE 2.21   The My Project window.

My Project is organized in tabs; each tab represents a specific area of the project, such as application-level properties, external references, deployment options, compile options, debugging options, and many more. At the moment you don't need to learn each tab of My Project because during the rest of the book we use it a lot, learning the meaning and purpose of each tab when appropriate. What you instead need now is to

▶ Understand what My Project is.

▶ Remember how you can open it.

▶ Learn the usage of the Application tab, which we will discuss first.

UNDERSTANDING MY PROJECT

Understanding My Project is also important for another reason: It provides most of the infrastructure for the `My` namespace that will be discussed in Chapter 19, "The My Namespace." Most of settings you can specify in My Project are then accessible by invoking `My`. In Chapter 3, "The Anatomy of a Visual Basic Project," we describe the structure of My Project, so carefully read how it is composed.

Application Tab

Each application has some settings. Application settings can be the executable's name, icon, or metadata that will be grabbed by the operating system, such as the program version, copyright information, and so on. The purpose of the Application tab in My Project is to provide the ability to edit these kinds of settings. The Application tab is shown by default when you first open My Project. Figure 2.21 shows the Application tab. Some settings are common to every kind of Visual Basic project, whereas other ones are related to specific project types. In this chapter you get an overview of the common settings, whereas specific ones will be discussed when required in the next chapters.

Assembly Name

The Assembly name field sets the name of the compiled assembly—that is, your executable. By default, Visual Studio assigns this setting based on the project name, but you can replace it as needed.

Root Namespace

This particular field sets the root-level namespace identifier. Namespaces will be discussed later in this book. You can think of the root namespace as the object that stores all that is implemented by your project. According to Microsoft specifications, the root namespace should be formed as follows: `CompanyName.ProductName.Version`. This convention is optimal when developing class libraries or components but might not be necessary when developing standalone executables. By default, Visual Studio sets the root namespace based on the project name.

Application Type

This represents the application type (for example, Console application, Class Library, Windows Forms application) and is automatically set by Visual Studio on the appropriate choice. To ensure you will avoid any problems, you should not change the default setting.

Icon

This field allows setting an icon for the executable file. You can browse the disk and select an existing .ico file as the executable icon.

NOTE ABOUT ICONS

Assigning an icon to the executable file will not automatically assign icons to Windows Forms windows or WPF windows when developing client applications. In such scenarios you need to explicitly assign icons for each window because the Icon item in the `Application` tab will just set the icon for the executable.

Startup Object

By setting the Startup Object field, you can specify which object will be executed first when running your application. For example, imagine you have a Windows Presentation Foundation application with more than one window. You might want to decide which window must be the application's main window. With the Startup Object field, you can make this decision. Notice that the startup object changes based on the project type. For example, in a WPF application the startup object is a `Window` object, whereas in a Console Application the default startup object is a `Module` in which the `Sub Main` method is located. The name of the field also changes based on the project type. In a WPF application it is called Startup URI, whereas in a Console Application it is called Startup Object.

CHANGING THE STARTUP OBJECT

Please be careful when changing the Startup Object. A wrong choice could cause errors on your application and prevent it from running.

Assembly Information

By clicking the Assembly Information button, you get access to a new window called Assembly Information, as shown in Figure 2.22.

FIGURE 2.22   The Assembly Information window.

From this window you can specify several properties for your executable that will be visible both to the .NET Framework and to the Windows operating system. Table 2.1 explains each property.

TABLE 2.1   Assembly Information Explained

Property	Description
Title	The title for your application, for example, "My First 2012 Program."
Description	The description for your application, for example, "My first application with VB 2012."
Company	Your company name.
Product	The product name, for example, "Suite of My New 2012 Applications."
Copyright	Copyright information on the author.
Trademark	Trademarks information.
Assembly version	Specifies the version number for the assembly in the style Major.Minor.Build.Revision. This information identifies the assembly for the .NET Framework.
File version	Specifies the version number for the executable in the style Major.Minor.Build.Revision. This information is visible to the Windows operating system.
GUID	A globally unique identifier assigned to the assembly. You can replace it with a new one or leave it as the GUID provided by the IDE.
Neutral language	Specifies what local culture is used as the neutral language.
Make assembly COM-Visible	.NET assemblies can be exposed to COM. By marking this flag, you can accomplish this task later.

The Assembly Information tool is important because it enables you to specify settings that you want to be visible to your customers and other settings needed by the .NET Framework. Behind the scenes, all this information is translated into Visual Basic code, which is discussed more in Chapter 3.

View Windows Settings

Starting from Windows Vista, Microsoft introduced to the Windows operating system an important component, known as User Account Control (UAC). When enabled, this mechanism requires the user to explicitly grant elevated permissions to applications being run. Because of this and starting from Visual Studio 2008, you have the ability of specifying the permissions level your application will require for the UAC. For example, if your application needs to write to the Program Files folder (this is just an example and rarely a good idea), you need to ask for elevated permissions to the UAC. You can specify UAC settings for your application by clicking the **View Windows Settings** button. At this point Visual Studio generates a new XML manifest that will be packaged into your executable and that you can edit within the IDE. This file contains information for UAC settings and

for specifying the operating systems that the application is designed to work for (see the
supportedOS node). Listing 2.2 shows an excerpt of the default content of the manifest,
related to the UAC settings.

LISTING 2.2   The UAC Manifest Content

```xml
<?xml version="1.0" encoding="utf-8"?>
<asmv1:assembly manifestVersion="1.0" xmlns="urn:schemas-microsoft-com:asm.v1"
xmlns:asmv1="urn:schemas-microsoft-com:asm.v1" xmlns:asmv2="urn:schemas-microsoft-
com:asm.v2" xmlns:xsi="http://www.w3.org/2001/XMLSchema-instance">
  <assemblyIdentity version="1.0.0.0" name="MyApplication.app"/>
  <trustInfo xmlns="urn:schemas-microsoft-com:asm.v2">
    <security>
      <requestedPrivileges xmlns="urn:schemas-microsoft-com:asm.v3">
        <!-- UAC Manifest Options
            If you want to change the Windows User Account Control level replace the
            requestedExecutionLevel node with one of the following.

          <requestedExecutionLevel  level="asInvoker" uiAccess="false" />
          <requestedExecutionLevel  level="requireAdministrator" uiAccess="false" />
          <requestedExecutionLevel  level="highestAvailable" uiAccess="false" />

            Specifying requestedExecutionLevel node will
            disable file and registry virtualization.
            If you want to utilize File and Registry Virtualization for backward
            compatibility then delete the requestedExecutionLevel node.
        -->
        <requestedExecutionLevel level="asInvoker" uiAccess="false" />
      </requestedPrivileges>
    </security>
  </trustInfo>

  <compatibility xmlns="urn:schemas-microsoft-com:compatibility.v1">
    <application>
      <!-- A list of all Windows versions that this application is designed
           to work with.
        Windows will automatically select the most compatible environment.-->

      <!-- If your application is designed to work with Windows Vista, uncomment the
following supportedOS node-->
        <!--<supportedOS Id="{e2011457-1546-43c5-a5fe-008deee3d3f0}"></supportedOS>-->

      <!-- If your application is designed to work with Windows 7, uncomment the
following supportedOS node-->
        <!--<supportedOS Id="{35138b9a-5d96-4fbd-8e2d-a2440225f93a}"/>-->
```

```
    <!-- If your application is designed to work with Windows 8, uncomment the
following supportedOS node-->
    <!--<supportedOS Id="{4a2f28e3-53b9-4441-ba9c-d69d4a4a6e38}"></supportedOS>-->

  </application>
 </compatibility>


 <!-- Enable themes for Windows common controls and dialogs (Windows XP and later)
-->
 <!-- <dependency>
   <dependentAssembly>
    <assemblyIdentity
        type="win32"
        name="Microsoft.Windows.Common-Controls"
        version="6.0.0.0"
        processorArchitecture="*"
        publicKeyToken="6595b64144ccf1df"
        language="*"
     />
   </dependentAssembly>
  </dependency>-->


</asmv1:assembly>
```

Notice how a huge number of comments help you understand the file content and how
you should manage the behavior of your application according to the Windows version
that your application is going to target. The requestedExecutionLevel element enables
you to specify which permission level must be requested to the UAC. You have three
possibilities, explained in Table 2.2.

TABLE 2.2   UAC Settings

Setting	Description
asInvoker	Runs the application with the privileges related to the current user. If the current user is a standard user, the application will be launched with standard privileges. If the current user is an administrator, the application will be launched with administrative privileges. This is the default selection in the manifest.
requireAdministrator	The application needs administrative privileges to be executed.
highestAvailable	Requires the highest privilege level possible for the current user.

To specify a privilege level, just uncomment the line of XML code corresponding to the desired level. You can also delete the `requestedExecutionLevel` node in case you want to use file and registry virtualization for backward compatibility with older versions of the Windows operating system.

PAY ATTENTION TO UAC REQUIREMENTS

Be careful of the combination of activities that you need to execute on the target machine and the user privileges because bad UAC settings could cause big problems. A good practice is selecting the `asInvoker` level and architecting your application in a way that it will work on user-level folders and resources. In some situations, you will need deeper control of the target machine and administrator privileges, but these should be considered exceptions to the rule.

The Application Framework

In the lower part of the screen is the Enable Application Framework group, a feature that allows executing special tasks at the beginning and at the end of the application lifetime. For Console applications it is not available, but it is relevant to other kinds of applications; for instance, in the Windows Forms application it enables the setting of a splash screen or establishing which form is the main application form. The application framework is discussed in Chapter 19.

Target Framework

From the Target Framework combo box, you can select the version of the .NET Framework that your application will target. The main difference with the same selection that you can do when creating a new project is that here you can target the .NET Framework Client Profile for versions 4.0, 3.5 Service Pack 1, and 3.5 Server Core. The .NET Framework Client Profile is a subset of the .NET Framework that provides the infrastructure for client applications and that can be included in your deployments instead of the full version. Microsoft removed the .NET Framework Client Profile in version 4.5.

NOTE FOR VISUAL STUDIO 2010 USERS

Until Visual Studio 2010, the Target Framework option was available in the Advanced Compile Options dialog box. In Visual Studio 2012 it has been moved to the Application tab of My Project.

Compiling Projects

Compiling a project (or *building* according to the Visual Studio terminology) is the process that produces a .NET assembly starting from your project and source code (according to the .NET architecture described in Chapter 1, "Introducing the .NET Framework 4.5"). An assembly can be a standalone application (.exe assembly) or a .NET class library

(.dll assembly). To compile your project into an assembly, you need to click the **Build** command in the Build menu. Notice that the Build command is followed by the name of your project. When invoking this command, Visual Studio launches, behind the scenes, the Visual Basic command-line compiler (Vbc.exe) and provides this tool all the necessary command-line options. For solutions containing different kinds of projects, Visual Studio launches MSBuild.exe, a command-line utility that can compile entire solutions containing several projects written in different languages and of different types. At the end of the build process, Visual Studio shows a log inside the Output window. Figure 2.23 shows the output log of the build process for the MyFirst2012Program sample application.

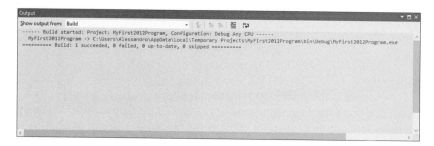

FIGURE 2.23   The Output window shows the compilation process results.

The compilation log shows useful messages that help you understand what happened. In this case there were no errors, but in situations in which the compilation process fails because of some errors in the code, you will be notified of the errors found by the compiler. The Error List window shows a complete list of error messages and warnings and enables you to easily understand where the errors happened by double-clicking the error message. This operation redirects you to the code that generated the error. The executable (or the executables, in the case of more than one project in the solution) will be put in a subfolder within the project's directory, called Bin\Debug or Bin\Release, depending on the output configuration you chose. Configurations are discussed next.

Debug and Release Configurations

Visual Studio provides two default possibilities for compiling your projects. The first one is related to the debugging phase in the development process and includes debug symbols that are necessary for debugging applications. The second one is related to the end of the development process and is the one you will use when releasing the application to your customers. Both ways are represented by configurations. By default, Visual Studio offers two built-in configurations: Debug and Release. When the Debug configuration is active, the Visual Basic compiler generates debug symbols that the Visual Studio debugger can process. Without these symbols, you cannot debug your applications with the Visual Studio debugger. The Release configuration basically excludes debug symbols from the build process. It is the configuration you will use when building the final version of your application—that is, the executable you will release to your customers. To set the current configuration, you have two possibilities:

▶ Use the combo box located on the Visual Studio toolbar.

▶ Access the Compile options inside the My Project window.

Figure 2.24 shows the Compile tab in My Project.

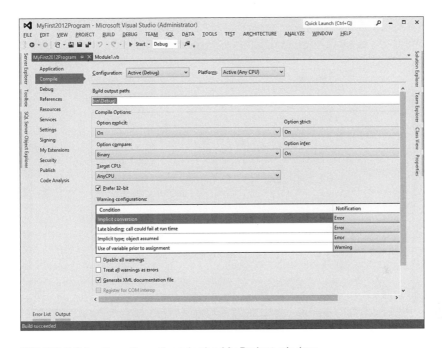

FIGURE 2.24   Compile options in the My Project window.

At the top of the window is a combo box called Configuration. There you can select the most appropriate configuration for you. By default, Visual Studio 2012 is set up on the Debug configuration. You could also consider building a custom configuration (although both Debug and Release can be customized instead of making new ones), which will be discussed next. For our purposes, it's suitable to leave unchanged the selection of the Debug configuration as the default because we will study the Visual Studio debugging features in depth.

Creating Custom Configurations with Configuration Manager

You might have situations in which both the Debug and Release configurations are not enough for your needs. As mentioned in the previous paragraph, with Visual Studio 2012 you can also create your custom configuration. To accomplish this, you need to access the Configuration Manager tool (see Figure 2.25), which is reachable using the Configuration

Manager command in the Build menu. There you can edit an existing configuration or create a new one.

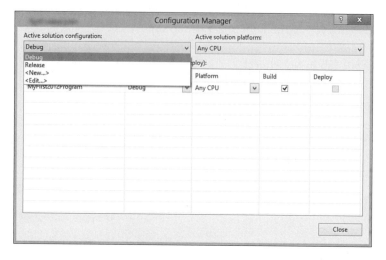

FIGURE 2.25   The Configuration Manager.

To create a new custom configuration, perform the following steps:

1. Click the **Active Solution Configuration** combo box and select the **New** option.

2. In the New Solution Configuration window, specify a name for the new configuration and select an existing configuration (such as Debug) from which settings will be copied. Figure 2.26 shows an example.

FIGURE 2.26   Creating a custom configuration that imports settings from an existing one.

3. When done, click **Close**.

4. Click the **Advanced Compiler Options** button in the Compile tab and specify which compile options must affect the new configuration. For example, you could decide to affect just compilations against 64-bit processors, so you would need to change the value in the Target CPU combo box. This is the point at which you can modify your real configuration settings and how your project should be built.

Such modification influences just the new configuration. Moreover, if you decide to use the new configuration, you will have a new subfolder under the Bin subfolder in your project's main folder, which takes the name of your custom configuration and contains the output of the build process made with that configuration. For our MyFirst2012Program sample, the project folder is named MyFirst2012Program and contains the Bin subfolder, which also contains the default Debug and Release subfolders. With your custom configuration, a new TestConfiguration subfolder will be available under Bin.

Background Compiler

Visual Basic 2012 offers a great feature: the background compiler. While you write your code, the IDE invokes the Visual Basic compiler that will immediately compile the code and notify you about errors that occur, writing messages in the Error List window. This is possible because the Visual Basic compiler can compile your code on-the-fly while you type. As you can imagine, this feature is important because you will not necessarily need to build your project each time to understand whether your code can be successfully compiled. Typical examples of the background compiler in action are error messages shown in the Error List window when typing code. Refer to Figure 2.19 to get an idea of this feature. You can double-click the error message to be redirected to the line of code that caused the error. Also, the IDE underlines code containing errors with squiggly lines so that it is easier to understand where the problem is.

Other Compile Options

Visual Studio 2012 enables developers to get deep control over the build process. With particular regard to Visual Basic, you can control other compile options that are specific to the language. Table 2.3 lists them in detail.

TABLE 2.3   Visual Basic Compile Options

Option	Meaning
Option Explicit	When set to On, the developer must declare an object before using it in code.
Option Strict	When set to On, the developer must specify the type when declaring objects. In other words, Object is not automatically assigned as the default type. Moreover, Option Strict On disallows late binding and conversions from one type to another where there is a loss of precision or data. You should always set Option Strict On unless required.
Option Compare	Determines which method must be used when comparing strings (Binary or Text). The Binary option enables the compiler to compare strings based on a binary representation of the characters, while the Text option enables string comparisons based on textual sorting, according to the local system international settings.
Option Infer	When set to On, enables local type inference (this feature is discussed in Chapter 20, "Advanced Language Features").

OPTION STRICT ON

By default, Option Strict is Off. You can set it to On each time you create a new project, but you can also change the default setting by clicking Tools, Options. Then in the Options dialog box expand the Projects and Solutions node; finally select the VB Defaults element and change the default setting.

Options shown in Table 2.3 are also considered by the background compiler, so you will be immediately notified when your code does not match these requirements. You can also specify how the Visual Basic compiler has to treat some kind of errors. This is what you see next.

Target CPU

You can specify the CPU architecture your applications will target. You can choose among 32-bit architectures (x86), 64-bit architectures (x64), Itanium processors, ARM (in the case of Windows Store Apps) or any architecture (AnyCPU). Until Visual Studio 2010 this setting was available in the Advanced Compile Options dialog box.

Warning Configurations

Warning configurations state how the Visual Basic compiler should notify the developer of some particular errors, if just sending warning messages (which will not prevent from compiling the project) or error messages (which will instead prevent from completing the build process).

DO NOT IGNORE WARNING MESSAGES

Even if warning messages will not prevent the completion of the build process, they should never be blindly ignored. They could be suggestions of potential exceptions at runtime. You should always accurately check why a warning message is thrown and, possibly, solve the issue that caused the warning. A typical example of when warnings could be ignored is when running code analysis on code that does not need to be compliant with Microsoft specifications (for example, the user interface side of a WPF application). In all other situations, you should be careful about warnings.

Depending on how you set the Visual Basic compile options discussed in the previous paragraph, Visual Studio will propose some default scenarios for sending notifications (and, consequently, influencing the build process). Table 2.4 lists the available warning conditions.

TABLE 2.4   Warning Condition Details

Condition	Description

Implicit conversion	Checked when trying to assign an object of a type to an object of another type. For example, the following code will cause the condition to be checked (implicit conversion from Object to String):
	`Dim anObject As Object = "Hi!"`
	`Dim aString As String = anObject`

Condition	Description
Late binding	Checked when trying to assign at runtime a typed object to another one of type `Object`.
Implicit type	Checked when not specifying the type for an object declaration. If Option Infers is on, this condition is checked only for declarations at class level. For example, the following class-level declaration would cause the condition to be checked: `Private Something` This condition is determined by `Option Strict On`.

Use of variable prior of assignment	Checked when attempting to use a variable that doesn't have a value yet. This is typical with instance variables. The following code causes this condition to be checked:
	
	`Dim p As Process`
	`Console.WriteLine(`
	`p.ProcessName.ToString)`
	
	In this case `p` must get an instance of the `Process` object before attempting to use it.

Function/operator without return value	Checked when a `Function` method or an operator definition performs actions without returning a value.
Unused local variable	Checked when a variable is declared but never used. It's a good practice to remove unused variables both for cleaner code and for memory allocation.
Instance variable accesses shared members	Checked when trying to invoke a member from an instance object that is instead a shared member.
Recursive operator or property access	Checked when trying to use a member (properties or operators) inside the code block that defines the member itself.

Duplicate or overlapping catch blocks	Checked when a `Catch` clause inside a `Try..Catch..End Try` code block is never reached because of inheritance. The following code causes the condition to be checked because the `FileNotFoundException` inherits from `Exception` and therefore should be caught before the base class; otherwise, `Exception` would be always caught before derived ones:
	
	`Try`
	
	`Catch ex As Exception`
	`Catch ex As FileNotFoundException`
	
	`End Try`

You also have the ability to change single notifications; just select the most appropriate notification mode for your needs. Based on the explanations provided in Table 2.4, be careful about the consequences that this operation could cause. If you are not sure about consequences, the best thing is leaving default options unchanged. Three other compile options are listed at the bottom of the Compile tab and described in Table 2.5.

TABLE 2.5   Additional Compile Options

Option	Description
Disable all warnings.	The Visual Basic compiler will not produce warning messages.
Treat all warnings as errors.	The Visual Basic compiler will treat all warning messages as if they were errors.
Generate XML documentation file.	When flagged, enables Visual Studio to generate an XML file for documenting the source code. If XML comments are included in the code, this file also contains descriptions and detailed documentation for the code. This is useful when you need to automate the documentation process for your class libraries.

Advanced Compile Options

You can specify advanced settings for the build process. To accomplish this, you need to click the **Advanced Compile Options** button.

COMPILER SETTINGS AND CONFIGURATIONS

Advanced compiler settings are at the configuration level. This means that the Debug configuration has its own advanced settings, the Release configuration has its own settings, and your custom configurations will have their own settings. Please remember this when providing advanced settings.

Figure 2.27 shows the Advanced Compiler Settings window.

FIGURE 2.27   The Advanced Compiler Settings window.

Here you can set compiler options to drive the build process. Next we discuss options in detail.

Optimizations

The Optimization tab offers options that would potentially lead to building a smaller and faster executable. This tab is composed of four options that we discuss.

Remove Integer Overflow Checks   When you make calculations in your code against `Integer` or `Integer`-style data types, the Visual Basic compiler checks that the result of the calculation falls within the range of that particular data type. By default, this option is turned off so that the compiler can do this kind of check. If you flag this check box, the compiler will not check for such overflows, and the application execution might result faster. Be careful about this choice, especially if your code implements calculations.

Enable Optimizations   When this check box is flagged, the compiler basically removes some opcodes that are required for interacting with the debugger. Moreover, the Just-In-Time compilation is optimized because the runtime knows that a debugger will not be attached. On the other hand, this can result in major difficulties when debugging applications. For example, you might not use breakpoints at specific lines of code and, consequently, perform debugging tasks although the optimization process could produce a smaller and faster executable.

DLL Base Address   This option is available when developing class libraries and user controls and provides the ability to specify the Base Address for the assembly. As you might know, the base address is the location in memory where a .dll file is loaded. By default, Visual Studio assigns a base address and represents it in hexadecimal format. If you need to provide a custom base address, this is the place where you can do it.

Generate Debug Information   Generating debug information when building your project allows you to use the debugger against your application. By default, this option is set to Full, which means that full debug information is generated so that the debugger can be fully used to debug an application. (This is the case of the Debug configuration.) If you set this option to None, no debug information will be generated; if you set this option to pdb-only, the compiler will produce just a .pdb file containing debug symbols and project state information.

Compilation Constants

You can use compilation constants to conditionally compile blocks of code. Conditional compilation relies on the evaluation to True of constants that will be included in the final assembly. The Visual Basic compiler defines some default constants you can evaluate within your code; you also have the ability to declare custom constants. In the Advanced Compiler Settings window, you can specify whether the compiler needs to include the `DEBUG` and `TRACE` constants. The first one enables you to understand if the application is running in debug mode; in other words, if the application has been compiled using the Debug configuration. The second one is also related to debugging tasks; particularly, the .NET Framework exposes a class called `Trace` that is used in debugging and that can send the tracing output to the Output window when the `TRACE` constant is defined. If not, no output is generated because invocations versus the `Trace` class are ignored. A full list of built-in constants can be found at MSDN Library at http://msdn.microsoft.com/en-us/library/dy7yth1w(VS.110).aspx. Evaluating constants in code is simple. You can use the `#If`, `#Else`, `#ElseIf`, and `#EndIf` directives. For example, if you want to evaluate whenever an application has been compiled with the Debug configuration, you could write the following code:

```
#If DEBUG Then
        Console.WriteLine("You are in Debug configuration")
#Else
        Console.WriteLine("You are not in Debug configuration")
#End If
```

which essentially verifies if the constant is defined and takes some action at that point. In our example, if the DEBUG constant is defined in the assembly, this means that it has been built via the Debug configuration.

Custom Constants   You can also define custom constants. This can be basically accomplished in two ways. The first is adding custom constants in the appropriate field of the Advanced compiler settings window. Each constant must have the form of Name="Value", and constants are separated by commas. The second way for providing custom constants is adding a #Const directive in your code. For example, the following line of code

```
#Const TestConstant = True
```

defines a constant named TestConstant whose value is set to True. The big difference in using a #Const directive is that it defines just private constants that have visibility within the code file that defines them.

Generate Serialization Assemblies

As we discuss in Chapter 41, "Serialization," serialization in .NET development is a technique that allows persisting the state of an object. Among several alternatives, this can be accomplished using a class called XmlSerializer. In such situations, the Visual Basic compiler can optimize applications that use the XmlSerializer class, generating additional assemblies for better performances. By default, this option is set to **Auto** so that Visual Studio generates serialization assemblies only if you are effectively using XML serialization in your code. Other options are On and Off.

Debugging Overview

In this section you get an overview of the debugging features in Visual Studio 2012 for Visual Basic applications. Although the debugger and debugging techniques are detailed in Chapter 5, "Debugging Visual Basic 2012 Applications," here we provide information on the most common debugging tasks, which is something that you need to know in this first part of your journey through the Visual Basic programming language.

Debugging an Application

To debug a Visual Basic application, you basically need to perform two steps:

▶ Enable the Debug configuration in the compile options.

▶ Press F5 to start debugging.

By pressing F5, Visual Studio runs your application and attaches an instance of the debugger to the application. Because the Visual Studio debugger needs the debug symbols to proceed, if you do not choose the Debug configuration, you cannot debug your applications. The instance of the debugger detaches when you shut down your application.

> **TIP**
>
> As an alternative you can click the Start button on the Visual Studio standard toolbar. If the Debug configuration is selected, this action will be the equivalent of pressing F5. If the Release configuration is selected, this is the equivalent of launching the application with CTRL + F5.

The debugger monitors your application's execution and notifies for runtime errors; it allows you to take control over the execution flow as well. Figure 2.28 shows our sample application running with the Visual Studio debugger attached.

FIGURE 2.28   Our sample application running with an attached instance of the Visual Studio debugger.

In the bottom area of the IDE, you can notice the availability of some tabs, such as Locals, Watch 1, Watch 2, Call Stack, Breakpoints, Command Window, Immediate Window, and Output. Each tab represents a tool window that has specific debugging purposes. Also, notice how the status bar becomes orange and an orange border is placed around the IDE, to remind the developer that the IDE is running in debugging mode. The Visual Studio debugger is a powerful tool; next you learn the most important tasks in debugging applications. Before explaining the tooling, it is a good idea to modify the source code of our test application so that we can cause some errors and see the debugger in action. We could rewrite the `Sub Main` method's code, as shown in Listing 2.3.

LISTING 2.3   Modifying the Sub Main for Debugging Purposes

```
Sub Main()

    'A text message
    Dim message As String = "Hello Visual Basic 2012!"

    Console.WriteLine(message)

    'Attempt to read a file that does not exist
    Dim getSomeText As String =
                    My.Computer.FileSystem.ReadAllText("FakeFile.txt")

    Console.WriteLine(getSomeText)
    Console.ReadLine()

End Sub
```

NEW TO VISUAL BASIC .NET?

If you are not an existing Visual Basic .NET developer, you may not know some of the objects and keywords shown in the code listings of this chapter. The code is the simplest possible, so it should be easy to understand; comments are also provided. The next chapters guide you to the details of the programming language, so everything used here will be explained. At the moment, it is important for you to focus on the instrumentation more than on the code.

The code simply declares a message object of type `String`, containing a text message. This message is then shown in the Console window. This is useful for understanding breakpoints and other features in the code editor. The second part of the code will try to open a text file, which effectively does not exist and store its content into a variable called `getSomeText` of type `String`. We need this to understand how the debugger catches errors at runtime, together with the edit and continue feature.

Breakpoints and Data Tips

Breakpoints enable you to control the execution flow of your application. A breakpoint breaks the execution of the application at the point where the breakpoint itself is placed so that you can take required actions (a situation known as *break mode*). You can then resume the application execution. To place a breakpoint on a specific line of code, just place the cursor on the line of code you want to debug and then press **F9**.

> **TIP**
>
> To add a breakpoint, you can also right-click the line of code you want to debug and select the Breakpoint, Insert breakpoint command from the pop-up menu or just click the left-most column in the code window.

A breakpoint is easily recognizable because it highlights in red the selected line of code (see Figure 2.29).

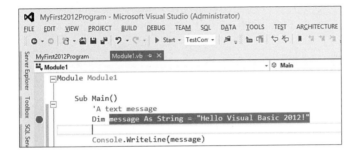

FIGURE 2.29   Placing a breakpoint in the code editor.

To see how breakpoints work, we can run the sample application by pressing **F5**. When the debugger encounters a breakpoint, it breaks the execution and highlights in yellow the line of code that is being debugged, as shown in Figure 2.30, before the code is executed.

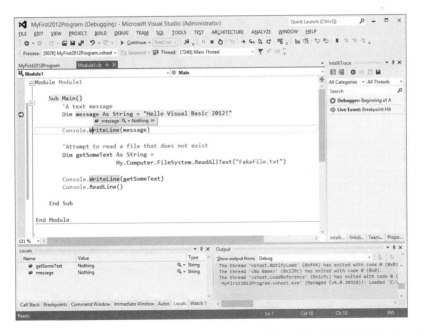

FIGURE 2.30   When encountering a breakpoint, Visual Studio highlights the line of code that is currently debugged.

If you take a look at Figure 2.30, you notice that, if you pass with the mouse pointer over the message variable, IntelliSense shows the content of the variable itself, which at the moment contains no value (in fact, it is set to Nothing). This feature is known as Data Tips and is useful if you need to know the content of a variable or of another object in a particular moment of the application execution.

THE VISUAL STUDIO HISTORICAL DEBUGGER

If you run the Microsoft Visual Studio 2012 Ultimate edition, you also notice another window called IntelliTrace. This window is also known as the Visual Studio Historical Debugger and is specific to the Visual Studio Ultimate instrumentation. It is discussed in Chapter 55, "Advanced Analysis Tools."

You can then execute just one line of code at a time, by pressing **F11**. For example, supposing we want to check if the message variable is correctly initialized at runtime. We could press F11 (which is a shortcut for the Step Into command in the Debug menu). The line of code where the breakpoint is placed will now be executed, and Visual Studio will highlight the next line of code. At that point, you can still pass the mouse pointer over the variable to see the assignment result, as shown in Figure 2.31.

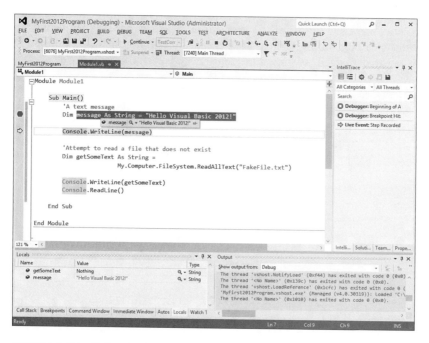

FIGURE 2.31   Using the Step Into command lets us check whether the variable has been assigned correctly.

When you finish checking the assignments, you can resume the execution by pressing **F5**. The execution of the application continues until another breakpoint or a runtime error is encountered. We discuss this second scenario next.

Runtime Errors

Runtime errors are particular situations in which an error occurs during the application execution. These are not predictable and occur due to programming errors that are not visible at compile time. Typical examples of runtime errors are when you create an application and you give users the ability to specify a filename, but the file is not found on disk, or when you need to access a database and pass an incorrect SQL query string. Obviously, in real-life applications you should predict such possibilities and implement the appropriate error handling routines (discussed in Chapter 6, "Handling Errors and Exceptions"), but for our learning purposes about the debugger, we need some code that voluntarily causes an error. Continuing the debugging we began in the previous paragraph, the application's execution resumption causes a runtime error because our code is searching for a file that does not exist. When the error is raised, Visual Studio breaks the execution as shown in Figure 2.32.

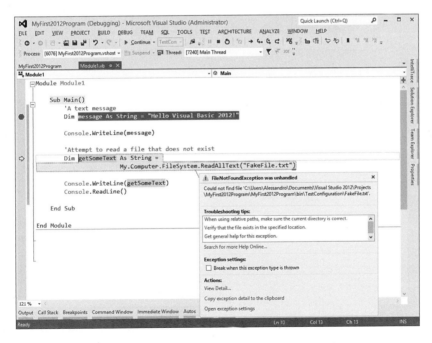

FIGURE 2.32   The Visual Studio debugger encounters a runtime error.

As you can see, the line of code that caused the error appears highlighted. You also can see a pop-up window that shows some information about the error. In our example, the code searched for a file that does not exist, so a `FileNotFoundException` was thrown and was not handled by error handling routines; therefore, the execution of the application was broken. Visual Studio also shows a description of the error message. (In our example it communicates that the code could not find the FakeFile.txt file.) Visual Studio also shows some suggestions. For example, the Troubleshooting tips suggest some tasks you could perform at this point, such as verifying that the file exists in the specified location, checking the pathname, or getting general help about the error. By clicking a tip, you are redirected to the MSDN documentation about the error. This can be useful when you don't exactly know what an error message means. There are other options within the Actions group. The most important is View Detail. This enables you to open the View Detail window, which is represented in Figure 2.33. Notice how the StackTrace item shows the hierarchy of calls to classes and methods that effectively produced the error. Another interesting item is the InnerException. In our example it is set to Nothing, but it's not unusual for this item to show a kind of exceptions tree that enables you to better understand what actually caused an error. For example, think of working with data. You might want to connect to SQL Server and fetch data from a database. You could not have sufficient rights to access the database, and the runtime might return a data access exception that does not allow you to immediately understand what the problem is. Browsing the InnerException can help you understand that the problem was caused by insufficient rights. Going back to the code, this is the point where you can fix it and where the Edit and Continue features comes in.

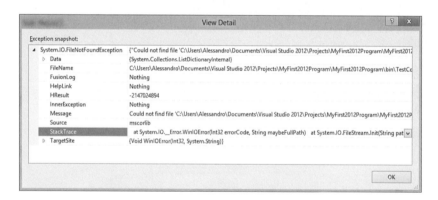

FIGURE 2.33   The View Detail window enables developers to examine what caused an exception.

Edit and Continue

The Edit and Continue features enable you to fix bad code and resume the application execution from the point where it was broken, without having to restart the application. You just need to run the application by pressing **F5**; then you can break its execution by pressing **Ctrl+Alt+Break** or either selecting the **Break All** command in the Debug menu or pressing Pause on the Debug toolbar.

> **AVAILABILITY OF EDIT AND CONTINUE**
>
> Generally, you can use the Edit and Continue features, but there are situations in which you will not. For example, if fixing your code might influence the general application behavior, you need to restart the application. Also, Edit and Continue is not available when running configurations that target 64-bit CPUs nor in Silverlight applications.

In our example we need to fix the code that searches for a not existing file. We can replace the line of code with this one:

```
Dim getSomeText As String = "Fixed code"
```

This replaces the search of a file with a text message. At this point we can press **F5** (or **F11** if we want to just execute the line of code and debug the next one) to resume the execution. Figure 2.34 shows how the application now runs correctly. The Edit and Continue feature completes the overview of the debugging features in Visual Studio. As we mentioned before, this topic is covered in detail in Chapter 6.

FIGURE 2.34   The sample application running correctly after fixing errors.

After this brief overview of the debugging features in Visual Studio 2012, it's time to talk about another important topic for letting you feel at home within the Visual Studio 2012 IDE when developing applications: getting help and documentation.

Browsing the Visual Basic and .NET Documentation

The *.NET Framework Base Class Library* is very large, and remembering all the objects that you can use in your applications (or the ones that .NET Framework relies on) is not possible. What is instead important is to know where to search for information. You have different tools available to browse the .NET Framework and its documentation, for Visual Basic, too. Because the goal of this chapter is to provide information on the primary tools you need for developing Visual Basic applications, getting help with the language and with the tooling is absolutely one of the primary necessities, as discussed next.

Online Help and the MSDN Library

Visual Studio 2012 ships with the MSDN Library, which is the place where you can find documentation for Visual Basic 2012 and the .NET Framework 4.5. There are basically two ways to access the MSDN Library: offline and online. To access the MSDN Library offline, you have the following alternatives:

▶ Click the **View Help** command from the Help menu in Visual Studio.

▶ Press **F1** from wherever you are.

▶ Open the **Microsoft Help Viewer** shortcut in Windows's Start, All Programs, Microsoft Visual Studio 2012 menu; this launches the local help viewer.

If you are writing code or performing a particular task on a tool within the IDE, pressing F1 is the best choice because you will be redirected to the help page related to that instruction, code statement, or tool. If you are instead searching for information about a particular technology or framework, such as WPF *or the* Visual Studio Tools for Office, you could consider one of the other choices. To access the MSDN Library online, you just need an Internet connection. Then you can specify to always use the online help by selecting **Help, Set Help Preference** and then clicking **Launch in Browser or Launch Help Viewer**, or you can manually open one of the following websites, which are the main points of interest for a Visual Basic developer:

▶ The MSDN Library portal at http://msdn.microsoft.com/en-us/library/default.aspx

▶ The .NET Framework reference at http://msdn.microsoft.com/en-us/library/w0x726c2(VS.110).aspx

▶ The Visual Basic page on the Visual Studio Developer Center at http://msdn.com/vbasic

You can also quickly find information on particular objects using built-in tools, such as the Object Browser.

MANAGING HELP CONTENTS

You can download additional documentation or remove documentation that is already on your system by selecting Help, Add or Remove Help Content.

Object Browser Window

The Object Browser is a special tool window that enables you to browse the .NET Framework class library as well as any referenced libraries and types defined in your projects. You can get a hierarchical view of the Base Class Library and of all the types defined in your solution, including types defined in referenced external assemblies. The Object Browser can be activated by pressing **CTRL+ALT+J**; it is useful because you can understand how a type is defined, which members it exposes, which interfaces it implements, and which other classes it derives from. If the types are documented, you can get a description for each object or member.

Figure 2.35 represents, as an example, the Object Browser showing members of the `System.Windows.ContentElement` class.

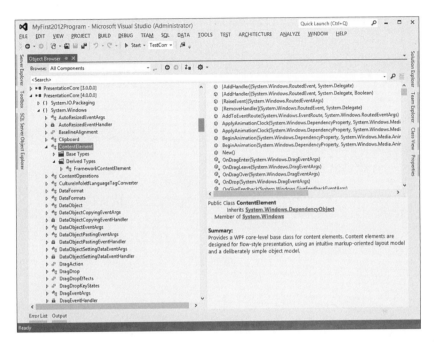

FIGURE 2.35   The Object Browser enables exploring .NET objects showing information.

The right side of the window lists methods and properties exposed by the selected object. When you click on a method or on a member of the object in the left side of the window, a short description of the object should appear in the bottom-right side of the Object Browser. If the description is not useful enough to understand the meaning of an object or of one of its members, you can press **F1**, and Visual Studio shows the online help (if available) for the object or member. The Object Browser also provides links to objects used by the one you are exploring. Considering the example shown in Figure 2.35, you not only can see the description of a method, but also can also click the parameters' identifiers to be redirected to the definition of the parameter. The Object Browser can also be invoked when writing code, as discussed next.

Invoking the Object Browser from the Code Editor
Often you need to know how particular .NET objects or members are structured or how they work. Visual Studio 2012 provides the ability of invoking the Object Browser directly from the code editor by right-clicking the object you want to browse and selecting the **Go to Definition** command from the pop-up menu. For example, imagine you

want to know how the `Console` class is defined. To accomplish this, you can revisit the MyFirst2012Program example. When in the code editor, right-click the `Console` object and select Go To Definition. By doing this, Visual Studio opens the Object Browser that automatically selects the `Console` class, showing its methods on the right side of the screen (see Figure 2.36).

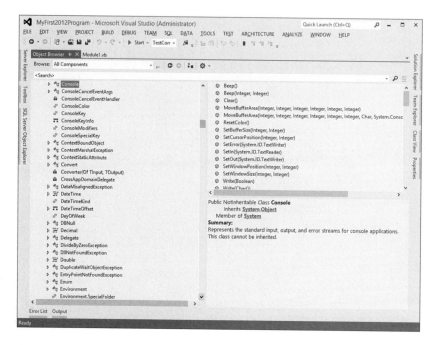

FIGURE 2.36   The Object Browser can be invoked from the code editor by clicking the Go to Definition command.

This technique works with shared classes or, more generally, with declarations of noninstance classes; however, in some situations you might want to learn about data types or instance members' definitions. For example, consider the following code:

```
Dim text As String
text = "Hi!"
```

If you try to run the Go to Definition command for the text identifier, you will be redirected to the first line of code, which effectively defines the text object. But what if you want to browse the `String` object? Fortunately there is another command you can choose in such situations—Go to Type Definition. It is still available in the pop-up menu. Invoking Go to Type Definition redirects to the definition of the type that characterizes the object you declared (in our example, `String`). The result will be the same as in Figure 2.36, of course referring to the selected type.

> **NOTE**
>
> Instance and shared members are discussed in detail in Chapter 7, "Class Fundamentals."

Although the Object Browser's purpose is not typically to provide help, it is a good place for learning about .NET objects, both if you need information on their structure and if you need descriptions on their usage.

Quick Launch Tool

Visual Studio 2012 introduces a new tool called Quick Launch. The purpose of this tool is making it easy to find commands, options, and recently opened files. The tool is available through a search box located at the upper right corner of the IDE. For example, imagine you need to launch the SQL Server Object Explorer window but do not remember where the command for launching such a window is and do not want to waste time browsing every menu. If you type "SQL" in the Quick Launch search box, Visual Studio will show all menu commands, options, and recently opened files (if any) containing the "SQL" word. As you can see from Figure 2.37 the SQL Server Object Explorer is the first search result, so you can simply click it to open the desired tool.

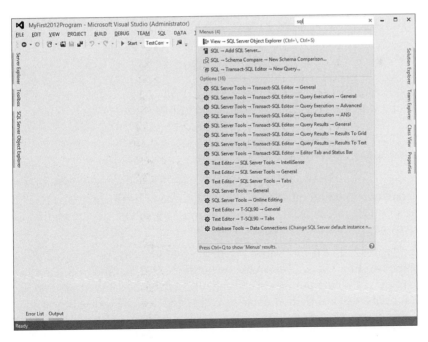

FIGURE 2.37   Finding commands and options with Quick Launch.

To understand how it works, repeat the search and select the SQL Server Tools -> General option from the list. You will see how Visual Studio will open the Options dialog box pointing to the requested setting. This is a useful tool that can save a lot of time in finding the necessary tools.

Showing the Hierarchy of Method Calls

Visual Studio 2012 brings to Visual Basic a tool window named Call Hierarchy, which was already introduced for Visual C# in Visual Studio 2010. As its name implies, Call Hierarchy enables the showing of the hierarchy of calls to and from one or more methods. To understand how it works, let's consider the following code:

```
Module Module1

  Sub Main()
    DoSomething()
  End Sub

  Sub DoSomething()
    DoSomethingElse()
  End Sub

  Sub DoSomethingElse()
    DoNothing()
  End Sub

  Sub DoNothing()
    '
  End Sub

End Module
```

The code defines some method, without performing any particular tasks, but it demonstrates a nested hierarchy of method calls. If you right-click one of the method's names and then select View Call Hierarchy from the pop-up menu, you will be able to see the method call hierarchy as demonstrated in Figure 2.38.

As you can see from Figure 2.38, the tool shows the first level hierarchy, but you can also expand method names to show the full hierarchy, including nested method calls. On the right side of the window is the line number in the code file where the selected method is defined. Also, if you double-click a method name in Call Hierarchy, the code editor will automatically focus on the method definition.

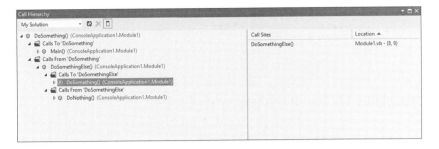

FIGURE 2.38   Analyzing method calls with Call Hierarchy.

Summary

In this chapter we discussed basic things you need to know as a Visual Basic developer to feel at home within the Visual Studio 2012 Integrated Development Environment. Tasks such as creating projects, compiling projects, debugging applications, and searching for documentation and tools are the most common in a developer's life, and this chapter offers a fast way to understand all the primary tools you need for building applications with Visual Basic 2012. You also saw some new tools introduced by Visual Studio 2012, such as Quick Launch and Call Hierarchy. Now that you know how you can move inside the IDE, it's time to begin working with the Visual Basic programming language.

CHAPTER 3

The Anatomy of a Visual Basic Project

Although you can create lots of kinds of projects both for Windows and the Web with Visual Basic 2012, there is a common set of files for each project. In this chapter you learn which files give the structure to each project and how the files influence the building of an application. You also get an overview of references, namespaces, classes, modules, and Visual Basic keywords.

Brief Overview of Types and Members

In the second part of this book, we discuss important topics related to object-oriented programming with Visual Basic 2012, and we explore features such as types, classes, modules, namespaces, interfaces, and class members. Before going into this, it would be a good idea to have at least an overview of classes, modules, namespaces, and class members because you will find these objects in code examples or in Visual Basic features that are shown prior to Chapter 7, "Class Fundamentals."

IF SOMETHING IS NOT CLEAR

The following is only a brief overview of some important topics. Don't be afraid if any of the following concepts are not clear or worry if things seem small. Starting in Chapter 4, "Data Types and Expressions," and continuing through Part II, "Object-Oriented Programming with Visual Basic 2012," of this book, all concepts are discussed in detail.

Classes

Classes in .NET development represent objects whose declaration is enclosed within `Class..End Class` blocks. The following is an example of class declaration:

```
Class Person
End Class
```

Classes are *reference types* (explained more in Chapter 4) and can expose members that influence the object's behavior, such as properties *and* methods. Classes can implement interfaces; they can also be static (or Shared according to the VB terminology) and can provide support for inheritance.

Properties

Properties are characteristics of a type. For example,, the previously shown class `Person` could have two properties, such as the first name and the last name:

```
Class Person
   Property FirstName As String
   Property LastName As String
End Class
```

PROPERTIES IN THE LATEST VERSIONS OF VISUAL BASIC

Visual Basic 2010 first introduced a new syntax for properties known as *auto-implemented properties*. To declare properties you need the Property keyword without explicitly specifying getters and setters. This is discussed further in Chapter 7.

Methods

Methods are the .NET representation of what in other programming environments you define as functions and procedures. A method can be a member of classes, structures, and modules. Methods that return a value are represented by `Function..End Function` blocks, such as the following:

```
Function DoSomething() As String
      Return "A text message"
End Function
```

Methods that do not return a value are represented by `Sub..End Sub` blocks, such as the following:

```
Sub DoSomething()
'write your code here
End Sub
```

Methods can receive parameters that can be processed within code blocks. Such parameters are called, using .NET terminology, *arguments*. The following code block shows an example of an argument named message:

```
Sub DoSomething(ByVal message As String)
    Console.Writeline(message)
End Sub
```

Modules

Modules are defined within a `Module..End Module` code block. Modules are basically `Shared` classes but, unlike classes, they cannot implement interfaces or use inheritance. The following is an example of a module:

```
Module Module1

    Sub DoSomething()
        'Code goes here
    End Sub
End Module
```

Members defined inside modules don't require the name of the module when invoked.

Structures

Structures are .NET objects represented by a `Structure..End Structure` code block. Structures are *value types*, which are described more in Chapter 4, and for classes, can expose properties, methods, and so on. The following is an example of a structure declaration:

```
Structure SomeValues

    Property FirstValue As Boolean
    Property SecondValue As Integer

    Sub DoSomething()

    End Sub
End Structure
```

Inheritance

Inheritance is one of the most important features of the .NET Framework. A class can inherit or derive from another class, meaning that the new class can have all properties, methods, and members exposed by the first class, which is called "the base class;" it can then define its own members. Inherited members can then be overridden to adapt their behavior to the new class's context. The .NET Framework provides one-level inheritance, meaning that a class can inherit from one other class per time. Each class derives implicitly from `System.Object`. The `Inherits` keyword is used to inherit classes. The following code provides an example of a base class named `Person` and of a derived class named `Customer`:

```
Public Class Person
    Public Property FirstName As String
    Public Property LastName As String

    'A new definition of System.Object.ToString
    Public Overrides Function ToString() As String
        Return String.Concat(FirstName, " ", LastName)
    End Function
End Class

Public Class Customer
    Inherits Person

    Public Property CompanyName As String

    Public Overrides Function ToString() As String
        Return CompanyName
    End Function

End Class
```

In the preceding example, the `Person` class overrides (that is, provides a new definition of) the `System.Object.ToString` method. The `Customer` class exposes a new `CompanyName` property whereas, via inheritance, it exposes the `FirstName` and `LastName` properties. Finally, the class also overrides the `Person.ToString` method. Inheritance is discussed in Chapter 12, "Inheritance."

Namespaces

A *namespace* is basically a container of types. This means that one namespace can contain multiple classes, multiple modules, multiple interfaces, multiple structures, and so on. The following is an example of a namespace exposing two classes, one module, one structure, and one interface:

```
Namespace Test

    Class Person
        Property FirstName As String
        Property LastName As String
    End Class
```

```
    Class Employee
        Inherits Person

        Property EmployeeID As Integer
    End Class

    Module Module1

        Sub DoSomething()

        End Sub
    End Module

    Interface ITest
        Sub TakeATest()
    End Interface

    Structure SomeValues
        Property FirstValue As Boolean
        Property SecondValue As Integer
    End Structure
End Namespace
```

Namespaces are important for a better organization of types, but there is another reason. You could have two classes with the same name (for example, `Employee`) but with different properties. Namespaces enable you to avoid conflicts in such scenarios. You can access types exposed by a namespace by writing its identifier followed by a dot and then by the type name. For example,, if you want to invoke the method `DoSomething` in Module1 you could write the following line of code:

```
Test.Module1.DoSomething()
```

Namespaces are described in detail in Chapter 9, "Organizing Types Within Namespaces," where you will also find a discussion about a new feature in Visual Basic 2012: global namespaces.

Accessing Members

Unless you declare shared objects, you need to instantiate classes and structures before you can use members and store information within those objects. You instantiate a class declaring a variable and using the `New` keyword as in the following line of code:

```
Dim testPerson As New Person
```

Then you can set properties for the new instance or eventually invoke other members such as methods. For example,, you could initialize `testPerson`'s properties as follows:

```
testPerson.FirstName = "Alessandro"
testPerson.LastName = "Del Sole"
```

When you need to invoke a member of a class, you type the name of the instance (in this example `testPerson`) followed by a dot and the name of the member. For shared members, you just write the name of the class or structure followed by a dot and the name of the member.

INITIALIZING MEMBERS

Since version 2008, Visual Basic offers an alternative way for initializing members' values when instantiating classes. This feature is known as Object Initializers and is discussed in Chapter 7.

`Imports` Directives

As you saw before, namespaces can expose objects that expose members. Moreover, namespaces can expose nested namespaces, exposing objects and so on. You often need to access members of objects exposed by nested namespaces. To avoid the need to type the entire name of long (or nested) namespaces and write long lines of code, the Visual Basic language offers the `Imports` directive. For example, consider the following lines of code that open a file on disk:

```
Dim myFile As New System.IO.FileStream("C:\test.bin",
                              IO.FileMode.Open)


myFile.Close()
```

The `FileStream` class is exposed by the `IO` namespace that is exposed by the `System` namespace. You could place the following directive at the beginning of the code:

```
Imports System.IO
```

At this point the first line of code could be rewritten as follows:

```
Dim myFile As New FileStream("C:\test.bin", FileMode.Open)
```

Since you might be using long namespaces, Visual Basic offers a feature known as namespace aliasing, which allows defining a custom identifier to represent the namespace. The following line demonstrates how to define a `GZip` identifier to import the `System.IO.Compression` namespace:

```
Imports GZip = System.IO.Compression
```

This is useful when you need to invoke members of the namespace in code, like in the following example:

```
'Instead of using System.IO.Compression.GZipStream,
'you can use a shortened format with namespace aliasing
Dim archive As GZip.GZipStream
```

`Imports` directives are useful because they help to handle a much clearer code. Just remember that such directives must be the first lines of each code file. The only exception is constituted by the `Option` clause that must precede the `Imports` directives and, of course, by comments.

Region Directives

Visual Basic provides an efficient way for organizing your code within regions. A region represents a collapsible area of the code editor that can contain any code and that takes advantage of the outlining feature of the Visual Studio 2012 code editor. Regions are defined with `#Region..#End Region` directives. The following code snippet shows how to define a region:

```
#Region "Private Members"

    Private firstItem As String
    Private secondItem As Integer

#End Region
```

The `#Region` directive requires the specification of a descriptive caption. When you declare regions, you can then collapse regions by clicking the - (minus) symbol on the left of the `#Region` directive. When collapsed, the region shows just the descriptive caption and can then be expanded again by clicking the + (plus) symbol. Also notice that the Visual Studio 2012 IDE allows collapsing a region by double-clicking anywhere on the `#Region..#End Region` connector line on the left side of the code window. Such directives will not be compiled and will not affect performance at all.

Attributes

Attributes are classes deriving from the `System.Attribute` class and provide declarative information to objects or members they are applied to, providing the capability to change their behavior. As a convention, applying an attribute is also known as *decorating* or *marking* a member. Attributes are basically class instances; you can apply attributes enclosing their names within < > symbols; moreover they can receive arguments. The following are examples of decorating members with attributes:

```
<Serializable()> Class Test

End Class

<CLSCompliant(True)> Class Test

End Class
```

In the preceding snippets, the `Serializable` attribute creates a new instance of the `System.SerializableAttribute` class that indicates to the compiler that the decorated class can take advantage of the serialization process. The `CLSCompliant` attribute, whose value is True, means that the decorated class is compliant to Microsoft's Common Language Specifications. Attributes are discussed in Chapter 47, "Coding Attributes," and you often find examples in this book that require code to be decorated with attributes.

Implicit Line Continuation

In versions of Visual Basic prior to 2010, if you needed to split a long line of code into more brief and readable lines of code in the editor, you had to add an underscore (_) character. This is no longer necessary due to a feature called *implicit line continuation*, which makes the underscore unnecessary. You can press Enter when you need to split a line of code, and the compiler will automatically recognize a line continuation, depending on the type of code you are writing. In some situations, implicit line continuation is not allowed; the following is a list of situations in which the implicit line continuation is allowed:

- ▶ Within LINQ queries
- ▶ Within embedded expressions in LINQ to XML queries
- ▶ After dots
- ▶ After commas
- ▶ After brackets
- ▶ When decorating members with attributes
- ▶ Before an assignment

Let's see how implicit line continuation works. The first code snippet shows a LINQ query:

```
Dim query = From proc In Process.GetProcesses.AsEnumerable
            Where (proc.ProcessName.StartsWith("A"))
            Select proc
```

Before Visual Basic 2010, you needed to add an underscore after the first and second lines of code. Fortunately, this is no longer necessary. The second code snippet shows a LINQ to XML query with embedded expressions without underscores:

```
Dim doc = <?xml version="1.0"?>
          <Processes>
```

```
<%= From proc In query
  Select <Process>
            <Name <%= proc.ProcessName %>/>
         </Process>
 %>
</Processes>
```

The third code snippet shows both commas and brackets without underscores:

```
Dim p As New List(Of Integer) From {
                                     1,
                                     2,
                                     3,
                                     4}
```

The fourth code snippet is about dots. In this case implicit line continuation can be useful when invoking methods or properties:

```
Dim appDataDir As String = My.Computer.FileSystem.
SpecialDirectories.AllUsersApplicationData()
```

The fifth code snippet shows implicit line continuation with attributes:

```
<CLSCompliant(True)>
Class Test

End Class
```

The sixth and last code snippet demonstrates how you can use implicit line continuation before an assignment:

```
Dim aValue As Integer
aValue =
        10
```

All the preceding code snippets are now perfectly legal. In all cases other than the preceding examples, implicit line continuation is not allowed. For example, you still must add an underscore after the Handles clause when handling events:

```
Private Sub AnEventHandler(ByVal sender As Object, ByVal e As EventArgs) _
                     Handles anObject.Disposed

End Sub
```

Of course, implicit line continuation is not mandatory: If you still prefer using the underscore when writing code, you can certainly do that.

Visual Basic 2012 Reserved Keywords

When writing code, you often define types or declare variables. Types and variables are recognizable via *identifiers*. An identifier is essentially the name of a type or of a variable and not necessarily a word that makes sense, although it is a good practice to assign human-readable identifiers. For example, an identifier such as *DoSomething* is much better than *DoSmt*. For this, there are some words in the Visual Basic lexical grammar that you cannot use as identifiers for your variables because they are reserved for the language.

IDENTIFIERS NAMING CONVENTIONS

.NET programming principles establish that identifiers must match some rules when writing code, including identifiers. Such naming conventions are stated by the Common Language Specifications, which are covered in Chapter 20, "Advanced Language Features." For now, keep in mind the best practice regarding human-readable identifiers. Later in the book you learn how identifiers should be correctly written.

Table 3.1 shows a list of the Visual Basic 2012 reserved words.

TABLE 3.1   Visual Basic 2012 Reserved Keywords

AddHandler	AddressOf	Alias	And
AndAlso	As	Boolean	ByRef
Byte	ByVal	Call	Case
Catch	CBool	CByte	CChar
CDate	CDbl	CDec	Char
CInt	Class	CLng	CObj
Const	Continue	CSByte	CShort
CSng	CStr	CType	CUInt
CULng	CUShort	Date	Decimal
Declare	Default	Delegate	Dim
DirectCast	Do	Double	Each
Else	ElseIf	End	EndIf
Enum	Erase	Error	Event
Exit	False	Finally	For
Friend	Function	Get	GetType
GetXmlNamespace	Global	GoSub	GoTo
Handles	If	Implements	Imports
In	Inherits	Integer	Interface
Is	IsNot	Let	Lib
Like	Long	Loop	Me
Mod	Module	MustInherit	MustOverride
MyBase	MyClass	Namespace	Narrowing

New	Next	Not	Nothing
NotInheritable	NotOverridable	Object	Of
On	Operator	Option	Optional
Or	OrElse	Overloads	Overridable
Overrides	ParamArray	Partial	Private
Property	Protected	Public	RaiseEvent
ReadOnly	ReDim	REM	RemoveHandler
Resume	Return	SByte	Select
Set	Shadows	Shared	Short
Single	Static	Step	Stop
String	Structure	Sub	SyncLock
Then	Throw	To	True
Try	TryCast	TypeOf	UInteger
ULong	UShort	Using	Variant
Wend	When	While	Widening
With	WithEvents	WriteOnly	Xor

USING RESERVED WORDS AS IDENTIFIERS

As an exception, you can use reserved words as identifiers, enclosing them in a couple of square brackets. For example, `New` is a reserved word and cannot be used whereas `[New]` can be accepted. Although allowed, this practice should be used only in particular cases because it could lead to confusion—especially if you are not an experienced developer.

Although the code editor is powerful enough to advise when you are attempting to use a reserved keyword as an identifier, having a reference is practical. In addition, a number of so-called *unreserved keywords* are available that are basically words you can use as identifiers but that the programming language keeps for its own usage with particular technologies or scenarios. Table 3.2 provides the full list of unreserved keywords. The suggestion is to always avoid the usage of unreserved keywords as identifiers for your objects or variables.

TABLE 3.2   Visual Basic 2012 Unreserved Keywords

Aggregate	Ansi	Assembly	Async
Auto	Await	Binary	Compare
Custom	Distinct	Equals	Explicit
From	Group By	Group Join	Into
IsFalse	IsTrue	Iterator	Join
Key	Mid	Off	Order By
Preserve	Skip	Skip While	Strict

Take	Take While	Text	Unicode
Until	Where	Yield	#Region
#ExternalSource			

VISUAL BASIC IS CASE-INSENSITIVE

When writing code, remember that Visual Basic is a case-insensitive programming language. This means that, unlike C#, writing Hello is the same of writing HELLO or hello or heLLo. Take care with this feature when assigning identifiers.

Understanding Project Files

Each Visual Basic project is composed of several code files. Some of them are by default visible to the developer and are the ones you need to edit to create your application. Additionally, some other files (which are hidden by default but can be made visible manually) can be considered as support files. To understand the kind of support these files offer, consider that most of the settings we can provide to our applications via the My Project window are represented with Visual Basic code. Particularly, Visual Basic translates into code the content of the Application, Resources, Settings and My Extensions tabs. In this chapter you get a detailed description of files that represent the Application tab in My Project; then you get an overview of files that represent other tabs. Although you seldom edit these code files manually because all of them have design time support from My Project (as detailed in Chapter 19, "The My Namespace," when describing the My namespace), there could be some situations in which you need to manually edit them. Thus, it's important to know something about them. Before continuing, you need to click the **Show All Files** button in Solution Explorer. This gives visibility to several code files that are hidden by default and that provide the main infrastructure for each Visual Basic project. Notice that Windows 8 projects for Windows 8 applications have a slightly different structure; because the focus of this book is not Windows 8 development, in this chapter you learn about the composition of Visual Basic projects except Windows 8 ones.

Dissecting My Project

In Chapter 2 we introduced the My Project window and showed how it offers graphical tools for specifying some settings when developing applications, such as application information and compile options. Understanding My Project is important because it also provides the infrastructure of the My namespace, offering the ability for specifying important settings that are discussed in Chapter 19. For now, you need to know that My Project offers a graphical representation of information stored in some code files. In Solution Explorer is an element named My Project. When you double-click this element, you are redirected to the My Project window. But when you enable the All Files view, you notice how the My Project element can be expanded. Within this element (which is a folder physically stored inside the project's folder and that contains all files described in this section), you can notice the presence of several files packaged into the assembly's meta-data when you build the project. We now describe such files and how they work.

MY PROJECT IS VERSATILE

Depending on the kind of application you develop, My Project can implement additional tabs or remove some. For example, if you develop a Silverlight application, you can find tabs in My Project that are specific for Silverlight and that will be discussed in the appropriate chapters.

Application.MyApp

The Application.myapp file is an XML representation of the project's main properties. Listing 3.1 shows the content of this file as it becomes available when you create a new Console application.

LISTING 3.1   The Content of Application.myapp

```
<?xml version="1.0" encoding="utf-8"?>
<MyApplicationData xmlns:xsi="http://www.w3.org/2001/XMLSchema-instance"
xmlns:xsd="http://www.w3.org/2001/XMLSchema">
  <MySubMain>false</MySubMain>
  <SingleInstance>false</SingleInstance>
  <ShutdownMode>0</ShutdownMode>
  <EnableVisualStyles>true</EnableVisualStyles>
  <AuthenticationMode>0</AuthenticationMode>
  <ApplicationType>2</ApplicationType>
  <SaveMySettingsOnExit>true</SaveMySettingsOnExit>
</MyApplicationData>
```

XML elements in this file are self-explanatory, and you might notice how each of them represents a particular item on the Application tab. The Application.myapp file is the brother of another file named Application.Designer.vb. Such a file stores information related to Windows Forms applications, such as the authentication mode and the shut-down mode. It is the complement for those application options that you can see in the Windows Application Framework Properties group in the Application tab. Listing 3.2 shows the content of the Application.Designer.vb as it is generated for a Windows Forms application.

WINDOWS FORMS COMPATIBILITY

Even if Windows Forms will not be discussed in this book because it is an obsolete presentation technology, this paragraph has some reference to Windows Forms for compatibility with existing applications and to provide a way to get a deeper knowledge of what you have developed in the past (or that you are currently building with that platform).

LISTING 3.2   The Content of Application.Designer.vb

```
Partial Friend Class MyApplication
        Public Sub New()
                MyBase.New(Global.Microsoft.VisualBasic.ApplicationServices.
    AuthenticationMode.Windows)
                Me.IsSingleInstance = false
                Me.EnableVisualStyles = true
                Me.SaveMySettingsOnExit = true
                Me.ShutDownStyle = Global.Microsoft.VisualBasic.ApplicationServices.
    ShutdownMode.AfterMainFormCloses
        End Sub


        Protected Overrides Sub OnCreateMainForm()
                Me.MainForm = Global.WindowsApplication1.Form1
        End Sub
End Class
```

For the sake of simplicity, in the preceding code some attributes are omitted that Visual Studio adds to class members and that are related to the debugger interaction. As you can see examining Listing 3.2, items in the Application tab of My Project have been mapped to Visual Basic properties. The Me identifier represents the instance of the current application. The OnCreateMainForm method establishes which window must be the startup one. In this case, Form1 is the default name that Visual Studio assigns to the main window when a new project is created. If you also examine the code inside the IDE, you can notice how some comments in the code advise that the code itself is auto-generated and that you should not edit it manually because you can use the My Project designer that will automatically map changes to the Visual Basic code. You might need to set custom actions for application events (such as Startup or Shutdown, which are usually handled in the ApplicationEvents.vb file), and **Application.designer.vb** is the right place.

AssemblyInfo.vb

In Chapter 2 we discussed the **Assembly Information** dialog box, describing how it is used for specifying information about applications. All the information is stored in a file named **AssemblyInfo.vb**. Listing 3.3 shows the content of this file as it is available when you create a new project.

LISTING 3.3   AssemblyInfo.vb Content

```
Imports System
Imports System.Reflection
Imports System.Runtime.InteropServices


' General Information about an assembly is controlled through the following
' set of attributes. Change these attribute values to modify the information
' associated with an assembly.
```

```
' Review the values of the assembly attributes

<Assembly: AssemblyTitle("WindowsApplication1")>
<Assembly: AssemblyDescription("")>
<Assembly: AssemblyCompany("")>
<Assembly: AssemblyProduct("WindowsApplication1")>
<Assembly: AssemblyCopyright("Copyright © 2009")>
<Assembly: AssemblyTrademark("")>


<Assembly: ComVisible(False)>


'The following GUID is for the ID of the typelib if this project is exposed to COM
<Assembly: Guid("5572d199-a7ca-48c3-98d3-56533cd6ba86")>


' Version information for an assembly consists of the following four values:
'
'       Major Version
'       Minor Version
'       Build Number
'       Revision
'
' You can specify all the values or you can default the Build and Revision Numbers
' by using the '*' as shown below:
' <Assembly: AssemblyVersion("1.0.*")>


<Assembly: AssemblyVersion("1.0.0.0")>
<Assembly: AssemblyFileVersion("1.0.0.0")>
```

In Listing 3.3, there are several items whose identifier begins with the word *Assembly*, such as `AssemblyTitle`, `AssemblyCompany`, and so on. Each item is in relationship with fields of the Assembly Information dialog box. Such items are marked with an attribute named `Assembly`. Attributes are discussed in Chapter 47. The reason it is useful to know about the previous file is because sometimes you'll need to edit this file manually. Examples are localization of WPF applications or marking an assembly as compliant to *Microsoft Common Language Specifications*.

Resources and the Resources.resx File

Visual Studio 2012 enables defining resources that you can embed in your assembly's metadata and use within your applications. Resources can include strings, icons, picture files, audio files, and so on. My Project offers a tab named Resources that provides a visual way for defining project level resources.

PRACTICAL USAGE OF RESOURCES

Although available in several kinds of projects, resources have to be used to fit particular scenarios. For example, resources can be successfully used in Windows applications such as Console and Windows Forms, but they are not the best choice for Windows Presentation Foundation applications. So you need to pay attention when using resources according to the particular situations.

Figure 3.1 shows the Resources designer with the definition of a `String` resource named `TextMessage` that has a value and a description. We revisit the Resources tab in Chapter 19, where we discuss My namespace, but if you are curious, you can play with the designer to see what types of resources you can add.

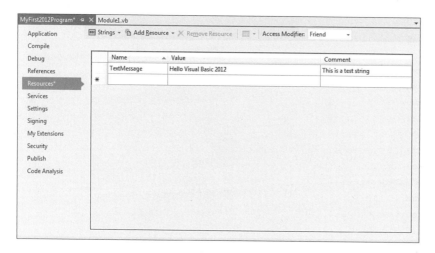

FIGURE 3.1   The My Resources designer.

Resources are supported by two files stored inside the My Project folder: Resources.resx and Resources.designer.vb. The first one is basically an XML schema used by Visual Studio for working with resources. Listing 3.4 shows the content of the schema.

LISTING 3.4   The Content of Resources.resx

```
<root>
  <xsd:schema id="root" xmlns="" xmlns:xsd="http://www.w3.org/2001/XMLSchema"
  xmlns:msdata="urn:schemas-microsoft-com:xml-msdata">
    <xsd:import namespace="http://www.w3.org/XML/1998/namespace" />
    <xsd:element name="root" msdata:IsDataSet="true">
      <xsd:complexType>
        <xsd:choice maxOccurs="unbounded">
          <xsd:element name="metadata">
            <xsd:complexType>
              <xsd:sequence>
```

```
              <xsd:element name="value" type="xsd:string" minOccurs="0" />
            </xsd:sequence>
            <xsd:attribute name="name" use="required" type="xsd:string" />
            <xsd:attribute name="type" type="xsd:string" />
            <xsd:attribute name="mimetype" type="xsd:string" />
            <xsd:attribute ref="xml:space" />
          </xsd:complexType>
        </xsd:element>
        <xsd:element name="assembly">
          <xsd:complexType>
            <xsd:attribute name="alias" type="xsd:string" />
            <xsd:attribute name="name" type="xsd:string" />
          </xsd:complexType>
        </xsd:element>
        <xsd:element name="data">
          <xsd:complexType>
            <xsd:sequence>
              <xsd:element name="value" type="xsd:string" minOccurs="0"
➥msdata:Ordinal="1" />
              <xsd:element name="comment" type="xsd:string" minOccurs="0"
➥msdata:Ordinal="2" />
            </xsd:sequence>
            <xsd:attribute name="name" type="xsd:string" use="required"
➥msdata:Ordinal="1" />
            <xsd:attribute name="type" type="xsd:string" msdata:Ordinal="3" />
            <xsd:attribute name="mimetype" type="xsd:string" msdata:Ordinal="4" />
            <xsd:attribute ref="xml:space" />
          </xsd:complexType>
        </xsd:element>
        <xsd:element name="resheader">
          <xsd:complexType>
            <xsd:sequence>
              <xsd:element name="value" type="xsd:string" minOccurs="0"
➥msdata:Ordinal="1" />
            </xsd:sequence>
            <xsd:attribute name="name" type="xsd:string" use="required" />
          </xsd:complexType>
        </xsd:element>
      </xsd:choice>
    </xsd:complexType>
  </xsd:element>
</xsd:schema>
<resheader name="resmimetype">
  <value>text/microsoft-resx</value>
</resheader>
<resheader name="version">
```

```
   <value>2.0</value>
  </resheader>
  <resheader name="reader">
    <value>System.Resources.ResXResourceReader, System.Windows.Forms,
     Version=4.0.0.0, Culture=neutral, PublicKeyToken=b77a5c561934e089</value>
  </resheader>
  <resheader name="writer">
    <value>System.Resources.ResXResourceWriter, System.Windows.Forms,
➥Version=4.0.0.0, Culture=neutral, PublicKeyToken=b77a5c561934e089</value>
  </resheader>
  <data name="TextMessage" xml:space="preserve">
    <value>Hello Visual Basic 2012!</value>
    <comment>This is a test string</comment>
  </data>
</root>
```

This schema establishes how a resource is defined, with names, values, comments, and a MIME (Multipurpose Internet Mail Extensions) type that identifies the file type. At the end of the XML markup code, you can see how resources are stored. Continuing with our example, you can see the name of the resource (inside the data element), its value, and the description we provided via the designer. This schema is used by Visual Studio for design time purposes. To work with resources in our applications, Visual Studio also needs to provide Visual Basic code support for resources. Such support is provided by a code file named Resources.designer.vb. This file handles a reference to a .NET object called ResourceManager that is responsible for managing resources in code. Listing 3.5 shows the content of Resources.designer.vb. (For the sake of simplicity, auto-generated attributes are not covered here.)

LISTING 3.5   Content of Resources.designer.vb

```
Friend Module Resources

        Private resourceMan As Global.System.Resources.ResourceManager

        Private resourceCulture As Global.System.Globalization.CultureInfo

        Friend ReadOnly Property ResourceManager() As
    Global.System.Resources.ResourceManager
            Get
                If Object.ReferenceEquals(resourceMan, Nothing) Then
                    Dim temp As Global.System.Resources.ResourceManager =
    New Global.System.Resources.ResourceManager("MyFirst2012Program.Resources",
    GetType(Resources).Assembly)
                    resourceMan = temp
                End If
                Return resourceMan
```

```
        End Get
    End Property

    Friend Property Culture() As Global.System.Globalization.CultureInfo
        Get
            Return resourceCulture
        End Get
        Set(ByVal value As Global.System.Globalization.CultureInfo)
            resourceCulture = value
        End Set
    End Property

    Friend ReadOnly Property TextMessage() As String
        Get
            Return ResourceManager.GetString("TextMessage", resourceCulture)
        End Get
    End Property
End Module
```

At this point in the book you don't effectively need to know what each type used in code refers to, although it is useful to know the existence of the `ResourceManager` property that points to the project resources. (See the declaration of the `temp` variable.) This handles a reference to the application-level ResourceManager that enables access to resources. There is another property named `Culture` that is of type `System.Globalization.CultureInfo`. This property sets or returns the current localization for resources. The last property in the code is named `TextMessage` and is the Visual Basic representation of the string resource defined in My Project. This is a read-only property because you cannot change it in code (you can change it only via designer); it returns a localized version of the resource invoking the `GetString` method of the `ResourceManager` class. `GetString` requires an object of type `CultureInfo` (in our code it's `resourceCulture`) that represents the culture to which the resource must be localized. The following line of code shows how you can access the preceding defined resource, which is discussed further in Chapter 19:

```
Dim myString As String = My.Resources.TextMessage
```

When you access resources, as shown in Chapter 19, you do not need to manually invoke this background code, but you need to know how it is structured to better understand what's happening behind the scenes. Resources are not the only feature in My Project that is supported by Visual Basic code for design time features. Settings are another one of these features.

Application Settings

Settings in Visual Basic development are particular objects that provide a managed way for manipulating applications and user-level settings. For example, you could provide users with the ability to customize options in the user interface of your application. To save and read such customizations to and from disk, you can use .NET Settings. My Project provides a tab named Settings that enables specifying information at the application or user level. Figure 3.2 shows an example.

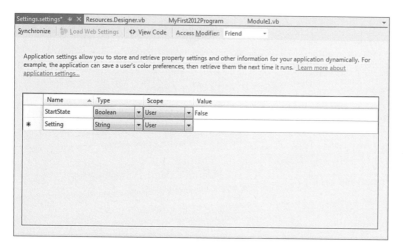

FIGURE 3.2   Settings tab in My Project.

As you can see in Figure 3.2, you can specify an identifier for each setting, a type (which you can understand better by reading Chapter 4), the scope, and the value. For the scope, User means that only the user who runs the application can use that setting. Application means that the setting is available at the application level, independently from the user who logged in to Windows (and therefore is available to all users). As with Resources, Settings are also described in detail in Chapter 19. Settings are represented by a simple XML file, named Settings.settings. Listing 3.6 shows the content of Settings.settings after the addition of the sample setting.

VIEWING THE SETTINGS.SETTINGS FILE WITH THE XML EDITOR

To view the XML content for the Settings.settings file, right-click the filename in Solution Explorer, select the Open With command, and select Xml (Text) Editor in the Open With dialog box.

LISTING 3.6   Settings.settings Content

```
<?xml version='1.0' encoding='utf-8'?>

<SettingsFile xmlns="http://schemas.microsoft.com/VisualStudio/2004/01/settings"
CurrentProfile="(Default)" GeneratedClassNamespace="My" GeneratedClass-
Name="MySettings" UseMySettingsClassName="true">
  <Profiles />
  <Settings>
    <Setting Name="StartState" Type="System.Boolean" Scope="User">
```

```
        <Value Profile="(Default)">True</Value>
      </Setting>
    </Settings>
</SettingsFile>
```

In the XML markup you can see the presence of a Settings node that stores as many Setting elements and as many settings that you specify in My Project. In our example there is just one Setting element that contains the name of the setting, the data type, the scope, and the default value (which means the value you specify in My Project). The Settings.settings file also has Visual Basic support, which is represented by another file named Settings.designer.vb. We do not need to examine all the content of this file when just a couple of parts of the code can be interesting for us. First, this file implements a property named Settings that is accessible via the My namespace, as detailed in Chapter 19. Listing 3.7 shows the definition of this property.

LISTING 3.7   Definition of the Settings Property

```
    Friend ReadOnly Property Settings() As
Global.MyFirst2012Program.My.MySettings
        Get
            Return Global.MyFirst2012Program.My.MySettings.Default
        End Get
    End Property
```

The Settings property represents the active instance of the Settings object that you can use in your applications. How the active instance is defined is beyond the scope of this chapter, but now you know that the Settings tab in My Project also has a counterpart in two support files. Just for your convenience, the following line of code shows how you can access settings and how we set them before:

```
Dim currentValue As Boolean = My.Settings.StartState
```

The value stored in the StartState setting will be assigned to a variable named currentValue. Examining the My namespace in Chapter 19 can clarify the usage of Settings and Resources and of many other interesting features.

Understanding References

The Base Class Library exposes types through several assemblies that are part of the .NET Framework, and you will often need to invoke types from those assemblies. Moreover, although very rich, the Base Class Library (BCL) cannot define types covering every aspect of application development. This means that you will often need to use types exposed by other assemblies, such as other projects in the same solution or external compiled assemblies.

NOTE

Each time you create a new project, Visual Studio automatically adds references to some .NET assemblies that are necessary for each kind of application and that expose the BCL's core part, such as System.dll and System.Core.dll.

To use types defined in external assemblies, you need to add a reference to the desired assembly in your project. To accomplish this, right-click the project name in Solution Explorer and click the **Add Reference** command from the pop-up menu or select the **References** tab in My Project and click **Add**. This activates the Reference Manager dialog box, as shown in Figure 3.3.

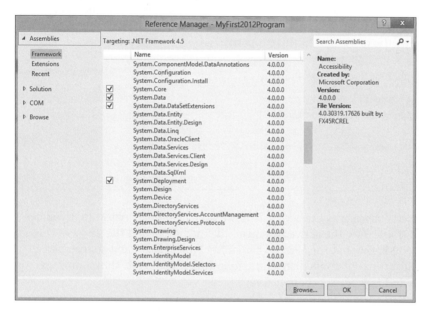

FIGURE 3.3   The Reference Manager dialog box.

You can select all the assemblies you want to reference; multiple selections are allowed by clicking the check box near the assembly name or by pressing **Ctrl** and then clicking the name of the required assembly. The Reference Manager dialog box is divided into several tabs. The default tab is named Assemblies and shows a list of all the available assemblies in the Global Assembly Cache through a group called Framework and a list of available assemblies exposed by installed extensions for Visual Studio through a group called Extensions.

WHAT IS THE GLOBAL ASSEMBLY CACHE?

The Global Assembly Cache (GAC) can be described as a repository for information and locations on installed assemblies. The .NET Framework knows where assemblies can be found by browsing the GAC, which also can distinguish between different versions of an assembly. The GAC is discussed in detail in Chapter 50, "Understanding the Global Assembly Cache."

The Reference Manager dialog box shows the version number of assemblies; this is useful because you can have different versions of an assembly with the same name. When you add a reference to an assembly, Solution Explorer updates the References node. For example, if you want to add security features to your applications, you need to add a reference to the System.Security.dll assembly (refer to Figure 3.3), which is part of the BCL. When added, Solution Explorer looks like Figure 3.4.

FIGURE 3.4   Solution Explorer is updated with the new reference.

You can use your code types exposed by the specified assemblies that have public visibility. The Reference Manager dialog box provides other tabs and groups. The Recent group in the Assemblies tab shows a list of all the most recently used assemblies for faster reuse. The Browse tab enables searching for assemblies that are not registered into the GAC. The Solution tab enables adding references to other projects in the solution. This is typically the case when you have a class library that exposes types you want to use inside a client application. Another tab, named COM, lets you add references to COM-type libraries as we discuss next.

Adding References to COM Libraries

You might come across situations in which you are required to use COM type libraries in your .NET applications, a scenario also known as COM Interop. This should be rare because .NET and COM are such different architectures, and the second one was not made to work within the first one. Visual Studio 2012 enables you to add references to old libraries. To accomplish this, you need to select the **COM** tab in the Reference Manager dialog box. All the registered COM-type libraries will be shown within the dialog box, and you can select the needed components (see Figure 3.5).

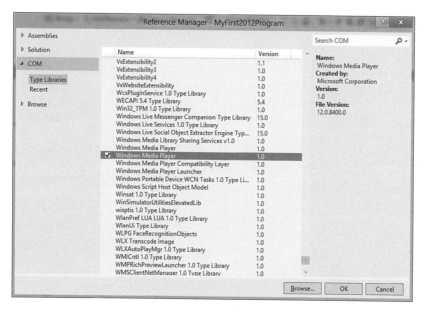

FIGURE 3.5   Adding a reference to a COM component.

For example, you might want to include the Windows Media Player functionalities in your application; to do this, you can select the **Windows Media Player** component and then click **OK** (see Figure 3.5). Visual Studio will show a reference named WMPLib.dll in Solution Explorer and generate an assembly named Interop.WMPLib.dll. This assembly is a managed wrapper for the Windows Media Player component and will provide managed access to types exposed by the type library. More generally, Visual Studio generates an Interop.AssemblyName.dll assembly (where AssemblyName is the original name of the assembly) for each referenced type library, which is known as Primary Interoperability Assembly (PIAs) and that allows interoperation between .NET and COM architectures. Different from previous versions of .NET Framework and Visual Studio, by default you no longer see the wrapper assemblies included in your build output because of a feature called Deploy Without Primary Interoperability Assemblies.

Deploy Without PIAs

When deploying applications that reference a COM library, you also must include in your distribution the primary interoperability assemblies. In our example, the PIA is Interop. WMPLib.dll. In Visual Studio 2012, you can avoid including primary interoperability assemblies in your distributions, although you reference those assemblies. This is possible because Visual Studio can embed in your executable only the types that you effectively use from the referenced assembly. This avoids the need of including the assembly itself in the build output and, consequently, in the deployment process. For our sample scenario about including the Windows Media Player component, we could write a small application that has the name of a media file provided by the user and then launches WMP. Listing 3.8 accomplishes this.

LISTING 3.8   Using a COM Component in Code

```
Module Module1
    Sub Main()

        Console.WriteLine("Type the name of a media file:")
        Dim fileName As String = Console.ReadLine

        Dim wmp As New WMPLib.WindowsMediaPlayer
        wmp.openPlayer(fileName)
    End Sub
End Module
```

In the preceding code, you need to take a look at this simple line:

```
Dim wmp As New WMPLib.WindowsMediaPlayer
```

Declaring an instance of the WMPLib.WindowsMediaPlayer class is sufficient for Visual Studio to embed the definition of the WindowsMediaPlayer object inside our executable so that it will not need to include the entire Interop.WMPLib.dll assembly in the build output. As you can imagine, this is a great feature because, if you have a large type library and you need to use only a few types, you can save space and preserve performances. The Deploy Without PIAs feature is enabled by default. If you instead prefer to avoid embedding types within your executable and including the primary interoperability assemblies in your build output, you need to right-click the referenced assembly in Solution Explorer and then click **Properties**. Continuing our example, you would need to select **WMPLib. dll** in Solution Explorer. The Properties window will show a property called Embed Interop Types that is set to True by default (see Figure 3.6).

If you change the value to False, types will no longer be embedded in your executable and the primary interoperability assemblies will be included in the build output.

VERIFYING TYPES EMBEDDING

If you are an experienced developer, you can easily verify whether types have been embedded in your executable via the Deploy Without PIAs feature by opening executables with tools such as Reflector or IL Disassembler.

FIGURE 3.6   Enabling the Deploy Without PIAs feature and setting the Embed Interop Types property.

Final Considerations

The first three chapters of this book provide a necessary overview of tools and features that you must understand before moving on. Now that you have completed the introductory steps, you are ready to get your hands dirty on the core of the Visual Basic 2012 programming language.

Summary

This chapter provided an overview of some important language features. You also got a complete list of the Visual Basic 2012 reserved words that you cannot use as identifiers for your variables. Another important topic discussed is how a Visual Basic project is structured and which files compose a Visual Basic project. Finally, you got an overview of references and why they are important in developing applications. In this discussion you learned about a new feature of Visual Studio 2012 and .NET Framework 4.5: the Deployment Without the Primary Interoperability Assemblies.

CHAPTER 4

Data Types and Expressions

Every programming task manipulates data. Data can be of different kinds; you will often work with strings, dates and time, numbers, files, and custom data. Each of them is represented by a data type. The .NET Framework 4.5 (but also the Windows Runtime for Windows 8) provides tons of built-in data types and enables developers to easily create their own custom data types. In this chapter you learn how the .NET Framework handles data types and how you can work with *value types* and *reference types*. When you gain knowledge of data types, you can learn how to use them with special Visual Basic language constraints such as loops, iterations, and special statements. This is a fundamental chapter, so you should pay particular attention to the concepts that you need to understand before we discuss the object-oriented programming with Visual Basic 2012.

Introducing the Common Type System

The .NET Framework provides a special way for manipulating data types, which is named *Common Type System*. The Common Type System is important, so you need to know something about it before reading discussions on data types. In its name, the word *Common* has two particular meanings. First, the Common Type System provides a unified model for exposing data types so that all the .NET languages, such as Visual Basic, Visual C#, and Visual F#, can consume the same data types. For example, a 32-bit integer is represented by the System.Int32 data type, and all the .NET languages can invoke the System.Int32 object for declaring integers because this type is provided by the

.NET Framework and is language-independent. Second, each data type is an object that inherits from the `System.Object` class as we discuss next.

Everything Is an Object

In the .NET development you might hear that everything is an object. This is because all the types in the .NET Framework, including built-in and custom types, inherit from the `System.Object` class. Inheritance is a concept that is part of the object-oriented programming topic and that is discussed later in the book. We can define it as a way for reusing and extending data types so developers can create their hierarchy of types. `System.Object` provides the primary infrastructure all .NET types must have. The .NET Framework ships with thousands of built-in data types that all derive from `System.Object`. But why is this class so important in the Common Type System? The answer is simple: the Common Type System ensures that all .NET types inherit from `System.Object`; particularly both *value types* and *reference types* inherit from `System.Object`. At this point an overview of value types and reference types is required before delving into both categories.

Introducing Value Types and Reference Types

Value types are those data types that store their data directly. Examples of value types are integers (`System.Int32`), Boolean (`System.Boolean`), and bytes (`System.Byte`). Value types are stored in a memory area called *Stack*. They are represented by (and defined via) structures that are enclosed in `Structure..End Structure` code blocks. The following is an example of a value type containing a value:

```
Dim anInteger As System.Int32 = 5
```

Reference types are instead data types that, as their name implies, are just a reference to the actual data. In other words, reference types store the address of their data in the Stack whereas the actual data is stored in the Managed Heap. Reference types are represented by classes. The following is an example of reference type:

```
Class Person
    Property FirstName As String
    Property LastName As String
End Class
```

DON'T BE AFRAID OF MEMORY LOCATIONS

This paragraph is just an overview of value types and reference types. If you never heard about the Stack and the Managed Heap, don't worry. Details will be provided later in this chapter, when discussing value and reference types.

Reference types inherit directly from `System.Object` or from other classes that derive from `Object`. This is because `System.Object` is a reference type. So the question that you will probably ask now is "If both value types and reference types have to inherit from `System.Object`, how can value types inherit from `System.Object` if it is a reference type?" The answer is that in the case of value types an intermediate type named `System.ValueType` inherits from `System.Object` and ensures that all deriving objects are treated as value types. This is possible because the Common Language Runtime can distinguish how types are defined and consequently can distinguish between value types and reference types.

NAMING `System.Object`

Object is also a reserved word of the Visual Basic programming language and is the representation of `System.Object`. Because of this, we refer indistinctly to `Object` as `System.Object`.

`System.Object` and `System.ValueType`

At this point, it is necessary to provide an overview of both `System.Object` and `System.ValueType`. Instead of showing a diagram of inheritance, it is a good idea to offer a Visual Studio–oriented view so you can better understand what happens within the development environment. This can be accomplished via the Object Browser tool window introduced in Chapter 2, "Getting Started with the Visual Studio 2012 IDE." You can browse for both classes by just writing their names in the search box. Figure 4.1 shows how `System.Object` is defined, which members it exposes, and a full description.

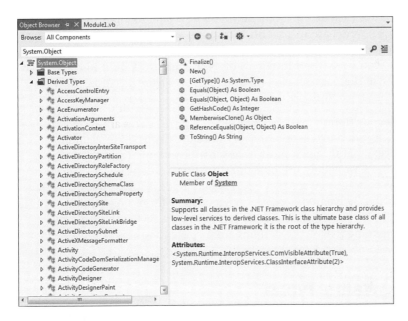

FIGURE 4.1   `System.Object` shown in detail in the Object Browser tool window.

Several things are worth mentioning. First, consider the class description. As you can see, `System.Object` is defined as the root of the type hierarchy, and all other classes within the .NET Framework derive from `System.Object`. This means that custom classes automatically inherit from `Object`. This class provides the infrastructure for all derived classes and exposes some methods. Because `System.Object` is important and because you will often invoke methods inherited from `Object`, it's convenient to get a simple reference for each method. Table 4.1 describes methods exposed by `System.Object`.

TABLE 4.1   Methods Exposed by `System.Object`

Method	Description
Equals	Compares two objects for equality
Finalize	Attempts to free up some resources during the object lifetime
New	Creates a new instance of the `Object` class
GetHashCode	Returns a hash code for the given object
GetType	Retrieves the qualified data type for the specified object
MemberwiseClone	Creates a shallow copy of the current `Object` instance
ReferenceEquals	Returns `true` if both the specified `Object` instances refer to the same instance
ToString	Provides a string representation of the `Object`

Methods listed in Table 4.1 are covered several times during the rest of the book, so don't be afraid if something is not clear at the moment. If you now refer to Figure 4.1, you can see how the `Object` class has no base types. This is because, as we said before, `Object` is the root in the type hierarchy. Considering this last sentence, if you instead try to expand the Derived types node, you see a list of hundreds of .NET Framework built-in classes that derive from `Object`. One of these classes is `System.ValueType`. Figure 4.2 shows how this class is represented in the Object Browser.

You should focus on the description first. As you can see, `System.ValueType` is the base class for all value types. It is declared as `MustInherit` (a clause discussed in detail in Chapter 12, "Inheritance") that means it must necessarily be inherited and that it can't work as a standalone object, providing the base infrastructure for derived value types. If you expand the Base types node, you see that `ValueType` is a derived class from `Object`. If you then try to expand the Derived types node, you get a large list of types that inherit from `ValueType`, such as `Boolean`, `Byte`, and other primitive data types. As mentioned before, the CLR can determine that a type deriving from `System.ValueType` must be treated as a value type and not as a reference type.

Understanding Value Types

Value types are data types that directly store data that they define. For example, a `System.Int32` object represents a value type that can store an integer number as in the following line of code:

```
Dim anInteger As System.Int32 = 5
```

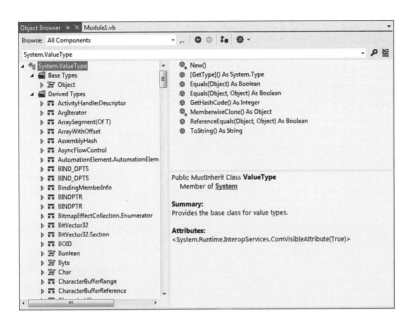

FIGURE 4.2 `System.ValueType` shown in detail in the Object Browser.

Among value types, the most common are numeric types that enable, for example, performing math operations or implementing counters or just storing a numeric value. Value types enable developers to choose the best data type according to the particular scenario. As we mentioned at the beginning of this chapter, value types are Structure objects. The .NET Framework provides several built-in value types that cover most needs in your development process, although you can create custom data types. In this section you learn about most common built-in value types and about building your own structures, including how value types are declared and used and how they are stored in memory.

.NET Framework Primitive Value Types

The .NET Framework Base Class Library provides lots of built-in value types that you can use according to your needs. Each value type is a structure exposed by the Base Class Library.

Visual Basic 2012 provides reserved words that are counterparts of the most common value type names. For example, the `System.Int32` value type has an alias in the `Integer` reserved word. The following two lines of code are perfectly equivalent:

```
Dim anInteger As System.Int32 = 0
Dim anInteger As Integer = 0
```

You might use indistinctly both .NET names and the Visual Basic reserved words when referring to built-in value types.

NAMING CONVENTIONS

Although you are allowed to invoke value types with both .NET names and the Visual Basic counterparts' keywords, it's a best practice to choose the .NET names when developing reusable class libraries according to the Microsoft Common Language Specification. We discuss this topic later in this chapter. In such a scenario it is a good practice because you should avoid language-dependent features and practices when developing assemblies bound to also work with other .NET languages; this will not change the results, but your code will be cleaner, and you will use a .NET-oriented approach instead of a language-oriented one.

Table 4.2 lists the most common value types in the .NET Framework, showing a description and the Visual Basic-related keywords.

TABLE 4.2   Most Common Value Types in the .NET Framework 4.5

Value Type	Description	Visual Basic Reserved Keyword
System.Int16	Represents a numeric value with a range between −32768 and 32767.	Short
System.Int32	Represents a numeric value with a range between −2147483648 and 2147483647.	Integer
System.Int64	Represents a numeric value with a range between −9223372036854775808 and 9223372036854775807.	Long
System.Single	Represents a floating point number with a range from −3.4028235E+38 to 3.4028235E+38.	Single
System.Double	Represents a large floating number (double precision) with a range from −1.79769313486232e308 to 1.79769313486232e308.	Double
System.Boolean	Accepts True or False values.	Boolean
System.Char	Represents a single Unicode character.	Char
System.IntPtr	Represents a pointer to an address in memory.	–
System.DateTime	Represents dates, times, or both in different supported formats (see following paragraphs).	Date
System.Numerics. BigInteger	Represents an arbitrarily large integer with no maximum and minimum value.	–
System.Byte	Represents an unsigned byte, with a range from 0 to 255.	Byte
System.SByte	Represents a signed byte, with a range from −128 to 127.	SByte
System.UInt16	Represents a numeric positive value with range between 0 and 65535.	UShort

Value Type	Description	Visual Basic Reserved Keyword
`System.UInt32`	Represents a numeric positive value with a range between 0 and 4294967295.	`UInteger`
`System.UInt64`	Represents a numeric positive value with a range between 0 and 18446744073709551615.	`ULong`
`System.Decimal`	Represents a decimal number in financial and scientific calculations with large numbers. A range between –79228162514264337593543950335 and 79228162514264337593543950335.	`Decimal`
`System.TimeSpan`	Represents an interval of time. The range is between -10675199.02:48:05.4775808 and 10675199.02:48:05.4775807 ticks.	
`System.TimeZone`	Represents time information according to the specific world's time zone.	
`System.Guid`	Allows generating *Globally Unique Identifiers*.	

UPGRADING FROM VISUAL BASIC 6

If you are upgrading from Visual Basic 6, you have to keep in mind that VB 6's `Long` is an `Integer` in .NET and that VB 6's `Integer` is `Short` in .NET.

As you might notice in Table 4.2, most built-in value types are exposed by the `System` namespace except for the `BigInteger` type that is instead exposed by the `System.Numerics` namespace.

MEMORY REQUIREMENTS

You might wonder what should influence your choice when working with value types. The answer is that it depends. Of course, you should take care of memory allocation. If you know that you need to work with a small number, you will probably do best if choosing a `Byte` instead of a `Short`. Regarding this, consider that `Byte` requires 8 bits, `Short` requires 16 bits, `Integer` and `Single` require 32 bits, `Long` and `Double` require 64 bits, and `Decimal` requires 128 bits. The Visual Basic compiler is optimized for 32-bit integers, so choosing `Integer` is of course a better choice than `Short`, but, in the case of very small numbers, choose `Byte` (1 byte) instead of `Integer` (4 bytes).

Using Value Types

In this paragraph you learn to use value types. The following demonstration assumes you have created a new Visual Basic project for the Console (see Chapter 2 for details).

Listing 4.1 shows how you can declare variables storing value types. You can write the code inside the `Main` method for learning purposes.

LISTING 4.1   Using Value Types

```
Sub Main()
    'Declares an Integer
    Dim anInteger As Integer = 2

    'Declares a double and stores the result of a calculation
    Dim calculation As Double = 74.6 * 834.1

    'Declares one byte storing a hexadecimal value
    Dim oneByte As Byte = &H0

    'Declares a single character
    Dim oneCharacter As Char = "a"c

    'Declares a decimal number
    Dim sampleDecimal As Decimal = 8743341.353531135D

    'Declares a Boolean variable
    Dim isTrueOrFalse As Boolean = True

    'Declares a BigInteger
    Dim arbitraryInteger As New System.Numerics.BigInteger(800000)

    Console.WriteLine(anInteger)
    Console.WriteLine(calculation)
    Console.WriteLine(oneByte)
    Console.WriteLine(oneCharacter)
    Console.WriteLine(isTrueOrFalse)
    Console.WriteLine(arbitraryInteger)
    Console.ReadLine()
End Sub
```

You can declare variables of the desired value types using the `Dim` keyword followed by the identifier of the variable and by the `As` clause that then requires the type specification.

NOTES ABOUT `Dim` AND `As`

`Dim` is the most important keyword for declaring variables and is commonly used in local code blocks. It is also worth mentioning that in .NET Framework you can declare different kinds of objects both with `Dim` and with other keywords according to the scope of the objects (such as fields, properties, and classes). This is discussed in Chapter 7, "Class Fundamentals." Then in Chapter 20, "Advanced Language Features," you learn about another important feature in .NET Framework known as the Local Type Inference that avoids the need to add the As clause in particular scenarios such as data access with LINQ.

You can also declare more than one variable within the same Dim statement. You can write something like this:

```
Dim anInteger As Integer = 2, calculation As Double = 3.14,
    TrueOrFalse As Boolean = True
```

You can also declare more than one variable of the same type just by specifying such a type once, as in the following line of code:

```
'Three integers
Dim anInteger, secondInteger, thirdInteger As Integer
```

If you upgrade from Visual Basic 6, this is a great change because in a declaration like the preceding one VB 6 automatically assigns Variant instead of the appropriate data type. Generally you do not need to specify the constructor (the New keyword) when declaring value types. This is because in such situations the constructor addition is implicit and provided by the compiler behind the scenes. An exception to this general rule is the BigInteger type that instead allows the constructor to be explicit, but it also allows inline initialization. Listing 4.1 also shows how you can get the value stored in value types. In our example values are written to the Console window, but you can use values the most appropriate way for you. Figure 4.3 shows the result of the code in Listing 4.1.

FIGURE 4.3   Using value types in our sample code produced this result.

Pay attention when using Char and String data types. Because both types require their content to be enclosed within quotes, the value of a Char must be followed by the c letter that tells the compiler to treat that value as a single character (if you are using Option Strict On). The Decimal data type also has a similar behavior. When you declare a decimal value (see Listing 4.1), you must ensure that the value is followed by the upper D character; otherwise, the compiler treats the number as a Double and raises an error.

Identifiers like c and d are also known as *literal type characters* and are available for a number of primitive types, as summarized in Table 4.3.

TABLE 4.3   Literal Type Characters

Character	Type	Sample
C	Char	oneChar = "s"c
D	Decimal	oneDec = 87.2D
F	Single	oneSingle = 87.2F
I	Integer	anInt = 18I
L	Long	oneLong = 1324L
R	Double	oneDouble = 1234R
S	Short	oneShort = 18S
UI	UInteger	anInt = 18UI
UL	ULong	oneLong = 1324UL
US	UShort	oneShort = 18US

Literal type characters are not available for the following types:

▶ Boolean

▶ Byte

▶ Date

▶ Object

▶ SByte

▶ String

Assigning Value Types

At the beginning of the section, we mentioned that value types directly store the data to which they refer. This can be easily verified with assignments. Consider the following code:

```
Sub DoAssignments()

    Dim anInteger As Integer = 10
    Dim anotherInteger As Integer = anInteger

    Console.WriteLine(anInteger)
    Console.WriteLine(anotherInteger)

    Console.ReadLine()

End Sub
```

This code produces the following output:

```
10
10
```

This is because the value of `anInteger` has been assigned to another variable of type `Integer`, named `anotherInteger`. `anotherInteger` is a copy of the first variable and lives its own life, independent from `anInteger`. If you now write the following line of code after `anotherInteger` assignment

```
anotherInteger = 5
```

the code produces the following output:

```
10
5
```

So you have changed the value of `anotherInteger` while you left unchanged the value of `anInteger` because they are two different objects with separate lives. Although this can appear obvious, it is important because it is the base for later understanding the different behavior in reference types. You might also use assignments in situations in which you need to get a result without knowing values that produce the result itself, such as in calculations that require an input from the user. With regard to this, consider the following code:

```
Dim firstNumber As Double = 567.43
Dim secondNumber As Double = 321.52

Dim result As Double = firstNumber * secondNumber

Console.WriteLine(result)
Console.ReadLine()
```

In the preceding code, you get the result of a multiplication given two numbers. In real scenarios, the two numbers would be provided by the user and the result variable would store the result of the calculation. Such calculations are performed not on numbers but on the value of variables that store numbers. This means that you do not need to know in advance the numbers; you just work on variables and assignments.

> **NOTE**
>
> You could probably expect a code example in which the input should be provided by the user. Reference types, conversion operators, and parsing methods have not been discussed yet—those will be discussed later. So here the goal was to avoid confusion because user input is provided as `String` objects. There will be appropriate code examples when needed, as in the next paragraph.

Analyzing the Content of Value Types

In most cases you will require users to enter an input that you will then need to elaborate, or you could simply read the content of a text file and then convert such content into the appropriate .NET value type. Typically, user input is provided as strings; you will also get strings when reading text files. In business applications you need to implement validation rules on the user input, but it is worth mentioning that value types offer common methods for analyzing the contents of a string and check whether such content matches a particular value type. Even if we have not discussed the `String` object (which is a reference type), yet the following code samples are easy to understand. For example, consider the following code that declares some strings:

```
Dim firstValue As String = "1000"
Dim secondValue As String = "True"
Dim thirdValue As String = "123.456"
```

The content of each string is a representation of a particular value type: `firstValue` content represents an integer, `secondValue` represents a Boolean, and `thirdValue` represents a `Double`. We could parse the content of each string and transform it into the appropriate value type as follows:

```
Dim anInteger As Integer = Integer.Parse(firstValue)
Dim aBoolean As Boolean = Boolean.Parse(secondValue)
Dim aDouble As Double = Double.Parse(thirdValue)
```

As you can see, value types expose a method called `Parse` that converts the string representation of a numeric or logical value into the correspondent value type. `Integer.Parse` converts the "1000" string into a 1000 integer and so on. If the compiler cannot perform the conversion, a `FormatException` error will be thrown and the application execution will be broken. To avoid possible errors, you could use another method called `TryParse` that returns `True` if the conversion succeeds or `False` if it fails. For example, consider the following code:

```
Dim testInteger As Integer
Dim result = Integer.TryParse(secondValue, testInteger)
```

The code attempts to convert a string that contains the representation of a Boolean value into an `Integer`. Because this is not possible, `TryParse` returns `False`. Notice that in this particular case you don't perform an assignment to another variable (such as in the case of `Parse`) because `TryParse` requires the variable that will store the value as the second argument, passed by reference (a more detailed explanation on passing arguments by reference is provided in Chapter 7).

VALUE TYPES METHODS

Because the purpose of this book is to examine the Visual Basic 2012 language features —and examining all the .NET Framework available types and members isn't possible—only methods common to all value types are described. Methods and members specific to some value types are left to you for future studies. Always remember that when you do not know an object member, IntelliSense and the Object Browser together with the MSDN documentation can be your best friends, providing useful information.

Value types (including `System.Char` and `System.DateTime`) also expose two properties named `MinValue` and `MaxValue` that contain the minimum accepted value and the maximum accepted value for each type, respectively. For example, the following line of code

```
Console.WriteLine(Integer.MinValue)
```

produces -2147483648 as the result. The following line of code

```
Console.WriteLine(Char.MaxValue)
```

produces the ? character as the result. Finally, the following line of code

```
Console.WriteLine(Date.MaxValue)
```

produces 12/31/9999 11:59:59PM as the result.

`MinValue` and `MaxValue` can be useful for two purposes: The first purpose is for times when you don't remember the minimum and maximum values accepted by a particular value type. The second purpose deals with comparisons—you might need to check whether a value or a number is in the range of accepted values by a particular data type. Now we have completed a general overview of value types. Next, we focus on optimizations and on using special value types such as `System.DateTime`.

Optimization Considerations

When working with value types, you should always choose the best type for your needs. For example, if you need to work with a number composed in the `Integer` range, you should not use a `Long` type. Moreover, the Visual Basic compiler (and, behind the scenes, the CLR) provides optimizations for the `System.Int32` and `System.Double` types, so you should always use these types when possible. For example, use an `Int32` instead of an `Int16`, although the number you work with is composed in the range of the `Int16`. Other considerations about unsigned value types are related to compliance with *Microsoft Common Language Specification*, which is a topic discussed later in this chapter.

NULLABLE TYPES

Sometimes you need to assign null values to value types—for example, when mapping SQL Server data types to .NET data types for fetching data. To accomplish this, the .NET Framework provides support for the nullable types. Because nullable types have the syntax of Generics objects, and because you first need to know how Generics work, they are discussed in Chapter 14, "Generics and Nullable Types."

Working with `BigInteger`

The `System.Numerics.BigInteger` is a value type exposed by the `System.Numerics` namespace and requires a reference to the System.Numerics.dll assembly. It represents a signed, arbitrarily large integer number. This means that it doesn't have minimum and maximum values, opposite of other value types such as `Integer` and `Long`. Instantiating a `BigInteger` is easy, as you can see from the following line of code:

```
Dim sampleBigInteger As New System.Numerics.BigInteger
```

You can assign any signed number to a `BigInteger` because it has no minimum and maximum values, as demonstrated by the following code snippet:

```
'Neither minimum nor maximum values
sampleBigInteger = Byte.MinValue
sampleBigInteger = Long.MaxValue
```

`Byte` and `Long` are the smallest and the biggest acceptable signed integers, respectively. `BigInteger` directly supports integer types such as `SByte`, `Byte`, `UInteger`, `Integer`, `UShort`, `Short`, `ULong`, and `Long`. You can also assign to a `BigInteger` the values of type `Double`, `Single`, and `Decimal`, but you do need to accomplish this passing the value as an argument to the constructor or performing an explicit conversion using `CType` (assuming that `Option Strict` is `On`). The following code demonstrates both situations:

```
'The constructor can receive arguments, Double is accepted
Dim sampleBigInteger2 As New _
                    System.Numerics.BigInteger(123456.789)


'Single is accepted but with explicit conversion
Dim singleValue As Single = CSng(1234.56)
Dim sampleBigInteger3 As New System.Numerics.BigInteger
sampleBigInteger3 = CType(singleValue, _
                    Numerics.BigInteger)
```

Notice that rounding will occur when converting floating types to `BigInteger`. Such structure also offers shared methods for performing arithmetic operations. You can add, subtract, divide, and multiply `BigIntegers` as in the following code:

```
'Assumes an Imports System.Numerics directive
'Sum
Dim sum As BigInteger =
    BigInteger.Add(sampleBigInteger, sampleBigInteger2)

'Subtract
Dim subtraction As BigInteger =
    BigInteger.Subtract(sampleBigInteger, sampleBigInteger2)
```

```
'Division
Dim division As BigInteger =
    BigInteger.Divide(sampleBigInteger, sampleBigInteger3)


'Multiplication
Dim multiplication As BigInteger =
    BigInteger.Multiply(sampleBigInteger2, sampleBigInteger3)
```

You can also perform complex operations, such as exponentiation and logarithm calculations as demonstrated here:

```
'Power
Dim powerBI As BigInteger = BigInteger.Pow(sampleBigInteger2, 2)


'10 base logarithm
Dim log10 As Double = BigInteger.Log10(sampleBigInteger3)


'natural base logarithm
Dim natLog As Double = BigInteger.Log(sampleBigInteger, 2)
```

As usual, IntelliSense can be your best friend when exploring methods from `BigInteger` and can help you understand what other math calculations you can perform.

Building Custom Value Types

Building custom value types is accomplished by creating *structures*. Because creating structures can also be a complex task and is part of the object-oriented programming topic, it is thoroughly discussed in Chapter 11, "Structures and Enumerations."

Understanding Reference Types

Reference types are represented by classes. Classes are probably the most important items in modern programming languages and are the basis of object-oriented programming. Reference types have one big difference versus value types. Variables that declare a reference type do not store the data of the type itself; they just store an address to the data. In other words, they are just pointers to the data. To better explain (and understand) this fundamental concept, let's look at an example. Consider the following class Person, which exposes two simple properties:

```
Class Person

    Property FirstName As String
    Property LastName As String


End Class
```

You need to create an instance of such a class so that you can store data (in this case, setting properties) and then manipulate the same data. This can be accomplished by the following lines of code:

```
Dim onePerson As New Person
onePerson.FirstName = "Alessandro"
onePerson.LastName = "Del Sole"
```

STRONGLY TYPED OBJECTS

In .NET development, you often encounter the words *strongly typed*. This definition can be explained with an example. The `onePerson` object in the preceding code is strongly typed because it is of a certain type, `Person`. This means that `onePerson` can accept an assignment only from compliant objects, such as other `Person` objects. Such restriction is important because it avoids errors and problems. Moreover, the compiler knows how to treat such a specialized object. A variable of type `Object` is instead not strongly typed because it is just of the root type and is not specialized. `Object` can accept anything, but without restrictions the usage of non-strongly typed objects could lead to significant problems. Chapter 14 discusses Generics, so you'll get a more thorough understanding of strongly typed objects.

Now you have an *instance* of the `Person` class, named `onePerson`. Consider the following line of code:

```
Dim secondPerson As Person = onePerson
```

A new object of type `Person` (`secondPerson`) is declared and is assigned with the `onePerson` object. Because of the equality operator, you would probably expect `secondPerson` to be an exact copy of `onePerson`. We could consider at this point some edits to the `secondPerson` object; for example, we could modify the first name:

```
secondPerson.FirstName = "Alex"
```

We can try to check the result of the previous operations by simply writing the output to the Console window. Let's begin by writing the result of `secondPerson`:

```
Console.WriteLine(secondPerson.FirstName)
Console.WriteLine(secondPerson.LastName)
Console.ReadLine()
```

As you might correctly expect, the preceding code produces the following result:

```
Alex
Del Sole
```

Now let's simply write the result for `onePerson` to the Console window:

```
Console.WriteLine(onePerson.FirstName)
Console.WriteLine(onePerson.LastName)
Console.ReadLine()
```

This code produces the following result:

```
Alex
Del Sole
```

As you can see, editing the first name in `secondPerson` also affected `onePerson`. This means that `secondPerson` is not a copy of `onePerson`. It is instead *a copy of the reference* to the actual data. Now you should have a better understanding of reference types. We can say that, as their name implies, reference types have an address in memory where data is stored and variables declaring and instantiating reference types just hold a reference to that data. To get a real copy of data, you should write something like this:

```
Dim secondPerson As New Person
secondPerson.FirstName = onePerson.FirstName
secondPerson.LastName = onePerson.LastName
```

Then you could edit `secondPerson`'s properties, ensuring that this will not affect the `onePerson` object. This kind of technique for creating a clone for a reference type is good with objects exposing only a few properties, but fortunately there are more interesting techniques to clone more complex objects. These are discussed in the "Deep Copy and Shallow Copy" section. As a clarification, notice that, in the .NET Framework, String is a reference type but it's actually treated as a value type, as I will explain in a few paragraphs.

.NET Framework Primitive Reference Types

The .NET Framework 4.5 ships with tons of reference types exposed by the Base Class Library (BCL) and that cover most needs. However, you will often use several reference types in the development process that many other reference types derive from. Table 4.4 lists the most common reference types.

TABLE 4.4   Most Common Built-In Reference Types in .NET Framework

Type	Description
System.Object	The root class in the object hierarchy
System.String	Represents a string
System.Array	Represents an array of objects
System.Exception	Represents an error occurring during the application execution
System.IO.Stream	The base class for accessing other resources such as files or in-memory data.

You can use a number of reference types when developing real-life applications, and most of them are discussed in subsequent chapters; however, the ones listed in Table 4.4 provide the basis for working with reference types. Most of them are the base infrastructure for other important derived classes. We previously discussed `System.Object`, so we will not do it again. It is instead worth mentioning how `System.String` is a reference type, although it seems natural to think about it as a value type. `System.String`, or simply `String`, is used as a value type, so it will not be difficult to build strings. By the way, strings are immutable (that means "read-only"), so each time you edit a string, the runtime creates a new instance of the String class and passes in the edited string. Because of this, editing strings using `System.String` can cause unnecessary usage of memory. To solve this problem, the .NET Framework provides more efficient ways, as you will see in the sections "Working with Strings," "Working with Dates," and "Working with Arrays."

Differences Between Value Types and Reference Types

Value types and reference types differ in several ways. In the previous sections we saw how they differ in assignment and how a value type can directly store data, whereas a reference type stores only the address to the actual data. We now explain such implementation and provide information on the other differences between value and reference types.

Memory Allocation

Value types and reference types are differently allocated in memory. Value types are allocated in the *Stack*. The Stack is a memory area where methods are executed according to the *last-in, first-out* manner. The first method *pushed* to the Stack is the application entry point; that is, the `Main` method. When `Main` invokes other methods, the CLR creates a sort of restore point and pushes those methods to the Stack. When the method needs to be executed, data required by that method is also pushed to the Stack. When a method completes, the CLR removes (*popping*) it from the Stack together with its data, restoring the previous state. Because of this ordered behavior, the Stack is efficient, and the Common Language Runtime can easily handle it. Consider the following line of code, declaring a variable of type `Integer`, therefore a value type:

```
Dim anInteger As Integer = 5
```

Figure 4.4 shows how the `anInteger` variable is allocated in the Stack.

On the contrary, reference types are allocated in a memory area named *Managed Heap*. Different from how objects are treated in the Stack, objects in the Managed Heap are allocated and deallocated randomly. This provides fast allocation but requires more work for the CLR. To keep things ordered, the CLR needs two instruments: the *Garbage Collector* and *Memory Manager*. We provide details about this architecture in Chapter 8, "Managing an Object's Lifetime." At the moment you need to understand how reference types and their data are allocated. Consider the following lines of code, declaring a new version of the `Person` class and an instance of this class:

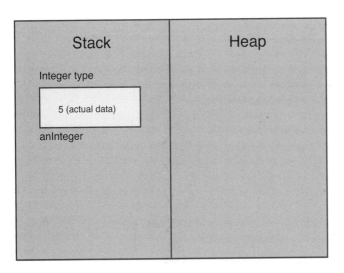

FIGURE 4.4   Value types are allocated in the Stack.

```
Class Person

    Property Name As String
    Property Age As Integer
End Class
Dim onePerson As New Person
onePerson.Name = "Alessandro Del Sole"
onePerson.Age = 35
```

As you can see, there is now a property in this class (Age) that is a value type. The instance of the class will be allocated in the Heap, and its reference (onePerson) will be allocated in the Stack. Figure 4.5 provides a visual representation of this scenario.

Because the Person class handles a value type in one of its properties, such value types stay in the Stack. Figure 4.6 completes this overview. In the second part of this book, you will have different opportunities to explore reference types and memory management when discussing the object's lifetime.

Object-Oriented Differences

There are a couple of differences with regard to principles related to object-oriented programming. Although these principles are discussed in detail in Part II, "Object-Oriented Programming with Visual Basic 2012," it's convenient to mention them here.

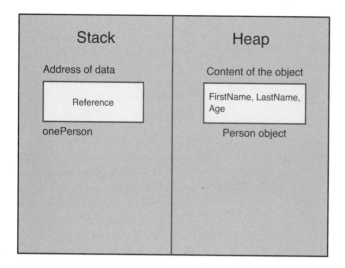

FIGURE 4.5   Reference types are allocated in the Heap, whereas their addresses reside in the Stack.

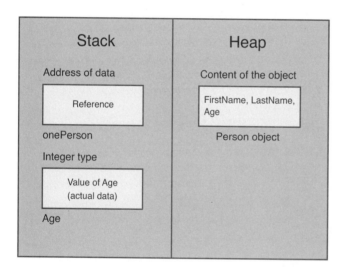

FIGURE 4.6   Complete overview of memory allocation for value and reference types.

Inheritance

The first principle deals with inheritance, which is covered in Chapter 12. Classes (that is, reference types) support inheritance, whereas structures (value types) do not. Consider the following code:

```
Class Person

    Property FirstName As String
    Property LastName As String

End Class

Class Developer
    Inherits Person

    Property UsedProgrammingLanguage As String

    Public Overrides Function ToString() As String
        Return Me.LastName
    End Function
End Class
```

In this example, the Person class is the base class and provides the basic properties
for representing a hypothetical person. The Developer class inherits from Person (see
the Inherits keyword), and this means that the Developer class will expose both the
FirstName and LastName properties plus the new one named UsedProgrammingLanguage.
It also redefines the behavior of the default ToString method so that it can return a more
significant name for the object. In Visual Basic 2012, you can inherit from only one object
at a time. Thus, Developer can inherit only from Person and not from any other object.
If you need multiple-level inheritance, you should architect your object's framework so
that a second class can inherit from the first one, the third one from the second one, and
so on. Structures do not support inheritance at all, except for the fact that they inherit by
nature from System.ValueType.

Interfaces Implementation

Both classes and structures provide support for interfaces implementation. For example,
you could implement the IComparable interface in both cases:

```
Class Person
    Implements IComparable

    Property FirstName As String
    Property LastName As String

    Public Function CompareTo(ByVal obj As Object) As Integer Implements
            System.IComparable.CompareTo
        'Write your code here
    End Function
End Class
```

```
Structure Dimension
    Implements IComparable

    Public Function CompareTo(ByVal obj As Object) As Integer Implements
            System.IComparable.CompareTo
        'Write your code here
    End Function


    Property X As Integer
    Property Y As Integer
    Property Z As Integer
End Structure
```

Inheritance and interfaces are discussed in Part II, so don't worry if something is not clear.

Constructors

When you declare a reference type, you need an instance before you can use it (with the exception of shared classes, which are discussed in Chapter 7). You create an instance by invoking the *constructor* via the `New` keyword. When you declare a value type, the new variable is automatically initialized to a default value; this is usually zero for numbers and `False` for `Boolean`. Because of this, value types do not need to have a default constructor invoked. The Visual Basic compiler still accepts declaring a value type and invoking the constructor, which also initializes the type with the default value. However, in this case you cannot initialize the value. The following code snippet demonstrates this:

```
'Declares an Integer and sets the value to zero
Dim anInt As New Integer
'Initialization not allowed with New
Dim anotherInt As New Integer = 1
'Allowed
Dim aThirdInt As Integer = 1
```

Finalizers

Finalizers are related to the object's lifetime, as discussed in Chapter 8. As for constructors, it's convenient having a small reference. We previously said that when methods using value types complete their execution, they are automatically removed from the Stack together with the data. This is managed by the CLR, and because of this ordered behavior, value types do not need to be finalized. In contrast, reference types are allocated on the Heap and have a different behavior. Deallocation from memory is handled by the Garbage Collector that needs finalizers on the reference type's side to complete its work.

Performance Differences

A lot of times value types store data directly, whereas reference types store only the address of the data. Although you can create and consume types according to your needs, there are some concerns with performance, particularly regarding methods. Methods can accept parameters, also known as *arguments*. Arguments can be value types or reference types. If you pass a value type to a method, you pass to that method all the data contained in the value type, which could be time-consuming and cause performance overhead. Passing a reference type passes only the address to the data, so it could be faster and more efficient. There could be situations in which you need to pass one or more value types to methods. This depends on your needs. Generally, the performance difference in such a scenario is not relevant, but it will depend on the size of the value type. If your method receives a large value type as an argument but is invoked only once, performance should not be affected. But if your method is invoked many times, perhaps passing a reference type would be better. Just be aware of this when implementing your methods.

What Custom Type Should I Choose?

Answering this question is not simple. It depends. If you need to implement a custom type that will act similarly to a value type (for example, a type that works with numbers), you should choose a `Structure`. If you need to implement an object for storing a large amount of data, it could be a good idea to choose a `class`. Such considerations are not mandatory, and their purpose is simply to let you think a little bit more about what you are going to implement and what your needs are.

Converting Between Value Types and Reference Types

In your developer life, you often need to convert one data type into another in different types of situations. For example, you might need to convert a value type into another one or just convert an instance of type `Object` into a strongly typed object. In this section, you learn how to convert between data types and about conversion operators, beginning with basic but important concepts, such as implicit conversions, boxing, and unboxing.

Understanding Implicit Conversions

Previously we discussed the `System.Object` class. As you might remember, such a class is the root in the class hierarchy. That said, you can assign both reference types and value types to an `Object` instance because they both inherit from `System.Object`. Consider the following lines of code:

```
Dim anInt As Object = 10
Dim onePerson As Object = New Person
```

The first line assigns a value type (`Integer`) to an `Object`, and the second one assigns an instance of the `Person` class to an `Object`. Visual Basic 2012 always enables such assignments because they are always safe. What is unsafe is trying to assign an `Object` to a strongly typed instance, such as assigning `Object` to an instance of the `Person` class. This is quite obvious because `Object` can represent whatever type, and the compiler cannot be sure if that type is a `Person`, which can cause errors. Consider the following line of code:

```
Dim onePerson As Person = New Object
```

The code is trying to assign an instance of the `Object` class to an instance of `Person`. The Visual Basic compiler enables handling such situations in two different ways, depending on how `Option Strict` is set. We discussed `Option Strict` in Chapter 2, and now you can see the first usage. If `Option Strict` is set to `On`, the preceding line of code causes an error. The Visual Basic compiler does allow an implicit conversion from `Object` to a strongly typed object, throwing an error message that you can see in the code editor. Figure 4.7 shows this error message.

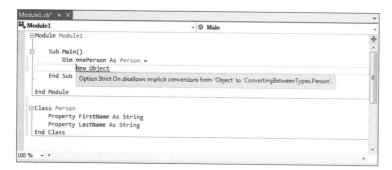

FIGURE 4.7   With `Option Strict On`, the Visual Basic compiler disallows implicit conversions.

This is useful because it prevents type conversion errors. If you want to perform an assignment of this kind, you need to explicitly convert `Object` into the appropriate data type. For example, this can be accomplished using the `CType` conversion operator, as in the following line of code:

```
Dim onePerson As Person = CType(New Object, Person)
```

A conversion operator offers another advantage: It communicates whether the conversion is possible; if it's not, you can handle the situation, particularly at runtime. The code editor also simplifies the addition of a `CType` conversion by offering a convenient correction pop-up you enable by clicking the small red line that appears under the bad object and that will automatically convert into the appropriate type (see Figure 4.8 for an example). It is worth mentioning that `CType` will work without throwing an exception only if the target type for the conversion is the correct type.

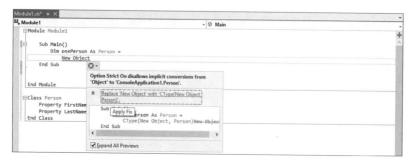

FIGURE 4.8   Using the error correction options to easily add `CType`.

By the way, the Visual Basic compiler provides a way to allow implicit conversions avoiding error messages. To accomplish this, you need to set `Option Strict` to `Off`. You can write the following line of code (preceding all the other code and Imports directives):

```
Option Strict Off
```

You could also adjust `Option Strict` settings in the Compiler tab of the My Project window, as shown in Chapter 2. Assigning an `Object` to a `Person`, as we did before, is perfectly legal. But please be careful: If you do not need to perform such assignments, please avoid `Option Strict Off` and instead use `Option Strict On`. This can ensure less runtime and compile time errors and enable you to write more efficient code.

`Option Strict Off`: WHEN?

You should almost never set `Option Strict` to `Off`. There is only one situation in which you should set `Option Strict` to `Off`—late binding. This topic is discussed in Chapter 46, "Reflection." Outside this particular scenario, never set `Option Strict` to `Off` so that you can be sure that you are working with strongly typed objects and that the compiler, debugger, and CLR will enable you to quickly find errors. The other reason you should not set `Option Strict` to `Off` is because performance will suffer. You'll learn about this, and other reasons, in Chapter 14. I suggest you set `Option Strict` to `On` as a default in the Visual Studio 2012 options.

Boxing and Unboxing

The Common Type System enables implicit conversions. It also enables conversions between reference types and value types, and vice versa, because both inherit from `System.Object`. You often need to work with two techniques, boxing and unboxing, when you have methods that receive arguments of type `Object`. See the tip at the end of this section for details.

Boxing

Boxing occurs when converting a value type to a reference type. In other words, boxing is when you assign a value type to an `Object`. The following lines of code demonstrate boxing:

```
Dim calculation As Double = 14.4 + 32.12
Dim result As Object = calculation
```

The calculation variable, which stores a value deriving from the sum of two numbers, is a `Double` value type. The result variable, which is of type `Object` and therefore a reference type, is allocated in the Heap and boxes the original value of calculation so that you now have two copies of the value, one in the Stack and one in the Heap. Figure 4.9 shows how boxing causes memory allocation.

Boxing requires performance overhead. This will be clearer when reading the next section.

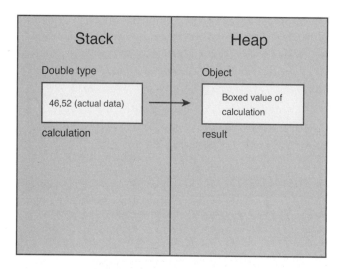

FIGURE 4.9   Boxing causes both Stack and Heap allocation.

Unboxing

Unboxing occurs when you convert a reference type to a value type. You perform unboxing when converting an `Object` into a value type. Continuing with the previous example, the following line of code demonstrates unboxing:

```
Dim convertedResult As Double = CType(result, Double)
```

Unboxing can cause another copy of the original value (the same stored in the calculation variable) to be created and allocated in the Stack. Figure 4.10 shows a representation of what happens when unboxing a value.

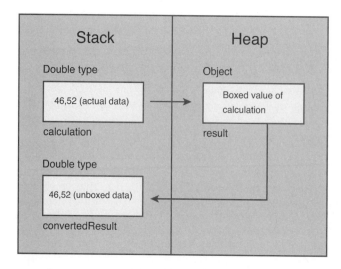

FIGURE 4.10   Unboxing causes a third copy of the original value to be created.

Boxing and unboxing also cause performance overhead, so they should always be avoided if not truly needed. This is because value types directly store the data they refer to and therefore create three copies of the data, which can consume more resources than necessary. If the value types you box and unbox are small, performance might not be influenced (or, better, you might not see the difference). But if the value types store a large amount of data, the loss of performance could be significant.

AVOIDING BOXING AND UNBOXING

Boxing and unboxing can be necessary if you have methods that receive arguments of type `Object`. There are a couple of best practices that you can take when implementing methods, such as using Generics or implementing overloads of methods that can accept multiple strongly typed arguments. Generics and overloads are discussed later in the book.

EARLY BINDING AND LATE BINDING

When talking about reference types, another important topic is early binding and late binding. Although this might be the right place to discuss them, I prefer to postpone such discussion until Chapter 46. This way, you first get a complete overview of reference types and then get real examples of the late binding technique.

Deep Copy and Shallow Copy

In the "Understanding Reference Types" section, you saw how reference type assignments differ from value type assignments and how assignments are not enough to create a copy of a reference type. We also provided one basic solution to this problem, which was to create a new instance of a specified reference type and then assign each property of the target instance with values coming from the original one. But this is not enough, both because it is not complete and because it can be good only with small classes. To create a complete clone of a reference type, in the .NET development we can take advantage of two techniques: *deep copy* and *shallow copy*. Both techniques require the implementation of the `ICloneable` interface. Although we discuss interfaces later, the concepts presented here are easy to understand. The `ICloneable` interface provides a unique method named `Clone` that enables developers to know that classes exposing such a method can easily be cloned. For example, consider the following implementation of the `Person` class that also implements the `ICloneable` interface:

```
Class Person
    Implements ICloneable

    Property FirstName As String
    Property LastName As String
    Property Work As Job
```

```
    Public Function Clone() As Object Implements System.ICloneable.Clone
        Return Me.MemberwiseClone
    End Function
End Class
```

The most interesting thing in the code is the `Clone` method required by the `ICloneable` interface. In the method body, you should write code that performs the real copy of the reference type. Fortunately, the `Object` class provides a method named `MemberwiseClone` that automatically returns a shallow copy of your reference type. The keyword Me indicates the current instance of the class. Because `Clone` must work with all possible types, it returns `Object`. (We see later how to convert this result.) The class exposes two `String` properties, `FirstName` and `LastName`. You might remember that, although `String` is a reference type behind the scenes, you will actually treat it as a value type. The class also exposes another property named `Work` of type `Job`. This is a new reference type representing a person's occupation. `Job` is implemented in the following way:

```
Class Job
    Property CompanyName As String
    Property Position As String
End Class
```

Given this implementation, we can simply create a *shallow copy*.

Shallow Copy

A shallow copy creates a new instance of the current object and copies values of members of the original to the new one but does not create copies of children (referenced) objects. Continuing the example of the preceding implementation, `Clone` creates a copy of the `Person` class into a new instance and copies members' values that are value types or `Strings`. Because `Job` is a pure reference type, the shallow copy provided by `Clone` will not also create a clone of `Job`. This is the explanation about what we said before, that a shallow copy creates a copy only of the specified instance but not of children objects. We can easily verify our assertions by writing the following code:

```
Sub Main()

    'The original person
    Dim firstPerson As New Person
    firstPerson.FirstName = "Alessandro"
    firstPerson.LastName = "Del Sole"

    'Defines a work for the above person
    Dim randomJob As New Job
    randomJob.CompanyName = "Del Sole Ltd."
    randomJob.Position = "CEO"

    'Assignment of the new job
    firstPerson.Work = randomJob
```

```
    'Gets a shallow copy of the firstPerson object
    Dim secondPerson As Person = CType(firstPerson.Clone, Person)


    'Check if they are the same instances

    'returns False, 2 different instances:
    Console.WriteLine(firstPerson.FirstName Is secondPerson.FirstName)

    'returns True (still same instance of Job!):
    Console.WriteLine(firstPerson.Work Is secondPerson.Work)
    Console.ReadLine()
End Sub
```

The preceding code first gets a new instance of the `Person` class, setting some properties such as a new instance of the `Job` class, too. Notice how the result of the `Clone` method, which is of type `Object`, is converted into a `Person` instance using `CType`. At this point we can check what happened. The `Is` operator enables comparing two instances of reference types and returns `True` if they are related to the same instance. For the `FirstName` property, the comparison returns `False` because the shallow copy created a new, standalone instance of the `Person` class. But if we do the same check on the `Work` property, which is a child reference type of the `Person` class, the comparison returns `True`. This means that `firstPerson.Work` refers to the same instance of the `Job` class as in `secondPerson.Work`. And this also means that a shallow copy did not create a new copy of the `Job` class to be assigned to the `secondPerson` object. This is where the *deep copy* comes in.

Deep Copy

Deep copy is something complex that can create perfect copies of an entire object's graph. If you need to perform a deep copy, you have some alternatives. The easiest (and the one we can show at this point of the book) is to perform a shallow copy of the main object and then manually copy the other properties of children reference types. The best one instead recurs to serialization, which is an advanced topic discussed in Chapter 41, "Serialization." At the moment we can focus on editing the previous implementation of the `Clone` method for performing a simple deep copy. We could also implement the `ICloneable` interface in the `Job` class, as follows:

```
Class Job
    Implements ICloneable

    Property CompanyName As String
    Property Position As String

    Public Function Clone() As Object Implements System.ICloneable.Clone
        Return Me.MemberwiseClone
    End Function
End Class
```

Now we can modify the `Clone` implementation inside the `Person` class, as follows:

```
Class Person
    Implements ICloneable

    Property FirstName As String
    Property LastName As String
    Property Work As Job

    Public Function Clone() As Object Implements System.ICloneable.Clone

        Dim tempPerson As Person = CType(Me.MemberwiseClone, Person)

        tempPerson.Work = CType(Me.Work.Clone, Job)

        Return tempPerson

    End Function
End Class
```

IMPLEMENTING `Icloneable`

Implementing `ICloneable` in referenced classes is not the only way of providing deep copies. We could also generate a new instance of the `Job` class and manually assign values read from the original instance. But because we are discussing `ICloneable` and `Clone`, the example was completed this way.

The code obtains first a shallow copy of the current instance of the `Person` class and then gets a shallow copy of the child instance of the `Job` class.

PAY ATTENTION TO RECURSIVE CLONE

Cloning objects with recursive calls to the `Clone` method could lead to a stack overflow if the hierarchy of your objects is particularly complex. Because of this, the previous implementation goes well with small classes and small objects graphs. If this is not the case, you should prefer serialization.

If we now try to run the same check again comparing the instances of `firstPerson` and `secondPerson`, the output will be the following:

```
False
False
```

This is because now the instances are different. We have two completely standalone instances of the `Person` class.

The `GetType` Keyword

Each time you create an instance of a class, the .NET runtime creates an instance behind the scenes of the `System.Type` class that represents your object. Because in the .NET development you have the ability to inspect instances of the `System.Type` class (known as Reflection) at runtime and to get a reference to that `System.Type`, the Visual Basic programming language offers the `GetType` keyword that enables you to accomplish both tasks. The `GetType` keyword has two different behaviors: The first one is an operator, the second one is a method. `GetType` is typically used to compare two instances of an object or to access metadata of a type at runtime. To understand `GetType`, here are a few examples. Consider this first code snippet:

```
'GetType here is related to the type
Dim testType As Type = GetType(Integer)

For Each method As System.Reflection.MethodInfo
            In testType.GetMethods
    Console.WriteLine(method.Name)
Next
Console.ReadLine()
```

In a few words, the preceding code retrieves all the information and metadata related to the `System.Int32` type; then it shows a list of all the methods exposed by such type, using Reflection. (`MethodInfo` is an object representing the methods' information.) This is useful if you need to retrieve information on a particular data type. If you instead need to retrieve information about metadata of a specific instance of a data type, you can use the `GetType` method, as shown in the following code:

```
'GetType here is related to an instance
Dim testInt As Integer = 123456
Dim testType As Type = testInt.GetType

For Each method As System.Reflection.MethodInfo
            In testType.GetMethods
    Console.WriteLine(method.Name)
Next
Console.ReadLine()
```

In this particular situation, you retrieve information of **an instance** of the `System.Int32` type and not of the type. You can also use `GetType` to compare two types for equality:

```
'Comparing two types
If testInt.GetType Is GetType(Integer) Then
    Console.WriteLine("TestInt is of type Integer")
End If
```

Understanding Conversion Operators

In the previous section we discussed converting between value types and reference types. These kinds of conversions are not the only ones allowed by the .NET Framework because you often need to perform conversions between two value types or two reference types. For example, imagine that you want to represent a number as a text message. In such a case, you need to convert an `Integer` into a `String`; you could also have an `Integer` value that must be passed to a method that instead receives an argument of type `Double`. Another common scenario is when you work with user controls in the user interface. Some controls such as `ListBox` and `DataGridView` on the Windows side or the `DataGrid` on the web side can store any kind of object. If you show a list of `Person` objects inside a `ListBox`, the control stores a list of `Object`, so you need to perform an explicit conversion from `Object` to `Person` each time you need to retrieve information on a single `Person`. In this section we show how conversions between types can be performed.

Widening and Narrowing Conversions

With the exception of boxing and unboxing, conversions are of two kinds: *widening* conversions and *narrowing* conversions. Their type depends on whether the conversion is explicit or implicit. This is explained next.

Widening Conversions

Widening conversions occur when you try to convert a type into another one that can include all values of the original type. A typical example of a widening conversion is converting from an `Integer` into a `Double`, as in the following lines of code:

```
'Widening conversion
Dim i As Integer = 1
Dim d As Double = i
```

As you might remember from Table 4.2, `Integer` represents a numeric value whereas `Double` represents a large floating number. Therefore, `Double` is greater than `Integer` and can accept conversions from `Integer` without loss of precision. Widening conversions do not need an explicit conversion operator, which instead happens for narrowing conversions.

Narrowing Conversions

The opposite of widening conversions, *narrowing conversions* occur when you attempt to convert a type into another that is smaller or with a loss of precision. For example, converting a `Double` into an `Integer` can cause a loss of precision because `Double` is a large floating number and `Integer` is just a numeric value, which is also smaller than `Double`. There are several ways to perform narrowing conversions, depending on how the types you need to convert are implemented. Visual Basic 2012, continuing what was already available in previous versions of the language, provides an easy way to perform conversions between base types wrapped by Visual Basic keywords. For example, if we need to convert a `Double` into an `Integer,` we could write the following lines of code:

```
Dim d As Double = 12345.678
Dim i As Integer = CInt(d)
```

The `CInt` function converts the specified `Object` into an `Integer`. In this particular case the value of `i` becomes 12346 because the conversion caused a loss of precision and the Visual Basic compiler produced an integer number that is the closest to the original value. Another example is when you need to convert a number into a string representation of the number itself. This can be accomplished by the following line of code:

```
Dim s As String = CStr(i)
```

The `CStr` function converts the specified `Object` into a string. With particular regard to string conversions, all .NET objects expose a method named `ToString` that performs a conversion of the original data into a new `String`. The last line of code could be rewritten as follows:

```
Dim s As String = i.ToString()
```

`ToString` is also useful because you can format the output. For example, consider the following line of code:

```
Dim i As Integer = 123456
Dim s As String = i.ToString("##,##.00")
```

The `ToString` method enables specifying how the string should be formatted. On my machine the code produces the following output:

```
123,456.00
```

The output depends on regional settings for your system, with particular regard to separators.

USE `ToString` INSTEAD OF `CStr`

Because it enables you to format the result, `ToString` should be preferred to `CStr`. You can override the standard implementation of `ToString` (provided by the `Object` class) so that you can provide your own conversion logic. This is discussed later, with regard to inheritance.

Table 4.5 shows the complete list of conversion functions provided by the Visual Basic grammar.

TABLE 4.5   Visual Basic Conversion Functions

Operator	Description
CInt	Converts an object into an Integer
CLng	Converts an object into a Long
CShort	Converts an object into a Short
CSng	Converts an object into a Single
CDbl	Converts an object into a Double
CBool	Converts an object into a Boolean
CByte	Converts an object into a Byte
CChar	Converts an object into a Char
CStr	Converts an object into a String
CObj	Converts an object into an instance of Object
CDate	Converts an object into a Date
CUInt	Converts an object into a UInteger
CULong	Converts an object into a ULong
CUShort	Converts an object into a UShort
CSByte	Converts an object into a SByte

REMEMBER THE LOSS OF PRECISION

Always take care when performing narrowing conversions because of the loss of precision, particularly with numeric values. Another particular case is when converting from String to Char. Such conversions retrieve only the first character of the specified string.

When narrowing conversions fail, an InvalidCastException is thrown by the compiler. An example of this situation occurs when you attempt to convert a String into an Integer. Because String is a valid object expression, you do not get an error at compile time, but the conversion would fail at runtime. Because of this, you should always enclose conversions within error handling code blocks (see Chapter 6, "Handling Errors and Exceptions," for details). There are also alternatives that are independent from the Visual Basic language and that are provided by the .NET Framework. The first way is using the System.Convert class that is available on objects that implement the IConvertible interface. Convert exposes a lot of methods, each for converting into a particular data type. For example, the following line of code converts a string representation of a number into an integer:

```
Dim c As Integer = System.Convert.ToInt32("1234")
```

If the string contains an invalid number, a FormatException is thrown. Methods exposed by the Convert class are well implemented because they do not only accept Object expressions, but also specific types, such as Integer, Boolean, String, and so on. IntelliSense can help you understand which types are supported. Table 4.6 provides an overview of the most common conversion methods exposed by `System.Convert`.

TABLE 4.6   System.Convert Most Commonly Used Methods

Method	Description
ToBool	Converts the specified type into a `Boolean`
ToByte	Converts the specified type into a `Byte`
ToChar	Converts the specified type into a `Char`
ToDateTime	Converts the specified type into a `Date`
ToDecimal	Converts the specified type into a `Decimal`
ToDouble	Converts the specified type into a `Double`
ToInt16	Converts the specified type into a `Short`
ToInt32	Converts the specified type into an `Integer`
ToInt64	Converts the specified type into a `Long`
ToSByte	Converts the specified type into a `SByte`
ToSingle	Converts the specified type into a `Single`
ToString	Converts the specified type into a `String`
ToUInt16	Converts the specified type into an `UShort`
ToUInt32	Converts the specified type into a `UInteger`
ToUInt64	Converts the specified type into an `ULong`

Notice that `System.Convert` also provides other methods that are not discussed here because they are related to particular situations that assume you have a deep knowledge of specific .NET topics and are out of the scope in a general discussion such as this one.

CType, DirectCast, TryCast

The Visual Basic programming language offers some other conversion operators that are probably the most commonly used because of their flexibility. The first one is `CType`. It converts from one type to another and, if the conversion fails, the Visual Basic compiler throws an exception. The good news is that the conversion is also performed by the background compiler, so if the target type's range exceeds the source one, you are immediately notified of the problem. For example, the compiler knows that converting a `Date` into an `Integer` is not possible, so in such a scenario you are immediately notified. If the conversion is legal (and therefore can compile) but types are populated at runtime with data that cannot be converted, an `InvalidCastException` is thrown. For example, the following code converts an `Integer` into a `Short`:

```
Dim i As Integer = 123456
Dim s As Short = CType(i, Short)
```

CType is also useful in unboxing. The following code converts from an Object that contains an Integer into a pure Integer:

```
Dim p As Object = 1
Dim result As Integer = CType(p, Integer)
```

Of course, it can also be used for converting between reference types:

```
Dim p As Object = New Person
Dim result As Person = CType(p, Person)
```

CType is specific to the Visual Basic runtime and enables widening and narrowing conversions from one type into another type that accepts the first one. For example, a Double can be converted to an Integer, although with loss of precision. Another couple of important operators, DirectCast and TryCast, can be used the same way, but they have different behavior. Both operators enable conversions when there is an inheritance or implementation relationship between the two types. For example, consider the following lines of code:

```
Dim d As Double = 123.456
Dim s As Short = CType(d, Short)
```

Converting from Double to Short using CType will succeed. Now consider the usage of DirectCast in the same scenario:

```
Dim d As Double = 123.456
Dim s As Short = DirectCast(d, Short)
```

This conversion will fail because Short does not inherit from Double and no implementation relationship exists between the two types. A conversion failure is notified via an InvalidCastException. This means you should use DirectCast only when you are sure that the inheritance or implementation conditions between types are satisfied. However, using DirectCast has some advantages in terms of performances because it relies directly on the .NET runtime. DirectCast conversions are also checked by the background compiler, so you are immediately notified if conversions fail via the Error List window. DirectCast works with both value and reference types. If you work with reference types, it's a best practice to check whether the two types are compliant so you can reduce the risks of errors:

```
'In this example P is of type Object but stores a Person
If TypeOf (p) Is Person Then
    Dim result As Person = DirectCast(p, Person)
End If
```

The TypeOf operator compares an object reference variable to a data type and returns True if the object variable is compatible with the given type. As you might imagine, such checks can require performance overhead. Another operator that works only with reference types is known as `TryCast`. This one works exactly like `DirectCast`, but instead of throwing an `InvalidCastException` in the case of conversion failure, it returns a null object (`Nothing`). This can be useful because you can avoid implementing an exceptions check, simplifying your code (that will only need to check for a null value) and reducing performance overhead. The last code snippet could be rewritten as follows:

```
'In this example P is of type Object but stores a Person
Dim result As Person = TryCast(p, Person)
```

If the conversion fails, `TryCast` returns `Nothing`, so you will just need to check such a result.

Working with .NET Fundamental Types

There are special types that you will often work with, such as strings, date and time, and arrays. Although you will often work with collections, too (see Chapter 16, "Working with Collections and Iterators"), understanding how such objects work is an important objective. The .NET Framework 4.5 simplifies your developer life because objects provide methods to perform the most common operations on the data.

NOTE ON EXTENSION METHODS

This section describes built-in methods from value and reference types. Because of the .NET infrastructure, all types provide the ability of invoking extension methods that could be potentially used for accomplishing some of the tasks proposed in this section. They will not be described because the scope of this chapter is to describe built-in members; you will need to understand extension methods, which are covered in Chapter 20.

Working with Strings

Working with strings is one of the most common developer activities. In the .NET Common Type System, `System.String` is a reference type. This might be surprising because strings actually behave like value types. The `String` class cannot be inherited, so you can't create a custom class derived from it. In addition, `String` objects are immutable, like value types. What does this mean? It means that when you create a new `String`, you cannot change it. Although you are allowed to edit a string's content, behind the scenes the CLR does not edit the existing string; it instead creates a new instance of the `String` object containing your edits. The CLR then stores such `String` objects in the Heap and returns a reference to them. We discuss how to approach strings in a more efficient way later; at the moment you need to understand how to work with them. The `System.String` classv provides lots of methods for working with strings without the need to write custom code. Assuming you understand the previous section relating to reference types, you can learn how to manipulate strings using the most common `System.String` methods.

System.String METHODS

System.String provides several methods for performing operations on strings. We discuss the most important of them. Each method comes with several overloads. Discussing every overload is not possible, so you learn how methods work; then you can use IntelliSense, the Object Browser, and the documentation for further information.

Comparing Strings

Comparing the content of two strings is an easy task. The most common way for comparing strings is taking advantage of the equality (=) operator, which checks whether two strings have the same value. The following is an example that compares strings for equality:

```
Dim stringOne As String = "Hi guys"
Dim stringTwo As String = "How are you?"
Dim stringThree As String = "Hi guys"
'Returns False
Dim result1 As Boolean = (stringOne = stringTwo)
'Returns True
Dim result2 As Boolean = (stringOne = stringThree)
```

You can also use the equality operator inside conditional blocks, as in the following snippet:

```
If stringOne = stringTwo Then
    'Do something if the two strings are equal
End If
```

You instead check for strings' inequality using the inequality operator (<>).

THE VISUAL BASIC COMPILER AND THE EQUALITY OPERATOR

When using the equality operator for string comparisons, the Visual Basic compiler works differently from other managed languages. In fact, behind the scenes it makes a call to the Microsoft.VisualBasic.CompilerServices.Operators.CompareString method, whereas other languages, such as C#, make an invocation to System.String.Equals.

The String class also exposes other interesting methods for comparing strings: Equals, Compare, CompareTo, and CompareOrdinal. Equals checks for strings equality and returns a Boolean value of True if the strings are equal or False if they are not (which is exactly like the equality operator). The following code compares two strings and returns False because they are not equal:

```
Dim firstString As String = "Test string"
Dim secondString As String = "Comparison Test"

Dim areEqual As Boolean = String.Equals(firstString, secondString)
```

Equals has several signatures allowing deep control of the comparison. For example, you could check if two strings are equal according to the local system culture and without being case-sensitive:

```
Dim areCaseEqual As Boolean =
    String.Equals(firstString, secondString,
    StringComparison.CurrentCultureIgnoreCase)
```

The `StringComparison` object provides a way for specifying comparison settings. IntelliSense provides descriptions for each available option. Then there is the `Compare` method. It checks whether the first string is minor, equal, or greater than the second and returns an `Integer` value representing the result of the comparison. If the first string is minor, it returns -1; if it is equal to the second one, the method returns zero; if the first string is greater than the second, `it` returns 1. The following code snippet demonstrates this kind of comparison:

```
Dim firstString As String = "Test string"
Dim secondString As String = "Comparison Test"

Dim result As Integer = String.Compare(firstString, secondString)
```

In this case `Compare` returns 1 because the second string is greater than the first one. `Compare` enables specifying several comparing options. For example, you could perform the comparison based on case-sensitive strings. The following code demonstrates this:

```
Dim caseComparisonResult As Integer =
    String.Compare(firstString, secondString, True)
```

For `Equals`, `Compare` also enables a comparison based on other options, such as the culture information of your system. The next method is `String.CompareTo`, whose return values are the same as `String.Compare`; however, `String.CompareTo` is an instance method. You use it like in the following code:

```
Dim firstString As String = "Test string"
Dim secondString As String = "Comparison Test"

Dim result As Integer = firstString.CompareTo(secondString)
```

The last valuable method is `String.CompareOrdinal`, which checks for casing differences via ordinal comparison rules, which means comparing the numeric values of the corresponding `Char` objects that the string is composed of. The following is an example:

```
Dim firstString As String = "test"
Dim secondString As String = "TeSt"

'Returns:
'0 if the first string is equal to the second
```

```
'< 0 if the first string is less than the second
'> 0 if the first string is greater than the second
Dim result As Integer = String.CompareOrdinal(firstString, secondString)
```

Checking for Empty or Null Strings

The System.String class provides a method named IsNullOrEmpty that easily enables checking if a string is null or if it does not contain any characters. You can use such a method as follows:

```
If String.IsNullOrEmpty(stringToCheck) = False Then
    'The string is neither null nor empty
Else
    'The string is either null or empty
End If
```

Of course, you could also perform your check against True instead of False. In such situations both conditions (null or empty) are evaluated. This can be useful because you often need to validate strings to check whether they are valid. There could be situations in which you need to just ensure that a string is null or not empty. In this case you should use the usual syntax:

```
If stringToCheck Is Nothing Then
    'String is null
End If
If stringToCheck = "" Then
    'String is empty
End If
```

Formatting Strings

Often you need to send output strings according to a particular format, such as currency, percentage, and decimal numbers. The System.String class offers a useful method named Format that enables you to easily format text. Consider the following code example, paying attention to comments:

```
'Returns "The cost for traveling to Europe is $1,000.00
Console.WriteLine(String.Format("The cost for traveling to Europe is {0:C}
                                dollars", 1000))
'Returns "You are eligible for a 15.50% discount"
Console.WriteLine(String.Format("You are eligible for a {0:P} discount",
                                15.55F))
'Returns "Hex counterpart for 10 is A"
Console.WriteLine(String.Format("Hex counterpart for 10 is {0:X}", 10))
```

The first thing to notice is how you present your strings; Format accepts a number of values to be formatted and then embedded in the main string, which are referenced with the number enclosed in brackets. For example, {0} is the second argument of Format, {1} is the third one, and so on. Symbols enable the format; for example, c stands for currency, p stands for percentage, and x stands for hexadecimal. Visual Basic 2012 offers the symbols listed in Table 4.7.

TABLE 4.7   Format Symbols Accepted

Symbol	Description
C or c	Currency
D or d	Decimal
E or e	Scientific
F or f	Fixed point
G or g	General
N or n	Number
P or p	Percentage
R or r	Roundtrip
X or x	Hexadecimal

ROUNDTRIP

Roundtrip ensures that conversions from floating point to String and that converting back are allowed.

You can format multiple strings in one line of code, as in the following example:

```
Console.Writeline(String.Format("The traveling cost is" &
                " {0:C}. Hex for {1} is '{1,5:X}'", 1000, 10))
```

The preceding code produces the following result:

```
The traveling cost is $1,000.00. Hex for 10 is '    A'
```

As you can see, you can specify a number of white spaces before the next value. This is accomplished by typing the number of spaces you want to add followed by a : symbol and then the desired format symbol. String.Format also enables the use of custom formats. Custom formats are based on the symbols shown in Table 4.8.

TABLE 4.8   Symbols You Can Use for Custom Formats

Symbol	Description
0	A numeric placeholder showing 0
#	A digit placeholder
%	Percentage symbol

Symbol	Description
.	Decimal dot
,	Thousands separator
;	Section separator
"ABC" or 'ABC'	String literals
\	Escape
E or e combined with + or −	Scientific

According to Table 4.7, we could write a custom percentage representation:

```
'Returns "Custom percentage %1,550"
Console.WriteLine(String.Format("Custom percentage {0:%##,###.##} ", 15.50))
```

Or you could write a custom currency representation. For example, if you live in Great Britain, you could write the following line for representing the Sterling currency:

```
Console.WriteLine(String.Format("Custom currency {0:£#,###.00} ", 987654))
```

Another interesting feature in customizing output is the ability to provide different formats according to the input value. For example, you can decide to format a number depending if it is positive, negative, or zero. At this regard, consider the following code:

```
Dim number As Decimal = 1000
Console.WriteLine(String.
            Format("Custom currency formatting:
            {0:£#,##0.00;*£#,##0.00*;Zero}",
            number))
```

Here you specify three different formats, separated by semicolons. The first format affects positive numbers (such as the value of the number variable); the second one affects negative numbers, and the third one affects a zero value. The preceding example therefore produces the following output:

```
Custom currency formatting: £1,000.00
```

If you try to change the value of the number to −1000, the code produces the following output:

```
Custom currency formatting: *£1,000.00*
```

Finally, if you assign number = 0, the code produces the following output:

```
Custom currency formatting: Zero
```

Creating Copies of Strings

Strings in .NET are reference types. Because of this, assigning a string object to another string to perform a copy will just copy the reference to the actual string. Fortunately, the `System.String` class provides two useful methods for copying strings: `Copy` and `CopyTo`. The first one creates a copy of an entire string:

```
Dim sourceString As String = "Alessandro Del Sole"
Dim targetString As String = String.Copy(sourceString)
```

`Copy` is a shared method and can create a new instance of `String` and then put into the instance the content of the original string. If you instead need to create a copy of only a subset of the original string, you can invoke the instance method `CopyTo`. Such method works a little differently from `Copy` because it returns an array of `Char`. The following code provides an example:

```
Dim sourceString As String = "Alessandro Del Sole"
Dim charArray(sourceString.Length) As Char
sourceString.CopyTo(11, charArray, 0, 3)
Console.WriteLine(charArray)
```

You first need to declare an array of `Char`—in this case as long as the string length. The first argument of `CopyTo` is the start position in the original string; the second is the target array. The third one is the start position in the target array, and the fourth one is the number of characters to copy. In the end, such code produces `Del` as the output.

`Clone` METHOD

The `String` class also offers a method named `Clone`. You should not confuse this method with `Copy` and `CopyTo` because it will just return a reference to the original string and not a real copy.

Inspecting Strings

When working with strings, you often need to inspect or evaluate their content. The `System.String` class provides both methods and properties for inspecting strings. Imagine you have the following string:

```
Dim testString As String = "This is a string to inspect"
```

You can retrieve the string's length via its `Length` property:

```
'Returns 27
Dim length As Integer = testString.Length
```

Another interesting method is `Contains`, which enables you to know whether a string contains the specified substring or array of `Char`. `Contains` returns a Boolean value, as you can see in the following code snippet:

```
'Returns True
Dim contains As Boolean = testString.Contains("inspect")
'Returns False
Dim contains1 As Boolean = testString.Contains("Inspect")
```

Just remember that evaluation is case-sensitive. In some situations, you might need to check whether a string begins or ends with a specified substring. You can verify both situations using StartsWith and EndsWith methods:

```
'Returns False, the string starts with "T"
Dim startsWith As Boolean = testString.StartsWith("Uh")
'Returns True
Dim endsWith As Boolean = testString.EndsWith("pect")
```

Often you might also need to get the position of a specified substring within a string. To accomplish this, you can use the IndexOf method. For example, you could retrieve the start position of the first "is" substring as follows:

```
'Returns 2
Dim index As Integer = testString.IndexOf("is")
```

The code returns 2 because the start index is zero-based and refers to the "is" substring of the "This" word. You do not need to start your search from the beginning of the string; you can specify a start index or specify how the comparison must be performed via the StringComparison enumeration. Both situations are summarized in the following code:

```
'Returns 5
Dim index1 As Integer = testString.IndexOf("is", 3,
                StringComparison.InvariantCultureIgnoreCase)
```

StringComparison ENUMERATION

You can refer to IntelliSense when typing code for further details on the StringComparison enumeration options. They are self-explanatory, and for the sake of brevity, all options cannot be shown here.

IndexOf performs a search on the exact substring. You might also need to search for the position of just one character of a set of characters. This can be accomplished using the IndexOfAny method as follows:

```
'Returns 1
Dim index2 As Integer = testString.
                IndexOfAny(New Char() {"h"c, "s"c, "i"c})
```

The preceding code has an array of Char storing three characters, all available in the main string. Because the first character in the array is found first, IndexOfAny returns its position. Generally, IndexOfAny returns the position of the character that is found first. There are counterparts to both `IndexOf` and `IndexOfAny`: `LastIndexOf` and `LastIndexOfAny`. The first two methods perform a search starting from the beginning of a string, whereas the last two perform a search starting from the end of a string. This is an example:

```
'Returns 5
Dim lastIndex As Integer = testString.LastIndexOf("is")
'Returns 22
Dim lastIndex1 As Integer = testString.LastIndexOfAny(New Char()
                               {"h"c, "s"c, "i"c})
```

Notice how `LastIndexOf` returns the second occurrence of the "is" substring if you consider the main string from the beginning. Indexing is useful, but this only stores the position of a substring. If you need to retrieve the text of a substring, you can use the `SubString` method that works as follows:

```
'Returns "is a string"
Dim subString As String = testString.Substring(5, 11)
```

You can also just specify the start index, if you need the entire substring starting from a particular point.

Editing Strings

The `System.String` class provides members for editing strings. The first method described is named `Insert` and enables adding a substring into a string at the specified index. Consider the following example:

```
Dim testString As String = "This is a test string"
'Returns
'"This is a test,for demo purposes only,string"
Dim result As String = testString.Insert(14, ",for demo purposes only,")
```

As you can see from the comment in the code, `Insert` adds the specified substring from the specified index but does not append or replace anything. `Insert`'s counterpart is `Remove`, which enables removing a substring starting from the specified index or a piece of substring from the specified index and for the specified number of characters. This is an example:

```
'Returns "This is a test string"
Dim removedString As String = testString.Remove(14)
```

Remember that you always need to assign the result of a method call that makes an edit to a string, because of the immutability of string types. In this case, invoking `Remove` does not change the content of `testString`, so you need to assign the result of the method call to a variable (new or existing).

Another common task is replacing a substring within a string with another string. For example, imagine you want to replace the "test" substring with the "demo" substring within the testString instance. This can be accomplished using the Replace method as follows:

```
'Returns
'"This is a demo string"
Dim replacedString As String = testString.Replace("test", "demo")
```

The result of Replace must be assigned to another string to get the desired result. (See "Performance Tips" at the end of this section.) Editing strings also contain splitting techniques. You often need to split one string into multiple strings, especially when the string contains substrings separated by a symbol. For example, consider the following code in which a string contains substrings separated by commas, as in CSV files:

```
Dim stringToSplit As String = "Name,Last Name,Age"
```

You might want to extract the three substrings, Name, Last Name, and Age, and store them as unique strings. To accomplish this, you can use the Split method, which can receive as an argument the separator character:

```
Dim result() As String = stringToSplit.Split(","c)
For Each item As String In result
    Console.WriteLine(item)
Next
```

The preceding code retrieves three strings that are stored into an array of String and then produces the following output:

```
Name
Last Name
Age
```

Split has several overloads that you can inspect with IntelliSense. One of these enables you to specify the maximum number of substrings to extract and split options, such as normal splitting or splitting if substrings are not empty:

```
Dim result() As String = stringToSplit.Split(New Char() {","c}, 2,
                StringSplitOptions.RemoveEmptyEntries)
```

In this overload you have to explicitly specify an array of Char; in this case there is just a one-dimension array containing the split symbol. Such code produces the following output, considering that only two substrings are accepted:

```
Name
Last Name, Age
```

Opposite to Split, there is also a Join method that enables joining substrings into a unique string. Substrings are passed as an array of String and are separated by the specified character. The following code shows an example:

```
'Returns "Name, Last Name, Age"
Dim result As String = String.Join(",",
                        New String() {"Name", "Last Name", "Age"})
```

Another way to edit strings is trimming. Imagine you have a string containing white spaces at the end of the string or at the beginning of the string, or both. You might want to remove white spaces from the main string. The `System.String` class provides three methods, `Trim`, `TrimStart`, and `TrimEnd`, that enable you to accomplish this task, as shown in the following code (see comments):

```
Dim stringWithSpaces As String = "    Test with spaces    "
'Returns "Test with spaces"
Dim result1 As String = stringWithSpaces.Trim
'Returns "Test with spaces    "
Dim result2 As String = stringWithSpaces.TrimStart
'Returns "    Test with spaces"
Dim result3 As String = stringWithSpaces.TrimEnd
```

All three methods provide overloads for specifying characters different from white spaces. (Imagine you want to remove an asterisk.) Opposite to `TrimStart` and `TrimEnd`, `System.String` exposes `PadLeft` and `PadRight`. The best explanation for both methods is a practical example. Consider the following code:

```
Dim padResult As String = testString.PadLeft(30, "*"c)
```

It produces the following result:

```
*********This is a test string
```

`PadLeft` creates a new string, whose length is the one specified as the first argument of the method and that includes the original string with the addition of a number of symbols that is equal to the difference from the length you specified and the length of the original string. In our case, the original string is 21 characters long, although we specified 30 as the new length. So, there are 9 asterisks. `PadRight` does the same, but symbols are added on the right side, as in the following example:

```
Dim padResult As String = testString.PadRight(30, "*"c)
```

This code produces the following result:

```
This is a test string*********
```

Both methods are useful if you need to add symbols to the left or to the right of a string.

PERFORMANCE TIPS

Because of its particular nature, each time you edit a string you are not actually editing the string—instead, you are creating a new instance of the `System.String` class. As you might imagine, this could lead to performance issues. That said, although it's fundamental to know how you can edit strings; you should always prefer the `StringBuilder` object, especially when concatenating strings. `StringBuilder` is discussed later in this chapter.

Concatenating Strings

Concatenation is perhaps the most common task that developers need to perform on strings. In Visual Basic 2012 you have some alternatives. First, you can use the addition operator:

```
Dim firstString As String = "Hello! My name is "
Dim secondString As String = "Alessandro Del Sole"

Dim result As String = firstString + secondString
```

Another, better, approach is the `String.Concat` method:

```
Dim concatResult As String =
               String.Concat(firstString, secondString)
```

Both ways produce the same result, but both ways have a big limitation; because strings are immutable, the CLR needs to create a new instance of the `String` class each time you perform a concatenation. This scenario can lead to a significant loss of performance. If you need to concatenate 10 strings, the CLR creates 10 instances of the `String` class. Fortunately, the .NET Framework provides a more efficient way for concatenating strings: the `StringBuilder` object.

The `StringBuilder` Object

The `System.Text.StringBuilder` class provides an efficient way for concatenating strings. You should always use `StringBuilder` in such situations. The real difference is that `StringBuilder` can create a buffer that grows along with the real needs of storing text. (The default constructor creates a 16-byte buffer.) Using the `StringBuilder` class is straightforward. Consider the following code example:

```
'Requires an Imports System.Text directive
Function ConcatenatingStringsWithStringBuilder() As String
        Dim result As New StringBuilder

        'Ensures that the StringBuilder instance
        'has the capacity of at least 100 characters
        result.EnsureCapacity(100)
        result.Append("Hello! My name is ")
        result.Append("Alessandro Del Sole")
        Return result.ToString
End Function
```

You simply instantiate the `StringBuilder` class using the `New` keyword and then invoke the `Append` method that receives as an argument the string that must be concatenated. In the end, you need to explicitly convert the `StringBuilder` to a `String` invoking the `ToString` method. This class is powerful and provides several methods for working with strings, such as `AppendLine` (which appends an empty line with a carriage return), `AppendFormat` (which enables you to format the appended string), and `Replace` (which enables you to replace all occurrences of the specified string with another string). The `EnsureCapacity` method used in the code example ensures that the `StringBuilder` instance can contain at least the specified number of characters. You can find in the `StringBuilder` class the same methods provided by the `String` class (`Replace`, `Insert`, `Remove`, and so on), so working with `StringBuilder` should be familiar and straightforward.

Working with Dates

Together with strings, you often need to handle dates and moments in time. To accomplish this, the .NET Framework 4.5 provides the `System.DateTime` value type.

> ### MinValue AND MaxValue
>
> Being a value type, `System.DateTime` has two shared fields: `MinValue` and `MaxValue`. These store the minimum accepted date and the maximum date, respectively. The minimum date is 01/01/0001 00:00:00 a.m., and maximum date is 12/31/9999 11:59:59 p.m.

Creating Dates

The Visual Basic grammar offers the `Date` keyword, which is a lexical representation of the `System.DateTime` object, so you can use both definitions. For consistency, we use the `Date` reserved keyword, but keep in mind that this keyword creates (or gets a reference to) an instance of the `System.DateTime` type. Working with dates is an easy task. You can create a new date by creating an instance of the `DateTime` class:

```
Dim myBirthDate As New Date(1977, 5, 10)
```

The constructor has several overloads, but the most common is the preceding one, where you can specify year, month, and day. For example, such values could be written by the user and then converted into a `DateTime` object. Another common situation in which you need to create a date is for storing the current system clock date and time. This can be easily accomplished using the `DateTime.Now` property as follows:

```
Dim currentDate As Date = Date.Now
```

Such code produces the following result, representing the moment when I'm writing this chapter:

```
5/28/2012 10:02:35 PM
```

When you get an instance of a `DateTime`, you can retrieve a lot of information about it. For example, consider the following code taking care of comments:

```
'Creates a new date; May 10th 1977, 8.30 pm
Dim myBirthDate As New Date(1977, 5, 10,
                            20, 30, 0)


'In 1977, May 10th was Tuesday
Console.WriteLine(myBirthDate.DayOfWeek.
                 ToString)


'8.30 pm
Console.WriteLine("Hour: {0}, Minutes: {1}",
                 myBirthDate.Hour,
                 myBirthDate.Minute)


'Is the date included within the Day Light Saving Time period?
Console.WriteLine("Is Day light saving time: {0}",
                 myBirthDate.IsDaylightSavingTime.
                 ToString)


'Is leap year
Console.WriteLine("Is leap: {0}",
                 Date.IsLeapYear(myBirthDate.Year).
                 ToString)
```

The code first creates the following date, representing my birth date: 5/10/1977 8:30:00 PM. Then it retrieves some information, such as the name of the day of the week (represented by the `DayOfWeek` enumeration), the hours, the minutes (via the `Hour` and `Minute` integer properties), and the specified date within Daylight Saving Time. The `DateTime` object also exposes a shared method named `IsLeapYear` that can establish whether the specified year is a leap year. In our example, the year is not passed directly but is provided via the `Year` property of the `myBirthDate` instance. The following is the result of the code:

```
Tuesday
Hour: 20, Minutes: 30
Is Day light saving time: True
Is leap: False
```

Finally, you can declare dates with the so-called date literals. The following is an example of how you can customize the date format:

```
Dim customDate As Date = #5/25/2012 8:00:00 PM#
```

Converting Strings into Dates

It is not unusual to ask the user to provide a date within an application. Typically, this is accomplished via the user interface and, if you do not provide a specific user control (such as the WPF `DatePicker` or the Win Forms `DateTimePicker`) for selecting dates in a graphical fashion, such input is provided in the form of a string. Because of this, you need a way of converting the string into a date, so that you can then manipulate the user input as an effective `DateTime` object (unless the string is invalid; then you need validation). To accomplish this kind of conversion, the `System.DateTime` class provides two methods that you already saw when discussing value types: `Parse` and `TryParse`. For example, consider the following code that receives an input by the user and attempts to convert such input into a `DateTime` object:

```
Sub ParsingDates()
    Console.WriteLine("Please specify a date:")
    Dim inputDate As Date
    Dim result As Boolean = Date.TryParse(Console.ReadLine, inputDate)

    If result = False Then
        Console.WriteLine("You entered an invalid date")
    Else
        Console.WriteLine(inputDate.DayOfWeek.ToString)
    End If
End Sub
```

The `TryParse` method receives the string to convert as the first argument (which in this case is obtained by the Console window) and the output object passed by reference (`inputDate`); it returns `True` if the conversion succeeds or `False` if it fails. The conversion succeeds if the input string format is accepted and recognized by the `DateTime` type. If you run this code and enter a string in the format 1977/05/10, the conversion succeeds because such format is accepted by `DateTime`. You can then manipulate the new date as you like. (In the preceding example, the code shows the day of the week for the specified date, which in my example is Tuesday.)

TIP

In many cases you work with data from a database. The ADO.NET engine and layered technologies, such as LINQ, map dates from databases directly into a `System.DateTime` object so that you will be able to work and manipulate such objects from and to data sources.

Formatting Dates

You need to present dates for several scenarios, and you might be required to perform this task in different ways. Fortunately, the `System.DateTime` provides many ways of formatting dates. The easiest way is invoking the `ToString` method, which accepts an argument that enables specifying how a date must be presented. For example, consider the following code snippet that writes the current date in both the extended (D) and the short (d) date formats:

```
Console.WriteLine(DateTime.Now.ToString("D"))
Console.WriteLine(DateTime.Now.ToString("d"))
```

Such code produces the following output:

```
Monday, May 28, 2012
5/28/2012
```

The result is based on the regional and culture settings of your system. Table 4.9 summarizes symbols you can use with the ToString method.

TABLE 4.9   Date Formatting Symbols with ToString

Symbol	Preview
D	Monday, May 28, 2012
d	5/28/2012
T	10:02:35 PM
t	10:02 PM
F	Monday, May 28, 2012 10:02:35 PM
f	Monday, May 28, 2012 10:02 PM
G	5/28/2012 10:02:35 PM
g	5/28/2012 10:02 PM
S	2012-05-28T22:2:35
U	Monday, May 28, 2012 10:02:35 PM
u	2012-05-28 22:2:35Z

ToString also recognizes date literals. The following is an example of how you can customize and write a date:

```
Console.WriteLine(Date.Today.ToString("dd/MM/yyyy"))
```

The previous code prints the current date in the Day/Month/Year format. System.DateTime provides a plethora of other useful methods you can use for formatting dates. Such methods also return different data types, depending on the scenario in which they have to be used in. Table 4.10 summarizes the most important methods you can always inspect with IntelliSense and the Object Browser.

TABLE 4.10   System.DateTime Useful Methods

Method	Description	Type Returned
ToLocalTime	Returns the full date representation according to regional settings	Date (System.DateTime)
ToLongDateString	Returns a long format date (without time)	String

Method	Description	Type Returned
`ToShortDateString`	Returns a short format date (without time)	`String`
`ToLongTimeString`	Returns a long format time (without date)	`String`
`ToShortTimeString`	Returns a short format time (without date)	`String`
`ToUniversalTime`	Returns a full date representation according to the Coordinated Universal Time specifications	`Date (System.DateTime)`
`ToOADate`	Returns an OLE Automation date format	`Double`
`ToFileTime`	Returns the Windows file time representation of a date	`Long`
`ToFileTimeUtc`	Returns the Windows file time representation of a date, according to the Coordinated Universal Time specifications	`Long`

The following code snippet uses all the preceding methods to demonstrate how the output differs depending on the method:

```
Console.WriteLine("Local time: {0}", Date.Now.ToLocalTime)
Console.WriteLine("Long date: {0}", Date.Now.ToLongDateString)
Console.WriteLine("Short date: {0}", Date.Now.ToShortDateString)
Console.WriteLine("Long time: {0}", Date.Now.ToLongTimeString)
Console.WriteLine("Short time: {0}", Date.Now.ToShortTimeString)
Console.WriteLine("Universal time: {0}", Date.Now.
                ToUniversalTime.ToString)
Console.WriteLine("File time: {0}", Date.Now.
                ToFileTime.ToString)
Console.WriteLine("File time UTC: {0}", Date.Now.
                ToFileTimeUtc.ToString)
Console.WriteLine("OLE Automation date: {0}", Date.Now.
                ToOADate.ToString)
```

The preceding code produces the following result, which you can compare with the methods described in Table 4.9:

```
Local time: 05/28/2012 19:27:22
Long date: Monday, May 28, 2012
Short date: 5/28/2012
Long time: 7:27:22 PM
Short time: 7:27 PM
Universal time: 5/28/2012 7:27:22 PM
```

```
File time: 129826997181439508
File time UTC: 129826997181439508
OLE Automation date: 41057.811552581
```

Subtracting Dates and Adding Time to Time

It's not unusual to need to know the amount of time spent between two dates. The `System.DateTime` enables this by invoking a `Subtract` method, which returns a `System.TimeSpan` value. For example, consider the following code that subtracts a date from another one:

```
Dim birthDate As Date = New Date(1977, 5, 10, 20, 30, 0)
Dim secondDate As Date = New Date(1990, 5, 11, 20, 10, 0)

Dim result As System.TimeSpan = secondDate.Subtract(birthDate)

'In days
Console.WriteLine(result.Days)
'In "ticks"
Console.WriteLine(result.Ticks)
```

You can subtract two `DateTime` objects and get a result of type `TimeSpan` (discussed next). You can then get information on the result, such as the number of days that represent the difference between the two dates or the number of ticks. The previous code produces the following result:

```
4748
4103124000000000
```

You can also add values to a date. For example you can edit a date by adding days, hours, minutes, seconds, or ticks or by incrementing the year. Consider the following code snippet:

```
Dim editedDate As Date = birthDate.AddDays(3)
editedDate = editedDate.AddHours(2)
editedDate = editedDate.AddYears(1)

Console.WriteLine(editedDate)
```

This code adds three days and two hours to the date and increments the year by one unit. In the end, it produces the following output:

```
5/13/1978 10:30:00 PM
```

You can use negative numbers to subtract values from a single date, which returns a `Date` object instead of a `TimeSpan` like in `Subtract`. For instance, the following code subtracts a day from the date represented by the `birthDate` variable:

```
'Returns 05/09/1977
Dim result As Date = birthDate.AddDays(-1)
```

Dates are important and, although they allow working with time, too, the .NET Framework provides an important structure specific for representing pieces of time: System.TimeSpan.

NOTE ABOUT OPERATORS

You can use standard operators such as the addition and subtraction operators when working with both DateTime and TimeSpan objects. This is possible because both objects overload the standard operators. Overloading operators is discussed in Chapter 11.

Working with Time

You often need to represent intervals of time in your applications, especially in conjunction with dates. The .NET Framework provides a structure—a value type named System.TimeSpan. This structure can represent time from a minimum value (one tick) until a maximum value (one day). A *tick* is the smallest unit for time representations and is equal to 100 nanoseconds. TimeSpan represents a summed amount of time between two given time values, and the time portion of a Date object represents a single specific moment in time.

MINIMUM AND MAXIMUM VALUES

As for other value types, System.TimeSpan also provides two shared properties named MinValue and MaxValue. MinValue returns -10675199.02:48:05.4775808, and MaxValue returns 10675199.02:48:05.4775807. For the sake of clarity, both values are respectively equal to System.Int64.MinValue and System.Int64.MaxValue.

You can find several places in which using TimeSpan is needed other than simply working with dates. For example, you might want to create your performance benchmarks using the StopWatch object that returns a TimeSpan. Or you might need such structure when working with animations in WPF applications. The following code example simulates a performance test; a System.StopWatch object is started, an intensive loop is performed, and then the StopWatch is stopped. The StopWatch class offers an Elapsed property that is of type TimeSpan and that can be useful for analyzing the amount of elapsed time:

```
Dim watch As New Stopwatch

watch.Start()
For i = 0 To 10000
    'Simulates intensive processing
    System.Threading.Thread.SpinWait(800000)
Next
watch.Stop()
```

```
Console.WriteLine(watch.Elapsed.Seconds)
Console.WriteLine(watch.Elapsed.Milliseconds)
Console.WriteLine(watch.Elapsed.Ticks)
```

The preceding code produced the following result on my machine, but it will be different on yours, depending on your hardware:

```
49
374
493746173
```

The `TimeSpan` structure is similar to the area of the `DateTime` type that is related to time. Notice that `TimeSpan` offers several similar properties, such as `Days`; `Hours`; `Minutes`; `Seconds`; `Milliseconds`; and methods such as `AddDays`, `AddHours`, `AddMinute`, and `Subtract`. `TimeSpan` is all about time; this means that although there are similarities, as mentioned before, with the time-related `DateTime` members, you cannot (obviously) work with dates. The following code provides an example of creating a `TimeSpan` instance starting from an existing date:

```
Sub TimeSpanInstance()
    Dim currentDate As Date = Date.Now
    'Because the System namespace is imported at project
    'level, we do not need an Imports directive
    Dim intervalOfTime As TimeSpan = currentDate.TimeOfDay

    Console.WriteLine("My friend, in the current date " &
                    "there are {0} days; time is {1}:{2}:{3}",
            intervalOfTime.Days,
            intervalOfTime.Hours,
            intervalOfTime.Minutes,
            intervalOfTime.Seconds)
End Sub
```

The preceding code produces the following result:

```
My friend, in the current date there are 0 days; time is 19:30
```

In the specified interval, there is only the current day, so the first argument returns zero. Take a look back at the section "Subtracting Dates and Adding Time to Time" to see an example of `TimeSpan` usage for an interval of time retrieved subtracting two dates.

Working with `TimeZone` and `TimeZoneInfo`

You might often ask what people are doing on the other side of world when in your country it's a particular time of the day. Working with time zones can also be important for your business if you need to contact people who live in different and faraway countries. The .NET Framework provides two types, `TimeZone` and `TimeZoneInfo`, which enable retrieving information on time zones. Both types are exposed by the `System` namespace. For example, imagine you want to retrieve information on the time zone of your country. This can be accomplished as follows (assuming regional settings on your machine are effectively related to your country):

```
Dim zone As TimeZone = TimeZone.CurrentTimeZone
```

`TimeZone` is a reference type and through its `CurrentTimeZone` property it provides a lot of information such as the name of the time zone or the Daylight Saving Time period as demonstrated here:

```
Console.WriteLine(zone.DaylightName)
Console.WriteLine(zone.StandardName)
Console.WriteLine(zone.IsDaylightSavingTime(Date.Now))
```

This code produces the following result on my machine:

```
W. Europe Daylight Time
W. Europe Standard Time
True
```

The official MSDN documentation states that using the `TimeZoneInfo` class should be preferred instead of `TimeZone`. This is because `TimeZoneInfo` also provides the ability of creating custom time zones. The following code shows how you can retrieve current time zone information using `TimeZoneInfo`:

```
Dim tz As TimeZoneInfo = TimeZoneInfo.Local
'Shows the current time zone Identifier
Console.WriteLine(tz.Id)
```

Creating a custom time zone is also a simple task, which is accomplished by the following code:

```
Dim customZone As TimeZoneInfo = TimeZoneInfo.
    CreateCustomTimeZone("CustomTimeZone",
    Date.UtcNow.Subtract(Date.Now),
    "Custom Zone", "Custom Zone")
```

All you need is to specify a custom identifier, the difference between the UTC time span and the local time span, a daylight identifier, and a standard identifier. `TimeZoneInfo` also provides another useful method for enumerating time zones recognized by the system, named `GetSystemTimeZones`; you can use it like this:

```
For Each timez As TimeZoneInfo In TimeZoneInfo.GetSystemTimeZones
    Console.WriteLine(timez.DisplayName)
Next
```

An excerpt of the output provided by this simple iteration is the following:

```
(UTC-12:00) International Date Line West
(UTC-11:00) Midway Island, Samoa
(UTC-10:00) Hawaii
(UTC-09:00) Alaska
(UTC-08:00) Pacific Time (US & Canada)
(UTC-08:00) Tijuana, Baja California
(UTC-07:00) Arizona
(UTC-07:00) Chihuahua, La Paz, Mazatlan
(UTC-07:00) Mountain Time (US & Canada)
(UTC-06:00) Central America
(UTC-06:00) Central Time (US & Canada)
(UTC-05:00) Eastern Time (US & Canada)
(UTC-05:00) Indiana (East)
(UTC-04:30) Caracas
(UTC-04:00) Santiago
(UTC-03:30) Newfoundland
(UTC-01:00) Cape Verde Is.
(UTC) Casablanca
(UTC) Coordinated Universal Time
(UTC) Dublin, Edinburgh, Lisbon, London
(UTC) Monrovia, Reykjavik
(UTC+01:00) Amsterdam, Berlin, Bern, Rome, Stockholm, Vienna
(UTC+02:00) Windhoek
(UTC+03:00) Baghdad
(UTC+03:00) Kuwait, Riyadh
(UTC+03:00) Moscow, St. Petersburg, Volgograd
(UTC+03:00) Nairobi
(UTC+06:00) Almaty, Novosibirsk
(UTC+06:00) Astana, Dhaka
(UTC+06:30) Yangon (Rangoon)
(UTC+07:00) Krasnoyarsk
(UTC+08:00) Beijing, Chongqing, Hong Kong, Urumqi
(UTC+08:00) Perth
(UTC+08:00) Taipei
(UTC+09:00) Yakutsk
(UTC+09:30) Adelaide
(UTC+10:00) Vladivostok
(UTC+11:00) Magadan, Solomon Is., New Caledonia
(UTC+12:00) Auckland, Wellington
(UTC+12:00) Fiji, Kamchatka, Marshall Is.
(UTC+13:00) Nuku'alofa
```

Thanks to this information, you could use the `TimeZoneInfo` class for converting between time zones. The following code demonstrates how to calculate the hour difference between Italy and Redmond, Washington:

```
'Redmond time; requires specifying the Time Zone ID
Dim RedmondTime As Date = TimeZoneInfo.
    ConvertTimeBySystemTimeZoneId(DateTime.Now, "Pacific Standard Time")

Console.WriteLine("In Italy now is {0} while in Redmond it is {1}",
                Date.Now.Hour,RedmondTime.Hour)
```

By invoking the `ConvertTimeBySystemZoneId` method, you can convert between your local system time and another time, based on the zone ID. If you don't know zone IDs, just replace the previous iterations for showing the content of the `timez.Id` property instead of `DisplayName`.

Working with GUIDs

How many times do you need to represent something with a unique identifier? Probably very often. Examples are items with the same name but with different characteristics. The .NET Framework enables creating unique identifiers via the `System.Guid` structure (therefore a value type). This lets you generate a unique, 128-bit string, identifier. To generate a unique identifier, invoke the `Guid.NewGuid` method, which works as follows:

```
'Declaring a Guid
Dim uniqueIdentifier As Guid

'A unique identifier
uniqueIdentifier = Guid.NewGuid
Console.WriteLine(uniqueIdentifier.ToString)

'Another unique identifier,
'although to the same variable
uniqueIdentifier = Guid.NewGuid
Console.WriteLine(uniqueIdentifier.ToString)
```

If you run the preceding code, you notice that each time you invoke the `NewGuid` method a new GUID is generated, although you assign such a value to the same variable. This makes sense because you use the GUID each time you need a unique identifier. On my machine the preceding code produces the following result:

```
46e0daca-db56-45b1-923e-f76cf1636019
6fd3a61d-ec17-4b6a-adec-6acfa9a0cb00
```

EXAMPLES OF GUIDS

The Windows operating system makes a huge usage of GUIDs. If you try to inspect the Windows Registry, you'll find lots of examples.

The `Guid.NewGuid` method provides auto-generated GUIDs. If you need to provide your own GUID, you can use the `New` constructor followed by the desired identifier:

```
'Specifying a Guid
uniqueIdentifier = New Guid("f578c96b-5918-4f79-b690-6c463ffb2c3e")
```

The constructor has several overloads, which enable generating GUIDs also based on byte arrays and integers. Generally, you use GUIDs each time you need to represent something as unique. Several .NET types accept GUIDs, so you need to know how you can create them in code, although this is not the only way.

Creating GUIDs with the Visual Studio Instrumentation

The Visual Studio IDE provides a graphical tool for generating GUIDs. You can run this tool by selecting the **Create GUID** command from the Tools menu. Figure 4.11 shows the Create GUID window.

FIGURE 4.11   The Create GUID tool from Visual Studio.

You can choose the format you need for your GUID, such as Windows-like GUIDs. When you get your GUID, you can copy it to the clipboard and then reuse it in your code.

Working with Arrays

As a developer, you know what arrays are. They are a place in which you can store a set of items, generally of the same type. In the .NET Framework 4.5 (as in older versions), arrays are reference types all deriving from the `System.Array` class and can be both one-dimensional and multidimensional.

ARRAYS VERSUS COLLECTIONS

Collections, especially generic ones, are more efficient than arrays. I always recommend working with collections instead of arrays, except when strictly needed. (For example, you might need jagged arrays.)

You can either declare an array and use it later in your code or declare it and assign it with objects. The following is an example of declaring an array of `String` objects, meaning that it can store only objects of type `String`:

```
Dim anArrayOfString() As String
```

In this line of code an array of `String` is declared. This array has no predefined bounds, so it is flexible and useful if you cannot predict how many items it needs to store. There is also an alternative syntax, which allows placing parentheses at the end of the type, as follows:

```
'Alternative syntax
Dim anArrayOfString As String()
```

You are free to use whichever syntax you like. For the sake of consistency, the first one is used.

IS `Option Strict` **ON?**

The preceding and the following code examples assume that `Option Strict` is set to `On`. If it is off, adding instances of `System.Object` is also allowed but might cause errors at runtime. It is recommended to set `Option Strict` to `On` to avoid implicit conversion, and this is one of those cases.

You can initialize arrays directly when declaring them, as in the following code that declares an array of strings and stores three instances of the `System.String` class:

```
'Inline initialization with implicit bounds
Dim anArrayOfThreeStrings() As String = New String() {"One", "Two", "Three"}
```

Notice how you assign an array using the `New` keyword followed by the type name and a couple of parentheses. Brackets contain the items to store. The declared array has no bounds limits, but actually after the assignment its upper bound is 2, so its bounds are determined by the number of values it is initialized with.

ARRAYS BASE

Arrays are zero-based. This means that an array with an upper bound of 2 can store three items (index of zero, index of one, and index of two). This also means that the upper bound will always be one less than the `Count` property of the array.

This approach works with arrays of other .NET types, too, as in the following code in which `Char` and `Byte` are used:

```
Dim anArrayOfChar() As Char = New Char() {"a"c, "b"c, "c"c}

Dim anArrayOfByte() As Byte = New Byte() {1, 2, 3}
```

If you already know how many items the array can store, you can specify the bounds limits. For example, imagine you want to store three instances of System.Byte into an array of Byte. This can be accomplished via the following code:

```
Dim anExplicitBoundArrayOfByte(2) As Byte
anExplicitBoundArrayOfByte(0) = 1
anExplicitBoundArrayOfByte(1) = 2
anExplicitBoundArrayOfByte(2) = 3
```

INLINE INITIALIZATION WITH EXPLICIT BOUNDS

Inline initialization is not allowed against arrays declared with explicit bounds. In such situations the only allowed syntax is the one shown in the previous code snippet.

The upper limit is enclosed in parentheses. Storing items is accomplished through indices. (The first one is always zero.) As with assignment, you can retrieve the content of a particular item using indices:

```
'Outputs 2
Console.WriteLine(anExplicitBoundArrayOfByte(1).ToString)
```

You can also perform tasks on each element in the array using a For Each loop, as in the following code snippet, which works the same on an array of Byte and on array of String:

```
For Each value As Byte In anExplicitBoundArrayOfByte
    Console.WriteLine(value)
Next
For Each value As String In anArrayOfThreeStrings
    Console.WriteLine(value)
Next
```

Another important task you should perform when working with not explicitly bound arrays is checking whether they contain something. You can accomplish this checking whether the array is Nothing:

```
If anArrayOfString Is Nothing Then
    'The array is not initialized
End If
```

This is because attempting to access a null array causes the runtime to throw an exception.

The ReDim Keyword

In some situations you need to increase the capacity of an array that you previously declared with explicit bounds. Let's retake one of the previous arrays:

```
Dim anExplicitBoundArrayOfByte(2) As Byte
anExplicitBoundArrayOfByte(0) = 1
anExplicitBoundArrayOfByte(1) = 2
anExplicitBoundArrayOfByte(2) = 3
```

At runtime you might need to store an additional `Byte`, so in this case you should first increase the array's size. To accomplish this, the Visual Basic grammar provides a special keyword named `ReDim`. `ReDim` redeclares an array of the same type with new bounds. But this keyword would also clean all the previously stored items; so what if you just need to add a new item to an existing list without clearing? Fortunately, the Visual Basic grammar provides another keyword named `Preserve` that is the best friend of `ReDim` in such situations and enables maintaining the previously stored values, preventing cleaning. The following code redeclares the preceding array without cleaning previous values:

```
ReDim Preserve anExplicitBoundArrayOfByte(3)
```

At this point, you can add a new item using the new available index:

```
anExplicitBoundArrayOfByte(3) = 4
```

Notice how you do not specify again the type of the array when using `ReDim`.

Multidimensional Arrays

Arrays can have multiple dimensions. Two-dimensional (also known as *rectangular*) and three-dimensional arrays are the most common situations. The following code declares a two-dimensional array with four values, but with no explicit dimensions specified:

```
Dim multiArray(,) As Integer = {{1, 2}, {3, 4}}
```

You can also specify dimensions as follows:

```
Dim multiArrayWithExplicitBounds(5, 1) As Integer
```

You cannot initialize arrays inline in the case of multidimensional arrays. You can then access indices as follows:

```
multiArrayWithExplicitBounds(1, 0) = 1
multiArrayWithExplicitBounds(2, 0) = 2
multiArrayWithExplicitBounds(1, 1) = 3
```

ARRAY LITERALS

Visual Basic also offers a specific feature for working with both multidimensional arrays and jagged arrays (discussed next), named Array Literals. This feature enables the compiler to infer the appropriate type for arrays. Because it requires that you are familiar with the Local Type Inference, Array Literals are discussed in Chapter 20.

Jagged Arrays

Jagged arrays are arrays of arrays and are similar to multidimensional arrays. However, they differ because each item of a dimension is an array. Here you see examples of jagged arrays of `Integer`. To declare a jagged array, you can use the following syntax:

```
'A 9-entry array on the left and
'an unbound array on the right
Dim firstJaggedArray(8)() As Integer
```

As you can see, a jagged array declaration is characterized by a double couple of parentheses. You can also declare a jagged array that is not explicitly bound, as in the following code snippet:

```
Dim unboundJaggedArray()() As Integer
```

Although you can perform inline initializations, this coding technique could become difficult with complex arrays. Because of this, it could be more convenient declaring the array and then assigning its indices as follows:

```
Dim oneIntArray() As Integer = {1, 2, 3}
Dim twoIntArray() As Integer = {4, 5, 6}
unboundJaggedArray = {oneIntArray, twoIntArray}
```

By the way, the following initialization is perfectly legal:

```
Dim unboundJaggedArray()() As Integer _
    = {New Integer() {1, 2, 3}, New Integer() {4, 5, 6}}
```

As I explain in Chapter 20, the Array Literals feature makes inline initialization easier. You can then normally access arrays (that is, items) in a jagged array—for example, performing a For..Each loop:

```
'Returns 1 2 3 4 5 6
        For Each arr As Integer() In unboundJaggedArray
            For Each item As Integer In arr
                Console.WriteLine(item.ToString)
            Next
        Next
```

Sorting, Creating, Copying, and Inspecting Arrays with the System.Array Class

As I mentioned at the beginning of this section, all arrays derive from the System.Array class and therefore are reference types. This is an important consideration because you have to know how to manipulate them. System.Array provides several static and instance members for performing tasks on arrays. Here we discuss the most important members and method overloads; they should be self-explanatory. IntelliSense can help by showing the necessary information. First, here's an example of an array of byte:

```
Dim anArrayOfByte() As Byte = New Byte() {1, 2, 3}
```

In this array, bounds are not explicit. Particularly at runtime, you might need to access array indices. To avoid IndexOutOfRange exceptions, though, you do need to know at least the upper bound. Just for clarification, imagine you want to perform a For..Next loop against an array. To accomplish this, you first need to know the bounds.

The `GetLowerBound` and `GetUpperBound` methods enable retrieving the lower and upper bounds of an array, as shown in the following code:

```
'Returns 0 and 2
Console.WriteLine("Lower bound {0}, upper bound {1}",
                anArrayOfByte.GetLowerBound(0).ToString,
                anArrayOfByte.GetUpperBound(0).ToString)
```

Both methods receive the dimension of the array as an argument. This is because they can work both on one-dimensional arrays and on multidimensional arrays. A zero dimension means that you are working with a one-dimensional array or with the first dimension of a multidimensional array. Another common task is sorting arrays. There are two methods that you can use, `Sort` and `Reverse`. `Sort` performs an ordering of arrays in an ascending way, whereas `Reverse` performs the ordering in a descending way. Starting from the `anArrayOfByte` array, the following code reverses the order:

```
'Array now contains 3, 2, 1
Array.Reverse(anArrayOfByte)
```

To sort the array back, you can simply invoke the `Sort` method:

```
Array.Sort(anArrayOfByte)
```

Both methods perform ordering according to the `IComparable(Of T)` interface. You can also search for a particular item within an array. For this purpose, you can use two methods: `IndexOf` and `BinarySearch`. Both return the index of the specified item, but the first one just stops searching when the first occurrence is found; the second one searches through the entire array, but only if the array is sorted according to the implementation of the `IComparable` interface. Their usage is very straightforward:

```
'A conversion to Byte is required
'Both return 1
Dim position As Integer = Array.IndexOf(anArrayOfByte, CByte(2))
Dim position2 As Integer = Array.BinarySearch(anArrayOfByte, CByte(2))
```

Both methods receive an `Object` as the second argument. But we have an array of `Byte`. Because just writing 2 tells the compiler to recognize such a number as an `Integer`, we need to explicitly convert it to `Byte`.

NOTE ON `System.Array` METHODS

`System.Array` also provides methods that take a lambda expression as arguments. Lambdas are discussed in Chapter 20, so we do not apply them to arrays in this chapter. A quick recap is done for your convenience in the appropriate place.

Another common task with arrays is copying. Because they are reference types, assigning an array to another just copies the reference. To create a real copy of an array, you can take advantage of the shared `Copy` method and of the instance `CopyTo` method. First, you need to declare a target array. Continuing the example about the `anArrayOfByte` array, you could declare the new one as follows:

```
'Declares an array to copy to,
'with bounds equals to the source array
Dim targetArray(anArrayOfByte.GetUpperBound(0)) As Byte
```

To ensure the upper bound is the same as in the original array, an invocation to the `GetUpperBound` method is made. Next, you can copy the array:

```
'Copies the original array into the target,
'using the original length
Array.Copy(anArrayOfByte, targetArray, anArrayOfByte.Length)
```

`Array.Copy` needs you to pass the source array, the target array, and the total number of items you want to copy. Supposing you want to perform a complete copy of the source array, you can just pass its length. The alternative is to invoke the instance method `CopyTo`:

```
anArrayOfByte.CopyTo(targetArray, 0)
```

The method receives the target array as the first argument and the index where copying must begin as the second argument. A third way for copying an array is invoking the `Clone` method, which is inherited from `System.Object`. Note that `Copy` and `CopyTo` provide more granularity and control over the copy process. The last scenario creates arrays on-the-fly. You could need to perform such a task at runtime given a number of items of a specified type—for example, when you receive several strings as the user input. The `System.Array` class provides a shared method named `CreateInstance`, which creates a new instance of the `System.Array` class. It receives two arguments: the `System.Type` that the array must be of and the upper bound. For example, the following code creates a new array of `String` that can store three elements:

```
Dim runTimeArray As Array = Array.CreateInstance(GetType(String), 2)
```

PAY ATTENTION TO CreateInstance

You should use `CreateInstance` with care because you can write code that is correctly compiled but that can cause runtime errors (for example, with regard to array bounds).

Because the first argument is the representation of the `System.Type` you want to assign to the array, you must use the `GetType` keyword to retrieve information about the type. You can assign items to each index invoking the `SetValue` method, which is an instance method. The following line of code assigns a string to the zero index of the previous array:

```
runTimeArray.SetValue(CStr("Test string"), 0)
```

If you want to retrieve your items, simply invoke the `GetValue` method specifying the index:

```
'Returns "Test string"
Console.WriteLine(runTimeArray.GetValue(0))
```

Common Operators

When working with data types, you often need to perform several tasks on them. Depending on which type you work with, the Visual Basic programming language offers different kinds of operators, such as arithmetic operators, logical and bitwise operators, and shift operators. In this section you learn about Visual Basic operators and how you can use them in your own code. Let's begin by discussing arithmetic operators, which are probably the operators you will use most frequently.

Arithmetic Operators

Visual Basic 2012 provides some arithmetic operators, listed in Table 4.11.

TABLE 4.11   Arithmetic Operators

Operator	Description
+	Addition operator
-	Subtraction operator
*	Multiplication operator
/	Division operator
\	Integer division operator
^	Exponentiation operator
Mod	Integer division remainder

The first three operators are self-explanatory, so I would like to focus on the other ones. First, an important consideration should be done on the division operators. As shown in Table 4.11, Visual Basic offers two symbols, the slash (/) and backslash (\). The first one can be used in divisions between floating-point numbers (such as `Double` and `Single` types), and the second can be used only in divisions between integer numbers. This backslash is fast when working with integers and truncates the result in case it is a floating-point number. The backslash accepts and returns just integers. To understand this concept, consider the following division between `Doubles`:

```
'Division between double: returns 2.5
Dim dblResult As Double = 10 / 4
```

The result of such calculation is 2.5. Now consider the following one:

```
'Division between integers: returns 2
Dim intResult As Integer = 10 \ 4
```

The result of this calculation is 2. This is because the \ operator truncated the result, due to its integer nature. If you try to use such operators in a division involving floating-point numbers, the Visual Basic compiler throws an exception, which is useful for avoiding subtle errors. By the way, such an exception occurs only with Option Strict On, which you should always set as your default choice.

SUPPORTED TYPES

The integer division operator supports the SByte, Byte, Short, UShort, Integer, UInteger, Long, and ULong data types, which are all numeric types that do not support a floating point.

For divisions between floating-point numbers, it's worth mentioning that divisions between Single and Double are also allowed but cause the compiler to perform some implicit conversions that should be avoided. In such situations, you should just perform an explicit conversion, as in the following code:

```
'Division between Single and Double
Dim singleValue As Single = 987.654
Dim doubleValue As Double = 654.321
Dim division As Single = singleValue / CSng(doubleValue)
```

The next interesting operator is the exponentiation operator. A simple example follows:

```
Dim result As Double = 2 ^ 4   'returns 16
```

The exponentiation operator returns a Double value. Because of this, even if operands are other types (such as Integer or Long), they will be always converted to Double. Behind the scenes, the ^ operator invokes the Pow method exposed by the System.Math class. So you could also rewrite the preceding line of code as follows:

```
Dim result As Double = System.Math.Pow(2,4)   'returns 16
```

The last built-in operator is Mod (which stands for *modulus*) that returns the remainder of a division between numbers. The following lines of code show an example:

```
'Mod: returns 0
Dim remainder As Integer = 10 Mod 2
'Mod: returns 1
Dim remainder As Integer = 9 Mod 2
```

A typical usage of Mod is for determining whether a number is an odd number. To accomplish this, you could create a function like the following:

```
Function IsOdd(ByVal number As Integer) As Boolean
  Return (number Mod 2) <> 0
End Function
```

If the remainder is different from zero, the number is odd and therefore returns True. Mod supports all numeric types, including unsigned types and floating-point ones. The .NET Framework offers another way for retrieving the remainder of a division, which is the System.Math.IEEERemainnder method that works as follows:

```
'Double remainder
Dim dblRemainder As Double = System.Math.IEEERemainder(10.42, 5.12)
```

Although both Mod and IEEERemainder return the remainder of a division between numbers, they use different formulas behind the scenes. Thus, the result can differ. According to the MSDN documentation, this is the formula for the IEEERemainder method:

```
IEEERemainder = dividend - (divisor * Math.Round(dividend / divisor))
```

This is instead the formula for the Modulus operator:

```
Modulus = (Math.Abs(dividend) - (Math.Abs(divisor) *
          (Math.Floor(Math.Abs(dividend) / Math.Abs(divisor))))) *
          Math.Sign(dividend)
```

You can see how calculations work differently, especially where Modulus gets the absolute value for dividend and divisor.

System.Math CLASS

This section provides an overview of the arithmetic operators built in to the Visual Basic 2012 programming language. The System.Math class provides lots of additional methods for performing complex calculations, but this is beyond the scope here.

Assignment Operators

You can use operators shown in the previous paragraph for incremental operations. Consider the following code:

```
Dim value As Double = 1

value += 1 'Same as value = value + 1

value -= 1 'Same as value = value - 1

value *= 2 'Same as value = value * 2

value /= 2 'Same as value = value / 2
```

```
value ^= 2 'Same as value = value ^ 2

Dim test As String = "This is"
test &= " a string" 'same as test = test & " a string"
```

You can abbreviate your code using this particular form when performing operations or concatenations. Also notice that += assignment operator works on strings as well.

Logical, Bitwise, and Shift Operators

Visual Basic 2012 offers logical, bitwise, and shift operators. Logical operators are special operators enabling comparisons between Boolean values and returning Boolean values. Bitwise and shift operators enable performing operations bit by bit. Next let's discuss both logical and bitwise operators.

Logical Operators

Visual Basic 2012 has eight logical/bitwise operators: Not, And, Or, Xor, AndAlso, OrElse, IsFalse, and IsTrue. In this section you learn about the first four; the other ones are covered in the next section. The first operator, Not, returns the opposite of the actual Boolean value. For example, the following lines of code return False because, although the 43 number is greater than 10, Not returns the opposite:

```
'Returns False
Dim result As Boolean = (Not 43 > 10)
```

Logical operators can also be used with reference types. For example, you can return the opposite of the result of a comparison between objects (see the section "Comparison Operators" for details):

```
Dim firstPerson As New Person
Dim secondPerson As New Person
'Returns True
result = (Not firstPerson Is secondPerson)
```

This code returns True; the comparison between firstPerson and secondPerson returns False because they point to two different instances of the Person class, but Not returns the opposite. The next operator is And, which compares two Boolean values or expressions and returns True if both values or expressions are True; otherwise, if at least one value is False, And returns False. Here is an example of And:

```
'Returns False
result = 10 > 15 and 30 > 15
'Returns True
result = 20 > 15 and 30 > 15
'Returns True
result = 20 > 15 and 15 = 15
```

And is also useful for comparing Boolean properties of objects. For example, you might want to check whether a text file exists on disk and that it is not zero-byte; you could write the following code:

```
If My.Computer.FileSystem.FileExists("C:\MyFile.txt") = True And
    My.Computer.FileSystem.ReadAllText("C:\MyFile.txt").Length > 0 Then
        'Valid file
End If
```

If both actions return True, And returns True. In our example this should mean that we encountered a valid text file. The next operator is Or. Such an operator works like this: if expressions or values are True, it returns True; if both are False, it returns False; and if one of the two expressions is True, it returns True. The following code demonstrates this scenario:

```
'Returns True
result = 10 > 15 or 30 > 15
'Returns True
result = 10 < 15 or 30 > 15
'Returns False
result = 10 > 15 or 30 < 15
```

The last operator is Xor (*eXclusive or*). Such an operator compares two Boolean expressions (or values) and returns True only if one of the two expressions is True; in all other cases it returns False. Continuing the first example, Xor returns the values described inside comments:

```
'Returns True
result = 10 > 15 Xor 30 > 15
'Returns False
result = 20 > 15 Xor 30 > 15
'Returns False
result = 20 > 15 Xor 15 = 15
```

Short-Circuiting Operators

Sometimes you do not need to perform the evaluation of the second expression in a Boolean comparison because evaluating the first one provides the result you need. In such scenarios, you can use two *short-circuiting operators*, AndAlso and OrElse. *Short-circuiting* means that code execution is shorter and performances are improved. Such operators are particularly useful when you need to invoke an external method from within an If..Then code block. Let's consider again the previous example for the And operator:

```
If My.Computer.FileSystem.FileExists("C:\MyFile.txt") = True And
    My.Computer.FileSystem.ReadAllText("C:\MyFile.txt").Length > 0 Then
        'Valid file
End If
```

The Visual Basic compiler performs both evaluations. What would happen if the file did not exist? It throws a `FileNotFoundException` when the `ReadAllText` method is invoked because the `And` operator requires both expressions to be evaluated. You should implement error-handling routines for such code, but this example is just related to operators. You can prevent your code from encountering the previously described problem using `AndAlso`. You need to replace `And` with `AndAlso`, as in the following code:

```
If My.Computer.FileSystem.FileExists("C:\MyFile.txt") = True AndAlso
My.Computer.FileSystem.ReadAllText("C:\MyFile.txt").Length > 0 Then
        'Valid file
    End If
```

`AndAlso` evaluates the first expression; if this returns `False`, the second expression is not evaluated at all. In this case, if the file does not exist, the code exits from the `If` block. `AndAlso`'s counterpart is `OrElse`, which evaluates the second expression only when the first one is False. Finally, in Visual Basic are two other operators named `IsTrue` and `IsFalse`. The first one works in conjunction with the `OrElse` operator, while the second works with the `AndAlso`. You cannot explicitly invoke these operators in your code because it is the job of the Visual Basic compiler to invoke them within an evaluation expression. This means that the types you want to be evaluated via `OrElse` or `AndAlso` must expose both of them. The following is a simple sample:

```
Public Structure myType
    Public Shared Operator IsFalse(ByVal value As myType) As Boolean
        Dim result As Boolean
        ' Insert code to calculate IsFalse of value.
        Return result
    End Operator
    Public Shared Operator IsTrue(ByVal value As myType) As Boolean
        Dim result As Boolean
        ' Insert code to calculate IsTrue of value.
        Return result
    End Operator
End Structure
```

Bitwise Operators

Performing bitwise operations means performing operations with two binary numbers, bit by bit. The problem here is that Visual Basic does not allow working directly with binary numbers, so you need to write code against decimal or hexadecimal numbers that the Visual Basic compiler will actually treat, behind the scenes, in their binary representation. However, you still need to write them in a comprehensible way.

CONVERTING BETWEEN DECIMAL AND BINARY

You can use the Windows Calculator in scientific mode to perform conversions between decimal/hexadecimal and binary numbers.

The bitwise operators in Visual Basic are still And, Or, Not, and Xor. Unlike logical operations, though, in which such operators evaluate expressions, bitwise operations are related to bit manipulations. You might wonder why you would need to perform bitwise operations in the era of WPF, Silverlight, and other high-level technologies. You could get multiple answers to this question, but the most useful one is probably providing the example of applications that interact with hardware devices in which you still need to work in a bit-by-bit fashion. Another common situation in Visual Basic is the combination of Enum flags. Let's see some examples. The And operator combines two operands into a result. Inside such a result, it puts a 1 value where both operands have 1 in a particular position; otherwise, it puts a zero. For a better explanation, consider the following code:

```
Dim result As Integer = 152 And 312
```

The binary counterpart for 152 is 10011000, whereas the binary counterpart for 312 is 100111000. The result variable's value is 24, whose binary counterpart is 11000. If you observe the following representation

```
 10011000
100111000
    11000
```

You can notice how the third line, which represents the result of the And operation, contains 1 only in positions in which both operands have 1. If you then convert the result back to a decimal number, you get 24. The Or operator works similarly: It combines two operands into a result; inside such a result, it puts a 1 value if at least one of the operands has a 1 value in a particular position. Consider this code:

```
Dim result As Integer = 152 Or 312
```

Both 152 and 312 binary counterparts are the same as the previous example. The Or operator produces 110111000 as a binary output, whose decimal counterpart is 440. To understand this step, take a look at this comparison:

```
 10011000
100111000
110111000
```

It's easy to see that the result contains 1 where at least one of the operands contains 1 in a particular position. The Xor operator combines two operands into a result; inside such a result, it puts a 1 value if at least one of the operands has a 1 value in a particular position, but not if both have 1 in that position. (In such a case it places 0.) Consider this bitwise operation:

```
Dim result As Integer = 152 Xor 312
```

The 152 and 312 binary counterparts are the same as in the preceding example. But this line of code returns 416, whose binary counterpart is 110100000. So let's see what happened:

```
 10011000
100111000
110100000
```

As you can see, Xor placed 1 where at least one of the operands has 1 in a particular position, but where both operands have 1, it placed 0. The Not operator is probably the easiest to understand. It just reverses the bits of an operand into a result value. For example, consider this line of code:

```
Dim result As Integer = Not 312
```

In the following comparison, the second line is the result of the preceding negation:

```
100111000
011000111
```

This result has –313 as its decimal counterpart.

BINARY NUMBERS

This book does not teach binary numbers, so the code shown in this and in the following section assumes that you are already familiar with binary representations of decimal numbers.

Shift Operators

Shift operators are also something that makes more sense with binary numbers than with decimal or hexadecimal numbers, although you need to provide them via their decimal representations. With shift operators, you can move (that is, shift) a binary representation left or right for the specified number of positions. The left-shift operator is <<, and the right-shift operator is >>. For example, consider the following Integer:

```
'Binary counterpart is
'101000100
Dim firstValue As Integer = 324
```

The binary representation for 324 is 101000100. At this point, we want to left-shift the binary for four positions. The following line accomplishes this:

```
'Returns 5184, which is
'1010001000000
Dim leftValue As Integer = firstValue << 4
```

With the left-shifting of four positions, the number 101000100 produces 1010001000000 as a result. Such binary representation is the equivalent of the 5184 decimal number, which is the actual value of the `leftValue` variable. The right-shift operator works the same but moves positions on the right:

```
'Returns 20, which is
'10100
Dim rightValue As Integer = firstValue >> 4
```

This code moves 101000100 for four positions to the right, so the binary result is 10100. Its decimal equivalent is then 20, which is the actual value of the `rightValue` variable.

SUPPORTED TYPES

Shift operators support `Byte`, `Short`, `Integer`, `Long`, `SByte`, `UShort`, `UInteger` and `ULong` data types. When using shift operators with unsigned types, there is no sign bit to propagate; therefore, the vacated positions are set to zero.

Concatenation Operators

As in the previous versions, Visual Basic 2012 still offers concatenation operators—the + and & symbols. The main difference is that the + symbol is intended for numeric additions, although it can also work with strings; the & symbol is defined only for strings, and should be preferred when concatenating strings so that you can avoid possible errors. Listing 4.2 shows an example of concatenation.

LISTING 4.2   Concatenation Operators

```
Module ConcatenationOperators
    Sub ConcatenationDemo()

        Dim firstString As String = "Alessandro"
        Dim secondString As String = "Del Sole"

        Dim completeString As String = firstString & secondString

        'The following still works but should be avoided
        'Dim completeString As String = firstString + secondString

    End Sub
End Module
```

Comparison Operators

As in its predecessors, Visual Basic 2012 still defines some comparison operators. Typically, comparison operators are of three kinds: numeric operators, string operators, and object operators. Let's see these operators in detail.

Numeric Comparison Operators

You can compare numeric values using the operators listed in Table 4.12.

TABLE 4.12   Numeric Comparison Operators

Operator	Description
=	Equality operator
<>	Inequality operator
<	Less than
>	Greater than
<=	Less than or equal to
>=	Greater than or equal to

These operators return a Boolean value that is `True` or `False`. The following code snippet shows an example (comments within the code contain the Boolean value returned):

```
Sub NumericOperators()

    Dim firstNumber As Double = 3
    Dim secondNumber As Double = 4
    Dim comparisonResult As Boolean = False

    'False
    comparisonResult = (firstNumber = secondNumber)
    'True
    comparisonResult = (secondNumber > firstNumber)
    'False
    comparisonResult = (secondNumber <= firstNumber)
    'True
    comparisonResult = (secondNumber <> firstNumber)
End Sub
```

String Comparison Operators

String comparison was discusses in the section "Working with Strings," so refer to that topic.

Objects Comparison Operators: `Is`, `IsNot`, and `TypeOf`

You can compare two or more objects to understand whether they point to the same instance or what type of object you are working with. The three operators for comparing objects are `Is`, `IsNot`, and `TypeOf`. `Is` and `IsNot` are used to understand whether two objects point to the same instance. Consider the following code:

```
Dim firstPerson As New Person
Dim secondPerson As New Person
```

```
'Returns True, not same instance
If firstPerson IsNot secondPerson Then

End If


'Returns False, not same instance
If firstPerson Is secondPerson Then

End If


'Returns True, same instance
Dim onePerson As Person = secondPerson
If secondPerson Is onePerson Then

End If
```

firstPerson and secondPerson are two different instances of the Person class. In the first comparison, IsNot returns True because they are two different instances. In the second comparison, Is returns False because they are still two different instances. In the third comparison, the result is True because you might remember that simply assigning a reference type just copies the reference to an object. In this case, both secondPerson and onePerson point to the same instance. The last example is related to the TypeOf operator. Typically, you use it to understand whether a particular object has inheritance relationships with another one. Consider the following code snippet:

```
'Returns True
Dim anotherPerson As Object = New Person
If TypeOf anotherPerson Is Person Then

End If
```

We have here an anotherPerson object of type Object, assigned with a new instance of the Person class. (This is possible because Object can be assigned with any .NET type.) The TypeOf comparison returns True because anotherPerson is effectively an instance of Person (and not simply object). TypeOf is useful if you need to check for the data type of a Windows Forms or WPF control. For example, a System.Windows.Controls.Button control in WPF inherits from System.Windows.Controls.FrameworkElement, and then TypeOf x is FrameworkElement and returns True.

OPERATORS PRECEDENCE ORDER

Visual Basic operators have a precedence order. For further information, refer to the MSDN Library: http://msdn.microsoft.com/en-us/library/fw84t893(v=vs.110).aspx.

Iterations, Loops, and Conditional Code Blocks

Hundreds of programming techniques are based on loops and iterations. Both loops and iterations enable the repetition of some actions for a specific number of times or when a particular condition is `True` or `False`. All these cases are discussed next.

Iterations

Iterations in Visual Basic 2012 are performed via the `For..Next` and `For Each` loops. Let's analyze them more in details.

For..Next

A `For..Next` loop enables repeating the same action (or group of actions) for a finite number of times. The following code shows an example in which the same action (writing to the Console window) is performed 10 times:

```
For i As Integer = 1 To 10
    Console.WriteLine("This action has been repeated {0} times", i)
Next
```

In such loops, you need to define a variable of a numeric type (`i` in the preceding example) that acts as a counter.

> **TIP**
>
> You can also assign the variable with another variable of the same type instead of assigning a numeric value.

The previous code produces the following result:

```
This action has been repeated 1 times
This action has been repeated 2 times
This action has been repeated 3 times
This action has been repeated 4 times
This action has been repeated 5 times
This action has been repeated 6 times
This action has been repeated 7 times
This action has been repeated 8 times
This action has been repeated 9 times
This action has been repeated 10 times
```

Notice that you can also initialize the counter with zero or with any other numeric value.

> **TIP**
>
> You can use the `Integer` or `UInteger` variables as counters in `For..Next` loops. This is because these data types are optimized for the Visual Basic compiler. Other numeric types are also supported but are not optimized, so you are encouraged to always use `Integer` or `UInteger`.

You can also decide how the counter must be incremented. For example, you could decide to increment the counter of two units instead of one (as in the previous example). This can be accomplished via the `Step` keyword:

```
For i As Integer = 1 To 10 Step 2
    Console.WriteLine("Current value is {0}", i)
Next
```

This code produces the following output:

```
Current value is 1
Current value is 3
Current value is 5
Current value is 7
Current value is 9
```

Step can also work with negative numbers and lets you perform a going-back loop:

```
For i As Integer = 10 To 1 Step -2
    Console.WriteLine("Current value is {0}", i)
Next
```

You can also decide to break a `For` loop when a particular condition is satisfied and you do not need to still perform the iteration. This can be accomplished with the `Exit For` statement, as shown in the following example:

```
For i As Integer = 1 To 10
    Console.WriteLine("Current value is {0}", i)
    If i = 4 Then Exit For
Next
```

In the preceding example, when the counter reaches the value of 4, the `For` loop is interrupted and control is returned to the code that immediately follows the `Next` keyword. There is also another way for controlling a `For` loop, such as when you need to pass the control directly to the next iteration of the loop when a particular condition is satisfied (which is the opposite of `Exit For`). This can be accomplished with the `Continue For` statement, as shown in the following code snippet:

```
For i As Integer = 1 To 10
    If i = 4 Then  'Ignore the 4 value
        i += 1 'Increments to 5
        Continue For  'Continues from next value, that is 6
    End If
    Console.WriteLine("Current value is  {0}", i)
Next
```

In the preceding example we are doing some edits on the counter. Notice that each time you invoke a `Continue For`, the counter itself is incremented one unit.

For Each

A `For Each` loop allows performing an action or a group of actions on each item from an array or a collection. Although collections are discussed in Chapter 16, I'm providing a code example with them because this is the typical usage of a `For Each` loop. For example, consider the following code:

```
'A collection of Process objects
Dim procList As List(Of Process) = Process.GetProcesses.ToList

For Each proc As Process In procList
    Console.WriteLine(proc.ProcessName)
    Console.WriteLine("      " & proc.Id)
Next
```

In the preceding code snippet is a collection containing references to all the running processes on the machine. Each process is represented by an instance of the `System.Diagnostics.Process` class; therefore, `List(Of Process)` is a collection of processes. Supposing we want to retrieve some information for each process, such as the name and the identification number, we can iterate the collection using a `For Each` statement. You need to specify a variable (also known as *control variable*) that is the same type of the item you are investigating. In the preceding code you are just performing reading operations, but you can also edit items' properties. For example, you might have a collection of `Person` objects and could retrieve and edit information for each `Person` in the collection, as in the following code:

```
'A collection of Person objects
Dim people As New List(Of Person)
'Populate the collection here..
'....
For Each p As Person In people
    p.LastName = "Dr. " & p.LastName
    Console.WriteLine(p.LastName)
Next
```

This code will add the `Dr.` prefix to the `LastName` property of each `Person` instance.

For Each AVAILABILITY

Behind the scenes, `For Each` can be used against objects that implement the `IEnumerable` or `IEnumerable(Of T)` interfaces. Such objects expose the enumerator that provides support for `For Each` iterations.

You can still use `Exit For` when you need to break out from a `For Each` statement. A `For Each` loop has better performances with collections than with arrays, but you can use it in both scenarios.

ITERATORS

Visual Basic 2012 introduces a new feature, the *iterators*. With iterators, you can return elements from the collection or the array to the caller code while the iteration is still in progress, so that such elements can be used by the caller without having to wait for the iteration to be completed. Iterators are typically used with collections, so this feature is discussed in Chapter 16.

Visual Basic 2012 Compiler Fixes

Until Visual Basic 2010, if you wrote a `For..Each` loop to iterate the result of a lambda expression or the content of a variable of type `IQueryable` or `IQueryable(Of T)`, you had to declare a temporary variable to avoid the following error message:

```
Using the iteration variable in a query might have unexpected results
```

The following code shows an example:

```
Private Function SearchProducts(ParamArray keywords As String()) As _
        IQueryable(Of Product)
  Dim query As IQueryable(Of Product) = dataContext.Products

  For Each keyword As String In keywords

    query = query.Where(Function(p) p.Description.Contains(keyword))

  Next
  Return query
End Function
```

As you can see, a lambda expression exists inside the loop, whose result is assigned to the `query` variable. Such a lambda is using the control variable (`keyword`) directly, and this was not allowed because only one slot of memory was allocated and every lambda expression or query was referring to the same variable. Because of this, until Visual Basic 2012 you had to rewrite the previous code as follows:

```
Private Function SearchProducts(ParamArray keywords As String()) As _
        IQueryable(Of Product)
  Dim query As IQueryable(Of Product) = dataContext.Products

  For Each keyword As String In keywords

    Dim temp As String = keyword
    query = query.Where(Function(p) p.Description.Contains(temp))
```

```
    Next
    Return query
End Function
```

By declaring a temporary variable (`temp` in the example), you could solve the problem. The Visual Basic 2012 compiler solves the memory allocation problem and makes it possible to use the control variable directly, without the need of declaring an intermediate variable. So, in Visual Basic 2012 you could write the previous example as in the first code snippet.

Loops

As in the previous versions of the language, Visual Basic 2012 offers two kinds of loops: `Do..Loop` and `While..End While`. In this section we take a look at both loops.

Do..Loop

The `Do..Loop` is the most frequently used loop in Visual Basic and the most flexible. This loop can have two behaviors: repeating a set of actions until a condition is false and repeating a set of actions until a condition is true. The first scenario is accomplished using a `Do While` statement, as demonstrated in Listing 4.3.

LISTING 4.3   Performing a `Do While` Loop

```
Sub LoopWhileDemo()
    Dim max As Integer = 0
    Do While max < Integer.MaxValue
        max += 1
        'Do something else here
        If max = 7000000 Then Exit Do
    Loop
    Console.WriteLine("Done: " & max.ToString)
End Sub
```

The code is quite easy: Whereas the value of max is less than the maximum value of the Integer type, increment max itself is one unit. `Do While` evaluates a `False` condition. (The loop goes on because max is less than `Integer.MaxValue`.) The code also demonstrates how you can exit from a loop using an `Exit Do` statement. This passes the control to the next statement after the `Loop` keyword. The other scenario is when you need to evaluate a `True` condition. This can be accomplished via a `Do Until` loop. Listing 4.4 demonstrates this.

LISTING 4.4   Demonstrating a `Do Until` Loop

```
Sub LoopUntilDemo()
    Dim max As Integer = 0
    Do Until max = Integer.MaxValue
        max += 1
```

```
        If max = 7000000 Then Exit Do
    Loop
    Console.WriteLine("Done: " & max.ToString)
End Sub
```

The difference here is that the loop ends when the condition is True—that is, when the value of max equals the value of Integer.MaxValue. As before, Exit Do can end the loop. The interesting thing in both cases is that you can evaluate the condition on the Loop side instead of the Do one. Listing 4.5 shows how you could rewrite both examples.

LISTING 4.5   Evaluating Conditions on the Loop Line

```
'Loop is executed at least once
Sub LoopUntilBottomDemo()
    Dim max As Integer = 0
    Do
        max += 1
        If max = 7000000 Then Exit Do
    Loop Until max = Integer.MaxValue
    Console.WriteLine("Done: " & max.ToString)
End Sub

'Loop is executed at least once
Sub LoopWhileBottomDemo()
    Dim max As Integer = 0
    Do
        max += 1
        If max = 7000000 Then Exit Do
    Loop While max < Integer.MaxValue
    Console.WriteLine("Done: " & max.ToString)
End Sub
```

Both loops behave the same way as previous ones, with one important difference: Here the loop is executed at least once.

PERFORMANCE TIPS

The For loops are faster than Do ones. Because of this, you should use For loops, particularly when you know that you will do a finite number of iterations.

While..End While

A While..End While loop performs actions when a condition is False. Listing 4.6 shows an example.

LISTING 4.6   While..End While Loop

```
Sub WhileEndWhileDemo()
    Dim max As Integer = 0
    While max < Integer.MaxValue
        max += 1

        If max = 7000000 Then Exit While
    End While
    Console.WriteLine("Done: " & max.ToString)
End Sub
```

The loop behaves the same as Do While because both evaluate the same condition.

> **NOTE**
>
> The While..End While loop is less efficient than a Do While and is deprecated, although it is still supported. You should therefore always use a Do While loop.

Conditional Code Blocks

If..Then..Else

The If..Then..Else is the most classical block for conditionally executing actions. An If evaluates an expression as True or False and, according to this, allows specifying actions to take place. Listing 4.7 shows an example.

LISTING 4.7   Demonstrating the If..Then..Else Block

```
Sub IfThenElseDemo()
    Console.WriteLine("Type a number")
    'Assumes users type a valid number
    Dim number As Double = CDbl(Console.ReadLine)

    If number >= 100 Then
        Console.WriteLine("Your number is greater than 100")
    ElseIf number < 100 And number > 50 Then
        Console.WriteLine("Your number is less than 100 and greater than 50")
    Else
        'General action
        Console.WriteLine("Your number is: {0}", number)
    End If
End Sub
```

If checks whether the condition is True; if so, it takes the specified action. You can also specify to evaluate a condition for False (for example, If something = False Then). You can also use an `ElseIf` to delimit the condition evaluation. If no expression satisfies the condition, the `Else` statement provides an action that will be executed in such a situation.

CODING TIP

The Visual Studio IDE offers a useful feature known as *code blocks delimiters selection*. Because you can nest different `If..Then` blocks or can have a long code file, when you place the cursor near either the If/Then keywords or the `End If` statement, the IDE highlights the related delimiter (`End If`, if you place the cursor on an `If`, and vice versa).

Notice how the code uses an `And` operator to evaluate the condition. You can use other operators such as logical and short-circuit operators as well. Another typical example is when you need to check whether a condition is false using the `Not` operator. The following is an example:

```
If Not number >= 100 Then
    'Number is False
End If
```

`Not` also requires the same syntax when working with reference types, but in this case you can also use the `IsNot` operator. The following example checks whether the instance of the `Person` class is not null:

```
Dim p As Person   'p is actually null

'You can check with IsNot
If p IsNot Nothing Then
    'p is not null
Else
    'p is null
End If
```

`IsNot` is not available with value types.

The `IIf` Operator

The `IIf` operator evaluates an expression and returns one of two objects, according to the evaluation result which can be true or false. The syntax for the `IIf` operator is the following:

```
Dim result As Object = IIf(Expression As Boolean, TruePart As Object,
                FalsePart As Object)
```

So the first argument of the operator is a Boolean expression. If the expression result is `True`, the operator returns the second argument (`TruePart`) otherwise it returns the third one (`FalsePart`). The following code demonstrates how to evaluate if the user input is null and show a text message according to the result:

```
Dim input As String = Console.ReadLine

Dim result As Object = IIf(input Is Nothing, "Enter something please",
                           String.Concat("You entered ", input))


Console.WriteLine(CStr(input))
```

Remember that the IIf operator and its arguments must return Object, so you will have to make the appropriate type conversions when needed.

Select Case

Select Case is a statement that allows evaluating an expression against a series of values. Generally, Select Case is used to check whether an expression matches a particular value in situations evaluated as True. Listing 4.8 provides an example.

LISTING 4.8   Using the Select Case Statement for Evaluating Expressions

```
Sub SelectCaseDemo()
    Console.WriteLine("Type a file extension (without dot):")
    Dim fileExtension As String = Console.ReadLine

    Select Case fileExtension.ToLower
        Case Is = "txt"
            Console.WriteLine("Is a text file")
        Case Is = "exe"
            Console.WriteLine("Is an executable")
        Case Is = "doc"
            Console.WriteLine("Is a Microsoft Word document")
        Case Else
            Console.WriteLine("Is something else")
    End Select
End Sub
```

The code in Listing 4.8 simply compares the string provided by the user with a series of values. If no value matches the string, a Case Else is used to provide a general result. Comparison is performed with the Is operator and the equality operator. The following syntax is also accepted:

```
Case "txt"
```

IntelliSense adds the Is = symbology by default. You can also break from a Select Case statement in any moment using an Exit Select statement. Select..Case also offers another syntax to apply when you want to check whether a value falls within a particular range. To accomplish this, you use the To keyword instead of the Is = operators, as in the following code that waits for the user to enter a number and then checks what range the number falls in:

```
Console.WriteLine("Enter a number from 1 to 50:")
Dim result As Integer = CInt(Console.ReadLine)
Select Case result
    'The user entered a number in the range from 1 to 25
    Case 1 To 25
        Console.WriteLine("You entered {0} which is a small number",
                          result.ToString)
        'The user entered a number in the range from 26 to 50
    Case 26 To 50
        Console.WriteLine("You entered {0} which is a high number",
                          result.ToString)
        'The user entered a number < 1 or > 50
    Case Else
        Console.WriteLine("You entered a number which is out of range")
End Select
```

In other words, considering the preceding example, `Case 1 To 25` means in case the value to check is in the range between the left value (1) and the right value (25), then take the nested action. You can also check for multiple items not ranged with the following syntax:

```
Select Case result
    'The user entered 1 or a value between 5 and 10 or 12
    'All other values are excluded
    Case Is = 1, 5 To 10, 12
        '...
End Select
```

CODING TIP

For the `If..End If` block, the code blocks delimiters selection feature is also available for `Select..End Select` blocks.

PERFORMANCE TIPS

The Visual Basic compiler evaluates expressions as a sequence. Because of this, in `Select Case` statements it evaluates all conditions until the one matching the value is found. Consequently, the first `Case` instructions in the sequence should be related to values considered the most frequent.

Constants

Constants provide a way for representing an immutable value with an identifier. There could be situations in which your applications need to use the same value (which can be of any .NET type); therefore, it can be convenient to define an easy-to-remember identifier instead of a value. What would happen if such a value were a Long number? You declare constants as follows:

```
Const defaultIntegerValue As Integer = 123456789
Const aConstantString As String = "Same value along the application"
```

Constants are read-only fields that can be declared only at the module and class level or within a method and must be assigned with a value when declared. Constants within methods have public visibility by default, whereas constants at the module and class level can have one of the .NET scopes, as in the following lines:

```
Private Const defaultIntegerValue As Integer = 123456789
Public Const aConstantString As String= "Same value along the application"
```

The reason constants must be assigned when declared is that the expression is evaluated at compile time. Starting from Visual Basic 2008, there are a couple of things to consider. Look at the following line of code:

```
Private Const Test = "Test message"
```

The type for the Test variable is not specified. Until Visual Basic 2005, with Option Strict Off, such a declaration would assign Object. In later versions of the language, if Option Infer is On, the compiler assigns String; if it is Off, the compiler goes back to assigning Object.

With..End With Statement

Visual Basic provides an alternative way for invoking object members—the With..End With statement. Consider the following code block, in which a new Person class is instantiated and then properties are assigned while methods are invoked:

```
Dim p As New People.Person
p.FirstName = "Alessandro"
p.LastName = "Del Sole"
Dim fullName As String = p.ToString
```

Using a With..End With statement, you just need to specify the name of the class once and then type a dot so that IntelliSense shows members you can use, as follows:

```
Dim p As New People.Person
With p
    .FirstName = "Alessandro"
    .LastName = "Del Sole"
    Dim fullName As String = .ToString
End With
```

There is no difference between the two coding techniques, so feel free to use the one you like most. With..End With offers the advantage of speeding up the code writing a little and can be useful if you have a lot of members to invoke or assign at one time.

With..End With

`With..End With` has no equivalent in other .NET languages, so if you have to interoperate, assigning members the normal way can be a good idea. Although the compiler translates the `With..End With` blocks as single members' invocations, in such scenarios the best approach is a .NET-oriented coding style instead of a VB-oriented one.

Summary

Every development environment relies on data types. The .NET Framework relies on two kinds of data types: value types and reference types. Both kinds of types are managed by the Common Type System, which provides a common infrastructure to .NET languages for working with types. In this chapter, you learned the important basics of the .NET development and the Visual Basic language, which can be summarized as follows:

- ▶ Common Type System

- ▶ Value types and reference types

- ▶ `System.Object` and inheritance levels in value types and reference types

- ▶ Memory allocation of both value types and reference types

- ▶ Converting between types and conversion operators

- ▶ Most common value types and reference types

- ▶ Common operators

You often need to work with and analyze data types. Visual Basic 2012 provides several ways for performing work on types and the data they store. To accomplish this, you can use

- ▶ Iterations, such as `For..Next` and `For..Each`

- ▶ Loops, such as `Do..Loop`

- ▶ Conditional code blocks, such as `If..End If` and `Select Case..End Select`

It's important to understand all the preceding features because they often recur in your developer life; these features appear extensively in the rest of the book. But you also might encounter errors when working with types. The next two chapters discuss two fundamental topics in the .NET development with Visual Basic: debugging and handling errors.

CHAPTER 5

Debugging Visual Basic 2012 Applications

Debugging is one of the most important tasks in your developer life. Debugging enables you to investigate for errors and analyze the application's execution flow over an object's state. Visual Studio 2012 offers powerful tools for making debugging an easier task. In this chapter you get details about the Visual Studio instrumentation and learn how to make your code interact better with the debugger. Microsoft introduced some specific enhancements to the debugger in Visual Studio 2012 for parallel debugging and the Task Parallel Library; these enhancements will eventually be described in the appropriate chapters. In this chapter you find information regarding the generality of Visual Basic applications. Chapter 2, "Getting Started with the Visual Studio 2012 IDE," provides an overview of the most common debugging tasks, but in this chapter you learn about more advanced debugging tools and techniques available in the IDE. Be sure you read Chapter 2 before continuing on with this one.

Preparing an Example

Most debugging features illustrated in this chapter require some code before you can use them. At the moment we are more interested in the Visual Studio 2012 instrumentation than in complex code, so we start with a simple code example that is a good base for understanding how the debugger works. You can create a new Visual Basic project for the Console and then type the code, as shown in Listing 5.1.

LISTING 5.1   Preparing the Base for the Debugger

```
Module Module1

    Sub Main()

        Console.WriteLine("Enter a valid string:")
        Dim lineRead As String = Console.ReadLine()

        Dim result As Boolean = Test(lineRead)

        Console.WriteLine("Is a valid string: " & result.ToString)
        Console.ReadLine()
    End Sub

    Function Test(ByVal name As String) As Boolean
        If String.IsNullOrEmpty(name) = False Then
            Return True
        Else
            Return False
        End If
    End Function
End Module
```

The code is quite simple. The application just asks the user to enter a string and then returns False if the string is null or is empty; it returns True if the string is valid. With such simple code, you can now begin learning the advanced debugging instrumentation available in Visual Studio 2012.

Debugging Instrumentation

The Visual Studio 2012 IDE offers several powerful tools for deeply debugging applications. These tools are part of the development environment instrumentation and are discussed in this section. Remember that when you debug an application, the status bar and the border of Visual Studio 2012 become orange.

Debugging in Steps

When the application execution breaks—for example, when the debugger finds a breakpoint—you can usually continue to execute the application running just one line of code per time or a small set of lines of code per time. In Chapter 2, you learned about the Step Into command; in this section we discuss other similar commands that cause different debugger behaviors.

HOW CAN I EXECUTE SUCH TECHNIQUES?

The debugging techniques described in this section can be accomplished by invoking commands available in the Debug menu of Visual Studio 2012. In the meantime, shortcuts are available for invoking the same commands using the keyboard. These are provided when discussing each command.

Step Into

The Step Into command executes one instruction per time. It is similar to Step Over, but if the instruction to be executed is a method, the method is executed one instruction per time and, when finished, the execution goes back to the caller. You can invoke Step Into by pressing **F11**.

NOTE ON KEYBOARD SHORTCUTS

The keyboard shortcuts in this chapter assume that you are using the Visual Studio default keyboard layout and can vary depending on the IDE configuration settings. The Debug menu shows the appropriate keyboard shortcuts for your active configuration.

Step Over

Similarly to Step Into, Step Over executes one instruction per time. The difference is that if the instruction to be executed is a method, the debugger does not enter the method and completes its execution before going back to the caller. You can invoke Step Over by pressing **F10**. This can be useful when you need to debug a portion of code that invokes several methods you already tested and that you do not need to delve into each time.

Step Out

Step Out works only within methods and enables executing all lines of code next to the current one, until the method completes. If you consider the code shown in Listing 5.1 and place a breakpoint on the `If` statement inside the `Test` method definition, invoking Step Out can cause the debugger to execute all the lines of code next to the If, completing the execution of the method. In this example, after Step Out completes, the control is returned to the second `Console.Writeline` statement in `Sub Main`. You can invoke Step Out by pressing **Shift+F11**.

Run to Cursor

You can place the cursor on a line of code, right-click the line of code, and tell the debugger to execute all the code until the selected line. This can be accomplished by selecting the **Run to Cursor** command on the pop-up menu.

Set Next Statement

Within a code block, you can set the next statement to be executed when resuming the application execution after a breakpoint or stop. Continuing the previous code example, if you place a breakpoint on the first `Console.Writeline` statement, inside the `Main` method, the application stops the execution at that point. Now imagine you want the debugger to resume debugging from the second `Console.Writeline` statement (therefore skipping the debugging of the `Test` method invocation) and execute the lines of code before. You can right-click the `Console.Writeline` statement and select **Set Next Statement** from the pop-up menu, and this line will be the first that you can step through. As an alternative, you can drag the yellow arrow in the IDE to the desired line.

Show Next Statement

This command moves the cursor to the next executable statement. This can be useful if you have long code files and breakpoints are not immediately visible. You can invoke it simply by right-clicking the code editor and selecting the **Show Next Statement** command from the pop-up menu.

Mixed Mode Debugging

You can debug Visual Basic applications built on both managed and native code with the Mixed Mode feature, which is available for both 32-bit and 64-bit applications. To enable mixed-mode debugging, follow these steps:

1. In Solution Explorer, select the project you want to debug.

2. Open My Project and select the **Debug** tab.

3. Select the **Enable Native Code Debugging** check box.

"Just My Code" Debugging

You might remember from Chapter 2 and Chapter 3, "The Anatomy of a Visual Basic Project," that every time you create a Visual Basic application the IDE generates some background code. Moreover, your code often invokes system code that you do not necessarily need to investigate. In Visual Basic the IDE offers the capability of debugging just your own code, excluding system and auto-generated code. This feature is also known as Just My Code debugging. This is useful because you can focus on your code. Just My Code is enabled by default in Visual Studio 2012. To disable it or enable it, open the Options window, select the **Debugging** node on the left, and then flag or unflag the **Enable Just My Code (Managed Only)** check box, as shown in Figure 5.1.

Behind the scenes, Just My Code adds (or removes) some .NET attributes to auto-generated code that can influence the debugger behavior. To see a simple example, open or create a project and then click the **Show All Files** button in Solution Explorer. After doing this, go to the Settings.designer.vb code file. Listing 5.2 shows the content of the `My` namespace definition inside the file.

LISTING 5.2   Understanding Just My Code Behind the Scenes

```
Namespace My

    <Global.Microsoft.VisualBasic.HideModuleNameAttribute(), _
    Global.System.Diagnostics.DebuggerNonUserCodeAttribute(), _
```

```
      Global.System.Runtime.CompilerServices.CompilerGeneratedAttribute()> _
    Friend Module MySettingsProperty


        <Global.System.ComponentModel.Design.HelpKeywordAttribute("My.Settings")> _
        Friend ReadOnly Property Settings() As
                        Global.DebuggingFeatures.My.MySettings
            Get
                Return Global.DebuggingFeatures.My.MySettings.Default
            End Get
        End Property
    End Module
End Namespace
```

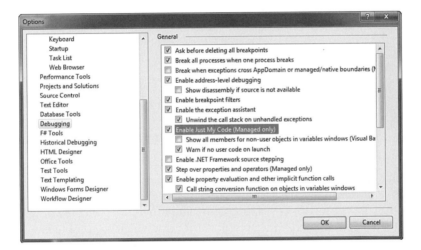

FIGURE 5.1   Enabling/disabling Just My Code debugging.

You can notice that the module MySettingsProperty is decorated with a particular attribute named System.Diagnostics.DebuggerNonUserCodeAttribute. This attribute indicates to the debugger that the code is not your code (user code) and that it will not be debugged when Just My Code is on. Three attributes influence the debugger's behavior in this feature. Table 5.1 shows the complete list.

TABLE 5.1   Just My Code Attributes

Attribute	Description
DebuggerNonUserCode	Indicates to the debugger that the code is not user code and therefore is treated as system code
DebuggerHidden	Indicates to the debugger that code will not be visible at all to the debugger and therefore will be excluded from debugging
DebuggerStepThrough	Indicates to the debugger that the Step Into procedure is not allowed

Of course, you can use attributes of your own so that you can influence the behavior of the debugger when Just My Code is disabled.

Working with Breakpoints and Trace Points

In Chapter 2, we introduced breakpoints and saw how we can break the application execution before some statements are executed. We now discuss some interesting features of breakpoints when debugging Visual Basic applications.

The Breakpoints Window

Using the Breakpoints window, you can manage all breakpoints in your solution. You can open such a window by pressing **Ctrl+Alt+B**. Supposing we placed three breakpoints in our sample application, Figure 5.2 shows how the Breakpoints window would look.

FIGURE 5.2   The Breakpoints window.

In the Breakpoints window, you can easily manage your breakpoints. For example, you could delete, temporarily disable, or enable again the breakpoints. You can also specify the behavior for each breakpoint, such as Hit count, Filter, and other functionalities that we describe next. Also, you can easily switch to the source code in which the breakpoint is located or to the disassembly view. (See Figure 5.9 in the "Call Stack Window" section later in this chapter.) An important opportunity is exporting and importing breakpoints; Visual Studio 2012, as well as its predecessor, can export to XML files the list of breakpoints or import a list from an XML file. If you have lots of breakpoints, you can search breakpoints according to specific criteria using the Label feature, which we focus on next. The Breakpoints window provides a graphical unified instrument for performing operations on breakpoints.

Editing Breakpoints Labels

You can add labels to breakpoints. Labels are a kind of identifier that can identify more than one breakpoint, and their purpose is categorizing breakpoints so that you can easily find and manage them within the Edit Breakpoint Label window. You can add a label to a breakpoint from the Edit Breakpoint Label window or by right-clicking the red ball on the left of the desired breakpoint in the code editor and then selecting the **Edit Labels** command from the pop-up menu. The Edit Breakpoint Labels window is shown in Figure 5.3.

FIGURE 5.3   The Edit Breakpoint Labels window enables categorizing breakpoints.

You need to specify labels and click **Add**. When you finish, select the label you want from the list and click **OK** so that the label is assigned to the breakpoint. You can assign the same label to multiple breakpoints performing the same steps, or you can assign multiple labels to a single breakpoint. Assigning labels to breakpoints can be reflected into the **Breakpoints** window in which you can search for breakpoints specifying labels in the search box.

Location

You can change the position of a breakpoint by right-clicking the breakpoint and then selecting the **Location** command from the pop-up menu. In the dialog box that opens, you need to specify the line of code and the character position to which you want the breakpoint to be moved. This can be useful because you can move a breakpoint without losing breakpoint settings.

Hit Count

With the *hit* term we mean each time a breakpoint is encountered and therefore the application execution should stop. You can control the hit's behavior. For example, imagine you have a cyclic code that contains a breakpoint, but you need to break the execution only when the cycle arrives at a particular point. By using the Hit Count command, you can specify when the debugger must break the application. For example, consider the following code snippet:

```
For i As Integer = 0 To 3
    Console.WriteLine("Breakpoint test")
Next
```

Imagine you place a breakpoint on the `Console.WriteLine` statement and that you want the debugger to break only starting from the second iteration. You can specify this condition by right-clicking the breakpoint and then selecting the **Hit Count** command. In the Breakpoint Hit Count dialog box, you need to specify the condition. The default setting is always break, which means that the debugger breaks the execution each time a breakpoint is encountered. For our example, set the condition to **Break When the Hit Count Is Greater Than or Equal To** with value of 2. Figure 5.4 shows the Hit Count window.

FIGURE 5.4   The Breakpoint Hit Count window enables customizing breakpoints' behavior.

With this setting, the previous code would break on the second iteration. It can be convenient when you need to debug your code only from a certain point.

When Hit

When Hit lets you specify a tracepoint. The difference between a breakpoint and a tracepoint is that in this second case, the debugger will not break the execution of the application and writes the information that you specify in the Output window. To set a hit condition, right-click a breakpoint and then select the **When Hit** command from the pop-up menu. This opens the When Breakpoint Is Hit window, which is shown in Figure 5.5.

FIGURE 5.5   Specifying tracepoint conditions.

You can set one of the special expressions indicated in the window to build a kind of log message that will be written to the Output window. A tracepoint is highly customizable, so you can also specify a Visual Basic macro and decide whether the execution needs to continue. This feature is useful when you prefer getting a log message about the application state instead of breaking the execution.

Condition

This command enables specifying whether a breakpoint must be hit, depending on whether the supplied expressions are evaluated to `True` or get changed. Information on conditions is provided by the following page of the MSDN Library: http://msdn.microsoft.com/en-us/library/za56x861(v=vs.110).aspx. When a condition is set, the debugger then steps into the Hit Count tool.

Locals Window

The Locals window shows the active local variables and their values. Considering the example in Listing 5.1, when stepping into the `Main` method the Locals window shows information about `lineRead` and `result` variables, as shown in Figure 5.6.

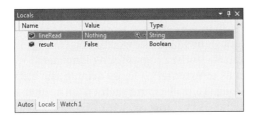

FIGURE 5.6   The Locals window shows information on local variables.

As you can see, the window shows names of the local variables, their types (in our example `Boolean` and `String`), and their actual values. When a variable is not initialized yet, the window shows the default value (for example, `Nothing` for reference types and zero for `Integers`). Moreover, if a variable represents an object such as a class or a collection, the variable can be expanded to show members and their values. You can also change variables' values by double-clicking each one. Some variables cannot be viewed without executing code, such as in-memory queries (they can be still viewed, though the IDE will run the code in memory to be able to display the results).

Command Window

The Command window enables evaluating expressions or running functions without running the application or continuing the debug. Figure 5.7 shows the Command window evaluating an `Integer.Parse` statement and an invocation to our `Test` method.

This can be useful because we do not need to run our application to see whether a method works, and we could also evaluate complex expressions before writing code. Just remember that only functions are allowed; procedures are not supported. Expressions can be constituted by several .NET objects and Visual Basic keywords, but not all of them are supported. You can get a complete list of supported keywords and expressions from the related MSDN web page available at http://msdn.microsoft.com/en-us/library/099a40t6(v=vs.110).aspx.

To evaluate an expression or test a function, you need to first write a question mark (?) symbol. Using a double question mark (??) causes the debugger to open a Quick Watch window, which is discussed later in this chapter. It is worth mentioning that the ? symbol works when either in debug mode or not, while the ?? symbol requires the IDE to be already in debug mode.

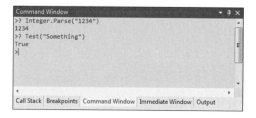

FIGURE 5.7   The Command window enables evaluating expressions and functions.

Call Stack Window

The Call Stack window shows the method calls stack frame. In other words, you can see how method calls run in the stack. The window can show the programming language that the method is written with and can display calls to external code. By default, the Call Stack window shows information about Just My Code. To understand method calls, press **F11** to step into the code. Figure 5.8 shows the Call Stack window related to Listing 5.1.

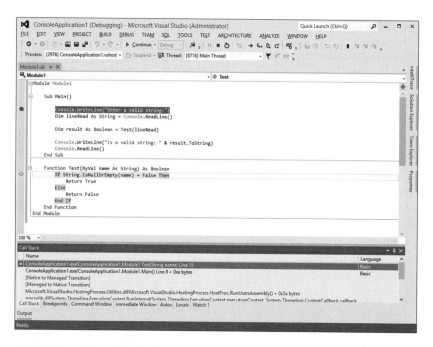

FIGURE 5.8   The Call Stack window shows method calls in the Stack.

The window shows the names of methods being executed and the programming language with which they were written. Calls to .NET Framework system methods are also shown. Another interesting feature is that you can see the assembly code for code execution. Right-click the window and select the **Go to Disassembly** command from the pop-up menu. As shown in Figure 5.9, you can see Visual Basic lines of code and the related underlying assembly code that you can step into by pressing **F11**.

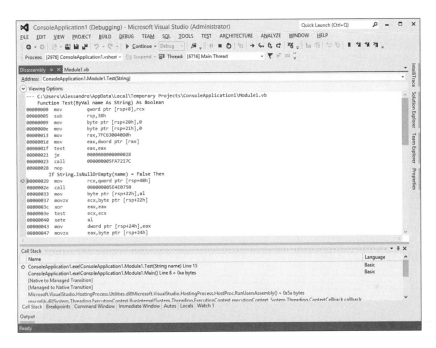

FIGURE 5.9   The assembly code execution shows in Call Stack.

You can also customize the type of information you want to visualize by expanding the View Options control. This feature provides great granularity on what's happening behind the scenes and allows understanding if method calls are executed correctly. You can invoke the Call Stack window by pressing **Ctrl+Alt+C**.

THREADS AND CALL STACK

The Call Stack window can show information only on the current thread. Therefore, method calls on other threads are ignored by the window.

Watch Windows

Watch windows enable monitoring object variables or expressions so that you can track what a variable is doing. There are four Watch windows available, enabling you to track different objects or expressions. To add items to a Watch window, when in break mode right-click the object in the code editor and then select the **Add Watch** command from the pop-up menu. Continuing our example of Listing 5.1, imagine you want to keep track of the Test method state. Run the application in Step Into mode by pressing **F11**. When the debugger breaks the application execution, right-click the Test method definition and then click **Add Watch**. The method is considered as an expression. The first available Watch window is shown and contains the Test item but advertises that no argument has been supplied, as shown in Figure 5.10.

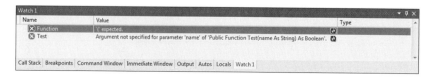

FIGURE 5.10   Adding an expression to a Watch window.

If you continue stepping into the code, you notice that when the debugger begins stepping into the Test method, the expression is first evaluated as False. (This is the default value for Boolean.) When the code completes the execution, the Watch window contains the actual evaluation of the expression; in our example, if the user writes a valid string in the Console window, the expression is evaluated as True, as shown in Figure 5.11.

In this way you can control whether your variables or methods are correctly executed.

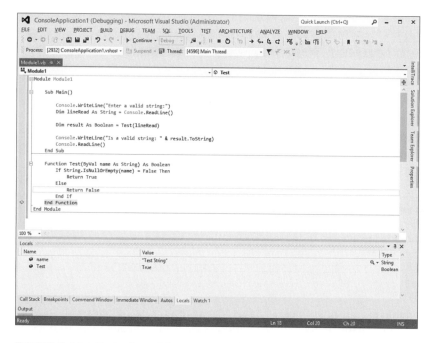

FIGURE 5.11   Evaluation of the expression is completed within the Watch window.

Quick Watch Window

The Quick Watch window is an additional Watch window that enables quickly evaluating one expression or variable per time, choosing between items you previously added to Watch windows or right-clicking an object in the code editor and then selecting the Quick Watch command. In this scenario, the expression or variable is evaluated considering its state at the moment you request the Quick Watch to appear. Figure 5.12 shows the Quick Watch window.

FIGURE 5.12   The Quick Watch window.

You can pick an expression from the Expression combo box. When you choose the expression, you can click **Reevaluate** to run the evaluation. Just remember that this dialog box is a modal dialog box, so you need to close it before you can go back to Visual Studio.

Threads Window

.NET applications can run multiple threads. This can happen with your applications, too. You can get a view of the running threads and debugging threads within the Threads window, which you can enable by pressing **Ctrl+Alt+H**. Figure 5.13 shows the Threads window open when the sample application is in break mode.

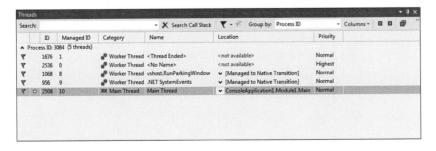

FIGURE 5.13   The Threads window.

The window shows a list of running threads and enables stepping into the Call Stack for the various threads. If the source code is available for threads other than the current one, you can step into this code. In our example, the main thread is the Console application. You can also organize and filter the view, search within the Call Stack, and get information on the thread's priority. The Threads window is particularly useful with multi-threaded applications. For applications that take advantage of the Task Parallel Library, the Visual Studio 2012 debugger provides other tools, which are described in Chapter 43, "Parallel Programming and Parallel LINQ."

CALL STACK

You can get the method call stack per thread by passing the mouse pointer over each thread in the window. The list of method calls is offered under the form of a tooltip.

Autos Window

The Autos window shows the variables used by the current statement and by the previous three and next three statements. Figure 5.14 shows an example of the Autos window.

FIGURE 5.14   The Autos window.

For the Autos window, you can change variables' values by double-clicking each one.

64-BIT SUPPORT

One of the new features in the Visual Studio 2012 debugger is that mixed mode with 64-bit applications debugging is now supported.

Inspecting Object Details with Debugger Visualizers

Debugger visualizers are built-in tools that enable viewing information on objects, controls, members, and variables (generally complex data) in a particular format. For example, if you place a breakpoint on the following line of code of the sample project

```
Dim result As Boolean = Test(lineRead)
```

you can then open the Locals window and select the lineRead variable. In the Value column, notice the small magnifying glass you can click. From there, you can choose how you want to visualize information on the `lineRead` variable, such as Text format, XML format, and HTML format. Of course, trying to view the content of plain text as XML content does not provide any benefits, but if you have a string representing XML data or HTML code, you could get an appropriate representation to understand what's happening. Visualizers are also useful when you have a large multiline string and you need to see how it is formatted. In our example, Figure 5.15 shows the Text visualizer for the `lineRead` variable.

FIGURE 5.15   Viewing information with debugger visualizers.

The visualizers' purpose is to provide a graphical tool for analyzing what's happening on expressions.

CUSTOM DEBUGGER VISUALIZERS

Visual Studio 2012 offers default debugger visualizers that are useful in common situations, but you might need custom visualizers. You can build custom visualizers, but this is beyond the scope of this chapter. Information on creating custom visualizers is available in the MSDN documentation at http://msdn.microsoft.com/en-us/library/e2zc529c(v=vs.110).aspx.

Debugging in Code

The .NET Framework offers the ability to interact with the debugger via managed code. You can use two classes, `System.Diagnostics.Debug` and `System.Diagnostics.Trace`, to verify conditions and evaluations that can be useful to provide feedback about your code if it is working correctly. Information generated by these classes can eventually be added to the application.

DEBUG AND TRACE ARE SINGLETON

Both `Debug` and `Trace` classes are single-instance shared classes and therefore expose only shared members.

The `Debug` Class

The `Debug` class, exposed by the `System.Diagnostics` namespace, provides interaction with the Visual Studio debugger and lets you know whether your code is working correctly via instrumentation that evaluates conditions at a certain point of your code. The `Debug` class exposes only shared methods and can display contents into the Output window so that you can programmatically interact with the debugger without the need to set breakpoints. Table 5.2 provides an overview of `Debug` methods.

TABLE 5.2   Debug Class Methods

Method	Description
Assert	Checks for a condition and shows a message if the condition is False
Close	Empties the buffer and releases trace listeners
Fail	Generates an error message
Flush	Empties the buffer and forces data to be written to underlying trace listeners
Indent	When writing to the Output window, increases the text indentation
Print	Writes the specified message to the listeners; supports text formatting
Unindent	When writing to the Output window, decreases the text indentation
Write	Writes the specified message to the listeners without a line terminator; supports text formatting
WriteIf	Writes the specified message to the listeners without a line terminator if the supplied condition is True; supports text formatting
WriteLine	Writes the specified message to the listeners with a line terminator; supports text formatting
WriteLineIf	Writes the specified message to the listeners with a line terminator if the supplied condition is True; supports text formatting

DEBUG OUTPUT

Saying that the `Debug` class can display contents to the Output window is true only in part. Developers can use other built-in outputs known as *trace listeners* to redirect the output. Later in this chapter we provide an overview of trace listeners.

Continuing the code example in Listing 5.1, try to add the following lines of code after the declaration and assignment of the `result` variable within the `Main` method:

```
Debug.WriteLine("Value of result is " & result.ToString)
Debug.WriteLineIf(result = True, "Result is valid because = True")
'If you type an empty or null string,
'then the condition "result=True" is False therefore
'shows an error message
Debug.Assert(result = True, "Needed a valid string")
```

Now run the application and type in a valid (nonempty) string. Figure 5.16 shows how the Output window appears when the runtime encounters the Debug methods.

FIGURE 5.16   Writing debug information to the Output window.

The first line shows the Boolean value of the `result` variable. The `WriteLine` method can be useful if you need to monitor objects' values without breaking the application. This method also adds a line terminator so that a new line can begin. The `Write` method does the same but does not add a line terminator. The `WriteLineIf` (and `WriteIf`) writes a message only if the specified condition is evaluated as `True`. If you enter a valid string, the `WriteLineIf` method writes a message. Notice that there is an invocation to the `Assert` method. This method causes the runtime to show a message box containing the specified message that is shown only if the specified expression is evaluated as `False`. According to this, if you enter a valid string in the sample application, the expression is evaluated as `True`; therefore, no message is shown. If you instead enter an empty string (that is, press **Enter**), the runtime shows the dialog box represented in Figure 5.17.

The `Fail` method, which is not shown in the example, shows a similar dialog box but without evaluating any condition. In Table 5.2, method descriptions mention trace listeners. We now provide an overview of the `Trace` class and then an overview of the particular objects.

The `Trace` Class

The `Trace` class, which is also exposed by the `System.Diagnostics` namespace, works exactly like the `Debug` class. One important difference influences the building process. The output of the `Debug` class is included in the build output only if the DEBUG constant is defined, but the `Trace` class's output is included in the build output only if the TRACE constant is defined. When you build your applications with the Debug configuration active, both constants are defined, so both outputs are included. The Release configuration defines only the TRACE constant, so it includes only this output.

FIGURE 5.17   The Assertion dialog box.

Understanding Trace Listeners

In the preceding examples related to the Debug class (and consequently related to the Trace class, too), you saw how to send the output of the debugger to the Output window. The .NET Framework enables sending the output to other targets, known as *trace listeners*. A trace listener is an object that "listens" to what is happening at debugging time and then collects information under various forms. For example, you could collect information as XML files or just send such information to the Output window. Both the Debug and Trace classes expose a property named Listeners that represents a set of built-in listeners. Table 5.3 groups the .NET Framework built-in listeners.

TABLE 5.3   .NET Built-In Trace Listeners

Listener	Description
DefaultTraceListener	Redirects the output to the Output window.
TextWriterTraceListener	Redirects the output to a text file.
XmlWriterTraceListener	Redirects the output to an XML file.
EventLogTraceListener	Redirects the output to the operating system's events log.
DelimitedListTraceListener	Redirects the output to a text file. Information is separated by a symbol.
EventSchemaTraceListener	Redirects the output to an XML schema that is formed on the supplied arguments.
ConsoleTraceListener	Redirects the output to the Console window.

SYSTEM.DIAGNOSTICS NAMESPACE REQUIRED

All listeners listed in Table 5.3 are exposed by the `System.Diagnostics` namespace, which is not mentioned for the sake of brevity. Usually this namespace is imported by default, according to the options set within My Project. If the background compiler advises that classes are not defined, you should add an `Imports System.Diagnostics` directive to your code.

When you invoke members from the `Debug` and `Trace` classes, by default the output is redirected to the output window. This is because the `DefaultTraceListener` is attached to the application by the debugger. Now suppose you want to redirect the output to a text file. This can be accomplished by writing the following lines of code:

```
Trace.Listeners.Clear()
Trace.Listeners.Add(New
     TextWriterTraceListener
     ("C:\users\alessandro\desktop\TraceOutput.txt"))

'This will ensure the file is closed when
'the debugger shuts down
Trace.AutoFlush = True
Trace.WriteLineIf(result = True, "You entered a valid string")
```

LISTENERS DO NOT OVERWRITE FILES

All built-in trace listeners that redirect output to a file do not overwrite the file itself if it already exists. They just append information to an existing file. If you need to create a new file each time from scratch, remember to remove the previous version (for example, invoking the `File.Delete` method).

The `Trace.Listener.Clear` method ensures that all previous information from other listeners gets cleared. You need to add a new instance of the `TextWriterTraceListener` class to listeners' collection. At this point you need to supply the name of the output file as an argument. If you add the preceding code after the declaration and assignment of the `result` variable within the `Main` method of our main example, the output is redirected to a text file, as shown in Figure 5.18.

The `AutoFlush` property set as `True` ensures that the text file is correctly closed when the debugger shuts down. In the end, you write evaluations as you would do when sending output to the Output window (see `WriteLineIf` method). A class named `DelimitedListTraceListener` inherits from `TextWriterTraceListener` and enables writing information to a file using a delimitation symbol. By default, this symbol is a comma (output files are Comma Separated Value [CSV] files that can be opened with Microsoft Excel), but you can set the `Delimiter` property value with another symbol. The usage remains the same as its base class. You also might want to redirect output to an XML file. This can be accomplished adding an instance of the `XmlWriterTraceListener` class, as shown in the following code:

```
Trace.Listeners.Clear()
Trace.Listeners.Add(New
     XmlWriterTraceListener
     ("C:\users\alessandro\desktop\TraceOutput.xml"))

'This will ensure the file is closed when
'the debugger shuts down
Trace.AutoFlush = True
Trace.WriteLineIf(result = True, "You entered a valid string")
```

FIGURE 5.18   The debugging output has been redirected to a text file.

The usage is the same as in the `TextWriterTraceListener` example. If you try to run the preceding code, you can obtain a well-formed XML document, as shown in Figure 5.19.

FIGURE 5.19   The output produced by the `XmlWriterTraceListener` class.

As you should understand, writing the output to an XML document is a more powerful task because of the amount of information collected. All the information persisted to the XML document is reflected by properties of the instance of the XmlWriterTraceListener class. Each property is named as the related information in the XML document. For example, the Computer property represents the name of the computer running the debugger, the ProcessName property represents the name of the process that the debugger is attached to, the ProcessID property represents the process identification number of the process, and the ThreadID property represents the thread identification number of the process. Another listener that you can use for producing XML files is named EventSchemaTraceListener. This object creates an XML schema starting from debugging information; the EventSchemaTraceListener constructor has several overloads that enable specifying how the schema will be formed. The following code shows an example:

```
Trace.Listeners.Add(New
        EventSchemaTraceListener("Test.xsd",
        "My listener",
        32768,
        TraceLogRetentionOption.LimitedCircularFiles,
        65536, 10))
```

Explaining this class in detail is beyond the scope of this book. If you would like to read further details on this class, you can read the official MSDN documentation at http://msdn.microsoft.com/en-us/library/system.diagnostics.eventschematracelistener(v=vs.110).aspx. The EventLogTraceListener class works similarly to the previous ones. The following lines of code attach a new instance of the class to the debugger, and the debug output is redirected to the Windows Event Log:

```
Trace.Listeners.Clear()
Trace.Listeners.Add(New EventLogTraceListener
                ("Chapter 5 - Debugging applications"))

'This will ensure the log resources are released when
'the debugger shuts down
Trace.AutoFlush = True
Trace.WriteLineIf(result = True, "You entered a valid string")
```

APPLICATION LOG REQUIRES ADMINISTRATOR

Writing to the application log requires administrative privileges. If you run Windows Vista or Windows 7 and you have the User Account Control active on your system, you should also run Visual Studio 2012 as an administrator.

The preceding code creates a new entry in the application log of the operating system. Figure 5.20 shows the content of the application log, which is reachable via the Event viewer shortcut of the Administrative tools menu.

FIGURE 5.20   Windows's Event viewer shows the application log containing our debug output.

> **My.Application.Log**
>
> Visual Basic 2012 offers an alternative to the `EventLogTraceListener` that is provided by the `My` namespace. As you see in Chapter 19, "The My Namespace," an object named `My.Application.Log` provides a simpler way for writing the trace output to the application log.

The last listener object is named `ConsoleTraceListener` and enables sending messages to the Console window. You use this object as the previous ones. At this point we should focus on an important feature of listeners: Hard-coding listeners in Visual Basic code is not mandatory. The good news is that you can add listeners to a configuration file that can be manually edited externally from Visual Studio.

Setting Listeners in Configuration Files

To set listeners to a configuration file, first you need one. In Solution Explorer, right-click the project name and then select the **Add New Item** command from the pop-up menu. When the Add New Item dialog box appears, you can search for the Application Configuration File template using the search box, as shown in Figure 5.21.

If you now double-click the configuration file in Solution Explorer, you notice a section that is named `System.Diagnostics`, as in the following snippet:

```
<system.diagnostics>
    <sources>
        <source name="DefaultSource" switchName="DefaultSwitch">
            <listeners>
                <add name="FileLog"/>
            </listeners>
```

```
                </source>
            </sources>
            <switches>
                <add name="DefaultSwitch" value="Information" />
            </switches>
        </system.diagnostics>
```

FIGURE 5.21   Adding a new configuration file to the project.

This section represents the same-named namespace and offers the capability to specify trace listeners. By default, a DefaultTraceListener is added. This can be understood examining the preceding code snippet. You might also add other listeners, such as a TextWriterTraceListener or an XmlWriterTraceListener. The following code snippet shows how you can add a TextWriterTraceListener to the App.config file, remembering that it must be nested into the System.Diagnostics node:

```
<trace autoflush="true">
  <listeners>
    <add name="DemoTestWriter"
         type="System.Diagnostics.TextWriterTraceListener"
         initializeData="output.txt"/>
    <!-- If you want to disable the DefaultTraceListener-->
    <remove name="Default"/>
  </listeners>
</trace>
```

As you can see, you need to supply a name, the type (that is, the class name), and the output file. The following code snippet shows instead how you can add an `XmlWriterTraceListener`:

```
<trace autoflush="true">
  <listeners>v
    <add name="DemoTestWriter"
        type="System.Diagnostics.XmlWriterTraceListener"
        initializeData="output.xml"/>
    <!-- If you want to disable the DefaultTraceListener-->
    <remove name="Default"/>
  </listeners>
</trace>
```

Of course, using configuration file is optional. This could be a good choice if another person who cannot edit your source code should change how the debugger information is collected because the configuration file can be edited externally from Visual Studio.

Using Debug Attributes in Your Code

In the section "'Just My Code' Debugging," I explained how some attributes can influence the debugger's behavior versus autogenerated code and that you can use that versus your own code. The .NET Framework also provides other attributes you can use to decorate your code for deciding how the debugger should behave versus such code. Table 5.4 lists other attributes that complete the list in Table 5.1.

TABLE 5.4   Debug Attributes

Attribute	Description
DebuggerVisualizer	Indicates to the IDE that the code implements a custom debugger visualizer.
DebuggerStepperBoundary	When a DebuggerNonUserCode attribute is also specified, this causes the debugger to run the code instead of stepping through.
DebuggerBrowsable	Establishes how data should be shown in the Data Tips windows.
DebuggerDisplay	Allows customizing strings and messages in Data Tips.
DebuggerTypeProxy	Allows overriding how data tips are shown for a particular type.

As previously described in this chapter, discussing custom debugger visualizers is beyond the scope of this book, so the `DebuggerVisualizer` attribute is not discussed here.

NOTE ON DEBUG ATTRIBUTES

The previous attributes are effectively used and useful when debugging the application from within Visual Studio. When you compile the application in Release mode, debug attributes are ignored and do not affect your code at runtime.

DebuggerStepperBoundary

This attribute is used only in multithreading scenarios and has effects only when a DebuggerNonUserCode is also specified. It is used to run code instead of stepping through it when you are stepping into user code that does not actually relate to the thread you were debugging. Due to its particular nature, this attribute is not discussed in detail. The MSDN Library provides additional information at this address: http://msdn.microsoft.com/en-us/library/system.diagnostics.debuggerstepperboundaryattribute(v=vs.110).aspx.

DebuggerBrowsable

You can use the DebuggerBrowsable attribute to establish how an item should be visualized in Data Tips or variables windows by specifying one of the following arguments exposed by the System.Diagnostics.DebuggerBrowsableState enumeration:

▶ Collapsed, which establishes that an item is collapsed and that you have to click the + symbol to expand it and see its children elements

▶ Never, which causes the specified item to never be visible in windows such as Autos and Locals

▶ RootHidden, which forces the debugger to show just the children elements of the specified item

For example, consider the following code snippet that retrieves an array of processes (each represented by an instance of the System.Diagnostics.Process class):

```
<DebuggerBrowsable(DebuggerBrowsableState.RootHidden)>
Private ProcessesList As Process()

Sub ShowProcesses()
    ProcessesList = Process.GetProcesses
End Sub
```

The preceding code causes the debugger to show only the children element of the array, excluding the root (ProcessesList), as shown in Figure 5.22.

DebuggerDisplay

The DebuggerDisplay attribute also enables you to establish how an item should be shown inside Data Tips. With this attribute, you can replace Visual Studio default strings and customize the description for an object within Data Tips. For example, imagine you have the code shown in Listing 5.3, in which a Person class and code creates a list of people.

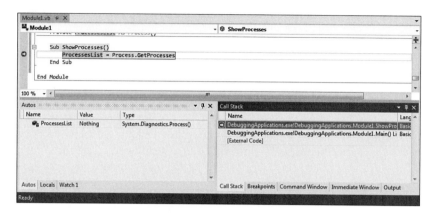

FIGURE 5.22   Using `DebuggerBrowsable`, you can establish how an object can be shown in debugger windows.

LISTING 5.3   Using the `DebuggerDisplay` Attribute

```
Module Module1

    Sub Main()

        Dim p As New List(Of Person)
        p.Add(New Person With {.FirstName = "Alessandro", .LastName = "Del Sole"})
        p.Add(New Person With {.FirstName = "MyFantasyName",
                               .LastName = "MyFantasyLastName"})

        Console.ReadLine()
    End Sub
End Module


<DebuggerDisplay("This person is {FirstName} {LastName}")>
Class Person
    Property FirstName As String
    Property LastName As String
End Class
```

At this point, it's not important to focus on how collections of objects are created. However, it's interesting to understand what the `DebuggerDisplay` attribute does. Now place a breakpoint on the `Console.ReadLine` statement and then run the application. If you pass the mouse pointer over the p object, Data Tips for this object will be activated. The debugger then displays data formatted the way we described in the `DebuggerDisplay` attribute. Figure 5.23 shows the result of our customization.

FIGURE 5.23   The `DebuggerDisplay` attribute enables customizing Data Tips messages.

DebuggerTypeProxy

As its name implies, the `DebuggerTypeProxy` enables you to override how debug information for a specific data type is shown within Data Tips. Listing 5.4 shows how you can implement such an attribute.

LISTING 5.4   Using the `DebuggerTypeProxy` Attribute

```
Module Module1

    Sub Main()

        Dim p As New List(Of Person)
        p.Add(New Person With {.FirstName = "Alessandro", .LastName = "Del Sole"})
        p.Add(New Person With {.FirstName = "MyFantasyName",
                               .LastName = "MyFantasyLastName"})

        Console.ReadLine()
    End Sub
End Module

<DebuggerTypeProxy(GetType(PersonProxy))>
Class Person
    Property FirstName As String
    Property LastName As String

End Class

Class PersonProxy
    Dim myProxy As Person

    Sub New(ByVal OnePerson As Person)
        myProxy = OnePerson
    End Sub
```

5

```
    ReadOnly Property Length As Integer
        Get
            Return String.Concat(myProxy.FirstName, " ", myProxy.LastName).Length
        End Get
    End Property
End Class
```

The `PersonProxy` class gets the instance of the `Person` class being debugged, reads the information from such instance, and returns via the `Length` property the length of the string composed by the `FirstName` and `LastName` properties. The `Length` property here is a basic example, but it is useful to understand where the real proxy is. To activate the proxy, you need to decorate the `Person` class with the `DebuggerTypeProxy` attribute whose argument is the Type representation of what you need to debug. This type is retrieved using a `GetType` keyword. If you now try to run the application, you can see that the debugger can display the new Length information, as shown in Figure 5.24.

FIGURE 5.24   The `DebuggerTypeProxy` enables customizing the debug information.

So you now have a powerful way to customize debug information.

Summary

Debugging is a primary task in developing applications. The Visual Studio 2012 IDE offers lots of useful tools that can enhance the debugging experience. In this chapter, you learned what Just My Code is and then learned how you can work with breakpoints and trace points, passing through debugging in steps. You also saw the debugger windows in action, enabling deep control over variables and objects. In the end, you learned how to customize your own code to take advantage of the Visual Studio debugging tools by decorating your code with debug attributes. But debugging is just one part in the development process that fights against errors. Exceptions are the other part, and they are discussed in Chapter 6, "Handling Errors and Exceptions."

CHAPTER 6

Handling Errors and Exceptions

Every application might encounter errors during its execution, even when you spend several nights on testing the application and all the possible execution scenarios. Runtime errors are especially unpredictable because the application execution is conditioned by user actions. Because of this, error handling is a fundamental practice that, as a developer, you need to know in depth. In this chapter you learn how the .NET Framework enables handling errors and how to get information to solve problems deriving such errors. In other words, you learn about .NET exceptions.

Introducing Exceptions

In development environments other than .NET, programming languages can handle errors occurring during the application execution in different ways. For example, the Windows native APIs return a 32-bit HRESULT number in case an error occurs. Visual Basic 6 uses the On Error statements, whereas other languages have their own error-handling infrastructures. As you can imagine, such differences cannot be allowed in the .NET Framework because all languages rely on the Common Language Runtime (CLR), so all of them must intercept and handle errors the same way. With that said, the .NET Framework identifies errors as *exceptions*. An exception is an instance of the System.Exception class (or of a class derived from it) and provides deep information on the error that occurred. Such an approach provides a unified way for intercepting and handling errors. Exceptions occur at runtime as well as during the application execution. Exceptions can be *thrown* by the Visual Basic compiler at compile time or by the background compiler when typing code. Errors occurring when designing the user interface of an application or when working within the Visual Studio 2012 IDE are typically called exceptions. This is because such tasks (and most of the Visual Studio IDE) are powered by the .NET Framework. In Chapter 2, "Getting Started with the Visual Studio 2012 IDE," we introduced the Visual Studio debugger and saw how it can be used for analyzing error messages provided by exceptions (see the "About Runtime Errors" section in Chapter 2). In that case, we did not implement any error-handling routine because we were just introducing the debugging features of Visual Studio during the development process. But what if an error occurs at runtime when the application has been deployed to your customer without implementing appropriate error-handling code? Imagine an application that attempts to read a file that does not exist and in which the developer did not implement error checks. Figure 6.1 shows an example of what could happen and what should never happen in a real application.

FIGURE 6.1   Without handling exceptions, solving errors is difficult.

As you can see from Figure 6.1, in case of an error the application stops its execution and no resume is possible. Moreover, identifying the type of error occurred can also be difficult. Because of this, as a developer it is your responsibility to implement code for intercepting exceptions and take the best actions possible to solve the problem—while keeping your users' choices in mind. The best way to understand exceptions is to begin to write some code that causes an error, so this is what we do in the next section.

Handling Exceptions

Visual Basic 2012 enables deep control over exceptions. With regard to this, an important concept is that you not only can check for occurring exceptions, but can also conditionally manage solutions to exceptions and raise exceptions when needed. In this section we discuss all these topics, providing information on how you can intercept and manage exceptions in your application.

Tips for Visual Basic 6 Migration

One of the (very few) commonalities between Visual Basic 6 and Visual Basic .NET and higher is the syntax approach. This should help a little more in migrating from Visual Basic 6 to 2012. Although Visual Basic 2012 (more precisely, VB.NET from 2002 to 2012) still enables the usage of the `On Error Goto` and `On Error Resume` statements, when developing .NET applications with Visual Basic, you should never use such statements for two reasons. First, exceptions are the only thing that enables interoperation with other .NET languages such as Visual C# and Visual F#. This is fundamental when developing class libraries or components that could potentially be reused from other languages than Visual Basic. The second reason is that the old-fashioned way for handling errors is not as efficient as handling .NET exceptions. If you decided to migrate, you should completely forget `On Error` and exclusively use exceptions.

`System.Exception`, Naming Conventions, and Specialization

`System.Exception` is the most general exception and can represent all kinds of errors occurring in applications. It is also the base class for derived exceptions, which are specific to situations you encounter. For example, the `System.IOException` derives from `System.Exception`, is thrown when the application encounters input/output errors when accessing the disk, and can be handled only for this particular situation. On the other hand, `System.Exception` can handle not only this situation, but also any other occurring errors. You can think of `System.Exception` as the root in the exceptions hierarchy. We explain later in code the hierarchy of exception handling. Classes representing exceptions always terminate with the word `Exception`. You encounter exceptions such as `FileNotFoundException`, `IndexOutOfRangeException`, `FormatException`, and so on. This is not mandatory, but a recommended naming convention. Generally, .NET built-in exceptions inherit from `System.Exception`, but because they are reference types, you find several exceptions inheriting from a derived exception.

Handling Exceptions with `Try..Catch..Finally` Blocks

You perform exception handling by writing a `Try..Catch..Finally` code block. The logic is that you say to the compiler, "Try to execute the code; if you encounter an exception, take the specified actions; whenever the code execution succeeds or it fails due to an exception, execute the final code." The most basic code for controlling the execution flow regarding exceptions is the following:

```
Try
    'Code to be executed
Catch ex As Exception
    'Code to handle the exception
End Try
```

IntelliSense does a great job here. When you type the `Try` keyword and then press **Enter**, it automatically adds the `Catch` statement and the `End Try` terminator. The `ex` variable gets the instance of the `System.Exception` that is caught, and that provides important information so that you can best handle the exception. To see what happens, consider the following code snippet:

```
Try
    Dim myArray() As String = {"1", "2", "3", "4"}

    Console.WriteLine(myArray(4))
Catch ex As Exception
    Console.WriteLine(ex.Message)
End Try
```

Here we have an array of strings in which the upper range of the array is 3. The `Try` block tries to execute code that attempts writing the content of the fourth index to the Console window. Unfortunately, such an index does not exist, but because the code is formally legal, it will be correctly compiled. When the application runs and the runtime encounters this situation, it throws an exception to communicate the error occurrence. So the `Catch` statement intercepts the exception and enables deciding which actions must be taken. In our example, the action to handle the exception is to write the complete error message of the exception. If the code within `Try` succeeds, the execution passes to the first code after the `End Try` terminator. In our example, the control transfers to the `Catch` block that contains code that writes to the Console window the actual error message that looks like the following:

```
Index was outside the bounds of the array
```

The runtime never throws a generic `System.Exception` exception. There are specific exceptions for the most common scenarios (and it is worth mentioning that you can create custom exceptions as discussed in Chapter 12, "Inheritance") that are helpful to identify what happened instead of inspecting a generic exception. Continuing our example, the runtime throws an `IndexOutOfRangeException` that means the code attempted to access and index greater or smaller than allowed. Based on these considerations, the code could be rewritten as follows:

```
Try
    Dim myArray() As String = {"1", "2", "3", "4"}

    Console.WriteLine(myArray(4))

Catch ex As IndexOutOfRangeException
    Console.WriteLine("There is a problem: probably you are "
            & Environment.NewLine &
            " attempting to access an index that does not exist")
```

```
Catch ex As Exception
    Console.WriteLine(ex.Message)

End Try
```

As you can see, the most specific exception needs to be caught before the most generic one. This is quite obvious because, if you first catch the `System.Exception`, all other exceptions will be ignored. Intercepting specific exceptions can also be useful because you can both communicate the user detailed information and decide which actions must be taken to solve the problem. Anyway, always adding a `Catch` block for a generic `System.Exception` is a best practice. This enables you to provide a general error-handling code in case exceptions you do not specifically intercept will occur. You could also need to perform some actions independently from the result of your code execution. The `Finally` statement enables executing some code either if the `Try` succeeds or if it fails, passing control to `Catch`. For example, you might want to clean up resources used by the array:

```
Dim myArray() As String = {"1", "2", "3", "4"}

Try
    Console.WriteLine(myArray(4))

Catch ex As IndexOutOfRangeException
    Console.WriteLine("There is a problem: probably you are "
            & Environment.NewLine &
            " attempting to access an index that does not exists")
Catch ex As Exception
    Console.WriteLine(ex.Message)
Finally
    myArray = Nothing
End Try
```

Notice how objects referred within the `Finally` block must be declared outside the `Try`.. `End Try` block because of visibility. The code within `Finally` will be executed no matter what the result of the `Try` block will be. This is important; for example, think about files. You might open a file and then try to perform some actions on the file that for any reason can fail. In this situation you would need to close the file, and `Finally` ensures you can do that if the file access is successful and even if it fails (throwing an exception). An example of this scenario is represented in Listing 6.1.

LISTING 6.1   Use `Finally` to Ensure Resources Are Freed Up and Unlocked

```
Imports System.IO

Module Module1

    Sub Main()
```

```vbnet
        Console.WriteLine("Specify a file name:")
        Dim fileName As String = Console.ReadLine

        Dim myFile As FileStream = Nothing

        Try
            myFile = New FileStream(fileName, FileMode.Open)
            'Seek a specific position in the file.
            'Just for example
            myFile.Seek(5, SeekOrigin.Begin)
        Catch ex As FileNotFoundException
            Console.WriteLine("File not found.")
        Catch ex As Exception
            Console.WriteLine("An unidentified error occurred.")
        Finally
            If myFile IsNot Nothing Then
                myFile.Close()
            End If
        End Try

        Console.ReadLine()
    End Sub
End Module
```

The code in Listing 6.1 is quite simple. First, it asks the user to specify a filename to be accessed. Accessing files is accomplished with a `FileStream` object. Notice that the `myFile` object is declared outside the `Try..End Try` block so that it can be visible within `Finally`. Moreover, its value is set to `Nothing` so that it has a default value, although it's null. If we did not assign this default value, `myFile` would just be declared but not yet assigned, so the Visual Basic compiler would throw a warning message. By the way, setting the default value to `Nothing` will not prevent a `NullReferenceException` at runtime unless the variable gets a value. The `Try` block attempts accessing the specified file. The `FileStream.Seek` method here is just used as an example needed to perform an operation on the file. When accessing files, there could be different problems, resulting in various kinds of exceptions. In our example, if the specified file does not exist, a `FileNotFoundException` is thrown by the runtime and the `Catch` block takes control over the execution. Within the block, we just communicate that the specified file was not found. If, instead, the file exists, the code performs a search. In both cases, the `Finally` block ensures that the file gets closed, independently on what happened before. This is fundamental because if you leave a file open, other problems would occur.

Exceptions Hierarchy

In Listing 6.1, we saw how we can catch a specific exception, such as `FileNotFoundException`, and then the general `System.Exception`. By the way, `FileNotFoundException` does not directly derive from `System.Exception`; instead, it derives from `System.IO.IOException`, which is related to general input/output problems. Although you are not obliged to also catch an `IOException` when working with files, adding it could be a good practice because you can separate error handling for disk input/output errors from other errors. In such situations, the rule is that you have to catch exceptions from the most specific to the most general. Continuing the previous example, Listing 6.2 shows how you can implement exceptions hierarchy.

LISTING 6.2   Understanding Exceptions Hierarchy

```
Imports System.IO

Module Module1

    Sub Main()

        Console.WriteLine("Specify a file name:")
        Dim fileName As String = Console.ReadLine

        Dim myFile As FileStream = Nothing

        Try
            myFile = New FileStream(fileName, FileMode.Open)
            'Seek a specific position in the file.
            'Just for example
            myFile.Seek(5, SeekOrigin.Begin)
        Catch ex As FileNotFoundException
            Console.WriteLine("File not found.")
        Catch ex As IOException
            Console.WriteLine("A general input/output error occurred")
        Catch ex As Exception
            Console.WriteLine("An unidentified error occurred.")
        Finally
            If myFile IsNot Nothing Then
                myFile.Close()
            End If
        End Try

        Console.ReadLine()
    End Sub
End Module
```

`FileNotFoundException` is the most specific exception, so it must be caught first. It derives from `IOException`, which is intercepted second. `System.Exception` is instead the base class for all exceptions and therefore must be caught last.

System.Exception **Properties**

The System.Exception class exposes some properties that are useful for investigating exceptions and then understanding what the real problem is. Particularly when you catch specialized exceptions, it could happen that such exception is just the last ring of a chain and that the problem causing the exception itself derives from other problems. System.Exception's properties enable a better navigation of exceptions. Table 6.1 lists the available properties.

TABLE 6.1   System.Exception's Properties

Property	Description
Message	Gets the complete error message generated from the exception
Source	Represents the name of the application or the object that threw the exception
TargetSite	Retrieves the method that actually throws the exception
Data	Stores a sequence of key/value pairs containing additional information on the exception
Help	Allows specifying or retrieving the name of the help file associated with the exception
InnerException	Gets the instance of the exception object that actually caused the current exception
StackTrace	Retrieves the method calls hierarchy in the Call Stack when the exception occurred

Listing 6.3 shows how you can retrieve deep information on the exception. In the example, information is retrieved for the System.IO.FileNotFoundException, but you can use these properties for any exception you like.

LISTING 6.3   Investigating Exceptions Properties

```
Imports System.IO

Module Module1

    Sub Main()
        Console.WriteLine("Specify a file name:")
        Dim fileName As String = Console.ReadLine

        Dim myFile As FileStream = Nothing

        Try
            myFile = New FileStream(fileName, FileMode.Open)
            'Seek a specific position in the file.
            'Just for example
            myFile.Seek(5, SeekOrigin.Begin)
```

```vb
    Catch ex As FileNotFoundException
        Console.WriteLine()
        Console.WriteLine("Error message: " & ex.Message & Environment.NewLine)
        Console.WriteLine("Object causing the exception: "
                        & ex.Source & Environment.NewLine)
        Console.WriteLine("Method where the exception is thrown; "
                        & ex.TargetSite.ToString & Environment.NewLine)
        Console.WriteLine("Call stack:" & ex.StackTrace & Environment.NewLine)

        Console.WriteLine("Other useful info:")
        For Each k As KeyValuePair(Of String, String) In ex.Data
            Console.WriteLine(k.Key & " " & k.Value)
        Next

    Catch ex As IOException
        Console.WriteLine("A general input/output error occurred")
    Catch ex As Exception
        Console.WriteLine(ex.Message)
    Finally
        If myFile IsNot Nothing Then
            myFile.Close()
        End If
    End Try

    Console.ReadLine()
    End Sub
End Module
```

If you run this code and specify a filename that does not exist, you can retrieve a lot of useful information. Figure 6.2 shows the result of the code.

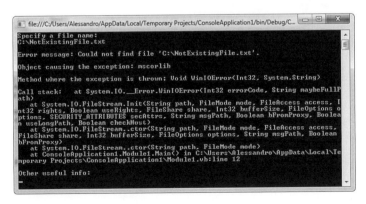

FIGURE 6.2   Getting information on the exception.

As you can see from Figure 6.2, the `Message` property contains the full error message. In production environments, this can be a useful way to provide customers a user-friendly error message. The `Source` property shows the application or object causing the exception. In our example, it retrieves Mscorlib, meaning that the exception was thrown by the CLR. The `Target` property retrieves the method in which the exception was thrown. It is worth mentioning that this property retrieves the native method that caused the error, meaning that the method was invoked by the CLR. This is clearer if we take a look at the content of the `Stack` property. We can see the hierarchy of method calls in descending order: the `.ctor` method is the constructor of the `FileStream` class, invoked within the `Main` method; the next method, named `Init`, attempts to initialize a `FileStream` and is invoked behind the scenes by the CLR. `Init` then invokes the native `WinIOError` function because accessing the file was unsuccessful. Analyzing such properties can be useful to understand what happened. Because there is no other useful information, iterating the `Data` property produced no result. By the way, if you just need to report a detailed message about the exception, you can collect most of the properties' content by invoking the `ToString` method of the `Exception` class. For example, you could replace the entire `Catch ex as FileNotFoundException` block as follows:

```
Catch ex As FileNotFoundException
    Console.WriteLine(ex.ToString)
```

This edit produces the result shown in Figure 6.3. As you can see, the result is a little different from the previous one. We can find a lot of useful information, such as the name of the exception, complete error message, filename, Call Stack hierarchy, and line of code that caused the exception.

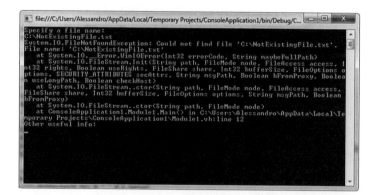

FIGURE 6.3   Invoking the `Exception.ToString` method offers detailed information.

Typically, you use `ToString` just to show information, whereas you use properties to analyze exception information.

NOTE ABOUT PERFORMANCE

Catching exceptions is necessary but is also performance consuming. Sometimes you could simply check the value of an object instead of catching exceptions. For example, you could check with an `If..Then` statement whether an object is null instead of catching a NullReference exception (when possible, of course). Exceptions are best left to handling "exceptional" situations that occur in code, so you should limit the use of them when possible.

F Catching Exception

You can also ignore exceptions by simply not writing anything inside a `Catch` block. For instance, the following code catches a `FileNotFoundException` and prevents an undesired stop in the application execution but takes no action:

```
Try
    testFile = New FileStream(FileName, FileMode.Open)


Catch ex As FileNotFoundException
End Try
```

Nested `Try..Catch..Finally` Blocks

You also have the ability to nest `Try..Catch..Finally` code blocks. Nested blocks are useful when you have to try the execution of code onto the result of another `Try..Catch` block. Consider the following code that shows the creation time of all files in a given directory:

```
Try
    Dim allFiles As String() =
        Directory.GetFiles("C:\TestDirectory")

    Try
        For Each f As String In allFiles
            Console.WriteLine(File.GetCreationTime(f).ToString())
        Next

    Catch ex As IOException

    Catch ex As Exception

    End Try

Catch ex As DirectoryNotFoundException

Catch ex As Exception
End Try
```

The first `Try..Catch` attempts reading the list of files from a specified directory. Because you can encounter directory errors, a `DirectoryNotFoundException` is caught. The result (being an array of `string`) is then iterated within a nested `Try..Catch` block. This is because the code is now working on files and then specific errors might be encountered.

`Exit Try` Statements

You can exit from within a `Try..Catch..Finally` block at any moment using an `Exit Try` statement. If a `Finally` block exists, `Exit Try` pulls the execution into `Finally` that otherwise resumes the execution at the first line of code after `End Try`. The following code snippet shows an example:

```
Try
    'Your code goes here
    Exit Try
    'The following line will not be considered
    Console.WriteLine("End of Try block")

Catch ex As Exception

End Try
'Resume the execution here
```

The `Throw` Keyword

In some situations you need to programmatically throw exceptions or you catch exceptions but do not want to handle them in the `Catch` block that intercepted exceptions. Programmatically throwing exceptions can be accomplished via the `Throw` keyword. For instance, the following line of code throws an `ArgumentNullException` that usually occurs when a method receives a null argument:

```
Throw New ArgumentNullException
```

You often need to manually throw exceptions when they should be handled by another portion of code, also in another application. A typical example is when you develop class libraries. A class library must be as abstract as possible, so you cannot decide which actions to take when an exception is caught; this is the responsibility of the developer who creates the application that references your class library. If both developers are the same person, this remains a best practice because you should always separate the logic of class implementations from the client logic (such as the user interface). To provide a clearer example, a class library cannot show a graphical message box or a text message into the Console window. It instead needs to send the code the exception caught to the caller, and this is accomplished via the Throw keyword. We can provide a code example. Visual Studio 2012 creates a new blank solution and then adds a new Class Library project that you could name, for example, TestThrow. Listing 6.4 shows the content of the class.

LISTING 6.4   Throwing Back Exceptions to Caller Code

```
Imports System.IO

Public Class TestThrow

    Public Sub TestAccessFile(ByVal FileName As String)
        If String.IsNullOrEmpty(FileName) Then
            Throw New ArgumentNullException("FileName",
                     "You passed an invalid file name")
        End If
        Dim testFile As FileStream = Nothing

        Try
            testFile = New FileStream(FileName, FileMode.Open)

        Catch ex As FileNotFoundException
            Throw New FileNotFoundException("The supplied file name was not found")
        Catch ex As Exception
            Throw
        Finally
            If testFile IsNot Nothing Then
                testFile.Close()
            End If
        End Try
    End Function
End Class
```

The `TestThrow` class's purpose is just attempting to access a file. This is accomplished
by invoking the `TestAccess` method that receives a `FileName` argument of type `String`.
The first check is on the argument: If it is null, the code throws back to the caller an
`ArgumentNullException` that provides the argument name and a description. In this
scenario, the method catches but does not handle the exception. This is thrown back to
the caller code, which is responsible to handle the exception (for example, asking the
user to specify a valid filename). The second check is on the file access. The `Try..Catch..`
`Finally` block implements code that tries to access the specified file and, if the file is not
found, it throws back the `FileNotFoundException` describing what happened. In this way
the caller code is responsible for handling the exception; for example, asking the user
to specify another filename. Also notice how a generic `System.Exception` is caught and
thrown back to the caller by simply invoking the `Throw` statement without arguments.
This enables the method to throw back to the caller the complete exception information.

RETHROWING EXCEPTIONS

Throwing back an exception to the caller code is also known as the *rethrow technique*.

Now we can create an application that can reference the TestThrow class library and handle exceptions on the client side. Add to the solution a new Visual Basic project for the Console and add a reference to the TestThrow class library by selecting **Project, Add Reference**. Adding a reference to another assembly enables you to use types exposed publicly from such an assembly. Finally, write the code shown in Listing 6.5.

LISTING 6.5   Handling Exceptions on the Client Side

```
Imports System.IO

Module Module1

    Sub Main()

        Console.WriteLine("Specify the file name:")
        Dim name As String = Console.ReadLine
        Dim throwTest As New TestThrow.TestThrow

        Try
            throwTest.TestAccessFile(name)
        Catch ex As ArgumentNullException
            Console.WriteLine(ex.ToString & Environment.NewLine &
                    "You passed an invalid argument")
        Catch ex As FileNotFoundException
            Console.WriteLine(ex.Message)
        Catch ex As Exception
            Console.WriteLine(ex.ToString)
        Finally
            Console.ReadLine()
        End Try
    End Sub
End Module
```

The code in Listing 6.5 first asks the user to specify a filename to access. If you press **Enter** without specifying any filename, the TestAccessFile method is invoked passing an empty string, so the method throws an ArgumentNullException, as shown in Figure 6.4.

If this situation happened inside a Windows application, you could provide a MessageBox showing the error message. With this approach, you maintain logics separately. If you instead specify a filename that does not exist, the caller code needs to handle the FileNotFoundException; the result is shown in Figure 6.5.

FIGURE 6.4   Passing an empty string as an argument causes an `ArgumentNullException`.

FIGURE 6.5   The caller code handles the `FileNotFoundException` and shows a user-friendly message.

The caller code writes the content of the `ex.Message` property to the Console window, which is populated with the error message provided by the `Thrown` statement from the class library. If any other kinds of exceptions occur, a generic `System.Exception` is handled and its content is shown to the user.

CATCHING TASK-SPECIFIC EXCEPTIONS

Depending on which tasks you perform within a `Try..Catch` block, always catch exceptions specific for those tasks. For example, if your code works with files, don't limit it to catch a `FileNotFoundException`. Consider file-related and disk-related exceptions, too. To get a listing of the exceptions that a class was designed to throw, you can read the MSDN documentation related to that class. The documentation describes in detail which exceptions are related to the desired object.

Performance Overhead

Invoking the `Throw` keyword causes the runtime to search through all the code hierarchy until it finds the caller code that can handle the exception. Continuing our previous example, the Console application is not necessarily the first caller code. There could be another class library that could rethrow the exception to another class that could then rethrow the exception to the main caller code. Obviously, going through the callers' hierarchy is a task that could cause performance overhead, so you should take care about how many callers are in your code to reduce the overhead. In the end, if the caller code is missing a `Catch` block, the result will be the same as what is shown in Figure 6.1, which should always be avoided.

The `When` Keyword

Sometimes you might need to catch an exception only when a particular condition exists. You can conditionally control the exception handling using the `When` keyword, which enables taking specific actions when a particular condition is evaluated as `True`. Continuing the example of the previous paragraph, the `TestThrow` class throws an `ArgumentNullException` in two different situations (although similar). The first one is if the string passed to the `TestAccessFile` method is empty; the second one is if the string passed to the method is a null value (`Nothing`). So it could be useful to decide which actions to take depending on what actually caused the exception. According to this, we could rewrite the code shown in Listing 6.5 as what is shown in Listing 6.6.

LISTING 6.6   Conditional Exception Handling with the `When` Keyword

```
Imports System.IO

Module Module1

    Sub Main()

        Console.WriteLine("Specify the file name:")
        Dim name As String = Console.ReadLine

        Dim throwTest As New TestThrow.TestThrow

        Try
            throwTest.TestAccessFile(name)

        Catch ex As ArgumentNullException When name Is Nothing
            Console.WriteLine("You provided a null parameter")
        Catch ex As ArgumentNullException When name Is String.Empty
            Console.WriteLine("You provided an empty string")
        Catch ex As FileNotFoundException
            Console.WriteLine(ex.Message)
        Catch ex As Exception
            Console.WriteLine(ex.ToString)
```

```
        Finally
            Console.ReadLine()
        End Try
    End Sub
End Module
```

As you can see from Listing 6.6, by using the `When` keyword you can conditionally handle exceptions depending if the expression on the right is evaluated as True. In this case, when handling the `ArgumentNullException`, the condition is evaluating the name variable. If name is equal to `Nothing`, the exception is handled showing a message saying that the string is null. If name is instead an empty string (which is different from a null string), another kind of message is shown. `When` can be applied only to `Catch` statements and works only with expressions. Of course, you can use the `When` keyword also with value types; for example, you might have a counter that you increment during the execution of your code and, in case of exceptions, you might decide which actions to take based on the value of your counter. The following code demonstrates:

```
Dim oneValue As Integer = 0
Try
    'perform some operations
    'on oneValue
Catch ex As Exception When oneValue = 1

Catch ex As Exception When oneValue = 2

Catch ex As Exception When oneValue = 3

End Try
```

Catching Exceptions Without a Variable

You do not always need to specify a variable in the `Catch` block. This can be the case in which you want to take the same action independently from the exception that occurred. For example, consider the following code:

```
Try
    Dim result As String =
        My.Computer.FileSystem.ReadAllText("C:\MyFile.txt")

Catch ex As Exception
    Console.WriteLine("A general error occurred")
End Try
```

The `ex` variable is not being used and no specific exceptions are handled. So the preceding code can be rewritten as follows, without the `ex` variable:

```
Try

    Dim result As String =
        My.Computer.FileSystem.ReadAllText("C:\MyFile.txt")

Catch
    Console.WriteLine("A general error occurred")
End Try
```

Whichever exception occurs, the code shows the specified message. This also works with regard to the rethrow technique. The following code simply rethrows the proper exception to the caller:

```
Try

    Dim result As String =
        My.Computer.FileSystem.ReadAllText("C:\MyFile.txt")

Catch
    Throw
End Try
```

Summary

Managing errors is something that every developer needs to take into consideration. The .NET Framework provides a unified system for managing errors, which is the exception handling. `System.Exception` is the root class in the exceptions hierarchy, and exceptions are handled using a `Try..Catch..Finally` block. You can create nested `Try..Catch..Finally` blocks and check exceptions conditionally using the `When` keyword. In the end, you can programmatically generate exceptions using the `Throw` keyword that is particularly useful in class libraries development. This chapter provided a high-level overview of exceptions; now you can decide which kinds of exceptions you need to handle for your code and how to take actions to solve errors.

Class Fundamentals

In your everyday life, you perform all sorts of activities using objects. You use a fork to eat; you drive your car to reach your office; and you spend money to buy things. Each of these objects has its own characteristics. There are hundreds of car models; they have different colors, different engines, and different accessories, but they all are cars. *Object-oriented programming (OOP)* is similar to this view of life. In fact, OOP relies on objects; for example, you can have an object that enables working on files or another object that enables managing pictures. In .NET development of an object is typically represented by a class. Structures are also objects, but their purpose is to represent a value more than to take actions. For car characteristics, objects have their own characteristics known as *properties*. But they also have some members that enable taking actions, known as *methods*. In this chapter you learn how classes in .NET development are structured and how to create your own classes, implementing all members that the .NET Framework enables in the context.

Declaring Classes

Classes in Visual Basic 2012 are declared with `Class..End Class` statements. Classes support the following visibility modifiers: `Public`, `Protected`, `Friend`, `Private`, and `Protected Friend`. Classes with `Public` can be reached from other assemblies, whereas classes with `Friend` visibility can be reached from within the assembly that defines them. Both modifiers are the only valid ones for non-nested classes, as you will see later in this chapter.

The following are the only acceptable class declarations:

```
Public Class Test

End Class
Friend Class Test

End Class
```

If you omit the qualifier (that is, `Public` or `Friend` keyword), the Visual Basic compiler assigns `Public` by default. Classes can define members, such as fields, properties, and methods (all covered in this chapter), but also other classes and structures. The next section covers members that can be defined within classes so that you can have a complete overview about creating your custom classes.

CLASS LIBRARIES

You can define classes in whatever code file you like. Usually developers assign a single code file to one class. If you plan to develop a reusable assembly, exposing classes or types' definitions only, you can use the Class Library project template that enables you to build a .dll assembly that can be referenced by other projects and applications, which is particularly useful for the modular development. Also, Visual Studio 2012 introduces the Portable Class Library project template that enables you to create class libraries that can be successfully reused across multiple platforms such as .NET Framework, Silverlight, Silverlight for Windows Phone, and .NET for Metro. The Portable Class Library template is discussed later in Chapter 17, "Creating Objects: Visual Tools and Portable Libraries," because it requires a deeper knowledge of concepts about OOP.

Nested Classes

You can organize classes within other classes. The following code snippet shows how you can define a nested class:

```
Public Class Test

    Friend Class NestedClass

    End Class

End Class
```

Nested classes can also be marked as `Private`, and this is the only situation in which the qualifier is enabled. If you make a class private, you cannot use that class outside the class that defines it. Continuing with the preceding example, if the `NestedClass` class were marked as `Private`, you could use it only within the `Test` class. If a nested class is not private, you can invoke it the usual way; you need to write the full name of the class as follows:

```
Dim nc As New Test.NestedClass
```

Typically, classes are organized within namespaces (as described in Chapter 9, "Organizing Types Within Namespaces"), but there can be situations in which you need to organize small frameworks of classes, and then nested classes are useless without the parent class.

Fields

Fields are the places in which you store information to and read information from. They are declared in the form of class-level variables and differ from local variables in that they are declared at the method or property level. The following code shows how simple it is to declare fields:

```
Class FieldsDemo

    'a private field
    Private counter As Integer

    'a public field
    Public publicCounter As Integer

    Public Sub DoSomething()

        'a local variable
        Dim localVariable As Integer = 0
    End Sub
End Class
```

Fields can be reachable from within the class and its members, and if you specify one of the appropriate qualifiers (such as Public), they can also be reached from the external world. Inside fields, you store the actual information your custom objects need.

USING FIELDS

With the introduction of auto-implemented properties (see next section) since Visual Basic 2010, fields are now typically used to store information at the class level. They lose part of their purpose regarding properties, although you can still use fields as a repository for property information when auto-implemented properties are not enough for your needs.

You can also provide inline initialization of fields, as in the following snippet:

```
Private counter As Integer = 2


'With reference types
Public inlineDemo As Person = New Person
```

Assigning a field inline or not is something that depends exclusively on your needs. Probably you will initialize fields at runtime when you receive an input from the user or with a value received from the constructor, whereas you might prefer inline initialization when you need to start from a certain value. Fields can also be read-only. When you need to provide a field with an immutable value, you can use read-only fields as follows:

```
'read-only fields
Private ReadOnly counter As Integer = 3
Private ReadOnly testReference As Person = New Person
```

A read-only value requires inline initialization. If not, zero will be assigned to value types and `Nothing` assigned to reference types. Read-only fields work similarly to constants with one big difference: Constants are evaluated at compile time; in contrast, read-only fields are evaluated at runtime, meaning that their initial value can be the result of a method call or value coming from some other runtime derived object.

SCOPE

Fields, as much as properties, have scope. To understand how you can limit or grant access to fields and properties using the appropriate qualifiers, see the "Scope" section in this chapter.

Avoiding Ambiguities with Local Variables

As previously mentioned, fields are at class level, unlike local variables which are at the method/property level. There could be situations in which a local variable has the same name of a field. For example, consider the following code in which two items are named counter: a class-level field and a local variable:

```
Public Class AvoidingAmbiguities
    Private counter As Integer

    Public Sub DoSomething()

        'a local variable
        Dim counter As Integer

        counter = CInt(Console.ReadLine)
    End Sub
End Class
```

The code will be correctly compiled; no conflict exists between the two counter members because the second one is enclosed within a method and has no external visibility. This also means that the assignment performed within the DoSomething method will not affect the counter private field. If you instead need to assign such a field, you need to use the Me keyword as follows:

```
Public Sub DoSomething()

    'a local variable
    Dim counter As Integer

    'Will assign the class level field
    Me.counter = CInt(Console.ReadLine)
End Sub
```

Properties

Properties are the public way that callers have to access data stored within fields. With properties, you decide the type of permissions users can have to read and write the actual information. Properties are typically used as fields, but they act as methods. Starting from Visual Basic 2010, properties have been completely revisited; in fact, until Visual Basic 2010, a typical property was implemented as follows:

```
Private _firstName As String

Public Property FirstName As String
    Get
        Return _firstName
    End Get
    Set(ByVal value As String)
        _firstName = value
    End Set
End Property
```

You had a private field in which you stored an incoming value and whose value you returned to the callers. Starting from Visual Basic 2010, the same property can be defined as follows:

```
Public Property FirstName As String
```

This feature is known as *auto-implemented properties*. You just need to specify the name and the type for the property. The Visual Basic compiler handles read-and-write operations for you. The resulting code is much cleaner, and you can avoid the need of writing several lines of code. If you had 10 properties, until Visual Basic 2010 you had to write 10 of the previously shown code blocks. Now, though, you need to write 10 lines of code-defining properties. Auto-implemented properties and fields might sound similar, but actually properties are definitely more robust and can be used in data-binding scenarios, while fields cannot. An interesting thing is that if you try to define a private field as in the old code and then an auto-implemented property, you receive this code:

```
'Error: field matching implicit
'auto-generated identifier
Private _firstName As String
Public Property FirstName As String
```

The Visual Basic compiler throws an exception because, behind the scenes, it creates a private field with the same name for handling read/write operations on the property. Of course, you can change the identifier if you need a private field for your purposes.

AUTO-IMPLEMENTED PROPERTIES IN THIS BOOK

Except when specifically needed, you should always use auto-implemented properties when providing code examples that require properties. This is because they provide a much cleaner way for writing code; moreover, code samples seldom need customizations of the read/write actions.

Auto-implemented properties are useful if you need a default behavior for your properties that store and return a value. In some situations you need to perform manipulations over a value before you return it; you store a value provided by the user (property Setter) and then return the value with some edits (property Getter). In this case, you cannot use auto-implemented properties, but you can still write properties the old-fashioned way. The following code snippet shows an example:

```
Public Class Woman

    Private Const Prefix As String = "Mrs."

    Private _firstName As String
    Public Property FirstName As String
        Get
            Return Prefix & Me._firstName
        End Get
        Set(ByVal value As String)
            Me._firstName = value
        End Set
    End Property
End Class
```

In the preceding code, the value stored by the property is edited before it is returned by adding a prefix. Because the default Visual Studio's behavior is all about auto-implemented properties, you do not gain a great advantage from IntelliSense in this scenario. To write code faster, if you do not need auto-implemented properties, follow these steps:

1. Write an auto-implemented property.

2. On the following line of code, type the **End Property** delimiter.

3. The Visual Basic compiler throws an error and Visual Studio suggests adding the missing getter and setter as a solution. Click this action and you're done.

As an alternative, you can type `Property` and then press Tab so that Visual Studio will add a property stub using a predefined code snippet.

In addition, sometimes you cannot use auto-implemented properties: read-only properties and write-only properties.

Read-Only Properties

It's not unusual to give a class the capability of exposing data but not of modifying such data. Continuing the example of the `Person` class, imagine you want to expose the `FirstName` and `LastName` properties plus a `FullName` property that returns the full name of the person. This property should be marked as read-only because only the `FirstName` and `LastName` properties should be editable and `FullName` is the result of the concatenation of these two properties. You can therefore define a read-only property as follows:

```
Public Class Person
    Public Property FirstName As String
    Public Property LastName As String

    Public ReadOnly Property FullName As String
        Get
            Return Me.FirstName & " " & Me.LastName
        End Get
    End Property
End Class
```

The `ReadOnly` keyword marks properties as read-only. As you can easily understand, auto-implemented properties cannot work here because you need a space to write code for returning a value.

Write-Only Properties

Opposite to read-only properties, you can also implement write-only properties. In real-life applications, write-only properties are uncommon, so you will probably never implement such members. It makes much more sense to provide read-only members than members that you can only write to but not read from. Anyway, you can implement write-only properties marking your properties with the `WriteOnly` keyword as demonstrated in the following code snippet:

```
Private _fictitiousCounter As Integer

Public WriteOnly Property FictitiousCounter As Integer
```

```
    Set(ByVal value As Integer)
        _fictitiousCounter = value
    End Set
End Property
```

You have different options here; one is storing the value received by the setter within a field that you can then eventually reutilize. Otherwise, you can perform some tasks directly within the setter.

Exposing Custom Types

Properties can expose both reference and value types, and they are not limited to built-in .NET types. Thus, you can expose your custom classes and structures through properties. The following code shows an `Order` class that exposes a property of type `Customer`; such type is another custom class representing a fictitious customer of your company:

```
Public Class Customer
    Public Property CompanyName As String
    Public Property ContactName As String
End Class


Public Class Order
    Public Property CustomerInstance As Customer
    Public Property OrderID As Integer
End Class
```

You can use the same technique for exposing custom structures. After all, you do nothing different from when you expose strings and integers. Remember that if you do not initialize properties with values, value types returned by properties will have a default value while reference types could result in null references causing runtime errors.

Accessing Properties

Accessing properties is a simple task. You access properties for both reading and writing information that a type needs. The following code demonstrates this:

```
Dim p As New Person

'Properties assignment (write)
p.FirstName = "Alessandro"
p.LastName = "Del Sole"

'Properties reading
If p.LastName.ToLower = "del sole" Then
    Console.WriteLine(p.LastName)
End If
```

Default Properties

Visual Basic language enables defining default properties. A *default property* is a property marked with the Default keyword that enables assignments to the objects defining the property without the need of invoking the property itself. Default properties are strictly related to data arrays and collections of objects because they provide the ability of managing an index. For example, imagine you have an array of strings defined within a class as follows:

```
Private listOfNames() As String = _
    {"Alessandro", "Del Sole", "VB 2012 Unleashed"}
```

A default property enables easy access to such an array, both for reading and writing. The following code demonstrates how you can implement a default property:

```
Default Public Property GetName(ByVal index As Integer) As String
    Get
        Return listOfNames(index)
    End Get
    Set(ByVal value As String)
        listOfNames(index) = value
    End Set
End Property
```

PARAMETER TYPES

The preceding example shows the most common use of default properties, where they accept a numeric index. By the way, default properties can accept any data type as the parameter, not only numeric types. The only rule is actually that the default property must have a parameter.

Notice the Default keyword and how the property accesses the array taking advantage of the index argument to return the desired item in the array. Supposing the preceding definition was contained within a class named TestDataAccess, the following code demonstrates how you can access the default property:

```
Dim t As New TestDataAccess
t(2) = "Visual Basic 2012 Unleashed"
Console.WriteLine(t(1))
Console.WriteLine(t(2))
```

As you can see, you do not need to specify the property name when performing assignments or invocations. The preceding code would produce the following result:

```
Del Sole
Visual Basic 2012 Unleashed
```

INDEXERS

Visual Basic default properties can be compared to Visual C# *indexers*. It's important to know this terminology because you will often hear about indexers.

Types and Members Visibility: Scope

All .NET types and their members have *scope*, which represents the level of visibility and accessibility that a type or its members can have. For example, the *public* scope enables members of classes or structure within a class library to be reachable by other classes or assemblies. On the other hand, the *private* scope can prevent members of classes or structures to be reached from outside the class or structure in which they are defined. You assign scope to your objects or members via *qualifiers*, which are special keywords or combination of keywords that establish how an object or its members can be reached from outside the object. Table 7.1 summarizes scope levels in Visual Basic 2012.

TABLE 7.1   Scope Levels in Visual Basic 2012

Qualifier	Description
Public	Allows types and members to be accessed from anywhere, also from external assemblies. It assigns no access restrictions.
Private	Types and members are visible only within the object in which they are defined.
Friend	Types and members are visible within the assembly that contains declarations.
Protected	Types and members are visible within the objects they are defined in and from derived classes.
Protected Friend	Types and members are visible within the assembly, within the objects they are defined in, and from derived classes.

The following code snippet gives you an alternative view of scope:

```
'The class is visible to other
'external assemblies.
Public Class ScopeDemo

    'This field is visible only
    'within the class
    Private counter As Integer

    'Visible within this assembly, this class,
    'derived classes, other assemblies: no restrictions
    Public Property FirstName As String
    Public Property LastName As String
```

```
    'Only within this class and derived classes
    Protected Property Age As Integer

    'Within this assembly
    Friend Property ReservedInformation As String

    'Within this assembly, this class and derived classes
    Protected Friend Function ReturnSomeInformation() As String
        Return FirstName & " " & LastName
    End Function

End Class
```

`Public` and `Private` qualifiers are self-explanatory, so you probably need some more information about the other ones. To make things easier, let's create a new class that derives from the preceding `ScopeDemo`, as in the following code snippet:

```
Public Class InheritedScopeDemo
    Inherits ScopeDemo

End Class
```

If you try to reach the base class's members, you notice that only the ones marked with `Friend`, `Protected Friend`, and `Protected` are visible to the new class (other than `Public`, of course). But this happens until you are working with one assembly—more precisely, with the assembly that defines all the preceding members. What about another assembly referencing the first one? If you have created a Visual Basic solution for testing the preceding code, add a new Visual Basic project to the solution, and to the new project add a reference to the previous one. In the new project, write the following code:

```
Dim testScope As New Scope.InheritedScopeDemo
```

If you try to invoke members of the `testScope` object, you can see only the `FirstName` and `LastName` properties because they were marked as `Public`. This qualifier is the only one allowing members to be reached from external assemblies. As you might imagine, establishing the appropriate scope is fundamental. For example, you might need a field for storing some data that you do not want to share with the external world; marking a field as `Private` prevents derived classes from reaching the field. So you should instead mark it as `Protected` or `Protected Friend` according to the access level you want to grant. Particularly when working with inheritance, scope is important.

Executing Actions with Methods

In the .NET terminology, *method* is the word that represents procedures in other programming languages; basically a *method* is a member that performs an operation. Methods are of two kinds: `Sub` (which does not return values) and `Function` (which returns a value). The following are minimal examples of methods:

```
Sub DoSomething()
    If IO.File.Exists("C:\SomeFile.txt") = False Then
        Throw New IO.FileNotFoundException
    Else
        Console.WriteLine("The file exists")
    End If

End Sub


Function DoSomethingElse() As Boolean

    Dim result As Boolean = IO.File.Exists("C:\SomeFile.txt")
    Return result
End Function
```

This book makes intensive use of methods, so detailed descriptions on implementations are provided across chapters.

SCOPE

Methods' visibility within types can be assigned using one of the qualifiers listed in Table 7.1. If no qualifier is specified, `Public` is assigned by default.

Invoking Methods

To invoke a method, you call its name. Continuing with the preceding example, you can invoke the `DoSomething` method by typing the following line:

```
DoSomething()
```

If the method is a Function, you should assign the invocation to a variable as follows:

```
Dim targetOfInvocation As Boolean = DoSomethingElse()
```

This is important if you need to evaluate the value returned by the method. If you do not need to evaluate the result, you can invoke Function as if it were Sub:

```
'Allowed
DoSomethingElse()
```

You can invoke functions anywhere you need a value. Continuing with the preceding example, the following code is acceptable:

```
Console.WriteLine(DoSomethingElse())
```

In the preceding examples, we act as if the method were defined within a module. If the method is exposed by a class, you need to add a dot symbol after the class name and then type the name of the method, as follows:

```
Public Class Person

    Public Sub DoSomething()

    End Sub
End Class
...
Dim p As New Person
p.DoSomething()
```

The Visual Basic grammar also provides the `Call` keyword, which enables invoking methods. This keyword is obsolete and deprecated, so you are strongly discouraged from using it; it is part of the language grammar, so this is the reason we mention it. You can use it as follows:

```
Call DoSomething()
```

Methods Arguments: `ByVal` and `ByRef`

Methods can receive parameters and can then work with data provided by parameters. In the .NET terminology, parameters are also known as *arguments*. We use the word *arguments* more often because it's the one that you typically find within the documentation about topics related to.NET development. The following code shows a simple sample of a method definition receiving an argument and subsequent invocation of that method passing an argument:

```
Public Sub PrintString(ByVal stringToPrint As String)
    Console.WriteLine(stringToPrint)
End Sub

Sub RunTest()
    PrintString("Visual Basic 2012 Unleashed")
End Sub
```

Arguments can be passed by value and by reference. Arguments are passed by value by adding the `ByVal` keyword, whereas they are passed by reference by specifying the `ByRef` keyword. In the previous versions of Visual Basic, if you did not specify either keyword, the code editor automatically added a `ByVal` keyword passing arguments by value as a default. Now in Visual Basic 2012, if you do not specify either `ByVal` or `ByRef`, the code editor does not add any keyword but the compiler assumes `ByVal` by default. So in Visual Basic 2012, the `PrintString` method of the preceding code snippet can be rewritten as follows:

```
Public Sub PrintString(stringToPrint As String)
    Console.WriteLine(stringToPrint)
End Sub
```

So, in this code the compiler assumes that the stringToPrint argument is passed by value. In this book we use both syntaxes. This will be useful to avoid confusion in case you have existing code that you want to analyze while reading this book. There are differences between passing arguments by value and by reference. Before providing code examples for a better understanding, these differences are all related to the variables you pass as arguments and can be summarized as follows:

▶ If you pass a value type by value, the compiler creates a copy of the original value so changes made to the argument are not reflected to the original data. If you pass a value type by reference, changes made to the argument are reflected to the original data because, in this case, the argument is the memory address of the data.

▶ If you pass a reference type by reference, the compiler passes in the memory pointer. If you pass a reference type by value, the compiler passes a copy of the memory pointer. In both cases, the original object will be modified regardless of how the parameter is passed.

Listing 7.1 shows how value types can be passed by value and by reference.

LISTING 7.1   Passing Arguments by Value

```
Module ByValByRefDemo

    Dim testInt As Integer = 10

    'Creates a copy of the original value(testInt)
    'and does not change it. Outputs 10
    Sub ByValTest(ByVal anInt As Integer)
        anInt = 20
        Console.WriteLine(testInt)
    End Sub

    'Gets the reference of the original value (testInt)
    'and changes it. Outputs 20
    Sub ByRefTest(ByRef anInt As Integer)
        anInt = 20
        Console.WriteLine(testInt)
    End Sub

    Sub Main()
        ByValTest(testInt)
        ByRefTest(testInt)
        Console.ReadLine()
    End Sub

End Module
```

Both the `ByValTest` and `ByRefTest` methods receive an argument of type `Integer`. Such an argument is the `testInt` variable. In the `ByValTest` method, the argument is passed by value, so the compiler creates a copy of the original data and changes made to the argument variable are not reflected to the original one—in fact, the code returns 10, which is the original value for the `testInt` variable. In the `ByRefTest` method, the argument is passed by reference. Thus, the compiler gets the memory address of the original value and changes made to the argument variable are also reflected to the original data—in fact, this code returns 20, which is the new value for the `testInt` variable. Now consider the following code that provides a similar demonstration for passing reference type both by value and by reference:

```
Dim testString As String = "Visual Basic 2012"
Sub ByValStringTest(ByVal aString As String)
    aString = "Visual Basic 2012 Unleashed"
    Console.WriteLine(testString)
End Sub

Sub ByRefStringTest(ByRef aString As String)
    aString = "Visual Basic 2012 Unleashed"
    Console.WriteLine(testString)
End Sub
```

Invoking the `ByValStringTest` method, passing the `testString` variable as an argument will not change the original value for the reasons previously explained. Invoking the `ByRefStringTest` method, still passing the `testString` variable as an argument, will also change the original value of the `testString` variable that now becomes `Visual Basic 2012 Unleashed`.

PASSING ARRAYS

When passing arrays as arguments, these will be affected by any modifications to their members, because they are reference types, regardless of whether you pass the array by value or by reference. As for other reference types, the most important thing to care about is that when you set the variable's reference in the method to `Nothing`, the original reference is not destroyed if the array is passed by value, whereas it is destroyed if the array is passed by reference.

`ParamArray` Arguments

Another way of supplying arguments to a method is the `ParamArray` keyword. As its name implies, the keyword enables specifying an array of a given type to be accepted by the method. Each item in the array is then treated as a single argument. The following example shows how to implement `ParamArray` arguments:

```
Sub ParamArrayTest(ByVal ParamArray names() As String)
    'Each item in the array is an
    'argument that you can manipulate
    'as you need
```

```
    For Each name As String In names
        Console.WriteLine(name)
    Next
End Sub
```

You can then invoke the method as follows:

```
ParamArrayTest("Alessandro", "Del Sole", "Visual Basic 2012 Unleashed")
```

This method produces the following result, considering that each string is an argument:

```
Alessandro
Del Sole
Visual Basic 2012 Unleashed
```

`ParamArray` arguments are always the last argument of a method definition and are always passed by value, and because they are real arrays, they are reference types. So in reality, arrays are passed by reference (and changes to the array values will persist). You can first declare an array and then pass it to the method invocation, like so:

```
Dim args() As String = {"Alessandro", "Del Sole",
                        "Visual Basic 2012 Unleashed"}
ParamArrayTest(args)
```

Because of being arrays, you can perform any other operations that these objects support. You can pass to methods an array as an argument or an arbitrary number of single arguments that, behind the scenes, are turned into an array. Finally, remember that you cannot pass an array with empty fields. The following code will not be compiled:

```
ParamArrayTest("Alessandro", , "Visual Basic 2012 Unleashed")
```

The Visual Basic background compiler shows an error message saying `Omitted Argument Cannot Match ParamArray Argument`.

Optional Arguments

Methods can receive optional arguments. Therefore, methods modify their behavior according to the number of arguments they received. Optional arguments are defined with the `Optional` keyword. The following code snippet shows how you can define optional arguments:

```
'Returns the full name of a person
Function FullName(ByVal FirstName As String,
                Optional ByVal LastName As String = "",
                Optional ByVal Title As String = "") As String

    'Assumes that the optional Title parameter
    'was not passed by comparing the default value
    If Title = "" Then Title = "Mr. "
```

```
    Dim result As New System.Text.StringBuilder
    result.Append(Title)
    result.Append(LastName)
    result.Append(FirstName)

    Return result.ToString
End Function
```

The purpose of the preceding `FullName` method is simple (and simplified). It should return the full name of a person, but the `LastName` and `Title` arguments are optional, meaning that the caller must provide at least the `FirstName`. Optional arguments must be assigned with a default value; in the preceding code, the default value is an empty string.

DEFAULT VALUES

Default values for optional arguments must be constant expressions. This is the reason I did not assign a `String.Empty` object but assigned a = "" value. The compiler provides the appropriate warnings if the default value is not good.

Default values are important for at least one reason: there are no other ways for understanding whether an optional argument were passed. A default value is therefore needed for comparison. Moreover, there could be situations in which a default value would be necessary—for example, for object initializations. In the preceding code, to check whether the optional `Title` parameter were passed, a comparison is performed against the `Title`'s value. If its value equals the default value, we can assume that the argument was not supplied. This example provides a custom value in case the argument was not passed. If we write the following invocation

```
Console.WriteLine(FullName("Alessandro"))
```

we would get the following result: `Mr. Alessandro`. Behind the scenes, the Visual Basic compiler generates a new invocation that includes all optional parameters with a default value, as follows: `FullName("Alessandro","","")`. Although useful, optional arguments are not always the best choice, and we do not recommend their usage. This is because other .NET languages implement them differently and so they are not compliant with Microsoft's Common Language Specifications. So if you produce class libraries, you should be aware of this. Instead, the .NET Framework provides a cleaner way for handling methods with different arguments and signatures that is powerful; it's known as *overloading* and is discussed next.

Optional Nullable Arguments

Visual Basic 2012 allows passing nullable types as optional arguments. The following code demonstrates this:

```
Sub NullableDemo(ByVal firstArgument As String,
                Optional ByVal secondArgument As _
                Nullable(Of Integer) = Nothing)
```

7

```
    If secondArgument Is Nothing Then
        'We can assume that the
        'optional argument was not supplied
    End If
End Sub
```

As you can see, nullable arguments are supported, but you are still required to provide a default value, which can also be null. Remember that optional nullable arguments can only go after nonoptional ones in the argument list. They are particularly useful when dealing with scenarios like Microsoft Office automation, where optional arguments are common.

Overloading Methods

One of the most powerful features in the object-oriented development with the .NET Framework is the capability of overloading methods. *Overloading* means providing multiple signatures of the same method, in which signature is the number and types of arguments a method can receive. The following code snippet demonstrates overloading:

```
Private Function ReturnFullName(ByVal firstName As String,
                                ByVal lastName As String) As String
    Return firstName & " " & lastName
End Function


Private Function ReturnFullName(ByVal firstName As String,
                                ByVal lastName As String,
                                ByVal Age As Integer) As String
    Return firstName & " " & lastName & " of age " & Age.ToString
End Function


Private Function ReturnFullName(ByVal title As String,
                                ByVal firstName As String,
                                ByVal lastName As String) As String
    Return title & " " & firstName & " " & lastName
End Function


Private Function ReturnFullName(ByVal title As String,
                                ByVal firstName As String,
                                ByVal lastName As String,
                                ByVal Age As Integer) As String
    Return title & " " & firstName & " " & lastName & _
            " of age " & Age.ToString
End Function
```

As you can see, there are four different implementations of one method named
ReturnFullName. Each implementation differs from the others in that it receives a different number of arguments. The preceding example is simple, and the arguments are
self-explanatory; each implementation returns the concatenation of the supplied arguments. You might wonder why you would need overloading and to provide four different implementations of a single method when you would obtain the same result with
optional arguments. The answer is that this approach is the only accepted method by the
Microsoft Common Language Specification and ensures that every .NET language can use
the different implementations, whereas optional arguments are not supported from other
.NET languages. Another good reason for using overloads is that you can return strongly
typed results from methods. If you need to work with specific data types, you can use
overloaded signatures instead of providing one signature that returns Object. The Visual
Basic grammar defines an Overloads keyword as one that can be used to define overloaded
signatures; the following example is an excerpt of the previous one, now using Overloads:

```
Private Overloads Function ReturnFullName(ByVal firstName As String,
                           ByVal lastName As String) As String
    Return firstName & " " & lastName
End Function

Private Overloads Function ReturnFullName(ByVal firstName As String,
                           ByVal lastName As String,
                           ByVal Age As Integer) As String
    Return firstName & " " & lastName & " of age " & Age.ToString
End Function
```

There's no difference in using the Overloads keywords. If you decide to use it, you must
decorate it with all other definitions. To support overloading, signatures must differ from
each other in some points:

▶ Signatures cannot differ only in ByVal or ByRef arguments. If two signatures have
  two arguments of the same type, the arguments cannot differ only in ByVal/ByRef
  even though they consist of different types.

▶ In the case of Function, overloaded implementations can return the same type or
  different types. If they return different types but have exactly the same arguments,
  the code cannot be compiled. This means that different implementations must have
  different arguments.

You invoke methods defined in this way as you would normally with other methods.
Moreover, IntelliSense provides a great help on finding the most appropriate overload for
your needs, as shown in Figure 7.1.

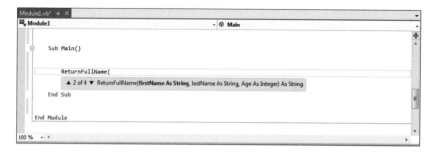

FIGURE 7.1   IntelliSense helps you choose among overloads.

Coercion

It can happen that an invocation to an overloaded method supplies a compliant type but not the same type established in the signature. Consider the following overloaded method:

```
Private Sub CoercionDemo(ByVal anArgument As Double)
    Debug.WriteLine("Floating point")
End Sub

Private Sub CoercionDemo(ByVal anArgument As Integer)
    Debug.WriteLine("Integer")
End Sub
```

The Visual Basic compiler can decide which signature is the most appropriate according to the argument passed. This is particularly important when working with numeric types. Moreover, the compiler can also handle coercion, meaning that it can perform conversion when there's no loss of precision. Consider the following code:

```
Dim testValue As Byte = 123
CoercionDemo(testValue)
```

The `CoercionDemo` overloads do not support `Byte`—only `Double` and `Integer`. Because `Byte` is basically an integer type, the Visual Basic compiler converts the object into an `Integer` type because this expansion conversion will always be successful. The compiler can also decide the best overload to fit the scenario.

Overload Resolution

Visual Basic 2012 introduces new rules in managing the precedence of the invocation of generic methods' overloads, where the generic type is an `IEnumerable(Of T)`.

WHAT ARE GENERICS?

Generic types are .NET types that can adapt their behavior to different kinds of objects without the need of defining a separate version of the type. Generics are discussed further in Chapter 14, "Generics and Nullable Types." If you already have experience with Visual Basic (since version 2005), you might already know about them. What you need to know about them here is that they are types that can represent a lot of other types.

For example, consider the following code:

```
Sub Demo()
    Dim x As New List(Of Integer)
    x.Add(1)
    x.Add(2)
    x.Add(3)
    Calculate(x.AsEnumerable)
End Sub

Sub Calculate(Of T)(x As T)
    'Perform your calculation here
End Sub

Sub Calculate(Of T)(x As IEnumerable(Of T))
    'Perform your calculation here
End Sub
```

We have two overloads of the `Calculate` method, and both can accept an `IEnumerable(Of T)` as the generic type. In this case, then, the compiler must be intelligent enough to understand which of the two overloads must be invoked from the `Demo` method. Until Visual Basic 2010, such a situation would cause some conflicts. Now in Visual Basic 2012, the compiler automatically invokes the overload where the generic parameter is more deeply nested; in this case it invokes the second overload (the one with a generic parameter of type `IEnumerable(Of T)`). You can easily verify this by placing a breakpoint on the second overload of the `Calculate` method and stepping into the code by pressing F11. Actually, this is one of those improvements required to make the compiler work better with the asynchronous programming patterns, but it is important that it exists.

Declaring Optional Parameter Overloads

Another new feature in Visual Basic 2012 is the possibility of defining optional arguments for method overloads. The following code, which would not work in Visual Basic 2010, is now legal in Visual Basic 2012:

```
Sub MyMethod(x As Integer)
End Sub

Sub MyMethod(x As Integer, Optional y As Integer = 0)
End Sub
```

You can specify an optional parameter inside a method overload; this solves a previous conflict that caused the second method to be exactly like the first one if the second argument were not passed. To make sure the correct method is selected, you add the comma for the optional parameter but provide no value. This is another improvement introduced for better supporting asynchronous programming, but it can be useful in different scenarios as well.

Overloading Properties

Now that you know what overloading is, you need to know that the technique is not limited to methods but can also be applied to properties. The following code snippet shows an example:

```
Property Test(ByVal age As Integer) As Integer
    Get

    End Get
    Set(ByVal value As Integer)

    End Set
End Property
Property Test(ByVal name As String) As String
    Get

    End Get
    Set(ByVal value As String)

    End Set
End Property
```

Because of their different implementations, in this scenario you cannot use auto-implemented properties, mainly because overloads cannot differ only because of their return type. To provide overloaded properties, you need to remember the same limitations listed for methods.

Exit from Methods

Methods execution typically completes when the `End Sub` or `End Function` statements are encountered. You often need to break methods execution before the execution completes. In the case of `Sub` methods, you can accomplish this using the `Exit Sub` statement. The following example checks the value of an integer and immediately breaks if the value is greater than 10. If not, it loops until the value is 10 and then breaks:

```
Sub TestingValues(ByVal anInteger As Integer)
    If anInteger > 10 Then
        Exit Sub
    ElseIf anInteger < 10 Then
        Do Until anInteger = 10
            anInteger += 1
        Loop
```

```
        Exit Sub
    End If
End Sub
```

You can also use the `Return` keyword without a value instead of `Exit Sub`. For Function methods, things are a little different because they return a value. When the methods execution completes regularly, you return a value via the `Return` keyword. Until now, you found several examples of methods returning values.

AVOID VISUAL BASIC 6 STYLE

If you migrate from Visual Basic 6, you probably return values from functions assigning the result to the name of the function itself. In .NET development, this is deprecated, although it will be compiled. The `Return` keyword is optimized for returning values and all .NET languages have a specific keyword, so you should always use this approach.

When you instead need to break the method execution, you can use the `Exit Function` statement, as shown in the following code snippet:

```
Function TestingValue(ByVal anInteger As Integer) As Boolean

    Dim result As Boolean

    If anInteger < 10 Then
        Do Until anInteger = 10
            anInteger += 1
        Loop
        result = True
        'Returns False
    ElseIf anInteger = 10 Then
        Exit Function
    Else
        result = False
    End If
    Return result
End Function
```

Keep in mind that Function methods always have to return something. Because of this, `Exit Function` returns the default value of the return data type. In the preceding example, the method returns `Boolean`, so `Exit Function` returns `False`. If the method returned `Integer` or another numeric type, `Exit Function` would return zero. If the method returned a reference type, `Exit Function` would return `Nothing`. Another best practice in returning value is to assign the result of the evaluation to a variable (result in the preceding example) and then provide a single invocation to the `Return` instruction because this can optimize the compilation process, as well as make coding easier.

Partial Classes

You can split the definition of a class across multiple parts using the *partial classes* feature. You do not actually create different classes; you create one class implemented within multiple parts, typically across multiple files. This feature was first introduced in Visual Basic 2005 for separating Visual Studio's auto-generated code from developer's code, but it is useful in various scenarios. To see a practical implementation of partial classes, create a new Windows Forms project. Then click the **Show All Files** button in Solution Explorer, expand the Form1.vb item, and double-click the **Form1.designer.vb** file. Inside this file you can find the definition of the Form1 class, as shown in Listing 7.2.

LISTING 7.2   Visual Studio Auto-Generated Partial Class

```
Partial Class Form1
    Inherits System.Windows.Forms.Form

    'Form overrides dispose to clean up the component list.
    <System.Diagnostics.DebuggerNonUserCode()> _
    Protected Overrides Sub Dispose(ByVal disposing As Boolean)
        Try
            If disposing AndAlso components IsNot Nothing Then
                components.Dispose()
            End If
        Finally
            MyBase.Dispose(disposing)
        End Try
    End Sub

    'Required by the Windows Form Designer
    Private components As System.ComponentModel.IContainer

    'NOTE: The following procedure is required by the Windows Form Designer
    'It can be modified using the Windows Form Designer.
    'Do not modify it using the code editor.
    <System.Diagnostics.DebuggerStepThrough()> _
    Private Sub InitializeComponent()
        components = New System.ComponentModel.Container()
        Me.AutoScaleMode = System.Windows.Forms.AutoScaleMode.Font
        Me.Text = "Form1"
    End Sub
End Class
```

As you can see, the class definition includes the `Partial` keyword. This indicates to the compiler that elsewhere in the project another piece of the class is defined within a different code file. In this case, the other piece is the Form1.vb file whose code is simple when you create a new project:

```
Public Class Form1

End Class
```

Both files implement one class. By the way, this approach makes your code much cleaner. In this example, partial classes help developers to concentrate on their own code, ensuring that auto-generated code will not be confusing. The Visual Studio IDE makes a huge usage of partial classes; LINQ to SQL and ADO.NET Entity Framework are just a couple examples. Following is a custom example of partial classes. Imagine you have this implementation of the `Person` class within a code file named Person.vb:

```
Public Class Person

    Public Property FirstName As String
    Public Property LastName As String
    Public Property Age As Integer

    Public Overrides Function ToString() As String
        Return String.Concat(FirstName, " ", LastName)
    End Function

    Public Sub New(ByVal Name As String, ByVal SurName As String,
                   ByVal Age As Integer)
        Me.FirstName = Name
        Me.LastName = SurName
        Me.Age = Age
    End Sub
End Class
```

Then you decide to implement the `ICloneable` interface to provide a custom implementation of the `Clone` method, but you want to separate the implementation from the rest of the class code. At this point, you can add a new code file to the project and write the following:

```
Partial Public Class Person
    Implements ICloneable

    Public Function Clone() As Object Implements System.ICloneable.Clone
        Return Me.MemberwiseClone
    End Function
End Class
```

This last code will be still part of the `Person` class; it has been defined in another place.

PARTIAL CLASSES TIPS

You can split your classes within multiple files. Generally, you create partial classes within just two files, but you have to know that you are allowed to create them within two or more files. Partial classes also take whatever scope you define in one of the partial class definitions.

Also notice how IntelliSense can improve your coding experience by showing a list of the partial classes you can complete (see Figure 7.2).

FIGURE 7.2   IntelliSense helps choose the available partial classes.

A partial approach can also be applied to Structures as follows:

```
Partial Structure Test

End Structure
```

PARTIAL CLASSES HOW-TO

Partial classes can be split across multiple parts—parts, not files. This is because one Visual Basic code file can contain the implementation of theoretically infinite types, so you can split a class definition within the same code file using partial classes. You can, but you probably will not. Partial classes are particularly useful for splitting definitions across multiple files, which is covered when discussing LINQ to SQL and the ADO.NET Entity Framework.

Partial classes indeed have a limitation: You cannot define them within other classes. For example, the following code will correctly be compiled, but it does not implement partial classes even though it creates two different classes:

```
Class TestPartial

    'Compiles, but creates a new partial class
    'instead of extending the previous Person
```

```
    Partial Class Person

    End Class
End Class
```

Partial Methods

Another interesting feature is partial methods. This feature has been introduced in LINQ to ADO.NET, but it can be used in different scenarios for other language features. The concept behind partial methods is the same as partial classes: Method implementations can be split across multiple parts. Partial methods have three particular characteristics: They must be `Private` methods, they cannot return values (that is, only `Sub` methods are allowed), and their bodies must be empty in the class in which methods are defined. Consider the following code, in which a class named `Contact` is split across partial classes and a partial method is defined:

```
Public Class Contact

    Public Property FirstName As String
    Public Property LastName As String
    Public Property EmailAddress As String

    Public Sub New(ByVal Name As String,
        ByVal LastName As String, ByVal Email As String)
        Me.FirstName = Name
        Me.LastName = LastName
        Me.EmailAddress = Email
    End Sub

    Partial Private Sub Validate(ByVal Email As String)
    End Sub

End Class
```

A partial method is marked with the `Partial` keyword. It has a `Private` scope, it returns no value, and its definition's body is empty. Suppose you want to implement the actual code for your method. For example, we could verify whether the Email address provided by the user is a valid address; to accomplish this, we can use regular expressions.

ABOUT REGULAR EXPRESSIONS

Regular expressions are an advanced way to work with text. The .NET Framework provides the `System.Text.RegularExpression` namespace that exposes classes for managing regular expressions with .NET languages.

The following code shows how you can implement a partial class in which the actual code for a partial method is provided:

```
Partial Public Class Contact

    Private Sub Validate(ByVal Email As String)

        Dim validateMail As String = _
        "^([\w-\.]+)@((\[[0-9]{1,3}\." &
        "[0-9]{1,3}\.)|(([\w-]+\.)+))" &
        "([a-zA-z]{2,4}|[0-9]{1,3})(\]?)$"

        If Text.RegularExpressions.
            Regex.IsMatch(Email, validateMail) _
            = False Then
            Throw New  _
            InvalidOperationException _
            ("The specified mail address is not valid")
        End If
    End Sub
End Class
```

When you effectively implement the partial method, you do not need to mark it again as `Partial`. This qualifier must be added only in the empty method definition. The preceding code checks whether the specified email address is valid; if it is not, it throws an `InvalidOperationException`.

PRACTICAL IMPLEMENTATIONS

Partial methods are mentioned when discussing LINQ to SQL so that you can get an overview of practical implementations of partial methods, which are particularly useful when you need to provide custom validation techniques.

To describe partial methods in another way, the concept is "to accomplish this particular task, you do need this particular method. But the implementation of the method is left to your choice."

Constructors

A constructor is a method you invoke to create a new instance of a class that is represented by the `New` keyword in Visual Basic. For instance, if you have the following `Contact` class

```
Public Class Contact

    Public Property FirstName As String
    Public Property LastName As String
```

```
      Public Property Email As String
      Public Property Address As String

      Public Sub New()

      End Sub
End Class
```

you can then create a new instance of the `Contact` class as follows:

```
'First syntax
Dim aContact As Contact
aContact = New Contact

'Second syntax
Dim aContact As New Contact

'Third syntax
Dim aContact As Contact = New Contact
```

All the three preceding syntaxes are enabled, so you can use the one you prefer. (I use the second one for better readability.) In other words, creating an instance means giving life to a new copy of the object so you can use it for your purposes, such as storing data or performing tasks. All classes must have a constructor. If you do not provide a constructor, Visual Basic provides one for you. The default constructor is hidden in the code editor, but it has public visibility and contains no code; it serves just for instantiating the object. If you want to make it visible, click the **Declaration** combo box in the code editor and select the **New** method, as shown in Figure 7.3.

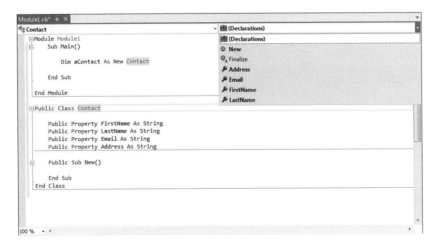

FIGURE 7.3   Making the default constructor visible.

Constructors are useful for initializing objects' members. Because of this, and because constructors are basically methods, they can receive arguments. For example, you could implement the constructor in a way that receives appropriate arguments for initializing the Contact class's properties:

```
Public Sub New(ByVal name As String,
               ByVal surName As String,
               ByVal emailAddress As String,
               ByVal homeAddress As String)

    Me.FirstName = name
    Me.LastName = surName
    Me.Email = emailAddress
    Me.Address = homeAddress
End Sub
```

In this way you can easily assign members of the class. You invoke the parameterized constructor as follows:

```
Dim aContact As New Contact("Alessandro",
                            "Del Sole",
                            "alessandro.delsole@visual-basic.it",
                            "5Th street")
```

At this point, your object is ready to be used and is populated with data. You might also want to add simple validations for arguments received by the constructor. This is important because, if you need data initialization, you also need valid data. You can throw an ArgumentException if arguments are invalid, as shown here:

```
Public Sub New(ByVal name As String,
               ByVal surName As String,
               ByVal emailAddress As String,
               ByVal homeAddress As String)

    If surName = "" Then _
        Throw New ArgumentException("surName")
    Me.FirstName = name
    Me.LastName = surName
    Me.Email = emailAddress
    Me.Address = homeAddress
End Sub
```

Continuing the discussion about members' initialization, you might have members (typically fields) with inline initialization. In this scenario, when you invoke the constructor, members' initialization is also performed even if the constructor contains no code about initialization. This is demonstrated by the following code snippet:

```
Public Class Contact

    Private ReadOnly InitializationDemo As Integer = 100

'Just for demo purposes!
    Public Sub New()
        Console.WriteLine(InitializationDemo.ToString)
        Console.ReadLine()
    End Sub
End Class
```

The constructor does not perform any initialization, but when the class gets instantiated, the value is assigned. The preceding code produces 100 as the output. Another interesting thing is that constructors are the only place in which you can initialize read-only fields. We can rewrite the preceding code as follows:

```
Public Class Contact

    Private ReadOnly InitializationDemo As Integer

    'Just for demo purposes!
    Public Sub New()
        InitializationDemo = 100
        Console.WriteLine(InitializationDemo.ToString)
        Console.ReadLine()
    End Sub
```

Notice that the code is correctly compiled and the produced output is 100. This technique is important if you plan to expose read-only members in your classes.

Overloading Constructors

Because constructors are effectively methods, they support the overloading feature. You can therefore provide multiple implementations of the New method, taking care of the limitations described for methods. You cannot use the Overloads keyword; the compiler does not need it. Continuing the example of the Contact class, we can provide different implementations of the constructor as follows:

```
Public Sub New()
    Me.FirstName = "Assigned later"
    Me.LastName = "Assigned later"
    Me.Email = "Assigned later"
    Me.Address = "Assigned later"
End Sub
```

```
Public Sub New(ByVal surName As String)
    If String.IsNullOrEmpty(surName) Then _
        Throw New ArgumentException("surName")


    Me.LastName = surName


    'Will be assigned later
    Me.FirstName = ""
    Me.Email = ""
    Me.Address = ""
End Sub


Public Sub New(ByVal name As String,
               ByVal surName As String,
               ByVal emailAddress As String,
               ByVal homeAddress As String)


    If surName = "" Then _
        Throw New ArgumentException("surName")
    Me.FirstName = name
    Me.LastName = surName
    Me.Email = emailAddress
    Me.Address = homeAddress
End Sub
```

The first overload receives no arguments and provides a default members' initialization. The second overload receives just an argument, initializing other members with empty strings. The last overload is the most complete and provides initialization features for all the properties exposed by the class.

Nested Invocations

Overloads are useful, but when working with constructors, you might want to consider a common place for initializing members. To accomplish this, you can invoke constructors' overloads from another overload. Consider the following code snippet:

```
Public Sub New(ByVal LastName As String)
    Me.New(LastName, "")
End Sub


Public Sub New(ByVal LastName As String, ByVal Email As String)
    Me.LastName = LastName
    Me.Email = Email
End Sub
```

The first overload can invoke the second overload, passing required arguments. In the preceding example, only an empty string is passed, but according to your scenario you could make a different elaboration before passing the argument. The good news in this technique is that you need to provide initialization code only once (in this case, in the second overload). By the way, take care about the hierarchical calls; the first overload can invoke the second one because this receives more arguments, but not vice versa. This kind of approach can be used because both overloads have an argument in common. For instance, say you instead had a `ContactID` property of type `Integer` that you wanted to initialize via the constructor and you had the following overloads:

```
Public Sub New(ByVal LastName As String)

End Sub


Public Sub New(ByVal ContactID As Integer)

End Sub
```

In this case the two overloads have no arguments in common; because of this, if you want to provide a common place for initializations, you need to implement a private constructor as follows:

```
Private Sub New()
    'Replace with your
    'initialization code
    Me.ContactID = 0
    Me.LastName = "Del Sole"
End Sub
```

Then you can redirect both preceding overloads to invoke a private constructor:

```
Public Sub New(ByVal LastName As String)
    Me.New()
    Me.LastName = LastName
End Sub


Public Sub New(ByVal ContactID As Integer)
    Me.New()
    Me.ContactID = ContactID
End Sub
```

PRIVATE CONSTRUCTORS

There is a little bit more to say about private constructors that is discussed later in this chapter in the section "Shared Members." At the moment, you need to remember that if you place a private constructor, you *must* remove the public one with the same signature. For example, if you have a `Private Sub New()`, you cannot also have a `Public Sub New()`.

Object Initializers

Starting from Visual Basic 2008 and .NET 3.5, the Visual Basic grammar offers another feature, named *object initializers,* that enables inline initialization of objects' members when creating an instance, without the need of providing specific constructors' overloads. For a better understanding, let's provide a practical example. We can implement the Contact class without implementing a constructor overload that receives any arguments for initialization:

```
Public Class Contact

    Public Property FirstName As String
    Public Property LastName As String
    Public Property Email As String
    Public Property Address As String

End Class
```

To instantiate the class and initialize its members, according to the classical, old-fashioned syntax, we should write the following code:

```
Dim aContact As New Contact
With aContact
    .FirstName = "Alessandro"
    .LastName = "Del Sole"
    .Email = "alessandro.delsole@visual-basic.it"
    .Address = "5Th street"
End With
```

The recent Visual Basic syntax instead enables the object initializers way, which works as in the following snippet:

```
Dim aContact As New Contact With {.LastName = "Del Sole",
    .FirstName = "Alessandro",
    .Email = "alessandro.delsole@visual-basic.it",
    .Address = "5Th street"}
```

You add the With keyword after the instance declaration. The keyword is followed by a couple of brackets. Within the brackets, you can easily assign members by writing members' names preceded by a dot symbol and separated by commas. This code demonstrates how you can provide inline initialization of members even if no constructor's overloads receive an appropriate number of arguments for the purpose of initialization. I will often write code using object initializers; this feature is important for advanced language features, which are covered in the next part of the book.

WHY OBJECT INITIALIZERS?

You might wonder why this feature has been introduced to the .NET languages, considering that there were already several ways for providing initialization. The reason is LINQ. As you see later in the book, object initializers provide a way for initializing objects within queries; another important feature known as *anonymous types* takes advantage of object initializers. Chapter 20, "Advanced Language Features," discusses anonymous types.

Shared Members

Classes can expose instance and shared members. Until now, all discussions used instance members for examples. It's important to understand the difference between instance and shared members because you can successfully use both of them in your classes. When you create a new instance of a class, you create a copy of that class with its own life and its own data. On the other hand, with shared members, you work with only one copy of a class and of its data. Classes can support different situations, such as all shared members or just a few shared members. For example, if you have a class exposing only shared members, you work with exactly one copy of the class. If you have only a few shared members within a class, all instances of that class access only one copy of the data marked as shared.

SHARED/STATIC

In Visual Basic we talk about *shared* members. This is because these members are marked with the `Shared` keyword. In other programming languages, such behavior is represented by the "static" definition; *shared* and *static* mean the same thing. Typically, the static definition is better when talking about interoperability with other .NET languages; both definitions refer to the same thing and we use the shared definition for consistency.

You expose only shared members in two main circumstances: with mere methods libraries or with classes that can exist in only one copy (known as *singleton*), such as the Application class in Windows Forms applications. Now we cover how to implement shared members within classes.

Shared Classes

Visual Basic, different from other .NET languages such as Visual C#, does not provide the capability of creating shared classes. To accomplish this, you have two alternatives: You can create a class the usual way and mark all members as shared, or you can create a module. Modules are a specific Visual Basic feature that work almost as shared classes (see Chapter 10, "Modules").

Shared Fields

Shared fields are useful to store information that is common to all instances of a class. For example, imagine you have a class named Document that represents a text document. You could implement a shared field acting as a counter of all the documents opened in your application:

```
Public Class Document

    Private Shared _documentCounter As Integer

    Public Sub New()
        _documentCounter += 1
    End Sub

End Class
```

The code in the example increments the counter each time a new instance is created. The documentCounter field is common to all instances of the Document class because it is marked with the Shared keyword.

Shared Properties

In an object-oriented approach, fields should be wrapped by properties that gain access to fields. This also happens with shared members. Continuing with the preceding example, a shared property would be implemented as follows:

```
Private Shared _documentCounter As Integer

Public Shared ReadOnly Property DocumentCounter As Integer
    Get
        Return _documentCounter
    End Get
End Property
```

In this case, the property is also marked as read-only because its value is incremented only when a new instance of the class is created, passing through the related field. However, shared properties support both Get and Set. Because the preceding code offers a read-only property, you cannot take advantage of the new auto-implemented properties feature. If you do not need a read-only property, you can declare a shared property as follows:

```
Public Shared Property DocumentCounter As Integer
```

By doing so, you can avoid the implementation of private shared fields.

Shared Methods

Shared methods can be invoked without the need of creating an instance of the class that defines them. As in the previous members, shared methods are decorated with the Shared keyword. A common use of shared methods is within class libraries that act as helper repositories of functions. For example, you can have a class that provides methods for compressing and decompressing files using the System.IO.Compression namespace.

In such a scenario, you do not need to create an instance of the class; in fact, shared methods just need to point to some files and not to instance data. The following code snippet provides an example of shared methods:

```
Public Class CompressionHelper

    Public Shared Sub Compress(ByVal fileName As String,
                                ByVal target As String)
        'Code for compressing files here
    End Sub

    Public Shared Sub Decompress(ByVal fileName As String,
                                  ByVal uncompressed As String)
        'Code for decompressing files here
    End Sub
End Class
...
Sub Test()

    CompressionHelper.Compress("Sourcefile.txt", "Compressedfile.gz")

    CompressionHelper.Decompress("Compressedfile.gz", "Sourcefile.txt")

End Sub
```

As you can see, you invoke shared methods by writing the name of the class instead of creating an instance and invoking methods onto the instance. This approach is useful for organizing functions in libraries according to their purpose (established via the class name). If you try to invoke shared methods from an instance, the Visual Basic compiler throws a warning message advising that such invocation might be ambiguous and will offer an autocorrect option to change the instance name to the class name, removing the potential ambiguity. Of course, you can remove such warnings by editing the Instance Variable Accesses Shared Member option in the Compiler tab within My Project. I suggest you leave the default setting unchanged because it can help you avoid ambiguous code. Shared methods also support overloading, so you can take advantage of this feature if necessary. When implementing shared methods, you should be aware of some considerations. First, you cannot work with instance members from within shared methods. For instance, the following code throws a compilation error:

```
'Instance field
Private instanceField As Integer

'Cannot refer to an instance member
Public Shared Function testSharedInstance() As Integer
    Return instanceField
End Function
```

To solve this error, you should mark as Shared the member you are working with (instanceField in the preceding example):

```
'Shared field
Private Shared sharedField As Integer

'Correct
Public Shared Function testSharedInstance() As Integer
    Return sharedField
End Function
```

The alternative is to change the method from shared to instance, removing the Shared keyword from the method definition. But this is not a game. You need to evaluate how your methods will behave and how they will use members exposed by your classes. According to this, you can decide whether methods can be shared or must be instance ones. Another consideration is related to classes exposing only shared methods. Because in this scenario the class does not need to be instantiated, a private empty constructor must be supplied as follows:

```
Private Sub New()
    'No code
End Sub
```

This constructor contains no code (but it could for initialization purposes) and is just necessary to prevent instance creation.

SHARED SUB MAIN

In all code examples shown to this point, you saw how console applications provide a module containing the entry point for applications, which is the Sub Main. Because modules are basically shared classes, you can supply a class containing shared members with a Shared Sub Main that works as in modules. Although modules are suggested instead of shared classes, because they cause less confusion and are a Visual Basic-specific feature, you need to know how to implement the Shared Sub Main within classes. If you ever use conversion tools from Visual C# to VB (or if you get code examples translated into VB by Visual C# folks), you will typically find a class named Program containing the previously mentioned shared entry point.

Shared Constructors

Classes can implement shared constructors, as shown in the following code:

```
'Private visibility
Shared Sub New()
    'Initialization of shared
    'members
    instanceField = 10
End Sub
```

Shared constructors are particularly useful for initializing shared members or for loading data that is common to all instances of a class. A shared constructor is invoked immediately before the normal constructor that creates a new instance of the class. With that said, the following code is appropriate and accepted by the compiler:

```
Shared Sub New()
    'Initialization of shared
    'members
    instanceField = 10
End Sub

Sub New()

End Sub
```

Another important thing to take care of is that shared constructors have `Private` visibility, and they are the only point in the class in which you can initialize a read-only field.

Common Language Specification

One of the most important features of the .NET Framework is the CLR, which offers a common infrastructure for various .NET languages. You might also remember from Chapter 1, "Introducing the .NET Framework 4.5," that all .NET compilers produce Intermediate Language (IL) code. Because of this, .NET languages can interoperate: An assembly produced with Visual Basic can be used by an application written in Visual C#, and vice versa. But different languages have, of course, different characteristics; so if developers use specific features of a language, the risk is that another language cannot use that produced assembly because they might encounter several errors. This can occur when companies produce reusable components, such as class libraries or user controls that you should be able to use from whatever .NET application written in whatever language you want without problems. To provide a common set of rules that developers should follow to ensure interoperability, Microsoft wrote the Common Language Specification (CLS) that are a set of rules that every developer has to follow to produce reusable assemblies. This chapter provides an overview of the CLS and gives you information about applying such rules to the topics discussed in this chapter. Each time a new topic is covered, tips for making code CLS-compliant are provided.

COMMON LANGUAGE SPECIFICATION WEBSITE

Microsoft offers a dedicated page to CLS on the MSDN portal that you should look at: http://msdn.microsoft.com/en-us/library/12a7a7h3(v=vs.110).aspx

Where Do I Need to Apply?

CLS is important when producing reusable components, such as class libraries or user controls. Because only public classes and public members from public classes can be used from other applications also written in different languages, the CLS applies only to

▶ Public classes

▶ Public members exposed by public classes, such as methods or properties, and members that can be inherited

▶ Objects used by public members, such as types passed as arguments to methods

In all other cases, such as private members, applying CLS is ignored by the compiler. Another situation when you do not need to apply CLS is when you do not produce reusable components. For example, the UI side of a Windows application (Win Forms or WPF) is not required to be CLS-compliant because external applications will not invoke the UI.

Marking Assemblies and Types as CLS-Compliant

Chapter 2, "Getting Started with the Visual Studio 2012 IDE," and Chapter 3, "The Anatomy of a Visual Basic Project," offer an overview of assemblies. When you produce a reusable component such as a class library or a user control such as a .dll assembly, you need to ensure that it is CLS-compliant. You can add the following attribute to the assembly definition:

```
<Assembly: CLSCompliant(True)>
```

This attribute tells the compiler to check whether a type used in your code is CLS-compliant. If the compiler finds a non–CLS-compliant type, it throws a warning message. Assembly members should also be marked as CLS-compliant if you plan that they will be. A class is defined CLS-compliant as follows:

```
<CLSCompliant(True)> Public Class Person
```

You might wonder why you should add this attribute at the class level if you specified one at the assembly level. The reason is that you might implement non–CLS-compliant classes (therefore assigning False to the CLSCompliant attribute). This is useful for communicating to both the compiler and code analysis tools that a non–CLS-compliant class should not be checked.

CODE ANALYSIS

There are different code analysis tools for checking whether code is CLS-compliant. The first one is the well-known Microsoft FxCop. The second one is the code analysis instrumentation available in Visual Studio 2012, which is covered in Chapter 55, "Advanced Analysis Tools." Both tools are important for finding errors about CLS compliance of your code.

Naming Conventions

Assigning comprehensible identifiers to types and members is a best practice in every development environment. This becomes a rule in .NET development, especially if you want your code to be CLS-compliant. To understand this, you need to first know that the Common Language Specification enables only two notations, Pascal and camel. If you are an old Visual Basic 6 or Visual C++ developer, you might be familiar with the Hungarian notation that is not supported by .NET rules. An identifier is Pascal-cased when the first letter of each word composing the identifier is uppercase. The following identifier is Pascal-case: `FirstName`. An identifier is instead defined as camel-case when the first character of the first word composing the identifier is lowercase. The following identifier is camel-cased: `firstName`. It's important to know this difference to understand where and when you should use one notation or the other one. You use the Pascal notation in the following situations:

▶ Namespaces' identifiers

▶ Identifiers of all public members within an assembly, such as classes, properties, methods, and custom types

Instead, use the camel notation in the following situations:

▶ Identifiers of all private members within an assembly, such as fields, methods, and so on. This is not actually a requirement (because private members are not affected by CLS in terms of naming conventions), but it's a good programming practice.

▶ Arguments' names for methods, both public and private.

No other naming notation is enabled in the Common Language Specification.

USING AN UNDERSCORE WITH PRIVATE VARIABLES

As a commonly accepted convention, often the name of private variables starts with an underscore (_). This is useful when you declare properties the extended way and need a backing field that holds the property value. Different from Visual C#, which is case-sensitive, in Visual Basic you cannot have two identifiers with the same name but with different casing, so an underscore at the beginning of the private variable's name solves the problem and is a standardized practice.

Obviously, if you do not plan to write CLS-compliant code, you can use any notation you like. However, it's preferable to use a .NET-oriented notation. Another important rule about naming conventions is in methods' names. You should first place the name of the verb and then the target of the action. For example, `CompressFile` is correct, whereas `FileCompress` is not. The following code shows an example of a well-formed class:

```
'Public members of an assembly
'are pascal cased
Public Class NamingConventionsDemo

    'private fields are camel-cased
    Private documentCounter As Integer = 0

    'public properties are pascal-cased
    Public Property FirstName As String
```

```
'public methods are pascal-cased
'arguments are camel-cased
Public Function CompressFile(ByVal sourceFile As String,
                        ByVal targetFile As String) As Boolean

End Function

'private methods are camel-cased
'arguments are camel-cased
Private Sub checkForFileExistance(ByVal fileName As String)

End Sub

End Class
```

Because of their importance, this book follows the preceding naming conventions, even for CLS-incompliant code.

Rules About Classes

The CLS influences classes' implementation with basically a few rules. The most rules are related to inheritance as much as for methods. Because inheritance hasn't been covered yet (discussed in Chapter 12, "Inheritance"), the only rule mentioned here is that if a class exposes only shared members, it must have an empty private constructor and must be marked as NotInheritable, as follows:

```
<CLSCompliant(True)> Public NotInheritable Class GzipCompress
    'Empty private constructor
    Private Sub New()

    End Sub

    Public Shared Sub Compress(ByVal fileName As String,
                          ByVal target As String)

    End Sub

    Public Shared Sub Decompress(ByVal fileName As String,
                            ByVal source As String)

    End Sub
End Class
```

The other rules about classes are described in Chapter 12.

Rules About Properties

The CLS provides a couple of rules about properties implementation:

▶ All properties exposed by a class must have the same access level, meaning that they must be all instance properties or all shared properties or all virtual properties. Virtual properties (that is, marked with the `MustOverride` keyword) are described in Chapter 12.

▶ `Get`, `Set`, and the property itself must return and receive the same type; the type must also be CLS-compliant. If the property returns `String`, both `Get` and `Set` must handle `String`, too. The type must be passed by value and not by reference.

Rules About Methods

CLS influences methods both for inheritance implementations and for declarations. You need to know that arguments with a nonfixed length must be specified only with the `ParamArray` keyword.

Rules About Arrays

For arrays, CLS rules are simple:

▶ Items within arrays must be CLS-compliant types.

▶ Arrays must have a fixed length greater than zero.

▶ Arrays must be zero-based. (This is mostly a rule for compilers.)

Summary

In this chapter, you learned several important concepts about object-oriented programming with Visual Basic 2012. You saw how classes are the most important item in the object-oriented programming; you also learned how to declare classes and how to expose members from classes, such as methods, properties, and fields. Summarizing these features, you might remember that fields are the real state of objects and properties are a way for ruling access to fields from the external world. You can also remember that methods are procedures that take actions. Methods are flexible due to the overloading technique that enables implementing different signatures of the same method. A special method known as constructor creates an instance of a class and gives the class the real life. Each time you create an instance of a class, you create a new copy of an object with its own life and data. But there are situations in which you need only one copy of an object and data, and that is where shared members come in. You also took a tour of interesting features such as partial classes and partial methods that enable a better organization of your classes' infrastructure. But as in all fantastic worlds, the risk of doing something wrong is always there, especially if you consider the CLR infrastructure that enables .NET languages to interoperate. Because of this, a set of rules named the Common Language Specification has been created to ensure that all classes and their members can be used from all .NET languages with the minimum risk of errors. After this overview of classes, it's time to understand how they live within memory.

CHAPTER **8**

Managing an Object's Lifetime

Real life is often a great place to get programming examples. Think of life: Humans are born; they grow up; they live their lives; they do tons of things; and, at a certain point, they die. Managing objects in programming environments works similarly. You give life to an object by creating an instance; then you use it in your own application while it is effectively useful to the application. But there is a point at which you do not need an object anymore, so you need to destroy it to free up memory and other resources, bringing an object to "death." Understanding how object lifetimes work in .NET programming is fundamental because it gives you the ability to write better code—code that can take advantage of system resources, to consume resources the appropriate way or return unused resources to the system.

Understanding Memory Allocation

Chapter 4, "Data Types and Expressions," discusses value types and reference types, describing how both of them are allocated in memory. Value types reside in the Stack, whereas reference types are allocated on the managed Heap. When you create a new instance of a reference type, via the New keyword, the .NET Framework reserves some memory in the managed Heap for the new object instance. Understanding memory allocation is fundamental, but an important practice is to also release objects and resources when they are unused or unnecessary. This returns free memory and provides better performance. For value types, the problem has an easy solution: Being allocated on the Stack, they are simply removed from memory when you assign the default zero value. The real problem is about reference types—you need to destroy the instance of an object. To accomplish this, you assign Nothing to the instance of a reference type.

When you perform this operation, the .NET Framework marks the object reference as no longer used and marks the memory used by the object as unavailable to the application. However, it does not immediately free up the Heap, and the runtime cannot immediately reuse such memory. Memory previously used by no-longer-referenced objects can be released by the .NET Framework after some time because the .NET Framework knows when it is the best moment for releasing resources. Such a mechanism is complex, but fortunately it is the job of the *garbage collector*.

Understanding Garbage Collection

In your applications, you often create object instances or allocate memory for resources. When you perform these operations, .NET Framework checks for available memory in the Heap. If available memory is not enough, .NET Framework launches a mechanism known as *garbage collection*, powered by an internal tool named *garbage collector*. The garbage collector can also be controlled by invoking members of the System.GC class, but the advantage is leaving the .NET Framework the job of handling the process automatically for you. The garbage collector first checks for all objects that have references from your applications, including objects referenced from other objects, enabling object graphs to be kept alive. Objects having any references are considered as used and alive, so the garbage collector marks them as in use and therefore will not clean them up. Any other objects in the Heap are considered as unused, and therefore the garbage collector removes these objects and references to them. After this, it compresses the Heap and returns free memory space that can be reallocated for other, new objects or resources. In all this sequence of operations, you do nothing. The garbage collector takes care of everything required. You can, however, decide to release objects when you do not need them anymore; you set their references to Nothing to free up some memory. The following snippet shows how you can logically destroy an instance of the Person class:

```
Dim p As New Person
p.FirstName = "Alessandro"
p.LastName = "Del Sole"


p = Nothing
```

When you assign an object reference with Nothing, the Common Language Runtime (CLR) automatically invokes the destructor (the Finalize method is covered in the next section) that any class exposes because the most basic implementation is provided by System.Object. At this point, there is a problem. The garbage collection behavior is known as *nondeterministic*, meaning that no one can predict the moment when the garbage collector is invoked. In other words, after you set an object reference to Nothing, you cannot know when the object will be effectively released. There can be a small delay, such as seconds, but there can also be a long delay, such as minutes or hours. This can depend on several factors; for example, if no additional memory is required during your application's lifetime, an object could be released at the application shutdown. This can be a problem of limited importance if you have only in-memory objects that do not access to external resources, such as files or the network. You do not have to worry about free memory because, when required, the garbage collector will kick in. Anyway, you can force a garbage collection process by invoking the System.GC.Collect method. The following is an example:

```
p = Nothing
'Forces the garbage collector
'so that the object is effectively
'cleaned up
System.GC.Collect()
```

Forcing the garbage collection process is not a good idea. As you can imagine, frequently invoking a mechanism of this type can cause performance overhead and significantly slow down your application performances. When you work with in-memory objects that do not access external resources, such as the Person class, leave the .NET Framework the job of performing a garbage collection only when required. The real problem is when you have objects accessing to external resources, such as files, databases, and network connections, which you want to be free as soon as possible when you set your object to Nothing and therefore you cannot wait for the garbage collection process to kick in. In this particular scenario, you can take advantage of two methods that have very similar behaviors: Finalize and Dispose.

OUT OF SCOPE OBJECTS

Objects that go out of scope will also be marked for garbage collection if they have no external reference to them, even if you don't set them explicitly to Nothing.

Understanding the `Finalize` Method

The Finalize method can be considered as a destructor that executes code just before an object is effectively destroyed, that is when memory should be effectively released. This method is inherited from System.Object; therefore any class can implement the method by declaring it as Protected Overrides, as follows:

```
Protected Overrides Sub Finalize()
    'Write your code here for releasing
    'such as closing db connections,
    'closing network connections,
    'and other resources that VB cannot understand

    MyBase.Finalize() 'this is just the base implementation
End Sub
```

If you need to destroy an object that simply uses memory, do not invoke `Finalize`. You need to invoke it when your object has a reference to something that Visual Basic cannot understand because the garbage collector does not know how to release that reference. Thus, you need to instruct it by providing code for explicitly releasing resources. Another situation is when you have references to something that is out of the scope of the object, such as unmanaged resources, network connections, and file references different from .NET streams. If an object explicitly provides a `Finalize` implementation, the CLR *automatically* invokes such a method just before removing the object from the Heap. This means that you *do not* need to invoke it manually. Notice that `Finalize` is not invoked immediately when you assign `Nothing` to the object instance you want to remove. Although `Finalize` enables you to control how resources must be released, it does not enable you to control when they are effectively released. This is due to the nondeterministic behavior of the garbage collector that frees up resources in the most appropriate moment, meaning that minutes or hours can be spent between the `Finalize` invocations and when resources are effectively released. However, invoking `Finalize` marks the object as no longer available. You could force the garbage collection process and wait for all finalizers to be completed, if you wanted to ensure that objects are logically and physically destroyed. Although this is not a good practice, because manually forcing a garbage collection causes performance overhead and loss of .NET Framework optimizations, you can write the following code:

```
'Object here is just for demo purposes
Dim c As New Object
c = Nothing
GC.Collect()
GC.WaitForPendingFinalizers()
```

Here are a few considerations on what `Finalize` should contain within its body:

▶ Do not throw exceptions within `Finalize` because the application cannot handle them and will crash.

▶ Invoke only shared methods except when the application is closing; this will avoid invocations on instance members from objects that can be logically destroyed.

▶ Continuing the previous point, do not access external objects from within `Finalize`.

To complete the discussion, it is worth mentioning that destruction of objects that explicitly provide `Finalize` require more than one garbage collection process. The reason destroyed objects are removed from the Heap at least at the second garbage collection is that `Finalize` could contain code that assigns the current object to a variable, keeping a reference still alive during the first garbage collection. This is known as *object resurrection* and is discussed in the section called "Restoring Objects with Object Resurrection." As a consequence, implementing `Finalize` can negatively impact performance and should be used only when strictly required.

Understanding `Dispose` and the `IDisposable` Interface

One of the issues of the `Finalize` destructor is that you cannot determine whether resources will be freed up and when an object will be physically destroyed from memory. This is because of the nondeterministic nature of the garbage collector—unused references will still remain in memory until the garbage collector kicks in, which is not a good idea. A better approach is to provide clients the ability to immediately release resources (such as network connections, data connections, or system resources) just before the object is destroyed, setting it to `Nothing`. The .NET Framework provides a way for releasing resources immediately and under your control, which is the `Dispose` method. Implementing `Dispose` avoids the need of waiting for the next garbage collection and enables you to clean up resources immediately, right before the object is destroyed. In contrast to `Finalize`, `Dispose` must be invoked manually. To provide a `Dispose` implementation, your class must implement the `IDisposable` interface. Visual Studio 2012 provides a skeleton of `IDisposable` implementation when you add the `Implements` directive (see Figure 8.1.) The code in Listing 8.1 shows the implementation.

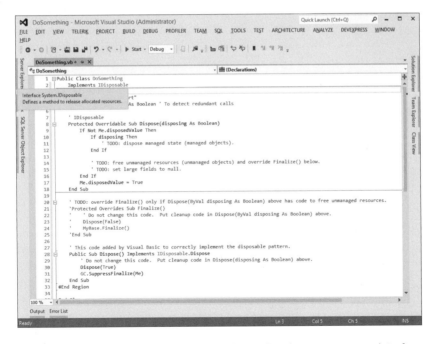

FIGURE 8.1   IntelliSense speeds up implementing the `IDisposable` interface providing a skeleton of required `members`.

LISTING 8.1   Implementing the IDisposable Interface

```vb
Class DoSomething
    Implements IDisposable

#Region "IDisposable Support"
    Private disposedValue As Boolean ' To detect redundant calls

    ' IDisposable
    Protected Overridable Sub Dispose(ByVal disposing As Boolean)
        If Not Me.disposedValue Then
            If disposing Then
                ' TODO: dispose managed state (managed objects).
            End If

            ' TODO: free unmanaged resources (unmanaged objects) and
            ' override Finalize() below.
            ' TODO: set large fields to null.
        End If
        Me.disposedValue = True
    End Sub

    ' TODO: override Finalize() only if Dispose(ByVal disposing As Boolean) above
    'has code to free unmanaged resources.
    'Protected Overrides Sub Finalize()
    'Do not change this code.  Put cleanup
    'code in Dispose(ByVal disposing As Boolean) above.
    '    Dispose(False)
    '    MyBase.Finalize()
    'End Sub

    ' This code added by Visual Basic to correctly implement the disposable pattern.
    Public Sub Dispose() Implements IDisposable.Dispose
        ' Do not change this code.  Put cleanup
        'code in Dispose(ByVal disposing As Boolean) above.
        Dispose(True)
        GC.SuppressFinalize(Me)
    End Sub
#End Region
End Class
```

Notice how Dispose is declared as Overridable so that you can provide different implementations in derived classes. Visual Studio is polite enough to provide comments showing you the right places for writing code that release managed or unmanaged resources. Also notice the implementation of Finalize that is enclosed in comments and is therefore inactive. Such a destructor should be provided only if you have to release unmanaged resources. You invoke the Dispose method before setting your object reference to nothing, as demonstrated here:

```
Dim dp As New DoSomething
'Do your work here...

dp.Dispose()
dp = Nothing
```

As an alternative, you can take advantage of the Using..End Using statement covered in the next section. When implementing the Dispose pattern, in custom classes you need to remember to invoke the Dispose method of objects they use within their bodies so they can correctly free up resources. Another important thing to take care of is checking whether an object has already been disposed when Dispose is invoked, but the auto-generated code for the Dispose method already keeps track of this for you.

Dispose AND INHERITANCE

When you define a class deriving from another class that implements IDisposable, you do not need to override Dispose unless you need to release additional resources in the derived class.

Using..End Using Statement

As an alternative to directly invoking Dispose, you can take advantage of the Using..End Using statement. This code block automatically releases and removes from memory the object that it points to, invoking Dispose behind the scenes for you. The following code shows how you can open a stream for writing a file and ensure that the stream will be released even if you do not explicitly close it:

```
Using dp As New IO.StreamWriter("C:\TestFile.txt", False)
    dp.WriteLine("This is a demo text")
End Using
```

Notice how you simply create an instance of the object via the Using keyword. The End Using statement causes Dispose to be invoked on the previously mentioned instance. The advantage of Using..End Using is that the resource is automatically released in cases of unhandled exceptions, and this can be useful.

Putting Dispose and Finalize Together

Implementing Dispose and Finalize cannot necessarily be required. It depends only on what kind of work your objects perform. Table 8.1 summarizes what and when you should implement.

TABLE 8.1   Implementing Destructors

What	When
No destructor	Objects that just work in memory and that reference other .NET in memory objects.
Finalize	Executing some code before the object gets finalized. The limitation is that you cannot predict when the garbage collector comes in.
Dispose	Your objects access external resources that you need to free up as soon as possible when destroying the object.
Finalize and Dispose	Your objects access unmanaged resources that you need to free up as soon as possible when destroying the object.

You already have seen examples about `Finalize` and `Dispose`, so here you get an example of their combination. Before you see the code, you have to know that you will see invocations to Win32 unmanaged APIs that you do not need in real applications, but these kinds of functions are useful to understand to know how to release unmanaged resources. Now take a look at Listing 8.2.

LISTING 8.2   Implementing `Dispose` and `Finalize`

```
Imports System.Runtime.InteropServices

Public Class ProperCleanup
    Implements IDisposable

    Private disposedValue As Boolean ' To detect redundant calls

    'A managed resource
    Private managedStream As IO.MemoryStream

    'Unmanaged resources
    <DllImport("winspool.drv")>
    Shared Function OpenPrinter(ByVal deviceName As String,
                               ByVal deviceHandle As Integer,
                               ByVal printerDefault As Object) _
                               As Integer
    End Function
    <DllImport("winspool.drv")>
    Shared Function _
    ClosePrinter(ByVal deviceHandle As Integer) _
             As Integer
    End Function

    Private printerHandle As Integer
```

```vb
'Initializes managed and unmanaged resources
Public Sub New()
    managedStream = New IO.MemoryStream
    OpenPrinter("MyDevice", printerHandle, &H0)
End Sub

'Just a sample method that does nothing
'particular except for checking if the object
'has been already disposed
Public Function FormatString(ByVal myString As String) As String
    If disposedValue = True Then
        Throw New ObjectDisposedException("ProperCleanup")
    Else
        Return "You entered: " & myString
    End If
End Function

' IDisposable
Protected Overridable Sub Dispose(ByVal disposing As Boolean)
    If Not Me.disposedValue Then
        If disposing Then
            ' TODO: dispose managed state (managed objects).
            managedStream.Dispose()
        End If

        ' TODO: free unmanaged resources (unmanaged objects)
        ' and override Finalize() below.
        ' TODO: set large fields to null.
        ClosePrinter(printerHandle)
    End If
    Me.disposedValue = True
End Sub

' TODO: override Finalize() only if Dispose(ByVal disposing As Boolean)
' above has code to free unmanaged resources.
Protected Overrides Sub Finalize()
    ' Do not change this code.  Put cleanup code in
    ' Dispose(ByVal disposing As Boolean) above.
    Dispose(False)
    MyBase.Finalize()
End Sub

' This code added by Visual Basic to correctly implement the disposable pattern.
Public Sub Dispose() Implements IDisposable.Dispose
    ' Do not change this code.  Put cleanup code
    ' in Dispose(ByVal disposing As Boolean) above.
```

```
        Dispose(True)
        GC.SuppressFinalize(Me)
    End Sub
End Class
```

The code in Listing 8.2 has some interesting points. First, notice how both managed resources (a `System.IO.MemoryStream`) and unmanaged resources (`OpenPrinter` and `ClosePrinter` API functions) are declared. Second, notice how the constructor creates instances of the previous resources. Because there are unmanaged resources, you need to override the `Finalize` method. Visual Basic is polite enough to show you comments describing this necessity, so you simply uncomment the `Finalize` block definition. This method invokes the `Dispose` one passing `False` as an argument; this can ensure that `Dispose` will clean up unmanaged resources as you can understand examining the conditional code block within the method overload that accepts a Boolean argument. Finally, notice how the other `Dispose` overload, the one accepting no arguments, invokes the other overload passing `True` (therefore requiring managed resources to be released); then it invokes the `GC.SuppressFinalize` method to ensure that `Finalize` is not invoked. There are no unmanaged resources to release at this point because `Finalize` was previously invoked to clean up unmanaged resources.

Restoring Objects with Object Resurrection

With the *object resurrection* phrase, we describe the scenario in which an object is restored after its reference was removed, although the object was not removed yet from memory. This is an advanced technique, but it is not very useful and Microsoft strongly discourages you from using it in your applications. It is helpful to understand something more about objects' lifetime. An object being finalized can store a self-reference to a global variable, and this can keep the object alive. In simpler words, a reference to a "died" object is restored when within the `Finalize` method the current object is assigned (using the `Me` keyword) to a class-level or module-level variable. Here's a small code example for demonstrating object resurrection. Keep in mind that the code is simple to focus on the concept more than on the code difficulty, but you can use this technique with more and more complex objects. You add this code to a module:

```
Public resurrected As ResurrectionDemo

Sub TestResurrection()
    Dim r As New ResurrectionDemo
    'This will invoke Finalize
    r = Nothing

End Sub
```

The resurrected variable is of type `ResurrectionDemo`, a class that will be implemented next. This variable holds the actual reference to the finalizing object so that it can keep it alive. The `TestResurrection` method creates an instance of the class and sets it to

Nothing, causing the CLR to invoke Finalize. Now notice the implementation of the ResurrectionDemo class and specifically the Finalize implementation:

```
Class ResurrectionDemo

    Protected Overrides Sub Finalize()
        'The object is resurrected here
        resurrected = Me
        GC.ReRegisterForFinalize(Me)
    End Sub
End Class
```

Notice how Finalize's body assigns the current object to the resurrected variable, which holds the reference. When an object is resurrected, Finalize cannot be invoked a second time because the garbage collector removed the object from the finalization queue. This is the reason the GC.ReRegisterForFinalize method is invoked. As a consequence, multiple garbage collections are required for a resurrected object to be cleaned up. At this point, just think of how many system resources this can require. Moreover, when an object is resurrected, previously referenced objects are also resurrected. This can result in application faults because you cannot know whether objects' finalizations already occurred. As mentioned at the beginning of this section, the object resurrection technique rarely takes place in real-life application because of its implications and because it can be successfully used only in scenarios in which you need to create pools of objects whose frequent creation and destruction could be time-consuming.

Advanced Garbage Collection

The garbage collection is a complex mechanism, and in most cases you do not need to interact with the garbage collector because, in such cases, you must be extremely sure that what you are doing is correct. The .NET Framework automatically takes care of what the CLR needs. Understanding advanced features of the garbage collector can provide a better view of objects' lifetime. The goal of this section is therefore to show such advanced features.

Interacting with the Garbage Collector

The System.GC class provides several methods for manually interacting with the garbage collector. In this chapter you already learned some of them. Remember these methods:

- ▶ Collect, which enables you to force a garbage collection

- ▶ WaitForPendingFinalizers which enables you to wait for all Finalize methods to be completed before cleaning up resources

- ▶ ReRegisterForFinalize which puts an object back to the finalization queue in object resurrection

- ▶ SuppressFinalize which is used in the Dispose pattern for avoiding unnecessary finalizations

There are other interesting members; for example, you can get an approximate amount of allocated memory as follows:

```
Dim bytes As Long = System.GC.GetTotalMemory(False)
```

You pass `False` if you do not want a garbage collection to be completed before returning the result. Another method is `KeepAlive` that adds a reference to the specified object preventing the garbage collector from destroying it:

```
GC.KeepAlive(anObject)
```

You can then tell the garbage collector that a huge amount of unmanaged memory should be considered within a garbage collection process; you accomplish this by invoking the `AddMemoryPressure` method. It requires the amount of memory as an argument. Next, you can tell the garbage collector that an amount of unmanaged memory has been released by invoking the `RemoveMemoryPressure` method. Other interesting members enable garbage collector interaction; these are covered in the next section for their relationship with the specific topic.

Understanding Generations and Operation Modes

The garbage collector is based on *generations* that are basically a counter representing how many times an object survived the garbage collection. The .NET Framework supports three generations. The first one is named `gen0` and is when the object is at its pure state. The second generation is named `gen1` and is when the object survived one garbage collection; the last generation is named `gen2` and is when the object survived two or more garbage collections. This is a good mechanism for figuring the garbage collector's performance because it first tries to remove objects at `gen2` instead of searching for all live references. The garbage collection process is available in two modes: server and workstation. The first one is intended for server applications, whereas the second mode is typically intended for standalone machines. The garbage collection can be executed on multiple threads, and this is known as *concurrent* garbage collection. Until .NET Framework 3.5 SP 1, concurrent garbage collection could perform collections on both `gen0` and `gen1` concurrently or most of a `gen2` without pausing managed code, but never `gen2` concurrently with the other ones. In .NET Framework 4.0, a new feature named *Background GC* was introduced and replaced concurrent garbage collection; this enables collecting all generations together and also enables allocating memory while collecting.

BACKGROUND GC IMPROVEMENTS

The .NET Framework 4.5 introduces an improvement that makes the background garbage collection available to the Server mode in addition to the Workstation mode. This removes a limitation that was part of its version in .NET 4.0.

The good news is that you can also take advantage of a feature that enables subscribing to garbage collection events, so that you can be notified once the `gen2` completes. The code in Listing 8.3 demonstrates this (read comments for explanations).

LISTING 8.3   Registering for Garbage Collection Events

```vb
Sub Main()
    Try
        'Registers for notification about gen2 (1st arg) and
        'large objects on the Heap (2nd arg)
        GC.RegisterForFullGCNotification(10, 10)

        'Notifications are handled via a separate thread
        Dim thWaitForFullGC As New Thread(New _
                                ThreadStart(AddressOf WaitForFullGCProc))
        thWaitForFullGC.Start()

    Catch ex As InvalidOperationException

        'Probably concurrent GC is enabled
        Console.WriteLine(ex.Message)
    End Try
End Sub


Public Shared Sub WaitForFullGCProc()
    While True
        'Notification status
        Dim s As GCNotificationStatus

        'Register for an event advising
        'that a GC is imminent
        s = GC.WaitForFullGCApproach()

        If s = GCNotificationStatus.Succeeded Then
            'A garbage collection is imminent

        End If

        'Register for an event advising
        'that a GC was completed
        s = GC.WaitForFullGCComplete()
        If s = GCNotificationStatus.Succeeded Then

            'A garbage collection is completed
        End If
    End While
End Sub
```

You can easily subscribe for garbage collection events by invoking `WaitForFullGCComplete` and `WaitForFullApproach`.

Summary

Understanding how memory and resources are released after object usage is fundamental in every development environment. In .NET, this is accomplished by the garbage collector, a complex mechanism that works after you set an object reference to `Nothing` or when you attempt to create new instances of objects but don't have any more memory available. You can also implement explicit destructors, such as `Finalize` or `Dispose`, according to specific scenarios in which you do need to release external or unmanaged resources before destroying an object. The garbage collection process has been improved in .NET Framework 4.5 so that it extends the Background GC, which enables you to execute the process across multiple threads in every generation step, to the Server mode.

CHAPTER 9

Organizing Types Within Namespaces

.NET Framework ships with many built-in types. Such an enormous quantity necessarily needs a hierarchical organization in which types must be divided into their areas of interest (data access, file manipulation, communications, and so on). Moreover, the .NET Framework provides an extensible platform, and companies can also build their own custom components exposing types that could have the same name of existing built-in types in .NET Framework. To avoid naming conflicts and to enable a hierarchical organization of the code, Visual Basic offers the *namespaces* feature discussed in this chapter.

Understanding Namespaces

Namespaces provide a way for a better organization of the code and avoiding conflicts between types with the same name. Consider a complex hierarchical framework of objects (such as .NET Framework) in which you have the need to expose more than one type with a particular identifier. The typical example is when software companies produce class libraries; different companies could need to provide their own implementation of the `Person` class, or the same company could provide different implementations of the `Person` class within the same assembly, so there could be ambiguities for developers when invoking a particular implementation of the `Person` class. To solve this coding problem, programming languages in the .NET family offer the capability of organizing types within namespaces. For example, imagine using assemblies from two companies, `Company1` and `Company2`, with both produced assemblies exposing their own implementation of the `Person` class. You would need to use one of the two implementations, but you would still need to reference both assemblies in your project. The following code

```
Dim p As New Person
```

can cause the Visual Basic compiler to throw an exception because it does not know which of the two implementations you want to invoke. By using namespaces, you can avoid this ambiguity as follows:

```
Dim p1 As New Company1.Person
Dim p2 As New Company2.Person
```

In this code example, `Company1` and `Company2` are namespaces that virtually encapsulate lots of types, whereas both `Company1.Person` and `Company2.Person` represent the full name of the Person class. The .NET Framework Base Class Library (BCL) relies heavily on namespaces. The main namespace in the BCL is `System`, which is the root in the BCL hierarchy. `System` exposes dozens of other namespaces, such as `System.Xml`, `System.Data`, `System.Linq`, and so on. Each of these namespaces exposes types and other nested namespaces, and in this way a hierarchical framework is more maintainable. Namespaces solve a coding problem and an object implementation problem. This is because namespaces are all about coding. The Common Language Runtime (CLR) does not recognize namespaces, but it does recognize only full class names, such as `Company2.Person` in the previous example or `System.Object` or `System.Console`. Namespaces are just a logical feature that helps developers write better-organized and reusable code. The CLR never encounters conflicts because it recognizes only full class names, but as you learn later in this chapter, as a developer you might encounter such conflicts. So, having some help in writing and organizing code will be necessary, especially when working with long named classes (see the "Imports Directives" section).

Organizing Types Within Namespaces

Namespaces are defined within `Namespace..End Namespace` blocks. Every namespace can expose the following types and members:

▶ Classes

▶ Structures

▶ Enumerations

▶ Modules

▶ Interfaces

▶ Delegates

▶ Nested namespaces

Listing 9.1 shows an example of a namespace exposing most of the preceding listed members.

LISTING 9.1   Organizing Types Within a Namespace

```vb
Namespace People

    Public Interface IContactable
        ReadOnly Property HasEmailAddress As Boolean
    End Interface

    Public MustInherit Class Person
        Public Property FirstName As String
        Public Property LastName As String

        Public Overrides Function ToString() As String
            Return FirstName & " " & LastName
        End Function
    End Class

    Public Enum PersonType
        Work = 0
        Personal = 1
    End Enum

    Public Class Contact
        Inherits Person
        Implements IContactable

        Public Property EmailAddress As String

        Public Overrides Function ToString() As String
            Return MyBase.ToString()
        End Function

        Public ReadOnly Property HasEmailAddress As Boolean _
                        Implements IContactable.HasEmailAddress
            Get
                If String.IsNullOrEmpty(Me.EmailAddress) Then
                    Return False
                Else
                    Return True
                End If
            End Get
        End Property
    End Class

    Public Class Employee
        Inherits Person
```

```
        Public Property Title As String

        Public Overrides Function ToString() As String
            Return Me.Title & " " & Me.FirstName & " " & Me.LastName
        End Function
    End Class


    Public Class Customer
        Inherits Person

        Public Property CompanyName As String
        Public Overrides Function ToString() As String
            Return Me.LastName & " from " & Me.CompanyName
        End Function

    End Class


    Module GlobalDeclarations
        Public Data As Object
    End Module


    Public Structure PersonInformation
        Public Property PersonCategory As PersonType
        Public Property HasEmailAddress As Boolean
    End Structure
End Namespace
```

As you can see in Listing 9.1, you can organize your custom objects within a namespace.
The code implements an abstract class (`Person`), three derived classes (`Contact`, `Employee`,
and `Customer`), an interface (which is then implemented by the `Contact` class), an enumeration (`PersonType`), a structure (`PersonInformation`), and a module (`GlobalDeclarations`).
The namespace becomes part of the full name of a type. For example, the full name for
the `Contact` class is `People.Contact`. Therefore, if you need to access a type defined within
a namespace, you need to refer to it by writing the full name, as in the following line
of code:

```
Dim firstContact As New People.Contact
```

ADDING IMPORTS

Later in this chapter we discuss the `Imports` directives, which can prevent the need to
add the namespace identifier to the full type name every time.

Namespaces can also expose partial classes. This is a common situation within .NET
Framework built-in namespaces.

Why Are Namespaces So Useful?

The purpose of namespaces is to enable a better organization of types. In some situations, an object's hierarchy could expose two different types with different behaviors, but with the same name. For example, imagine you have two Person classes; the first one should represent business contacts, and the second one should represent your friends. Of course, you cannot create two classes with the same name within one namespace. Because of this, you can organize such types in different namespaces and thus avoid conflicts. The code in Listing 9.2 shows how you can define two Person classes within two different namespaces.

LISTING 9.2   Avoiding Conflicts with Different Namespaces

```vb
Namespace People

    Public Class Person
        Public Property FirstName As String
        Public Property LastName As String

        Public Overrides Function ToString() As String
            Return FirstName & " " & LastName
        End Function
    End Class
End Namespace

Namespace MyFriends
    'Will not conflict with People.Person
    Public Class Person
        Public Property FirstName As String
        Public Property LastName As String
        Public Property Sibling As String

        Public Overrides Function ToString() As String
            Return FirstName & " " & LastName & ": " & Sibling
        End Function
    End Class
End Namespace
```

This is the way two classes with the same name can coexist within the same assembly. To access both of them, you just need to invoke their full names, as follows:

```vb
Dim aFriend As New MyFriends.Person
Dim aContact As New People.Person
```

NOTE

The `Person` class is just an example. You can refer to inheritance as in Listing 9.1 instead of providing different namespaces, but the `Person` class is the simplest example for demonstrating topics, which is the reason to continue to use such a class.

Nested Namespaces

You can nest namespaces within namespaces to create a complex hierarchy of namespaces. However, you should be careful in creating complex hierarchies of namespaces because this can lead to particular complexity in your code that can cause difficulties in maintainability and reuse. You nest a namespace within another one by adding a new `Namespace..End Namespace` block. For example, in Listing 9.1 there are two different kinds of people: personal contact and businesspeople (which includes `Customer` and `Employee`). You could then consider defining a new namespace for your business objects and one for your personal objects. Listing 9.3 shows a shorter version of the first example, in which nested namespaces expose the two kinds of classes.

LISTING 9.3   Implementing Nested Namespaces

```
Namespace People

    Public Interface IContactable
        ReadOnly Property HasEmailAddress As Boolean
    End Interface

    Public MustInherit Class Person
        Public Property FirstName As String
        Public Property LastName As String

        Public Overrides Function ToString() As String
            Return FirstName & " " & LastName
        End Function
    End Class
Namespace Work
    Public Class Customer
        Inherits Person

        Public Property CompanyName As String
        Public Overrides Function ToString() As String
            Return Me.LastName & " from " & Me.CompanyName
        End Function

    End Class
```

```
        Public Class Employee
            Inherits Person

            Public Property Title As String

            Public Overrides Function ToString() As String
                Return Me.Title & " " & Me.FirstName & " " & Me.LastName
            End Function
        End Class
    End Namespace

    Namespace Personal
        Public Class Contact
            Inherits Person
            Implements IContactable

            Public Property EmailAddress As String

            Public Overrides Function ToString() As String
                Return MyBase.ToString()
            End Function

            Public ReadOnly Property HasEmailAddress As Boolean _
                        Implements IContactable.HasEmailAddress
                Get
                    If String.IsNullOrEmpty(Me.EmailAddress) Then
                        Return False
                    Else
                        Return True
                    End If
                End Get
            End Property
        End Class
    End Namespace
End Namespace
```

As you can see from Listing 9.3, nesting namespaces is an easy task. Creating complex hierarchies can lead to problems in code readability because of several possible indentations. Luckily, Visual Basic enables an alternative syntax for defining nested namespaces without writing indented code. Listing 9.4 shows how you can create nested namespace with the alternative syntax.

LISTING 9.4   Nesting Namespace Without Indented Code

```
Namespace People

    Public Interface IContactable
        ReadOnly Property HasEmailAddress As Boolean
    End Interface

    Public MustInherit Class Person
        Public Property FirstName As String
        Public Property LastName As String

        Public Overrides Function ToString() As String
            Return FirstName & " " & LastName
        End Function
    End Class
End Namespace

Namespace People.Work
    Public Class Employee
        Inherits Person

        Public Property Title As String

        Public Overrides Function ToString() As String
            Return Me.Title & " " & Me.FirstName & " " & Me.LastName
        End Function
    End Class

    Public Class Customer
        Inherits Person

        Public Property CompanyName As String
        Public Overrides Function ToString() As String
            Return Me.LastName & " from " & Me.CompanyName
        End Function
    End Class
End Namespace

Namespace People.Personal
    Public Class Contact
        Inherits Person
        Implements IContactable

        Public Property EmailAddress As String
```

```
        Public Overrides Function ToString() As String
            Return MyBase.ToString()
        End Function

        Public ReadOnly Property HasEmailAddress As Boolean _
                    Implements IContactable.HasEmailAddress
            Get
                If String.IsNullOrEmpty(Me.EmailAddress) Then
                    Return False
                Else
                    Return True
                End If
            End Get
        End Property
    End Class
End Namespace
```

As you can see from Listing 9.4, you can nest namespaces by adding a dot after the parent namespace and then specifying the child namespace name without having to nest namespaces on the code side. This produces the same result, but your code is more readable. By the way, you are free to use both methodologies.

Scope

Namespaces have scope of visibility. As a rule, namespaces have public visibility because they can be recognized within the project, from other projects that reference the project defining the namespace and from external assemblies. Because of this behavior, namespace declarations can be adorned neither with qualifiers nor with attributes. Members defined within namespaces can only be `Friend` or `Public`. If you do not want the external world to use some members defined within a namespace, you need to mark such members as `Friend`. By default, Visual Basic considers members within namespaces as `Friend`. If you want them to be of public access, you need to explicitly mark them as `Public`.

Root Namespace

Each application has a root namespace that contains all types defined in the application. When you create a new project, Visual Studio automatically assigns the root namespace (also known as the *first-level namespace*) with the name of the project. This is important to understand, for several reasons. First, if you develop class libraries or reusable components, the root namespace must follow the naming conventions of the Common Language Specification (CLS). Second, you must know how your types and auto-generated code are organized within your project. For example, the project containing the code of this chapter is named `OrganizingTypesWithinNamespaces`. By default, Visual Studio assigned the root namespace identifier with the `OrganizingTypesWithinNamespaces` identifier. Continuing the previous example, you access the `People` namespace in this way:

6

`OrganizingTypesWithinNamespaces.People`. You then get access to `People`'s objects as follows:

```
OrganizingTypesWithinNamespaces.People.Person
```

To replace the identifier for your root namespace, you need to open the My Project window and open the Application tab. You find a text box named Root namespace, which is represented in Figure 9.1.

FIGURE 9.1   Checking and editing the root namespace.

Here you can change the root namespace. If you develop class libraries, the root namespace should have the following form: `CompanyName.ProductName` (for this particular scenario, you should also consider the Global namespace feature discussed at the end of this chapter).

ROOT NAMESPACE

When invoking a member defined inside the root namespace, you do not need to include the name of the namespace. This is the only exception when invoking members. For example, if you need to access the `People` namespace we defined in the code example, type People and not `OrganizingTypesWithinNamespaces.People`.

Imports Directives

It often happens that you need to invoke types defined within long-named, nested namespaces. To invoke types, you need to write the full name of the type, which includes the identifier of the namespace that defines a particular type, as in the following code:

```
Dim aFile As New System.IO.FileStream("C:\test.txt",
                System.IO.FileMode.Open)
Dim onePerson As New ImportsDirectives.People.Work.Customer
```

Although IntelliSense has been highly improved from previous versions and it helps in writing code, it can result quite annoyingly in typing long-named namespaces. To help developers write code faster, Visual Basic enables the usage of Imports directives. Such directives enable developers to avoid having to write the full namespace identifier preceding the types' names. The preceding code can be rewritten as follows:

```
Imports System.IO
Imports ImportsDirectives.People.Work
...
        Dim aFile As New FileStream("C:\test.txt", FileMode.Open)
        Dim onePerson As New Customer
```

POSITION IN CODE OF `Imports` DIRECTIVES

`Imports` directives can be added to each code file you need. They *must* be the first lines of code, preceding any other code except comments, the `Option Strict`, `Option Compare`, `Option Explicit`, and `Option Infer` directives that are the only lines of code always on the top.

You can now invoke types exposed by the `System.IO` namespace without having to write the namespace identifier each time. In this particular code example, we had just two invocations of members from the namespace, but in an application that manipulates files, you could have hundreds of invocations; with a single `Imports` directive. You do not need to write the namespace identifier before the types' names each time. `System.IO` is a .NET built-in namespace, but the same applies to your own namespaces (in our example, the `ImportsDirectives.People.Work`). You can also take advantage of another technique that enables assigning an identifier to a long namespace so that invocations can be smarter (a feature known as *namespace alias*):

```
Imports work = ImportsDirectives.People.Work
...
        Dim onePerson As New work.Customer
```

IMPORTING XML NAMESPACES

Starting from Visual Basic 2008, `Imports` directives also enable importing XML namespaces. This feature is discussed in Chapter 27, "Manipulating XML Documents with LINQ and XML Literals," for LINQ to XML.

`Imports` directives also enable importing class names. This enables invoking only shared members without the need of writing the full class name. Consider the following code, which deletes a file from disk:

```
System.IO.File.Delete("C:\text.txt")
```

Delete is a shared method exposed by the `System.IO.File` class. You can rewrite the previous code as follows:

```
Imports System.IO.File
...
        Delete("C:\text.txt")
```

This can be useful if you need to invoke lots of shared members from a particular class.

Project-Level Default Imports

By default, Visual Studio 2012 adds some auto-generated Imports directives each time you create a new Visual Basic project, so you do not need to manually add such statements. Default Imports are specific to the project type, so if you create a Console application, there will be Imports related to these kinds of applications. If you create a web application, there will be Imports related to the most common namespaces for web applications and so on. You can easily add project-level namespaces via the My Project window. In the References tab, you can find a group box named Imported namespaces, as shown in Figure 9.2.

FIGURE 9.2   Setting project-level namespaces.

You can click the check box corresponding to each available namespace to add project-level Imports directives. This avoids the need of manually typing such Imports.

Additionally, if a particular namespace is not available in the list, you can manually enter its name and it will be added.

TIP

You can add a namespace alias in the Imported namespaces list. For example, if you want to import the System.Windows.Forms namespace, you can type something like F = System.Windows.Forms and then access namespace members as if you wrote the alias in the code (for example, F.TextBox).

Avoiding Ambiguities

You might have situations in which you need to access objects with the same name, coming from different namespaces. For example, both Windows Forms and Windows Presentation Foundation technologies provide a MessageBox class. In interoperability scenarios, where you have both references to Windows Forms and WPF assemblies, invoking such objects could result in ambiguities. Consider the following code:

```
Imports System.Windows.Forms
Imports System.Windows
Class Window1
```

```
    Public Sub MyMethod()
        MessageBox.Show("")
    End Sub
End Class
```

Both `System.Windows` and `System.Windows.Forms` namespaces expose a `MessageBox` class, but you need those Imports for working with other classes. In such situations, adding Imports directives can cause the background compiler to throw an exception. This is because the code is ambiguous in invoking the `MessageBox` class, since it is not clear which of the two classes the runtime should invoke. In this case, you can avoid ambiguities by writing the full name of the class:

```
'Invokes the WPF MessageBox
System.Windows.MessageBox.Show("")
```

You could also solve this ambiguity by using namespace aliasing. Another example is the one provided by Listing 9.2. There we have two different implementations of the `Person` class, so adding an Imports directive would lead to ambiguities. Thus, in that case, you have to invoke members with their full names. Generally, when you have multiple namespaces defining classes with the same name, you should write the full class name including the namespace. This is probably one of the best examples for understanding why namespaces are so useful.

Namespaces and Common Language Specification

The Common Language Specification provides a couple of simple rules about namespaces. The first rule is that namespaces identifiers must be Pascal-cased. For example, `MyCustomTypes` is a well-formed namespace identifier. The second rule establishes that to be CLS-compliant, a namespace must expose at least five types (classes, structures, enumerations, delegates, and so on). If this is not your case, you should prefer single classes or modules or consider merging types within another namespace already containing other types.

Global Namespaces and the `Global` Keyword

A common scenario in .NET development is creating class libraries that will be reused in other projects or given (or sold) to other developers. In these situations, it is convenient defining one or more first-level namespaces that can expose types or other namespaces. However, when you create a new project, Visual Basic also defines the root namespace (refer to Figure 9.1 for an example). This implies that defining a custom namespace like this:

```
Namespace MyUtilities
  Public Class Utility1
    'Your implementation goes here...
  End Class
End Namespace
```

causes the Visual Basic compiler to include the new namespace inside the root one whose name is, by default, the same as the project name (unless you change it manually). Continuing the example, the full name for the new namespace becomes `OrganizingTypesWithinNamespaces.MyUtilities`, which can be easily verified through the Object Browser window, as represented in Figure 9.3.

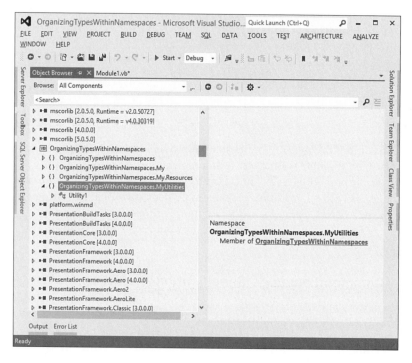

FIGURE 9.3   New namespaces are nested in the root namespace by default.

So the need at this point is abstracting custom namespaces from the root namespace, so that custom namespaces can be at the first-level like the root one. Until Visual Basic 2010, this was possible only by deleting the content of the Root Namespace box in My Project and then adding the required `Namespace..End Namespace` statements in every code file. In real-world solutions, this was impossible because a developer or a team could have hundreds or thousands of code files. Fortunately, Visual Basic 2012 introduces the feature of **Global Namespaces**, which allows you to bring custom namespaces to the same level of the root namespace by using the `Global` keyword. This is not a new keyword in Visual Basic, but in previous versions it was used to avoid conflicts with system namespaces. You place the `Global` keyword before the name of the namespace as follows:

```
Namespace Global.MyUtilities
    Public Class Utility1
        'Your implementation goes here...
    End Class
End Namespace
```

In this way, you can define standalone namespaces that are independent from the project's root namespace, as you can easily verify again via the Object Browser (see Figure 9.4).

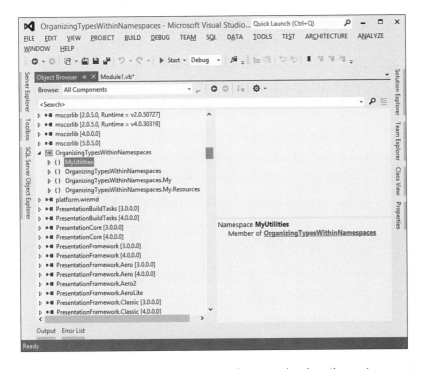

FIGURE 9.4   Global namespaces are at the same level as the root namespace.

This should also make it easy to understand that this technique allows extending the .NET Framework's namespaces from others without having the source code. The following code demonstrates how to extend the internal `System.String` type with a new extension method, passing through the `Global` namespace:

```
Imports System.Runtime.CompilerServices

Namespace Global.System

    'You can also use the following syntax:
    'Namespace Global
    '    Namespace System

    Public Module Extensions

        <Extension()>
        Public Function Parse(element As String) As String
```

```
      Return element + " is made of " + CStr(element.Length) + " characters"
   End Function

  End Module
End Namespace
```

Extension methods are discussed in more detail in Chapter 20, "Advanced Language Features," but the code should make you understand how an internal type in .NET is extended. Notice that the compiler assumes the `System` namespace as the default if no namespace identifier is specified after the `Global` keyword, so the following line:

```
Namespace Global
```

means `Namespace Global.System`. The suggestion is therefore to always specify the full name of the namespace to avoid confusion. The following code demonstrates how to extend another namespace, more precisely `System.Text`, with a new class:

```
Namespace Global.System.Text

  Public Class CustomStringBuilder

    Private _builder As StringBuilder
    Public ReadOnly Property Builder As StringBuilder
      Get
        Return _builder
      End Get
    End Property


    'Storing the original string into a new string builder
    'This is just for demo
    Public Sub New(startString As String)
      Me._builder.AppendLine(startString)
    End Sub

  End Class
End Namespace
```

The purpose of the code is just to show how to extend a namespace, so it is very simple. The new type is being added to the `System.Text` namespace via the namespace declaration and demonstrating this is easy:

```
Sub Demo()
  'Using the new class from the extended namespace
  Dim txt As New System.Text.CustomStringBuilder("Starting string")
  Console.WriteLine(txt.Builder.ToString)
End Sub
```

In summary, the `Global` namespace allows abstracting custom namespaces from the project's root namespace and extending existing namespaces.

Summary

.NET Framework Base Class Library ships with many built-in types that are organized within namespaces. As a developer, you can build your custom types; therefore, you can organize them in namespaces. Namespaces are also a way to have different implementations of objects with the same name within a complex framework hierarchy. Because they are visible to other projects or assemblies, namespaces have a `Public` or `Friend` scope. Namespaces are also flexible; you can implement complex hierarchies nesting namespaces, and you can use whatever identifier you like. Finally, you saw a new feature in Visual Basic 2012—the Global namespace—and the usage of the `Global` keyword with this new feature. You have to deal with namespaces many times in object-oriented programming, so this chapter gives you the basis for feeling at home with this important feature of the .NET Framework.

CHAPTER 10

Modules

IN THIS CHAPTER

▶ Modules Overview

▶ Differences Between Modules and Classes

Visual Basic programming language provides a simplified way for working with shared classes. Modules have been a part of Visual Basic since the beginning, so it is the real reason why Visual Basic .NET has modules versus C# which has shared classes. In this brief chapter you learn about the module feature.

Modules Overview

Modules are a specific feature of the Visual Basic programming language. You can think of modules as classes exposing only shared members; each module is defined within a `Module..End Module` code block. The following code provides an example of a module:

```
Module Module1

    Sub Main()
        'DoSomething is a method defined elsewhere
        DoSomething()
    End Sub

End Module
```

Differently from Visual C#, Visual Basic does not directly support shared classes; it provides support for classes with only shared members. According to this, the preceding module is the Visual Basic representation of the following class:

```
Class Program
    Shared Sub Main()
        'DoSomething is a method defined elsewhere
```

```
        DoSomething()
    End Sub
End Class
```

If you had any other member in this class, it should be marked as `Shared`. Modules are particularly useful when you want to implement objects and members that can be easily shared across your application and that do not need an instance.

Multiple modules can be defined in one code file, or multiple code files can define one or more modules as well. The following module defines a field and a property that you can reach from anywhere in your project:

```
'From anywhere in your project you'll be able
'to reach the two objects
Module Declarations

    Friend myFirstField As String
    Friend Property myFirstProperty As Integer

End Module
```

Because you cannot create an instance of a module, you have just one copy in memory of both the field and the property. The following example instead defines a method that assigns variables defined inside a different module:

```
Module Methods
    Friend Sub DoSomething()
        myFirstField = "A string"
        myFirstProperty = 0
    End Sub
End Module
```

It is worth mentioning that, different from classes, you do not need to invoke methods by writing first the name of the class that defines methods. For example, if the `DoSomething` method were defined within a class named Program, you should use the following syntax:

```
Program.DoSomething()
```

With modules, this is not necessary—you simply need to invoke the method name:

```
DoSomething()
```

This is true unless a conflict exists with the method name and a local method of the same name.

Scope

Typically, modules are required within a project and are not exposed to the external world. Because of this, the default scope qualifier for modules is `Friend`. But because of their particular nature, modules are also allowed to be `Public`—but neither `Private` nor `Protected/Protected Friend`. Members defined within modules can be also marked as `Private`.

ABOUT PUBLIC MODULES

There is a particular exception to the previous discussion: creating a custom extension methods library. Because in Visual Basic you define extension methods within modules, if you want to export such methods, you need to mark them as `Public`. Extension methods are discussed in Chapter 20, "Advanced Language Features."

Differences Between Modules and Classes

There are some differences between modules and classes. This brief section looks at those differences.

No Constructor

As previously mentioned, modules can be considered as shared classes, although Visual Basic provides support for classes with only shared members and not direct support for shared classes. Because of their shared nature, as a general rule modules do not support the constructor (`Sub New`). An exception is that you can declare a `Sub New` in a module that will be private and any code in the private constructor will be executed the first time any call to the module is made.

No Inheritance Support

Modules cannot inherit from other modules or classes or be inherited. Therefore, the `Inherits`, `NotInheritable`, and `MustInherit` keywords are not supported by modules.

INHERITANCE AND SHARED MEMBERS

Although it is not a good programming practice, it is legal to create a `NotInheritable` `Class` that exposes only shared members.

No Interface Implementation

Modules cannot implement interfaces. If you need to implement interfaces, you should consider developing a class with shared members instead of a module.

Summary

Modules are an alternative for working with shared members and data. Although they have some limitations compared to classes, they are useful for exchanging information across the project. In this chapter you got an overview of modules and saw the differences between modules and classes.

CHAPTER 11

Structures and Enumerations

So far, we have discussed a lot of important concepts about .NET development with Visual Basic. Just to mention some key topics, we have covered class fundamentals, objects' lifetime, types' organization, and exception handling. We applied all these concepts to reference types (classes). But in your developer life, you will often work with value types, both built-in and custom ones. In Chapter 4, "Data Types and Expressions," you started with the most important built-in value types in the .NET Framework. To complete your skills, though, you now need to know how to implement your own value types. In this chapter you get this information. You first understand structures and how to create them. Then you learn how to extend structures with custom versions of operators. Finally, you learn about enumerations, another kind of value type in the .NET Framework. This is not just a simple illustration because you also gain information on memory allocation to get a complete overview of this development area.

Understanding Structures

Structures in .NET development are the way to create custom value types. You find a lot of similarities between classes and structures, although this section explains some important differences. You create structures using a `Structure..End Structure` block. The following code provides an example of a structure representing a fictitious order received by your company:

```
Public Structure Order

    Public Property OrderID As Integer
    Public Property OrderDate As Date
    Public Property ShippedDate As Date
    Public Property CustomerID As Integer
    Public Property EmployeeID As Integer
    End Sub
End Structure
```

`Structure` can expose several members, such as fields, properties, and methods, as it happens for classes. The first important difference has to do with constructors. First, to create an instance of a structure, you aren't required to use the `New` keyword as you are for classes. The following code shows how you can instantiate a structure:

```
Dim o As Order
Dim o1 As New Order
```

Both syntaxes are legal. The only difference is that if you don't use the `New` keyword, the variable will be marked as unused until you assign a value and the VB compiler will show a warning message about this. Then you can assign (or invoke) members of the structure by typing the name followed by a dot:

```
o.OrderDate = Date.Now
o.OrderID = 1
'Other assignments..
```

Notice that, when you declare a structure without assigning its members, the compiler assigns the structure members a default value (which is usually zero for value types and `Nothing` for reference types). You can also utilize the object initializers feature discussed in Chapter 7, "Class Fundamentals," to initialize members of a structure. The following syntax is allowed but requires the specification of the `New` keyword:

```
Dim o As New Order With {.OrderID = 1, .OrderDate = Date.Now,
    .ShippedDate = Date.Now.AddDays(1), .CustomerID = 1,
    .EmployeeID = 1}
```

The second difference is that Visual Basic automatically provides an implicit constructor with no parameters, and you are not enabled to explicitly provide a constructor that receives no parameters; if you try, the Visual Basic compiler throws an error. You are instead enabled to provide a constructor that receives arguments, as follows:

```
Public Sub New(ByVal Id As Integer,
               ByVal OrderDate As Date,
               ByVal ShippedDate As Date,
               ByVal CustomerId As Integer,
               ByVal EmployeeId As Integer)
```

```
        Me.OrderID = Id
        Me.OrderDate = OrderDate
        Me.ShippedDate = ShippedDate
        Me.CustomerID = CustomerId
        Me.EmployeeID = EmployeeId
    End Sub
```

As previously stated, structures can expose methods and fields but also shared members. Consider the following new implementation of the structure:

```
Public Structure Order

    Private Shared orderCount As Integer

    Public Property OrderID As Integer
    Public Property OrderDate As Date
    Public Property ShippedDate As Date
    Public Property CustomerID As Integer
    Public Property EmployeeID As Integer

    Public Sub New(ByVal Id As Integer,
                   ByVal OrderDate As Date,
                   ByVal ShippedDate As Date,
                   ByVal CustomerId As Integer,
                   ByVal EmployeeId As Integer)

        Me.OrderID = Id
        Me.OrderDate = OrderDate
        Me.ShippedDate = ShippedDate
        Me.CustomerID = CustomerId
        Me.EmployeeID = EmployeeId

        orderCount += 1
    End Sub

    Public Shared Function Count() As Integer
        Return orderCount
    End Function
End Structure
```

As you can see, now a private shared field exists that provides a counter for the instances of the type. Moreover, a shared method named Count returns the number of instances of the structure. The following code snippet demonstrates how the method works:

```
Dim firstOrder As New Order(1, Date.Now, Date.Now, 1, 1)
Dim secondOrder As New Order(2, Date.Now, Date.Now, 1, 1)
'Returns 2
Console.WriteLine(Order.Count)
```

The preceding code returns 2 because there are two active instances of the structure. Notice that the code would not work if you initialized the structure using object initializers because the `orderCount` field is incremented in the parameterized constructor.

Assigning Structures to Variables

Because structures are value types, assigning an instance of a structure to a variable declared as of that type creates a full copy of the data. The following brief code demonstrates this:

```
'Creates a real copy of firstOrder
Dim thirdOrder As Order
thirdOrder = firstOrder
```

In the preceding code, `thirdOrder` is a full copy of `firstOrder`. You can easily check this by using the data tips feature of the Visual Studio Debugger or adding the variable to a Watch window.

Passing Structures to Methods

Structures can be passed to methods as arguments. For example, consider the following method that simulates an order process taking an instance of the previously shown `Order` structure:

```
Private Sub ShowOrderInfo(ByVal orderInstance As Order)
    Console.WriteLine("Order info:")
    Console.WriteLine("ID: {0}, Date received: {1}",
                    orderInstance.OrderID,
                    orderInstance.OrderDate)
    Console.ReadLine()
End Sub
```

You can then invoke the method, passing the desired instance as follows:

```
Dim firstOrder As New Order(1, Date.Now, Date.Now, 1, 1)
ShowOrderInfo(firstOrder)
```

The preceding code produces an output that looks like this:

```
ID: 1, Date received: 05/30/2012 22:44:11
```

Members' Visibility

Structures' members require you to specify a scope qualifier. Structures accept only the `Private`, `Public`, and `Friend` qualifiers. If no qualifier is specified, `Public` is provided by default. Only fields can be declared using the `Dim` keyword, and they are equivalent to `Public`. The following line demonstrates this:

```
Public Structure Order
'Means Public:
    Dim orderCount As Integer
```

Inheritance Limitations and Interface Implementation

As for other built-in value types, structures implicitly inherit from the `System.ValueType` type that inherits from `System.Object`. This is the only inheritance level allowed for structures. This means that, different from reference types (classes), structures can neither inherit nor derive from other structures. Therefore, the `Inherits` keyword is not allowed within structures. Because structures derive from `System.Object`, they inherit only from classes such as the `Equals`, `GetHashCode`, and `ToString` methods that can also be overridden within structures. Chapter 12, "Inheritance," provides detailed information on inheritance and overriding. Structures can instead implement interfaces; therefore, the `Implements` keyword is enabled. Chapter 13, "Interfaces," discusses interfaces.

Memory Allocation

Structures are value types. This means they are allocated in the stack. Such behavior provides great efficiency to structures because when they are no longer necessary, the Common Language Runtime (CLR) removes them from the Stack and avoids the need of invoking the garbage collector as happens for reference types. But this is just a general rule. Structures' members can expose any kind of .NET type and therefore reference types, too. The following revisited implementation of the `Order` structure provides an example, exposing an `OrderDescription` property of type `String` that is a reference type:

```
Public Structure Order

    Public Property OrderID As Integer
    Public Property OrderDate As Date
    Public Property ShippedDate As Date
    Public Property CustomerID As Integer
    Public Property EmployeeID As Integer


    Public Property OrderDescription As String
End Structure
```

In this scenario, the garbage collection process is invoked to free up memory space when the `OrderDescription` is released and causes an increase in performance overhead. With that said, value types are faster and more efficient than reference types only if they do not expose members that are reference types. Another important consideration is that when you pass or assign a structure to a method or variable, the actual value and data of the structure are passed (or copied in assignments) unless you pass the structure to a method by reference. If the data you want to represent is large, you should consider reference types.

Organizing Structures

You can optimize structures' efficiency with a little bit of work. This work is related to the order in which you implement members within a structure. For example, consider the following code:

```
Public Structure VariousMembers
    Public Property anInteger As Integer
    Public Property aByte As Byte
    Public Property aShort As Short
End Structure
```

Notice in which order the members are exposed. Because of their memory allocation in bytes, it's preferable to expose members in the order of bytes they require. This is a revisited, more efficient version of the structure:

```
Public Structure VariousMembers
    Public Property aByte As Byte
    Public Property aShort As Short
    Public Property anInteger As Integer
End Structure
```

If you are in doubt, don't worry. The .NET Framework offers an interesting attribute named StructLayout, exposed by the System.Runtime.InteropServices namespaces, which tells the compiler to organize a structure in the most appropriate way and that you can use as follows:

```
'Requires
'Imports System.Runtime.InteropServices
<StructLayout(LayoutKind.Auto)>
Public Structure VariousMembers
    Public Property aByte As Byte
    Public Property aShort As Short
    Public Property anInteger As Integer
End Structure
```

IMPORTANT NOTE

Remember that if you use the StructLayout attribute, you cannot pass your structure to unmanaged code such as Windows APIs. If you try, the compiler throws an exception. This is because the Windows APIs expect members to be presented in a predefined order and not reorganized at compile time.

Overloading Operators

In Chapter 4 you learned about operators offered by the Visual Basic grammar. Although Visual Basic does not enable creating new custom operators, it offers the possibility of *overloading* existing operators. In other words, you have the ability to extend existing operators with custom versions. You might wonder when and why this could be necessary. You get an answer to this question with the following code. Consider the simple structure that represents a three-dimensional coordinate:

```
Public Structure ThreePoint

    Public Property X As Integer
    Public Property Y As Integer
    Public Property Z As Integer

    Public Sub New(ByVal valueX As Integer, ByVal valueY As Integer,
                   ByVal valueZ As Integer)
        Me.X = valueX
        Me.Y = valueY
        Me.Z = valueZ
    End Sub
End Structure
```

Now imagine that, for any reason, you want to sum two instances of the structure using the + operator. If you try to write the following code

```
'Won't compile, throws an error
Dim result As ThreePoint = t1 + t2
```

the Visual Basic compiler throws an error saying that the + operator is not defined for the ThreePoint structure. You should begin understanding why operator overloading can be a good friend. The same situation is for other operators. In Visual Basic, you overload operators using a `Public Shared Operator` statement within your type definition. The following code overloads the + and - operators:

```
Public Shared Operator +(ByVal firstValue As ThreePoint,
                         ByVal secondValue As ThreePoint) As ThreePoint
    Return New ThreePoint With {.X = firstValue.X + secondValue.X,
                                .Y = firstValue.Y + secondValue.Y,
                                .Z = firstValue.Z + secondValue.Z}
End Operator

Public Shared Operator -(ByVal firstValue As ThreePoint,
                         ByVal secondValue As ThreePoint) As ThreePoint
    Return New ThreePoint With {.X = firstValue.X - secondValue.X,
                                .Y = firstValue.Y - secondValue.Y,
                                .Z = firstValue.Z - secondValue.Z}
End Operator
```

Of course, this is just an example, and you might want to perform different calculations. Both overloads return a ThreePoint structure whose members have been populated with the sum and the difference between the x, Y, and z properties, respectively, from both initial instances. When overloading operators, you need to remember that some of them require you to also overload the negation counterpart. For example, the equality = operator cannot be overloaded alone but requires the overloading of the inequality <> operator. You will be informed by the Visual Basic background compiler when an operator can't be overloaded alone. The following code shows an overloading example of equality and inequality operators for the ThreePoint structure:

```
Public Shared Operator =(ByVal firstValue As ThreePoint,
                         ByVal secondValue As ThreePoint) As Boolean
    Return (firstValue.X = secondValue.X) _
           AndAlso (firstValue.Y = secondValue.Y) _
           AndAlso (firstValue.Z = secondValue.Z)
End Operator


Public Shared Operator <>(ByVal firstValue As ThreePoint,
                          ByVal secondValue As ThreePoint) As Boolean
    Return (firstValue.X <> secondValue.X) _
           OrElse (firstValue.Y <> secondValue.Y) _
           OrElse (firstValue.Z <> secondValue.Z)
End Operator
```

IntelliSense can help you understand which operators can be overloaded. For your convenience, a list of operators that can be overloaded is provided in Table 11.1.

TABLE 11.1   Operators That Can Be Overloaded

Operator	Type
+	Unary/Binary
-	Unary/Binary
Not	Unary
IsTrue	Unary
IsFalse	Unary
*	Binary
/	Binary
\	Binary
&	Binary
^	Binary
Mod	Binary
Like	Binary
CType	Unary
=	Logical
<>	Logical

Operator	Type
>, >=	Logical
<, =<	Logical
And/Or/Xor	Logical
<<	Shift
>>	Shift

OPERATORS CONTEXT

Overloading operators is discussed in this chapter because operators such as sum and subtraction make more sense with value types. However, this technique is also allowed with classes—for example, for comparison operators. You can certainly overload operators within reference types, too.

Overloading CType

The CType operator also can be overloaded to provide appropriate mechanisms for converting to and from a custom type. The interesting thing in overloading CType is that you have to consider both situations studied in Chapter 4, known as *widening* and *narrowing* conversions (see that topic for further details). Continuing the previous example of the ThreePoint structure, the following code snippet offers a special implementation of CType, enabling conversions to and from an array of integers:

```
'From ThreePoint to Array of Integer
Public Shared Narrowing Operator CType(ByVal instance As ThreePoint) _
                                As Integer()

    Return New Integer() {instance.X,
                          instance.Y,
                          instance.Z}
End Operator


'From Integer() to ThreePoint
Public Shared Widening Operator CType(ByVal instance As Integer()) _
                                As ThreePoint

    If instance.Count < 3 Then
        Throw New ArgumentException("Array is out of bounds",
                                    "instance")
    Else
        Return New ThreePoint With {.X = instance(0),
                                    .Y = instance(1),
                                    .Z = instance(2)}

    End If
End Operator
```

The code is quite simple. Notice how you must specify a keyword corresponding to the effective kind of conversion (Widening and Narrowing) and how, within the Widening definition, the code performs a basic validation ensuring that the array of integers contains at least three items.

CType CONVENTIONS

As a convention, your type should implement an overload of CType that converts from a String into the custom type. Such conversion should also be offered implementing two methods conventionally named as Parse and TryParse that you saw in action in Chapter 4 with several primitive types.

Structures and Common Language Specification

The Common Language Specification (CLS) has established specific rules for structures. If you want your structure to be CLS-compliant, you need to overload the equality and inequality operators and redefine the behavior of the Equals and GetHashCode methods inherited from Object. Listing 11.1 shows an example of a CLS-compliant structure.

LISTING 11.1   Building a CLS-compliant Structure

```
<CLSCompliant(True)>
Public Structure CLSCompliantStructure

    Public Shared Operator =(ByVal obj1 As CLSCompliantStructure,
                            ByVal obj2 As CLSCompliantStructure) As Boolean
        Return obj1.Equals(obj2)
    End Operator

    Public Shared Operator <>(ByVal obj1 As CLSCompliantStructure,
                            ByVal obj2 As CLSCompliantStructure) As Boolean
        Return Not obj1.Equals(obj2)
    End Operator

    Public Overrides Function Equals(ByVal obj As Object) As Boolean
        Return Object.Equals(Me, obj)
    End Function

    Public Overrides Function GetHashCode() As Integer
        Return Me.GetHashCode
    End Function
End Structure
```

If you are not already familiar with overriding, you can read the next chapter and then take a look back at the preceding code.

Enumerations

Enumerations are another kind of value type available in the .NET Framework. They represent a group of constants enclosed within an `Enum..End Enum` code block. An enumeration derives from `System.Enum`, which derives from `System.ValueType`. The following is an example of enumeration:

```
'These are all Integers
Public Enum Sports
     Biking        '0
     Climbing      '1
     Swimming      '2
     Running       '3
     Skiing        '4
End Enum
```

By default, enumerations are sets of integer values. The preceding code defines a `Sports` enumeration of type `Integer`, which stores a set of integer constants. The Visual Basic compiler can also automatically assign an integer value to each member within an enumeration, starting from zero, as indicated in comments. You can eventually manually assign custom values, but you should avoid this when possible because the standard behavior ensures that other types can use your enumeration with no errors. The following code shows how you can change the result type of an enumeration instead:

```
Public Enum LongSports As Long
     Biking
     Climbing
     'and so on...
End Enum
```

IntelliSense can help you understand that enumerations support only numeric types, such as `Byte`, `Short`, `Integer`, `Long`, `UShort`, `UInteger`, `ULong`, and `SByte`. Notice that enumerations can be made of mixed numeric data types if assigned with values of different numeric types.

WRITING ENUMERATIONS

Enumerations are easy to use and fast to implement. They are essentially read-only groups of read-only constants. Because of this, use them when you are sure that those values need no modifications; otherwise, consider implementing a structure instead.

Using Enumerations

You use enumerations as any other .NET type. For example, consider the following method that receives the `Sports` enumeration as an argument and returns a response depending on which value has been passed:

```
Private Sub AnalyzeSports(ByVal sportsList As Sports)
    Select Case sportsList
        Case Is = Sports.Biking
            Console.WriteLine("So, do you really like biking my friend?")
        Case Is = Sports.Climbing
            Console.WriteLine("I do not like climbing like you!")
        Case Else
            Console.WriteLine("Every sport is good!")
    End Select
End Sub
```

The following code snippet then declares a variable of type Sports, assigns a value, and then invokes the method by passing the variable:

```
Dim mySport As Sports = Sports.Climbing
AnalyzeSports(mySport)
```

Notice how IntelliSense comes in when you need to specify a value whose type is an enumeration. Figure 11.1 shows the IntelliSense pop-up window related to our custom enumeration.

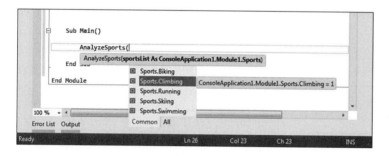

FIGURE 11.1   IntelliSense provides flexibility in choosing and assigning enumerations.

Useful Methods from System.Enum

As mentioned at the beginning of this section, all enumerations derive from the System. Enum class. Such a type exposes some shared methods that enable performing operations on enumerations. This subsection explains how you can take advantage of methods for working on enumerations.

GetValues and GetNames

The first two methods described are GetValues and GetNames. Both enable retrieving an array of items stored within an enumeration, but GetValues gets an array of integers corresponding to the numeric values of enumerations' items, whereas GetNames retrieves an array of strings storing the names of the enumerations' items. Continuing the example of the Sports enumeration, consider the following code:

```
For Each item As Integer In System.Enum.GetValues(GetType(Sports))
    Console.WriteLine(item)
Next
```

This code's output is the following list:

```
0
1
2
3
4
```

GetNames works similarly except that it returns an array of strings:

```
For Each item As String In System.Enum.GetNames(GetType(Sports))
    Console.WriteLine(item)
Next
```

And this code produces the following output:

```
Biking
Climbing
Swimming
Running
Skiing
```

Notice how both methods require a System.Type argument instead of a System.Enum; therefore, you must invoke the GetType operator. Another interesting thing about the syntax is that the System.Enum class full name for invoking its methods is used here because the Enum class is exposed by the System namespace that is always imported at project level. Technically, you could just write invocations as follows: Enum.GetNames. But this is not allowed in Visual Basic because of conflicts with the Enum reserved keyword. To use the simplified syntax, you can enclose the Enum work within square brackets as follows:

```
[Enum].GetNames(GetType(Sports))
```

The Visual Basic compiler enables this syntax perfectly equivalent to the previous one. Notice that the IDE will add the square brackets for you when typing Enum. Now, let's discover other useful methods.

GetName

GetName works similarly to GetNames, except that it returns just a single name for a constant. Consider the following code:

```
'Returns Climbing
Console.WriteLine(System.Enum.GetName(GetType(Sports), 1))
```

You need to pass the type instance and the value in the enumeration whose name you want to retrieve.

IsDefined

`IsDefined` checks whether the specified constant exists within an enumeration and returns a Boolean value. The following code looks first for an existing value and then for a nonexisting one:

```
'Returns True
Console.WriteLine(System.Enum.IsDefined(GetType(Sports), "Climbing"))
'Returns False
Console.WriteLine(System.Enum.IsDefined(GetType(Sports), "Soccer"))
```

ToString and Parse

`System.Enum` also provides two methods for converting to and from string. The `ToString` method is inherited from `System.Object` and is redefined so that it can provide a string representation of the specified value. Consider the following code snippet:

```
'Sports.Climbing
Dim mySport As Sports = CType(1, Sports)
Console.WriteLine(mySport.ToString)
```

Such code returns `Climbing`, which is the string representation of the specified constant value. Also notice how, if `Option Strict` is `On`, you must explicitly convert the value into a `Sports` enumeration using `CType`. `Parse` is the opposite of `ToString` and gets the corresponding numeric value within an enumeration depending on the specified string. The following code provides an example:

```
Console.WriteLine("Enter your favorite sport:")
Dim sport As String = Console.ReadLine
Dim result As Sports = CType(System.Enum.Parse(GetType(Sports),
                       sport, True), Sports)
'Returns 2
Console.WriteLine("The constant in the enumeration for {0} is {1}",
               sport.ToString, CInt(result))
Console.ReadLine()
```

The previous code requires the input from the user, who has to enter a sport name. Using `Parse`, the code obtains the element in the enumeration corresponding to the entered string. For example, if you enter `Swimming`, the code produces the following output:

```
The constant in the enumeration for Swimming is 2
```

Notice how `Parse` can receive a third argument of type Boolean that enables specifying if the string comparison must ignore casing.

ASSIGNING ENUMS TO INTEGERS

You can assign an enumeration variable to an `Integer` type without a conversion operator.

Using Enums As Return Values from Methods

A common usage of enumerations is representing different results from methods that return a numeric value, as often happens for methods that return a number for communicating the result of the code. Consider the following code, which defines an enumeration that a method uses to communicate the result of a simple elaboration on a file:

```
Public Enum Result
    Success = 0
    Failed = 1
    FileNotFound = 2
End Enum


Public Function ElaborateFile(ByVal fileName As String) As Result
    Try
        Dim text As String = My.Computer.FileSystem.ReadAllText(fileName)

        'Do some work here on your string

        Return Result.Success

    Catch ex As IO.FileNotFoundException
        Return Result.FileNotFound
    Catch ex As Exception
        Return Result.Failed
    End Try
End Function
```

Each `Return` statement returns an `Integer` value from 0 to 2 depending on the method result, but using an enumeration provides a more convenient way for understanding the result, as demonstrated in the following code:

```
Sub OpenFile()
    Dim res As Result = ElaborateFile("myfile.txt")
    'Success = 0
    If res = Result.Success Then
        Console.WriteLine("Success")
        'FileNotFound = 2
    ElseIf res = Result.FileNotFound Then
        Console.WriteLine("File not found")
        'Failed = 1
```

```
    ElseIf res = Result.Failed Then
        Console.WriteLine("The elaboration failed")
    End If
End Sub
```

Enum Values As Bit Flags

Enumerations can be designed for supporting bitwise operations by marking them with the Flags attribute. This allows combining enumeration values with bitwise operators such as OR. Consider the following implementation of the Sports enumeration that was described previously:

```
<Flags>
Public Enum Sports
    Biking
    Climbing
    Swimming
    Running
    Skiing
End Enum
```

By applying the Flags attribute, the values for each enumeration value now become bitflag patterns that have a binary representation such as the following:

```
00000000
00000001
00000010
00000100
00001000
```

Combining all values with the OR operator will result in a 11111111 binary value. For example, you could perform an evaluation like the following:

```
'sportsTest is 0000010
Dim sportsTest As Sports =
    Sports.Biking And Sports.Climbing Or Sports.Swimming
```

This kind of approach is useful when you want to be able to perform bitwise operations and comparisons.

Enumerations and Common Language Specification

When introducing enumerations, you learned that they support only numeric types. There is another limitation if you plan to implement CLS-compliant enumerations. Only CLS-compliant types can characterize CLS-compliant enumerations; therefore, the SByte, UShort, UInteger, and ULong types cannot be used within CLS-compliant enumerations. Another important consideration is that CLS-compliant enumerations must be decorated with the Flag attribute. The following is an example of a CLS-compliant enumeration:

```
<Flags()> Public Enum ClsCompliantEnum As Byte
    FirstValue = 0
    SecondValue = 1
    ThirdValue = 2
End Enum
```

NOTE

The `Flag` attribute indicates to the compiler that an enumeration has to be considered as a bit field.

Summary

In this chapter you saw another important part of .NET development with Visual Basic, which is related to creating custom value types. Structures are the .NET way of building custom value types and can expose methods, properties, and fields. There are several similarities with classes, but structures are value types allocated in the Stack and cannot inherit or derive from other structures but can implement interfaces. Because of their nature, structures are susceptible to operations. This requires, in certain situations, the need for specific operators. The .NET Framework enables overloading operators to provide custom implementations of unary, binary, and logical operators—a technique that is allowed for classes. Another kind of value types is enumeration, which represent a group of read-only constants and that are optimized for `Integer` values, offering several shared methods for performing operations on constants composing the enumeration. An overview of how Common Language Specification rules the implementation of structures and enumerations completed the chapter.

CHAPTER 12

Inheritance

Inheritance is the feature that enables you to design classes that *derive* from simpler classes, known as *base classes*. Derived classes implement members defined within the base class and have the possibility of defining new members or of redefining inherited members. Members that a derived class inherits from the base one can be methods, properties, and fields, but such members must have `Public`, `Protected`, `Friend`, or `Protected Friend` scope. (See Chapter 7, "Class Fundamentals," for details about scopes.) In .NET development, inheritance represents a typical *"is-a"* relationship. For a better understanding, let's consider real life. When you say "person," you identify a general individual. Every one of us is a person, with a first name and a last name. But a person also has a gender, either man or woman. In such a situation, a single person is the base class and a woman is a derived class because it inherits the name and last name attributes from the person but also offers a gender attribute. But this is only the first layer. Each man and each woman can have a job, and jobs are made of roles. So a woman can be employed by a company; therefore, as an employee she will have an identification number, a phone number, and an office room number. In this representation there is a deeper inheritance; because a person can be compared to a base class, a woman can be compared to an intermediate base class (also deriving from the person), and the employee is the highest level in the inheritance hierarchy. If we want to go on, we could still define other roles, such as lawyer, program manager, law clerk, pharmacist, and so on. Each of these roles could be represented by a class that derives from the employee role. As you can see, this articulate representation is something that in a development environment such as the .NET Framework enables defining a complex but powerful framework of objects. In this chapter you get a complete overview of the inheritance features in .NET Framework with Visual Basic 2012, and you will learn how you can take advantage of inheritance for both building hierarchical frameworks of custom objects and more easily reusing your code.

Applying Inheritance

Before explaining how inheritance is applied in code, a graphical representation can be useful. Figure 12.1 shows how you can create robust hierarchies of custom objects with inheritance.

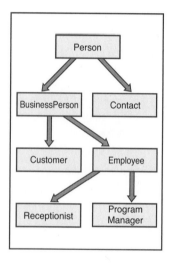

FIGURE 12.1   A graphical representation of a custom framework of objects using inheritance.

You derive a class from a base class using the `Inherits` keyword. For example, consider the following implementation of the `Person` class that exposes some basic properties:

```
Public Class Person

    Public Property FirstName As String
    Public Property LastName As String

    'A simplified implementation
    Public Function FullName() As String
        If FirstName = "" And LastName = "" Then
          Throw New _
          InvalidOperationException("Both FirstName and LastName are empty")
```

```
      Else
           Return String.Concat(FirstName, " ", LastName)
      End If
   End Function
End Class
```

Inherits System.Object

In the .NET Framework development, every class inherits from `System.Object`. Due to this, there is no need to add an inherits directive each time you implement a custom type because the Visual Basic compiler will do this for you behind the scenes.

The class also offers a `FullName` method that returns the concatenation of the two `FirstName` and `LastName` properties, providing a simplified and basic validation that is here for demonstration purposes. Now we can design a new class that inherits from `Person`, and in this scenario `Person` is the *base class*. The new class is named `Contact` and represents a personal contact in our everyday life:

```
Public Class Contact
    Inherits Person

    Public Property Email As String
    Public Property Phone As String
    Public Property BirthDate As Date
    Public Property Address As String

End Class
```

`Contact` is the *derived class*. It receives all public members from `Person` (in this example both the `FirstName` and `LastName` properties and the `FullName` method) and provides implementation of custom members. This is a typical application of .NET inheritance, in which one derived class inherits from the base class. The .NET Framework does not enable inheriting from multiple classes. You can create a derived class from only a base class. But in some situations multiple levels of inheritance would be required. Continuing the example of the `Person` class, you will meet several kinds of people in your life, such as customers, employees of your company, and personal contacts. All these people will have common properties, such as the first name and the last name; therefore, the `Person` class can be the base class for each of them, providing a common infrastructure that can then be inherited and customized. But if you consider a customer and an employee, both people will have other common properties, such as a title, a business phone number, and an email address. They will differ in the end because of the proper characteristics of their roles. For this purpose, you can implement intermediate classes that are derived classes from a first base class and base classes for other and more specific ones. For example, you could implement an intermediate infrastructure for both customers and employees. The following code snippet provides a class named BusinessPerson that inherits from Person:

```
Public Class BusinessPerson
    Inherits Person

    Public Property Email As String
    Public Property Title As String
    Public Property BusinessPhone As String

End Class
```

This class inherits the FirstName and LastName properties from Person (other than methods such as ToString and other public methods exposed by System.Object) and exposes other common properties for classes with a different scope. For example, both a customer and an employee would need the preceding properties, but each of them needs its own properties. Because of this, the BusinessPerson class is the intermediate derived class in the hierarchic framework of inheritance. Now consider the following classes, Customer and Employee:

```
Public Class Customer
    Inherits BusinessPerson

    Public Property CustomerID As Integer
    Public Property CompanyName As String
    Public Property Address As String
    Public Property ContactPerson As String

End Class

Public Class Employee
    Inherits BusinessPerson

    Public Property EmployeeID As Integer
    Public Property HomePhone As String
    Public Property MobilePhone As String
    Public Property HireDate As Date

End Class
```

Both classes receive the public properties from BusinessPerson, and both implement their custom properties according to the particular person they intend to represent. We can summarize the situation as follows:

`Customer` exposes the following properties:

- ▶ `FirstName` and `LastName`, provided at a higher level by `Person`

- ▶ `Email`, `Title`, and `BusinessPhone` provided by `BusinessPerson`

- ▶ `CustomerID`, `CompanyName`, `Address`, and `ContactPerson` provided by its implementation

`Employee` exposes the following properties:

- ▶ `FirstName` and `LastName`, provided at a higher level by `Person`

- ▶ `Email`, `Title`, and `BusinessPhone` provided by `BusinessPerson`

- ▶ `EmployeeID`, `HomePhone`, `MobilePhone`, and `HireDate` provided by its implementation

At a higher level, we also exposed a method named `FullName`, which has public visibility, so this method is also visible from derived classes.

MEMBERS' SCOPE AND INHERITANCE

Remember that only the `Public`, `Protected`, `Friend`, and `Protected Friend` members can be inherited within derived classes.

When available, you can use derived classes the same way as you would do with any other class, even if you do not know at all that a class derives from another one. The following, simple code demonstrates this:

```
'Employee inherits from BusinessPerson
'which inherits from Person
Dim emp As New Employee With {.EmployeeID = 1,
    .Title = "Dr.",
    .LastName = "Del Sole",
    .FirstName = "Alessandro",
    .Email = "alessandro.delsole@visual-basic.it",
    .BusinessPhone = "000-000-000000",
    .HomePhone = "000-000-000000",
    .MobilePhone = "000-000-000000",
    .HireDate = New Date(5 / 30 / 2012)}
```

Until now, you've seen only properties in an inheritance demonstration. Methods are also influenced by inheritance and by interesting features that make them powerful.

INHERITANCE AND COMMON LANGUAGE SPECIFICATION

The Common Language Specification (CLS) establishes that a CLS-compliant class must inherit only from another CLS-compliant class; otherwise, it will not be CLS-compliant.

Illustrating `System.Object` in Detail

As you should remember from Chapter 4, "Data Types and Expressions," in.NET development all types implicitly derive from `System.Object`, considering both reference and value types. Because of the inheritance relationship, custom types also inherit some methods, so you have to know them. Table 12.1 summarizes inherited methods.

TABLE 12.1   `System.Object` Methods

Member	Description
Finalize	Performs cleanup operations; already described in Chapter 8, "Managing an Object's Lifetime"
GetType	Returns the `System.Type` object related to the instance of the class
GetHashCode	Returns the hash code for the current instance
New	Creates an instance of the class
Equals	Checks for equality between instances of the class
MemberwiseClone	Provides a shallow copy of a class instance
ReferenceEquals	Checks whether the two specified instances are the same instance
ToString	Provides a string representation of the current object

You need to understand which members are exposed by `System.Object` because they will all be inherited by your custom classes and by all built-in classes in the .NET Framework. I already discussed `GetType` and `Finalize` methods in Chapter 4 and Chapter 8, respectively. Such methods are inherited by all .NET types. The `GetHashCode` method returns the hash that is assigned at runtime by the CLR to a class instance. The following code provides an example:

```
Dim p As New Object

Dim hashCode As Integer = p.GetHashCode
Console.WriteLine(hashCode.ToString)
```

On my machine the code produces the following result: `33156464`. This is useful to uniquely identify a class's instance. `New` is the constructor, as described in Chapter 7. When creating custom classes, a constructor is inherited and implicitly defined within classes and constitutes the default constructor. `Object` also exposes two shared members—`Equals` and `ReferenceEquals`—which return a Boolean value. It's worth mentioning that shared methods are also inherited by derived classes, but they cannot be overridden (as better described in next section). For example, the following code establishes whether both specified objects are considered the same instance:

```
'Two different instances
Dim firstObject As New Object
Dim secondObject As New Object
```

```
'Returns False
Dim test As Boolean = Object.ReferenceEquals(firstObject, secondObject)
```

Next, the code instead checks whether two instances are considered equal by the compiler:

```
'Returns False
Dim test As Boolean = Object.Equals(firstObject, secondObject)
```

There is also an overload of the Equals method that is instead an instance method. The following code shows an example of instance comparisons using Equals:

```
'Returns False
Console.WriteLine(firstObject.Equals(secondObject))
'Copies the reference to the instance
Dim testObject As Object = firstObject
'Returns True
Console.WriteLine(testObject.Equals(firstObject))
```

For assignments, you can always assign any type to an Object instance, as demonstrated here:

```
Dim aPerson As New Person
Dim anObject As Object = aPerson
```

Because Object is the mother of all classes, it can receive any assignment. The last method in System.Object (that you will often use) is ToString. This method provides a string representation of the object. Because System.Object is the root in the class hierarchy, this method just returns the pure name of the class. Therefore, the following line of code returns System.Object:

```
Console.WriteLine(firstObject.ToString)
```

But this is not appropriate for value types, in which you need a string representation of a number, or for custom classes, in which you need a custom representation. Taking the example of the famous Person class, it would be more useful to get a string composed by the last name and the first name instead of the name of the class. Fortunately, the .NET Framework inheritance mechanism provides the capability to change the behavior of inherited members as it is exposed by base classes; this is known as *overriding*.

Introducing Polymorphism

Polymorphism is another key concept in object-oriented programming (OOP). As its name implies, polymorphism enables an object to assume different forms. In .NET development, it means you can treat an object as another one, due to the implementation of common members. A first form of polymorphism is when you assign base classes with derived classes. For example, both `Contact` and `Customer` classes are derived of the `Person` class. Now consider the following code:

```
Dim c As New Contact
Dim cs As New Customer

'C is of type Contact
Dim p As Person = c
```

The new instance of the `Person` class receives an assignment from an instance of the `Contact` class. This is always possible because `Person` is the parent of `Contact` (in which base is the parent of derived). Therefore, you might also have the following assignment:

```
'Cs is of type Customer
Dim p As Person = cs
```

In this scenario, `Person` is polymorphic in that it can "impersonate" multiple classes that derive from itself.

RETRIEVING THE ACTUAL TYPE

Use the `TypeOf` operator, discussed in Chapter 4, to check whether the polymorphic base class is representing a derived one.

Polymorphism is useful when you need to work with different kinds of objects using one common infrastructure that works the same way with all of them. Now let's continue with the preceding example. The `Person` class exposes the usual `FirstName` and `LastName` properties also common to `Contact` and `Customer`. At this point, you can remember how our previous implementations of the `Person` class offered a method named `FullName` that returns the concatenation of both the `LastName` and `FirstName` properties. For the current discussion, consider the following simplified version of the `FullName` method, as part of the `Person` class:

```
Public Function FullName() As String
    Return String.Concat(FirstName, " ", LastName)
End Function
```

All classes deriving from `Person` inherit this method. All deriving classes do need a method of this kind for representing the full name of a person, but they would need different implementations. For example, the full name for a customer should include the company name, whereas the full name for a personal contact should include the title. This means that all classes deriving from `Person` will still need the `FullName` method (which is part of the commonalities mentioned at the beginning of this section) but with a custom implementation fitting the particular need. For this, the .NET Framework enables realizing polymorphism by *overriding* members, as the next section describes.

NOTE ON POLYMORPHISM

Overriding is the most important part of polymorphism in .NET development, but interfaces also play a role. Chapter 13, "Interfaces," explains how interfaces complete polymorphism.

Overriding Members

When a class derives from another one, it inherits members and the members behave as they are defined in the base class. (For this purpose, remember the scope.) As for other .NET languages, Visual Basic enables redefining inherited methods and properties so that you can change their behavior. This technique is known as *overriding* and requires a little work on both the base class and the derived class. If you want to provide the ability of overriding a member, in the base class you have to mark the member as Overridable. Let's continue the example of the Person class, defined as follows:

```
Public Class Person

    Public Property FirstName As String
    Public Property LastName As String

    'Simplified version, with no validation
    Public Function FullName() As String
        Return String.Concat(LastName, " ",
                        FirstName)
    End Function

End Class
```

The goal is providing derived classes the capability of overriding the FullName method so that they can provide a custom and more appropriate version. The method definition must be rewritten as follows:

```
Public Overridable Function FullName() As String
```

At this point, we could provide a simplified version of the Contact class, inheriting from Person. Such implementation will override the FullName method to provide a custom result. Let's begin with the following code:

```
Public Class Contact
    Inherits Person

    Public Property Email As String

    Public Overrides Function FullName() As String
        'By default returns the base class'
        'implementation
```

```
        Return MyBase.FullName()
    End Function
End Class
```

Two things are important here. First, the `Overrides` keyword enables you to redefine the behavior of a member that has been marked as Overridable in the base class. Second, Visual Studio automatically provides an implementation that is the behavior established in the base class, due to the `MyBase` keyword, which is discussed later. IntelliSense is powerful in this situation, too, because when you type the `Overrides` keyword, it shows all overridable members, making it easier to choose what you have to override (see Figure 12.2).

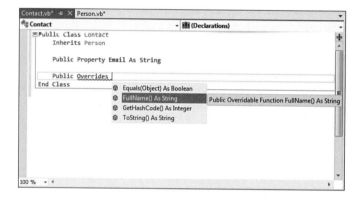

FIGURE 12.2   IntelliSense helps you choose overridable members.

Figure 12.2 can also help you understand which members from `System.Object` are overridable. The instance overload of `Equals`, `GetHashCode`, and `ToString` are methods you can redefine. You cannot instead override (neither mark as `Overridable`) shared members, and this is demonstrated by the fact that the shared overload of `Equals` and `ReferenceEquals` are not available in the IntelliSense pop-up window. At this point, we could provide a new implementation of the `FullName` method specific for the `Contact` class:

```
Public Overrides Function FullName() As String
    'A simplified implementation
    'with no validation
    Dim result As New Text.StringBuilder
    result.Append(Me.FirstName)
    result.Append(" ")
    result.Append(Me.LastName)
    result.Append(", Email:")
    result.Append(Me.Email)

    Return result.ToString
End Function
```

Now you can create a new instance of the `Contact` class and invoke the `FullName` method to understand how overriding changed its behavior:

```
Dim testContact As New Contact With _
    {.FirstName = "Alessandro",
     .LastName = "Del Sole",
     .Email = "Alessandro.delsole@visual-basic.it"}
Console.WriteLine(testContact.FullName)
```

The preceding code produces the following result:

```
Alessandro Del Sole, Email:Alessandro.delsole@visual-basic.it
```

Such a result is, of course, more meaningful if related to the specific kind of class. Another common situation is redefining the behavior of the `ToString` method that is inherited from `Object` and that is marked as `Overridable`. For example, in the `Contact` class we could override `ToString` as follows:

```
Public Overrides Function ToString() As String
    Dim result As New Text.StringBuilder
    result.Append(Me.FirstName)
    result.Append(" ")
    result.Append(Me.LastName)
    result.Append(", Email:")
    result.Append(Me.Email)

    Return result.ToString

End Function
```

We can then invoke this method as follows:

```
Console.WriteLine(testContact.ToString)
```

Typically, overriding `ToString` is more appropriate if you need to return a string representation of a class, as in the preceding example. The `FullName` method is just an example of how you can override a custom method that is defined in a base class and that is not inherited from `System.Object`.

OVERRIDDEN IS OVERRIDABLE

When a member is overridden using the `Overrides` keyword, the member is also implicitly `Overridable`. Because of this, you cannot use the `Overridable` keyword on a member marked with `Overrides`; the compiler would throw an error message, requiring you to remove the `Overridable` keyword.

NotOverridable Keyword

You can mark an overridden method or property as NotOverridable so that derived classes cannot override them again. The NotOverridable keyword cannot be used versus methods or properties that do not override a base member. Continuing the example of the Contact class previously defined, the NotOverridable keyword can be used as follows:

```
Public NotOverridable Overrides Function FullName() As String
    Return String.Concat(MyBase.FullName(), ": ", Email)
End Function
```

In this way the FullName method within the Contact class overrides the base class, but derived classes cannot override it again. NotOverridable is used only within derived classes that override the base class's members because in a base class the default behavior for members is that they cannot be overridden unless you explicitly mark them as Overridable.

Overloading Derived Members

You can use the overloading technique described in Chapter 7 within derived classes, with a few differences. You saw in Chapter 7 how overloaded members must not be marked with the Overloads keyword within a class. Instead, a derived class using the Overloads keyword is mandatory if you implement a new overload of a member with a different signature. The following code provides an example of overloading the FullName method within the Contact class you previously saw:

```
Public Overloads Function FullName(ByVal Age As Integer)
    Return MyBase.FullName & " of age: " & Age.ToString
End Function
```

If another signature of the member is available within the derived class, the Overloads keyword is required; otherwise, the compiler throws a warning message saying that another signature is declared as Overrides or Overloads. If, instead, no other signatures are available within the derived class, the Overloads keyword is required to prevent from shadowing the base class's member. Shadowing is discussed at the end of this chapter, in the section "Shadowing."

Conditioning Inheritance

Inheritance is an important feature in OOP with .NET. You might have situations in which inheritance is not a good option—for example, when you want to prevent others from accessing members in the base class. Or there could be custom frameworks implementations in which a high-level class should not be used directly, and therefore it should be always inherited. The Visual Basic language enables accomplishing both scenarios via special keywords, as discussed in the next section.

NotInheritable **Keyword**

There are situations in which you might want to prevent inheritance from your classes. This can be useful if you do not want a client to modify in any way the base object's behavior and its members. To accomplish this, you simply need to mark a class with the NotInheritable keyword. The following code shows an example of a class that cannot be derived:

```vb
Public NotInheritable Class BusinessPerson
    Inherits Person

    Public Property Email As String
    Public Property Title As String
    Public Property BusinessPhone As String
End Class
```

As you can see, the BusinessPerson class is marked as NotInheritable and cannot be derived by other classes. It can still inherit from other classes but, obviously, members cannot be marked as Overridable because they are not inheritable. Another typical example of classes that cannot be inheritable is when you have a class exposing only shared members, as shown in the following code:

```vb
<CLSCompliant(True)>
Public NotInheritable Class CompressionHelper

    Private Sub New()

    End Sub

    Public Shared Sub CompressFile(ByVal source As String,
                                   ByVal target As String)
        'Your code goes here
    End Sub

    Public Shared Sub DecompressFile(ByVal compressed As String,
                                     ByVal original As String)
        'Your code goes here
    End Sub
End Class
```

The class is also decorated with the CLSCompliant attribute because such a situation is explicitly established by the Common Language Specification. NotInheritable is the Visual Basic counterpart of the sealed keyword in Visual C#. It's important to know the C# representation because in .NET terminology not-inheritable classes are defined as sealed and many analysis tools use this last word. NotInheritable classes provide better performance; the compiler can optimize the usage of this type of classes, but you cannot blindly use classes that cannot be inherited only to avoid a small overhead. You should always design classes that fit your needs.

> **NOTE**
>
> As a better programming practice, developers should always mark classes with `NotInheritable` unless they explicitly plan for the class to be inheritable by a consuming class.

MustInherit and MustOverride **Keywords**

Inheritance is powerful because it enables building custom objects' frameworks. In this context, an object can represent the base infrastructure for different kinds of classes. We saw how the `Person` class is the base infrastructure for the `Customer`, `Employee`, and `Contact` derived classes. Because of its implementation, the `Person` class does nothing special. It has a generic behavior, and you will probably never create instances of that class; it is more likely that you will create instances of its derived classes. In this scenario, therefore, when you have a general-purpose base class that acts just as a basic infrastructure for derived classes, you can force a class to be inherited so it cannot be used directly. To accomplish this, Visual Basic provides the `MustInherit` keyword that states that a class will work only as a base class and cannot be used directly unless you create a derived class.

> **ABSTRACT CLASSES**
>
> In .NET terminology, classes marked as `MustInherit` are also known as *abstract* classes. This is important to remember because you will often encounter this term within the documentation and in several analysis tools.

The following code shows a new implementation of the `Person` class:

```
Public MustInherit Class Person

    Public Property FirstName As String
    Public Property LastName As String
End Class
```

Now you can derive classes only from `Person`. Another interesting feature is the capability to force members to be overridden. This can be accomplished using the `MustOverride` keyword on methods and properties. Continuing with the example of the `Person` class, we can rewrite the `FullName` method definition as follows:

```
Public MustOverride Function FullName() As String
```

When you mark a method with `MustOverride`, the method has no body. This makes sense because, if it must be redefined within a derived class, it would not be very helpful providing a base implementation. The same thing happens with properties, meaning that you will have only a declaration.

Inheriting from an Abstract Class

When you create a class that inherits from an abstract class (that is, marked as MustInherit), the only thing you need to pay particular attention to is overriding members. To help developers in such a scenario, the Visual Studio IDE automatically generates members' stubs for methods and properties marked as MustOverride in the base abstract class. So, if you create a new implementation of the Contact class, when you press **Enter** after typing the Inherits line of code, Visual Studio generates an empty stub for the FullName method as follows:

```
Public Class Contacts
    Inherits Person

    Public Overrides Function FullName() As String

    End Function
End Class
```

Now you can be sure that all MustOverride members have an implementation. In our example you might want to complete the code by adding the implementation shown in the "Overriding Members" section in this chapter.

Abstract Classes and Common Language Specification

The Common Language Specification contains a small rule regarding abstract classes. This rule establishes that to be CLS-compliant, members in abstract classes must explicitly be marked as CLSCompliant. The following code provides an example:

```
<CLSCompliant(True)>
Public MustInherit Class Person

    <CLSCompliant(True)> Public Property FirstName As String
    <CLSCompliant(True)> Public Property LastName As String

    <CLSCompliant(True)> Public MustOverride Function FullName() As String

End Class
```

Accessing Base Classes Members

Sometimes you need to access the base classes' members from derived classes. There are several reasons for doing this, so you need to know how. Visual Basic provides two special keywords for invoking base members, MyBase and MyClass. Both are discussed in this section.

MyBase Keyword

When you need to get a reference to the base class of the derived class you are working on, you can invoke the MyBase keyword. This keyword represents an instance of the base class and enables you to work on members as they are exposed by the base class, instead of the ones exposed by the derived class. Consider the following implementation of the Person class, in which a FullInformation method provides a representation of all the information supplied to the class:

```
Public Class Person

    Public Property FirstName As String
    Public Property LastName As String
    Public Property Age As Integer

    Public Overridable Function FullInformation() As String
        Dim info As New Text.StringBuilder

        info.Append("Name: ")
        info.Append(Me.FirstName)
        info.Append(" Last name: ")
        info.Append(Me.LastName)
        info.Append(" Age: ")
        info.Append(Me.Age.ToString)
        Return info.ToString
    End Function
End Class
```

Now we can create a new implementation of the Contact class, inheriting from Person. A new class needs to override the FullInformation method from the base class. When you type the Overrides keyword, Visual Studio generates a default implementation that looks like the following:

```
Public Overrides Function FullInformation() As String
    Return MyBase.FullInformation
End Function
```

The code returns the result offered by the FullInformation method as it is implemented in the base class, which is accomplished via the MyBase keyword. We can now rewrite the complete code for the Contact class as follows:

```
Public Class Contact
    Inherits Person

    Public Property Title As String

    Public Overrides Function FullInformation() As String
        Dim firstInfo As String = MyBase.FullInformation

        Dim newInfo As New Text.StringBuilder
        newInfo.Append(firstInfo)
```

```
        newInfo.Append(" Title: ")
        newInfo.Append(Me.Title)
        Return newInfo.ToString
    End Function
End Class
```

Notice that the overridden method does not perform a complete string concatenation while it invokes first the `MyBase.FullInformation` method. This is a best practice because one of inheritance's purposes is favoring code reusability; therefore, this invocation is better than rewriting the code from scratch. The following code snippet shows how you can interact with both base class and derived class properties, assuming that `FirstName` and `LastName` have been declared as `Overridable` in the base class and overridden within the derived class:

```
Public Sub New(ByVal name As String,
              ByVal surName As String,
              ByVal age As Integer,
              ByVal title As String)

    'Goes to the base class properties
    MyBase.FirstName = name
    MyBase.LastName = surName

    'Current instance properties
    Me.Age = age
    Me.Title = title
End Sub
```

Me AND MyBase

The `Me` keyword refers to the instance of the current class, whereas `MyBase` refers to the base class from which the current class derives. This difference is evident when a member is overridden, but if members are not redefined, both keywords refer to the same code.

The next section details a few things you need to know about constructors within derived classes.

`MyClass` Keyword

Another way of accessing the base classes' members is the `MyClass` keyword. Imagine you have a base class exposing some overridable members, such as properties or methods; then you have a derived class that overrides those members. The `MyClass` keyword avoids the application of overriding and invokes members on the derived class as if they were `NotOverridable` on the base class. In other words, `MyClass` enables executing members of a base class in the context of a derived class, ensuring that the member version is the one in the base class. Listing 12.1 shows an example.

LISTING 12.1   Demonstrating the `MyClass` Keyword

```
Public Class BaseClassDemo

    Public Overridable ReadOnly Property Test As String
        Get
            Return "This is a test in the base class"
        End Get
    End Property

    Public Function DoSomething() As String
        Return MyClass.Test
    End Function
End Class

Public Class DerivedClassDemo
    Inherits BaseClassDemo

    Public Overrides ReadOnly Property Test As String
        Get
            Return "This is a test in the derived class"
        End Get
    End Property
End Class
Module Module1
    Sub Main()

        Dim derived As New DerivedClassDemo

        'Invokes the member within the derived
        'class but as if it was not overridden
        Dim result As String = derived.DoSomething
    End Sub
End Module
```

The `BaseClassDemo` base class exposes an overridable property that returns a text message, for demo purposes. It also exposes a public method that just shows the text stored within the `Test` property. Within the derived `DerivedClassDemo`, the `Test` property is overridden but the `DoSomething` method is not. This method is still available when you create an instance of the `DerivedClassDemo` class. Because the method is defined within the base class and then is executed within the derived class's context, if you implemented the method as follows:

```
Public Function DoSomething() As String
    Return Me.Test
End Function
```

it would return the content of the derived `Test` property. In some situations, though, you might want to ensure that only base class members are used within other members that are not overridden; this can be accomplished using the `MyClass` keyword. If you run the code shown in Listing 12.1, the result variable contains the string `"This is a test in the base class"`, although the `DoSomething` method has been invoked on an instance of the derived class. You can still use the overridden `Test` property for other purposes in your derived class. `MyClass` is similar to `Me` in that both get a reference to the instance of the current class, but `MyClass` behaves as if members in the base class were marked as `NotOverridable` and therefore as if they were not overridden in the derived class.

Constructors' Inheritance

The previous section discussed the `MyBase` keyword and how it can be used to access members from a base class. The keyword also has another important purpose when it comes to constructors. Consider the following constructor, which is implemented within the `Person` class (that is, the base class) shown in the previous section:

```
Public Sub New(ByVal firstName As String,
               ByVal lastName As String,
               ByVal age As Integer)

    Me.FirstName = firstName
    Me.LastName = lastName
    Me.Age = age
End Sub
```

The problem now is in derived classes. The rule is that if you have a constructor receiving arguments in the base class, you do need to provide a constructor receiving arguments also within a derived class, and the constructor needs to invoke the base class. The following code shows how a constructor needs to be implemented within the `Contact` class:

```
Public Sub New(ByVal name As String,
               ByVal surName As String,
               ByVal age As Integer,
               ByVal title As String)

    MyBase.New(name, surName, age)
    Me.Title = title
End Sub
```

As you can see from the preceding code snippet, the first line of code is an invocation to the constructor of the base class—and this is a rule that you *must* follow. After that line of code, you can provide any other initialization code. This particular requirement is necessary if you plan to provide a constructor that receives arguments within the base class, although it's not necessary if you implement a constructor that does not receive arguments or if you do not provide any constructor (which is implicitly provided by the Visual Basic compiler).

Shadowing

The beginning of this chapter explained that classes can inherit from base classes exposed by class libraries such as .dll assemblies and that you do not necessarily need the source code. You could create a class deriving from another class exposed by a compiled assembly and implement a new member. In addition, the publisher of the compiled base class could release a new version of the class, providing a member with the same name of your custom member. In this case, you would not be able to edit the base class because you wouldn't have the source code. Visual Basic 2012 provides an interesting way of dealing with such a situation known as *shadowing*. Although the Visual Basic compiler still enables compiling (it throws warning messages), your class needs to "shadow" the member with the same name of your custom one. This is accomplished using the `Shadows` keyword. Consider this particular implementation of the `Person` class, exposing a `Title` property, of type `String`:

```
Public Class Person

    Public Property FirstName As String
    Public Property LastName As String
    Public Property Title As String

End Class
```

Now consider the following implementation of the `Contact` class, which requires a value defined within the `Titles` enumeration:

```
Public Class Contact
    Inherits Person

    Public Property Title As Titles
End Class

Public Enum Titles
    Dr
    Mr
    Mrs
End Enum
```

The `Contact` class exposes a `Title` property, but its base class already has a `Title` property; therefore, the Visual Basic compiler shows a warning message related to this situation. If you want your code to use the derived `Title` property, you need to mark your member with `Shadows` as follows:

```
Public Class Contact
    Inherits Person

    Public Shadows Property Title As Titles
End Class
```

You can accomplish the same result by marking the property within the derived class as `Overloads`:

```
Public Overloads Property Title As Titles
```

In this particular example we can use auto-implemented properties. If the property within the derived class returned the same type of the one within the base class, it would make more sense using old-fashioned properties so that you have the ability to customize the behavior.

BE VERY CAREFUL WHEN SHADOWING

If you have a derived class that shadows some property or method (like `Contact` in the example above), and you pass an instance to a method that accepts an argument of the base class type (like `Person`), if the method makes calls to something that was shadowed, it will take the base implementation, even though you passed in the derived type. This can lead to unexpected results, so be very careful when shadowing.

Overriding Shared Members

Shared members cannot be overridden. This means that you can only use them as they have been inherited from the base class or provide a shadowing implementation for creating a new definition from scratch. For example, consider this simplified implementation of the `Person` class, which exposes a shared `Counter` property:

```
Public Class Person

    Public Shared Property Counter As Integer
End Class
```

If you now create a `Contact` class that inherits from `Person`, you can use the `Counter` property as previously implemented, or you can shadow the base definition as follows:

```
Public Class Contact
    Inherits Person

    Public Shared Shadows Property Counter As Integer
End Class
```

If you intend to provide an overloaded member with a different signature, you can use overloading as follows:

```
Public Shared Shadows Property Counter As Integer
Public Shared Shadows Property Counter(ByVal maximum As Integer) As Integer
    Get

    End Get
    Set(ByVal value As Integer)

    End Set
End Property
```

Another limitation of shared members is that you cannot invoke the `MyBase` and `MyClass` keywords within them. Moreover, you cannot invoke shared members using the `MyBase` keyword. So, if you were to assign the `Counter` shared property defined in the person class, you would have to write `Person.Counter = 0` instead of `MyBase.Counter = 0`.

Practical Inheritance: Building Custom Exceptions

In Chapter 6, "Handling Errors and Exceptions," you learned about exceptions in .NET development; you saw what exceptions are and how you can intercept them at runtime to create well-formed applications that can handle errors. The .NET Framework ships with hundreds of exceptions related to many aspects of .NET development. You might encounter a situation where you need to implement custom exceptions. You can build custom exceptions due to inheritance. A custom exception can inherit from the root `System.Exception` class or from another exception (such as `System.IO.IOException`) that necessarily inherits from `System.Exception`. Custom exceptions should always be CLS-compliant. Let's look at the `Person` class implementation again, adding a method that returns the full name of the person and that requires at least the last name:

```
Public Class Person

    Public Property FirstName As String
    Public Property LastName As String

    Public Function FullName() As String

        If String.IsNullOrEmpty(Me.LastName) Then
            Throw New MissingLastNameException("Last name not specified")
        Else
            Return String.Concat(LastName, " ", FirstName)
        End If
    End Function
End Class
```

As you can see, if the `LastName` property contains an empty or null string, the code throws a `MissingLastNameException`. This exception is custom and must be implemented.

NAMING CONVENTIONS

Remember that every exception class's identifier must terminate with the `Exception` word. Microsoft naming convention rules require this.

The `MissingLastNameException` is implemented as follows:

```
<Serializable()>
Public Class MissingLastNameException
    Inherits Exception

    Public Sub New()
        MyBase.New()
    End Sub

    Public Sub New(ByVal message As String)
        MyBase.New(message)
    End Sub

    Public Sub New(ByVal message As String, ByVal inner As Exception)
        MyBase.New(message, inner)
    End Sub

    Protected Sub New(ByVal info As Runtime.Serialization.SerializationInfo,
                      ByVal context As _
                      Runtime.Serialization.StreamingContext)
        MyBase.New(info, context)
    End Sub
End Class
```

There is a series of considerations:

▶ As a custom exception, it inherits from `System.Exception`.

▶ The class is decorated with the `Serializable` attribute; this is one of the CLS establishments, and it enables developers to persist the state of the exception to disk (see Chapter 41, "Serialization").

▶ Custom exceptions expose three overloads of the base constructors plus one overload marked as `Protected` that is therefore available to eventually derive classes and that receives information on serialization.

▶ Custom exceptions are caught exactly as any other built-in exception.

When you have your custom exception, you can treat it as other ones:

```
Try
    Dim p As New Person
    'Will cause an error because
    'the LastName was not specified
    Console.WriteLine(p.FullName)
Catch ex As MissingLastNameException
    Console.WriteLine("ERROR: please specify at least the last name")
Catch ex As Exception
    Console.WriteLine("Generic error")
    Console.WriteLine(ex.ToString)
Finally
    Console.ReadLine()
End Try
```

The preceding code intentionally causes an exception to demonstrate how the MissingLastNameException works, by not assigning the LastName property in the Person class instance.

AVOID COMPLEX INHERITANCE CHAINS

Building a complex inheritance chain is something that should be carefully considered because as the chain grows, the child classes will be tied and rely on the base classes not changing, at risk of disrupting the inheritance chain.

Summary

Inheritance is a key topic in the object-oriented programming with Visual Basic and the .NET Framework. In this chapter, you learned lots of important concepts. First, you learned what inheritance is and how you can take advantage of it for creating frameworks of custom objects. Then you saw how to derive classes from base classes using the Inherits keyword and how your derived classes automatically inherit some members from System.Object, which is the root in the class hierarchy. When deriving classes, you need to consider how constructors and shared members behave; the chapter also provided an overview. But inheritance would be of less use without polymorphism. You learned how polymorphism requires implementing one common infrastructure for multiple objects, taking advantage of the capability to redefine inherited members' behavior. For this purpose, the .NET Framework enables the overriding technique that you can use to modify the behavior of derived members. Additionally, with shadowing you can override a member from a class of which you do not have the source code. You often want to condition inheritance, establishing when classes should be sealed (NotInheritable) or abstract (MustInherit). In inheritance scenarios, you also often need to have access to base class members; therefore, you need the MyBase and MyClass keywords. But you seldom work with theories. Because of this, the chapter closed with a practical demonstration of inheritance, showing how you can build custom exceptions to use in your applications.

CHAPTER 13

Interfaces

Most people have a car. Cars have an engine, four wheels, several gears, and other instrumentation. A lot of different companies produce cars, and each company makes several models. All companies have to build car models adhering to some particular specifications established by the law, and such specifications provide information on what minimal components will compose cars, including a list of those components that are therefore common to every car. In .NET development we can compare interfaces to the previously described law specifications. Interfaces provide a list of members that an object must implement to accomplish particular tasks in a standardized way. They are also known as *contracts* because they rule how an object must behave to reach some objectives. You saw an example in Chapter 8, "Managing an Object's Lifetime," for the `IDisposable` interface that must be implemented if an object wants to provide the capability to release resources that are not only in-memory objects, according to a standardized way. This means that the .NET Framework knows that the `Dispose` method from `IDisposable` is required to free up resources. In this chapter you first learn how to define and implement custom interfaces; then you get an overview of the most common interfaces in .NET Framework. You also learn why interfaces are important—because you will surely wonder why you should use them.

Defining Interfaces

An *interface* is a reference type defined within an `Interface..End Interface` block. Interfaces define only signatures for members that classes will then expose and are a set of the members' definitions. Imagine you want to create an interface that defines members for working with documents. This is accomplished with the following code:

```
Public Interface IDocument

    Property Content As String
    Sub Load(ByVal fileName As String)
    Sub Save(ByVal fileName As String)

End Interface
```

The interface is marked as `Public` because the default scope for interfaces is `Friend`. Assigning public visibility ensures that external assemblies use the interface (which is a common scenario).

INTERFACES SCOPE

Interfaces can be declared `Private`, `Protected`, or `Protected Friend` only if they are defined within a type such as a class.

As a convention, interface identifiers begin with a capital `I`. This is not mandatory (except when creating interfaces that are compliant with the Common Language Specification), but I strongly recommend you follow the convention. The most important consideration is that the interface definition contains only members' definitions with no body. For both the `Load` and `Save` methods' definitions, there is only a signature but not the method body and implementation, which are left to classes that implement the interface. Members defined within interfaces cannot be marked with one of the scope qualifiers, such as `Public`, `Friend`, and so on. By default, members defined by interfaces are `Public`. Finally, being reference types, interfaces need to be treated as such. See Chapter 4, "Data Types and Expressions," for further information on reference types.

NESTED CLASSES

Interfaces can define classes. A class defined within an interface is a typical `Class..End Class` block, as you would normally define one. This is an uncommon scenario and can be useful when you want to avoid naming conflicts with other classes, but you have to know that it is possible.

Implementing and Accessing Interfaces

Implementing interfaces means telling a class that it needs to expose all members defined within the interface. You do this by using the `Implements` keyword followed by the name of the interface. IntelliSense will offer a list of available interfaces, as demonstrated in Figure 13.1. The following code snippet shows how to implement the `IDocument` interface within a `Document` class:

```
Public Class Document
    Implements IDocument

    Public Property Content As String Implements IDocument.Content

    Public Sub Load(ByVal fileName As String) Implements IDocument.Load
    End Sub

    Public Sub Save(ByVal fileName As String) Implements IDocument.Save
    End Sub

End Class
```

FIGURE 13.1   Choosing from available interfaces.

You'll notice that, when pressing Enter, the Visual Studio IDE automatically generates members' templates for you, as represented in Figure 13.2.

This is useful because it saves you from having to waste your time writing members' signatures. You'll also notice that when a member is defined within a class because of the interface implementation, the `Implements` keyword is also added at the end of the member followed by the related element in the interface.

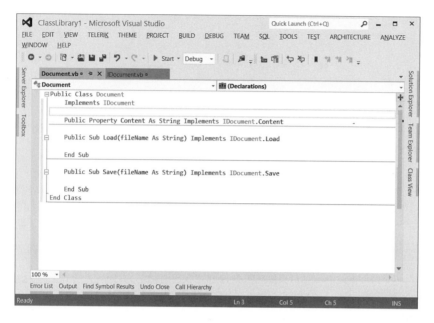

FIGURE 13.2   Visual Studio generates a skeleton for members based on the interface.

MULTIPLE IMPLEMENTATIONS

Different from inheritance, classes and structures can implement more than one interface. You see an example later in the chapter when discussing `IEnumerable` and `IEnumerator`.

The `Document` class is basic and is for demo purposes only. To complete the implementation example, we can write code to populate methods for performing operations established in the interface, as shown in Listing 13.1.

LISTING 13.1   Implementing Interfaces

```
Public Class Document
    Implements IDocument

    Public Property Content As String Implements IDocument.Content

    'Gets the content of a text document
    Public Sub Load(ByVal fileName As String) Implements IDocument.Load
        Try
            Content = My.Computer.FileSystem.ReadAllText(fileName)
        Catch ex As Exception
            Throw
        End Try
    End Sub
```

```
'Saves a text document to file
Public Sub Save(ByVal fileName As String) Implements IDocument.Save
    Try
        My.Computer.FileSystem.WriteAllText(fileName,
                                       Content, False)

    Catch ex As Exception
        Throw
    End Try
End Sub
```

```
End Class
```

When you implement interfaces, you need to populate members' templates with your own code. This can ensure that your object is respecting the contract established by the interface. When a class implements an interface, it also needs to access members it defines. You have two alternatives for this purpose. The first one is simple and intuitive and consists of creating an instance of the class that implements the interface. Continuing with the example of the Document class shown in Listing 13.1, the following code shows how you can accomplish this:

```
Dim myDocument As New Document
myDocument.Load("SomeDocument.txt")

Console.WriteLine(myDocument.Content)
```

The code invokes instance members of the class with no differences for normal classes' implementations. The second alternative is declaring an *interface variable*. You declare a variable whose type is the interface; the variable receives the result of an explicit conversion from the class that implements the interface to the interface itself. More than words, code can provide a good explanation:

```
Dim myDocument As IDocument = CType(New Document, IDocument)
myDocument.Load("SomeDocument.txt")

Console.WriteLine(myDocument.Content)
```

The result is the same. You often find code that makes use of interface variables, so spend a little time becoming familiar with this approach. After this discussion, you will probably wonder why you need to define and implement interfaces because you just need to write code as you would do without them. The answer is *polymorphism*.

Passing Interfaces as Method Arguments

One of the most powerful features when working with interfaces is that methods can receive interfaces as parameters. This means that you can pass in any object as these parameters so long as it implements the given interface. The following example shows a method that accepts an argument of type ILList, meaning that any object implementing the ILList interface can be accepted:

```
'Interfaces as parameters
Public Class WorkWithLists
    Public Function Elaborate(ByVal items As IList) As Integer
        'Just for demo, returns 0 if the list contains something
        If items.Count > 0 Then
            Return 0
        Else
            'if not, adds a new object to the list
            Dim item As New Object
            items.Add(item)
            Return -1
        End If
    End Function


End Class
```

This is with no doubt one of the most important features in programming by contracts with interfaces.

Interfaces and Polymorphism

Chapter 12, "Inheritance," discusses polymorphism, which offers a common infrastructure to different types of objects. In the discussion, interfaces find their natural habitat. They provide a common set of members that classes need to implement if they need to perform a particular series of tasks. A typical example is the IDisposable interface that you met in Chapter 8. All classes that need to provide a mechanism for releasing resources implement that interface, which exposes a set of common members. Another example is the ICloneable interface that defines a Clone method that classes can implement to provide the capability to copy a class instance. You can easily understand that interfaces are generic; they are not specific to any class but are instead as generic as possible so that the widest variety of classes can implement them. To provide a code example, let's reexamine the IDocument interface proposed in the previous section. This interface was implemented by a Document class. But the same interface can be implemented in other kinds of classes. For example, we can define an Invoice class that can implement the same IDocument interface because it exposes a common set of members that can be easily used within the Invoice class. Then the new class can provide new members specific to its particular needs and behavior. The following code demonstrates this:

```
Public Class Invoice
    Implements IDocument

    Public Property Content As String Implements IDocument.Content

    Public Sub Load(ByVal fileName As String) Implements IDocument.Load
```

```
    End Sub

    Public Sub Save(ByVal fileName As String) Implements IDocument.Save

    End Sub

    Public Property InvoiceNumber As Integer

    Public Function CalculateDiscount(ByVal price As Decimal,
                             ByVal percent As Single) As Decimal

    End Function

End Class
```

As you can see, the `IDocument` interface can serve the `Invoice` class with its members; then the class defines new members (`InvoiceNumber` and `CalculateDiscount`) strictly related to its behavior. By the way, the `IDocument` interface provides polymorphic code that can be used in different situations and objects with a common infrastructure.

Interfaces Inheritance

Two situations are related to both inheritance and interfaces. The first scenario occurs when you create a class that derives from another one that implements an interface. In such a scenario, the derived class also inherits members implemented through an interface and does not need to implement the interface again. Moreover, if the base class contains members that are marked as overridable and implemented via an interface, the derived class can override such members if not private. The second scenario is a pure interface inheritance, in which an interface can inherit from another one. Continuing the previous examples, we can consider creating an `IInvoice` interface that inherits from `IDocument` and provides some more specific members to represent an invoice. The following code demonstrates this:

```
Public Interface IInvoice
    Inherits IDocument

    'New members
    Property InvoiceNumber As Integer
    Function CalculateDiscount(ByVal price As Decimal,
                             ByVal percent As Single) As Decimal

End Interface
```

As you can see, the `Inherits` keyword is used also for interface inheritance. In this example, the new interface inherits all members' definitions from the `IDocument` interface and adds two new members—the `InvoiceNumber` property and the `CalculateDiscount` method. After this, you could rewrite the `Invoice` class as follows:

```
Public Class Invoice
    Implements IInvoice

    Public Property Content As String Implements IInvoice.Content

    Public Sub Load(ByVal fileName As String) Implements IInvoice.Load

    End Sub

    Public Sub Save(ByVal fileName As String) Implements IInvoice.Save

    End Sub

    Public Property InvoiceNumber As Integer Implements IInvoice.InvoiceNumber

    Public Function CalculateDiscount(ByVal price As Decimal,
                            ByVal percent As Single) As Decimal Implements
IInvoice.CalculateDiscount

    End Function
End Class
```

It is worth mentioning that, due to inheritance, members exposed by the base interface can be implemented using the name of the base interface, instead of the derived one. For example, in the previous code snippet the `Content` property is implemented like this:

```
Public Property Content As String Implements IInvoice.Content
```

Because this property is exposed by the `IDocument` interface and inherited by `IInvoice`, the compiler also accepts the following implementation:

```
Public Property Content As String Implements IDocument.Content
```

Defining CLS-Compliant Interfaces

The Common Language Specification (CLS) also provides rules for interfaces. The first rule is that if you mark an interface as CLS-compliant, you cannot use CLS-noncompliant types within signatures. The following interface is not correct because it is marked as `CLSCompliant` but uses a noncompliant type:

```
'Incorrect: UInteger is not CLS compliant
<CLSCompliant(True)> Public Interface ITest
```

```
    Property Counter As UInteger

End Interface
```

The second rule is that a CLS-compliant interface cannot define shared members. The last rule is that all members must be explicitly marked with the `CLSCompliant` attribute. The following is an example of a CLS-compliant interface:

```
<CLSCompliant(True)> Public Interface IClsCompliant

    <CLSCompliant(True)> Property Counter As Integer
    <CLSCompliant(True)> Function DoSomething() As Boolean

End Interface
```

NAMING CONVENTIONS

It is an implicit rule that identifiers for all CLS-compliant interfaces *must* begin with a capital `I`. `IDocument` is a correct identifier, whereas `MyDocumentInterface` is not. Identifiers cannot contain the underscore character (_) and are written according to the Pascal-casing conventions.

Most Common .NET Interfaces

Because of their importance in polymorphism, the .NET Framework defines a large quantity of interfaces implemented by most types within the Framework. You need to understand the most common built-in interfaces because they provide great flexibility in your code, and in several situations you need to implement such interfaces in your objects that need to perform particular tasks. Table 13.1 summarizes the most common .NET interfaces.

TABLE 13.1   Most Common Interfaces

Interface	Description
ICloneable	Its purpose is to provide methods for cloning objects.
IDisposable	It's implemented when a class needs to provide methods for releasing resources.
IEnumerable	It's implemented to provide the enumerator, which enables objects to be iterated.
IComparable	When an object wants to provide the capability of sorting, it must implement this interface.
IConvertible	To be implemented if an object enables conversion.
IFormattable	It provides support for formatting data.

The `ICloneable` interface is discussed in Chapter 4, and the `IDisposable` interface is discussed in Chapter 8. This chapter therefore does not revisit these interfaces. Instead, you'll learn how you can implement the other ones in your code.

The `IEnumerable` Interface

You implement the `IEnumerable` interface each time you want your class to support `For..Each` loops. Each time you iterate an object (typically a collection) using `For Each`, it is because that object implements `IEnumerable`. The .NET Framework offers lots of collections (including generic ones) and enables you to create custom collections inheriting from built-in ones; therefore, implementing `IEnumerable` will probably be spared for you. It's important to understand how the interface works, especially for its intensive usage when working with LINQ. `IEnumerable` provides one method, named `GetEnumerator`, which generally is implemented as follows:

```
Public Function GetEnumerator() As System.Collections.IEnumerator _
    Implements System.Collections.IEnumerable.GetEnumerator
    Return CType(Me, IEnumerator)


End Function
```

As you can see, the method returns the result of the conversion of the class instance to an `IEnumerator` object; this means that `IEnumerable` must be implemented together with another interface. It's named `IEnumerator` and offers methods and properties for moving between items in a collection and for providing information on the current item. To provide an example, imagine you have a class named `Contacts` that acts as a repository of items of type `Contact` and that implements `IEnumerable` to provide iteration capabilities. Listing 13.2 shows how this is accomplished in code, including a sample loop performed invoking `For..Each`.

LISTING 13.2   Implementing IEnumerable and IEnumerator

```
Public Class Contacts
    Implements IEnumerable, IEnumerator

    Public Function GetEnumerator() As System.Collections.IEnumerator _
        Implements System.Collections.IEnumerable.GetEnumerator
        Return CType(Me, IEnumerator)
    End Function

    Private position As Integer = -1

    Public ReadOnly Property Current As Object _
        Implements System.Collections.IEnumerator.Current
        Get
            Return Items(position)
        End Get
    End Property
```

```vb
    Public Function MoveNext() As Boolean _
        Implements System.Collections.IEnumerator.MoveNext
        position += 1
        Return (position < Items.Length)
    End Function

    Public Sub Reset() Implements System.Collections.IEnumerator.Reset
        position = -1
    End Sub

    Private Items() As Contact = New Contact() {New Contact With _
                                    {.FirstName = "Alessandro",
                                    .LastName = "Del Sole",
                                    .Email = "alessandro.delsole" & _
                                            "@visual-basic.it",
                                    .PhoneNumber = "000-0000-00"},
                                    New Contact With _
                                    {.FirstName = "Robert",
                                    .LastName = "Green",
                                    .Email = "email@something.com",
                                    .PhoneNumber = "000-0000-00"} _
                                    }

End Class

Public Class Contact

    Public Property FirstName As String
    Public Property LastName As String
    Public Property Email As String
    Public Property PhoneNumber As String

End Class
Module Module1

    Sub Main()

        Dim c As New Contacts
        'Returns "Del Sole", "Green"
        For Each Cont As Contact In c
            Console.WriteLine(Cont.LastName)
        Next

        Console.ReadLine()
    End Sub
End Module
```

The `Contacts` class stores an array of `Contact` objects and provides a private field, position, which is used for returning information. The `Current` property returns the item in the array corresponding to the current position, whereas the `MoveNext` method increments the position variable and returns `True` if the position number is still less than the upper bound in the array. In the end, `Reset` just restores the initial value for position. You also notice how, within the `Sub Main` in `Module1`, a simple `For..Each` loop is given for demonstration purposes. If you run the code, you see that it correctly returns last names for both actual contacts within the `Contacts` class.

IEnumerable(Of T)

As for other interfaces, a generic version of `IEnumerable` supports specific types. Because Chapter 15, "Delegates and Events," discusses generics, this chapter shows the non-generic version that works the same, except that it is related to `Object`.

The `IComparable` Interface

You implement the `IComparable` interface when you want to offer custom comparison instrumentation to your objects. `IComparable` requires you to implement a `CompareTo` method that returns an `Integer` value that is less than zero if the instance is less than the compared object, is zero if the instance equals the compared object, and is greater than zero if the instance is greater than the compared object. For example, imagine you want to provide a comparison to the `Person` class based on the length of the `LastName` property. Listing 13.3 shows how you can accomplish this.

LISTING 13.3   Implementing the `IComparable` Interface

```
Public Class Person
    Implements IComparable

    Public Property FirstName As String
    Public Property LastName As String
    Public Property Email As String


    Public Function CompareTo(ByVal obj As Object) As Integer Implements
➥System.IComparable.CompareTo
        If Not TypeOf (obj) Is Person Then
            Throw New ArgumentException
        Else

            Dim tempPerson As Person = DirectCast(obj, Person)

            If Me.LastName.Length < tempPerson.LastName.Length Then
                Return -1
            ElseIf Me.LastName.Length = tempPerson.LastName.Length Then
```

```
                    Return 0
            Else
                    Return 1
            End If


        End If
    End Function
End Class
Module Module1

    Sub Main()
        Dim p1 As New Person With {.LastName = "Del Sole",
                                   .FirstName = "Alessandro"}
        Dim p2 As New Person With {.LastName = "AnotherLastName",
                                   .FirstName = "AnotherFirstName"}

        Dim c As New ComparableHelper(p1)
        Console.WriteLine(c.CompareTo(p2))
        Console.ReadLine()
    End Sub


End Module
```

You might notice that a first check is performed on the object type, which must be Person. If not, the code throws an ArgumentException (meaning that the argument is not valid). The comparison is accomplished in a simple way using unary operators. Next, to perform the comparison, you just need to create an instance of the Person class and then invoke its CompareTo method, passing the Person you want to compare to the current instance.

IComparer INTERFACE

If you want to provide custom sorting for arrays, you need to implement the IComparer interface. The following article in the Microsoft Knowledge Base provides a good example that is extensible to Visual Basic 2012: http://support.microsoft.com/kb/321292/en-us

---

Utilizing the Generic IComparable(Of T)

Although Chapter 15 discusses generics, this is a good point for showing something interesting about them. Many interfaces within the .NET Framework have a generic counterpart. For example, there is an IEnumerable(Of T) or IComparable(Of T), in which T is a specific .NET type instead of Object, which would require conversions and, therefore, performance overhead. We could rewrite the Person class shown in Listing 13.3 using the IComparable(Of T) interface to provide support for Person objects. This is accomplished with the following code:

```
Public Class Person
    Implements IComparable(Of Person)

    Public Property FirstName As String
    Public Property LastName As String
    Public Property Email As String

    Public Function CompareTo(ByVal other As Person) As Integer _
            Implements System.IComparable(Of Person).CompareTo
        If Me.LastName.Length < other.LastName.Length Then
            Return -1
        ElseIf Me.LastName.Length = other.LastName.Length Then
            Return 0
        Else
            Return 1
        End If
    End Function

End Class
```

You will soon notice how `DirectCast` conversions disappear and how the `CompareTo` method receives an argument of type `Person` instead of `Object`. This means less code and more precision. In Chapter 15 and Chapter 16, "Working with Collections and Iterators," you gain detailed information about generics and generic collections.

The `IConvertible` Interface

Objects implementing the `IConvertible` interface expose a series of `ToXXX` methods exactly as the `Convert` class does so that such objects can easily be converted into another type. This example uses a structure instead of a class, for the sake of simplicity. Listing 13.4 shows how the `IConvertible` interface can be implemented.

LISTING 13.4   Implementing the `IConvertible` Interface

```
Public Structure ThreePoint
    Implements IConvertible

    Public Function GetTypeCode() As System.TypeCode Implements _
        System.IConvertible.GetTypeCode

        Return TypeCode.Object
    End Function

    'Just a custom return value
    Public Function ToBoolean(ByVal provider As System.IFormatProvider) _
        As Boolean Implements System.IConvertible.ToBoolean
        Return X > Y
```

```
End Function

Public Function ToByte(ByVal provider As System.IFormatProvider) _
    As Byte Implements System.IConvertible.ToByte
    Return Convert.ToByte(SumPoints)
End Function

Public Function ToChar(ByVal provider As System.IFormatProvider) _
    As Char Implements System.IConvertible.ToChar
    Return Convert.ToChar(SumPoints)
End Function

Public Function ToDateTime(ByVal provider As System.IFormatProvider) _
    As Date Implements System.IConvertible.ToDateTime
    Return Convert.ToDateTime(SumPoints)
End Function

Public Function ToDecimal(ByVal provider As System.IFormatProvider) _
    As Decimal Implements System.IConvertible.ToDecimal
    Return Convert.ToDecimal(SumPoints)
End Function

Public Function ToDouble(ByVal provider As System.IFormatProvider) _
    As Double Implements System.IConvertible.ToDouble
    Return Convert.ToDouble(SumPoints)
End Function

Public Function ToInt16(ByVal provider As System.IFormatProvider) _
    As Short Implements System.IConvertible.ToInt16
    Return Convert.ToInt16(SumPoints)
End Function

Public Function ToInt32(ByVal provider As System.IFormatProvider) _
    As Integer Implements System.IConvertible.ToInt32
    Return SumPoints()
End Function

Public Function ToInt64(ByVal provider As System.IFormatProvider) _
    As Long Implements System.IConvertible.ToInt64
    Return Convert.ToInt64(SumPoints)
End Function

Public Function ToSByte(ByVal provider As System.IFormatProvider) _
    As SByte Implements System.IConvertible.ToSByte
    Return Convert.ToSByte(SumPoints)
End Function
```

```vb
Public Function ToSingle(ByVal provider As System.IFormatProvider) _
    As Single Implements System.IConvertible.ToSingle
    Return Convert.ToSingle(SumPoints)
End Function


'Required "Overloads"
Public Overloads Function ToString(ByVal provider As System.IFormatProvider) _
    As String Implements System.IConvertible.ToString
    Return String.Format("{0}, {1}, {2}", Me.X, Me.Y, Me.Z)
End Function


Public Function ToType(ByVal conversionType As System.Type, _
                       ByVal provider As System.IFormatProvider) _
                       As Object Implements System.IConvertible.ToType
    Return Convert.ChangeType(SumPoints, conversionType)
End Function


Public Function ToUInt16(ByVal provider As System.IFormatProvider) _
    As UShort Implements System.IConvertible.ToUInt16

    Return Convert.ToUInt16(SumPoints)
End Function


Public Function ToUInt32(ByVal provider As System.IFormatProvider) _
    As UInteger Implements System.IConvertible.ToUInt32
    Return Convert.ToUInt32(SumPoints)
End Function


Public Function ToUInt64(ByVal provider As System.IFormatProvider) _
    As ULong Implements System.IConvertible.ToUInt64
    Return Convert.ToUInt64(SumPoints)
End Function


Public Property X As Integer
Public Property Y As Integer
Public Property Z As Integer

Public Sub New(ByVal valueX As Integer, _
               ByVal valueY As Integer, _
               ByVal valueZ As Integer)
    Me.X = valueX
    Me.Y = valueY
    Me.Z = valueZ
End Sub
```

```
      Public Function SumPoints() As Integer
          Return (Me.X + Me.Y + Me.Z)
      End Function
End Structure
```

The `ThreePoint` structure is simple; it exposes three integer properties (x, y, and z) whose sums are returned via a `SumPoints` method. The goal of the `IConvertible` implementation is therefore to enable returning the result of the method converted into different types. Each conversion method invokes the corresponding one of the `Convert` class, with some exceptions. The first one is the `ToBoolean` method, which returns a customized result depending on the value of x and y, but this is just for demonstration purposes. (You can invoke the `Convert.ToBoolean` as well.) The second exception is the `ToString` method. When you implement an interface that provides a method already existing in the class (even because of inheritance), Visual Studio renames the interface's method by adding a 1 in the end. For example, every class exposes `ToString` because it is inherited from `System.Object`. Thus, the `ToString` version provided by the interface is automatically renamed to `ToString1`. But this is not elegant. A better technique is overloading because the method is marked with `Overloads` and named correctly.

IMPORTANT NOTICE

`IConvertible` does not adhere to the CLS because it makes use of CLS-incompliant types, such as `UInt16`, `UInt32`, and so on. You should be aware of this if you plan to develop objects that need to be CLS-compliant.

The `IFormattable` Interface

The `IFormattable` interface enables implementing a new overload of the `ToString` method to provide customized string formatting with deep control over the process, also defining custom qualifiers. Listing 13.5 shows how you can implement the `IFormattable` interface.

LISTING 13.5   Implementing the `IFormattable` Interface

```
Imports System.Globalization

Public Class Person
    Implements IFormattable

    Public Property FirstName As String
    Public Property LastName As String
    Public Property Email As String

    Public Overloads Function ToString(ByVal format As String,
                    ByVal formatProvider As System.IFormatProvider) _
                    As String Implements System.IFormattable.ToString
```

```
        If String.IsNullOrEmpty(format) Then format = "G"
        If formatProvider Is Nothing Then formatProvider = _
                                    CultureInfo.CurrentCulture

    Select Case format
        'General specifier. Must be implemented
        Case Is = "G"
            Return String.Format("{0} {1}, {2}",
                    Me.FirstName, Me.LastName, Me.Email)
        Case Is = "F"
            Return FirstName
        Case Is = "L"
            Return LastName
        Case Is = "LF"
            Return String.Format("{0} {1}", Me.LastName, Me.FirstName)
        Case Else
            Throw New FormatException
    End Select
    End Function
End Class


Module Module1
    Sub Main()
        Dim p As New Person With {.FirstName = "Alessandro",
            .LastName = "Del Sole",
            .Email = "alessandro.delsole@visual-basic.it"}

        Console.WriteLine("{0:G}", p)
        Console.WriteLine("{0:L}", p)
        Console.WriteLine("{0:F}", p)
        Console.WriteLine("{0:LF}", p)
        Console.ReadLine()
    End Sub
End Module
```

Listing 13.5 shows a particular implementation of the `Person` class, which exposes the `FirstName`, `LastName`, and `Email` properties. It implements the `IFormattable` interface that offers a new overload of the `ToString` method. This method receives two arguments; the first one, format, represents the qualifier. For example, in standard formatting, the letter *c* represents currency. Here you can specify your own qualifiers. Because of this, the first check is whether the format is null or empty. In such case, a `G` qualifier is assigned by default. `G` stands for `General` and is the only qualifier that *must* be implemented. When you provide `G`, you can create your own qualifiers. The next check is on `formatProvider` that represents the culture for string formatting. If it's null, the code assigns the local system culture. The subsequent `Select..End Select` block takes into consideration some identifiers as custom qualifiers. `L` stands for `LastName`, `F` stands for `FirstName`, and `LF` stands for `LastName + FirstName`. You can change or extend this code by intercepting your custom identifiers within this block. Running the code shown in Listing 13.5 produces the following result:

```
Alessandro Del Sole, alessandro.delsole@visual-basic.it
Del Sole
Alessandro

Del Sole Alessandro
```

You can easily compare the output result with the code and understand how custom formatting works.

Summary

This chapter focused on interfaces, another key topic in the object-oriented programming. Interfaces, which are defined within `Interface..End Interface` blocks, provide signatures of sets of members that an object must implement to accomplish specific tasks. You might remember the example of the `IDisposable` interface that must be implemented by objects that need to provide methods for freeing up resources. You saw how to create and implement custom interfaces in your code via the `Implements` keyword and then how to invoke objects that implement interfaces both by creating class instances and via interface variables. You found out why interfaces are important and why the .NET Framework makes an intensive usage of interfaces, talking about polymorphism and how interfaces can contribute to provide standardized infrastructures for multiple objects. It's important to adhere to the Common Language Specification when defining interfaces, so you got information about this. Finally, code examples have been provided for the most common .NET built-in interfaces, to provide a deeper understanding of how things happen behind the scenes and to reuse those interfaces in your code.

13

Generics and Nullable Types

When you organize your home, you probably place things according to their type. For example, you have a place for food that is different from the place where you put clothes. But foods are also different. You do not treat fish like candy or pizza and so on. So you need safe places for each kind of food, avoiding the risks derived from treating all foods the same way; the same is true for clothes and any other item in your home. The .NET development would be similar without Generics. Consider groups of .NET objects of different types, all grouped into a collection of `Object`. How can you be sure to treat an item in the collection as you should if the collection stores different types that you identify as `Object`? What if you want to create just a collection of strings? Generics solve this problem. In this chapter you learn what Generics are. In Chapter 16, "Working with Collections and Iterators," you learn about generic collections and see why Generics are so useful. This chapter also introduces nullable types, which are generic on their own.

Introducing Generics

Generic types are .NET types that can adapt their behavior to different types of objects without the need of defining a separate version of the type. In other words, you can implement a generic type to work with integers, strings, custom reference types, and any other .NET type with a single implementation. Generics offer several advantages:

▶ **Strongly typed programming techniques**—Generic objects can hold only the specified type and avoid accidents of handling objects of different types within the same group.

▶ **Better performances**—Because Generics enable you to handle only the specified type, they avoid the need of boxing and unboxing from and to `System.Object`, and this retains for performance overhead.

▶ **Code reuse**—As you will see in a few moments, Generics enable you to create objects that behave the same way and that have the same infrastructure whatever kind of .NET type you pass them.

▶ **The ability of writing better code**—Avoiding working with nongeneric `System.Object`, you not only get all IntelliSense features for the specified type, but also can take advantages from not using late-binding techniques.

Generally, the use of Generics is related to the creation of strongly typed collections for storing groups of items of the same type. Because of this, there are two considerations: the first one is that you should check whether the .NET Framework provides a built-in generic collection suiting your needs before creating custom ones (read Chapter 16); the second consideration is that code examples shown in this chapter will be related to creating a generic collection so you know how to create one if .NET built-in Generics are not sufficient for you.

Creating and Consuming Generics

Creating a generic type is accomplished by providing a parameterized type definition. The following is an example:

```
Class CustomType(Of T)

End Class
```

The `Of` keyword is followed by the type that the new object can handle. `T` is the *type parameter* and represents the .NET type you want to be held by your generic type. The type parameter's name is left to your own choosing, but `T` is often used as a common name in the .NET Framework Base Class Library (BCL). At this point, you must write code to manipulate the `T` type in a way that will be convenient for possibly every .NET type. Now imagine you want to build a custom collection that you want to reuse with any .NET type. Listing 14.1 shows how to accomplish this.

LISTING 14.1   Building a Custom Generic Type

```
Public Class CustomType(Of T)

    Private items() As T

    Public Sub New(ByVal upperBound As Integer)
        ReDim items(upperBound - 1)
    End Sub
```

```
    Private _count As Integer = 0
    'Cannot provide auto-implemented properties when read-only
    Public ReadOnly Property Count As Integer
        Get
            Return _count
        End Get
    End Property

    Public Sub Add(ByVal newItem As T)
        If newItem IsNot Nothing Then
            Me.items(Me._count) = newItem
            Me._count += 1
        End If
    End Sub

    Default Public ReadOnly Property Item(ByVal index As Integer) As T
        Get
            If index < 0 OrElse index >= Me.
                Count Then Throw New IndexOutOfRangeException
            Return items(index)
        End Get
    End Property
End Class
```

WHY ARRAYS?

You notice that the code in Listing 14.1 uses arrays to store objects. Arrays do not support removing objects or, at least, this cannot be done easily. This is the reason you only find an Add method. By the way, in this particular case you do not need to focus on how to add and remove items (Chapter 16 covers this), but you need to understand how to handle the generic type parameter.

The code shows how simple it is to manage the type parameter. It can represent any .NET type but, as in the previous example, an array can be of that type and store objects of that type. Because arrays cannot be empty, the constructor receives the upper bound that is then used by ReDim. The Add method equally receives an argument of type T whose value is pushed into the array. This introduces another important concept: generic methods. In generic methods, methods can accept generic parameters (named *type argument*). Notice how a Count property returns the number of items in the array. In this particular scenario, auto-implemented properties cannot be used because a read-only property needs an explicit Get block. Finally, the Item property enables retrieving the specified object in the array at the given index. The new class therefore can handle different types with the same infrastructure.

WHAT CAN BE GENERICS?

You can define as generic the following types: classes, interfaces, delegates, structures, and methods.

Consuming Generic Types

To instantiate and consume generic types, you pass to the constructor the type you want to be handled. For example, the following code creates a new instance of the `CustomType` class, enabling it to handle only integers or types that are converted to `Integer` via a widening conversion:

```
Dim integerCollection As New CustomType(Of Integer)(2)
integerCollection.Add(0)
integerCollection.Add(1)
'Writes 1
Console.WriteLine(integerCollection(1).ToString)
```

You pass the desired type to the constructor after the `Of` keyword. When invoking the `Add` method, you can notice how IntelliSense tells you that the method can receive only `Integer` (see Figure 14.1).

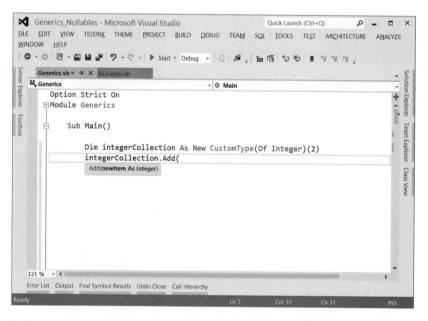

FIGURE 14.1   IntelliSense shows what type is accepted by the generic method.

If you pass a different type, you get an error message. But this does not work only with .NET common types. You can use this technique with custom types, too. For example, you can create a generic collection of Person objects (supposing you have defined a Person class in your code) as follows:

```
Dim onePerson As New Person
onePerson.FirstName = "Alessandro"
onePerson.LastName = "Del Sole"

Dim secondPerson As New Person
secondPerson.FirstName = "Robert"
secondPerson.LastName = "White"

Dim personCollection As New CustomType(Of Person)(2)
personCollection.Add(onePerson)
personCollection.Add(secondPerson)
'Returns 2

Console.WriteLine("How many people are there?")
Console.WriteLine("The answer is {0}", personCollection.Count)
```

This code produces the result shown in Figure 14.2.

FIGURE 14.2   Demonstrating the usage of custom generic types.

Generics' purpose should be clearer now. Their purpose is to provide reusable infrastructures for different types, avoiding mixed groups of objects in favor of strongly typed objects.

Implementing Generic Methods

In Listing 14.1 you saw how to implement a method that receives a generic type parameter. Generic methods are something more. You can add the Of keyword to a generic method to parameterize the method, other than getting generic-type parameters. The following code provides an example, where two arrays of integers are swapped:

```
'Arrays are passed by reference in this case
Public Sub Swap(Of T1)(ByRef array1() As T1, ByRef array2() As T1)
    Dim temp() As T1
    temp = array1
    array1 = array2
    array2 = temp

End Sub
```

Continuing the executive code shown in the "Consuming Generic Types" section, the following snippet shows how you can invoke the previous generic method to swap the content of two arrays of integers:

```
Dim arr1() As Integer = {1, 2, 3}
Dim arr2() As Integer = {4, 5, 6}
integerCollection.Swap(Of Integer)(arr1, arr2)


'Demonstrates that arr2 now
'contains values previously
'stored in arr1
For Each item In arr2
    Console.WriteLine(item)
Next
```

Similarly, you could have arrays of Person objects and invoke the Swap method on the personCollection class, demonstrating how generic methods can work with different types. For instance, the following code creates a new instance of the Person class continuing the previous example and defines two arrays of Person. Next, it invokes Swap(Of Person) on the personCollection class:

```
Dim thirdPerson As New Person
thirdPerson.FirstName = "Neil"
thirdPerson.LastName = "Rowe"

Dim personArray1() As Person = {onePerson, secondPerson}
Dim personArray2() As Person = {thirdPerson}
personCollection.Swap(Of Person)(personArray1,
                        personArray2)
```

This demonstrates how different types can be targeted with generic methods.

Understanding Constraints

With constraints, you can control Generics' behavior, and both provide additional functionalities and limit the implementation to specific data types. Let's begin by understanding constraints on methods.

Methods Constraints

Imagine you want the ability to compare two items within an array. To accomplish this, you need to take advantage of the IComparable interface, and because of this, you want to require that the type argument implements the IComparable interface. The following code demonstrates this:

```
Public Function CompareItems(Of T As IComparable)(ByVal sourceArray() As T,
                                    ByVal index1 As Integer,
                                    ByVal index2 As Integer)
                                As Integer

    Dim result As Integer = _
                sourceArray(index1).CompareTo(sourceArray(index2))

    Return result
End Function
```

Notice how the As clause in the method argument requires the type to implement the IComparable interface. If the type does not implement the interface, the generic method cannot be used. This simplifies how objects can be compared, in that you can directly invoke the CompareTo method on the first item in the array. This approach is useful for another reason: If you did not specify the IComparable constraint, you could attempt a conversion from T to IComparable at runtime, but this would throw an InvalidCastException if the object does not implement the interface. Therefore, by using constraints you can ensure that your objects suit your needs.

Type Constraints

At a higher level, you can apply constraints to generic objects' definitions. For example, you can require the type parameter to implement the IComparable interface as follows:

```
Public Class CustomType(Of T As IComparable)

End Class
```

You can specify which interfaces the object must implement or which class it has to inherit from. This is an example that accepts types deriving from System.IO.Stream:

```
Public Class CustomType(Of T As System.IO.Stream)

End Class
```

In this example, acceptable types would be StreamWriter, StreamReader, BinaryWriter, and BinaryReader objects.

New Constraints

You can combine the As New keywords to require the type argument to expose an explicit parameterless constructor. This is accomplished by the following definition:

```
Public Class CustomType(Of T As New)
    Public Sub TestInstance()
        Dim instance As New T
    End Sub
End Class
```

The TestInstance method is an example of how you can instantiate the T type. This approach gives you the ability to create new instances of the type and prevents the type from being an interface or an abstract (MustInherit) class.

Providing Multiple Constraints

You can combine multiple constraints to provide a series of requirements in your generic types. Multiple constraints are enclosed in curly braces and separated by commas. The following code defines a generic type accepting only reference types that implement the ICloneable interface and an explicit parameterless constructor:

```
Public Class CustomType(Of T As {Class, ICloneable, New})

End Class
```

INHERITANCE CONSTRAINT

You can also provide inheritance constraints other than interfaces constraint, as described at the beginning of this section. You provide the name of the abstract or base class you require to be inherited in the type parameter.

The Class keyword in the constraint indicates that only reference types are accepted. You use the Structure keyword if you want to accept only value types, keeping in mind that in such a scenario you cannot combine it with the New keyword. The following code demonstrates how you can directly access the Clone method because of the ICloneable implementation constraint:

```
Public Sub TestConstraint()
    Dim newObj As New T
    Dim clonedObj As Object = newObj.Clone()
End Sub
```

NESTED TYPES

The type parameter can be used only within the body of the generic type. Nested types can still take advantage of the type parameter as well, so you can create complex infrastructures in your generic types.

Overloading Type Parameters

You can overload generic definitions providing different signatures for the type parameter, similar to what happens in method overloads. The following code provides an example:

```
Public Class CustomType

End Class


Public Class CustomType(Of T1, T2)

End Class


Public Class CustomType(Of T As {Class, ICloneable, New})

End Class
```

It is worth mentioning that providing a nongeneric version of your class is not necessary. You can provide different implementations for your generic types. Now consider the following overloading attempt:

```
Class CustomType(Of T1, T2)

End Class

'Fails at compile time

Class CustomType(Of T1 As IComparable, T2 As ICloneable)

End Class
```

This code is not compiled because, although in the second definition some constraints are defined, the type implementation is considered by the compiler with the same, identical signature. Similarly, you can provide overloaded methods using techniques learned in Chapter 7, "Class Fundamentals," but against generic methods as demonstrated in the following code:

```
Sub DoSomething(Of T1, T2)(ByVal argument1 As T1, ByVal argument2 As T2)

End Sub


Sub DoSomething(Of T)(ByVal argument As T)

End Sub
```

Overloading provides great granularity over Generics implementation, and you will often see examples in built-in generic collections.

Introducing Nullable Types

As we mentioned when talking about value types and reference types, value types have a default value that is zero, whereas reference types have a default value that is Nothing. This is because a reference type can store null values, but value types cannot. Attempting to assign a null value to a value type would result in resetting to the default value for that type. This is a limitation because there are situations in which you need to store null values in value types, such as when fetching data from a SQL Server database. You can have a hypothetical Orders table where the Ship date column enables null values. SQL Server has its own data types, one of which is the DBNull that enables null values. Because Visual Basic 2012 enables mapping SQL Server data types to .NET data types, as you see in Part IV, "Data Access with ADO.NET and LINQ," it could be a problem trying to map a NULL type in SQL Server into a DateTime type in VB. To avoid such problems, starting from .NET Framework 2.0, Microsoft introduced the *Nullable types*.

WHY NULLABLE TYPES IN THIS CHAPTER?

Nullable types are covered in this chapter because they are generic types and are required in the next chapters.

Nullable types were first introduced with Visual Basic 2005 and differ from other types because they can have both a value and have a null value. Nullable types are generic types, and variables are declared as Nullable(Of T) or by adding a question mark just after the type name. You declare a nullable value type as follows:

```
Dim nullInt As Nullable(Of Integer)
```

The following syntax is also supported:

```
Dim nullInt as Integer?
```

You can also add inline initialization:

```
Dim nullInt As Nullable(Of Integer) = Nothing
```

Nullable types expose two properties, HasValue and Value. The first one is of type Boolean and allows understanding if a variable stores a value so that you can avoid using it if it is null. The second one returns the actual value of the type. For example, the following code checks whether the preceding declared nullInt variable has a value and shows its value if it has one:

```
'Has no value, so WriteLine is not executed
If nullInt.HasValue Then
    Console.WriteLine(nullInt.Value)
End If
```

Because we assigned `Nothing`, `HasValue` is `False`. The next example declares a `Boolean` nullable and demonstrates how you can use the value (the alternative syntax with the question mark is used):

```
Dim nullBool As Boolean? = False
If nullBool.HasValue Then
    Console.WriteLine(nullBool.Value)
End If
```

Nullable types also expose a method called `GetValueOrDefault`, which returns the current value for the type instance if the `HasValue` property is `True`. If `HasValue` is `False`, the method returns the default value for the type or the specified default value. The following code describes how you use `GetValueOrDefault`:

```
Dim anInt As Integer? = 10
'HasValue is True, so returns 10
Dim anotherInt As Integer = anInt.GetValueOrDefault

Dim anInt As Integer?
'HasValue is False, so returns 0
'which is the default Value for Integer
Dim anotherInt As Integer = anInt.GetValueOrDefault

Dim anInt As Integer?
'HasValue is False, so returns the default value
'specified as the method argument
Dim anotherInt As Integer = anInt.GetValueOrDefault(10)

Dim anInt As Integer? = 5
'HasValue is True, so returns the current value
'while the method argument is ignored
Dim anotherInt As Integer = anInt.GetValueOrDefault(10)
```

Using nullables will make your life easier in lots of scenarios.

Summary

Generics are a great benefit in the .NET development with Visual Basic 2012. Generics are .NET types that can adapt their behavior to different kinds of objects without the need of defining a separate version of the type. So, you can implement a generic type to work with integers, strings, custom reference types, and any other .NET type with a single implementation. They provide several benefits, including strongly typed programming, IntelliSense support, and better performance. Generics require the `Of` keyword to specify the type parameter that you can manipulate in your object body.

Within Generics definition, you can implement your own custom methods both in the usual fashion and as generic methods, which still require the `Of` keyword followed by the type specification. Generics are also very flexible thanks to the constraints feature. It allows them to accept only types that adhere to the specified requirements, such as interfaces implementation, inheritance, or the presence of an explicit constructor. Nullable types are special generic types that allow null values for value types. They work like other types but expose a `HasValue` property for checking whether the object is null or populated. During the rest of the book, you will find hundreds of Generics usages, especially after Chapter 16 where collections and generic collections will be covered.

CHAPTER 15

Delegates and Events

So far, you have seen how to create and manipulate your objects, working with the result of operations performed onto object instances or shared members. All the work up to now does not provide a way for understanding the moment when a particular thing happens or for being notified of a happening. In .NET development, as with many other programming environments, getting notifications for occurrences and knowing the moment when something happens is accomplished by handling *events*. Events are information that an object sends to the caller, such as the user interface or a thread, about its state so that the caller can make decisions according to the occurred event. Events in .NET programming are powerful and provide great granularity about controlling each happening. This granularity can take place because of another feature named *delegates*, which provide the real infrastructure for event-based programming. Because of this, we discuss delegates first before going into the events discussion.

Understanding Delegates

Delegates are *type-safe* function pointers. The main difference between classic function pointers (such as C++ pointers) and delegates is that function pointers can point anywhere, which can be dangerous. Delegates, on the other hand, can point only to those methods that respect delegates' signatures. Delegates hold a reference to a procedure (its address) and enable applications to invoke different methods at runtime, but such methods must adhere to the delegate signature. Delegates also enable you to invoke a method from another object. This is important according to the main purpose of delegates, which is offering an infrastructure for handling events.

WHERE ARE DELEGATES USED?

Delegates are used in event-handling architectures, but they are powerful and can be used in other advanced techniques. You find examples of delegates being used in multithreading or in LINQ expressions. In Chapter 20, "Advanced Language Features," you learn about lambda expressions that enable implementing delegates on-the-fly.

Delegates are reference types deriving from System.Delegate. Because of this, they can also be defined at namespace level, as you might recall from Chapter 9, "Organizing Types Within Namespaces." They can also be defined at the class and module level. In the next section, you learn to define delegates. Pay attention to this topic because delegates have a particular syntax for being defined and that can be a little bit confusing.

Declaring Delegates

A delegate is defined via the Delegate keyword followed by the method signature it needs to implement. Such a signature can be referred to as a Sub or as a Function and might or might not receive arguments. The following code defines a delegate that can handle a reference to methods able to check an email address, providing the same signature of the delegate:

```
Public Delegate Function IsValidMailAddress(ByVal emailAddress _
                                    As String) As Boolean
```

DELEGATES SUPPORT GENERICS

Delegates support generics, meaning that you can define a Delegate Function (Of T) or Delegate Sub(Of T).

Notice that IsValidMailAddress is a type and not a method as the syntax might imply. emailAddress is a variable containing the email address to check while any methods respecting the signature return a Boolean value depending on the check result. To use a delegate, you need to create an instance of it. The delegate's constructor requires you to specify an AddressOf clause pointing to the actual method that accomplishes the required job. After you get the instance, the delegate points to the desired method that you can call using the Invoke method. The following code demonstrates the described steps:

```
'The method's signature is the same as the delegate: correct
Function CheckMailAddress(ByVal emailAddress As String) As Boolean

    'Validates emails via regular expressions, according to the
    'following pattern
    Dim validateMail As String = "^([\w-\.]+)@((\[[0-9]{1,3}\." & _
        "[0-9]{1,3}\.)|(([\w-]+\.)+))([a-zA-z]{2,4}|[0-9]{1,3})(\]?)$"
```

```
        Return Text.RegularExpressions.Regex.IsMatch(emailAddress,
                                                     validateMail)

End Function

Sub Main()
    'Creates an instance of the delegate and points to
    'the specified method
    Dim mailCheck As New IsValidMailAddress(AddressOf CheckMailAddress)

    'You invoke a delegate via the Invoke method
    Dim result As Boolean = mailCheck.
                        Invoke("alessandro.delsole@visual-basic.it")
    Console.WriteLine("Is valid: {0}", result)
End Sub
```

At this point, you might wonder why delegates are so interesting if they require so much code just for a simple invocation. The first reason is that you can provide as many methods as you like that respect the delegate signature and decide which of the available methods to invoke. For example, the following code provides an alternative (and much simplified) version of the CheckMailAddress method, named CheckMailAddressBasic:

```
Function CheckMailAddressBasic(ByVal emailAddress As String) As Boolean
    Return emailAddress.Contains("@")

End Function
```

Although different, the method still respects the delegate signature. Now you can invoke the new method by changing the AddressOf clause, without changing code that calls Invoke for calling the method:

```
'Alternative syntax: if you already declared
'an instance, you can  do this assignment
mailCheck = AddressOf CheckMailAddressBasic

'No changes here!
Dim result As Boolean = mailCheck.
                        Invoke("alessandro.delsole@visual-basic.it")
Console.WriteLine("Is valid: {0}", result)
```

If you still wonder why all this can be useful, consider a scenario in which you have hundreds of invocations to the same method. Instead of replacing all the invocations, you can change what the delegate is pointing to. Invoke is also the default member for the Delegate class, so you can rewrite the previous invocation as follows:

```
Dim result As Boolean = mailCheck("alessandro.delsole@visual-basic.it")
```

This also works against methods that do not require arguments.

15

ADVANCED DELEGATES TECHNIQUES

Starting with Visual Basic 2008, the .NET Framework introduced new language features such as lambda expressions and relaxed delegates. Both are intended to work with delegates (and in the case of lambda expressions, to replace them in some circumstances), but because of their strict relationship with LINQ, they are discussed in Chapter 20, which is preparatory for the famous data access technology.

Combining Delegates: Multicast Delegates

A delegate can hold a reference (that is, the address) to a method. It is possible to create delegates holding references to more than one method by creating multicast delegates. A multicast delegate is the combination of two or more delegates into a single delegate, providing the delegate the capability to make multiple invocations. The following code demonstrates how to create a multicast delegate, having two instances of the same delegate pointing to two different methods:

```vb
'The delegate is defined at namespace level
Public Delegate Sub WriteTextMessage(ByVal textMessage As String)


'....
Private textWriter As New WriteTextMessage(AddressOf WriteSomething)
Private complexWriter As New WriteTextMessage(AddressOf _
                                    WriteSomethingMoreComplex)

Private Sub WriteSomething(ByVal text As String)
    Console.WriteLine(" report your text: {0}", text)
End Sub

Private Sub WriteSomethingMoreComplex(ByVal text As String)
    Console.WriteLine("Today is {0} and you wrote {1}",
                Date.Today.ToShortDateString, text)
End Sub

'Because Combine returns System.Delegate, with Option Strict On
'an explicit conversion is required.
Private CombinedDelegate As WriteTextMessage = CType(System.Delegate.
                                    Combine(textWriter,
                                    complexWriter),
                                    WriteTextMessage)

'....
CombinedDelegate.Invoke("Test message")
```

In this scenario, you have two methods that behave differently, but both respect the delegate signature. A new delegate (`CombinedDelegate`) is created invoking the `System.Delegate.Combine` method that receives the series of delegates to be combined as arguments. It is worth mentioning that `Combine` returns a `System.Delegate`; therefore, an explicit conversion via `CType` is required with `Option Strict On`. With a single call to `CombinedDelegate.Invoke`, you can call both `WriteSomething` and `WriteSomethingMoreComplex`. The preceding code produces the following output:

```
report your text: Test message
Today is 05/31/2012 and you wrote Test message
```

Delegate KEYWORD AND `System.Delegate`

`Delegate` is a reserved keyword in Visual Basic. Because of this, to invoke the `System.Delegate.Combine` shared method, the full name of the class has been utilized. You can still take advantage of the shortened syntax including `Delegate` within square brackets. In other words, you can write something like this: `[Delegate].Combine(params())`. This works because the `System` namespace is imported by default, and square brackets make the compiler consider the enclosed word as the identifier of a class exposed by one of the imported namespaces, instead of a reserved keyword.

15

Handling Events

Events are members that enable objects to send information on their state to the caller. When something occurs, an event tells the caller that something occurred so that the caller can make decisions on what actions to take. You handle events in UI-based applications, although not always. The .NET Framework takes a huge advantage from delegates to create event infrastructures, and this is what you can do in creating your custom events. In this section you first learn how to catch existing events, and then you get information on creating your own events. This approach is good because it provides a way to understand how delegates are used in event handling.

Registering for Events: `AddHandler` and `RemoveHandler`

To provide your applications the capability of intercepting events raised from any object, you need to register for events. Registering means giving your code a chance to receive notifications and to take actions when it is notified that an event was raised from an object. To register for an event notification, you use the `AddHandler` keyword that requires two arguments: The first one is the event exposed by the desired object, and the second is a delegate pointing to a method executed when your code is notified of an event occurring. The code in Listing 15.1 shows an example using a `System.Timers.Timer` object.

LISTING 15.1   Registering and Catching Events

```
Public Class EventsDemo
    'Declares a Timer
    Private myTimer As Timers.Timer

    'A simple counter
    Private counter As Integer
```

```
    'Interval is the amount of time in ticks
    Public Sub New(ByVal interval As Double)
        'Register for notifications about the Elapsed event
        AddHandler myTimer.Elapsed, AddressOf increaseCounter
        'Assigns the Timer.Interval property
        Me.myTimer.Interval = interval
        Me.myTimer.Enabled = True
    End Sub


    'Method that adheres to the delegate signature and that is
    'executed each time our class gets notifications about
    'the Elapsed event occurring
    Private Sub increaseCounter(ByVal sender As Object,
                            ByVal e As Timers.ElapsedEventArgs)
        counter += 1
    End Sub
End Class
```

Comments within Listing 15.1 should clarify the code. Notice how the `AddHandler`
instruction tells the runtime which event from the `Timer` object must be intercepted
(`Elapsed`). Also notice how, via the `AddressOf` keyword, you specify a method that
performs some action when the event is intercepted. `AddHandler` at this particular point
requires the method to respect the `ElapsedEventHandler` delegate signature. With this
approach, the `increaseCounter` method is executed every time the `System.Timers.Timer.`
`Elapsed` event is intercepted. `AddHandler` provides great granularity on controlling events
because it enables controlling shared events and works within a member body, too. The
`AddHandler` counterpart is `RemoveHandler`, which enables deregistering from getting notifications. For example, you might want to deregister before a method completes its execution. Continuing with the example shown in Listing 15.1, you can deregister before you
stop the timer:

```
RemoveHandler myTimer.Elapsed, AddressOf increaseCounter
Me.myTimer.Enabled = False
```

As you see in the next section, this is not the only way to catch events in Visual Basic.

Declaring Objects with the `WithEvents` Keyword

By default, when you declare a variable for an object that exposes events, Visual Basic
cannot see those events. This is also the case with the previous section's example, where
you declare a `Timer` and then need to explicitly register for event handling. A solution to
this scenario is to declare an object with the `WithEvents` keyword, which makes events
visible to Visual Basic. Thanks to `WithEvents`, you do not need to register for events and
can take advantage of the `Handles` clause to specify the event a method is going to handle.
The code in Listing 15.2 demonstrates this, providing a revisited version of the `EventsDemo`
class.

LISTING 15.2   Catching Events with `WithEvents` and `Handles`

```
Public Class WithEventsDemo

    Private WithEvents myTimer As Timers.Timer

    Private counter As Integer

    Public Sub New(ByVal interval As Double)
        Me.myTimer.Interval = interval
        Me.myTimer.Enabled = True
    End Sub

    Private Sub increaseCounter(ByVal sender As Object,
                               ByVal e As Timers.ElapsedEventArgs) _
                               Handles myTimer.Elapsed

        counter += 1
    End Sub
End Class
```

Notice that if you do not specify a `Handles` clause, the code cannot handle the event, although it respects the appropriate delegate's signature. It is worth mentioning that languages such as Visual C# do not have a `WithEvents` counterpart, so you might prefer using `AddHandler` and `RemoveHandler` if you plan to write code that will be translated into or compared to other .NET languages.

PLATFORM EXCEPTIONS

Exceptions to the last sentence are Windows Presentation Foundation (WPF), Silverlight, and WinRT. Because of the particular events' infrastructure (routed events), the code can catch events even if you do not explicitly provide a `Handles` clause. Of course, take care in this situation.

Offering Events to the External World

In the previous section, you learned how to handle existing events. Now it's time to get your hands dirty on implementing and raising custom events within your own objects. Visual Basic provides two ways for implementing events: the `Event` keyword and custom events. Let's examine both of them.

Raising Events

You declare your own events by using the `Event` keyword. This keyword requires you to specify the event name and eventually a delegate signature. Although not mandatory (`Event` allows specifying no arguments), specifying a delegate signature is useful so that you can take advantage of `AddHandler` for subsequently intercepting events. The code in

Listing 15.3 shows an alternative implementation of the `Person` class in which an event is raised each time the `LastName` property is modified.

LISTING 15.3   Implementing and Raising Events

```
Public Class Person
    Public Event LastNameChanged(ByVal sender As Object,
                                 ByVal e As EventArgs)

    Public Property FirstName As String

    Private _lastName As String
    Public Property LastName As String

        Get
            Return _lastName
        End Cct
        Set(ByVal value As String)
            If value <> _lastName Then
                _lastName = value
                RaiseEvent LastNameChanged(Me, EventArgs.Empty)
            End If
        End Set
    End Property

End Class
```

Notice that in this particular case you need to implement the `LastName` property the old-fashioned way, so you can perform subsequent manipulations. The code checks that the property value changes; then the `LastNameChanged` event is raised. This is accomplished via the `RaiseEvent` keyword. Also notice how the `LastNameChanged` event definition adheres to the `EventHandler` delegate signature. This can be considered as the most general delegate for the events infrastructure. The delegate defines two arguments: The first one, which is named sender, is of type `Object` and represents the object that raised the event. The second is an argument, named `e`, of type `System.EventArgs` that is the base type for classes containing events information. You get a deeper example in the next section. At this point, intercepting the event is simple. You just need to register for event notifications or create an instance of the `Person` class with `WithEvents`. The following code demonstrates this:

```
Sub TestEvent()
    Dim p As New Person
    AddHandler p.LastNameChanged,
            AddressOf personEventHandler
    p.LastName = "Del Sole"
```

```
      Console.ReadLine()
End Sub

Private Sub personEventHandler(ByVal sender As Object,
                              ByVal e As EventArgs)
      Console.WriteLine("LastName property was changed")
End Sub
```

Now every time you change the value of the `LastName` property, you can intercept the edit.

PROPERTY CHANGE NOTIFICATION IN THE REAL WORLD

The .NET Framework provides the `INotifyPropertyChanged` interface, which is used to send notifications to the caller when the value of a property changes, by raising the `PropertyChanged` event exposed by the interface. The current example shows a different technique because it is useful to make you understand how events work at a more general level.

Passing Event Information

In the previous code example, you got a basic idea about passing event information via the base `System.EventArgs` class. In the .NET Framework, you can find hundreds of classes that inherit from `System.EventArgs` and that enable passing custom event information to callers. This is useful whenever you need additional information on what happened during the event handling. Continuing with the previous example, imagine you want to check whether the `LastName` property value contains blank spaces while you raise the `LastNameChanged` event, sending this information to callers. This can be accomplished by creating a new class that inherits from `System.EventArgs`. Listing 15.4 shows how you can implement the class and how you can take advantage of it in the `Person` class.

LISTING 15.4   Providing Custom Event Information

```
Public Class LastNameChangedEventArgs
      Inherits EventArgs

      Private _lastName As String
      Public ReadOnly Property LastName As String
          Get
              Return _lastName
          End Get
      End Property

      Public ReadOnly Property ContainsBlank As Boolean
          Get
              Return Me.LastName.Contains(" ")
```

15

```
        End Get
    End Property


    Public Sub New(ByVal lastName As String)
        Me._lastName = lastName
    End Sub
End Class


Public Class Person
    Private _lastName As String
    Public Property LastName As String
        Get
            Return _lastName
        End Get
        Set(ByVal value As String)
            If value <> _lastName Then
                _lastName = value
                Dim e As New LastNameChangedEventArgs(value)
                RaiseEvent LastNameChanged(Me, e)
            End If
        End Set
    End Property


    Public Event LastNameChanged(ByVal sender As Object,
                        ByVal e As LastNameChangedEventArgs)

End Class
```

Notice how the `LastNameChangedEventArgs` class exposes the public properties representing information you want to return to the caller. When raising the event in the `Person` class, you create a new instance of the `LastNameChangedEventArgs` and pass the required information elaborated by the instance. Now you can change the event handler described in the previous section as follows:

```
Private Sub personEventHandler(ByVal sender As Object,
                            ByVal e As LastNameChangedEventArgs)
    Console.WriteLine("LastName property was changed")
    Console.WriteLine("Last name contains blank spaces: " &
                    e.ContainsBlank)
End Sub
```

In this way, you can easily handle additional event information. Finally, it is important to understand how you can get the instance of the object that raised the event because it is something that you will often use in your applications. You accomplish this by converting the sender into the appropriate type. The following code shows how to get the instance of the `Person` class that raised the previous `LastNameChanged` event:

```
Dim raisingPerson As Person = DirectCast(sender, Person)
```

Creating Custom Events

Starting from Visual Basic 2005, you have had the ability to define your own events by implementing the *custom events*. Custom events are useful because they provide a kind of relationship with a delegate. They are also useful in multithreaded applications. You declare a custom event via the `Custom Event` keywords combination, supplying the event name and signature as follows:

```
Public Custom Event AnEvent As EventHandler
    AddHandler(ByVal value As EventHandler)

    End AddHandler

    RemoveHandler(ByVal value As EventHandler)

    End RemoveHandler

    RaiseEvent(ByVal sender As Object, ByVal e As System.EventArgs)

    End RaiseEvent
End Event
```

IntelliSense is very cool here because, when you type the event declaration and press **Enter**, it adds a skeleton for the custom event that is constituted by three members (see Figure 15.1): `AddHandler` is triggered when the caller subscribes for an event with the `AddHandler` instruction; `RemoveHandler` is triggered when the caller removes an event registration; and `RaiseEvent` is triggered when the event is raised. In this basic example, the new event is of the type `EventHandler`, which is a delegate that represents an event storing no information—and that is the most general delegate.

Now take a look at the following example that demonstrates how to implement a custom event that can affect all instances of the `Person` class:

```
Public Delegate Sub FirstNameChangedHandler(ByVal info As String)

Dim handlersList As New List(Of FirstNameChangedHandler)

Public Custom Event FirstNameChanged As FirstNameChangedHandler
    AddHandler(ByVal value As FirstNameChangedHandler)
        handlersList.Add(value)
        Debug.WriteLine("AddHandler invoked")
    End AddHandler
```

```
RemoveHandler(ByVal value As FirstNameChangedHandler)
    If handlersList.Contains(value) Then
        handlersList.Remove(value)
        Debug.WriteLine("RemoveHandler invoked")
    End If
End RemoveHandler

RaiseEvent(ByVal info As String)
    'Performs the same action on all instances
    'of the Person class
    For Each del As FirstNameChangedHandler In handlersList
        'del.Invoke(info ......
    Next
    End RaiseEvent
End Event
```

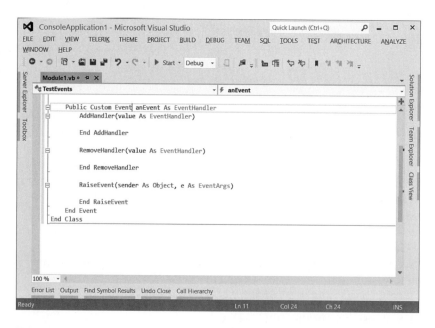

FIGURE 15.1   IntelliSense generates a skeleton for all members of custom events.

This code provides an infrastructure for handling changes on the FirstName property in the Person class. In this case, we build a list of delegates that is populated when the caller registers with AddHandler. When the caller invokes RemoveHandler, the delegate is popped from the list. The essence of this resides in the RaiseEvent stuff, which implements a loop for performing the same operation on all instances of the delegate and therefore of the Person class. To raise custom events, you use the RaiseEvent keyword. For this, you need to edit the FirstName property implementation in the Person class as follows:

```
Private _firstName As String
Public Property FirstName As String

    Get
        Return _firstName
    End Get
    Set(ByVal value As String)
        If value <> _firstName Then
            _firstName = value
            RaiseEvent FirstNameChanged(FirstName)
        End If
    End Set
End Property
```

You raise the event the same way for non-custom events, with the difference that custom events provide deep control over what is happening when the caller registers, deregisters, or raises the event.

Summary

Delegates are type-safe function pointers that store the address of a `Sub` or `Function`, enabling different methods to be invoked at runtime. Delegates are reference types declared via the `Delegate` keyword; they enable invoking methods via the `Invoke` method. They can be used in different programming techniques, but the most important scenario where you use delegates is within event-based programming. Events take advantage of delegates in that the objects require their signature to be respected. Coding events is something that can be divided into main areas, such as catching events and exposing events from your objects. To catch events, you can register and deregister via the `AddHandler` and `RemoveHandler` keywords, or you can declare objects by exposing events via the `WithEvents` reserved word. Then you can provide event handlers respecting the appropriate delegate signature and adding the `Handles` clause. You instead define your own events in two ways: via the `Event` keyword or with custom events. The advantage of providing custom events is that you can have deep control over the event phases, such as registering and deregistering. In this discussion, it is important to remember that you can provide custom event information by creating classes that inherit from `System.EventArgs` where you can store information useful to the caller.

CHAPTER 16

Working with Collections and Iterators

Applications often require working with data. Until now you got information on how to store data within classes and structures, but it is common to need to create groups of data. In .NET development, this is accomplished using special classes known as *collections*, which enable storing a set of objects within one class. The .NET Framework provides a lot of collections, each one specific to a particular need or scenario. The main distinction is between nongeneric collections and generic collections, but all of them can store a set of objects. Collections are not merely groups of data. They are the backend infrastructure for engines such as the ADO.NET Entity Framework and LINQ, so understanding collections is an important task. At a higher level, collections' infrastructure is offered by the `System.Collections` namespace and by some interfaces that bring polymorphism to collections. After you have stored data in collections, it is not uncommon for you to analyze the content of such collections; this task is often performed via (but not limited to) `For..Each` or `For..Next` loops. Continuing the goal of helping developers write better and more responsive code, the .NET Framework 4.5 brings to Visual Basic a feature called *iterators*. Iterators make loops more responsive through a background asynchrony. In this chapter you learn about the .NET Framework's collections, both nongeneric and generic ones. You also learn how to create and consume custom collections, and you get an overview of concurrent collections. Finally, you learn about iterators in Visual Basic 2012, an important new addition to the language.

Understanding Collections Architecture

Collections are special classes that can store sets of objects; the .NET Framework offers both nongeneric and generic collections. Whatever kind of collection you work on, collections implement some interfaces. The first one is ICollection that derives from IEnumerable and provides both the enumerator (which enables For..Each iterations) and special members, such as Count (which returns the number of items within a collection) and CopyTo (which copies a collection to an array). Collections also implement IList or IDictionary; both inherit from ICollection and expose members that enable adding, editing, and removing items from a collection. The difference is that IDictionary works with key/value pairs instead of single objects as IList. The previously mentioned interfaces are about nongeneric collections. If you work with generic collections, the collections implement the generic counterpart of those interfaces such as ICollection(Of T), IList(Of T), and IDictionary(Of TKey, TValue). It's important to understand this implementation because this provides similarities between collections so that you can learn members from one collection and be able to reuse them against other kinds of collections.

USE THE OBJECT BROWSER

Remember that the Object Browser tool can provide thorough information on objects' architecture, meaning that if you don't remember which members are exposed by a collection, this tool can be your best friend.

Working with Nongeneric Collections

The System.Collections namespace defines several nongeneric collections. The namespace also defines interfaces mentioned in the previous section. Here you learn to work with nongeneric collections so that in the next section you can easily understand why generic ones are more efficient.

The ArrayList Collection

System.Collections.ArrayList is the most common nongeneric collection in the .NET Framework and represents an ordered set of items. By *ordered*, we mean that you add items to the collection one after the other, which is different from sorting. ArrayList collections can store any .NET type because, at a higher level, it accepts items of type Object. The following code shows how you can create a new ArrayList and can set the number of items it can contain by setting the Capacity property:

```
Dim mixedCollection As New ArrayList
mixedCollection.Capacity = 10
```

Adding new items to an ArrayList is a simple task. To do this, you invoke the Add method that receives as an argument the object you want to add, as demonstrated by the following snippet:

```
mixedCollection.Add(35)
mixedCollection.Add("35")
mixedCollection.Add("Alessandro")
mixedCollection.Add(Date.Today)
```

The preceding code adds an `Integer`, two `Strings`, and a `Date`. Of course, you can also add composite custom types. Always be careful when using an `ArrayLists`. The first two items' value is 35, but the first one is an `Integer` whereas the second is a `String`. If you want to compare such items or iterate them, you should explicitly convert from `String` to `Integer`, or vice versa. This would require boxing/unboxing operations. You work with collections of a single type, so I suggest you avoid nongeneric collections in favor of generic ones. For example, if you have to work with a set of strings, you should use the `List(Of String)`. The second part of this chapter discusses generic collections.

WHY YOU SHOULD PREFER GENERICS

The second part of this chapter is about generic collections. You should use this kind of collection for two reasons; the first is that generic collections are strongly typed and prevent the possibility of errors that can be caused when working with items of type `Object`. The second reason is that each time you add a value type to a nongeneric collection, the type is first subject to boxing (that was discussed in Chapter 4, "Data Types and Expressions"), which can cause performance overhead and does not provide the best object management.

You can also add a block of items in a single invocation using the `AddRange` method. The following code shows how you can add an array of strings to the existing collection:

```
Dim anArray() As String = {"First", "Second", "Third"}
mixedCollection.AddRange(anArray)
```

`Add` and `AddRange` add items after the last existing item. You might want to add items at a specified position. This can be accomplished via the `Insert` and `InsertRange` methods whose first argument is the position; the second one is the object. The following code demonstrates this:

```
mixedCollection.Insert(3, "New item")
mixedCollection.InsertRange(3, anArray)
```

You can remove items from the collection using one of two methods. `Remove` enables you to remove a specific object, and `RemoveAt` enables you to remove the object at the specified position:

```
'Removes the string "35"
mixedCollection.RemoveAt(1)
'Removes 35

mixedCollection.Remove(35)
```

One interesting method is `TrimToSize`; it enables you to resize the collection based on the number of items effectively stored. For example, consider the following code:

```
Dim mixedCollection As New ArrayList
mixedCollection.Capacity = 10

mixedCollection.Add(32)
mixedCollection.Add("32")
mixedCollection.Add("Alessandro")
mixedCollection.Add(Date.Today)

mixedCollection.TrimToSize()
```

When created, the `ArrayList` can store up to 10 items. After the `TrimToSize` invocation, `Capacity`'s value is 4, which is the number of items effectively stored. If you have a large collection, the `ArrayList` provides a `BinarySearch` method that enables searching the collection for a specified item, returning the index of the item itself:

```
'Returns 2
Dim index As Integer = mixedCollection.BinarySearch("Alessandro")
```

If the item is not found within the collection, the return value is a negative number. If the collection contains more than one item matching the search criteria, `BinarySearch` returns only one item—which is not necessarily the first one. This collection also exposes other interesting members that are summarized in Table 16.1.

TABLE 16.1   `ArrayList` Members

Member	Description
Count	Returns the number of items within the collection.
CopyTo	Copies the `ArrayList` instance into an array.
Contains	Returns `True` if the specified item exists within the collection.
ToArray	Copies the content of the `ArrayList` into an array of `Object`.
IndexOf	Returns the zero base index of the specified item.
GetRange	Creates a new `ArrayList` that is just a subset of the initial one, based on the specified criteria.
Sort	Performs a sorting operation over the collection.
Reverse	Performs a descending sorting operation over the collection.
Item	Property that gets or sets an item at the specified index. This is the default property of the `ArrayList` class.
Clear	Removes all items from the collection.

You can access an item from the `ArrayList` using the index as follows:

```
Dim anItem As Object = mixedCollection(0)
```

You need to perform a conversion into the appropriate type, which is something you can accomplish inline if you already know the type:

```
Dim anItem As Integer = CInt(mixedCollection(0))
```

If the conversion fails, an `InvalidCastException` is thrown. The `ArrayList` implements the `IList` interface and thus can take advantage of the enumerator; therefore, you can iterate it via a `For..Each` loop as follows:

```
For Each item As Object In mixedCollection
    Console.WriteLine(item.ToString)

Next
```

You just need to pay attention to the fact that each item is treated as an `Object`, so you must be aware of conversions. The `ArrayList` collection provides members that you find in other kinds of collections. This is the reason the most common members are discussed here.

The `Queue` Collection

The `System.Collections.Queue` collection works according to the FIFO (First-In, First-Out) paradigm, meaning that the first item you add to the collection is the first pulled out of the collection. `Queue` exposes two methods: `Enqueue` adds a new item to the collection, and `Dequeue` removes an item from the collection. Both methods receive an argument of type `Object`. The following code provides an example:

```
Sub QueueDemo()

    Dim q As New Queue
    q.Enqueue(1)
    q.Enqueue(2)

    'Returns
    '1
    '2
    Console.WriteLine(q.Dequeue)
    Console.WriteLine(q.Dequeue)

End Sub
```

You just need to invoke the `Dequeue` method to consume and automatically remove an item from the collection. You can also invoke the `Peek` method, which returns the first item from the collection without removing it. Be careful when adding items to a queue because you are working in a fashion that is not strongly typed. If you plan to work with objects of a specified type (for example, you need a collection of `Integer`), consider using a `Queue(Of T)` that behaves the same way except that it is strongly typed. The collection also exposes a `Count` property that returns the number of items in the collection. The constructor provides an overload that enables specifying the capacity for the collection.

The `Stack` Collection

The `System.Collections.Stack` collection mimics the same-named memory area and works according to the LIFO (Last-In, First-Out) paradigm meaning that the last item you add to the collection is the first that is pulled out from the collection. `Stack` exposes three important methods: `Push` adds an item to the collection, `Pop` enables the consuming of and removing of an item from the collection, and `Peek` returns the top item in the collection without removing it. The following is an example:

```
Dim s As New Stack


s.Push(1)
s.Push(2)


'Returns 2 and leaves it in the collection
Console.WriteLine(s.Peek)
'Returns 2 and removes it
Console.WriteLine(s.Pop)
'Returns 1 and removes it
Console.WriteLine(s.Pop)
```

As for `Queue`, here you work with `Object` items. Although this enables pushing different kinds of objects to the collection, it is not a good idea. You should use the generic counterpart (`Stack(Of T)`) that enables you to work with a single type in a strongly typed fashion. The `Stack` collection also exposes the `Count` property, which returns the number of objects that it stores.

The `HashTable` Collection

The `System.Collections.HashTable` collection can store items according to a key/value pair, where both key and value are of type `Object`. The `HashTable` peculiarity is that its items are organized based on the hash code of the key. The following code provides an example:

```
Dim ht As New Hashtable
ht.Add("Alessandro", "Del Sole")
ht.Add("A string", 35)
ht.Add(3.14, New Person)


'Number of items
Console.WriteLine(ht.Count)
'Removes an item based on the key
ht.Remove("Alessandro")
```

Items within a `HashTable` can be accessed by the key, as shown in the last line of code in the preceding example. It also offers two methods named `ContainsKey` and `ContainsValue` that check whether a key or a value exists within the collection, as demonstrated here:

```
'Checks if a key/value exists
Dim checkKey As Boolean = ht.ContainsKey("A string")
Dim checkValue As Boolean = ht.ContainsValue(32)
```

Note that if you do not check whether a key already exists, as in the preceding example, and attempt to add a key that already exists, then an `ArgumentException` is thrown. This is because keys must be unique. A single item within the collection is of type `DictionaryEntry` that exposed two properties, `Key` and `Value`. For example, you can iterate a `HashTable` as follows:

```
'iterate items
For Each item As DictionaryEntry In ht
    Console.WriteLine("{0} {1}", item.Key, item.Value)
Next
```

`HashTable` also offers two other properties named `Keys` and `Values` that return an `ICollection` containing keys in the key/value pair and values in the same pair, respectively. This is demonstrated here:

```
'iterate keys
For Each key As Object In ht.Keys
    Console.WriteLine(key)
Next
```

It is recommend that you use a strongly typed `Dictionary(Of T, T)` that provides more efficiency. (And this suggestion is appropriate when discussing other dictionaries.)

The `ListDictionary` Collection

The `System.Collections.Specialized.ListDictionary` collection works exactly like `HashTable` but differs in that it is more efficient until it stores up to 10 items. It is not preferred after the item count exceeds 10.

The `OrderedDictionary` Collection

The `System.Collections.Specialized.OrderedDictionary` collection works like `HashTable` but differs in that items can be accessed via either the key or the index, as demonstrated by the following code:

```
Dim od As New OrderedDictionary
od.Add("a", 1)


'Access via index
Dim item As DictionaryEntry = CType(od(0), DictionaryEntry)
Console.WriteLine(item.Value)
```

The `SortedList` Collection

The `System.Collections.SortedList` collection works like `HashTable` but differs in that items can be accessed via the key or the index items are automatically sorted based on the key. For example, look at the following code:

```
Dim sl As New SortedList
sl.Add("Del Sole", 2)
sl.Add("Alessandro", 1)

For Each item As String In sl.Keys
    Console.WriteLine(item)
Next
```

It sorts items based on the key; therefore, it produces the following result:

```
Alessandro
Del Sole
```

The `HybridDictionary` Collection

The `System.Collections.Specialized.HybridDictionary` collection is a dynamic class in that it implements a `ListDictionary` until the number of items is small and then switches to `HashTable` if the number of items grows large. Technically, it works like `HashTable`.

The `StringCollection` Collection

The `System.Collections.Specialized.StringCollection` is similar to the `ArrayList` collection except that it is limited to accepting only strings. The following code provides an example:

```
Dim stringDemo As New StringCollection

stringDemo.Add("Alessandro")
stringDemo.Add("Del Sole")

'Returns True
Dim containsString As Boolean = stringDemo.Contains("Del Sole")

stringDemo.Remove("Alessandro")
```

You can use the same members of `ArrayList` and perform the same operations.

The `StringDictionary` Collection

The `System.Collections.Specialized.StringDictionary` collection works like the `HashTable` collection but differs in that it accepts only key/value pairs of type `String`, meaning that both keys and values must be `String`. The following is a small example:

```
Dim stringDemo As New StringDictionary

stringDemo.Add("Key1", "Value1")
stringDemo.Add("Alessandro", "Del Sole")

'Simple iteration
For Each value As String In stringDemo.Values
    Console.WriteLine(value)
Next
```

You can recall the `HashTable` collection for a full member listing.

The `NameValueCollection` Collection

The `NameValueCollection` behaves similarly to the `StringDictionary` collection, but it differs in that `NameValueCollection` enables accessing items via either the key or the index. The following code snippet provides a brief demonstration:

```
Dim nv As New NameValueCollection

nv.Add("First string", "Second string")

Dim item As String = nv(0)
```

The `Add` method also provides an overload accepting another `NameValueCollection` as an argument.

The `BitArray` Collection

The `System.Collections.BitArray` collection enables storing bit values represented by Boolean values. A `True` value indicates that a bit is on (1), whereas a `False` value indicates that a bit is off (0). You can pass to the `BitArray` arrays of `Integer` numbers or Boolean values, as demonstrated by the following code:

```
Dim byteArray() As Byte = New Byte() {1, 2, 3}
'Length in zero base
Dim ba As New BitArray(byteArray)

For Each item As Object In ba
    Console.WriteLine(item.ToString)
Next
```

This code produces the output shown in Figure 16.1, which is a human-readable representation of the bits in the collection.

The constructor also accepts a length argument that enables specifying how large the collection must be.

FIGURE 16.1   Human-readable representation of bits in a `BitArray` collection.

The `Bitvector32` Collection

`System.Collections.Specialized.BitVector32` has the same purpose of `BitArray` but differs in two important elements; the first one is that `BitVector32` is a structure that is a value type and therefore can take advantage of a faster memory allocation. On the other hand, the collection manages only 32-bit integers. All data is stored as 32-bit integers that are affected by changes when you edit the collection. The most important (shared) method is `CreateMask` that enables creating a mask of bits. The method can create an empty mask (which is typically for the first bit) or create subsequent masks pointing to the previous bit. When done, you can set the bit on or off by passing a Boolean value. The following code provides an example:

```
'Passing zero to the constructor
'ensures that all bits are clear
Dim bv As New BitVector32(0)

Dim bitOne As Integer = BitVector32.CreateMask
Dim bitTwo As Integer = BitVector32.CreateMask(bitOne)
Dim bitThree As Integer = BitVector32.CreateMask(bitTwo)

bv(bitOne) = True
bv(bitTwo) = False
bv(bitThree) = True
```

The `Data` property stores the actual value of the collection, as demonstrated here:

```
'Returns 5 (the first bit + the second bit = the third bit)
Console.WriteLine(bv.Data)
```

If you instead want to get the binary representation of the data, you can use the name of the instance. The following code demonstrates this:

```
Console.WriteLine(bv)
```

This code produces the following result:

```
BitVector32{00000000000000000000000000000101}
```

MEMBERS AND EXTENSION METHODS

Collections provide special members, such as properties and methods, and are extended by most of the built-in extension methods. Providing a thorough discussion on each member is not possible; IntelliSense can point you in the right direction to provide explanations for each member. Each member has a self-explanatory identifier; therefore, it is easy to understand what a member does when you understand the high-level logic. In this chapter you are introduced to the most important members from collections so that you can perform the most common operations.

Working with Generic Collections

The .NET Framework offers generic counterparts of the collections described in the previous section. Moreover, it offers new generic collections that are specific to particular technologies such as WPF. In this section, you learn to work with generic built-in collections and how you can take advantage of a strongly typed fashion. Generic collections are exposed by the `System.Collections.Generic` namespace, but a different namespace is explained.

The `List(Of T)` Collection

The `System.Collections.Generic.List(Of T)` collection is a generic ordered list of items. It is a strongly typed collection, meaning that it can accept only members of the specified type. It is useful because it provides support for adding, editing, and removing items within the collection. For example, imagine you need to store a series of `Person` objects to a collection. This can be accomplished as follows:

```
Dim person1 As New Person With {.FirstName = "Alessandro",
                                .LastName = "Del Sole",
                                .Age = 35}
Dim person2 As New Person With {.FirstName = "XXXXX",
                                .LastName = "ZZZZZZZZ",
                                .Age = 44}
```

```
Dim person3 As New Person With {.FirstName = "YYYYY",
                                .LastName = "DDDDDDDD",
                                .Age = 18}

Dim personList As New List(Of Person)
personList.Add(person1)
personList.Add(person2)
personList.Add(person3)
```

You notice that the `List(Of T)` has lots of members in common with its nongeneric counterpart—the `ArrayList`. This is because the first one implements the `IList(Of T)` interface, whereas the second one implements `IList`. The following code shows how you can access an item within the collection using the `IndexOf` method and how you can remove an item invoking the `Remove` method, passing the desired instance of the `Person` class:

```
'Returns the index for Person2
Dim specificPersonIndex As Integer = personList.IndexOf(person2)

'Removes person3
personList.Remove(person3)
```

The `List(Of T)` still provides members such as `Capacity`, `AddRange`, `Insert`, and `InsertRange`, but it exposes a method named `TrimExcess` that works like the `ArrayList.TrimToSize`. Because the `List(Of T)` implements the `IEnumerable(Of T)` interface, you can then iterate the collection using a classic `For..Each` loop, but each item is strongly typed, as demonstrated here:

```
For Each p As Person In personList
    Console.WriteLine(p.LastName)
Next
```

If you need to remove all items from a collection, you can invoke the `Clear` method, and when you do not need the collection anymore, you assign it to `Nothing`:

```
personList.Clear()
personList = Nothing
```

In this case, the code simply assigns `Nothing` to the list because this does not implement the `IDisposable` interface. If it did, you have to be sure to invoke the `Dispose` method before clearing and destroying the collection to avoid locking resources. There are also other interesting ways to interact with a collection, such as special extension methods. Extension methods are discussed in Chapter 20, "Advanced Language Features." For now, you need to know that they are special methods provided by the `IEnumerable(Of T)` interface that enables performing particular operations against a collection. For example, the Single method enables retrieving the unique instance of a type that matches the specified criteria:

```
'Returns a unique Person whose LastName
'property is Del Sole
Dim specificPerson As Person = personList.Single(Function(p) _
                            p.LastName = "Del Sole")
```

This method receives a lambda expression as an argument that specifies the criteria. Lambda expressions are also discussed in Chapter 20. Another interesting method is `FindAll`, which enables the generation of a new `List(Of T)` containing all the type instances that match a particular criteria. The following snippet retrieves all the `Person` instances whose `LastName` property starts with the letter *D*:

```
'Returns a new List(Of Person) storing
'all Person instances whose LastName starts
'with "D"
Dim specificPeople = personList.FindAll(Function(p) _
                            p.LastName.StartsWith("D"))
```

As usual, IntelliSense can be your best friend in situations such as this. Because all members from each collection cannot be described here, that technology can help you understand the meaning and the usage of previously mentioned members whose names are always self-explanatory.

INVESTIGATING COLLECTIONS AT DEBUG TIME

Chapter 5, "Debugging Visual Basic 2012 Applications," discussed the Data Tips features of the Visual Studio debugger. They are useful if you need to investigate the content of collections while debugging, especially if you need to get information on how collections and their items are populated.

Working with Collection Initializers

Visual Basic 2012 implements a language feature known as *collection initializers*. This feature works like the object initializers, except that it is specific for instantiating and populating collections inline. To take advantage of collection initializers, you need to use the `From` reserved keyword enclosing items within brackets, as demonstrated in the following code:

```
'With primitive types
Dim listOfIntegers As New List(Of Integer) From {1, 2, 3, 4}
```

The preceding code produces the same result as the following:

```
Dim listOfIntegers As New List(Of Integer)

listOfIntegers.Add(1)
listOfIntegers.Add(2)
listOfIntegers.Add(3)
listOfIntegers.Add(4)
```

16

You can easily understand how collection initializers enable writing less code that's more clear. This feature can also be used with any other .NET type. The following code snippet shows how you can instantiate inline a `List(Of Person)`:

```
'With custom types
Dim person1 As New Person With {.FirstName = "Alessandro",
                                .LastName = "Del Sole",
                                .Age = 35}
Dim person2 As New Person With {.FirstName = "XXXXX",
                                .LastName = "ZZZZZZZZ",
                                .Age = 44}
Dim person3 As New Person With {.FirstName = "YYYYY",
                                .LastName = "DDDDDDDD",
                                .Age = 18}


Dim people As New List(Of Person) From {person1,
                                        person2,
                                        person3}
```

The code also shows how you can take advantage of implicit line continuation if you have long lines for initializations. When you have an instance of the new collection, you can normally manipulate it. Of course, this feature works with any other collection type.

NON GENERIC COLLECTIONS

Collection initializers are also supported by nongeneric collections using the same syntax.

The `ReadOnlyCollection(Of T)` Collection

The `System.Collections.ObjectModel.ReadOnlyCollection(Of T)` is the read-only counterpart of the `List(Of T)` class. Being read-only, you can add items to the collection only when you create an instance, but then you cannot change it. The constructor requires an argument of type `IList(Of T)` so that the new collection will be generated starting from an existing one. The following code demonstrates how you can instantiate a new ReadonlyCollection:

```
Dim person1 As New Person With {.FirstName = "Alessandro",
                                .LastName = "Del Sole",
                                .Age = 35}
Dim person2 As New Person With {.FirstName = "XXXXX",
                                .LastName = "ZZZZZZZZ",
                                .Age = 44}
Dim person3 As New Person With {.FirstName = "YYYYY",
                                .LastName = "DDDDDDDD",
                                .Age = 18}
```

```
Dim people As New List(Of Person) From {person1, person2, person3}

Dim readonlyPeople As New ReadOnlyCollection(Of Person)(people)
```

As an alternative, you can create a `ReadonlyCollection` invoking the `List(Of T).AsReadOnly` method, as shown in the following code:

```
'Same as above
Dim readonly As ReadOnlyCollection(Of Person) = people.AsReadOnly
```

Invoking `AsReadOnly` produces the same result of creating an explicit instance.

The `Dictionary(Of TKey, TValue)` Collection

The `System.Collections.Generic.Dictionary(Of TKey, TValue)` collection is the generic counterpart for the `HashTable`. Each item within a `Dictionary` is a key/value pair; therefore, the constructor requires two arguments (`TKey` and `TValue`) where the first one is the key and the second one is the value. The following code shows instantiating a `Dictionary(Of String, Integer)` in which the `String` argument contains a person's name and the `Integer` argument contains the person's age:

```
Dim peopleDictionary As New Dictionary(Of String, Integer)
peopleDictionary.Add("Alessandro", 35)
peopleDictionary.Add("Stephen", 27)

peopleDictionary.Add("Rod", 44)
```

A single item in the collection is of type `KeyValuePair(Of TKey, TValue)`, and both arguments reflect the collection's ones. For a better explanation, take a look at the following iteration that performs an action on each `KeyValuePair`:

```
For Each item As KeyValuePair(Of String, Integer) In peopleDictionary
    Console.WriteLine(item.Key & " of age " & item.Value.ToString)

Next
```

The previous code will produce the following output:

```
Alessandro of age 35
Stephen of age 27
Rod of age 44
```

Each `KeyValuePair` object has two properties, `Key` and `Value`, which enable separated access to parts composing the object. You can then manipulate the `Dictionary` like you would other collections.

16

The `SortedDictionary(Of TKey, TValue)` Collection

The `System.Collections.Generic.SortedDictionary(Of TKey, TValue)` works exactly like the `Dictionary` collection, except that items are automatically sorted each time you perform a modification. You can rewrite the code shown in the section about the `Dictionary(Of TKey, TValue)` collection as follows:

```
Dim peopleDictionary As New SortedDictionary(Of String, Integer)

peopleDictionary.Add("Alessandro", 35)
peopleDictionary.Add("Stephen", 27)
peopleDictionary.Add("Rod", 44)

For Each item As KeyValuePair(Of String, Integer) In peopleDictionary
    Console.WriteLine(item.Key & " of age " & item.Value.ToString)

Next
```

This code will produce the following result:

```
Alessandro of age 35
Rod of age 44
Stephen of age 27
```

Notice how the result has a different order than the one we added items to the collection with. In fact, items are sorted alphabetically. This collection performs sorting based on the `Key` part.

The `ObservableCollection(Of T)` Collection

The `System.Collections.ObjectModel.ObservableCollection(Of T)` is a special collection that is typically used in WPF, Silverlight, and Windows Store applications. Its main feature is that it implements the `INotifyPropertyChanged` interface and can therefore raise an event each time its items are affected by any changes, such as adding, replacing, or removing. Thanks to this mechanism, the `ObservableCollection` is the most appropriate collection for the WPF and Silverlight data-binding because it provides support for two-way data-binding in which the user interface gets notification of changes on the collection and is automatically refreshed to reflect those changes. Although a practical example of this scenario is offered in the chapters about WPF, this section shows you how the collection works. The `ObservableCollection` is exposed by the `System.Collections.ObjectModel` namespace, meaning that you need to add an `Imports` directive for this namespace. Notice that in the .NET Framework 4.5 the `ObservableCollection` has been moved to the System.dll assembly from the WindowsBase.dll assembly. This makes it usable not only in WPF applications, but also in other kinds of applications (and this is why you do not need to add any reference manually as you would do in previous versions). Now consider the following code snippet:

```
Dim people As New ObservableCollection(Of Person)
AddHandler people.CollectionChanged, AddressOf CollectionChangedEventHandler
```

The people variable represents an instance of the collection, and its purpose is to store a set of Person class instances. Because the collection exposes a CollectionChanged event, which enables intercepting changes to items in the collection, we need an event handler to understand what is happening. The following code shows an example of event handler implementation:

```
Private Sub CollectionChangedEventHandler(ByVal sender As Object,
                        ByVal e As Specialized.
                        NotifyCollectionChangedEventArgs)

    Select Case e.Action
        Case Is = Specialized.NotifyCollectionChangedAction.Add
            Console.WriteLine("Added the following items:")
            For Each item As Person In e.NewItems
                Console.WriteLine(item.LastName)
            Next
        Case Is = Specialized.NotifyCollectionChangedAction.Remove
            Console.WriteLine("Removed or moved the following items:")
            For Each item As Person In e.OldItems
                Console.WriteLine(item.LastName)
            Next
    End Select
End Sub
```

The System.Collections.Specialized.NotifyCollectionChangedEventArgs type exposes some interesting properties for investigating changes on the collection. For example, the Action property enables you to understand if an item was added, moved, replaced, or removed by the collection via the NotifyCollectionChangedAction enumeration. Next, the collection exposes other interesting properties such as NewItems, which returns an IList object containing the list of items that were added, and OldItems, which returns an IList object containing the list of items that were removed/moved/replaced. The NewStartingIndex and the OldStartingIndex provide information on the position where changes (adding and removing/replacing/moving, respectively) occurred. Now consider the following code, which declares three new instances of the Person class and then adds them to the collection and finally removes one:

```
Dim person1 As New Person With {.FirstName = "Alessandro",
                        .LastName = "Del Sole",
                        .Age = 35}
Dim person2 As New Person With {.FirstName = "XXXXX",
                        .LastName = "ZZZZZZZZ",
                        .Age = 44}
```

16

```
Dim person3 As New Person With {.FirstName = "YYYYY",
                                .LastName = "DDDDDDDD",
                                .Age = 18}
```

```
people.Add(person1)
people.Add(person2)
people.Add(person3)
people.Remove(person1)
```

The `ObservableCollection` works like the List one; therefore, it exposes methods such as `Add`, `Remove`, `RemoveAt`, and so on and supports extension methods. The good news is that each time a new item is added or an item is removed, the `CollectionChanged` event is raised and subsequently handled. Because of our previous implementation, if you run the code, you get the following output:

```
Added the following items:
Del Sole
Added the following items:
ZZZZZZZZ
Added the following items:
DDDDDDDD
Removed or moved the following items:
Del Sole
```

Because of its particularity, the `ObservableCollection(Of T)` can also be useful in scenarios different from WPF, Silverlight, and WinRT, though they remain the best places where you can use it.

The `ReadonlyObservableCollection(Of T)` Collection

As for the `List(Of T)` and also for the `ObservableCollection(Of T)`, there is a read-only counterpart named `ReadonlyObservableCollection(Of T)` that works like the `ReadonlyCollection(Of T)` plus the implementation of the `CollectionChanged` event. The collection is also exposed by the `System.Collections.ObjectModel` namespace.

The `LinkedList(Of T)` Collection

Think of the `System.Collections.Generic.LinkedList(Of T)` collection as a chain in which each ring is an item in the collection that is linked to the others. In other words, an item is linked to the previous one and the next one and points to them. Each item in the collection is considered as a `LinkedListNode(Of T)`, so if you decide to create a `LinkedList(Of Person)`, each `Person` instance will be represented by a `LinkedListNode(Of Person)`. Table 16.2 summarizes the most common methods and properties for the collection over the ones that you already know (derived from `IList(Of T)`).

TABLE 16.2 `LinkedList` Members

Member	Type	Description
AddFirst	Method	Adds a new item as the first in the collection
AddLast	Method	Adds a new item as the last in the collection
AddBefore	Method	Adds a new item before the specified node
AddAfter	Method	Adds a new item after the specified node
Clear	Method	Clears all items in the collection
Contains	Method	Checks if the specified item exists in the collection
CopyTo	Method	Copies the collection into an array
Count	Property	Returns the number of items in the collection
First	Property	Returns the first node in the collection
Last	Property	Returns the last node in the collection
Remove	Method	Removes the specified item from the collection
RemoveFirst	Method	Removes the first item from the collection
RemoveLast	Method	Removes the last item from the collection

The following code provides an example of creating and consuming a `LinkedList(Of Person)` collection (see comments for explanations):

```vb
Dim person1 As New Person With {.FirstName = "Alessandro",
                                .LastName = "Del Sole",
                                .Age = 35}
Dim person2 As New Person With {.FirstName = "XXXXX",
                                .LastName = "ZZZZZZZZ",
                                .Age = 44}
Dim person3 As New Person With {.FirstName = "YYYYY",
                                .LastName = "DDDDDDDD",
                                .Age = 18}

'Creates a new LinkedList
Dim linkedPeople As New LinkedList(Of Person)

'Creates a series of nodes
Dim node1 As New LinkedListNode(Of Person)(person1)
Dim node2 As New LinkedListNode(Of Person)(person2)
Dim node3 As New LinkedListNode(Of Person)(person3)

'The first item in the collection
linkedPeople.AddFirst(node1)

'The last one
linkedPeople.AddLast(node3)
```

16

```
'Add a new item before the last one and after
'the first one
linkedPeople.AddBefore(node3, node2)

'Removes the last item
linkedPeople.RemoveLast()
'Gets the instance of the last item
'(person2 in this case)
Dim lastPerson As Person = linkedPeople.Last.Value

'Determines if person1 is within the collection
Dim isPerson1Available As Boolean = linkedPeople.Contains(person1)
```

The most important difference between this collection and the other ones is that items are linked. This is demonstrated by an Enumerator structure exposed by every instance of the collection that enables moving between items, as demonstrated in the following code snippet:

```
Dim peopleEnumerator As LinkedList(Of Person).
    Enumerator = linkedPeople.GetEnumerator

Do While peopleEnumerator.MoveNext
    'Current is a property that is of type T
    '(Person in this example)
    Console.WriteLine(peopleEnumerator.Current.LastName)
Loop
```

This code demonstrates that items in the collections are linked and that each one points to the next one (see Figure 16.2).

FIGURE 16.2   Demonstrating linked items in a LinkedList collection.

The Queue(Of T) and Stack(Of T) Collections

The .NET Framework offers generic versions of the Queue and Stack collections, known as System.Collections.Generic.Queue(Of T) and System.Collections.Generic.Stack(Of T). Their behavior is the same as nongeneric version, except that they are strongly typed. Because of this, you already know how to work with generic versions, so they are not discussed here.

Building Custom Collections

Built-in collections are good for most scenarios. In some situations you might need to implement custom collections. You have two options: creating a collection from scratch or recur to inheritance. The first choice can be hard. You create a class implementing the `ICollection(Of T)` and `IList(Of T)` (or `IDictionary`) interfaces, but you need to manually write code for performing the most basic actions onto items. The other choice is inheriting from an existing collection. This is a good choice for another reason: You can create your custom base class for other collections. Imagine you want to create a custom collection that stores sets of `FileInfo` objects, each one representing a file on disk. It would not be useful to reinvent the wheel, so inheriting from `List(Of T)` is a good option. The following code inherits from `List(Of FileInfo)` and extends the collection implementing a new `ToObservableCollection` method, which converts the current instance into an `ObservableCollection(Of FileInfo)` and overrides `ToString` to return a customized version of the method:

```
Public Class FileInfoCollection
    Inherits List(Of FileInfo)


    Public Overridable Function ToObservableCollection() As _
            ObservableCollection(Of FileInfo)
        Return New ObservableCollection(Of FileInfo)(Me)
    End Function

    Public Overrides Function ToString() As String
        Dim content As New StringBuilder

        For Each item As FileInfo In Me
            content.Append(item.Name)
        Next
        Return content.ToString
    End Function
End Class
```

Now you have a strongly typed collection working with `FileInfo` objects. Plus, you extended the collection with custom members.

Concurrent Collections

The .NET Framework 4.5 includes the Task Parallel Library (TPL), which offers support for multicore CPU architectures. The library exposes specific generic collections, via the `System.Collections.Concurrent` namespace that was introduced by .NET 4.0. Table 16.3 gives you a list of the new classes.

TABLE 16.3   Concurrent Collections

Name	Description
ConcurrentStack(Of T)	A thread-safe stack collection
ConcurrentQueue(Of T)	A thread-safe queue collection
ConcurrentDictionary(Of TKey, TValue)	A thread-safe strongly typed dictionary of key/value pairs
ConcurrentBag(Of T)	A thread-safe list of objects
ConcurredLinkedList(Of T)	A thread-safe collection in which items are linked to one another

You get an overview of these collections in the appropriate chapters, but for completeness, you now have a full list of available collections.

Iterators in Visual Basic

The concept of iterators is not new in modern programming language—for example, Visual C# has had iterators since version 2005. However, version 2012 is the first time this feature becomes part of the Visual Basic programming language. Technically speaking, iterators are used to step through a collection and iterator functions perform custom iterations over a collection. They can have only an IEnumerable, IEnumerable(Of T), IEnumerator, or IEnumerator(Of T) as their return type. Iterators use the new Yield keyword to return the item that is currently iterated to the caller code; then the iteration stops at that point. After Yield executes, the iteration restarts from that point. With this kind of approach, an iteration over a collection is more responsive and makes items in the collection immediately available to the caller code right after they have been returned. If this technical explanation can seem difficult, let's provide an easier one. Imagine you have a For..Each loop that iterates through a collection and returns a list of elements; such a loop is invoked from within a method that needs to make further elaborations over the list of elements returned by the loop. This is a common situation, and the caller method needs to wait until the For..Each loop completes the iteration and populates the list of elements before it can use it. If the collection that For..Each is iterating is very large, this task can take a lot of time and the caller code will need to wait a while. With iterators, things change for the better—in fact, if you use iterators to loop through a collection, every item in the collection will be immediately sent to the caller via Yield so that the caller can start its elaboration, while the loop is still in progress and goes to completion. In this way an application is faster and more responsive. In the next paragraphs you get more detailed explanations about iterators via some code examples.

ITERATOR FUNCTIONS' SCOPE

Because they are methods, iterator functions can have the same scope of methods. So they can be Private, Public, Friend, Protected, or Protected Friend (except for when they are implemented in Module, where they can be Private, Friend, or Public).

Understanding the Benefits of Iterators in Code

Iterators have plenty of usages, and this chapter describes them all in detail. Before studying the many ways iterators can be useful, though, a better idea is understanding why they allow you to write better and more responsive code. Let's imagine we have a collection of items of type `Person` and a method that iterates through the collection the way you know. Listing 16.1 demonstrates how to reproduce this simple scenario in code.

LISTING 16.1   Iterating Through a Collection the Usual Way

```
Public Class Person
    Public Property FirstName As String
    Public Property LastName As String
    Public Property Age As Integer
End Class

Public Class People
    Inherits List(Of Person)



End Class

Module Module1
    Dim somePeople As New People

    Sub Main()
        'Populates the collection with a million items, for demo purposes
        For i As Integer = 1 To 1000000
            somePeople.Add(New Person With {.FirstName = "First Name: " &
➥i.ToString,
                                            .LastName = "Last Name: " & i.ToString,
                                            .Age = i})
        Next

        For Each item As Person In GetPeople()
            Console.WriteLine("{0}, {1} of age: {2}", item.FirstName,
                            item.LastName, item.Age.ToString)
        Next
        Console.ReadLine()
    End Sub

    Function GetPeople() As IEnumerable(Of Person)
        Dim p As New People
        For Each item As Person In somePeople
```

```
            p.Add(item)
            Threading.Thread.Sleep(10)
        Next
        Return p
    End Function
End Module
```

Notice how a sample collection called `People` is created and populated with a million items for demo purposes. The `GetPeople` method iterates through the `People` collection and returns the result to the caller code (the `Main` method in this example). The code execution is delayed for 10 milliseconds (via `Threading.Thread.Sleep`) to force a small delay and provide a demonstration of performance improvement with iterators (in-memory collections are faster than other collections such as database tables, where you could instead face long running query operations). If you run this code, you will see that `GetPeople` needs to populate the local `p` collection before returning it as a result to the caller, so you will have to wait for this before being able to iterate the result and see the list of elements in the Console window. We can now rewrite the `GetPeople` method using iterators, as follows:

```
Iterator Function GetPeople() As IEnumerable(Of Person)
    For Each item As Person In somePeople
        Yield item
        Threading.Thread.Sleep(10)
    Next
End Function
```

This is an iterator function. It requires the `Iterator` modifier in its definition and returns an object of type `IEnumerable(Of T)`, where `T` is now `Person`. If you run the edited code, you will see how every item of type `Person` is returned from `GetPeople` immediately and made available to the caller code for further elaborations, while the iteration continues its progress. Figure 16.3 shows a moment of the operation progress. In other words, you will not have to wait for all the iteration to complete before elaborating items that it stores. As a consequence, the whole process is faster and the application is more responsive.

MEASURING PERFORMANCES

You can add a `System.Diagnostics.StopWatch` object to the code and use its `Start` and `Stop` method to measure how much time the process takes and make comparisons between both implementations of `GetPeople`.

Now that you have understood the benefits of iterators, it is time to discuss them in more detail.

FIGURE 16.3   Iterators return items while the loop is still in progress.

Simple Iterators

You can return elements from iterator functions with multiple `Yield` invocations. The following code demonstrates how to perform a loop over an iterator that returns a collection of strings:

```vb
Iterator Function StringSeries() As IEnumerable(Of String)
    Yield "First string"
    Yield "Second string"
    Yield "Third string"
    '...
End Function


Sub Main()
    For Each item As String In StringSeries()
        Console.WriteLine(item)
    Next
    Console.ReadLine()
End Sub
```

You can also use a single `Yield` statement inside a `For..Each` or `For..Next` loop. The following code demonstrates how to retrieve the list of odd numbers in a sequence of integers:

```vb
Iterator Function OddNumbers(first As Integer,
            last As Integer) As IEnumerable(Of Integer)
    For number As Integer = first To last
```

```
            If number Mod 2 <> 0 Then
                'is odd
                Yield number
            End If
        Next
    End Function


    Sub Main()
        'Prints 1, 3, 5, 7, 9
        For Each number As Integer In OddNumbers(1, 10)
            Console.WriteLine(number)
        Next

        Console.ReadLine()
    End Sub
```

In this case the caller code in the Sub Main will not need to wait for a collection of integers to be populated before the iteration occurs; instead, each number that comes from the Yield invocation is immediately printed to the Console window.

Exiting from Iterators

You can break the execution of an iterator by using either an Exit Function or a Return statement. The following snippet demonstrates how to exit from an iterator function:

```
Iterator Function StringSeries() As IEnumerable(Of String)
    Yield "First string"
    Yield "Second string"
    Exit Function 'Return is also accepted
    Yield "Third string"
    '...
End Function
```

Iterators with Try..Catch..Finally

Unlike Visual C#, in Visual Basic the Yield statement can be executed from within a Try statement of a Try..Catch..Finally block. The following code demonstrates how to rewrite the OddNumbers iterator function including error handling:

```
Iterator Function OddNumbers(first As Integer,
                last As Integer) As IEnumerable(Of Integer)
    Try
        For number As Integer = first To last
            If number Mod 2 <> 0 Then
                'is odd
                Yield number
            End If
```

```
        Next
    Catch ex As Exception
        Console.WriteLine(ex.Message)
    Finally
        Console.WriteLine("Loop completed.")
    End Try
End Function
```

As you can see, the `Yield` statement is allowed inside the `Try` block.

Anonymous Iterators

Iterators can also be implemented as anonymous methods. These are discussed in more detail in Chapter 20, but for now all you need to know is that they are methods with no name and are defined on-the-fly inside a code block. The following code snippet demonstrates how to implement the previous iterator as an anonymous method:

```
'Type of oddSequence is inferred by the compiler
Dim oddSequence = Iterator Function(first As Integer,
                                last As Integer) As IEnumerable(Of Integer)
            Try
                For number As Integer = first To last
                    If number Mod 2 <> 0 Then
                        'is odd
                        Yield number
                    End If
                Next
            Catch ex As Exception
                Console.WriteLine(ex.Message)
            Finally
                Console.WriteLine("Loop completed.")
            End Try
        End Function

For Each number As Integer In oddSequence(1, 10)
    Console.WriteLine(number)
Next
```

As you can see, the iterator is defined as an in-line method without an explicit name and its result is assigned to a variable whose type is inferred by the compiler (in this case `IEnumerable(Of Integer)`).

Implementing an Iterator Class

Iterators can be useful in creating classes that act like lists. By implementing the `IEnumerable` interface and the `GetEnumerator` method of this interface, you can write efficient code that takes advantage of iterator functions to yield the content of a list. Listing

16.2 demonstrates how to create a class called `BottlesOfWine` that stores a list of bottles of wine given a name and a color of the wine (red or white). Internally it uses a `List(Of BottleOfWine)` instance, but instead of invoking the usual `GetEnumerator` method of the `List` class (provided by the `IEnumerable` interface that the `List` implements), it returns the list of bottles via an iterator function. It also returns a list of bottles based on their color.

LISTING 16.2   Implementing a Collection Class That Uses Iterators

```
Public Class BottleOfWine
    Property Brand As String
    Property Color As WineColor
End Class


Public Enum WineColor
    Red
    White
End Enum


Public Class BottlesOfWine
    Implements IEnumerable(Of BottleOfWine)

    Private _bottles As New List(Of BottleOfWine)

    Public Function GetEnumerator1() As IEnumerator Implements
➥IEnumerable.GetEnumerator
        Return Me._bottles.GetEnumerator
    End Function

    Public Iterator Function GetEnumerator() As IEnumerator(Of BottleOfWine)
➥Implements IEnumerable.GetEnumerator(Of BottleOfWine)

        'Use Yield instead of List.GetEnumerator
        For Each bottle As BottleOfWine In Me._bottles
            Yield bottle
        Next
    End Function

    Private Iterator Function BottlesByColor(ByVal color As WineColor) As
➥IEnumerable _
            (Of BottleOfWine)
        For Each bottle As BottleOfWine In Me._bottles
            If bottle.Color = color Then
```

```
                Yield bottle
            End If
        Next
    End Function


    Public ReadOnly Property RedBottles As IEnumerable(Of BottleOfWine)
        Get
            Return BottlesByColor(WineColor.Red)
        End Get
    End Property


    Public ReadOnly Property WhiteBottles As IEnumerable(Of BottleOfWine)
        Get
            Return BottlesByColor(WineColor.White)
        End Get
    End Property


    Public Sub AddRedBottle(ByVal name As String)
        Me._bottles.Add(New BottleOfWine With {.Brand = name, .Color =
➥WineColor.Red})
    End Sub


    Public Sub AddWhiteBottle(ByVal name As String)
        Me._bottles.Add(New BottleOfWine With {.Brand = name, .Color =
➥WineColor.White})
    End Sub
End Class
```

By returning with `Yield` the result of both the `GetEnumerator` and of `BottlesByColor`
methods, the code is more responsive. You can then use the code easily—for example,
creating a list of bottles of red wine and then iterating the list in a way that is efficient
because the result takes advantage of iterators, as in the following code:

```
Dim bottles As New BottlesOfWine
bottles.AddRedBottle("Chianti")
bottles.AddRedBottle("Cabernet")

'Result is returned via an iterator function
For Each bottle As BottleOfWine In bottles
    Console.WriteLine(bottle.Brand)
Next
```

ITERATORS ARE AN OPPORTUNITY, NOT THE RULE

Iterators provide an additional opportunity to write efficient code, but of course they are not necessary everywhere. You typically use iterators with large collections of objects and over long-running operations. So, they are not a new rule for iterating collections. For this reason, in this book you will find code examples for collections that are not based on iterators, which is instead the general rule. In particular circumstances, samples based on iterators are offered.

Summary

Applications often require data access. You store data within classes and structures, but often you need to group a set of data and collections to help you in this task. The .NET Framework offers both nongeneric collections (such as `ArrayList`, `Queue`, `Stack`, and `HashTable`) and generic ones (such as `List(Of T)`, `ObservableCollection(Of T)`, `Dictionary(Of TKey, TValue)`, `Queue(Of T)`, and `Stack(Of T)`). In both cases you can add, remove, and edit items within collections using the same members (due to the interfaces implementations). Moreover, with the feature of *collection initializers*, you can instantiate and populate collections inline. Although you typically use collections for manipulating data, the .NET Framework provides some special read-only collections, such as `ReadonlyCollection(Of T)`. You learned to create custom collections, which is not an uncommon scenario, and finally you learned a new efficient way to iterate over collections via iterator functions and the `Yield` keyword.

CHAPTER 17

Creating Objects: Visual Tools and Portable Libraries

Visual Studio 2012 is the best version ever of the premier developer tool from Microsoft. It offers a powerful code editor with the presence of IntelliSense that dramatically simplifies your coding experience. Writing code and architecting objects before writing code have the same importance, and for this reason Visual Studio lets you reach both objectives easily. On one side, it enables you to graphically design objects for your applications and contextually write code related to such objects. The built-in tool that enables you to perform this task is known as *Class Designer*, and in this chapter you get a high-level overview of it. On the other side, it is not uncommon for you as a developer to realize that you need to implement new objects on-the-fly—objects that you did not previously consider but that later become necessary or existing objects that must be extended. In this chapter, you also learn how to use this instrumentation and get the most out of its capabilities. Finally, Visual Studio 2012 introduces the *Portable Class Library* tooling that makes it easier to share the same code across multiple platforms, which is so important in a world where different kinds of applications and frameworks need to communicate with one another. So, in this chapter you also learn how to create portable code with the new instrumentation.

Visual Studio Class Designer

Visual Studio 2012 offers an instrument known as Visual Studio Class Designer that you should already know if you have experience with previous versions. You can design objects in a visual way by taking advantage of a graphical tool. You design objects; Visual Studio generates code. In this chapter, you learn how to design objects according to object-oriented principles using the Class Designer to create a new implementation of the Person class and of a couple of derived classes. Before continuing to read, create a new, empty VB project for the Console. This is the base for your subsequent work.

Enabling the Class Designer

To enable the Visual Studio Class Designer, you need to right-click the project name in Solution Explorer and then select **View Class Diagram**. When ready, the Class Designer appears as a new window within the IDE and shows a graphical representation of the main application module, including the definition of the Main method. All tasks you can perform on the Class Designer can be accomplished by invoking commands exposed by the context menu that you get when right-clicking the designer's surface. Figure 17.1 shows the previously mentioned representation of Module1 and the available commands.

FIGURE 17.1   The Visual Studio Class Designer when launched, plus available commands for design operations.

Figure 17.1 also shows the Add command expanded; it provides a list of available objects that you can add to the diagram. Such objects include classes, enumerations, interfaces, structures, delegates, and modules. You can also select the **Comment** command to add sticky notes on the designer's surface. Table 17.1 summarizes the goal of other commands in the context menu.

TABLE 17.1   Commands List for the Class Designer

Command	Description
Add	Provides subcommands for adding objects to the designer's surface.
Zoom	Enables you to zoom the designer surface for a better visualization.
Group Members	Establishes how objects' members must be grouped. By Kind means that members are divided in types groups (for example, properties, methods, and so on). By Access means that members are grouped according to their scope (for example, all public members, all private members, and so on). Sorted Alphabetically means that objects' members are listed in alphabetical order with no grouping options.
Change Members Format	Sets how members' names appear.
Layout Diagram	Rearranges items on the designer's surface for a better view.
Adjust Shapes Width	Automatically adapts objects' width so that their members' names are more readable.
Export Diagram as Image	Enables you to export the generated diagram as an image, in different formats such as .bmp, .jpg, .png, and .tiff.

CLASS DIAGRAMS FILES

Class diagrams generated with the Visual Studio Class Designer are stored within a .cd file that becomes part of the solution. By default, the file is named ClassDiagram1.cd, but you can rename it as you like via Solution Explorer.

Now it's time to use the Class Designer. Your goal is to design an IPerson interface that an abstract class named Person can implement and that will also be the base class for two other derived classes—Customer and Contact, both created with this interesting graphical tool.

Adding and Designing Objects

The first step to perform is creating an interface. To accomplish this, follow these steps:

1. Right-click the designer surface (see Figure 17.1) and select the **Add, Interface** command.

2. When the New Interface dialog box appears, specify the IPerson name and leave all other options unchanged, which are self-explanatory. Figure 17.2 shows the dialog box. This adds a new item on the designer, representing an interface.

FIGURE 17.2   The New Interface dialog box enables you to specify the name of the new interface and other settings as the access level and the filename.

3. Right-click the new interface and select the **Add, | Property** command. For each object type, the context menu provides specific commands related to members the particular object can contain. Figure 17.3 shows how you can accomplish this. When the new property is added to the interface, it is focused and highlighted for renaming, so rename it `FirstName`. Notice that the default type for members is `Integer`; therefore, you need to open the Properties window (by pressing **F4**) and write the appropriate type in the Type field.

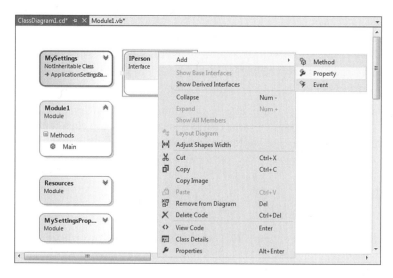

FIGURE 17.3   Adding members to the new interface.

4. Repeat the previous step to add a new `LastName` property and a `FullName` method, both of type `String`. The Class Designer implements `Sub` methods by default that are switched to `Function` when you specify a return type via the Properties window. This step is shown in Figure 17.4.

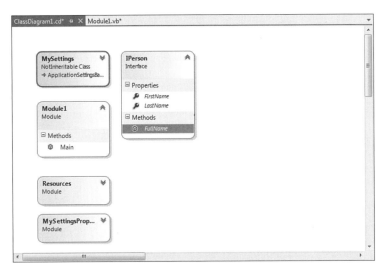

FIGURE 17.4   Specifying a return type for methods and the new completed interface.

If you now double-click the new interface, Visual Studio 2012 shows the code that it generated behind the scenes, as shown in Listing 17.1.

LISTING 17.1   IPerson Interface with Code Generated by Visual Studio

```
Public Interface IPerson
    Property LastName As String
    Property FirstName As String
    Function FullName() As String
End Interface
```

The next step is to add an abstract class named Person, which serves as the base class for subsequent classes. To accomplish this, right-click the designer and select the **Add, Abstract Class** command. Name the new class Person and, when ready, notice within the designer that is marked as MustInherit. Next, double-click the new class and add an Implements IPerson statement below the class declaration. This ensures that the new class is going to implement the IPerson interface. This is reflected in the class diagram and confirmed by the appearance of properties and methods defined within the interface inside the new class and by a rounded symbol that identifies an interface relationship. Figure 17.5 shows the result of the preceding operations.

Listing 17.2 shows the full code for the Person class.

LISTING 17.2   Code for an Abstract Class

```
Public MustInherit Class Person
    Implements IPerson
```

```
    Public Property FirstName As String Implements IPerson.FirstName
    Public MustOverride Function FullName() As String Implements IPerson.FullName
    Public Property LastName As String Implements IPerson.LastName
End Class
```

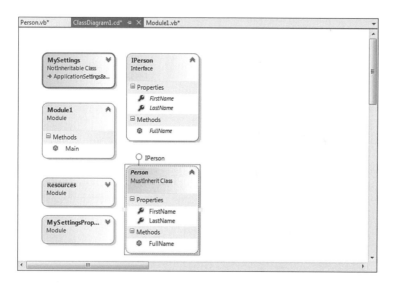

FIGURE 17.5   A new abstract class that implements an interface.

The `FullName` method is declared as `MustOverride`. The Properties window offers deep control to classes. Table 17.2 summarizes the most important properties except those related to filenames and locations.

TABLE 17.2   Class Control Properties

Property	Description
Access	Used to set class's scope
Name	The class name
Custom attributes	Used to decorate the class with attributes
Inheritance modifiers	Set to `MustInherit` for an abstract class, to `NotInheritable` for a sealed class, or to `None` for a general implementation

The Properties window also offers the Remarks and Summary fields that enable you to specify descriptions under the form of XML comments. This feature is available for all members, not just classes. Also, the Properties window shows the Generic, Implements, and Inherits fields, which are disabled by design.

Implementing Derived Classes

The Class Designer is powerful enough to provide support for class inheritance. Suppose you want to create two classes deriving from `Person`—for example, `Contact` and `Customer`. To create a `Contact` class that inherits from `Person`, follow these steps:

1. Right-click the designer surface and select the **Add, Class** command. When the New Class dialog box appears, specify the class name and leave the other properties unchanged.

2. When the new class is added to the designer's surface, select Inheritance from the Toolbox and connect a line between the Person class and the new class. This establishes an inheritance relationship between the two classes. You notice that the designer does not show inherited properties while it is limited to show overridden methods (`FullName` in our example).

3. Add two new properties, `Age` of type `Integer` and `Email` of type `String`, using skills gained in the previous subsection. The result of this implementation is shown in Figure 17.6.

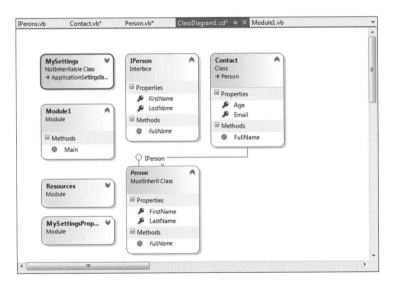

FIGURE 17.6   The implementation of a derived class.

Now create a new `Customer` class that still inherits from `Person` following the previous listed steps, adding two new properties: `CompanyName` of type `String` and `CustomerID` of type `Integer`. The result of this new implementation is shown in Figure 17.7.

To understand how Visual Studio interpreted your operations, click both the `Customer` and `Contact` classes. For your convenience, the code of both classes is shown in Listing 17.3.

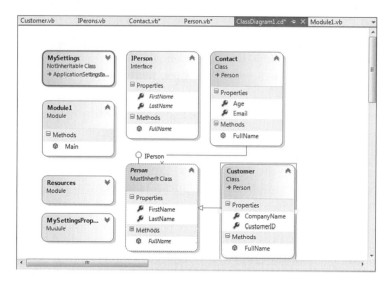

FIGURE 17.7   The implementation of a second derived class.

LISTING 17.3   Code for Derived Classes Generated by the IDE

```
Public Class Contact
    Inherits Person

    Public Property Age As Integer
    Public Property Email As String

    Public Overrides Function FullName() As String
    End Function
End Class
Public Class Customer
    Inherits Person

    Public Property CustomerID As Integer
    Public Property CompanyName As String
    Public Overrides Function FullName() As String
    End Function
End Class
```

It's worth noticing how the IDE correctly wrote inheritance code and marked as Overrides the FullName method in both classes. The generated code can be considered as a mere template; therefore, you have to populate it your own way. To complete your work, you need to write the methods body for FullName in both classes. The following is an example related to the Contact class:

```
Public Overrides Function FullName() As String
    Return String.Format("{0} {1}, of age: {2}",
                         Me.LastName,
                         Me.FirstName,
                         Me.Age.ToString)
End Function
```

On the other hand, the following is the implementation for the `Customer` class:

```
Public Overrides Function FullName() As String
    Return String.Format("Customer {0} is {1}",
                         Me.CustomerID,
                         Me.CompanyName)
End Function
```

In this section you have seen an alternative way for designing classes in Visual Basic 2012. That is important, particularly to get a hierarchical representation. Most of all, such work has been completed with a few mouse clicks.

Creating Multiple Diagrams

You are not limited to creating one diagram. You can add multiple class diagrams to your project so that you can have a graphical representation of a complex hierarchical object's structure. To add diagrams to your project, right-click the project name in Solution Explorer and select the **Add New Item** command. When the Add New Item dialog box appears, select the **Class Diagram** item in the Common Items list (see Figure 17.8).

FIGURE 17.8   Adding a new class diagram to the project.

This can be useful if you have to graphically represent complex frameworks, and if you need large design surfaces.

Exporting the Diagram

As a respectable graphical tool, the Class Designer can export diagrams as images. The tool supports the following image formats:

▶ Windows Bitmap (24 bit)

▶ Portable Network Graphics (.png)

▶ JPEG

▶ Tag Image File Format (.tiff)

▶ Graphics Interchange Format (.gif)

To export diagrams to images, right-click the designer's surface and select the **Export Diagram as Image** command. Figure 17.9 shows the Export Diagram as Image dialog box.

FIGURE 17.9   Exporting diagrams to images.

You can select multiple diagrams if available. You need to select the location, which by default points to the project's folder. The combo box at the bottom of the dialog box enables you to choose the image format.

Class View Window

Since the previous versions of Visual Studio, the IDE offers another graphical tool for managing objects, known as the Class View window. To enable this tool, you can press

Ctrl+Shift+C if it's not already available as a floating window. It's a browsing tool that shows a graphical representation of the objects' hierarchy in your solution and enables you to search for specific members or get information about types being part of your project, including base types. Figure 17.10 shows this tool window in action, pointing to the same project used in the previous section.

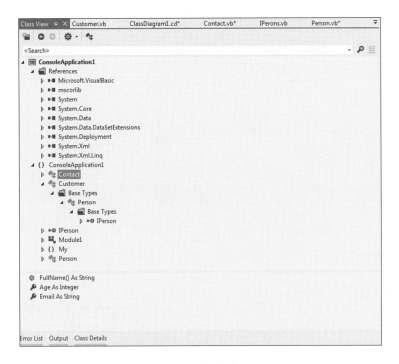

FIGURE 17.10   The Class View tool window.

As you can see in Figure 17.10, the Class View enables you to browse custom objects in your projects (including base types such as interfaces) and built-in objects invoked by your project. Moreover, you can browse references to assemblies and expand them so that you can still get information on members for your custom objects. The Class View window also provides a Settings command that enables you to specify which kind of objects will be shown. (For example, you can decide if the view must include base types.)

Generate from Usage

One great feature in the code editor that Visual Studio 2012 inherits from its predecessor is the ability to generate on-the-fly objects that do not exist yet. This feature is known as Generate from Usage. To understand how it works, create a new Console application named `GenerateFromUsage` and, within the `Main` method, type the following code:

```
Sub Main()
    Dim p As New Person

End Sub
```

Because the `Person` class has not been implemented, the Visual Basic compiler throws an exception, offering the usual pop-up button that suggests solutions, as shown in Figure 17.11.

FIGURE 17.11   Suggestions on how to create the Person class.

As you can see in Figure 17.11, the IDE provides the ability of generating a new Person class directly when writing code offering a Generate 'Class Person' command. There is also another choice named Generate, which is discussed later in this chapter. Now focus on the first choice and click the Generate 'Class Person' command. Visual Studio then creates a new code file named Person.vb that you can find in Solution Explorer as part of the project. This code file contains a basic definition for the Person class that is declared as follows:

```
Class Person
End Class
```

DEFAULT ACCESSIBILITY

When generating objects on-the-fly, Visual Studio assigns the default visibility to both objects and members. If you want to provide a different scope, you need to do it by writing qualifiers manually or by selecting the Generate Other command.

Now go back to the `Main` method; you notice that the error message disappeared. Type the following assignment:

```
p.LastName = "Del Sole"
```

Because the `LastName` property is not exposed by the `Person` class, the Visual Basic compiler throws a new error still offering solutions, as shown in Figure 17.12.

FIGURE 17.12   Generating members on-the-fly.

The IDE correctly recognizes the assignment and proposes adding a new property or a new field in the `Person` class. Click the Generate property stub to add a new property that is implemented in the Person class as follows:

```
Class Person
    Property LastName As String
```

The IDE also correctly specifies the data type to the property (`String` in the preceding example) based on the assignment content. Repeat this last step to add a second property named `FirstName` of type `String` using your first name for convenience. My code looks like the following:

```
p.LastName = "Del Sole"
p.FirstName = "Alessandro"
```

Now we should provide a method that returns the full name for the person. Generating a method stub is also an easy task. Write the following:

```
Dim fullName As String = p.FullName
```

Now the IDE offers three solutions, as shown in Figure 17.13.

You can choose to generate a method, property, or field. The IDE can distinguish which kind of solutions it can propose in that particular coding scenario. Click the Generate method stub command, and Visual Studio implements the `FullName` method as follows:

```
Function FullName() As String
    Throw New NotImplementedException
End Function
```

17

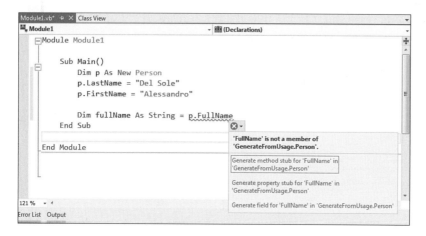

FIGURE 17.13   Generating a new method stub.

The new method throws a `NotImplementedException`; therefore, you need to replace it with your code. All examples shown so far in this book provide the following implementation:

```
Function FullName() As String
    Return String.Concat(LastName, " ", FirstName)
End Function
```

Now you have generated your definitely working `Person` class without exiting from the code editor. This is the most basic approach to the new feature, but this tooling is powerful and enables you to define different kinds of objects according to the context in which you are writing code. This is what the next sections discuss.

Generating Shared Members

Visual Studio is intelligent enough to understand whenever you try to define a shared member. For example, imagine you want to implement a method that returns the number of active instances of the `Person` class. If you type the following code:

```
Person.ReturnInstanceCount()
```

and then select the Generate method stub correction option, Visual Studio generates the following code:

```
Shared Sub ReturnInstanceCount()
    Throw New NotImplementedException
End Sub
```

On-the-Fly Code and Object Initializers

You might often use object initializers to create objects instances in line; generating code on-the-fly is powerful. Consider the following declaration:

```
Dim p As New Person With {.FirstName = "Alessandro",
                          .LastName = "Del Sole"}
```

When you write this code, the `Person` class and its `FirstName` and `LastName` properties do not exist. At this point, you can open the correction options and select the Generate Class command. Visual Studio automatically associates the previous assignments with the class that is initialized in line and generates the appropriate members. Code generation for the previous code snippet produces the following result:

```
Class Person
    Property LastName As String
    Property FirstName As String

End Class
```

With a single mouse click, you have accomplished a task that would normally require a couple more steps, as described in the previous section.

Generating Complex Objects

You can now generate new objects on-the-fly by using default solutions proposed by Visual Studio. You are not limited to generating previously described classes and members. Visual Studio enables you to generate the following types:

▶ Classes

▶ Structures

▶ Interfaces

▶ Delegates

▶ Enumerations

The following is instead the list of members you can generate for the preceding types:

▶ Methods

▶ Properties

▶ Fields

You can generate objects on-the-fly by running the New Type dialog box that you can activate by choosing Generate Other solution instead of Generate Class. For example,

17

imagine you want to generate a new structure on-the-fly. First, type the following line of code:

```
Dim threeDim As New ThreePoint
```

Because the `ThreePoint` type does not exist, Visual Studio 2012 throws an error proposing fixes. At this point, click the Generate New Type solution, as shown in Figure 17.14.

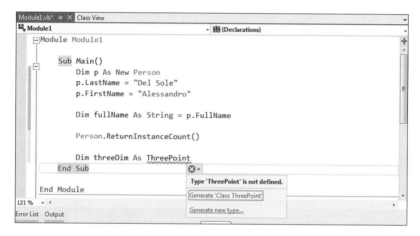

FIGURE 17.14   Selecting the Generate New Type command for constructing different types.

The Generate New Type window displays, which enables you to get deeper control over the type generation, as shown in Figure 17.15.

FIGURE 17.15   The Generate New Type dialog box.

Several options are available for generating a new type. First, the Access combo box enables you to specify the accessibility level that can be Public, Friend, or the default level for the selected type. The Kind combo box enables you to specify which type you intend to generate. Figure 17.15 also shows a list of available types. For our example, leave the default settings unchanged. In the lower part of the dialog box, you can establish where the type must be declared and in which file. You can select which project (if the solution contains more than one project) defines the new type and which code file declares the new type.

Here it's worth mentioning that you can decide to create a new file (default choice) or to add the code to an existing one using the Add to Existing File control box. When you click **OK**, the new type is created. Visual Studio generates the following structure declaration:

```
Public Structure ThreePoint

End Structure
```

Now you can repeat the steps you performed when you added members to the `Person` class in the first section of this chapter. For example, first write the following code:

```
ThreePoint.X = 10
ThreePoint.Y = 20
ThreePoint.Z = 30
```

None of the X, Y, and Z properties has been implemented yet within the `ThreePoint` structure; therefore, you can add them via the correction options. (Refer to Figure 17.12 for a recap.)

Interfaces Additions

The Visual Studio 2012 IDE offers default solutions according to naming conventions it finds in your code. This is particularly true if you want to generate interfaces instead of other types. For example, if you type

```
Dim interfaceVariable as ITestInterface
```

The IDE notices that `ITestInterface`'s identifier begins with the letter *I* and is followed by another capital letter; therefore, it assumes you want to generate an interface (if the second letter is not capital, it would offer to generate a class). Because of this, the default solution in the correction options will not be Generate Class, but Generate Interface. The stub for the new interface is the following:

```
Interface ITestInterface
End Interface
```

If you want to change the accessibility level for the new interface, you need to generate it invoking the Generate New Type window or writing the appropriate qualifier manually.

Creating Portable Classes

During the previous years a number of platforms built upon subsets of the .NET Framework have been produced, such as (but not limited to) Silverlight, Windows Phone, and the Windows Runtime for Windows 8. Because of this, one of the biggest concerns for developers is creating class libraries that can share the same code across multiple platforms. So far, developers have had to remember which assemblies and what kind of types were supported in each of those platforms and then manually create and arrange class library projects to make them reusable. Fortunately, Visual Studio 2012 helps Visual Basic developers solve this problem by introducing a new project template called Portable Class Library. This project template enables you to create portable libraries that only reference assemblies that are common to the following platforms:

- ▶ .NET Framework 4.5

- ▶ Silverlight 4 and 5

- ▶ Windows Phone 7 and 7.1 SDK

- ▶ .NET for Windows 8 Store Apps

- ▶ Xbox 360

You will not be able to take advantage of all the types and members offered by a specific platform, but you will be sure that what you have available in a portable class library will run on all the aforementioned platforms with no effort. You create a portable class library by selecting **File**, **New**, **Project** and then selecting the Portable Class Library project template in the Add New Project dialog box, as demonstrated in Figure 17.16.

FIGURE 17.16   Creating a new portable class library.

After specifying a name for the project and clicking OK, Visual Studio will ask you to select the target platforms. By default, the project will target .NET 4.5, Silverlight 4 and 5, Windows Phone 7 and 7.1 SDK, and .NET for Windows 8 Store Apps as represented in Figure 17.17.

FIGURE 17.17   Specifying platforms that the portable library will target.

At a higher level, a portable class library project includes references to the following assemblies:

- ▶ MsCorLib.dll
- ▶ System.dll
- ▶ System.Core.dll
- ▶ System.ComponentModel.Composition.dll
- ▶ System.ComponentModel.Annotations.dll
- ▶ System.Net.dll
- ▶ System.Runtime.Serialization.dll
- ▶ System.ServiceModel.dll
- ▶ System.Xml.dll
- ▶ System.Xml.Linq.dll
- ▶ System.Xml.Serialization.dll
- ▶ System.Windows.dll

You can easily see which assemblies and namespaces are part of a portable library by expanding the References node in Solution Explorer and then double-clicking the .NET Portable Subset item, which will be opened in the Object Browser (see Figure 17.18).

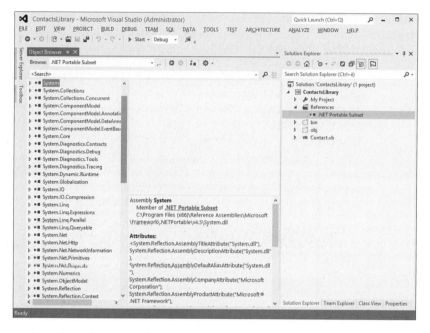

FIGURE 17.18   Investigating the portable assemblies' subset.

Not all the assemblies are supported on all the platforms—for example, the System. ComponentModel.Composition.dll, which exposes the Managed Extensibility Framework (MEF), is not supported on Windows Phone and Xbox 360. For a full comparison between platforms and supported assemblies, visit: http://msdn.microsoft.com/en-us/library/ gg597391(v=vs.110).aspx. Visual Studio 2012 adds references only to assemblies that are supported by all the selected platforms. If you try to add a reference to an assembly that is not supported by all the selected platforms, then you will get a warning.

Creating a Sample Portable Library

WHAT WE ASSUME ABOUT YOU IN THIS SECTION

The sample demonstrated in this section assumes you already have experience with either WPF or Silverlight (or both), and the reason is that here we explain concepts such as the MVVM pattern that requires existing knowledge of how the data-binding works in XAML code, of what a command is in those technologies, and knowledge of other concepts specific to WPF and Silverlight that it is not possible to summarize in a short chapter.

Even if having an opportunity of sharing the same code across multiple platforms is obviously a great benefit at a more general level, the Portable Class Library template has a couple of specific purposes: making interaction with Windows Communication Foundation (WCF) services easier and providing portable implementations of the

Model-View-ViewModel (MVVM) pattern. This pattern has been very popular among WPF and Silverlight developers in the past years because it enables them to achieve a high level of separation between data business objects (the model), the business logic (view models), and the user interface (the view) built upon XAML. So, even though you can create portable libraries for different purposes, the most common is making MVVM-based objects as reusable as possible. The MVVM pattern is not typically intended for beginners, so this section shows an example that is intended for an intermediate audience with existing experience on the WPF or Silverlight platform. That said, create a new project based on the Portable Class Library template and name it ContactLibrary. The goal of the library is exposing a simplified contact management framework. When creating the project, ensure you are targeting the default platforms.

The Model

When the project is ready in Visual Studio 2012, add a new class called `Contact`; see the code in Listing 17.4.

LISTING 17.4   Defining the Model—A Contact Class

```vb
Public Class Contact
    Public Property ContactID() As Integer
    Public Property FirstName() As String
    Public Property LastName As String
    Public Property EmailAddress As String
    Public Property PhysicalAddress As String
    Public Property Phone() As String
End Class
```

The class is a simplified business object to represent a contact. Next, add a class called `Contacts`, which is a collection of `Contact` objects. The code shown in Listing 17.5 demonstrates its implementation.

LISTING 17.5   Defining the Model—A Collection of Contacts

```vb
Public Class Contacts
    Private _contacts As ObservableCollection(Of Contact)

    Public Sub New()
        Me._contacts = New ObservableCollection(Of Contact)
        'Create some sample data
        Me._contacts.Add(New Contact With {.ContactID = 1, .FirstName =
➡"Alessandro",
                                        .LastName = "Del Sole",
                                        .EmailAddress = _
                                        "alessandro.delsole@visual-basic.it",
                                        .Phone = "111-111-111",
                                        .PhysicalAddress = "Cremona"})
```

17

```vb
        Me._contacts.Add(New Contact With {.ContactID = 2, .FirstName = "Renato",
                                .LastName = "Marzaro",
                                .EmailAddress = _
                                "renato.marzaro@visual-basic.it",
                                .Phone = "222-111-111",
                                .PhysicalAddress = "Varese"})

        Me._contacts.Add(New Contact With {.ContactID = 3, .FirstName = "Diego",
                                .LastName = "Cattaruzza",
                                .EmailAddress = _
                                "dcattaruzza@visual-basic.it",
                                .Phone = "222-222-111",
                                .PhysicalAddress = "Trieste"})

        Me._contacts.Add(New Contact With {.ContactID = 4, .FirstName = "Antonio",
                                .LastName = "Catucci",
                                .EmailAddress = _
                                "antonio.catucci@visual-basic.it",
                                .Phone = "222-111-222",
                                .PhysicalAddress = "Milan"})

    End Sub

    Public Function GetContacts() As ObservableCollection(Of Contact)
        Return Me._contacts
    End Function

    Public Sub DeleteContact(currentContact As Contact)
        Me._contacts.Remove(currentContact)
    End Sub

End Class
```

The code in Listing 17.5 creates some sample contacts in the constructor and populates a collection of type `ObservableCollection(Of Contact)`. Assuming you already have experience with WPF or Silverlight, you might know that this is the most appropriate collection for binding data to the user interface because it supports change notification. Both the `Contact` and `Contacts` class represent our data, so they are the *Model* in the MVVM implementation. In a typical MVVM implementation, you need to implement a class called `RelayCommand` (by convention), which implements the `ICommand` interface. Such an interface is typical in WPF and Silverlight and enables you to implement commands— that is, actions that can be executed in the desired circumstance. Implementing `ICommand` requires exposing a method called `Execute` (which represents the action to take when the command is invoked) and another method called `CanExecute` (which returns `Boolean` and establishes whether the command can be executed). With the `RelayCommand` class, the code relays the command logic by implementing a generic handler that will launch the action required by every command in the library. The code in Listing 17.6 demonstrates how to implement the `RelayCommand` class.

LISTING 17.6   Relaying the Command Logic

```vb
Imports System.Windows.Input

Public Class RelayCommand
    Implements ICommand

    Private _isEnabled As Boolean
    Private ReadOnly _handler As Action

    Public Sub New(ByVal handler As Action)
        _handler = handler
    End Sub

    Public Event CanExecuteChanged As EventHandler
➥Implements ICommand.CanExecuteChanged

    Public Property IsEnabled() As Boolean
        Get
            Return _isEnabled
        End Get
        Set(ByVal value As Boolean)
            If (value <> _isEnabled) Then
                _isEnabled = value
                RaiseEvent CanExecuteChanged(Me, EventArgs.Empty)
            End If
        End Set
    End Property

    Public Function CanExecute(parameter As Object) As Boolean Implements
➥ICommand.CanExecute
        Return IsEnabled
    End Function

    Public Sub Execute(parameter As Object) Implements ICommand.Execute
        _handler()
    End Sub

End Class
```

Notice how the `CanExecute` method returns a Boolean value that is set by the caller code. Finally, notice how `Execute` invokes a generic handler under the form of an instance of the `Action` class—that is the actual command.

View Models

You now need an intermediate layer that contains the business logic and that exposes data and commands to the user interface. The goal is in fact separating the business logic from the user interface so that the latter will not interact directly with the data. The reason for this separation is making data and business logic abstracted from the UI and, therefore, reusable. By convention, you create a `ViewModelBase` class that is the base class for all other view models. The code in Listing 17.7 demonstrates how to create the `ViewModelBase` class and how to create a derived view model specific for the `Contacts` collection, which exposes data and commands (see comments in the code for explanations).

LISTING 17.7   Defining View Models

```vb
Imports System.ComponentModel
Imports System.Collections.ObjectModel

'Generic View Model
Public MustInherit Class ViewModelBase
    Implements INotifyPropertyChanged

    Public Event PropertyChanged As PropertyChangedEventHandler Implements
INotifyPropertyChanged.PropertyChanged

    'Raise a property change notification
    Protected Overridable Sub OnPropertyChanged(propname As String)
        RaiseEvent PropertyChanged(Me, New PropertyChangedEventArgs(propname))
    End Sub
End Class


Public Class ContactViewModel
    Inherits ViewModelBase

    Private _contacts As ObservableCollection(Of Contact)
    Private _currentContact As Contact
    Private _contactList As Contacts
    Private _deleteContactCommand As RelayCommand

    Public Sub New()
        Me._contactList = New Contacts
        Me._contacts = Me._contactList.GetContacts

        SetupCommands()
    End Sub
```

```vb
'Set up commands by creating instances of RelayCommand
'and passing the appropriate delegate
Private Sub SetupCommands()
    DeleteContactCommand = New RelayCommand(AddressOf DeleteContact)
End Sub


'Expose the command
Public Property DeleteContactCommand() As RelayCommand
    Get
        Return _deleteContactCommand
    End Get
    Private Set(value As RelayCommand)
        _deleteContactCommand = value
    End Set
End Property


'Expose the list of contact
Public Property Contacts() As ObservableCollection(Of Contact)
    Get
        Return Me._contacts
    End Get
    Set(value As ObservableCollection(Of Contact))
        Me._contacts = value
    End Set
End Property


'Represents the currently selected contact
'Raise a property change notification
'Enable the command
Public Property CurrentContact() As Contact
    Get
        Return _currentContact
    End Get
    Set(value As Contact)
        _currentContact = value
        OnPropertyChanged("CurrentContact")
        DeleteContactCommand.IsEnabled = True
    End Set
End Property


'Delete the specified contact
Public Sub DeleteContact()
    Me._contactList.DeleteContact(CurrentContact)
End Sub


End Class
```

17

It is important to remember that a good view model exposes collections of data only via ObservableCollection(Of T) objects.

The View

The View represents the user interface in a client application and is typically based on XAML code, which means WPF, Silverlight, or Metro-style Windows applications. The goal of the example is to demonstrate how two different clients can share not only the same implementation of the model and view model, but also the same XAML code. For a better understanding, add a WPF project and a Silverlight (version 5) project to the current solution, both for Visual Basic. In both projects, add a reference to the ContactsLibrary project (for the Silverlight project the reference must be added to the client project, not the web one). Both applications will show a data grid and a button that will enable you to delete the selected contact in the data grid. In the WPF project, the XAML code for the main window is represented in Listing 17.8.

LISTING 17.8   Defining a View in WPF

```
<Window x:Class="MainWindow"
    xmlns="http://schemas.microsoft.com/winfx/2006/xaml/presentation"
    xmlns:x="http://schemas.microsoft.com/winfx/2006/xaml"
    Title="MainWindow" Height="350" Width="525">
    <Grid>
        <Grid.RowDefinitions>
            <RowDefinition/>
            <RowDefinition Height="40"/>
        </Grid.RowDefinitions>
        <DataGrid Name="ContactsDataGrid" ItemsSource="{Binding Contacts}"
                AutoGenerateColumns="True" SelectedItem="{Binding
➥CurrentContact}"/>
        <Button Name="DeleteButton" Command="{Binding DeleteContactCommand}"
                Width="100" Height="30" Grid.Row="1"
                Content="Delete"/>
    </Grid>
</Window>
```

The DataGrid control is data-bound to the Contacts collection of the view model, and the SelectedItem property is bound to the CurrentContact property of the same view model. The Button control does not work with a Click event; instead it is bound to the DeleteContactCommand command. This makes it so the user interface does not have to work directly against the data. Listing 17.9 shows the user interface in the Silverlight client.

LISTING 17.9   Defining a View in Silverlight

```
<UserControl
    xmlns="http://schemas.microsoft.com/winfx/2006/xaml/presentation"
    xmlns:x="http://schemas.microsoft.com/winfx/2006/xaml"
    xmlns:d="http://schemas.microsoft.com/expression/blend/2008"
    xmlns:mc="http://schemas.openxmlformats.org/markup-compatibility/2006"
    xmlns:sdk="http://schemas.microsoft.com/winfx/2006/xaml/presentation/sdk"
x:Class="SilverlightApplication1.MainPage"
    mc:Ignorable="d"
    d:DesignHeight="300" d:DesignWidth="400">

    <Grid x:Name="LayoutRoot" Background="White">

        <Grid.RowDefinitions>
            <RowDefinition/>
            <RowDefinition Height="40"/>
        </Grid.RowDefinitions>
        <sdk:DataGrid Name="ContactsDataGrid" ItemsSource="{Binding Contacts}"
                AutoGenerateColumns="True" SelectedItem="{Binding
➥CurrentContact}"/>
        <Button Name="DeleteButton" Command="{Binding DeleteContactCommand}"
                Width="100" Height="30" Grid.Row="1"
                Content="Delete"/>
    </Grid>
</UserControl>
```

Notice that both listings are almost identical—there's just a difference in the fact that the Silverlight client uses a `UserControl` object instead of `Window` and that the `DataGrid` control requires importing the `sdk` namespace.

The final step is creating an instance of the view model in the code-behind. The following code shows how to implement the constructor in both projects, exactly in the same way:

```
Public Sub New()

    ' This call is required by the designer.
    InitializeComponent()

    ' Add any initialization after the InitializeComponent() call.
    Me.DataContext = New ContactLibrary.ContactViewModel

End Sub
```

17

If you now run both the applications, you will see how they show a similar user interface and how they are able to perform exactly the same operations against the data collection, which has been possible due to the portable class library and the MVVM pattern. Figure 17.19 shows the WPF application in action, whereas Figure 17.20 shows the Silverlight one.

FIGURE 17.19 The WPF client in action.

FIGURE 17.20 The Silverlight client in action.

You might now understand why it is so important to have an opportunity to share code across different platforms and how the Portable Class Library project template makes it easy in Visual Studio 2012.

DEPLOYING PORTABLE LIBRARIES

Deploying portable libraries requires adding libraries themselves as dependencies in the setup procedure you create. Visual Studio 2012 enables you to deploy applications via InstallShield limited edition and ClickOnce, as you discover in Chapter 51, "Setup and Deployment Projects with InstallShield and for Visual Studio," and Chapter 52, "Deploying Applications with ClickOnce." You can find information on adding dependencies inside those chapters but also in the MSDN documentation, which also explains some hints for Silverlight clients, available at the following address: http://msdn.microsoft.com/en-us/library/gg597391(v=vs.110).aspx.

Summary

In this chapter you saw how to design objects for your application using the built-in Visual Studio tool known as Visual Studio Class Designer. This tool enables you to design objects via a specific designer that offers support for adding all kinds of .NET objects, such as classes, structures, interfaces, delegates, enumerations, and modules. Behind the scenes, this tool generates code related to design operations. You saw how easily you can implement interfaces, abstract classes, and derive classes by learning steps that you will be required to perform for other objects. Completing the topic, the chapter provided information on creating multiple diagrams and exporting diagrams to images.

An overview about one of the most important IDE features in Visual Studio 2012, known as Generate from Usage, was also presented. You learned how you can generate objects on-the-fly, first writing code and then generating objects that you invoke with just a couple of mouse clicks. You also saw how you can generate customized objects running the Generate New Type dialog box that provides deep control over types to be generated on-the-fly. Finally, you learned how Visual Studio 2012 offers the perfect environment in which to create objects that can be shared across multiple platforms via the Portable Class Library addition, with an advanced example based on the Model-View-ViewModel pattern that was useful to demonstrate how the same code can run on WPF and Silverlight.

17

Manipulating Files and Streams

Manipulating files, directories, drives, and pathnames has always been one of the most common requirements for every role in IT for home users. Since MS-DOS, you have probably had this necessity tons of times. In application development for the .NET Framework with Visual Basic 2012, manipulating files is even more straightforward because you have two opportunities: accessing system resources with the usual ease due to self-explanatory classes and members and because of the Common Language Runtime (CLR) as a supervisor. In this chapter, you learn how to manipulate files, directories, and drives by using specific .NET classes. Moreover, you learn about transporting such simplicity into more general data exchange objects, known as streams.

Manipulating Directories and Pathnames

The .NET Framework makes it easier to work with directories and pathnames, providing the `System.IO.Directory` and `System.IO.Path` classes. These classes offer shared methods for accessing directories and directory names, enabling deep manipulation of folders and names. To be honest, `System.IO.Path` also provides members for working against filenames, and due to its nature, it is included in this section. In some situations, you need to work against single directories as instances of .NET objects, and this is where the `System.IO.DirectoryInfo` class comes in. In this section, you learn to get the most from these classes for directory manipulation.

> **TIP**
>
> All the code examples provided in this chapter require an `Imports System.IO` directive to shorten lines of code.

The `System.IO.Path` Class

Often you need to work with pathnames, directory names, and filenames. The .NET Framework provides the `System.IO.Path` class, offering shared members that enable you to manipulate pathnames. For example, you might want to extract the filename from a pathname. This is accomplished by invoking the `GetFileName` method as follows:

```
'Returns "TextFile.txt"
Dim fileName As String = Path.GetFileName("C:\TextFile.txt")
```

The `GetExtension` method returns instead only the file extension and is used as follows:

```
'Returns ".txt"
Dim extension As String = Path.GetExtension("C:\TextFile.txt")
```

To ensure that a filename has an extension, you can also invoke the `HasExtension` method that returns `True` if the filename has one. In some situations you need to extract the filename without considering its extension. The `GetFileNameWithoutExtension` accomplishes this:

```
'Returns "TextFile"
Dim noExtension As String = Path.
                    GetFileNameWithoutExtension("C:\TextFile.txt")
```

Another common situation is retrieving the directory name from a full pathname that includes a filename, too. The `GetDirectoryName` method enables you to perform this:

```
'Returns "C:\Users\Alessandro\My Documents"
Dim dirName As String =

    Path. GetDirectoryName("C:\Users\Alessandro\My Documents\Document.txt")
```

When working with filenames, you might want to replace the extension. This is accomplished by invoking the `ChangeExtension` method as follows:

```
'Returns "MyFile.Doc"
Dim extReplaced As String = Path.ChangeExtension("MyFile.Txt", ".doc")
```

Notice that such a method returns a string that contains the required modification but does not rename the file on disk (which is covered later). Path is also useful when you need to create temporary files or to store files in the Windows temporary folder. You invoke the `GetTempFileName` method to get a unique temporary file:

```
Dim temporaryFile As String = Path.GetTempFileName
```

The method returns the filename of the temporary file so that you can easily access it and treat it like any other file, being sure that its name is unique. If you instead need to access Windows temporary folder, you can invoke the `GetTempPath` method as follows:

```
Dim temporaryWinFolder As String = Path.GetTempPath
```

You could combine both temporary folder name and temporary filename to create a temporary file in the temporary folder. Combining pathnames is accomplished by invoking the `Combine` method, which takes two arguments such as the first pathname and the second one, or a parameter array containing strings representing pathnames. You can also generate a random filename invoking the `GetRandomFileName` method:

```
Dim randomFile As String = Path.GetRandomFileName
```

The difference with `GetTempFileName` is that this one also creates a physical file on disk, returning the full path. `System.IO.Path` offers two other interesting methods: `GetInvalidFileNameChars` and `GetInvalidPathChars`. These both return an array of `Char` storing unaccepted characters within filenames and within directory names, respectively. They are useful if you generate a string that will then be used as a filename or folder name.

The `System.IO.Directory` Class

To access directories, you use the `System.IO.Directory` class that offers shared members that enable you to perform common operations on folders. All members should be self-explanatory. For example, you can check whether a directory already exists and, if not, create a new one as follows:

```
If Not Directory.Exists("C:\Test") Then
    Directory.CreateDirectory("C:\Test")
End If
```

The `Move` method enables you to move a directory from one location to another; it takes two arguments, the source directory name and the target name:

```
Directory.Move("C:\Test", "C:\Demo")
```

If the target directory already exists, an `IOException` is thrown. You can easily get or set attribute information for directories by invoking special methods. For example, you can get the directory creation time by invoking the `GetCreationTime` method that returns a `Date` type or the `SetCreationTime` that requires a date specification, to modify the creation time:

```
Dim createdDate As Date = Directory.GetCreationTime("C:\Demo")
Directory.SetCreationTime("C:\Demo", New Date(2009, 5, 10))
```

18

Table 18.1 summarizes members for getting/setting attributes.

TABLE 18.1   Members for Getting/Setting Attributes

Method	Description
GetAccessControl/ SetAccessControl	Gets/Sets the ACL entries for the specified directory via a System.Security.AccessControl.DirectorySecurity object
GetCreationTime/ SetCreationTime	Gets/Sets the creation time for the directory
GetCreationTimeUtc/ SetCreationTimeUtc	Gets/Sets the directory creation time in the Coordinated Universal Time format
GetLastAccessTime/ SetLastAccessTime	Gets/Sets the directory last access time
GetLastAccessTimeUtc/ SetLastAccessTimeUtc	Gets/Sets the directory last access time in the Coordinated Universal Time format
GetLastWriteTime/ SetLastWriteTime	Gets/Sets the directory last write time
GetLastWriteTimeUtc/ SetLastWriteTimeUtc	Gets/Sets the directory last write time in the Coordinated Universal Time format

You can easily get other information, such as the list of files available within the desired directory. You can get the list of files from a directory by invoking the GetFiles method, returning an array of string (each one is a filename), which works like this:

```
'Second argument is optional, specifies a pattern for search
Dim filesArray() As String = Directory.GetFiles("C:\", "*.exe")
```

As an alternative, you can invoke the EnumerateFiles that returns an IEnumerable(Of String) and that works like this:

```
'get files
Dim filesEnumerable As IEnumerable(Of String) = _
                    Directory.EnumerateFiles("C:\", "*.exe")

For Each item In filesEnumerable
    Console.WriteLine("File name: {0}", item)
Next
```

This difference probably does not make much sense at this particular point of the book, but you learn later that IEnumerable objects are LINQ-enabled; therefore, you can write LINQ queries against sequences of this type. Similarly to GetFiles and EnumerateFiles, you invoke GetDirectories and EnumerateDirectories to retrieve a list of all subdirectories' names within the specified directory. Next, the GetFiles and EnumerateFiles return a list of all filenames and subdirectory names within the specified directory. Actually there is another difference between GetXXX and EnumerateXXX methods, which is about perfor-mance: The latter starts enumerating as the Framework is still gathering files/directories, making things faster and more efficient.

To delete a directory, you invoke the Delete method. It works only if a directory is empty and requires the directory name:

```
'Must be empty
Directory.Delete("C:\Demo")
```

If the folder is not empty, an IOException is thrown. Delete has an overload that accepts a Boolean value if you want to delete empty subdirectories, too. The Directory class also provides the capability of retrieving a list of available drives on your machine. This is accomplished by invoking the GetLogicalDrives method that returns an array of String, which you can then iterate:

```
Dim drivesOnMyMachine() As String = Directory.
                              GetLogicalDrives

For Each drive In drivesOnMyMachine
    Console.WriteLine(drive)

Next
```

On my machine the preceding code produces the output shown in Figure 18.1.

FIGURE 18.1   Enumerating the list of drives on the current system.

The last example is about retrieving the current directory, which is accomplished by invoking the `GetCurrentDirectory` method:

```
Dim currentFolder As String = Directory.GetCurrentDirectory
```

You can also set the current folder by invoking the shared `SetCurrentDirectory` method, passing the folder name as an argument. Accessing directories via the `Directory` class is straightforward, but in some circumstances you have no access to specific information. For this, a more flexible class that enables you to work on specific directories is `DirectoryInfo`.

The `System.IO.DirectoryInfo` Class

The `System.IO.DirectoryInfo` class represents a single directory. More precisely, an instance of the `DirectoryInfo` class handles information about the specified directory. It inherits from `System.IO.FileSystemInfo`, which is a base class that provides the basic infrastructure for representing directories or files. You create an instance of the `DirectoryInfo` class by passing the desired directory name as an argument to the constructor:

```
Dim di As New DirectoryInfo("C:\Demo")
```

You have the same members that you already learned about for the `Directory` class, with some differences. First, now members are instance members and not shared. Second, methods summarized in Table 18.1 are now properties. Third, members are invoked directly on the instance that represents the directory; therefore, you do not need to pass the directory name as an argument. For example, you remove an empty directory by invoking the instance method `Delete` as follows:

```
di.Delete()
```

An interesting property is `DirectoryInfo.Attributes`, which enables you to specify values from the `System.IO.FileAttributes` enumeration and that determine directory behavior. For example, you can make a directory hidden and read-only setting bitwise flags as follows:

```
di.Attributes = FileAttributes.Hidden Or FileAttributes.ReadOnly
```

When you specify values from such enumeration, IntelliSense can help you understand what the value is about; it's worth mentioning that such values are self-explanatory. Sometimes you do not programmatically create instances of `DirectoryInfo`; instead you receive an instance from some other objects. For example, the `Directory.CreateDirectory` shared method returns a `DirectoryInfo` object. In such cases, you can get further information as the directory name invoking the `FullName` property, which returns the full pathname of the folder, or the `Name` property that just returns the name without path. Both work like this:

```
Dim directoryFullName As String = di.FullName
Dim directoryName As String = di.Name
```

Use the `DirectoryInfo` class each time you need to store information for specific directories—for example, within collections.

The `System.IO.DriveInfo` Class

Similarly to `System.IO.DirectoryInfo`, `System.IO.DriveInfo` provides access to drives information. Using this class is straightforward; it provides information on the disk type, disk space (free and total), volume label, and other self-explanatory properties that you can discover with IntelliSense. The following example shows how you can create an instance of the class and retrieve information on the specified drive:

```
Sub DriveInfoDemo()
    Dim dr As New DriveInfo("C:\")

    Console.WriteLine("Drive type: {0}", dr.DriveType.ToString)
    Console.WriteLine("Volume label: {0}", dr.VolumeLabel)
    Console.WriteLine("Total disk space: {0}", dr.TotalSize.ToString)
    Console.WriteLine("Available space: {0}",
                        dr.AvailableFreeSpace.ToString)
    dr = Nothing
End Sub
```

Handling Exceptions for Directories and Pathnames

When working with directories and pathnames, encountering exceptions is not so uncommon. Table 18.2 summarizes directory-related exceptions.

TABLE 18.2   Directory-Related Exceptions

Exception	Description
IOException	General exception that happens when operations on directories fail (such as creating existing directories, deleting nonempty directories, and so on)
DirectoryNotFoundException	Thrown when the directory is not found
PathTooLongException	Thrown when the pathname exceeds the size of 248 characters for folders and 260 for filenames
UnauthorizedAccessException	Thrown if the caller code doesn't have sufficient rights to access the directory
ArgumentNullException	Thrown when the supplied argument is Nothing
ArgumentException	Thrown when the supplied argument is invalid

18

It is important to implement `Try..Catch` blocks for handling the previously described exceptions and provide the user the ability to escape from such situations.

Manipulating Files

Manipulating files is a daily task for every developer. Luckily, the .NET Framework provides an easy infrastructure for working with files. In this section, you learn about the `System.IO.File` and `System.IO.FileInfo` classes that also represent some important concepts before you go into streams.

The `System.IO.File` Class

The `System.IO.File` class provides access to files on disk exposing special shared members. For example, you can easily create a text file invoking two methods: `WriteAllText` and `WriteAllLines`. Both create a new text file, put into the file the given text, and then close the file; however, the second one enables you to write the content of an array of strings into multiple lines. The following code provides an example:

```
File.WriteAllText("C:\Temp\OneFile.txt", "Test message")


Dim lines() As String = {"First", "Second", "Third"}
File.WriteAllLines("C:\Temp\OneFile.txt", lines)
```

Such methods are useful because they avoid the need to manually close files on disk when you perform the writing operation. You can also easily create binary files by invoking the `WriteAllBytes` method that works like the previous ones but requires the specification of an array of byte instead of text. The following is a small example:

```
File.WriteAllBytes("C:\Temp\OneFile.bin", New Byte() {1, 2, 3, 4})
```

Reading files' content is also easy. There are reading counterparts of the previously described method. `ReadAllText` and `ReadAllLines` enable you to retrieve content from a text file; the first one returns all content as a `String`, whereas the second one returns the content line-by-line by putting in an array of `String`. This is an example:

```
Dim text As String = File.ReadAllText("C:\Temp\OneFile.txt")
Dim fileLines() As String = File.ReadAllLines("C:\Temp\OneFile.txt")
```

Similarly you can read data from binary files invoking `ReadAllBytes`, which returns an array of `Byte`, as follows:

```
Dim bytes() As Byte = File.ReadAllBytes("C:\Temp\OneFile.bin")
```

For text files, you can also append text to an existing file. You accomplish this by invoking `AppendAllText` if you want to put an entire string or `AppendAllLines` if you have a sequence of strings. This is an example:

```
Dim lines As IEnumerable(Of String) = _
              New String() {"First", "Second", "Third"}.AsEnumerable
File.AppendAllLines("C:\Temporary\Test.txt", lines)
File.AppendAllText("C:\Temporary\Text.txt",
                "All text is stored within a string")
```

Notice how an array of strings is converted into an `IEnumerable(Of String)` invoking the `AsEnumerable` extension method, which is discussed in Chapters 20, "Advanced Language Features," and 23, "LINQ to Objects." `AppendAllLines` takes an `IEnumerable(Of String)` as a parameter, but you can also pass an array of strings because arrays are actually enumerable. After reading and writing, copying is also important. The `Copy` method enables you to create copies of files, accepting two arguments: the source file and the target file. This is an example:

```
File.Copy("C:\OneFolder\Source.txt", "C:\AnotherFolder\Target.txt")
```

You can also move a file from a location to another by invoking `Move`. Such a method is also used to rename a file and can be used as follows:

```
File.Move("C:\OneFolder\Source.txt", "C:\AnotherFolder\Target.txt")
```

Another useful method is `Replace`. It enables you to replace the content of a file with the content of another file, making a backup of the first file. You use it as follows:

```
File.Replace("C:\Source.Txt", "C:\Target.txt", "C:\Backup.txt")
```

You are not limited to text files. The `File` class offers two important methods that provide a basic encryption service, `Encrypt` and `Decrypt`. `Encrypt` makes a file accessible only by the user who is currently logged into Windows. You invoke it as follows:

```
File.Encrypt("C:\Temp\OneFile.txt")
```

If you try to log off from the system and then log on with another user profile, the encrypted file will not be accessible. You need to log on again with the user profile that encrypted the file. To reverse the result, invoke `Decrypt`:

```
File.Decrypt("C:\Temp\OneFile.txt")
```

Finally, you can easily delete a file from disk. This is accomplished with the simple `Delete` method:

```
File.Delete("C:\Temp\OneFile.txt")
```

The `File` class also has members similar to the `Directory` class. Consider the summarization made in Table 18.1 about the `Directory` class's members. The `File` class exposes the same members with the same meaning; the only difference is that such members now affect files. Those members are not covered again because they behave the same on files.

MEMBERS RETURNING STREAMS

The `System.IO.File` class exposes methods that return or require streams, such as `Create` and `Open`. Such members are not covered here for two reasons: The first one is that the streams discussion will be offered later in this chapter; the second one is that streams provide their own members for working against files that do the same as file members and therefore a more appropriate discussion is related to streams.

The `System.IO.FileInfo` Class

Similarly to what I explained about the `System.IO.DirectoryInfo` class, there is also a `System.IO.FileInfo` counterpart for the `System.IO.File` class. An instance of the `FileInfo` class is therefore a representation of a single file, providing members that enable you to perform operations on that particular file or get/set information. Because `FileInfo` inherits from `System.IO.FileSystemInfo` like `DirectoryInfo`, you can find the same members. You create an instance of the `FileInfo` class by passing the filename to the constructor, as demonstrated here:

```
Dim fi As New FileInfo("C:\MyFile.txt")
```

You can set attributes for the specified file assigning the `Attributes` property, which receives a value from the `System.IO.FileAttributes` enumeration:

```
fi.Attributes = FileAttributes.System Or FileAttributes.Hidden
```

You can still perform operations by invoking instance members that do not require the filename specification, such as `CopyTo`, `Delete`, `Encrypt`, `Decrypt`, or `MoveTo`: the `FileInfo`, such as `Length` (of type `Long`) that returns the file size in bytes; `Name` (of type `String`) that returns the filename and that is useful when you receive a `FileInfo` instance from somewhere else; `FullName` that is the same as `Name` but also includes the full path; `Exists` that determines if the file exists; and `IsReadOnly` that determines if the file is read-only. Using `FileInfo` can be useful if you need to create collections of objects, each representing a file on disk. Consider the following custom collections that stores series of `FileInfo` objects:

```
Class MyFileList
    Inherits List(Of FileInfo)

End Class
```

Now consider the following code that retrieves the list of executable filenames in the specified folder and creates an instance of the `FileInfo` class for each file, pushing it into the collection:

```
Module FileInfoDemo

    Sub FileInfoDemo()

        'An instance of the collection
        Dim customList As New MyFileList

        'Create a FileInfo for each .exe file
        'in the specified directory
        For Each itemName As String In _
            Directory.EnumerateFiles("C:\", "*.exe")
```

```
            Dim fileReference As New FileInfo(itemName)
            customList.Add(fileReference)
        Next


        'Iterate the collection
        For Each item In customList
            Console.WriteLine("File: {0}, length: {1}, created on: {2}",
                              item.Name, item.Length, item.CreationTime)
        Next
    End Sub
End Module
```

In this particular case enclosing the code within a module is just for demonstration purposes. Notice how you can access properties for each file that you could not know in advance. Just like `DirectoryInfo`, `FileInfo` also exposes properties that are counterparts for methods summarized in Table 18.1 and that this time are related to files. Refer to that table for further information.

Handling File Exceptions

Refer to Table 18.2 for exceptions that can occur when working with files. Other than those exceptions, you may encounter a `FileNotFoundException` if the specified file does not exist.

Understanding Permissions

The .NET Framework provides a high-level security mechanism over system resources, so it can happen that you attempt to access, in both reading or writing, directories or files but you do not have the required rights. To prevent your code from failing at runtime, you can check whether you have permissions. When working with files and directories, you need to check the availability of the `System.Security.FileIOPermission` object. For example, the following code asks the system (`Demand` method) if it has permissions to read local files:

```
Dim fp As New FileIOPermission(PermissionState.None)
fp.AllLocalFiles = FileIOPermissionAccess.Read
Try
    fp.Demand()
Catch ex As Security.SecurityException
    Console.WriteLine("You have no permission for local files")
Catch ex As Exception
End Try
```

If your code has no sufficient permissions, a `SecurityException` is thrown. Checking for permission is absolutely a best practice and should be applied where possible. In Chapter 45, "Working with Assemblies," you get some more information about the security model in the .NET Framework.

18

Introducing Streams

Streams are sequences of bytes exchanged with some kind of sources, such as files, memory, and network. A stream is represented by the abstract `System.IO.Stream` class that is the base class for different kinds of streams and that implements the `IDisposable` interface. The `Stream` class exposes some common members that you find in all other streams. Table 18.3 summarizes the most important common members.

TABLE 18.3   Streams Common Members

Member	Description
Close	Closes the stream and releases associated resources
Write	Writes the specified sequence of bytes to the stream
WriteByte	Writes the specified byte to the stream
Read	Reads the specified number of bytes from the stream
ReadByte	Reads a byte from the stream
Length	Returns the stream's dimension (property)
Seek	Moves to the specified position in the stream
Position	Returns the current position (property)
CanRead	Determines if the stream supports reading (property)
CanWrite	Determines if the stream supports writing (property)
CanSeek	Determines if the stream supports seeking (property)
BeginRead	Starts an asynchronous reading operation
BeginWrite	Starts an asynchronous writing operation
EndRead	Waits for an asynchronous operation to be completed

Now that you have a summarization of common members, you are ready to discover specific kinds of streams that inherit from `Stream`.

Reading and Writing Text Files

You create text files by instantiating the `StreamWriter` class, which is a specific stream implementation for writing to text files. The following code, which will be explained, provides an example:

```
Dim ts As New StreamWriter("C:\Temporary\OneFile.txt",
                       False, System.Text.Encoding.UTF8)

ts.WriteLine("This is a text file")
ts.WriteLine("with multi-line example")
ts.Close()
```

The constructor provides several overloads; the one used in the code receives the file name to be created—a Boolean value indicated whether the text must be appended if the file already exists and how the text is encoded. `WriteLine` is a method that writes a string and then puts a line terminator character. When you are done, you must close the stream invoking `Close`. You can also invoke `Write` to put in just one character. The reading counterpart is the `StreamReader` that works in a similar way, as demonstrated here:

```
Dim rf As New StreamReader("C:\Temporary\OneFile.txt",
                           System.Text.Encoding.UTF8)
Dim readALine As String = rf.ReadLine
Dim allContent As String = rf.ReadToEnd

rf.Close()
```

`StreamReader` provides the ability to read one line (`ReadLine` method), one character per time (`Read` method), or all the content of the stream (`ReadToEnd` method) putting such content into a variable of type `String`. In both `StreamWriter` and `StreamReader`, the constructor can receive an existing stream instead of a string. This is exemplified by the following code:

```
Dim fs As New FileStream("C:\Temporary\OneFile.txt", FileMode.Create)
Dim ts As New StreamWriter(fs)

'Work on your file here..
ts.Close()

fs.Close()
```

First, you need an instance of the `FileStream` class, which enables you to open a communication with the specified file and with the mode specified by a value of the `FileMode` enumeration (such as `Create`, `Append`, `CreateNew`, `Open`, and `OpenOrTruncate`). This class provides support for both synchronous and asynchronous operations. Then you point to the `FileStream` instance in the constructor of the `StreamWriter`/`StreamReader` class. Remember to close both streams when you are done.

Reading and Writing Binary Files

You can read and write data to binary files using the `BinaryReader` and `BinaryWriter` classes. Both require a `FileStream` instance and enable you to read and write arrays of bytes. The following is an example of creating a binary stream:

```
Dim fs As New FileStream("C:\Temporary\OneFile.bin", FileMode.CreateNew)
Dim bs As New BinaryWriter(fs)

Dim bytesToWrite() As Byte = New Byte() {128, 64, 32, 16}

bs.Write(bytesToWrite)
bs.Close()
fs.Close()
```

18

The `Write` method enables you to write information as binary, but it also accepts base .NET types such as integers and strings, all written as binary. It provides several overloads so that you can also specify the offset and the number of bytes to be written. To read a binary file, you instantiate the `BinaryReader` class. The following example retrieves information from a file utilizing a `Using..End Using` block to ensure that resources are correctly freed up when no longer necessary:

```
fs = New FileStream("C:\Temporary\OneFile.bin", FileMode.Open)
Using br As New BinaryReader(fs)
    If fs IsNot Nothing AndAlso fs.Length > 0 Then
        Dim buffer() As Byte = br.ReadBytes(CInt(fs.Length))
    End If
End Using
fs.Close()
```

In this case the `ReadBytes` method, which is used to retrieve data, reads a number of bytes corresponding to the file length. Because binary data can have different forms, `ReadBytes` is just one of a series of methods for reading .NET types such as `ReadChar`, `ReadInt32`, `ReadString`, `ReadDouble`, and so on.

ASYNCHRONOUS PROGRAMMING

The .NET Framework 4.5 introduces a new pattern for asynchronous programming techniques based on the Async/Await keywords. This pattern has some new features for working with streams asynchronously as well. Because you first need to know how this pattern works, examples on asynchronous operations over streams will be provided in Chapter 44, "Asynchronous Programming."

Using Memory Streams

Memory streams are special objects that act like file streams but that work in memory, providing the ability to manipulate binary data. The following code creates a `MemoryStream` with 2 Kbytes capacity and puts in a string:

```
Dim ms As New MemoryStream(2048)

Dim bs As New BinaryWriter(ms)
bs.Write("Some text written as binary")
bs.Close()
ms.Close()
```

To retrieve data, you use a `BinaryReader` pointing to the `MemoryStream` as you saw in the paragraph for binary files. So, in this example, you can invoke `ReadString` as follows:

```
'The stream must be still open
Using br As New BinaryReader(ms)
    If ms IsNot Nothing AndAlso ms.Length > 0 Then
```

```
        Dim data As String = br.ReadString

    End If
End Using
ms.Close()
```

Using Streams with Strings

Although not often utilized, you can use `StringReader` and `StringWriter` for manipulating strings. The following example generates a new `StringBuilder` and associates it to a new `StringWriter`. Then it retrieves the list of filenames in the C:\ directory and puts each string into the writer. You notice that because of the association between the two objects, changes are reflected to the `StringBuilder`. Try this:

```
Dim sBuilder As New Text.StringBuilder
Dim sWriter As New StringWriter(sBuilder)

For Each name As String In Directory.GetFiles("C:\")
    sWriter.WriteLine(name)
Next
sWriter.Close()

Console.WriteLine(sBuilder.ToString)
```

To read strings, you can use the `StringReader` object, whose constructor requires a string to be read. To continue with the example, we can read the previously created `StringBuilder` line-by-line:

```
Dim sReader As New StringReader(sBuilder.ToString)
Do Until sReader.Peek = -1
    Console.WriteLine(sReader.ReadLine)

Loop
```

You notice lots of similarities between string streams and `StreamWriter`/`StreamReader` because both work with text.

Compressing Data with Streams

One of the most interesting features of streams is the ability to compress and decompress data utilizing the `GZipStream` and `DeflateStream` objects. Both are exposed by the `System.IO.Compression` namespace, and they both compress data using the GZip algorithm. The only difference is that the `GZipStream` writes a small header to compressed data. The interesting thing is that they work similarly to other streams, and when you write or read data into the stream, data is automatically compressed or decompressed by the runtime. The good news is that you are not limited to compressing files, but any other kind of stream. Compressing and decompressing data is quite a simple task. In some situations you need more attention according to the kind of data you need to access for files. To make comprehension easier, take a look at the code example provided in Listing 18.1 that contains comments that explain how such streams work. The purpose of the example is to provide the ability to compress and decompress files that is a common requirement in applications. You are encouraged to read comments within the code that can help you get started with the GZipStream.

LISTING 18.1   Compressing and Decompressing Streams

```vb
Imports System.IO
Imports System.IO.Compression

Module Compression

    Sub TestCompress()
        Try
            Compress("C:\Temp\Source.Txt",
                     "C:\Temp\Compressed.gzp")
        Catch ex As FileNotFoundException
            Console.WriteLine("File not found!")
        Catch ex As IOException
            Console.WriteLine("An input/output error has occurred:")
            Console.WriteLine(ex.Message)
        Catch ex As Exception
            Console.WriteLine(ex.Message)
        End Try
    End Sub

    Sub TestDecompress()
        Try
            Decompress("C:\Temp\Compressed.gzp",
                       "C:\Temp\Original.txt")

        Catch ex As FileNotFoundException
            Console.WriteLine("File not found!")
        Catch ex As IOException
            Console.WriteLine("An input/output error has occurred:")
            Console.WriteLine(ex.Message)
        Catch ex As Exception
            Console.WriteLine(ex.Message)
        End Try
    End Sub


    Public Sub Compress(ByVal inputName As String, ByVal outputName As String)
```

```vbnet
'Instantiates a new FileStream
Dim infile As FileStream

Try
    'The Stream points to the specified input file
    infile = New FileStream(inputName, FileMode.Open, FileAccess.Read, _
                            FileShare.Read)

    'Stores the file length in a buffer
    Dim buffer(CInt(infile.Length - 1)) As Byte

    'Checks if the file can be read and assigns to the "count"
    'variable the result of reading the file
    Dim count As Integer = infile.Read(buffer, 0, buffer.Length)

    'If the number of read byte is different from the file length
    'throws an exception
    If count <> buffer.Length Then
        infile.Close()
        Throw New IOException
    End If
    'closes the stream
    infile.Close()
    infile = Nothing

    'Creates a new stream pointing to the output file
    Dim ms As New FileStream(outputName, FileMode.CreateNew, _
                             FileAccess.Write)

    'Creates a new GZipStream for compressing, pointing to
    'the output stream above leaving it open
    Dim compressedzipStream As New GZipStream(ms, _
                                              CompressionMode.Compress, _
                                              True)
    'Puts the buffer into the new stream, which is
    'automatically compressed
    compressedzipStream.Write(buffer, 0, buffer.Length)

    compressedzipStream.Close()
    ms.Close()
    Exit Sub
Catch ex As IO.FileNotFoundException
    Throw
Catch ex As IOException
    Throw
Catch ex As Exception
```

18

```vb
            Throw
        End Try
    End Sub

    Public Sub Decompress(ByVal fileName As String, ByVal originalName As String)

        Dim inputFile As FileStream

        'Defining the stream for decompression
        Dim compressedZipStream As GZipStream

        'Defining a variable for storing compressed file size
        Dim compressedFileSize As Integer

        Try

            'Reads the input file
            inputFile = New FileStream(fileName,
                                    FileMode.Open,
                                    FileAccess.Read,
                                    FileShare.Read)

            'Reads input file's size
            compressedFileSize = CInt(inputFile.Length)

            'Creates a new GZipStream in Decompress mode
            compressedZipStream = New GZipStream(inputFile,
                                        CompressionMode.Decompress)

            'In compressed data the first 100 bytes store the original
            'data size, so let's get it
            Dim offset As Integer = 0
            Dim totalBytes As Integer = 0

            Dim SmallBuffer(100) As Byte

            'Reads until there are available bytes in the first 100
            'and increments variables that we'll need for sizing
            'the buffer that will store the decompressed file
            Do While True

                Dim bytesRead As Integer = compressedZipStream.
                                        Read(SmallBuffer, 0, 100)
                If bytesRead = 0 Then
```

```
        Exit Do
    End If

    offset += bytesRead
    totalBytes += bytesRead
Loop

compressedZipStream.Close()
compressedZipStream = Nothing

'Creates a new FileStream for reading the input file
inputFile = New FileStream(fileName,
                    FileMode.Open,
                    FileAccess.Read,
                    FileShare.Read)

'and decompress its content
compressedZipStream = New GZipStream(inputFile,
                            CompressionMode.Decompress)

'Declares the buffer that will store uncompressed data
Dim buffer(totalBytes) As Byte

'Reads from the source file the number of bytes
'representing the buffer length, taking advantage
'of the original size
compressedZipStream.Read(buffer, 0, totalBytes)

compressedZipStream.Close()
compressedZipStream = Nothing

'Creates a new file for putting uncompressed
'data
Dim ms As New FileStream(originalName,
                    FileMode.Create,
                    FileAccess.Write)

'Writes uncompressed data to file
ms.Write(buffer, 0, buffer.Length)
ms.Close()
ms = Nothing
Exit Sub
```

```
            'General IO error
        Catch ex As IOException
            Throw
        Catch ex As Exception
            Throw
            Exit Try
        End Try
    End Sub
End Module
```

TIP

You use `GZipStream` and `DeflateStream` the identical way. The only difference is about the header in the compressed stream. If you need further information on the difference, here is the official MSDN page: http://msdn.microsoft.com/en-us/library/system. io.compression.deflatestream(VS.110).aspx.

Notice how, at a higher level, you just instantiate the stream the same way in both compression and decompression tasks. The difference is the `CompressionMode` enumeration value that determines whether a stream is for compression or decompression. With this technique, you can invoke just the two custom methods for compressing and decompressing files, meaning that you could apply it to other kinds of data, too.

New in Visual Basic 2012: Working with Zip Archives

The .NET Framework 4.5 introduces new features to the `System.IO.Compression` namespace, which provide an opportunity of working with classic Zip archives. Until this version of the Framework, it was not possible to work directly with the famous Zip algorithm because only the GZip one was supported. Technically speaking, in .NET 4.5 applications you add a reference to the System.IO.Compression.FileSystem.dll assembly. This extends the `System.IO.Compression` namespace with new types that will be described shortly. The real thing you have to take care about is that the new features offer basic ways for working with Zip archives and so there could be some situations in which you might need more advanced libraries, such as the famous DotNetZip (http://dotnetzip. codeplex.com) or SharpZipLib (http://sharpziplib.com) available for free on the Internet. For example, currently the new classes do not enable you to enter passwords when extracting archives or specify one to protect archives. Also, full compatibility is not always guaranteed. Notice that these new types are not available for Metro-style apps in Windows 8, where you will still use streams described previously. In the .NET Framework 4.5, you can now use the `ZipFile` class, which exposes two shared methods, `CreateFromDirectory` and `ExtractToDirectory`. The first method creates a Zip archive containing all files in the specified directory, whereas the second one extracts the content of a Zip archive into the specified directory. The following example demonstrates how to create and extract a Zip archive:

```
ZipFile.CreateFromDirectory("C:\temp", "C:\ZippedTemp.zip",
        CompressionLevel.Optimal, True)
ZipFile.ExtractToDirectory("C:\ZippedDemo.zip", "C:\temp")
```

In the previous example, `CreateFromDirectory` generates a compressed archive called ZippedTemp.zip, which stores the content of a folder called C:\Temp. The third argument (called `compressionLevel`) represents the compression level and requires one value from the `CompressionLevel` enumeration. You choose among `Optimal`, `NoCompression`, and `Fastest`. The fourth argument (called `includeBaseDirectory`) is instead a Boolean value that, when `True`, enables you to include the base directory in the archive. Using `ExtractToDirectory` is even simpler because you just specify the archive to decompress and the target directory. Both methods have an overload that provides an argument called `entryNameEncoding` of type `System.Text.Encoding` which enables you to specify the encoding to use with file entries for compatibility with Zip archives that do not support UTF-8. The System.IO.Compression namespace also offers the `ZipArchive` and `ZipArchiveEntry` classes, representing a Zip archive and one entry inside the compressed archive, respectively. These classes provide better control over Zip files. The following code demonstrates how to show the list of files inside a Zip archive:

```
Using zipArc As ZipArchive = ZipFile.Open("C:\temp\Northwind.zip",
➥ZipArchiveMode.Read)
    For Each item As ZipArchiveEntry In zipArc.Entries
        Console.WriteLine("{0}, Compressed size: {1}, ",
                        item.FullName,
                        item.CompressedLength.ToString)
    Next
End Using
```

Because the `ZipArchive` class implements the `IDisposable` interface, it can be convenient to enclose the code within a `Using..End Using` block. Notice that the `ZipArchive` instance receives the result of another method from the `ZipFile` class, `Open`. Every item in the archive is an instance of the `ZipArchiveEntry` class; a collection called `Entries`, of type `ReadOnlyCollection(Of ZipArchiveEntry)`, can be iterated to get the list of items that are stored inside the Zip archive. It is also easy to create a new Zip file with `ZipArchive` and `ZipFile.Open`. The following code demonstrates this:

```
Using zipArc As ZipArchive = ZipFile.Open("C:\Temp\NewZipped.zip",
                ZipArchiveMode.Create)
    zipArc.CreateEntry("C:\Temp\Northwind.sdf", CompressionLevel.NoCompression)
End Using
```

Here you use the `ZipArchiveMode.Create` mode for opening the Zip file, since you want to create a new one. Then you use the `CreateEntry` instance method of the `ZipArchive` class to add entries to the zipped archive. Notice that the entry is actually added to the archive when the `Using` block gets finalized. You can also update an existing archive by adding or deleting entries. The following code demonstrates how to add an entry to an existing archive and how to remove an existing entry:

```
Using zipArc As ZipArchive = ZipFile.Open("C:\Temp\NewZipped.zip",
                ZipArchiveMode.Update)
    zipArc.CreateEntry("C:\Temp\AnotherFile.txt", CompressionLevel.Fastest)
    'Get the specified entry
    Dim entry As ZipArchiveEntry = zipArc.GetEntry("Northwind.sdf")
    'Delete the entry from the archive
    entry.Delete()
End Using
```

You use `GetEntry` to get the instance of the `ZipArchiveEntry` that you want to remove, by specifying the name. Then you invoke the `Delete` method on the retrieved instance.

Networking with Streams

The .NET Framework provides functionalities for data exchange through networks using streams; in particular, it exposes the `System.Net.Sockets.NetworkStream` class. Reading and writing data via a `NetworkStream` instance passes through a `System.Net.Sockets.TcpClient` class's instance. Code in Listing 18.2 shows how you can both write and read data in such a scenario. See comments in code for explanations.

LISTING 18.2   Networking with `NetworkStream`

```
Imports System.Net.Sockets
Imports System.Text

Module Network

    Sub NetStreamDemo()
        'Instantiating TcpClient and NetworkStream
        Dim customTcpClient As New TcpClient()
        Dim customNetworkStream As NetworkStream

        Try
            'Attempt to connect to socket
            '127.0.0.1 is the local machine address
            customTcpClient.Connect("127.0.0.1", 587) 'Port
            'Gets the instance of the stream for
            'data exchange
            customNetworkStream = customTcpClient.GetStream()

            'The port is not available
        Catch ex As ArgumentOutOfRangeException
            Console.WriteLine(ex.Message)
            'Connection problem
```

```
        Catch ex As SocketException
            Console.WriteLine(ex.Message)
        End Try

        'Gets an array of byte from a value, which is
        'encoded via System.Text.Encoding.Ascii.GetBytes
        Dim bytesToWrite() As Byte = _
            Encoding.ASCII.GetBytes("Something to exchange via TCP")

        'Gets the stream instance
        customNetworkStream = customTcpClient.GetStream()
        'Writes the bytes to the stream; this
        'means sending data to the network
        customNetworkStream.Write(bytesToWrite, 0,
                            bytesToWrite.Length)

        'Establishes the buffer size for receiving data
        Dim bufferSize As Integer = customTcpClient.
                            ReceiveBufferSize
        Dim bufferForReceivedBytes(bufferSize) As Byte

        'Gets data from the stream, meaning by the network
        customNetworkStream.Read(bufferForReceivedBytes, 0,
                            bufferSize)

        Dim result As String = Encoding.ASCII.GetString(bufferForReceivedBytes,
                            0, bufferSize)
    End Sub
End Module
```

There are several ways for data exchange, and this is probably one of the most basic ones in the era of Windows Communication Foundation. This topic is related to streams, so an overview was necessary.

Summary

Working with files, directories, and drives is a common requirement for each application. The .NET Framework provides two main classes for working with directories: `System.IO.Directory` and `System.IO.Path`. The first one enables you to perform operations such as creating, moving, renaming, and investigating for filenames. The second one is about directory and filename manipulation other than gaining access to Windows temporary folder. Similar to `Directory`, the `System.IO.DirectoryInfo` class provides access to directory operations and information, but the difference is that an instance of such a class represents a single directory. If you instead need to get information on physical drives on your machine, create an instance of the `System.IO.DriveInfo` class. Similar to `Directory` and `DirectoryInfo`, the `System.IO.File` and `System.IO.FileInfo` classes provide access to files on disk, and their members are the same as for directory classes except that they enable you to work with files. The last part of the chapter is about streams. Streams are sequences of bytes that enable you to exchange different kinds of data. All stream classes inherit from `System.IO.Stream`. `StreamReader` and `StreamWriter` enable you to read and write text files. `BinaryReader` and `BinaryWriter` enable you to read and write binary files. `MemoryStream` enables you to read and write in-memory binary data. `StringReader` and `StringWriter` enable you to manage in-memory strings. `GZipStream` and `DeflateStream` enable you to compress data according to the `GZip` algorithm (you saw new features in .NET 4.5 about Zip compression). `NetworkStream` enables you to exchange data through a network. Writing and reading data can often require several lines of code. Luckily the Visual Basic language offers an important alternative known as the `My` namespace that is covered in the next chapter.

The My Namespace

The great debate is always the same: which is better—Visual Basic or Visual C#? Because of the .NET Framework, the Common Language Runtime (CLR), and the IL language, the languages' evolution brought both VB and C# to do the same things. Of course, there are some differences, and one language has some features that the other one does not have. One example is void lambdas in C#, which weren't introduced in VB until this last version, or VB's XML literals that C# does not have. Differences are obvious. One of the Visual Basic features that does not have commonalities with other managed languages is the My namespace, belonging to VB starting from Visual Basic 2005. In this chapter we examine the My namespace that can write productive code, according to the philosophy of "less code, more productivity." Keep in mind that what you learn in this chapter does not apply to Metro-style apps for Windows 8; in fact, even if the My namespace still exists in that platform, for Metro it does not expose anything. This is an important clarification and will no longer be repeated through the chapter.

Introducing the My Namespace

The My namespace provides shortcuts for accessing several common objects in .NET development. My exposes classes that wrap existing built-in objects and offers them again in a way that's easier to use. By using My, you can access lots of development areas and write less code than you would if you used traditional techniques. At a higher level My exposes the following members:

▶ `My.Application`, a property exposing members that allows access to other properties of the current application

▶ `My.Computer`, a property exposing members that provides shortcuts to common operations with your machine, such as the file system or the Registry

▶ `My.Settings`, a property that provides code support for the Settings tab in My Project and that also enables the use of settings from your application

▶ `My.Resources`, a namespace that defines several objects providing support for the Resources tab in My Project and allowing handling resources in code

▶ `My.User`, a property providing members for getting or setting information about the current user that logged into the operating system

▶ `My.WebServices`, a property that enables the retrieval of information on web services consumed by your application

The preceding listed My members are the most general, and you can find them in every kind of Visual Basic application (except for Metro apps, as stated at the beginning of the chapter). There are also specific extensions for the My namespace related to specific applications, such as WPF. (A description is provided at the end of this chapter.) My is interesting because it can be also be extended with custom members providing great flexibility to your applications. If something within My does not satisfy you, you can change it. After all, My is a namespace, meaning that it is implemented in code.

"MY" IS A RESERVED KEYWORD

Due to its particular role within the Visual Basic programming language, although it just refers to a namespace, My is also a reserved word in Visual Basic.

My.Application

The My.Application properties expose members for retrieving information on the running instance of the application. This information can be divided into three major groups: application information at assembly level, culture for localization and deployment, and environment information. Let's examine all these features.

APPLICATION FRAMEWORK

In specific kinds of applications, such as Windows Forms and WPF applications, My. Application also provides support for the application framework and application events. This is discussed in the last section of this chapter.

Retrieving Assembly Information

My.Application maps the same-named tab within My Project. Because of this, it provides the ability of investigating in-code assemblies' information. This can be accomplished via the `My.Application.Info` property (of type `Microsoft.VisualBasic.ApplicationServices.AssemblyInfo`) that retrieves information about the current assembly, such as the name, version, company name, copyright, and so on. The following code shows how you can accomplish this:

```
'Assembly information
Console.WriteLine("Assembly name: {0}",
                  My.Application.Info.AssemblyName)
Console.WriteLine("Assembly version: {0}",
                  My.Application.Info.Version)
Console.WriteLine("Company name: {0}",
                  My.Application.Info.CompanyName)
'Returns the directory where the application is running from
Console.WriteLine("Running from: {0}",
                  My.Application.Info.DirectoryPath)
```

Another interesting feature is that you can get information on all referenced assemblies, as shown in the following iteration:

```
Console.WriteLine("References:")
For Each item In My.Application.Info.LoadedAssemblies
    Console.WriteLine(item)
Next
```

The `LoadedAssemblies` property is of type `ReadonlyCollection(Of System.Reflection.AssemblyInfo)`, so you become more skilled after reading Chapter 46, "Reflection."

Working with Cultures

In Chapter 33, "Localizing Applications," you get more information about localizing applications, but at this particular point of the book, you can get an interesting taste using `My`. Two cultures are settable for your application: the thread's culture, which is about string manipulation and formatting, and the user interface culture, which is about adapting resources to the desired culture. You can get information on both by invoking the `Culture` and `UICulture` properties from `My.Application`; then you can set different cultures for both the main culture and UI culture by invoking the `ChangeCulture` and `ChangeUICulture` methods. The following code demonstrates this:

```
Dim culture As CultureInfo = My.Application.Culture
Console.WriteLine("Current culture: {0}", culture.Name)

Dim UICulture As CultureInfo = My.Application.UICulture
Console.WriteLine("Current UI culture: {0}", UICulture.Name)

My.Application.ChangeCulture("it-IT")
My.Application.ChangeUICulture("it-IT")
```

```
Console.WriteLine("New settings: {0}, {1}",
                   My.Application.Culture.Name,
                   My.Application.UICulture.Name)
```

First, the code retrieves information about cultures. Such information is of type `System.Globalization.CultureInfo`. This object provides lots of information on cultures, but in this case we use `Name` that returns the culture name. Notice how you can change cultures by invoking `ChangeCulture` and `ChangeUICulture` just by passing a string representing the culture's name. On my machine the preceding code produces the following result:

```
Current culture: en-US
Current UI culture: en-US
New settings: it-IT, it-IT
```

If you need to pass a custom culture, you should create a new `CultureInfo` object and then pass the name of the new culture. Typically, you will not remember each culture name, so if you want to investigate available cultures, you can write a simple iteration taking advantage of the shared `GetCultureInfo` method:

```
For Each c In CultureInfo.GetCultures(CultureTypes.AllCultures)
    Console.WriteLine(c.Name)
Next
```

Deployment and Environment Information

The `My.Application` property allows managing the following environment information:

- ▶ Getting information on the ClickOnce deployment for the current application
- ▶ Retrieving environment variables
- ▶ Writing entries to the Windows Applications log
- ▶ Retrieving command line arguments

Next you see in detail how you can get/set such information using `My.Application`.

Deployment Information

It can be useful to get information on the state of the deployment if your application has been installed via the ClickOnce technology (discussed in detail in Chapter 52, "Deploying Applications with ClickOnce"). You might want to provide the ability of downloading files on-demand or to implement additional behaviors according to the updates status. You can use the `IsNetworkDeployed` property to know if an application has been deployed to a network via ClickOnce and the `My.Application.Deployment` property (which wraps `System.Deployment.Application.ApplicationDeployment`) to make other decisions. The following code shows information on the deployment status only if the application has been deployed to a network:

```
'Deployment and environment information
If My.Application.IsNetworkDeployed = True Then
    Console.
    WriteLine("Application deployed to a network via ClickOnce")

    Console.WriteLine("Current deployment version: {0}",
            My.Application.Deployment.CurrentVersion)
    Console.WriteLine("The application runs from: {0}",
            My.Application.Deployment.ActivationUri)
    Console.WriteLine("Is first time run: {0}",
            My.Application.Deployment.IsFirstRun)
End If
```

The `CurrentVersion` property is useful to understand the current *deployment* version, while `ActivationUri` is the address from which the application manifest is invoked. You can also programmatically check for updates invoking specific methods, such as `CheckForUpdate`, `CheckForUpdateAsync`, and `CheckForUpdateAsyncCancel`. The following is an example:

```
My.Application.Deployment.CheckForUpdate()
```

Luckily, `My.Application.Deployment` members' names are self-explanatory, and with the help of IntelliSense and a little bit of curiosity, you have in your hands all the power of such an object.

Retrieving Environment Variables

There are situations where you need to retrieve the content of the operating system's environment variables. This can be accomplished by invoking the `GetEnvironmentVariable` that receives the name of the variable as an argument. The following code shows how to retrieve the content of the `PATH` environment variable:

```
Dim PathEnvironmentVariable As String = My.Application.
                                GetEnvironmentVariable("PATH")
```

Writing Entries to the Windows' Applications Log

The .NET Framework provides several ways of interacting with the operating system logs, but the `My` namespace offers an easy way to write information to the Windows application log. `My.Application` offers a `Log` property, of type `Microsoft.VisualBasic.Logging.Log`, which exposes members for writing information. The following code snippet shows how you can write a message to the application log invoking the `WriteEntry` method:

```
My.Application.Log.WriteEntry("Demonstrating My.Application.Log",
                    TraceEventType.Information)
```

The first argument is the message, and the second one is a member of the `TraceEventType` enumeration whose members are self-explanatory, thanks to IntelliSense, and allow specifying the level of your message. Alternatively, you can write the content of an entire exception invoking the `WriteException` method:

```
Try

Catch ex As Exception
    My.Application.Log.WriteException(ex)
End Try
```

You can also get control over the listeners and the file used by the .NET Framework by utilizing the `TraceSource` and `DefaultFileLogWriter`.

Retrieving Command-Line Arguments

If you need to retrieve command-line arguments for your application, `My.Application` offers a convenient way. To complete the following demonstration, go to the Debug tab of My Project and set whatever command-line arguments you like in the Command Line Arguments text box. `My.Application` offers a `CommandLineArgs` property, which is a `ReadOnlyCollection(Of String)` that stores such arguments. Each item in the collection represents a command-line argument. The following code shows how you can iterate such collection and check for available command-line arguments:

```
For Each argument As String In My.Application.CommandLineArgs
    Console.WriteLine(argument)
Next
```

My.Computer

`My.Computer` provides lots of shortcuts for accessing features on the local system, starting from the clipboard arriving at the Registry, passing through audio capabilities. This is a class exposing several properties, each one related to a computer area. This is a list of `My.Computer` properties:

▶ **FileSystem**—Provides members for accessing files, directories, and other objects on disk

▶ **Clipboard**—Provides members for setting data to and getting data from the system clipboard

▶ **Audio**—Allows playing audio files

▶ **Mouse**—Allows retrieving information on the installed mouse

▶ **Keyboard**—Provides members for getting information on the state of keys in the keyboard

▶ **Registry**—Provides members for getting and setting information to Windows Registry

▶ **Network**—Offers members for performing operations within the network that the computer is connected to

▶ **Ports**—Allows retrieving information on the computer's serial ports

▶ **Screen**—Allows retrieving information on the screen properties (Windows Forms only)

▶ **Info**—Provides a series of information about the running machine

As usual, IntelliSense provides detailed information on each member from the preceding properties. In the next section you learn to access your machine information with `My.Computer`, but providing examples for each member is not possible. Because of this, members for the biggest areas are summarized and code examples for the most important members are provided.

Working with the File System

`My.Computer` provides lots of shortcuts for performing most common operations on files and directories via the `FileSystem` property. Members are self-explanatory and easy to understand, so you can always take advantage of IntelliSense. To demonstrate how easy it is to work with the file system, let's go through some examples. The following code copies a directory into another one, then it creates a new directory, and finally it retrieves the current directory:

```
My.Computer.FileSystem.CopyDirectory("C:\Source", "C:\Target")
My.Computer.FileSystem.CreateDirectory("C:\Temp")
Dim currentDir As String = My.Computer.FileSystem.CurrentDirectory
```

You can also get information on Windows' special directories via the `SpecialDirectories` property as follows:

```
'Gets My Pictures path
Dim picturesFolder As String =
    My.Computer.FileSystem.SpecialDirectories.MyPictures
```

Working with files is also easy. For example, you can read or create a text file in one line of code:

```
'Read the content of a text file
Dim content As String =
    My.Computer.FileSystem.ReadAllText("C:\ADocument.txt")
```

```
'Creates a new text file
My.Computer.FileSystem.WriteAllText("C:\ADocument.txt", "File content",
                                    append:=False)
```

This can be useful if you do not need to create a text file dynamically—for example, line by line. For files, you can iterate a directory to get an array of strings storing all filenames as follows:

```
For Each item As String In My.Computer.FileSystem.GetFiles("C:\")
    'Do something here
Next
```

This last example allows extracting the filename of a full path name:

```
'Returns MyFile.txt
Dim parsedString As String =
    My.Computer.FileSystem.GetName("C:\Temp\MyFile.txt")
```

`My.Computer.FileSystem` is powerful and simplifies access to the file system resources avoiding the need to write lots of lines of code.

Working with the Clipboard

The `My.Computer.Clipboard` property provides members for working with the system clipboard. Table 19.1 summarizes the members.

TABLE 19.1   `My.Computer.Clipboard` Members

Member	Description
Clear	Clears the clipboard content
ContainsAudio	Checks if the clipboard contains an audio file
ContainsData	Checks if the clipboard contains data according to the specified format
ContainsFileDropList	Checks if the clipboard contains a file drop-down list
ContainsImage	Checks if the clipboard contains an image
ContainsText	Checks if the clipboard contains some text
GetAudioStream	Gets an audio file from the clipboard as a stream
GetData	Gets data from the clipboard according to the specified format
GetDataObject	Gets data from the clipboard as `IDataObject`
GetImage	Retrieves an image from the clipboard
GetFileDropDownList	Retrieves a file drop-down list from the clipboard
GetText	Retrieves text from the clipboard
SetAudio	Copies the specified audio to the clipboard
SetData	Copies the specified custom data to the clipboard
SetDataObject	Copies the specified `System.Windows.Forms.DataObject` to the clipboard
SetImage	Copies the specified image to the clipboard
SetText	Copies the specified text to the clipboard

The following code shows how you can clear the clipboard and then copy some text; in the end the code checks if some text is available and, if so, returns the text:

```
My.Computer.Clipboard.Clear()
My.Computer.Clipboard.SetText("This is some text")

If My.Computer.Clipboard.ContainsText Then
    Console.WriteLine(My.Computer.Clipboard.GetText)
End If
```

Playing Audio Files

`My.Computer.Audio` provides three methods for audio files reproduction. The first one is `Play`, which can play a .Wav file. The following is an example:

```
My.Computer.Audio.Play("C:\MySound.Wav", AudioPlayMode.WaitToComplete)
```

You need to pass at least the filename as the first argument; as an alternative, you can pass the .wav file as a byte array or a `FileStream`. The `AudioPlayMode` enumeration enables you to specify how the audio file needs to be played. `WaitToComplete` means that no other code will be executed until the reproduction ends; `Background`, which is the default setting, means that the audio is reproduced asynchronously; last, `BackgroundLoop` means that the audio file is reproduced in the loop until you explicitly invoke the `Stop` method as follows:

```
My.Computer.Audio.Play("C:\MySound.Wav",
                       AudioPlayMode.BackgroundLoop)
'Other code...
My.Computer.Audio.Stop()
```

The last method is `PlaySystemSound`, whose first argument is the system sound to reproduce, which works like this:

```
My.Computer.Audio.PlaySystemSound(Media.SystemSounds.Exclamation)
```

Sounds examples other than `Exclamation` are `Asterisk`, `Beep`, `Hand`, and `Question`.

Managing the Keyboard

You can check for the state of some keyboard keys. `My.Computer.Keyboard` lets you accomplish this via six properties. Three are about the Caps-lock, Num-lock, and Scroll-lock keys, whereas the other three let you get the state (pressed or not) of Alt, Shift, and Ctrl. The following code provides a complete example:

```
'All Boolean values
Console.WriteLine(My.Computer.Keyboard.AltKeyDown)
Console.WriteLine(My.Computer.Keyboard.CtrlKeyDown)
Console.WriteLine(My.Computer.Keyboard.ShiftKeyDown)
Console.WriteLine(My.Computer.Keyboard.CapsLock)
Console.WriteLine(My.Computer.Keyboard.NumLock)
Console.WriteLine(My.Computer.Keyboard.ScrollLock)
```

Working with the Registry

`My.Computer` provides fast access to Windows Registry. It exposes a `Registry` property wrapping lots of functionalities of `Microsoft.Win32.Registry` class for faster work. `My.Computer.Registry` offers some properties, of type `Microsoft.Win32.RegistryKey`, representing the most important areas of the Registry, such as HKEY_LOCAL_MACHINE (wrapped by the `LocalMachine` property), HKEY_ USERS (wrapped by `Users`), HKEY_ CURRENT_USER (wrapped by `CurrentUser`), and HKEY_CLASSES_ROOT (wrapped by `ClassesRoot`). All of them provide methods for creating subkeys, querying, deleting, and setting values within subkeys. For example, the following code (which requires an `Imports Microsoft.Win32` directive) creates a subkey in the HKEY_CURRENT_USER\Software key, providing a company name and the application name. The code also sets permissions for writing/reading the key and its eventual subkeys:

```
Dim regKey As RegistryKey = My.Computer.Registry.
             CurrentUser.CreateSubKey("Software\DelSole\MyApplication",
             RegistryKeyPermissionCheck.ReadWriteSubTree,
             RegistryOptions.None)
```

Because the `CreateSubKey` returns a `RegistryKey` object, you can invoke instance members from this type. For example, you can add values to the new key by invoking the `SetValue` method as follows:

```
'Value-name, actual value
regKey.SetValue("MyValue", 1)
```

You get the value of the desired subkey by invoking the `GetValue` method as follows:

```
'Returns "1"
Dim value As String = CStr(My.Computer.Registry.
    GetValue("HKEY_CURRENT_USER\Software\DelSole\MyApplication",
                             "MyValue",
                             Nothing))
```

Remember that `GetValue` returns `Object`, so you need to perform an explicit conversion according to the value type you expect. You also have the ability to determine what kind of value is associated to a value name. This can be accomplished by getting a `RegistryValueKind` value, such as `DWord`, `Binary`, `String`, and `QWord`, (which is an enumeration from `Microsoft.Win32`) via the `GetValueKind` method so that you can also be more precise when requiring values:

```
'Returns DWORD
Dim valueKind As RegistryValueKind = regKey.GetValueKind("MyValue")

If valueKind = RegistryValueKind.DWord Then
         Dim value2 As Integer = _
             CInt(My.Computer.
             Registry.
```

```
GetValue("HKEY_CURRENT_USER\Software\DelSole\MyApplication",
        "MyValue", Nothing))
End If
```

In addition, a `GetNames` method returns an array of strings, each representing a value in the specified subkey if more than one value is stored within the subkey. The following code instead removes the previously created value:

```
regKey.DeleteValue("MyValue")
```

Remember to close (and dispose) the Registry key when you do not use it anymore:

```
regKey.Close()
```

```
regKey.Dispose()
```

Finally, you can delete a subkey by invoking the `DeleteSubKey` as follows:

```
My.Computer.Registry.
    CurrentUser.DeleteSubKey("Software\DelSole\MyApplication",
    True)
```

Other than the mentioned properties about Registry areas, `My.Computer.Registry` exposes just two interesting methods, `SetValue` and `GetValue`, which require you to specify long strings and that usually can be replaced by the same-named methods of the instance of `RegistryKey`. By the way, with `My.Computer.Registry` you can perform lots of tasks onto the system Registry writing code easier and faster.

Accessing the Network

If your machine is connected to a network, you can use the `My.Computer.Network` property that wraps some functionalities of the `System.Net` namespace. The most interesting members are the `IsNetworkAvailable` property that returns `True` if the machine is connected, the `DownloadFile` method that allows downloading a file from the network, `UploadFile` that allows uploading a file to the specified target on the network, and `Ping` that sends a ping to the specified address. The following code checks first for network availability, then sends a ping to my English language blog, and in the end attempts to download a file from the Italian VB Tips & Tricks community (where I'm a team member) passing credentials as strings:

```
If My.Computer.Network.IsAvailable Then
    Try

        '2000 is the timeout
        Dim available As Boolean = My.Computer.
                                   Network.
Ping("http://community.visual-basic.it/AlessandroEnglish",
                    2000)
```

19

```
                        My.Computer.Network.DownloadFile("http://www.visual-
➥basic.it/scarica.asp?ID=1016",

                                    "C:\WpfDemo.zip",
                                    "MyUserName",
                                    "MyPassword")

            Catch ex As System.Net.WebException

            Catch ex As Exception

            End Try
        End If
```

Notice how a `System.Net.WebException` is caught in case there are any network problems, especially with the `DownloadFile` method. The `DownloadFile` requires you to specify the source as the first argument and the target file as the second one. You can also specify the source as a `System.Uri`; the method can also download html contents. `UploadFile` works similarly, in that it requires the name of the file to be uploaded and the address, also allowing credentials specifications. Both methods offer several overloads that IntelliSense explains in detail. About `Ping`, the methods returns `True` if the website is reachable.

Getting Computer Information

`My.Computer` provides the ability of retrieving information on the current machine. The first information is the machine name, which is available from `My.Computer.Name`, a property of type `String`. Second is the `My.Computer.Info` property of type `Microsoft .VisualBasic.Devices.ComputerInfo`, which collects information such as the total and available memory, both physical and virtual or the name, platform, and version of the operating system. The following code shows how you can get some information on the system:

```
Console.WriteLine("Computer name {0}: ", My.Computer.Name)
Console.WriteLine("Total physical memory {0}: ",
                My.Computer.Info.TotalPhysicalMemory)
Console.WriteLine("Available physical memory {0}: ",
                My.Computer.Info.AvailablePhysicalMemory)
Console.WriteLine("Operating system full name {0}: ",
                My.Computer.Info.OSFullName)
Console.WriteLine("Operating system version: {0}",
                My.Computer.Info.OSVersion)
Console.WriteLine("Installed User Interface culture: {0}",
                My.Computer.Info.InstalledUICulture.Name)
```

`My.Computer` also exposes a `Clock` property that offers three subproperties: `GmtTime` that returns the local date and time expressed as GMT, `LocalTime` that returns the local date and time, and `TickCount` that returns the number of ticks considering the machine timer. This is how you can use it:

```
Console.WriteLine("GMT Time for local machine: {0}",
                  My.Computer.Clock.GmtTime.ToString)
```

You can interact with system hardware with two other properties, `Mouse` and `Screen`. The first one allows knowing if your mouse has a wheel, if buttons' functionalities are swapped, or how many lines the scroll will be each time you move the wheel. This is an example:

```
Console.WriteLine("Mouse buttons are swapped: {0}",
                  My.Computer.Mouse.ButtonsSwapped.ToString)
Console.WriteLine("Mouse has wheel: {0}",
                  My.Computer.Mouse.WheelExists.ToString)
```

`Screen` is also interesting because it enables the retrieval of information on your display, such as the resolution, the device name, or the actual working area, but it is only available for Windows Forms applications. The following is an example, assuming you have a form with three `Label` controls:

```
Private Sub Form1_Load(sender As Object, e As EventArgs) Handles MyBase.Load
    Me.Label1.Text = "Screen resolution: " &
        My.Computer.Screen.Bounds.Width.ToString & _
        " x " & My.Computer.Screen.Bounds.Height.ToString
    Me.Label2.Text = "Bits per pixel: " & _
        My.Computer.Screen.BitsPerPixel.ToString
    Me.Label3.Text = "Working area: " &
        My.Computer.Screen.WorkingArea.Width.ToString & _
        " x " & My.Computer.Screen.WorkingArea.Height.ToString
End Sub
```

Figure 19.1 shows the global result of the preceding code running on my machine.

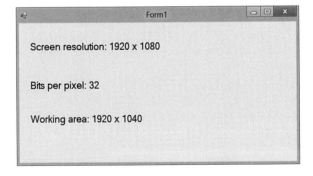

FIGURE 19.1   Information on the local machine using `My.Computer`.

You can obtain detailed information about both the computer and the operating system, including localization properties. `My.Computer` members for retrieving information are always self-explanatory, but you can always take advantage of IntelliSense and the Object Browser tool.

My.Settings

One of the most common requirements for applications is providing the ability of storing user preferences, such as the graphic theme, personal folders, options, and so on. Generally, there are two kinds of settings that the .NET Framework lets you save within the application configuration file: application-level settings and user-level settings. Application-level settings are related to the general behavior of the application, and users will not have the ability of providing modifications. User-level settings are related to each user profile that runs the applications and allows storing and editing preferences. My namespace provides a class named My.Settings, which offers members that easily allow working with settings at both levels, but only user-level settings can be written. At a higher level My.Settings is the code representation of the Settings tab in My Project. Because of this we start discussing My.Settings by talking about the Settings designer and then explaining how you can work with settings in code. Create a new Console project (if not yet done) and open My Project; then click the **Settings** tab. Figure 19.2 shows the Settings designer.

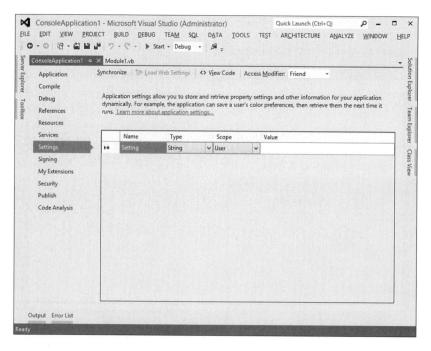

FIGURE 19.2   Settings designer.

Each setting is represented by a variable that can be of any .NET type (as long as it is marked as serializable) storing the desired value. This variable can be provided at both application level and user level, with the condition that only user-level variables can be also written. You now learn how to design settings and then how to use them in code. Imagine you want to provide a simple way for checking if the application is running for the first time. In the Name column replace the default Settings identifier with IsFirstTimeRun. In the Type column choose the Boolean type from the combo box, and in the Scope column ensure that User is selected. In the Value column choose True from the combo box.

Notice that Visual Studio can provide appropriate values depending on the setting type; for Boolean values, it offers True and False. After this sequence, your Settings Designer looks like Figure 19.3.

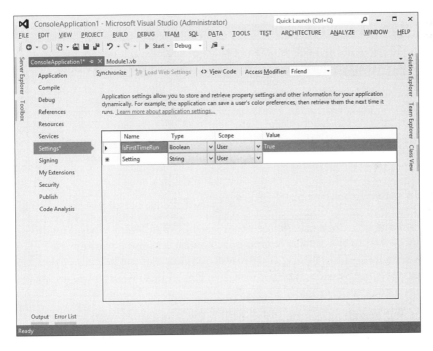

FIGURE 19.3   Providing a Boolean user-level setting.

You can now write some code to check if the application is running for the first time and, if so, set the IsFirstTimeRun setting to False as follows:

```vb
Sub UserSettingsDemo()

    If My.Settings.IsFirstTimeRun = True Then
        Console.WriteLine("The application is running for the first time")
        My.Settings.IsFirstTimeRun = False
        My.Settings.Save()
```

```
    Else
        Console.
        WriteLine("The application is already familiar with your system!")
    End If

End Sub
```

When you first launch the application, you get the following result:

```
The application is running for the first time
```

The code also changed the `IsFirstTimeRun` setting from `True` to `False`; this is possible because it is a user-level setting. If it were an application-level setting, it would be offered as a read-only property.

APPLICATION-LEVEL ONLY SETTINGS

With the Settings Designer you can define different kinds of settings, both at application level and user level. Among these settings, Connection Strings and Web Services URL are only available at application level to avoid modifications in code. In this way, only the appropriate personnel can make the right modifications if needed.

Notice also that you have to invoke the `Save` method; otherwise changes will not be saved. To check that everything works, rerun the application; you should now get the following message:

```
The application is already familiar with your system!
```

With the same technique you can easily define other settings of different types. You are not limited to types shown in the default combo box. You can choose any other .NET type that supports serialization by clicking the **Browse** command at the bottom of the combo box. This displays the Select a Type window (see Figure 19.4) where you can make your choice.

Settings definitions and default values are stored within the application configuration (app.config) file as XML definition. If your project does not already contain a configuration file, Visual Studio 2012 adds one.

User-level settings are defined within a section named `userSettings`. The following is an excerpt from the app.config file for the demo project showing the definition of the previously described `IsFirstTimeRun` setting:

```
<userSettings>
    <MyNamespace.My.MySettings>
        <setting name="IsFirstTimeRun" serializeAs="String">
            <value>True</value>
        </setting>
    </MyNamespace.My.MySettings>
</userSettings>
```

FIGURE 19.4   Selecting a nondefault .NET type for designing settings.

Notice how each setting is defined by a setting node that also defines the setting's name and way of serialization. (Although serialized as a string, based on its value, the .NET Framework can recognize the setting as Boolean.) Each setting node has a child node named value that stores the default value for the setting.

CONFIGURATION FILE NAMING

Your application configuration file is named app.config as long as it is included in your project folder. When the application is built in to the target folder (such as the default Debug and Release subfolders), the configuration file takes the complete name of the executable (for example, MyApplication.exe) plus the .config extension (for example, MyApplication.exe.config).

Similarly, application-level settings are stored within a section named applicationSettings. The following is the excerpt related to the test setting previously shown:

```
<applicationSettings>
    <MyNamespace.My.MySettings>
        <setting name="Setting" serializeAs="String">
            <value>test</value>
        </setting>
    </MyNamespace.My.MySettings>
</applicationSettings>
```

Settings also have a Visual Basic code counterpart. Each setting is mapped to a Visual Basic property. To understand this, click the **Show All Files** button in Solution Explorer and then expand the My Project folder; double-click the **Settings.designer.vb** file under Settings.Settings. Among the code that defines My.Settings, you can also find the definition for your custom settings. The `IsFirstTimeRun` setting defined in the previous example is mapped to a VB property as follows:

```
<Global.System.Configuration.UserScopedSettingAttribute(), _
 Global.System.Diagnostics.DebuggerNonUserCodeAttribute(), _
 Global.System.Configuration.DefaultSettingValueAttribute("True")> _
Public Property IsFirstTimeRun() As Boolean
    Get
        Return CType(Me("IsFirstTimeRun"), Boolean)
    End Get
    Set(ByVal value As Boolean)
        Me("IsFirstTimeRun") = Value
    End Set
End Property
```

The `System.Configuration.UserScopedSettingAttribute` tells the compiler that the setting has user-level scope, whereas the `System.Configuration.DefaultSettingValueAttribute` tells the compiler that the default value for the property is `True`. Notice how an explicit conversion with `CType` is performed to avoid any problems when deserializing. Now you know how and where settings are defined, but you still probably do not know where they are actually stored when you run the application outside Visual Studio (for example, in production environments). The .NET Framework creates a folder for the application within the AppData\Local folder in Windows, which has user-level scope. If you consider the current example, named MyNamespace on my machine, the .NET Framework created the following folders structure (on Windows 8, Windows 7, and Windows Vista): C:\Users\Alessandro\AppData\Local\MyNamespace\MyNamespace.vshost.exe_Url_wizb0ypr4ultyjhh1g1o352espg4ehdd\1.0.0.0. This auto-generated folder contains a file named user.config that contains the following, simple markup:

```
<?xml version="1.0" encoding="utf-8"?>
<configuration>
    <userSettings>
        <MyNamespace.My.MySettings>
            <setting name="IsFirstTimeRun" serializeAs="String">
                <value>False</value>
            </setting>
        </MyNamespace.My.MySettings>
    </userSettings>
</configuration>
```

As you can see, it is the same piece of XML code that was originally defined within the application configuration file, but now it stays as a single file within a user-level folder. This file is the place where changes to an application's settings are effectively saved. Visual Studio provides a convenient way for restoring such files to the default settings' value by just clicking the **Synchronize** button in the Settings Designer.

`My.Settings` Events

`My.Settings` provides some interesting events that allow understanding of what is happening behind the scenes. Here are the following four events:

- ▶ `SettingChanging`, which is raised just before a setting value is changed

- ▶ `PropertyChanged`, which is raised just after a setting value has been changed

- ▶ `SettingsLoaded`, which is raised just after settings values are loaded

- ▶ `SettingsSaving`, which is raised just before settings values are persisted to disk

To handle such events you need to double-click the **Settings.Designer.vb** file in Solution Explorer.

Creating event handlers is not a difficult task. When the Settings.Designer.vb file is open, select the **MySettings events** item in the upper-left combo box and select the event you want to handle in the upper right, as shown in Figure 19.5. When selected, Visual Studio 2012 automatically generates an event handler stub.

For example, imagine you want to validate a setting before changes are saved. To accomplish this, add a new `String` setting in the Settings Designer and name the setting as `ValidationTest`. The goal is to avoid saving the string value if it is null. The following code accomplishes this:

```
Private Sub MySettings_SettingsSaving(ByVal sender As Object,
                           ByVal e As
               System.ComponentModel.CancelEventArgs) _
                     Handles Me.SettingsSaving

    If My.Settings.ValidationTest Is Nothing Then
        Throw New NullReferenceException("Cannot save a null string")
```

19

```
            e.Cancel = True
        End If
End Sub
```

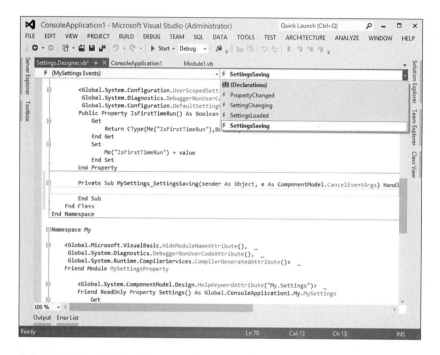

FIGURE 19.5   Handling `My.Settings` events.

The `SettingsSaving` event allows performing some checks before values are saved.

The `e` variable of type `System.ComponentModel.CancelEventArgs` provides a `Cancel` property that cancels saving when set to `True`. The following example shows instead how you can handle the `SettingChanging` event that is raised before a setting value gets changed:

```
Private Sub MySettings_SettingChanging(ByVal sender As Object,
                                ByVal e As _
                                System.Configuration.
                                SettingChangingEventArgs) _
                                Handles Me.SettingChanging
    Console.WriteLine("About to change the settings values")
    'Waits for one second
    System.Threading.Thread.Sleep(1000)
End Sub
```

`My.Settings` provides a convenient way for managing user settings in a strongly typed way offering a modern infrastructure that is more efficient than older .ini files.

My.Resources

Visual Studio and the .NET Framework enable you to include resources within your application. Resources are different kinds of information that would usually be available from external files, such as sounds, images, and text. You can embed in your application all resources you want using My.Resources and the Resources Designer.

WPF RESOURCES

Things behave a little differently in WPF, Silverlight (including Phone), and Metro applications. Because of their particular infrastructures, embedding resources using the Resources Designer is a practice that you must avoid. To understand how WPF resources work, take a look at the official page in the MSDN Library: http://msdn.microsoft.com/en-us/library/ms750613(VS.110).aspx. This chapter describes resources with Console and Windows Forms applications for backward compatibility with existing code you might have written in the past.

Differently from other My members, My.Resources is a namespace defining subsequent members that can wrap in code resources that you define in the designer. At this point, you need to open **My Project** and then select the **Resources** tab. Figure 19.6 shows the Resources Designer.

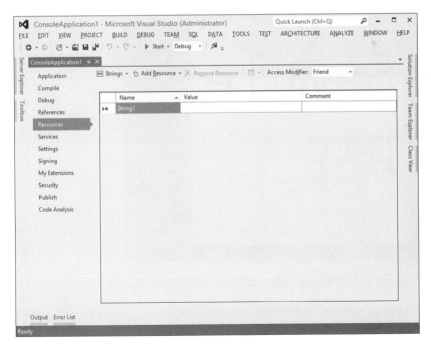

FIGURE 19.6   The Resources Designer.

Each time you add a new resource, Visual Studio generates a .NET property that provides managed access to the resource itself. For example, in the Name column replace the String1 default identifier with TestString and type **Resources demonstration** in the Value column. If you like, you can also provide a comment. Visual Studio generates a TestString property of type String and Friend visibility that you can access like any other property, as in the following code:

```
Console.WriteLine(My.Resources.TestString)
```

The interesting thing is that the Visual Basic compiler will try to format the string according to the current culture settings. By clicking the **Add Resource** button, you will be prompted with a series of file types to add as resources. If you add a text file, the file will be represented by a String property. You can add both existing or new files. For example, click the **Add Resource** button and select the **New Image, JPEG Image...** command. After you specify the new image name, Visual Studio 2012 shows the image editor where you can leverage your drawing ability. Figure 19.7 shows an editor in action.

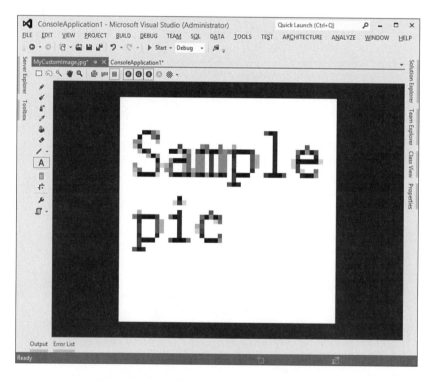

FIGURE 19.7   The Visual Studio 2012's built-in image editor.

After you create your image, or even if you add an existing one from disk, the IDE generates a property of type System.Drawing.Bitmap pointing to the image. If you have a Windows Forms application, you could recall your image as follows:

```
'PictureBox1 is a Windows Forms "PictureBox" control
'MyCustomImage is the name of the new custom image
Me.PictureBox1.Image = My.Resources.MyCustomImage
```

You can then pick images from resources if you need to populate a PictureBox control at design time by clicking the **Browse** button from the Properties window to set the Image property. Figure 19.8 shows how you can select an image directly from resources.

FIGURE 19.8   Assigning an image to a PictureBox picking from resources.

The same is true for icons—you can create and draw a new icon with the Visual Studio Designer and then assign it to a Windows Forms `Icon` property. For audio files, you can add only `.Wav` files to ensure that they are automatically recognized as audio files. Such files are then mapped as `System.IO.UnmanagedMemoryStream` objects and can be played via `My.Computer` as follows:

```
My.Computer.Audio.Play(My.Resources.
                    AnAudioFile,
                    AudioPlayMode.WaitToComplete)
```

You can also add files other than text, pictures, icons, and audio. When Visual Studio cannot recognize a file type, it returns it from resources as byte array (`System.Byte()`), so you should implement code to analyze the particular resource. Visual Studio also creates a project-level folder named Resources where it stores resource files. Another interesting thing is to understand how resources are defined in code. Each time you add a resource via the designer, the IDE generates a Visual Basic property for it. For example, the following code shows how the new .jpeg image is mapped in code:

```
Friend ReadOnly Property MyCustomImage() As System.Drawing.Bitmap
    Get
        Dim obj As Object = ResourceManager.
                    GetObject("MyCustomImage", resourceCulture)
```

```
        Return CType(obj, System.Drawing.Bitmap)
    End Get
End Property
```

And this is how the first string resource is mapped:

```
Friend ReadOnly Property TestString() As String
    Get
        Return ResourceManager.
                GetString("TestString", resourceCulture)
    End Get
End Property
```

The `ResourceManager` class provides methods for retrieving resources according to the specified culture that by default is the system one. Such properties are available in the Resources.designer.vb file that should never be edited manually.

Getting Resources by Name in Code

Sometimes you need to access resources by name in code. This can be accomplished via the Reflection, which is discussed in Chapter 46. The following code provides an example:

```
'Returns the specified resource of type String
'usage:
'Dim myRes As String = GetResourceByName("TestString")
Function GetResourceByName(ByVal resourceName As String) As String
    'An example for [Application Name].[Resource File]
    'is the current app:
    'MyNamespace.Resources.resx
    Dim rm As New ResourceManager("[Application Name].[Resource File]",
                              Assembly.GetExecutingAssembly)

    Return rm.GetString(resourceName)
End Function
```

In this case the method returns resources of type `String`, but you can implement methods that return a different type.

`My.User`

`My.User` is a property that allows getting information on the user who logged in to the Windows operating system and that is running the application. Such a property is of type `Microsoft.VisualBasic.ApplicationServices.User` and is a wrapper of this last mentioned one, meaning that you can invoke both and obtain the same results. Utilizing `My.User` is straightforward because it offers just a few but easy-to-understand members, as summarized in Table 19.2.

TABLE 19.2 `My.User` Members

Member	Type	Description
`CurrentPrincipal`	Property	Retrieves information on the current user based on the System.Security.Principal implementation for a role-based security
`InitializeWithWindowsUser`	Method	Associates the application with the current principal that logged into Windows
`Name`	Property	A string that stores the name of the currently logged user
`IsAuthenticated`	Property	A Boolean value representing if the current user is authenticated
`IsInRole`	Method	Returns True if the current user belongs to the specified role

Listing 19.1 shows how you can get information on the current user that runs the application. Notice how an invocation to `InitializeWithWindowsUser` is required to associate the current user to the application.

LISTING 19.1   Using `My.User` to Get Information on the Current User

```
Module Module1

    Sub Main()
        MyUserInformation()
        Console.ReadLine()
    End Sub

    Sub MyUserInformation()
        My.User.InitializeWithWindowsUser()
        Console.WriteLine("Current user is: {0}", My.User.Name)
        Console.WriteLine("User is authenticated: {0}", My.User.IsAuthenticated)
        Console.WriteLine("Application is running as Administrator: {0}",
                    My.User.IsInRole("BUILTIN\Administrators"))
        Console.WriteLine(My.User.CurrentPrincipal.
                    Identity.AuthenticationType.ToString)
    End Sub

End Module
```

The code shown in Listing 19.1 produces, on my machine, the following output:

```
Current user is: DELSOLELAPTOP\Alessandro
User is authenticated: True
Application is running as Administrator: False
NTLM
```

Notice how the username is provided as "Computer name\user name" and also how the role for the `IsInRole` method requires the name of the machine. (BUILTIN is a default value for all machines.) The authentication type is determined via the `CurrentPrincipal.Identity.AuthenticationType` property. Here, `Identity` is a `System.Security.Principal.IIdentity` object that provides information about a user, considering the role-based security system in the .NET Framework (for more information, check the MSDN documentation). With a few lines of code, you can get information about the current user without the need of dealing with classes and members from the `Microsoft.VisualBasic.ApplicationServices.User` object.

My.WebServices

When you have in your application references to web services, you can easily reach members provided by the proxy classes using `My.WebServices`. For example, if you have a proxy class named `DataAccess` exposing a `GetCustomers` method, you can write the following line:

```
My.WebServices.DataAccess.GetCustomers()
```

This is a rapid way for invoking members from referenced web services (as long as they are in the same solution of your application).

Extending My

One of the most interesting features of the `My` namespace is that it is extensible with custom members. You can both extend `My` at the root level or extend existing members such as `Application` and `Computer`. The first goal of this section is to show how you can extend `My` at the higher level, implementing functionalities for working with collections, such as a property that allows converting from a generic collection into an `ObservableCollection(Of T)`. We need to mimic how Visual Basic 2012 handles the `My` namespace, so first add a new module to the project and name it **MyCollectionsUtils**. Each member you want to be added to `My` must start with the **My** letters; this is the reason for using the `MyCollectionsUtils` identifier. The compiler can then distinguish that this member belongs to `My` if you enclose it within such a namespace. Add a reference to the WindowsBase.dll assembly (not required in WPF applications) and then write the code shown in Listing 19.2.

LISTING 19.2   Extending My at Root Level

```
Imports System.Collections.ObjectModel

Namespace My

    <Global.Microsoft.VisualBasic.HideModuleName(),
     Global.System.Diagnostics.DebuggerNonUserCode()>
    Module MyCollectionsUtils
```

```
        Private helper As New _
                ThreadSafeObjectProvider(Of ObservableCollectionHelper)

        Friend ReadOnly Property CollectionsUtils _
                As ObservableCollectionHelper
            Get
                Return helper.GetInstance
                helper = Nothing
            End Get
        End Property
    End Module

End Namespace

Class ObservableCollectionHelper

    Public Function ConvertToObservableCollection(Of T) _
                        (ByVal collection As ICollection(Of T)) _
                        As ObservableCollection(Of T)
        Return New ObservableCollection(Of T)(collection)
    End Function
End Class
```

FRIEND VISIBILITY

Module's members are marked as `Friend` to reproduce the default Visual Basic behavior.

There are some tasks to perform after examining Listing 19.2. First, notice how the `ObservableCollectionHelper` class exposes a public method that effectively converts an `ICollection(Of T)` into a new `ObservableCollection`. Also notice how there is the need to explicitly provide a `Namespace My..End Namespace` declaration, which encloses custom members for `My`. The `MyCollectionsUtils` module exposes members that are effectively accessible via `My`. To replicate the VB default behavior, the module is marked as `System.Diagnostics.NonUserCode` so that the debugger does not step into such code (if you instead need debugger support, remove this attribute) and as `Microsoft.VisualBasic.HideModuleName` that prevents the module name to be shown by IntelliSense when invoking your custom members. Then notice how the helper field is of type `ThreadSafeObjectProvider(Of T)`. According to the Microsoft documentation, this is a best practice because it ensures that each thread invoking `My.CollectionsUtils` has access to a separate instance. The read-only property `CollectionsUtils` then wraps the `ObservableCollectionHelper.ConvertToObservableCollection` method being exposed through the `GetInstance` invocation. When you have created your extension, you can use it in a simple way. The following code shows how you can convert a `List(Of Integer)` into an `ObservableCollection` using your custom `My.CollectionsUtils` member:

```
Dim someInts As New List(Of Integer) From {1, 2, 3}

Dim obs As ObservableCollection(Of Integer) =

        My.CollectionsUtils.ConvertToObservableCollection(someInts)

For Each number As Integer In obs
    Console.WriteLine(number)
Next
```

After seeing how you can extend My at the root level, let's now see how you can customize existing members.

Extending My.Application and My.Computer

Extending existing members such as Application and Computer is straightforward because both are implemented as partial classes, so you can add your own partial classes without the need of editing auto-generated code. Previous considerations remain unchanged, meaning that your partial classes' names need to start with My (such as MyApplication and MyComputer) and that both must be enclosed within an explicit declaration of a Namespace My..End Namespace code block. For example, imagine you want to extend My.Application with a method that associates a file extension with your application so that each time you double-click a file with that particular extension it will be opened by your application. Listing 19.3 accomplishes this (notice that if you run Windows Vista, Windows 7, or Windows 8 you need to start Visual Studio with administrative rights).

LISTING 19.3   Extending My.Application

```
Imports Microsoft.Win32

Namespace My

    Partial Friend Class MyApplication

        Public Function AssociateExtension(ByVal extension As String,
                                ByVal mimeType As String) As Boolean
            Try
                'Creates a registry entry for the extension
                My.Computer.Registry.ClassesRoot.
                CreateSubKey(extension).SetValue("",
                mimeType, RegistryValueKind.String)

                'Creates a registry entry for the Mime type
                'Environment.GetCommandLineArgs(0) returns
                'the executable name for Console applications
                My.Computer.Registry.ClassesRoot.
                CreateSubKey(mimeType & "\shell\open\command").
```

```
            SetValue("", Environment.GetCommandLineArgs(0) & " ""%1"" ",
            RegistryValueKind.String)

                Return True
            Catch ex As Exception
                Return False
            End Try
        End Function
    End Class
End Namespace
```

Notice how the `MyApplication` class is marked as `Partial Friend`. This is required to match the definition provided by Visual Basic to `My.Application`. Now you can use the extension as you normally would do with `My.Application`. The following is an example:

```
Dim succeeded As Boolean =
    My.Application.AssociateExtension(".ale",
    "AlessandroDelSole/document")
```

Extending `My.Computer` works similarly. For example, we could implement a property that returns the MIME type for the specified filename. Code in Listing 19.4 demonstrates this.

LISTING 19.4   Extending `My.Computer`

```
Imports Microsoft.Win32

Namespace My
    Partial Friend Class MyComputer

        Public ReadOnly Property MimeType(ByVal fileName As String) As String
            Get
                Return getMimeType(fileName)
            End Get
        End Property

        Private Function getMimeType(ByVal fileName As String) As String

            Dim mimeType As String = String.Empty

            Dim fileExtension = System.IO.Path.
                            GetExtension(fileName).ToLower()
            Dim registryKey = Registry.ClassesRoot.
                            OpenSubKey(fileExtension)

            If registryKey IsNot Nothing And _
                            registryKey.GetValue("Content Type") _
                            IsNot Nothing Then
```

19

```
          mimeType = registryKey.
                    GetValue("Content Type").ToString
        Else
            mimeType = ""
        End If
        Return mimeType
    End Function


    End Class
End Namespace
```

You still need to mark the class as Partial Friend by enclosing it within the My namespace declaration. At this point, you can use your extension as usual—for example, to retrieve the MIME type of a text file:

```
Dim mimeType As String = My.Computer.MimeType("Testfile.txt")
```

Of course, you are not limited to extending Application and Computer; you can also extend Settings and Resources.

Extending My.Resources and My.Settings

Extending My.Resources and My.Settings is also possible, although with a few differences. Resources is a namespace, so you need to declare it as follows:

```
Namespace My.Resources
    Friend Module MyResources
        'Your code here
    End Module
End Namespace
```

Generally, you do not need custom extensions to Resources; you could decide to offer alternative localized versions of some contents. Extending My.Settings works more similarly to Application and Computer, but you do not need to provide custom extensions here because the Visual Studio 2012 Designer provides a graphical environment for performing all operations you need and selecting all available .NET types.

My in Different Applications

Now that you know how My can be customized, you can easily understand why different kinds of Visual Basic applications have their own customizations, provided by the IDE. For example, Windows Presentation Foundation applications provide a My.Windows property that allows access to windows' instances, as follows:

```
'Get the instance of the Main window
 Dim aWindows As Window = My.Windows.MainWindow
```

This is mainly due to the support offered in code by the My namespace to the Application Framework feature. This feature enables you to execute special tasks at the beginning and at the end of the application lifetime, such as showing splash screens or establishing what form is the main application form normally. In Windows Forms applications the application framework is enabled by default, and you can get in touch with it by opening My Project and selecting the **Application** tab, as shown in Figure 19.9.

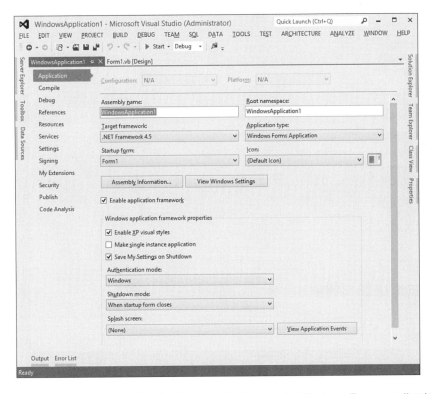

FIGURE 19.9   The application framework designer for Windows Forms applications.

Enabling the application framework allows you to visually manage features with no lines of code, although you are allowed to customize the related auto-generated code. For example, the following line manually establishes that My.Settings has to be saved when the application shuts down:

```
My.Application.SaveMySettingsOnExit = True
```

The following line shows how you instead can set the minimum number of milliseconds for a splash screen to be shown:

```
My.Application.MinimumSplashScreenDisplayTime = 1000
```

19

For WPF applications the application framework is slightly different, as shown in Figure 19.10.

FIGURE 19.10   The application framework for WPF applications.

The following lines show how you can take advantage of `My.Application` in WPF to retrieve some information:

```
'The main Window XAML's uri
Dim startup As String = My.Application.StartupUri.ToString


'Main Window
Dim mainWindow As Window = My.Application.MainWindow


'Application resources
Dim appResources As ResourceDictionary = My.Application.Resources
```

All members are self-explanatory, so IntelliSense can be a great friend to you in this situation, too. In both Windows Forms and WPF applications, the **View Application Events** button redirects you to the appropriate file for defining application events (Application.xaml.vb in WPF and Application.Designer.vb in Win Forms). For web applications, Silverlight applications do not support the `My` namespace, and ASP.NET applications do not offer the `My.Application` and `My.WebServices` members; they instead expose the

`My.Response` and `My.Request` properties that respectively wrap members from `System.Web.HttpResponse` and `System.Web.HttpRequest`.

Understanding Application Events

Applications that provide support for the application framework can be also managed with application events. This is the typical case of client applications such as Windows Forms and WPF applications. Windows Forms applications provide the following events:

- ▶ `NetworkAvailabilityChanged`, which is raised when the network becomes available or the connection is no longer available

- ▶ `ShutDown`, which is raised when the application shuts down

- ▶ `Startup`, which is raised when the application starts

- ▶ `StartupNextInstance`, which is raised when another instance of the application starts up

- ▶ `UnhandledException` which is raised when the application encounters an unhandled exception during tasks that involve the application framework

Application events are handled within the code file that implements `My.Application` customizations, which by default is Application.designer.vb. The following example shows how you can intercept the network state change:

```
Private Sub MyApplication_NetworkAvailabilityChanged(ByVal sender As Object,
                                ByVal e As Microsoft.VisualBasic.
                                Devices.
                                NetworkAvailableEventArgs) _
                                Handles
                                Me.NetworkAvailabilityChanged

    If e.IsNetworkAvailable = False Then
        'Network no longer available
    Else
        'Network available
    End If
End Sub
```

In WPF applications you have more events that you can handle. First, application events in WPF are handled in the Application.xaml.vb file. You have the following events available:

- ▶ `Activated`, which is raised when the application gets the foreground focus

- ▶ `Deactivated`, which is raised when the application loses the foreground focus

- ▶ `DispatcherUnhandledException`, which is raised when the `Dispatcher` object encounters an unhandled exception

▶ Exit, which is raised when the application shuts down

▶ LoadCompleted, Navigated, Navigating, NavigationFailed, NavigationProgress, and NavigationStopped, which are raised in case of navigation applications, which is self-explanatory if you think of navigation between pages

▶ Startup, which is raised when the application starts up and specifies the main UI object

▶ FragmentNavigation, which is raised when navigating to a specific XAML Uri

▶ SessionEnding, which is raised when the user logs off from Windows or is shutting down the system

The following example shows how you can intercept the SessionEnding event and decide to back up your work if the e.ReasonSessionEnding property has value ReasonSessionEnding.Shutdown:

```
Private Sub Application_SessionEnding(ByVal sender As Object,
                              ByVal e As _
                              SessionEndingCancelEventArgs) _
                              Handles Me.SessionEnding

    If e.ReasonSessionEnding = ReasonSessionEnding.Shutdown Then
        'Backup your files here
    End If
End Sub
```

Application events provide a great way for getting information on what happens behind the scenes of the application lifetime.

Summary

The My namespace is a unique feature of Visual Basic language that offers lots of shortcuts to most common operations. It was first made available in VB 2005. In this chapter you saw how you can interact with your application with My.Application and how you can perform operations on your system with My.Computer, including file operations, Registry operations, and clipboard operations. You then got information about an important feature provided by My.Settings, which has the capability to save and load user preferences using the Visual Studio Designer and managed code; this is a convenient way if compared to old initialization files. Next you saw about My.Resources, a special place for embedding files in your executable—typically for Console and Windows Forms applications. Finally, you got in touch with one of the most important features in My: the ability to extend the namespace with custom members, both at root level and existing members.

CHAPTER 20

Advanced Language Features

Back in 2008, the .NET Framework 3.5 introduced revolutionary technologies such as LINQ. Because of its complex infrastructure, all .NET languages (especially VB and C#) required new keywords, syntaxes, and constructs to interact with LINQ but that could be successfully used in lots of other scenarios. Visual Basic 2010 introduced even more features to make the coding experience better and Visual Basic 2012 not only continues to support those language features but also applies some fixes to small bugs. Most of the language features discussed in this chapter are important for the comprehension of the next chapters, so I recommend you pay particular attention to the topics presented here.

Local Type Inference

Local type inference is a language feature that allows you to omit specifying the data type of a local variable even if Option Strict is set to On. The Visual Basic compiler can deduce (*infer*) the most appropriate data type depending on the variable's usage. The easiest way to understand and hopefully appreciate local type inference is to provide a code example. Consider the following code and pay attention to the comments:

```
Sub Main()
    'The compiler infers String
    Dim oneString = "Hello Visual Basic 2012!"

    'The compiler infers Integer
    Dim oneInt = 324
```

```
    'The compiler infers Double
    Dim oneDbl = 123.456


    'The compiler infers Boolean


    Dim oneBool = True
End Sub
```

As you can see, the code doesn't specify the type for all variables because the compiler can infer the most appropriate data type according to the usage of a variable. To ensure that the VB compiler inferred the correct type, pass the mouse pointer over the variable declaration to retrieve information via a useful tooltip, as shown in Figure 20.1.

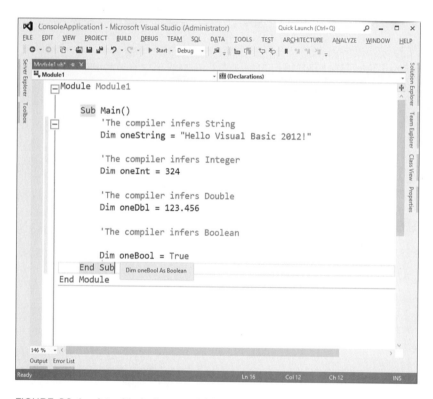

FIGURE 20.1   A tooltip indicates which type the Visual Basic compiler inferred to local variables.

BEHIND THE SCENES OF LOCAL TYPE INFERENCE

Types' inference is determined via the *dominant type* algorithm. This was described perfectly (and is still valid) in the Visual Basic 10.0 language specifications document, available at http://www.microsoft.com/en-us/download/details.aspx?id=15039.

The local type inference also works with custom types, as demonstrated by the following example:

```
Dim p As New Person With {.FirstName = "Alessandro",
                          .LastName = "Del Sole"}
'The compiler infers Person
Dim onePerson = p
```

You can also use local type inference within loops or in any other circumstance you like:

```
'The compiler infers System.Diagnostic.Process
For Each proc In Process.GetProcesses
    Console.WriteLine(proc.ProcessName)
Next
```

`Option Infer` Directive

To enable or disable local type inference, the Visual Basic grammar provides the `Option Infer` directive. `Option Infer On` enables inference, whereas `Option Infer Off` disables it. You do not need to explicitly provide an `Option Infer` directive because it is offered at the project level by Visual Studio. By default, `Option Infer` is `On`. If you want to change the default settings for the current project, open My Project and then switch to the **Compile** tab. There you can find the Visual Basic compiler options, including `Option Infer`. If you instead want to change settings for each new project, select the **Options** command from the Tools menu. When the Options dialog box appears, move to the **Projects and Solutions** tab and select the **VB defaults** item, as shown in Figure 20.2.

FIGURE 20.2 Changing the default behavior for `Option Infer`.

You then need to add an `Option Infer On` directive if you want to switch back to local type inference.

Local Type Inference Scope

The word *local* in the local type inference definition has a special meaning. Local type inference works only with local variables defined within code blocks and does not work with class-level declarations. For example, consider the following code:

```
Class Person

    Property LastName As String
    Property FirstName As String

    Function FullName() As String
        'Local variable: local type inference works
        Dim completeName = Me.LastName & " " & Me.FirstName
        Return completeName
    End Function
End Class
```

Local type inference affects the `completeName` local variable, which is enclosed within a method. Now consider the following code:

```
'Both Option Strict and Option Infer are On
Class Person
    'Local type inference does not work with
    'class level variables. An error will be
    'thrown.
    Private completeName
```

The preceding code will not be compiled because local type inference does not affect class-level declarations; therefore, the Visual Basic compiler throws an error if `Option Strict` is `On`. If `Option Strict` is `Off`, the `completeName` class-level variable will be considered of type `Object` but still won't be affected by local type inference. So be aware of this possible situation. The conclusion is that you always need to explicitly provide a type for class-level variables, whereas you can omit the specification with local variables.

WHY LOCAL TYPE INFERENCE?

If you are an old-school developer, you probably will be surprised and perhaps unhappy by local type inference because you always wrote your code the most strongly typed possible. You will not be obliged to declare types by taking advantage of local type inference except when you need to generate *anonymous types*, which are discussed later in this chapter. I always use (and suggest) the local type inference because it's straightforward and avoids the need of worrying about types while still providing type safety, especially with different kinds of query result when working with LINQ. I often use this feature in the rest of the book.

Array Literals

The array literals feature works like the local type inference but is specific to arrays. It was first introduced in Visual Basic 2010. Consider this array of strings declaration as you would write it in Visual Basic 2008:

```
Dim anArrayOfStrings() As String = {"One", "Two", "Three"}
```

In Visual Basic 2010 and 2012 you can write it as follows:

```
'The compiler infers String()
Dim anArrayOfStrings = {"One", "Two", "Three"}
```

According to the preceding code, you are still required to place only a couple of parentheses, but you can omit the type that is correctly inferred by the compiler as you can easily verify by passing the mouse pointer over the variable declaration. Of course, array literals work with value types, too, as shown here:

```
'The compiler infers Double
Dim anArrayOfDouble = {1.23, 2.34, 3.45}
'The compiler infers Integer
Dim anArrayOfInteger = {4, 3, 2, 1}
```

Array literals also support mixed arrays. For example, the following array is inferred as an array of Object:

```
'Does not work with Option Strict On
Dim mixedArray = {1.23, "One point Twentythree"}
```

The preceding code will not be compiled if Option Strict is On, and the compiler will show a message saying that the type cannot be inferred, which is a situation that can be resolved explicitly by assigning the type to the array. You could therefore explicitly declare the array as Dim mixedArray() As Object, but you need to be careful in this because mixed arrays could lead to errors.

Bug Fix: Return Type in Array Literals

Visual Basic 2012 fixes a bug related to the return type in array literals. Strictly related to the previous code snippet about mixed arrays, the following code in Visual Basic 2010 would result in an error because the type returned by the Return statement would be considered as Object():

```
Function oneMethod(i As Integer) As Integer()
   If i = 0 Then Return {}
   Return {1, 2, i}
End Function
```

This has been fixed in Visual Basic 2012 and the compiler is now capable of inferring the appropriate type (Integer in this case).

Multidimensional and Jagged Arrays

Array literals also affect multidimensional and jagged arrays. The following line of code shows how you can declare a multidimensional array of integers by taking advantage of array literals:

```
Dim multiIntArray = {{4, 3}, {2, 1}}
```

In this case, you do not need to add parentheses. The Visual Basic compiler infers the type as follows:

```
Dim multiIntArray(,) As Integer = {{4, 3}, {2, 1}}
```

Figure 20.3 shows how you can check the inferred type by passing the mouse pointer over the declaration, getting a descriptive tooltip.

FIGURE 20.3   Type inference for a multidimensional array.

Array literals work similarly on a jagged array. For example, you can write a jagged array of strings as follows:

```
Dim jaggedStringArray = {({"One", "Two"}),
                         ({"Three", "Four"})}
```

This is the same as writing:

```
Dim jaggedStringArray()() As String = {({"One", "Two"}),
                                       ({"Three", "Four"})}
```

And the same as for multidimensional arrays in which the code editor can provide help on type inference, as shown in Figure 20.4.

Array literals can help in writing more elegant and shorter code.

FIGURE 20.4   Type inference for a jagged array.

Extension Methods

Extension methods are a feature that Visual Basic 2012 inherits from its predecessors. As for other features discussed in this chapter, their main purpose is being used with LINQ, although they can also be useful in hundreds of scenarios. Extension methods are special methods that can extend the data type they are applied to. The most important thing is that you can extend existing types even if you do not have the source code and without the need to rebuild class libraries that expose types you go to extend—and this is important. For example, you can extend .NET built-in types, as you see in this section, although you do not have .NET source code.

We now discuss extension methods in two different perspectives: learning to use existing extension methods exposed by .NET built-in types and implementing and exporting custom extension methods. The first code example retrieves the list of processes running on the system and makes use of an extension method named ToList:

```
Dim processList = Process.GetProcesses.ToList
```

ToList converts an array or an IEnumerable collection into a strongly typed List(Of T), in this case into a List(Of Process) (notice how the assignment works with local type inference). Extension methods are easily recognizable within IntelliSense because they are characterized by the usual method icon plus a blue down arrow, as shown in Figure 20.5.

They are also recognizable because the method definition is marked as <Extension> as you can see from the descriptive tooltip shown in Figure 20.5, but this will also be discussed in creating custom methods. The next example uses the AsEnumerable method for converting an array of Process into an IEnumerable(Of Process):

```
Dim processEnumerable As IEnumerable(Of Process) =
                     Process.GetProcesses.AsEnumerable
```

20

FIGURE 20.5   Recognizing extension methods within IntelliSense.

Extension methods can execute hundreds of tasks, so it is not easy to provide a general summarization, especially because they can be customized according to your needs. At a higher level, .NET built-in extension methods accomplish three main objectives: converting types into other types, data filtering, and parsing. The most common built-in .NET extension methods are provided by the `System.Linq.Enumerable` class and are summarized in Table 20.1.

TABLE 20.1   Built-in Extension Methods

Method	Description
Aggregate	Accumulates items of a sequence.
All	Checks whether elements within a sequence satisfy a condition.
Any	Checks whether any elements within a sequence satisfy a condition.
AsEnumerable	Converts a sequence of elements into an `IEnumerable(Of T)`.
Average	Retrieves the result of the average calculation from the members of a sequence.
Cast	Performs the conversion from an `IEnumerable(Of T)` into the specified type. It is used explicitly when the compiler cannot infer the appropriate type.
Concat	Returns the concatenation of two sequences.
Contains	Checks if a sequence contains the specified item.
Count	Returns the number of items in a sequence.
DefaultIfEmpty	Returns the elements of the specified sequence or the type parameter's default value in a singleton collection if the sequence is empty.
Distinct	Ensures that no duplicates are retrieved from a sequence or removes duplicates from a sequence.
ElementAt	Obtains the object in the sequence at the specified index.
ElementAtOrDefault	Like `ElementAt` but returns a default value if the index is wrong.

Method	Description
Except	Given two sequences, creates a new sequence with elements from the first sequence that are not also in the second one.
First	Gets the first element of a sequence.
FirstOrDefault	Like `First` but returns a default value if the first element is not what you are searching for.
GroupBy	Given a criteria, groups elements of a sequence into another sequence.
GroupJoin	Given a criteria, joins elements from two sequences into one sequence.
Intersect	Creates a sequence with common elements from two sequences.
Join	Joins elements from two sequences based on specific criteria, such as equality.
Last	Retrieves the last item in a sequence.
LastOrDefault	Like `Last` but returns a default value if the specified instance is not found.
LongCount	Returns the number of items in a sequence under the form of Long (`System.Int64`) type.
Max	Retrieves the highest value in a sequence.
Min	Retrieves the minimum value in a sequence.
OfType	Filters an `IEnumerable` collection according to the specified type.
OrderBy	Orders elements in a sequence using the specified criteria.
OrderByDescending	Orders elements in a sequence using the specified criteria in a descending order.
Reverse	Reverses the order of items in a sequence.
Select	Puts an item into a sequence for queries.
SelectMany	Puts more than one item into a sequence for queries.
SequenceEquals	Determines whether two sequences are equal by comparing the elements by using the default equality comparer for their type or using a specified comparer.
Single	Returns the only item from a sequence that matches the specified criteria.
SingleOrDefault	Like `Single` but returns a default value if the specified item could not be found.
Skip	When creating a new sequence, skips the specified number of items and returns the remaining items from the starting sequence.
SkipWhile	Like `Skip` but only while the specified condition is satisfied.
Sum	In a sequence of numeric values, returns the sum of numbers.
Take	Returns the specified number of items starting from the beginning of a sequence.

20

Method	Description
TakeWhile	Like `Take` but only while the specified condition is satisfied.
ThenBy	After invoking `OrderBy`, provides the ability of a subsequent ordering operation.
ThenByDescending	After invoking `OrderBy`, provides the ability of a subsequent ordering operation in a descending way.
ToArray	Converts an `IEnumerable(Of T)` into an array.
ToDictionary	Converts an `IEnumerable(Of T)` into a `Dictionary(Of T, T)`.
ToList	Converts an `IEnumerable(Of T)` into a `List(Of T)`.
ToLookup	Converts an `IEnumerable(Of T)` into a `LookUp(Of TSource, TKey)`.
Union	Creates a new sequence with unique elements from two sequences.
Where	Filters a sequence according to the specified criteria.

ARGUMENTS AS LAMBDAS

In most cases you use lambda expressions as arguments for extension methods. Lambda expressions are discussed later in this book; therefore, examples where lambdas are not used are provided.

In the next part of this book, which is dedicated to data access with LINQ, you see how extension methods are used for filtering, ordering, and parsing data. The following code snippet shows an example of filtering data using the `Where` extension method:

```
'A real app example would use
'a lambda expression instead of a delegate
Dim filteredProcessList = Process.GetProcesses.
    Where(AddressOf EvaluateProcess).ToList

Private Function EvaluateProcess(ByVal p As Process) As Boolean
    If p.ProcessName.ToLowerInvariant.StartsWith("e") Then Return True
End Function
```

The preceding code adds `Process` objects to a list only if the process name starts with the letter *e*. The evaluation is performed through a delegate; although in this chapter you learn how to accomplish this using the lambda expression. Table 20.1 cannot be exhaustive because the .NET Framework offers other extension methods specific to some development areas that are eventually discussed in the appropriate chapters. IntelliSense provides help about extension methods not covered here. By reading Table 20.1, you can also understand that extension methods from `System.Linq.Enumerable` work on or return results from a *sequence of elements*. This notion is important because you use such methods against a number of different collections (that is, sequences of elements of a particular type), especially when working with LINQ.

EXTENSION METHODS BEHAVIOR

Although extension methods behave as instance methods, the Visual Basic compiler translates them into static methods. This is because extension methods are defined within modules (or static classes if created in Visual C#).

Coding Custom Extension Methods

One of the most interesting things when talking about extension methods is that you can create your custom extensions. This provides great power and flexibility to development because you can extend existing types with new functionalities, even if you do not have the source code for the type you want to extend. There are a set of rules and best practices to follow in coding custom extension methods; the first considerations are the following:

▶ In Visual Basic, extension methods can be defined only within modules because they are considered as shared methods by the compiler.

▶ Only `Function` and `Sub` methods can be coded as extensions. Properties and other members cannot work as extensions.

▶ Methods must be decorated with the `System.Runtime.CompilerServices.Extension` attribute. Decorating modules with the same attribute is also legal but not required.

▶ Extension methods can be overloaded.

▶ Extension methods can extend reference types, value types, delegates, arrays, interfaces, and generic parameters but cannot extend `System.Object` to avoid late binding problems.

▶ They must receive at least an argument. The first argument is always the type that the extension method goes to extend.

For example, imagine you want to provide a custom extension method that converts an `IEnumerable(Of T)` into an `ObservableCollection(Of T)`. The `ObservableCollection` is a special collection exposed by the `System.Collections.ObjectModel` namespace from the WindowsBase.dll assembly, which is usually used in WPF applications. (You need to add a reference to WindowsBase.dll.) The code in Listing 20.1 shows how this can be implemented.

LISTING 20.1   Implementing Custom Extension Methods

```
Imports System.Runtime.CompilerServices
Imports System.Collections.ObjectModel

<Extension()> Module Extensions
    <Extension()> Function ToObservableCollection(Of T) _
                    (ByVal List As IEnumerable(Of T)) _
                    As ObservableCollection(Of T)
        Try
```

```
            Return New ObservableCollection(Of T)(List)
        Catch ex As Exception
            Throw
        End Try
    End Function

End Module
```

The code in Listing 20.1 is simple. Because the ObservableCollection is generic, the ToObservableCollection extension method is also generic and goes to extend the generic IEnumerable type, which is the method argument. The constructor of ObservableCollection provides an overload that accepts an IEnumerable to populate the new collection and then returns an instance of the collection starting from the IEnumerable data. Using the new method is straightforward:

```
Dim processCollection = Process.GetProcesses.ToObservableCollection
```

Now suppose you want to extend the String type to provide an extension method that can check whether a string is a valid email address. In such a situation the best check can be performed using regular expressions. The following code shows how you can implement this extension method:

```
'Requires an Imports System.Text.RegularExpressions statement
<Extension()> Function IsValidEMail(ByVal EMailAddress As String) _
            As Boolean
    Dim validateMail As String = _
    "^([\w-\.]+)@((\[[0-9]{1,3}\.[0-9]{1,3}\.)" & _
    "|(([\w-]+\.)+))([a-zA-z]{2,4}|[0-9]{1,3})(\]?)$"


    Return Regex.IsMatch(EMailAddress, _
                         validateMail)

End Function
```

The goal is not to focus on the comparison pattern via regular expressions, which is complex. Just notice how the result of the comparison (Regex.IsMatch) is returned by the method that extends String because such type is the first (and only) argument in the method. You can then use the method as follows:

```
Dim email As String = "Alessandro.delsole@visual-basic.it"
If email.IsValidEMail Then
    Console.WriteLine("Valid address")
Else
    Console.WriteLine("Invalid address")
End If
```

You may remember that extension methods are shared methods but behave as instance members; this is the reason the new method is available on the email instance and not on the String type.

Overloading Extension Methods

Extension methods support the overloading technique and follow general rules already described in Chapter 7, "Class Fundamentals," especially that overloads cannot differ only because of their return types but must differ in their signatures.

Exporting Extension Methods

You can create libraries of custom extension methods and make them reusable from other languages. This could be useful if you need to offer your extension methods to other applications written in different programming languages. To accomplish this, you need to be aware of a couple of things. First, the module defining extensions must be explicitly marked as Public, and the same is true for methods. Second, you need to write a public sealed class with an empty private constructor because the Common Runtime Language (CLR) provides access to extension methods through this class, to grant interoperability between languages. Listing 20.2 shows a complete example.

LISTING 20.2 Building an Extension Methods Library

```
Imports System.Runtime.CompilerServices
Imports System.Collections.ObjectModel
Imports System.Text.RegularExpressions


<Extension()> Public Module Extensions
    <Extension()> Public Function ToObservableCollection(Of T) _
                    (ByVal List As IEnumerable(Of T)) _
                    As ObservableCollection(Of T)
        Try
            Return New ObservableCollection(Of T)(List)
        Catch ex As Exception
            Throw
        End Try
    End Function


    <Extension()> Public Function IsValidEMail(ByVal EMailAddress As String) _
            As Boolean
        Dim validateMail As String = _
        "^([\w-\.]+)@((\[[0-9]{1,3}\.[0-9]{1,3}\.)" & _
        "|(([\w-]+\.)+))([a-zA-z]{2,4}|[0-9]{1,3})(\]?)$"


        Return Regex.IsMatch(EMailAddress, _
                        validateMail)
```

```
      End Function
End Module


Public NotInheritable Class MyCustomExtensions

      Private Sub New()

      End Sub
End Class
```

Creating a public sealed class is necessary because modules are a specific feature of Visual Basic; therefore, such a class is the bridge between our code and other languages. By compiling the code shown in Listing 20.2 as a class library, .NET languages can take advantage of your extension methods.

TESTING CUSTOM EXTENSION LIBRARIES

If you want to be sure that class libraries exposing custom extension methods work correctly, create a new Visual C# project (a VB one is good as well) and add a reference to the new assembly. Then write code that invokes extended types and check via IntelliSense whether your custom methods are effectively available.

EXPORTING EXTENSION METHODS TIPS

Exporting extension methods requires a little bit of attention. For example, extending types in which you do not own the source code can be dangerous because it may lead to conflicts if, in the future, the original author adds extensions with the same name. Instead consider encapsulating extensions within specific namespaces. Microsoft created a document containing a series of best practices that can be found at the following address: http://msdn.microsoft.com/en-us/library/bb384936(VS.110).aspx

Anonymous Types

As their name implies, *anonymous types* are .NET objects that have no previously defined type in the .NET Framework or your code and can be generated on-the-fly. They were first introduced with .NET Framework 3.5, and their main purpose is collecting data from LINQ queries. You prefer named types to anonymous types outside particular LINQ scenarios; however, it's important to understand how anonymous types work. Declaring an anonymous type is straightforward, as shown in the following code snippet:

```
Dim anonymous = New With {.FirstName = "Alessandro",
                          .LastName = "Del Sole",
                          .Email = "",
                          .Age = 32}
```

As you can see, no name for the new type is specified, and a new instance is created just invoking the `New With` statement. Creating an anonymous type takes advantage of two previously described features, object initializers and local type inference. Object initializers are necessary because anonymous types must be generated in one line, so they do need such a particular feature. Local type inference is fundamental because you have no other way for declaring a new type as an anonymous type, meaning that only the compiler can do it via local type inference. This is the reason declaring an anonymous type cannot be accomplished using the `As` clause. For example, the following code throws an error and will not be compiled:

```
'Throws an error: "the keyword does not name a type"
Dim anonymous As New With {.FirstName = "Alessandro",
                          .LastName = "Del Sole",
                          .Age = 35}
```

Local type inference is also necessary for another reason. As you can see, you can assign *but not declare* properties when declaring an anonymous type. (`FirstName`, `LastName`, `Age`, and `Email` are all properties for the new anonymous type that are both implemented and assigned.) Therefore, the compiler needs a way to understand the type of a property and then implement one for you, and this is only possible due to the local type inference. In the preceding example, for the `FirstName`, `LastName`, and `Email` properties, the compiler infers the `String` type, whereas for the `Age` property it infers the `Integer` type. When you have an anonymous type, you can use it like any other .NET type. The following code provides an example:

```
'Property assignment
anonymous.Email = "alessandro.delsole@visual-basic.it"
'Property reading
Console.WriteLine("{0} {1}, of age: {2}",
                  anonymous.FirstName,
                  anonymous.LastName,
                  anonymous.Age.ToString)
```

As previously mentioned, you can work with an anonymous type like with any other .NET type. The difference is that anonymous types do not have names. Such types can also implement read-only properties. This can be accomplished using the Key keyword with a property name, as demonstrated here:

```
'The Age property is read-only and can
'be assigned only when creating an instance
Dim anonymousWithReadOnly = New With {.FirstName = "Alessandro",
                                     .LastName = "Del Sole",
                                     Key .Age = 35}
```

In this example, the `Age` property is treated as read-only and thus can be assigned only when creating an instance of the anonymous type. You probably wonder why anonymous types can be useful. You get more practical examples in Part IV, "Data Access with ADO. NET and LINQ."

Relaxed Delegates

When you code methods that are pointed to by delegates, your methods must respect the delegate's signature. An exception to this rule is when your method receives arguments that are not effectively used and therefore can be omitted. Such a feature is known as *relaxed delegates*. The simplest example to help you understand relaxed delegates is to create a WPF application. After you've created your application, drag a **Button** control from the toolbox onto the main window's surface. Double-click the new button to activate the code editor so that Visual Studio generates an event handler stub for you and type the following code:

```
Private Sub Button1_Click(ByVal sender As Object,
                          ByVal e As RoutedEventArgs) _
                          Handles Button1.Click
    MessageBox.Show("It works!")
End Sub
```

As you can see, the method body shows a text message but does not make use of both sender and e arguments received by the event handler (which is a method pointed by a delegate). Because of this, Visual Basic allows an exception to the method signature rule, and therefore the preceding method can be rewritten as follows:

```
'Relaxed delegate
Private Sub Button1_Click() Handles Button1.Click
    MessageBox.Show("It works! - relaxed version")
End Sub
```

The code still works correctly because the compiler can identify the preceding method as a relaxed delegate. This feature can be useful especially in enhancing code readability.

Lambda Expressions

Lambda expressions have existed in .NET development since Visual Basic 2008. Because of their flexibility, they are one of the most important additions to .NET programming languages. The main purpose of lambda expressions, as for other language features, is related to LINQ, as you see in the next chapters. They can also be successfully used in many programming scenarios. Lambda expressions in Visual Basic are anonymous methods that can be generated on-the-fly within a line of code and can replace the use of delegates. The easiest explanation of lambdas is that you can use a lambda wherever you need a delegate.

UNDERSTANDING LAMBDA EXPRESSIONS

Lambda expressions are powerful, but they are probably not easy to understand at first. Because of this, several steps of explanations are provided before describing their common usage, although this might seem unnecessary.

You create lambda expressions using the `Function` keyword. When used for lambda expressions, this keyword returns a `System.Func(Of T, TResult)` (with overloads) delegate that encapsulates a method that receives one or more arguments of type `T` and returns a result of type `TResult`. `System.Func` is defined within the `System.Core.dll` assembly and can accept as many `T` arguments for as many parameters that are required by the anonymous method. The last argument of a `System.Func` type is always the return type of a lambda. For example, the following line of code creates a lambda expression that accepts two `Double` values and returns another `Double` constituted by the multiplication of the first two numbers:

```
Dim f As Func(Of Double, Double, Double) = Function(x, y) x * y
```

As you can see, the `Function` keyword does not take any method name. It just receives two arguments, and the result is implemented after the last parenthesis. Such a lambda expression returns a `System.Func(Of Double, Double, Double)` in which the first two doubles correspond to the lambda's arguments, whereas the third one corresponds to the lambda's result type. You can then invoke the obtained delegate to perform a calculation, as in the following line:

```
'Returns 12
Console.WriteLine(f(3, 4))
```

Of course, this is not the only way to invoke the result of a lambda expression, but it is an important starting point. The code provides a lambda instead of declaring an explicit delegate. Now consider the following code that rewrites the previously shown lambda expression:

```
Function Multiply(ByVal x As Double, ByVal y As Double) As Double
    Return x * y
End Function
Dim f As New Func(Of Double, Double, Double)(AddressOf Multiply)


'Returns 12
Console.WriteLine(f(3, 4))
```

As you can see, this second code explicitly creates a method that performs the required calculation that is then passed to the constructor of the `System.Func`. Invoking the delegate can then produce the same result. The difference is that using a lambda expression brought major elegance and dynamicity to our code. `System.Func` can receive up to 16 arguments; independently from how many arguments you need, remember that the last one is always the return value. Another common scenario is a lambda expression that evaluates an expression and returns a Boolean value. To demonstrate this, we can recall the `IsValidEMail` extension method that was described in the "Extension Methods" section to construct complex code. Listing 20.3 shows how you can invoke extension methods for a lambda expression to evaluate whether a string is a valid email address, getting back True or False as a result.

20

LISTING 20.3   Complex Coding with Lambda Expressions

```
Module TestLambda

    Sub ComplexEvaluation()
        Dim checkString As Func(Of String, Boolean) = Function(s) s.IsValidEMail
        Console.WriteLine(checkString("alessandro.delsole@visual-basic.it"))
    End Sub
End Module


<Extension()> Module Extensions
    <Extension()> Public Function IsValidEMail(ByVal EMailAddress As String) _
            As Boolean
        Dim validateMail As String = _
        "^([\w-\.]+)@((\[[0-9]{1,3}\.[0-9]{1,3}\.)" & _
        "|(([\w-]+\.)+))([a-zA-z]{2,4}|[0-9]{1,3})(\]?)$"

        Return Regex.IsMatch(EMailAddress, _
                            validateMail)
    End Function
End Module
```

If you look at Listing 20.3, you notice that the `checkString` delegate takes a `String` to evaluate and returns `Boolean`. Such an evaluation is performed invoking the `IsValidEMail` extension method.

OK, BUT WHY LAMBDAS?

You might wonder why you need lambda expressions instead of invoking methods. The reason is code robustness offered by delegates, as you will remember from Chapter 15, "Delegates and Events." Therefore if you decide to use delegates, using lambda expressions is a good idea while it becomes a necessity if you access data with LINQ.

You often use lambda expressions as arguments for extension methods. The following code shows how you can order the names of running processes on your machine, including only names starting with the letter *e*:

```
Dim processes = Process.GetProcesses.
                OrderBy(Function(p) p.ProcessName).
                Where(Function(p) p.ProcessName.ToLowerInvariant.
                StartsWith("e"))
```

The `OrderBy` extension method receives a lambda expression as an argument that takes an object of type `System.Diagnostics.Process` and orders the collection by the process name, whereas the `Where` extension method still receives a lambda as an argument pointing to the same `Process` instance and that returns `True` if the process name starts with the letter *e*. To get a complete idea of how the lambda works, the best way is rewriting code without using the lambda. The following code demonstrates this concept; and the first lambda remains to provide an idea of how code can be improved using such a feature:

```
'An explicit method that evaluates the expression
Private Function EvaluateProcess(ByVal p As Process) As Boolean
    If p.ProcessName.ToLowerInvariant.StartsWith("e") Then
        Return True
    Else
        Return False
    End If
End Function
    Dim processes = Process.GetProcesses.
                    OrderBy(Function(p) p.ProcessName).
                    Where(AddressOf EvaluateProcess)
```

As you can see, avoiding the usage of lambda expressions requires you to implement a method that respects the signature of the `System.Func` delegate and that performs the required evaluations. Such a method is then pointed via the `AddressOf` keyword. You can easily understand how lambda expressions facilitate writing code and make code clearer, especially if you compare the `OrderBy` method that still gets a lambda expression. For the sake of completeness, it's important to understand that lambda expressions improve the coding experience, but the Visual Basic compiler still translates them the old-fashioned way, as explained later in the "Lexical Closures" section. All the examples provided until now take advantage of the local type inference feature and leave to the VB compiler the work of inferring the appropriate types. The next section discusses this characteristic.

Type Inference and Lambda Expressions

At a higher level, lambda expressions fully support local type inference so that the Visual Basic compiler can decide for you the appropriate data type. For lambdas, there is something more to say. Type inference is determined by how you write your code. Consider the first lambda expression at the beginning of this section:

```
Dim f As Func(Of Double, Double, Double) = Function(x, y) x * y
```

In the preceding code, local type inference affects both arguments and the result of the `Function` statement. The compiler can infer `Double` to the x and y parameters and therefore can determine `Double` as the result type. This is possible only because we explicitly provided types in the delegate declaration—that is, `Func(Of Double, Double, Double)`. Because a local type inference is determined by the compiler using the *dominant algorithm*, something must be explicitly typed. For a better understanding, rewrite the preceding code as follows:

```
'The compiler infers Object
Dim f = Function(x, y) x * y
```

20

In this case because no type is specified anywhere, the compiler infers `Object` for the `f` variable, but in this special case it also throws an exception because operands are not supported by an `Object`. Thus, the code will not be compiled if `Option Strict` is `On`. If you set `Option Strict Off`, you can take advantage of late binding. In such a scenario both the result and the arguments will be treated as `Object` at compile time, but at runtime the CLR can infer the appropriate type depending on the argument received by the expression. The other scenario is when the type result is omitted but arguments' types are provided. The following code demonstrates this:

```
Dim f = Function(x As Double, y As Double) x * y
```

In this case the result type for the f variable is not specified, but arguments have been explicitly typed so that the compiler can infer the correct result type.

Multiline Lambdas

With multiline lambdas, you have the ability to write complete anonymous delegates within a line of code, as demonstrated in the following snippet:

```
Console.WriteLine("Enter a number:")
Dim number = CDbl(Console.ReadLine)

Dim result = Function(n As Double)
                 If n < 0 Then
                     Return 0
                 Else
                     Return n + 1
                 End If
             End Function


Console.WriteLine(result(number))
```

In this particular case, the compiler can infer the `System.Func(Of Double, Double)` result type because the n argument is of type `Double`. Within the method body, you can perform required evaluations, and you can also explicitly specify the return type (take a look at the first lambda example) to get control over the `System.Func` result. Another example is for multiline lambdas without variable declarations, as in the following code:

```
Dim processes = Process.GetProcesses.
                Where(Function(p)
                    Try
                        'Returns True
                        p.ProcessName.ToLowerInvariant.
                        StartsWith("e")
                    Catch ex As Exception
                        Return False
                    End Try
                End Function)
```

This code performs the same operations described in the "Lambda Expressions" section, but now you have the ability to write more complex code—for example, if you need to provide error handling infrastructures as previously shown.

Sub **Lambdas**

So far you have seen lambda expressions that were represented only by functions that could return a value and that were realized via the Function keyword. You can also use *Sub lambdas* that C# developers know as *anonymous methods*. This feature lets you use the Sub keyword instead of the Function one so that you can write lambda expressions that do not return a value. The following code demonstrates this:

```
Dim collection As New List(Of String) From {"Alessandro",
                                "Del Sole",
                                alessandro.delsole@visual-basic.it"}


collection.ForEach(Sub(element) Console.WriteLine(element))
```

The preceding code iterates a List(Of String) collection and sends to the console window the result of the iteration. A Sub lambda is used because here no return value is required.

Array.Foreach AND List(Of T).Foreach

The System.Array and the System.Collections.Generic.List(Of T) classes offer a ForEach method that allows performing loops similarly to the For..Each statement described in Chapter 4, "Data Types and Expressions." The difference is that you can take advantage of lambda expressions and eventually of delegates to iterate elements.

Consider that trying to replace Sub with Function causes an error. (That makes sense because Console.WriteLine does not return values while Function does.) Like Function, arguments' types within Sub can be inferred by the compiler. In this case the element is of type String because it represents a single element in a List(Of String) collection. You can use Sub lambdas each time a System.Action(Of T) is required, opposite to the System.Func(Of T, T) required by Function. System.Action(Of T) is a delegate that represents a method accepting just one argument and that returns no value. Sub lambdas can also be implemented as multiline lambdas. The following code shows a multiline implementation of the previous code, where a simple validation is performed onto every string in the collection:

```
' "collection" has the same previous implementation
collection.ForEach(Sub(element)
                Try
                    If String.IsNullOrEmpty(element) = False Then
                        Console.WriteLine(element)
                    Else
                        Console.
```

```
                              WriteLine("Cannot print empty strings")
                    End If
            Catch ex As Exception

            End Try
        End Sub)
```

In this way you can also implement complex expressions, although they do not return a value.

Lexical Closures

To provide support for lambda expressions, the Visual Basic compiler implements a background feature known as *lexical closures*. Before going into the explanation, remember that you will not use closures in your code because they are typically generated for compiler use only. However, it's important to know what they are and what they do. Lexical closures allow access to the same class-level variable to multiple functions and procedures. A code example provides a better explanation. Consider the following code, in which the Divide method takes advantage of a lambda expression to calculate the division between two numbers:

```
Class ClosureDemo

    Sub Divide(ByVal value As Double)
        Dim x = value
        Dim calculate = Function(y As Double) x / y
        Dim result = calculate(10)
    End Sub
End Class
```

Because both the Divide method and its lambda expression have access to the x local variable, the compiler internally rewrites the preceding code in a more logical way that looks like the following:

```
Class _Closure$__1

    Public x As Double

    Function _Lambda$__1(ByVal y As Double) As Double
        Return x * y
```

```
      End Function
End Class

Class ClosureDemo

    Sub Divide(ByVal value As Double)
        Dim closureVariable_A_8 As New _
            _Closure$__1
        _Closure$__1.closureVariable_A_8 = value

        Dim calculate As Func(Of Double, Double) _
        = AddressOf _Closure$__1._Lambda$__1
        Dim result = calculate(10)

    End Sub
End Class
```

Identifiers are not easy to understand, but they are generated by the compiler that is the only one responsible for their handling. The lexical closure feature creates a new public class with a public field related to the variable having common access. It also generated a separate method for performing the division that is explicitly accessed as a delegate (and here you will remember that lambdas can be used every time you need a delegate) from the Divide method. In conclusion, lexical closures provide a way for a logical organization of the code that provides behind-the-scenes support for lambda expressions but, as stated at the beginning of this section, they are exclusively the responsibility of the Visual Basic compiler.

Ternary If Operator

The ternary If operator is used with lambda expressions and allows evaluating conditions on-the-fly. With this operator, you can evaluate a condition and return the desired value either in case the condition is True or if it is False. Imagine you have a Person class exposing both FirstName and LastName string properties and that you want to first verify that an instance of the Person class is not Nothing and, subsequently, that its LastName properties are initialized. The following code shows how you can accomplish the first task (see comments):

```
Sub EvaluatePerson(ByVal p As Person)
    'Check if p (a Person instance) is Nothing
    'If it is Nothing, returns False else True
    'The result is returned as a delegate
    Dim checkIfNull = If(p Is Nothing, False, True)

    'If False, p is Nothing, therefore
    'throws an exception
    If checkIfNull = False Then
```

20

```
        Throw New ArgumentNullException("testPerson")
    End If

End Sub
```

As you can see, the `If` operator receives three arguments: The first one is the condition to evaluate; the second is the result to return if the condition is `True`; the third is the result to return if the condition is `False`. In this specific example, if the `Person` instance is null the code returns `False`; otherwise, it returns `True`. The result of this code is assigned to a Boolean variable (`checkIfNull`) that contains the result of the evaluation. If the result is `False`, the code throws an `ArgumentNullException`. You could write the preceding code in a simpler way, as follows:

```
If p Is Nothing Then
    'do something
Else
    Throw New ArgumentNullException
End If
```

The difference is that, with the ternary operator, you can perform inline evaluations also with lambda expressions, and this scenario is particularly useful when working with LINQ queries. Now it's time to check whether the `LastName` property was initialized. The following code snippet shows an example that returns a `String` instead of a `Boolean` value:

```
Dim executeTest = If(String.IsNullOrEmpty(p.LastName) = True,
                    "LastName property is empty",
                    "LastName property is initialized")
```

The explanation is simple: If the `LastName` property is an empty string or a null string, the code returns a message saying that the property is empty. Otherwise, it returns a message saying that the property has been correctly initialized. You could rewrite the code in the classic fashion as follows:

```
If String.IsNullOrEmpty(p.LastName) = True Then
    'LastName property is empty
Else
    'LastName property is initialized
End If
```

The following lines show how you can test the preceding code:

```
'Throws an ArgumentNullException
EvaluatePerson(Nothing)
'A message says that the LastName property is initialized
EvaluatePerson(New Person With {.LastName = "Del Sole"})
```

Generic Variance

The concept of generic variance was introduced in Visual Basic 2010 and is divided into two areas: covariance and contra variance. This concept is related to inheritance versus generics and generic collections; a couple of examples are provided next for a better explanation.

Covariance

Covariance enables you to assign strongly typed collections (such as List) of derived classes to IEnumerable collections of abstract classes. The code in Listing 20.4 shows how covariance works.

LISTING 20.4   Covariance in Visual Basic 2012

```
Module Covariance

    Sub Main()

        'Using collection initializers
        Dim stringsCollection As New List(Of String) _
                        From {"Understanding ", "covariance ", "in VB 2010"}

        'This code is now legal
        Dim variance As IEnumerable(Of Object) = stringsCollection

        For Each s In variance
            Console.WriteLine(s)
        Next

        Console.ReadLine()
    End Sub
End Module
```

If you examine Listing 20.4, you see that the variance variable is generic of type IEnumerable(Of Object) and receives the assignment of a generic List(Of String) content, in which Object is the base class of String. Until Visual Basic 2008, this code was illegal and would therefore throw a compile exception. In Visual Basic 2010 and 2012, this code is legal but works only with IEnumerable(Of T) collections. If you try to replace IEnumerable(Of Object) with List(Of Object), the compiler still throws an error suggesting that you use an IEnumerable. By the way, you assigned a collection of String to a collection of Object, and this is how covariance works. The For..Each loop correctly recognizes items in the IEnumerable as String and therefore produces the following, simple output:

```
Understanding
covariance
in VB 2010
```

20

Contra Variance

Contra variance works the opposite of covariance: From a derived class, we can take advantage of an abstract class or of a base class. To understand how contra variance works, the best example is to create a client application in which two events of the same control are handled by the same event handler. For this, create a new Windows Presentation Foundation application and write the following XAML code to define a simple `Button` control:

```
<Button Content="Button" Height="50" Name="Button1" Width="150" />
```

CREATING WPF APPLICATIONS

If you are not familiar with WPF applications, you notice one important thing when creating such projects: The designer provides a graphical editor and the code editor for the XAML code (which is XML-styled). You can write the previous snippet within the XAML code editor or drag a `Button` control from the toolbox onto the Window, which is not a problem. You can also notice, in Solution Explorer, the presence of the code-behind file that has an .xaml.vb extension. There you can write the code shown next. Chapter 28, "Creating WPF Applications," discusses WPF applications in detail.

Like other controls, the `Button` control exposes several events. For example, let's consider the `MouseDoubleClick` event and the `KeyUp` event and decide that it would be a good idea to handle both events writing a unique event handler. To accomplish this, we can take advantage of contra variance. Consider the following code, which explicitly declares handlers for events:

```
Public Sub New()

    ' This call is required by the Windows Form Designer.
    InitializeComponent()

    ' Explicitly specify handlers for events
    AddHandler Button1.KeyUp, AddressOf CommonHandler
    AddHandler Button1.MouseDoubleClick, AddressOf CommonHandler
End Sub
```

Both events point to the same delegate, which is implemented as follows:

```
Private Sub CommonHandler(ByVal sender As Object,
                          ByVal e As EventArgs)
    MessageBox.Show("You did it!")
End Sub
```

The `KeyUp` event should be handled by a delegate that receives a `System.Windows.Input.KeyEventArgs` argument, whereas the `MouseDoubleClick` should be handled by a delegate that receives a `System.Windows.Input.MouseButtonEventArgs` argument. Because both objects inherit from `System.EventArgs`, we can provide a unique delegate that receives an argument of such type and that can handle both events. If you now try to run the application, you see that the message box is correctly shown if you either double-click the button or press a key when the button has the focus. The advantage of contra variance is that we can use abstract classes to handle the behavior of derived classes.

Summary

In this chapter, you got the most out of some advanced language features that provide both special support for the LINQ technology and improvements to your coding experience. Local type inference enables developers to avoid specifying types in local variables assignment because the Visual Basic compiler automatically provides the most appropriate one. Array literals extend local type inference to arrays. Extension methods allow extending existing objects, even if you do not own the source code (such as in case of the .NET Framework) with custom methods. Anonymous types enable you to generate on-the-fly no-name types that you often use within LINQ queries. Relaxed delegates provide the ability to write code smarter and faster because you are authorized to not respect delegates' signatures if you do not use arguments. Lambda expressions strengthen your code by introducing anonymous delegates that can be generated on-the-fly, improving your code quality and efficiency. Sub lambdas can be used to handle anonymous delegates that do not return a value. Generic covariance and contra variance provide further control over generic `IEnumerable` collections when you work with inheritance.

CHAPTER 21

Introducing ADO.NET and DataSets

Working with data is one of the primary tasks that an application must accomplish. Over the years, the .NET Framework has evolved, offering various kinds of data access platforms, but at a higher level the way you work with data is based only on two ways: connected or disconnected modes. For the disconnected mode, DataSets still play an important role today because many developers build or maintain applications based on DataSets—you are one of them! But times change and technology advances. New data platforms, such as the ADO.NET Entity Framework and LINQ to SQL, have been introduced to the .NET world, and the classic approach is becoming obsolete. If you think of Silverlight applications, you cannot use DataSets. You instead use LINQ. Of course, in some situations you can still take advantage of the old approach (such as the connected mode), and this is left to your strategy. Because of these considerations, the purpose of this chapter is to provide a quick recap on connected mode and disconnected mode with DataSets. We focus on what is new in data access with LINQ in the following chapters. Basically, you get information that can put you on the right track for comparing and appreciating the power of LINQ.

System Requirements

This chapter and the next ones are all about data. For this reason, you need to set up a development environment for testing code that works with data. Microsoft Visual Studio 2012 ships with a new edition of SQL Server 2012, called Local DB. This is a reduced edition of SQL Server Express, which is dedicated to developers who need to test data on their development machines. However, some compatibility issues exist with Local DB when using the old Data Readers.

Even though it is appropriate on a development machine, it does not completely allow simulating a real-world database engine. For this reason, the current chapter and the next ones require you to install Microsoft SQL Server 2012 Express Edition, which is still available for free. You can download it from the following address: http://www.microsoft.com/ sqlserver/en/us/editions/2012-editions/express.aspx. After you have downloaded, installed, and configured SQL Server 2012 Express, you are required to install the famous Northwind sample database, which is also available for free at http://archive.msdn.com/Northwind. You will need to open the InstNwnd.sql file in Visual Studio 2012 and execute the script against the specified SQL Server instance.

Introducing ADO.NET

ADO.NET is the .NET Framework area that provides the capability to access data from databases, and can be thought of as the .NET version of ActiveX Data Objects (ADO), which was the data access technology prior to .NET, based on the COM architecture. ADO.NET can be observed from two perspectives, known as connected and disconnected modes. It can access data from different data sources thanks to data providers. In the next sections, you learn about providers and connection modes and how you can access data in a connected environment.

After completing these procedures, a recap on DataSets is offered before discussing LINQ in the next chapter.

Data Providers

Data providers are .NET objects that allow the .NET Framework to speak with data sources. Data sources are generally databases, such as SQL Server, Oracle, and Access, but also include Microsoft Excel spreadsheets. The .NET Framework includes several built-in data providers exposed by the System.Data namespace. Table 21.1 summarizes built-in data providers.

TABLE 21.1   .NET Data Providers

Provider	Namespace
SQL Server	System.Data.SqlClient
OleDb	System.Data.OleDb
ODBC	System.Data.Odbc
Oracle	System.Data.Oracle (requires reference to the System.Data.Oracle.dll assembly)
EntityClient	System.Data.EntityClient (allows data access with the ADO.NET Entity Framework, which is covered in Chapter 26, "Introducing ADO.NET Entity Framework")

These are the most common providers, but several companies provided their own, such as MySQL or PostgreSQL. Notice how the OleDb provider is available to provide support for data sources such as Microsoft Access databases or Excel spreadsheets. In this book, for this chapter and the ones dedicated to LINQ, Visual Basic topics using the SQL Server provider are covered. There are obviously some differences when writing code for each provider; however, you also find several similarities in connecting to data sources and manipulating data. Such operations are discussed in the next sections.

Connection Modes

ADO.NET provides support for both connected and disconnected modes. The big difference between the two modes is that in a connected mode, you explicitly open and close connections against a data source so that you can work with data. This is something you accomplish with the `Connection`, `DataReader`, and `Command` objects. In a disconnected environment, you work against in-memory data that is later persisted to the underlying data source. This is achieved with DataSets, although you see starting from Chapter 24, "LINQ to SQL," how such an approach is the same in LINQ to ADO.NET. I'm sure that you already worked with both modes in your developer experience, so here's just a quick recap so that you appreciate the difference between what you learn in this chapter and what you learn studying LINQ.

Understanding Connections and Data Readers

To establish a connection to a database, you need to create an instance of the `SqlConnection` class by passing the connection string as an argument. Then you invoke the `Open` method to open the connection so you can perform your data operations. Finally, you invoke `Close` to close the connection. The following code, which requires an `Imports System.Data.SqlClient` directive, demonstrates how you establish a connection to the Northwind database:

```
Using myConnection As New _
       SqlConnection("Data Source=SERVERNAME\SQLEXPRESS;Initial Catalog=Northwind;" &
                "Integrated Security=True;MultipleActiveResultSets=True")
       myConnection.Open()


End Using
```

Utilizing a `Using..End Using` block ensures that the connection will be correctly released without the need of invoking `Close`. You have to replace SERVERNAME with the name of the SQL Server to which you are connecting.

Inserting Data

To perform an insert operation, you create an instance of the `SqlCommand` class by passing the SQL instructions that perform the actual insertion. The constructor also requires the connection to be specified. The following code demonstrates this:

```
Using myConnection As New _
       SqlConnection("Data Source=SERVERNAME\SQLEXPRESS;Initial Catalog=Northwind;" &
                "Integrated Security=True;MultipleActiveResultSets=True")
```

```
      myConnection.Open()

   Using addCustomer As New SqlCommand("INSERT INTO CUSTOMERS(CompanyName, "&
                                  "CustomerID) VALUES (@COMPANYNAME,
                                  @CUSTOMERID)",
                                  myConnection)
         addCustomer.Parameters.AddWithValue("@COMPANYNAME", "Del Sole")
         addCustomer.Parameters.AddWithValue("@CUSTOMERID", "DELSO")
         addCustomer.ExecuteNonQuery()
   End Using
End Using
```

Notice how you can provide parameterized query strings specifying values with the `SqlCommand.Parameters.AddWithValue` method. The code adds a new customer to the Customers table in the database, specifying two fields, `CompanyName`, and `CustomerID`. The `ExecuteNonQuery` method enables the execution of a Transact-SQL operation instead of a simple query.

Updating Data

Updating data works similarly to inserting, in that you write the same code, changing the SQL instructions in the query string. The following code provides an example affecting the previously added customer:

```
Using updateCustomer As New SqlCommand("UPDATE CUSTOMERS SET " &
                                  "COMPANYNAME=@NAME WHERE
                                   CUSTOMERID=@ID",
                                  myConnection)
      updateCustomer.Parameters.AddWithValue("@NAME", "Alessandro Del Sole")
      updateCustomer.Parameters.AddWithValue("@ID", "DELSO")
      updateCustomer.ExecuteNonQuery()
End Using
```

So, you simply use an `Update` SQL instruction.

Deleting Data

Deletion works the same as other operations, differing only when it comes to the SQL code that uses a `Delete` statement. The following code demonstrates this:

```
Using deleteCustomer As New SqlCommand("DELETE FROM WHERE CUSTOMERID=@ID",
                                  myConnection)
      deleteCustomer.Parameters.AddWithValue("@ID", "DELSO")
      deleteCustomer.ExecuteNonQuery()
End Using
```

Querying Data

Querying data is the last operation; it is important because it demonstrates a fundamental object: the `SqlDataReader`. The object enables the retrieval of a series of rows from the specified database object. The following code demonstrates how you can retrieve a series of customers:

```
Using myConnection As New _
      SqlConnection("Data Source=SERVERNAME\SQLEXPRESS;Initial Catalog=Northwind;" &
                    "Integrated Security=True;MultipleActiveResultSets=True")

    myConnection.Open()

    Using queryCustomers As New SqlCommand("SELECT * FROM CUSTOMERS",
                                            myConnection)

        Dim reader As SqlDataReader = queryCustomers.ExecuteReader()

        While reader.Read
            Console.WriteLine("Customer: {0}", reader("CompanyName"))
        End While

    End Using
End Using
```

The query string contains a projection statement that enables the querying of data. The `ExecuteReader` method sends the reading query string to the data source and retrieves the desired information. Now that you have recalled the ways for working with data in a connected mode, it is time to recall the disconnected mode and DataSets.

Introducing DataSets

A `DataSet` is basically an in-memory database that lets you work in a disconnected mode. Being disconnected means that first a connection is open, data is read from the data source and pushed to the `DataSet`, and finally the connection is closed and you work against in-memory data stored by the `DataSet`. DataSets introduced a first attempt of typed programming against in-memory data, a concept that has been unleashed in the modern data access layers such as LINQ to SQL and ADO.NET Entity Framework. Now you get a quick recap on DataSets with Visual Basic before facing LINQ.

Creating DataSets

You create DataSets starting from a database and adding a new data source to your project. This is accomplished by clicking the **Add New Data Source** command from the Data menu in Visual Studio 2012. This launches the Data Source Configuration Wizard where you choose the Database source, as shown in Figure 21.1.

When you proceed, you are prompted to specify whether you want to create a DataSet or an Entity Data Model. Select DataSet and click Next. At this point, you are prompted to specify the database connection. For example, with the Northwind database available on SQL Server, your connection looks similar to the one shown in Figure 21.2, which represents what I have on my machine.

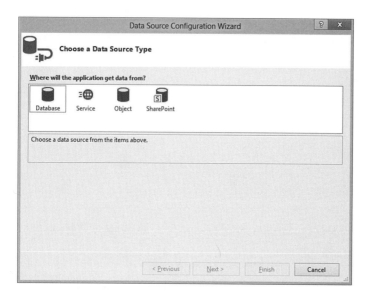

FIGURE 21.1   The first step of the Data Source Configuration Wizard.

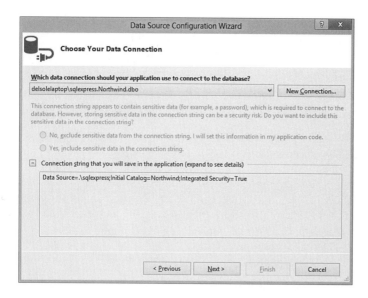

FIGURE 21.2   Specifying the database connection.

Next, you are prompted to specify the database objects you want to be represented by the new `DataSet`. Choose the number of tables you like, but be sure that the `Products` table is also selected, to complete the next code examples. When the wizard completes, Visual Studio generates a DataSet that you can manage via the designer, represented in Figure 21.3.

FIGURE 21.3   The DataSet designer.

The designer shows how database objects have been mapped into the DataSet. Each table is represented by a DataTable object. Each record in a table is represented by a DataRow object, and each field is a property having its own data type. DataSets use Data Adapters to read and write data. A Data Adapter is actually a bridge between the data source and the DataSet. Each DataTable works with a specific adapter; with more than one adapter, an object must take care of all of them, which is the job of the TableAdapterManager. If you work with Windows Forms and WPF applications, Visual Studio generates all adapters for you. For Console applications, as in the following example, you must perform a few steps manually. When you have your DataSet, you need an instance of the DataSet and of table adapters:

```
'DataSet here is also the project name
Imports DataSet.NorthwindDataSetTableAdapters
...
    Dim WithEvents NWindDataSet As New NorthwindDataSet
    Dim WithEvents ProductsTblAdapter As New ProductsTableAdapter
    Dim WithEvents TblAdapterManager As New TableAdapterManager
```

Then you populate the DataSet's object by invoking the adapter Fill method. In the meantime, you also assign a TableAdapterManager if you have more than one adapter:

```
ProductsTblAdapter.Fill(NWindDataSet.Products)
TblAdapterManager.ProductsTableAdapter = ProductsTblAdapter
```

The next paragraphs recap the insert/update/delete operations. For the moment, remember that you can save back changes to your data source by invoking the adapter's Update method as follows:

```
ProductsTblAdapter.Update(NWindDataSet.Products)
```

Inserting Data

Each DataTable exposes a NewTableRow method, where Table is the name of the DataTable. In the example of the Products table, the method is named NewProductsRow. This method returns a new instance of the ProductRow object that you can fill with your information. Finally, you invoke the AddProductsRow method to send your data to the DataSet. Of course, each table has a corresponding Add method. The following code demonstrates how you can insert a new product:

```
'Insert
Dim row As NorthwindDataSet.ProductsRow = NWindDataSet.
                                          Products.NewProductsRow
row.ProductName = "Italian spaghetti"
row.Discontinued = False

NWindDataSet.Products.AddProductsRow(row)
ProductsTblAdapter.Update(NWindDataSet.Products)
```

Generally, when performing create/read/update/delete (CRUD) operations, you work against rows.

Updating Data

To update a row, you first retrieve the instance of the corresponding DataRow so that you can perform manipulations. Then you can update your data. The following snippet demonstrates this:

```
'Update
Dim getRow As NorthwindDataSet.ProductsRow
getRow = NWindDataSet.Products.FindByProductID(1)

getRow.Discontinued = True
ProductsTblAdapter.Update(NWindDataSet.Products)
```

Notice how the instance has been retrieved via the FindByProductID method. When you create a DataSet, Visual Studio generates a FindByXXX method that allows you to retrieve the instance of the specified row.

Deleting Data

Deleting a row is simple. You get the instance of the row and then invoke the `DataRow.Delete` method. The following code demonstrates this:

```
'Delete
Dim delRow As NorthwindDataSet.ProductsRow
delRow = NWindDataSet.Products.FindByProductID(1)
delRow.Delete()


ProductsTblAdapter.Update(NWindDataSet.Products)
```

To delete an object, you could also invoke the `TableAdapter.Delete` method. However, this would require the complete specification of the row's properties.

Querying Data

You query data from DataSets by writing query strings. This is the old approach, though; in Visual Basic 2012 a more convenient way is to use LINQ to DataSets, which is covered in Chapter 25, "LINQ to DataSets."

Summary

ADO.NET is the .NET Framework area providing the data access infrastructure for data access. With ADO.NET, you access data in two modes: connected and disconnected. For the connected mode, you create `Connection` objects to establish a connection, `Command` objects to send SQL query strings to the data source, and `DataReader` for fetching data; finally, you close the `Connection` object. In a disconnected environment, you take advantage of DataSets that are in-memory representations of databases and where each table is a `DataTable` object, each record is a `DataRow` object, and `TableAdapter` objects act like a bridge between the database and the `DataSet`. You perform CRUD operations invoking the `Add`, `Delete`, `Update`, and `New` methods of `DataTable` objects, although a better technique for querying data is offered by LINQ to DataSets in Chapter 25. After this brief recap on the old-fashioned data access techniques, you are ready to start a new journey through the LINQ technology.

CHAPTER 22

Introducing LINQ

Developers create applications that in most cases need to access data sources and manipulate data. Over the years, hundreds of data sources and file formats saw the light, and each of them has its own specifications, requirements, and language syntaxes. Whenever an application requires accessing data from a database or parsing a structured file, in most cases manipulation commands are supplied as strings, making it difficult to reveal bugs at compile time. LINQ solves all these problems in one solution, changing how developers write code and improving productivity. This chapter provides an overview of this revolutionary technology that is reprised and discussed in detail in the next chapters.

What Is LINQ?

The LINQ project has been the most important new feature in the .NET Framework 3.5, affecting both Visual Basic 2008 and Visual C# 3.0. LINQ stands for *Language INtegrated Query* and is a project Microsoft began developing in 2003. The first beta versions saw the light in 2005 and eventually became part of the Common Language Runtime (CLR) with .NET 3.5 and later versions. As its name implies, LINQ is a technology that allows querying data directly from the programming language. LINQ is very important and revolutionary because most real-world applications need to access data by querying, filtering, and manipulating that data. The word *data* has several meanings. In the modern computer world, there are hundreds of different data sources, such as databases, XML documents, Microsoft Excel spreadsheets, web services, in-memory collections, and so on. And each of these kinds of data sources can be further differentiated. For example, there is not just one kind of database; there are lots of databases, such as Microsoft SQL Server, Microsoft Access, Oracle, MySQL, and so on. Each of these databases has its own infrastructure, its own administrative tools, and its own syntax. As you can imagine, developers need to adopt different programming techniques and syntaxes according to the specific data source they are working on, and this can be complex. Accessing an XML document is completely different from accessing a SQL Server database; therefore, there is the need for specific types and members for accessing such data sources, and one is different from the other one. So, the first thing that Microsoft considered is related to the plethora of programming techniques to adopt depending on the data source. The next part of this discussion is related to practical limitations of the programming techniques before LINQ came in. For example, consider accessing a SQL Server database with DataSets. Although powerful, this technique has several limitations that can be summarized as follows:

▶ You need to know both the SQL Server syntax and the Visual Basic/Visual C# syntax. Although preferable, this is not always possible, and in some cases it can lead to confusion.

▶ SQL queries are passed to the compiler as strings. This means that if you write a bad query (for example, because of a typo), this will not be visible at compile time—only when your application runs. IntelliSense support is not provided when writing SQL syntax; therefore, typos can easily occur. The same is true for possibly bad query logical implementations. Both scenarios should be avoided, but often they can be subtle bugs to identify.

▶ In most cases the developer will not also deeply know the database structure if she is not also an administrator. This means that she cannot necessarily know which data types are exposed by the database, although it is always a preferable situation.

Now consider querying in-memory collections of .NET objects. Before LINQ, you could only write long and complex `For` and `For..Each` loops or conditional code blocks (such as `If..Then` or `Select..Case`) to access collections. The last example is related to XML documents: Before LINQ, you had two ways of manipulating XML files. You could treat them as text files, which is one of the worst things in the world; or you could recur to the `System.Xml` namespace, which makes things difficult when you need to simply read and write a document. All these considerations caused Microsoft to develop LINQ; so again we ask the question, "What is LINQ?" The answer is the following: LINQ provides a unified programming model that allows accessing, querying, filtering, and manipulating different kinds of data sources, such as databases, XML documents, and in-memory collections, using the same programming techniques independently from the data source. This is accomplished via special keywords of typical SQL derivation that are integrated into .NET languages and that allow working in a completely object-oriented way. Developers can take advantage of a new syntax that offers the following returns:

▶ The same techniques can be applied to different kinds of data sources.

▶ Because querying data is performed via new keywords integrated in the language, this enables you to work in a strongly typed way, meaning that eventual errors can be found at compile time. This keeps you from having to spend a large amount of time investigating problems at runtime.

▶ Full IntelliSense support.

LINQ syntax is powerful, as you see in this chapter and in the following ones, and it can deeply change how you write your code.

LINQ IN THIS BOOK

LINQ is a big technology and has lots of features, so discussing the technology in deep detail would require another dedicated book. What you find in this book is first the Visual Basic syntax for LINQ. Second, you learn how to use LINQ for querying and manipulating data, which is the real purpose of LINQ. You will not find dedicated scenarios such as LINQ in WPF, LINQ in Silverlight, and so on. Just keep in mind that you can bind LINQ queries to every user control that supports the `IEnumerable` interface or convert LINQ queries into writable collections (which is shown here) to both present and edit data via the user interface (UI). For example, you can directly assign (or first convert to a collection) a LINQ query to a Windows Forms `BindingSource` control, a WPF `CollectionViewSource`, or an ASP.NET `DataGrid`.

LINQ Examples

To understand why LINQ is revolutionary, the best way is to begin with some code examples. In the next chapters, you see a huge quantity of code snippets, but this chapter offers basic queries to provide a high-level comprehension. Imagine you have a `Person` class exposing the `FirstName`, `LastName`, and `Age` properties. Then, imagine you have a collection of `Person` objects, of type `List(Of Person)`. Last, imagine you want to extract from the collection all `Person` instances whose `LastName` property begins with the letter *D*. This scenario is performed via the following code snippet that uses a LINQ query:

```
' "people" is of type List(Of Person)
Dim peopleQuery = From pers In people
                  Where pers.LastName.StartsWith("D")
                  Order By pers.Age Descending
                  Select pers
```

This form of code is known as *query expression* because it extracts from a data source only a subset of data according to specific criteria. Notice how query expressions are performed using some keywords that recall the SQL syntax, such as `From`, `Where`, `Order By`, and `Select`. Such keywords are also known as *clauses*, and the Visual Basic grammar offers a large set of clauses that is examined in detail in the next chapters. The first consideration is that, while typing code, IntelliSense speeds up your coding experience, providing the usual appropriate suggestions. This is due to the integration of clauses with the language. Second, because clauses are part of the language, you can take advantage of the background compiler that determines whether a query expression fails before running the application. Now let's examine what the query does. The `From` clause specifies the data source to be queried, in this case a collection of `Person` objects, which allows specifying a condition that is considered if evaluated to `True`. In the previous example, each `Person` instance is taken into consideration only if its `LastName` property begins with the letter D. The `Order By` clause allows sorting the result of the query depending on the specified criteria; here it's the value of the `Age` property in descending order. The `Select` clause extracts objects and pulls them into a new `IEnumerable(Of Person)` collection that is the type for the `peopleQuery` variable. Although this type has not been explicitly assigned, local type inference is used, and the Visual Basic compiler automatically infers the appropriate type as the query result. Another interesting consideration is that queries are now strongly typed. You are not writing queries as strings because you work with reserved keywords and .NET objects, and therefore your code can take advantage of the Common Language Runtime (CLR) control, allowing better results at both compile time and at runtime. Working in a strongly typed way is one of the greatest LINQ features thanks to its integration with the CLR.

IMPLICIT LINE CONTINUATION

Unlike Visual Basic 2008 and starting from Visual Basic 2010, you can omit the underscore (_) character within LINQ queries as demonstrated by the previous code.

The same result can be obtained by querying a data source with extension methods. The following code demonstrates this:

```
Dim peopleQuery2 = people.Where(Function(pers) pers.LastName.
                        StartsWith("D")).OrderBy(Function(pers) pers.Age).
                        Select(Function(pers) pers)
```

The .NET Framework offers extension methods that replicate Visual Basic and Visual C# reserved keywords and that receives lambda expressions as arguments pointing to the data source.

Language Support

In Chapter 20, "Advanced Language Features," you got an overview of some advanced language features in the Visual Basic 2012 language. Some of those features were already introduced with Visual Basic 2008 and have the purpose of providing support for LINQ. Particularly, the language support to LINQ is realized via the following features:

- ▶ Local type inference
- ▶ Anonymous types
- ▶ Lambda expressions
- ▶ Extension methods

- ▶ If ternary operator

- ▶ Nullable types

- ▶ Xml literals

- ▶ Object initializers

The addition of keywords such as From, Where, and Select complete the language support for this revolutionary technology. In the next chapters, you see LINQ in action and learn how to use all the language features and the dedicated keywords.

Understanding Providers

The .NET Framework 4.5 provides the ability of using LINQ against six built-in kinds of data sources, which are summarized in Table 22.1.

TABLE 22.1   LINQ Standard Providers

Provider Name	Description
LINQ to Objects	Allows querying in-memory collections of .NET objects
LINQ to DataSets	Allows querying data stored within DataSets
LINQ to SQL	Allows querying and manipulating data from an SQL Server database via a specific object relational mapping engine
LINQ to XML	Allows querying and manipulating XML documents
LINQ to Entities	Allows querying data exposed by an Entity Data Model (see ADO. NET Entity Framework for details)
Parallel LINQ	An implementation that allows querying data using the Task Parallel Library

A specific LINQ implementation exists, according to the data source (objects, datasets, SQL databases, and XML documents). Such implementations are known as *standard providers*. Due to their importance, each provider is covered in a specific chapter (but Parallel LINQ is covered in Chapter 43, "Parallel Programming and Parallel LINQ," because it requires some concepts about the parallel programming first). LINQ implementation is also referred to as providers or standard providers. There could be situations in which you need to use a custom data source and would like to take advantage of the LINQ syntax. Luckily, LINQ is also extensible with custom providers that can allow access to any kind of data source; this is possible due to its particular infrastructure. (A deep discussion on LINQ infrastructure is out of the scope here, and you might want to consider a specific publication, while the focus is on the Visual Basic language for LINQ.) Custom implementations such as LINQ to CSV, LINQ to Windows Desktop Search, and LINQ to NHibernate give a good idea about the power of this technology.

EXTENDING LINQ

The following document in the MSDN Library can help you get started with extending LINQ with a custom provider: http://msdn.microsoft.com/en-us/library/bb546158(v=vs.110).aspx.

Overview of LINQ Architecture

Providing detailed information on the LINQ architecture is out of the scope of this book. Getting a high-level overview can help you understand how LINQ works. Basically, LINQ is the last layer of a series, as shown in Figure 22.1.

FIGURE 22.1   LINQ is at the top of a layered infrastructure.

At the bottom is the Common Language Runtime that provides the runtime infrastructure for LINQ. The next layer is constituted by the managed languages that offer support to LINQ with special reserved keywords and features. The next layer is all about data and is represented by the data sources LINQ allows querying. The last layer is LINQ itself with its standard providers. You may or may not love architectures built on several layers, but LINQ has one big advantage, particularly when working with databases: It will do all the work behind the scenes for sending the SQL commands to the data source and avoid the need for you to perform it manually. This also offers several high-level classes and members for accessing data in a completely object-oriented way. You see practical demonstrations of this discussion in the appropriate chapters.

Summary

In this chapter you got a brief overview of Language INtegrated Query, which is discussed in more depth in the next chapters. You learned what LINQ is and how it can improve querying data sources thanks to integrated reserved keywords and taking advantage of a strongly typed approach. You got an overview of the built-in LINQ providers and information on the specific language support for LINQ. Now you are ready to delve into LINQ in the next chapters.

22

CHAPTER 23

LINQ to Objects

L INQ changes the way you write code. This is something that you will often hear when talking about LINQ. It provides the ability to query different data sources and take advantage of the same syntax, background compiler, IntelliSense, and Common Language Runtime (CLR) control with its intuitive programming model. LINQ's syntax is so straightforward that you become familiar with the technology quickly. In this chapter you learn about LINQ to Objects, which is the starting point of every LINQ discussion. You see how easy querying .NET objects, such as in-memory collections, is. In the next chapters, you'll find out how you can use the same approach against different data sources and LINQ providers. Take your time to read this chapter; it's important—especially the second part, which is about standard query operators. It explains concepts that pervade every LINQ provider and will not be explained again in other chapters, except where expressly required.

Introducing LINQ to Objects

In the previous chapter, I provided an overview of the LINQ technology and told you that it provides a unified programming model for querying various types of data sources using the same syntax constructs. You got a few examples of LINQ syntax, but now you'll get to see LINQ in action in different scenarios and with more examples. This chapter is about LINQ to Objects, which is the standard provider for querying in-memory objects. This definition considers collections, arrays, and any other object that implements the `IEnumerable` or `IEnumerable(Of T)` interface (or interfaces deriving from them). LINQ to Objects can be considered as the root of LINQ providers, and it's important to understand how it works because the approach is essentially the same in accessing databases and XML documents. We focus on code more than on introducing the provider with annoying discussions, so let's start.

Querying in Memory Objects

LINQ to Object's purpose is querying in-memory collections in a strongly typed fashion using recently added keywords that recall SQL instructions syntax and that are now integrated in the Visual Basic language. This enables the compiler to manage your actions at compile time. Before querying data, you need a data source. For example, imagine you have the following `Product` class that represents some food products of your company:

```
Class Product
    Property ProductID As Integer
    Property ProductName As String
    Property UnitPrice As Decimal
    Property UnitsInStock As Integer
    Property Discontinued As Boolean
End Class
```

CODING TIP: USING OBJECT INITIALIZERS

In this chapter and the next ones dedicated to LINQ, you notice that in most cases classes do not implement an explicit constructor. You see the advantages of object initializers in both normal code and in LINQ query expressions, which is the reason custom classes have no explicit constructors. This is not a mandatory rule; instead it is an approach specific to LINQ that you need to be familiar with.

At this point consider the following products, as a demonstration:

```
Dim prod1 As New Product With {.ProductID = 0,
                               .ProductName = "Pasta",
                               .UnitPrice = 0.5D,
                               .UnitsInStock = 10,
                               .Discontinued = False}

Dim prod2 As New Product With {.ProductID = 1,
                               .ProductName = "Mozzarella",
                               .UnitPrice = 1D,
                               .UnitsInStock = 50,
                               .Discontinued = False}
```

```
Dim prod3 As New Product With {.ProductID = 2,
                               .ProductName = "Crabs",
                               .UnitPrice = 7D,
                               .UnitsInStock = 20,
                               .Discontinued = True}

Dim prod4 As New Product With {.ProductID = 3,
                               .ProductName = "Tofu",
                               .UnitPrice = 3.5D,
                               .UnitsInStock = 40,
                               .Discontinued = False}
```

The code is simple; it just creates several instances of the `Product` class populating its properties with some food names and characteristics. Usually, you collect instances of your products in a typed collection. The following code accomplishes this, taking advantage of collection initializers:

```
Dim products As New List(Of Product) From {prod1,
                                           prod2,
                                           prod3,
                                           prod4}
```

Because the `List(Of T)` collection implements `IEnumerable(Of T)`, it can be queried with LINQ. The following query shows how you can retrieve all non-discontinued products in which the `UnitsInStock` property value is greater than 10:

```
Dim query = From prod In products
            Where prod.UnitsInStock > 10 _
            And prod.Discontinued = False
            Order By prod.UnitPrice
            Select prod
```

CODING TIP: IMPLICIT LINE CONTINUATION

In LINQ queries, you can take advantage of the feature known as *implicit line continuation* that avoids the need of writing the underscore character at the end of a line. An exception in LINQ queries is when you use logical operators, as in the preceding code snippet, in which the underscore is required. The code provides an easy view of this necessity. As an alternative, you can place the logical operator (`And`, in the example) on the preceding line to avoid the underscore.

This kind of LINQ query is also known as *query expression*. The `From` keyword points to the data source; the `prod` identifier represents one product in the products list. The `Where` keyword allows filtering data in which the specified condition is evaluated to `True`; the

Order By keywords allow sorting data according to the specified property. Select pushes each item that matches the specified Where conditions into an IEnumerable(Of T) result. Notice how local type inference avoids the need of specifying the query result type that is inferred by the compiler as IEnumerable(Of Product). Later in this chapter you will see why type inference is important in LINQ queries for anonymous types' collections. At this point, you can work with the result of your query; for example, you can iterate the preceding query variable to get information on the retrieved products:

```
For Each prod In query
    Console.WriteLine("Product name: {0}, Unit price: {1}",
                    prod.ProductName, prod.UnitPrice)
Next
```

This code produces on your screen a list of products that are not discontinued and where there is a minimum of 11 units in stock. For your convenience, Listing 23.1 shows the complete code for this example, providing a function that returns the query result via the Return instruction. Iteration is executed later within the caller.

LISTING 23.1   Querying In-Memory Collections with LINQ

```
Module Module1

    Sub Main()

        Dim result = QueryingObjectsDemo1()

        For Each prod In result
            Console.WriteLine("Product name: {0}, Unit price: {1}",
                            prod.ProductName, prod.UnitPrice)
        Next
        Console.Readline()
    End Sub



    Function QueryingObjectsDemo1() As IEnumerable(Of Product)

        Dim prod1 As New Product With {.ProductID = 0,
                                        .ProductName = "Pasta",
                                        .UnitPrice = 0.5D,
                                        .UnitsInStock = 10,
                                        .Discontinued = False}

        Dim prod2 As New Product With {.ProductID = 1,
                                        .ProductName = "Mozzarella",
                                        .UnitPrice = 1D,
                                        .UnitsInStock = 50,
                                        .Discontinued = False}
```

```
            Dim prod3 As New Product With {.ProductID = 2,
                                           .ProductName = "Crabs",
                                           .UnitPrice = 7D,
                                           .UnitsInStock = 20,
                                           .Discontinued = True}

            Dim prod4 As New Product With {.ProductID = 3,
                                           .ProductName = "Tofu",
                                           .UnitPrice = 3.5D,
                                           .UnitsInStock = 40,
                                           .Discontinued = False}

            Dim products As New List(Of Product) From {prod1,
                                                       prod2,
                                                       prod3,
                                                       prod4}

        Dim query = From prod In products
                    Where prod.UnitsInStock > 10 _
                    And prod.Discontinued = False
                    Order By prod.UnitPrice
                    Select prod

        Return query
    End Function
End Module


Class Product
    Property ProductID As Integer
    Property ProductName As String
    Property UnitPrice As Decimal
    Property UnitsInStock As Integer
    Property Discontinued As Boolean
End Class
```

If you run the code in Listing 23.1, you get the following result:

```
Product name: Mozzarella, Unit price: 1
Product name: Tofu, Unit price: 3.5
```

Such a result contains only those products that are not discontinued and that are available in more than 11 units. You can perform complex queries with LINQ to Objects.

23

USING ITERATORS WITH LINQ

In Chapter 16, "Working with Collections and Iterators," you learned about the new feature of Iterators in Visual Basic 2012 and the `Yield` keyword. LINQ queries are the perfect candidates for using iterator functions because, in most cases, you will write `For..Each` loops against query results. You can rewrite the sample shown in Listing 23.1 by decorating the `QueryingObjectsDemo1` method with the Iterator modifier and then replace the `Return` statement with the following code:

```
For Each item In query
     Yield item
Next
```

In this way, your code will be much more efficient and responsive in case of very large in-memory collections.

The following example provides a LINQ to Objects representation of what you get with relational databases and LINQ to SQL or LINQ to Entities. Consider the following class that must be added to the project:

```
Class ShippingPlan
    Property ProductID As Integer
    Property ShipDate As Date
End Class
```

The purpose of the `ShippingPlan` is storing the ship date for each product, represented by an ID. Both the `ShippingPlan` and `Product` classes expose a `ProductID` property that provides a basic relationship. Now consider the following code that creates four instances of the `ShippingPlan` class, one for each product and a collection of items:

```
Dim shipPlan1 As New ShippingPlan With {.ProductID = 0,
                                        .ShipDate = New Date(2012, 1, 1)}
Dim shipPlan2 As New ShippingPlan With {.ProductID = 1,
                                        .ShipDate = New Date(2012, 2, 1)}
Dim shipPlan3 As New ShippingPlan With {.ProductID = 2,
                                        .ShipDate = New Date(2012, 3, 1)}
Dim shipPlan4 As New ShippingPlan With {.ProductID = 3,
                                        .ShipDate = New Date(2012, 4, 1)}

Dim shipPlans As New List(Of ShippingPlan) From {
                                        shipPlan1,
                                        shipPlan2,
                                        shipPlan3,
                                        shipPlan4}
```

At this point, the goal is to retrieve a list of product names and the related ship date. This can be accomplished as follows:

```
Dim queryPlans = From prod In products
    Join plan In shipPlans On plan.ProductID Equals prod.ProductID
    Select New With {.ProductName = prod.ProductName,
                      .ShipDate = plan.ShipDate}
```

As you can see, the Join clause enables the joining of data from two different data sources having in common one property. This works similarly to the JOIN SQL instruction. Notice how you can take advantage of anonymous types to generate a new type on-the-fly that stores only the necessary information, without the need of creating a custom class for handling that information. The problem is now another one. If you need to use such a query result within a method body, no problem. The compiler can distinguish which members and how many members an anonymous type exposes so that you can use these members in a strongly typed way. The problem is when you need to return a query result that is the result of a function. You cannot declare a function as an IEnumerable(Of anonymous type), so you should return a nongeneric IEnumerable, which returns an IEnumerable(Of Object). Therefore, you cannot invoke members from anonymous types except if you recur to late binding. This makes sense because anonymous types' members have visibility only within the parent member that defines them. To solve this problem, you need to define a custom class holding query results. For example, consider the following class:

```
Class CustomProduct
    Property ProductName As String
    Property ShipDate As Date
End Class
```

It stores information from both Product and ShippingPlan classes. Now consider the following query:

```
Dim queryPlans = From prod In products
    Join plan In shipPlans On plan.ProductID Equals prod.ProductID
    Select New CustomProduct With {.ProductName = prod.ProductName,
                      .ShipDate = plan.ShipDate}
```

It creates an instance of the CustomProduct class each time an object matching the condition is encountered. In this way, you can return the query result as the result of a function returning IEnumerable(Of CustomProduct). This scenario is represented for your convenience in Listing 23.2.

LISTING 23.2   Complex LINQ to Objects Queries

```
Function QueryObjectsDemo2() As IEnumerable(Of CustomProduct)
    Dim prod1 As New Product With {.ProductID = 0,
                      .ProductName = "Pasta",
                      .UnitPrice = 0.5D,
                      .UnitsInStock = 10,
                      .Discontinued = False}
```

```vb
Dim prod2 As New Product With {.ProductID = 1,
                               .ProductName = "Mozzarella",
                               .UnitPrice = 1D,
                               .UnitsInStock = 50,
                               .Discontinued = False}

Dim prod3 As New Product With {.ProductID = 2,
                               .ProductName = "Crabs",
                               .UnitPrice = 7D,
                               .UnitsInStock = 20,
                               .Discontinued = True}

Dim prod4 As New Product With {.ProductID = 3,
                               .ProductName = "Tofu",
                               .UnitPrice = 3.5D,
                               .UnitsInStock = 40,
                               .Discontinued = False}

Dim products As New List(Of Product) From {prod1,
                                           prod2,
                                           prod3,
                                           prod4}

Dim shipPlan1 As New ShippingPlan With {.ProductID = 0,
                                        .ShipDate = New Date(2012, 1, 1)}
Dim shipPlan2 As New ShippingPlan With {.ProductID = 1,
                                        .ShipDate = New Date(2012, 2, 1)}
Dim shipPlan3 As New ShippingPlan With {.ProductID = 2,
                                        .ShipDate = New Date(2012, 3, 1)}
Dim shipPlan4 As New ShippingPlan With {.ProductID = 3,
                                        .ShipDate = New Date(2012, 4, 1)}

Dim shipPlans As New List(Of ShippingPlan) From {
                                            shipPlan1,
                                            shipPlan2,
                                            shipPlan3,
                                            shipPlan4}

Dim queryPlans = From prod In products
                 Join plan In shipPlans On _
                 plan.ProductID Equals prod.ProductID
                 Select New CustomProduct _
                 With {.ProductName = prod.ProductName,
                       .ShipDate = plan.ShipDate}
```

```
        Return queryPlans
    End Function
    Sub QueryPlans()
        Dim plans = QueryObjectsDemo2()
        For Each plan In plans
            Console.WriteLine("Product name: {0} will be shipped on {1}",
                                plan.ProductName, plan.ShipDate)
        Next
        Console.ReadLine()
    End Sub

'If you invoke the QueryPlans method, you get the following output:
'Product name: Pasta will be shipped on 01/01/2012
'Product name: Mozzarella will be shipped on 02/01/2012
'Product name: Crabs will be shipped on 03/01/2012
'Product name: Tofu will be shipped on 04/01/2012
```

You would obtain the same result with anonymous types if the iteration were performed within the method body and not outside the method itself. This approach is always useful and becomes necessary in scenarios such as LINQ to XML on Silverlight applications. LINQ to Objects offers a large number of operators, known as *standard query operators*; these are discussed in this chapter. An important thing you need to consider is that you can also perform LINQ queries via extension methods. Language keywords for LINQ have extension methods counterparts that can be used with lambda expressions for performing queries. The following snippet provides an example of how the previous query expression can be rewritten invoking extension methods:

```
Dim query = products.Where(Function(p) p.UnitsInStock > 10 And _
            p.Discontinued = False).
            OrderBy(Function(p) p.UnitPrice).
            Select(Function(p) p)
```

Notice how extension methods are instance methods of the data source you are querying. Each method requires a lambda expression that returns instances of the `Product` class, letting you perform the required tasks. Before studying operators, there is an important concept that you must understand; it's related to the actual moment when queries are executed.

Understanding Deferred Execution

When the Common Language Runtime (CLR) encounters a LINQ query, the query is not executed immediately. LINQ queries are executed only when they are effectively used. This concept is known as *deferred execution* and is part of all LINQ providers you encounter, both standard and custom ones. For example, consider the query that is an example in the previous discussion:

```
Dim query = From prod In products
            Where prod.UnitsInStock > 10 _
            And prod.Discontinued = False
            Order By prod.UnitPrice
            Select prod
```

This query is not executed until you effectively use its result. If the query is defined within a function and is the result of the method, the Return instruction causes the query to be executed:

```
Dim query = From prod In products
            Where prod.UnitsInStock > 10 _
            And prod.Discontinued = False
            Order By prod.UnitPrice
            Select prod
'The query is executed here:
Return query
```

Iterating the result also causes the query to be executed:

```
Dim query = From prod In products
            Where prod.UnitsInStock > 10 _
            And prod.Discontinued = False
            Order By prod.UnitPrice
            Select prod
'The query is executed here, the Enumerator is invoked
For Each prod In query
    Console.WriteLine("Product name: {0}, Unit price: {1}",
                    prod.ProductName, prod.UnitPrice)
Next
```

Another example of query execution is when you just invoke a member of the result as in the following example:

```
Console.WriteLine(query.Count)
```

You can also force queries to be executed when declared, invoking methods on the query itself. For example, converting a query result into a collection causes the query to be executed, as demonstrated here:

```
Dim query = (From prod In products
            Where prod.UnitsInStock > 10 _
            And prod.Discontinued = False
            Order By prod.UnitPrice
            Select prod).ToList 'the query is executed here
```

This is also important at debugging time. For example, consider the case where you have a query and want to examine its result while debugging, taking advantage of Visual Studio's data tips. If you place a breakpoint on the line of code immediately after the query and then pass the mouse pointer over the variable that receives the query result, the data tips feature pops up a message saying that the variable is an in-memory query and that clicking to expand the result processes the collection. This is shown in Figure 23.1.

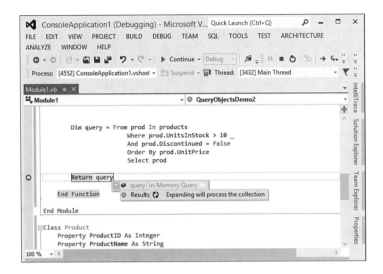

FIGURE 23.1   Visual Studio data tips show how the query has not been executed yet.

At this point, the debugger executes the query in memory. When executed, you can inspect the query result before it is passed to the next code. Data tips enable you to examine every item in the collection. Figure 23.2 demonstrates this.

FIGURE 23.2   The debugger executes the query so that you can inspect its result.

Deferred execution is a key topic in LINQ development, and you always need to keep in mind how it works to avoid problems in architecting your code.

Introducing Standard Query Operators

Querying objects with LINQ (as much as XML documents and ADO.NET models) is accomplished via the standard query operators that are a set of Visual Basic keywords allowing performing both simple and complex tasks within LINQ queries. This chapter covers standard query operators illustrating their purpose. For this, remember that this topic is important because you need operators in other LINQ providers as well. You can also notice that standard query operators have extension methods counterparts that you can use as well.

Projection Operators

LINQ query expressions extract values from data sources and then push results into a sequence of elements. This operation of pushing items into a sequence is known as *projection*. select is the projection operator for LINQ queries. Continuing the example of products shown in the previous section, the following query creates a new sequence containing all product names:

```
Dim productNames = From prod In products
                   Select prod.ProductName
```

The query result is now an IEnumerable(Of String). If you need to create a sequence of objects, you can select each single item as follows:

```
Dim productSequence = From prod In products
                      Select prod
```

This returns an IEnumerable(Of Product). You can also pick more than one member for an item:

```
Dim productSequence = From prod In products
                      Select prod.ProductID, prod.ProductName
```

This returns an `IEnumerable(Of Anonymous type)`. Of course, for an anonymous type, you can use the extended syntax that also allows specifying custom properties names:

```
Dim productSequence = From prod In products
                      Select ID = prod.ProductID,
                      Name = prod.ProductName
```

This is the equivalent of the following:

```
Dim productSequence = From prod In products
                      Select New With {.ID = prod.ProductID,
                      .Name = prod.ProductName}
```

An extension counterpart exists for `Select`, which is the `Select` extension method that receives a lambda expression as an argument that allows specifying the object or member that must be projected into the sequence and that works like this:

```
'IEnumerable(Of String)
Dim prodSequence = products.Select(Function(p) p.ProductName)
```

Query expressions can require more complex projections, especially if you work on different sources. Another projection operator known as `SelectMany` is an extension method, but it can be performed in expressions, too. To continue with the next examples, refer to the "Querying In-Memory Objects" section and retake the `ShippingPlan` and `Product` classes and code that populates new collections of such objects. After you've done this, consider the following query:

```
Dim query = From prod In products
            From ship In shipPlans
            Where prod.ProductID = ship.ProductID
            Select prod.ProductName, ship.ShipDate
```

With nested `From` clauses, we can query different data sources, and the `Select` clause picks data from both collections, acting as `SelectMany` that has an extension method counterpart that accepts lambda expressions as arguments pointing to the desired data sources.

Restriction Operators

LINQ offers an operator named `Where` that allows filtering query results according to the specified condition. For example, continuing with the previous examples of a collection of products, the following code returns only non-discontinued products:

```
Dim query = From prod In products
            Where prod.Discontinued = False
            Select prod
```

The same result can be accomplished by invoking a same-named extension method that works as follows:

```
Dim result = products.Where(Function(p) p.Discontinued = False).
             Select(Function(p) p)
```

Where supports lots of operators on the line that are summarized in Table 23.1.

TABLE 23.1   Operators Supported by Where

Operator	Description
<, >	Major and minor operators that return True if the value is smaller or greater than the other one, respectively
=, <>	Equality and inequality operators for value types comparisons
Is	Returns True if the comparison between two objects succeeds
IsNot	Returns True if the comparison between two objects does not succeed
And	Allows specifying two conditions and returns True if both conditions are true
AndAlso	Allows specifying two conditions and returns True if both conditions are true; but if the first one is False, the second one is skipped
Or	Allows specifying two conditions and returns True if at least one of the conditions is evaluated to True
OrElse	Allows specifying two conditions and returns True if both conditions are True
Like	Compares a string to a pattern and returns True if the string matches the pattern
Mod	Returns the remainder of a division between numbers

The following code provides a more complex example of filtering using Where and logical operators to retrieve the list of executable files that have been accessed within two dates:

```
Dim fileList = From item In My.Computer.FileSystem.
                         GetDirectoryInfo("C:\").GetFiles
               Where item.LastAccessTime < Date.Today _
               AndAlso item.LastAccessTime > New Date(2009, 9, 10) _
               AndAlso item.FullName Like "*.exe"
               Select item
```

The preceding code uses AndAlso to ensure that the three conditions are True. Using AndAlso shortcircuiting offers the benefit of making evaluations more efficient in one line. Notice how Like is used to provide a pattern comparison with the filename. You find a lot of examples about Where in this book, so let's discuss other operators.

Aggregation Operators

Aggregation operators allow performing simple mathematic calculations on a sequence's items using the Aggregate and Into clauses. The combination of such clauses can affect the following methods:

▶ Sum, which returns the sum of values of the specified property for each item in the collection

▶ Average, which returns the average calculation of values of the specified property for each item in the collection

▶ Count and LongCount, which return the number of items within a collection, respectively as Integer and Long types

▶ Min, which returns the lowest value for the specified sequence

▶ Max, which returns the highest value for the specified sequence

For example, you can get the sum of unit prices for your products as follows:

```
'Returns the sum of product unit prices
Dim totalAmount = Aggregate prod In products
                Into Sum(prod.UnitPrice)
```

You need to specify the object property that must be affected by the calculation (UnitPrice in this example) and that also works the same way in other aggregation operators. The following code shows how you can retrieve the average price:

```
'Returns the average price
Dim averagePrice = Aggregate prod In products
                Into Average(prod.UnitPrice)
```

The following snippet shows how you can retrieve the number of products in both Integer and Long formats:

```
'Returns the number of products
Dim numberOfItems = Aggregate prod In products
                Into Count()
```

```
'Returns the number of products as Long
Dim longNumberOfItems = Aggregate prod In products
                Into LongCount()
```

The following code shows how you can retrieve the lowest and highest prices for your products:

```
'Returns the lowest value for the specified
'sequence
Dim minimumPrice = Aggregate prod In products
                Into Min(prod.UnitPrice)
```

```
'Returns the highest value for the specified
'sequence
Dim maximumPrice = Aggregate prod In products
                Into Max(prod.UnitPrice)
```

All the preceding aggregation operators have extension method counterparts that work similarly. For example, you can compute the minimum unit price as follows:

```
Dim minimum = products.Min(Function(p) p.UnitPrice)
```

Such extension methods require you to specify a lambda expression pointing to the member you want to be part of the calculation. Other extension methods work the same way.

> **NOTE**
>
> When using aggregation operators, you do not get back an `IEnumerable` type. You instead get a single value type.

Understanding the `Let` Keyword

The Visual Basic syntax offers a keyword named `Let` that can be used for defining temporary identifiers within query expressions. The following code shows how you can query Windows Forms controls to get a sequence of text boxes:

```
Dim query = From ctrl In Me.Controls _
            Where TypeOf (ctrl) Is TextBox _
            Let txtBox = DirectCast(ctrl, TextBox) _
            Select txtBox.Name
```

The `Let` keyword enables the defining of a temporary identifier so that you can perform multiple operations on each item of the sequence and then invoke the item by its temporary identifier.

Conversion Operators

LINQ query results are returned as `IEnumerable(Of T)` (or `IQueryable(Of T)`, as you see in the next chapters), but you often need to convert this type into a most appropriate one. For example, query results cannot be edited unless you convert them into a typed collection. To do this, LINQ offers some extension methods whose job is converting query results into other .NET types such as arrays or collections. Let's consider the `Products` collection of the previous section's examples and first perform a query expression that retrieves all products that are not discontinued:

```
Dim query = From prod In products
            Where prod.Discontinued = False
            Select prod
```

The result of this query is `IEnumerable(Of Product)`. The result can easily be converted into other .NET types. First, you can convert it into an array of `Product` invoking the `ToArray` extension method:

```
'Returns Product()
Dim productArray = query.ToArray
```

Similarly, you can convert the query result into a `List(Of T)` invoking `ToList`. The following code returns a `List(Of Product)` collection:

```
'Returns List(Of Product)
Dim productList = query.ToList
```

You can perform a more complex conversion with `ToDictionary` and `ToLookup`. `ToDictionary` generates a `Dictionary(Of TKey, TValue)` and receives only an argument that, via a lambda expression, specifies the key for the dictionary. The value part of the key/value pair is always the type of the query (`Product` in this example). This is an example:

```
'Returns Dictionary(Of Integer, Product)
Dim productDictionary = query.ToDictionary(Function(p) _
                                    p.ProductID)
```

Because the value is a typed object, the `Value` property of each `KeyValuePair` in the `Dictionary` is an instance of your type; therefore, you can access members from `Value`. The following snippet demonstrates this:

```
For Each prod In productDictionary
    Console.WriteLine("Product ID: {0}, name: {1}", prod.Key,
                    prod.Value.ProductName)
Next
```

The next operator is `ToLookup` that returns an `ILookup(Of TKey, TElement)`, where `TKey` indicates a key similarly to a `Dictionary` and `TElement` represents a sequence of elements. Such a type can be used in mapping one-to-many relationships between an object. Continuing the example of the Product class, we can provide an elegant way for getting the product name based on the ID. Consider the following code snippet that returns an `ILookup(Of Integer, String)`:

```
Dim productLookup = query.ToLookup(Function(p) p.ProductID, _
                            Function(p) p.ProductName & " has " & _
                            p.UnitsInStock & " units in stock")
```

We can now query the products sequence based on the `ProductID` property and extract data such as product name and units in stock. Because of the particular structure of `ILookup`, a nested `For..Each` loop is required and works like the following:

```
For Each prod In productLookup
    Console.WriteLine("Product ID: {0}", prod.Key)

    For Each item In prod
        Console.WriteLine("     {0}", item)
    Next
Next
```

`Prod` is of type `IGrouping(Of Integer, String)`, a type that characterizes a single item in an `ILookup`. If you run this code, you get the following result:

```
Product ID: 0
      Pasta has 10 units in stock
Product ID: 1
      Mozzarella has 50 units in stock
Product ID: 3
      Tofu has 40 units in stock
```

Opposite from operators that convert into typed collections or arrays, two methods convert from typed collections into `IEnumerable` or `IQueryable`. They are named `AsEnumerable` and `AsQueryable`, and their usage is pretty simple:

```
Dim newList As New List(Of Product)
'Populate your collection here..

Dim anEnumerable = newList.AsEnumerable
Dim aQueryable = newList.AsQueryable
```

Another operator filters a sequence and retrieves only items of the specified type, generating a new sequence of that type. It is named `ofType` and is considered a conversion operator. The following code provides an example in which from an array of mixed types only `Integer` types are extracted and pushed into an `IEnumerable(Of Integer)`:

```
Dim mixed() As Object = {"String1", 1, "String2", 2}
Dim onlyInt = mixed.OfType(Of Integer)()
```

This is the equivalent of using the `TypeOf` operator in a query expression. The following query returns the same result:

```
Dim onlyInt = From item In mixed
              Where TypeOf item Is Integer
              Select item
```

It is not uncommon to need to immediately convert a query result into a collection, so you can invoke conversion operators directly in the expression as follows:

```
Dim query = (From prod In products
             Where prod.Discontinued = False
             Select prod).ToList
```

Remember that invoking conversion operators causes the query to be executed.

Generation Operators

Most of LINQ members are offered by the `System.Enumerable` class. This also exposes two shared methods, `Range` and `Repeat`, which provide the capability to generate sequences of elements. `Range` allows generating a sequence of integer numbers, as shown in the following code:

```
'The sequence will contain 100 numbers
'The first number is 40
Dim numbers = Enumerable.Range(40, 100)
```

It returns `IEnumerable(Of Integer)`, so you can then query the generated sequence using LINQ. `Repeat` enables you to generate a sequence where the specified item repeats the given number of times. `Repeat` is generic in that you need to specify the item's type first. For example, the following code generates a sequence of 10 Boolean values and `True` is repeated 10 times:

```
Dim stringSequence = Enumerable.Repeat(Of Boolean)(True, 10)
```

Repeat returns `IEnumerable(Of T)`, where `T` is the type specified for the method itself.

Ordering Operators

Ordering operators allow sorting query results according to the given condition. Within LINQ queries, this is accomplished via the `Order By` clause. This clause allows ordering query results in both ascending and descending order, where ascending is the default. The following example sorts the query result so that products are ordered from the one that has the lowest unit price to the one having the highest unit price:

```
Dim query = From prod In products
            Order By prod.UnitPrice
            Select prod
```

To get a result ordered from the highest value to the lowest, you use the `Descending` keyword as follows:

```
Dim queryDescending = From prod In products
                      Order By prod.UnitPrice Descending
                      Select prod
```

This can shape the query result opposite of the first example. You can also provide more than one `Order By` clause to get subsequent ordering options. Using extension methods provides a bit more granularity in ordering results. For example, you can use the `OrderBy` and `ThenBy` extension methods for providing multiple ordering options, as demonstrated in the following code:

```
Dim query = products.OrderBy(Function(p) p.UnitPrice).ThenBy(Function(p)
➡p.ProductName)
```

As usual, both methods take lambdas as arguments. In addition, the `OrderByDescending` and `ThenByDescending` extension methods order the result from the highest value to the lowest. The last ordering method is `Reverse` that reverses the query result and that you can use as follows:

```
Dim revertedQuery = query.Reverse()
```

Set Operators

Set operators let you remove duplicates and merge sequences and exclude specified elements. For instance, you could have duplicate items within a sequence or collection; you can remove duplicates using the `Distinct` operator. The following provides an example on a simple array of integers:

```
Dim someInt = {1, 2, 3, 3, 2, 4}
'Returns {1, 2, 3, 4}
Dim result = From number In someInt Distinct
             Select number
```

The result is a new `IEnumberable(Of Integer)`. In real scenarios, you could find this operator useful in LINQ to SQL or the Entity Framework for searching duplicate records in a database table. The next operator is `Union`, which is an extension method and merges two sequences into a new one. The following is an example:

```
Dim someInt = {1, 2, 3, 4}
Dim otherInt = {4, 3, 2, 1}

Dim result = someInt.Union(otherInt)
```

The preceding code returns an `IEnumerable(Of Integer)` containing 1, 2, 3, 4, 4, 3, 2, 1. The first items in the new sequences are those from the collection that you invoke `Union` on. Next operator is `Intersect`, which is another extension method. This method creates a new sequence with elements that two other sequences have in common. The following code demonstrates this:

```
Dim someInt = {1, 2, 3, 4}
Dim otherInt = {1, 2, 5, 6}

Dim result = someInt.Intersect(otherInt)
```

The new sequence is an `IEnumerable(Of Integer)` containing only 1 and 2 because they are the only values that both original sequences have in common. The last set operator is `Except` that generates a new sequence taking only those values that two sequences do not have in common. The following code is an example, which then requires a further explanation:

```
Dim someInt = {1, 2, 3, 4}
Dim otherInt = {1, 2, 5, 6}
Dim result = someInt.Except(otherInt)
```

Surprisingly, this code returns a new IEnumerable(Of Integer) containing only 3 and 4, although 5 and 6 also are values that the two sequences do not have in common. This is because the comparison is executed only on the sequence that you invoke Except on, and therefore all other values are excluded.

Grouping Operators

The grouping concept is something that you already know if you ever worked with data. Given a products collection, dividing products into categories would provide a better organization of information. For example, consider the following Category class:

```
Class Category
    Property CategoryID As Integer
    Property CategoryName As String
End Class
```

Now consider the following review of the Product class, with a new CategoryID property:

```
Class Product
    Property ProductID As Integer
    Property ProductName As String
    Property UnitPrice As Decimal
    Property UnitsInStock As Integer
    Property Discontinued As Boolean
    Property CategoryID As Integer
End Class
```

At this point we can write code that creates instances of both classes and populates appropriate collections, as in the following snippet:

```
Sub GroupByDemo()

    Dim cat1 As New Category With {.CategoryID = 1,
                                   .CategoryName = "Food"}

    Dim cat2 As New Category With {.CategoryID = 2,
                                   .CategoryName = "Beverages"}

    Dim categories As New List(Of Category) From {cat1,
                                                  cat2}

    Dim prod1 As New Product With {.ProductID = 0,
                                   .ProductName = "Pasta",
                                   .UnitPrice = 0.5D,
                                   .UnitsInStock = 10,
                                   .Discontinued = False,
                                   .CategoryID = 1}
```

```
Dim prod2 As New Product With {.ProductID = 1,
                               .ProductName = "Wine",
                               .UnitPrice = 1D,
                               .UnitsInStock = 50,
                               .Discontinued = False,
                               .CategoryID = 2}

Dim prod3 As New Product With {.ProductID = 2,
                               .ProductName = "Water",
                               .UnitPrice = 0.5D,
                               .UnitsInStock = 20,
                               .Discontinued = False,
                               .CategoryID = 2}

Dim prod4 As New Product With {.ProductID = 3,
                               .ProductName = "Tofu",
                               .UnitPrice = 3.5D,
                               .UnitsInStock = 40,
                               .Discontinued = True,
                               .CategoryID = 1}

Dim products As New List(Of Product) From {prod1,
                                           prod2,
                                           prod3,
                                           prod4}
```

To make things easier to understand, only two categories have been created. Notice also how each product now belongs to a specific category. To group foods into the Food category and beverages into the Beverages category, you use the Group By operator. This is the closing code of the preceding method, which is explained just after you write it:

```
Dim query = From prod In products
            Group prod By ID = prod.CategoryID
            Into Group
            Select CategoryID = ID,
                   ProductsList = Group

' "prod" is inferred as anonymous type
For Each prod In query
    Console.WriteLine("Category {0}", prod.CategoryID)

    ' "p" is inferred as Product
    For Each p In prod.ProductsList
        Console.WriteLine("    Product {0}, Discontinued: {1}",
                          p.ProductName, p.Discontinued)
```

```
        Next
    Next
End Sub
```

The code produces the following result:

```
Category 1
      Product Pasta, Discontinued: False
      Product Tofu, Discontinued: True
Category 2
      Product Wine, Discontinued: False
      Product Water, Discontinued: False
```

`Group By` requires you to specify a key for grouping. This key is a property of the type composing the collection you are querying. The result of the grouping is sent to a new `IEnumerable(Of T)` sequence represented by the `Into Group` statement. Finally, you invoke `Select` to pick up the key and items grouped according to the key; the projection generates an `IEnumerable(Of anonymous type)`. Notice how you need a nested `For..Each` loop. This is because each item in the query result is composed of two objects: the key and a sequence of object (in this case sequence of `Product`) grouped based on the key. The same result can be accomplished using extension methods' counterpart that works like this:

```
Dim query = products.GroupBy(Function(prod) prod.CategoryID,
                             Function(prod) prod.ProductName)
```

Union Operators

You often need to create sequences or collections with items taken from different data sources. If you consider the example in the previous "Grouping Operators" section, it would be interesting to create a collection of objects in which the category name is also available so that the result can be more human-readable. This is possible in LINQ using union operators (not to be confused with the union `Set` operator keyword), which perform operations that you know as *joining*. To complete the following steps, recall the previously provided implementation of the `Product` and `Category` classes and the code that populates new collections of products and categories. The goal of the first example is to create a new sequence of products in which the category name is also available. This can be accomplished as follows:

```
Dim query = From prod In products
            Join cat In categories On _
            prod.CategoryID Equals cat.CategoryID
            Select CategoryName = cat.CategoryName,
                   ProductName = prod.ProductName
```

The code is quite simple to understand. Both products and categories collections are queried, and a new sequence is generated to keep products and categories whose `CategoryID` is equal. This is accomplished via the `Join` keyword in which the `On` operator requires the condition to be evaluated as `True`. Notice that `Join` does not accept the equality operator (=), but it does require the `Equals` keyword. In this case the query result is an `IEnumerable(Of Anonymous type)`. You could, however, create a helper class exposing properties to store the result. You can then iterate the result to get information on your products, as in the following snippet:

```
For Each obj In query
    Console.WriteLine("Category: {0}, Product name: {1}",
                        obj.CategoryName, obj.ProductName)
Next
```

The code produces the following output:

```
Category: Food, Product name: Pasta
Category: Beverages, Product name: Wine
Category: Beverages, Product name: Water
Category: Food, Product name: Tofu
```

This is the simplest joining example and is known as *Cross Join*, but you are not limited to this. For example, you might want to group items based on the specified key, which is known as *Group Join*. This allows you to rewrite the same example of the previous paragraph but taking advantage of joining can get the category name. This is accomplished as follows:

```
Dim query = From cat In categories
            Group Join prod In products On _
            prod.CategoryID Equals cat.CategoryID
            Into Group
            Select NewCategory = cat,
                NewProducts = Group
```

Notice that now the main data source is `Categories`. The result of this query is generating a new sequence in which groups of categories store groups of products. This is notable if you take a look at the `Select` clause, which picks sequences instead of single objects or properties. The following iteration provides a deeper idea on how you access information from the query result:

```
For Each obj In query
    Console.WriteLine("Category: {0}", obj.NewCategory.CategoryName)

    For Each prod In obj.NewProducts
        Console.WriteLine("    Product name: {0}, Discontinued: {1}",
                            prod.ProductName, prod.Discontinued)
    Next
Next
```

Such nested iteration produces the following output:

```
Category: Food
    Product name: Pasta, Discontinued: False
    Product name: Tofu, Discontinued: True
Category: Beverages
    Product name: Wine, Discontinued: False
    Product name: Water, Discontinued: False
```

The *Cross Join with Group Join* technique is similar. The following code shows how you can perform a cross group join to provide a simplified version of the previous query result:

```
Dim query = From cat In categories
            Group Join prod In products On _
            prod.CategoryID Equals cat.CategoryID
            Into Group
            From p In Group
            Select CategoryName = cat.CategoryName,
                   ProductName = p.ProductName
```

Notice that by providing a nested `From` clause pointing to the group, you can easily select what you need from both sequences—for example, the category name and the product name. The result, which is still a sequence of anonymous types, can be iterated as follows:

```
For Each item In query
    Console.WriteLine("Product {0} belongs to {1}",
                      item.ProductName,
                      item.CategoryName)
Next
```

It produces the following output:

```
Product Pasta belongs to Food
Product Tofu belongs to Food
Product Wine belongs to Beverages
Product Water belongs to Beverages
```

The last union operator is known as *Left Outer Join*. It is similar to the cross group join, but it differs in that you can provide a default value in case no item is available for the specified key. Consider the following code:

```
Dim query = From cat In categories
            Group Join prod In products On _
            prod.CategoryID Equals cat.CategoryID
            Into Group
            From p In Group.DefaultIfEmpty
            Select CategoryName = cat.CategoryName,
                   ProductName = If(p IsNot Nothing,
                   p.ProductName, "No available product")
```

23

Notice the invocation of the `Group.DefaultIfEmpty` extension method that is used with the `If` ternary operator to provide a default value. You can then retrieve information from the query result as in the cross group join sample.

Equality Operators

You might want to compare two sequences to check whether they are perfectly equal. The `SequenceEqual` extension method allows performing this kind of comparison. It compares whether a sequence is equal considering both items and the items order within a sequence, returning a Boolean value. The following code returns `True` because both sequences contain the same items in the same order:

```
Dim first = {"Visual", "Basic", "2010"}
Dim second = {"Visual", "Basic", "2010"}
'Returns True
Dim comparison = first.SequenceEqual(second)
```

The following code returns instead `False` because, although both sequences contain the same items, they are ordered differently:

```
Dim first = {"Visual", "Basic", "2010"}
Dim second = {"Visual", "2010", "Basic"}
'Returns False
Dim comparison = first.SequenceEqual(second)
```

Quantifiers

LINQ offers two interesting extension methods for sequences, `Any` and `All`. `Any` checks whether at least one item in the sequence satisfies the specified condition. For example, the following code checks whether at least one product name contains the letters "of":

```
Dim result = products.Any(Function(p) p.ProductName.Contains("of"))
```

The method receives a lambda as an argument that specifies the condition and returns `True` if the condition is matched. `All` checks whether all members in a sequence match the specified condition. For example, the following code checks whether all products are discontinued:

```
Dim result = products.All(Function(p) p.Discontinued = True)
```

As previously noted, the lambda argument specifies the condition to be matched.

IMPROVING CODE PERFORMANCES WITH ANY

Very often you will need to know if a collection contains at least one element (that is, not empty). A common error is using the following syntax:

```
If myCollection.Count > 0 Then ...
```

This had to be used prior to LINQ (and lots of Visual Basic 6 users migrating to .NET use that), but with LINQ you can write:

```
If myCollection.Any Then...
```

The difference is huge: if you use Count, the runtime will move the iterator through all the elements in the collection. But if you use Any, the runtime will move the iterator just one position, which is enough to return True or False. This dramatically increases performance, especially if the collection has hundreds or thousands of elements.

Concatenation Operators

Sequences (that is, IEnumerable(Of T) objects) expose a method named Concat that enables the creation of a new sequence containing items from two sequences. The following code shows an example in which a new sequence of strings is created from two existing arrays of strings:

```
Dim firstSequence = {"One", "Two", "Three"}
Dim secondSequence = {"Four", "Five", "Six"}

Dim concatSequence = firstSequence.Concat(secondSequence)
```

The result produced by this code is that the concatSequence variable contains the following items: "One", "Two", "Three", "Four", "Five", and "Six". The first items in the new sequence are taken from the one you invoke the Concat method on.

Elements Operators

Some extension methods enable you to get the instance of a specified item in a sequence. The first one is Single, and it gets the instance of only the item that matches the specified condition. The following code gets the instance of the only product whose product name is Mozzarella:

```
Try
    Dim uniqueElement = products.Single(Function(p) p.
                                    ProductName = "Mozzarella")

Catch ex As InvalidOperationException
    'The item does not exist
End Try
```

Single takes a lambda expression as an argument in which you can specify the condition that the item must match. It returns an InvalidOperationException if the item does not exist in the sequence (or if more than one element matches the condition). As an alternative, you can invoke SingleOrDefault, which returns a default value if the item does not exist instead of throwing an exception. The following code returns Nothing because the product name does not exist:

```
Dim uniqueElement = products.SingleOrDefault(Function(p) p.
                ProductName = "Mozzarell")
```

The next method is First. It can return either the first item in a sequence or the first item that matches a condition. You can use it as follows:

```
'Gets the first product in the list
Dim firstAbsolute = products.First

Try
    'Gets the first product where product name starts with P
    Dim firstElement = products.First(Function(p) p.ProductName.
                                                  StartsWith("P"))
Catch ex As InvalidOperationException
    'No item available
End Try
```

The previous example is self-explanatory: If multiple products have their names start-ing with the letter *P*, `First` returns just the first one in the sequence or throws an `InvalidOperationException` if no item is available. Additionally, a `FirstOrDefault` method returns a default value, such as `Nothing`, if no item is available. `Last` and `LastOrDefault` return the last item in a sequence and that work like the preceding illus-trated ones.

Partitioning Operators

Partitioning operators enable you to use a technique known as *paging*, which is common in data access scenarios. There are two main operators in LINQ: `Skip` and `Take`. `Skip` avoids selecting the specified number of elements, and `Take` puts the specified number of elements into a sequence. The code in Listing 23.3 shows an example of paging imple-mentation using the two operators.

LISTING 23.3   Implementing a Basic Paging Technique

```
Module Partitioning

    Private pageCount As Integer
    Private Products As List(Of Product)

    Sub PopulateProducts()
        Dim prod1 As New Product With {.ProductID = 0,
                                       .ProductName = "Pasta",
                                       .UnitPrice = 0.5D,
                                       .UnitsInStock = 10,
                                       .Discontinued = False}


        Dim prod2 As New Product With {.ProductID = 1,
                                       .ProductName = "Mozzarella",
                                       .UnitPrice = 1D,
                                       .UnitsInStock = 50,
                                       .Discontinued = False}
```

```vbnet
        Dim prod3 As New Product With {.ProductID = 2,
                                       .ProductName = "Crabs",
                                       .UnitPrice = 7D,
                                       .UnitsInStock = 20,
                                       .Discontinued = True}

        Dim prod4 As New Product With {.ProductID = 3,
                                       .ProductName = "Tofu",
                                       .UnitPrice = 3.5D,
                                       .UnitsInStock = 40,
                                       .Discontinued = False}

        Products = New List(Of Product) From {prod1,
                                              prod2,
                                              prod3,
                                              prod4}
    End Sub

    Function QueryProducts() As IEnumerable(Of Product)

        Dim query As IEnumerable(Of Product)
        'If pageCount = 0 we need to retrieve the first 10 products
        If pageCount = 0 Then
            query = From prod In Products _
                    Order By Prod.ProductID _
                    Take 10

        Else
            'Skips the already shown products
            'and takes next 10
            query = From prod In Products _
                    Order By Prod.ProductID _
                    Skip pageCount Take 10

        End If

        'In real applications ensure that query is not null
        Return query
    End Function
End Module
```

The private field pageCount acts as a counter. According to its value, the query skips the number of elements already visited, represented by the value of pageCount. If no elements were visited, the query skips nothing. The code invoking QueryProducts increases or decreases the pageCount value by 10 units depending on whether you want to move forward or backward to the collection items.

Summary

In this chapter, you got a high-level overview of LINQ key concepts. In this particular discussion, you got information about LINQ to Objects as the built-in provider for querying in-memory collections. We showed LINQ in action via specific Visual Basic keywords that recall the SQL syntax, such as `From`, `Select`, `Where`, and `Join`. You can build LINQ queries while writing Visual Basic code, taking advantage of the background compiler, IntelliSense, and CLR control. Such queries written in the code editor are known as *query expressions*. Query expressions return an `IEnumerable(Of T)` but are not executed immediately. According to the key concept of deferred execution, LINQ queries are executed only when they are effectively utilized. This is something that you find in subsequent LINQ providers. With LINQ, you can build complex query expressions to query your data sources via the standard query operators, which were covered in the last part of the chapter. LINQ to Objects is the basis of LINQ, and most of the concepts shown in this chapter will be revisited in the next ones.

LINQ to SQL

How many times did you face runtime errors when sending SQL instructions to your databases for querying or manipulating data? Your answer is probably "several times." Sending SQL instructions in the form of strings has been, for years, the way of accessing data in the .NET development, but one of the main disadvantages was the lack of compile time control over your actions. Experienced developers can also remember when they had to work against databases in a connected environment taking care of everything that happened. LINQ to SQL solves several of these issues, providing both a disconnected way for working with data, where data is mapped into an object model that you work with until you decide to save back data, and a strongly typed programming fashion that improves your productivity by checking queries and CRUD operations at compile time. In this chapter you explore the most important LINQ to SQL functionalities, learning the basics of data access with such technology.

PREFER THE ADO.NET ENTITY FRAMEWORK

Although powerful, Microsoft is no longer investing in LINQ to SQL (but it is supported), and it should not be used in new projects. We discuss it because it is still a standard LINQ provider and because you might have existing code relying on this provider. Last but not least, as per today LINQ to SQL is the only way to access local databases when developing applications for Windows Phone 7.x. You are encouraged to use the ADO.NET Entity Framework and LINQ to Entities in new desktop or web applications, but keep LINQ to SQL for your mobile apps.

Introducing LINQ to SQL

LINQ to SQL is an object relational mapping engine for Microsoft SQL Server databases. In has been the first built-in LINQ provider for SQL Server when LINQ first shipped in the .NET Framework 3.5, offering not only the capability of querying data (as instead LINQ to DataSet is limited to) but also a complete infrastructure for manipulating data, including connections, queries, and *CRUD* (Create/Read/Update/Delete) operations. LINQ to SQL is another layer in the data access architecture, but it is responsible for everything starting from opening the connection until closing. One of the advantages from LINQ to SQL is that you will query your data using the usual LINQ syntax thanks to the unified programming model offered by the technology. But this is not the only advantage. Being an object relational mapping engine makes LINQ to SQL mapping databases' tables and relationships into .NET objects. This allows working in a disconnected way and in a totally strongly typed fashion so that you can get all the advantages of the CLR management. Each table from the database is mapped into a .NET class, whereas relationships are mapped into .NET properties, providing something known as *abstraction*. This enables you to work against a conceptual model instead of against the database, and you will work with objects until you finish your edits that will be persisted to the underlying data source only when effectively required. This provides several advantages: First, you work with strongly typed objects, and everything is managed by the Common Language Runtime (CLR). Second, you do not work connected to the database, so your original data will be secure until you send changes after validations. According to the LINQ terminology, classes mapping tables are called *entities*. A group of entities is referred to as an *entity set*. Relationships are instead called *associations*. You access LINQ to SQL features by creating specific classes that are described in next section.

LINQ INTERNALS

This is a language-focused book, so discussing LINQ to SQL internals and architecture is not possible. A discussion of this kind would probably require a specific book. Here you will instead learn of manipulating and querying data with LINQ to SQL and the Visual Basic language, getting the fundamental information about architecture when necessary.

Prerequisites and Requirements for This Book

This chapter assumes that you have installed Microsoft SQL Server 2012, at least the Express Edition, or possibly the "With Tools" version that also includes SQL Server Management Studio Express. If you did not install it yet, you can download it from here: http://www.microsoft.com/express/sql/default.aspx.

If you installed SQL Server Management Studio (Express or higher), it is a good idea to attach the Northwind database to the SQL Server instance so you can simulate a production environment.

Understanding LINQ to SQL Classes

To access SQL Server databases with LINQ to SQL, you need a LINQ to SQL class. This kind of class is generated by Visual Studio when you select members for the new object model and contains all the Visual Basic code that represents tables, columns, and relationships. Adding a LINQ to SQL class is also necessary to enable the Visual Studio OR/M Designer for LINQ to SQL. To understand what these sentences mean, follow these preliminary steps:

▶ Create a new project for the Console and name it **LinqToSql**.

▶ Establish a connection to the Northwind database either via the Server Explorer tool window or via the new SQL Server Object Explorer tool window.

▶ In Solution Explorer, right-click the project name and select **Add, New Item**. When the Add New Item dialog box appears move to the Data folder and select the **LINQ to SQL Classes** item, replacing the default name with **Northwind.dbml**. Figure 24.1 shows this scenario.

FIGURE 24.1   Adding a new LINQ to SQL class to the project.

When you click **Add**, after a few seconds the Visual Studio 2012 IDE shows the LINQ to SQL Object Relational Designer that appears empty, as shown in Figure 24.2.

The designer provides a brief description of its job, requiring you to pick items from either the Server Explorer window or from the toolbox. You need to pick tables from the Northwind database, passing them to Visual Studio to start the mapping process. Look at Figure 24.3 and then expand Server Explorer (or SQL Server Object Explorer) to show the Northwind database structure; then expand the Tables folder.

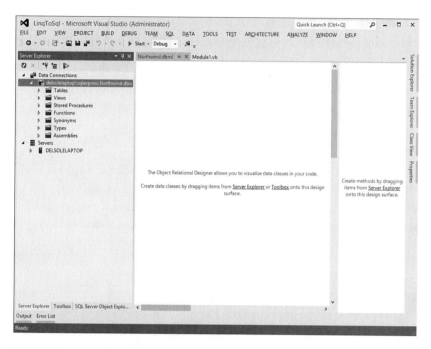

FIGURE 24.2   The LINQ to SQL designer popping up for the first time.

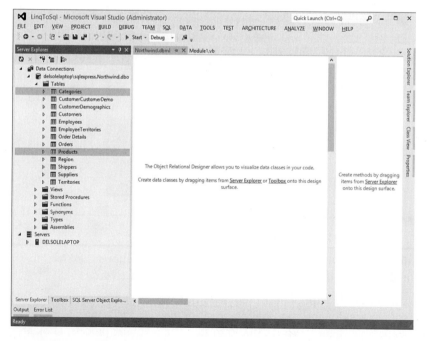

FIGURE 24.3   Preparing to pick tables from the Northwind database.

Now keep the Ctrl key pressed and click both the **Categories** and **Products** tables. Our goal is to provide an example of a master-details relationship. When selected, drag the tables onto the designer surface until you get the result shown in Figure 24.4.

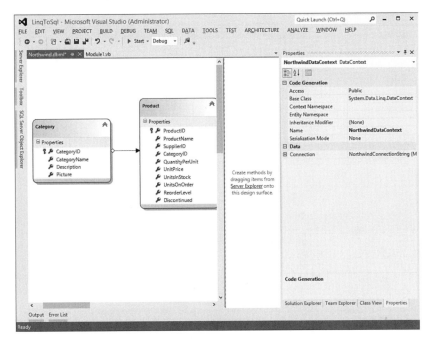

FIGURE 24.4   The LINQ to SQL designer is now populated.

At this point, we can begin making some considerations. Visual Studio generated a diagram that is the representation of Visual Basic code. This diagram contains the defini- tion of two entities, `Category` and `Product`. Each of them is mapped to Visual Basic classes with the same name. If you inspect the diagram, you notice that both classes expose properties. Each property maps a column within the table in the database. Figure 24.4 also shows the Properties window opened to show you a new, important concept, the `System.Data.Linq.DataContext` class. Every LINQ to SQL object model defines a class that inherits from `DataContext` and which is the main entry point of a LINQ to SQL class. It is, in other words, an object-oriented reference to the database. It is responsible for

▶ Opening and closing connections

▶ Handling relationships between entities

▶ Keeping track, with a single instance, of all changes applied to entities during all the object model lifetimes

▶ Translating Visual Basic code into the appropriate SQL instructions

▶ Managing entities' lifetimes, no matter how long

Visual Studio generates a new `DataContext` class by forming its name and concatenating the database name with the `DataContext` phrase. So in our example, the class is named `NorthwindDataContext`. This class, as you can see in Figure 24.4, exposes some properties including the connection string, base class, and access modifier.

INHERITANCE AND SERIALIZATION

Although this chapter also covers advanced LINQ to SQL features, some things are beyond the scope in this language-focused book, such as inheritance and serialization of data contexts. Such features are better described in the MSDN documentation at the following address: http://msdn.microsoft.com/en-us/library/bb386976(v=vs110).aspx

Now click the `Category` item in the designer that represents an entity described in Figure 24.5 within the Properties window.

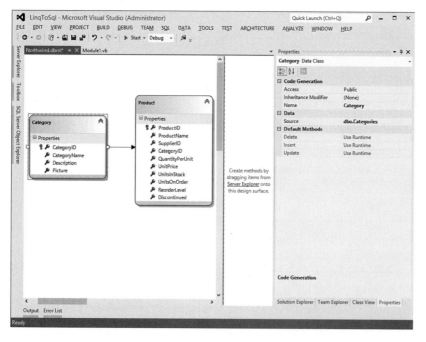

FIGURE 24.5   Examining the `Category` class.

It is interesting to understand that such a class has public access that requires code (Use Runtime definition) to support Insert/Update/Delete operations. The `Source` property also tells us what the source table in the database is. Now click on the arrow that establishes the relationship. Figure 24.6 shows how the Properties window describes such an object.

Notice how a one-to-many relationship is represented. The Child property shows the "many" part of the one-to-many relationship, whereas the Parent property shows the "one" part of the relationship.

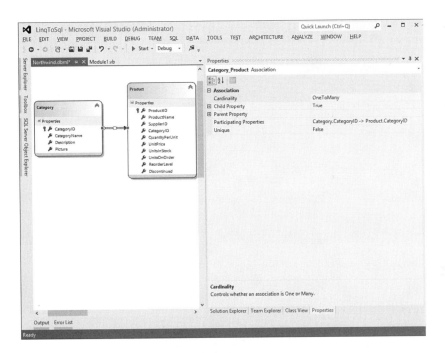

FIGURE 24.6   Examining associations.

RELATIONSHIPS

LINQ to SQL does not support many-to-many relationships. For this purpose, you should use the ADO.NET Entity Framework.

Now that you have a clearer idea about LINQ to SQL classes in a graphical way, it's time to understand the architecture. This kind of a class is referred via a .dbml file that groups nested files. To see nested files, you need to activate the **View All Files** view in Solution Explorer. The first nested file has a .dbml.layout extension and contains the XML definition for the class diagram that we just saw in the Visual Studio Designer. All edits, including Visual Studio-generated items, are performed onto the designer and then reflected into a .designer.vb file (in our example, Northwind.designer.vb). This file is fundamental because it stores code definitions for the DataContext, entities, and associations classes. Understanding how this file is defined is important, although you should never edit it manually. Listing 24.1 shows the definition of the NorthwindDataContext class:

LISTING 24.1   The NorthwindDataContext Class Definition

```
<Global.System.Data.Linq.Mapping.DatabaseAttribute(Name:="Northwind")> _
Partial Public Class NorthwindDataContext
    Inherits System.Data.Linq.DataContext
```

```vbnet
Private Shared mappingSource As System.Data.Linq.Mapping.MappingSource = _
                        New AttributeMappingSource()

Partial Private Sub OnCreated()
End Sub
Partial Private Sub InsertCategory(instance As Category)
End Sub
Partial Private Sub UpdateCategory(instance As Category)
End Sub
Partial Private Sub DeleteCategory(instance As Category)
End Sub
Partial Private Sub InsertProduct(instance As Product)
End Sub
Partial Private Sub UpdateProduct(instance As Product)
End Sub
Partial Private Sub DeleteProduct(instance As Product)
End Sub

Public Sub New()
    MyBase.New(Global.LinqToSql.My.MySettings.Default.
            NorthwindConnectionString, mappingSource)
    OnCreated
End Sub

Public Sub New(ByVal connection As String)
    MyBase.New(connection, mappingSource)
    OnCreated
End Sub

Public Sub New(ByVal connection As System.Data.IDbConnection)
    MyBase.New(connection, mappingSource)
    OnCreated
End Sub

Public Sub New(ByVal connection As String,
            ByVal mappingSource As System.Data.Linq.
            Mapping.MappingSource)
    MyBase.New(connection, mappingSource)
    OnCreated()
End Sub

Public Sub New(ByVal connection As System.Data.IDbConnection,
            ByVal mappingSource As System.Data.Linq.
            Mapping.MappingSource)
```

```
        MyBase.New(connection, mappingSource)
        OnCreated()
    End Sub

    Public ReadOnly Property Categories() As System.Data.Linq.Table(Of Category)
        Get
            Return Me.GetTable(Of Category)
        End Get
    End Property
    Public ReadOnly Property Products() As System.Data.Linq.Table(Of Product)
        Get
            Return Me.GetTable(Of Product)
        End Get
    End Property
End Class
```

The class is marked with the `DataBase` attribute and inherits from `DataContext`, meaning
that it has to be a managed reference to the database. The constructor provides several
overloads, most of them accepting a connection string if you do not want it to be stored
in the configuration file (which is the default generation). Two properties are important,
`Categories` and `Products` of type `System.Data.Linq.Table(Of T)`. This type offers a
.NET representation of a database table. The `GetTable` method invoked within properties creates `Table(Of T)` objects based on entities. Notice how several partial methods
for Insert/Update/Delete operations are defined and can be extended later. Similar to
the `DataContext` class, both `Product` and `Category` classes have a Visual Basic definition within the same file. As a unified example, Listing 24.2 shows the definition of the
`Category` class.

LISTING 24.2   The `Category` Class Definition

```
<Global.System.Data.Linq.Mapping.TableAttribute(Name:="dbo.Categories")> _
Partial Public Class Category
    Implements System.ComponentModel.INotifyPropertyChanging,
                System.ComponentModel.INotifyPropertyChanged

    Private Shared emptyChangingEventArgs As PropertyChangingEventArgs = _
                New PropertyChangingEventArgs(String.Empty)

    Private _CategoryID As Integer

    Private _CategoryName As String

    Private _Description As String

    Private _Picture As System.Data.Linq.Binary
```

```vb
Private _Products As EntitySet(Of Product)


Partial Private Sub OnLoaded()
End Sub
Partial Private Sub OnValidate(action As System.Data.Linq.ChangeAction)
End Sub
Partial Private Sub OnCreated()
End Sub
Partial Private Sub OnCategoryIDChanging(value As Integer)
End Sub
Partial Private Sub OnCategoryIDChanged()
End Sub
Partial Private Sub OnCategoryNameChanging(value As String)
End Sub
Partial Private Sub OnCategoryNameChanged()
End Sub
Partial Private Sub OnDescriptionChanging(value As String)
End Sub
Partial Private Sub OnDescriptionChanged()
End Sub
Partial Private Sub OnPictureChanging(value As System.Data.Linq.Binary)
End Sub
Partial Private Sub OnPictureChanged()
End Sub


Public Sub New()
    MyBase.New
    Me._Products = New EntitySet(Of Product)(AddressOf Me.attach_Products,
                                        AddressOf Me.detach_Products)
    OnCreated
End Sub


<Global.System.Data.Linq.Mapping.ColumnAttribute(Storage:="_CategoryID",
        AutoSync:=AutoSync.OnInsert, DbType:="Int NOT NULL IDENTITY",
        IsPrimaryKey:=True, IsDbGenerated:=True)> _
Public Property CategoryID() As Integer
    Get
        Return Me._CategoryID
    End Get
    Set(ByVal value As Integer)
        If ((Me._CategoryID = Value) _
            = False) Then
            Me.OnCategoryIDChanging(Value)
            Me.SendPropertyChanging()
            Me._CategoryID = Value
            Me.SendPropertyChanged("CategoryID")
```

```vb
                Me.OnCategoryIDChanged()
            End If
        End Set
    End Property


    <Global.System.Data.Linq.Mapping.ColumnAttribute(Storage:="_CategoryName",
          DbType:="NVarChar(15) NOT NULL", CanBeNull:=False)> _
    Public Property CategoryName() As String
        Get
            Return Me._CategoryName
        End Get
        Set(ByVal value As String)
            If (String.Equals(Me._CategoryName, Value) = False) Then
                Me.OnCategoryNameChanging(Value)
                Me.SendPropertyChanging()
                Me._CategoryName = Value
                Me.SendPropertyChanged("CategoryName")
                Me.OnCategoryNameChanged()
            End If
        End Set
    End Property


    <Global.System.Data.Linq.Mapping.ColumnAttribute(Storage:="_Description",
          DbType:="NText", UpdateCheck:=UpdateCheck.Never)> _
    Public Property Description() As String
        Get
            Return Me._Description
        End Get
        Set(ByVal value As String)
            If (String.Equals(Me._Description, Value) = False) Then
                Me.OnDescriptionChanging(Value)
                Me.SendPropertyChanging()
                Me._Description = Value
                Me.SendPropertyChanged("Description")
                Me.OnDescriptionChanged()
            End If
        End Set
    End Property


    <Global.System.Data.Linq.Mapping.ColumnAttribute(Storage:="_Picture",
          DbType:="Image", UpdateCheck:=UpdateCheck.Never)> _
    Public Property Picture() As System.Data.Linq.Binary
        Get
            Return Me._Picture
        End Get
        Set(ByVal value As System.Data.Linq.Binary)
```

24

```vb
            If (Object.Equals(Me._Picture, Value) = False) Then
                Me.OnPictureChanging(Value)
                Me.SendPropertyChanging()
                Me._Picture = Value
                Me.SendPropertyChanged("Picture")
                Me.OnPictureChanged()
            End If
        End Set
    End Property


    <Global.System.Data.Linq.Mapping.AssociationAttribute(Name:="Category_Product", _
            Storage:="_Products", ThisKey:="CategoryID", OtherKey:="CategoryID")> _
    Public Property Products() As EntitySet(Of Product)
        Get
            Return Me._Products
        End Get
        Set(ByVal value As EntitySet(Of Product))
            Me._Products.Assign(Value)
        End Set
    End Property


    Public Event PropertyChanging As PropertyChangingEventHandler Implements _
                System.ComponentModel.INotifyPropertyChanging.PropertyChanging

    Public Event PropertyChanged As PropertyChangedEventHandler Implements _
                System.ComponentModel.INotifyPropertyChanged.PropertyChanged


    Protected Overridable Sub SendPropertyChanging()
        If ((Me.PropertyChangingEvent Is Nothing)  _
                    = false) Then
            RaiseEvent PropertyChanging(Me, emptyChangingEventArgs)
        End If
    End Sub


    Protected Overridable Sub SendPropertyChanged(ByVal propertyName As [String])
        If ((Me.PropertyChangedEvent Is Nothing)  _
                    = false) Then
            RaiseEvent PropertyChanged(Me, _
                                New PropertyChangedEventArgs(propertyName))
        End If
    End Sub


    Private Sub attach_Products(ByVal entity As Product)
        Me.SendPropertyChanging
        entity.Category = Me
    End Sub
```

```
    Private Sub detach_Products(ByVal entity As Product)
        Me.SendPropertyChanging
        entity.Category = Nothing
    End Sub
End Class
```

The class is marked with the `System.Data.Linq.TableAttribute` attribute, meaning that it has to represent a database table. It implements both the `INotifyPropertyChanging` and `INotifyPropertyChanged` interfaces to provide the ability of notifying the user interface of changes about entities. It then defines partial methods that you can extend and customize when a particular event occurs. (This is covered when discussing data validation.) Each property is decorated with the `System.Data.Linq.Mapping.ColumnAttribute` that represents a column within a database table. This attribute takes some arguments that are self-explanatory. The most important of them are `Storage`, which points to a private field used as a data repository, and `DbType`, which contains the original SQL Server data type for the column. It is worth mentioning that Visual Basic provides an appropriate type mapping according to the related SQL data type. A primary key requires two other attributes, `IsPrimaryKey = True` and `AutoSync`. The second one establishes that it has to be auto-incremented and synchronized when a new item is added. In the end, notice how Set properties members perform a series of actions, such as raising events related to the beginning of property editing, storing the new value, and finally raising events related to the property set completion. This is auto-generated code from Visual Studio, and you should never change it manually. You are instead encouraged to use the LINQ to SQL designer that reflects changes in code. The last file for a LINQ to SQL class has a .dbml. layout extension and is just related to the diagram layout. Now that you are a little bit more familiar with LINQ to SQL classes, you can begin querying data with LINQ to SQL.

Behind the Scenes of LINQ to SQL Classes

The Visual Studio 2012 IDE generates LINQ to SQL classes invoking a command-line tool named SQLMetal.exe that is part of the Windows SDK for .NET. The following is an example of the command line for performing a manual generation of LINQ to SQL classes for the Northwind database and Visual Basic:

```
SQLMetal.exe /Server:.\SQLExpress /DataBase:Northwind /dbml:Northwind.dbml
/language:VisualBasic
```

SQLMetal.exe offers other command-line options for generating LINQ to SQL classes, but in most cases you do not need such manual generation because the IDE will do all the appropriate work for you. There is only one scenario in which you need to manually create a LINQ to SQL class—when mapping SQL Server Compact Edition 3.5 databases. This is discussed at the end of this chapter (and that also applies to Windows Phone development). For further information on SQLMetal, visit the official page on MSDN: http://msdn.microsoft.com/en-us/library/bb386987(VS.110).aspx.

24

Querying Data with LINQ to SQL

Before you begin querying data with LINQ to SQL, you need to instantiate the `DataContext` class. Continuing with the console application example started in the previous section, you can declare such an instance at the module level as follows:

```
Private northwind As New NorthwindDataContext
```

REAL-WORLD LINQ - CLASS LEVEL DECLARATION

In this example, the instance is declared at the module level because a console application is covered. In most cases, you work with client applications such as WPF or Windows Forms; therefore, the instance will be generated at the class level. Also, in my client applications, I used to follow this approach: I'd provide a class-level declaration of the `DataContext` but instantiate the object within the constructor. This allows handling exceptions that could occur at runtime while attempting to connect to the database, other than performing other initialization actions.

Declaring a single instance at the module or class level allows one `DataContext` to manage entities for all the object model lifetimes. When you create such an instance, the `DataContext` connects to the database and provides required abstraction so that you can work against the object model instead of working against the database. The `DataContext` class's constructor also accepts a connection string if you want it to be hard-coded instead of storing it within a configuration file. You have different alternatives for querying data. For example, you might want to retrieve the complete list of products that is accomplished as follows:

```
'Returns Table(Of Product)
Dim allProduct = northwind.Products
```

This code returns a `System.Data.Linq.Table(Of Product)` that is an object inheriting from `IQueryable(Of T)` and that represents a database table. `IQueryable(Of T)` is the general type returned by LINQ to SQL queries and inherits from `IEnumerable(Of T)` but also offers some more members specific for data manipulation. Although this type can be directly bound to user interface controls for presenting data as much as `IEnumerable`, it does not support data editing. A `Table(Of T)` instead supports adding, removing, and saving objects. To perform LINQ queries using filtering, ordering, and projection operators, you use the LINQ keywords and the same programming techniques provided by the unified programming model of this technology. A little difference from LINQ to Objects is that LINQ to SQL queries return an `IQueryable(Of T)` instead of `IEnumerable(Of T)`. For example, the following LINQ query returns the list of products in which the unit price is greater than 10:

```
'Returns IQueryable(Of Product)
Dim queryByPrice = From prod In northwind.Products
                   Where prod.UnitPrice > 10
                   Select prod
```

You can also convert a query into an ordered collection such as the `List(Of T)` using extension methods:

```
'Returns List(Of Product)
Dim queryByPrice = (From prod In northwind.Products
                    Where prod.UnitPrice > 10
                    Select prod).ToList
```

Remember that *LINQ queries are effectively executed only when used*; therefore, the first example does not run the query until you invoke something on it. The second query is instead executed immediately because of the `ToList` invocation. For example, the following iteration would cause the first query to be executed when the enumerator is invoked:

```
'Returns IQueryable(Of Product)
Dim queryByPrice = From prod In northwind.Products
                   Where prod.UnitPrice > 10
                   Select prod


'Query is executed now
For Each prod In queryByPrice
    Console.WriteLine(prod.ProductName)
Next
```

This iteration shows the list of product names. You can also perform more complex queries that are probably what you will do in your real applications. The following method queries products for the specified category, given the category name taking only products that are not discontinued, finally ordering the result by the number of units in stock for product:

```
Function QueryByCategoryName(ByVal categoryName As String) _
        As List(Of Product)

    Dim query = From categories In northwind.Categories
                Where categories.CategoryName = categoryName
                Join prod In northwind.Products
                On prod.CategoryID Equals categories.CategoryID
                Where prod.Discontinued = False
                Order By prod.UnitsInStock
                Select prod


    Return query.ToList
End Function
```

You can invoke the method and iterate the result as follows:

```
Dim productsList = QueryByCategoryName("Seafood")

For Each prod In productsList
    Console.WriteLine("Product name: {0}, unit price: {1}",
                      prod.ProductName,
                      prod.UnitPrice)
Next
```

The preceding code produces the following result:

```
Product name: Rogede sild, unit price: 9.5000
Product name: Nord-Ost Matjeshering, unit price: 24.8900
Product name: Gravad lax, unit price: 26.0000
Product name: Konbu, unit price: 6.0000
Product name: Ikura, unit price: 31.0000
Product name: Carnarvon Tigers, unit price: 62.5000
Product name: Escargots de Bourgogne, unit price: 13.2500
Product name: Jack's New England Clam Chowder, unit price: 9.6500
Product name: Spegesild, unit price: 12.0000
Product name: Röd Kaviar, unit price: 15.0000
Product name: Inlagd Sill, unit price: 19.0000
Product name: Boston Crab Meat, unit price: 18.4000
```

In other cases, you need to data-bind your result to user interface controls. If you work with Windows Forms applications, a good idea is returning a System.ComponentModel. BindingList(Of T) that is a collection specific for data-binding. So the preceding method could be rewritten as follows:

```
Function QueryByCategoryName(ByVal categoryName As String) _
        As System.ComponentModel.BindingList(Of Product)

    Dim query = From categories In northwind.Categories
                Where categories.CategoryName = categoryName
                Join prod In northwind.Products
                On prod.CategoryID Equals categories.CategoryID
                Where prod.Discontinued = False
                Order By prod.UnitsInStock
                Select prod

    Return New System.ComponentModel.
                BindingList(Of Product)(query.ToList)
End Function
```

Similarly, for WPF applications you would return an `ObservableCollection(Of T)`:

```
Function QueryByCategoryName(ByVal categoryName As String) _
         As System.ObjectModel.ObservableCollection(Of Product)

    Dim query = From categories In northwind.Categories
                Where categories.CategoryName = categoryName
                Join prod In northwind.Products
                On prod.CategoryID Equals categories.CategoryID
                Where prod.Discontinued = False
                Order By prod.UnitsInStock
                Select prod

    Return New System.ObjectModel.ObservableCollection(query)
End Function
```

IMPORTANT NOTE ON LINQ TO SQL QUERIES

When performing LINQ to SQL queries (and LINQ to Entities queries in the next chapter); they can execute only members that have a corresponding type or function in SQL Server and the SQL syntax; otherwise, an exception will be thrown. For example, try to invoke the `ToLowerInvariant` method on the `categories.CategoryName` statement within the Where clause in the previous method. The Visual Basic compiler correctly compiles the code because the .NET Framework correctly recognizes all members. But SQL Server does not have a function that does the same, so a `NotSupportedException` will be thrown at runtime. Therefore, always ensure that .NET members you invoke have a counterpart in SQL Server. Keep in mind this rule also for the next chapter.

You could also take advantage of anonymous types for collecting data from different tables into a unique collection. The following code obtains a list of products for the given category name, picking up some information:

```
Dim customQuery = From prod In northwind.Products
                  Join cat In northwind.Categories On
                  prod.CategoryID Equals cat.CategoryID
                  Order By cat.CategoryID
                  Select New With {.CategoryName = cat.CategoryName,
                                   .ProductName = _
                                   prod.ProductName,
                                   .UnitPrice = prod.UnitPrice,
                                   .Discontinued = _
                                   prod.Discontinued}
```

This query, when executed, returns an `IQueryable(Of Anonymous type)`. As you already know, lists of anonymous types can be iterated or also bound to user interface controls for presenting data but cannot be edited. If you need to create custom objects from query results, such as collecting data from different tables, you first need to implement a class that groups all required data as properties. Consider the following class:

```
Class CustomObject
    Property CategoryName As String
    Property ProductName As String
    Property UnitPrice As Decimal?
    Property Discontinued As Boolean?
End Class--
```

Now you can rewrite the preceding query as follows, changing the Select clause allowing generating a new CustomObject instance:

```
Dim customQuery = From prod In northwind.Products
                  Join cat In northwind.Categories On
                  prod.CategoryID Equals cat.CategoryID
                  Order By cat.CategoryID
                  Select New CustomObject _
                      With {.CategoryName = cat.CategoryName,
                            .ProductName = prod.ProductName,
                            .UnitPrice = prod.UnitPrice,
                            .Discontinued = prod.Discontinued}
```

Now the query returns an IQueryable(Of CustomObject). You can convert it into a typed collection according to your needs or iterate it as in the following example:

```
For Each obj In customQuery
    Console.WriteLine("Category name: {0}, Product name: {1},
                      Unit price: {2}, Discontinued: {3}",
                      obj.CategoryName, obj.ProductName,
                      obj.UnitPrice, obj.Discontinued)
Next
```

Providing this approach instead of working against anonymous types can allow you to bind your collections to user interface controls and provide two-way data binding, or simpler, can provide the ability of programmatically coding Insert/Update/Delete operations as explained in the next section.

Insert/Update/Delete Operations with LINQ

LINQ to SQL is not just querying data but is also a complete infrastructure for data manipulation. This means that you can perform Insert/Update/Delete operations against your object model using LINQ. Let's discuss first how a new entity can be added to an entity set.

Inserting Entities

You instantiate a new entity as any other .NET class and then set its properties. The following code shows how you can add a new `Product` to the `Products` entity set. Notice how the method receives the belonging category as an argument, which is required for setting the one-to-many relationship:

```
Sub AddProduct(ByVal categoryReference As Category)
    Dim aProduct As New Product

    aProduct.ProductName = "Italian spaghetti"
    aProduct.Discontinued = False
    aProduct.QuantityPerUnit = "10"
    aProduct.UnitPrice = 0.4D

    'Setting the relationship
    aProduct.Category = categoryReference

    'Adding the new product to the object model
    northwind.Products.InsertOnSubmit(aProduct)
End Sub
```

You set property values as you would in any other .NET class. Here you have to pay attention to add a non-null value to non-nullable members. In the previous example, `QuantityPerUnit` is a non-nullable and therefore must be assigned with a valid string. You can then omit assigning nullable members. LINQ to SQL can provide auto-increment functionalities on primary keys that in the original SQL Server database implement such a feature. In this example, `ProductID` is not assigned because it is an auto-incrementable primary key. You set a one-to-many relationship assigning the property referring to the other part of the relationship (`Category` in the preceding example) with the instance of the entity that completes the relationship. When this is performed, you invoke the `InsertOnSubmit` method on the instance of the entity set that receives the new entity (respectively `Products` and `Product` in our example). This method saves the new data into the object model, but it does not send data to the underlying database until you invoke the `SubmitChanges` method, as follows:

```
Sub SaveChanges()
    Try
        northwind.SubmitChanges()

    Catch ex As SqlClient.SqlException

    Catch ex As Exception

    End Try
End Sub
```

This saves data to the database. If something fails, you need to handle a `SqlClient.SqlException` exception. Now add an invocation to the custom `SaveChanges` method after the `InsertOnSubmit` one. At this point you can invoke the custom `AddProduct` method for programmatically adding a new product that must be bound to a specific category because of the one-to-many relationship. Working with a Console application, you can add such an invocation within the `Main` method. The following code demonstrates this:

```
Dim cerealsCategory As Category = _
    northwind.Categories.Single(Function(cat) _
    cat.CategoryName = "Grains/Cereals")


AddProduct(cerealsCategory)
```

You need the instance of the category you want to pass to the method. To accomplish this, you can invoke the `Single` extension method on the categories' collection to get the unique category with the specified name, taking advantage of a lambda expression. As an alternative, you can directly pass a lambda as an argument as follows:

```
AddProduct(northwind.Categories.
        Single(Function(cat) cat.CategoryName = "Grains/Cereals"))
```

Both solutions accomplish the same result.

GETTING INSTANCES IN CLIENT APPLICATIONS

In client applications such as Windows Forms, WPF, or Silverlight, getting an instance of an entity is even simpler. You just need to retrieve the current element of the data control (for example, `ComboBox`, `DataGrid`, or `DataGridView`) or, even better, the current selected item in the data source bridge control, such as `BindingSource` or `CollectionViewSource`.

If you run this code and everything works fine, your new product is added to the `Products` table of the `Northwind` database when the `DataContext.SubmitChanges` method is invoked and a relationship with the `Grains/Cereals` category is also set. You can easily verify this by opening Server Explorer and then expanding the Northwind Tables folder; then right-click the **Products** table and select **Show Table Data**. (If you have a local copy of the Northwind database instead, you need to double-click the database copy available in the Bin\Debug or Bin\Release folder to open it in Server Explorer.) As an alternative, you can open the new SQL Server Object Explorer tool window, expand the Northwind database, and then right-click the Products table and select View data. Figure 24.7 reproduces the scenario, showing also the new product, this time in SQL Server Object Explorer.

One thing that you need to remember is to check whether an entity already exists to prevent malicious runtime exceptions. To accomplish this, you can take advantage of the `Single` extension method that throws an exception if the specified entity does not exist; therefore, it can be added. The `AddProduct` method can be rewritten as follows (see comments in code):

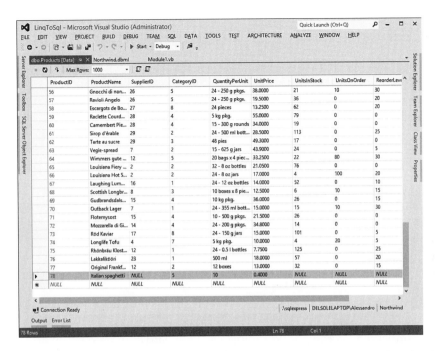

FIGURE 24.7   Checking that the new product has been correctly saved to the database.

```vb
Sub AddProduct(ByVal categoryReference As Category)
    Try
        Dim productCheck = northwind.Products.
                            Single(Function(prod) _
                            prod.ProductName = "Italian spaghetti")
        productCheck = Nothing


        'the Product does not exist, so add it
    Catch ex As InvalidOperationException
        Dim aProduct As New Product

        aProduct.ProductName = "Italian spaghetti"
        aProduct.Discontinued = False
        aProduct.QuantityPerUnit = "10"

aProduct.UnitPrice = 0.4D
        aProduct.CategoryID = categoryReference.CategoryID

        'Setting the relationship
        aProduct.Category = categoryReference
```

```
'Adding the new product to the object model
northwind.Products.InsertOnSubmit(aProduct)
SaveChanges()


    End Try
End Sub
```

Now that you know how to create and save data, it's also important to understand how
updates can be performed.

Updating Entities

Updating existing entities is even easier than adding new ones. First, you need to obtain
the instance of the entity you want to update. When you get the instance, you edit its
properties and then invoke the `DataContext.SubmitChanges` method. The following code
provides an example:

```
Sub UpdateProduct(ByVal productInstance As Product)

    'Throws an exception if a null value is passed
    If productInstance Is Nothing Then
        Throw New NullReferenceException
    Else
        With productInstance
            .ProductName = "Italian Linguine"
            .UnitsInStock = 100
        End With
    End If


    SaveChanges()
End Sub
```

This method requires an instance of the `Product` entity to be updated. To get an instance
of the desired product, you can still take advantage of a lambda, but this time exception
handling is reverted, as you can see from the following snippet:

```
Try
    UpdateProduct(northwind.Products.
                Single(Function(prod) prod.
```

```
                ProductName = "Italian spaghetti"))

    'The specified product does not exist
Catch ex As InvalidOperationException

End Try
```

When the `NorthwindDataContext.SubmitChanges` method is invoked, data is updated to the underlying database. Notice that you can update multiple entities and the `SubmitChanges` method sends changes all at once. You can easily check for correct updates following the steps shown in the previous paragraph and summarized in Figure 24.7.

Deleting Entities

Deleting an entity works similarly to update, at least for retrieving the entity instance. Deletion is performed by invoking the `DeleteOnSubmit` method, which works opposite to the `InsertOnSubmit`. The following is an example, which also checks whether the entity exists:

```
Sub DeleteProduct(ByVal productInstance As Product)

    If productInstance Is Nothing Then
        Throw New NullReferenceException
    Else
        northwind.Products.DeleteOnSubmit(productInstance)
        SaveChanges()
    End If
End Sub
```

Remember how the custom `SaveChanges` method invokes the `NorthwindDataContext.SubmitChanges` one. The following code shows invoking the previous method for performing a product deletion:

```
Try
    DeleteProduct(northwind.Products.
              Single(Function(prod) prod.
              ProductName = "Italian spaghetti"))

    'The specified product does not exist
Catch ex As InvalidOperationException

End Try
```

Similarly to `InsertAllOnSubmit`, you can also invoke `DeleteAllOnSubmit` to remove multiple entities from the object model.

Mapping Stored Procedures

LINQ to SQL allows mapping stored procedures from the SQL Server database into a .NET method that you can use within your object model and that is managed by the running instance of the `DataContext`. In this way, you do not lose the advantage of stored procedures when working with LINQ. To map a stored procedure, go back to the Visual Studio Designer for LINQ to SQL and ensure that the Methods pane is opened on the right side of the designer; then open Server Explorer, expand the database structure, and expand the Stored Procedures folder. After you've done this, drag the stored procedure you need onto the Methods pane. Figure 24.8 shows how to accomplish this against the Northwind database of the current example.

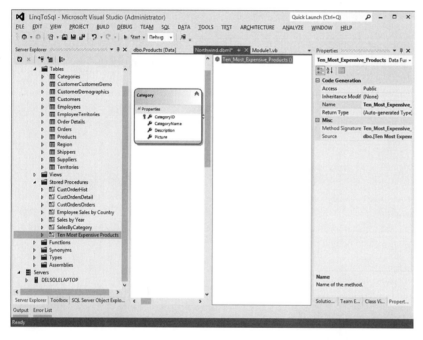

FIGURE 24.8   Mapping a stored procedure to a .NET method in LINQ to SQL.

Notice also how the Properties window shows method properties, such as access qualifier and signature. The Return type property is set as auto-generated because the result is determined according to the stored procedure type. Some procedures return a single result value, and therefore the returned type is `ISingleResult(Of T)`. Other ones can return multiple result values, and therefore the returned type is `IMultipleResult(Of T)`. Behind the scenes, a stored procedure is mapped into a method, but such a method also requires a support class mapping types used by the stored procedure. The following code is excerpted from the Northwind.designer.vb file and shows the class definition:

```vb
Partial Public Class Ten_Most_Expensive_ProductsResult

    Private _TenMostExpensiveProducts As String

    Private _UnitPrice As System.Nullable(Of Decimal)

    Public Sub New()
        MyBase.New
    End Sub

    <Global.System.Data.Linq.Mapping.
            ColumnAttribute(Storage:="_TenMostExpensiveProducts",
            DbType:="NVarChar(40) NOT NULL", CanBeNull:=False)> _
    Public Property TenMostExpensiveProducts() As String
        Get
            Return Me._TenMostExpensiveProducts
        End Get
        Set(ByVal value As String)
            If (String.Equals(Me._TenMostExpensiveProducts, value) = False)
            Then
                Me._TenMostExpensiveProducts = value
            End If
        End Set
    End Property

    <Global.System.Data.Linq.Mapping.ColumnAttribute(Storage:="_UnitPrice",
            DbType:="Money")> _
    Public Property UnitPrice() As System.Nullable(Of Decimal)
        Get
            Return Me._UnitPrice
        End Get
        Set(ByVal value As System.Nullable(Of Decimal))
            If (Me._UnitPrice.Equals(Value) = False) Then
                Me._UnitPrice = Value
            End If
        End Set
    End Property
End Class
```

The class works like other auto-generated classes in that it sets or returns values taken from the data source. The method that actually performs the action is mapped as follows within the `NorthwindDataContext` class definition:

```vb
<Global.System.Data.Linq.Mapping.
        FunctionAttribute(Name:="dbo.[Ten Most Expensive Products]")> _
Public Function Ten_Most_Expensive_Products() As _
```

```
        ISingleResult(Of Ten_Most_Expensive_ProductsResult)
    Dim result As IExecuteResult = Me.ExecuteMethodCall(Me,
                                CType(MethodInfo.GetCurrentMethod,
                                MethodInfo))
    Return CType(result.ReturnValue,
            ISingleResult(Of Ten_Most_Expensive_ProductsResult))
End Function
```

The `System.Data.Linq.Mapping.FunctionAttribute` attribute decorates the method signature with the original stored procedure name. As you can see, this particular method returns an `ISingleResult(Of T)`, and invocation to the stored procedure is performed via reflection. Invoking in code, a stored procedure is as simple as in other methods usage. The following code takes an `ISingleResult(Of T)`:

```
'Gets the list of the ten most expensive
'products from the Products table
Dim result = northwind.Ten_Most_Expensive_Products
```

You can then iterate the result to get a list of the products as in the following example:

```
For Each r In result
    Console.WriteLine(r.UnitPrice)
Next
```

This simple iteration produces the following result:

```
263,5000
123,7900
97,0000
81,0000
62,5000
55,0000
53,0000
49,3000
46,0000
45,6000
```

Notice that an `ISingleResult` can be iterated only once; otherwise, you get an `InvalidOperationException`. If you plan to access this result multiple times, the only way is to convert the result into a generic collection such as the `List(Of T)`. The following code converts the stored procedure result into a `List`, making possible iterations more than once:

```
'Gets the list of the ten most expensive
'products from the Products table into
'a List(Of T)
Dim result = northwind.Ten_Most_Expensive_Products.ToList
```

Also notice that converting to `IQueryable(Of T)` will not allow the result to be accessed more than once.

Using the Log

LINQ to SQL sends SQL instructions each time it has to perform an operation on our demand. This is accomplished via its complex infrastructure that relies on the .NET Framework. By the way, as a developer you may be interested in understanding what really happens behind the scenes and in getting information about the real SQL instructions sent to SQL Server. Luckily, you can use a SQL log that allows showing SQL instructions. You need to set the `DataContext.Log` property as follows, before taking actions you want to inspect:

```
northwind.Log = Console.Out
```

If you want to monitor everything happening, add the preceding code after the creation of the `DataContext` instance. If you apply this code before running the first example shown in the "Insert/Update/Delete operations with LINQ" section, you get the result shown in Figure 24.9.

FIGURE 24.9   Showing the LINQ to SQL log result.

As you can see, this is useful because you get an idea about the actual SQL instructions sent by LINQ to SQL to SQL Server. The `DataContext.Log` property is of type `System.IO.TextWriter`; therefore, you can assign it with a stream pointing to a file on disk if you want the SQL output to be redirected to a file instead of the Console window.

Advanced LINQ to SQL

While you become familiar with LINQ to SQL, you understand how it allows performing usual data operations in a strongly typed way. Because of this, you also see the need to perform other operations that you are used to making in classical data development, such as data validation and handling optimistic concurrency. The next section describes this but also something more.

Custom Validations

Validating data is one of the most important activities in every data access system, so LINQ to SQL provides its own methodologies, too. To accomplish data validation, you can take advantage of partial methods. You might remember that in Chapter 20, "Advanced Language Features," you got a practical example of partial methods when discussing LINQ to SQL. Validation rules are useful in LINQ to SQL for two main reasons: The first one is that they enable you to understand whether supplied data is compliant to your requirements; the second one is that they allow you to check whether supplied data has a SQL Server type counterpart. The following code example demonstrates both examples. Imagine you want to add a new product to the object model and then save changes to the database, as you already did following the steps in the first part of the previous section. If you take a look at the `QuantityPerUnit` property—for example, recurring to the Visual Studio Designer—you notice that it is mapped to a `string` .NET type, but its SQL Server counterpart type is `NVarChar(20)`, meaning that the content of the property is a string that must not be longer than 20 characters; otherwise, saving changes to SQL Server will be unsuccessful. To provide validation rules, the first step is to add a partial class. With that said, right-click the project name in Solution Explorer, then select **Add New Class**, and, when requested, supply the new class name, for example **Product.vb**. When the new class is added to the project, add the `Partial` keyword as follows:

```
Partial Public Class Product


End Class
```

At this point we can implement a partial method that performs validation. Because partial methods' signatures are defined within the Northwind.designer.vb code file, here we can implement the full method body as follows:

```
Private Sub OnQuantityPerUnitChanging(ByVal value As String)
    If value.Length > 20 Then Throw New _
        ArgumentException _
        ("Quantity per unit must be no longer than 20 characters")
End Sub
```

Notice that you have to handle methods whose names end with `Changing`, which maps an event that is raised before changes are sent to the object model. The code checks for the length of the supplied value, and if it does not match the `NVarChar(20)` type of SQL Server, it throws an `ArgumentException`. To understand how it works, consider the following code that creates a new product and then attempts to write changes:

```
Sub AddProduct(ByVal categoryReference As Category)
    Try
        Dim productCheck = northwind.Products.
                        Single(Function(prod) _
                        prod.ProductName = "Italian spaghetti")
        productCheck = Nothing
```

```
          'the Product does not exist, so add it
     Catch ex As InvalidOperationException

        Try
            Dim aProduct As New Product

            aProduct.ProductName = "Italian spaghetti"
            aProduct.Discontinued = False

            'The string is 22 characters long
            aProduct.QuantityPerUnit = "1000000000000000000000"
            aProduct.UnitPrice = 0.4D
            aProduct.CategoryID = categoryReference.CategoryID

            'Setting the relationship
            aProduct.Category = categoryReference

            'Adding the new product to the object model
            northwind.Products.InsertOnSubmit(aProduct)
            SaveChanges()

        Catch e As ArgumentException
            Console.WriteLine(e.Message.ToString)
            Exit Try
        Catch e As Exception

        End Try
    End Try
End Sub
```

Notice how a nested `Try..End Try` block has been provided to handle eventual `ArgumentNullException` errors coming from validation. You can still invoke the `AddProduct` method in the previous section as follows:

```
AddProduct(northwind.Categories.
           Single(Function(cat) cat.CategoryName = "Grains/Cereals"))
```

If you now try to run the code, you get an error message advising that the `QuantityPerUnit` content cannot be longer than 20 characters. In this way, you can control the content of your data but also ensure that data matches the related SQL Server type. By using this technique, you can perform validation on each data you want.

DATA VALIDATION AND THE UI

One common scenario is implementing the `IDataErrorInfo` interface in partial classes so that its members can send notifications to the user interface. Windows Forms and WPF applications can take advantage of notifications for presenting error messages in ways different from a simple messages box. The official documentation for the interface is available here: http://msdn.microsoft.com/en-us/library/system.componentmodel. idataerrorinfo(VS.110).aspx.

Handling Optimistic Concurrency

Optimistic concurrency is a scenario in which multiple clients send changes to the database simultaneously. LINQ to SQL allows resolving optimistic concurrency with the `DataContext.ChangeConflicts.ResolveAll` method. Such method receives an argument that is an enumeration of type `System.Data.Linq.RefreshMode` and allows resolving the exception with one of the enumeration members summarized in Table 24.1.

TABLE 24.1   RefreshMode Enumeration Members

Member	Description
KeepCurrentValues	If any changes, keeps original values in the database
KeepChanges	If any changes, keeps changes but other values are updated with original database values
OverwriteCurrentValues	Overrides all current values with original values from database

The following is an example of handling optimistic concurrency, providing a revisited version of the previously utilized `SaveChanges` custom method:

```
Sub SaveChanges()
    Try
        northwind.SubmitChanges()

    Catch ex As System.Data.Linq.ChangeConflictException

        northwind.ChangeConflicts.ResolveAll(Data.Linq.RefreshMode.
                                    KeepCurrentValues)
        northwind.SubmitChanges()
    Catch ex As SqlClient.SqlException

    Catch ex As Exception

    End Try
End Sub
```

Notice first how a `ChangeConflictException` is handled. Here the `ChangeConflicts.ResolveAll` method is required to resolve concurrency. The `KeepCurrentValues` argument allows keeping original values in the database. Also notice how a subsequent invocation to `SubmitChanges` is made. This is necessary because the first invocation caused the exception; therefore, another execution must be attempted.

Using SQL Syntax Against Entities

LINQ to SQL also allows writing SQL code against entities so that you can still take advantage of the object model if you prefer the old-fashioned way of manipulating data. The `DataContext` class offers an instance method named `ExecuteQuery(Of T)` that allows sending SQL instructions in string form. For example, the following code retrieves a list of products for the `Grain/Cereals` category, ordered by product name:

```
Sub DirectSqlDemo()

    Dim products = northwind.
        ExecuteQuery(Of Product)("SELECT * FROM PRODUCTS WHERE " & _
                                 "CATEGORYID='5' ORDER BY PRODUCTNAME")


    For Each prod In products
        Console.WriteLine(prod.ProductName)
    Next
End Sub
```

`ExecuteQuery(Of T)` returns an `IEnumerable(Of T)` that you can then treat as you like, according to LINQ specifications. You can also send SQL instructions directly to the database, invoking the `ExecuteCommand` method. This method returns no value and allows performing Insert/Update/Delete operations against the data. For example, the following code updates the product name of a product:

```
northwind.ExecuteCommand("UPDATE PRODUCTS SET " & _
        "PRODUCTNAME='Italian mozzarella' WHERE PRODUCTID='72'")
```

If you then want to check that everything work correctly, get the instance of the product and get information:

```
Dim updatedProduct = _
    northwind.Products.First(Function(prod) prod.ProductID = 72)

'Returns "Italian mozzarella"
Console.WriteLine(updatedProduct.ProductName)
```

Remember: Sending SQL instructions can prevent you from taking advantage of compile-time checking offered by the LINQ syntax and exposes your code to possible runtime errors. Be aware of this.

LINQ to SQL with SQL Server Compact Edition 3.5

LINQ to SQL is not limited to querying and manipulating data from SQL Server databases, but you can also perform the same operations against SQL Server Compact Edition 3.5 databases (with .sdf extensions). There are some reasons to mention SQL Server Compact with LINQ to SQL. The first reason is that you might want to use a lightweight local database in your applications and SQL Compact is a good choice. The second reason is that

SQL Server Compact 3.5 can be used also in Windows Phone 7.5 apps for local data access. In Chapter 38, "Building Apps for Windows Phone 7.5," we introduce the development for this operating system; it is important to know how to create LINQ to SQL classes for SQL Compact. Visual Studio 2012 ships with SQL Server Compact Edition 4.0, but this new version does not support LINQ to SQL (more precisely, the SQLMetal.exe command line tool does not support SQL Compact 4.0). So you will be able to use LINQ with SQL Server Compact 3.5, which is also the one you still use with Windows Phone. If you have installed Visual Studio 2010 on your machine you already have version 3.5, otherwise you can download it from http://www.microsoft.com/en-us/download/details.aspx?id=5783. The big difference is that generating LINQ to SQL classes for this engine is not supported by the IDE, so you have to perform a couple of steps manually. First, run the Visual Studio command prompt; if you run Windows 7, it is under **Start**, **All Programs**, **Microsoft Visual Studio 2012, Visual Studio Tools**. If you run Windows 8, you can use the Search charm and type VS 2012; the one you will select is the **VS 2012 Cross Tools** one. When you get the command line, move to the folder where the SQL Compact database is available. For example, you can play with the Northwind database in the compact edition version. Type the following command line:

```
CD C:\Program Files\Microsoft SQL Server Compact Edition\v3.5\Samples
```

Next, type the following command line:

```
SQLMetal /dbml:Northwind.dbml /language:VisualBasic Northwind.sdf
```

This step generates a .dbml file, which is a complete LINQ to SQL class. To create a LINQ to SQL project supporting your .sdf database, you create a Visual Basic project, right-click the project name in Solution Explorer, and then select the Add Existing Item command. When the dialog box appears, select the newly created LINQ to SQL class and you're done. Remember that you can use all LINQ to SQL possibilities with SQL Server Compact Edition databases as well, so everything you learned in this chapter is also applicable to SQL Compact files. Of course, there are limitations due to the database's structure (for example SQL Compact databases do not support stored procedures), but this is something that is related more to SQL Server than Visual Basic. By the way, LINQ to SQL is the same in both SQL Server and SQL Compact.

LOCAL DATA ACCESS IN WINDOWS PHONE WITH LINQ TO SQL

The author of this book has published a detailed article on the Visual Basic Developer Center, explaining how to use SQL Compact 3.5 and LINQ to SQL in Windows Phone 7.5 apps. It is available at this address: http://msdn.microsoft.com/en-us/vstudio/hh758260.aspx.

SQL COMPACT 3.5 AND VISUAL STUDIO 2012

Visual Studio 2012 provides full support for SQL Server Compact 4.0 but does not support SQL Compact 3.5. This means that you will have no limitations in using SQL Compact 4.0 in both client and web applications (in VS 2010 with Service Pack 1 only web applications were allowed), but you will not be able to use SQL Compact 3.5 directly. Limitations with the IDE exist, but you can write code that establishes a connection to SQL Compact 3.5 manually as it is for the current example.

Writing the Connection String

Different from classic LINQ to SQL, when you work with SQL Compact databases, you need to manually pass the connection string to the database; this is because the class generation could not take advantage of the IDE automation. This means that when you declare an instance of the `DataContext` class, you need to pass the connection string. For example, instantiating the `DataContext` for Northwind would be something like this:

```
Private NorthwindContext As New _
        Northwind("Data Source=C:\My Folder\Northwind.sdf")
```

Summary

LINQ to SQL is a built-in object relational mapping engine for Microsoft SQL Server databases. The engine maps database information such as tables and columns into .NET objects such as classes and properties, enabling you to work in a disconnected fashion against an object model rather than against the database. Mapped classes are known as entities. Adding LINQ to SQL classes to your projects can provide the ability of using LINQ for both querying entities and performing CRUD operations via specific methods offered by the `DataContext` class. This is responsible for managing the connection and entities during an application's lifetime, including keeping track of changes that can be submitted to the database in one shot. LINQ to SQL also offers a trace log to understand which SQL instructions were sent to the database and provides the ability of handling optimistic concurrency as much as validating data by taking advantage of partial methods. Finally, you can still write your queries the old-fashioned way by sending SQL instructions directly to the data source. LINQ to SQL is useful if you need to work with a lightweight and if you are limited to SQL Server databases. If you instead need something more flexible and powerful, you should consider the ADO.NET Entity Framework discussed in Chapter 26.

LINQ to DataSets

For many years datasets have been the main data access technology for .NET developers, including Visual Basic programmers. Although the most recent versions of the .NET Framework introduced new object relational mapping technologies such as LINQ to SQL and ADO.NET Entity Framework, datasets are still very diffused especially in older applications. Because of this, Microsoft produced a LINQ standard provider that is specific for querying datasets: *LINQ to DataSets*. In this chapter you do not find information on manipulating datasets (refer to Chapter 21, "Introducing ADO.NET and DataSets"); instead you learn to query existing datasets using LINQ, and you become familiar with some peculiarities of this provider that are not available in the previous ones.

Querying Datasets with LINQ

LINQ to DataSets is the standard LINQ provider for querying datasets and is offered by the `System.DataSet. DataSetExtensions` namespace. Querying means that LINQ can only get information for datasets but not for manipulating them. If you need to add, remove, replace, or persist data versus datasets, you need to use old-fashioned techniques. Instead you can improve getting information using LINQ. You use datasets in Windows or web applications (except for Silverlight applications that do not support datasets). This chapter shows you code within a Console application. This is because we need a high level of abstraction so that all the code you see here can be used in both Windows and web applications. To complete the proposed examples, follow these steps:

▶ Create a new Console application and name the project **LinqToDataSets**.

▶ Establish a connection to the Northwind database via the **Server Explorer** window.

▶ Add a new dataset including the Customers, Orders, and Order Details tables.

When done, you need to manually write some code that populates the dataset. Usually such tasks are performed by Visual Studio if you generate a dataset within Windows Forms or WPF applications; however, in this case you need to do it. Write the following code that declares three TableAdapter objects and populates them with data coming from tables:

```
Imports LinqToDataSets.NorthwindDatasetTableAdapters

Module Module1

    Dim NwindDataSet As New NorthwindDataSet

    Dim NorthwindDataSetCustomersTableAdapter As CustomersTableAdapter _
        = New CustomersTableAdapter()
    Dim NorthwindDataSetOrdersTableAdapter As OrdersTableAdapter _
        = New OrdersTableAdapter()
    Dim NorthwindDataSetOrderDetailsTableAdapter As _
        Order_DetailsTableAdapter _
        = New Order_DetailsTableAdapter

    Sub Main()
        NorthwindDataSetCustomersTableAdapter.Fill(NwindDataSet.Customers)
        NorthwindDataSetOrdersTableAdapter.Fill(NwindDataSet.Orders)
        NorthwindDataSetOrderDetailsTableAdapter.
                Fill(NwindDataSet.Order_Details)
    End Sub
End Module
```

Now you are ready to query your dataset with LINQ. LINQ syntax is the same as for other providers but with a few exceptions:

▶ LINQ queries DataTable objects, each representing a table in the database.

▶ LINQ to DataSets queries return EnumerableRowCollection(Of DataRow) instead of IEnumerable(Of T) (or IQueryable(Of T)), in which DataRow is the base class for strongly typed rows. The only exception is when you create anonymous types within queries. In such situations, queries return IEnumerable(Of Anonymous type).

You can use LINQ to retrieve a list of objects. For example, consider the following code that retrieves the list of orders for the specified customer:

```
Private Sub QueryOrders(ByVal CustomerID As String)

    Dim query = From ord In NwindDataSet.Orders
              Where ord.CustomerID = CustomerID
              Select ord
End Sub
```

As you can see, the syntax is the same as other providers. The query variable type is inferred by the compiler as `EnumerableRowCollection(Of OrdersRow)`. There is a particular difference: The query result is not directly usable if you want to provide the ability of editing data. As it is, the query can only be presented; you need first to convert it into a `DataView` using the `AsDataView` extension method. The following code rewrites the preceding query, providing the ability of binding data to a control:

```
Dim query = (From ord In NwindDataSet.Orders
            Where ord.CustomerID = CustomerID
            Select ord).AsDataView
```

When you invoke `AsDataView`, you can bind a LINQ query to any user control that supports data binding, such as the Windows Forms `BindingSource`. Don't invoke instead `AsDataView` if you simply need to get information without the need of manipulating data (for example, with a `For..Each` loop). You can use other query operators to get different information; the following code shows how you can get the number of orders made by the specified customer using the `Aggregate` clause:

```
Private Function QueryOrders(ByVal CustomerID As String) As Integer

    Dim ordersByCustomer = Aggregate ord In NwindDataSet.Orders
                         Where ord.CustomerID = CustomerID
                         Into Count()

    Return ordersByCustomer
End Function
```

STANDARD QUERY OPERATORS

LINQ to DataSets allows the querying of datasets using standard query operators offered by LINQ to Objects; because of this, the chapter does not explore standard operators. It also provides some additions discussed in the next section.

Building Complex Queries with Anonymous Types

Same as you would do with other LINQ providers, you can build complex queries taking advantage of anonymous types in LINQ to DataSets. The following code shows how you can join information from the `Orders` and `Order_Details` tables retrieving information on order details for each order made by the given customer. Projection is accomplished by generating anonymous types:

```
Private Sub QueryOrderDetails(ByVal CustomerID As String)

    Dim query = From ord In NwindDataSet.Orders
                Where ord.CustomerID = CustomerID
                Join det In NwindDataSet.Order_Details
                On det.OrderID Equals ord.OrderID
                Select New With {.OrderID = ord.OrderID,
                                 .OrderDate = ord.OrderDate,
                                 .ShippedDate = ord.ShippedDate,
                                 .ShipCity = ord.ShipCity,
                                 .ProductID = det.ProductID,
                                 .Quantity = det.Quantity,
                                 .UnitPrice = det.UnitPrice}
End Sub
```

The query variable is of type `IEnumerable(Of Anonymous type)`, which is different from normal queries. Remember that `IEnumerable` results cannot be edited; therefore, you are limited to presenting data through specific controls such as `BindingSource`. In LINQ to DataSets `IEnumerable(Of Anonymous type)`, queries do not support `AsDataView`; therefore, you should consider creating a new `DataTable`, which is shown in the first example of the next section.

LINQ to DataSets' Extension Methods

As a specific provider for datasets, LINQ to DataSets exposes some special extension methods generally required when converting from data rows collections into other objects. In this section you get an overview of methods and their usage.

Understanding `CopyToDataTable`

Tables from databases are represented within datasets via `DataTable` objects. You can create custom tables in code using a special extension method named `CopyToDataTable`, which can convert from `EnumerableRowCollection (Of T)` into a new `DataTable`. Imagine you want to create a subset of orders from the `Orders` table and that you want to create a new table with this subset of information. The following code accomplishes this:

```
Dim query = (From ord In NwindDataSet.Orders
            Where String.IsNullOrEmpty(ord.ShipCountry) = False
            Select ord).CopyToDataTable
query.TableName = "FilteredOrders"
NwindDataSet.Tables.Add(query)
```

The query retrieves only the orders where the `ShipCountry` property contains something and creates a new `DataTable` with this piece of information. The query variable's type is `DataTable`; therefore, you can treat this new object as you would versus a classical table as demonstrated by assigning the `TableName` property and by the addition of the new table to the dataset. You can also create custom tables with more granularities by taking advantage of anonymous types. For example, imagine you want to create a table that wraps information from both the `Orders` and `Order_Details` tables. You need to manually create a new table, add columns, perform the query, and then add rows. The following code demonstrates this:

```
Private Function CreateCustomTable() As DataTable

    'Create a new table
    Dim customTable As New DataTable("Custom_orders")

    'Add columns
    With customTable
        With .Columns
            .Add("OrderID", GetType(Integer))
            .Add("Quantity", GetType(Short))
            .Add("UnitPrice", GetType(Decimal))
        End With
    End With

    'Retrieve data from different sources
    Dim query2 = From ord In NwindDataSet.Orders,
                     det In NwindDataSet.Order_Details
                 Where det.Quantity > 50
                 Select New With {.OrderID = ord.OrderID,
                                  .Quantity = det.Quantity,
                                  .UnitPrice = det.UnitPrice}

    'Add rows
    For Each item In query2
        customTable.Rows.Add(New Object() {item.OrderID,
                                           item.Quantity,
                                           item.UnitPrice})
    Next

    Return customTable
End Function
```

Notice how the new table is created in code and how columns are added. The `Columns`. `Add` method allows specifying the type (via the `GetType` keyword) for each column. We just want to retrieve the `OrderID`, `Quantity`, and `UnitPrice` information only for those products whose quantity is greater than 50. The LINQ query returns an `IEnumerable(Of`

`Anonymous types`). Because of this, you need to iterate the collection and instantiate a new array of `Object` for each row, containing the specified information. When you have the new table populated, you can add it to the dataset and use it as any other table.

Understanding `Field(Of T)` and `SetField(Of T)`

The `Field` generic extension method allows retrieving a strongly typed form for all values from a given column within a table. `Field` receives as an argument the column name or the column index and then tries to convert values in a column into the specified type. Because of this, when using `Field` you should also predict some exceptions, such as `InvalidCastException` that can occur if the conversion fails, `NullReferenceException` if `Field` attempts to access a non-`Nullable` null value, and `IndexOutOfRangeException` if you pass an invalid index for the column. The following code retrieves all strongly typed versions of orders' data:

```
Private Sub FieldDemo()

    Try

        Dim query = From ord In NwindDataSet.Orders
                    Where ord.Field(Of Date)("ShippedDate") < Date.Today
                    Select New With {
                                .OrderID = ord.
                                        Field(Of Integer)("OrderID"),
                                .OrderDate = ord.
                                        Field(Of Date)("OrderDate"),
                                .ShipCountry = ord.
                                        Field(Of String) _
                                        ("ShipCountry")
                            }
    Catch ex As InvalidCastException
        'Conversion failed

    Catch ex As NullReferenceException
        'Attempt to access to a non nullable
        'null object

    Catch ex As IndexOutOfRangeException
        'Wrong index

    Catch ex As Exception

    End Try
End Sub
```

In addition; a `SetField` method enables you to put a strongly typed value into the specified field, and that works like this:

```
ord.SetField(Of Date)("OrderDate",Date.Today)
```

Summary

Although Microsoft is making lots of investments in much more modern technologies such as ADO.NET Entity Framework, datasets are a data source that you can find in tons of applications. Because of this, the .NET Framework provides the LINQ to DataSets provider to enable the querying of datasets via the LINQ syntax. Datasets are particular; therefore, there are specific extension methods that you can use versus datasets, such as `CopyToDataTable` that generates a new `DataTable` from a LINQ query and `Field` that allows getting strongly typed information from columns. In this chapter you got an overview of how LINQ works over datasets, and how you can use retrieved information in your applications.

25

CHAPTER 26

Introducing ADO.NET Entity Framework

Most applications require accessing data. This is a sentence that you already read in this book and probably in many other places, but it is so important. Before the .NET Framework 3.5, developers had to access data using DataSets or they were required to work directly against the database; then they had a new opportunity with LINQ to SQL. This was revolutionary because it proposes a conceptual object model that enables you to work with managed objects, being responsible for whatever is necessary in managing also the underlying database. But it has some limitations. It supports only SQL Server databases; it does not support many-to-many relationships; and it does not provide support for modeling data before creating a database. To provide a modern data platform based on the idea of the conceptual object model, Microsoft created the ADO. NET Entity Framework that was first introduced as a library in .NET Framework 3.5 SP 1 and that has become part of the .NET Framework since version 4.0. In this chapter you get started with the Entity Framework by learning to perform the most common operations on data and understanding the basics of such a platform, also learning some new APIs that change the way data models are generated and that make code much cleaner and simpler.

Introducing Entity Framework

ADO.NET Entity Framework is a modern data platform included in .NET Framework 4.5, also known as EF 5. It is an object relational mapping engine, but it is powerful, absolutely more flexible and powerful than LINQ to SQL. It enables you to create conceptual object models, known as Entity Data Models (EDMs) that provide a high level of abstraction from the underlying data source. Abstraction means that tables and tables' columns within a database are mapped into .NET classes and properties, meaning that you do not work against the database but with .NET objects that represent the database so that you can take advantage of manipulating .NET objects under the Common Language Runtime (CLR) control, with IntelliSense support and the background compiler check. You do not need to have knowledge of the database infrastructure, although this is always suggested because the Entity Framework is responsible for communications between the object model and the data source. It provides the entire necessary infrastructure so that you can focus only on writing code for manipulating and querying data. Working with an abstractive object model means taking advantage of all the .NET Framework's power and all available Visual Studio instrumentation. The .NET Framework 4.5 introduces new programming patterns to the Entity Framework, more specifically it introduces the so-called Code First approach, which enables you coding your model independently from the database, that can be generated later. Differently from its predecessor, Visual Studio 2012 now generates Entity Data Models based on Code First's APIs. In the next section, you start with the EF by understanding Entity Data Models and the new classes provided by the .NET Framework 4.5. In the second part of this chapter, you will see how to code your data models and you will get a recap about the previous APIs. In fact, these are still important in scenarios like the WCF RIA Services for Silverlight.

Understanding Entity Data Models

The best way to understand EDMs is to create one. First, create a new Visual Basic project for the Console and name it **EntityFramework**. Save the new project immediately, so that all references required by the EF are updated. The next steps require the Northwind database that you installed in Chapter 21, "Introducing ADO.NET and DataSets." Right-click on the project name in Solution Explorer and select **Add New Item**. When the Add New Item dialog box appears, move to the Data Node, select the **ADO.NET Entity Data Model** item template, and name it **Northwind.edmx**, as shown in Figure 26.1.

When you click **Add**, the Entity Data Model Wizard starts. In the first screen you need to specify the source for the EDM. With EF 4 and EF 5, you can create EDMs starting from an existing database or modeling custom EDMs from scratch. Select the existing database options, as shown in Figure 26.2. This is also known as Database First.

The next screen is important because it requires the specification of the database. You can click **New Connection** or select one of the favorite connections from the appropriate combo box. Figure 26.3 shows how on my machine the connection points to Northwind as it is available on SQL Server.

Notice how the connection string is represented in the dialog box. Also notice that this is not the usual connection string because it contains metadata information that will be clearer when the EDMs' infrastructure is explained. You decide whether to save the string in the configuration file. The next step is crucial because you have to select what database objects you want to be mapped into the EDM. Figure 26.4 shows the dialog box.

FIGURE 26.1   Adding a new Entity Data Model.

FIGURE 26.2   Creating an EDM from an existing database.

FIGURE 26.3   Choosing the database and connection settings.

FIGURE 26.4   Selecting objects for the new EDM.

FOREIGN KEY COLUMNS SUPPORT

The ADO.NET Entity Framework supports mapping foreign keys from the database into the model. This is the reason you find a check box in the Entity Data Model wizard, as shown in Figure 26.4. Select the check box to add the foreign key's support.

Also notice how you are required to specify a model namespace. This is important because the namespace stores Visual Basic definitions for objects that are mapped to database objects, which are explained later. You can write your own or leave the default identifier unchanged. At the moment, just choose the `Categories` and `Products` tables and then Click `Finish`. After a few moments, when Visual Studio generates the code for the object model, the EDM Designer opens as shown in Figure 26.5.

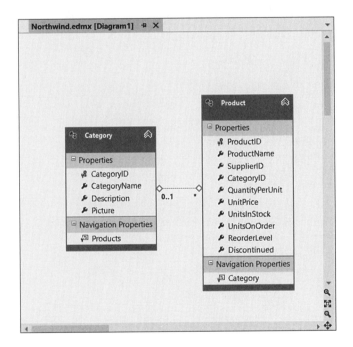

FIGURE 26.5   The EDM Designer for Visual Studio.

The object model available in the Visual Studio designer is, behind the scenes, defined by a new XML document that is the schema for the Entity Data Model. This XML file is the one with the .edmx extension, in our case Northwind.edmx. The schema is divided into three sections that are summarized in Table 26.1.

TABLE 26.1   Sections of the Entity Data Model

Section Name	Description
Conceptual Schema Definition Language	Defines entities, relationships, and inheritance. .NET classes are generated based on this section.
Store Schema Definition Language	Provides a representation of the original database.
Mapping Specification Language	Maps entities as they are defined in the CSDL against db objects as they are defined in the SSDL.

To understand how an EDM is composed, in Solution Explorer right-click the Northwind.
edmx file; then select **Open With**, and when the Open With dialog box appears, double-
click the **XML editor** option. At this point, Visual Studio shows the content of the EDM as
an XML file instead of the designer. The file contains three sections as described in Table
26.1. Listing 26.1 shows the CSDL definition (which is actually the second section in the
XML file).

LISTING 26.1   Conceptual Schema Definition Language

```
<!-- CSDL content -->
<edmx:ConceptualModels>
      <Schema Namespace="NorthwindModel" Alias="Self"
➥p1:UseStrongSpatialTypes="false" xmlns :annotation="http://schemas.microsoft.com/
➥ado/2009/02/edm/annotation" xmlns:p1="http
://schemas.microsoft.com/ado/2009/02/edm/annotation"
➥xmlns="http://schemas.microsoft.com /ado/2009/11/edm">
        <EntityContainer Name="NorthwindEntities" p1:LazyLoadingEnabled="true">
          <EntitySet Name="Categories" EntityType="NorthwindModel.Category" />
          <EntitySet Name="Products" EntityType="NorthwindModel.Product" />
          <AssociationSet Name="FK_Products_Categories"
➥Association="NorthwindModel.FK_Products_Categories">
            <End Role="Categories" EntitySet="Categories" />
            <End Role="Products" EntitySet="Products" />
          </AssociationSet>
        </EntityContainer>
        <EntityType Name="Category">
          <Key>
            <PropertyRef Name="CategoryID" />
          </Key>
          <Property Name="CategoryID" Type="Int32" Nullable="false"
➥p1:StoreGeneratedPattern="Identity" />
          <Property Name="CategoryName" Type="String" Nullable="false"
➥MaxLength="15" Unicode="true" FixedLength="false" />
          <Property Name="Description" Type="String" MaxLength="Max"
➥Unicode="true" FixedLength="false" />
```

```
          <Property Name="Picture" Type="Binary" MaxLength="Max"
➥FixedLength="false" />
          <NavigationProperty Name="Products"
➥Relationship="NorthwindModel.FK_Products_Categories" FromRole="Categories"
➥ToRole="Products" />
        </EntityType>
        <EntityType Name="Product">
          <Key>
            <PropertyRef Name="ProductID" />
          </Key>
          <Property Name="ProductID" Type="Int32" Nullable="false"
➥p1:StoreGeneratedPattern="Identity" />
          <Property Name="ProductName" Type="String" Nullable="false"
➥MaxLength="40" Unicode="true" FixedLength="false" />
          <Property Name="SupplierID" Type="Int32" />
          <Property Name="CategoryID" Type="Int32" />
          <Property Name="QuantityPerUnit" Type="String" MaxLength="20"
➥Unicode="true" FixedLength="false" />
          <Property Name="UnitPrice" Type="Decimal" Precision="19" Scale="4" />
          <Property Name="UnitsInStock" Type="Int16" />
          <Property Name="UnitsOnOrder" Type="Int16" />
          <Property Name="ReorderLevel" Type="Int16" />
          <Property Name="Discontinued" Type="Boolean" Nullable="false" />
          <NavigationProperty Name="Category"
➥Relationship="NorthwindModel.FK_Products_Categories" FromRole="Products"
➥ToRole="Categories" />
        </EntityType>
        <Association Name="FK_Products_Categories">
          <End Role="Categories" Type="NorthwindModel.Category"
➥Multiplicity="0..1" />
          <End Role="Products" Type="NorthwindModel.Product" Multiplicity="*" />
          <ReferentialConstraint>
            <Principal Role="Categories">
              <PropertyRef Name="CategoryID" />
            </Principal>
            <Dependent Role="Products">
              <PropertyRef Name="CategoryID" />
            </Dependent>
          </ReferentialConstraint>
        </Association>
      </Schema>
    </edmx:ConceptualModels>
```

Entities (`EntityType`) are defined along with scalar properties (`Property`), relationships
(`Association`), entity sets (`EntitySet`), and a container named `NorthwindEntities`. The

next section that we consider is the SSDL, which is constituted by the XML markup code shown in Listing 26.2 and which is actually the first section in the XML file.

LISTING 26.2   The Store Schema Definition Language

```
<edmx:StorageModels>
      <Schema Namespace="NorthwindModel.Store" Alias="Self" Provider="System.Data.
➥SqlClient"ProviderManifestToken="2008" xmlns:store="http://schemas.microsoft.com/
➥ado/2007/12/ edm/EntityStoreSchemaGenerator" xmlns="http://schemas.microsoft.com/
➥ado/2009/11/ edm/ssdl">
      <EntityContainer Name="NorthwindModelStoreContainer">
        <EntitySet Name="Categories" EntityType="NorthwindModel.Store.Categories"
➥store:Type="Tables" Schema="dbo" />
        <EntitySet Name="Products" EntityType="NorthwindModel.Store.Products"
➥store:Type="Tables" Schema="dbo" />
        <AssociationSet Name="FK_Products_Categories"
➥Association="NorthwindModel.Store.FK_Products_Categories">
          <End Role="Categories" EntitySet="Categories" />
          <End Role="Products" EntitySet="Products" />
        </AssociationSet>
      </EntityContainer>
      <EntityType Name="Categories">
        <Key>
          <PropertyRef Name="CategoryID" />
        </Key>
        <Property Name="CategoryID" Type="int" Nullable="false"
➥StoreGeneratedPattern="Identity" />
        <Property Name="CategoryName" Type="nvarchar" Nullable="false"
➥MaxLength="15" />
        <Property Name="Description" Type="ntext" />
        <Property Name="Picture" Type="image" />
      </EntityType>
      <EntityType Name="Products">
        <Key>
          <PropertyRef Name="ProductID" />
        </Key>
        <Property Name="ProductID" Type="int" Nullable="false"
➥StoreGeneratedPattern="Identity" />
        <Property Name="ProductName" Type="nvarchar" Nullable="false"
➥MaxLength="40" />
        <Property Name="SupplierID" Type="int" />
        <Property Name="CategoryID" Type="int" />
        <Property Name="QuantityPerUnit" Type="nvarchar" MaxLength="20" />
        <Property Name="UnitPrice" Type="money" />
```

```
            <Property Name="UnitsInStock" Type="smallint" />
            <Property Name="UnitsOnOrder" Type="smallint" />
            <Property Name="ReorderLevel" Type="smallint" />
            <Property Name="Discontinued" Type="bit" Nullable="false" />
        </EntityType>
        <Association Name="FK_Products_Categories">
            <End Role="Categories" Type="NorthwindModel.Store.Categories"
➥Multiplicity="0..1" />
            <End Role="Products" Type="NorthwindModel.Store.Products"
➥Multiplicity="*" />
            <ReferentialConstraint>
              <Principal Role="Categories">
                <PropertyRef Name="CategoryID" />
              </Principal>
              <Dependent Role="Products">
                <PropertyRef Name="CategoryID" />
              </Dependent>
            </ReferentialConstraint>
        </Association>
      </Schema>
    </edmx:StorageModels>
```

This schema is similar to the previous schema, except that it represents the database structure as you can see from type definition within `Property` elements. The last schema is the
Mapping Definition Language that is illustrated in Listing 26.3.

LISTING 26.3   Mapping Definition Language

```
<edmx:Mappings>
      <Mapping Space="C-S" xmlns="http://schemas.microsoft.com/ado/2009/11/
➥mapping/cs">
        <EntityContainerMapping StorageEntityContainer=
➥"NorthwindModelStoreContainer" Cd mEntityContainer="NorthwindEntities">
          <EntitySetMapping Name="Categories">
            <EntityTypeMapping TypeName="NorthwindModel.Category">
              <MappingFragment StoreEntitySet="Categories">
                <ScalarProperty Name="CategoryID" ColumnName="CategoryID" />
                <ScalarProperty Name="CategoryName" ColumnName="CategoryName" />
                <ScalarProperty Name="Description" ColumnName="Description" />
                <ScalarProperty Name="Picture" ColumnName="Picture" />
              </MappingFragment>
            </EntityTypeMapping>
          </EntitySetMapping>
          <EntitySetMapping Name="Products">
            <EntityTypeMapping TypeName="NorthwindModel.Product">
```

```
                  <MappingFragment StoreEntitySet="Products">
                    <ScalarProperty Name="ProductID" ColumnName="ProductID" />
                    <ScalarProperty Name="ProductName" ColumnName="ProductName" />
                    <ScalarProperty Name="SupplierID" ColumnName="SupplierID" />
                    <ScalarProperty Name="CategoryID" ColumnName="CategoryID" />
                    <ScalarProperty Name="QuantityPerUnit"
➥ColumnName="QuantityPerUnit" />
                    <ScalarProperty Name="UnitPrice" ColumnName="UnitPrice" />
                    <ScalarProperty Name="UnitsInStock" ColumnName="UnitsInStock" />
                    <ScalarProperty Name="UnitsOnOrder" ColumnName="UnitsOnOrder" />
                    <ScalarProperty Name="ReorderLevel" ColumnName="ReorderLevel" />
                    <ScalarProperty Name="Discontinued" ColumnName="Discontinued" />
                  </MappingFragment>
                </EntityTypeMapping>
              </EntitySetMapping>
            </EntityContainerMapping>
          </Mapping>
        </edmx:Mappings>
```

The content of the MDL is quite simple, in that each `ScalarProperty` represents an entity's property and establishes mapping between the property and the related column name in the database table.

Understanding the `DbContext` Class: The Visual Basic Mapping

Schemas in the Entity Data Model have a Visual Basic counterpart that enables you to write code to work against entities. To understand this, enable the **View All Files** view in Solution Explorer and expand the **Northwind.edmx** file. You will see two files with a .tt extension, Northwind.Context.tt and Northwind.tt. Files with a .tt extension are templates that Visual Studio uses for code generation and that are useful to the IDE to generate classes that allow developers to interact with the object model. Regardless of their content, which you are not required to understand for this chapter, start expanding the Northwind.Context.tt file, which contains another file called Northwind.Context.vb. Similar to the `DataContext` class in LINQ to SQL, the ADO.NET Entity Framework provides a class named `System.Data.Entity.DbContext`. This class, also referred to as the object context, is new in the Entity Framework 5 and is also the basis of the Code First pattern; It acts as a reference to the Entity Data Model and encapsulates the entities' definition so that you can work with entities. It is also responsible for opening and closing connections, persisting data, keeping track of changes, and persisting data back to the database. `DbContext` is just the base class (as the `DataContext` is in LINQ to SQL) that every entity data model inherits from. Listing 26.4 shows how the object context is defined in our specific scenario.

LISTING 26.4   `DbContext` **Definition**

```
Imports System
Imports System.Data.Entity
Imports System.Data.Entity.Infrastructure

Partial Public Class NorthwindEntities
    Inherits DbContext

    Public Sub New()
        MyBase.New("name=NorthwindEntities")
    End Sub

    Protected Overrides Sub OnModelCreating(modelBuilder As DbModelBuilder)
        Throw New UnintentionalCodeFirstException()
    End Sub

    Public Property Categories() As DbSet(Of Category)
    Public Property Products() As DbSet(Of Product)
End Class
```

The code is easy to understand. There is only one constructor that creates an instance of the object model. Next, notice the `Categories` and `Products` properties: `DbSet(Of Category)` and `DbSet(Of Product)`. A `System.Data.Entity.DbSet(Of T)` represents an entity set and provides several methods and members for manipulating entities, such as the `Add` or `Remove` methods. Properties of type `DbSet` handle references to a series of objects. Such objects are defined in separate code files, one for each entity, all nested inside the Northwind.tt file. For the sake of simplicity, Listing 26.5 shows only the definition of the `Category` class in the Category.vb file whereas the `Product` class is left out, being substantially defined using the same concepts.

LISTING 26.5   **The Category Entity Definition**

```
Imports System
Imports System.Collections.Generic

Partial Public Class Category
    Public Property CategoryID As Integer
    Public Property CategoryName As String
    Public Property Description As String
    Public Property Picture As Byte()

    Public Overridable Property Products As _
            ICollection(Of Product) = New HashSet(Of Product)
End Class
```

Each entity class represents a database object, but differently from the previous versions of the Entity Framework, the entity definition is now made of only a few lines of code and relies on the Plain Old CLR Object (POCO) definition. This means that there is no platform-specific code, but normal classes that you could use not only inside an object model definition. You can easily compare the example shown in the previous edition of this book with the current example to see how much cleaner the code now is.

Navigation Properties in Code

Finally, notice how those things named Navigation Properties in the EDM are also defined within entity classes. A navigation property is a .NET property of type `ICollection(Of T)`, in the case of the "many" part of the relationship, or of the entity type that the current entity is associated with for the "one" part of the relationship (in the case of the `Product` entity, the navigation property is of type `Category`). Navigation properties typically represent foreign keys in the database.

Now that you have a clearer idea of what Visual Basic requires behind the scenes, you are ready to understand the usage of some interesting design-time tools.

Entity Designer Tool Windows

When the EDM designer is active, you notice that some new tool windows appear in the IDE. The first one is the Mapping Details tool window, which shows how database objects are mapped to .NET types. Figure 26.6 shows the Mapping Details window.

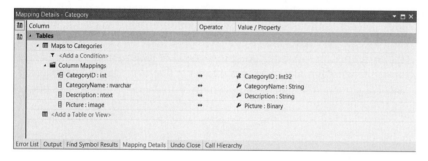

FIGURE 26.6   The Mapping Details tool window.

As you can see in Figure 26.6, on the left side of the window, you can find the original SQL definition and on the right side of the window, you can find the .NET type utilized to map SQL types into the EDM. You can manually edit such mapping, but the suggestion is you leave unchanged what the IDE proposes by default unless you understand that a bad mapping from SQL to .NET has been performed. The second tool is the Model Browser, which provides a hierarchical graphical view of the object model so that you can easily browse both the conceptual model and the store model. Figure 26.7 shows the tool window.

FIGURE 26.7   The Model Browser tool window.

Such a tool window also simplifies performing operations on the entity data model, such as updating the model itself, as explained later in this chapter with regard to stored procedures. Other than these tool windows, you can take advantage of the Properties window for getting information on the objects that compose the entity data model. For example, if you click the blank space in the designer, the Properties window shows high-level information on the EDM, such as the database schema name, the entity container name (that is, the object context), or the model namespace. Figure 26.8 provides an overview.

Similarly, you can get information on the entities' definition by clicking the desired entity name in the designer. Figure 26.9 represents the Properties window showing information about the Category entity.

The window shows information about the class implementation, such as the class name, the inheritance level, or the access level other than the related entity set container name. If you instead try to click a navigation property, the Properties window provides information on how relationships are handled. For example, the name of the foreign key, the return type, and multiplicity type is shown in a human-readable fashion, as demonstrated in Figure 26.10.

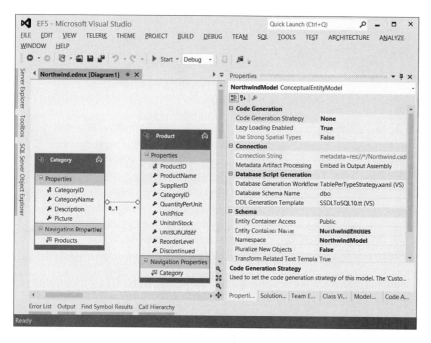

FIGURE 26.8   Getting model information via the Properties window.

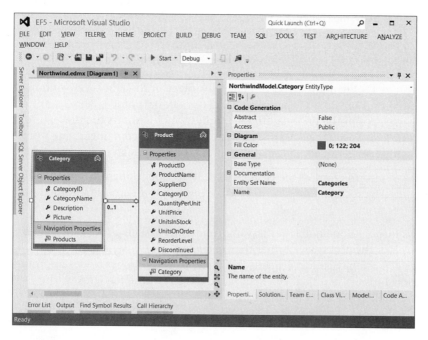

FIGURE 26.9   Getting entity information with the Properties window.

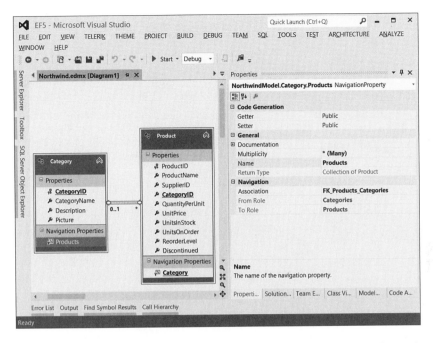

FIGURE 26.10   Getting information on navigation properties with the Properties window.

Useful information can also be retrieved on relationships. If you click the association line that conjuncts entities in the designer, the Properties window not only shows how the relationship is defined, but also enables you to choose custom behavior when deleting entities (for example, Cascade). Of course, this must be supported (or just enabled) in the underlying database. In the case of SQL Server databases, you can modify associations' behaviors using SQL Server Management Studio. Figure 26.11 shows such a scenario.

The last use of the Properties window is getting and setting values for scalar properties. For example, click the **QuantityPerUnit** property in the `Product` entity. Figure 26.12 shows how the Properties window displays.

Properties are self-explanatory, and you can get more information by clicking the property you are interested in; the tool window will be updated with information. Consider two properties: `Entity Key`, which establishes whether the scalar property represents a primary key, and `StoreGeneratedPattern`, which provides the ability to autogenerate the column in the database during insert and update operations. This tooling is particularly useful because here you can manually change the entities' behavior without the need to edit the autogenerated Visual Basic code; this job belongs to Visual Studio and you should always let it do this for you.

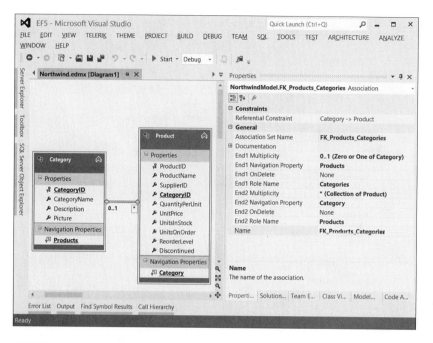

FIGURE 26.11   Getting associations information via the Properties window.

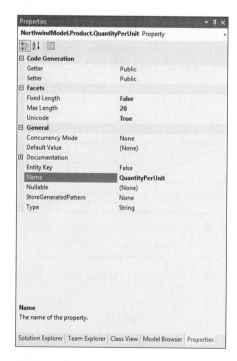

FIGURE 26.12   Getting information on scalar properties.

Insert/Update/Delete Operations for Entities

The ADO.NET Entity Framework offers a complete infrastructure for manipulating data, meaning that it offers the ability to add, update, and remove data to and from the object model and subsequently from the database. Let's discover these features.

Instantiating the `DbContext`

The first task you need to accomplish when working with the ADO.NET Entity Framework in code is to get an instance of the `DbContext` class. At the beginning of this chapter you were told to create a new Visual Basic project for the Console, so let's continue on this path. At module level (or class level, in most common scenarios), declare a variable of type `NorthwindEntities` that represents our object context as follows:

```
Private northwindContext As NorthwindEntities
```

Within the `Sub Main` (or in the constructor if you work with classes), create the actual instance:

```
Sub Main()
    Try
        northwindContext = New NorthwindEntities
    Catch ex As SqlClient.SqlException
        'Handle a SqlException here...
    Catch ex As Exception
        'Handle general exceptions here...


    End Try

End Sub
```

Notice how a `System.Data.SqlClient.SqlException` general exception is handled in case of problems.

CODING TIPS ON THE OBJECT CONTEXT

It is usually a good idea to provide a class-level declaration for a variable that holds the instance of the DbContext class, so that the variable can be reached by all code in your class (or classes if the variable is Friend) but also for another reason: you can handle exceptions when creating the actual instance within the code block that performs this action. I do not personally like code examples in which the instance is generated at the class level, but this is just a suggestion.

When you have the object context instance, you can read and write data on your object model.

Adding Entities

Adding entities against an entity data model requires you to pass the instance of the entity to the `Add` method exposed by the entity set. For example, in our demonstration scenario we have a `Products` entity set exposing an `Add` method. The following code shows how you can programmatically create a new product and add it to the object model:

```vb
Sub AddProduct(ByVal categoryReference As Category)
    Try

        Dim check = northwindContext.Products.
                    Single(Function(p) p.
                    ProductName = "Italian spaghetti")

    Catch ex As InvalidOperationException

        Try
            Dim prod As New Product
            With prod
                .ProductName = "Italian spaghetti"
                .QuantityPerUnit = "10 packs"
                .Discontinued = True
                .SupplierID = 4
                .UnitPrice = 0.5D
                .UnitsInStock = 100
                .UnitsOnOrder = 50

                .Category = categoryReference
            End With

            northwindContext.Products.Add (prod)
            northwindContext.SaveChanges()

        Catch e As Exception
        'Exception handling when saving changes
        End Try

    Catch ex As Exception
        'Handle general exceptions here
    End Try
End Sub
```

First, the code checks whether the product already exists based on the specified condition. This is accomplished by invoking the `Single` extension method. It is something that you already saw in LINQ to SQL and is not discussed thoroughly here. Notice how you set properties for the new product. The custom method receives a `Category` instance as an argument. This is necessary for setting a one-to-many relationship between the new product and the desired category. Setting the relationship just requires you to assign the `Category` property with the category instance. When done, you invoke the `northwindContext.Products.Add` method by passing the new product and then invoke the `SaveChanges` method for sending changes to the database.

TRACKING CHANGES

Remember that the `DbContext` instance can keep track of changes during the application lifetime, so its `SaveChanges` method will persist all pending changes.

In Chapter 24, you saw how to use Visual Studio to inspect the database for checking if changes were correctly submitted to the database. The good news is that the same technique can be also used when working with EDMs.

Deleting Entities

Deleting entities is also a simple task. You first need to get the instance of the entity you want to remove and then invoke the `DbSet(Of T).Remove` method. The following code shows how to get the instance of the specified product and then to remove it first from the model and then from the database:

```
Sub DeleteProduct()

    Try
        Dim check = northwindContext.Products.
                    Single(Function(p) p.
                    ProductName = "Italian spaghetti")

        northwindContext.Products.Remove(check)
        northwindContext.SaveChanges()

        'Does not exist
    Catch ex As InvalidOperationException

    End Try
End Sub
```

Same as in previous code, we take advantage of the `Single` method that throws an `InvalidOperationException` if the object does not exist.

DELETING ENTITIES WITH RELATIONSHIPS

In this chapter you see simplified examples focusing on the technology. In some situations you need to delete entities with relationships; for example, imagine you have an `Order` class with associated `OrderDetails`. When you delete the order, you probably want to remove associated details. To accomplish this, you need to work at the database level and enable it to cascade the deletion. For SQL Server databases, you can accomplish this within SQL Server Management Studio, changing properties for the foreign key related to the relationship.

Updating Entities

Updating entities is a little bit different from adding and deleting in that there is no Update method in either the DbContext or the DbSet classes. You get the instance of the object you want to update, change its properties, and then invoke SaveChanges. The following code demonstrates this:

```
Sub UpdateProduct()

    Try
        Dim check = northwindContext.Products.
                    Single(Function(p) p.
                    ProductName = "Italian spaghetti")

        check.Discontinued = True
        check.UnitsInStock = 30
        northwindContext.SaveChanges()

        'Product does not exist
    Catch ex As InvalidOperationException

    Catch ex As UpdateException
    End Try
End Sub
```

Just remember to check whether the product exists before trying an update. Notice also how an UpdateException is caught; this is thrown when there is some problem in sending updates to the data source.

Handling Optimistic Concurrency

Of course, the ADO.NET Entity Framework provides the ability to handle optimistic concurrency exceptions. You need to intercept eventual System.Data.Entity. Infrastructure.DbUpdateConcurrencyException instances. When intercepted, you need to determine what entries were not updated in the database by using the Entries property of the exception instance and make an appropriate decision. The following code revisits the UpdateProduct custom method described in the "Updating Entities" subsection, providing the first example:

```
Sub UpdateProduct()

    Try
        Dim check = northwindContext.Products.
```

```
                Single(Function(p) p.
                ProductName = "Italian spaghetti")


        check.Discontinued = True
        check.UnitsInStock = 30
        northwindContext.SaveChanges()


        'Product does not exist
    Catch ex As InvalidOperationException


        'Handle optimistic concurrency
    Catch ex As DbUpdateConcurrencyException
        ex.Entries.Single.Reload()
    Catch ex As UpdateException
    End Try
End Sub
```

If an `DbUpdateConcurrencyException` is thrown, you can invoke the `Reload` method on the instance of the entity that was not updated and reload original values from the database, overwriting the current entity values. This is the first possible way to solve concurrency blocks and is known as *database wins*. The second possibility is known as *client wins* and is the opposite, which means that you can force to overwrite database values with the current entity's values. This requires a particular technique, which will set the original values for the entity with values from the database.

The following code demonstrates this:

```
Catch ex As DbUpdateConcurrencyException
    Dim entry = ex.Entries.Single
    entry.OriginalValues.SetValues(entry.GetDatabaseValues)
```

The `OriginalValues.SetValues` method takes an argument of type `DbPropertyValues`, which is a collection of properties for an entity. The `GetDatabaseValues` returns a collection of current properties from the database. What you have to keep in mind when working with optimistic concurrency is that you handle the `Entries` property and retrieve the instance of the entity that could not be updated; of course there are additional techniques that the MSDN documentation describes in more detail at: http://msdn.microsoft.com/en-us/data/jj592904.aspx.

NOTE ABOUT CURRENT AND ORIGINAL VALUES

When an entity is attached to the object context, the Entity Framework keeps track of two values for each property: The current value that is the current value of the property in the entity. The original value is instead the value that the property had when the entity was queried from the database or attached to the context. The MSDN documentation shows additional ways to work with entity properties at: http://msdn.microsoft.com/en-us/data/jj592677.

26

Of course, in this book it is not possible to reproduce a real concurrency scenario, but now you know what the main objects are for handling this situation.

Validating Data

Differently from the past, with Entity Framework 5 and the new APIs you no longer need to use partial methods in order to validate the data. Data validation now consists in decorating entities and their properties with some attributes from the System.ComponentModel. DataAnnotations and System.ComponentModel.DataAnnotations.Schema namespaces (from the System.ComponentModel.DataAnnotations.dll assembly). Each attribute provides additional information or validation rules to types. This is not new: if you have developed Silverlight applications with WCF RIA Services in the past, you used data annotations frequently. The following code demonstrates how to add some validation rules to the Product entity using data annotations:

```
Imports System.ComponentModel.DataAnnotations

Partial Public Class Product
    Public Property ProductID As Integer
    'The product name length must be at least 5 and no more than 15 characters
    'A custom error message is provided
    <StringLength(15, ErrorMessage:="String length not within the expected range",
        ErrorMessageResourceName:=Nothing,
        ErrorMessageResourceType:=Nothing,
        MinimumLength:=5)> Public Property ProductName As String
    <Required> Public Property SupplierID As Nullable(Of Integer)
    Public Property CategoryID As Nullable(Of Integer)
    'QuantityPerUnit is now a mandatory field, minimum length is 4
    <Required>Public Property QuantityPerUnit As String
    Public Property UnitPrice As Nullable(Of Decimal)
    Public Property UnitsInStock As Nullable(Of Short)
    Public Property UnitsOnOrder As Nullable(Of Short)
    Public Property ReorderLevel As Nullable(Of Short)
    Public Property Discontinued As Boolean

    Public Overridable Property Category As Category

End Class
```

The Required attribute marks a property as mandatory, so the user must supply a value for it. The StringLength attribute allows specifying a minimum and a maximum length for a string, including a custom error message and resources. Notice that all values are optional except the first argument, which is the maximum length. Useful attributes are also MaxLength and MinLength which instead determine the maximum and the minimum length of an array of String respectively. The validation mechanism can run in two ways. The first way is automatic and is when the runtime executes the DbContext.SaveChanges method. This causes the runtime to check if an entity adheres to validation rules; If not, a

`DbEntityValidationException` is thrown. The second way is checking for validation errors programmatically, before attempting to save changes. You can check for all validation errors in the current object context, or you can check a single entity or a single property. The following code demonstrates how to check for any validation errors in the model instance by invoking the `DbContext.GetValidationErrors` method:

```
If northwindContext.GetValidationErrors.Any Then
    'There is at least one validation error
End If
```

This method returns a collection of `DbEntityValidationResult` objects, each containing detailed information on the error. You can also validate a single entity on demand, by invoking the `DbEntityEntry.GetValidationResult` method on the specified entity like in the following code:

```
'Validate an entity
Dim result As DbEntityValidationResult = _
            northwindContext.Entry(prod).GetValidationResult
For Each validationError In result.ValidationErrors
    Console.WriteLine("Property {0} raised the following message: {1}",
                    validationError.PropertyName,
                    validationError.ErrorMessage)
Next
```

The method returns an object of type `DbEntityValidationResult`, whose `ValidationErrors` property contains a list of validation errors pending on the specified entity instance. Notice that such an instance must be attached to the current context. Each error is represented by an instance of the `DbValidationError` class, which exposes two properties: `PropertyName` and `ErrorMessage`; the first property stores the name of the entity property that raised the validation error, whereas the second one contains a descriptive error message. Finally you can validate a single property of an entity, like in the following example:

```
'Validate a single property
Dim productNameProperty As DbPropertyEntry = _
    northwindContext.Entry(prod).Property(Function(p) p.ProductName)
For Each validationError In productNameProperty.GetValidationErrors
    Console.WriteLine("Property {0} raised the following message: {1}",
                    validationError.PropertyName,
                    validationError.ErrorMessage)
Next
```

You first retrieve the property you want to validate via the `DbEntityEntry.Property` method. You need to pass the property name you want to validate and this can be done by passing the property name as a string or via a lambda expression, like in the above code, which takes advantage of the background compiler and IntelliSense to determine the property name correctly. `GetValidationErrors` and its results remain the same as in the previous example. Actually the `System.ComponentModel.DataAnnotations` namespace provides additional attributes that are instead useful when using the Code First approach to create the model and to generate the database. These are discussed in the section called "Using Data Annotations" later in this chapter.

Querying EDMs with LINQ to Entities

LINQ to Entities is the standard LINQ provider for querying entities within an Entity Data Model. You use the same LINQ syntax for querying entities, too, so you will not encounter particular difficulties.

USING STANDARD QUERY OPERATORS

LINQ to Entities supports standard query operators described in Chapter 23, "LINQ to Objects," to perform complex query expressions.

The one big difference is about eager loading, which is explained after showing the code. As in LINQ to SQL, LINQ to Entities queries return an `IQueryable(Of T)`, unless you convert the result into a different type using extension methods at the end of the query. The following code returns the list of products for the specified category, taking only those products that are not discontinued and sorting the result by unit price:

```
Sub LINQtoEntitiesDemo(ByVal CategoryName As String)

    Dim query = From prod In northwindContext.Products.
                Include("Category")
                Where prod.Category.CategoryName = CategoryName _
                And prod.Discontinued = False
                Order By prod.UnitPrice
                Select prod

    Console.WriteLine("Category: {0}",
                      CategoryName)

    For Each prod In query
        Console.WriteLine("Product name: {0}, Unit price: {1:c}",
                          prod.ProductName, prod.UnitPrice)
    Next
End Sub
```

As you can see, the LINQ syntax works similarly to other LINQ providers except that here the `Include` method has been invoked on the entity set instance. This method requires an argument of type `String`, which is the name of the navigation property mapped to the entity being queried—that is, the name of the entity set with which the queried entity has a relationship. `Include` performs that technique known as *eager loading* that enables you to load related entities. This is necessary if you want to perform comparisons as in the preceding example, where an evaluation must be done on the category name to which the current product belongs. In other words, if you do not invoke `Include`, you will have available only `Products` information but not `Categories` information while you need this to perform the comparison. You can take advantage of standard query operators described in Chapter 23 to accomplish complex LINQ queries against entities as well. You can also use iterators for efficient code in long running query operations. For instance, you can rewrite the last code example as follows:

```
Sub LINQtoEntitiesDemo(ByVal CategoryName As String)
    Console.WriteLine("Category: {0}",
                      CategoryName)


    For Each prod In GetProducts(CategoryName)
        Console.WriteLine("Product name: {0}, Unit price: {1:c}",
                          prod.ProductName, prod.UnitPrice)
    Next
End Sub


Iterator Function GetProducts(categoryName As String) As IEnumerable(Of Product)
    Dim query = From prod In northwindContext.Products.
        Include("Category")
        Where prod.Category.CategoryName = categoryName _
        And prod.Discontinued = False
        Order By prod.UnitPrice
        Select prod


    For Each prod In query
        Yield prod
    Next
End Function
```

Querying EDMs with Entity SQL

LINQ to Entities is not the only way to query data exposed by EDMs. An important alternative named Entity SQL enables you to query entity data models by providing both the ability to send SQL instructions to the data source and to treat query results as managed entities. To accomplish this, the `DbSet` class exposes a method named `SqlQuery` that queries the EDM via the specified set of SQL instructions. The following example shows how you can retrieve a list of products for the `Grains/Cereals` category in Northwind, sorting the result by the product name:

```
Sub EntitySQLDemo()
    Try
        Dim grainProducts = northwindContext.Products.
        SqlQuery("SELECT * FROM PRODUCTS WHERE " & _
                "CATEGORYID='5' ORDER BY PRODUCTNAME")
```

```
Catch ex As EntitySqlException
    Console.WriteLine("An error occurred in column: {0}",
                        ex.Column.ToString)
Catch ex As Exception
    Console.WriteLine(ex.ToString)
End Try
End Sub
```

`SqlQuery` returns a `DbSqlQuery` object that represents a strongly typed query against entities. As with any other LINQ query, Entity SQL queries are executed when they are effectively used, for example in `For..Each` loops, when converting to collections. By default, entities returned by the method are tracked by the instance of the `DbContext` class. You can change this by invoking the `AsNoTracking` method on the returned collection.

Mapping Stored Procedures

The Entity Framework enables you to import stored procedures from a SQL Server database into the object model and Visual Studio 2012 makes thing easier than its predecessor. In this section you learn to add stored procedure mappings to the entity data model. To accomplish this, first open the Visual Studio designer by double-clicking the Northwind. edmx file in Solution Explorer. When ready, right-click the designer and select the **Update Model from Database** command. This launches again the wizard that enables you to select database objects not included yet in the entity data model. Now, expand the Stored Procedures item and select the **Ten Most Expensive Products** stored procedure, as shown in Figure 26.13.

FIGURE 26.13 Adding a stored procedure to the EDM.

You can follow these steps to add database objects to the EDM if you did not do it before. This operation provides mappings for the stored procedure. The mapping lets the stored procedure to be mapped into a .NET method that returns a value; therefore, you need to know which kind of value such methods must return. To accomplish this, open either the Server Explorer or the SQL Server Object Explorer tool window, expand the Northwind database structure, and then expand the Stored Procedures folder (if you use the SQL Object Explorer this folder is under Programmability); finally double-click the **Ten Most Expensive Products** stored procedure. Now the Visual Studio 2012 IDE shows the SQL instructions for the previously selected stored procedure, as shown in Figure 26.14.

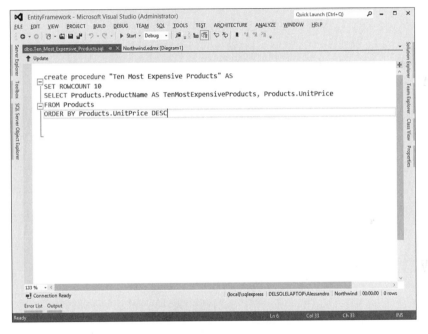

FIGURE 26.14   Examining SQL instructions for the stored procedure.

SCRIPT FILES

When Visual Studio shows SQL code for database objects, it also generates a .sql script file that can be saved for your later reuse. The SQL code editor points in fact to a newly generated script file that contains the code you see on screen.

Examining the SQL code, you can see that the stored procedure returns a list of product names. Now switch back to the EDM designer so that the Model Browser tool window becomes active. Inside the window expand the NorthwindModel, Function Imports item. You will notice the presence of an element called `Ten_Most_Expensive_Product` (see Figure 26.15 for a reference). This is nothing but a .NET method that Visual Studio 2012 has automatically generated to map the requested stored procedure. Because it is a method that returns a set of records, it must also have a return type. Visual Studio 2012 automatically generated a complex type (which means neither a scalar type like `String`, `Integer`, and so on, nor an entity type like `Product` or `Category`, but a specific type that includes information from specific columns) called `Ten_Most_Expensive_Product_Result`, as you can see by expanding the NorthwindModel, Complex Types node in the Model Browser (see Figure 26.15).

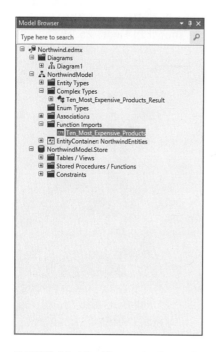

FIGURE 26.15   The method mapping the stored procedure and its return type.

The `Ten_Most_Expensive_Products_Result` complex type is a class exposing two auto-generated properties, one called `TenMostExpensiveProducts` of type `String` that stores the product name and one called `UnitPrice` of type `Nullable(Of Decimal)`. You are now ready to invoke your stored procedure as a .NET method being part of the entity data model, exposed by the `NorthwindEntities` class. For example, if you want to retrieve the list of the ten most-expensive products, you can write something like this:

```
For Each prod In northwindContext.Ten_Most_Expensive_Products
'Print the names of the ten most expensive products
    Console.WriteLine(prod.TenMostExpensiveProducts)
Next
```

Behind the scenes, mapping a stored procedure is something that Visual Basic accomplishes by adding the following invocation to the `ExecuteFunction(Of T)` method to the `NorthwindEntities` class definition:

```
Public Overridable Function Ten_Most_Expensive_Products() As  _
        ObjectResult(Of Ten_Most_Expensive_Products_Result)
    Return DirectCast(Me, IObjectContextAdapter).
            ObjectContext.ExecuteFunction(Of Ten_Most_Expensive_Products_Result) _
            ("Ten_Most_Expensive_Products")
End Function
```

By completing this, you have the basic knowledge for working with the ADO.NET Entity Framework; you can learn more from the MSDN documentation.

> **MODIFYING AUTO-GENERATED FUNCTION IMPORTS AND COMPLEX TYPES**
>
> You might want to make some edits over autogenerated function imports or complex types. In the Model Browser window you can right-click the function import name (such as `Ten_Most_Expensive_Products` of the current example) and then select Properties in the pop-up menu. The Properties window will provide an opportunity of changing the function name and of editing the complex type as well, by clicking the buttons with three dots near the Return Type property. This enables the Edit Function Import dialog box, where you can rename the function and assign a new complex type as the return type. To accomplish this, you first need to click Get Column Information and then Create New Complex Type.

Introducing the Code First Approach

So far, you have seen how the Entity Framework enables you to create applications that access data based on a model-centric approach, in which an abstraction layer enables you to map to .NET objects an existing database (Database First), via convenient tools and designers. Back in Visual Studio 2010, Microsoft also introduced the so-called Model First approach, which enables you to generate an empty model without having a database; here you design your entities and associations in the Entity Framework designer and can finally generate a database with the Generate Database from Model command that is available when you right-click the designer. You can easily experiment with Model First on your own by selecting the Empty Model option when adding a new Entity Data Model. Both approaches are well made and can take advantage of a convenient designer, but they have the following limitations:

▶ Database First requires an existing database. You can still model your entities in the designer, but you must be sure of the perfect correspondence between a managed environment (the Entity Framework) and the data store (SQL Server).

▶ Model First enables you to model your entities in a convenient designer, but this can be difficult and tiring when the model gets complex.

▶ Both have dependencies on the EDMX file.

To make things faster and to avoid dependencies, Microsoft introduced a new approach called Code First with Entity Framework 4.3.1 and that is still available in version 5—the one that we discuss in this chapter. As its name implies, with Code First you model your data only writing code; the IntelliSense and the power of the Visual Studio's code editor will help you write your entities quickly and all the power of the Entity Framework will remain unchanged. Before providing some examples, it is necessary to install some components.

Downloading Additions to the Entity Framework 5

The .NET Framework 4.5 includes Entity Framework 5, and Visual Studio 2012 provides support for this version. At the time this chapter was written, the core of the Entity Framework 5 is included in the .NET Framework but some additions like Code First are not included by default, so you need to download specific packages from the Internet. Such additions are available via NuGet, the famous library manager included in Visual Studio 2012 that enables you to download libraries and all the necessary dependencies. The requirement is for you to have a project before downloading required libraries, so first create a new Console application called CodeFirst. Then follow these steps:

1. Select Project, Manage NuGet Packages.

2. When the Manage NuGet Packages dialog box appears (see Figure 26.16), select the Online node on the left.

3. In the search box in the upper-right corner, type Entity Framework 5.

4. When the Entity Framework 5 package appears in the list, click Install and accept the license agreement when the download completes.

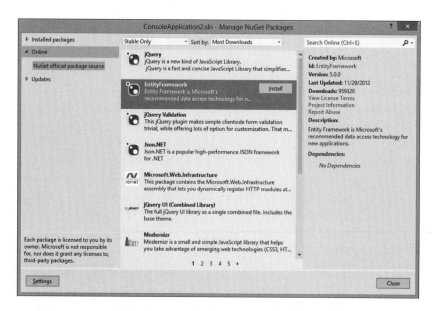

FIGURE 26.16   Searching for Entity Framework 5 additions with NuGet.

At this point, Visual Studio 2012 adds a reference to a new assembly called
EntityFramework.dll assembly, as you can easily verify in Solution Explorer. Now that you
have set up the environment, you are ready to start with Code First.

Coding Your Model

As you learned previously, with the Code First approach you define entities and associations in code. Let's provide a simple example, in which we implement business objects
like an Author class and a Book class representing two entities. Listing 26.6 shows how to
define both entities.

LISTING 26.6   Coding Two Entities in Code First

```
Public Class Author
    Public Property AuthorId As Integer
    Public Property FirstName As String
    Public Property LastName As String

    Public Property Books As ICollection(Of Book)
End Class


Public Class Book
    Public Property BookId As Integer
    Public Property Title As String
    Public Property Author As Author
    Public Property ISBN As String
    Public Property Price As Decimal
End Class
```

There is nothing difficult in Listing 26.6 because it is a normal class definition and you are
probably now remembering the definition of the Product and Category classes generated
by Visual Studio in the example about the Northwind database. Notice how the Author
class exposes a Books property of type ICollection(Of Book). The ICollection(Of T)
type is typical in Code First to represent a navigation property for the "many" part of a
one-to-many relationship. In this example, we are in fact simulating a one-to-many relationship in which an author has multiple books. In real-world applications, you should
implement a many-to-many relationship for a scenario like this (because multiple authors
can write many books), but for making it easier to understand how Code First works, a

26

one-to-many is enough. The next step is defining a context class. In Code First, you still have the `System.Data.Entity.DbContext` class described previously. So you have to define a class that inherits from `DbContext` like the following:

```
Public Class BookStoreContext
    Inherits DbContext


    Public Property Books As DbSet(Of Book)
    Public Property Authors As DbSet(Of Author)
End Class
```

The `BookStoreContext` class inherits from `DbContext` all the necessary infrastructure for working with data, plus it exposes two properties of type `DbSet(Of T)`, each representing a collection of entities as defined in Listing 26.6. So now you have a basic model definition (that will be extended later). Before using the model and entities, you need to supply a connection string to the database. Because Code First's main goal is simplicity, the connection string must be supplied in the simplest form possible. The new connection string must be added in the `ConnectionStrings` section of the application configuration file, so open App.config in the code editor (when adding the Entity Framework package, Visual Studio 2012 automatically adds the configuration file if not found). By convention, the name of the new connection string should match the name of the context class—in our example `BookStoreContext`. This is not mandatory but is a good practice. The following code demonstrates how to specify a connection string:

```
<connectionStrings>
  <add name="BookStoreContext"
   connectionString="data source=SERVERNAME;
   initial catalog=BookStoreDatabase;Integrated Security=SSPI"
   providerName="System.Data.SqlClient" />
</connectionStrings>
```

Inside the `connectionString` attribute, you must first specify the server name (which can be a local engine like LocalDB or SQL Express or a production server) and the name of the database that will be used, in this case `BookStoreDatabase`. Both the model and the connection string are ready, so you can now perform operations against data.

Generating the Database and Executing Data Operations

So far, you have created your data model in code, but you do not have a database yet. The power of Code First is that the Entity Framework checks whether the database exists and, if not, it automatically creates one for you with the name specified in the connection string, without writing a single line of code. After the database is ready, data operations can be performed. The goal is now to generate some `Author` and `Book` entities and populate the database. This is an Insert operation. The `DbSet(Of T)` class is a collection, and therefore it exposes `Add` and `Remove` methods for adding and removing entity instances—that is, data into and from the database. You will use the same techniques learned previously with EDMs. Listing 26.7 demonstrates how to add a new author and two books per that author; finally the code demonstrates how you still use LINQ to Entities for querying the data model.

LISTING 26.7   Querying the Model and Executing Insert Operations

```
Sub Main()
    Using db As New BookStoreContext
        Dim _author As New Author With {.FirstName = "Alessandro",
                                        .LastName = "Del Sole"}
        db.Authors.Add(_author)

        Dim LSBook As New Book With {.Title = "Visual Basic LightSwitch Unleashed",
                                     .Author = _author,
                                     .ISBN = "978-0672335532",
                                     .Price = 31.49D}
        db.Books.Add(LSBook)

        Dim VB2010Book As New Book With {.Title = "Visual Basic Basic " _
                                         + " 2010 Unleashed",
                                         .Author = _author,
                                         .ISBN = " 978-0672331008",
                                         .Price = 31.49D}
        db.Books.Add(VB2010Book)

        db.SaveChanges()

        Dim authorInstance = db.Authors.
            Single(Function(a) a.LastName = "Del Sole")
        Console.WriteLine(authorInstance.FirstName + " " + authorInstance.LastName)

        For Each item In authorInstance.Books
            Console.WriteLine("     published ""{0}"", ISBN: {1}",
                              item.Title,
                              item.ISBN)
        Next

    End Using
    Console.ReadLine()
End Sub
```

You can notice in Listing 26.7 how you perform Insert operations by generating new entity instances and sending such instances to the model with the Add method of the desired collection. In this particular example, we use the Single extension method to retrieve the specified Author instance and then iterate the Books collection. If you run the code, you will get the result shown in Figure 26.17.

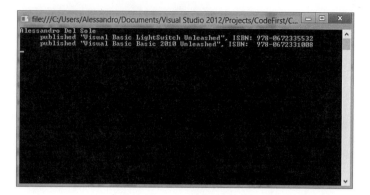

FIGURE 26.17   Adding and querying data against the database.

It is really interesting to see how data has been sent somewhere, even if we did not create a database. As you were told previously, the Entity Framework created the database for you at the moment in which the code started and determined that the database did not exist yet. You can either use Server Explorer or SQL Server Object Explorer to see how the database was created and attached to the instance of the server that was specified in the connection string. Figure 26.18 shows how the database appears in SQL Server Object Explorer.

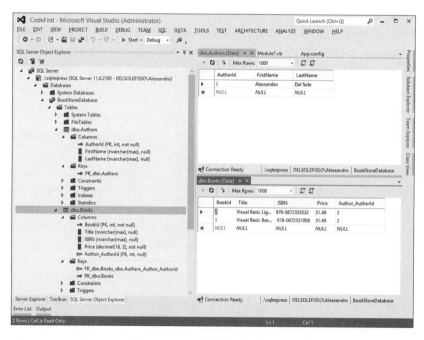

FIGURE 26.18   The structure of the autogenerated database, with data.

If you expand the structure of the database, you can see how Books and Authors tables have been created based on our Code First approach, including columns and keys for relationships. You can also show the tables' content (see Figure 26.18) to demonstrate that the code has sent data to the database correctly.

THE MAGIC OF CONVENTIONS

You might wonder how Entity Framework was also capable of generating primary keys if we did not decorate the code in any manner. The `Author` entity has an `AuthorId` property, and the `Book` entity has a `BookId` property, both property names contain the `Id` suffix. By convention, EF 5 considers an entity property named `Id` or containing the `Id` suffix or prefix as the primary key. Similarly, EF behaves for foreign keys. The relationship between `Author` and `Books` is defined via an `ICollection` object whose generic type is an entity. Based on this, it generates the appropriate keys.

You have seen how convenient the Code First approach is for working with data, but it has some limitations as it is. For example, you cannot specify some primary validation rules or you cannot customize the mapping to meet specific database requirements. Fortunately, the EF 5 provides two ways to make this possible: Data Annotations and the Fluent APIs.

Introducing Data Annotations

Data Annotations consists in decorating entities and their properties with some attributes from the `System.ComponentModel.DataAnnotations` and `System.ComponentModel.DataAnnotations.Schema` namespaces (from the System.ComponentModel.DataAnnotations.dll assembly). You already saw a particular usage of data annotations when talking about data validation previously, but you can also provide additional information to types, not just validation rules. The following code demonstrates how to rewrite the `Book` entity using data annotations:

```
<Table("OneBook")>
Public Class Book
    'Primary key
    <Key> Public Property BookNumber As Integer

    'Forced to be mandatory,
    'minimum length is 20 characters,
    'maximum length is 150
    <Required> <MinLength(20)> <StringLength(150)>
    Public Property Title As String

    'Determine the name of the foreign key
    'for the relationship
    <ForeignKey("Books_Author")> Public Property Author As Author
```

```
'Force the type in SQL Server to be 'char(10)'
<Column(TypeName:="char"), StringLength(10)> Public Property ISBN As String

'Force the type in SQL Server to be 'money'
<Column(TypeName:="money")> Public Property Price As Decimal
End Class
```

By reading the comments in the code, you can understand how attributes enable you to better customizations over the model and, consequently, over the database. For instance, using the Table attribute to mark the class will cause the database to contain a table called OneBook instead of Book, but in your code you will still use Book. The Key attribute marks a property as a primary key and is useful if you do not want to use a conventional name (that is, containing the Id literal). It is worth mentioning that you can force the mapping of a .NET type into a SQL type in the data store by using the Column attribute and then specifying the SQL type, like for ISBN and Price properties in the previous code. Table 26.2 summarizes the most common data annotations attributes.

TABLE 26.2 Data Annotations Attributes

Attribute	Description
Table	Enables you to specify the table name in the database.
Key	Enables you to specify the name of the primary key, based on the property that is decorated with the attribute.
Required	Marks a property as non-nullable. This is particularly useful with reference types, like String, since value types are non-nullable by default unless you define them as nullable using the Nullable(Of T) syntax or the question mark after the type name.
StringLength	Specifies the maximum length for a string.
MinLength, MaxLength	Enable you to specify the minimum and maximum length of a string, respectively (MaxLength is equivalent to StringLength).
ForeignKey	Enables you to specify the name for a navigation property representing a relationship.
Column	Enables you to specify the SQL Server data type that will be used to map the property's .NET type.

Using Data Annotations will not change the way the EF 5 checks for the database existence and creation if not found. Data Annotations are very useful but rely on a huge amount of attributes. You have an alternative for manipulating entities without using attributes, based on the Fluent APIs.

Handling Changes on the Database Schema

If you use the Code First approach and let the Entity Framework generate the database for you the first time you run the code that defines your model, the next time you make edits to your model you might also need to re-create your database. This is a common situation at development time and of course should never occur with production data. The reason is that the database schema could no longer match the model in some situations like adding/removing relationships, changing table definitions, and so on. In fact it might happen that you encounter an `InvalidOperationException` if you attempt to let EF 5 access the database after breaking changes in your model, which means you need to re-create the database. You can delete the database manually—for example, using Server Explorer or SQL Server Object Explorer in Visual Studio 2012—but you can also take advantage of the `Database` class that Entity Framework provides to decide in code how and when the database should be re-created. You have two options. The first option is re-creating the database every time you run the code; the second option is re-creating the database only when some differences exist between the database and classes that constitute the model. To accomplish this, you use the `Database.SetInitializer` shared method. The following code snippet demonstrates both options :

```
'Recreate the database only in case of changes
'between the model and the database schema
Database.SetInitializer(New DropCreateDatabaseIfModelChanges(Of BookStoreContext))

'Always recreate the database
Database.SetInitializer(New DropCreateDatabaseAlways(Of BookStoreContext))
```

The method's parameter can be either a new instance of the `DropCreateDatabaseIfModelChanges` class or a new instance of the `DropCreateDatabaseAlways` class. Both are generic classes, and the type parameter is the name of the context class.

The line of code that establishes how to re-create the database must come before the initialization of the context class. **Remember to remove the line of code when the application goes to production.** There is another class called `CreateDatabaseIfNotExists`, which is the default behavior and that you can omit.

CODE FIRST MIGRATIONS

The ADO.NET Entity Framework Team at Microsoft realized that making changes on the model and then sending those changes to the database schema is in most cases a complex task. For this reason, they are offering a migration mechanism called Code First Migrations that is available via NuGet and that is explained in the MSDN Library at the following page: http://msdn.microsoft.com/en-US/data/jj591621 http://msdn.microsoft.com/en-us/library/hh770484(v=vs.110).aspx

---

Introducing the Fluent APIs

There is an interesting alternative for customizing the model mapping in code, based on the Fluent APIs. As the name implies, this technique enables customizations only writing fluent code, without additional attributes or external mapping files. To use the Fluent APIs, you need to override the `OnModelCreating` method in the context class and, inside

26

the method body, apply edits via lambda expressions. The following code demonstrates how to rewrite the Book class using fluent code:

```
Public Class BookStoreContext
    Inherits DbContext

    Public Property Books As DbSet(Of Book)
    Public Property Authors As DbSet(Of Author)

    Protected Overrides Sub OnModelCreating(modelBuilder As DbModelBuilder)
        'Define the primary key
        modelBuilder.Entity(Of Book).HasKey(Function(b) b.BookNumber)

        'Define a one-to-many relationship
        modelBuilder.Entity(Of Book).HasRequired(Function(b) b.Author).WithMany()

        modelBuilder.Entity(Of Book)() _
            .Property(Function(b) b.Title).
            IsRequired.HasMaxLength(150)

        modelBuilder.Entity(Of Book)() _
            .Property(Function(b) b.ISBN).HasColumnType("char").
            HasMaxLength(10).IsFixedLength()

        modelBuilder.Entity(Of Book)() _
            .Property(Function(b) b.Price).
            HasColumnType("money")
    End Sub
End Class
```

Following is a list of interesting notes:

▶ The method's argument is an instance of the DbModelBuilder class, which is responsible to translate .NET code into a database schema.

▶ The generic Entity(Of T) method of the DbModelBuilder class takes the entity you want to edit as the type parameter.

▶ Entity(Of T) exposes a method called Property, whose argument is a lambda expression in which you specify the entity property you want to edit.

▶ You can set the primary key using the HasKey method, passing to the lambda expression the property that you want to be the primary key.

▶ You can set foreign keys using the HasRequired method, passing to the lambda expression the type that you want to be the other part of the relationship. You specify WithMany to create a one-to-many relationship (see the previous example).

▶ You can use multiple mapping methods over the specified properties, method names are self-explanatory, and IntelliSense helps you choose the appropriate methods.

The same rules for the database recreation apply to the Fluent APIs.

Additional Fluent Methods

Because the goal of the Fluent APIs is making it possible to write cleaner code, the Entity Framework provides specific members that make data manipulation easier. All members are exposed by the `DbSet(Of T)` class. The `Find` method enables you to retrieve the specific entity instance based on its primary key:

```
Dim anAuthor = db.Authors.Find(1)
```

The `Local` property enables you to work against in-memory data, which is the data currently stored in the model (except for those objects marked for deletion) without querying the database again:

```
Dim myBooks = From aBook In db.Books.Local
              Select aBook
              Order By aBook.Price Descending
```

The `Include` method, that you saw against EDMs, in Code First offers a generic implementation so that you no longer need to type the name of the entity. You use it with a lambda expression like this:

```
Dim myBooks = db.Authors.Include(Function(b) b.Books)
```

Finally, the `Load` extension method immediately executes a query against the database, avoiding the deferred execution. This is the equivalent of writing code to use a query at least once to make its result available. You use it like this:

```
db.Authors.Load()
```

All these members provide additional efficient ways to work with data in the Code First approach. You can also use the Object Browser and IntelliSense to see other members exposed by the `DbContext` and `DbSet` classes, and you will discover that most of them have a similar behavior of counterparts exposed by `ObjectContext` and `ObjectSet` classes that you met when talking about Entity Data Models. This makes migrating from one approach to another definitely easier.

MORE ABOUT CODE FIRST IN ENTITY FRAMEWORK

This chapter provided an overview of Code First, so you might want to check out the Data Developer Center at http://msdn.microsoft.com/en-us/data/aa937723, where you can find additional information and learning resources about Entity Framework and related development techniques. Also, the Entity Framework team at Microsoft has released a free extension for Visual Studio 2012 called Entity Framework Power Tools, which adds

26

design-time functionalities for generating DbContext classes. At the time in which this chapter is being written, it is available for C# only and as a beta, but you can check out the following page for future updates: http://visualstudiogallery.msdn.microsoft.com/72a60b14-1581-4b9b-89f2-846072eff19d

Compatibility with the Past and with Other Technologies

Before .NET 4.5 and Visual Studio 2012, Entity Data Models were generated with a different code generation strategy, so the context class and entities were very different and more complex if compared to the result that you get now with the new APIs. However, the previous code generation strategy and the related APIs have not been deprecated, so not only can they be a good alternative, but also they are required in specific scenarios. So it is a good idea to summarize the most important points in the previous code generation strategy:

▶ The context class is `System.Data.Objects.ObjectContext(Of T)` and the constructor allows specifying a connection string in code other than in the configuration file.

▶ Collection of entities are represented by the `System.Data.Objects.ObjectSet(Of T)` class.

▶ Classes defining entities are much more complex because of a number of attributes used for mapping database objects.

▶ Adding and removing items in a collection is performed via the `AddObject` and `DeleteObject` from the `ObjectSet(Of T)` class.

▶ Optimistic concurrency is handled by intercepting the `System.Data.OptimisticConcurrencyException`.

▶ Data validation is performed via partial methods declared in the entity definition.

▶ The .edmx had only one Visual Basic code file related, whose name finishes with .designer.vb.

It is not the goal of this chapter to provide a full explanation of the aforementioned objects, because the goal is instead introducing the new APIs, but it is very important to know that you can still convert Entity Data Models generated with the new code generation strategy so that they can use the old approach. To accomplish this, follow these steps:

1. Open the Entity Framework designer in Visual Studio 2012.

2. Right-click the designer and select Properties.

3. Change the value of the **Code Generation Strategy** property from None to Default.

4. In Solution Explorer, remove both the .tt files under the .edmx file.

5. Save and recompile the project.

By doing so you will be able to use the old code generation strategy and, consequently, the old APIs. The reason why this is useful is that not all of the platforms shipping with the .NET Framework 4.5 support the DbContext class. As an example, WCF RIA Services still need to use the ObjectContext class, as also shown in Chapter 36, "Building Rich Internet Applications with Silverlight 5."

Summary

In this chapter you got a high-level overview of ADO.NET Entity Framework in .NET 4.5, also known as EF 5. Entity Framework is a modern data platform providing a high abstraction layer from the database that enables you to work with a conceptual model instead of working directly with the data source. Database objects are mapped to the .NET equivalent into an Entity Data Model object model. Entities are a key concept in the EF and are classes representing database tables, as much as scalar properties represent tables' columns and navigation properties represent relationship. The DbContext class is responsible for managing the EDM lifetime, including the execution of Insert/Update/Delete operations that can be performed by invoking specific methods from entities. Querying data is instead accomplished via LINQ to Entities, a specific LINQ provider for the EF, and Entity SQL. You also saw how Visual Studio 2012 makes it easier to map stored procedures to the object model. Finally, you got started with the new Code First approach, which requires you to write some more code but which also enables you to maintain code cleaner and provides more controls over the generated data model.

26

Manipulating XML Documents with LINQ and XML Literals

With the growing diffusion of the Internet during the years, one of the most common needs has been establishing standards for information exchange across computers in different parts of the world. For such an exchange, the XML file format was introduced to provide a unified standard that was specific to structured data. Because of its flexibility, the XML file format became popular among developers, and the .NET Framework has always offered a built-in way for manipulating XML documents: the System.Xml namespace. With the advent of LINQ in Visual Basic 2008, things have been improved. Although the System.Xml namespace still exists for several reasons, a more efficient way of manipulating XML documents is now available in Visual Basic due to important features such as LINQ to XML and XML literals that are also integrated into the language syntax. In this chapter you learn about manipulating XML documents using LINQ to XML and XML literals, and you discover how much more powerful this opportunity is when compared to the System.Xml namespace.

KNOWLEDGE OF XML

The goal of this chapter is not explaining XML syntax and document structure, so you are required to be familiar with XML syntax and implementation.

Introducing LINQ to XML

LINQ to XML is the standard LINQ provider for reading, creating, and manipulating XML documents with the .NET languages starting from Visual Basic 2008 and Visual C# 3.0. Such a provider is implemented in the System.Xml.Linq.dll assembly and supports all operators available in LINQ to Objects with a few differences due to the XML document structure and other specific language features. The good news is that you can take advantage of the unified programming model offered by LINQ to perform XML manipulations via the classical LINQ syntax that you already know. Visual Basic 2012, like its predecessors, offers particular syntax paradigms for LINQ to XML that is also described in this chapter. You first learn how to create and manipulate XML documents using managed objects; in the second part of this chapter, you become skillful with XML literals that can allow you to write code more quickly and cleanly.

The `System.Xml.Linq` Namespace

The System.Xml.Linq namespace exposes objects for creating, reading, and manipulating XML documents. All objects inherit from System.Xml.Linq.XObject. Table 27.1 summarizes and describes available objects.

TABLE 27.1   Objects Available in the System.Xml.Linq Namespace

Object	Description
XDocument	Represents an entire XML document
XElement	Represents an XML element with attributes
XAttribute	Represents an XML attribute
XComment	Represents a comment within an XML document
XDeclaration	Represents the XML declaration, including version number and encoding
XNode	Represents an XML node which is made of an XML element and children elements
XName	Provides a name to an XML element or attribute
XCData	Represents a CData section
XText	Represents a text node
XContainer	Represents a container for node
XNamespace	Declares an XML namespace
XDocumentType	Represents a Document Type Definition (DTD) typically for XML schemas

You create an XML document declaring an instance of the XDocument class:

```
Dim myDocument As New XDocument
```

When you have the instance, you can add all acceptable objects mentioned in Table 27.1. The first required element is the XML declaration that can be added as follows and that is mandatory:

```
myDocument.Declaration = New XDeclaration("1.0", "utf-8", "no")
```

If you want to add comments to your XML documents, you can create as many instances of the XComment class for as many comments as you need to add:

```
myDocument.Add(New XComment("My first Xml document with LINQ"))
```

The next step is creating a first-level XElement that stores nested XElement objects:

```
Dim mainElement As New XElement("Contacts")
```

Now you can create nested elements and specify some attributes, as demonstrated in the following code:

```
'An Xml element with attributes
Dim firstNestedElement As New XElement("Contact")
Dim attribute1 As New XAttribute("LastName", "Del Sole")
Dim attribute2 As New XAttribute("FirstName", "Alessandro")
Dim attribute3 As New XAttribute("Age", "35")
firstNestedElement.Add(attribute1)
firstNestedElement.Add(attribute2)
firstNestedElement.Add(attribute3)

Dim secondNestedElement As New XElement("Contact")
Dim attribute4 As New XAttribute("LastName", "White")
Dim attribute5 As New XAttribute("FirstName", "Robert")
Dim attribute6 As New XAttribute("Age", "40")
secondNestedElement.Add(attribute4)
secondNestedElement.Add(attribute5)
secondNestedElement.Add(attribute6)

'In-line initialization with an array of XAttribute
Dim thirdNestedElement As New XElement("Contact", New XAttribute() {
                            New XAttribute("LastName", "Red"),
                            New XAttribute("FirstName", "Stephen"),
                            New XAttribute("Age", "41")})
```

When you create an XAttribute you need to invoke the XElement.Add instance method to assign the new attribute. Creating elements and assigning attributes is a simple task because classes are self-explanatory, and IntelliSense helps you understand which arguments the constructors need. But if you take a look at the last instance, you can see that

27

things can become difficult, especially if you think that you could create an array of `XElement` with nested `XElement` definitions, with nested `XAttribute` definitions. You see later in this chapter how XML literals make things easier; for now let's focus on fundamentals. The next step is to add all nested `XElement` objects to the main `XElement` as follows:

```
With mainElement
    .Add(firstNestedElement)
    .Add(secondNestedElement)
    .Add(thirdNestedElement)
End With
```

`mainElement` now stores a sequence of XML elements that must be added to the document as follows:

```
myDocument.Add(mainElement)
```

In the end, you can save your XML document to disk by invoking the `Save` method:

```
myDocument.Save("C:\Contacts.xml")
```

This method has several overloads that also enable the specifying of a stream instead of a string of file options for controlling formatting. If you just want to check your result, invoke `XDocument.ToString` as follows:

```
Console.WriteLine(myDocument.ToString)
```

This line of code allows you to see how your document is formed. The output follows:

```
<!--My first Xml document with LINQ-->
<Contacts>
  <Contact LastName="Del Sole" FirstName="Alessandro" Age="32" />
  <Contact LastName="White" FirstName="Robert" Age="40" />
  <Contact LastName="Red" FirstName="Stephen" Age="41" />
</Contacts>
```

Creating an XML document with the `System.Xml.Linq` namespace is more intuitive than the older `System.Xml` namespace, but things can go better as you see later. At the moment you need to know how to load and parse existing documents.

Loading and Parsing Existing XML Documents

To load an existing XML document, you invoke the shared `XDocument.Load` method as follows:

```
Dim myDocument = XDocument.Load("C:\Contacts.xml")
```

You can get a new instance of `XDocument` and get access to its members via numerous methods and properties that the class offers. Table 27.2 summarizes the most important members.

TABLE 27.2   Most Important Members of the `XDocument` Class

Member	Type	Description
AddAfterSelf	Method	Adds the specified content just after the node whose instance is invoking the method itself
AddBeforeSelf	Method	Adds the specified content just before the node whose instance is invoking the method itself
AddFirst	Method	Adds the specified content as the first node in the document
ReplaceWith	Method	Replaces the node whose instance is invoking the method with the specified content
Root	Property	Returns the root `XElement`
Remove	Method	Removes the node from its parents
RemoveNodes	Method	Removes children nodes from the object instance that is invoking the method
Element	Method	Retrieves an `XElement` instance of the specified XML element
Descendants	Method	Returns an `IEnumerable(Of XElement)` collection of descendant `XElement` objects
FirstNode/LastNode/ NextNode/PreviousNode	Properties	Return the instance of the node which position is indicated by the property name

Notice that both `XDocument` and `XElement` classes expose methods in Table 27.2, and `XElement` can also load and save XML content as much as `XDocument`. Both `XDocument` and `XElement` classes also allow parsing strings containing XML representation to get an appropriate object. This is accomplished invoking the `Parse` method as in the following example:

```
Dim document As String = "<?xml version=""1.0""?>" & Environment.NewLine & _
                "    <Contacts>" & Environment.NewLine & _
                "        <Contact FirstName=""Alessandro"" Last
                    Name=""Del Sole"" Age=""35""/>" & _
            Environment.NewLine & _
                "        <Contact FirstName=""Robert"" Last
                    Name=""White"" Age=""40""/>" & _
            Environment.NewLine & _
                "    </Contacts>"

Dim resultingDocument As XDocument = XDocument.Parse(document)
resultingDocument.Save("C:\Contacts.xml")
```

This can be useful if you need to get a real XML document from a simple string.

27

Querying XML Documents with LINQ

You can take advantage of the LINQ syntax for querying XML documents. Consider the following XML file:

```
<Contacts>
  <Contact LastName="Del Sole" FirstName="Alessandro" Age="35" />
  <Contact LastName="White" FirstName="Robert" Age="40" />
  <Contact LastName="Red" FirstName="Stephen" Age="41" />
</Contacts>
```

Now imagine you want to get a list of last names for people with an age greater than or equal to 40. This can be accomplished by the following query:

```
Dim query = From element In myDocument.Descendants("Contact")
            Where Integer.Parse(element.Attribute("Age").Value) >= 40
            Select element.Attribute("LastName").Value
```

The `Descendants` method returns an `IEnumerable(Of XElement)` and stores all `XElement` objects whose `XName` is the one specified as the argument. To get the value of an attribute about comparisons as in our situation, you invoke the `XElement.Attribute()`. `Value` property that contains the actual value of the `XAttribute` instance whose name is specified within `Attribute("")`. Notice how an explicit conversion is required from `String` to `Integer` to perform an evaluation on numbers. The preceding query returns an `IEnumerable(Of String)`. If you need to generate custom results, you can take advantage of anonymous types as in the following query that get only the `LastName` and `Age` values:

```
Dim query = From element In myDocument.Descendants("Contact")
            Let age = Integer.Parse(element.Attribute("Age").Value)
            Where age >= 40
            Select New With {.LastName = element.
                                        Attribute("LastName").Value,
                      .Age = age}
```

The preceding query returns `IEnumerable(Of anonymous type)`. Notice how the `Let` keyword is used to provide a temporary identifier that can be used both for performing a comparison and for assignment to the anonymous type's `Age` property. With the exception of anonymous types, as you remember from the LINQ to Objects discussion, you can bind results of LINQ to XML queries directly to user interface controls, such as the `BindingSource` in Windows Forms or the `CollectionViewSource` in WPF. By the way, remember that, if you do not select just one attribute per element (which would return an `IEnumerable(Of String)`), this would work as collections of `XElement`; therefore, it is not the best approach because you need to work against your business objects and not against `XElement` instances. Just to provide a simple example, if you need an iteration over your query, iterating an `IEnumerable(Of XElement)` would not probably make much sense; though it instead would with a `List(Of Contact)`. The appropriate approach is creating a class that maps each element within the XML document. For example, consider the following simplified implementation of the `Contact` class:

```
Class Contact
    Property FirstName As String
    Property LastName As String
    Property Age As Integer
End Class
```

At this point, you can write a LINQ query that generates a collection of `Contact` and that can be both mapped to a user interface control and that can be edited:

```
'Returns a List(Of Contact)
Dim contactCollection = (From element In myDocument.Descendants("Contact")
                        Let age = Integer.Parse(element.
                                                Attribute("Age").Value)
                        Select New Contact With {.FirstName = element.

                                             Attribute("FirstName").Value,
                                             .LastName = element.

                                             Attribute("LastName").Value,
                                             .Age = age}).ToList
```

Now you have a `List(Of Contact)` that can be both used for presenting data or for editing. On the contrary, you could create an XML document starting from a collection of objects, but this is something you see in a more efficient way in the discussion of XML literals in the next section.

Writing XML Markup in VB with XML Literals

The `System.Xml.Linq` namespace is powerful. Manipulating complex XML documents that store a lot of data can lead to writing less elegant and more complex code. Luckily the Visual Basic language provides a powerful feature for manipulating XML documents, known as *XML literals*. You can write XML markup together with the Visual Basic code. The following code provides an example:

```
'The compiler infers XDocument
Dim Contacts = <?xml version="1.0"?>
            <Contacts>
                <Contact LastName="Del Sole"
                    FirstName="Alessandro"
                    Age="35"
                    email="alessandro.delsole@visual-basic.it"/>
                <!- Fantasy name->
                <Contact LastName="White"
                    FirstName="Robert"
                    Age="45"
                    email="address1@something.com"/>
            </Contacts>
```

This means that you can write entire XML documents integrating XML markup and Visual Basic code. Here IntelliSense features are less powerful than in the classic Visual Studio XML editor, but they are good enough to provide syntax colorization and code indentation. Figure 27.1 shows what the preceding code looks like in the Visual Basic code editor.

FIGURE 27.1   XML literals in the Visual Basic code editor.

Just think that you can paste from the clipboard the content of long and complex XML documents, such as Microsoft Excel workbooks or Open XML documents, and take advantage of XML literals. The Visual Basic compiler can then map XML nodes to the appropriate .NET type. In the previous example, Contacts and Contact are mapped to XElement objects, whereas properties of each Contact element are mapped to XAttribute objects. The previous example also takes advantage of local type inference. In such a scenario, the Visual Basic compiler infers the XDocument type for the Contacts variable. This is because the XML markup contains the XML declaration. If you do not specify such a declaration, the XML markup is mapped to an XElement, as in the following code:

```
'The compiler infers XElement
Dim Contacts = <Contacts>
                 <Contact LastName="Del Sole"
                     FirstName="Alessandro"
                     Age="32"
                     email="alessandro.delsole@visual-basic.it"/>
               </Contacts>
```

If you do not want to use local type inference, you need to pay attention to which type the XML markup is mapped. For example, both the following code snippets throw an `InvalidCastException`:

```
'Throws an InvalidCastException
'Cannot assign to XElement markup that
'ships with the Xml declaration
Dim Contacts As XElement = <?xml version="1.0"?>
                           <Contacts>
                             <Contact LastName="Del Sole"
                               FirstName="Alessandro"
                               Age="35"
                               email="alessandro.delsole@visual-basic.it"/>
                                   <!-- Fantasy name-->
                             <Contact LastName="White"
                               FirstName="Robert"
                               Age="45"
                               email="address1@something.com"/>
                           </Contacts>
'Throws an InvalidCastException
'Cannot assign to XDocument markup that
'does not have the Xml declaration
Dim Contacts As XDocument = <Contacts>
                             <Contact LastName="Del Sole"
                               FirstName="Alessandro"
                               Age="35"
                               email="alessandro.delsole@visual-basic.it"/>
                             <!-- Fantasy name-->
                             <Contact LastName="White"
                               FirstName="Robert"
                               Age="45"
                               email="address1@something.com"/>
                           </Contacts>
```

XML literals are powerful because they allow you to write more elegant code and provide a view of your XML documents as you would within an XML editor that is better than generating nodes, elements, and attributes the old-fashioned way. The preceding code has one limitation: It is hard-coded, meaning that values have been added manually. This would be a big limitation because you often need to dynamically generate XML documents (for example, generating elements for each member within a data source). Luckily, XML literals make this easier, providing the ability to embed local variables' values and LINQ queries within the XML markup, as shown in the next section.

27

BEHIND THE SCENES

The Visual Basic compiler parses XML documents, elements, and attributes written with XML literals into the appropriate .NET types, such as XDocument, XElement, and XAttribute. Comments are included in such a mapping and converted into XComment objects and so on. Please refer to Table 27.1 for available objects.

LINQ Queries with XML Literals

XML literals provide an alternative syntax for LINQ to XML queries in Visual Basic code. Let's look at the first XML document used in the "System.Xml.Linq Namespace" section again, which looks like the following but with a slight modification:

```
<?xml version="1.0" encoding="utf-8"?>
<Contacts>
  <Contact FirstName="Alessandro"
          LastName="Del Sole"
          Age="35"
          Email="alessandro.delsole@visual-basic.it">
  </Contact>
  <!--The following are fantasy names-->
  <Contact FirstName="Stephen"
          LastName="Red"
          Age="40"
          Email="address1@something.com">
  </Contact>
  <Contact FirstName="Robert"
          LastName="White"
          Age="41"
          Email="address2@something.com">
  </Contact>
  <Contact FirstName="Luke"
          LastName="Green"
          Age="42"
          Email="address3@something.com">
  </Contact>
  <Person FirstName="Alessandro"
          LastName="Del Sole">
  </Person>
</Contacts>
```

There is a Person element that we want to be excluded. The goal is querying all Contact elements whose age is greater than or equal to 40. Instead of recurring to the classical syntax, you can write the following code:

```
Dim doc = XDocument.Load("Contacts.xml")

Dim query = From cont In doc.<Contacts>.<Contact>
            Where Integer.Parse(cont.@Age) >= 40
            Select cont
```

The preceding code uses new symbols for querying documents known as *XML Axis
Properties*. Table 27.3 summarizes XML axis.

TABLE 27.3   XML Axis

Symbol	Description
...<>	XML Axis Descendants Property. Returns all descendant elements of the XML document named as the identifier enclosed within the symbols.
.<>	XML Axis Child Property. Returns children of an XElement or XDocument.
.@	XML Axis Attribute Property. Returns the value of an attribute within an XML element.

The preceding query can be described by this sentence: "Process all Contacts' children
Contact elements." The difference with the XML Axis Descendants Properties can be
explained with another example. Consider the following document that is just a revalida-
tion of the previous one:

```
<?xml version="1.0" encoding="utf-8"?>
<Contacts>
  <Contact>
    <FirstName>Alessandro</FirstName>
    <LastName>Del Sole</LastName>
    <Age>35</Age>
    <Email>alessandro.delsole@visual-basic.it</Email>
  </Contact>
  <Contact>
    <FirstName>Stephen</FirstName>
    <LastName>Red</LastName>
    <Age>40</Age>
    <Email>address1@something.com</Email>
  </Contact>
  <Person>
    <FirstName>Robert</FirstName>
    <LastName>White</LastName>
  </Person>
</Contacts>
```

27

Now each `Contact` element has sub-elements. If you wanted to get a collection of all `LastName` elements for all elements, you could use the XML Axis Descendants property as follows:

```
'Returns a collection of all <LastName></LastName>
'elements within the document
Dim onlyLastNames = From cont In doc...<LastName>
```

It's worth mentioning that such a query also includes results from the `Person` element because it exposes a `LastName` attribute. So if you need to filter results depending on the root element, you should invoke the Axis Descendants property. Notice also how in both the previous code examples an explicit conversion is required when you need a comparison against non-String data. In this particular case the comparison is done against an integer number (40); therefore, you can invoke the `Integer.Parse` method—because you expect that the `Age` attribute contains the string representation of a number. XML Axis properties provide a simplified and cleaner way for querying XML documents. Just remember that, as discussed in the previous section, *you will need helper classes for mapping each XElement content into a .NET type* to provide data-binding features to your code.

WHY `Option Strict On` IS IMPORTANT

One of the last code snippets had an explicit conversion using `Integer.Parse`. If you set `Option Strict On` and forget to perform such a conversion, the compiler throws an exception requiring you to perform an appropriate conversion, which is always good. If you instead set `Option Strict Off`, no conversion is required at compile time, but in all cases you encounter errors at runtime except if you assign the value of an attribute to a `String` variable. You should always keep `Option Strict On`.

Understanding Embedded Expressions

With embedded expressions, you can include local variables or perform dynamic queries within XML literals. Let's look again at the first example about XML literals, where an XML document contains a couple of contacts. Imagine you want to generate a contact starting from some variables (that you could populate at runtime with different values) instead of hard-coding the last name, first name, and age. This can be accomplished as follows:

```
'All with type inference
Dim FirstName = "Alessandro"
Dim LastName = "Del Sole"
Dim Age = 35

Dim Contacts = <?xml version="1.0"?>
               <Contacts>
                   <Contact LastName=<%= LastName %>
                       FirstName=<%= FirstName %>
                       Age=<%= Age %>
```

```
                  email="alessandro.delsole@visual-basic.it"/>
           <!-- Fantasy name-->
           <Contact LastName="White"
                FirstName="Robert"
                Age="45"
                email="address1@something.com"/>
      </Contacts>
```

Although the second contact in the list is equal to the first example, the first contact is generated with embedded expressions. You create an embedded expression including an expression within <%= and => symbols. While you write the expression after the opening tag, IntelliSense works to improve your coding experience. In this way, you can create elements dynamically. But this code works just for one element. What if you need to dynamically generate as many elements for as many items stored within a collection or within a database table? Imagine you have a Contact class that is implemented as follows:

```
Class Contact
     Property FirstName As String
     Property LastName As String
     Property Age As Integer
     Property EmailAddress As String
End Class
```

Now imagine that within a method body you create a collection of Contact. For demo purposes, four instances of the Contact class are created and then pushed into a new collection:

```
Dim firstContact As New Contact With {.FirstName = "Alessandro",
                 .LastName = "Del Sole",
                 .EmailAddress = "alessandro.delsole@visual-basic.it",
                 .Age = 35}


'Now fantasy names
Dim secondContact As New Contact With {.FirstName = "Stephen",
                 .LastName = "Red",
                 .EmailAddress = "address1@something.com",
                 .Age = 40}
Dim thirdContact As New Contact With {.FirstName = "Robert",
                 .LastName = "White",
                 .EmailAddress = "address2@something.com",
                 .Age = 41}
Dim fourthContact As New Contact With {.FirstName = "Luke",
                 .LastName = "Green",
                 .EmailAddress = "address3@something.com",
                 .Age = 42}
```

27

```
Dim people As New List(Of Contact) From {
                    firstContact,
                    secondContact,
                    thirdContact,
                    fourthContact}
```

Our goal is to generate an XML document that contains all the preceding created contacts as XML nodes. This is accomplished by the following code:

```
Dim newDocument = <?xml version="1.0"?>
                    <Contacts>
                        <%= From cont In people
                            Where cont.Age > 35
                            Select <Contact
                                        FirstName=<%= cont.FirstName %>
                                        LastName=<%= cont.LastName %>
                                        Age=<%= cont.Age %>
                                        Email=<%= cont.EmailAddress %>>
                                    </Contact>
                            %>
                    </Contacts>


newDocument.Save("C:\Contacts.xml")
```

Embedding an expression means that you can also embed a LINQ query. Notice how the query is part of the first embedded expression and how the Select clause allows the creation of a new XElement object using XML literals where nested embedded expressions can provide advantage of local variables. The previous code can produce the following result (remember that only people with an age greater than 35 have been included):

```
<Contacts>
  <Contact FirstName="Stephen" LastName="Red" Age="40"
        Email="address1@something.com"></Contact>
  <Contact FirstName="Robert" LastName="White" Age="41"
        Email="address2@something.com"></Contact>
  <Contact FirstName="Luke" LastName="Green" Age="42"
        Email="address3@something.com"></Contact>
</Contacts>
```

Using XML literals and embedded expressions, you dynamically created an XML document that can contain an infinite number of elements. This example was related to a simple generic collection, but you can easily understand what kinds of results you can reach if you need to generate XML documents from database tables. If you work with LINQ to SQL or with ADO.NET Entity Framework, the code remains the same; the only exception is that the data source in the From clause is the DataContext instance for LINQ to SQL or the ObjectContext or DbContext classes in the ADO.NET Entity Framework.

Iterators and XML Literals

The new Visual Basic feature of iterators can be used inside XML literals code blocks. Specifically, you can use the anonymous iterators (or iterator lambdas). The following code shows how to use an anonymous iterator to retrieve only the `LastName` property for each item in the `People` collection created previously and creates an XML document where each contact has only the `LastName` attribute:

```
Dim doc = <?xml version="1.0"?>
          <Contacts>
              <%= (Iterator Function()
                      For Each person In people
                          Yield person
                      Next
                  End Function)().
                  Select(Function(c) <Contact LastName=<%= c.LastName %>>
                                     </Contact>) %>
          </Contacts>
```

By using the iterator lambda you can write more responsive code, whose result can be elaborated while the rest of processing is still in progress.

XML Schema Inference

LINQ to XML and XML literals are both powerful features, but they have a limitation: Within embedded expressions or when using the literals symbols in queries, IntelliSense support is not as good as usual, especially when you need to invoke XML attributes. This means that in most situations you need to remember and manually write code that maps attributes with no IntelliSense support. This can lead to errors because elements and attributes within XML documents are case-sensitive, so typing `age` instead of `Age` results in a runtime error. To solve this issue, Visual Basic offers the XML Schema Inference Wizard, which is a tool integrated in the IDE and that is specific for Visual Basic. The tool enables the generating of an XML schema from the XML document you query and allows enabling IntelliSense support. First, you need an XML document. The following is a simplified list of customers that is the base document:

```
<?xml version="1.0" encoding="utf-8" ?>
<Customers xmlns="DelSole.Customers">
  <Customer CustomerID="DELSO" CompanyName="Del Sole Ltd."
```

27

```
            Country="Italy" Address="Unspecified"
            Email="alessandro.delsole@visual-basic.it"/>

  <!- Not real names ->
  <Customer CustomerID="GREEN" CompanyName="Green Corp."
            Country="Italy" Address="Unspecified"
            Email="address1@something.com"/>

  <Customer CustomerID="WHITE" CompanyName="White Corp."
            Country="Italy" Address="Unspecified"
            Email="address2@something.com"/>
</Customers>
```

Notice how an XML namespace declaration has been added to the `Customers` node. This is important and is explained later. Save the file as **Customers.xml**. When you get the document, right-click the project name in Solution Explorer and select **Add New Item**. When the Add New Item dialog box appears, select the **XML to Schema** template and name it **CustomersSchema.xsd**, as shown in Figure 27.2.

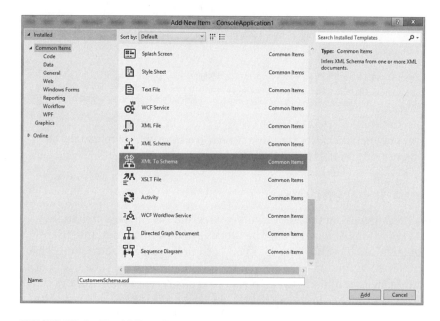

FIGURE 27.2   The XML to Schema item template.

After you click **Add**, a dialog box named Infer XML Schema Set from XML Documents appears, requiring you to specify the XML document as the base. You are not limited to specifying existing XML documents; you can manually write the document (or paste it from the clipboard) or specify an XML document that is available on a network. This can be useful if you want to generate schemas for RSS feeds. Click the **Add from File** button and select the **Customers.xml** document. (You can notice that Visual Studio automatically points to the project folder making the selection easier.) Figure 27.3 shows the dialog box.

FIGURE 27.3   Selecting the XML document for generating XML schemas from.

The good news is that you are not limited to just one document; you can add multiple documents to generate multiple schemas at one time. When you finish and click **OK**, Visual Studio generates an .Xsd document whose content is the following:

```
<?xml version="1.0" encoding="utf-8"?>
<xs:schema attributeFormDefault="unqualified"
           elementFormDefault="qualified"
           targetNamespace="DelSole.Customers"
           xmlns:xs="http://www.w3.org/2001/XMLSchema">
  <xs:element name="Customers">
    <xs:complexType>
      <xs:sequence>
        <xs:element maxOccurs="unbounded" name="Customer">
          <xs:complexType>
            <xs:attribute name="CustomerID" type="xs:string"
                      use="required" />
            <xs:attribute name="CompanyName" type="xs:string"
                      use="required" />
```

27

```
           <xs:attribute name="Country" type="xs:string"
                         use="required" />
           <xs:attribute name="Address" type="xs:string"
                         use="required" />
           <xs:attribute name="Email" type="xs:string"
                         use="required" />
         </xs:complexType>
       </xs:element>
     </xs:sequence>
   </xs:complexType>
  </xs:element>
</xs:schema>
```

The schema is simple because the structure of our starting document is simple. Notice how the schema declaration contains a `targetNamespace` attribute that maps the XML namespace we provided within the original document. You can also get a visual representation of the new schema via the XML Schema Explorer tool window that is available by clicking **View, XML Schema Explorer**. The tool window is shown in Figure 27.4.

FIGURE 27.4   The XML Schema Explorer tool window.

This window is helpful to understand the hierarchical structure of an XML schema. For the newly created schema, notice the custom namespace at the root level and then the root document node, named `Customers`. Within the child node, `Customer`, you can see nested attributes and mappings to data types. Also notice how Visual Studio tells us that `Customer` is part of a one-to-many relationship (1..*).

XML SCHEMA DESIGNER

Visual Studio 2012 offers a specific designer for XML schemas that is also enabled each time you work with such documents. The editor is now based on WPF and allows generating or editing schemas with a powerful designer. This tool is not described here, but you can easily understand how to take advantage of its instrumentation to edit schemas the first time you see it.

At this point, you are ready to write Visual Basic code. The first thing to do is to add an `Imports` directive pointing to the XML namespace. This is possible because the `Imports` keyword can import XML namespaces, too, as follows:

```
Imports <xmlns:ds="DelSole.Customers">
```

IMPORTING XML NAMESPACES

Each time you need to work with XML documents or schemas that define an XML namespace, you need to import that namespace. This is because, otherwise, you should rewrite the XML namespace declaration every time you write an XML element within your document. By importing the namespace, you do not need to worry anymore about XML namespaces. Microsoft Excel's workbooks or XAML markup code are good examples of this.

This is the point where IntelliSense can provide support for your schemas. Now you can understand why the addition of an XML namespace within the original document was necessary. At this point you could write whatever query you need. The following query is simple, but its purpose is not to show how you can query data; instead its purpose is to demonstrate IntelliSense capabilities in XML literals after the addition of an XML schema:

```
Dim custDoc = XDocument.Load("Customers.xml")

Dim customers = From cust In custDoc...<ds:Customer>
                Select cust.@CompanyName
```

At the point at which you type the `...<` symbols, IntelliSense shows all the available options for the schema allowing the selection of available nodes. Figure 27.5 shows IntelliSense in action.

As you can imagine, this is helpful because now you are not required to remember every element in the XML document and to type it manually. And this works not only with XML elements, but also with XML attributes, which is what you get when beginning to write the `.@` symbols. Figure 27.6 represents such a situation.

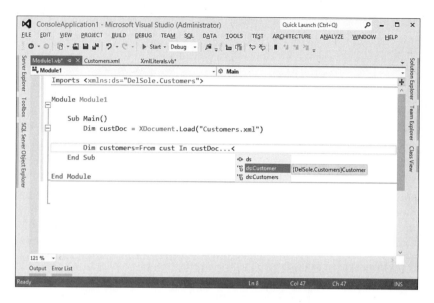

FIGURE 27.5   XML Schema Inference enables IntelliSense in LINQ queries with XML literals.

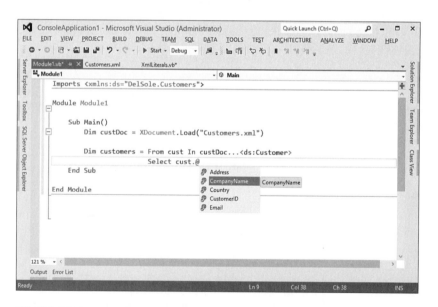

FIGURE 27.6   IntelliSense also allows you to select attributes.

If you have multiple schemas or multiple namespaces, IntelliSense can provide support for all of them making your coding experience straightforward.

Summary

The .NET Framework offers a special LINQ provider named LINQ to XML that enables working with XML documents. Via the `System.Xml.Linq` namespace, this provider allows creating and manipulating XML documents in an efficient way. Classes such as `XDocument`, `XElement`, `XAttribute`, `XComment`, and `XDeclaration` are self-explanatory and allow easy generation of XML documents. To query XML documents, you just write LINQ queries using the unified syntax that you already know, with a few additions such as the `Descendants` or `Attribute` property. Although efficient, `System.Xml.Linq` can be confusing when XML documents become larger. Luckily, Visual Basic provides the XML literals feature that enables the writing of XML markup code directly into the VB code editor. To make things real, with embedded expressions you can generate documents putting local variables, expressions, and LINQ queries within XML literals so that you can generate XML documents dynamically. Visual Basic also takes care of your coding experience and provides the XML Schema Inference Wizard that generates an XML schema starting from the XML document you want to query with LINQ to XML and allows enabling IntelliSense for that particular document, avoiding the risk of typos.

27

CHAPTER 28

Creating WPF Applications

Over the years, the requirement for high-quality applications has dramatically increased. Modern technologies enable users to perform even more complex tasks; technology and computers are a significant part of users' lives. Computer applications need to respond to such requests. The user experience is something that cannot be disregarded anymore, even if an application works perfectly on data access. The more complex the task an application can perform, the more important is the need of an interactive user interface that enables the user to easily perform tasks through the application. And this is something that is strictly related to different kinds of applications: business applications, home applications, and multimedia and entertainment applications. Windows 8 Store Apps are the most recent examples of great user interfaces. For many years, .NET developers could build user interfaces based on the Windows Forms, which has been a good and important framework for creating user experiences with the .NET technology. Windows Forms has big limitations, especially if you need to create dynamic interfaces or complex data-bindings. Also, .NET Framework 4.0 signaled the last point in which some enhancements have been added to Windows Forms, but Microsoft stopped investing in that platform, even if it's still supported. With the purpose of providing a unified programming model for building advanced user interfaces, being suitable for combining data access, dynamic interfaces, multimedia, and documents capabilities, Microsoft created the Windows Presentation Foundation technology (WPF), which dramatically increases developer productivity and offers a great environment for styling the application layout by a professional designer. WPF combines in one framework all you need to build new generation applications. If you are an experienced WPF developer, maybe this chapter is just a quick recap for you. If you are new to WPF, this and the following chapters give you the basics for beginning to build modern applications with Visual Basic 2012.

What Is WPF?

Windows Presentation Foundation (WPF) is the premier framework from Microsoft for building user interfaces in desktop applications for Windows 8, Windows 7, and Windows Vista. WPF is not intended to be a replacement for Windows Forms; it can be considered as a revolutionary alternative for building rich client applications. Windows Presentation Foundation offers several advantages that make user interface development straightforward. First, it is built on the top of the Microsoft DirectX graphic libraries, meaning that WPF applications can embed audio, videos, pictures, animations, and 3D graphics, all in a .NET-oriented fashion, with few lines of code. You can create rich client applications continuing to write Visual Basic code as you are already used to doing. WPF takes advantage of the GPU support of a graphics card, but it is also fully compatible with software rendering and can fall back on that when a GPU is not available (although it is actually expensive in terms of performance). Second, WPF has a powerful data-binding engine that makes it easier to build data-oriented applications. Third, it provides a separation layer between the developer and the designer so that professional designers can completely restyle the application's layout with specific tools, improving what the developer built. WPF completely changes the way you think of your user interfaces but does not change the way you write Visual Basic code. WPF has some big differences with Windows Forms in its architecture; therefore, you need a different approach to some problems. As an example, WPF handles events via the routed events that are completely different from the event infrastructure in Windows Forms. You can handle events in WPF the same way you do in Windows Forms. The way you write code is the same, on the top of different technologies. WPF has been the first platform using the XAML markup language for declaring the user interface; XAML was later brought to Silverlight, Silverlight for Windows Phone, and now to Metro-style apps for Windows 8 (with some small differences due to their different contexts). This means that all the investments you made (or you are ready to make) in learning WPF are also valid in a number of other development platforms; by using the same programming approach you can quickly be productive against different platforms and scenarios. This should be enough to convince you why learning WPF is so important.

PERSONAL SUGGESTIONS ON APPROACHING WPF

I delivered several technical speeches on Windows Presentation Foundation, and one thing I noticed is that lots of developers do not approach WPF correctly. This is because the Internet is full of impressive demo applications with enhanced user interfaces and graphical experience and lots of presentation demos are built to show advanced WPF topics. Seeing a 3D application with animations is surely impressive, but it can be quite frustrating if you try to reproduce it after a few days' experience with WPF. Because of this, often developers do not continue studying WPF. The best approach is instead to understand what one needs to work with WPF even if the UI is not so impressive. When you know how user controls work and how they are built, you can easily search within the MSDN library to make them nicer.

Improvements in WPF 4.5

If you already have experience with WPF, you might be interested in getting some hints about improvements in the new version. The Visual Studio 2012 designer has been significantly improved to make your experience even better. A plethora of improvements is strictly related to data-binding; in most cases you will not see performance improvements but it is worth mentioning that you can now control the behavior of the `VirtualizingStackPanel` object by setting its `ScrollUnit` attached property. You can set the `Delay` property of a data-binding to avoid a data source to be updated immediately (think of a slider moving continuously and causing performance overhead). You can now perform data-binding against static properties. Data sources can now automatically reflect to the user interface the result of a filter or of a sorting operation. Last but not least, a `RibbonControl` has been introduced in order to make it easier to create applications that mimic the Office 2007 and 2010 layout (and of some applications included in Windows 7 and Windows 8). The full list of improvements that are part of WPF 4.5 is available at this address of the MSDN library: http://msdn.microsoft.com/en-us/library/bb613588(v=vs.110).aspx.

In the next sections you learn the foundations of WPF and learn about specific features of this interesting technology.

> **NOTE**
>
> This is a language-oriented book; therefore, covering every aspect of the WPF technology is not possible. If you want to learn more about the WPF technology, consider *Windows Presentation Foundation Unleashed* from Sams Publishing.

WPF and Windows 8: The Future of Desktop Development

Since the first developer preview of Windows 8, one of the biggest concerns for developers has been related to the future of WPF and, more generally, of the desktop development for Windows. The reason is that Windows 8 Store Apps are a real revolution for an operating system like Windows, and Microsoft is pushing this kind of development so much that some developers got confused, thinking that only Store Apps will be the development platform on the new operating system. As you might know, Windows 8 on a PC can work both as Desktop and with apps. This implies that not only the Desktop is still alive and will survive for a long time, but also that WPF is the one platform that developers will use to build applications for the Desktop in Windows 8, although only for x86 and x64 processors. Developing for ARM processors only allows building Windows Store Apps. Also, do not forget Windows 7 and Windows Vista: You can still use WPF 4.5 to build client applications for those operating systems. All the investments you made in WPF will be still there, ready for Windows 8's desktop. So, don't be afraid if you are migrating from Windows Forms or if you made previous investments: The present and future of the desktop development is Windows Presentation Foundation.

Introducing the WPF Architecture

WPF relies on a layered architecture that is represented in Figure 28.1. The first layer is the Windows operating system. The second layer is constituted by the combination of two communicating layers: User32, which is the part of the operating system responsible for exchanging messages with applications, and the DirectX libraries, which are the real power of WPF. The next layer is named Milcore and is written in unmanaged code. It is responsible for integrating the unmanaged area of the architecture with the managed architecture that starts from the next layer, the Common Language Runtime (CLR), which is the root of every managed activity or layer. The PresentationCore is the first WPF layer that is responsible for implementing several important features such as the XAML language (covered later) or the integration with media contents. The next layer is the PresentationFramework, which is fundamental because it exposes all namespaces and classes that developers can take advantage of for building applications (and that are also utilized by Visual Studio when generating new projects).

FIGURE 28.1   Windows Presentation Foundation architecture.

PresentationFramework exposes namespaces and classes through a complex hierarchy of inheritance, in which the root class is `System.Object`. The hierarchy provides the infrastructure for the user interface elements. This hierarchy is composed of the following list of classes, where each class inherits from the previous one:

- `System.Object`

- `System.Threading.DispatcherObject`

- `System.Windows.DependencyObject`

- `System.Windows.Media.Visual`

- `System.Windows.UIElement`

- `System.Windows.FrameworkElement`

- `System.Windows.Controls.Control`

The `System.Threading.DispatcherObject` is responsible for threading and messages that WPF relies on. The dispatcher takes advantage of the User32 messages for performing cross-thread calls. The WPF architecture is also based on a complex properties infrastructure that in most cases replaces methods and events. This is because a property-based architecture is preferable for showing contents of UI controls and because they better integrate with other development models. To provide this infrastructure, the WPF architecture exposes the `System.Windows.DependencyObject` class that implements a common set of properties for derived objects. The main capability of this class is keeping track of property changes so that bound objects can automatically update their statuses according to those changes. `System.Windows.Media.Visual` is responsible for the graphic rendering of all elements belonging to the user interface, under the form of a tree (known as Visual Tree that is covered later). `System.Windows.UIElement` adds other functionalities to the infrastructure, such as the capability to receive input from the user and other overridable members. `System.Windows.FrameworkElement` is important, exposing special features of WPF such as objects lifetime, styles, animations, and the data-binding engine. The last class is `System.Windows.Controls.Control`, which is the base class for WPF user controls and that adds further functionalities that empower base controls and custom user controls. Now that you have a basic knowledge of the WPF architecture, it is time to create the first application.

Building WPF Applications with Visual Studio 2012

You create WPF applications in Visual Studio 2012 by selecting one of the available project templates. WPF project templates are available in the Windows section of the New Project window, as shown in Figure 28.2, and are summarized in Table 28.1 (for your convenience, the list of project templates in Figure 28.2 has been restricted to WPF ones by using the search box, as the figure itself demonstrates).

TABLE 28.1   WPF Project Templates

Template	Description
WPF Application	Allows creating a WPF desktop application for Windows
WPF Browser Application	Allows creating a WPF application that can be run within a web browser
WPF User Control Library	Allows creating WPF user controls
WPF Custom Control Library	Allows redefining WPF controls at code level

This chapter shows you WPF in action with a desktop Windows application. Select the **WPF application** template and name the new project **WPFDemo_Chapter28**. After a few seconds, the IDE shows the code editor, so in Solution Explorer double-click the MainWindow.xaml file so you access the designer, as shown in Figure 28.3.

FIGURE 28.2   Available project templates for WPF applications.

FIGURE 28.3   The IDE is ready on a new WPF project.

As you can see, things are a little different from a Windows Forms project. In the upper part of the IDE, you can see the designer showing the main window of the new application. On the left side is the Toolbox; this is a tool that you already understand and that contains specific WPF controls. In the lower part of the IDE is a special code editor for the *eXtensible Application Markup Language* (XAML, pronounced as *ZAMEL*) that you must know as a WPF developer. The next section describes XAML and explains how it works. In Solution Explorer, you can see a new kind of file, with the .xaml extension. Each .xaml file can represent a window, control (or set of controls), or set of resources. For each .xaml file there is a Visual Basic code-behind file (with a .xaml.vb extension) that you can access by expanding the filename. The reason for this separation between the .xaml file and the .xaml.vb file is part of a key concept in the WPF development, which is the separation of roles between developers and designers that is described better in the next section.

MY PROJECT

WPF applications enable you to take advantage of the My Project designer similarly to other kinds of client applications. If you examine the window, you see these similarities, and you also see how different options are self-explanatory.

Understanding the eXtensible Application Markup Language

In Windows Presentation Foundation applications, the user interface is defined via the *eXtensible Application Markup Language* (*XAML*), which is a markup language that allows defining the interface in a declarative mode and that derives from the XML language. This markup language is revolutionary because it allows the separation of the roles of designers and developers. Professional designers can style the application's layout by using specific tools that allow generating and editing XAML without the need of knowing the programming fundamentals, leaving unchanged the code that empowers the application.

NOTE ON DESIGNER TOOLS

Designers typically use professional tools such as Microsoft Expression Blend for styling WPF and Silverlight applications. Because this book's focus is developer-oriented, the usage of Expression Blend for manipulating XAML is not covered, whereas the focus is on what you do need to know as a developer from within Visual Studio 2012.

This discussion provides an explanation that for each .xaml file there is a VB code-behind file. The .xaml file contains XAML code that defines the user interface, whereas the .xaml.vb code-behind file contains Visual Basic code that makes the user interface alive with the rest of the application. XAML logic is simple: Each XML element represents a user control, and each XML attribute represents a property to a control. Because of the special XML syntax, XAML refers to a specific XML schema for WPF controls.

XAML AND SILVERLIGHT

You need to learn how XAML works if you are also interested in developing rich Internet applications with Microsoft Silverlight or mobile applications with Silverlight for Windows Phone. As explained in Chapter 36, "Building Rich Internet Applications with Silverlight 5" and in Chapter 38, "Building Apps for Windows Phone 7.5," Silverlight and its mobile counterpart are also based on XAML for the UI side.

Now take a look at Listing 28.1 that contains the code generated by Visual Studio 2012 when a new project is created.

LISTING 28.1   XAML Default Code for a WPF Project

```
<Window x:Class="MainWindow"
    xmlns="http://schemas.microsoft.com/winfx/2006/xaml/presentation"
    xmlns:x="http://schemas.microsoft.com/winfx/2006/xaml"
    Title="MainWindow" Height="240" Width="500">
    <Grid>

    </Grid>
</Window>
```

In WPF applications, every window is wrapped by a `System.Windows.Window` control. The root element in the XAML code is a `Window` element. The `x:Class` attribute (which is actually a property) points to the Visual Basic class that handles the Window on the runtime side. The `Title` property contains text shown on the window's title bar. `Width` and `Height` are self-explanatory properties that define the window's size. Also notice how XML schemas are imported via `xmlns` tags. These schemas have two purposes: enabling IntelliSense in the XAML code editor and ensuring that only valid elements are used in the XAML code. `Grid` is one of the WPF *panels*. Unlike Windows Forms, user controls in WPF are arranged within panels; the last part of this introduces them better. Now you understand better what was explained at the beginning of this section: In XAML every element (except for resources) represents a control with properties (attributes). XAML offers a hierarchical organization of controls. For example, a `Window` can contain one or more panels that can contain other panels that can contain controls, and so on. This hierarchical logic is versatile because it enables great customizations of the interface, as you see in this chapter and subsequent ones. As previously stated, the XAML editor fully supports IntelliSense. You can check this out by writing code, as demonstrated in Figure 28.4.

You are not obliged to manually type XAML code to design your user interface. Every time you drag a control from the Toolbox onto the designer, Visual Studio generates the related XAML code for you and you can assign event handlers in the Properties window. In some circumstances manually editing the XAML code is a good task to fix a control's position. Moreover, although initially writing XAML can seem annoying, when you understand its hierarchical logic, it becomes straightforward, also due to IntelliSense. What you perform manually writing XAML can be accomplished with the design tools.

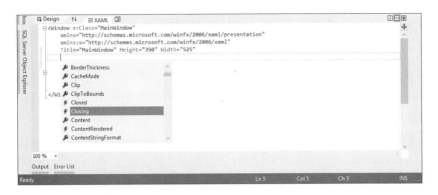

FIGURE 28.4   The XAML code editor fully supports IntelliSense.

Declaring and Using Controls with the Designer and XAML

To add controls to the user interface, you have two possibilities: dragging controls from the Toolbox onto the designer surface or manually writing XAML. For a better understanding, we first show you how to drag from the Toolbox. With the Toolbox open, click the **Button** control and drag it onto the designer. When you release it, the IDE should look like Figure 28.5.

FIGURE 28.5   Dragging controls and generating XAML.

As you can see from Figure 28.5, Visual Studio also generates the XAML code for the controls you add to the UI. For the new button, this is the XAML code generated:

```
<Button Content="Button" Height="23"
        HorizontalAlignment="Left"
        Margin="90,84,0,0" Name="Button1"
        VerticalAlignment="Top" Width="75" />
```

Confirming that each control is represented as an XML element, the most interesting properties here are Name, which assigns an identifier to the control, and Content, which stores the control's content. To manage your controls you now have two choices: editing its XAML code or using the Properties window, which is represented in Figure 28.6.

FIGURE 28.6   Managing controls with the Properties window.

If you are not familiar with WPF, probably you can find lots of properties that you do not know yet. You can learn most of these properties in this book and in your further studies; what is important here is to understand how the designer can control the UI members. The Properties window for WPF controls also offers a special tab that you can enable by clicking the **Events** button (in the upper side of the tool window); that enables associating event handlers to each event exposed by that specific control (see Figure 28.7). Obviously, event handlers are written in Visual Basic code; the next section explains how you handle events.

FIGURE 28.7   The Properties window enables the selecting of event handlers. Click the combo near the desired event and pick an event handler.

Declarative and Imperative Modes

Writing (or letting Visual Studio generate) XAML code is known as *declarative mode*. This is because XAML allows declaring elements required by the user interface but does not allow them taking actions. By the way, an important statement is that with Visual Basic (or Visual C# as well) you can do anything you do in XAML, meaning that you can declare user interface elements in Visual Basic code and add them to the user interface at runtime. Moreover, managing controls with Visual Basic allows them taking actions. This is the *imperative mode*. For a better explanation, consider the following XAML code that declares a simple button:

```
<Button Content="Button" Height="30"
        Name="Button1"
        Width="100"/>
```

The same thing can be also accomplished in Visual Basic. The following code demonstrates this:

```
Dim Button1 As New Button
With Button1
    .Width = 100
    .Height = 30
```

28

```
    .Content = "Button1"
End With
Me.Grid1.Children.Add(Button1)
```

The difference is that in Visual Basic you need to explicitly add your control to a panel in
the user interface.

Understanding Visual Tree and Logical Tree

When talking about WPF applications, you will often hear about the Logical Tree and the
Visual Tree. The Logical Tree is a tree representation of the .NET classes for user interface
controls. Consider the following XAML code:

```
<Window>
    <StackPanel Orientation="Horizontal" Margin="5">
        <TextBlock Text="Sample controls" Margin="5"/>
        <Button Content="Test button" Margin="5"/>
    </StackPanel>
</Window>
```

This code uses .NET objects within a hierarchical structure that can be reconfigured in a
Logical Tree, as shown in Figure 28.8.

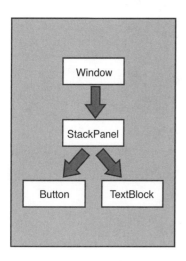

FIGURE 28.8   The Logical Tree provides a hierarchical view of the UI elements.

You can investigate the Logical Tree in a more convenient way, with the Document
Outline tool window (you find it in **View, Other Windows**) that provides a hierarchical
view of the interface (see Figure 28.9).

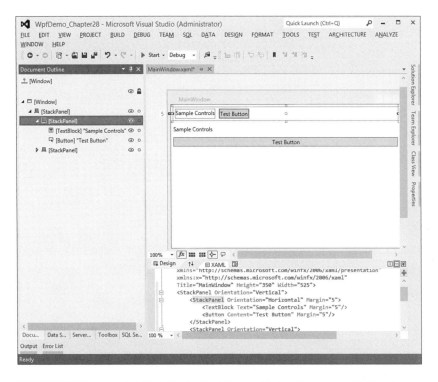

FIGURE 28.9   Investigating the Logical Tree with the Document Outline tool.

The Visual Tree is a more complex concept that is important. As explained in the next chapters, WPF controls are the result of the aggregation of primitive elements, and they can be completely redefined with control templates. For example, a default `Button` is made of `Chrome`, `ContentPresenter`, and `TextBlock` controls. The combination of these elements creates a `Visual`, which represents a visual element in the user interface. The Visual Tree is thus the representation of all the visual elements in the UI that are rendered to the screen, plus their components. Consider the following simple XAML:

```
<StackPanel Orientation="Horizontal" Margin="5">
    <Button Content="Test button" Margin="5"/>
</StackPanel>
```

The visual tree representation is reported in Figure 28.10.

Understanding the Visual Tree is important for understanding another key concept in the WPF development—routed events. These are described just after introducing how you handle events in WPF.

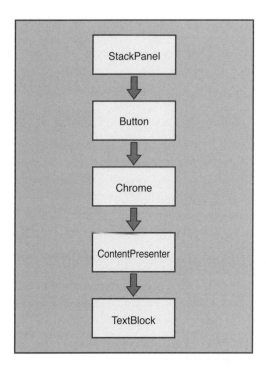

FIGURE 28.10   The Visual Tree representation for UI elements.

Handling Events in WPF

You handle events in WPF the same way you do in other kinds of applications: You code a Visual Basic event handler and associate the handler to a control event. What actually changes is the way you assign the handler to the event. For example, you can assign an event handler to a control event directly within the XAML code editor. To accomplish this, you type the name of the event you want to handle (events are recognizable within IntelliSense with the Lightning icon) and then press Tab when IntelliSense shows the <New Event Handler> pop-up command (see Figure 28.11 for details).

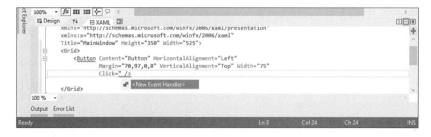

FIGURE 28.11   Generating a new event handler with IntelliSense.

This generates an event handler stub in your code-behind file. Continuing the example of the previous button, Visual Studio first assigns a new identifier to the *Click* event in XAML, which looks like this:

```
Click="Button1_Click"
```

As you can see, the IDE generates the event handler's identifier considering the control's name. Now right-click the event handler's name and select the **Navigate to Event Handler** command from the pop-up menu. This redirects to the Visual Basic event handler generated for you, which looks like this:

```
Private Sub Button1_Click(ByVal sender As System.Object,
                    ByVal e As System.Windows.RoutedEventArgs)

End Sub
```

It is worth mentioning two aspects. The first one is that the event handler signature requires an argument of type `RoutedEventArgs`. WPF introduces the concept of routed events that is covered in the next section. The second one is that in this case there is no `Handles` clause. This is because the IDE added an `AddHandler` instruction behind the scenes in the Window1.g.vb file (which is generated at compile time). Notice that such a filename depends on the current `Window` name, in this case `Window1`. As an alternative, you can specify the `Handles` clause the same way you would do in other kinds of applications. However, in this case you must not specify the event handler in XAML, to avoid an event being caught twice. You can also double-click a control in the designer to generate an event handler for the default event. For instance, say a button's default event is `Click`, so double-clicking a button in the designer generates an event handler stub for handling the `Click` event. The default event for a `TextBox` control is `TextChanged`, so double-clicking a text box generates an event handler stub for the `TextChanged` event, and so on. When you add event handlers by double-clicking controls, such handlers use the `Handles` clause on the method name. As previously mentioned, the last alternative is to assign an existing event handler to a control's event with the Properties window.

A More Thorough Discussion: Introducing the Routed Events

WPF introduces a revolutionary way to generate and handle events, known as *routed events*. When a user's interface element generates an event, the event passes along through the entire Visual Tree, rethrowing the event for each element in the tree. The WPF runtime can then understand what element first generated the event that is the actual handled event. Event handlers whose job is managing a routed event must include an object of type `System.Windows.RoutedEventArgs` in their signature. For a better understanding, consider the following basic XAML code that implements three buttons:

```
<StackPanel Button.Click="OnClick">
    <Button Width="100" Height="30"
            Content="Button One" Name="Button1" />
    <Button Width="100" Height="30"
            Content="Button Two" Name="Button2" />
```

28

```
<Button Width="100" Height="30"
        Content="Button Three" Name="Button3" />
</StackPanel>
```

Notice how no event handler is specified for buttons, whereas a unique handler is speci-fied within the `StackPanel` definition taking advantage of the `Button.Click` attached event. This enables the establishing of one event handler for each button in the `StackPanel`'s children. In the code-behind file, write the following handler:

```
Private Sub OnClick(ByVal sender As Object, ByVal e As RoutedEventArgs)

    Dim element As FrameworkElement = CType(e.Source, _
                                            FrameworkElement)

    Select Case element.Name
        Case Is = "Button1"
            MessageBox.Show("You clicked Button1")
        Case Is = "Button2"
            MessageBox.Show("You clicked Button2")
        Case Is = "Button3"
            MessageBox.Show("You clicked Button3")
    End Select
End Sub
```

Thanks to routed events, we can write just one common handler. To get the instance of the element that actually generated the event, you need to convert the `e.Source` property (which is of type `Object`) into the appropriate type. In this case the conversion could be with a `Button` type, but `FrameworkElement` is utilized to include various kinds of elements or controls. This is because with routed events you can intercept events from each element in the Visual Tree (such as the `ContentPresenter` for buttons), thus not only user controls.

Introducing Routing Strategies: Direct, Tunneling, and Bubbling

Routed events are implemented according to three modes, known as *routing strategies*. Strategies are implemented by the `System.Windows.RoutingStrategy` enumeration and can be summarized as follows:

▶ **Direct**—The event is generated directly against the target object. This is what usually happens in other kinds of .NET applications, such as Windows Forms, and is the most uncommon strategy in WPF.

▶ **Tunnel**—In the tunneling strategy, an event is generated from the root object and passes through the entire Visual Tree until getting to the target object.

▶ **Bubble**—The bubbling strategy is opposite to the tunneling one, meaning that an event starts from the target object and passes back through the Visual Tree.

In most cases, such as the preceding code example, you face tunneling routed events or bubbling ones. Offering a thorough discussion on routed events is beyond the scope of this chapter; you can refer to the MSDN official page that you can find at http://msdn. microsoft.com/en-us/library/ms742806(VS.110).aspx.

Arranging Controls with Panels

WPF changes the way you arrange controls on the user interface. This is because one goal of WPF is to provide the ability to create dynamic interfaces that can be rearranged according to the user's preferences or when the user resizes the interface. Because of this, WPF controls are arranged within special containers, known as panels. WPF provides several panels, each allowing different arrangement possibilities. This is different from Windows Forms, where you place controls on the user interface, but the controls are not flexible. Although some types of panels are available, Windows Forms panels are not as versatile as WPF panels. In this section you learn about WPF panels and how you use them to arrange controls. The most important thing that you have to keep in mind is that WPF controls have a hierarchical logic; therefore, you can nest multiple panels to create complex user experiences. Panels are all exposed by the `System.Windows.Controls` namespace from the PresentationFramework.dll assembly.

The `Grid` Panel

The `Grid` is one of the easiest panels to understand in WPF. It allows creating tables, with rows and columns. In this way you can define cells and each cell can contain a control or another panel storing nested controls. The `Grid` is versatile in that you can just divide it into rows or into columns or both. The following code defines a `Grid` that is divided into two rows and two columns:

```
<Grid>
    <Grid.RowDefinitions>
        <RowDefinition />
        <RowDefinition />
    </Grid.RowDefinitions>
    <Grid.ColumnDefinitions>
        <ColumnDefinition />
        <ColumnDefinition />
    </Grid.ColumnDefinitions>

</Grid>
```

`RowDefinitions` is a collection of `RowDefinition` objects, and the same is true for `ColumnDefinitions` and `ColumnDefinition`. Each item represents a row or a column within the `Grid` respectively. You can also specify a `Width` or a `Height` property to delimit row and column dimensions; if you do not specify anything, both rows and columns are dimensioned at the maximum size available, and when resizing the parent container, rows and columns are automatically rearranged. The preceding code creates a table with four cells. The Visual Studio 2012 Designer offers a convenient way for designing rows and columns. When the cursor is within the `Grid` definition in the XAML code editor or when the `Grid` has the focus in the designer, you use the `Rows` and `Columns` properties in the Properties

28

window. Figure 28.12 shows how you add columns to the Grid and how you can set properties for each column. Adding rows works exactly the same.

FIGURE 28.12   Adding columns with design tools.

To place controls in the Grid, you specify the row and column position. The following code places two buttons, the first one in the upper-left cell and the second one in the upper-right cell:

```
<Button Width="100" Height="50" Grid.Column="0"
        Grid.Row="0" Name="Button1" Content="First button"/>
<Button Width="100" Height="50" Grid.Column="1"
        Grid.Row="0" Name="Button2" Content="Second button"/>
```

To place controls, you select the column via the Grid.Column property, whose index is zero-based, meaning that 0 is the first column from the left. This kind of property is known as *attached property* and allows setting a property of a parent container from within the current object. Specifying the row works similarly, in that you assign the row via the Grid.Row attached property. The property's index is also zero-based, meaning that 0 represents the first row from the top. You can place nested containers within a cell or a single row or column. The following code shows how to nest a grid with children control into a single cell:

```
<Grid Grid.Row="1" Grid.Column="0">
    <Grid.ColumnDefinitions>
        <ColumnDefinition />
```

```
        <ColumnDefinition />
    </Grid.ColumnDefinitions>
    <Grid.RowDefinitions>
        <RowDefinition />
        <RowDefinition />
    </Grid.RowDefinitions>

    <Button Width="50" Height="50" Grid.Column="0"
        Grid.Row="0" Name="Button3" Content="Button3"/>
    <Button Width="50" Height="50" Grid.Column="1"
        Grid.Row="0" Name="Button4" Content="Button4"/>
</Grid>
```

If you run the code shown in this section, you get the result shown in Figure 28.13. This should give you an idea on how controls can be placed within a `Grid`.

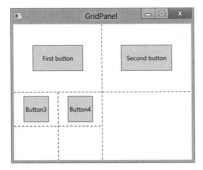

FIGURE 28.13   Arranging controls within a `Grid`.

SHOWING GRID LINES

Grid lines are not shown by default. To make them visible, add a `ShowGridLines` property to the `Grid` element and set its value to `True`.

PERSONAL SUGGESTION

Each time you study a WPF container, try to resize the application windows or controls so that you can get a good idea of how panels work.

The `StackPanel` Panel

The `StackPanel` panel allows placing controls near each other, as in a stack that can be arranged both horizontally and vertically. As with other containers, the `StackPanel` can

28

contain nested panels. The following code shows how you can arrange controls horizontally and vertically. The root `StackPanel` contains two nested panels:

```
<StackPanel Orientation="Vertical">
    <StackPanel Orientation="Horizontal" Margin="5">
        <TextBlock Text="Sample controls" Margin="5"/>
        <Button Content="Test button" Margin="5"/>
    </StackPanel>

    <StackPanel Orientation="Vertical" Margin="5">
        <TextBlock Text="Sample controls" Margin="5"/>
        <Button Content="Test button" Margin="5"/>
    </StackPanel>
</StackPanel>
```

The `Orientation` property can be set as `Horizontal` or `Vertical`, and this influences the final layout. One of the main benefits of XAML code is that element names and properties are self-explanatory, and this is the case of `StackPanel`'s properties, too. Remember that controls within a `StackPanel` are automatically resized according to the orientation. If you do not like this behavior, you need to specify `Width` and `Height` properties. If you run this code, you get the result shown in Figure 28.14.

FIGURE 28.14   Arranging controls within `StackPanels`.

If you want to provide a dynamic user interface, you need to take care of some considerations. If you do not provide static `Width` and `Height` values, your controls will be resized along with the `StackPanel`, which also automatically adapts to its parent container. Alternatively, controls arranged within a `StackPanel` are not resized, but they have the limitation of being hidden when decreasing the parent's container size, as better represented in Figure 28.15.

If you predict that your application will encounter such a situation, you should implement a `WrapPanel` panel, which is covered in the next subsection.

FIGURE 28.15   Resizing fixed controls within a StackPanel causes them to be hidden.

The WrapPanel Panel

The WrapPanel container works like StackPanel, but it differs in that it can rearrange controls on multiple lines in the interface so that they are never hidden. Figures 28.16 and 28.17 show how the WrapPanel enables the rearranging of controls when resizing the parent container (a Window, in our examples).

FIGURE 28.16   WrapPanel arranges controls similarly to the StackPanel.

FIGURE 28.17   WrapPanel rearranges controls dynamically making them always visible, as if they were implemented line-by-line.

In code terms, the panel is represented by a `WrapPanel` element in XAML. The following code reproduces what you saw in the previous figures:

```
<WrapPanel>
    <TextBlock Text="WrapPanel test" Margin="5"/>
    <Button Width="140" Height="30" Content="Test Button"
            Margin="5"/>
    <TextBlock Text="Second test" Margin="5"/>
</WrapPanel>
```

The `VirtualizingStackPanel` Control

In some situations you need to show a big number of elements in your user interface. This is the case of the `DataGrid` or `ListBox` controls, which can display hundreds of elements within a single control. This would heavily affect the application performances if you were using a classic `StackPanel`, which would show all the available items. The `VirtualizingStackPanel` control offers a valid alternative that can calculate how many items can appear in a particular moment and then arranges controls according to the calculation result. You do not need to implement the `VirtualizingStackPanel` manually (it is the default item template of data controls) but, if you need to, you write the following definition:

```
<VirtualizingStackPanel>
    <!--Nest controls here...-->
</VirtualizingStackPanel>
```

This kind of panel works like the `StackPanel`, with the previously described difference.

The `Canvas` Panel

Most WPF containers allow the dynamic rearrangement of controls within the user interface. This is useful when you want your user to adjust interface settings, but it can complicate things when you need to place controls in a fixed, unchangeable place (as happens in Windows Forms). To accomplish this, you use the `Canvas` container, which allows absolute placement, meaning that it allows specifying the position of nested controls. When you place controls into a `Canvas` container, you specify the absolute position with some attached properties: `Canvas.Left`, `Canvas.Top`, `Canvas.Right`, and `Canvas.Bottom`. The following code shows how you place a button that never changes its position in the user interface, thanks to the `Canvas.Left` and `Canvas.Top` attached properties:

```
<Canvas>
    <Button Width="100" Height="50" Content="Test Button"
            Canvas.Left="30" Canvas.Top="50"/>
</Canvas>
```

The `DockPanel` Panel

The `DockPanel` container has some similarities with the `StackPanel` in that it allows arranging child controls near each other. The main difference in `DockPanel` is that child controls are docked to the panel sides according to the direction you specify, and they are docked to each other and you can establish the position and size for each child control. The most common usage of the `DockPanel` panel is creating interfaces for placing menus and toolbars. The following example shows how you can dock multiple toolbars and their buttons within a `DockPanel`:

```
<DockPanel VerticalAlignment="Top"
           LastChildFill="True">
    <ToolBar DockPanel.Dock="Top"
             Name="MainToolbar" >
        <Button Content="First Button"/>
        <Button Content="Second Button"/>
    </ToolBar>

    <ToolBar DockPanel.Dock="Top"
             Name="NextToolbar" >
        <Button Content="First Button"/>
        <Button Content="Second Button"/>
    </ToolBar>
</DockPanel>
```

You set the `DockPanel` orientation by specifying either the `VerticalAlignment` property or `HorizontalAlignment`. The `LastChildFill` is a property that indicates whether child controls must completely fill the available blank space in the container. Notice how within child controls (such as the Toolbars) you specify the docking position by taking advantage of an attached property named `DockPanel.Dock`, whose value indicates where the control must be docked within the `DockPanel`. This is because child controls are not limited to being docked into one side of the `panel` but can be docked into any of the four sides. The preceding code produces the result shown in Figure 28.18.

FIGURE 28.18   Docking controls within a `DockPanel`.

The `ViewBox` Panel

The `ViewBox` panel allows adapting nested controls to its size, including the content of controls. For example, consider the following code:

```
<Viewbox>
    <Button Width="150" Height="75">
        ViewBoxed button
    </Button>
</Viewbox>
```

You immediately notice how the button's text is expanded to best fit the button size. This also happens if you decrease or increase the window size, as demonstrated in Figure 28.19.

FIGURE 28.19   The `ViewBox` panel in action.

In a few words, the `ViewBox` allows resizing controls and their content.

Managing Windows

WPF allows managing windows similarly to Windows Forms, although there are some obvious differences, such as the fact that WPF windows can be considered as the root container for all other child panels when arranging UI elements. Whatever way you decide to apply windows properties, at design time such properties are addressed in XAML code, but you are also allowed to set them at runtime in Visual Basic code. Available properties enable the establishing of the window startup position, its resize mode, its appearance on the task bar, and so on. Table 28.2 summarizes the most important available properties.

TABLE 28.2   Window's Properties

Name	Description
Title	Specifies text for the window title bar
WindowStartupLocation	Specifies the position for the window when it is first loaded (can be Manual, CenterScreen, or CenterOwner)

Name	Description
WindowState	Specifies the window state when loaded (can be `Normal`, `Maximized`, or `Minimized`)
WindowStyle	Specifies the window layout style (`None`, `SingleBorderWindow`, `ThreeDBorderWindow`, or `ToolWindow`)
TopMost	Makes the window always visible on top
ShowInTaskBar	Makes the window title visible in the operating system task bar
Background	Allows specifying a brush for the background color (see Chapter 30, "Brushes, Styles, Templates, and Animations in WPF")
BorderBrush	Specifies a color or brush for the Window border
BorderThickness	Specifies how thick the border is

You can take advantage of the Properties tool window for setting the previously mentioned properties at design time. The following XAML code snippet shows how you can set some window properties:

```
<!-- The following code sets the Window as Maximized,
     its startup position at the center of the screen,
     its style as a Window with 3D borders and keeps it
     always on top. It also replaces the default title-->
<Window x:Class="MainWindow"
    xmlns="http://schemas.microsoft.com/winfx/2006/xaml/presentation"
    xmlns:x="http://schemas.microsoft.com/winfx/2006/xaml"
    Title="Chapter 31 demonstration" Height="240" Width="500"
    WindowStartupLocation="CenterScreen"
    WindowState="Maximized" WindowStyle="ThreeDBorderWindow"
    Topmost="True">
</Window>
```

This is what you do at design time. The same result can be accomplished in managed code as follows:

```
'Me is the current Window
With Me
    .Title = "Chapter 31 demonstration"
    .WindowStartupLocation = Windows.WindowStartupLocation.
                            CenterScreen
    .WindowState = Windows.WindowState.
                   Maximized
    .WindowStyle = Windows.WindowStyle.
                   ThreeDBorderWindow
    .Topmost = True
End With
```

28

To add more `Window` objects to your project you select the **Project, Add Window** command and assign the filename in the New Item dialog box. Remember that every Window in the project inherits from `System.Windows.Window`. When you have multiple windows in your project, you can also establish which of them must be the startup object. To accomplish this, go to My Project and select the new window in the Startup URI combo box. Figure 28.20 shows how to accomplish this.

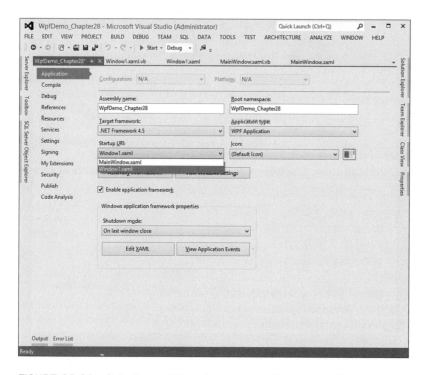

FIGURE 28.20   Selecting a different `Window` as the startup object.

The window is specified via the related XAML file address (Uri).

Instantiating Windows at Runtime

Creating and displaying windows at runtime is a common task in every client application. To do this, you create an instance of a `System.Windows.Window` and then invoke the `Show` or `ShowDialog` methods, depending on whether the `Window` must be considered a modal dialog box. The following Visual Basic code demonstrates how you create and show a new `Window`:

```
Dim aWindow As New Window
'Set your Window properties here...
aWindow.ShowDialog()
'....
aWindow.Close()
```

In the preceding code, a new Window is generated from scratch, so this requires specifying all properties. In most cases you can instead create and show instances of existing windows that you implemented at design time; for this, in the above code you just replace Window with the name of your custom window. This works the same as Windows Forms, although all the backend technology is completely different. This approach helps you when moving your Windows Forms applications to WPF.

Introducing the `Application` Object

As for Windows Forms, WPF also provides an `Application` class that allows interacting with your application instance. The class exposes several methods and properties that allow the getting or assigning of settings available within My Project. First, you need to get the instance of the running application. You accomplish this by assigning the `Application.Current` property to a variable as follows:

```
Dim myApp As Application = CType(Application.Current, Application)
```

When you get the instance of the application, you can get or set required information. The following code shows how you can retrieve the startup Uri (which corresponds to the startup object referred to in a XAML file), the main application window, and assembly information:

```
'Gets the startup object under the form of a XAML file
Dim startupObject As Uri = myApp.StartupUri

'Gets (but also allows setting) the application main window
Dim mainWindow As Window = myApp.MainWindow

'Get assembly information
With myApp.Info
    Dim companyName As String = .CompanyName
    Dim appName As String = .ProductName

    'get other info here...
End With
```

The `Application` class does not directly expose a `Close` method as instead happens in Windows Forms. If you want to programmatically shut down your application, you invoke the `Current.ShutDown` shared method as follows:

```
Application.Current.Shutdown()
```

28

Table 28.3 summarizes the most important members of the `Application` class.

TABLE 28.3   Application Class's Most Important Members

Member	Type	Description
Current	Property	Returns the instance of the running application.
Dispatcher	Property	Returns the instance of the `Dispatcher` for the current application. The `Dispatcher` is responsible for managing threads.
FindResource	Method	Searches for the specified resource (which is at XAML level).
Info	Property	Returns a collection of assembly information.
LoadComponent	Method	Loads a XAML file from the specified Uri and then converts the resulting object into an instance that is added to the application.
Main	Method	The application entry point.
MainWindow	Property	Returns the instance of the Window object that is first run at startup.
Resources	Property	Returns a collection of resources.
Run	Method	Runs a WPF application.
Shutdown	Method	Shuts down the application.
ShutdownMode	Property	Gets or sets how an application must shut down.
StartupUri	Property	Returns the Uri of the XAML file that is loaded at startup.
Windows	Property	Returns a collection of `Window` objects that have been instantiated in the application.

TIP

Chapter 19, "The My Namespace," discussed the `My` namespace. WPF applications provide a special extension of `My` that allows interacting with the application by invoking the `My.Application` property.

The `Application` class is also important for another reason: It contains the entry point (that is, the `Sub Main`) that effectively runs your application and is the place where you control application events, such as the startup or the shutdown. This class is implemented as a partial class. In Solution Explorer, you can find the Application.xaml file that can store application-level resources; the file has a code-behind counterpart named Application.xaml.vb where you can write code that influences the entire application instead of single elements of the user interface. The following code shows how you can handle the `startup` and `Exit` events that represent the initial and final moments of the application lifetime:

```
Class Application

    ' Application-level events, such as Startup, Exit,
    ' and DispatcherUnhandledException
    ' can be handled in this file.

    Private Sub Application_Startup(ByVal sender As Object,
                                   ByVal e As System.Windows.
                                               StartupEventArgs) _
                                   Handles Me.Startup
        MessageBox.Show("Application is starting up")
    End Sub

    Private Sub Application_Exit(ByVal sender As Object,
                                ByVal e As System.Windows.ExitEventArgs) _
                                Handles Me.Exit
        MessageBox.Show("Application is closing")
    End Sub
End Class
```

You use the `Application` class for controlling specific moments in the lifetime; when you instead need to set application properties, the best choice is opening the My Project designer.

Brief Overview of WPF Browser Applications

Since the first version of WPF, developers have been allowed to build applications that can run within a web browser, such as Microsoft Internet Explorer or Mozilla Firefox. This kind of application is named WPF Browser Applications (formerly known as Xaml Browser Applications) or XBAP. Several differences exist between a client application and an XBAP; first, Browser Applications can only be executed online (from the Internet or an intranet). Second, they are executed with the limitations of the Internet Zone of the .NET Framework's Code Access Security rules. Because of this, Browser Applications cannot perform several tasks. The main advantage is instead that, keeping in mind the previously mentioned limitations, you can use the same programming model.

28 (margin tab)

CHOOSE SILVERLIGHT

WPF Browser Applications were first introduced when the real web counterpart of WPF, Silverlight, was not at today's levels. Silverlight is the real .NET offering for creating rich Internet applications, with both multimedia and business capabilities. You should use Silverlight applications instead of Browser Applications. Browser Applications are kept for compatibility reasons, but situations where you should use them are limited. If your company needs an online application with WPF capabilities but with a small number of functionalities, Browser Applications could do well, but Silverlight provides a full-featured environment for each kind of rich web application.

You create an application of this kind by selecting the **WPF Browser Application** project template from the New Project window. Then, create a new Browser Application naming the project **WpfBrowserApplication_Chapter28.** When the project is ready, you soon notice another difference from classic WPF applications. In the XAML code editor, you can see how the root object is now a `Page` instead of a `Window`. This is required for applications to work within a web browser. The second difference is the presence of a strong name file (with .pfx extension) in Solution Explorer. This is required because of the CAS rules. At this point we can implement some features to see the application in action. The goal of the example is to create an application that can validate an email address showing the validation result. Listing 28.2 shows the user interface implementation, which is simple.

LISTING 28.2   Defining the XBAP's Interface

```
<Page x:Class="Page1"
      xmlns="http://schemas.microsoft.com/winfx/2006/xaml/presentation"
      xmlns:x="http://schemas.microsoft.com/winfx/2006/xaml"
      xmlns:mc="http://schemas.openxmlformats.org/markup-compatibility/2006"
      xmlns:d="http://schemas.microsoft.com/expression/blend/2008"
      mc:Ignorable="d"
      d:DesignHeight="300" d:DesignWidth="300"
      Title="Page1">
    <StackPanel>
        <Label Content="Enter the e-mail address to validate:" Margin="5"/>
        <TextBox Name="MailTextBox" Margin="5"/>
        <Button Width="100" Height="30" Content="Validate" Margin="5"
                Name="Button1" />
    </StackPanel>
</Page>
```

On the Visual Basic side, we need to implement a method that validates the user input and an event handler for the button's `Click` event. Code in Listing 28.3 shows how to accomplish this.

LISTING 28.3   Providing Actions for the XAML Browser Application

```
Imports System.Text.RegularExpressions

Class Page1

    Private Sub Button1_Click(ByVal sender As System.Object,
                              ByVal e As System.Windows.RoutedEventArgs) _
                              Handles Button1.Click

        If String.IsNullOrEmpty(Me.MailTextBox.Text) = True Then Exit Sub
```

```
        MessageBox.Show("Is a valid address: " & IsValidEMail(Me.MailTextBox.Text))

    End Sub

    Function IsValidEMail(ByVal EMailAddress As String) _
                As Boolean
        Dim validateMail As String = _
        "^([\w-\.]+)@((\[[0-9]{1,3}\.[0-9]{1,3}\.)" & _
        "|(([\w-]+\.)+))([a-zA-z]{2,4}|[0-9]{1,3})(\]?)$"

        Return Regex.IsMatch(EMailAddress, _
                        validateMail)

    End Function
End Class
```

Notice how you handle a routed event the same way you would in a Windows application. The `IsValidEmail` method is already explained in this book; it uses regular expressions for validation. If you run the application, you get the result shown in Figure 28.21.

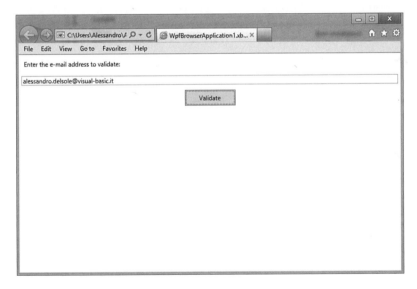

FIGURE 28.21   The WPF Browser Application running in the default web browser.

When the application is launched from the Visual Studio debugger, the default web browser is launched and points to the application.

XBAP DEPLOYMENT

Deploying an XBAP is a task that you should perform through ClickOnce. This technology, which is covered in Chapter 52, "Deploying Applications with ClickOnce," is perfect for this purpose because it can deploy the application to a web server, manage CAS settings, and deploy an application as "online" (a required scenario for XBAPs). Finally, ClickOnce cannot install assemblies to the GAC, and thus you can be sure that the target machine will not be affected.

Summary

In this chapter you took a first look at the Windows Presentation Foundation technology. You saw what WPF is and how it is architected. You then saw how to create your first WPF application with Visual Studio 2012, getting a high-level introduction of the XAML markup language and the interaction with managed code. For the architecture, you learned about some concepts such as the Logical Tree and the Visual Tree. For the Visual Tree, understanding this led you to another key concept: routed events. These events enable the generating of cascade events through the hierarchical structure of the user interface. After this, you made a contact with WPF, understanding how you arrange controls within panels, getting also a first overview of all available panels. Last, you saw another kind of client application in action with WPF: Browser Applications. You saw how this kind of application can run within a web browser, although with some limitations due to their nature. With these basics, you are now ready to take some more control over WPF. This is the goal of the next chapters.

CHAPTER 29

WPF Common Controls

Being a technology for Windows desktop applications, Windows Presentation Foundation offers built-in controls that you can immediately use in your applications to build rich user interfaces. You can also build your own custom controls. WPF 4.5 offers a good standard toolbox, provided by the System.Windows.Controls namespace. If you are new to WPF and you come from the Windows Forms experience, you can certainly find differences in controls implementation between the two technologies, but, fortunately, you will feel at home because of the names. Look for WPF controls that are counterparts to Windows Forms interface elements. In this chapter you first learn some important features in WPF controls; next, you take a tour through the most common user controls so you can start building your user interface.

Introducing WPF Controls Features

Before using WPF controls, you need to understand some behaviors. In Chapter 28, "Creating WPF Applications," you learned that UI elements, including controls, are declared in XAML code. You also saw how to assign a name to controls to interact with them in Visual Basic code. XAML allows you to declare and implement controls even if you do not assign a name. For example, the following Button declaration is legal:

```
<Button Width="100" Height="50" Click="OnClick"/>
```

The control declared in this way works normally as you would expect, also raising click events that you can handle in managed code. This is possible because of the particular WPF architecture part that implements routed events discussed in Chapter 28. When an unnamed control raises an event, the event passes through the entire Visual Tree, and the WPF runtime can intercept the event independently from the control name. Providing a name therefore is useful when you need to assign properties in managed code or when you want to assign an event handler to a specific visual element. Another interesting feature is that WPF controls are defined as *lookless*. This means that WPF controls are classes that expose a series of properties defining the behavior of controls while the look is assigned via a *template*. When you drag a WPF control from the toolbox to the designer, the control takes advantage of a standard template that defines its layout, but templates can be completely customized or overridden with the so-called *control templates*. Chapter 30, "Brushes, Styles, Templates, and Animations in WPF," provides more examples and explanations, but you need to understand the concept before examining common controls. Basing controls' layout on templates enables roles separation between developers and designers and is the reason Microsoft created a tool such as Expression Blend. Another fundamental feature in WPF control is that it can contain almost any visual elements. This is possible with the ContentControl item, which is the subject of the next section.

WPF CONTROLS AND SILVERLIGHT CONTROLS

Understanding WPF controls is useful for Silverlight development, too. In most cases, controls described here have a counterpart in Silverlight, and this is why a similar discussion is not provided for Silverlight.

Understanding the ContentControl

One of the biggest presentation benefits in WPF is the capability for controls to show more than simple text. Particularly, all controls exposing a Content property can nest complex visual elements to offer special effects with or without text. For example, consider the following button whose content is just text:

```
<Button Name="Button1" Width="100" Height="100" Content="Click me!"/>
```

The Content property can be declared in a hierarchical fashion so that you can take advantage of the XAML logic for nesting complex elements. The following example shows how you can replace the button text with a movie:

```
<Button Name="Button1" Width="100" Height="100">
    <Button.Content>
        <MediaElement Source="MyVideo.wmv" LoadedBehavior="Play"/>
    </Button.Content>
</Button>
```

At this point your button plays a video instead of showing the Click me! text. This is possible because of a special element named ContentControl that provides the capability to embed complex visual elements within controls offering the Content property. It is an invisible element, but its presence is noticeable when you can get these results.

Another example is nesting multiple elements within a panel as the child element of the `ContentControl`. The following example shows how you can embed text and video together:

```
<Button Name="Button1" Width="100" Height="100">
    <Button.Content>
    <StackPanel>
        <MediaElement LoadedBehavior="Play"
                    Source="MyVideo.wmv"/>
        <TextBlock Text="Click me!"/>
    </StackPanel>
    </Button.Content>
</Button>
```

It is fundamental to understand the existence of the `ContentControl` because even the most classic controls can be enriched with complex visual elements with a couple lines of code.

Understanding Common Controls

In this section you learn about the most common controls in Windows Presentation Foundation. In most cases, we provide XAML implementation because this is the place where you define your user interface; remember that everything you do in XAML is reproducible in Visual Basic code for runtime handling (refer to Chapter 28).

The `Border` Control

Consider the `Border` control as a special container that draws a border around the child control, with the specified color, thickness, and corner radius. The following XAML code draws a red border with a depth of 3 around a rectangle:

```
<Border BorderBrush="Red" BorderThickness="3"
        CornerRadius="8">
    <Rectangle Height="100"/>
</Border>
```

Changes are immediately visible in the Visual Studio designer. Notice that the `Border` can nest just one child element, so if you want to add multiple visual elements, you need to encapsulate them within a container such as the `Grid` or `StackPanel`. Figure 29.1 shows the result of the preceding code.

SPECIFYING DIFFERENT BRUSHES

In the preceding code the `BorderBrush` is assigned with a `SolidColorBrush` (Red), but according to the hierarchical logic of XAML, you could set it with a different brush, such as `LinearGradientBrush`.

29

FIGURE 29.1   Drawing a border.

The `Button` Control

In Chapter 28 you saw some `Button` examples in action, so we do not cover this again here.

Showing Dates with the `Calendar` Control

The `Calendar` control shows a calendar where you can select a particular day in the specified month and year. The following XAML code defines a calendar with a custom border and a `TextBox` that contains the selected date to be assigned programmatically:

```
<StackPanel Orientation="Horizontal">
    <Calendar Name="Calendar1" Margin="5"
        BorderBrush="Blue" BorderThickness="3"
        SelectedDatesChanged="Calendar1_SelectedDatesChanged">
    </Calendar>
    <TextBox Name="TextBox1" Margin="5" Height="30" Width="200"/>
</StackPanel>
```

The `SelectedDatesChanged` event is raised when the user clicks a different date. The following is instead the event handler that gets the instance of the calendar and sends the selected date to the text box:

```
Private Sub Calendar1_SelectedDatesChanged(ByVal sender As Object,
                                ByVal e As Windows.Controls.
                                SelectionChangedEventArgs)

    Dim currentCalendar = CType(sender, Calendar)
    Me.TextBox1.Text = currentCalendar.SelectedDate.Value.ToString

End Sub
```

Figure 29.2 shows the result of our work.

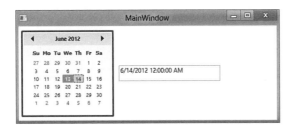

FIGURE 29.2   Implementing a `Calendar` control.

You can also programmatically assign the `SelectedDate` property with an object of type `Date` to change the date shown in the `Calendar` control with a different one.

Items Selection with the `CheckBox` Control

The WPF `CheckBox` control works like any other same-named controls in other technologies. Take a look at the following XAML code:

```
<CheckBox Name="Check1" Content="I will do this"
          Margin="5" Checked="Check1_Checked"
          Unchecked="Check1_Unchecked"/>
```

The `CheckBox`'s text is set via the `Content` property. Setting `Content` also means that you can fill the control with visual elements other than text. It exposes two events, `Checked` and `Unchecked`, that are raised when you place or remove the flag from the control and that can be handled as follows:

```
Private Sub Check1_Checked(ByVal sender As System.Object,
                           ByVal e As System.Windows.RoutedEventArgs)
    MessageBox.Show("Checked")
End Sub

Private Sub Check1_Unchecked(ByVal sender As Object,
                             ByVal e As System.Windows.RoutedEventArgs)
    MessageBox.Show("Unchecked")
End Sub
```

Finally, you invoke the `IsChecked` Boolean property for verifying whether the control is checked. Figure 29.3 shows the control.

29

FIGURE 29.3　Implementing a CheckBox.

Selecting Values from a List with the ComboBox Control

The WPF ComboBox also works the same as in other technologies. The following XAML snippet shows how you implement a sample ComboBox showing a list of hypothetical customers:

```
<ComboBox Name="CustomerNamesCombo"
          Width="200" Height="30"
          SelectionChanged="CustomerNamesCombo_SelectionChanged">
    <ComboBox.Items>
        <ComboBoxItem Content="Alessandro"/>
        <ComboBoxItem Content="Brook"/>
    </ComboBox.Items>
</ComboBox>
```

Each item in the control is represented by a ComboBoxItem object whose Content property sets the item's content that can be also something different from text. (For example, you might embed a video through a MediaElement control.) The SelectionChanged event is raised when the user selects an item.

DESIGNER TOOLS FOR ADDING ITEMS

You can add items to a ComboBox by clicking the button on the Items property in the Properties window. This displays a dialog box where you can take advantage of the Visual Studio designer tools.

This control is powerful because it also supports data-binding. The next example renames the `ComboBox` into `ProcessNamesCombo`, setting the `ItemsSource` property as follows:

```
<ComboBox Name="ProcessNamesCombo"
          Width="200" Height="30" ItemsSource="{Binding}"
          SelectionChanged="CustomerNamesCombo_SelectionChanged">
```

This ensures that items will be populated at runtime via data-binding. The following Visual Basic code shows how you populate the `ComboBox` via a LINQ query with the list of running processes' names:

```
Private Sub MainWindow_Loaded(ByVal sender As Object,
                              ByVal e As RoutedEventArgs) _
                        Handles Me.Loaded
    Dim procList = From proc In Process.GetProcesses
                   Select proc.ProcessName

    'Assuming the Combo's name is now ProcessNamesCombo
    Me.ProcessNamesCombo.ItemsSource = procList
End Sub
```

If you want to handle items selection, you write an event handler such as the following:

```
Private Sub CustomerNamesCombo_SelectionChanged(ByVal sender As Object,
                             ByVal e As SelectionChangedEventArgs)

    Dim selectedProcess = CType(CType(sender, ComboBox).SelectedItem,
                          String)

    MessageBox.Show("You selected " & selectedProcess)
End Sub
```

You need to get the instance of the selected item (`ComboBox.SelectedItem`) and then convert it into the appropriate type, which in this case is `String`. If you bounded a list of `Process` objects, instead of their names, conversion would return `Process`. You would need to add a `DisplayMemberPath` attribute on the XAML side pointing to the property you wanted to show (for example, `ProcessName`). Figure 29.4 shows the result of the data-bound `ComboBox`.

Presenting Tabular Data with the `DataGrid` Control

The `DataGrid` control enables you to present and edit tabular data. A complete example is available in Chapter 32, "Introducing Data-Binding."

29

FIGURE 29.4   Binding a ComboBox to a list of objects.

Selecting Dates with the DatePicker Control

The DatePicker control shows a pop-up calendar where you can pick a date; the date is then bound to a text box placed near the control. The DatePicker is used in data-binding techniques (see Chapter 32). The following XAML code shows how you can implement a DatePicker; the selection, which is mapped by the SelectedDate property of type Date, is then bound to a second, external text box to demonstrate how the value can be consumed by other user controls:

```
<StackPanel Orientation="Horizontal">
    <DatePicker Name="DatePicker1" Margin="5"
          SelectedDateChanged="DatePicker1_SelectedDateChanged" />
    <TextBox Name="TextBox2" Margin="5"
          Text="{Binding ElementName=DatePicker1,
                    Path=SelectedDate}"
          Height="30" Width="200"/>

</StackPanel>
```

Figure 29.5 shows how the DatePicker appears.

The DatePicker exposes an event called SelectedDateChanged that is raised when the user selects another date. The following event handler shows an example of handling the event:

```
Private Sub DatePicker1_SelectedDateChanged(ByVal sender As Object,
                                    ByVal e As _
                                    SelectionChangedEventArgs)

    'Use the "e" object to access the DatePicker control
    '(Source represents
    'the instance)
    MessageBox.Show("The new date is " & CType(e.Source,
                DatePicker).SelectedDate.
                Value.ToLongDateString)
End Sub
```

FIGURE 29.5   Implementing a `DatePicker`.

Viewing XPS Documents with the `DocumentViewer` Control

The `DocumentViewer` control enables viewing flow documents. A complete example is available in Chapter 31, "Manipulating Media and Documents."

Drawing Shapes: The `Ellipse`

The `Ellipse` element is not properly a user control because it is actually a geometric shape. It is useful to understand how the element works because you can use it when creating your custom control templates. The following XAML code declares an `Ellipse`:

```
<Ellipse Width="150" Height="80" Stroke="Red"
        StrokeThickness="3" Fill="Orange"/>
```

The most important properties are `Width` and `Height` that define dimensions. `Stroke` defines the color that surrounds the ellipse, and `StrokeThickness` is a value indicating the stroke depth. As with other geometric shapes, `Ellipse` background can be assigned via the `Fill` property. Figure 29.6 shows the drawn ellipse.

29

FIGURE 29.6   Drawing and filling an ellipse.

Organizing Controls with the `Expander`

The `Expander` control is a special kind of control container that can be expanded or collapsed and that is useful for organizing your controls. The following is an example of `Expander` with nested controls:

```
<Expander Name="Expander1" Header="Expand to view controls"
         Background="LightBlue">
    <StackPanel>
        <ComboBox Name="Combo1" Margin="10">
            <!- Add your items here...->
        </ComboBox>
        <ListBox Name="List1" Margin="10">
            <!- Add your items here...->
        </ListBox>
    </StackPanel>
</Expander>
```

You must use a panel, as in the preceding example, if you want to add multiple visual elements because the `Expander`'s `Content` property supports just one element. You access members by invoking their names as if they were not nested inside the `Expander`. Figure 29.7 shows the `Expander` in action.

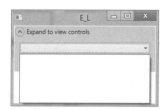

FIGURE 29.7   Implementing the `Expander` and nesting controls.

`Frame`

The `Frame` control enables showing Html contents, including web pages. The most basic usage is assigning its `Source` property with an `Uri`, as in the following example:

```
<Frame Source="http://msdn.com/vbasic" />
```

Figure 29.8 shows how the website appears in the `Frame` control.

FIGURE 29.8   Opening a website with a `Frame` control.

This control exposes a `Navigate` method that enables programmatically browsing HTML contents and/or web pages as in the following snippet:

```
Frame1.Navigate(New Uri("Http://msdn.com/vbasic"))
```

You can also point to an html file on disk; just remember that each content name must be converted into `Uri`.

USING `Webbrowser`

Later this chapter discusses the `WebBrowser` control that provides better functionalities for browsing web pages. Frame should be considered as an HTML document viewer more than a real browsing control.

Organizing Controls with the `GroupBox` Control

The WPF `GroupBox` control has the same purpose for same named controls in other technologies, offering a container with a header and a border for grouping nested controls. The following code shows how you can implement a `GroupBox`, assigning its headers and nesting controls:

```
<GroupBox Name="Group1" Margin="5">
    <GroupBox.Header>
        <TextBlock Text="Set your options"/>
    </GroupBox.Header>
    <StackPanel Margin="10">
        <CheckBox Name="Check3" Content="Set a single option"/>
        <RadioButton Name="Radio3" Content="Use this"/>
        <RadioButton Name="Radio4" Content="Use that"/>
    </StackPanel>
</GroupBox>
```

Figure 29.9 shows the output of this code.

FIGURE 29.9   Grouping controls with a GroupBox.

Notice that in this example the Header property is defined in the hierarchical fashion, meaning that you can add to the header complex visual elements other than simple text. For example, you can add a StackPanel nesting an image with text.

Displaying Images with the Image Control

The Image control enables presenting images. A complete example is available in Chapter 31.

Displaying Text Messages with the Label Control

The Label control shows a text message, as in the following code example:

```
<Label Name="Label1" Content="A sample value"/>
```

WPF offers the TextBlock control that provides deeper customizations features for text, so you should use the one covered in more detail later in this chapter.

Presenting Data with the ListBox Control

The ListBox control enables listing a series of items. The good news is that you are not limited to text items but can also add complex items. Each item is represented by a ListBoxItem object, nested in the ListBox. The following example shows how you can declare a ListBox in XAML code:

```
<ListBox Name="ListBox1">
    <ListBoxItem Content="Item 1"/>
    <ListBoxItem Content="Item 2"/>
    <!- Creating a complex item,
        with text and picture ->
    <ListBoxItem>
        <ListBoxItem.Content>
            <StackPanel>
                <TextBlock Text="Item 3 with image"/>
                <Image Source="MyImage.jpg" />
            </StackPanel>
        </ListBoxItem.Content>
    </ListBoxItem>
</ListBox>
```

A `ListBox` is populated at runtime via data-binding. These concepts are the same as illustrated for the `ComboBox` control, so take a look there for a recap. To accomplish data-binding, specify the `ItemsSource` markup extension as follows:

```
<ListBox Name="ListBox1" ItemsSource="{Binding}"/>
```

Then in Visual Basic code, you assign the `ItemsSource` property with a data-source as demonstrated in the following LINQ query that returns a list of names about running processes:

```
Dim procList = From proc In Process.GetProcesses
               Select proc.ProcessName

Me.ListBox1.ItemsSource = procList
```

You access items in the `ListBox` via some properties such as the following:

▶ `SelectedItem`, of type `Object`, which returns the instance of the selected item in the `ListBox`. The returned object must be converted into the appropriate type.

▶ `Items`, which returns a read-only collection of items in the control.

In Chapter 32 you see a more extensive example of data-binding using the `ListBox`. Figure 29.10 shows the result for the data-bound implementation.

DATA-BINDING

The `ListBox` control is intended for presenting data, even if you can customize items' template with `TextBox` controls. For two-way data-binding, use the `DataGrid` control described in Chapter 32.

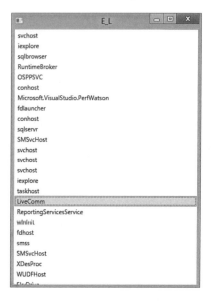

FIGURE 29.10   A data-bound `ListBox`.

Presenting Data with the `ListView` Control

The `ListView` control offers a higher customization level if compared to the `ListBox` and can also be used for receiving user input other than just presenting data. Same as for the `ListBox`, you might want to consider the `DataGrid` control for advanced data-binding techniques. To present a series of items, the `ListView` can be declared the same way as the `ListBox`. Things are better when you instead use this control with columns, such as in a grid. Consider the following XAML code that declares a `ListView` data-bound to the list of running processes:

```
<ListView Name="ListView1" ItemsSource="{Binding}">
    <ListView.View>
        <GridView>
            <GridViewColumn Header="Process ID">
                <GridViewColumn.CellTemplate>
                    <DataTemplate>
                        <TextBlock Text="{Binding Path=Id}"/>
                    </DataTemplate>
                </GridViewColumn.CellTemplate>
            </GridViewColumn>
            <GridViewColumn Header="Process name">
                <GridViewColumn.CellTemplate>
                    <DataTemplate>
                        <TextBlock
                        Text="{Binding Path=ProcessName}"/>
                    </DataTemplate>
```

```
        </GridViewColumn.CellTemplate>
    </GridViewColumn>

</GridView>
</ListView.View>
</ListView>
```

The `View` property establishes how the control will look. The `GridView` creates a nested grid with column definitions. Each `GridViewColumn` represents a single column where you can customize cells by defining the `CellTemplate` item. A `DataTemplate` item is nested that actually stores one or more visual elements that show how each object in the `ListView` appears. See Chapter 32 for more details on data-binding; at the moment consider that the `Binding Path` extension points to the specified property of the associated data source. Then you assign the `ItemsSource` property, as in the following Visual Basic code that retrieves the list of running processes:

```
Me.ListView1.ItemsSource = Process.GetProcesses.AsEnumerable
```

This populates the `ListView` that just shows two properties from the data source. Figure 29.11 shows the result of the code.

FIGURE 29.11   The result for the data-bound `ListView`.

Playing Audio and Video with the `MediaElement` Control

The `MediaElement` control enables playing multimedia files. A complete example is available in Chapter 31.

Building Effective User Interfaces with the `Menu` Control

WPF still enables creating user interfaces based on menus via the `Menu` control. You nest inside the `Menu` control many `MenuItem` objects and as many commands as you need; you can also nest `MenuItem` objects into other `MenuItems` to create submenus. Menus in WPF are highly customizable because you can specify background and foreground colors, add images and other visual elements, and set different fonts for specific menu items. The following example shows how to accomplish this:

```xml
<DockPanel LastChildFill="True" VerticalAlignment="Top">
    <Menu DockPanel.Dock="Top">

        <MenuItem Header="First menu" IsEnabled="True"
                DockPanel.Dock="Top">

            <MenuItem Header="_TestMenu"/>
            <Separator/>
            <MenuItem IsEnabled="True" Name="Copy"
                    Click="Copy_Click">
                <MenuItem.Header>_Copy</MenuItem.Header>
            </MenuItem>
            <MenuItem IsEnabled="True" Name="Paste"
                    Click="Paste_Click"
                    ToolTip="Paste your text">
                <MenuItem.Header>_Paste</MenuItem.Header>
            </MenuItem>
            <Separator />

            <MenuItem Name="FontMenuItem" Header="Item with another font"
                FontFamily="Tahoma" FontSize="16" FontStyle="Italic"
                FontWeight="Bold"
                />
        </MenuItem>

        <MenuItem Header="Second menu" DockPanel.Dock="Top"
                Background="Blue" Foreground="White">

            <!--<MenuItem Header="Item with bitmap image">
                <MenuItem.Icon>

                    <Image Source="Immages/MyImage.png" />
                </MenuItem.Icon>
            </MenuItem>-->

            <MenuItem Header="Checkable item" IsCheckable="True"
                    IsChecked="True" />
```

```
        <MenuItem Header="Disabled item" IsEnabled="False"
                    Name="DisabledMenuItem"/>


        </MenuItem>
    </Menu>
</DockPanel>
```

You can set a lot of properties within menus. Table 29.1 summarizes the most important ones that were used in the preceding code.

TABLE 29.1   Most Common Properties in `Menu` and `MenuItems`

Property	Description
Header	Sets the content of the item
IsEnabled	Sets the item enabled or disabled (`True` or `False`)
Name	Assigns an identifier so that you can interact in VB code
Tooltip	Provides a description over the item when the mouse passes over
IsCheckable	Sets the item to be flagged via a check box
Icon	Sets the menu item's icon

By assigning the `Click` property for each `MenuItem`, you can handle the click event, as in the following code snippet:

```
Private Sub Copy_Click(ByVal sender As System.Object,
                    ByVal e As System.Windows.RoutedEventArgs)
    MessageBox.Show("You clicked Copy")
End Sub


Private Sub Paste_Click(ByVal sender As System.Object,
                    ByVal e As System.Windows.RoutedEventArgs)
    MessageBox.Show("You clicked Paste")
End Sub
```

Notice that the main `Menu` item is placed inside a `DockPanel` container that provides better arrangement for this kind of control. Figure 29.12 shows the result of the menu implementation.

Entering Passwords with the `PasswordBox` Control

The `PasswordBox` control is a special text box intended for entering passwords and that automatically hides characters. The following code snippet shows an example:

```
<StackPanel Orientation="Horizontal">
    <PasswordBox Name="PasswordBox1" Margin="5"
                Width="150" MaxLength="20"
```

29

```
                    PasswordChar="*"/>
    <Button Name="PasswordButton" Width="100" Height="30"
            Margin="5" Content="Check password"
            Click="PasswordButton_Click"/>
</StackPanel>
```

FIGURE 29.12   Implementing menus and submenus.

By default, characters are hidden with a dot, but you can replace it via the PasswordChar property (optional). The MaxLength property limits the password length (optional). Such control exposes the Password property of type String that is the entered password, as demonstrated by the following code:

```
Private Sub PasswordButton_Click(ByVal sender As Object,
                                    ByVal e As RoutedEventArgs)
    Dim myPassword = "TestPassword"
    If PasswordBox1.Password = myPassword Then
        MessageBox.Show("Password matches")
    Else
        MessageBox.Show("Password does not match")
    End If
End Sub
```

Figure 29.13 shows the result of the code.

FIGURE 29.13   Implementing a PasswordBox.

The main event in the `PasswordBox` is `PasswordChanged` that is raised when the control's content changes.

Showing the Progress of an Operation with the `ProgressBar` Control

The `ProgressBar` control requires you to set some start properties, such as `Minimum`, `Maximum`, and `Value`. Then you can increase the value at runtime. The following XAML code declares a `ProgressBar`:

```
<ProgressBar Name="ProgressBar1" Height="30"
             Value="0"
             Minimum="0" Maximum="10000"/>
```

To update the progress value, a good approach is making this asynchronously. This can be accomplished by invoking the `Dispatcher`, which is the WPF object responsible for managing threads. This points to the `ProgressBar.SetValue` to update the progress value. So the first step is to create a custom delegate that matches `SetValue`'s signature:

```
Private Delegate Sub updateDelegate(ByVal depProperty As _
                System.Windows.DependencyProperty, _
                ByVal value As Object)
```

The next step is to provide code that updates the progress value. This is just a demonstration loop that invokes the dispatcher while increasing the progress value:

```
Private Sub HandleProgressBar()
    Dim value As Double = ProgressBar1.Value

    Dim updateProgressBar As New _
        updateDelegate(AddressOf _
                             ProgressBar1.SetValue)

    Do Until ProgressBar1.Value = ProgressBar1.Maximum
        value += 1

        Dispatcher.Invoke(updateProgressBar, _
            System.Windows.Threading.DispatcherPriority.Background, _
            New Object() {ProgressBar.ValueProperty, value})
    Loop
End Sub
```

The `Dispatcher.Invoke` method invokes the delegate, which does nothing but invoke `ProgressBar.SetValue`. The other interesting argument is an array of `Object` storing the dependency property to be updated (`ProgressBar.ValueProperty`), which will be reflected onto `Value`, and its value. Figure 29.14 shows the result of the code.

FIGURE 29.14   The `ProgressBar` value increasing.

USING `Dispatcher.InvokeAsync`

WPF 4.5 introduces some new methods for the `Dispatcher` class. It is worth mentioning `InvokeAsync`. Different from `Invoke`, which you saw in the previous example and which works synchronously, `InvokeAsync` executes the specified thread asynchronously on the thread the Dispatcher is associated with.

Accepting User Choices with the `RadioButton` Control

The `RadioButton` control works similarly to the `CheckBox`, differing in that this enables one choice among several alternatives, but it exposes the same properties. The following XAML code declares two `RadioButton` controls:

```
<StackPanel>
    <RadioButton Name="Radio1" Content="First option"/>
    <RadioButton Name="Radio2" Content="Second option"/>
</StackPanel>
```

Each instance exposes the `IsChecked` property and the `Checked` and `Unchecked` events. For this, take a look back at the `CheckBox` discussion. Figure 29.15 shows how the controls look.

FIGURE 29.15   Adding `RadioButton` selection.

Drawing Shapes: The `Rectangle`

The `Rectangle` element is another common geometric shape that you can utilize in custom control templates. Drawing a rectangle is easy, as demonstrated in the following code example:

```
<Rectangle Width="150" Height="50"
          Fill="Orange" Stroke="Red"
          StrokeThickness="3"/>
```

You define its dimensions, specifying `Stroke` and `StrokeThickness` as for the ellipse (optional). Figure 29.16 shows how the object is drawn.

FIGURE 29.16   Drawing a rectangle.

`Rectangle` also has the `RadiusX` and `RadiusY` properties that you can assign to round corners.

Editing Text with the `RichTextBox` Control

WPF 4.5 offers a `RichTextBox` control that works differently from Windows Forms and requires you to understand flow documents. This topic will be discussed in Chapter 31.

Extended View with the `ScrollBar` Control

You can implement scrollbars with the `ScrollBar` control. The following code provides an example:

```
<ScrollBar Name="Scroll1" Maximum="100" Minimum="0"
          Value="50" Scroll="Scroll1_Scroll"/>
```

The implementation is simple because you just have to provide the `Minimum`, `Maximum`, and current `Value`. The `Scroll` event is instead raised when the selector position changes. The event handler is then implemented as follows:

```
Private Sub Scroll1_Scroll(ByVal sender As System.Object,
                           ByVal e As Primitives.
                           ScrollEventArgs)

End Sub
```

WPF offers a more versatile control, named ScrollViewer, as described in the next section.

Scrolling the Visual Tree with the `ScrollViewer` Control

The ScrollViewer element enables scrolling its entire content with both horizontal and vertical scrollbars. This can be easily understood directly at design time. Type the following XAML code:

```
<ScrollViewer VerticalScrollBarVisibility="Auto"
              HorizontalScrollBarVisibility="Auto">
    <StackPanel>
        <TextBlock Width="1000"/>
        <TextBlock Height="2000"/>
    </StackPanel>
</ScrollViewer>
```

You notice that, because of the big width and height values, the ScrollViewer provides both scrollbars, as demonstrated in Figure 29.17.

FIGURE 29.17   Implementing a ScrollViewer.

This control is useful when you need to arrange multiple elements in a fixed fashion and still want to provide the ability of scrolling them within the window.

Separating Visual Elements with the `Separator` Control

The Separator control is used for drawing a separation line between visual elements. I provided an example previously when discussing the Menu control.

Value Selection with the `Slider` Control

The `Slider` control provides a selector you can use to set a particular value that is bound to another control. Chapter 31 provides an example binding a `Slider` to a `MediaElement` for controlling the volume; however, at the moment consider the following code:

```
<Slider Name="Slider1"
        Maximum="10" Minimum="0" Value="5"
        AutoToolTipPlacement="BottomRight"
        TickPlacement="TopLeft" TickFrequency="1"
        />
<TextBlock Text="{Binding ElementName=Slider1,
        Path=Value}"/>
```

A `Slider` requires a `Minimum` and `Maximum` value, whereas Value is the current selected value. You can place tool tips reporting the value (`AutoToolTipPlacement`) that specify the position (`TopLeft` or `BottomRight`). Moreover, you can place ticks so that visualization is clearer and decide how many ticks to place (`TickFrequency`). For example, the preceding code can produce 10 ticks (1 per possible value). The `TextBlock` shows the value of the slider via data-binding, which is the preferred way of binding a `Slider` value to another control. This object raises a `ValueChanged` event when the user moves the selector to another value. Figure 29.18 shows the result of the preceding code.

FIGURE 29.18   Setting values with a `Slider`.

Displaying Information with the `StatusBar` Control

WPF enables you to place status bars at the bottom of a `Window`. This is accomplished by declaring a `StatusBar` object that nests `StatusBarItems` elements. The good news is that you are not limited to adding text to a `StatusBar` because you can add several kinds of visual elements. The following example shows adding text and a `ProgressBar` into a `StatusBar`:

```
<StatusBar>
    <StatusBarItem Name="Item1" Content="Ready"/>
    <StatusBarItem Name="Item2">
```

```
    <ProgressBar Name="Progress1"
        Minimum="0" Maximum="200" Value="50"
        Width="50" Height="15" />
    </StatusBarItem>
</StatusBar>
```

Figure 29.19 shows the result of the preceding code. You access members in the bar at the Visual Basic level via their identifiers.

FIGURE 29.19   A StatusBar with nested controls.

Organizing User Interfaces with the TabControl Control

The TabControl enables you to split an area into tabs. Each tab is represented by a TabItem object, and tabs are enclosed within a TabControl.TabItems collection. The following code demonstrates how you can implement a TabControl with both standard and customized tabs:

```
<TabControl>
    <TabControl.Items>
        <TabItem Header="Tab1">
            <!- Nest your controls here.. ->
        </TabItem>
        <TabItem Foreground="Blue"
                Background="Orange">
            <TabItem.Header>
                <StackPanel Orientation="Horizontal">
                    <TextBlock Text="Tab2"/>
                    <!- Replace with a valid image
                    <Image Source="MyImage.jpg"/>->
                </StackPanel>
            </TabItem.Header>
        </TabItem>
    </TabControl.Items>
</TabControl>
```

You set the tab header content assigning the `Header` property for each `TabItem` and then nest controls within the element. Notice how you can customize tabs by setting `Foreground` and `Background` and declaring the `Header` in a hierarchical fashion to place multiple elements. Figure 29.20 shows the `TabControl` implementation.

FIGURE 29.20   Implementing a `TabControl`.

You can also customize the header with text and an image, as you can check in the comment placed in the code. Then you access nested controls via their names as you would do in any other situation.

Presenting Text with the `TextBlock` Control

The `TextBlock` control enables showing text messages. Its purpose is similar to the `Label`'s purpose, but it differs in that `TextBlock` offers deeper control over text customization. The following example demonstrates how you can present customized text using the `TextBlock`:

```
<TextBlock Name="TextBlock1" FontFamily="Tahoma"
           FontSize="20" FontStyle="Italic"
           FontWeight="Bold"
           Text="Sample text with TextBlock">
    <TextBlock.Foreground>
        <LinearGradientBrush>
            <GradientStop Offset="0" Color="Blue"/>
            <GradientStop Offset="0.5" Color="Violet"/>
            <GradientStop Offset="1" Color="Green"/>
        </LinearGradientBrush>
    </TextBlock.Foreground>
</TextBlock>
```

Font properties are of particular interest. `FontFamily` indicates the font name, `FontStyle` indicates whether the font is normal or oblique, and `FontWeight` sets the font depth. IntelliSense enables easy selections for available members on each of the previously mentioned properties. Figure 29.21 shows the result of the preceding code.

29

FIGURE 29.21   Drawing a `TextBlock`.

Because of its flexibility, the `TextBlock` control is often used in custom control templates that require customizing text. You can also set the `TextBlock` text at runtime by assigning the `Text` property.

Entering Text with the `TextBox` Control

Another typical control that is also provided by WPF is the `TextBox`. You declare one as follows:

```
<TextBox Name="TextBox1"
         TextChanged="TextBox1_TextChanged"/>
```

The most common event is `TextChanged` that is raised when the text is modified and that can be handled as follows:

```
Private Sub TextBox1_TextChanged(ByVal sender As System.Object,
                                 ByVal e As System.Windows.Controls.
                                 TextChangedEventArgs)

End Sub
```

The e object of type `TextChangedEventArgs` offers a `Changes` collection property that can be iterated to get a list of changes that affect the control's content. The `TextBox` control provides support for undo actions (that is, Ctrl+Z) and a `SelectedText` property that enables you to easily retrieve in VB code the currently selected text in the control.

Offering Commands with the `ToolBar` Control

The `ToolBar` control enables you to create toolbars for your WPF applications. You can add multiple `ToolBar` objects within a `ToolBarTray` object. The following XAML code shows how you can define a simple toolbar; you have to replace image files with valid ones:

```
<ToolBarTray>
    <ToolBar>
        <Button Name="NewButton"
                Click="NewButton_Click">
            <Image Source=NewDocument.png" />
        </Button>
        <Button Name="OpenButton"
                Click="OpenButton_Click">
            <Image Source="OpenFolder.png" />
        </Button>
        <Button Name="SaveButton"
                Click="SaveButton_Click">
            <Image Source="Save.png" />
        </Button>
    </ToolBar>
</ToolBarTray>
```

Notice how the code implements primitive `Button` controls that you can manage in Visual Basic code with classic event handlers for the `Click` event. Following this logic, you can place additional `ToolBar` objects inside the `ToolBarTray`. Figure 29.22 shows the `ToolBar`.

FIGURE 29.22   Implementing a `ToolBar`.

Presenting Hierarchical Data with the `TreeView` Control

The `TreeView` is another important control, and WPF provides its own implementation that exposes a `TreeView.Items` collection where you nest nodes. Each node is represented by a `TreeViewItem` object. You can build complex items as in the following example:

```
<TreeView Name="TreeView1">
    <TreeView.Items>
        <TreeViewItem Header="Root Node" Name="RootNode"
                      Tag="Information for this node">
            <TreeViewItem Header="Node0" Name="Node0"/>
            <TreeViewItem Header="Node1" Name="Node1">
```

29

```
            <TreeViewItem Header="SubNode"
                          Name="SubNode"/>
        </TreeViewItem>
      </TreeViewItem>
    </TreeView.Items>
</TreeView>
```

The text in the node is specified with the Header property, while you can assign additional information with the Tag property. Assigning the Name property is also useful because you can interact with nodes in managed code. To add nodes at runtime, you create an instance of the TreeViewItem class and then add it to the specified node as demonstrated here:

```
Dim nt As New TreeViewItem
With nt
    .Header = "New sub node"
    .Tag = "Runtime added"
End With

Node0.Items.Add(nt)
```

Figure 29.23 shows the result for all the preceding code.

FIGURE 29.23   Implementing and populating a TreeView.

The TreeView can also be populated via data-binding with the ItemsSource property; it exposes the SelectedItem property, exactly as it happens for the ComboBox and ListBox controls. Thus, you can apply the same techniques.

Accessing the Web with the WebBrowser Control

The WebBrowser control provides specific functionalities for browsing websites. You add it to the user interface by declaring a WebBrowser element as follows:

```
<WebBrowser Name="Browser1"/>
```

Then you can control the `WebBrowser` behavior from Visual Basic code; the following are methods exposed by the `WebBrowser` allowing navigation:

```
'Open the specified website
Browser1.Navigate(New Uri("Http://msdn.com/vbasic"))
'Back to the previous page
Browser1.GoBack()
'Forward to the next page
Browser1.GoForward()
'Refresh the page
Browser1.Refresh()
```

The `WebBrowser` also exposes some events; the most important is `LoadCompleted`, which is raised when the control completes loading a web page. This can be handled to get useful information on the visited website, as in the following code snippet:

```
Private Sub Browser1_LoadCompleted(ByVal sender As Object,
                         ByVal e As NavigationEventArgs) _
                         Handles Browser1.Navigated
    MessageBox.Show(e.Uri.ToString)
End Sub
```

The object of type `NavigationEventArgs` provides properties that retrieve information such as the website URL or the `WebResponse` instance.

Windows Forms Interoperability with the `WindowsFormsHost` Control

The `WindowsFormsHost` control enables interoperability with the Windows Forms technology and provides a way for hosting Win Forms user controls within a WPF application.

> **INTEROPERABILITY TIPS**
>
> I often answer questions in online forums about WPF, and one of the most common questions is about interoperability between Windows Forms and WPF, especially for developers who are moving their applications to WPF. So many architectural differences exist between the two technologies that interoperability is not a task that I suggest. You should use interoperability only when there is no other way of rewriting a WPF version of a Windows Form control, which is improbable.

To host a Windows Forms control, you drag the `WindowsFormsHost` element from the Toolbox onto the Window surface. The next step is adding a reference to the System.Windows.Forms.dll assembly. If you want to host Windows Forms controls built in the .NET Framework, you need to add an XML namespace declaration at the Window level; the following line of XAML code demonstrates this:

```
xmlns:wf="clr-namespace:System.Windows.Forms;assembly=System.Windows.Forms"
```

At this point, you can nest the desired control inside the `WindowsFormsHost` declaration, as in the following example that adds a `System.Windows.Forms.PictureBox`:

```
<WindowsFormsHost Height="100"
                  Name="WindowsFormsHost1"
                  Width="200">
    <wf:PictureBox x:Name="Picture1"/>
</WindowsFormsHost>
```

Notice that you need to provide the `x:Name` attribute to make the control reachable from the Visual Basic code. Now you can interact with the `PictureBox` like you would in any other Windows Forms application by invoking its identifier—as demonstrated in the following code snippets where the code loads an image file and assigns it to the `PictureBox`. This particular example also requires a reference to the System.Drawing.dll assembly:

```
'This is Windows Forms code inside a WPF application
Me.Picture1.Image = System.Drawing.Image.
                    FromFile("C:\Picture.jpg")
```

This technique works with custom user controls as well; you just need to add an XML namespace reference pointing to the appropriate assembly exposing the custom user control (including the current project). Then you can use the control itself.

Using Common Dialogs

In WPF 4.5, as well as its predecessors, common dialogs are wrappers of Win32 dialogs. They are exposed by the `Microsoft.Win32` namespace and are `OpenFileDialog` and `SaveFileDialog`. (WPF also provides a `PrintDialog` control exposed by the `System.Windows.Controls` namespace.) The following code demonstrates how you instantiate both dialogs:

```
'Instantiating an OpenFileDialog
Dim od As New Microsoft.Win29.OpenFileDialog
With od
    .Title = "Your title here..."
    .Filter = "All files|*.*"
    .ShowReadOnly = True

    If .ShowDialog = True Then
        Dim fileName As String = .FileName
    End If
End With

'Instantiating a SaveFileDialog
Dim sd As New Microsoft.Win29.SaveFileDialog
With sd
```

```
        .Title = "Your title here..."
        .InitialDirectory = "."
        .Filter = "All files|*.*"
        If .ShowDialog = True Then
            Dim fileName As String = .FileName
        End If
    End With
```

Notice that the ShowDialog method returns a Nullable(Of Boolean), in which True means that the user clicks **OK**, False when she clicks **Cancel**, and Nothing when she closes the dialog.

Summary

In this chapter you got an overview of WPF's most commonly used controls, which you can use in your client applications, understanding how they can be both implemented in XAML or VB code. Also we covered some particular aspects about them, such as their so-called lookless implementation, understanding why they can also be nameless because of routed events.

29

Brushes, Styles, Templates, and Animations in WPF

Building rich user experiences has become an important business. Functionalities are no longer the only requirement, even in business applications, because an attractive user interface (UI) also plays a fundamental role. Windows Presentation Foundation (WPF) offers the ideal platform for enriching the user interface with interactive content, such as animations, media files, dynamic documents, and graphical effects. WPF is also the ideal platform for building graphics manipulation applications, in which geometry or 3D graphics can run. Before you learn such important features, it is important to know about some graphics fundamentals so that you can enrich visual elements. It is worth mentioning that one of the biggest benefits of WPF is that you can take complete control over UI elements' customization. You can fill them with impressive gradients; you can completely rewrite their layout while keeping their behavior safe; and you can animate them along the UI, ensuring that they will still work as you expect. The goal of this chapter is to illustrate customization so that you can make your UI more and more attractive.

Introducing Brushes

At one time or another, you have probably wanted to fill your UI controls with interesting background textures or gradients or set a particular color, maybe as the background or the foreground. In WPF, you fill visual elements with brushes. WPF defines several kinds of brushes, all deriving from `System.Windows.Media.Brush`. The following list summarizes available brushes:

▶ **SolidColorBrush**—Enables you to fill a graphical object with a single color. Colors are exposed as static properties from the `System.Windows.Media.Colors` class.

▶ **LinearGradientBrush**—Enables you to fill a graphical object with a linear gradient composed of multiple colors.

▶ **RadialGradientBrush**—Similar to the previous one, but the gradient is circular.

▶ **ImageBrush**—Enables you to fill a graphical object with a picture.

▶ **DrawingBrush**—Enables you to fill a graphical object with geometrical shapes or pen drawings.

▶ **SelectionBrush**—Enables you to define the highlighting color when selecting text in specific controls.

▶ **CaretBrush**—Enables you to define the mouse pointer color in particular controls. Actually, `CaretBrush` is a property exposed by controls such as `TextBox` and `RichTextBox`, which accept `Brush` objects.

▶ **VisualBrush**—Enables you to fill a graphical object with the content of another element in the user interface.

▶ **BitmapCacheBrush**—Enables you to cache a visual element instead of rendering it again and is useful when you need to recall the same visual elements multiple times.

You can apply brushes to properties in visual elements exposing a `Background`, `Foreground`, or `Fill` property, such as user controls and geometrical shapes. In the next sections, you learn to fill your UI elements with the previously listed brushes. Before providing examples, let's create a new WPF project with Visual Basic 2012. Divide the default `Grid` into eight rows and adjust `Window`'s size as follows:

```
<Window x:Class="MainWindow"
    xmlns="http://schemas.microsoft.com/winfx/2006/xaml/presentation"
    xmlns:x="http://schemas.microsoft.com/winfx/2006/xaml"
    Title="MainWindow" Height="550" Width="550">
    <Grid>
        <Grid.RowDefinitions>
            <RowDefinition />
            <RowDefinition />
            <RowDefinition />
            <RowDefinition />
            <RowDefinition />
            <RowDefinition />
            <RowDefinition />
            <RowDefinition />
        </Grid.RowDefinitions>
    </Grid>
</Window>
```

ABBREVIATING LINES OF CODE

To make lines of code shorter, add an `Imports System.Windows.Media` directive in the Visual Basic code behind the file.

Applying a `SolidColorBrush`

The `System.Windows.Media.SolidColorBrush` object enables you to fill an object with a single color. The color is applied to the `Fill` property of geometric shapes and to the `Background` or `Foreground` properties in UI controls. The following code demonstrates how to apply a `SolidColorBrush`:

```
<Rectangle Grid.Row="0" Width="200" Margin="5">
    <Rectangle.Fill>
        <SolidColorBrush Color="Red"/>
    </Rectangle.Fill>
</Rectangle>
```

The `Color` property receives a value of type `System.Windows.Media.Color`. Colors are exposed by the `System.Windows.Media.Colors` class as shared properties. The result of this color brush is shown in Figure 30.1.

FIGURE 30.1   Applying a `SolidColorBrush`.

30

Applying a color at runtime in Visual Basic code is also a simple task. The following snippet shows how you can set it within the code-behind file:

```
Dim rect As New Rectangle

Dim scb As New SolidColorBrush(Colors.Red)
rect.Fill = scb
```

Applying a `LinearGradientBrush`

A `LinearGradientBrush` enables you to apply a gradient color to fill a visual element. Valid targets are the `Fill` property for geometric shapes—`Background` and `Foreground` properties for user controls. The following code draws a `Rectangle` and demonstrates that the gradient is applied both as background color (`Fill` property) and as foreground (`Stroke`):

```
<Rectangle Grid.Row="1" Width="200" Margin="5" Name="GradientRectangle"
                StrokeThickness="3">
  <Rectangle.Fill>
    <LinearGradientBrush StartPoint="0,0" EndPoint="0,1">
        <GradientStop Offset="0" Color="Orange"/>
        <GradientStop Offset="0.5" Color="Red"/>
        <GradientStop Offset="0.9" Color="Yellow"/>
    </LinearGradientBrush>
  </Rectangle.Fill>
  <Rectangle.Stroke>
    <LinearGradientBrush StartPoint="0,0" EndPoint="0,1">
        <GradientStop Offset="0" Color="Blue"/>
        <GradientStop Offset="0.5" Color="Green"/>
        <GradientStop Offset="0.9" Color="Violet"/>
    </LinearGradientBrush>
  </Rectangle.Stroke>
</Rectangle>
```

First, it is worth mentioning that the `StrokeThickness` property of `Rectangle` specifies the shape's border size. Each color in the gradient is represented by a `GradientStop` element. Its `Offset` property requires a value from 0 to 1 and specifies the color position in the gradient, whereas the color property accepts the color name or the color hexadecimal representation. Also notice how the `StartPoint` and `EndPoint` properties in the `LinearGradientBrush` enable you to influence the gradient direction. Figure 30.2 shows the result of the preceding code.

You can define a `LinearGradientBrush` in Visual Basic code for runtime appliance. This is accomplished by the following code:

```
Dim lgb As New LinearGradientBrush
lgb.GradientStops.Add(New GradientStop With {.Offset = 0,
                                    .Color = Colors.Red})
```

```
lgb.GradientStops.Add(New GradientStop With {.Offset = 0,
                                             .Color = Colors.Yellow})
lgb.GradientStops.Add(New GradientStop With {.Offset = 0,
                                             .Color = Colors.Orange})

'rect is a Rectangle instance
rect.Fill = lgb
```

FIGURE 30.2   Applying a LinearGradientBrush.

Notice how you add instances of the GradientStop class to the GradientStops collection.
Each GradientStop requires both Offset (of type Double) and Color (of type System.
Windows.Media.Color) properties to be set. Colors are exposed by the System.Windows.
Media.Colors class as shared properties.

Applying a `RadialGradientBrush`

The `RadialGradientBrush` brush works exactly like the `LinearGradientBrush`, except that it creates a circular gradient. The following code shows how you can apply such a brush to an `Ellipse`:

```
<Ellipse Width="100" Margin="5" Grid.Row="2" Stroke="Black"
        StrokeThickness="2" >
    <Ellipse.Fill>
        <RadialGradientBrush>
                <GradientStop Offset="0" Color="Blue"/>
                <GradientStop Offset="0.5" Color="Green"/>
                <GradientStop Offset="0.9" Color="Violet"/>
        </RadialGradientBrush>
    </Ellipse.Fill>
</Ellipse>
```

You are not limited to the `Ellipse` shape, but for demo purposes it is the one that best fits the example. Figure 30.3 shows the result of the brush applied.

The Visual Basic code for applying the brush at runtime is similar to the one for the linear gradient. The following code snippet provides an example:

```
Dim ragb As New RadialGradientBrush
ragb.GradientStops.Add(New GradientStop With {.Offset = 0,
                                              .Color = Colors.Red})
ragb.GradientStops.Add(New GradientStop With {.Offset = 0,
                                              .Color = Colors.Yellow})
ragb.GradientStops.Add(New GradientStop With {.Offset = 0,
                                              .Color = Colors.Orange})
rect.Fill = ragb
```

Applying an `ImageBrush`

You can fill a visual element with an image file by using the `ImageBrush` brush. This object is useful even if you want to fill text with image textures. The following code snippet shows how to apply an `ImageBrush` as a button background and as the text foreground color:

```
<StackPanel Grid.Row="3" Orientation="Horizontal">
    <Button Width="100" Margin="5" Content="Hello!"
        Foreground="Yellow">
        <Button.Background>
            <ImageBrush Opacity="0.5"
                ImageSource=
           "/StylesBrushesTemplatesAnimations;component/Images/Avatar.jpg" />
        </Button.Background>
    </Button>
```

```
    <TextBlock Margin="5"
              FontFamily="Segoe UI" FontSize="40" Text="Hello!"
              FontWeight="Bold" >
        <TextBlock.Foreground>
          <ImageBrush ImageSource=
          "/StylesBrushesTemplatesAnimations;component/Images/Avatar.jpg"/>
        </TextBlock.Foreground>
    </TextBlock>
</StackPanel>
```

FIGURE 30.3   The result of the `RadialGradientBrush`.

NOTE

In the previous code, the Avatar.jpg file is just a sample picture of me. I suppose you might prefer to replace my face with one of your favorite pictures!

The image is specified by assigning the ImageSource property with the image's Uniform Resource Identifier (URI). The previous code produces the result shown in Figure 30.4 (see the last row).

FIGURE 30.4   Applying an ImageBrush as the background and foreground color.

If you want to add your images to the application resources so that you can easily refer to them when applying the ImageBrush, follow these steps:

1. Write the ImageBrush element in the XAML code editor.

2. Add image files to the project (Project, Add Existing Item).

3. In the XAML code editor, select the previously added ImageBrush object and then press F4 to open the Properties window.

4. Select the ImageSource property and expand the drop-down box, as shown in Figure 30.5. Pick up the desired picture that will be assigned to the selected brush. When added, its address will be assigned to the ImageProperty in the XAML code under the form of a packed Uri.

Applying an ImageBrush in Visual Basic code is also a simple task, demonstrated by the following code snippet:

```
Dim myButton As New Button
Dim imgb As New ImageBrush
imgb.ImageSource = New BitmapImage _
```

```
    (New _
    Uri("/StylesBrushesTemplatesAnimations;component/Images/Avatar.jpg",
    UriKind.Relative))
myButton.Background = imgb
```

FIGURE 30.5   Selecting an image with the designer tools.

Notice how, in Visual Basic code, you specify the image by creating first an instance of the `BitmapImage` class whose constructor receives an argument of type `Uri` pointing to the actual image file.

Applying `SelectionBrush` and `CaretBrush`

WPF 4.5 offers two special objects, `SelectionBrush` and `CaretBrush`, which are properties of type `System.Windows.Media.Brush` and that accept brushes to be assigned to them. The first one enables you to apply a brush to the highlighting color when selecting text, whereas the second one applies a brush to the mouse caret within the control. Controls that can receive application of these brushes are `TextBox` and `PasswordBox`. `SelectionBrush` can also be applied to `FlowDocumentPageViewer`, `FlowDocumentReader`, and `FlowDocumentScrollViewer`. You apply both brushes as child nodes of the desired control. The following code demonstrates how to apply a linear gradient color for both the highlighting selection color and the caret color:

```
<TextBox Grid.Row="4" Margin="5"
        FontSize="20" FontWeight="Bold"
        Name="TextBox1">
    <TextBox.SelectionBrush>
        <LinearGradientBrush>
            <GradientStop Offset="0" Color="Chartreuse"/>
            <GradientStop Offset="0.5" Color="Violet"/>
            <GradientStop Offset="1" Color="Blue"/>
        </LinearGradientBrush>
    </TextBox.SelectionBrush>

    <TextBox.CaretBrush>
        <LinearGradientBrush>
            <GradientStop Offset="0" Color="Red"/>
            <GradientStop Offset="0.5" Color="Yellow"/>
            <GradientStop Offset="1" Color="Orange"/>
        </LinearGradientBrush>
    </TextBox.CaretBrush>
</TextBox>
```

Figure 30.6 shows the result of this code, although the caret gradient is not visible at this point, but you will see there are no problems on your screen.

FIGURE 30.6   Applying SelectionBrush and CaretBrush.

You can apply different kinds of brushes, such as `ImageBrush` or `VisualBrush`, as described in the next section.

Applying a `VisualBrush`

The `VisualBrush` enables you to fill an object with the content of another visual element in the user interface. For example, you could set a button's background with the content of a `MediaElement` that is playing a video. Applying a `VisualBrush` is simple, in that you just need to assign its `Visual` property with the name of the visual element you want to bind. The following code example shows how you can assign another visual element currently in the user interface as the background of a button:

```
<Button Width="100" Margin="5" Grid.Row="5">
    <Button.Background>
        <VisualBrush Visual="{Binding ElementName=GradientRectangle}"/>
    </Button.Background>
</Button>
```

The requirement is that the source visual element has a `Name` property set. You assign the visual element with the `Binding` markup extension, whose `ElementName` property points to the actual visual element. You learn more about the `Binding` extension in Chapter 32, "Introducing Data-Binding." The previous example produces the result shown in Figure 30.7.

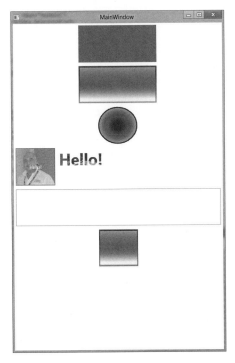

FIGURE 30.7   Applying a `VisualBrush`.

30

The button's background typically is not a color but is a rectangle with all its properties. So, if you make modifications to the binding source, the changes will be reflected into the VisualBrush. This is the real power of this brush. For example, try to use a TextBox as the source element; when you write in the TextBox, your text will be reflected into the VisualBrush.

Applying a DrawingBrush

The DrawingBrush brush enables you to paint an area with a so called *drawing*. A drawing, according to the MSDN documentation, can be a shape, an image, a video, text, or another item and is an instance of the System.Windows.Media.Drawing class. The following code sample fills a rectangle with a DrawingBrush defining a drawing where two ellipses intersect each other:

```
<Rectangle Width="100"
           Grid.Row="6">
    <Rectangle.Fill>
        <DrawingBrush>
            <DrawingBrush.Drawing>
                <GeometryDrawing>
                    <GeometryDrawing.Brush>
                        <LinearGradientBrush>
                            <GradientStop Offset="0" Color="Blue"/>
                            <GradientStop Offset="0.7" Color="LightBlue"/>
                        </LinearGradientBrush>
                    </GeometryDrawing.Brush>
                    <GeometryDrawing.Geometry>
                        <GeometryGroup>
                            <EllipseGeometry RadiusX="0.1" RadiusY="0.5"
                                             Center="0.5,0.5" />
                            <EllipseGeometry RadiusX="0.5" RadiusY="0.1"
                                             Center="0.5,0.5" />
                        </GeometryGroup>
                    </GeometryDrawing.Geometry>
                </GeometryDrawing>
            </DrawingBrush.Drawing>
        </DrawingBrush>
    </Rectangle.Fill>
</Rectangle>
```

Other than the brush, it is interesting here how ellipses are declared via EllipseGeometry objects that are the geometric representation of ellipses and are enclosed within a GeometryGroup that can group different kinds of geometric representations, such as LineGeometry or RectangleGeometry. (These classes derive from System.Windows.Media. Geometry, for your further studies.) Figure 30.8 shows the result of the previous snippet.

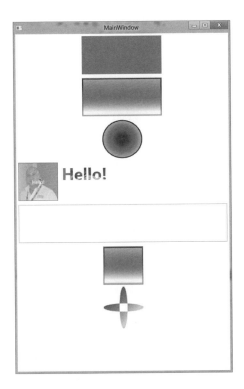

FIGURE 30.8   Applying a `DrawingBrush`.

Applying a `BitmapCacheBrush`

WPF 4.5 has the concept of *cached composition*, which was introduced back in WPF 4 and that lets you store a visual element to a cache so that redrawing an element is faster and provides better performance instead of rendering the graphic element each time it needs to be used. Among the others, with cached composition you can cache images to apply as a brush. This is accomplished by first declaring a `BitmapCache` object that establishes the rules for caching the desired object and then by applying a `BitmapCacheBrush` to the visual element. The following code demonstrates how to apply a `BitmapCacheBrush` as the background of two `TextBlock` controls, by using cached composition (comments in the code will help you understand better):

```
<StackPanel Grid.Row="7">
    <StackPanel.Resources>
        <!— an image pointing to the previously added
            resource —>
        <Image x:Key="cachedImage"
Source="/StylesBrushesTemplatesAnimations;component/Images/Avatar.jpg">
            <!— supposing we'll use the same image multiple
                times, we can cache it instead of
```

30

```
                rendering each time -->
          <Image.CacheMode>
              <!-- RenderAtScale = 1 means that it is cached
                   at its actual size (no zoom) -->
              <BitmapCache RenderAtScale="1"
                           EnableClearType="False"
                           SnapsToDevicePixels="False"/>
          </Image.CacheMode>
      </Image>
      <!-- Applying the cached image as a brush -->
      <BitmapCacheBrush x:Key="cachedBrush"
          Target="{StaticResource cachedImage}"/>
    </StackPanel.Resources>

    <TextBlock Text="Text one..." FontSize="24"
               Height="60" Foreground="Blue"
               FontWeight="Bold"
               Background="{StaticResource cachedBrush}"/>
    <TextBlock Text="Text two..." FontSize="24"
               Height="60" Foreground="Green"
               FontWeight="Bold"
               Background="{StaticResource cachedBrush}"/>
</StackPanel>
```

The `BitmapCache.RenderAtScale` property establishes when the visual element has to be cached. If assigned with 1, as in the preceding example, the visual element is cached at its natural size. For example, you could assign such a property with 2 in case you want to cache the visual element only when it is zoomed at the double of its size. The `BitmapCache.EnableClearType` property lets you decide whether you want to apply Clear Type precision to the visual elements, but it is useful only with text. The `BitmapCache.SnapsToDevicePixels` property should be assigned with `True` when you need precise pixel-alignment and takes the same value of the `EnableClearType` property. Finally, notice how the `BitmapCacheBrush` object points to the image via the `Target` property and how it is applied to `TextBlock` controls via the `Background` property pointing to the new resource. The preceding code produces the result shown in Figure 30.9. Now that you know about WPF brushes, you are ready to get an overview of another great feature: styles.

Introducing Styles

One of the biggest benefits of WPF user controls is that their layout is completely customizable. As explained further in the "Introducing Control Templates" section, you can completely redefine their layout and behavior using templates. In some situations, you have multiple controls of the same type and want them to have the same properties. For example, you might want to implement three buttons, with each button having the same width, height, and font as the other ones. To avoid the need of applying the same properties for each control, which can be annoying if you have dozens of controls, you can define a *style*. A style is an instance of the `System.Windows.Style` class and enables you to define a set of common properties for the specified type of control. Styles are defined within the `Resources` section of a `Window`, of panels, or at the application level (Application.xaml file). Each style must have an identifier assigned via the `x:Key` attribute and is applied to controls assigning their `Style` property. The code in Listing 30.1 defines a style for buttons and applies the style to three buttons in the interface.

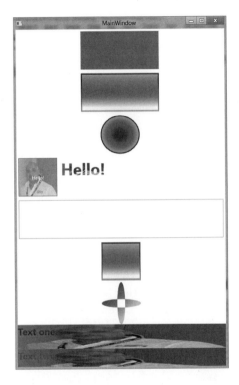

FIGURE 30.9   Applying `BitmapCachedBrush` objects.

LISTING 30.1   Defining and Assigning a Style for Buttons

```
<Window x:Class="Styles"
    xmlns="http://schemas.microsoft.com/winfx/2006/xaml/presentation"
    xmlns:x="http://schemas.microsoft.com/winfx/2006/xaml"
    Title="Styles" Height="300" Width="300">
    <StackPanel>
        <StackPanel.Resources>
            <Style x:Key="ButtonStyle" TargetType="Button">
                <Setter Property="Width" Value="100"/>
                <Setter Property="Height" Value="40"/>
                <Setter Property="Foreground" Value="Blue"/>
                <Setter Property="FontFamily" Value="Verdana"/>
```

30

```
                <Setter Property="Margin" Value="5"/>
                <Setter Property="Background">
                    <Setter.Value>
                        <LinearGradientBrush>
                            <GradientStop Offset="0.2" Color="Orange"/>
                            <GradientStop Offset="0.8" Color="Red"/>
                        </LinearGradientBrush>
                    </Setter.Value>
                </Setter>
            </Style>
        </StackPanel.Resources>

        <Button Style="{StaticResource ButtonStyle}" Content="Hello!"/>
        <Button Style="{StaticResource ButtonStyle}" Content="Another styled"/>
        <Button Style="{StaticResource ButtonStyle}" Content="Button three"/>
    </StackPanel>
</Window>
```

Understanding the scope of styles is important. In the code example, the style is defined at the panel level, meaning that buttons outside the panel cannot get the style applied. Notice how the `TargetType` property enables you to specify the target control type. If it's not specified, WPF assumes `FrameworkElement` as the target. Properties are specified via `Setter` elements. Each setter requires the target Property specification and its value. You can also define a complex value by splitting its definition to create a `Setter.Value` node, which can store multiple lines of XAML code. This was shown in Listing 30.1, where the technique is used to define a `LinearGradientBrush` gradient. Finally, notice how the new style is assigned to buttons setting the `Style` property, pointing to the style identifier via an XAML markup extension named `StaticResource`.

STATICRESOURCE AND DYNAMICRESOURCE

In different situations you can often find controls pointing to resources via `StaticResource` or `DynamicResource` markup extensions. The difference is that a `StaticResource` is something defined in the XAML that will not change during the application lifetime. It will be assigned only once, even before its actual point of use. A `DynamicResource` instead is assigned when its value is required and if its content changes during the application lifetime, its changes are reflected to the caller.

Running the code can produce the interesting result shown in Figure 30.10.

On the Visual Basic side, you create and apply a style as in the following code snippet:

```
Dim buttonStyle As New Style
'Need to specify the System.Type
buttonStyle.TargetType = GetType(Button)
'The Setter.Property member is assigned with a dependency property exposed
```

```
'by the System.Type
buttonStyle.Setters.Add(New Setter With {.Property = Button.WidthProperty,
                                          .Value = "100"})

Button1.Style = buttonStyle
```

FIGURE 30.10   Styling multiple controls of the same type with Styles.

This can be particularly useful if you need to generate a style at runtime, although you define styles at design time. Therefore, declaring and applying them via XAML is the most preferable way (so that designers can eventually take advantage of XAML for their work).

Styles Inheritance

You can define a style that inherits from another one to extend it with new settings. This is accomplished by specifying the BasedOn property as follows:

```
<Style x:Key="InheritedStyle" TargetType="Button"
       BasedOn="{StaticResource ButtonStyle}">
    <Setter Property="FontWeight" Value="ExtraBold"/>
</Style>
```

If you now assign this new style to a button, it can take all the style properties of the base style plus the FontWeight value.

Understanding Triggers

Until now, you saw how styles can be applied to controls without condition. This is useful, but it is more useful for deciding when to apply a style. The easiest example is to consider a button; you apply a background color that you might want to change when the mouse pointer passes over the button, and this behavior should be replicated for each button in the UI via styles. To conditionally apply styles, you use *triggers*. A trigger essentially represents a condition that enables you to apply a particular style when the condition is evaluated as True. Triggers are defined within a Style.Triggers collection, and each of them requires you to specify the property affected by the condition and a Boolean value (True or False) that determines when the trigger has to be executed. The code in

Listing 30.2 retakes the first style example, adding a trigger condition in the final part of the code.

LISTING 30.2   Applying a Single Trigger Condition

```
<Style x:Key="ButtonStyle" TargetType="Button">
    <Setter Property="Width" Value="100"/>
    <Setter Property="Height" Value="40"/>
    <Setter Property="Foreground" Value="Blue"/>
    <Setter Property="FontFamily" Value="Verdana"/>
    <Setter Property="Margin" Value="5"/>
    <Setter Property="Background">
        <Setter.Value>
            <LinearGradientBrush>
                <GradientStop Offset="0.2" Color="Orange"/>
                <GradientStop Offset="0.8" Color="Red"/>
            </LinearGradientBrush>
        </Setter.Value>
    </Setter>

    <Style.Triggers>
        <Trigger Property="IsMouseOver" Value="True">
            <Setter Property="Background">
                <Setter.Value>
                    <LinearGradientBrush>
                        <GradientStop Offset="0.2" Color="Red"/>
                        <GradientStop Offset="0.8" Color="Yellow"/>
                    </LinearGradientBrush>
                </Setter.Value>
            </Setter>
        </Trigger>
    </Style.Triggers>
</Style>
```

Applying the trigger described in code can cause buttons to have a different background color when the mouse pointer passes over them. In this way we applied a style according to just one condition, but sometimes multiple conditions have to be evaluated. For example, continuing the Button control discussion, we could decide to apply a style when the mouse pointer passes over the control and also if the button is enabled. This can be accomplished using a MultiTrigger object. A MultiTrigger can contain multiple condition specifications and as many setters for as many properties as we want to apply in the style. The following code snippet demonstrates how to declare a MultiTrigger for the preceding implemented style:

```
<Style.Triggers>
    <MultiTrigger>
        <MultiTrigger.Conditions>
            <Condition Property="IsMouseOver" Value="True"/>
            <Condition Property="IsEnabled" Value="True"/>
        </MultiTrigger.Conditions>
        <Setter Property="Background">
            <Setter.Value>
                <LinearGradientBrush>
                    <GradientStop Offset="0.2" Color="Red"/>
                    <GradientStop Offset="0.8" Color="Yellow"/>
                </LinearGradientBrush>
            </Setter.Value>
        </Setter>
    </MultiTrigger>
</Style.Triggers>
```

In this case the new background is applied only when both conditions are evaluated as True.

Introducing Control Templates

WPF controls have a particular structure, in which the layout system is separated from the behavior. When searching resources about WPF controls, you often find a definition stating that they are *lookless*. This means that WPF controls have no default aspect, whereas they expose a common set of properties that can be assigned for defining the layout and the behavior. This common set is referred to as the *control template*. The WPF system provides a default control template for each available control in the Base Class Library (BCL). You can then override the existing template or create a custom one. Control templates are so versatile because you can completely redesign the control look while keeping its original behavior, but you can also improve the behavior. For example, you can use an `Ellipse` as a control template for a `Button`. The new `Button` will look like an `Ellipse`, but your user can still click it and you can still handle button events.

USE EXPRESSION BLEND

Even if the XAML designer has been enhanced even more in Visual Studio 2012, creating custom control templates can be a hard task to accomplish with the IDE only. This is a developer tool and therefore cannot offer advanced design features as Expression Blend does. If you plan to make intensive use of custom control templates, use Blend. Use Visual Studio if your custom templates are basic implementations. In the next examples, you see something easy to implement with Visual Studio, although the logic of control templates is fully implemented.

30

Control templates are implemented as styles, but actually they are not simple styles. The difference between styles and templates is that styles affect existing properties within an existing template, whereas a control template can completely override or replace the properties and layout of a control. Talking in code terms, a control template is defined within a `Style` definition, setting the `Template` property and assigning the `Value` of this property. The code in Listing 30.3 shows how to utilize an `Ellipse` as the control template for buttons, where the background gradient color changes when the button is pressed or when the mouse pointer flies over it.

LISTING 30.3   Building a Control Template

```
<Window.Resources>
    <Style x:Key="ButtonStyle1" TargetType="{x:Type Button}">
        <Setter Property="Template">
            <Setter.Value>
                <ControlTemplate TargetType="{x:Type Button}">
                    <Grid>
                        <Ellipse x:Name="ellipse" Stroke="Black">
                            <Ellipse.Fill>
                                <LinearGradientBrush EndPoint="0.5,1"
                                                     StartPoint="0.5,0">
                                    <GradientStop Color="Black" Offset="0"/>
                                    <GradientStop Color="White" Offset="1"/>
                                </LinearGradientBrush>
                            </Ellipse.Fill>
                        </Ellipse>
                        <ContentPresenter HorizontalAlignment=
                         "{TemplateBinding HorizontalContentAlignment}"
                         VerticalAlignment=
                         "{TemplateBinding VerticalContentAlignment}"
                         SnapsToDevicePixels=
                         "{TemplateBinding SnapsToDevicePixels}"
                         RecognizesAccessKey="True"/>
                    </Grid>
                    <ControlTemplate.Triggers>
                        <Trigger Property="IsFocused" Value="True"/>
                        <Trigger Property="IsDefaulted" Value="True"/>
                        <Trigger Property="IsMouseOver" Value="True">
                            <Setter Property="Fill" TargetName="ellipse">
                                <Setter.Value>
                                    <LinearGradientBrush EndPoint="0.5,1"
                                                         StartPoint="0.5,0">
                                        <GradientStop Color="White" Offset="0"/>
                                        <GradientStop Color="Black" Offset="1"/>
                                    </LinearGradientBrush>
                                </Setter.Value>
```

```
                                    </Setter>
                                </Trigger>
                                <Trigger Property="IsPressed" Value="True">
                                    <Setter Property="Fill" TargetName="ellipse">
                                        <Setter.Value>
                                            <LinearGradientBrush EndPoint="0.5,1"
                                                                 StartPoint="0.5,0">
                                                <GradientStop Color="#FF4F4F4F"
                                                              Offset="0"/>
                                                <GradientStop Color="#FF515050"
                                                              Offset="1"/>
                                                <GradientStop Color="White"
                                                              Offset="0.483"/>
                                            </LinearGradientBrush>
                                        </Setter.Value>
                                    </Setter>
                                </Trigger>
                                <Trigger Property="IsEnabled" Value="False"/>
                            </ControlTemplate.Triggers>
                        </ControlTemplate>
                    </Setter.Value>
                </Setter>
            </Style>
        </Window.Resources>
```

TIP: RESTYLING WINDOWS

Control templates are not limited to user controls, but they can be successfully implemented for completely restyling `Window` objects layout so that you can create custom
windows while still taking advantage of their behavior. The template's `TargetType` is
therefore `Window`.

If you look at the code, you can notice how the button default aspect is replaced by an
`Ellipse` within the `ControlTemplate` value of the `Template` property. Probably some
concepts you learned about styles help you understand what is happening. Triggers enable
you to change the background color according to specific mouse actions. Don't forget to
add the `ContentPresenter` element in your custom templates because it enables you to
show text or other UI elements within your control. Control templates are assigned to
controls using the `DynamicResource` markup extension. The following XAML line assigns
the previous custom control template to a button:

```
<Button Click="Button_Click" Name="Button1"
        Style="{DynamicResource ButtonStyle1}"
        Width="100" Height="80" Content="Button"/>
```

30

Changes will be automatically reflected at design time. You can also assign an event handler for the Click event to ensure that everything is working fine:

```
Private Sub Button_Click(ByVal sender As System.Object,
                         ByVal e As System.Windows.RoutedEventArgs)
    MessageBox.Show("You clicked!")
End Sub
```

Figure 30.11 shows how the button looks within the running application when the mouse pointer passes over it.

FIGURE 30.11   The custom control template designs a button as an ellipse.

RECOMMENDATION

Control templates enable you to create amazing control layouts, but this is not necessarily a good choice. Remember that users prefer to easily associate a simple control shape to a particular action more than having colored and funny controls that they cannot easily recognize.

Introducing Transformations

Transformations are special objects that modify the appearance of visual elements of type FrameworkElement, applying interesting effects such as rotation or translation, keeping unchanged the visual element's functional behavior. For example, with transformations you can rotate a ListBox 180°, but it will still work as usual; only the layout changes. Transformations are important to understand if you intend to apply animations to visual elements. I cover animations in the next section. Keep in mind that when you apply animations, you animate transformation objects that affect visual elements. You apply transformations by adding a RenderTransform node for your visual element at the XAML level. I explain this by dividing a Grid into four cells, where each cell must contain a ListBox. To accomplish this, write the following XAML code that divides the grid and provides a common set of properties for ListBox instances via a style:

```
<Grid Name="Grid1">
    <Grid.RowDefinitions>
        <RowDefinition/>
        <RowDefinition/>
    </Grid.RowDefinitions>
    <Grid.ColumnDefinitions>
        <ColumnDefinition/>
        <ColumnDefinition/>
    </Grid.ColumnDefinitions>
    <Grid.Resources>
        <Style x:Key="ListStyle" TargetType="ListBox">
            <Setter Property="Margin" Value="5"/>
            <Setter Property="Width" Value="160"/>
            <Setter Property="Height" Value="160"/>
            <Setter Property="ItemsSource" Value="{Binding}"/>
        </Style>
    </Grid.Resources>
</Grid>
```

At this point, each cell contains a ListBox, as explained in the next sections. Before going into that, switch to the code behind file and handle the Window.Loaded event as follows:

```
Private Sub Transforms_Loaded(ByVal sender As Object,
                        ByVal e As System.Windows.RoutedEventArgs) _
                        Handles Me.Loaded

    'Gets a list of names for running processes
    'and populates the Grid.DataContext so that children
    'elements will pick up data from it
    Me.Grid1.DataContext = From proc In Process.GetProcesses
                        Select proc.ProcessName
End Sub
```

The DataContext property is the data-source for a given container, and all children controls pick up data from it. In this case, assigning the Grid1.DataContext property populates all children ListBoxes.

CHECKING THE SAMPLES RESULT

For the sake of simplicity, and because the design actions are reflected to the designer, only one figure will be provided about the transformations result. Figure 30.12 shows the complete results. The interesting thing is that ListBox controls continue working independently of their skew or position on the screen.

30

Rotating Visual Elements with `RotateTransform`

`RotateTransform` is a transformation that enables you to rotate a visual element for the specified number of degrees and at the specified position. The following code adds a `ListBox` in the upper-left cell, and it is rotated 180°:

```
<ListBox Name="RotateListBox" Grid.Row="0" Grid.Column="0"
        Style="{StaticResource ListStyle}">
    <ListBox.RenderTransform>
        <RotateTransform Angle="180" CenterX="80" CenterY="80"/>
    </ListBox.RenderTransform>
</ListBox>
```

Notice how the `Angle` property specifies the degrees, whereas `CenterX` and `CenterY` represent the position of rotation. In the preceding example, the rotation comes in at the center of the `ListBox` (both values are the half of `Width` and `Height`). Transformations are automatically reflected to the designer, so you should see the result of what you are doing. Figure 30.12 shows the result of this transformation (see the upper-left cell). Notice also how the control is working normally even if it is in an unusual position.

Dynamically Resizing Visual Elements with `ScaleTransform`

`ScaleTransform` enables you to dynamically resize a control. The following code demonstrates how a `ListBox` can be scaled to different dimensions:

```
<ListBox Name="ScaleListBox" Grid.Row="0" Grid.Column="1"
        Style="{StaticResource ListStyle}">
    <ListBox.RenderTransform>
        <ScaleTransform CenterX="0" CenterY="0" ScaleX="0.6" ScaleY="0.6"/>
    </ListBox.RenderTransform>
</ListBox>
```

Notice how scaling is expressed in percentage with the `ScaleX` and `ScaleY` properties. A value of 0.6 means that the control is scaled to 60% of its original dimensions. A value of 1 means 100% (that is, the original size), whereas a value bigger than 1 enlarges the visual element. Take a look at the upper-right cell in Figure 30.12 to get an idea about the result. With animations, `ScaleTransform` enables you to animate visual elements by making them larger or smaller.

Changing Visual Elements' Angles with `SkewTransform`

`SkewTransform` enables you to skew a visual element for the specified angles on both the X-axis and Y-axis, simulating 3D depth for 2D objects. The following code demonstrates how to apply to a `ListBox` a horizontal skew of 15° and a vertical skew of 30°, where the center point is established by `CenterX` and `CenterY` properties:

```
<ListBox Name="SkewListBox" Grid.Row="1" Grid.Column="0"
        Style="{StaticResource ListStyle}">
    <ListBox.RenderTransform>
```

```
        <SkewTransform AngleX="15" AngleY="30" CenterX="50" CenterY="50" />
    </ListBox.RenderTransform>
</ListBox>
```

Skewing is probably the most impressive transform if you then try to use visual elements and controls, discovering that they work exactly as if they were not transformed. Figure 30.12 shows the result of skewing (see the bottom-left cell).

Dynamically Moving Visual Elements with `TranslateTransform`

`TranslateTransform` enables you to move a visual element from a position to another one in the layout system. This is useful if you want to build animations capable of moving visual elements. The following example shows how you can translate a `ListBox` of 50 points on the X-axis and of 100 points on the Y-axis:

```
<ListBox Name="TranslateListBox" Grid.Row="1" Grid.Column="1"
        Style="{StaticResource ListStyle}">
    <ListBox.RenderTransform>
        <TranslateTransform X="50" Y="100" />
    </ListBox.RenderTransform>
</ListBox>
```

The result of this translation is shown in Figure 30.12 (see the bottom-right cell).

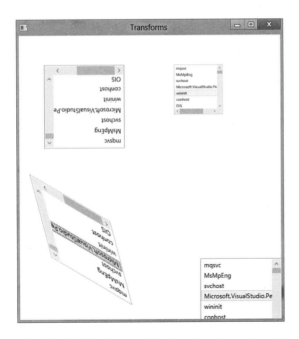

FIGURE 30.12   The result of applying transformations.

Applying Multiple Transforms

You can apply multiple transformations by contextually implementing a `TransformGroup` as a nested node of `RenderTransform`. The following code demonstrates how you can both rotate and skew a visual element:

```
<ListBox Name="SkewListBox" Grid.Row="1" Grid.Column="0"
        Style="{StaticResource ListStyle}">
    <ListBox.RenderTransform>
        <TransformGroup>
            <SkewTransform AngleX="15" AngleY="30" CenterX="50"
                        CenterY="50" />
            <RotateTransform Angle="180" CenterX="80" CenterY="80"/>
        </TransformGroup>
    </ListBox.RenderTransform>
</ListBox>
```

A COUPLE OF IMPORTANT NOTES

Another transformation named `MatrixTransform` is available and enables you to build custom transformations. This is quite a complex object and is beyond of the scope of this book. Visit the official MSDN page at http://msdn.microsoft.com/en-us/library/system. windows.media.matrixtransform(VS.110).aspx.

Next, `RenderTransform` is not the only place for putting transformations. Another node named `LayoutTransform` requires a transformation to be applied before the WPF layout system comes in. This can be useful only when you need the parent of the affected element to adjust the transformed size, but in all other cases use `RenderTransform` because it offers better performance, especially with animations.

Introducing Animations

WPF offers lots of interesting features about graphics and multimedia to provide a great user experience with rich client applications. Animations are one of these features. They enable visual elements (or just some portions of them) to move along the UI or to dynamically change their aspects during the specified interval. Subsequent sections explain how you can apply animations to WPF visual elements. There are different kinds of animations in WPF; we cover the most common of them—`DoubleAnimation` and `ColorAnimation`.

NOTE

A special type of animation based on timelines is available, but it is not easy to implement with Visual Studio. However, it is the easiest animation that you can realize with Expression Blend. With that said, from a developer perspective, this chapter covers animations based on storyboards.

Animations are cool in that they can be eventually controlled by pausing, removing, stopping, and manually playing and are represented by `System.Windows.Media.Animation`.

`Storyboard` objects. Each `Storyboard` can define one or more `DoubleAnimation` or
`ColorAnimation` that applies to transformations (see the previous section for details). To
decide the time when animations need to come in, you define them within the control's
triggers specifying an `EventTrigger` that requires you to specify the event representing the
moment for the animation to run. For example, if you want an animation to start when a
window is loaded, the `EventTrigger` points to `Window.Loaded`. Before providing any code
example, add a new window to your current WPF project or create a new project from
scratch. When the new window is ready, divide the default `Grid` into four cells by typing
the following XAML:

```
<Grid Name="Grid1">
        <Grid.RowDefinitions>
            <RowDefinition/>
            <RowDefinition/>
        </Grid.RowDefinitions>

        <Grid.ColumnDefinitions>
            <ColumnDefinition/>
            <ColumnDefinition/>
        </Grid.ColumnDefinitions>
</Grid>
```

Applying `DoubleAnimation`

A `DoubleAnimation` object enables you to animate the specified transform property; it also
enables you to revert the motion, specify the duration, and specify whether the animation needs to be repeated unlimitedly. The first example animates an image, applying the
animation to a `SkewTransform` and to a `ScaleTransform` contextually. The code in Listing
30.4 shows how to accomplish this.

LISTING 30.4   Applying a `DoubleAnimation` to an Image

```
        <Image Grid.Row="0" Grid.Column="0" Name="Image1"
Source="/StylesBrushesTemplatesAnimations;component/Images/Avatar.jpg">

            <Image.RenderTransform>
                <TransformGroup>
                    <SkewTransform x:Name="SkewImage"/>
                    <ScaleTransform x:Name="ScaleImage"/>
                </TransformGroup>
            </Image.RenderTransform>

            <Image.Triggers>
                <EventTrigger RoutedEvent="Image.Loaded">
                    <EventTrigger.Actions>
                        <BeginStoryboard>
                            <Storyboard>
```

30

```
                              <DoubleAnimation Storyboard.TargetName="SkewImage"
                                               Storyboard.TargetProperty="AngleY"
                                               From="0" To="15" Duration="0:0:3"
                                               AutoReverse="True"
                                               RepeatBehavior="Forever" />
                              <DoubleAnimation Storyboard.TargetName="ScaleImage"
                                               Storyboard.TargetProperty="ScaleX"
                                               From="1" To="0.3" Duration="0:0:3"
                                               AutoReverse="True"
                                               RepeatBehavior="Forever" />
                              <DoubleAnimation Storyboard.TargetName="ScaleImage"
                                               Storyboard.TargetProperty="ScaleY"
                                               From="1" To="0.3" Duration="0:0:3"
                                               AutoReverse="True"
                                               RepeatBehavior="Forever" />
                        </Storyboard>
                      </BeginStoryboard>
                    </EventTrigger.Actions>
                  </EventTrigger>

            </Image.Triggers>
          </Image>
```

The code first applies to transformations. They are empty, with no properties set, therefore with no changes to the Image. But they have a name so that they can be referred to from the storyboard. The EventTrigger within triggers specifies the Image.Loaded routed event, which establishes that the animation will run when the image is loaded. The BeginStoryboard object is a container for children Storyboard objects. In the code example there is just one Storyboard that contains multiple DoubleAnimation objects. Notice how each DoubleAnimation refers to a transformation via the Storyboard. TargetName attached property and to the particular transformation's property via the Storyboard.TargetProperty attached property. From and To specify the starting and finish points of the animation, respectively. In the case of the SkewTransform, they specify the angle degrees, whereas in the case of the ScaleTransform they specify the scaling percentage. Duration is a property for specifying how many hours:minutes:seconds the animation will last; AutoReverse specifies whether the animation has to be repeated back, and RepeatBehavior specifies how long the animation will last (Forever is self-explanatory). At this point, run the application to have your image skewed and scaled via the animation. Refer to Figure 30.13 to see an approximate result. (Figures cannot show animations running!) Next, the code example about DoubleAnimation is applied to a TextBlock object for animating text. In this case you see the conjunction of a RotateTransform and SkewTransform. The code in Listing 30.5 provides the previously mentioned example.

LISTING 30.5   Applying DoubleAnimation to a TextBlock

```xml
<TextBlock Grid.Row="0" Grid.Column="1" Text="Animated Text" FontSize="24"
          FontFamily="Verdana" FontWeight="Bold"
          HorizontalAlignment="Center"
          VerticalAlignment="Center" RenderTransformOrigin="0.5 0.5">

<TextBlock.Foreground>
  <LinearGradientBrush>
    <GradientStop Offset="0" Color="Red" />
    <GradientStop Offset="0.5" Color="Yellow" />
    <GradientStop Offset="1" Color="Orange"/>
  </LinearGradientBrush>
</TextBlock.Foreground>

<TextBlock.RenderTransform>
    <TransformGroup>
        <RotateTransform x:Name="RotateText" />
        <SkewTransform x:Name="SkewText"/>
    </TransformGroup>
</TextBlock.RenderTransform>

<TextBlock.Triggers>
  <EventTrigger RoutedEvent="TextBlock.Loaded">
    <BeginStoryboard>
      <Storyboard Name="TextAnimation">
        <DoubleAnimation Storyboard.TargetName="RotateText"
                         Storyboard.TargetProperty="Angle"
                         From="0" To="360" Duration="0:0:5"
                         RepeatBehavior="Forever" />

        <DoubleAnimation Storyboard.TargetName="SkewText"
                         AutoReverse="True"
                         Storyboard.TargetProperty="AngleX"
                         From="0" To="45" Duration="0:0:5"
                         RepeatBehavior="Forever" />

      </Storyboard>
    </BeginStoryboard>
  </EventTrigger>
</TextBlock.Triggers>
</TextBlock>
```

The logic is the same, with the EventTrigger and transformations. The first
DoubleAnimation is applied to a RotateTransform that affects rotation degrees. Run the
code to get an idea of the result and refer to Figure 30.13 for a graphical representation.

Applying `ColorAnimation`

A `ColorAnimation` enables you to animate colors within a brush, such as `LinearGradientBrush` and `RadialGradientBrush`. A color is replaced with another one passing through a gradient. The next example is a little bit particular because it will be applied to a `DataGrid` control to demonstrate that business controls can receive animations. The `DataGrid` exposes an `AlternatingRowBackground` property that enables you to specify a different color for alternating rows. The goal of the example is animating colors in the background of such rows. For this, code in Listing 30.6 shows how to apply the described color animation.

LISTING 30.6   Applying a `ColorAnimation`

```xml
<DataGrid Name="CustomerDataGrid" AutoGenerateColumns="True"
        Grid.Row="1" Grid.Column="1" Margin="5">
    <DataGrid.AlternatingRowBackground>
        <LinearGradientBrush EndPoint="0.5,1" StartPoint="0.5,0">
            <GradientStop Color="Black" Offset="0" />
            <GradientStop Color="Black" Offset="1" />
            <GradientStop Color="White" Offset="0.4" />
            <GradientStop Color="White" Offset="0.6" />
        </LinearGradientBrush>
    </DataGrid.AlternatingRowBackground>
    <DataGrid.Triggers>
        <EventTrigger RoutedEvent="DataGrid.Loaded">
            <EventTrigger.Actions>
                <BeginStoryboard>
                    <Storyboard>
                        <ColorAnimation From="Black" To="Violet"
                                Duration="0:0:2"
                                Storyboard.TargetProperty=
                            "AlternatingRowBackground.GradientStops[0].Color"
                                AutoReverse="True"
                                RepeatBehavior="Forever"/>
                        <ColorAnimation From="Black" To="Chartreuse"
                                Duration="0:0:2"
                                AutoReverse="True"
                                RepeatBehavior="Forever"
                                Storyboard.TargetProperty=
                            "AlternatingRowBackground.GradientStops[3].Color"/>
                    </Storyboard>
                </BeginStoryboard>
            </EventTrigger.Actions>
        </EventTrigger>
    </DataGrid.Triggers>
</DataGrid>
```

As you can see, this type of animation works like DoubleAnimation except that From and To require you to specify the source and target colors. When referring to a GradientStop, you enclose its index within square parentheses. (Remember that the index is zero-based.) To complete the example, you need to populate the DataGrid with some data. Switch to the code behind file and write the code in Listing 30.7, which defines a Customer class, creates some instances of the class, and creates a List(Of Customer) collection that is the data source.

LISTING 30.7   Populating the DataGrid

```
Public Class Animations

    Private Sub Animations_Loaded(ByVal sender As Object,
                            ByVal e As System.Windows.RoutedEventArgs) _
                            Handles Me.Loaded

        Dim cust1 As New Customer With {.Address = "7Th street",
                .CompanyName = "Del Sole", .ContactName = "Alessandro Del Sole"}
        Dim cust2 As New Customer With {.Address = "5Th street",
                .CompanyName = "Fictitious Red & White",
                .ContactName = "Robert White"}

        Dim custList As New List(Of Customer) From {cust1, cust2}
        Me.CustomerDataGrid.ItemsSource = custList
    End Sub
End Class


Public Class Customer
    Public Property CompanyName As String
    Public Property Address As String
    Public Property ContactName As String
End Class
```

Run the application. You get the result represented in Figure 30.13.

Working with Animation Events

Storyboard objects expose events that can help you get control over the animations. The first step is assigning a name to the desired storyboard, as in the following example:

```
<Storyboard Name="ImageStoryBoard">
```

After you assign a name to the Storyboard, you can handle events summarized in Table 30.1.

FIGURE 30.13   The result of applied animations.

TABLE 30.1   Storyboard Events

Event	Occurs When
Completed	The animation completes.
Changed	An object is modified.
CurrentGlobalSpeedInvalidated	The time progress rate changes.
CurrentStateInvalidated	The CurrentState property of the animation clock changes.
CurrentTimeInvalidated	The CurrentTime property of the animation clock changes.
RemoveRequested	The animation clock is removed.

You handle the Completed event to make an action when an animation completes, as in the following code snippet:

```
Private Sub ImageStoryBoard_Completed(ByVal sender As Object,
                          ByVal e As System.EventArgs) _
                          Handles ImageStoryBoard.Completed
    'Write code for the animation completion
End Sub
```

Notice how animations do not throw routed events, whereas they raise standard events. `Storyboard` objects also expose some methods that enable controlling the animation in code, such as `Begin`, `Stop`, `Pause`, `Seek`, and `Resume`, which are all self-explanatory. Moreover, you can set in Visual Basic code some animation properties that I explained through XAML code, as in the following code snippet:

```
With ImageStoryBoard
    .AutoReverse = True
    .RepeatBehavior = System.Windows.Media.Animation.
                      RepeatBehavior.Forever
    .Duration = New TimeSpan(0, 0, 5)
End With
```

Animations can also be applied to 3D graphics that are beyond the scope of this book but that you can explore through the MSDN documentation.

Creating Animations with Visual Basic

Maybe you understood that XAML is the best way for creating, customizing, and managing visual elements. Writing VB code is something that you should practice only when there is an effective need to apply effects at runtime. This can also be the case of animations. The code in Listing 30.8 shows how to create at runtime a new button and how to apply an animation that increases and decreases the button's height. The code is not difficult to understand when you have a clear idea of the sequence of elements required within an animation.

LISTING 30.8   Creating an Animation in VB Code

```
Public Class Animations
    Private myAnimation As Animation.DoubleAnimation
    Private WithEvents aButton As Button
    Private heightAnimationStoryboard As Animation.Storyboard

    Private Sub CreateRuntimeAnimation()

        'An instance of a new Button
        aButton = New Button With {.Width = 150, .Height = 50,
                                   .Content = "Runtime button",
                                   .Name = "RuntimeButton"}

        'Associates the button's name to the Window names collection
        '(required at runtime)
        Me.RegisterName(aButton.Name, aButton)

        'Adds the Button to the Grid at the given row/column
        Grid.SetColumn(aButton, 0)
```

30

```vb
        Grid.SetRow(aButton, 1)
        Grid1.Children.Add(aButton)

        'Creates a new DoubleAnimation, with properties
        myAnimation = New Animation.DoubleAnimation
        With myAnimation
            .AutoReverse = True
            'From and To are Nullable(Of Double)
            .From = 50
            .To = 15
            .RepeatBehavior = Animation.RepeatBehavior.Forever
            .Duration = New TimeSpan(0, 0, 3)
        End With

        'Sets the target control via its name
        Animation.Storyboard.SetTargetName(myAnimation, aButton.Name)
        'Sets the target property
        Animation.Storyboard.SetTargetProperty(myAnimation,
                                        New PropertyPath(Button.
                                            HeightProperty))

        'Create a new storyboard instance and adds the animation
        'to the storyboard's collection of animations
        heightAnimationStoryboard = New Animation.Storyboard
        heightAnimationStoryboard.Children.Add(myAnimation)
    End Sub

    'Starts the animation when the button is loaded
    Private Sub aButton_Loaded(ByVal sender As Object, ByVal e As RoutedEventArgs) _
                        Handles aButton.Loaded
        heightAnimationStoryboard.Begin(aButton)
    End Sub
End Class
```

The one thing you have to pay attention to is registering the button name because, otherwise, it will not be accessible at runtime by the animation. Another thing that is worth mentioning regards how you set the storyboard target property. This is accomplished via the StoryBoard.SetTargetProperty shared method that requires the animation instance and a PropertyPath instance that receives a dependency property as an argument. Figure 30.14 represents a particular moment of the animation running.

FIGURE 30.14   The application runs the Visual Basic-generated animation.

Summary

Windows Presentation Foundation offers great benefits for customizing user interface elements. In this chapter you got a high-level overview of the modes allowed for customizing elements and for making them more interesting to the final user. First, you got information about brushes and saw how many brushes are offered by WPF and how you can apply them for coloring or filling visual elements. Next, you learned about styles, understanding how you can use them for setting a common set of properties for the specified control type. Subsequently, you got an overview of control templates, learning how you can completely redefine the graphical aspect of a user control while keeping its behavior safe. You also got information on transformations, learning how they can dynamically change controls' appearance. Finally, you took a tour of animations, seeing how you can enrich your user interface with cool animations that take advantage of transformations. In the next chapter, we discuss other important features of WPF—the ability to create dynamic documents and manage media contents.

30

CHAPTER 31

Manipulating Media and Documents

W indows Presentation Foundation (WPF) offers native controls for working with media content and manipulating documents. This last topic is also important because documents are one of the most common requirements in modern applications, and WPF provides a way for creating and managing documents that can be dynamically arranged to offer a better user experience. In this chapter you learn how to use media contents to enrich your applications and to manipulate dynamic documents through built-in controls exposed by the .NET Framework.

Viewing Images

You use the `System.Windows.Controls.Image` control to show images. To see how the control works, create a new WPF project that will be used for all examples in this chapter and name it **DocumentsAndMedia**. When ready, drag an `Image` control from the toolbox onto the new `Window`; then set its dimensions as you like. To view an image, you need to set the `Source` property that points to a `Uri`, but you might want to add some images to your project first. As for any other kind of project, it is a good idea to organize contents into subfolders based on their types. So, in Solution Explorer create a new project subfolder called Images. Right-click this folder and then select Add, Existing Item. When the dialog box appears, select the number of image files you want to be added to the project. At this point, select the `Image` control either in the XAML designer or in the XAML code editor and open the Properties window by pressing **F4**. Select the Source property and expand the drop-down box for this property (see Figure 31.1). Here you can pick up an image from a list of image files and the image will be assigned to the Image control.

FIGURE 31.1   Adding images to the project.

Visual Studio automatically sets the Source property in XAML, taking advantage of the packed Uri, as demonstrated by the following line of XAML code:

```
<Image Source="Images/IMG006.jpg"
       Stretch="Fill" Name="Image1" />
```

The Stretch property enables you to establish how pictures will be tiled inside the Image control. Fill, which is the default value, dynamically adapts the picture to fill the entire Image control, but when you resize the control you can lose the original aspect ratio. If you instead use Uniform, you can keep the aspect ratio and dynamically adapt the picture. While setting UniformToFill, the picture will work like Uniform except that it will clip the source image so that the layout will be based on the Image control size. If you assign the Stretch property with None, the source image will be shown in its original size. Figure 31.2 shows how the image looks with Stretch set as Fill. You can also assign the Source property at runtime from Visual Basic code so you can provide users the capability to select different pictures. Unlike the XAML code, in VB you need to first create an instance of the BitmapImage class and assign some of its properties as follows:

```
Private Sub LoadPicture(ByVal fileName As String)

    Dim img As New BitmapImage
    With img
        .BeginInit()
        .BaseUri = New Uri("MyPicture.jpg")
```

```
      .EndInit()
   End With

   Image1.Source = img
End Sub
```

FIGURE 31.2   Showing images with the `Image` control.

You invoke `BeginInit` to start editing; then you set `BaseUri` pointing to the desired file and finally invoke `EndInit` to finish editing. When you perform these steps, you can assign the new instance to the `Image.Source` property.

Playing Media

Windows Presentation Foundation enables you to easily reproduce media files, such as audio and videos, through the `System.Windows.Controls.MediaElement` control. This enables reproducing, among others, all media contents supported by the Windows Media Player application, such as .wmv, .wma, .avi, and .mp3 files. This section shows you how to build a simple media player using `MediaElement` and Visual Basic 2012. Now add a new `Window` to an existing project, setting this as the main window. The goal of the next example is to implement a media player and buttons for controlling media reproduction. Code in Listing 31.1 declares the user interface (UI).

LISTING 31.1   Defining the User Interface for a Simple Media Player

```xml
<Window x:Class="PlayingMedia"
    xmlns="http://schemas.microsoft.com/winfx/2006/xaml/presentation"
    xmlns:x="http://schemas.microsoft.com/winfx/2006/xaml"
    Title="PlayingMedia" Height="300" Width="600">
    <Grid>
        <Grid.RowDefinitions>
            <RowDefinition />
            <RowDefinition Height="50" />
        </Grid.RowDefinitions>
        <MediaElement Name="Media1" Grid.Row="0" LoadedBehavior="Manual"
                    Volume="{Binding ElementName=VolumeSlider, Path=Value}"
                    MediaFailed="Media1_MediaFailed"
                    MediaEnded="Media1_MediaEnded"/>

        <StackPanel Orientation="Horizontal" Grid.Row="1">
            <Button Name="PlayButton" Width="70" Height="40"
                    Margin="5" Click="PlayButton_Click"
                    Content="Play"/>

            <Button Name="PauseButton" Width="70" Height="40"
                    Margin="5" Click="PauseButton_Click"
                    Content="Pause"/>

            <Button Name="StopButton" Width="70" Height="40"
                    Margin="5" Click="StopButton_Click"
                    Content="Stop"/>

            <Button Name="BrowseButton" Width="40" Height="40"
                    Margin="5" Content="..."
                    Click="BrowseButton_Click"/>

            <Slider Name="VolumeSlider" Width="80" Margin="5"
                    Minimum="0" Maximum="1" Value="0.5"
                    TickFrequency="0.1"
                    AutoToolTipPlacement="TopLeft"
                    TickPlacement="BottomRight"
                    ToolTip="Adjust volume"/>
        </StackPanel>
    </Grid>
</Window>
```

The MediaElement control has no look, so when you place it onto the user interface, it has a dark gray background and border, although you can replace this with your custom background and border. The LoadedBehavior property enables you to establish how the media file needs to be reproduced. For example, Play means that the associated video will be automatically played when the control is loaded; Manual means that playing will be started via Visual Basic code at the specified moment. (IntelliSense can help you to choose the most appropriate self-explanatory option.) You associate a media file to the MediaElement by assigning the Source property, but this is not mandatory because you can accomplish this later in code. The Volume property enables you to adjust reproduction volume, and its range is between 0 and 1. In this example the Volume value is bound to the VolumeSlider.Value property. The control also offers some events such as MediaFailed and MediaEnded that are raised when an error occurs when attempting to open the media file and when the reproduction completes, respectively. The MediaElement control also provides some methods for controlling reproduction in code, such as Play, Pause, and Stop. The code in Listing 31.2 shows how to implement the features and how to enable media selection from disk.

LISTING 31.2 Controlling the MediaElement in Code

```
Public Class PlayingMedia

    Dim sourceMedia As String = String.Empty

    Private Sub Media1_MediaEnded(ByVal sender As System.Object,
                                  ByVal e As System.Windows.
                                  RoutedEventArgs)
        'Playing completed
    End Sub

    Private Sub Media1_MediaFailed(ByVal sender As System.Object,
                                   ByVal e As System.Windows.
                                   ExceptionRoutedEventArgs)
        MessageBox.Show(e.ErrorException.Message)
    End Sub

    Private Sub PlayButton_Click(ByVal sender As System.Object,
                                 ByVal e As System.Windows.RoutedEventArgs)
        If String.IsNullOrEmpty(Me.sourceMedia) = False Then
            Me.Media1.Play()
        End If
    End Sub

    Private Sub PauseButton_Click(ByVal sender As System.Object,
                                  ByVal e As System.Windows.RoutedEventArgs)
        If String.IsNullOrEmpty(Me.sourceMedia) = False Then
            Me.Media1.Pause()
        End If
    End Sub

    Private Sub StopButton_Click(ByVal sender As System.Object,
                                 ByVal e As System.Windows.RoutedEventArgs)
```

```
        If String.IsNullOrEmpty(Me.sourceMedia) = False Then
            Me.Media1.Stop()
        End If
    End Sub


    Private Sub BrowseButton_Click(ByVal sender As System.Object,
                        ByVal e As System.Windows.RoutedEventArgs)
        Dim dialog As New Microsoft.Win32.OpenFileDialog

        With dialog
            .Title = "Select a media file"
            .Filter = "Avi & Wmv|*.avi;*.wmv|Audio|*.wma;*.mp3|All files|*.*"
            If .ShowDialog = True Then
                Me.sourceMedia = .FileName
                Me.Media1.Source = New Uri(sourceMedia,
                                    UriKind.RelativeOrAbsolute)
            End If
        End With
    End Sub
End Class
```

Notice how the `MediaFailed` event handler shows an error message in case an exception is thrown and how the media file is assigned under the form of a Uri to the `MediaElement.Source` property. This also means that you can assign a Uri such as a web address to play media content stored on a website. Now you can run the application, click the Browse button to select your media content, and click Play. Figure 31.3 shows the application playing a video. The `MediaElement` control also offers a `Position` property (of type `TimeSpan`) that provides the capability to seek the desired position within the media content.

FIGURE 31.3   The sample application playing a video.

Manipulating Documents

One of the most important requirements in modern applications is the ability to manage documents. WPF offers the `System.Windows.Documents` namespace that exposes objects so you can create flexible and dynamic documents that can adapt their layouts dynamically to the user interface. These kinds of documents use the Clear Type technology and are hosted inside `FlowDocument` objects. A `FlowDocument` is composed of `Paragraph` objects where you can place and format your text. Paragraphs are powerful because they enable you to add figures, bulleted lists, fully functional hyperlinks, and text formatting. To present and browse a flow document, you need to add a `FlowDocumentReader` control to the user interface. Flexibility and dynamicity are just two benefits of flow documents. Another cool feature in flow documents is that users can interact with documents as if they were reading a book, so they can add annotations and highlights that can be stored to disk for later reuse. Annotations are provided by the `System.Windows.Annotations` namespace that needs to be imported at the XAML level. The goals of the next code example are

▶ Illustrating how you can create flow documents

▶ Illustrating how you can add and format text within flow documents

▶ Implementing features for adding annotations to documents and saving them to disk

Add a new `Window` to the current one, setting it as the startup page. When ready, write the XAML code shown in Listing 31.3 that implements the UI side of the application. The code is explained at the end of the listing.

> **NOTE**
>
> The content of the sample flow document is just an excerpt of the content of Chapter 28, "Creating WPF Applications," which is provided as an example, but you can replace it with a more complete text of your own.

LISTING 31.3   Implementing Flow Documents

```
<Window x:Class="ManipulatingDocuments"
    xmlns="http://schemas.microsoft.com/winfx/2006/xaml/presentation"
    xmlns:x="http://schemas.microsoft.com/winfx/2006/xaml"
    xmlns:ann="clr-namespace:System.Windows.Annotations;assembly=
➥PresentationFramework"
    Title="ManipulatingDocuments" Height="480" Width="600">
    <Grid>
        <Grid.RowDefinitions>
            <RowDefinition />
            <RowDefinition Height="40"/>
        </Grid.RowDefinitions>
```

31

```xml
<StackPanel Grid.Row="1" Orientation="Horizontal">
<StackPanel.Resources>
    <Style x:Key="ButtonStyle" TargetType="Button">
        <Setter Property="Width" Value="100"/>
        <Setter Property="Height" Value="30"/>
        <Setter Property="Margin" Value="5"/>
    </Style>
</StackPanel.Resources>

    <Button Command="ann:AnnotationService.CreateTextStickyNoteCommand"
            CommandTarget="{Binding ElementName=FlowReader1}"
            Style="{StaticResource ButtonStyle}">
            Add note</Button>
    <Separator/>
    <Button Command="ann:AnnotationService.CreateInkStickyNoteCommand"
            CommandTarget="{Binding ElementName=FlowReader1}"
            Style="{StaticResource ButtonStyle}">
        Add Ink
    </Button>
    <Separator/>
    <Button Command="ann:AnnotationService.DeleteStickyNotesCommand"
            CommandTarget="{Binding ElementName=FlowReader1}"
            Style="{StaticResource ButtonStyle}">
            Remove note
    </Button>
    <Separator/>
    <Button Command="ann:AnnotationService.CreateHighlightCommand"
            CommandTarget="{Binding ElementName=FlowReader1}"
            Style="{StaticResource ButtonStyle}">
            Highlight
    </Button>
    <Separator/>
    <Button Command="ann:AnnotationService.ClearHighlightsCommand"
            CommandTarget="{Binding ElementName=FlowReader1}"
            Style="{StaticResource ButtonStyle}">
            Remove highlight
    </Button>
</StackPanel>

<FlowDocumentReader Grid.Row="0"  BorderThickness="2" Name="FlowReader1">
    <FlowDocument Name="myDocument"
        TextAlignment="Justify"
        IsOptimalParagraphEnabled="True"
        IsHyphenationEnabled="True"
        IsColumnWidthFlexible="True"
        ColumnWidth="300"
```

31

```
ColumnGap="20">
<Paragraph FontSize="36" FontWeight="Bold"
        FontStyle="Oblique">Chapter 28</Paragraph>
<Paragraph FontSize="24" FontWeight="Bold">Introducing
        WPF</Paragraph>
<Paragraph>
    Windows Presentation Foundation relies on a layered architecture
    that is represented in Figure 28.1. The first layer is the
    Windows operating system. The second layer is constituted by the
    combination of two communicating layers:
    User32, which is the part of the operating system responsible
    for exchanging messages with applications, and the DirectX
    libraries which are the real power of WPF.
    <!- Add other text here.... ->
    <Figure Width="300">
        <BlockUIContainer>
            <StackPanel>
                <!-Replace the image file with a valid one->
                <Image
        Source="/DocumentsAndMedia;component/Images/28fig01.tif"
                    Width="200"
                    Height="300"
                    Stretch="Fill" />
                <Separator></Separator>
                <TextBlock VerticalAlignment="Center"
                        Width="220" TextWrapping="Wrap"
                        FontSize="10" FontStyle="Italic">
                    Figure 28.1 - WPF architecture
                </TextBlock>
            </StackPanel>
        </BlockUIContainer>
    </Figure>
    <Bold>PresentationFramework</Bold> exposes namespaces
    and classes
    through a complex hierarchy of inheritance,
    where the root class is System.Object.
    Such hierarchy provides the infrastructure for the user
    interface elements.
    This hierarchy is composed by the following list of classes,
    where each class inherits from the previous one:
</Paragraph>
<List>
    <ListItem>
        <Paragraph
        FontFamily="Courier New">System.Object</Paragraph>
    </ListItem>
```

```xml
            <ListItem>
                <Paragraph
                 FontFamily="Courier New">
                 System.Threading.DispatcherObject</Paragraph>
            </ListItem>
            <ListItem>
                <Paragraph FontFamily="Courier New">
                 System.Windows.DependencyObject</Paragraph>
            </ListItem>
            <ListItem>
                <Paragraph
                 FontFamily="Courier New">
                 System.Windows.Media.Visual</Paragraph>
            </ListItem>
        </List>
        <Paragraph>
            The
            <Hyperlink
                NavigateUri="http://msdn.microsoft.com/en-
                us/library/ms750441(VS.110).aspx
                #System_Threading_DispatcherObject">
                System.Threading.DispatcherObject</Hyperlink>
            is responsible for threading and messages which
            WPF relies on. The dispatcher takes advantage
            of the User32 messages for performing
            cross thread calls.
        </Paragraph>
    </FlowDocument>
    </FlowDocumentReader>
    </Grid>
</Window>
```

Let's begin by illustrating the FlowDocumentReader control. It provides a container for flow documents and automatically implements buttons for browsing multiple-page documents and controlling documents' layout, as you see later in Figure 31.4. The FlowDocument object instead contains the document and exposes some interesting properties. The previous code uses the most important ones. TextAlignment enables specifying how the text must be aligned within the document and can have one of the following values: Center, Right, Left, or Justify. IsOptimalParagraph set as True enables paragraph layout optimization. IsHyphenationEnable set as True enables word hyphenation in the document. IsColumnWidthFlexible set as True means that the value of the ColumnWidth property is not fixed. This last property takes place when you enable the document view by columns. The ColumnGap property indicates the spacing between columns. A complete list of properties is available in the MSDN Library: http://msdn.microsoft.com/en-us/library/system.

windows.documents.flowdocument.aspx. For the document content, notice the following techniques:

▶ You divide the content into multiple `Paragraph` objects to provide different paragraph formatting.

▶ You can add inline formatting. For example, the following line contains bold formatting within a paragraph:

```
<Bold>PresentationFramework</Bold> exposes namespaces and classes
```

▶ You can also add fully functional hyperlinks as in the following sample line:

```
<Hyperlink
 NavigateUri="http://msdn.microsoft.com/en-
us/library/ms750441(VS.110).aspx#System_Threading_DispatcherObject">
    System.Threading.DispatcherObject</Hyperlink>
```

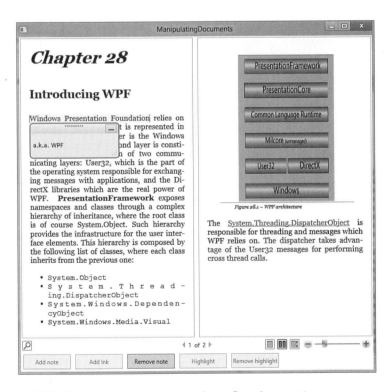

FIGURE 31.4   Viewing and annotating a flow document.

The sample document also shows how to implement bulleted lists via a `List` object that contains `ListItem` elements. It is interesting how flow documents also support figure insertion via a `Figure` element that contains a `BlockUIContainer` object nesting an `Image` control that stores the figure and a `TextBlock` control describing the figure. Each paragraph and subparagraph can be customized by setting font properties different from other paragraphs.

Switching the discussion to buttons implementation, instead of handling `Click` events, the code uses a technique known as *commanding* that takes advantage of built-in commands associated to specific actions. Each button is associated to one of the built-in actions for the annotation service via the `Command` property and points to the flow document as the target of the action (`CommandTarget`). At this point, you need to write code that enables the annotation service at the application startup so that the user can annotate or highlight text and then save annotations to disk for later reuse. The annotation service relies on the `System.Windows.Annotations` namespace that provides an `AnnotationService` class whose instance enables you to edit the document. Next, the `System.Windows.Annotations.Storage` namespace provides objects for storing annotations to XML files for later reuse. The code in Listing 31.4 shows how to implement the annotation service with Visual Basic. The code must be written to the code-behind file for the current window and contains comments for better reading.

LISTING 31.4   Implementing the Annotation Service

```
Imports System.Windows.Annotations
Imports System.Windows.Annotations.Storage
Imports System.IO


Public Class ManipulatingDocuments

    Dim annotationStream As FileStream

    Private Sub ManipulatingDocuments_Initialized(ByVal sender As Object,
                                     ByVal e As System.EventArgs) _
                                     Handles Me.Initialized

        'Gets the instance of the AnnotationService pointing to the FlowDocument
        Dim annotationServ As AnnotationService = _
            AnnotationService.GetService(FlowReader1)

        'Declares a store for annotations
        Dim annotationArchive As AnnotationStore

        'If no annotation service already exists for
        'the current flow document...
        If annotationServ Is Nothing Then
            '...creates a new service
            ' and a new store to an Xml file
            annotationStream = New FileStream("annotations.xml",
                                     FileMode.OpenOrCreate)
            annotationServ = New AnnotationService(FlowReader1)
```

```
            'Gets the instance of the stream
            annotationArchive = New XmlStreamStore(annotationStream)

            'Enables the document
            annotationServ.Enable(annotationArchive)
        End If
    End Sub

    Private Sub ManipulatingDocuments_Closed(ByVal sender As Object,
                                ByVal e As System.EventArgs) _
                                Handles Me.Closed
        Dim annotationServ As AnnotationService = _
            AnnotationService.GetService(FlowReader1)

        'If an instance of the annotation
        'service is available
        If annotationServ IsNot Nothing And _
            annotationServ.IsEnabled Then

            'shuts down the service
            'and releases resources
            annotationServ.Store.Flush()
            annotationServ.Disable()
            annotationStream.Close()
        End If
    End Sub
End Class
```

The annotation service startup is placed inside the `Window.Initialized` event handler, whereas the annotation service shutdown is placed inside the `Window.Closed` event handler. Now run the demo application by pressing **F5**. As you can see on the screen, if you resize the window, the flow document content is automatically and dynamically adapted to the window's layout. Moreover, you can decide, using the appropriate controls on the `FlowDocumentReader`, how the document has to be viewed (for example, if one or two pages appear on the window or with zoom enabled). The best way for getting a feel about how this works is to resize the window. Figure 31.4 shows how the application looks, including an example of annotation.

APPLYING ANNOTATIONS AND HIGHLIGHT

You apply annotations or highlights by selecting the desired text and then clicking one of the related buttons. You write the annotation text just after clicking the green box. Annotations are editable when reloaded.

You can also add ink annotations to your documents. Figure 31.5 shows how ink annotations look and how text is exposed with fonts other than the standard one. Also notice how the hyperlink is correctly highlighted and functional so that if you click it, you will be redirected to the related web page associated via the `NavigateUri` property in the XAML code.

FIGURE 31.5   Adding ink notes and viewing formatted text.

Annotations are automatically stored into an XML file, as implemented in code. Remember to resize the window to understand the flexibility of flow documents and of the `FlowDocumentReader` control.

Understanding the `RichTextBox` Control

WPF offers a `RichTextBox` control that works as you would expect for some aspects, thus enabling advanced formatting and image support. However, it differs from other technologies in that this control stores its content as a flow document. This is the reason for discussing this control in the current chapter. In XAML code the control definition looks like this:

```
<RichTextBox Name="RichTextBox1">
    <!- add your flow document here ->
</RichTextBox>
```

You could nest within the control the flow document shown in the previous section to get a fully editable document or write your text into the control, where such text takes standard formatting settings. You can also load an existing file into the RichTextBox, which requires some lines of code. The following method shows how to load a document as text:

```
Private Sub LoadDocument(ByVal fileName As String)

    Dim range As TextRange

    If File.Exists(fileName) Then
        range = New TextRange(RichTextBox1.Document.ContentStart,
                        RichTextBox1.Document.ContentEnd)

        Using documentStream As New FileStream(fileName,
                                        FileMode.
                                        OpenOrCreate)
            range.Load(documentStream,
                    System.Windows.DataFormats.Text)
        End Using
    End If
End Sub
```

The TextRange class represents the text area, and the code takes the entire area from start to end. Then the code invokes the TextRange.Load method to open the specified stream and converts the file content into a System.Windows.DataFormats.Text format that is acceptable for the RichTextBox. Notice that the previous example loads a text document that is then converted into XAML by the runtime. You can also load contents from XAML files using the DataFormats.Xaml option. To save the document content, you need to invoke the TextRange.Save method. The following method shows an example:

```
Private Sub SaveDocument(ByVal fileName As String)
    Dim range As New TextRange(Me.RichTextBox1.Document.ContentStart,
                        Me.RichTextBox1.Document.ContentEnd)

    Using documentStream As New FileStream(fileName,
                                    FileMode.Create)
        range.Save(documentStream, DataFormats.Xaml)
    End Using

End Sub
```

In this case the document content is saved under the form of XAML content, but you can still use the Text option to save such content as text, although this can cause a loss of formatting settings due to the restrictive conversion.

Implementing Spell Check

The RichTextBox control provides built-in spell check support. This can be enabled by setting the SpellCheck.IsEnabled property as follows:

```
<RichTextBox Name="RichTextBox1" SpellCheck.IsEnabled="True">
```

When enabled, when the user types unrecognized words in the English language the words are highlighted in red. By right-clicking the highlighted word, a list of valid alternatives is suggested, similar to what happens in applications such as Microsoft Word. Figure 31.6 shows how the spell check feature can help users fix typos in their documents.

FIGURE 31.6   The built-in spell check feature helps users fix typos.

Viewing XPS Documents

Starting from Windows Vista, Microsoft introduced a new file format known as XPS that is a portable file format for documents and is useful because you can share documents without having installed the application that generated that type of document because you need a viewer. WPF offers full support for XPS documents, also offering a DocumentViewer control that enables developers to embed XPS viewing functionalities in their applications. Support for XPS documents is provided by the ReachFramework. dll assembly (so you need to add a reference) that exposes the System.Windows.Xps. Packaging namespace. For code, you drag the DocumentViewer control from the toolbox onto the Window surface so that the generated XAML looks like the following:

```
<DocumentViewer Name="DocumentViewer1" />
```

At design time, this control offers a number of buttons for adjusting the document layout, zooming, and printing. XPS documents are fixed documents, unlike flow documents, so you need to create an instance of the XpsDocument class and get a fixed sequence of sheets to be assigned to the Document property of the viewer. This is demonstrated in the following code snippet that enables loading and presenting an XPS document:

```
Dim documentName As String = "C:\MyDoc.xps"
Dim xpsDoc As XpsDocument

xpsDoc = New XpsDocument(documentName, IO.FileAccess.ReadWrite)
DocumentViewer1.Document = xpsDoc.GetFixedDocumentSequence
```

Figure 31.7 shows a sample XPS document opened in the `DocumentViewer` control.

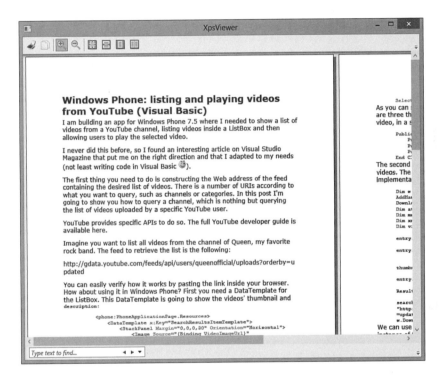

FIGURE 31.7   Viewing XPS documents through the `DocumentViewer` control.

So with a few steps, you can embed XPS functionalities in your applications.

Summary

This chapter was an overview about manipulating media and documents in WPF 4.5. You saw how you can present pictures with the `Image` control and how to reproduce media contents—such as videos and audio—through the `MediaElement` control, which also exposes events that you can intercept to understand the state of reproduction. Then flow documents and the `FlowDocumentReader` and `RichTextBox` controls were covered, examining how documents can be produced for dynamic arrangement within the user interface. Finally, we discussed WPF support for XPS documents through the `DocumentViewer` control and the `XpsDocument` class.

CHAPTER 32

Introducing Data-Binding

Many developers erroneously used to think of Windows Presentation Foundation (WPF) as just a multimedia platform, especially when the first versions came out. WPF is instead a complete framework for rich client applications development, including datacentric applications. This technology offers a powerful data-binding engine, and version 4.5 provides the ideal environment for building great business applications. This chapter provides a high-level introduction to the data-binding in WPF 4.5 with Visual Basic 2012, discussing the most important .NET objects that you can explore in further studies by applying WPF-specific patterns such as Model-View-View Model (MVVM).

SYSTEM REQUIREMENTS

Code examples are provided that require the Northwind database to be installed and made available on SQL Server 2012 Express or higher. You should already have done this if you read the chapters about LINQ.

In this case, this note is just a quick reminder.

Introducing the Data-Binding in WPF

Windows Presentation Foundation offers a powerful data-binding engine, held by the `System.Windows.Data` namespace, which makes binding data to the user interface (UI) and receiving input from the user even simpler. At a higher level, you perform data-binding between a user control and a data source making use of the `Binding` markup extension, which a lot of controls enable. It is worth mentioning that in WPF, a data source can be a collection of .NET objects but also a property from another user control. The following examples show you both scenarios. Particularly, you receive an explanation of the `DataGrid` control for tabular data representations and the `ObservableCollection(Of T)` in action for binding to a collection. Before going on, create a new WPF project with Visual Basic and name it `IntroducingDataBinding`. When the code editor is ready, write the following XAML code that divides the root `Grid` into two columns and adds some controls that will be necessary for the next examples:

```
<Grid Name="Grid1">
    <Grid.ColumnDefinitions>
        <ColumnDefinition Width="200" />
        <ColumnDefinition />
    </Grid.ColumnDefinitions>

    <StackPanel Grid.Column="0">
        <TextBox Name="ValueTextBox"
                Margin="5"/>

        <Slider Name="ValueSlider" Margin="5"
                Minimum="0" Maximum="10"/>
    </StackPanel>
    <StackPanel Grid.Column="1">
        <DataGrid Name="DataGrid1"
                Height="150"/>
        <TextBox Margin="5" Foreground="Red"
                Name="LogBox"
                Height="100"/>
    </StackPanel>
</Grid>
```

Utilized user controls now have no other properties than the ones necessary for defining their layout, which are set in code in the next sections.

Binding UI Elements with the `Binding` Markup Extension

You perform data-binding between a user control and a data source via the `Binding` XAML markup extension. Such an extension requires specifying two properties: `ElementName`, which is the source item name, and `Path`, which is the property containing the actual data to bind and whose name must be exposed by the object assigned to `ElementName`. The following example, in which you have to substitute to the first `TextBox` in the earlier example, shows how to bind the context of a `TextBox` to the value of a `Slider` control so that when the user moves the selector, the slider value is reflected into the `TextBox`:

```
<TextBox Text="{Binding ElementName=ValueSlider,
                    Path=Value}"
        Name="ValueTextBox"
        Margin="5"/>
```

Binding has to be applied to the property that will present bound data—in this case `Text`. If you now run the application and move the selector on the slider, you see how its value is reflected as the `TextBox.Text` content, as demonstrated in Figure 32.1.

FIGURE 32.1   Binding a control's property to another control's content.

This is the most basic data-binding example and can be considered as the one-way mode because the binding is performed only from the data-source (the `Slider.Value` property) to the UI control (the `TextBox`). In fact, the data-binding does not return a value from the `TextBox` to the `Slider`. To accomplish this, which means updating the `Slider` value according to the `TextBox` content, we need the two-way data-binding that enables binding from and to the data source. You apply for two-way data-binding by adding the `Mode=TwoWay` assignment within the `Binding` markup extension. The following code demonstrates this:

```
<TextBox Text="{Binding ElementName=ValueSlider,
                        Path=Value, Mode=TwoWay}"
         Name="ValueTextBox"
         Margin="5"/>

<Slider Name="ValueSlider" Margin="5"
        Minimum="0" Maximum="10"
        Value="{Binding ElementName=ValueTextBox,
        Path=Text, Mode=TwoWay}"/>
```

Notice how both controls need to set binding on the two-way mode so that they can reflect each other's value. If you run the application, you can see how the slider's selector value is updated according to the text box content. One-way and two-way are not the only allowed modes. Table 32.1 summarizes available data-binding modes in WPF, exposed by the `System.Windows.Data.BindingMode` enumeration.

TABLE 32.1   Available Data-Binding Modes

Mode	Description
OneWay	The data-binding is performed only from the data source to the UI. Changes on the data source are reflected to the UI, but not vice versa.
TwoWay	The data-binding is performed from the data source to the UI, and vice versa. Changes on the data source are reflected to the UI and changes via the UI are reflected to the data source.
OneWayToSource	Changes on the UI are reflected to the data source, but not vice versa. This is the opposite of OneWay.
OneTime	The data-binding is performed from the data source to the UI only once. When performed, changes are ignored and the UI is not updated. This is useful for presenting data, where you are sure that you will not update the data source.
Default	Applies the most convenient mode according to the user control. For example, the TextBox supports the two-way mode and thus this is the default mode. When you do not specify a different mode, this is the default.

Creating Bindings with Visual Basic

In case you need to create data-binding expressions at runtime, you need to write some Visual Basic code. You need an instance of the System.Windows.Data.Binding class setting some of its property and then pass such instance to the target control. The following snippet reproduces the data-binding expression described in the previous section, this time utilizing Visual Basic code:

```
Dim bind As New Binding
'Instead of ElementName, use Source assigning the control
bind.Source = ValueSlider
bind.Path = New PropertyPath("Value")
bind.Mode = BindingMode.TwoWay
'You set the binding considering a dependency property
Me.ValueTextBox.SetBinding(TextBox.TextProperty, bind)
```

Until now you saw the most basic data-binding technique that can be useful when you need to make controls depend on other controls' properties. In the next section you will see data-binding techniques against data sources based on .NET collections.

Understanding the DataGrid and the ObservableCollection

In most cases you perform data-binding operations against .NET collections, even when fetching data from databases. WPF offers a different binding mechanism, such as user controls like the new DataGrid, the ListView, or the ListBox; you can bind specific data to single controls like `TextBox` (for example, when building master-details representations). In this book, which targets Visual Basic 2012 and .NET 4.5, you get an example of how to take advantage of the new `DataGrid` control, which offers a convenient and fast way for tabular data. The goal of the next example is binding a collection of objects to a `DataGrid` enabling you to insert/update/delete operations onto the collection. First, add a new implementation of the `Person` class to the project as follows:

```
Public Class Person

    Public Property FirstName As String
    Public Property LastName As String
    Public Property Age As Integer

End Class
```

Now add a new `People` class, which inherits from `ObservableCollection(Of Person)` as follows:

```
Imports System.Collections.ObjectModel

Public Class People
    Inherits ObservableCollection(Of Person)

End Class
```

This new collection is the data source for binding to the `DataGrid`. Now go to the VB code behind the file for the main window. You need to declare a variable of type `People` and handle the `Window_Loaded` event to instantiate some `Person` objects to populate the collection. The following code accomplishes this:

```
Private WithEvents source As People

Private Sub MainWindow_Loaded(ByVal sender As Object,
                        ByVal e As System.Windows.
                        RoutedEventArgs) Handles Me.Loaded

    Dim personA As New Person With {.FirstName = "Alessandro",
                            .LastName = "Del Sole",
                            .Age = 35}
    'fantasy name
    Dim personB As New Person With {.FirstName = "Robert",
                            .LastName = "White",
                            .Age = 38}

    source = New People From {personA, personB}
```

```
    Me.Grid1.DataContext = source

    'If you plan to data-bind only the DataGrid:
    'Me.DataGrid1.ItemsSource = source
End Sub
```

You easily created an instance of the `People` collection with collection initializers. The most important thing here is the assignment of the `Grid.DataContext` property. As a general rule, `DataContext` is a property that points to a data source, and all children controls within the panel that exposes the `DataContext` property will populate by picking up data from this property. This also means that `DataContext` has scope; for example, the `Window.DataContext` property can share data to all controls in the user interface, whereas the `DataContext` from a particular panel can share data only with controls nested in that particular panel. In the previous code example, only controls nested in the `Grid` (including thus the `DataGrid`) can populate picking data from the `DataContext`. This is not mandatory. If you have a single control that you want to bind, you do not need to assign the `DataContext`, but you can assign the specific control data property. For instance, the `DataGrid` control exposes an `ItemsSource` property (like `ListView` and `ListBox`) that populates the control. Data-binding to user interface controls in WPF is possible thanks to the implementation of the `INotifyPropertyChanged` interface. Controls can reflect changes from data sources that implement that interface. The `ObservableCollection(Of T)` generic collection also implements behind the scenes and therefore can notify the user interface of changes so that it can be refreshed automatically. This is the reason we use such a collection in the example. This specialized collection is also interesting because it enables you to get information on what changed on data. It exposes a `CollectionChanged` event that offers an argument of type `NotifyCollectionEventArgs` that offers some useful information. For example, it enables intercepting when an item is added or removed or retrieving a collection of added items. Continuing with the example, suppose you want to create a sort of log to write a message each time an item is added or removed from the source collection. This is useful for demonstrating that the collection is effectively updated with changes performed through the user interface. The second `TextBox` in the user interface of the sample application is the place where log messages will be put. According to this, consider the following code snippet that provides an event handler for the `CollectionChanged` event:

```
'Requires an Imports System.Collections.Specialized directive    Private Sub
source_CollectionChanged(ByVal sender As Object,
                                 ByVal e As _
                                 NotifyCollectionChangedEventArgs) _
                                 Handles source.CollectionChanged


        Me.LogBox.Text += e.Action.ToString & Environment.NewLine
    End Sub
```

The code sends to the text box the current value of the `System.Collection.Specialized.NotifyCollectionChangedAction` enumeration, which can be one of the following:

`Add`, `Remove`, `Move`, `Replace`, or `Reset`. If you perform multiple CRUD operations on an `ObservableCollection` instance, you might also be interested in the `NewItems` and `OldItems` properties. They represent a collection of items added to the data source and a collection of items affected by a remove, replace, or move operation, respectively. Before running the application, it is necessary to perform a couple of operations on the `DataGrid` at the XAML level; therefore, switch back to the XAML code editor. Extend the `DataGrid` declaration as follows:

```
<DataGrid Name="DataGrid1"
          AutoGenerateColumns="True"
          AlternatingRowBackground="LightGreen"
          ItemsSource="{Binding}"
          Height="150"/>
```

First, the `DataGrid` automatically generates columns for you according to each property exposed by a single item (`Person`) in the bound collection (`People`). Second, the `ItemsSource`, which populates the control, is set to `Binding` with no arguments—meaning that the data-binding will be performed at runtime. Notice how the `AlternatingRowBackground` property enables specifying a color (which you can eventually replace with a brush) for the background in alternating rows. Now run the application. You get the result shown in Figure 32.2.

FIGURE 32.2   The data-bound `DataGrid` enables you to present and manipulate data.

Datagrid BINDING TIPS

Different from controls such as the `ListView` and the `ListBox`, the `DataGrid` enables you to bind any collection implementing `IList` or `IBindingList`. This is because such control requires a place for editing, other than presenting. So remember this requirement when you try to bind the result of LINQ queries to a `DataGrid`, which requires conversion into a generic collection. For LINQ, if you try to bind LINQ to XML, query results also remember to create a class for holding objects, just like the `Person` class and `People` collection instead of directly binding the query result.

If you play with the `DataGrid`, you can easily understand how it enables adding, removing, and editing items. The log text box stores messages each time you perform an operation, confirming that the underlying collection is actually affected by changes performed through the user interface. You can then plan to implement some code for saving your data. The `DataGrid` exposes other interesting properties:

▶ `SelectedItem`, which returns the instance of the selected object in the control

▶ `CurrentCell`, which returns the content of the selected cell

▶ `CanUserAddRows` and `CanUserRemoveRows`, which provide (or not) the user the ability of adding and deleting rows, respectively

▶ `CanUserReorderColumns`, `CanUserResizeColumns`, `CanUserSortColumns`, which provide (or not) the ability of changing the order of resizing and sorting columns

▶ `CanUserResizeRows`, which provides (or not) the ability of resizing rows

▶ `RowStyle`, which enables you to override the style for rows

So far, you've seen simple data-binding tasks, although the last code example provides a good way for understanding the mechanism. WPF data-binding is even more complex and the .NET Framework offers specific objects that are important in more articulate scenarios. The next section describes such objects taking advantage of new Visual Studio features.

Discussing the Drag'n'Drop Data-Binding

Visual Studio 2012 retakes from its predecessor the feature of the drag'n'drop data-binding, something that was already available in Windows Forms for many years. The drag'n'drop data-binding enables developers to quickly build data forms in WPF by dragging items from the Data Sources window, and Visual Studio will generate all the code for you, including master-details scenarios. This section explains how you can take advantage of the WPF drag'n'drop data-binding to easily build data forms, explaining the meaning and behavior of the autogenerated code.

> **TIP**
>
> The drag'n'drop data-binding has some limitations, and in many cases you need to put your hands over the autogenerated code or write your own data-binding code from scratch. This new technique offers several advantages: The result is completely customizable, as in the style of WPF applications; second, if you are new to data-binding in WPF, it enables you to understand how things work against a more complex data-source (such as an EDM or a DataSet). Finally, it also provides the ability of separating the data-source from the user interface, although this is something that you will probably need to edit according to your application logic.

To complete the next code examples, follow these steps:

1. Create a new WPF project for Visual Basic.

2. Add a new Entity Data Model based on the Northwind sample database, ensuring that you include the `Customers` and `Orders` tables. If you need a recap, take a look at Chapter 26, "Introducing ADO.NET Entity Framework."

After this brief introduction, it is time to understand how easy building data forms is with WPF 4.5.

Creating Tabular Data Forms

The goal of the next example is to show how simple it is to create tabular data representations, also taking a look at necessary objects for performing data-binding in code. To accomplish this, first divide the default Grid into two columns as follows:

```
<Grid>
    <Grid.ColumnDefinitions>
        <ColumnDefinition Width="200"/>
        <ColumnDefinition/>
    </Grid.ColumnDefinitions>
</Grid>
```

Next, add a `ListBox` control either by dragging it from the Toolbox or by writing the following code (for better layout purposes, ensure that you place it in the left column):

```
<ListBox Name="CustomersListBox"
         Grid.Column="0"/>
```

This `ListBox` stores a list of customers' names that will be added shortly. Now open the Data Sources window by clicking **Shift+Alt+D**. The result looks similar to Figure 32.3, depending on how many entities you added to the Entity Data Model.

The default icon near each entity name indicates that data will be represented as tabular, but you can replace this representation with a list view or with a details view by selecting the appropriate value from the combo box on the right side of each entity name. (At the moment, leave the default selection unchanged.) Now, expand the `Customers` entity (as shown in Figure 32.3) and select the `CompanyName` item; then drag it onto the `ListBox` and release the mouse. When you release the mouse, you will not notice anything new on the designer surface, but look at what happened in the XAML code editor:

```
<Window.Resources>
    <CollectionViewSource x:Key="CustomersViewSource"
                          d:DesignSource=
                          "{d:DesignInstance my:Customer,
                                              CreateList=True}" />
</Window.Resources>
<Grid DataContext="{StaticResource CustomersViewSource}">
    <Grid.ColumnDefinitions>
```

```
        <ColumnDefinition Width="200"/>
        <ColumnDefinition/>
    </Grid.ColumnDefinitions>
    <ListBox Name="CustomersListBox"
            Grid.Column="0" DisplayMemberPath="CompanyName"
            ItemsSource="{Binding}" />
</Grid>
```

FIGURE 32.3   The Data Source window lists entities from the EDM.

Visual Studio generates some code, both XAML and Visual Basic, each time you perform some drag'n'drop action. For now, it generated a CollectionViewSource object within the window's resources. You can compare the WPF CollectionViewSource to the Windows Forms' BindingSource control, which acts like a bridge between the underlying data collection and the user interface. The code states that such CollectionViewSource is populated via a list (CreateList=True) of Customer instances. This statement is accomplished via the d:DesignInstance custom markup extension, exposed by the d XML namespace that points to Microsoft Expression Blend schema for WPF. This is useful because it provides resources for design-time data-binding. Notice also how Visual Studio added a DataContext property for the default Grid, whose source is the previously described CollectionViewSource. In this way, all child controls will populate by picking data from the CollectionViewSource. You can get an example of this by taking a look at the ListBox overridden definition: It is populated with data-binding (ItemsSource property) and shows just the value of the `CompanyName` property (`DisplayMemberPath`) for each item in the bound collection. Now drag onto the form the `Orders` item from the Data Sources window, ensuring that you drag the one nested within `Customers`. When dragged and dropped, the result should look like Figure 32.4.

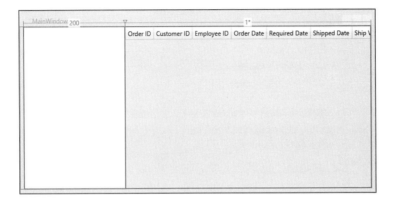

FIGURE 32.4   The result of the drag'n'drop operations in the Visual Studio designer.

First, notice how the new `DataGrid` control enables you to build tabular data representations. By dragging the data source, Visual Studio generated all the necessary items for you. If you now take a look at the XAML code editor, you will first notice a second `CollectionViewSource` referring to the `Orders` data:

```
<CollectionViewSource x:Key="CustomersOrdersViewSource"
                      Source="{Binding Path=Orders,
                      Source={StaticResource CustomersViewSource}}" />
```

Notice how the source for the data-binding is the `Orders` collection from the previously generated `CustomersViewSource` object of type `CollectionViewSource`. Next, Visual Studio also generated markup code for the `DataGrid`. For this, it did not take advantage of columns autogeneration; it instead created specific columns for each property in the bound collection. This enables the IDE to also generate custom cell templates that can show data with the appropriate control. The following is the XAML code for the `DataGrid`:

```
<DataGrid AutoGenerateColumns="False"
          EnableRowVirtualization="True"
          Grid.Column="1"
          ItemsSource="{Binding
          Source={StaticResource CustomersOrdersViewSource}}"
          Name="OrdersDataGrid"
          RowDetailsVisibilityMode="VisibleWhenSelected">
    <DataGrid.Columns>
        <DataGridTextColumn x:Name="OrderIDColumn"
                            Binding="{Binding Path=OrderID}"
```

```xml
                              Header="Order ID"
                              Width="SizeToHeader" />
<DataGridTextColumn x:Name="CustomerIDColumn"
                    Binding="{Binding Path=CustomerID}"
                    Header="Customer ID"
                    Width="SizeToHeader" />
<DataGridTextColumn x:Name="EmployeeIDColumn"
                    Binding="{Binding Path=EmployeeID}"
                    Header="Employee ID"
                    Width="SizeToHeader" />
<DataGridTemplateColumn x:Name="OrderDateColumn"
                        Header="Order Date"
                        Width="SizeToHeader">
    <DataGridTemplateColumn.CellTemplate>
        <DataTemplate>
            <DatePicker
              SelectedDate="{Binding Path=OrderDate}" />
        </DataTemplate>
    </DataGridTemplateColumn.CellTemplate>
</DataGridTemplateColumn>
<DataGridTemplateColumn x:Name="RequiredDateColumn"
                        Header="Required Date"
                        Width="SizeToHeader">
    <DataGridTemplateColumn.CellTemplate>
        <DataTemplate>
            <DatePicker
              SelectedDate="{Binding Path=RequiredDate}" />
        </DataTemplate>
    </DataGridTemplateColumn.CellTemplate>
</DataGridTemplateColumn>
<DataGridTemplateColumn x:Name="ShippedDateColumn"
                        Header="Shipped Date"
                        Width="SizeToHeader">
    <DataGridTemplateColumn.CellTemplate>
        <DataTemplate>
            <DatePicker
              SelectedDate="{Binding Path=ShippedDate}" />
        </DataTemplate>
    </DataGridTemplateColumn.CellTemplate>
</DataGridTemplateColumn>
<DataGridTextColumn x:Name="ShipViaColumn"
                    Binding="{Binding Path=ShipVia}"
                    Header="Ship Via"
                    Width="SizeToHeader" />
<DataGridTextColumn x:Name="FreightColumn"
                    Binding="{Binding Path=Freight}"
```

```xml
                             Header="Freight"
                             Width="SizeToHeader" />
        <DataGridTextColumn x:Name="ShipNameColumn"
                             Binding="{Binding Path=ShipName}"
                             Header="Ship Name"
                             Width="SizeToHeader" />
        <DataGridTextColumn x:Name="ShipAddressColumn"
                             Binding="{Binding Path=ShipAddress}"
                             Header="Ship Address"
                             Width="SizeToHeader" />
        <DataGridTextColumn x:Name="ShipCityColumn"
                             Binding="{Binding Path=ShipCity}"
                             Header="Ship  City"
                             Width="SizeToHeader" />
        <DataGridTextColumn x:Name="ShipRegionColumn"
                             Binding="{Binding Path=ShipRegion}"
                             Header="Ship Region"
                             Width="SizeToHeader" />
        <DataGridTextColumn x:Name="ShipPostalCodeColumn"
                             Binding="{Binding Path=ShipPostalCode}"
                             Header="Ship Postal Code"
                             Width="SizeToHeader" />
        <DataGridTextColumn x:Name="ShipCountryColumn"
                             Binding="{Binding Path=ShipCountry}"
                             Header="Ship Country"
                             Width="SizeToHeader" />
    </DataGrid.Columns>
</DataGrid>
```

The `DataGrid` data source is set via the `ItemsSource` property pointing to the `CustomersOrdersViewSource` object, which includes information from both `Customers` and related `Orders`. The rest of the code is quite simple to understand. Each column has a cell template, which is of type `DataGridTextColumn` for text fields. Other built-in types are `DataGridHyperLinkColumn` for displaying hyperlinks, `DataGridCheckBoxColumn` for displaying Boolean values with a check box control, and `DataGridComboBoxColumn` for selecting items from within a combo box. It is worth mentioning that for data types, the `DataGrid` has no default counterpart. Visual Studio generates a custom cell template with `DataGridTemplateColumn` objects. In this case the custom template has been generated for embedding `DatePicker` controls for setting and displaying dates within cells.

DESIGNING COLUMNS

The IDE provides a convenient way for designing columns with the designer instrumentation. Select the `DataGrid` and in the Properties window, click Columns. Figure 32.5 shows how you can edit existing columns or add new ones, also setting data-binding at design time.

FIGURE 32.5   Designing columns with Visual Studio.

This is not enough, of course, in that some Visual Basic code is also required for fetching data and assigning the data to the user interface for presenting. If you now open the Visual Basic code behind the file for the current `Window`, you get the result shown in Listing 32.1.

LISTING 32.1   The VB Auto-Generated Code for the Drag'n'Drop Data-Binding

```
'Add an Imports directive followed by the project namespace
Imports IntroducingDataBinding
Class MainWindow

    Private Function GetCustomersQuery(ByVal NorthwindEntities As NorthwindEntities)_
                    As System.Data.Objects.ObjectQuery(Of Customer)

        Dim CustomersQuery As System.Data.Objects.ObjectQuery(Of Customer) = _
                    NorthwindEntities.Customers
        'Update the query to include Orders data in Customers.
        'You can modify this code as needed.
        CustomersQuery = CustomersQuery.Include("Orders")
```

```
        'Returns an ObjectQuery.
        Return CustomersQuery
    End Function

    Private Sub Window_Loaded(ByVal sender As System.Object,
                            ByVal e As System.Windows.RoutedEventArgs) _
                            Handles MyBase.Loaded

        Dim NorthwindEntities As NorthwindEntities = New NorthwindEntities()
        'Load data into Customers. You can modify this code as needed.
        Dim CustomersViewSource As System.Windows.Data.CollectionViewSource = _
            CType(Me.FindResource("CustomersViewSource"),
            System.Windows.Data.CollectionViewSource)
        Dim CustomersQuery As System.Data.Objects.ObjectQuery(Of Customer) = _
            Me.GetCustomersQuery(NorthwindEntities)
        CustomersViewSource.Source = CustomersQuery.Execute(System.Data.Objects.
                                            MergeOption.AppendOnly)

    End Sub
End Class
```

The `GetCustomersQuery` method returns the full list of customers and related orders, returning a new Entity Framework object, `ObjectQuery(Of T)`. Such an object type represents a typed query and is also capable of receiving data back. Such a query is a default one; therefore, you can customize it according to your needs. When the window is loaded, other than the `ObjectContext` instance, notice how the code retrieves the instance of the `CustomersViewSource` (of type `CollectionViewSource`) via the FindResource method, which enables searching for a resource declared in XAML. This instance will finally receive the executed query so that its result will be reflected to the user interface. The process is the following: The query fetches data; data is assigned to a `CollectionViewSource` instance; because this instance is bound to a UI control (such as the `DataGrid`), fetched data is reflected to the UI, and vice versa. This is also because the `DataGrid` control provides support for the two-way data-binding, and is also allowed by the `ObjectQuery(Of T)` class. At this point, you can run the application to see the result shown in Figure 32.6.

With a few mouse clicks, you can build an application that can present tabular data. You can click inside the `DataGrid` for editing existing data or for adding new rows. If you want to save data to the underlying database, you should implement a control, such as a `Button`, whose `Click` event handler invokes the `ObjectContext.SaveChanges` method, and you are done. But you see this example in the next section, which is interesting but that requires a little bit of manual work.

FIGURE 32.6   The tabular data application running.

Creating Master-Details Forms

Similarly to what already happened in Windows Forms, creating master-details forms in WPF 4.5 is also straightforward. This also enables you to understand other important concepts for the data-binding. Add a new window to the current project and name it **MasterDetails**. Divide the default `Grid` into four cells, so that you can also add special buttons, as follows:

```
<Grid>
    <Grid.ColumnDefinitions>
        <ColumnDefinition Width="200"/>
        <ColumnDefinition/>
    </Grid.ColumnDefinitions>
    <Grid.RowDefinitions>
        <RowDefinition/>
        <RowDefinition Height="50"/>
    </Grid.RowDefinitions>
</Grid>
```

Repeat the step of adding a `ListBox` and binding the customer's `CompanyName` property, just as in the first part of the previous subsection. Ensure that the `ListBox` is placed in the upper-left column. Visual Studio 2012 generates exactly the same XAML code of the previous example for you. Now go to the Data Sources window, select the **Orders** item nested within Customers; then from the combo box, select **Details**. Next, drag **Orders** onto the upper-right cell of the window. Figure 32.7 shows the result of this operation.

FIGURE 32.7   The result of the master-details drag'n'drop.

Notice how Visual Studio generated a series of controls, which are couples of
Label/TextBlock. Also notice how the IDE can recognize the bound data type and add the
appropriate controls. For example, for dates, it adds to the form some DatePicker controls.
Instead of a DataGrid, the autogenerated XAML code contains a new Grid with a series of
children controls. Listing 32.2 shows an excerpt of the content of the new Grid.

LISTING 32.2   Excerpt of the Autogenerated XAML Code for Details

```xaml
<Grid DataContext="{StaticResource CustomersOrdersViewSource}"
      Grid.Column="1"
      Grid.Row="0" Name="Grid1" >
  <Grid.ColumnDefinitions>
      <ColumnDefinition Width="Auto" />
      <ColumnDefinition Width="Auto" />
  </Grid.ColumnDefinitions>
  <Grid.RowDefinitions>
      <RowDefinition Height="Auto" />
      <RowDefinition Height="Auto" />
      <RowDefinition Height="Auto" />
      <RowDefinition Height="Auto" />
      <RowDefinition Height="Auto" />
      <RowDefinition Height="Auto" />
      <RowDefinition Height="Auto" />
      <RowDefinition Height="Auto" />
      <RowDefinition Height="Auto" />
```

```xml
            <RowDefinition Height="Auto" />
            <RowDefinition Height="Auto" />
            <RowDefinition Height="Auto" />
            <RowDefinition Height="Auto" />
            <RowDefinition Height="Auto" />
        </Grid.RowDefinitions>
        <Label Content="Order ID:" Grid.Column="0" Grid.Row="0"
               HorizontalAlignment="Left" Margin="3"
               VerticalAlignment="Center" />
        <TextBox Grid.Column="1" Grid.Row="0" Height="23"
                 HorizontalAlignment="Left" Margin="3" Name="OrderIDTextBox"
                 Text="{Binding Path=OrderID}"
                 VerticalAlignment="Center" Width="120" />
        <Label Content="Customer ID:" Grid.Column="0" Grid.Row="1"
               HorizontalAlignment="Left" Margin="3"
               VerticalAlignment="Center" />
        <TextBox Grid.Column="1" Grid.Row="1" Height="23"
                 HorizontalAlignment="Left" Margin="3" Name="CustomerIDTextBox"
                 Text="{Binding Path=CustomerID}"
                 VerticalAlignment="Center" Width="120" />
        <Label Content="Employee ID:" Grid.Column="0" Grid.Row="2"
               HorizontalAlignment="Left" Margin="3"
               VerticalAlignment="Center" />
        <TextBox Grid.Column="1" Grid.Row="2" Height="23"
                 HorizontalAlignment="Left"
                 Margin="3" Name="EmployeeIDTextBox"
                 Text="{Binding Path=EmployeeID}"
                 VerticalAlignment="Center" Width="120" />
        <Label Content="Order Date:" Grid.Column="0" Grid.Row="3"
               HorizontalAlignment="Left" Margin="3"
               VerticalAlignment="Center" />
        <DatePicker Grid.Column="1" Grid.Row="3" Height="25"
                    HorizontalAlignment="Left" Margin="3"
                    Name="OrderDateDatePicker"
                    SelectedDate="{Binding Path=OrderDate}"
                    VerticalAlignment="Center" Width="115" />
        <!--Following other controls... -->
    </Grid>
</Grid>
```

The code implements pairs of labels/text. For dates, you can notice the presence of
DatePicker controls whose SelectedDate property is bound to the date property from
the data source. If you take a look at the Visual Basic autogenerated code, you see no
differences with the one shown in the first example. Now there is some other work to do.
Building a master-details form requires providing controls for navigating, adding, deleting,

and saving items. Now, you need to add the following XAML code, which implements some buttons whose meanings should be self-explanatory:

```xml
<StackPanel Grid.Row="1" Grid.Column="1" Orientation="Horizontal">
    <StackPanel.Resources>
        <Style TargetType="Button" x:Key="ButtonStyle">
            <Setter Property="Width" Value="80"/>
            <Setter Property="Height" Value="40"/>
            <Setter Property="Margin" Value="5"/>
        </Style>
    </StackPanel.Resources>
    <Button Style="{StaticResource ButtonStyle}" Content="Save"
            Name="SaveButton" Click="SaveButton_Click"/>
    <Button Style="{StaticResource ButtonStyle}" Content="Add"
            Name="AddButton" Click="AddButton_Click"/>
    <Button Style="{StaticResource ButtonStyle}" Content="Delete"
            Name="DeleteButton" Click="DeleteButton_Click"/>
    <Button Style="{StaticResource ButtonStyle}" Content="Next"
            Name="NextButton" Click="NextButton_Click"/>
    <Button Style="{StaticResource ButtonStyle}" Content="Back"
            Name="BackButton" Click="BackButton_Click"/>
</StackPanel>
```

Now switch to the Visual Basic code. The first task is moving the ObjectContext declaration at class level, to make it reachable from within other methods. Replace the NorthwindEntities variable declaration with the northwindContext name to avoid conflicts, move it to class level, and edit the first line of the Window_Loaded event as follows:

```vb
Private northwindContext As NorthwindEntities

Private Sub Window_Loaded(ByVal sender As System.Object,
                          ByVal e As System.Windows.RoutedEventArgs) _
                          Handles MyBase.Loaded

    Me.northwindContext = New NorthwindEntities
```

The first button that can be handled is the SaveButton. The Click event handler is the following:

```vb
Private Sub SaveButton_Click(ByVal sender As System.Object,
                             ByVal e As System.Windows.
                             RoutedEventArgs)
    'Handle your logic here, such as exceptions
    'and optimistic concurrency
```

```
    Try

        Me.northwindContext.SaveChanges()
    Catch ex As Exception


    End Try
End Sub
```

The second task is moving to class level the `CollectionViewSource` objects declarations so that we can invoke them within event handlers. They actually are enclosed in the `Window_Loaded` event handler and thus have no external visibility. Moreover, we also need to manually declare and get the instance of the `CustomersOrdersCollectionViewSource` object because the application needs to provide the ability of adding and removing items only to the `Orders` collection. (Performing this on `CustomersViewSource` would affect `Customers`, too.) The code in Listing 32.3 summarizes the edits that you need to do manually at this point.

LISTING 32.3   Moving `CollectionViewSource` Declarations at Class Level

```
Private CustomersViewSource As CollectionViewSource
Private CustomersOrdersViewSource As CollectionViewSource

Private Sub Window_Loaded(ByVal sender As System.Object,
                          ByVal e As System.Windows.RoutedEventArgs) _
                          Handles MyBase.Loaded

    Me.northwindContext = New NorthwindEntities
    'Load data into Customers. You can modify this code as needed.
    Me.CustomersViewSource = CType(Me.FindResource("CustomersViewSource"),
                             CollectionViewSource)
    Me.CustomersOrdersViewSource =
                          CType(Me.FindResource("CustomersOrdersViewSource"),
                          CollectionViewSource)

    Dim CustomersQuery As System.Data.Objects.
                          ObjectQuery(Of IntroducingDataBinding.Customer) = _
                          Me.GetCustomersQuery(northwindContext)
    CustomersViewSource.Source = CustomersQuery.
                          Execute(System.Data.Objects.
                          MergeOption.AppendOnly)
End Sub
```

The next buttons require explaining other concepts, which the next sections cover.

Understanding Views and Binding Lists

`CollectionViewSource` objects expose an interesting property named `View`. It provides the ability of filtering, sorting, and navigating through a bound collection of items.

To understand how a view works, the best example in our scenario is handling the `Next` and `Back` buttons. The following code snippet shows how easy it is to navigate back and forward through items:

```
Private Sub NextButton_Click(ByVal sender As System.Object,
                            ByVal e As System.Windows.RoutedEventArgs)
    If Me.CustomersOrdersViewSource.View.CurrentPosition < _
        CType(Me.CustomersOrdersViewSource.View, CollectionView).
        Count - 1 Then
        Me.CustomersOrdersViewSource.View.MoveCurrentToNext()
    End If
End Sub


Private Sub BackButton_Click(ByVal sender As System.Object,
                            ByVal e As System.Windows.RoutedEventArgs)
    If Me.CustomersOrdersViewSource.View.CurrentPosition > 0 Then
        Me.CustomersOrdersViewSource.View.MoveCurrentToPrevious()
    End If
End Sub
```

The code calculates the position and enables moving back or forward only if there are any other items that can be navigated. Notice how the `CustomersOrdersViewSource.View` property exposes the `Count` property, representing the current position being examined in the collection. Methods such as `MoveCurrentToNext` and `MoveCurrentToPrevious` enable moving back and forward to another item. Other interesting members from views are self-explanatory and are summarized in Table 32.2.

TABLE 32.2   Views' Most Common Members

Member	Type	Description
CanSort	Property	Returns a Boolean value indicating whether the collection can be sorted.
CanFilter	Property	Returns a Boolean value indicating whether the collection can be filtered.
CanGroup	Property	Returns a Boolean value indicating whether the collection can be grouped.
MoveCurrentTo	Method	Sets the specified item as the current item in the collection.
MoveCurrentToFirst	Method	Sets the first item in the collection as the current item.
MoveCurrentToLast	Method	Sets the last item in the collection as the current item.
MoveCurrentToNext	Method	Sets the next item in the collection as the current item.

Member	Type	Description
MoveCurrentToPrevious	Method	Sets the previous item in the collection as the current item.
CurrentItem	Property	Returns the instance of the current item in the collection. Because it is of type Object, it must be converted into the appropriate type.
CurrentPosition	Property	Returns an index corresponding to the current item in the collection.

To retrieve the items count, a CType operator converts from CollectionViewSource.View into a CollectionView object. This last one represents a single view, and the conversion is required because Option Strict is On and the View property is of type ICollectionView. Views from CollectionViewSource objects are straightforward because they also support data-binding but have several limitations. As you can see from Table 32.2, no member is exposed for adding, editing, or removing items in the underlying data collection. To provide the ability of CRUD operations, the best approach is utilizing a System.Window. Data.Binding ListCollectionView, which also offers a reference to data collections but provides more capabilities. At class level, declare the following variables:

```
Private WithEvents CustomerView As BindingListCollectionView
Private CustomersOrdersView As BindingListCollectionView
```

Now, in the Window_Loaded event handler, add the following lines as the last lines of code in the method:

```
Me.CustomerView = CType(Me.CustomersViewSource.View, _
                       BindingListCollectionView)
Me.CustomersOrdersView = CType(Me.CustomersOrdersViewSource.View, _
                       BindingListCollectionView)
```

This converts views references to two BindingListCollectionView objects. Now with these you can perform insert/update/delete operations to the underlying collection, which is picked up from the CollectionViewSource associations and is data-bound to the BindingListCollectionView, too. To understand how this works, write the following handler for the Click event about the Add button so that we can provide the capability of adding a new order:

```
Private Sub AddButton_Click(ByVal sender As System.Object, _
                       ByVal e As System.Windows.RoutedEventArgs)
    'A new order
    Dim newOrder As Order

    'Adds a new order to the view and assigns the instance
    'to the newly declared order
    newOrder = CType(Me.CustomersOrdersView.AddNew(), Order)
```

```
        'If I need to assign properties to newOrder before
        'it is sent to the collection, then this is the place

        'Sends the new order to the view
        Me.CustomersOrdersView.CommitNew()
End Sub
```

The AddNew method adds an instance of the specified object type to the view, and the addition is automatically reflected to the bound user interface controls. The CType conversion is required because the method returns Object; therefore, converting to the appropriate type returns the effective instance of the order. This is not actually required, but it is useful if you want to set some default properties before the object is sent to the underlying collection. Notice that this code submits the new item to the underlying collection, but the new object will not persist to the underlying database until you invoke the ObjectContext.SaveChanges method. Removing items works similarly, in that you retrieve the current object instance and invoke one of the enabled methods. The following event handler for the Delete button demonstrates this:

```
Private Sub DeleteButton_Click(ByVal sender As System.Object,
                               ByVal e As System.Windows.
                               RoutedEventArgs)
    If Me.CustomersOrdersView.CurrentPosition > -1 Then

        Dim result = MessageBox.Show("Are you sure?",
                                     "", MessageBoxButton.YesNo)
        If result = MessageBoxResult.Yes Then
            Me.CustomersOrdersView.
                RemoveAt(Me.CustomersOrdersView.CurrentPosition)
        Else
            Exit Sub
        End If
    End If
End Sub
```

In this case I'm using RemoveAt to remove the item at the current position, but you can also invoke Remove, which requires the instance of the current object. RemoveAt requires fewer lines of code. Before running the application, there is one thing that you need to take care of—and that is the fact that the BindingListCollectionView content needs to be refreshed each time you move to another item in the master part of the master-details relationships. Considering our code example, you need to remember the BindingListCollectionView referred to orders each time you select a different customer. To accomplish this, you handle the CurrentChanged event in the master part of the relationship, as demonstrated by the following code:

```
Private Sub CustomerView_CurrentChanged(ByVal sender As Object,
                        ByVal e As System.EventArgs) _
                        Handles CustomerView.CurrentChanged
```

```
Me.CustomersOrdersView = CType(Me.CustomersOrdersViewSource.View,
                                BindingListCollectionView)
End Sub
```

The preceding event handler is invoked when you click a different customer in the user interface and refreshes the `CustomersOrdersView` (of type `BindingListCollectionView`) object pointing to the actual orders collection referred by the underlying `CollectionViewSource`. That keeps the data-binding alive. Now you can run the application and get the result summarized in Figure 32.8.

FIGURE 32.8   The master-details application running.

BINDING TO DATASETS

The drag'n'drop data-binding works the same with DataSets, and you can still take advantage of `CollectionViewSource` and `BindingListCollectionView` objects. The code remains the same as the previously shown examples, whereas the difference is where you need to persist data to the database or fetch data, where you can use DataSet methods and LINQ to DataSets, respectively.

You can now play with additional controls such as `Add`, `Delete`, `Next`, and `Back`. When you are done, try to save changes to ensure that new or edited data is correctly persisted to the database. This sample application can be enhanced in several other ways. For example, you can implement entities validation or showing details for a single order using LINQ. These topics are beyond the scope of an introductory chapter about data-binding, but you can further explore them with the help of the MSDN documentation. Particularly, I suggest you read this blog post by Beth Massi from Microsoft, where she discusses WPF validation on entities: http://blogs.msdn.com/bethmassi/archive/2009/07/07/ implementing-validation-in-wpf-on-entity-framework-entities.aspx. Although the blog post targets the .NET Framework 3.5 SP 1, this technique is convenient on .NET 4.0 and 4.5, too.

Implementing String Formatters and Value Converters

The need to represent strings in a more appropriate format when binding data to the user interface is not uncommon. For example, you might want to present money values or percentages. In WPF, you can accomplish this in two modes: string formatters and the IValueConverter interface. This section describes both, showing how they can be used for better presentation purposes.

Implementing String Formatters

You can apply string formats directly in the XAML Binding markup extension that performs data-binding. This enables you to express a particular value type in a more convenient string format. For a better understanding, consider Figure 32.8. Notice how the Freight field is shown as a decimal number. However, you probably want to display it with your currency symbol. Locate the XAML code that implements the Freight textbox and apply the StringFormat property as shown in the following code snippet:

```
<TextBox Grid.Column="1" Grid.Row="7" Height="23"
        HorizontalAlignment="Left" Margin="3"
        Name="FreightTextBox"
        Text="{Binding Path=Freight, StringFormat=c}"
        VerticalAlignment="Center" Width="120" />
```

The BindingBase.StringFormat property is applied within the Binding markup extension and requires the specification of the formatter. Figure 32.9 shows how the Freight field is now represented with a currency symbol.

Table 32.3 summarizes the most common StringFormat values.

TABLE 32.3   Most Common Formatters' Values

Value	Description
c or C	Represents a value as a string with currency symbol.
p or P	Formats a value as a string with percentage representation.
D	Formats a date value as an extended string representation (for example, Monday, 21 October 2009).
d	Formats a date value as a short string representation (for example, 10/21/2009).
F	Provides a string representation of a decimal number with floating point. It is followed by a number that establishes how many numbers follow the floating point (for example, 3.14 can be represented by F2).

Value	Description
E	Scientific formatting.
X	Hexadecimal formatting.
G	General.

FIGURE 32.9   Representing strings with `StringFormat`.

The good news is that string formatters also provide converting the user input. For the `Freight` example, if you type a value into the field, it is represented as a currency in the user interface, but it is correctly saved to the data source according to the required type. `StringFormat` also enables string formatting as it happens in Visual Basic code. Consider the following code:

```
<TextBox Name="FreightTextBox"
         Text="{Binding Path=Freight, StringFormat=Amount: {0:c}}"/>
```

In the preceding code, the `Amount` word takes the place of 0 at runtime. So the result will be `Amount: $1.21`. There is another useful technique known as *multibinding*. The following code demonstrates how you can apply multiple formatters with `MultiBinding`:

```
<!--Applies date and currency formatting-->
<TextBlock>
  <TextBlock.Text>
    <MultiBinding StringFormat="Order date: {0:D}, Cost: {1:C}">
      <Binding Path="OrderDate"/>
      <Binding Path="OrderPrice"/>
    </MultiBinding>
  </TextBlock.Text>
</TextBlock>
```

Several user controls, such as `Button` and `Label`, also offer a `ContentStringFormat` property that enables you to apply formatting to the control's content the same way as `StringFormat` works. The following is an example:

```
<Label ContentStringFormat="C" Content="200"/>
```

Similarly, controls such as `ListView`, `ListBox`, and `DataGrid` offer the `HeaderStringFormat` and `ItemStringFormat` properties that enable you to format the header content for columns and items in the list, respectively. String formatters are straightforward, but in some situations you need more extensive control over value representation, especially when you need to actually convert from one data type to another. This is where `IValueConverter` comes in.

Implementing the `IValueConverter` Interface

Sometimes default conversions provided by string formatters are not enough, especially if you have to implement your custom logic when converting from the user input into another type. With `IValueConverter`, you can implement your custom logic getting control over the conversion process from and to the data source. To follow the next steps, create a new class and name it `CustomConverter`. When the new class is ready, implement the `IValueConverter` interface. The resulting code will be the following:

```
Public Class CustomConverter
    Implements IValueConverter

    Public Function Convert(ByVal value As Object,
                            ByVal targetType As System.Type,
                            ByVal parameter As Object,
                            ByVal culture As
                            System.Globalization.CultureInfo) _
                            As Object Implements _
                            System.Windows.Data.IValueConverter.Convert

    End Function

    Public Function ConvertBack(ByVal value As Object,
                                ByVal targetType As System.Type,
                                ByVal parameter As Object,
```

```
                            ByVal culture As System.Globalization.
                            CultureInfo) As Object _
                            Implements _
                            System.Windows.Data.IValueConverter.
                            ConvertBack

        End Function
End Class
```

The interface implementation requires two methods, `Convert` and `ConvertBack`. The first one manages data when applying from the data source to the user interface, and the second one manages the conversion when getting back from the user interface to the data source. The most important argument in the `Convert` method is `parameter`, which represents how data must be converted. Such data is stored by the `value` argument. Implementing `Convert` is quite easy, in that you need to format value as a string according to parameter's establishment. This can be accomplished taking advantage of the current culture. The following is the standard `Convert` implementation:

```
Public Function Convert(ByVal value As Object,
                        ByVal targetType As System.Type,
                        ByVal parameter As Object,
                        ByVal culture As _
                        System.Globalization.CultureInfo) _
                        As Object Implements System.Windows.Data.
                        IValueConverter.Convert

    If parameter IsNot Nothing Then
        Return String.Format(culture, parameter.ToString, value)
    End If

    Return value
End Function
```

This ensures that on the XAML side a valid converter property (reflected by parameter), which is described later, has been provided and that it is not null. In this case the method returns the string representation of the value according to the system culture. If no converter is specified, the method returns the value. `ConvertBack` is a little bit more complex because it has to convert strings (that is, the user input) into a more appropriate type. The goal of this example is providing conversion from `String` to `Decimal`, for money fields. The following code snippet implements the method (see comments for explanations):

```
Public Function ConvertBack(ByVal value As Object,
                            ByVal targetType As System.Type,
                            ByVal parameter As Object,
                            ByVal culture As System.Globalization.
                            CultureInfo) As Object _
```

```vb
            Implements System.Windows.Data.
            IValueConverter.ConvertBack

    'If the type to send back to the source is Decimal or Decimal?
    If targetType Is GetType(Decimal) OrElse targetType _
            Is GetType(Nullable(Of Decimal)) Then

        Dim resultMoney As Decimal = Nothing

        'Checks if the input is not null
        If Decimal.TryParse(CStr(value), resultMoney) = True Then
            'in such case, it is returned
            Return CDec(value)
            'if it is empty, returns Nothing
        ElseIf value.ToString = String.Empty Then
            Return Nothing
        Else
            'If it is not empty but invalid,
            'returns a default value
            Return 0D
        End If
    End If


    Return value
End Function
```

It is worth mentioning that you need to provide conversion for nullable types, as in the preceding code, if you work against an Entity Data Model (EDM). If your user interface presents data but does not receive input from the user, you can implement `ConvertBack` by putting a `Throw New NotImplementedException` as the method body. The MSDN official documentation suggests an interesting best practice when implementing custom converters. This requires applying the `ValueConversion` attributes to the class; this attribute enables you to specify data types involved in the conversion, as in the following line that has to be applied to the `CustomConverter` class:

```vb
<ValueConversion(GetType(String), GetType(Decimal))>
```

The first attribute's argument is the type you need to convert from, and the second one is the type you need to convert to. Custom converters must be applied at XAML level. This requires first adding an XML namespace pointing to the current assembly that defines the class. For the previous example, add the following namespace declaration within the `Window` element definition, taking care to replace the `IntroducingDataBinding` name with the name of your assembly (IntelliSense will help you choose):

```xml
xmlns:local="clr-namespace:IntroducingDataBinding"
```

When you have a reference to the assembly, which can be useful for utilizing other classes at the XAML level, you need to declare a new resource that points to the custom converter. Within the `Window.Resources` element, add the following line:

```
<local:CustomConverter x:Key="customConverter"/>
```

Now that the converter has an identifier and can be used at the XAML level, you pass it to the bound property you want to convert. For example, suppose you want to format and convert the `Freight` property from the `Order` class. The following code demonstrates how to apply the converter:

```
<TextBox Grid.Column="1" Grid.Row="7" Height="23"
        HorizontalAlignment="Left" Margin="3"
        Name="FreightTextBox"
        Text="{Binding Path=Freight,
            Converter={StaticResource customConverter},
            ConverterParameter='\{0:c\}'}"
        VerticalAlignment="Center" Width="120" />
```

You pass the converter identifier to the `Converter` property of the `Binding` markup extension. The `ConverterParameter` receives the conversion value, which are the same in Table 32.3. If you run the application, you get the result shown in Figure 32.9—the difference is that with custom converters you can control how the conversion and formatting processes behave.

Summary

The data-binding is a key concept in every kind of application, and this is true for WPF, too. In the first part of this chapter, you learned how to apply data-binding to simple controls with the `Binding` markup extension in XAML code, to bind some properties to the value of other controls or to a .NET data source. For this, you got an overview of the `DataGrid` control and of the `ObservableCollection(Of T)` generic class (which you already studied), this time applied to WPF. You found out how the `DataGrid` supports the two-way data-binding also due to the underlying support for the technique offered by the `ObservableCollection`. In the second part of the chapter, we covered the drag'n'drop data-binding and how easily you can create data forms. After this discussion, the `StringFormat` and `IValueConverter` objects were presented for formatting and converting objects to and from `string`. There is much more to say about data access in WPF, but it is beyond the scope here. The next chapter is the last one on WPF and is related to another important topic: localization.

CHAPTER 33

Localizing Applications

Limiting applications' user interfaces (UIs) to just one language means limiting your business. If you want to increase the possibilities of your applications being sold worldwide, you need to consider creating user interfaces that support multiple languages and the culture specifications of your users. Of course, you can give users the option to select the desired language or provide localized interfaces for a particular country, but the main concept is that localization is a common requirement in modern applications. The .NET Framework helps developers in localizing applications with several kinds of resources. In this chapter, you learn how to localize desktop applications and explore Windows Forms and WPF applications to understand the fundamentals of localization in both technologies. Specific techniques are available for web, Windows Phone, and Windows 8 Store applications, but these are beyond the scope of this book.

AVAILABLE TECHNIQUES

Localizing applications is something that you can accomplish in several ways in both Windows Forms and WPF. This chapter discusses the most commonly used techniques—just remember that they are not the only ones.

Introducing .NET Localization

The .NET Framework provides the infrastructure for application localization via the `System.Globalization` namespace. The most important class in this namespace is the `CultureInfo` class that allows getting or setting information on the current application culture or on new

custom settings. This class works with the `System.Threading.Thread.CurrentThread`
class that provides access to the thread representing your executable and that exposes
the `CurrentCulture` and `CurrentUICulture` properties you can assign with a `CultureInfo`
object. The following code demonstrates how to get information on the current thread
culture and how to set a new `CultureInfo`:

```
'Requires an Imports System.Globalization directive


'Gets the current culture and shows information
Dim culture As CultureInfo = System.Threading.Thread.
                            CurrentThread.CurrentCulture
Console.WriteLine(culture.DisplayName)


'Creates an instance of the CUltureInfo class
'based on the Italian culture and sets it as
'the current culture
Dim customCulture As New CultureInfo("it-IT")
System.Threading.Thread.CurrentThread.
      CurrentCulture = customCulture
```

The `CultureInfo` class provides lots of properties that enable applications to adhere to the
required culture specifications. For example, `DisplayName` shows the name of the culture
as it appears on the system, `DateTimeFormat` specifies the appropriate format for date and
time in the specified culture, and `NumberFormat` provides specifications on how numbers
and percentage need to be formatted in the specified culture. In this chapter you learn
how to localize smart client applications, thus Windows Forms and WPF.

Windows Forms Localization

WHY WINDOWS FORMS?

As for other code examples provided throughout the book, even if Windows Forms is no
longer explained, localization is discussed because such a platform is still popular and
common to have to maintain in the industry.

If you are an experienced Windows Forms developer, maybe you already faced the localization problem with this technology. There are different ways for localizing a Windows
Forms application, but basically all of them rely on managed resources. The easiest way
for localizing a Windows Forms application is to use the Visual Studio Designer so that
the IDE generates the appropriate resources files for you. An example is the best way for
providing explanations; the goal of this example is to localize a Windows Forms application in both English and Italian. Run Visual Studio 2012, create a new Windows Forms
project with Visual Basic 2012, and name it **WindowsFormsLocalization**. Follow
these steps:

1. Drag a `Button` from the toolbox onto the new form surface, and set its `Text` property as `Localized button`.

2. Drag a `Label` from the toolbox onto the new form surface, and set its `Text` property as `Localized label`.

3. Select the form, and in the Properties window, set its `Localizable` property as `True`; then set its `Language` property as `Italian`.

4. Select the `Button` and set its `Text` property as `Pulsante localizzato` (in Italian).

5. Select the `Label` and set its `Text` property as `Etichetta localizzata`.

6. Build the project and enable the **Show All Files** view in Solution Explorer.

Visual Studio has now generated a new **it-IT** subfolder under Bin\Debug (or Bin\Release) containing a satellite assembly where localized resources are stored. Moreover, Visual Studio generated a new localized resources file for the current form named Form1.it-IT. resx, storing the localized information for design time. If you try to run the application, you notice that it is still localized in English. This is because you need to explicitly assign the new localized culture in code. You can do this by adding the following code (which requires an `Imports System.Globalization` directive) at the beginning of the application startup, which is typically the constructor, before the `InitializeMethod` is invoked:

```
Public Sub New()

    With Threading.Thread.CurrentThread
        .CurrentUICulture = New CultureInfo("it-IT")
        .CurrentCulture = New CultureInfo("it-IT")
    End With
    ' This call is required by the designer.
    InitializeComponent()

    ' Add any initialization after the InitializeComponent() call.

End Sub
```

The code assigns to the current thread the new culture information that will be retrieved from the related subfolder and satellite assembly. Figure 33.1 shows how the application looks with localized controls.

Localizing Windows Forms applications is an easy task because you can use the Visual Studio Designer. Unfortunately, this is not the same in WPF applications, where a number of manual steps are required, as explained in the next section.

FIGURE 33.1   The localized Windows Forms application in action.

WPF Localization

In WPF, the localization process is also based on resources but with different steps. Also, there are some alternative techniques for accomplishing localization, but we cover only the most common.

NOTE ON INSTALLED CULTURE

The code examples shown in this section assume that your system's regional settings are based on the en-US (English-United States) culture. If your system is based on different regional settings, replace en-US with the culture information that suits your system.

When you compile a WPF project, the XAML code is parsed into a more efficient file format known as Binary Application Markup Language (BAML). Each BAML file represents a resource that is then linked into the executable storing all resources. To localize a WPF application, you need to localize BAML objects and put the result in a satellite assembly. This is accomplished using a command-line tool named LocBaml.exe, which is available for free from the MSDN. It is distributed as C# source code, so you need to open it inside Visual Studio and compile it. At the time this chapter is being written, LocBaml source code is available for .NET Framework versions prior to 4.5. Thus, in order to make it work with the next examples, you need to perform some steps that are described in the next subsection.

LOCBAML FOR .NET 4.5

You can check for the availability of a new version of LocBaml targeting .NET 4.5 at the following address: http://msdn.microsoft.com/en-us/library/ms771568(VS.110).aspx. When Microsoft makes it available, you can skip the next section and go to the "Localizing a WPF Application" section.

Preparing the LocBaml Tool

Until a new version of LocBaml is available for .NET 4.5, you can download version 4.0 and upgrade it manually. To accomplish this, follow these steps:

1. If not installed, install Visual C# on your machine (the Express Edition is also supported).

2. Download the LocBaml source code from this address: http://go.microsoft.com/fwlink/?LinkID=160016

3. Uncompress the downloaded archive into any folder you like.

4. Start Visual Studio 2012 and create a new Console Application with Visual C#, naming the project as LocBaml.

5. Save the new project into a different folder than the downloaded source code.

6. Remove the Program.cs and AssemblyInfo.cs code file from the project. Notice that the second file is just a duplicate of the one generated by the IDE and so can be safely removed.

7. Using the **Project, Add Existing Item** command, add all the code files (with .cs extension) from the downloaded source code folder to the current project folder.

8. Add a reference to the following assemblies: WindowsBase.dll, PresentationCore.dll, and PresentationFramework.dll

9. In the new project, add a folder named Resources and add to this new folder the StringTable.resText file, which you can pick from the same-named folder of the original LocBaml code.

10. After you've added the file, open the Properties window and set the Build Action property as **Embedded Resource**.

11. Open the LocBaml.csproj project file with the Windows Notepad and add the following lines (if not already available) within an `ItemGroup` node:

```
<EmbeddedResource Include="Resources\StringTable.resText">
  <LogicalName>Resources.StringTable.resources</LogicalName>
</EmbeddedResource>
```

12. In Solution Explorer, click Properties and ensure that the BamlLocalization.LocBaml is set as the startup object in the Application tab.

Now build the project. At this point you have a new version of LocBaml.exe that targets the .NET Framework 4.5.

Localizing a WPF Application

When you have completed the steps required to prepare LocBaml, imagine you want to create a localized version for the Italian culture of a WPF application based on English as the primary culture. Create a new WPF project with Visual Basic and name it as

WpfLocalization, and add the code shown in Listing 33.1 on the XAML side. The goal is to provide a WPF counterpart of the Windows Forms example shown in the previous section.

LISTING 33.1   Preparing the User Interface Before Localization

```
<Window x:Class="MainWindow"
    xmlns="http://schemas.microsoft.com/winfx/2006/xaml/presentation"
    xmlns:x="http://schemas.microsoft.com/winfx/2006/xaml"
    Title="MainWindow" Height="350" Width="525">
    <StackPanel>
        <Button Name="Button1" Width="100" Margin="5"
                Height="40" Content="Localized button"/>
        <TextBlock Text="Localized text"
                Margin="5"
                Name="TextBlock1"/>
    </StackPanel>
</Window>
```

The first step required to localize a WPF application is to specify the neutral-language specification at assembly level. Click the **Show All Files** button in Solution Explorer, expand **My Project**, and double-click **AssemblyInfo.vb**; finally uncomment the following line of code:

```
<Assembly: NeutralResourcesLanguage("en-US",
        UltimateResourceFallbackLocation.Satellite)>
```

This is required because the application looks for localization resources inside external satellite assemblies, and at least one culture must be provided as neutral. This is the culture you are writing code with. The next step is to open the project file, thus click the **File, Open, File** command and browse the project folder; then open the **WpfLocalization. vbproj** file. At this point you need to add the following line of XML markup inside one of the PropertyGroup items:

```
<UICulture>en-US</UICulture>
```

This works with the neutral language specification and ensures that a satellite assembly for current culture resources will be generated. The successive step is marking UI elements in XAML as localizable. This is accomplished by adding an x:Uid attribute to each localizable member, assigning an identifier equal or similar to the element name. This task can be accomplished manually but can be difficult if you have a lot of elements to mark as localizable, so the most common option is running the **MSBuild** compiler that automates this for you. Save the project, and then open a command prompt pointing to the project folder. Next, write the following command lines after the exact sequence shown:

```
msbuild /t:updateuid WpfLocalization.vbproj
msbuild /t:checkuid WpfLocalization.vbproj
```

The first command line adds an `x:Uid` attribute to each UI element possible (`updateuid`), whereas the second one performs a check to verify that all localizable members have an `x:Uid`. When MSBuild completes, you notice how visual elements have been marked as localizable, as shown in Listing 33.2.

LISTING 33.2   The XAML Code Marked as Localizable by MsBuild

```
<Window x:Uid="Window_1" x:Class="MainWindow"
    xmlns="http://schemas.microsoft.com/winfx/2006/xaml/presentation"
    xmlns:x="http://schemas.microsoft.com/winfx/2006/xaml"
    Title="MainWindow" Height="350" Width="525">
    <StackPanel x:Uid="StackPanel_1">
        <Button x:Uid="LocalizedButton" Name="LocalizedButton" Margin="5"
                Width="140" Height="40"
                Content="Localized button"/>
        <TextBlock x:Uid="LocalizedTextBlock" Name="LocalizedTextBlock" Margin="5"
                Text="Localized text"/>
    </StackPanel>
</Window>
```

Now build the project again in Visual Studio. You now notice that the project output folder (Bin\Debug or Bin\Release) contains a new subfolder named **en-US**, which contains a WpfLocalization.Resources.dll satellite assembly with localized resources for the en-US culture. The goal now is to create a similar folder/assembly structure per culture. In this case, you see how to create a localized satellite assembly for the Italian culture, but you can replace it with a different one. A subsequent step requires invoking LocBaml. The need is to extract resources information and edit the information with localized ones. The following command line parses the neutral-language resources and creates an editable .CSV file in which you can place custom information:

```
LocBaml.exe /parse en-US\WpfLocalization.resources.dll /out:WpfLocalization.csv
```

When ready, open the generated WpfLocalization.csv file with an appropriate editor, such as Microsoft Excel or Visual Studio. Figure 33.2 shows how the contents of the file appear in Microsoft Excel.

If you inspect the contents of the file, you'll notice the content of UI elements. For example, row 2 contains the `Window` title, row 9 contains the `Button` text as the last word, and row 12 contains the `TextBlock` text. Now you need to replace the original values with new ones. Continuing the example of the Italian localization, perform the following replacements:

▶ In row 2, replace `MainWindow` with `Finestra principale`.

▶ In row 9, replace `Localized button` with `Pulsante localizzato`.

▶ In row 12, replace `Localized text` with `Testo localizzato`.

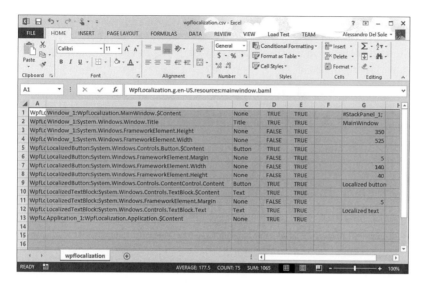

FIGURE 33.2   The extracted resources information opened in Excel.

Figure 33.3 shows the file after edits.

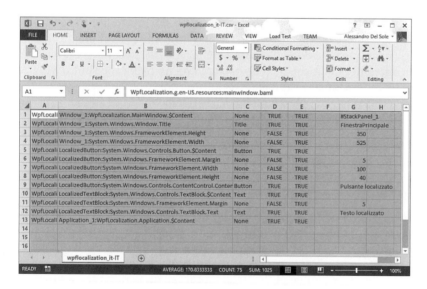

FIGURE 33.3   Resources information is edited for localization.

Now save the file with a different name—for example, **WpfLocalization_it-IT.csv**.
When done, manually create a new directory where the new localized resources will be
published; then create a folder named **it-IT** inside the same folder of en-US. You still
need to invoke LocBaml to build the localized satellite assembly, so write the following
command line:

```
LocBaml.exe /generate en-US\WpfLocalization.resources.dll /trans: WpfLocalization
_it-IT.csv /out:c:\ /cul:it-IT
```

The `/generate` option tells LocBaml to generate a new satellite assembly, translating
(`/trans`) the specified .csv file into the desired culture (`/cul`). The `/out` option enables
you to specify the target directory that in this example is the hard drive root folder. When
ready, move the newly generated WpfLocalization.resources.dll assembly from C:\ into
the it-IT subfolder you created before. The last step is to initialize the desired culture information at the application startup. In Application.xaml.vb provide a constructor as follows:

```
Imports System.Globalization
Imports System.Threading


Class Application


    Public Sub New()
        Thread.CurrentThread.CurrentUICulture = _
            New CultureInfo("it-IT")
        Thread.CurrentThread.CurrentCulture = _
            New CultureInfo("it-IT")
    End Sub
End Class
```

This is different from Windows Forms because in WPF the Application class is the actual
application entry point. If you now run the application, you get the result shown in
Figure 33.4, where you can see how UI elements have been localized.

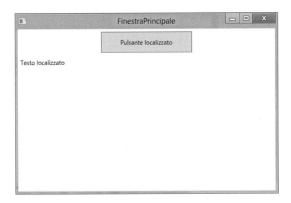

FIGURE 33.4   Localized UI elements in the WPF sample application.

Summary

In this chapter we covered localization; first we discussed information on how the .NET Framework provides objects for application localization at a general level. Next, the discussion focused on Windows Forms applications localization, using the Visual Studio Designer and managed resources files. Finally, you learned how localization works in WPF applications and how a number of manual steps are required, such as adding the neutral-language resource and culture information to the project file, running MSBuild to mark visual elements as localizable, and running LocBaml to generate satellite resources assemblies.

CHAPTER 34

Building ASP.NET Web Applications

Many of the most common activities in everyday life are often performed via the Internet and websites. You book a flight via airline companies' websites; you buy tickets for the theater via ticketing websites; and you can pay your bills via your bank's website. Also, most companies (and probably yours, too) have local networks running internal web applications for several kinds of purposes, such as office automation, storing data, and so on. Being a complete technology, the .NET Framework offers its own web platform for developing websites based on .NET, which is named ASP.NET. This is an engine for websites running on the server side, which enables building robust web applications using managed code. Even though several technologies came out in the past years for building web applications, including Microsoft platforms, this is still the most valid choice. In this chapter you start with the ASP. NET programming model and build web applications with Visual Basic 2012, also leveraging some of the new features typical of ASP.NET 4.5.

Introducing the ASP.NET Model

So far, we've discussed several kinds of client applications, such as Console, Windows Forms, and WPF. For this last technology, the discussion was deeper because WPF is the premier technology for building desktop clients. Developing web applications for ASP.NET with Visual Basic 2012 is different. If you are a web developer, this chapter will probably just be an overview of some new features introduced by .NET 4.5. However, if you are new to ASP.NET, although you can find lots of similarities with the client world in writing managed code and creating applications, the code in the web environment runs differently. So you need to under-stand where the code is running and why scaling applications is fundamental; therefore, you also need to understand the concept of the stateless nature of the Web so you can handle it in your applications. This is discussed next.

Understanding Page Requests

When you create a web application, the application will be hosted on a web server. This is the place where your Visual Basic compiled code actually resides. When the code is executed, the ASP.NET engine renders it as HTML so it can be consumed on the client side by a web browser such as Internet Explorer or Firefox, which can interpret Hypertext Markup Language (HTML) and display web pages. When you type a website address into your browser, it sends a web page request. This is then translated into an address that searches for the server hosting the requested page. When the server receives the request, the installed web server software catches the request and, if this is about an ASP.NET web page, passes the request to the ASP.NET engine so this can render the result as HTML and return it to the calling browser. Samples of web server software include Internet Information Services (IIS) and the Cassini Web Server. Visual Studio 2012 ships with its own two web servers: IIS Express and the ASP.NET Development Server. Both of these enable you to simulate a web server environment on the development machine for testing applications. The default option is IIS Express, but you can select a different server in the project's properties.

One key point is that you do not only write HTML markup; instead, you also write Visual Basic code that is compiled into an assembly residing on the server. So the ASP.NET engine sends requests to your code for processing and then returns the processing result as HTML that can be consumed by client browsers. All these operations are fine, but there is a problem: In a desktop environment, you have one user running one instance of the application that works against its set of data and information; even if you have hundreds of database records to load, the application will be responsive in most cases. The same is not true for web applications if you think that one web application hosted on a server could potentially receive hundreds of concurrent requests. Therefore, elaborating hundreds of data requests concurrently can cause a bottleneck with hard performance problems. Fortunately, ASP.NET provides a mechanism for scalability that lets the application solve performance problems the best way possible.

Scalability and Performance

Scalability is the capability of an application to serve requests well without getting too slow or crashing when the amount of work increases. As described before, in a single-user environment such as desktop applications, scalability is a plus but not a requirement. But it is a requirement in a web environment, where multiple requests can come to a web page. Because you do not want your application to get too slow or to crash when a large number of simultaneous requests come in, you instead want requests to be served in a small amount of time. So, you need to be aware of scalability and performance. Luckily, ASP.NET has its own mechanism that serves for application scalability. Think of desktop applications for a moment: in such environment all the work is in memory, when you load data into variables. Variables are instances of managed objects that you release when no more are needed so that the garbage collection process frees up unused resources. In a web environment, this is not possible because the application resides on one server and serving a large number of requests would soon lead to out-of-memory errors. Thus, the mechanism of state management must be necessarily different. The following is the list of operations that occur against the code when ASP.NET receives a request:

1. ASP.NET creates an instance of the `Page` object, which is the web counterpart of `Form` and `Window`.

2. Because `Page` is a managed object, when ASP.NET processes the request, it releases the reference of the page instance.

3. The Garbage Collection process clears from the managed heap all objects that no longer have any reference, including released `Page` objects.

This is cool because, when an object completes its work, it is soon removed from memory, and this improves scalability. The problem is that if the object is no longer available, then data exposed by that object is also no longer available. This means that if the same user sends another request to the same page (that is, creating a new instance of the `Page` object), the page will result empty. This occurs frequently, if you think of web pages that require filling in some fields before they make available other controls that require the page to be reloaded. So, this is the reason ASP.NET needs a different state management, which is provided by the `Application` and `Session` state objects that will be discussed later.

Another problem that travels hand-in-hand with scalability is performance. Each time you send a page request, you have to wait a few seconds. This is normal because sending the request takes time and waiting for the server to respond also takes time. Plus, elaborating complex data requires additional time because the number of bytes to transfer is increased. With complex web applications, performance can become a problem, but fortunately ASP.NET 4.5 includes a number of performance improvements such as (but not limited to) the following:

▶ **Multicore JIT compilation**—The .NET Framework 4.5 can use all the available processors to compile a website for the Just-In-Time compilation, so that this process becomes faster.

▶ **Optimized garbage collection for website hosting.**

▶ **Sharing common assemblies**—Multiple websites can share the same helper assemblies so that memory consumption is reduced.

▶ **Support for asynchronous requests based on the new Async/Await pattern**—See Chapter 44, "Asynchronous Programming," for more details.

You will not interact manually with the aforementioned improvements (except for asynchronous programming techniques), so they are not discussed further in this book. You now get started in getting some skills on ASP.NET that will also be useful when talking about Silverlight applications. The first step for acquiring such skills is starting to create your first web project with VB 2012.

Available Project Templates

Visual Studio 2012 offers a number of project templates for building ASP.NET web applications based on different frameworks. This chapter discusses the ASP.NET Web Forms model, which is the most important from a learning perspective. But the IDE also enables you to build applications based on the ASP.NET MVC (Model-View-Controller) framework, ASP.NET Ajax controls, and ASP.NET Dynamic Data Entities projects. It is not possible in this chapter to provide detailed information on each framework because they are all complex. To create web applications, you can either select File, New Project or select File, New Web Site. In the first case, you access the so-called web application templates, whereas in the second case you access website templates. Several differences exist between the two categories, but the major differences follow:

▶ A website template has no project file, whereas a web application has one. Choosing this second template brings more familiarity for other Visual Studio projects.

▶ A website template produces no compiled assemblies and requires the source code to be deployed, whereas a web application template allows building a compiled assembly and no source code is required.

▶ A website is simpler in its structure than a web application project template.

Due to their natures, this chapter shows examples based on the web application template. There are multiple templates for web projects, specific to particular scenarios. They are all available in the web folder of the New Project dialog box, as shown in Figure 34.1.

FIGURE 34.1   Web application project templates available with VB 2012.

The most basic project template is the ASP.NET Web Forms Application one. You can see templates dedicated to ASP.NET MVC and ASP.NET Dynamic Data applications, other than templates for building user controls. When building a complete working example later in this chapter, we use the ASP.NET Web Forms Application template that provides a skeleton of a web application with preconfigured pages. For the first experiments, create a new project based on the ASP.NET Empty Web Application. This generates a new empty project, where the first thing you have to do is add some pages. Pages in ASP.NET are represented by web forms.

Web Forms and Master Pages

ASP.NET web applications are made of pages. These can be standalone pages or ones providing common elements for each page. Standalone pages are known as *web forms*, while the other kind is known as a *master page*.

Web Forms

A web form represents a page in ASP.NET (a file with an .aspx extension) and is composed of markup code known as Extensible Hypertext Markup Language (XHTML) and of a code-behind part made of Visual Basic code. (XHTML is intended as an enhancement of classic HTML.) The concept is similar to the WPF development where the XAML code is for the user interface and the Visual Basic code makes the UI alive. The same is true for web forms, but the difference is that the UI is provided via XHTML code. The XHTML code in a web form contains markup for page layout, user controls, and eventually scripts. Each web application needs at least a Default.aspx page, so right-click the project name in Solution Explorer and select **Add New Item**. In the Add New Item dialog box, select the Web Form template, name it **Default.aspx**, and then click **OK**. When ready, the new page is made of some XHTML code. The following is the basic code of a web form, including a `Label` control for demonstrating some concepts:

```
<%@ Page Language="vb" AutoEventWireup="false"
        CodeBehind="Default.aspx.vb"
        Inherits="webApplication1._Default" %>

<!DOCTYPE html PUBLIC "-//W3C//DTD XHTML 1.0 Transitional//EN"
        "http://www.w3.org/TR/xhtml1/DTD/xhtml1-transitional.dtd">

<html xmlns="http://www.w3.org/1999/xhtml">
<head runat="server">
    <title></title>
</head>
<body>
    <form id="form1" runat="server">
    <div>
        <asp:Label ID="Label1" runat="server" Text="Label"></asp:Label>
```

```
    </div>
    </form>
</body>
</html>
```

The most important thing you need to remember is that code is executed on the server, so it is fundamentally adding a `runat="server"` attribute for each control; otherwise, it will not be correctly consumed by client browsers.

STYLING TIPS

ASP.NET enables you to style and apply themes to web forms via Cascade Style Sheets (CSS) files. A simpler way of styling controls is by selecting the `AutoFormat` option that's available when you click the smart tag.

Notice how the markup code contains classic HTML items that will be correctly rendered to client browsers. Each web form has a code-behind file, which you can find in Solution Explorer by enabling the Show All Files view and then expanding the desired web page file. When you double-click the Visual Basic code-behind file on a new web form, you can see that it is nothing but a class providing an event handler for the `Page.Load` event. As explained in the next subsection, a web form has a lifetime that is established by events.

Page Lifetime and Page Events

Each page has a lifetime that you need to understand so you can ensure changes you made through a postback are not ignored or overwritten. Page lifetime is articulated in events, each of them representing a particular moment. Although starting from ASP.NET 2.0 the `Page` class offers a bigger number of events, the most important are the following:

▶ `Init`, which is where the page initializes controls

▶ `Load`, which is when the page is loaded and you can play with controls

▶ `PreRender`, which occurs just before the page is rendered as HTML

Cached and Postback Events

Earlier in this chapter you learned that the biggest difference between the ASP.NET programming model and the client one is that in the ASP.NET development you cannot keep objects in memory and that, for scalability purposes, a page is reloaded each time you need to process some data. Reloading a page happens when you interact with controls on the page. Such controls raise events depending on the actions you took on them. These actions are divided into two categories: cached events and postback events. *Cached* events occur on controls that do not require an immediate page reload. The typical example is the `TextBox` control in which a `TextChanged` event is raised every time you edit the text but the page is not reloaded at each edit. *Postback* events occur on controls that cause an immediate page reload, such as `Button` and `ComboBox`. This is convenient because you expect immediate data processing when you click the `Button` or select a combo box item.

Cached events will also be elaborated at the page reload. Reloading a page means destroying the instance of the current page and then creating a new instance of the current page. This is good because you avoid overhead when working with big amounts of data, but the problem is that all objects and values held by the previous instance are lost, so you need a mechanism for restoring the original object values. This mechanism is typically the ViewState object that is covered later in more details; at the moment look at how you store an object value (such as the text stored in a TextBox) inside the ViewState before the page is reloaded at the Button click:

```
Protected Sub Page_Load(ByVal sender As Object,
                        ByVal e As System.EventArgs) _
                        Handles Me.Load
    If Not Page.IsPostBack Then
        Me.TextBox1.Text = CStr(Me.ViewState("MyText"))
    End If
End Sub

Protected Sub Button1_Click(ByVal sender As Object,
                            ByVal e As EventArgs) _
                            Handles Button1.Click
    Me.ViewState("MyText") = Me.TextBox1.Text
End Sub
```

The only situation when a postback event does not occur is when you open the website, meaning that the page is loaded for the first time. You can check whether the page is being loaded for the first time in the Page_Load event handler, where you read the value of the Page.IsPostBack property. If true, you can retrieve the content of the ViewState property to restore the original values.

TIP

If you use the ComboBox control, remember to set its AutoPostBack property as True so that it will cause a postback each time you select an item, when such behavior is desired.

Considering cached and postback events, the following is the updated list for the page lifetime:

1. Init

2. Load

3. Cached events

4. Postback events

5. PreRender

ASP.NET Controls

ASP.NET offers both server and HTML controls. Server controls run on the server side and emulate or are built upon existing HTML tags, but they provide more advanced features and usability. They also are object-oriented controls and support events, whereas HTML controls don't. Generally, HTML controls are more and more limited if compared to ASP. NET controls, although they can be still processed on the server by adding the usual `runat="server"` tag. The next sections list the most common controls from both types.

Server Controls

Server controls are typically user interface objects that users can use when running a web application on clients. You can notice that in most cases, ASP.NET server controls are counterparts of HTML controls but provide a fully object-oriented development environment and full support for managed code. Table 34.1 summarizes the most common server controls.

TABLE 34.1   Most Common Server Controls

Control	Description
AdRotator	Shows a series of advertisements.
BulletedList	Shows a bulleted list of items.
Button	A button that can be clicked.
Calendar	Provides a monthly calendar.
CheckBox	A check box control for Boolean check state.
CheckBoxList	A group of multiselection check boxes.
DataList	A drop-down list with database data.
DetailsView	Can show a single record of data.
DropDownList	A drop-down list enabling single selection.
FileUpload	Provides the capability of uploading files. ASP.NET 4.5 introduces the possibility of uploading multiple files in web browsers that support HTML5.
GridView	Enables tabular data representations.
HiddenField	Keeps data that will be hidden in the UI.
HyperLink	A hyperlink to open other websites.
Image	Shows a picture.
ImageButton	A button containing a picture instead of text.
ImageMap	Enables creating image regions that can be clicked.
Label	Enables presenting static text.
LinkButton	A button with hyperlink functionalities.
ListBox	Enables scrolling a list of items.
MultiView	Provides the capability of creating tabbed user interfaces.
Panel	A container for other controls.

Control	Description
RadioButton	A button with single option choice.
RadioButtonList	A group of radio button controls.
RangeValidator	Checks if the specified entry is between upper and lower bounds.
RequiredFieldValidator	Checks for the existence of an entry.
Substitution	A control that does not enable storing its content in cache.
Table	Enables presenting data within tables.
TextBox	A control that accepts text. In ASP.NET 4.5 its TextMode property supports HTML5's input types like email and datetime.
View	One item in a Multiview control.
Wizard	Enables creating wizards.
Xml	Provides combination between Xml and XSLT objects.

All controls in Table 34.1 are then rendered as their HTML equivalent so they can be consumed by web browsers.

NOTE

Server controls are not the only ones available. If you take a look at the Visual Studio toolbox, you notice the presence of different tabs. Remaining controls are typically data controls used for data-binding or navigation, validation, and login controls that will not necessarily be placed on the user interface.

HTML Controls

HTML controls in ASP.NET are representations of their classic HTML. Also, ASP.NET 4.5 introduces improvements to some controls for better HTML5 support. Table 34.2 summarizes the most common among available HTML controls.

WHAT IS HTML5?

You have probably heard a lot about HTML5 during the last couple of years, so you might be wondering what HTML5 actually is. It is the fifth version of the standard specifications of HTML, and it introduces some new rules that browsers will respect with particular regard to videos, audios, geolocation, JavaScript support for animation, media contents, and an information storage system called Web Storage that enables the local storing of more information than with cookies. Visual Studio 2012 and ASP.NET 4.5 support HTML5 in a number of ways, including IntelliSense improvements for JavaScript code and control enhancements. Your approach as a web developer will not change; you will only have new features and more powerful applications as web browsers will fully support the new HTML standard. Take a look at the World Wide Web Consortium (W3C) for updates about the HTML5 standard at http://www.w3.org/html.

TABLE 34.2   HTML Controls

Control	Description
HtmlAnchor	Allows accessing the `<a>` HTML element on the server
HtmlButton	A button that can be clicked
HtmlForm	A form control
HtmlGenericControl	An element that cannot be mapped to any specific HTML control
Image	A control showing a picture
HtmlInputButton	Expects input via a button
HtmlInputCheckBox	Expects input via a Checkbox
HtmlInputFile	Expects input from a file
HtmlInputHidden	Hides its content
HtmlInputImage	Expects an image as the input
HtmlInputRadioButton	Expects input via a RadioButton
HtmlInputText	Expects input via some text
HtmlTable	Represents a table
HtmlTableCell	Represents a cell within a table
HtmlTableRow	Represents a row within a table
HtmlTextArea	Represents an area of text

The main difference between HTML controls and their ASP.NET counterparts is that ASP.
NET versions can be accessed on the server side with managed code by adding an ID attribute and the `runat="server"` attribute, although HTML controls actually work on the
server side. It is worth mentioning that, with ASP.NET 4.5, those HTML controls having a
URL property now support `runat="server"`.

Handling Events

Due to the code-behind logic, handling events in ASP.NET applications looks similar to
what you saw with WPF. This means that a user control is implemented on the XHTML
side and an event handler in the Visual Basic side.

HANDLING EVENTS TIP

If you need to catch events from objects that are not user controls, such as business
objects or collections, you just write the event handler in Visual Basic code the usual way.

For example, consider the following XHTML code that provides a Button and a Label:

```
<form id="form1" runat="server">
<div>
    <asp:Button ID="Button1" runat="server" Text="Button"/>
```

```
    <asp:Label ID="Label1" runat="server"></asp:Label>
</div>
</form>
```

You can handle the `Button.Click` as usual—for example, with the following code that writes a message to the `Label`:

```
Protected Sub Button1_Click(ByVal sender As Object,
                            ByVal e As EventArgs) Handles Button1.Click
    Me.Label1.Text = "You clicked!"
End Sub
```

Notice that you can also specify the event handler in the XHTML code, avoiding the `Handles` clause on the VB side, exactly as in WPF. The `Click` event handler is specified with the `OnClick` attribute:

```
<asp:Button ID="Button1" runat="server" Text="Button"
OnClick="Button1_Click" />
```

And then you write the event handler without `Handles`:

```
Protected Sub Button1_Click(ByVal sender As Object,
                            ByVal e As EventArgs)
    Me.Label1.Text = "You clicked!"
End Sub
```

Understanding State Management

As I told you at the beginning of this chapter, ASP.NET applications have to manage their states in a different way than client applications. State is managed via some special objects: `Application`, `Cache`, `Context`, `Session`, and `ViewState`. All of them work with the `Object` type, and you use them like dictionaries because they accept key/value pairs. The next subsections explain this and provide examples.

The `Application` State

One of the most common situations with websites is that you have many people using the website concurrently. If you want to hold shared information across all the application instances, you use the `Application` state. The following is an example:

```
Application("SharedKey") = "Shared value"

Dim sharedString As String = CStr(Application("SharedKey"))
```

Notice the key/value semantics and how you need to perform an explicit conversion from `Object` to `String`. You will not use `Application` often because each application instance runs on a separate thread that could modify the information and therefore could corrupt the values, too.

The Cache State

The ASP.NET Cache has the same scope of Application, meaning that both can be accessed by all page requests. The primary difference is that Cache enables holding information in memory, which avoids the need of re-creating and retrieving objects. This is good if you want to maintain updatable objects but could cause overhead (always considering that the bigger the amount of data to transfer, the lower the performance) because it requires memory. So, it should be used only when needed or when you ensure that performance is acceptable. The following is an example of storing and retrieving information with Cache:

```
Cache("MyUpdatableDataKey") = "My updatable data"
Dim myUpdatableData As String = CStr(Cache("MyUpdatableDataKey"))
```

In addition, an alternative way for adding objects to the cache is the Cache.Add method. It provides the ability of setting advanced settings for the object, as demonstrated in this code:

```
Protected Sub Page_Load(ByVal sender As Object,
                        ByVal e As System.EventArgs) _
                        Handles Me.Load

    Dim callBack As New CacheItemRemovedCallback( _
        AddressOf Cache_ItemRemoved)

    'Sets the key, adds the data, sets the CacheDependency,
    'sets the expiration mode, expiration time, priority
    'and delegate to invoke when the item is removed
    Cache.Add("MyUpdatableDataKey", "My updatable data", Nothing,
            Cache.NoAbsoluteExpiration, New TimeSpan(0, 0, 45),
            CacheItemPriority.High, callBack)

    'Removes the item
    Cache.Remove("MyUpdatableDataKey")
End Sub

Private Sub Cache_ItemRemoved(ByVal key As String,
                             ByVal item As Object,
                             ByVal reason As CacheItemRemovedReason)
    'The item has been removed
End Sub
```

The most interesting settings are the expiration mode and the priority. The first one can be Cache.NoAbsoluteExpiration (like in the preceding code), which means that the data will always be available during the page lifetime Cache.SlidingExpiration, on the other hand, means that the data will be removed after it is not accessed for the specified amount of time. Priority is also important in case you have lots of objects in memory and ASP.NET is about to encounter out-of-memory problems. At this point, ASP.NET begins evicting items according to their priority. (An object with lower priority is evicted before another one with high priority.)

The `Context` State

You use the `Context` state when you want to hold state only for the lifetime of a single request. This is useful when you need to have information in memory for a long period of time and need to ensure that keeping such information does not affect scalability. This is an example:

```
Context.Items("MyStringKey") = "My string value"
Dim contextString As String = CStr(Context.Items("MyStringKey"))
```

The context information is accessed at the page level and will not be available again on the next request.

Using Cookies for Saving Information

Cookies are pieces of information that a user's browser can hold and that can have a maximum size of 4 Kbytes. Each time the browser opens your web application, it recalls all cookies provided by the website. The following are examples of writing and reading cookies:

```
'Write a cookie
Dim aCookie As New HttpCookie("MyCookie")
aCookie.Value = "Information to store"
aCookie.Expires = New DateTime(10, 10, 2010)
Response.Cookies.Add(aCookie)


'Read a cookie
Dim getCookie As HttpCookie = Request.Cookies("MyCookie")
Dim cookieVale As String = getCookie.Value
```

Notice that the `Expires` property of type `Date` is required to specify that the cookie information will no longer be valid after that date, whereas the `Value` property is of type `String` so that you can store information without conversions.

The `Session` State

ASP.NET provides the ability of holding per-user information via the `Session` object. When a user opens the website, ASP.NET creates a cookie with a session identifier and then manages the session for that user based on the ID. The only issue is that you have no way of knowing when the user leaves the website, so a `Session` state expires after 20 minutes as a default. The following is an example:

```
Session("MyKey") = "User level information"
Dim userInfo As String = CStr(Session("MyKey"))
```

The `ViewState` State

To provide support for the work that a page needs to do in its lifetime, ASP.NET provides a mechanism known as `ViewState`. It provides the infrastructure that serializes values for each control in the page. For example, when a page is rendered, a control has a particular value. When this value changes, and such change raises an event, ASP.NET makes a comparison between the `ViewState` and form variables so that it can update the control value. (The `TextBox` control with its `TextChanged` event is the most common example.) Such a mechanism is available behind the scenes, but you can also use the `ViewState` by yourself. The following is an example that makes an object available at page level:

```
ViewState("MyPageDataKey") = "Page-level information"
Dim myPageData As String = CStr(ViewState("MyPageDataKey"))
```

Making this information available at the page level means also making it available when the page is posted back, but that decreases performance because the size of bytes to transfer is bigger. Excluding the user controls necessary to your web form, you should use `ViewState` for your needs with care.

Creating a Web Application with VB 2012 with Navigation and Data-Binding

Visual Basic 2012 makes it easy to create web applications with navigation capabilities because the Web Forms Application project template provides a master page implementation with default pages and designer tools for adding further elements. If you want to create a data-centric web application, the .NET Framework 4.5 offers specific controls that enable you to supply a data source and data-binding capabilities with a few mouse clicks. This section shows you how to reach this objective. Select **File, New Project** and from the web projects folder, select the **ASP.NET Web Forms Application** template; name the new project **NorthwindOrders**, and then click **OK**. When the project is available in Solution Explorer, notice the presence of some web pages (Default.aspx and About.aspx) and of the master page (the Site.Master file). Now click the **Site.Master** file. You now see the simplest example of a master page, as shown in Figure 34.2.

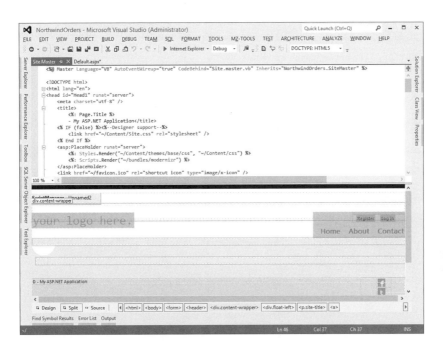

FIGURE 34.2   The default master page for the new web application.

Master Pages

A master page is a special page with .master extension, which provides a template containing a set of common elements for each page in the application. A master page typically contains elements such as headers, footers, and navigation elements so that you can implement a number of elements that each page can contain all at once. Visual Studio provides a specific item template for creating a master page, but the simplest way to understand how it works is to examine a basic one. When you create a new project using the ASP.NET Web Forms Application template, such as in the current example, the IDE adds a master page for you. As you can see, Visual Studio implements by default a couple of links for navigating between pages, such as Home and About. Both links have related web pages in the project, which are Default.aspx and About.aspx. Also notice the Login link that points to a Login.aspx page stored in the Account folder, which also contains other autogenerated pages for registering to the web application and for password management. The most basic code for designing a master page is the following:

```
<%@ Master Language="VB" AutoEventWireup="true" CodeBehind="Site.master.vb"
Inherits="NorthwindOrders.SiteMaster" %>

<!DOCTYPE html>
<html lang="en">
<head id="Head1" runat="server">
    <meta charset="utf-8" />
```

```
    <title>
        <%: Page.Title %>
        - My ASP.NET Application</title>
    <% IF (false) %><%--Designer support--%>
        <link href="~/Content/Site.css" rel="stylesheet" />
    <% End If %>
    <asp:PlaceHolder runat="server">
        <%: Styles.Render("~/Content/themes/base/css", "~/Content/css") %>
        <%: Scripts.Render("~/bundles/modernizr") %>
    </asp:PlaceHolder>
    <link href="~/favicon.ico" rel="shortcut icon" type="image/x-icon" />
    <meta name="viewport" content="width=device-width" />
    <asp:ContentPlaceHolder runat="server" ID="HeadContent" />
</head>
<body>
    <form runat="server">
    <asp:ScriptManager runat="server" AjaxFrameworkMode="Explicit">
        <Scripts>
            <asp:ScriptReference Name="MsAjaxBundle" />
            <asp:ScriptReference Name="jquery" />
            <asp:ScriptReference Name="jquery.ui.combined" />
            <asp:ScriptReference Name="webForms.js" Assembly="System.web"
➡Path="~/Scripts/webForms/webForms.js" />
            <asp:ScriptReference Name="webUIValidation.js" Assembly="System.web"
➡Path="~/Scripts/webForms/webUIValidation.js" />
            <asp:ScriptReference Name="MenuStandards.js" Assembly="System.web"
➡Path="~/Scripts/webForms/MenuStandards.js" />
            <asp:ScriptReference Name="GridView.js" Assembly="System.web"
➡Path="~/Scripts/webForms/GridView.js" />
            <asp:ScriptReference Name="DetailsView.js" Assembly="System.web"
➡Path="~/Scripts/webForms/DetailsView.js" />
            <asp:ScriptReference Name="TreeView.js" Assembly="System.web"
➡Path="~/Scripts/webForms/TreeView.js" />
            <asp:ScriptReference Name="webParts.js" Assembly="System.web"
➡Path="~/Scripts/webForms/webParts.js" />
            <asp:ScriptReference Name="Focus.js" Assembly="System.web"
➡Path="~/Scripts/webForms/Focus.js" />
            <asp:ScriptReference Name="webFormsBundle" />
        </Scripts>
    </asp:ScriptManager>
    <header>
        <div class="content-wrapper">
            <div class="float-left">
                <p class="site-title">
                    <a runat="server" href="~/">your logo here.</a></p>
            </div>
```

```
            <div class="float-right">
                <section id="login">
                    <asp:LoginView runat="server" ViewStateMode="Disabled">
                        <AnonymousTemplate>
                            <ul>
                                <li><a id="registerLink" runat="server"
➥href="~/Account/Register.aspx">Register</a></li>
                                <li><a id="loginLink" runat="server"
➥href="~/Account/Login.aspx">Log in</a></li>
                            </ul>
                        </AnonymousTemplate>
                        <LoggedInTemplate>
                            <p>
                                Hello, <a runat="server" class="username"
➥href="~/Account/ChangePassword.aspx" title="Change password">
                                    <asp:LoginName runat="server"
➥CssClass="username" />
                                </a>!
                                <asp:LoginStatus runat="server"
➥LogoutAction="Redirect" LogoutText="Log off" LogoutPageUrl="~/" />
                            </p>
                        </LoggedInTemplate>
                    </asp:LoginView>
                </section>
                <nav>
                    <ul id="menu">
                        <li><a runat="server" href="~/">Home</a></li>
                        <li><a runat="server" href="~/About.aspx">About</a></li>
                        <li><a runat="server" href="~/Contact.aspx">Contact</a></li>
                    </ul>
                </nav>
            </div>
        </div>
    </header>
    <div id="body">
        <asp:ContentPlaceHolder runat="server" ID="FeaturedContent" />
        <section class="content-wrapper main-content clear-fix">
            <asp:ContentPlaceHolder runat="server" ID="MainContent" />
        </section>
    </div>
    <footer>
        <div class="content-wrapper">
            <div class="float-left">
                <p>
                    &copy;
```

34

```
                <%: DateTime.Now.Year %>
                - My ASP.NET Application
            </p>
        </div>
        <div class="float-right">
            <ul id="social">
                <li><a href="http://facebook.com" class="facebook">Facebook
➥</a></li>
                <li><a href="http://twitter.com" class="twitter">Twitter</a>
➥</li>
            </ul>
        </div>
    </div>
    </footer>
    </form>
</body>
</html>
```

Notice how, unlike in the past, the template now includes shortcuts to social networks such as Twitter and Facebook, which you will want to replace with links to your (or your company's) online profiles. The goal of the sample application is fetching the list of orders from the Northwind database, showing the list in a `GridView` control (with editing capabilities), and adding navigation features to the master page. So, in the next section you see how to add the data source and data-bound controls. ASP.NET 4.5 introduces new, interesting features to work with data, so at the end of this discussion you will also get some hints about strongly typed data controls *and* model binding.

Adding the Data Model

The first thing to add in the web project is the data source. This can be of different kinds—for example, both LINQ to SQL classes and Entity Data Models are supported. The example will be based on the Entity Framework, thus you should add a new entity data model named Northwind.edmx and add to the model the Orders table from the database. Such steps have been described a lot of times in this book (refer to Chapter 26, "Introducing ADO.NET Entity Framework," for a full discussion), so we will not show them again in detail. When you have the data, you need a place for presenting and editing the data, so you need a new web form.

Adding a New Web Form

To add a new web form to the project, right-click the project name in Solution Explorer and select **Add New Item**. When the same-named dialog box appears, click the **Web** folder. Among all available items, you see options to add a Web Form (which is just a web page) or a Web Form Using Master Page. This second template is useful if you want to show the new page within a master page, unlike the first template which is instead for free pages. Select the second template so that we can link the new page to the master page, and name the new page **Orders.aspx** (see Figure 34.3); then click **OK**.

FIGURE 34.3   Adding a new web form using a master page.

At this point, Visual Studio asks you to indicate a master page from the project to link the new web form. In our case only one master page is available, so select it on the right side of the dialog box, as shown in Figure 34.4.

FIGURE 34.4   Specifying the master page to be associated to the new web form.

If you now double-click the **Orders.aspx** page, you get a new empty page linked to the master page, thus having navigation features. Now that we have a page, we can bind it to the data source.

Adding Data Controls

ASP.NET 4.5 offers a number of data controls that can be used to bind a data source to user controls and that act like a bridge. In particular, a control called `EntityDataSource` enables binding an entity data model to a graphic control.

ENABLING THE DESIGNER

By default, Visual Studio shows the HTML code for the pages. To enable the Visual Studio designer, click the Design button for switching to the full designer view or the Split button to get both the designer and the HTML code on the same view.

In the toolbox, expand the Data tab and drag the `EntityDataSource` control onto the Orders page until you get the result shown in Figure 34.5.

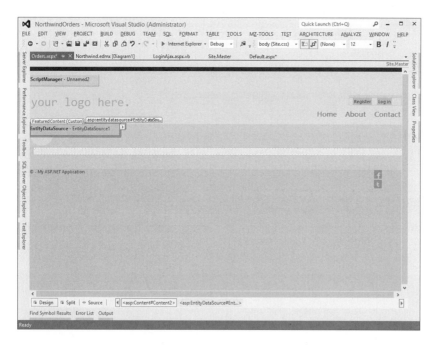

FIGURE 34.5   Adding an `EntityDataSource` control to the page.

The good news is that you can configure the control and bind it to a data source without writing a single line of code. Build the project so that all data references are updated, and then click the right arrow on the `EntityDataSource`. Next, click the **Configure data-source** item. This launches the Configure Data Source Wizard, whose first dialog box is shown in Figure 34.6. You need to specify the source entity data model in the first combo box and then the container name you want to associate to the data control in the lower combo box; then click **Next** to access the second dialog box of the wizard.

FIGURE 34.6   Associating the entity data model to the `EntityDataSource` control.

In the second dialog box, you can select the entity you want to be mapped into the `EntityDataSource`. There you can select only a desired number of columns or all columns, as shown in Figure 34.7.

FIGURE 34.7   Choosing entity and entity columns for mapping into the `EntityDataSource`.

This is all you need to configure the data source. Now a control for viewing and editing data is necessary. In the toolbox, double-click a `GridView` control so that it will be added to the page under the `EntityDataSource`. When ready, click the right arrow to access configuration properties. This shows the `GridView` Tasks pop-up window; here you specify the `EntityDataSource1` control in the Choose Data Source field to enable data-binding. Also select the **Enable Paging**, **Enable Sorting**, and **Enable Selection** check boxes. Figure 34.8 provides a graphical representation of this series of operations.

FIGURE 34.8   Applying data-binding and data options in the GridView Tasks pop-up.

With a few mouse clicks, you configured your new web form to present and edit data without writing a single line of Visual Basic code. If you take a look at the XHTML code for the page, you will notice that Visual Studio 2012 automatically configured the data source and generated columns for the `GridView` control:

```
<asp:EntityDataSource ID="EntityDataSource1" runat="server"
ConnectionString="name=NorthwindEntities" DefaultContainerName="NorthwindEntities"
EnableFlattening="False" EntitySetName="Orders">
</asp:EntityDataSource>
<asp:GridView ID="GridView1" runat="server" AllowPaging="True" AllowSorting="True"
    AutoGenerateColumns="False"
    DataKeyNames="OrderID" DataSourceID="EntityDataSource1">
  <Columns>
      <asp:CommandField ShowSelectButton="True" />
      <asp:BoundField DataField="OrderID" HeaderText="OrderID" ReadOnly="True"
          SortExpression="OrderID" />
      <asp:BoundField DataField="CustomerID" HeaderText="CustomerID"
          SortExpression="CustomerID" />
      <asp:BoundField DataField="EmployeeID" HeaderText="EmployeeID"
          SortExpression="EmployeeID" />
      <asp:BoundField DataField="OrderDate" HeaderText="OrderDate"
          SortExpression="OrderDate" />
      <asp:BoundField DataField="RequiredDate" HeaderText="RequiredDate"
          SortExpression="RequiredDate" />
      <asp:BoundField DataField="ShippedDate" HeaderText="ShippedDate"
          SortExpression="ShippedDate" />
```

```
        <asp:BoundField DataField="ShipVia" HeaderText="ShipVia"
            SortExpression="ShipVia" />
        <asp:BoundField DataField="Freight" HeaderText="Freight"
            SortExpression="Freight" />
        <asp:BoundField DataField="ShipName" HeaderText="ShipName"
            SortExpression="ShipName" />
        <asp:BoundField DataField="ShipAddress" HeaderText="ShipAddress"
            SortExpression="ShipAddress" />
        <asp:BoundField DataField="ShipCity" HeaderText="ShipCity"
            SortExpression="ShipCity" />
        <asp:BoundField DataField="ShipRegion" HeaderText="ShipRegion"
            SortExpression="ShipRegion" />
        <asp:BoundField DataField="ShipPostalCode" HeaderText="ShipPostalCode"
            SortExpression="ShipPostalCode" />
        <asp:BoundField DataField="ShipCountry" HeaderText="ShipCountry"
            SortExpression="ShipCountry" />
    </Columns>
</asp:GridView>
```

This is possible because the ASP.NET data controls implement all functionalities required to access and edit data by assigning some properties. Our page is ready for showing and editing orders from the database. I want to show you another couple of features for filtering data that can also help you understand how powerful ASP.NET is.

RUNTIME DATA-BINDING TIP

Most of ASP.NET data controls expose a DataSource property that can be assigned at runtime with a custom data source, such as a List(Of T). When assigned this property, you invoke the control's DataBind method to perform the binding.

Adding Filtering Capabilities

It would be interesting having filtering capabilities—for example, we could implement a filter that enables fetching all orders with the ShipCity property value that starts with the specified text. Thus, in the toolbox double-click a TextBox and a Button. These controls will be automatically placed onto the page (they will be placed at the top if that is where the cursor is in the designer). Now replace the Name property value of the TextBox with FilterTextBox. In the Button properties, change the Name value with FilterButton and the Text property with Filter. To provide filtering capabilities over the data source, ASP.NET offers the QueryExtender control that you can find within data controls in the toolbox. Add it to the page and then assign its TargetControlID property with EntityDataSource1, which is the name of the data control to be queried or filtered. Now you need to specify an expression for filtering; these kinds of expressions are known as *search expressions*. ASP.NET offers more than one search expression, but the simplest and most appropriate for our purposes is SearchExpression. This object requires the specification of the search type and of the columns to be interrogated, but this is not sufficient.

34

A `ControlParameter` element needs to be nested so you can specify the control where the search criteria are inserted (in our case the textbox) and the .NET type involved in the expression. Talking in code terms, you need to manually write the following code inside the `QueryExtender`:

```
<asp:QueryExtender ID="QueryExtender1" runat="server"
    TargetControlID="EntityDataSource1">
    <asp:SearchExpression DataFields="ShipCity" SearchType="StartsWith">
        <asp:ControlParameter ControlID="FilterTextBox" Type="String" />
    </asp:SearchExpression>
</asp:QueryExtender>
```

The only Visual Basic code we need to write is the event handler for the `Page.Loaded` event to check the `PostBack` state. This is accomplished by writing the following code in the Orders.aspx.vb code file:

```
Protected Sub Page_Load(ByVal sender As Object,
                        ByVal e As System.EventArgs) _
                        Handles Me.Load
    If Not Page.IsPostBack Then
        FilterTextBox.Text = ""
    End If
End Sub
```

This is all we need, no other code. Before running the sample web application, let's make the new web form reachable from the master page.

Adding Navigation Controls

Open the master page in the designer. You see the availability of two buttons named Home and About. These are menu items inside a Menu control that point to the associated web form. If you split the view so that the source code is visible, you can easily add menu items inside the `nav` element. The following XHTML code demonstrates how to add a new button pointing to the Orders.aspx page, after the existing buttons:

```
<nav>
    <ul id="menu">
        <li><a runat="server" href="~/">Home</a></li>
        <li><a runat="server" href="~/About.aspx">About</a></li>
        <li><a runat="server" href="~/Contact.aspx">Contact</a></li>
        <li><a runat="server" href="~/Orders.aspx">Orders</a></li>
    </ul>
</nav>
```

As you can see, the `href` tag holds a relative URI that points to the page, while the `a` element contains the description of the button. Now in the master page you can see a new Orders button associated to the same-named web page.

Running the Application

You can run the demo application by pressing **F5**. Figure 34.9 shows the Orders page, with a list of orders filtered according to the given search criteria. Also notice how paging features have been correctly implemented. Finally, try clicking the page buttons that provide navigation capabilities.

FIGURE 34.9   The sample web application running.

New in ASP.NET 4.5: Strongly Typed Data Controls and Model Binding

The previous code example demonstrated how to data-bind a collection of objects to a control of the user interface only using design tools and writing no code. In the real world, you will often need to write some code to perform data-binding. For example, if you have a `GridView` control like in the previous sample application, you can perform runtime binding by assigning the `DataSource` property and then invoking the `DataBind` method explicitly like this:

```
Me.GridView1.DataSource = northwind.Orders
Me.GridView1.DataBind()
```

ASP.NET 4.5 has some new goodies to help you write both declarative and runtime data-binding code, offering strongly typed data controls and model binding.

Strongly Typed Data Controls

In the previous versions of the .NET Framework, to bind data at runtime you needed to use an `Eval` expression for one-way binding and a `Bind` expression for two-ways binding. Listings 34.1 and 34.2 show an example of one-way and two-ways bindings, respectively, the old way. They use a `FormView` control which allows representing details of an object.

LISTING 34.1   One-way Binding in ASP.NET Prior to Version 4.5

```
<asp:FormView ID="FormView1" runat="server">
    <ItemTemplate>
        <li>
            Order ID: <%# Eval("OrderID")%><br />
            Ship City: <%# Eval("ShipCity")%><br />
        </li>
    </ItemTemplate>
</asp:FormView>
```

LISTING 34.2   Two-way Binding in ASP.NET Prior to Version 4.5

```
<asp:FormView ID="FormView1" runat="server">
    <EditItemTemplate>
    <div>
        <asp:Label ID="Label1" runat="server" AssociatedControlID="firstName">
            First Name:</asp:Label>
        <asp:TextBox ID="firstName" runat="server"
            Text='<%#Bind("FirstName") %>' />
    </div>
    <div>
        <asp:Label ID="Label2" runat="server" AssociatedControlID="lastName">
            First Name:</asp:Label>
        <asp:TextBox ID="lastName" runat="server"
            Text='<%#Bind("LastName") %>' />

    <asp:Button ID="Button1" runat="server" CommandName="Update"/>
    </EditItemTemplate>
</asp:FormView>
```

This kind of approach works fine but has two limitations: it necessarily invokes Reflection at runtime to determine the data-bound object's properties and has no support for IntelliSense or background compilation. So if you are writing bad property names, you will get no errors until you run the application. To solve both problems, in Visual Studio 2012 you can use a new feature called *Strongly Typed Data Controls*, which lets you declare the type of the data to which the control is bound. This can be done by assigning the new `ItemType` property with the data type (notice that, during the assignment, IntelliSense will help you choose among the available types with a convenient drop-down list). Next, you use an `Item` expression like in the following code:

```
<asp:FormView ID="FormView1" runat="server" ItemType="NorthwindOrders.Order">
    <ItemTemplate>
        <li>
            Order ID: <%# Item.OrderID%><br />
            Ship City: <%# Item.ShipCity%><br />
        </li>
    </ItemTemplate>
</asp:FormView>
```

When you type the dot after `Item`, you will see that IntelliSense lists all available members from the selected object type. This will avoid a lot of runtime errors due to bad writing and will use both IntelliSense and the background compiler so that errors will be immediately shown in the Errors tool window at compile time.

Model Binding

ASP.NET 4.5 extends web forms data controls with the model binding, which enables you to work with code-focused models like EDMs or Code First. You assign the `SelectMethod` property of data controls with the name of a method that returns a collection of objects, so you will no longer need to invoke `DataBind` explicitly. Let's see an example with a `GridView` that shows a reduced number of columns from the `Orders` table from the Northwind database:

```
<asp:GridView ID="GridView1" runat="server" AutoGenerateColumns="false"
    ItemType="NorthwindOrders.Order" SelectMethod="GetOrders">
    <Columns>
        <asp:BoundField DataField="OrderDate" HeaderText="OrderDate"
            SortExpression="OrderDate" />
        <asp:BoundField DataField="RequiredDate" HeaderText="RequiredDate"
            SortExpression="RequiredDate" />
        <asp:BoundField DataField="ShippedDate" HeaderText="ShippedDate"
            SortExpression="ShippedDate" />
        <asp:BoundField DataField="ShipVia" HeaderText="ShipVia"
            SortExpression="ShipVia" />
        <asp:BoundField DataField="Freight" HeaderText="Freight"
            SortExpression="Freight" />
    </Columns>
</asp:GridView>
```

You first use the strongly typed approach described previously by assigning the `ItemType` property. Then you specify a query method that returns the collection of data for the `SelectMethod` property. This method must be defined in the page's code-behind and must return an `IQueryable` or `IQueryable(Of T)`. In our case, the method can be defined as follows:

34

```
Public Function GetOrders() As IQueryable(Of Order)
    'Where 'northwind' is an instance of the EDM
    Return northwind.Orders
End Function
```

Because query methods return IQueryable or its generic flavor, you can either write LINQ queries or set the GridView's properties (or other data controls' properties) to allow filtering and sorting options. The following imperative code demonstrates how to execute a LINQ query to return a filtered and ordered collection of orders:

```
Public Function GetOrders() As IQueryable(Of Order)
    'Where 'northwind' is an instance of the EDM
    Dim query = From ord In northwind.Orders
                Where ord.OrderDate < Date.Today
                Order By ord.ShipCity
                Select ord
    Return query
End Function
```

With this code, the GridView will hold data-binding to the filtered and sorted collection without the need of invoking DataBind explicitly. Similarly, you can work directly on the XHTML code. The following snippet demonstrates how to enable paging and sorting directly on the GridView definition:

```
<asp:GridView ID="GridView1" runat="server" AutoGenerateColumns="false"
    ItemType="NorthwindOrders.Order" DataKeyNames="OrderID"
    AllowPaging="true" PageSize="100" AllowSorting="true"
    SelectMethod="GetOrders">
    <Columns>
        <asp:BoundField DataField="OrderDate" HeaderText="OrderDate"
            SortExpression="OrderDate" />
        <asp:BoundField DataField="RequiredDate" HeaderText="RequiredDate"
            SortExpression="RequiredDate" />
        <asp:BoundField DataField="ShippedDate" HeaderText="ShippedDate"
            SortExpression="ShippedDate" />
        <asp:BoundField DataField="ShipVia" HeaderText="ShipVia"
            SortExpression="ShipVia" />
        <asp:BoundField DataField="Freight" HeaderText="Freight"
            SortExpression="Freight" />
    </Columns>
</asp:GridView>
```

Notice how you enable paging by setting AllowPaging with true and by specifying the number of items per page with PageSize. Sorting is enabled by setting AllowSorting with true and with DataKeyNames, which contains the column(s) name used for sorting. Model binding also enables you to update data other than read-only query operations. For this purpose, you assign the UpdateMethod property on the data control. If you do not create a method first and choose the option to generate a new method via IntelliSense, Visual Studio will create a method stub (with a lot of useful comments) that you will have to change to make your changes to the selected object. For example, the following method has been generated by choosing the new method option with IntelliSense and demonstrates how to retrieve the instance of the selected order and how to send changes to the data source:

```
' The id parameter name should match the DataKeyNames value set on the control
Public Sub GridView1_UpdateItem(ByVal id As Integer)
    Dim item As NorthwindOrders.Order = northwind.Orders.
                FirstOrDefault(Function(o) o.OrderID = id)
    ' Load the item here, e.g. item = MyDataLayer.Find(id)
    If item Is Nothing Then
        ' The item wasn't found
        ModelState.AddModelError("",
                String.Format("Item with id {0} was not found", id))
        Return
    End If

    'Make your changes:
    item.ShipVia = 1

    'Update your model:
    TryUpdateModel(item)
    If ModelState.IsValid Then
        ' Save changes here, e.g. MyDataLayer.SaveChanges()
        northwind.SaveChanges()
    End If
End Sub
```

If you now assign UpdateMethod="GridView1_UpdateItem" on the GridView, this will always use the specified method to perform edits on the selected object.

Configuring a Web Application for Security

The sample web application that was illustrated in the previous section has one important limitation: It can be accessed by anonymous users who can access important data. If your application just presents information, anonymous access is typically fine. But if your application has the purpose of managing data or restricted information, you need to force users to log in with their own credentials, such as a username and password. ASP. NET provides a convenient and easy way for configuring web applications to require login credentials by storing user information inside a SQL Server database and using roles and registration; another interesting thing is that Visual Studio 2012 generates a login page for you when creating the project. To start configuring security for your web application, select Project, ASP.NET Configuration. This runs the ASP.NET Web Site Administration Tool, a web application executed in your web browser (see Figure 34.10).

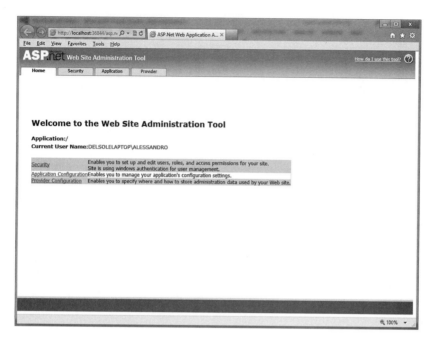

FIGURE 34.10   The ASP.NET Administration Tool.

This tool enables the configuring of different parts in the web application, but for the current example just click the Security tab. When you click this tab, you can access different security options, including setting users and roles. You can also utilize a guided procedure to configure the application security; thus, click the Use the Security Setup Wizard to Configure Security Step by Step hyperlink. You'll need to complete seven steps, but the first one is just a welcome message, so you can click Next. Starting from the second step, execute the following tasks:

1. Specify the access method by selecting either **From the Internet** and **From a Local Area Network**. The first option is more restrictive and requires users to register with their credentials, such as a username and password. This is particularly useful when you do not know who will access the website and want a user to log in with credentials. Moreover, if a website is available on the Internet, it can be reached by non-Windows environments and therefore Windows authentication is not appropriate. Instead, the local intranet option should be used only when the web application runs only inside of your company because it relies on Windows and domain authentication only, although this simplifies your work because you will not have to configure users. For the current example, where user administration is also covered, select the Internet security and then click **Next**.

2. Click **Next** at step 3 because you do not need to change storage information (such as the database provider).

3. Click the **Enable Roles for This website** check box, and then click **Next**. This is important because securing the web application requires at least one role. Typically, a website includes at least an administration role, so in the **New Role Name** textbox, type **Administrator** and then click **Add Role**. The new role will be added to the roles list, so click **Next**.

4. Sign up for a new account by providing required information. This is important because the web application requires at least one user who later will be associated to the role. When ready, click **Create User**. You will be told that adding the new user was successful, so click **Next**.

5. Specify access rules to the web application by allowing or denying access permissions to specific roles or users. You can allow all registered users and roles to access the whole application, but you can create custom rules granting permissions to selected users/roles. For example, you can select a folder of the application by first expanding the root folder on the left and then selecting the permission (Allow or Deny) for the users or roles in the **Rules Applies To** item. When this is set, click **Next**. Figure 34.11 shows an example.

6. In the last step, click **Finish**.

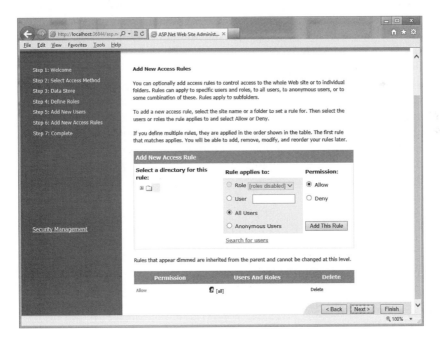

FIGURE 34.11   Configuring rules for users and roles for folder permissions.

SQL SERVER DATABASE

When you configure users or when users register to claim access to the web application, the user information is stored inside a default SQL Server database that Visual Studio generates for you. If you want to use a SQL Server database different from the default one, use the Aspnet_regsql.exe command-line tool that creates the appropriate tables.

With a few steps, you quickly configured your application for requesting registration and login. The last step before running the application is associating the main user to the Administrator role. To accomplish this, click **Manage Users** and then **Edit User**. When the user administration page appears, click the check box for **Administrator**. Finally, click **Save**. Now close the configuration tool, run the application, and try to open the Orders page. As you see, you cannot view the requested page until you log in with the previously created user's credentials. When you log in, you can browse the application. The really cool thing is that the Login page generated for you by Visual Studio 2012 is bound to the SQL Server database where user information is stored, so you do not need to write code to check whether a user has permissions to access. This is performed for you behind the scenes by the application that takes advantage of autogenerated elements.

Summary

In this chapter, we made an overview of the ASP.NET technology and of how you can build websites based on the technology. You read about important concepts on the ASP.NET model and how it maintains the application state; then you learned how to create a web application with Visual Basic 2012. For this, you first learned what web forms are and how the logic is divided into XHTML code for the user interface side and into Visual Basic code for performing executive tasks. You took a look at available user controls, both server and HTML controls; then you put your hands on a sample web application to manage data exposed from an Entity Data Model. Finally, you learned the steps necessary to configure security for websites implementing login credentials.

CHAPTER 35

Publishing ASP.NET Web Applications

To make your web application reachable by other users, you need to deploy it to a host web server, either on the Internet or on a local area network, such as your company's network. ASP.NET 4.5 and Visual Studio 2012, as in the previous version, make the deployment experience for web applications even simpler, via a special tool named MSDeploy. They also introduce some simplifications for publishing profiles. In this chapter you learn how to publish an ASP.NET 4.5 application using a number of available techniques and get some information about what's new in version 4.5.

Deployment Overview

Deploying a web application can be accomplished directly from within Visual Studio 2012, as it was for its predecessors. You can publish a web application to the following destinations:

▶ A web server with Internet Information Services 7 or higher installed

▶ A website with the FrontPage extensions installed

▶ An FTP site

▶ The local file system

▶ The local Internet Information Services

Visual Studio 2012 retakes some important changes brought by version 2010, which made the deployment experience different but certainly better as you discover in a few moments.

The 1-Click Deployment

Visual Studio 2012 retakes and follows the logic of deployment simplification with *1-Click deployment* introduced by its predecessor. What does it mean?

It means that you supply the required information such as web address and credentials; then you just click once on a button and Visual Studio will do the rest of the work for you, independently from the destination type. The reason for this important new way to deploy web applications is the presence of a tool named MSDeploy, which is described later and that can deploy articulated web applications. For now, let's begin to see how you can deploy web applications to FTP sites and IIS servers with the 1-Click deployment.

Classic Publishing

Visual Studio 2012 still provides the capability of publishing web applications the usual way, so it supports direct deployment to FTP sites, websites with FrontPage extensions enabled, the file system, and the local Internet Information Services, although some innovations are available in the graphical user interface of the deployment window. For example, you might want to deploy the NorthwindOrders web application, created in Chapter 34, "Building ASP.NET Web Applications," to an FTP site. In Solution Explorer, right-click the project name and then click **Publish**. This launches the Publish Web dialog box; here you must specify a new profile or import an existing one. Assuming you do not have an existing profile, expand the combo box and select New. At this point, you will be prompted to enter a name for the new profile—for example, **MyFirstProfile**. The Connection tab is now enabled and you will have to specify settings for the new profile. Select **FTP** in the Publish Method combo box. Figure 35.1 shows the dialog box.

FIGURE 35.1   Publishing a web application to an FTP site.

Click **Publish** so that Visual Studio 2012 publishes your web application to the specified FTP, or click Validate Connection if you want to be sure that supplied credentials can establish a successful connection. If you click Settings on the left side of the dialog box before publishing, you will be able to specify which project configuration will be published (Debug, Release, or any other available configuration) and whether files of a previous version of the application will be erased on the target machine when publishing the new one.

PROVIDERS' FIREWALL

Several Internet service providers or hosts enable firewalls to avoid unrecognized incoming connections. If you want to publish web applications to a website or FTP site, you need to ensure that the host's firewall accepts connections from Visual Studio 2012.

Another example is publishing the application to IIS, which can be also particularly useful for testing purposes. You accomplish this by setting the File System option in the Publish Method combo box and then typing the IIS instance address, as demonstrated in Figure 35.2. Publishing to the local IIS requires Visual Studio 2012 to be launched with administrative privileges.

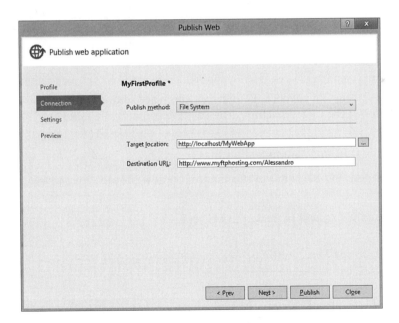

FIGURE 35.2   Publishing the web application to Internet Information Services.

You can click the Browse button (the one with three dots) to select an existing web folder or create a new one inside IIS.

MSDeploy Publish

One of the most interesting features in deploying web applications is the Microsoft Web Deployment Tool, also known as MSDeploy. It is a command-line tool included in the .NET Framework 4.5 and can build advanced deployment scripts. MSDeploy is an advanced tool in that it can

▶ Publish web applications and their settings

▶ Deploy SQL Server databases

▶ Direct advanced deployment to Internet Information Services web servers

▶ Publish GAC, COM, and Registry settings

MSDeploy is a complex tool, and writing the appropriate command lines can be annoying. Fortunately, Visual Studio 2012 enables you to publish web applications via MSDeploy through the Publish Web dialog box, as demonstrated later. Before getting into that, you need to know how web applications are packaged before deployment.

Understanding Packages

When you deploy a web application via MSDeploy, the application is first packaged into one archive that makes deployment easier. The package contains all the required information about the host web server and files and settings required by the application. You set package information in the Package/Publish Web tab of My Project, as shown in Figure 35.3.

Here you can find default settings for the local IIS, but you can place settings provided by the system administrator of the target machine. The package contains the following elements:

▶ The package containing the application and settings

▶ The destination manifest, which contains information on how to reach the target server

▶ The command-line script that will be passed to MSDeploy

When you have specified your package's settings, you are ready to deploy it with MSDeploy.

PRECOMPILING APPLICATIONS

A new feature in ASP.NET 4.5 enables you to precompile a web application by selecting the **Precompile the application before publishing** box in the package properties (refer to Figure 35.3). With this option enabled, Visual Studio precompiles the application and merges all the site's content when you publish it. You can control a number of options by clicking the Advanced button that becomes available after the option is selected, such as merging all the site's content into one or multiple assemblies.

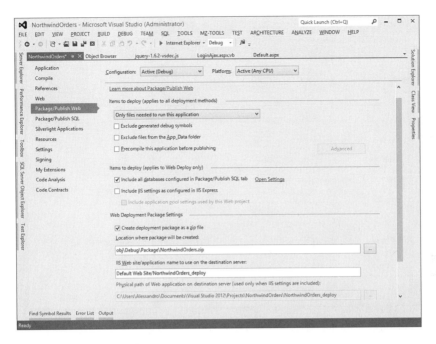

FIGURE 35.3   Setting options for packaging web applications for deployment.

Web Deploy with MSDeploy

Visual Studio 2012 provides the opportunity to deploy web applications with MSDeploy through its instrumentation in two alternative ways:

▶ Direct publishing to a web server

▶ Generation of a package that can be manually installed later on the server

In this chapter we examine both options, starting by the direct publishing. To publish a web application directly to a web server, right-click the project name in Solution Explorer and then click **Publish**. When the Publish Web dialog box appears, select the **Web Deploy** option from the Publish Method combo box in the Connection tab. Figure 35.4 shows the dialog box.

You need to provide some settings to deploy the web application with MSDeploy, and most of them are given to you by the Administrator of the target server. Table 35.1 summarizes the required settings.

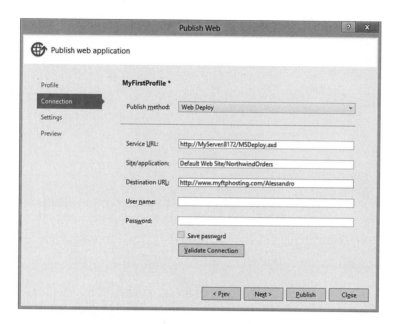

FIGURE 35.4   Setting options for the MSDeploy publish.

TABLE 35.1   Required Settings for MSDeploy Publish

Option	Tab	Description
Service URL	Connection	The URL of the MSDeploy service provided by the host or administrator. If you are publishing to your local IIS on the development machine for testing purposes, enter http://localhost; otherwise, see Figure 35.4 for an example of how the URL should be composed.
Site/Application	Connection	The name of the site and application on the target IIS. Here you can include subfolders.
Destination URL	Connection	The target URL of the web application after it is deployed
Allow Untrusted Certificate	Connection	Allows host and administrator to use self-signed certificates, according to the administrator instructions.
Username/Password	Connection	Credentials required to access the target IIS, provided by the server administrator.
Configuration	Settings	The project output you want to deploy based on the configuration (Debug, Release).
Remove additional files at destination	Settings	Enables you to remove files that are no longer part of the deployment when publishing a new version.

Option	Tab	Description
Databases	Settings	This is a group of connection strings and can vary depending on how many database connections you have in your project. Specify the appropriate connection string for each database (see Figure 35.5 for an example).

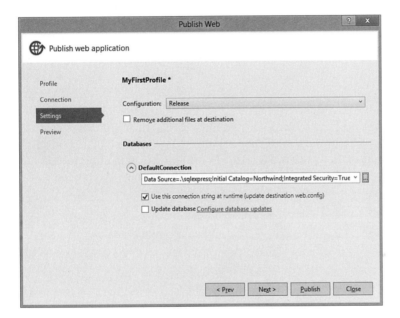

FIGURE 35.5   Specifying database connections.

If you choose to validate your credentials, Visual Studio will also check whether a valid certificate is available. Also, if you want to see how many files will be deployed to the web server, select the Preview tab in the Publish Web dialog box. This is especially useful when you are updating an existing application and want to see which files are going to be replaced with new versions. When you provide all required settings, click **Publish** to get your application deployed to the web server with MSDeploy—remembering that this tool provides the opportunity to deploy additional requirements such as SQL Server databases and GAC settings.

Packaging Web Applications for Manual Installation

MSDN REFERENCES

The goal of this chapter is explaining how to publish web applications from a developer perspective, so here you learn how to generate packages. However, in this section we are assuming that the installation is made by another person such as the server administrator. For this reason (and because explaining the process in detail would be beyond the scope of this book), here you learn how to generate a package. You will be invited to read the appropriate MSDN documentation to understand how to perform a manual installation of the package on the server.

The steps described in the previous paragraph enable you to automate the generation of a package that is automatically deployed to a web server. This is convenient but presents a couple of problems:

▶ You must have administrative privileges on the server to which you are deploying the application.

▶ The server administrator might need to customize the installation process because of some company's policies.

For this reason, Visual Studio allows you to generate a package as a .zip file that can be later installed manually on the server by another person. To accomplish this, you select the Web Deploy Package option in the Connection tab of the Publish Web dialog box and then specify some basic information that can be edited during the installation process. Figure 35.6 shows how you specify the target folder for the .zip package and the destination on the server.

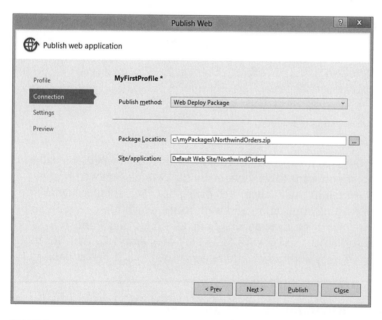

FIGURE 35.6   Specifying settings for manual package generation.

The Settings tab works like in the Web Deploy option. When you click Publish, Visual Studio generates several files into the folder that you specified, but the most important of them are the .zip package and a .deploy.cmd file (whose name starts with the application's name). These enable you to install the package locally or remotely. So, now you have two options for installing the package onto the web server:

▶ Launch the .deploy.cmd file. The MSDN documentation has specific explanations about this at http://msdn.microsoft.com/en-us/ff356104(v=vs.110).aspx.

▶ Import the package through the Internet Information Services Manager, which must be enabled on the server. Further information can be found at www.iis.net/learn/publish/using-web-deploy/import-a-package-through-iis-manager.

With both options, administrators can control the package installation and make the appropriate decisions based on the company's policies.

Summary

In this chapter, we discussed how to deploy ASP.NET web applications in both the classic fashion and a new one based on the Microsoft Web Deployment tool. Now you know how to use the 1-Click publish deployment system for quickly deploying your web applications directly from Visual Studio 2012. You also learned how the IDE provides options to generate packages that can be installed manually by administrators.

35

CHAPTER 36

Building Rich Internet Applications with Silverlight 5

The evolution of the Internet over the years has had the consequence of requiring web applications to be even more powerful and interactive, with the addition of multimedia, animations, high-quality graphics, and even business capabilities. Although powerful for its business productivity, ASP.NET has lacked in terms of interactivity and media features. If you think of the Adobe Flash plug-in for a web browser, you'll have a good idea of how multimedia and interactivity can improve the success of web applications. A few years ago, Microsoft realized that it should create a plug-in for a web browser with media, interactivity, and business features for the .NET platform integrating the coolest WPF graphic characteristics into web applications produced on the robust ASP.NET platform. This is where Microsoft Silverlight comes in. In this chapter you learn about building rich Internet applications (RIAs) with Silverlight and Visual Basic 2012 and take a tour of the most important features of this technology. You also learn about the most important new features in version 5 (for a full list of additions, check out the MSDN documentation at: `http://msdn.microsoft.com/en-us/library/gg986857(v=vs.95).aspx`). This chapter is also important because the overview you get of Silverlight here will be particularly useful in Chapter 38, "Building Apps for Windows Phone 7.5," where you learn that developing for that device relies on a specific version of Silverlight 4.

Introducing Silverlight

Microsoft Silverlight is a cross-browser, cross-platform, and cross-device plug-in for building rich Internet applications that offers the best from WPF and ASP.NET. Silverlight is a plug-in for web browsers that needs to be installed on the client side to run new generation web applications, and its size is about 5 megabytes. By installing Silverlight, you allow your web browser to run cool applications where data access, multimedia, and rich contents can be linked together. As you see later in this chapter, developing Silverlight applications can be easier if you are already familiar with WPF. Silverlight can be considered as a WPF subset for the web, meaning that you can create the user interface with XAML and write Visual Basic code to execute the application tasks. Before continuing to read this chapter, you need to install the Silverlight plug-in and the latest updates of the Visual Studio tools. You need the following components:

- ▶ **Silverlight tools for Visual Studio**—This installs the Silverlight runtime and enables the IDE to the Silverlight development. These tools are included in the Visual Studio 2012 setup, so you should not need to install them manually. It is worth mentioning that such tools are also available for Visual Studio 2010 with Service Pack 1 as a separate download from `http://silverlight.net`.

- ▶ **Silverlight Toolkit** (`http://silverlight.codeplex.com`)—This contains additional user controls to improve your development experience.

This chapter focuses on Silverlight 5, which is the latest (and probably the last) version available. What makes Silverlight so powerful is that you can still write code the way you know, thus taking advantage of your existing .NET Framework and Visual Basic skills without the need to write in different languages and on different technologies.

THE HTML5 STORY

There has been an incredible growth of the diffusion of mobile devices in the last years, such as smartphones and tablet devices, with different operating systems, different hardware, different requirements, and different audiences targeted, but all of them have one thing in common—making it easy to browse the Internet and connect with social networks. So web designers and web application developers know that their websites must run on a plethora of platforms, which means being portable. Plug-ins like Microsoft Silverlight and Adobe Flash Player are not portable, or at least they are only partially portable because they can run on different operating systems but not on all operating systems. They can run on some web browsers but not on all available web browsers, neither can they run on all the various hardware available today. For all these reasons, HTML has come back as the preferred choice for building web applications because it is the only language supported everywhere. Microsoft is strongly investing in HTML5 and JavaScript to enable developers to build rich web applications that are as portable as possible. In summary, if you plan to build web applications that run on Windows and Apple machines, Silverlight is still a reasonable and valid choice. But if your need is building rich Internet applications that not only run on Windows and Apple, but also on iPad, iPhone, Android devices, and Windows 8 devices, you are strongly encouraged to have a look at the HTML5/JavaScript pair (or at ASP.NET for more business-oriented applications).

Creating Silverlight Projects with Visual Basic 2012

One of the greatest benefits of Microsoft Silverlight is that you can create applications with Visual Basic 2012 the same way you create .NET applications. When you select **File, New Project** in the New Project dialog box, you have a project templates folder named Silverlight and a number of available project templates, as shown in Figure 36.1.

FIGURE 36.1   Selecting a Silverlight project template.

The project template for general purposes is the Silverlight Application. Ensure this is selected and then follow these steps:

1. Leave the project name unchanged, and then click **OK**.

2. You will be asked to specify how the new Silverlight application will be hosted. Silverlight applications are based on user controls that need to be hosted by an ASP. NET web application, such as a website or an MVC application. Also you can host your Silverlight applications inside existing web applications instead of specifying a new one. When the dialog box appears, leave the default selection on a new web application unchanged (see Figure 36.2 for details). Notice how you can also select the Silverlight runtime version and enable the application for RIA Services, which is introduced later in this chapter. Click **OK**.

After a few seconds, the new project is ready. Visual Studio now looks similar to WPF projects, as demonstrated in Figure 36.3.

FIGURE 36.2   Specifying a host project and runtime version.

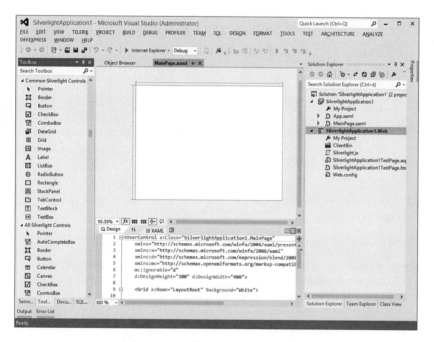

FIGURE 36.3   The IDE is ready on the new Silverlight project.

There are several differences from WPF; first, in the XAML code editor, the root element is a `UserControl`. This is because you essentially develop Silverlight controls to be hosted by an ASP.NET application. Next, notice the presence of two projects in Solution Explorer. The first one is the actual Silverlight application, which will be executed on the client side. The structure of the project is similar to WPF projects, with XAML files and Visual Basic code behind files.

TIP ON WPF AND SILVERLIGHT

Silverlight applications work within a web context, although the current version has full-trust support. Considering web limitations imposed by the Silverlight Base Class Library (BCL), you will see several similarities with the WPF programming model (such as user interface elements and user controls); this is the reason multiple chapters were devoted about WPF.

The second project is the web application that hosts the Silverlight user control. Notice the presence of a .js file that contains the JavaScript code that makes the control reachable from the ASP.NET application. Also, an .aspx web page shows the Silverlight control, and an HTML page exists for hosting the Silverlight application for testing. When you have your project, you are ready to add and manage user interface (UI) elements.

Adding Controls and Handling Events

Adding controls and UI elements to a Silverlight user control is an easy task and looks like what was already described about WPF. While you go through adding controls, you can also notice how Silverlight properties are in most cases the same as WPF properties. Replace the Background property value in the main Grid from White to SteelBlue. This provides better visibility of the user control in the web browser. You can still apply brushes as in WPF. Next, add a TextBlock control and place it at the top of the user control. Set its properties so that the foreground color is white and the font size is 24. Finally, drag a Button control from the toolbox onto the user control surface. Also notice how Visual Studio also generated the appropriate XAML code for each of the operations accomplished. To handle events, you still write event handlers as you are used to doing in other .NET applications. In this case, double-click the Button and write the following simple handler:

```
Private Sub Button1_Click(ByVal sender As System.Object,
                          ByVal e As System.Windows.RoutedEventArgs) _
                          Handles Button1.Click
    MessageBox.Show("You clicked a Silverlight button!")
End Sub
```

It is important that Silverlight still offers the routed events infrastructure as in WPF, so handling events in both technologies is identical. It is worth mentioning that Silverlight 5 adds support for multiclick events. This means you can determine how many clicks have been made over a control and decide to take an action based on the number of clicks. The following code provides an example:

```
Private Sub Button1_MouseLeftButtonUp(sender As Object, e As MouseButtonEventArgs) _
    Handles Button1.MouseLeftButtonUp
    Select Case e.ClickCount
        Case Is = 1
            'One click, take an action here...
        Case Is = 2
```

36

```
            'Double-click, this should be the default...
        Case Is = 3
            'Triple-click, take a different action...
    End Select
End Sub
```

You check the value of the `MouseButtonEventArgs.ClickCount` property to determine how many clicks the control has received. The `MouseButtonEventArgs` class is not available for the `Click` event—only with `MouseLeftButtonUp`, `MouseLeftButtonDown`, `MouseDown`, `MouseUp`, `MouseRightButtonUp`, and `MouseRightButtonDown`. Now press **F5** to start the application with an instance of the Visual Studio debugger attached. Figure 36.4 shows how the application runs inside the web browser.

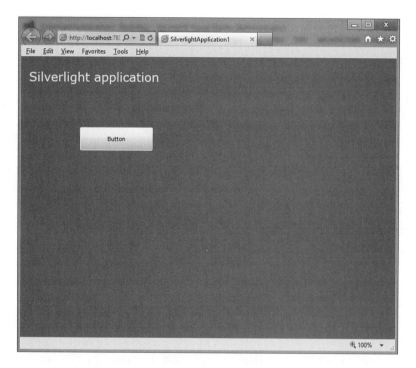

FIGURE 36.4 The Silverlight application running.

New features in Silverlight 5 enable you to customize lines of text within `TextBlock` and `TextBox` controls. With the `CharacterSpacing` property, you can specify the distance between characters; such a distance is measured by the 1000th of the current font size. This means that if your font is 24 and you specify a distance of 200, it will be (24 * 200)/1000 = 4.8 pixel. The following code shows an example:

```
<TextBlock Height="45" CharacterSpacing="200"
        Name="TextBlock1" Text="Silverlight application"
        FontSize="24" Foreground="White" />
```

You can also specify the line height with the `LineHeight` property in multiline text controls and, differently from `CharacterSpacing`, it is measured in pixels. It works like this:

```
<TextBlock Margin="5" LineHeight="30">
  Lorem ipsum dolor sit amet, consectetur adipiscing elit.
  <LineBreak />
  Lorem ipsum dolor sit amet, consectetur adipiscing elit.
  <LineBreak />
  Lorem ipsum dolor sit amet, consectetur adipiscing elit.
</TextBlock>
```

A technique called Line Stacking Strategy is also available and allows you to specify how each line is formatted. The following code provides an example:

```
<TextBlock Margin="25" FontSize="12">
  Lorem ipsum <Span FontSize="20">dolor sit amet</Span>, ...
  <LineBreak />
  Proin aliquam augue quis ipsum <Span FontSize="38">rhoncus</Span> ...
  <LineBreak />
  Quisque eleifend ante vitae velit vehicula luctus. ...
</TextBlock>
```

Next, you use a `Span` element within each `LineBreak` and specify the `FontSize` and other properties such as `LineHeight`. Now that you have built and run your first rich Internet application and learned a bunch of new features of Silverlight 5 for text controls, you need to learn how Silverlight applications are packaged and deployed.

How Silverlight Applications Are Packaged

When you create a Silverlight application, in the web host project is a folder named ClientBin. When you compile the project, this folder contains the build output of the Silverlight client project (not the web project). For this, you need to know that Silverlight applications are packaged into .xap files, which contain the actual application and its resources. Thus, when the build process is complete, the ClientBin folder contains the generated .xap file. When you run the application by pressing F5, it will be packaged and deployed on the local file system and will be hosted by the ASP.NET development server so that you can run it in your web browser. Because of all these operations, you can deploy the application with existing web deploying techniques.

DEPLOYING SILVERLIGHT APPLICATIONS

Silverlight applications are hosted inside an ASP.NET web application, so to publish a Silverlight application, you follow the same rules as for ASP.NET. For instance, you can right-click the web project in Solution Explorer and then select Publish from the pop-up menu.

36

Playing Media

As in WPF, Silverlight provides its implementation of the `MediaElement` control that enables media reproduction and streaming from networks. This means that you can interact with the control the same way as in WPF. Right-click the Silverlight project in Solution Explorer and then select **Add New Item**. (You could also create a new project from scratch, but you need to know how to change the default page.) In the dialog box, select the **Silverlight User Control** item template, as shown in Figure 36.5.

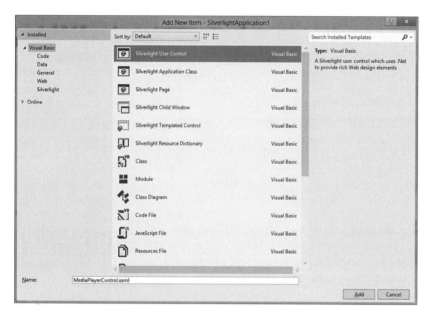

FIGURE 36.5   Adding a new user control.

The goal of the example is implementing a basic media player. When ready, write the XAML code shown in Listing 36.1—notice how the implementation is identical to WPF.

LISTING 36.1   Implementing a Basic Media Player with Silverlight

```
<UserControl x:Class="SilverlightApplication1.MediaPlayerControl"
    xmlns="http://schemas.microsoft.com/winfx/2006/xaml/presentation"
    xmlns:x="http://schemas.microsoft.com/winfx/2006/xaml"
    xmlns:d="http://schemas.microsoft.com/expression/blend/2008"
    xmlns:mc="http://schemas.openxmlformats.org/markup-compatibility/2006"
    mc:Ignorable="d"
    d:DesignHeight="300" d:DesignWidth="400">

    <Grid x:Name="LayoutRoot" Background="White">
        <Grid.RowDefinitions>
            <RowDefinition/>
```

```
            <RowDefinition Height="40"/>
        </Grid.RowDefinitions>

        <!-- Set the MediaElement.Source property
        pointing to a video on a web server-->
        <MediaElement Grid.Row="0" Name="Media1"
         Source="http://www.mywebsite.com/MyVideo.wmv"/>
        <StackPanel Grid.Row="1" Orientation="Horizontal">
            <StackPanel.Resources>

                <!—Using a style for buttons—>
                <Style x:Key="ButtonStyle" TargetType="Button">
                    <Setter Property="Width" Value="80"/>
                    <Setter Property="Height" Value="30"/>
                    <Setter Property="Margin" Value="5"/>
                </Style>
            </StackPanel.Resources>

            <Button Name="PlayButton" Style="{StaticResource ButtonStyle}"
                    Content="Play"/>
            <Button Name="PauseButton" Style="{StaticResource ButtonStyle}"
                    Content="Pause"/>
            <Button Name="StopButton" Style="{StaticResource ButtonStyle}"
                    Content="Stop"/>
        </StackPanel>
    </Grid>
</UserControl>
```

Just remember to assign the `MediaElement.Source` property with a valid media content address from a web server. Before implementing reproduction capabilities, it is worth mentioning that Silverlight 5 introduces support for remote control devices via the `System.Windows.Media.MediaCommand` enumeration and the `MediaElement.MediaCommand` event. Assuming your hardware supports receiving signals from remote controls, when a remote control sends a command to the Silverlight application, the `MediaElement.MediaCommand` is raised. This stores information inside an instance of the `MediaCommandEventArgs` class, including a property of type `MediaCommand` that determines the action sent from the remote device. Table 36.1 summarizes the list of values exposed by such an enumeration.

TABLE 36.1   Values of the `System.Windows.Media.MediaCommands` Enumeration

Value	Description
Play	Start playing media
Pause	Pause media
TogglePlayPause	Switch between media playback and temporarily stop the playback

Value	Description
Stop	Stop playing media
Record	Start capturing a video signal
FastForward	Accelerate the speed of the media
Rewind	Reverse the media at an accelerated speed
NextTrack	Move to the next track in the current media
PreviousTrack	Move to the previous track in the current media
IncreaseVolume	Increase the audio volume
DecreaseVolume	Decrease the audio volume
ChannelUp	Increment the channel
ChannelDown	Decrement the channel
MuteVolume	Silence the audio
Menu	Display a menu if available
Title	Show the title of the current media
Info	Show system information
Display	Change the media display
Guide	Show the television schedule
TV	Change the input focus to the television

Now switch to the code-behind file and write the Visual Basic code shown in Listing 36.2 that can provide reproduction capabilities.

LISTING 36.2   Enabling the Media Player to Content Reproduction

```
Partial Public Class MediaPlayerControl
    Inherits UserControl
    Public Sub New()
        InitializeComponent()
    End Sub

    'If you plan to set the MediaElement.Source property
    'in code, ensure its value is not Nothing
    Private Sub PlayButton_Click(ByVal sender As System.Object,
                        ByVal e As System.Windows.
                            RoutedEventArgs) Handles PlayButton.Click
        Me.Media1.Play()
    End Sub

    Private Sub PauseButton_Click(ByVal sender As System.Object,
                        ByVal e As System.Windows.
                            RoutedEventArgs) Handles PauseButton.Click
```

```
            Me.Media1.Pause()
        End Sub


        Private Sub StopButton_Click(ByVal sender As System.Object,
                            ByVal e As System.Windows.
                            RoutedEventArgs) Handles StopButton.Click
            Me.Media1.Stop()
        End Sub


        Private Sub Media1_MediaFailed(ByVal sender As Object,
                            ByVal e As System.Windows.
                            ExceptionRoutedEventArgs) Handles Media1.
                            MediaFailed
            MessageBox.Show(e.ErrorException.Message)
        End Sub
        Private Sub Media1_MediaCommand(sender As Object,
                    e As MediaCommandEventArgs) Handles Media1.MediaCommand
            Select Case e.MediaCommand
                Case Media.MediaCommand.Play
                    Me.Media1.Play()
                Case Media.MediaCommand.Stop
                    Me.Media1.Stop()
                Case Media.MediaCommand.Pause
                    Me.Media1.Pause()
            End Select
        End Sub
    End Class
```

Notice that only a few values from the MediaCommand enumeration have been handled here due to a limited number of features that the sample media player is offering. However, you are free to extend the code with additional values. Figure 36.6 shows new user control after implementing the user interface.

Before running the application, you need to replace the startup object with the new user control. You do this by replacing the code in the Application.Startup event handler available in the App.xaml.vb code file. The original event handler looks like this:

```
Private Sub Application_Startup(ByVal o As Object,
                            ByVal e As StartupEventArgs) _
                            Handles Me.Startup
    Me.RootVisual = New MainPage()
End Sub
```

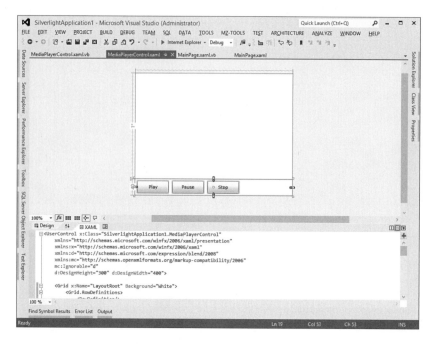

FIGURE 36.6   The new media player control within the Visual Studio Designer.

The `RootVisual` property (of type `UIElement`) represents the root element in the user inter-face and is assigned with an instance of the desired page. According to this, replace the `RootVisual` assignment as follows:

```
Me.RootVisual = New MediaPlayerControl
```

Finally, ensure that you have supplied a valid media URL for the `MediaElement.Source` property and then run the application by pressing **F5** to play/pause/stop the media file. Notice that Silverlight's version of the `MediaElement` control cannot play all media directly; instead, it supports only some specific encoding formats, which are described in detail at the following MSDN page: `http://msdn.microsoft.com/en-us/library/cc189080(VS.95).aspx`.

CAPTURING CAMERA

Silverlight 4 introduced interesting graphic APIs that enable accessing the webcam installed on your machine and microphone so that you can capture the cam output. These APIs are still available in Silverlight 5, and you can use them to enrich your media applica-tions. You can check out the MSDN documentation about the `System.Windows.Media.VideoCaptureDevice` class and the following article written by the author of this book: "Using Silverlight 4 APIs to Interact with Webcams and Microphones," available at `http://www.informit.com/articles/article.aspx?p=1608134`.

Silverlight 5 has also some new and interesting features for media reproduction. For instance, you can easily control the media speed by using the `PlaybackRate` property:

```
'Normal speed
Me.Media1.PlaybackRate = 1
'5 times faster
Me.Media1.PlaybackRate = 5
'2 times slower
Me.Media1.PlaybackRate = -2
```

Now you also have an opportunity of playing low-latency audio files—that is, .wav files, without the need of complex conversion operations. This is possible because Silverlight 5 includes libraries from the XNA Game Studio platform, so you just need to add a reference to the Microsoft.Xna.Framework.dll assembly. The following code demonstrates how to play a .wav file directly (this requires an `Imports Microsoft.Xna.Framework.Audio` directive):

```
'Replace with a valid .wav file Uri
Dim resource As StreamResourceInfo = Application.GetResourceStream _
    (New Uri("tada.wav",UriKind.RelativeOrAbsolute))

Dim effect As SoundEffect = SoundEffect.FromStream(resource.Stream)
effect.Play()
```

With a few lines of code, you can play a .wav file without the need of a complex analysis and elaboration of the file itself, as happened in the previous versions of Silverlight.

Animating UI Elements

Silverlight enables animating elements in the user interface similarly to what happens in WPF, so this section provides a brief and fast description of animations. Read Chapter 30, "Brushes, Styles, Templates, and Animations in WPF," for further details. Several kinds of animations are available, such as `DoubleAnimation`, `PointAnimation`, and `ColorAnimation`. They all come from the `System.Windows.Media.Animations` namespace. To understand how animations work in Silverlight, look at the code shown in Listing 36.3.

LISTING 36.3   Implementing Double Animations

```
<UserControl x:Class="SilverlightApplication1.AnimatingUIElements"
    xmlns="http://schemas.microsoft.com/winfx/2006/xaml/presentation"
    xmlns:x="http://schemas.microsoft.com/winfx/2006/xaml"
    xmlns:d="http://schemas.microsoft.com/expression/blend/2008"
    xmlns:mc="http://schemas.openxmlformats.org/markup-compatibility/2006"
    mc:Ignorable="d"
    d:DesignHeight="300" d:DesignWidth="400">
```

```xml
<Grid x:Name="LayoutRoot" Background="White">
    <Grid.ColumnDefinitions>
        <ColumnDefinition/>
        <ColumnDefinition/>
    </Grid.ColumnDefinitions>

    <!-- Replace with a valid image file -->
    <Image Grid.Column="0" Name="Image1"
            Source="/SilverlightApplication1;component/Images/AnImageFile.jpg">

        <Image.RenderTransform>
            <TransformGroup>
                <SkewTransform x:Name="SkewImage"/>
                <ScaleTransform x:Name="ScaleImage"/>
            </TransformGroup>
        </Image.RenderTransform>

        <Image.Triggers>
            <EventTrigger RoutedEvent="Image.Loaded">
                <EventTrigger.Actions>
                    <BeginStoryboard>
                        <Storyboard x:Name="ImageStoryBoard">
                            <DoubleAnimation Storyboard.TargetName="SkewImage"
                                             Storyboard.TargetProperty="AngleY"
                                             From="0" To="15" Duration="0:0:3"
                                             AutoReverse="True"
                                             RepeatBehavior="Forever" />
                            <DoubleAnimation Storyboard.TargetName="ScaleImage"
                                             Storyboard.TargetProperty="ScaleX"
                                             From="1" To="0.3" Duration="0:0:3"
                                             AutoReverse="True"
                                             RepeatBehavior="Forever" />
                            <DoubleAnimation Storyboard.TargetName="ScaleImage"
                                             Storyboard.TargetProperty="ScaleY"
                                             From="1" To="0.3" Duration="0:0:3"
                                             AutoReverse="True"
                                             RepeatBehavior="Forever" />
                        </Storyboard>
                    </BeginStoryboard>
                </EventTrigger.Actions>
            </EventTrigger>

        </Image.Triggers>
    </Image>
```

```xml
<TextBlock Grid.Column="1" Text="Animated Text" FontSize="24"
        FontFamily="Verdana" FontWeight="Bold"
        HorizontalAlignment="Center"
        VerticalAlignment="Center" RenderTransformOrigin="0.5 0.5">

<TextBlock.Foreground>
  <LinearGradientBrush>
    <GradientStop Offset="0" Color="Red" />
    <GradientStop Offset="0.5" Color="Yellow" />
    <GradientStop Offset="1" Color="Orange"/>
  </LinearGradientBrush>
</TextBlock.Foreground>

<TextBlock.RenderTransform>
    <TransformGroup>
        <RotateTransform x:Name="RotateText" />
        <SkewTransform x:Name="SkewText"/>
    </TransformGroup>
</TextBlock.RenderTransform>

<TextBlock.Triggers>
  <EventTrigger RoutedEvent="TextBlock.Loaded">
    <BeginStoryboard>
      <Storyboard x:Name="TextAnimation">
        <DoubleAnimation Storyboard.TargetName="RotateText"
                      Storyboard.TargetProperty="Angle"
                      From="0" To="360" Duration="0:0:5"
                      RepeatBehavior="Forever" />

        <DoubleAnimation Storyboard.TargetName="SkewText"
                      AutoReverse="True"
                      Storyboard.TargetProperty="AngleX"
                      From="0" To="45" Duration="0:0:5"
                      RepeatBehavior="Forever" />

      </Storyboard>
    </BeginStoryboard>
  </EventTrigger>
</TextBlock.Triggers>
</TextBlock>
    </Grid>
</UserControl>
```

You can specify some transformations for user interface elements you want to
animate, and then you can establish the event that will launch the animation with an

EventTrigger element within a Control.Triggers property node. The actual animation is provided by a StoryBoard object that contains one or more DoubleAnimation objects to animate the desired transformations. Figure 36.7 shows the result of the animation running.

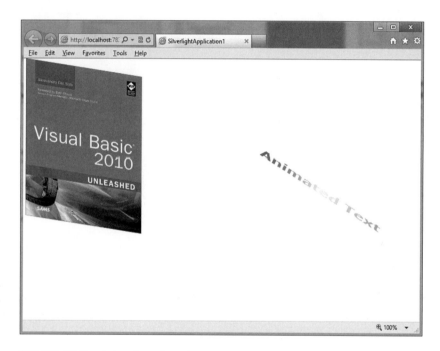

FIGURE 36.7   Animations in action.

SILVERLIGHT 5 AND 3-D GRAPHICS

Silverlight 5 introduces for the first time the support for 3D graphics. This is an extraordinary addition that reduces the gap with WPF even more and is made possible via a number of libraries that are part of the Microsoft XNA Game Studio platform, which are also included in Silverlight 5's runtime. You can find additional information in the MSDN documentation at http://msdn.microsoft.com/en-us/library/gg197424(v=XNAGameStudio.35).aspx.

Introducing Navigation Applications

Silverlight enables you to create applications for the Web, and in most cases a web application is not made of just one page. To provide support for navigation between pages, in a master page/details pages approach, Silverlight offers an infrastructure called Navigation Framework. This offers the capability of having a master page and then navigating different pages with different user controls. To create a navigation application, select

File, New Project and then the **Silverlight Navigation Application** project template in the Silverlight templates folder, as shown in Figure 36.8.

FIGURE 36.8   Creating a new navigation application.

When the project is ready, you can notice that the main page offers a page skeleton with borders and buttons. This can be considered as the master page. If you take a look at the XAML code, you notice the presence of the following lines, among others:

```
<navigation:Frame x:Name="ContentFrame"
                  Style="{StaticResource ContentFrameStyle}"
                  Source="/Home"
                  Navigated="ContentFrame_Navigated"
                  NavigationFailed="ContentFrame_NavigationFailed">
  <navigation:Frame.UriMapper>
    <uriMapper:UriMapper>
      <uriMapper:UriMapping Uri="" MappedUri="/Views/Home.xaml"/>
      <uriMapper:UriMapping Uri="/{pageName}"
       MappedUri="/Views/{pageName}.xaml"/>
    </uriMapper:UriMapper>
  </navigation:Frame.UriMapper>
</navigation:Frame>
```

The `System.Windows.Controls` namespace provides a `Frame` control that has an infrastructure for navigating between pages via a relative Uri that contains the folder and filename for the page to be browsed. This is accomplished by setting properties in the

`Frame.UriMapper` property. Among the number of files in the project, pages are stored in the Views subfolder. A couple of predefined pages are available, such as Home.xaml and About.xaml. The goal is now showing how you can add and browse a new page. Right-click the **Views** subfolder and select **Add New Item**. When the dialog box appears, select the **Silverlight Page** item template in the Silverlight folder and leave the Page1.xaml filename unchanged. When the new page is ready, add a simple text message to the main grid:

```
<Grid x:Name="LayoutRoot">
    <TextBlock Text="This is a secondary page"
            FontSize="32"/>
</Grid>
```

This is just a simple sample, but this is the place where you can provide your complex user interface. Now go back to the MainPage.xaml file and add the following button just above the other ones:

```
<HyperlinkButton x:Name="CustomLink" Style="{StaticResource LinkStyle}"
            NavigateUri="/Page1" TargetName="ContentFrame"
            Content="page1"/>
```

This can take advantage of an existing style for hyperlinked buttons and launch the new page specified via the `NavigateUri` property. What happens behind the scenes when you require browsing a new page is determined by the `ContentFrame_Navigated` event handler that appears as follows in the code-behind file:

```
Private Sub ContentFrame_Navigated(ByVal sender As Object,
        ByVal e As NavigationEventArgs) Handles ContentFrame.Navigated
    For Each child As UIElement In LinksStackPanel.Children
        Dim hb As HyperlinkButton = TryCast(child, HyperlinkButton)
        If hb IsNot Nothing AndAlso hb.NavigateUri IsNot Nothing Then
            If hb.NavigateUri = e.Uri Then
                VisualStateManager.GoToState(hb, "ActiveLink", True)
            Else
                VisualStateManager.GoToState(hb, "InactiveLink", True)
            End If
        End If
    Next
End Sub
```

The code gets the instance of `HyperlinkButton` controls and invokes the `GoToState` method to browse the specified page inside the `Frame` control. Now run the application by pressing **F5**. When ready, click the page1 hyperlink at the top of the page. This redirects to the new custom page, as shown in Figure 36.9.

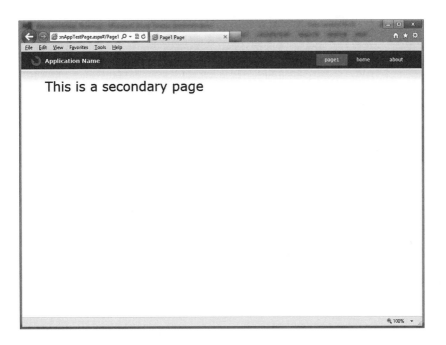

FIGURE 36.9   The custom page being browsed via the navigation framework.

Take a look at the Uri in the address bar of your web browser and look how it is formed by the relative path of the loaded page separated by a # symbol. Click **Home** or **About** to show predefined pages or go back to Visual Studio for editing your code and adding new custom pages. Finally, you can press the back and forward buttons in your browser to navigate pages. This is possible thanks to the System.Windows.Navigation. NavigationService object that provides, behind the scenes, support for browsing and loading pages into the Frame and for maintaining the URL history. Another important class in navigation applications is System.Windows.Navigation.NavigationContext, which is responsible for keeping track of the page context such as the URL and parameters passed in query string.

Introducing WCF RIA Services

WCF RIA Services (formerly known as .NET RIA Services) are a specific framework, offered by the System.Windows.Controls.Ria.dll assembly, for exposing data through networks that can then be consumed by Silverlight applications and that typically are implemented as a middle-tier for business applications. In this section you learn how to create a Silverlight business application consuming data from an Entity Data Model (EDM) exposed through RIA Services.

DATA ACCESS AND SILVERLIGHT

WCF RIA Services provide a well-structured and fast way of building line-of-business applications, but they are not the only way you can access data from Silverlight. Generally
speaking, you can implement your logic within a WCF service and expose data that a
Silverlight application can consume, such as Entity Data Models or LINQ to SQL models.

To create a business application based on WCF RIA Services, create a new project by selecting the **Silverlight Business Application** project template, as shown in Figure 36.10.

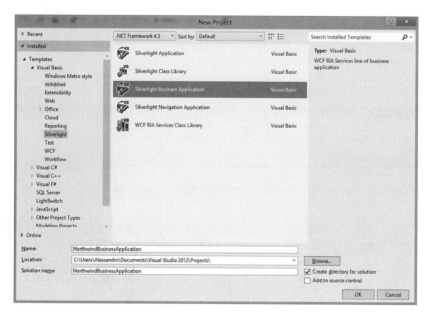

FIGURE 36.10   The WCF RIA Services project template.

Name the new project as **NorthwindBusinessApplication** and click **OK**. When the project
is ready, in Solution Explorer you notice a plethora of files and folders. This is because
RIA Services projects have an interesting structure based on models and views, other than
providing login and authentication infrastructure. Also, when opening the designer, the
new project is based on the navigation application template as described in the previous
section, so this can help you build complex user interfaces. The first thing to do now is
add a data source containing data you want to expose through the network.

Adding the Data Source

To add a data source based on the Northwind database (used in several other code examples in this book), follow these steps:

1. Right-click the **NorthwindBusinessApplication.Web** project and select **Add New
Item**; in the dialog box, select the **ADO.NET Entity Data Model** template, name it
Northwind.edmx, and click **OK**.

2. When the wizard starts, choose to generate the model from an existing database, and then select the Northwind database available on SQL Server as the data source.

3. When the list of database objects is available, select at least the **Orders** table and then click Finish.

4. Very important: because in Visual Studio 2012 by default Entity Data Models are based on the `DbContext` class instead of the `ObjectContext` class, and because at the moment WCF RIA Services do not support the `DbContext`, you have to change the model generation so that the `ObjectContext` is used. This can be done by right-clicking the Entity Data Model's designer and then selecting Properties; then you change the value of the Code Generation Strategy property from `None` to `Default`. Finally, in Solution Explorer you have to expand the .edmx file and remove both .tt files. When you rebuild the project, the Entity Data Model will re-generate code files based on the `ObjectContext` class.

TIP

The web application project represents the server-side application that exposes data through services. Remember that Silverlight applications act on the client side and will consume data from services, so this is why you just added the data model (and will add domain services) to the server-side application.

You now have a data source you can expose. Remember to build the project, so that it will be updated with references to the new EDM. As a final note, remember that Silverlight has full support for the Model-View-ViewModel (MVVM) pattern because it has been exposing the `ICommand` interface since version 4. In this chapter, we do not cover the MVVM pattern because we prefer to show how Silverlight works rather than discussing scenarios that are not specific to this technology; anyway you got a brief example of creating an MVVM-based Silverlight application when we talked about the Portable Class Library projects in Chapter 17, "Creating Objects: Visual Tools and Portable Libraries."

Adding the Domain Service Class

To make the data model consumable from clients, you need to implement your business logic. In WCF RIA Services-based applications, this is accomplished by implementing a Domain Service Class. Such kinds of classes inherit from `LinqToEntitiesDomainService(Of T)` and expose queries and methods for performing create/read/update/delete (CRUD) operations and can contain other custom logic. To add one, right-click the **Services** folder and select **Add New Item**. In the Add New Item dialog box, select the **Domain Service Class** template and name it **OrdersDomainService.vb**. The goal is to provide logic for accessing the `Orders` entity set (see Figure 36.11).

At this point, the IDE requires you to specify entities you want to be mapped into the domain service class and the access level. Figure 36.12 represents the dialog box that Visual Studio 2012 shows to provide such specifications.

FIGURE 36.11   The item template for adding a domain service class.

FIGURE 36.12   Specifying settings for the new domain service class.

Ensure that the **Enable Client Access** check box is flagged so that Silverlight applications can consume data. Select the entity data model from the combo box, and then choose one or more entities you want to be exposed by the domain service class. Also check the corresponding **Enable Editing** check box if you want to provide the ability of data editing. After you click **OK**, Visual Studio generates a domain service class that looks like the code shown in Listing 36.4.

LISTING 36.4   The Domain Service Class

```
Imports System
Imports System.Collections.Generic
Imports System.ComponentModel
Imports System.ComponentModel.DataAnnotations
Imports System.Data
Imports System.Linq
Imports System.Web.DomainServices
Imports System.Web.DomainServices.Providers
Imports System.Web.Ria
Imports System.Web.Ria.Services


'Implements application logic using the NorthwindEntities context.
' TODO: Add your application logic to these methods or in additional methods.
' TODO: Wire up authentication (Windows/ASP.NET Forms) and uncomment the following
➥to disable anonymous access
' Also consider adding roles to restrict access as appropriate.
'<RequiresAuthentication> _
<EnableClientAccess()> _
Public Class OrdersDomainService
    Inherits LinqToEntitiesDomainService(Of NorthwindEntities)

    'TODO: Consider
    ' 1. Adding parameters to this method and constraining returned results, and/or
    ' 2. Adding query methods taking different parameters.
    Public Function GetOrders() As IQueryable(Of Order)
        Return Me.ObjectContext.Orders
    End Function

    Public Sub InsertOrder(ByVal order As Order)
        If ((order.EntityState = EntityState.Added) _
                = false) Then
            If ((order.EntityState = EntityState.Detached) _
                    = false) Then
                Me.ObjectContext.ObjectStateManager.
                    ChangeObjectState(order, EntityState.Added)
            Else
                Me.ObjectContext.AddToOrders(order)
            End If
        End If
    End Sub
```

```
Public Sub UpdateOrder(ByVal currentOrder As Order)
    If (currentOrder.EntityState = EntityState.Detached) Then
        Me.ObjectContext.AttachAsModified(currentOrder,
                        Me.ChangeSet.GetOriginal(currentOrder))
    End If
End Sub


Public Sub DeleteOrder(ByVal order As Order)
    If (order.EntityState = EntityState.Detached) Then
        Me.ObjectContext.Attach(order)
    End If
    Me.ObjectContext.DeleteObject(order)
End Sub
End Class
```

Listing 36.4 shows how Visual Studio 2012 automatically implements logic for querying, adding, updating, and removing orders in the Orders entity set, working against an instance of the `ObjectContext` class from the Entity Framework. You can eventually add your own logic or edit the default one. For example, replace the `GetOrders` default method with the following that sorts orders by customer ID (adding an `OrderBy` clause is also mandatory if you plan to add data paging as we are going to do in a few minutes):

```
Public Function GetOrders() As IQueryable(Of Order)
    Return Me.ObjectContext.Orders.OrderBy(Function(ord) ord.CustomerID)
End Function
```

Then add the following simple method for saving changes, remembering that you can use your existing Entity Framework skills:

```
Public Sub SaveChanges()
    Me.ObjectContext.SaveChanges()
End Sub
```

Comments added by the IDE give you some suggestions to improve the class logic—for example, by providing authentication applying the `RequiresAuthentication` attribute. When you have the domain service class, which actually returns data, you first need to build the project again; then you are ready to bind such data to the appropriate controls in the user interface.

Data-Binding to Controls

The drag'n'drop data-binding techniques that you saw in WPF are also available in Silverlight projects. This is useful in WCF RIA Services applications because it enables easily generating data-oriented web pages. You now need to add user controls for showing data within the desired page. In the Silverlight project, expand the **Views** folder and double-click the **Home.xaml** page. You could consider adding a dedicated page, but for the sake of simplicity, an existing one can do the work the same. When the page is opened inside the Visual Studio designer, build the project and then open the Data Sources window by selecting the **Data, Show Data Sources** command. In the Data Sources window, you find some business objects produced by the generation of the RIA Services application, including the `Order` entity. Drag this onto the `DataGrid` and when you release the mouse, you notice that Visual Studio 2012 has generated the following XAML code:

```
<riaControls:DomainDataSource AutoLoad="True"
            d:DataContext="{d:DesignInstance my:Order,
            CreateList=true}" Height="0"
            Name="OrderDomainDataSource"
            QueryName="GetOrdersQuery" Width="0">
    <riaControls:DomainDataSource.DomainContext>
        <my:OrdersDomainContext />
    </riaControls:DomainDataSource.DomainContext>
</riaControls:DomainDataSource>
<sdk:DataGrid AutoGenerateColumns="False" Height="200"
            ItemsSource=
            "{Binding ElementName=OrderDomainDataSource,
            Path=Data}" Name="OrderDataGrid"
            RowDetailsVisibilityMode="VisibleWhenSelected"
            Width="400">
    <sdk:DataGrid.Columns>
        <sdk:DataGridTextColumn x:Name="CustomerIDColumn"
            Binding="{Binding Path=CustomerID}"
            Header="Customer ID"
            Width="SizeToHeader" />
        <sdk:DataGridTextColumn x:Name="EmployeeIDColumn"
            Binding="{Binding Path=EmployeeID}"
            Header="Employee ID" Width="SizeToHeader" />
        <sdk:DataGridTextColumn x:Name="FreightColumn"
            Binding="{Binding Path=Freight}"
            Header="Freight" Width="SizeToHeader" />
        <sdk:DataGridTemplateColumn x:Name="OrderDateColumn"
            Header="Order Date" Width="SizeToHeader">
            <sdk:DataGridTemplateColumn.CellTemplate>
                <DataTemplate>
                    <sdk:DatePicker
                        SelectedDate=
                        "{Binding Path=OrderDate,
                        Mode=TwoWay,
                        NotifyOnValidationError=true,
                        TargetNullValue=''}" />
                </DataTemplate>
            </sdk:DataGridTemplateColumn.CellTemplate>
        </sdk:DataGridTemplateColumn>
        <sdk:DataGridTextColumn x:Name="OrderIDColumn"
```

36

```
        Binding="{Binding Path=OrderID}"
        Header="Order ID" Width="SizeToHeader" />
<sdk:DataGridTemplateColumn
    x:Name="RequiredDateColumn"
    Header="Required Date" Width="SizeToHeader">
    <sdk:DataGridTemplateColumn.CellTemplate>
        <DataTemplate>
            <sdk:DatePicker
                SelectedDate=
                "{Binding Path=RequiredDate,
                Mode=TwoWay,
                NotifyOnValidationError=true,
                TargetNullValue=''}" />
        </DataTemplate>
    </sdk:DataGridTemplateColumn.CellTemplate>
</sdk:DataGridTemplateColumn>
<sdk:DataGridTextColumn x:Name="ShipAddressColumn"
    Binding="{Binding Path=ShipAddress}"
    Header="Ship Address" Width="SizeToHeader" />
<sdk:DataGridTextColumn x:Name="ShipCityColumn"
    Binding="{Binding Path=ShipCity}"
    Header="Ship City" Width="SizeToHeader" />
<sdk:DataGridTextColumn x:Name="ShipCountryColumn"
    Binding="{Binding Path=ShipCountry}"
    Header="Ship Country" Width="SizeToHeader" />
<sdk:DataGridTextColumn x:Name="ShipNameColumn"
    Binding="{Binding Path=ShipName}"
    Header="Ship Name" Width="SizeToHeader" />
<sdk:DataGridTemplateColumn
    x:Name="ShippedDateColumn"
    Header="Shipped Date"
    Width="SizeToHeader">
    <sdk:DataGridTemplateColumn.CellTemplate>
        <DataTemplate>
            <sdk:DatePicker
                SelectedDate=
                "{Binding Path=ShippedDate,
                Mode=TwoWay,
                NotifyOnValidationError=true,
                TargetNullValue=''}" />
        </DataTemplate>
    </sdk:DataGridTemplateColumn.CellTemplate>
</sdk:DataGridTemplateColumn>
<sdk:DataGridTextColumn
    x:Name="ShipPostalCodeColumn"
    Binding="{Binding Path=ShipPostalCode}"
```

```
            Header="Ship Postal Code"
            Width="SizeToHeader" />
        <sdk:DataGridTextColumn
            x:Name="ShipRegionColumn"
            Binding="{Binding Path=ShipRegion}"
            Header="Ship Region"
            Width="SizeToHeader" />
        <sdk:DataGridTextColumn
            x:Name="ShipViaColumn"
            Binding="{Binding Path=ShipVia}"
            Header="Ship Via"
            Width="SizeToHeader" />
    </sdk:DataGrid.Columns>
</sdk:DataGrid>
```

The `DataGrid` is now data-bound to a `DomainDataSource` control, which is the design-time representation of the domain service class, whereas the `DomainDataSource.DomainContext` property represents the data context for querying, loading, and submitting data. Notice how, similarly to what happens in Windows Presentation Foundation, the IDE generated `DataGrid` columns specific for the bound data type. At this point, you must build the project. Further considerations on executing the application are discussed in the next subsection. To make things even better, you can take advantage of the DataPager control, which allows the paging of data and provides better performance. To accomplish this, add the following row definitions to the `LayoutRoot` grid:

```
<Grid.RowDefinitions>
    <RowDefinition/>
    <RowDefinition Height="40"/>
</Grid.RowDefinitions>
```

Next, drag the `DataPager` control from the toolbox onto the newly created row in the current page and then edit the code removing all margins and spacing properties, so that it appears like this:

```
<sdk:DataPager PageSize="10" Grid.Row="1" />
```

The `DataPager` also supports the drag'n'drop data-binding, which means you can drag the `Orders` collection from the Data Sources window onto the control and Visual Studio will automatically bind the data source to the `DataPager` as well as to the `DataGrid`. Once you perform this operation, the code looks like the following:

```
<sdk:DataPager PageSize="10" Grid.Row="1" Source="{Binding Data,
            ElementName=OrderDomainDataSource}" />
```

The `PageSize` property determines how many items per page are loaded. To make a better example, replace 10 (which is the default) with 50.

Running the Application

After implementing business logic and providing data-binding for UI data controls, you are ready to run the application, so press **F5**. After a few seconds, you can see how the list of orders is correctly shown within the DataGrid in the Home page and how you can browse data with the DataPager control visible at the bottom of the page, as demonstrated in Figure 36.13.

FIGURE 36.13   The application based on WCF RIA Services shows requested data.

You could create a different page for showing data and making it reachable via the navigation framework, as described in the dedicated section of this chapter.

Filtering Data with the PivotViewer Control

Silverlight 5 introduces a new data-bound control called PivotViewer, which allows displaying data based on some filters and sorting conditions. To understand how it works, add a new page to the project or remove the DataGrid and DataPager control definitions from the home page of the previous example. First, you need a PivotViewer instance that you can drag from the toolbox onto the page in the designer. The control's definition in the XAML code looks like this:

```
<sdk:PivotViewer HorizontalAlignment="Left" Margin="0,10,0,0"
VerticalAlignment="Top"
             Height="430" Width="640" ItemsSource="{Binding Data,
             ElementName=OrderDomainDataSource}">
</sdk:PivotViewer>
```

Then you need a `DomainDataSource` control, which holds the list of data you want to be shown, in this case the list of orders (if you are editing the previous example you already have an instance):

```
<riaControls:DomainDataSource x:Name="OrderDomainDataSource" AutoLoad="True"
                Height="0" QueryName="GetOrdersQuery" Width="0">
    <riaControls:DomainDataSource.DomainContext>
        <local:OrdersDomainContext/>
    </riaControls:DomainDataSource.DomainContext>
</riaControls:DomainDataSource>
```

The `PivotViewer` control requires specifying three things:

▶ The data source that will be displayed

▶ Which elements from the data source will be included in the data view

▶ How elements from the data source will be presented

The first item in the previous bulleted list is represented by the `DomainDataSource` instance. The second item is represented by a group called `PivotViewer.PivotProperties`, which contains a number of objects representing columns in the database table. The following code, which you include inside the `PivotViewer` definition, provides an example:

```
<sdk:PivotViewer.PivotProperties>
    <sdk:PivotViewerStringProperty Id="OID" Options="CanFilter" DisplayName="Order
➡ID"
        Binding="{Binding OrderID}" />
    <sdk:PivotViewerDateTimeProperty Id="ODate" Options="CanFilter"
        DisplayName="Order Date" Binding="{Binding OrderDate}" />
    <sdk:PivotViewerStringProperty Id="CID" Options="CanFilter"
        DisplayName="Customer ID" Binding="{Binding CustomerID}" />
</sdk:PivotViewer.PivotProperties>
```

The `PivotViewer` control has a large number of properties and options, but you need to know how to represent types. The `PivotViewerStringProperty` object enables you to represent string values, whereas the `PivotViewerDateTimeProperty` object enables you to represent date/time items. Other available objects are `PivotViewerLinkProperty` (to show links) and `PivotViewerNumericProperty` (to show numbers).

CONTROL PROPERTIES AND CUSTOM DATA REPRESENTATION

Because I can't cover every possible property available in the `PivotViewer` control and how to implement custom types presentation, I suggest you have a look at the official MSDN documentation for the control available at `http://msdn.microsoft.com/en-us/library/system.windows.controls.pivot.pivotviewer(v=vs.95).aspx`.

36

Notice how every object is data-bound via the `Binding` markup extension to the specified property in the data source, exactly as you did in the `DataGrid` control with columns. The third item to supply is how elements from the data source will be presented—an item template. The following group, which you include in the control's definition and that is taken from the MSDN documentation, represents items from the collection with a blue box and white text:

```
<sdk:PivotViewer.ItemTemplates>
    <sdk:PivotViewerItemTemplate>
        <Border Width="200" Height="200" Background="Blue">
            <StackPanel Orientation="Vertical">
                <TextBlock Text="{Binding OrderID}"
                        FontSize="16" Foreground="White" />
                <TextBlock Text="{Binding OrderDate}"
                        FontSize="16" Foreground="White" />
                <TextBlock Text="{Binding CustomerID}"
                        FontSize="16" Foreground="White" />
            </StackPanel>
        </Border>
    </sdk:PivotViewerItemTemplate>
</sdk:PivotViewer.ItemTemplates>
```

If you now run the application, you will see how data can be filtered and sorted based on the columns you specified in code. Figure 36.14 shows an example in which the application displays orders from customer QUEEN for the year 1997.

FIGURE 36.14   Filtering and sorting data with the `PivotViewer` control.

It is easy to experiment with the various options offered by the control. This is definitely a useful addition to line-of-business applications.

"Out-of-Browser" Applications

You have the possibility of locally installing Silverlight applications so that they can be run in a desktop environment. This kind of application is generally known as "out of browser." Typically, you use this feature if you want to have a local copy of the application that does not need to be connected to a network for most of its requirements or in particular scenarios in which you need elevated permissions to access local resources. To make a Silverlight application be installable, you need to enable out-of-browser settings. To demonstrate how this works, create a new Silverlight project with Visual Basic 2012. When the new project is ready, in the main page type the following XAML:

```
<Grid x:Name="LayoutRoot" Background="White">
    <StackPanel>
        <Button Content="Get status" Height="40"
                HorizontalAlignment="Left" Margin="5"
                Name="Button1" VerticalAlignment="Top"
                Width="150" />
        <TextBlock Height="30" HorizontalAlignment="Left"
                Margin="5" Name="TextBlock1"
                VerticalAlignment="Top" Width="340"
                FontSize="16" />

    </StackPanel>
</Grid>
```

The goal is programmatically understanding whether the application is running inside or outside a web browser, so when the user clicks the button, a text message will be shown. Now in the code-behind file, handle the `Button.Click` event as follows:

```
Private Sub Button1_Click(ByVal sender As System.Object,
                    ByVal e As System.Windows.
                    RoutedEventArgs) Handles Button1.Click

    Me.TextBlock1.Text = "Running out of browser: " & _
    App.Current.IsRunningOutOfBrowser.ToString
End Sub
```

The `App.Current` property, of type `Application`, provides access to several application-level objects, including some for working with out-of-browser features. The `IsRunningOutOfBrowser` property returns `True` or `False` according to the execution context. Before running the demo application, you need to enable specific settings, so click **My Project** in Solution Explorer; then ensure the Silverlight tab is selected and check the **Enable Running Application out of the Browser** check box. Next, click the

36

Out-of-Browser Settings button that launches the same-named dialog box where you can customize settings for your offline application, as shown in Figure 36.15.

FIGURE 36.15   Customizing settings for out-of-browser applications.

These settings should be self-explanatory. If you do not want a default icon to be used, you can supply your own. You can also provide a shortcut name because you can choose to add a shortcut to the desktop or to the Start menu to the offline application. Now you can run the application. When ready, click the button so that you can verify that the code can determine that the application is running inside the browser, as shown in Figure 36.16. To install the application locally, right-click in the browser window and select the **Install ApplicationName onto This Computer** command, as shown in Figure 36.16. At this point, the Install Application dialog box will ask you to specify where you want to place shortcuts for running the application locally, such as the Desktop, the Start menu, or both (see Figure 36.17 for an example).

After it's installed, the application will be automatically launched out of the browser. Figure 36.18 shows how the demo application looks. Notice that you can uninstall the application by right-clicking inside the local window and then choosing the **Remove** command.

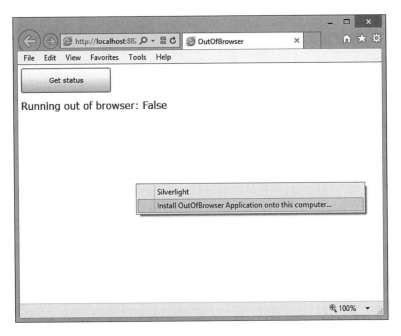

FIGURE 36.16   Running the application and selecting the local installation option.

FIGURE 36.17   Installing the application locally.

FIGURE 36.18   The application running out of the browser, locally.

36

Elevated Permissions and Security Considerations

Silverlight applications are normally considered partial-trust because they run on the Web and therefore cannot access resources on the local machine. This is the default behavior, but Silverlight 4 introduced support for COM Automation, which is particularly useful if you want to interact with Microsoft Office's applications. Other than COM Automation, Silverlight 4 introduced support for accessing the local file system and printers. All these possibilities require elevated privileges, which is why Silverlight 4 provided out-of-browser applications: by running on the desktop, an application can be full-trust and can interact with local resources. This could be annoying because you needed to deploy your application under the form of a desktop application, losing the benefits of offering your app through the Web. Fortunately, Silverlight 5 removes this limitation, introducing elevated permissions for in-browser applications as well. This new version lets you mark an in-browser application as full-trust, so that it can have elevated permissions and access local resources. To accomplish this, you need to go to the Silverlight's project properties and enable the **Require elevated trust when running In-browser** option. This works fine on the development machine, but the application must be signed with a valid X.509 certificate after you publish it.

ACCESSING THE LOCAL FILE SYSTEM

With Silverlight 4, an out-of-browser application could access the local file system, but this is true only for folders at the user level such as My Documents or My Music. Attempting to access different folders would result in a `SecurityException`. This limitation has been removed in Silverlight 5, so now you can access other folders as well, but remember that the application inherits the rights the current user has. So, if the current user does not have enough permissions to access a specified folder, the runtime will throw an exception even if Silverlight 5 has support for the local file system.

XAML Debugging

Probably the most interesting new feature in Silverlight 5 is the possibility of placing breakpoints directly inside the XAML code editor to enable debugging of data-binding assignments. To understand how it works, open the project called NorthwindBusinessApplication that you created while reading the section called "Introducing WCF RIA Services." Open the Home.xaml file and locate the assignment of the `ItemsSource` property of the `DataGrid` control. Select the line of code and press **F9**. Visual Studio will add a breakpoint on the `Binding` markup extension, as demonstrated in Figure 36.19.

When you run the application and the runtime starts loading the data, Visual Studio will break the execution on the specified breakpoint. If you open the Locals window, you will see a `BindingState` value representing the progress of the data-binding operation (see Figure 36.20). This contains a lot of useful information such as the `BindingExpression` value and the progress of the `UpdateTarget` operation, or the `ValidationErrors` collection. You will find the `Error` value that describes any data-binding error particularly useful because it will help you solve data-binding problems within a convenient debugging environment.

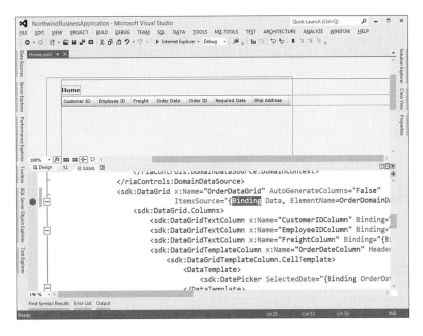

FIGURE 36.19   XAML debugging with breakpoints.

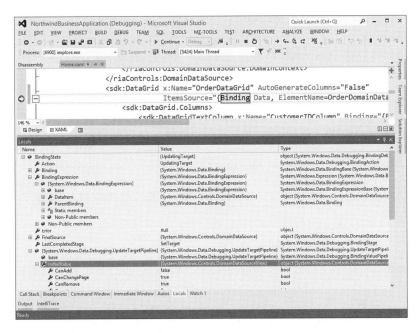

FIGURE 36.20   The debugger breaks the execution and shows the current state of data-binding.

Additional New Features in Silverlight 5

Following is a list of additional new features in Silverlight 5 that you might find useful and that are described in detail in the MSDN documentation:

▶ P/Invoke support. With the aforementioned improvements about elevated permissions, Silverlight 5 applications can invoke Windows APIs like any other desktop application. P/Invokes are discussed in Chapter 48, "Platform Invokes and Interoperability with the COM Architecture."

▶ Support for 64-bit browsers.

▶ Support for multiple windows via the `Window` class.

▶ Direct support for Windows Azure.

▶ Performance improvements in several areas such as startup, XAML parsing, and thread contention.

Before completing this chapter, it is very important for you to know that as of today, Microsoft has not yet talked about public plans for a sixth version of Silverlight. With the introduction of Windows 8 and the Windows Runtime, it is reasonable to think that Microsoft will not produce Silverlight 6, even if the current and the previous versions are supported and your investments are still valid.

Summary

In this chapter, you saw that Silverlight is a cross-browser, cross-platform, and cross-device plug-in for building rich internet applications based on the .NET Framework. You found out the many similarities that exist between Silverlight and WPF in both creating projects and in writing code (XAML and Visual Basic). You saw how Silverlight programming is based on the concept of user control and how you add user controls to the user interface and handle events. Next, you learned some common scenarios, such as playing media contents and animations. You also took a tour inside some important features for the business: navigation applications, which provide a framework for browsing pages as if you had master page and subpages, WCF RIA Services, a recent data framework for building business applications, drag'n'drop data-binding, and the new `PivotViewer` control. You saw how to make an application run on the desktop via the out-of-browser feature that offers the possibility of locally installing a Silverlight application. You also got an overview of security enhancements and how to debug your data-bindings directly in XAML with the support of breakpoints.

CHAPTER 37

Building and Deploying Applications for Windows Azure

Maintaining servers and data centers has costs and requires a company to have people specifically working on maintenance and administration. To reduce costs, a new way of thinking about data and web applications working on data is *cloud computing*. The idea of cloud computing is that you eliminate physical servers and data centers from your company's location and deploy your web applications to servers that are elsewhere in the world and maintained by another company, using network connections for accessing your data. Microsoft has been working hard since 2008 on its own cloud computing platform, known as Windows Azure Platform, which is now a mature platform. This platform is composed of several services, such as applications hosted on a 64-bit operating system, SQL Server data access, and .NET services. A deep discussion on Azure would certainly require an entire book; in this chapter you learn what Windows Azure is and how you can build and deploy Visual Basic web applications to Azure using Visual Studio 2012; further discussions on the numerous offered services are available in the MSDN official documentation.

Overview of the Windows Azure Platform

The Windows Azure Platform is the cloud computing platform from Microsoft. It offers an infrastructure for scaling applications on the Internet where services and applications are hosted on Microsoft data centers. With Windows Azure, you do not need physical servers in your company because data and applications are hosted by Microsoft servers. Windows Azure is instead just a part of the Azure Platform and is a 64-bit operating system providing the runtime and the environment for hosting your applications and the platform's services and for managing the applications' lifecycle. You are not limited to .NET applications; you can host PHP, Java, and other kinds of web applications on Azure as well. In this chapter, though, you learn only about .NET. One of the biggest benefits in developing for Windows Azure is that you can keep your existing skills in developing ASP.NET and Silverlight web applications and WCF services with just slight modifications due to the platform infrastructure, still utilizing Visual Studio 2012 as the development environment. The goal of this chapter is introducing you to developing and deploying your Visual Basic applications to the Azure platform. In-depth discussions are not possible here, although it is important to understand how you use Visual Studio 2012 to build and deploy Visual Basic applications. The Windows Azure Platform offers several services other than the Windows Azure operating system, which can be summarized as follows:

▶ **Websites**—These represent ASP.NET web applications, and their development fully integrates with Visual Studio and is available for several programming languages, not only in the .NET family, such as PHP, Java, and Python. With Websites, Windows Azure offers a service hosting space that runs applications and a Storage Account service where you place your data.

▶ **Cloud Services**—These include, among the others, a full SQL relational database (formerly known as SQL Azure) and APIs to connect public cloud networks with private networks.

▶ **Virtual Machines**—An environment to easily migrate existing Windows or Linux virtual machines to Windows Azure without the need of changing existing code, it also enables you to connect an on-premise network to virtual machines running on the cloud.

▶ **Application Building Blocks**—These include a number of useful additions to the platform such as media streaming, Cloud Storage (see the following bulleted list), identity support for corporate log-ins, the Windows Azure Marketplace (an easy way to sell your applications or data sets), and content delivery based on network availability.

With particular regard to Application Building Blocks, the Cloud Storage, which is enabled when you create your account, is composed by the following areas:

▶ **Blob Storage**—Here, you can place files and streams that you can reach via HTTP and HTTPS addresses.

▶ **Tables Storage**—Here, you can organize data within tables.

▶ **Local Storage**—The space on the disk in the virtual machine hosting your Windows Azure applications that your code can access for your needs.

▶ **Windows Azure Drives**—Virtual VHD disks that your code running on the virtual machine can mount and that are backed by a blob.

▶ **Queues Storage**—Service for sending and receiving messages on the network.

The Blob Storage is particularly useful when you need to store some files, which can be of any kind, to use in your applications. The Windows Azure Developer Center contains hundreds of learning resources about all the previously mentioned services. You can find it here: http://msdn.microsoft.com/en-us/azure/default.aspx. This chapter explains the tools necessary for building and deploying web applications to Azure, but before getting your hands dirty writing code, it is important to mention how you can register to the Windows Azure Platform.

Registering for the Windows Azure Developer Portal

To deploy hosted applications to Windows Azure, you first need to register and get an account. Windows Azure and related services are paid services, and you pay only for resources that you actually consume, which is the biggest benefit of a cloud-based solution (pay-per-use). Fortunately, you can request a 90-day free trial and decide to purchase a subscription later. You can request your free trial at http://www.windowsazure.com/en-us/pricing/free-trial/. At the expiration of the trial period, if you are interested in Microsoft cloud computing and in purchasing services, ensure you read this page about pricing first: http://www.windowsazure.com/en-us/pricing/purchase-options/. Only if you decide to pay for cloud computing services, follow the instructions provided in the Azure's website. Assuming you have chosen either a trial subscription or a paid subscription, you need to log in with a valid Windows Live ID. After you've logged in, follow the instructions shown to get your tokens. You will also receive an email with instructions to follow to activate your token on Windows Azure. Only when you are a registered user can you visit the Windows Azure Developer portal that is located at the following address: https://manage.windowsazure.com. Your new account will give you access to three main features: the Cloud Services, which is where you will publish your applications; SQL Databases, which represents the SQL database instance that hosts your databases on the cloud; and the Storage account, where you will have access to the blog storage, queues, and tables. Later in this chapter you see how to manage applications within the Windows Azure Developer Portal. Before going into that, you need to enable Visual Studio 2012 for cloud development.

Downloading and Installing Tools for Visual Studio

Visual Studio 2012 is the premier development environment for Windows Azure. To enable the IDE, you need to download and install Windows Azure SDK for .NET and Visual Studio 2012. You can find it at the following link: https://www.windowsazure.com/en-us/develop/net/. Click the **Install** button and choose the version of Visual Studio (2010 or 2012) you want to target. Installing the SDK will make some tools for Visual Studio available on your machine, which enables you to create and manage projects the usual way, and the Windows Azure SDK. The Windows Azure SDK is composed by the Compute Emulator, a tool that locally reproduces the hosting services on the cloud and that is required for running your applications locally; the Storage Emulator, which reproduces locally the environment for publishing blobs, queues, and messages; and the documentation. The Windows Azure SDK also contains sample applications with full source code for further studies. Also be sure to periodically check out the official Cloud Computing tools team blog from Microsoft, available here: http://blogs.msdn.com/cloud/.

USING VISUAL STUDIO 2012 EXPRESS FOR WEB

You can use the free Visual Studio 2012 Express for Web to build applications for Windows Azure using Visual Basic. This edition is free of charge and can be downloaded and installed (including the Windows Azure SDK for .NET) via the Web Platform Installer, available at http://www.microsoft.com/web/downloads/platform.aspx.

Additional Tools

With the growing diffusion of Windows Azure, lots of tools are coming out. Particularly there is a need for client tools for managing the Cloud Storage, especially when you need to manage files in the Blob Storage both locally and online. Following is a list of client applications that provide the ability to easily manage the cloud storage:

▶ **Cloud Storage Studio from Cerebrata**—A professional WPF application that manages not only blobs, but also tables and queues; it also enables you to manage permissions, show analytics, and handle multiple accounts. This application is paid, but it is probably the most complete and professional. Download a trial at: http://www.cerebrata.com/products/CloudStorageStudio.

▶ **CloudBerry Explorer for Windows Azure**—A freeware client that enables you to manage blobs and that supports synchronization between local files and online blobs. You can find it at http://www.cloudberrylab.com/free-microsoft-azure-explorer.aspx.

▶ **Azure Blob Studio 2011**—A free client written by me and available for free on CodePlex.com. This client is available both as a standalone WPF application and as an add-on for Visual Studio. It supports Blob Storage only, but it is completely written in Visual Basic. You can find it at http://azureblobstudio.codeplex.com.

▶ **Azure Storage Explorer**—Another free client with source code available on CodePlex (http://azurestorageexplorer.codeplex.com), which enables you to manage blobs, queues, and tables.

It is important for you to have one of these applications in your toolbox because you will often need to manage your cloud storage in case you want to start developing professional applications for Windows Azure.

Creating a Demo Project

SUPPORTED FRAMEWORKS

At the time this chapter is being written, Windows Azure does not support the .NET Framework 4.5 yet. This means that you can certainly use Visual Studio 2012 to build cloud-based applications, but the current chapter will provide an example based on the .NET Framework 4.0. This example will be still useful when .NET 4.5 is supported by Azure.

Creating applications for Windows Azure is something that affects a plethora of scenarios because you can build and deploy any kind of web applications. This chapter provides an example of a Silverlight web application to show how different technologies (ASP.NET, Silverlight, and Azure) can coexist in the cloud development. With that said, run Visual Studio 2012 and open the New Project dialog box.

VISUAL STUDIO REQUIRES ELEVATED PRIVILEGES

To test your Windows Azure applications locally, Visual Studio needs to be run with elevated privileges (Run as Administrator). This is required because Visual Studio needs to launch the Development Fabric, which also needs to be run with elevated privileges.

Click the Visual Basic folder, click the **Cloud** subfolder, and select the **Windows Azure Cloud Service** project template. Name the new project as **AzureBookstore**. See Figure 37.1 for details.

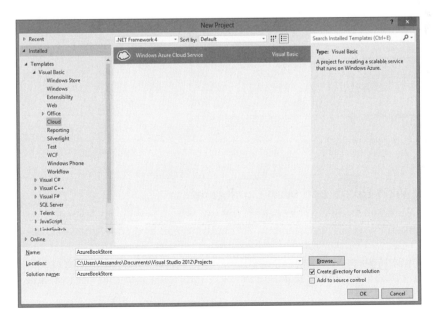

FIGURE 37.1   Creating the new project.

After you click OK, another dialog box displays requesting you to specify the application type. You can select different kinds of projects, such as ASP.NET Web Role, ASP.NET MVC Web Roles, WCF Services, Worker Roles, and Silverlight business applications. The ASP. NET Web Role is the most common template for classic ASP.NET applications; you learn more about roles in the next subsection. In this dialog box, select the **Silverlight Business Application** option and press the right arrow so that everything appears as in Figure 37.2. Notice that Visual Studio 2012 generates Silverlight 5 projects at this point. Move the mouse pointer over the item in the right column and click the pencil icon to rename the project into BookStore; finally click OK. After this, Visual Studio generates a new solution storing two projects: The first project is the Cloud service that stores information for the Windows Azure hosting service. The second project is the ASP.NET web application that you actually work on. As you know, Silverlight projects include an ASP.NET web application to host the rich client. Before putting hands on the code, an explanation about both projects is required.

FIGURE 37.2   Selecting the project type.

Understanding Web Roles and Web Configuration

A key concept in Windows Azure development is the *role*, which is typically a single component running in the Azure environment and built in managed code. Roles can be of two types: web roles and worker roles. A *web* role is an ASP.NET web application, like the case of our sample scenario in which a Silverlight application is hosted within an ASP. NET website. As you might remember from Figure 37.2, additional web roles are available for WCF applications. You might instead think of *worker* roles as services running behind the scenes, like in the case of Windows services, in the cloud. An Azure project can have multiple roles and multiple instances of one role; moreover, you can configure roles as required. When you create new cloud projects, the new solution will contain a web role project (an ASP.NET web project) and a service project where you can configure role properties. To access roles configuration, in Solution Explorer right-click the **BookStore. Web** role and select **Properties**. At this point, a special implementation of the **My Project** designer will pop up. Figure 37.3 shows what you will see on the screen.

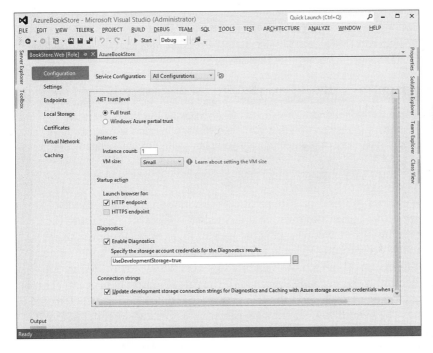

FIGURE 37.3   Accessing role configuration options.

The **Configuration** tab enables you to first set the .NET trust level for roles. By default, the trust level is **Full Trust**. The Windows Azure **Partial Trust** level has some limitations and denies your role access to some resources, such as the Registry, isolated storage, printing, and OleDb connections. The full restrictions list is available here: http://msdn. microsoft.com/en-us/library/dd573355.aspx. The **Instance Count** field enables you to set how many instances of the role are permitted, and **VM Size** enables you to specify the size of the virtual machine hosting your service. The virtual machines' size and power have changed during the years and will probably evolve as time goes on, so you should take a look at the official website for detailed information: http://www.windowsazure.com/en-us/ pricing/calculator/?scenario=virtual-machines

Just remember that a small virtual machine is a good choice if you have an MSDN subscription with Windows Azure benefits included. The Startup action group enables you to specify whether debugging should be launched via an HTTP or HTTPS endpoint (which must be defined in the Endpoints tab). In the Settings tab, you can define settings that you can access via the Windows Azure SDK Runtime API. By default, each role has a DiagnosticsConnectionString that defines whether you need access to the local storage or the online services. In the Endpoints tab, you can define endpoints for your application (you can retrieve endpoints in the Management Portal). Deciding to apply for an HTTPS endpoint also requires a valid SSL certificate. You add certificates to your deployment via the Certificates tab. The Local Storage tab enables you to configure the file system storage resources local for each instance. All the preceding options and settings are reflected into the ServiceConfiguration.cscfg and ServiceDefinition.csdef files that you can see in Solution Explorer and that are XML representations of settings.

ADDING MULTIPLE ROLES AND 64-BIT CONSIDERATIONS

You can add multiple web roles and worker roles by right-clicking the Roles folder in Solution Explorer. Another consideration that you need to keep in mind is that Windows Azure is a 64-bit operating system, so take care if you plan to invoke unmanaged code that might fail.

The Certificates tab allows you to configure certificate installation for the instance of the currently selected role; certificates must be uploaded to Windows Azure using the Management Portal. The Virtual Network tab enables you to activate Windows Azure Connect, which enables connecting the role to local computers. Click the appropriate hyperlink to get information about Windows Azure Connect. Finally, the Caching tab enables in-memory caching for multiple instances of the role for faster data access. This is not needed for the current example, and the IDE shows a hyperlink you can click to get further information. The default role for the new project is associated with the ASP.NET project that will actually run the application. You can therefore build your application directly within the web project or add a Silverlight project, as explained in next section.

Building the Silverlight 5 Project

The goal of this chapter is building a Silverlight application capable of showing and editing a list of books within a DataGrid control and providing the ability to read and save data to XML using the isolated storage. Visual Studio 2012 generated a full Silverlight 5 project, so you need to write some code and generate the user interface. Because we use LINQ to XML for listing and saving books, and because this will be accomplished using a DataGrid control, add references to the System.XML.Linq.dll and System.Windows. Controls.Data.dll assemblies. Both assemblies are available in the Extension node of the Reference Manager dialog box, as shown in Figure 37.4.

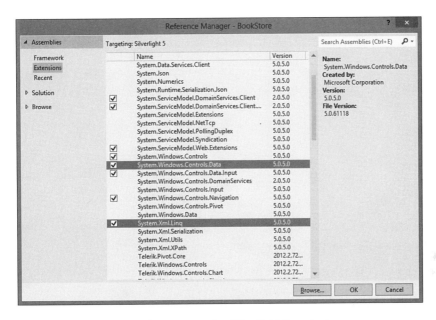

FIGURE 37.4   Adding references to the Silverlight 5 project.

You now need to implement a `Book` class representing one book and a `BooksCollection` class representing a typed collection of books, so add a new code file to the Silverlight project named Book.vb. The code in Listing 37.1 demonstrates this.

LISTING 37.1   Implementing Classes for Representing Books

```vb
Imports System.Collections.ObjectModel

Public Class Book

    Public Property Title As String
    Public Property Author As String
    Public Property DatePublished As Date
    Public Property ISBN As String

End Class

Public Class BooksCollection
    Inherits ObservableCollection(Of Book)

    Public Sub New(ByVal source As IEnumerable(Of Book))
        For Each b As Book In source
```

37

```
            Me.Add(b)
        Next
    End Sub


    Public Sub New()

    End Sub
End Class
```

For the sake of clarity, open the Home.xaml page (which is stored in the Views folder) and implement just a DataGrid and a Button for saving data. The following XAML code must replace the Grid definition:

```
<Grid x:Name="LayoutRoot">
    <ScrollViewer x:Name="PageScrollViewer" Style="{StaticResource
➥PageScrollViewerStyle}">

        <StackPanel x:Name="ContentStackPanel" Style="{StaticResource
➥ContentStackPanelStyle}">

            <TextBlock x:Name="HeaderText" Style="{StaticResource HeaderTextStyle}"
                Text="{Binding Strings.HomePageTitle, Source={StaticResource
➥ApplicationResources}}"/>

            <Grid Background="Green">
                <Grid.RowDefinitions>
                    <RowDefinition/>
                    <RowDefinition Height="50"/>
                </Grid.RowDefinitions>
                <sdk:DataGrid Name="BooksGrid" Grid.Row="0" ItemsSource="{Binding}"
                AutoGenerateColumns="True" />
                <StackPanel Grid.Row="1" Orientation="Horizontal">
                    <Button Width="100" Height="40" Margin="5"
                Content="Save" Name="SaveButton"/>
                </StackPanel>
            </Grid>
        </StackPanel>
    </ScrollViewer>
</Grid>
```

The DataGrid is defined within the System.Windows.Controls.Data namespace; because of this, you need to add the following XML namespace declaration at page level to use it:

```
xmlns:sdk="http://schemas.microsoft.com/winfx/2006/xaml/presentation/sdk"
```

Now it is time to write Visual Basic code. Our goal is reading data from an XML file containing the books' definitions, which is stored in the Silverlight's isolated storage. If the file is not found, which is the case of the first run, an empty books collection is defined. Finally, the code provides the capability of saving data to the isolated storage. Listing 37.2 shows all these operations (read comments within code for explanations).

LISTING 37.2   Defining Code for Retrieving, Showing, and Saving Books Definitions

```vb
Imports System.Windows.Controls
Imports System.Windows.Navigation
Imports System.Xml.Linq
Imports System.IO.IsolatedStorage
Imports System.IO

''' <summary>
''' Home page for the application.
''' </summary>
Partial Public Class Home
    Inherits Page

    ''' <summary>
    ''' Creates a new <see cref="Home"/> instance.
    ''' </summary>
    Public Sub New()
        InitializeComponent()

        Me.Title = ApplicationStrings.HomePageTitle
    End Sub

    ''' <summary>
    ''' Executes when the user navigates to this page.
    ''' </summary>
    Protected Overloads Overrides Sub OnNavigatedTo(ByVal e As NavigationEventArgs)
    End Sub


    'Declaring a books collection
    Private MyBooks As BooksCollection

    'Required for understanding if the DataGrid
    'is in edit mode
    Private isEditing As Boolean = False
    'Used to generate data if the data file is not
    'found
    Private Function CreateData() As BooksCollection
        Dim b As New Book With {.ISBN = "0000000"}
```

```vb
        Dim bc As New BooksCollection
        bc.Add(b)
        Return bc
    End Function


    'Attempts to read the data file from the isolated storage
    'If found, with a LINQ to Xml query a new books collection
    'is returned. If not found, a new empty collection is
    'generated and returned
    Private Function GetBooks() As BooksCollection
        Try
            Dim doc As XDocument

            Using store As IsolatedStorageFile = IsolatedStorageFile.
                                                    GetUserStoreForApplication
                Dim st As IsolatedStorageFileStream = _
                        store.OpenFile("Books.xml", FileMode.Open)
                doc = XDocument.Load(st)
                st.Close()
            End Using

            Dim query = From pbook In doc...<Book>
                    Select New Book With {.Author = pbook.@Author,
                                    .Title = pbook.@Title,
                                    .DatePublished = Date.
                                    Parse(pbook.@DatePublished),
                                    .ISBN = pbook.@ISBN
                        }

            Return New BooksCollection(query)


        Catch ex As Exception
            Return CreateData()
        End Try
    End Function


    'Saves data to the isolated storage. The Xml data is generated
    'with LINQ to Xml embedded-expressions
    Private Sub SaveButton_Click(ByVal sender As System.Object,
                            ByVal e As System.Windows.
                            RoutedEventArgs) Handles SaveButton.Click
        Dim data = <?xml version="1.0" encoding="utf-8"?>
                <Books>
                    <%= From b In MyBooks
                        Select <Book Author=<%= b.Author %>
                                Title=<%= b.Title %>
```

```
                         ISBN=<%= b.ISBN %>
                         DatePublished=<%= b.DatePublished.
                                         ToString %>/>
              %>
           </Books>

    Using store As IsolatedStorageFile = IsolatedStorageFile.
                                    GetUserStoreForApplication
        Dim st As IsolatedStorageFileStream = _
              store.OpenFile("Books.xml", FileMode.Create)
        data.Save(st)
        st.Close()
    End Using
End Sub


Private Sub Home_Loaded(sender As Object, e As RoutedEventArgs) Handles
➥Me.Loaded
        'Populates data
        Me.MyBooks = GetBooks()
        'Sets data-binding
        Me.DataContext = Me.MyBooks

End Sub


Private Sub BooksGrid_BeginningEdit(ByVal sender As Object,
                         ByVal e As System.Windows.Controls.
                         DataGridBeginningEditEventArgs) _
                         Handles BooksGrid.BeginningEdit
    isEditing = True
End Sub


'Allows DataGrid editing
Private Sub BooksGrid_KeyDown(ByVal sender As Object,
                         ByVal e As System.Windows.Input.
                         KeyEventArgs) Handles BooksGrid.KeyDown
    If isEditing = False Then
        'If the user press Delete, removes the selected item
        If e.Key = Key.Delete Then

            If Me.BooksGrid.SelectedItem IsNot Nothing Then
                Me.MyBooks.Remove(CType(Me.BooksGrid.SelectedItem, Book))
            End If
            'If the user press Insert, adds a new empty item to the collection
        ElseIf e.Key = Key.Insert Then
            Dim b As New Book With {.DatePublished = Today}
```

37

```
                Dim index As Integer = MyBooks.IndexOf(CType(Me.BooksGrid.
                                                     SelectedItem, Book))


                MyBooks.Insert(index + 1, b)
                BooksGrid.SelectedIndex = index
                BooksGrid.BeginEdit()
            End If
        End If
    End Sub


    Private Sub BooksGrid_RowEditEnding(ByVal sender As Object,
                            ByVal e As System.Windows.Controls.
                            DataGridRowEditEndingEventArgs) _
                            Handles BooksGrid.RowEditEnding

        isEditing = False
    End Sub


End Class
```

Our application is now ready to be started. One of the biggest benefits of the Windows
Azure SDK tools is that you can test your application locally before you deploy it to the
cloud. This is possible because of the Windows Azure debugging environment that is a
full-featured environment locally reproducing the cloud system.

Testing the Application Locally

When you run an Azure application locally for the first time, the environment needs to
be initialized. Fortunately, Visual Studio and the Windows Azure SDK will do the work
for you. When you press **F5**, the Windows Azure debugging environment is started and
a local developer account is created to replicate on your development machine what you
can activate on the online services. After the build process completes, you can see the
application correctly running in your web browser. Figure 37.5 demonstrates this.

You can now try to add or delete other books and finally save changes. So we reached
our objective locally. The next step should be deploying the application to the cloud,
but before doing this, here's some brief information about the Debugging Environment
tools. The Debugging Environment is essentially composed of two main tools: the Storage
Emulator, which is used for locally storing blobs, tables, and queues, and the Compute
Emulator, which is useful for monitoring running services. This environment provides a
tray bar icon that you can right-click to access both tools. Figure 37.6 displays how the
Compute Emulator gives information about the running application.

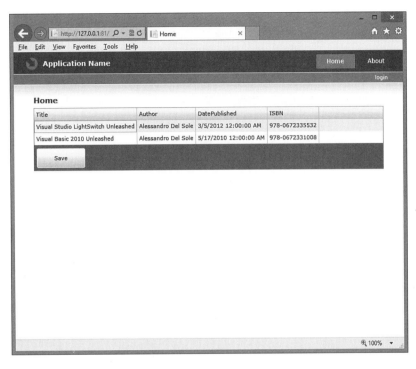

FIGURE 37.5   The application running locally.

FIGURE 37.6   The Compute Emulator shows services information.

It is worth mentioning that the Compute Emulator can show information about multiple running Azure services. Figure 37.7 instead shows the Storage Emulator UI. Here you can just enable or disable endpoints for blobs, tables, and queues, but the suggestion is to leave the default settings unchanged.

FIGURE 37.7   The Storage Emulator user interface.

Because the application runs correctly, we can now deploy it to the cloud environment of Windows Azure.

Deploying Applications to Windows Azure

Deploying applications to Windows Azure has been dramatically simplified in Visual Studio 2012 so that the IDE will do most of the work for you, avoiding several manual operations in the Management Portal as was required in the past. To deploy an application, you have to right-click the Cloud project in Solution Explorer (in our example it is AzureBookStore) and then click Publish in the pop-up menu. This will launch the Publish Windows Azure Application wizard, where you must enter both subscription and application settings. In the first dialog box, click **Sign in to download credentials**, so that Visual Studio will open the Windows Azure website, allowing you to download your subscription information without the need of entering such information manually. You will be asked to enter your Windows Live ID and your password; then the website will automatically invite you to download a file containing settings of your subscription. Figure 37.8 shows things at this point.

At this point, go back to Visual Studio 2012 and click Import. Then select the downloaded settings file. Figure 37.9 shows the dialog box, demonstrating how subscription settings have been imported.

FIGURE 37.8   Downloading subscription information from Windows Azure.

FIGURE 37.9   Settings for your Windows Azure subscription have been automatically imported.

If you did not import your settings in this way, you had to create a new profile manually, entering all the subscription information such as the subscription ID, which would probably involve opening the Management Portal and, consequently, wasting time. Visual Studio 2012 enables you to manage multiple subscriptions by selecting the Manage item in the Choose Your Subscription combo box. Click Next to access the Settings tab. Here you have to specify settings for your cloud service, which is the application. If this is the first time you deploy an application to Azure, you will have to create a new service. Expand the Cloud Service combo box and select Create New. In the Create Windows Azure Services dialog box, enter a name for your service and select the nearest location to you (in my case I chose West Europe because I live in Italy), as shown in Figure 37.10.

FIGURE 37.10   Creating a new cloud service.

When you click OK, the Common Settings tab shows basic information about the deployment. In this case you should change the value of the Environment combo box from Production to Staging. The Staging deployment is intended for configuration and testing purposes. This change is useful to show how to use the Management Portal because otherwise you could publish the application to production without any interaction with the portal (which is very different from the past). Figure 37.11 shows how Common Settings appear now.

FIGURE 37.11   Common Settings for the current cloud service.

You can also make a local deployment by replacing the value of the Service configuration combo box from Cloud to Local, and you can enable remote desktop connections for roles in the solution. The Advanced Settings tab lets you enable a number of interesting features (see Figure 37.12).

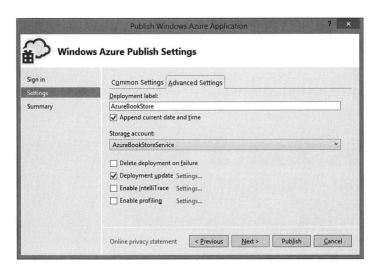

FIGURE 37.12   Advanced Settings for the current cloud project.

The Deployment Label is a name used to identify the deployment among all the deployments you have in your subscription. When you deploy an application to Azure, Visual Studio 2012 automatically generates a new storage account, which is necessary to host application files. If you have existing storage accounts, you can choose one of them instead of generating a new one. You can specify the way your application will be updated (one instance at a time or all instances); you can also enable IntelliTrace and profiling tools. Both IntelliTrace and the Profiler are discussed in Chapter 55, "Advanced Analysis Tools." If you click Next you go to the Summary page, which is just a summary of the deployment settings, as represented in Figure 37.13.

When ready, click Publish. Visual Studio 2012 now starts deploying your Visual Basic application to Windows Azure. The duration of the process might vary depending on the strength of your Internet connection and on the size of your application. The Windows Azure Activity Log tool window will keep you informed on the deployment progress. When this task is completed, a tool window highlights its status as Completed and shows information, including the website URL. Figure 37.14 provides an example based on the current project.

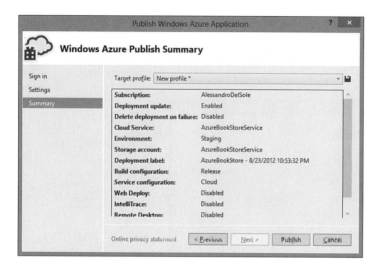

FIGURE 37.13   Deployment summary information.

FIGURE 37.14   The Windows Azure Activity Log window shows information on the deployment progress.

Remember that you are in a staging environment, so the URL you see is temporary; however, you can use it to ensure that the application works correctly (and remember to add the name of the BookStoreTestPage.aspx at the end of the URL). Assuming you have checked that your application is working well, you can move it to the Production state. You have two ways for moving an application from Staging to Production:

▶ Republish the application from Visual Studio, changing the environment from Staging to Production in the Settings dialog box.

▶ From within the Windows Azure Management Portal.

Although with specific regard to the current simple example, the first way could be easier; I want instead to introduce the Management Portal.

Introducing the Windows Azure Management Portal

A NEW MANAGEMENT PORTAL

In this chapter we cover the new version of the Management Portal, which is actually still a preview but that has been built with HTML5. If you worked with previous recent versions of the portal, you know they were Silverlight-based applications. The reason we cover the preview of the new portal is that it will be available in the future with full features and it can be accessed from any device (due to HTML portability).

That said, open your web browser and launch the portal by typing the following address: https://manage.windowsazure.com. The first thing you see when you access the portal is the full list of cloud services, storage accounts, and SQL databases running inside your subscription. Figure 37.15 shows an example based on my subscription, where you can see how the current sample application is running (sensitive information has been removed for privacy reasons in this figure and the next ones).

FIGURE 37.15   List of running items in the Windows Azure subscription.

In whatever page of the management portal you are, you can promote an application from staging to deployment by clicking the Swap button at the bottom of the page. When you click this button, Windows Azure will ask your confirmation, providing some information about what it is going to do, as represented in Figure 37.16.

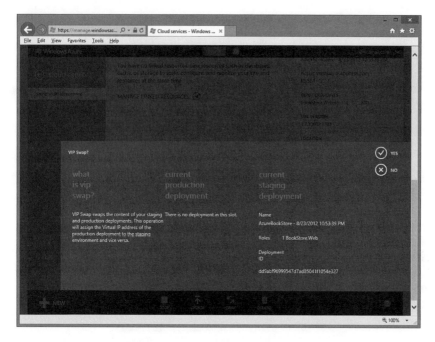

FIGURE 37.16   Promoting applications from staging to production.

Click **Yes** and wait for the process to complete. A specific page will be shown at the end of the process. You can now launch the application using the URL generated for you. Remember that, if you do not provide a Default.aspx page in your web project (as in the current case), you will have to supply the full URL including the page name. This means that the application can be launched with the following URL: http://azurebookstoreservices.cloudapp.net/BookStoreTestPage.aspx.

This will show the application running in your web browser and working as expected, as demonstrated in Figure 37.17.

REPLACING THE DEFAULT.ASPX PAGE

If you want to make your Silverlight application start automatically, in Solution Explorer rename the test page for Silverlight (in our example it is named BookStoreTestPage.Aspx) into Default.Aspx and set it as the start page.

With a few steps, you successfully published a web application to Windows Azure making it reachable from the Internet. If you plan on building datacentric applications requiring SQL Server database, be sure to visit the Windows Azure Developer Center where you can find lots of information about creating and consuming databases on the cloud. You can find the portal here: http://www.windowsazure.com/en-us/develop/overview/. After the application is running in production, the management portal offers a number of useful tools. For instance, you can use the Monitor tab to see the CPU usage percentage (see Figure 37.18) or the Dashboard tab to see more complex usage metrics, enable Team Foundation Server on the cloud, and get information on your cloud application.

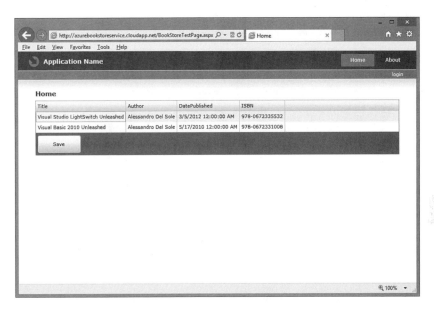

FIGURE 37.17   The sample application finally running in the cloud.

FIGURE 37.18   Understanding the virtual machine's CPU usage.

You can also easily configure the number of instances for your roles and the virtual machine size through the Instances tab, as shown in Figure 37.19. Be particularly careful when making changes in this place: Remember that increasing the number of instances and the size of your virtual machine can also change the costs of your services.

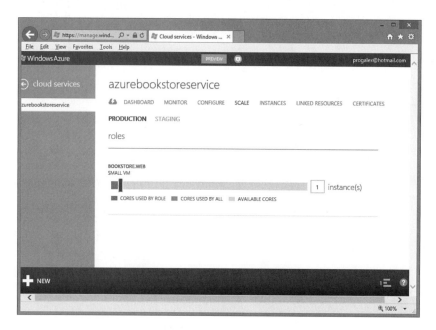

FIGURE 37.19   Configuring the role instances and virtual machine size.

The Management Portal offers a huge number of useful tools to configure and maintain your applications running on Windows Azure, but you got a good overview of what you can do without having a physical server, a networking infrastructure, and personnel working for maintenance of an on-premise solution.

DELETE YOUR TEST CLOUD SERVICES!

Do not forget to completely delete cloud services, databases, and storage accounts that you no longer use to avoid the risk of paying extra money. Also, remember that you will still be charged for services that are stopped. The only way to avoid the risk of paying extra money is by deleting services.

Summary

The Windows Azure platform is the cloud computing platform by Microsoft and includes several services such as the Windows Azure operating system, a SQL database, websites, and application building blocks. Windows Azure is a 64-bit operating system enabling web applications to be hosted and running in a cloud environment. To develop applications for the cloud, you use Visual Studio 2012, which must be enabled by installing the appropriate tools. After you install these tools and register for the Windows Azure services, you can begin developing and deploying applications. You can create ASP.NET web applications or Silverlight applications that can be deployed to Azure. You can test your applications locally before deployment, due to the presence of the Windows Azure Debugging Environment that includes tools for locally running applications with the same environment that is on the cloud. This tooling is installed together with the Windows Azure SDK for .NET and Visual Studio 2012. To publish a web application to the Azure platform, you use Visual Studio instrumentation; then you can still use the IDE or the Windows Azure Management Portal to edit, configure, and maintain your applications and data on the cloud.

37

Building Apps for Windows Phone 7.5

Today people want and need to stay connected even more than in the past; also they do more dynamic jobs and often need to check for work emails, browse the Internet, and run business tools when traveling or when not at the office. Mobile phones have become personal assistants, with calendars, appointments, and applications (also known as *apps* when referring to mobile phones) that can solve an infinite number of problems, or be used for personal entertainment. The so-called smartphones play a fundamental role in the everyday life for both business and personal purposes. Microsoft's offer for modern mobile phones is called Windows Phone, and in this chapter you learn how to build applications for version 7.5 of this operating system and see how easy it can be due to the opportunity of reusing existing skills based on WPF and Silverlight. Windows Phone development can be an important business opportunity, and Visual Basic offers all the power you need to build awesome apps.

Introducing Windows Phone

Windows Phone is the operating system from Microsoft for mobile phones of the new generation. Windows Phone was first released in October 2010 under the name of Windows Phone 7; a major upgrade, known as Windows Phone "Mango" (version 7.5) was released in mid-2011. In this chapter we target Windows Phone 7.5 because it is the most recent version.

EXPECTATIONS FOR WINDOWS PHONE 8

At the time this chapter is being written, Microsoft unveiled Windows Phone 8. From what we know, the company is still working on the new version of the operating system and rumors say that it will share the runtime infrastructure with Windows 8's kernel. No release date has been announced at the moment, which is why in this book you learn about Windows Phone 7.5. We only know that the future version of the developer tools for Windows Phone 8 will also enable you to create apps for Windows Phone 7.5 with Visual Studio 2012. It makes perfect sense to talk about Windows Phone 7.5 apps in this book because existing devices running this version of the operating system will not be eligible to upgrade to the new version, so you will still be able to build applications for a large number of existing users. Also, apps built for Windows Phone 7.5 will still run on Windows Phone 8 so investments made in these apps are also extended to the new platform.

Windows Phone is specifically designed for devices with touchscreens and that support multiple orientations, position locator (GPS), accelerometer, push notifications, cameras, and sensors. It is particularly innovative for at least two reasons:

▶ It introduces the Modern style interface (formerly known as Metro), which focuses on people first rather than the device and is a return to simplicity. This interface is important for Microsoft because it empowers Windows Phone and Windows 8 and is an inspiration for styling other recent tools such as Visual Studio 2012.

▶ It enables you to use apps' icons to update their contents based on notifications or events, so that the user can be notified of content updates without the need of opening the app, but seeing its icon. This is known as Live Tiles.

Going into the details of this modern design language and principles is beyond the scope of this chapter, so you will get specific information when required. For further details, you can read an interesting explanation available on Wikipedia: http://en.wikipedia.org/wiki/Metro_(design_language)

Developer Registration to the Windows Phone Marketplace

Before you go on reading this chapter and do some work, there is some information that you must be aware of as a developer. To publish your applications to the Windows Phone Marketplace, no matter if they are free or paid, you must be a registered developer. Registering is a paid service unless you have an MSDN Subscription, which entitles you to claim a complimentary developer account. Register only if you are really sure that you will be publishing apps to the Windows Phone Marketplace; otherwise, do not register and use the developer tools for local testing with the device emulator. Detailed information on the registration process and on pricing can be found at http://create.msdn.com/en-US/home/about/developer_registration_walkthrough. This chapter will describe application development based on the device emulator, so that you will not need to register to the Marketplace. Only the last part of this chapter describes the submission process, which requires a developer account, but you can read it without registering.

Downloading the Developer Tools

To provide programmers the best development experience possible, Microsoft created the Windows Phone SDK 7.1 that targets both Windows Phone 7 and Windows Phone 7.5. Internally, Windows Phone 7.5 is version 7.1 of the operating system. This explains the SDK versioning and makes it clear that calling it 7.5 was more for marketing purposes. The Windows Phone SDK includes, among the others, the following tools:

▶ **Visual Studio Express for Windows Phone**—A lightweight and free-of-charge edition of the Visual Studio environment specifically designed for building apps for Windows Phone with Visual Basic and Visual C#. This special edition of Visual Studio is also used in this chapter.

▶ **An add-in for Visual Studio 2010 Professional or higher**—This includes project templates and tooling for building apps for Windows Phone within major editions of the IDE.

▶ **The XNA Game Studio**—A specific environment and set of tools that developers can use to build games for the Windows Phone and Xbox platforms.

▶ **The Device Emulator**—A virtual machine representing a device that you use to test your apps on the development machine inside a software environment.

▶ **Application Deployment tool**—Enables you to deploy apps to both the device emulator and your physical device.

▶ **Windows Phone Registration tool**—Enables you to associate your physical devices to your Windows Live ID.

▶ **Expression Blend for Windows Phone**—Expression Blend is the premier environment for designers, and this version has specific tools for Windows Phone.

You can download the Windows Phone SDK 7.1 from the following location: http://www.microsoft.com/en-us/download/details.aspx?id=27570. You can choose to download a web installer or a full ISO image. If you are installing the tools on Windows 8, you must follow these steps:

1. Install the Games for Windows Live client, available at http://www.xbox.com/en-US/LIVE/PC/DownloadClient.

2. Install the Windows Phone SDK 7.1 (see the previous link).

3. Install the Windows Phone SDK 7.1.1 update available from http://www.microsoft.com/en-us/download/details.aspx?id=29233.

Microsoft also released a Community Technology Preview (CTP) of the Async libraries (see Chapter 44, "Asynchronous Programming"), which also target Windows Phone and that is available at http://www.microsoft.com/en-us/download/details.aspx?displaylang=en&id=9983. Note that this is unsupported and is not the same as the final release shipping with .NET 4.5, but with this library you can use both the asynchronous programming patterns and iterators.

38

WINDOWS PHONE 8 SDK AVAILABILITY

While this chapter is under revision, Microsoft has released the Windows Phone 8 SDK which includes developer tools for building apps for the upcoming Windows Phone 8. These tools are not discussed in this chapter both for timing reasons and because there is no physical device available at the moment that you could use for testing. Moreover, building apps for Windows Phone 8 relies on the Windows Runtime for Windows Phone, not Silverlight so it would be necessary to make an overview of WinRT which is beyond the scope of this book. You can download the Windows Phone 8 SDK for your own testing purposes from http://dev.windowsphone.com/en-us/downloadsdk. Similar to the previous version, this new SDK still includes a free Express edition of Visual Studio for Windows Phone, the Emulator, and deployment tools and also includes an add-on for Visual Studio 2012 that makes it possible to build apps for both Windows Phone 7.5 and Windows Phone 8 with the new version of the IDE.

Training and Learning Resources

Additional learning resources are available for Visual Basic developers on MSDN. In particular, you can download:

▶ **Code Samples for Windows Phone**—This covers all the possible areas in developing for this operating system. Such samples are available for free at: http://msdn.microsoft.com/en-us/library/ff431744(VS.92).aspx.

▶ **Windows Phone 7.5 Training Kit**—This includes a number of hands-on labs that guide you through the process of creating a complete application and that you can find at http://www.microsoft.com/en-us/download/details.aspx?id=28564.

Also, do not forget to periodically check out the Windows Phone Developer Center, available at http://dev.windowsphone.com/en-us/home, where you can get new samples, tools, and news about the development platform.

The Windows Phone 7.5 Programming Model

The application programming model for Windows Phone 7.5 is based on a specific version of Silverlight 4 for this kind of device, known as Silverlight for Windows Phone. This means that you will still design the user interface with XAML code and the imperative code in Visual Basic. This is a tremendous benefit because most of your existing skills with technologies like WPF and Silverlight will still be valid, with some obvious differences and limitations due to the specific platform. Also, most of .NET programming concepts and the language syntax are totally available. What you actually have to learn is how to interact with devices' functionalities and how to manage the application lifetime. This chapter cannot cover every possible opportunity in building apps for Windows Phone, but it is a good "get started" guide. The Windows Phone programming model relies on the following elements:

▶ **The Silverlight framework**—Enables developers to build rich user interfaces; you already discovered this in Chapter 36, "Building Rich Internet Applications with Silverlight 5."

▶ **The XNA Framework**—Provides a full set of APIs, services, and resources that developers can use to easily and quickly build games for multiple targets including Windows Phone, Xbox, and Zune. In particular, XNA includes specific APIs for sprite generation, 3D graphics, media interaction, and special gestures for games. Silverlight for Windows Phone and XNA can be combined into a single application and enable you to generate high-quality games that leverage all the device's functionalities.

▶ **Data and I/O**—Based on the well-known concept of Isolated Storage, which reserves some space to each application for data storage and file operation, but prevents apps from accessing the operating system's resources.

▶ **Location services**—Enable you to access (with the agreement of the user) the current physical position of the device so you can build apps that provide information of what it is around.

▶ **Push notifications**—Enable you to use Internet services to send notifications to the phone and update contents.

▶ **Media**—Includes not only the ability of playing animations and drawing complex graphics, but also interaction with videos and pictures on and from the device.

Windows Phone also uses some cloud-based services for tile notifications and other updates and provides a good support for interaction with the Windows Azure platform.

Creating Apps with Visual Basic

WHAT YOU FIND IN THIS CHAPTER AND WHAT YOU DO NOT FIND

Developing apps for Windows Phone 7.5 is something very exciting and interesting but would require an entire book to explain. For this reason, the goal of this chapter is teaching you how to start building apps with Visual Basic from zero to the submission to the Marketplace, providing information on the most common topics. So here you learn how to create and debug an app, how to write XAML and VB code, how to call built-in apps for common tasks and local storage, and how to customize and prepare an app for publication. You will not find topics like Live Tiles, sensors, push notifications, or location services. After you have the basics provided in this chapter, all these topics will be easier to study through the learning resources suggested previously.

You can create apps for Windows Phone 7.5 with the Visual Basic programming language by launching Visual Studio Express for Windows Phone that is available on your machine after you install the Windows Phone SDK 7.1. As usual, you must first create a new project by selecting **File**, **New Project**. The New Project dialog box (see Figure 38.1) shows a number of available project templates and the VB templates are available under Other Languages, Visual Basic. Notice how projects are also divided into two categories: Silverlight for Windows Phone and XNA Game Studio 4.0.

FIGURE 38.1   Creating a new Windows Phone project.

AGENTS AND STREAMING

Windows Phone 7.5 introduced the so-called *agents*, which enable you to execute tasks in the background and that you can compare to Windows' services. Agents are used to send notifications to applications or to play media contents in the background. Figure 38.1 shows how Visual Studio offers specific project templates to create agent-enabled applications. The MSDN Library provides information about how to implement such agents.

Let's start by creating a simple app, so you can understand how the environment works. You can select the Windows Phone Application template and leave the default name for the project unchanged; then click **OK**. Visual Studio will ask you to specify the operating system version, between 7.0 and 7.1. Notice that version 7.1 reflects the SDK version number, but actually it targets Windows Phone 7.5 so this must be your selection (see Figure 38.2).

FIGURE 38.2   Selecting the target version of Windows Phone.

After a few seconds the new project is generated and the IDE shows the Windows Phone designer and the XAML code editor. You should feel at home with this kind of approach because you find the surface where you design the UI and the place where you make adjustments in XAML, exactly as you do in WPF and Silverlight. Figure 38.3 shows the designer and the toolbox with common controls.

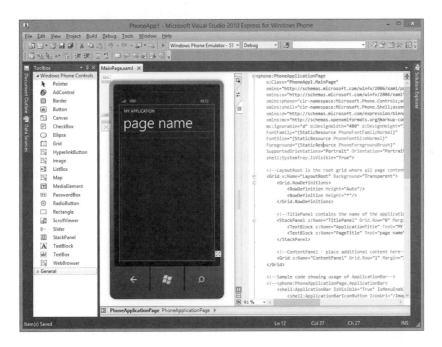

FIGURE 38.3   The Windows Phone designer in Visual Studio, with the XAML editor.

This first sample app will enable users to enter the URL of a website and view it inside an embedded web browser. As you can see in the XAML editor, two auto-generated `TextBlock` controls describe the application name and the page name, both contained inside a

StackPanel control. They are not mandatory but can be useful to help you understand how the UI works, so replace the Text property for the ApplicationTitle control with WEB SITE VIEWER and the Text property for the PageTitle control with home page. Next, drag from the toolbox onto the device designer the following controls:

▶ A StackPanel container that stores the following controls

▶ A TextBlock that contains an informative message

▶ A TextBox control where users will type the URL of the website

▶ A Button for launching the action

▶ A WebBrowser control that will show the desired website

After this, make some edits to the XAML code to adjust controls' sizing and spacing, like in the following code snippet:

```
<!--ContentPanel - place additional content here-->
<Grid x:Name="ContentPanel" Grid.Row="1" Margin="12,0,12,0">
    <StackPanel>
        <TextBlock Text="Type an URL:" Margin="5" />
        <TextBox Name="AddressBox" Margin="5"/>
        <Button Width="110" Height="80" Name="GoButton" Content="Go!"
                Click="GoButton_Click" />
        <phone:WebBrowser Name="Browser1" Height="424" />
    </StackPanel>
</Grid>
```

The next step is handling the button's Click event, where some code will launch the specified website. The Click event also responds to the touch of the user, which is known as a *tap*. You can double-click the Button in the designer so that Visual Studio will generate a Click event handler you could write as follows:

```
Private Sub GoButton_Click(sender As System.Object, e As
                           System.Windows.RoutedEventArgs)
    Try
        If String.IsNullOrEmpty(Me.AddressBox.Text) = False Then
            Me.Browser1.Navigate(New Uri(Me.AddressBox.Text))
        End If
    Catch ex As Exception
        MessageBox.Show(ex.Message)
    End Try

End Sub
```

You can notice how Silverlight for Windows Phone still uses routed events like WPF and Silverlight; also, it is easy to see how normal .NET programming techniques are used. The WebBrowser control exposes a Navigate method that receives an argument of type

`System.Uri` and that will open the specified website. You will now learn how to debug your apps and how to see them in action inside the local device emulator.

Starting and Debugging Windows Phone Apps

All the instrumentation that Visual Studio offers for debugging Visual Basic applications can be used with Windows Phone apps as well—for example, you can use breakpoints, data tips, and tool windows for debugging. Put succinctly, all the notions you learned in Chapter 5, "Debugging Visual Basic 2012 Applications," are still valid in Windows Phone. The real difference is how you execute apps for debugging and testing. In fact, you can either test and debug your apps on the local device emulator or perform debugging on the physical device. However, if you want to test your app on your device, this must be *developer unlocked*, which means it can be used for development purposes only if the associated Windows Live ID has been registered as a developer account. The standard toolbar of Visual Studio contains a combo box that enables you to specify the execution environment, as represented in Figure 38.4.

FIGURE 38.4   Selecting the execution environment for testing Windows Phone apps.

Choosing the Windows Phone Emulator with 512 MB of RAM is an appropriate choice, but you can choose 256 MB as well to see how your app works with less advanced devices. You can also switch between the classic Debug and Release configurations; as usual, you use the latter when the application is going to be released to the public. You can now press F5 so that the application will be compiled into a Silverlight XAP file and deployed to the target environment. The Windows Phone Emulator is actually a virtual machine specific for this kind of operating system; because of this, every time you shut down the emulator and then press F5 again, the operating system is loaded again. You can therefore leave the emulator open during your testing activities because Visual Studio will update the XAP file every time you start debugging. After a few seconds, the Emulator shows the application running, as demonstrated in Figure 38.5.

The keyboard displays after you enter the `TextBox`. It is worth mentioning that the Emulator is touch-enabled, so if you have a multitouch display, you can test how the application will work in reality. Enter the URL of a website and then tap the button. Figure 38.6 shows an example of the result of this action.

Understanding Pages, Orientations, and the Navigation Framework

Each Windows Phone app is made of at least one page, like in the previous example. A page is the root container of UI controls that the user interacts with. You can add multiple pages, so that you can show all the contents you need. Every page is an instance of the `PhoneApplicationPage` class. To browse between pages, Silverlight for Windows Phone offers its own Navigation Framework, which is exposed by shared methods of the

`NavigationService` class. The most important method of this class is `Navigate`, which enables you to move to the specified page in the application. Table 38.1 summarizes the most important members of this class.

FIGURE 38.5 The Windows Phone Emulator shows the application running.

FIGURE 38.6 The app is showing the specified website.

TABLE 38.1 The Most Important Members of the `NavigationService` Class

Member Name	Member Type	Data Type	Description
Navigate	Method		Opens the specified page in the application
GoBack	Method		Goes to the previous page
GoForward	Method		Goes to the next page
StopLoading	Method		Aborts loading the specified page
CanGoBack	Property	Boolean	Returns `True` if the navigation framework can return to the previous page

Member Name	Member Type	Data Type	Description
CanGoForward	Property	Boolean	Returns True if the navigation framework can go to the next page
Source	Property	System.Uri	Gets the URI of the content that is being navigated
Navigating	Event		Raised when the navigation framework starts opening a page
Navigated	Event		Raised when a page has been opened due to the invocation of Navigate, GoBack, or GoForward
NavigationFailed	Event		Raised if navigating to the specified page failed
NavigationStopped	Event		Raised when the navigation stopped due to the invocation of StopLoading

Pages in Windows Phone support two orientations: Portrait and Landscape. This is because of the device's orientation sensor, which enables you to rotate the content of a page. Typically, pages can also support both orientations, in case your contents can fit well in the available space in both portrait and landscape modes. Orientations are offered by the Microsoft.Phone.Controls.PageOrientation enumeration, and you set the value directly in XAML at design time. To understand all these concepts, select **Project, Add New Item**. In the Add New Item dialog box, you can see a number of page templates; for the sake of simplicity, select the Windows Phone Portrait Page template. Then name the new item as SecondPage.xaml (see Figure 38.7).

Visual Studio will add a new page to the project that you will see both in the designer and in Solution Explorer. If you take a look at the page definition, you will notice the availability of the following two lines:

```
SupportedOrientations="Portrait"
Orientation="Portrait"
```

So, by default the page is supporting only the portrait orientation. SupportedOrientations enables you to specify which orientations are supported, whereas Orientation establishes which orientation is used when the page is first loaded. You can support both portrait and landscape orientations by changing the first line as follows:

```
SupportedOrientations="PortraitOrLandscape"
```

Now drag a Button onto the page and handle its Click event as follows:

```
Private Sub Button1_Click(sender As System.Object,
                e As System.Windows.RoutedEventArgs) _
                Handles Button1.Click
```

38

```
If NavigationService.CanGoBack Then
    NavigationService.GoBack()
End If
End Sub
```

FIGURE 38.7   Adding a new page.

This will make the app return to the main page. Now double-click MainPage.xaml in Solution Explorer, and add a new button after the existing one, by typing the following XAML:

```
<Button Width="110" Height="80" Name="Page2Button" Content="Next"
                Click="Page2Button_Click" />
```

The `Click` event handler of this button invokes the `NavigationService.Navigate` method to move to the previously added page:

```
Private Sub Page2Button_Click(sender As System.Object,
                         e As System.Windows.RoutedEventArgs)
    NavigationService.Navigate(New Uri("/SecondPage.xaml",
                             UriKind.Relative))
End Sub
```

The page's address is a relative URI, so you do not need to specify the full address because the page is inside the application. Instead, you specify the filename of the page. If you now run the application, you can see how moving between pages is easy, by using the built-in navigation framework's members.

Using System Functionalities with Launchers

More often than not, you will need to create apps that interact with some system's functionalities such as the email client, the media player, Internet Explorer, or Bing Maps, or you might need to programmatically prepare a phone call or an SMS. In Silverlight for Windows Phone, you can easily access all these features via the *launchers*. Launchers are represented by classes from the `Microsoft.Phone.Tasks` namespace; each class enables you to access a specific feature, as summarized in Table 38.2.

TABLE 38.2   Summary of Launchers in Windows Phone

Class	Description
BingMapsDirectionsTask	Enables you to activate built-in Bing Maps and obtain directions for the given coordinates
BingMapsTask	Enables you to activate Bing Maps and search for the specified address
ConnectionSettingsTask	Enables you to access network connections settings
EmailComposeTask	Starts the email client and enables you to specify recipients and the email body
MarketPlaceDetailsTask	Opens the Marketplace pointing to the specified application, via the app ID
MarketPlaceHubTask	Opens the Marketplace, either for apps or for music
MarketPlaceReviewTask	Opens the Marketplace pointing to the rating page for the specified application, via the app ID
MarketPlaceSearchTask	Opens the search page in the Marketplace
MediaPlayerLauncher	Starts the built-in media player pointing to the given address
PhoneCallTask	Starts the phone application and enables you to specify the number to be called and a display name
SearchTask	Searches the Web for the specified terms through the built-in search feature
ShareLinkTask	Enables you to share a link to the specified social networks
ShareStatusTask	Enables you to share a personal message to the specified social networks
SmsComposeTask	Starts the SMS app with the specified telephone number and message body
WebBrowserTask	Starts an instance of Internet Explorer, pointing to the specified URL

38

Every launcher class exposes a `Show` method that must be invoked after assigning property values. The biggest benefit of using launchers is that you do not need to implement pages or custom controls to use some system features. For a better understanding, create a new blank Windows Phone project like you did in the previous section. You should replace the `Grid` container named `ContentPanel` with a `ScrollViewer` control, which enables you to scroll the page content with the finger if it does not fit the available space and list a number of buttons, each of them starting a specific launcher. So the new `ContentPanel` element looks like this:

```
<ScrollViewer x:Name="ContentPanel" Grid.Row="1" Margin="12,0,12,0">
    <StackPanel>
        <Button Width="250" Margin="5" Name="IEButton"
        Click="IEButton_Click">Internet Explorer</Button>
        <Button Width="250" Margin="5" Name="MPButton"
        Click="MPButton_Click">Media Player</Button>
        <Button Width="250" Margin="5" Name="BingButton"
        Click="BingButton_Click">Bing Maps</Button>
        <Button Width="250" Margin="5" Name="ConnectionButton"
        Click="ConnectionButton_Click">Connection</Button>
        <Button Width="250" Margin="5" Name="EmailButton"
        Click="EmailButton_Click">Email</Button>
        <Button Width="250" Margin="5" Name="CallButton"
        Click="CallButton_Click">Phone call</Button>
        <Button Width="250" Margin="5" Name="SearchButton"
        Click="SearchButton_Click">Search</Button>
        <Button Width="250" Margin="5" Name="SmsButton"
        Click="SmsButton_Click">SMS</Button>
        <Button Width="250" Margin="5" Name="StatusButton"
        Click="StatusButton_Click">Share Status</Button>
        <Button Width="250" Margin="5" Name="LinkButton"
        Click="LinkButton_Click">Share Link</Button>
        <Button Width="250" Margin="5" Name="MarketButton"
        Click="MarketButton_Click">Hub</Button>
    </StackPanel>
</ScrollViewer>
```

Go to the code-behind file so that you can write Visual Basic code to enable launchers.

The `WebBrowserTask`

The simplest launcher is the `WebBrowserTask`, which opens an instance of Internet Explorer pointing to the specified URL. You set the `Uri` property with the web address you want to visit and then invoke Show. The following code provides an example:

```
Private Sub IEButton_Click(sender As System.Object,
                           e As System.Windows.RoutedEventArgs)
    Dim browserTask As New WebBrowserTask
    browserTask.Uri = New Uri("http://www.microsoft.com", UriKind.Absolute)
    browserTask.Show()
End Sub
```

Figure 38.8 shows the result of the previous code. Tap the Back button of the Emulator to go back to the main page.

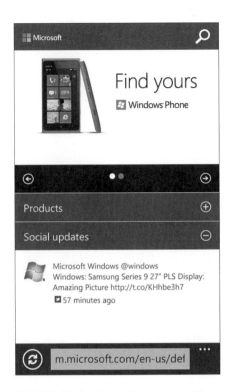

FIGURE 38.8   Launching Internet Explorer with the `WebBrowserTask`.

The `MediaPlayerLauncher`

The `MediaPlayerLauncher` starts the built-in media player and enables you to stream media contents. You can only stream videos and provide the address under the form of a `System.Uri` object. The following code provides an example:

```
Private Sub MPButton_Click(sender As System.Object,
                           e As System.Windows.RoutedEventArgs)
    Dim mediaTask As New MediaPlayerLauncher
    mediaTask.Media = New Uri("http://www.mysite.com/myvideo.wmv", UriKind.Absolute)
    mediaTask.Show()
End Sub
```

Windows Phone only supports video codecs specified in the following page of the MSDN Library: http://msdn.microsoft.com/en-us/library/windowsphone/develop/ff462087(v=vs.92).aspx

The `BingMapsTask`

You use the `BingMapsTask` to open the built-in Bing Maps app and search for the specified address. The following code demonstrates how to assign the `SearchTerm` property and the invocation of `Show`:

```
Private Sub BingButton_Click(sender As System.Object,
                            e As System.Windows.RoutedEventArgs)
    Dim bingTask As New BingMapsTask
    bingTask.SearchTerm = "Redmond, WA, One Microsoft Way"
    bingTask.Show()
End Sub
```

Figure 38.9 shows how the specified address is found with Bing Maps.

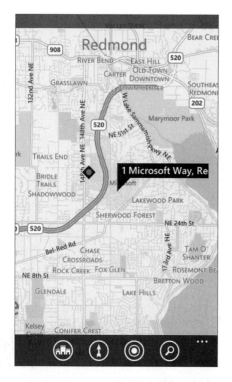

FIGURE 38.9   Finding an address with Bing Maps and the `BingMapsTask`.

The `ConnectionSettingsTask`

The `ConnectionSettingsTask` launcher allows programmatic access to network connections settings. The following code provides an example:

```
Private Sub ConnectionButton_Click(sender As System.Object,
                                   e As System.Windows.RoutedEventArgs)
    Dim connectionSettingsTask As ConnectionSettingsTask = _
                        New ConnectionSettingsTask()
    connectionSettingsTask.ConnectionSettingsType = ConnectionSettingsType.WiFi
    connectionSettingsTask.Show()
End Sub
```

You have to specify the type of network connection you want to check. This is done by assigning the `ConnectionSettingsType` property with one value from the `Microsoft.Phone.Tasks.ConnectionSettingsType` enumeration (`WiFi`, `AirPlane`, `Cellular`, `BlueTooth`). Figure 38.10 shows the result of the previous code.

FIGURE 38.10   Programmatic access to network connections settings.

The EmailComposeTask
The `EmailComposeTask` enables you to create an email message and send it to the built-in email client. The following code provides an example:

```
Private Sub EmailButton_Click(sender As System.Object,
                              e As System.Windows.RoutedEventArgs)
    Dim emailTask As New EmailComposeTask

    emailTask.To = "alessandro.delsole@visual-basic.it"
    emailTask.Subject = "Meeting tomorrow"
    emailTask.Cc = "alessandro.delsole@hotmail.com"
    emailTask.Bcc = "someoneelse@something.com"
    emailTask.Body = "This is a reminder about our meeting tomorrow at 10 a.m."
    emailTask.Show()
End Sub
```

As you can see, all the properties are self-explanatory and easy to use. The Windows Phone Emulator cannot be configured with a valid email account, so you will only be able to test this code on a physical device.

Making Phone Calls and Sending Messages with `PhoneCallTask` and `SmsComposeTask`

You can interact with typical features such as the phone app and the SMS app by using the `PhoneCallTask` and the `SmsComposeTask` launchers. The first launcher requires you to specify the phone number to call and a display name. Once started, the app will ask the user to choose whether she want to start the call or cancel the operation. The following code provides an example:

```
Private Sub CallButton_Click(sender As System.Object,
                             e As System.Windows.RoutedEventArgs)
    Dim callTask As New PhoneCallTask
    callTask.PhoneNumber = "+391122333"
    callTask.DisplayName = "Technical support"
    callTask.Show()
End Sub
```

For text messaging, you instead specify the message body and the target phone number:

```
Private Sub SmsButton_Click(sender As System.Object,
                            e As System.Windows.RoutedEventArgs)
    Dim smsTask As New SmsComposeTask
    smsTask.To = "+391122333"
    smsTask.Body = "Wanna meet tonight?"
    smsTask.Show()
End Sub
```

The text message will not be sent automatically; the user will decide whether to send the message or not.

The `SearchTask`

Implementing search functionalities is a common need in modern apps. Silverlight for Windows Phone offers the `SearchTask` launcher, which starts Bing and searches for the specified search term. The following code provides an example:

```
Private Sub SearchButton_Click(sender As System.Object,
                               e As System.Windows.RoutedEventArgs)
    Dim searchTask As New SearchTask
    searchTask.SearchQuery = "visual basic"
    searchTask.Show()
End Sub
```

You need to assign the `SearchQuery` property with a string containing the search terms. Figure 38.11 shows search results in the Emulator.

FIGURE 38.11   Searching with Bing from an app.

Social Networking with `ShareStatusTask` and `ShareLinkTask`

The Windows Phone operating system has deep integration with social networking platforms such as Facebook, Windows Live, Twitter, and LinkedIn. To make sharing messages and links easier, Silverlight for Windows Phone offers the `ShareStatusTask` and `ShareLinkTask` launchers. The first launcher enables you to share a text message to supported social networks, whereas the second one enables you to share a link. The `ShareStatusTask` requires you to assign the `Status` property with a string:

```
Private Sub StatusButton_Click(sender As System.Object,
                               e As System.Windows.RoutedEventArgs)
    Dim statusTask As New ShareStatusTask
    statusTask.Status = "I'm writing a new app for Windows Phone"
    statusTask.Show()
End Sub
```

The `ShareLinkTask` requires you to set the `LinkUri` property with the link, the `Title` property with a title, and the `Message` property with a description. The following code provides an example:

38

```
Private Sub LinkButton_Click(sender As System.Object,
                            e As System.Windows.RoutedEventArgs)
    Dim shareLink As New ShareLinkTask
    shareLink.LinkUri = _
            New Uri("http://www.informit.com/store/product.aspx?isbn=0672335530",
                    UriKind.Absolute)
    shareLink.Title = _
        "Visual Studio LightSwitch Unleashed"
    shareLink.Message = _
        "Official page for the Visual Studio LightSwitch Unleashed book"
End Sub
```

Both launchers will not post their content automatically. Instead, the operating system will first ask to which social networks the user wants to publish the content.

Launching the Marketplace with the `MarketPlaceHubTask`

You have several alternatives to opening the Marketplace in code, but the simplest is using the `MarketPlaceHubTask`. It enables you to open the store for either apps or music. The following code provides an example:

```
Private Sub MarketButton_Click(sender As System.Object,
                               e As System.Windows.RoutedEventArgs)
    Dim marketHubTask As New MarketplaceHubTask
    marketHubTask.ContentType = MarketplaceContentType.Applications
    marketHubTask.Show()
End Sub
```

You assign the `ContentType` property with a value from the `Microsoft.Phone.Tasks.MarketplaceContentType` enumeration, which can be `Applications` or `Music`.

Showing Multiple Contents with the `Panorama` Control

Sometimes applications need to show multiple contents and the physical size of the device's screen is not enough to contain all the information. Microsoft solved this problem by introducing the `Panorama` control, which is made of a long horizontal canvas that the user can scroll horizontally to see all the available contents in one page. Visual Studio provides a specific project template for creating panoramic applications, which you can see in Figure 38.12. Create a new project using the Windows Phone Panorama Application template.

Once created, add a reference to the System.Xml.Linq.dll assembly that is required later. The `Panorama` control presents as many `PanoramaItem` elements as you want to display. You will now build a sample application that downloads RSS feeds from a couple of websites. The project template implements sample data and a basic UI definition that you do not need at this point. For this reason, remove the following elements from the project:

▶ In Solution Explorer, the ViewModels and SampleData folders

▶ In the code-behind file of the main page, the `MainPage_Loaded` event handler and the `DataContext` assignment in the constructor

▶ In the XAML code editor, both the auto-generated `PanoramaItem` elements

▶ In the App.xaml.vb file, the `_viewModel` field and the `ViewModel` property; also the method body of the `Application_Activated` event handler

FIGURE 38.12   Creating a new panoramic application.

Now imagine you want to display the latest blog posts from the Visual Basic Team at Microsoft and the latest messages on Twitter from the same Team. This is accomplished by downloading the appropriate RSS feeds. In the MainPage.xaml file, add the following two `PanoramaItem` controls inside the root `PanoramaItem`:

```
<controls:PanoramaItem Header="VB Team" Name="VBTeamItem">
    <!--Double line list with image placeholder and text wrapping-->
    <ListBox Margin="0,0,-12,0"
            ItemsSource="{Binding}"
            SelectionChanged="ListBox_SelectionChanged">
        <ListBox.ItemTemplate>
            <DataTemplate>
                <StackPanel Margin="0,0,0,17" Width="432">
                    <TextBlock Tag="{Binding Path=Link}" Foreground="White"
                            Text="{Binding Path=Title}"
```

```
                                            TextWrapping="Wrap"
                                            Style="{StaticResource PhoneTextLargeStyle}"
                                            >
                            </TextBlock>
                            <TextBlock Text="{Binding Creator}" Foreground="White"
                                            TextWrapping="Wrap" Margin="12,2,12,0"
                                            Style="{StaticResource
                                                    PhoneTextSubtleStyle}"/>
                            <TextBlock Text="{Binding pubDate}"  Foreground="White"
                                            TextWrapping="Wrap" Margin="12,2,12,0"
                                            Style="{StaticResource
                                            PhoneTextSubtleStyle}"/>
                    </StackPanel>
                </DataTemplate>
            </ListBox.ItemTemplate>
        </ListBox>
</controls:PanoramaItem>


<controls:PanoramaItem Header="VB Tweets" Name="VBTweetsItem">
    <!--Double line list with image placeholder and text wrapping-->
    <ListBox Margin="0,0,-12,0"
            ItemsSource="{Binding}"
            SelectionChanged="ListBox_SelectionChanged">
        <ListBox.ItemTemplate>
            <DataTemplate>
                <StackPanel Margin="0,0,0,17" Width="432">
                    <TextBlock Tag="{Binding Path=Link}" Foreground="White"
                                    Text="{Binding Path=Title}"
                                    TextWrapping="Wrap"
                                    Style="{StaticResource PhoneTextLargeStyle}"
                                    >
                    </TextBlock>
                    <TextBlock Text="{Binding Creator}" Foreground="White"
                                    TextWrapping="Wrap" Margin="12,2,12,0"
                                    Style="{StaticResource
                                            PhoneTextSubtleStyle}"/>
                    <TextBlock Text="{Binding pubDate}"  Foreground="White"
                                    TextWrapping="Wrap" Margin="12,2,12,0"
                                    Style="{StaticResource
                                    PhoneTextSubtleStyle}"/>
                </StackPanel>
            </DataTemplate>
        </ListBox.ItemTemplate>
    </ListBox>
</controls:PanoramaItem>
```

Notice how each `PanoramaItem` contains a `ListBox` that will present news from RSS feeds. Each item in the `ListBox` will be displayed via a `ListBox.ItemTemplate` composed by a number of `TextBlock` controls, each data-bound to a property of a `FeedItem` class that will be defined in moments. Also, notice how the `ListBox` is data-bound to some data that will be passed at runtime (`ItemsSource="{Binding}"`). Now add a new class to the project, called `FeedItem`. This class will represent each item retrieved from the RSS feeds and will provide a shared method that loads contents from the specified feed. Listing 38.1 shows the code for this class (comments in the code will make reading easier).

LISTING 38.1   Implementing RSS Feed Reading with LINQ

```
Imports System.Xml.Linq
Imports <xmlns:dc="http://purl.org/dc/elements/1.1/">
Imports System.Windows.Threading

Public Class FeedItem

    'Content title
    Public Property Title As String
    'Date published
    Public Property pubDate As String
    'Content link
    Public Property Link As Uri
    'Content creator
    Public Property Creator As String

    Public Shared Event ErrorThrown()

    'Read RSS contents from the given Uri and assign
    'the result to the specified PanoramaItem
    Public Shared Sub ReadContentsRss(ByVal rssUri As Uri,
                ByVal panoramaElement As PanoramaItem)
        'The WebClient class enables you to async downloading
        Dim wclient As New WebClient()

        'The statement lambda is a replacement for AddressOf
        AddHandler wclient.OpenReadCompleted, Sub(sender As Object,
                                e As OpenReadCompletedEventArgs)
                            If e.Error IsNot Nothing Then
                                'If e.Error contains some ¡value,
                                'an error occurred.
                                MessageBox.Show(e.Error.Message)
                                RaiseEvent ErrorThrown()
                                Exit Sub
                            End If
```

38

```vb
                                        'Open the XML stream with LINQ
                                        Dim str As IO.Stream = e.Result
                                        Dim xdoc As XDocument =
                                            XDocument.Load(str)

                        ' take results from each item element in the XML feed
                        Dim rssFeedsItems = (From item In xdoc...<item>
                        Let tempPublished =
                            Convert.ToDateTime(item.Element("pubDate").Value)
                        Let published = "Published " + _
                                    CStr(tempPublished.Day) + "/" + _
                                    CStr(tempPublished.Month) + "/" + _
                                    CStr(tempPublished.Year)
                        Let title = item.<title>.Value
                        Let postLink = item.<link>.Value
                        Let creator = item.<dc:creator>.Value
                        Select New FeedItem With {.Link = New Uri(postLink,
                                        UriKind.Absolute),
                                        .pubDate = published,
                                        .Creator = creator,
                                        .Title = title}).ToList

                                        ' close the stream
                                        str.Close()
                                        ' add results to listbox
                                        ' an invocation to the Dispatcher
                                        ' is required for threading management
                                        Deployment.Current.Dispatcher.
                                            BeginInvoke(Sub() panoramaElement.
                                                    DataContext =
                                                    rssFeedsItems)
                                    End Sub
            wclient.OpenReadAsync(rssUri)
        End Sub
    End Class
```

Now that you have a data model for representing feed items and a method that loads RSS contents, you need to invoke this method in the appropriate place and enable users to open the link of the selected content. In the MainPage.xaml.vb file, first handle the ListBox_ SelectionChanged event as follows:

```vb
Private Sub ListBox_SelectionChanged(sender As System.Object,
                            e As System.Windows.Controls.
                            SelectionChangedEventArgs)
    If e.AddedItems.Count > 0 Then
        Dim item = CType(e.AddedItems(0), FeedItem)
```

```
        Dim wbt As New WebBrowserTask
        wbt.Uri = item.Link
        wbt.Show()
    End If
End Sub
```

If at least one item has been added to the selected `ListBox`, the selected item is converted into an instance of the `FeedItem` class and then the `WebBrowserTask` launcher is started to open the content inside Internet Explorer. The next step is writing a method that loads contents from RSS feeds. Consider the following code:

```
Private Sub LoadData()
    System.
        Threading.
        ThreadPool.
            QueueUserWorkItem(Sub()
                                FeedItem.
                                ReadContentsRss(New
                                Uri("http://blogs.msdn.com/b/vbteam/rss.aspx"),
                                                        VBTeamItem)
                                FeedItem.
                                ReadContentsRss(New
                                Uri("http://twitter.com/statuses/" _
                                + "user_timeline/visualbasicteam.rss"),
                                                        VBTweetsItem)
                              End Sub)
End Sub
```

The code is running the `ReadContentRss` method from the `FeedItem` class in another thread. This will make the application's user interface responsive when it is loading data. You can still use threading programming techniques from .NET, and a thread pool is available in Windows Phone. More on threading is explained in Chapter 42, "Processes and Multithreading." The result of the invocation of the method is sent to the appropriate `PanoramaItem` for data-binding. The invocation of `LoadData` can be performed in the `Loaded` event of the page, as follows:

```
Private Sub MainPage_Loaded(sender As Object,
                        e As System.Windows.RoutedEventArgs) _
                        Handles MyBase.Loaded
    LoadData()
End Sub
```

Finally, you have to handle connection lack or latency as required by the certification guidelines. The simplest way is to add some logic in the constructor via the `NetworkInformation.NetworkInterface.GetIsNetworkAvailable` method:

```
' Constructor
Public Sub New()
    InitializeComponent()

    If NetworkInformation.NetworkInterface.
        GetIsNetworkAvailable = False Then
        'Provide your logic if no connection is available
        'This is required by the certification process
    End If
End Sub
```

If you now run the application, other than seeing news from the specified RSS feeds, you will be able to scroll the panoramic view horizontally, as demonstrated in Figure 38.13.

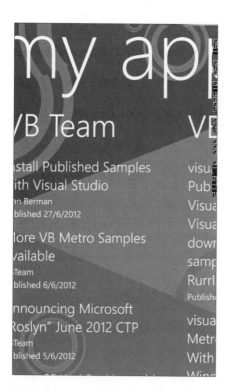

FIGURE 38.13   Showing Multiple Contents in One Page with the `Panorama` Control.

Local Data Storage

Windows Phone apps can certainly save and load data that they need to work with. However, for security reasons, they cannot interact with the operating system and with the device's disk. Because apps run inside a sandboxed environment, they have some reserved space that they can use for their needs, called *isolated storage*. This is a well-known concept in the .NET development and has been extended to Silverlight for Windows Phone. The isolated storage is offered by the `System.IO.IsolatedStorage` namespace. In your apps, you first need to get the instance of the app's isolated storage via the `IsolatedStorageFile.GetUserStoreForApplication` shared method:

```
Dim store As IsolatedStorageFile

' Constructor
Public Sub New()
    InitializeComponent()
    Me.store = IsolatedStorageFile.GetUserStoreForApplication
End Sub
```

After you have the instance, you use the `IsolatedStorageFileStream` class for both reading and writing operations. The usage of this stream is similar to others that you already know. For example, the following code demonstrates how to write a string to a text file:

```
Private Sub WriteToStorage()
    Using sf As New IsolatedStorageFileStream("MyInfo.txt",
                                       IO.FileMode.Create, store)
        Using sw As New IO.StreamWriter(sf)
            sw.WriteLine("Some data")
        End Using
    End Using
End Sub
```

A `StreamWriter` object points to the instance of the `IsolatedStorageFileStream` class and is used to send information to the file. The following code demonstrates how to read from the isolated storage:

```
Private Sub ReadFromStorage()
    Using sf As New IsolatedStorageFileStream("MyInfo.txt", IO.FileMode.Open, store)
        Using sw As New IO.StreamReader(sf)
            Dim theData As String = sw.ReadLine
        End Using
    End Using
End Sub
```

You still use the `IO.FileMode` enumeration to establish whether the file must be opened for reading or for writing.

LOCAL DATA ACCESS WITH SQL SERVER 3.5 COMPACT EDITION

Windows Phone 7.5 introduced support for local databases based on SQL Server 3.5 Compact Edition and LINQ to SQL. This is a more complex topic, so I suggest you read an article I published in the Visual Studio Developer Center at the following address: http://msdn.microsoft.com/en-us/vstudio/hh758260.aspx

38

Understanding the Application Bar

Every page can offer additional actions through the application bar, represented by the ApplicationBar class. This enables you to store up to four small buttons (represented by ApplicationBarIconButton objects), which are horizontally aligned, and items (represented by ApplicationBarMenuItem objects), which are vertically aligned. Both buttons and items can respond to Click events. Page item templates in Windows Phone provide a basic stub of the application bar, made of commented lines of code, at the bottom of the XAML code editor. The following code extends the autogenerated code, to demonstrate how you can specify an x:Name identifier to buttons and items and how they can respond to Click events:

```
<phone:PhoneApplicationPage.ApplicationBar>
    <shell:ApplicationBar IsVisible="True" IsMenuEnabled="True">
        <shell:ApplicationBarIconButton Click="ApplicationBarIconButton_Click"
                                        x:Name="Button1"
            IconUri="/Images/appbar_button1.png" Text="Button 1"/>
        <shell:ApplicationBarIconButton IconUri="/Images/appbar_button2.png"
                                        Text="Button 2"/>
        <shell:ApplicationBar.MenuItems>
            <shell:ApplicationBarMenuItem Text="MenuItem 1"
                                          Click="ApplicationBarMenuItem_Click" />
            <shell:ApplicationBarMenuItem Text="MenuItem 2"/>

        </shell:ApplicationBar.MenuItems>
    </shell:ApplicationBar>
</phone:PhoneApplicationPage.ApplicationBar>
```

You should also provide meaningful icons for buttons and set them via the IconUri property. Figure 38.14 shows an example of the app bar.

Accessing the Pictures Hub

The *Pictures Hub* in Windows Phone is the place where pictures are stored. It is organized in albums and shows pictures from both linked social network accounts and folders on the device. You can programmatically access the Pictures Hub via a convenient class called Microsoft.Phone.Tasks.PhotoChooserTask. You handle the Completed event of this class, which is raised after the user selects a picture, by getting the instance of the selected picture under the form of a stream that you can elaborate further. For example, imagine you have a new empty project and want to show a picture selected from the hub inside an Image control. Drag an Image control from the toolbox onto the main page of the application. Next, enable the app bar (so that you do not need to add a button to the app's surface) as follows:

```
<phone:PhoneApplicationPage.ApplicationBar>
    <shell:ApplicationBar IsVisible="True" IsMenuEnabled="True">
        <shell:ApplicationBarIconButton x:Name="GetImageButton"
            Click="GetImageButton_Click"
```

```
        IconUri="/Images/appbar_button1.png" Text="Button 1"/>
    </shell:ApplicationBar>
</phone:PhoneApplicationPage.ApplicationBar>
```

FIGURE 38.14   The app bar enables you to access additional actions and shortcuts.

Now move to the page's code-behind file. Listing 38.2 demonstrates how easily you can pick pictures from the hub and assign the result to the Image control.

LISTING 38.2   Accessing the Pictures Hub

```vb
Imports Microsoft.Phone.Tasks
Imports System.Windows.Media.Imaging

Partial Public Class MainPage
    Inherits PhoneApplicationPage

    ' Constructor
    Public Sub New()
        InitializeComponent()
    End Sub
```

38

```vb
Private Sub GetImageButton_Click(sender As System.Object,
                                e As System.EventArgs)
    'Open the Pictures Hub
    Dim photo As New PhotoChooserTask
    AddHandler photo.Completed, AddressOf photo_Completed
    'Allow users to take a new
    'picture from the camera
    photo.ShowCamera = True
    'Start the task
    photo.Show()
End Sub


Private Sub photo_Completed(Sender As Object,
                           e As PhotoResult)
    'If a picture has been selected
    If e.ChosenPhoto IsNot Nothing Then
        'Create a new BitmapImage
        Dim bmp As New BitmapImage
        'Set the image's source with
        'the stream representing the picture
        bmp.SetSource(e.ChosenPhoto)

        'Assign the Image.Source property
        Me.Image1.Source = bmp
    End If
End Sub
End Class
```

It is important to understand that you must set the `PhotoChooserTask.ShowCamera` property as `True` to allow users to pick a new photo from the camera and how the `PhotoResult.ChosenPhoto` property contains a reference to the selected picture via a stream.

Understanding the Execution Model

Although Windows Phone 7.5 introduced multitasking support, which is typically used to support agents, the main concept is that only one application at a time can be executed. The `App` class (available in the App.xaml.vb file) handles events that respond to moments of the application lifetime. The following numbered list provides the series of steps that constitute an app's execution:

1. The app is selected from the list of installed apps or from Start. From a "not running" state, the app switches to a "running" state. When the app is launching, the `Application.Launching` event is raised. After the app is brought to the foreground, the `Application.Activated` event is raised.

2. If the user taps the Back button of the device, the application is closed. At this point, the `Application.Closing` event is raised. After the app is brought to the background, the `Application.Deactivated` event is raised.

3. If the user holds the Back button to switch to another app or the user presses Start, the application is brought to the background but is not closed. It is deactivated and put to sleep. The `Application.Deactivating` event is raised.

As a developer, you are responsible for saving the state of the application when it is put to sleep and for restoring the last state after the application is resumed. This technique is called *tombstoning*. Because you typically work with pages, to perform tombstoning you override the `OnNavigatedFrom` and `OnNavigatedTo` methods. The following code refers to the first sample app and demonstrates how to store the content of the `TextBox` where the user enters the website address to visit when the application is put to sleep and how the same information is restored after the application is brought to the foreground:

```
'The app is going to sleep
'Save the content of the TextBox
Protected Overrides Sub OnNavigatedFrom(e As System.Windows.
                                        Navigation.NavigationEventArgs)
    Me.State.Add("webSiteAddress", Me.AddressBox.Text)
End Sub


'The app is resumed
'Restore the content of the TextBox
Protected Overrides Sub OnNavigatedTo(e As System.Windows.
                                      Navigation.NavigationEventArgs)
    Dim webAddress As Object = Nothing
    If Me.State.TryGetValue("webSiteAddress", webAddress) Then
        Me.AddressBox.Text = CStr(webAddress)
    End If
End Sub
```

The `Page` object exposes a `State` property, which is a `Dictionary(Of String, Object)`. You can store information by providing a key to identify such information; this is done when the app is being put to sleep by invoking the dictionary's `Add` method. When the app is resumed, the dictionary is queried via the `TryGetValue` method to see whether the specified key exists and, if it does, the stored information is converted into the appropriate type and sent to the user interface.

Setting Properties, Icons, and Splash Screen

You can customize your Windows Phone apps by replacing three default images:

▶ **The splash screen**—This must be a .jpeg image of size 480 × 800 and is shown when the application is being loaded. In Solution Explorer, you can see a file called

SplashScreenImage.jpg, which represents the default splash screen and that you can replace with your own image.

▶ **The application icon**—This must be a 62×62 PNG image file and is used to identify the app in the list of installed apps. In Solution Explorer, the default application icon is represented by the ApplicationIcon.png file.

▶ **The background image**—This must be a 173×173 PNG image file and is used when you pin the app to the Windows Phone's Start menu. In Solution Explorer, the default background image is represented by the BackgroundImage.png file.

After you have created your custom images, you can replace the default ones by accessing the project properties, as shown in Figure 38.15.

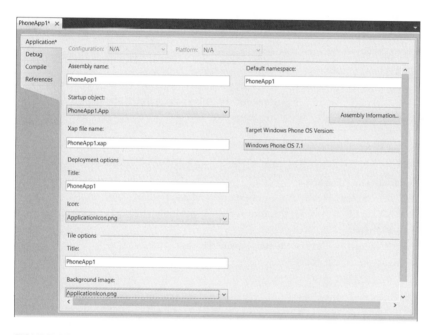

FIGURE 38.15   Customizing the Windows Phone app's properties.

Two other properties should be customized:

▶ **The Title field in the Deployment options group**—This contains the app name as it will be displayed in the list of installed apps and should represent the full app name.

▶ **The Title field in the Tile options group**—This contains text that will be displayed on the app tile when you pin it to the Start menu.

Additionally, you must customize the Assembly Information, as you already know. In particular, be sure you edit both the Company and Copyright fields because by default they contain the Microsoft identifier. This means that if they are not replaced with your information, the application will not pass certification.

Submitting Apps to the Marketplace

APPLICATION CERTIFICATION REQUIREMENTS

Before you submit your apps to the Windows Phone Marketplace, you must be sure they adhere to the certification policies. For this reason, bookmark the certification requirements page on MSDN because this will be one of your closest friends for avoiding rejections: http://msdn.microsoft.com/en-us/library/windowsphone/develop/hh184843(v=vs.92).aspx

---

When you have finished developing and testing your app, it is time for the Marketplace submission so that other users will be able to download your app on their devices. To submit an app, you need to access the Windows Phone Dev Center at http://dev.windowsphone.com and sign in with your registered Windows Live ID. After you are signed in, click **Dashboard** and then **Submit App**. You will be required to specify some information, such as the app's XAP file and submission details. Figure 38.16 shows the first step of the submission.

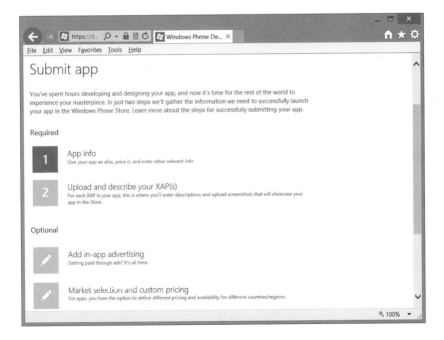

FIGURE 38.16   Starting the submission process.

If you click 1 – App info, you will be asked to specify the app name, the category, pricing, and worldwide distribution or distribution only to those marketplaces with no restriction rules. Figure 38.17 provides an example.

FIGURE 38.17   Specifying the application's details.

You can specify the price for your app, which can be 0.00 (free) or paid. Actually, the Windows Phone Marketplace and the development platform support a trial mode. Implementing the trial experience in code is easy, and if you click the appropriate link in the pricing box, you will be redirected to the MSDN documentation that explains how to accomplish this. If you expand More Options, you will have an opportunity to decide whether the app will be published as soon as it passes the certification process. This avoids the need of manually publishing the app later. After completing the first step, you will be asked to upload the XAP file of your app in step 2. Click Browse and locate the app's XAP file. After the XAP file has been uploaded, you will have a chance to provide additional details such as the version number. This is useful when you release application updates and represents the submission version number, so it is not the same number as the XAP file version number. In the same page, you must also specify the app language and description. The language must match the neutral language information that you supplied in the Assembly Information properties in Visual Studio, and the description will enable users to understand what your app does when they find it in the Marketplace (see Figure 38.18).

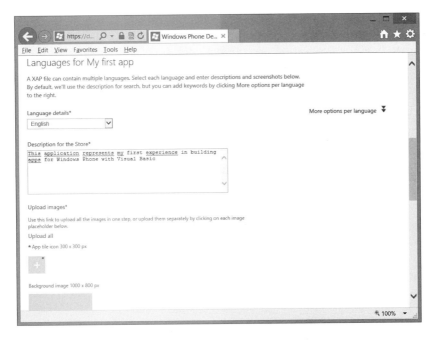

FIGURE 38.18   Supplying language, details, and images.

This is also the place where you have to specify a number of images that will be used in the Marketplace to identify your app, such as screenshots, app tile icon, and so on. Be sure you respect the required image sizes. When you complete this step, you have an opportunity to customize two additional settings: creating an advertising account so that apps will show advertising in exchange for some money (read the information available on the Dev Center carefully) and of choosing different pricing options for different markets. After you have completed all the required steps, you can submit the app for certification. When Microsoft completes reviewing the app, they will send you an email telling you whether the app was successfully certified and published or if it failed certification. If your app fails, the attached document will help you to identify the problem and how to fix it.

Summary

Windows Phone 7.5 is the most important operating system for mobile phones from Microsoft, and building apps for this platform relies on a special version of Silverlight 4. This makes developing applications easier because you can reuse existing skills on XAML and managed code. This chapter explained how to create a simple app interacting with the XAML and managed code editors. Next, you saw how to enable built-in device functionalities by taking advantage of launchers, which enable you to use Bing Maps, Internet Explorer, the built-in Media Player, the email client, and telephone and messaging apps.

38

You saw how to display multiple contents in one page by implementing the `Panorama` control. You learned how to leverage the app bar and how to interact with the Pictures Hub. You then learned how the application execution model works and, finally, saw how to customize the application and start the submission process to the Windows Phone Marketplace.

CHAPTER **39**

Creating and Consuming WCF Services

During the last several years, many technologies were developed for distributed applications that communicate over networks. The idea is that client applications can exchange information with a service via a network protocol such as Hypertext Transport Protocol (HTTP) or Transmission Control Protocol (TCP), just to mention some. Among these technologies there are SOAP (an XML-based information exchange system), Microsoft Messaging Queue (a message-based system), the well-known web services, and the .NET Remoting (which connects applications based on the .NET Framework). Although powerful, all these technologies have one limitation: Two or more applications can connect only if all of them rely on the same technology. Just for clarification, an application based on MSMQ cannot communicate with another one based on SOAP. To avoid this limitation, Microsoft created the Windows Communication Foundation (WCF) technology that was first introduced with the .NET Framework 3.0. It is a unified programming model for distributed applications. With WCF, developers can write code for exchanging data and information between services and clients without worrying about how data is transmitted because this is the job of the .NET Framework. WCF is another large technology, and covering every single aspect would require an entire book; therefore, in this chapter you learn about implementing, configuring, hosting, and consuming WCF services with Visual Basic 2012.

Introducing Windows Communication Foundation

WCF is a technology that enables data and information exchange between services and clients through messages. The service exposes information through the network and is nothing but a .NET assembly. Then the client receives that information and can send back other information or data. In this section, you learn how data exchange between the service and clients works before creating your first WCF service. This is important because you need to know some fundamentals about WCF infrastructure before putting your hands on the code. If you ever developed .NET Web Services (.asmx), you'll notice several similarities with WCF, at least in the implementation. However, several things under the hood make WCF more powerful. Moreover, although web services are obviously still allowed and supported in .NET Framework 4.5, WCF is the main technology for data exchange through networks and is intended to be a replacement of web services, even though WCF provides fully integrated support with client and web applications, such as WPF and Silverlight.

WCF 4.5

Windows Communication Foundation in .NET Framework 4.5 is also known as WCF 4.5, although this is actually the fourth version. There are some improvements in the new version of WCF, and a lot of work has been done to simplify the way services are developed and maintained. We, however, focus on them only when required, preferring to illustrate how you implement and consume services. For further information about what's new in WCF 4.5, read the MSDN Library at: http://msdn.microsoft.com/en-us/library/dd456789(v=vs.110).aspx.

Understanding Endpoints

A WCF service is a .NET assembly (in the form of dll) relying on the `System.ServiceModel` namespace and exposing objects and members like any other class library. Thus, client applications can invoke members and use objects exposed by services. Behind the scenes, this happens through message exchanges. Client and services exchange messages through *endpoints*. An endpoint is the place where client and service meet and is where both applications exchange their information, so it can be considered like a communication port. Each WCF service offers at least one endpoint; multiple endpoints serve as communication ports for different data types (for example, .NET objects and messages). But every endpoint needs to be configured with some other information to be a functional place for meeting the needs of service and clients. The configuration is provided by the `Address`, `Binding`, and `Contract` as explained in the next section.

Address, Binding, Contract: The ABC of WCF

When a client application attempts to reach a service, it needs to know some information for finding the service and for data exchange. The service exposes such information via the ABC, which represents the *Address*, *Binding*, and *Contract* properties in the service. The *Address* is the physical URI where the service is running. For example, on the local

machine the Address could be http://localhost/MyService.svc or http://www.something.
com/MyService.svc if the service is running on the Internet. The *Binding* property is a
complex object and is responsible for

▶ Establishing how service and clients communicate (with a `Behavior` object)

▶ Establishing which protocol and credentials must be used within the communication

▶ Handling data transmission to the target (via a `Channel` object), converting data
  into an acceptable format, and transmitting data via the specified protocol (such as
  HTTP, HTTPS, and so on)

The *Contract* is probably the most significant item in the ABC. It establishes what data can
be exchanged and which .NET objects/members are exposed by the service and that the
client must accept; this is defined as platform-independent because clients will just accept
the contract without worrying about the code that implemented objects on the server
side. If you think of classic managed class libraries, when you add a reference to a class
library, you want to use its members, but in most cases you will not worry about the code
that implemented those members. With WCF, it is the same thing. For code, a contract
is a .NET interface that defines public members available from the service to clients. Such
an interface is then implemented by a class that actually makes members available to the
external world. All these concepts will be explained in code. There are different contract
types in WCF, but the most important are summarized in Table 39.1.

TABLE 39.1   WCF Contracts

Contract	Description
ServiceContract	Provides the service skeleton and defines methods that will be available to the public
DataContract	Defines classes that will be available to the public as data objects
MessageContract	Used to exchange data with SOAP-based applications and serializes data into SOAP messages

As you see in the next section, contracts are applied with special .NET attributes. The good
news about the ABC is that all information is typically stored inside the configuration file
and therefore can be edited with any text editor by system and network administrators,
too, without the need of recompiling the source code. This makes services administration
simpler. At this point, you are ready to create your first WCF service with Visual
Basic 2012.

39

Implementing WCF Services

Visual Studio 2012 offers some project templates for creating WCF projects. Table 39.2
lists them all.

TABLE 39.2   WCF Project Templates

Template	Description
WCF Service Application	Used for creating a self-hosted WCF service
WCF Service Library	Used for creating a WCF service to be manually hosted and configured
WCF Workflow Service Application	Enables you to create a WCF service with integration with Workflow Foundation
WCF Syndication Library	Generates a WCF service enabled for RSS syndication
WCF RIA Services Class Library	Only available within Silverlight projects, enables you to add a WCF service with Silverlight integration

This book covers the WCF Service Application template, which is useful because it provides service self-hosting. A WCF service cannot be run or consumed as a standalone and must be hosted inside a .NET application. Host applications can be of several types: Console applications, Internet Information Services (including the Express edition), and ASP.NET Development Server are all valid host applications. The WCF Service Application template provides hosting inside the Internet Information Services (IIS) Express development server, which is something new in Visual Studio 2012. IIS Express is a lightweight version of the famous IIS web server and is typically used on development machines for testing purposes. In Visual Studio 2012, IIS Express is the default setting for WCF 4.5, but you can still use the ASP.NET Development Server (see Figure 39.6 to locate the host selection). Select the **File, New Project** command, and in the **New Project** dialog box, select the **WCF Service Application** template, as shown in Figure 39.1. Name the new project **BookService** and then click **OK**.

The goal of the example is to offer a way for validating books' information, such as ISBN code, title, and author. The service exposes a `Book` class representing a single book and a method named `ValidateBook` that provides the validation logic. Before writing custom code, you should take a look at the autogenerated code to understand what WCF needs. Visual Studio 2012 generated a web project visible in Solution Explorer. The new project contains the following files:

▶ IService1.vb, which defines the contract interface

▶ Service1.svc.vb (nested into Service1.svc as a code-behind file), which defines the class that implements the contract

▶ Service1.svc, which is the actual service that exposes data and that is to be consumed by clients

▶ Web.config, which provides definitions for the ABC

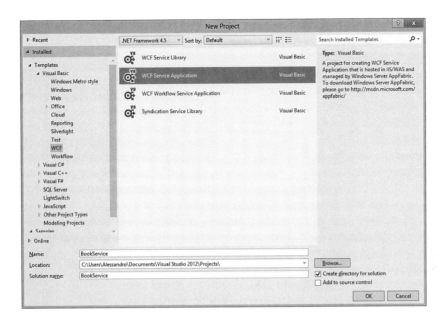

FIGURE 39.1   Creating a new WCF project.

NOTE ON THE WEB.CONFIG FILE

Starting with the .NET Framework 4.0 and Visual Studio 2010, the Web.config file no longer contains a WCF metadata definition in case you use the default settings because they are considered as implicit. This is important with regard to the current example. If you decide to implement custom settings instead, the Web.config stores the metadata definition. Because configuration files in client applications reflect Web.config files from services, later in this chapter you see the client-side metadata definition mapping the implicit metadata of the current sample service.

Let's take a look at the IService1.vb file, which is reported in Listing 39.1 and that defines a couple of contracts.

LISTING 39.1   Autogenerated Contracts

```
' NOTE: You can use the "Rename" command on the "Refactor" menu
' to change the interface name "IService1" in both code and
' config file together.
<ServiceContract()>
Public Interface IService1

    <OperationContract()>
    Function GetData(ByVal value As Integer) As String
```

39

```
    <OperationContract()>
    Function GetDataUsingDataContract(ByVal composite As _
                                CompositeType) As CompositeType


        ' TODO: Add your service operations here

End Interface


' Use a data contract as illustrated in the sample below
' to add composite types to service operations.
<DataContract()>
Public Class CompositeType


    <DataMember()>
    Public Property BoolValue() As Boolean

    <DataMember()>
    Public Property StringValue() As String
End Class
```

The IService1 interface is decorated with the ServiceContract attribute, meaning that it establishes which members the service defines and makes available to the public. The interface defines two methods, both decorated with the OperationContract attribute. This attribute makes methods visible to the external world and consumable by clients. You need to remember that, in WCF, marking a method as Public is not sufficient to make it available to clients; it needs to be marked as OperationContract to be visible. Methods exposed by WCF services are also known as *service operations*, and this definition will be recalled in the next chapter with regard to WCF Data Services. Notice how the GetDataUsingDataContract method receives an argument of type CompositeType. This type is a custom class declared as DataContract, so the WCF service can exchange data of this type. Members from this class also need to be marked as DataMember to be visible to the external world. As for service operations, marking a member as Public is not sufficient; you need to decorate members with the DataMember attribute. The Service1 class shows an example of implementing the contract and the logic for service operations. Listing 39.2 shows the autogenerated sample code.

LISTING 39.2   Autogenerated Contracts Implementation

```
' NOTE: You can use the "Rename" command on the "Refactor" menu to
' change the class name "Service1" in code, svc and config file together.
Public Class Service1
    Implements IService1

    Public Sub New()
    End Sub
```

```
    Public Function GetData(ByVal value As Integer) As String _
                Implements IService1.GetData
        Return String.Format("You entered: {0}", value)
    End Function

    Public Function GetDataUsingDataContract(ByVal composite As CompositeType) As _
                CompositeType Implements IService1.GetDataUsingDataContract
        If composite Is Nothing Then
            Throw New ArgumentNullException("composite")
        End If
        If composite.BoolValue Then
            composite.StringValue &= "Suffix"
        End If
        Return composite
    End Function
End Class
```

The class implements the contract interface and provides logic for service operations working like any other .NET class. The content of the .svc file is discussed later; for now let's make some edits to the code replacing the autogenerated one with custom implementation.

Implementing Custom Logic for the WCF Service

Rename the IService1.vb file to **IBookService.vb**; then switch to the code editor. Right-click the `IService1` identifier and select **Rename**. Next, provide the new `IBookService` identifier and click **OK**. Visual Studio will prompt for confirmation and will rename the instances in code as well. This is important to update all references inside the project to the interface, including references inside the .svc file. Now delete the code for the `CompositeType` class and replace the entire code with the one shown in Listing 39.3.

LISTING 39.3   Implementing Custom Contracts

```
<ServiceContract()>
Public Interface IBookService

    <OperationContract()>
    Function ValidateBook(ByVal bookToValidate As Book) As String

End Interface

<DataContract()>
Public Class Book

    <DataMember()>
    Public Property Title As String
```

39

```
<DataMember()>
Public Property ISBN As String

<DataMember()>
Public Property Author As String

<DataMember()>
Public Property DatePublished As Date?
End Class
```

The IBookService contract defines a ValidateBook method that will be invoked for validating a book. A single book is represented by the Book class, which exposes four self-explanatory properties. Now switch to the Service1 class and, following the steps described before, rename the Service1 identifier into BookService. Then replace the auto-generated code with the one shown in Listing 39.4.

LISTING 39.4   Implementing the Service Logic

```
Imports System.Text.RegularExpressions
Public Class BookService
    Implements IBookService

    Private Const isbnPattern As String = _
    "ISBN(?:-13)?:?\x20*(?=.{17}$)97(?:8|9)([ -])\d{1,5}\1\d{1,7}\1\d{1,6}\1\d$"

    Public Function ValidateBook(ByVal bookToValidate As Book) As _
                String Implements IBookService.ValidateBook

        Dim isValidIsbn As Boolean = Regex.IsMatch(String.Concat("ISBN-13: ",
                                        bookToValidate.ISBN),
                                        isbnPattern)

        If isValidIsbn = False Then
            Return "Invalid ISBN"
        End If

        Dim isValidAuthor As Boolean = String.IsNullOrEmpty(bookToValidate.Author)
        If isValidAuthor = True Then
            Return "Author not specified"
        End If

        Dim isValidTitle As Boolean = String.IsNullOrEmpty(bookToValidate.Title)
        If isValidTitle = True Then
```

```
        Return "Title not specified"
    End If

    If bookToValidate.DatePublished Is Nothing Then
        Return "Book data is valid but date published was not specified"
    End If

    Return "Valid book"
  End Function
End Class
```

The code for the `ValidateBook` method is simple. It uses a regular expression for checking whether the ISBN code is valid and then checks for valid properties in the Book class instance that must be validated.

NOTE ON THE REGULAR EXPRESSION PATTERN

The regular expression pattern for checking ISBNs is from the RegExLibrary website at the following address: http://regexlib.com/REDetails.aspx?regexp_id=1748. A lot of patterns for validating ISBNs are available; the one used in this book is just an example. You can replace it with a different one.

Now right-click the **BookService.svc** file in Solution Explorer, and select **View in Browser**. In a few seconds, the WCF service will be hosted by the ASP.NET Development Server and will run inside the web browser, as demonstrated in Figure 39.2.

This test is required to ensure that the service works correctly. Notice how information is provided on how consuming the service is. The web page shows information explaining that you should invoke the **SvcUtil.exe** command-line tool pointing to the wdsl metadata of the service.

WHAT IS WSDL?

Web-service Definition Language (WSDL) is a standard format and is an XML representation of how a web service works (including WCF services), describing document information and procedure information, including endpoints and messages. WSDL explains how a service must work—for example, how information has to be transmitted, which protocol must be used, and how it interacts in scenarios such as REST and SOAP. Such information is known as *service metadata* and in WCF it plays an important role.

39

SvcUtil is described in the next section. Click the link available near SvcUtil.exe. By doing so, you access metadata offered by the WCF service, including contracts and members, as reported in Figure 39.3.

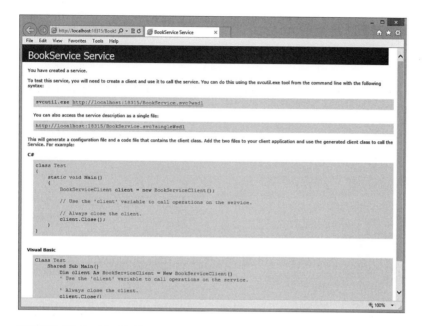

FIGURE 39.2   The WCF service has been hosted by the ASP.NET Development Server and is now running.

FIGURE 39.3   Exploring the service's metadata.

Client applications invoke service members passing through the service metadata. The next section explains how you invoke service members through a proxy class, but before going into that, let's take a look at the BookService.svc file.

EXPOSING GENERICS IN WCF

Because WCF services metadata are exposed via WSDL, some issues with generics are not supported by this. I suggest you read this blog post by MVP Jeff Barnes that provides explanations and workarounds: http://bit.ly/4CzGv3. Another suggestion is to investigate how WCF Data Services work for exposing entities (see Chapter 40, "Implementing and Consuming WCF Data Services," for information about Data Services).

Right-click this file and select **View Markup**. The XHTML code for this file is the following:

```
<%@ ServiceHost Language="VB" Debug="true"
    Service="BookService.BookService" CodeBehind="BookService.svc.vb" %>
```

This file defines the service entry point. It states that the BookService class is the service entry point because it defines the real logic that implements the contract. There is some other information such as the programming language used and the code-behind the file, but the Service tag is absolutely the most important. After this overview of the service implementation, it's time to consume the service from a client application.

EXPOSING ENTITY DATA MODELS AND LINQ TO SQL CLASSES

WCF services are also used to expose Entity Data Models (EDM) and LINQ to SQL classes via serialization. Entities and their members in EDMs are marked by default with the DataContract and DataMember attributes, respectively. LINQ to SQL classes, on the other hand, have to be enabled for serialization by setting the Serialization Mode property of the DataContext class as Unidirectional and then marking entities with DataContract. In Chapter 40 you learn about WCF Data Services, which provide an easy implementation of WCF services by exposing data models without the need of making such customizations manually. Thus, you should create custom WCF services for exposing data models only when you need to handle special scenarios that require implementing different business logic than the one offered by Data Services.

39

Consuming WCF Services

Clients can easily consume WCF services by adding a service reference directly from Visual Studio 2012. In the next example, you create a simple Console client application for validating ISBNs by invoking objects from the WCF service implemented in the previous section.

Creating the Client and Adding a Service Reference

Add a new Console project to the current solution and name it **BookClient**. The first step you have to accomplish is adding a service reference to the WCF service. Right-click the new project name in Solution Explorer and select **Add Service Reference**. This brings up the Add Service Reference dialog box, where you need to enter the full web address of your service. If the service you want to add a reference to is available in the current solution, as in the current example, click **Discover**. The service appears in the dialog box, as shown in Figure 39.4.

FIGURE 39.4   The Add Service Reference dialog box enables you to add a reference to a WCF service.

Click the service name on the left to enable the development server to correctly host the service and discover its members. At this point, the dialog box lists available contracts (IBookService in this case) and their members. Replace the Namespace identifier with BookServiceReference.

Understanding the Proxy Class

The WCF service is exposed through the network via a WSDL. To consume objects and data exposed by the WSDL, the client needs a proxy class that is responsible for translating WSDL information into managed code that you can reuse. This is accomplished via a command-line tool named SvcUtil.exe, which is part of the .NET Framework. Fortunately, you do not need to run SvcUtil manually because Visual Studio will do the work for you. When you click **OK** from the Add Service Reference dialog box, Visual Studio invokes SvcUtil and generates a proxy class. In Solution Explorer, a new folder named Service references appears. This folder contains all service references and, for the current example, stores a new item named BookServiceReference. This new item

provides all the metadata information required to consume the service and especially
the proxy class. Click the **Show All Files** button in Solution Explorer and expand the
Reference.svcmap file; then double-click the **Reference.vb** file. This code file exposes
the `BookServiceReference` namespace to provide client-side code for accessing members
exposed from the service. This namespace exposes client-side implementations of the
`Book` class and the `IBookService` interface. The most important class exposed by the
namespace is named `BookServiceClient` and is the actual proxy class, which inherits
from `System.ServiceModel.ClientBase` and is responsible for connecting to the service
and closing the connection. It is also responsible for exposing service members such as
the `ValidateBook` that was implemented on the service side. The namespace also exposes
the `IBookServiceChannel` interface that inherits from `IClientChannel`, which provides
members for the request/reply infrastructure required by WCF services. You instantiate
the proxy class to establish a connection with the WCF service, and you interact with the
proxy class for accessing members from the service, as explained in the next section.

Invoking Members from the Service

To invoke service members, you need to create an instance of the proxy class, which in
our example is named `BookClient.BookServiceReference.BookServiceClient`. Creating
an instance of the class can establish a connection to the WCF service and give you access
to public members. Continuing with the previous example, the client application could
have an instance of the `Book` class and invoke the `ValidateBook` method for checking
whether the `Book` instance is correct according to our needs. The code in Listing 39.5
shows how to accomplish this.

LISTING 39.5   Instantiating the Proxy Class and Invoking Service Members

```
Imports BookClient.BookServiceReference

Module Module1

    Sub Main()
        'Creates an instance of the proxy class
        'and automatically establishes a connection
        'to the service
        Dim client As New BookServiceClient

        'A new book
        'Note that the RegEx pattern requires to write the ISBN in the form
        'provided below, so like: 000-0-0000-0000-0 including the minus
        'character
        Dim myBook As New Book
        With myBook
            .Author = "Alessandro Del Sole"
            .Title = "Visual Studio LightSwitch Unleashed"
            .ISBN = "978-0-6723-3553-2"
```

```
            .DatePublished = Date.Today
        End With

        'Invokes the ValidateBook method from
        'the service
        Console.WriteLine(client.ValidateBook(myBook))
        Console.WriteLine("Done")
        Console.ReadLine()
        client.Close()

    End Sub
End Module
```

In the client you can invoke all public members from the service, where *public* means functions decorated with the OperationContract attribute and data classes decorated with the DataContract attribute. Running the code in Listing 39.5 produces the result shown in Figure 39.5, but you can try to change the ISBN code to check how the application works with different values.

FIGURE 39.5   The client application validated a book.

Remember to close the connection to the service invoking the Close method on the proxy class. This ensures that the service will be shut down.

Understanding the Configuration File

When you add a proxy class to your WCF service, Visual Studio also updates the configuration file to provide information on how to reach and interact with the service. The most important information is stored in the System.ServiceModel section of the **app.config** file. Listing 39.6 shows the most interesting excerpt.

LISTING 39.6   Configuration Settings for the Client

```xml
<?xml version="1.0" encoding="utf-8" ?>
<configuration>
    <startup>
        <supportedRuntime version="v4.0" sku=".NETFramework,Version=v4.5" />
    </startup>
    <system.serviceModel>
        <bindings>
            <basicHttpBinding>
                <binding name="BasicHttpBinding_IBookService" />
            </basicHttpBinding>
        </bindings>
        <client>
            <endpoint address="http://localhost:18315/BookService.svc"
                    binding="basicHttpBinding"
                    bindingConfiguration="BasicHttpBinding_IBookService"
                    contract="BookServiceReference.IBookService"
                    name="BasicHttpBinding_IBookService" />
        </client>
    </system.serviceModel>
</configuration>
```

The app.config file maps the related nodes in the Web.config file from the service. This is important to remember in case you want to implement a custom configuration different from the default one. The bindings node defines how data and information are transferred. The `basicHttpBinding` binding is the simplest way and uses HTTP and Text or XML as the encoding format. WCF offers lots of other bindings specific for particular needs, such as secured communications or peer-to-peer applications. Table 39.3 summarizes built-in bindings.

WCF SIMPLIFICATION IN .NET 4.5

Several simplification features in .NET 4.5 are specific for WCF. Among them, Visual Studio 2012 simplifies the generated app.config file for clients when you add a service reference. Such a simplification avoids the explicit specification of binding property values if they have the default value, making the XML code simpler. For example, a binding has the `openTimeOut` and `closeTimeOut` properties that, until Visual Studio 2010, were explicitly added to the binding with a value of 00:01:00 seconds. Because this is their default value, in Visual Studio 2012 they are no longer added explicitly in code and the runtime assumes they already have a value of 00:01:00. You will instead specify explicitly a binding property value only if such a property has a value different from the default one. This is the reason Listing 39.6 shows a simplified configuration file (if you purchased the previous edition of this book, you can easily check this out).

39

TABLE 39.3   WCF Built-In Bindings

Binding	Description
BasicHttpBinding	Used for ASP.NET-based web services. It uses the HTTP protocol and text or XML for messages encoding.
WSHttpBinding	Used for secured communications in non-duplex service contracts.
WSDualHttpBinding	Used for secured communications in duplex service contracts including SOAP.
WSFederationHttpBinding	Used for secured communications according to the WS-Federation protocol that provides an easy authentication and authorization system within a federation.
NetTcpBinding	Used for secured communications between WCF applications distributed across multiple machines.
NetNamedPipeBinding	Used for secured communications between WCF applications on the same machine.
NetMsmqBinding	Used for messaging communications between WCF applications.
NetPeerTcpBinding	Used for peer-to-peer applications.
MsmqIntegrationBinding	Used for communications between WCF applications and MSMQ applications across multiple machines.
BasicHttpContextBinding	Similar to BasicHttpBinding but with the capability of enabling cookies.
NetTcpContextBinding	Used for communications between WCF applications that need to use SOAP headers for data exchange across multiple machines.
WebHttpBinding	Used for WCF services exposed via endpoints requiring HTTP requests instead of SOAP endpoints.
WSHttpContextBinding	Similar to WsHttpBinding with the ability of enabling SOAP headers for information exchange.

In addition to built-in bindings, WCF enables defining custom bindings, but this is beyond the scope of this chapter.

IMPLEMENTING SECURE BINDINGS ON BOTH SERVICE AND CLIENTS

The current code example uses, on both the service side and client side, the basicHttp-Binding, which is the simplest binding available. Using a different binding depends on the particular scenario you need to work on. Because of this, look at the official MSDN documentation related to built-in bindings, which also provides examples and explanations on when each binding should be used. The documentation is located at the following address: http://msdn.microsoft.com/en-us/library/ms730879(v=vs.110).aspx.

You can also customize timeouts by specifying the `closeTimeout, openTimeout, send-Timeout`, and `receiveTimeOut` properties; you could change the maximum size for data exchange by setting `maxBufferSize` and `maxReceivedMessageSize`. These two are important because you might be required to increase the default size in case your application transfers large amounts of data. Now take a look at the `client` node. This defines the endpoint's ABC, such as the address pointing to the physical URI of the service, the binding transport protocol, and the contract interface (`BookServiceReference.IBookService`). Notice that when moving the service to production, the address URI must be replaced with the Internet/intranet address of your service. This can be accomplished by replacing the `address` item in the configuration file without the need of rebuilding the application.

Handling Exceptions in WCF

WCF applications can throw communication exceptions that both services and clients need to handle. Typically, the most common exception in the WCF development is the `System.ServiceModel.FaultException`; it offers a generic, strongly typed flavor and a nongeneric one. The exception needs to first be handled in the WCF service, but the nongeneric implementation is less useful than the generic one because it provides less detailed information. Because of this, we now consider how to handle the `FaultException(Of T)`. Replace the `ValidateBook` method definition in the `IBookService` interface as follows:

```
<OperationContract()> <FaultContract(GetType(Book))>
Function ValidateBook(ByVal bookToValidate As Book) As String
```

The `FaultContract` attribute receives the type that might encounter processing errors during the invocation of the service operation. This can enable the `FaultException` to throw detailed SOAP information for that type. To accomplish this, replace the `ValidateBook` method implementation in the `BookService` class with the following:

```
Public Function ValidateBook(ByVal bookToValidate As Book) As _
            String Implements IBookService.ValidateBook

    Try
        Dim isValidIsbn As Boolean = Regex.IsMatch(String.
                            Concat("ISBN-13: ",
                            bookToValidate.ISBN), isbnPattern)


        If isValidIsbn = False Then
            Return "Invalid ISBN"
        End If


        Dim isValidAuthor As Boolean = _
            String.IsNullOrEmpty(bookToValidate.Author)
```

```
        If isValidAuthor = True Then
            Return "Author not specified"
        End If


        Dim isValidTitle As Boolean = _
            String.IsNullOrEmpty(bookToValidate.Title)
        If isValidTitle = True Then
            Return "Title not specified"
        End If


        If bookToValidate.DatePublished Is Nothing Then
            Return _
            "Book data is valid but date published was not specified"
        End If


        Return "Valid book"

    Catch ex As FaultException(Of Book)
        Throw New FaultException(Of Book)(bookToValidate,
                                    ex.Reason, ex.Code)
    Catch ex As Exception
        Throw
    End Try
End Function
```

The intercepted `FaultException` is rethrown to the caller specifying the instance of the `Book` class that caused the error, a `Reason` property that contains a SOAP description of the problem, and a `Code` property that returns a machine-readable identifier used for understanding the problem. With these pieces of information, client applications can understand what the problem was during the communication.

Hosting WCF Services in Internet Information Services

Host applications for WCF services can be of various kinds. Besides the IIS Express or the ASP.NET Development Server, you can host services inside managed applications, Windows services, and Internet Information Services as well. In most cases, you will need to deploy to IIS so we will cover this scenario. To host your WCF service in IIS on your development machine, follow these steps:

1. Restart Visual Studio 2012 under administrator privileges.

2. Go to the My Project designer for the WCF service project and select the **Web** tab.

3. Check the **Use Local IIS Web Server** option, but uncheck the Use IIS Express option and specify, if required, a different directory; then rerun the WCF service (see Figure 39.6).

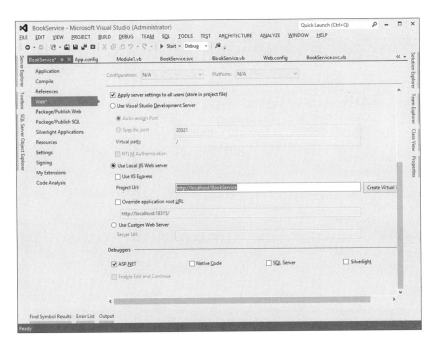

FIGURE 39.6   Setting IIS as the deployment web server.

Visual Studio will request your permission for creating and configuring a virtual directory on IIS, so you just need to accept it. When this is done, remember to replace the endpoint address in the client application configuration file with the new service URI. To host a WCF service on a nondevelopment machine, you need to create a directory under the Default Website and link the physical folder to the folder where the .svc file is placed together with the compiled dll service. You do this via the Internet Information Services Manager administrative tools available in the Windows operating system.

Configuring Services with the Configuration Editor

WCF services enable high-level customizations over their configuration. This task can be complex if you consider that there are hundreds of options that you should translate into XML. Fortunately, the .NET Framework offers a graphical tool called WCF Service Configuration Editor that you can also launch from the Tools menu in Visual Studio. In this section, you see how this tool can be used to enable tracing for WCF services. Tracing is useful because it lets you record into log file (with .svclog extension) events occurring during the WCF service running time. When launched, open the Web.config file for your service. When ready, click the **Diagnostics** folder on the left and then click the **Enable Tracing** command under the Tracing title on the right (see Figure 39.7).

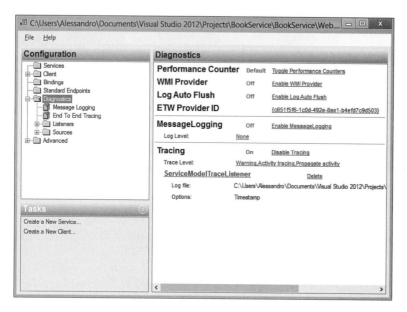

FIGURE 39.7   Enabling tracing for WCF services.

By default, tracing records messages classified at least as warnings. To modify this behavior, click the **Trace Level** link. If you click the **ServiceModelTraceListener** link, you can also specify additional information to be tracked, such as the process ID, the call stack, and the Thread ID. To view the log of recorded information, you need to run the Service Trace Viewer tool located in the C:\Program Files (x86)\Microsoft SDKs\Windows\v8.0A\ bin\NETFX 4.0 Tools folder on 64-bit machines (or C:\Program Files\Microsoft SDKs\ Windows\v8.0A\bin\NETFX 4.0 Tools on 32-bit systems). When the tool is running, open the .svclog file, which usually resides in the service folder. Figure 39.8 shows an example of log analysis. The tool provides tons of information about every event occurring at the service level and is helpful if you encounter any problems.

FIGURE 39.8   The Service Trace Viewer tool in action.

Summary

Windows Communication Foundation is a unified programming model for distributed applications that share information across networks. In this chapter, you got an introductory overview and then learned the basics about metadata. You learned that WCF services expose endpoints to be accessible from clients and that each endpoint exposes the ABC (Address-Binding-Contract). The contract is a .NET interface (marked with the `ServiceContract` attribute) that establishes service operations that can be consumed by clients. Services expose information and data through a class that implements the contract, which is the main entry point in the service. WCF services can also expose objects marked with the `DataContract` attribute and that represent data that services and clients can exchange. Next, you found out how to consume WCF services from clients by adding service references and creating proxy classes to access service members. The last part of this chapter provided an overview of exceptions handling and configurations with specific tools such as the Configuration Editor and the Service Trace Viewer.

39

Implementing and Consuming WCF Data Services

The growth of networks such as the Internet or local intranets increased the need to implement infrastructures for data exchange between companies or among users. Windows Communication Foundation (WCF) introduced an important unified programming model for information exchange over networks, but implementing a custom logic is not always an easy task. For this, Microsoft created an extraordinary platform named WCF Data Services, which uses the WCF technology and the Open Data Protocol serialization for exposing and consuming data over networks with a unified programming model that can propagate various kinds of data sources based on the .NET Framework and that can offer such infrastructure to the most common client applications types. In this chapter, you start to build REST-enabled, data-oriented applications with WCF Data Services.

What Are Data Services?

WCF Data Services is a framework for exposing data through networks such as the Internet or a local intranet and are based on the Windows Communication Foundation technology. In Visual Studio 2012 and .NET 4.5, you work with version 5.0 of WCF Data Services, which introduces a number of new features. At a higher level, data services are REST-enabled WCF services in that they support the REpresentational State Transfer programming model that enables querying data via HTTP requests. WCF data services can propagate through networks several types of data sources, such as entity data models or in-memory collections that can be consumed by several kinds of client applications, both Windows and web. These include WPF, Windows Forms, Silverlight, and ASP.NET Web Forms or MVC. This data access technology is particularly useful when you need an easy and fast way for implementing data exchange between a server and several clients, which can reach the service just with a web reference, through a unified programming model that can simplify your life—especially when you do not need deep customizations on the business logic. Clients can access data in two ways: via a uniform resource identifier (URI), with HTTP requests, or via a specific LINQ provider known as LINQ to WCF data services. Clients can perform C.R.U.D. operations using LINQ as well. In this chapter you learn to implement WCF data services exposing data from entity data models and consuming them from client applications using both URI and LINQ approaches. As I said before, WCF data services can expose several types of data sources, but the most common scenario (and the most modern) is exposing data from entity data models based on the Entity Framework, as shown in the examples in this chapter.

Querying Data via HTTP Requests

WCF data services can be queried via HTTP requests. This is possible because of the REST approach offered by this particular kind of WCF service, which is a special XML serialization format for data exchange. XML is perfect at this point because it enables you to standardize how data is exchanged in both directions. Querying a Data Service is performed by writing a URI in your web browser addresses bar or in managed code. For example, suppose you have a Data Service exposing data from the Northwind database. When deployed, the service has the following address:

```
http://localhost:4444/Northwind.svc
```

HTTP requests sent to a Data Service are represented by the HTTP verbs: GET, (read), POST (update), PUT (insert), and DELETE. The following URI sends a GET request and demonstrates how you can query the Customers collection and get all the Customer objects:

```
http://localhost:4444/Northwind.svc/Customers
```

As you will see later when discussing service implementation, this HTTP request can show the full customer list. You can then filter your query results. For example, you can retrieve all orders from the ANATR customer as follows:

```
http://localhost:4444/Northwind.svc/Customers('ANATR')/Orders
```

Finally, you could also perform other operations such as ordering via the query string. For instance, the following URI contains a query string that retrieves the same orders as previously mentioned but ordered according to the OrderDate property:

```
http://localhost:4444/Northwind.svc/Customers('ANATR')/Orders?orderby=OrderDate
```

For entity data models, a URI can be summarized as follows:

```
http://website/ServiceName.svc/EntitySetName/NavigationProperty(PrimaryKey)
```

So far, you have seen how you can use URIs to query a Data Service, but you do not know yet which infrastructure makes this possible. This is something important to know because you need to understand which libraries you will use and because such an infrastructure can open up your mind to new business scenarios. So, it is time to talk about the Open Data Protocol.

Open Data Protocol for WCF Data Services

To accept queries or data operations via HTTP, WCF data services use the *Open Data Protocol (OData)* by using the REST approach. I suggest you bookmark the OData official website, www.odata.org, because you will find documentation, tutorials, and libraries about data exchange with this protocol. OData is a web protocol for querying and updating data and uses ATOM (that is, XML) and JavaScript Object Notation (JSON, a text-based format used in AJAX applications) serialization modes, and it can be used in an infinite number of scenarios because it is based on a pure web approach rather than on a specific technology. OData exposes data as resources that can be reached via URIs. Clients access and update data by using standard HTTP verbs such as GET, PUT, POST, and DELETE. OData exposes resources as *feeds* and implements the entity-relationship conventions of the Entity Data Models (EDMs) so that data services can expose entity sets and related data under the form of resources that are related by associations.

A number of libraries make it easier for client applications to access OData resources by using an object-oriented approach rather than sending HTTP requests directly (an updated list is available at http://www.odata.org/libraries). The .NET Framework 4.5 includes a library called Microsoft.Data.OData.dll, which is a client library for accessing OData feeds in managed code and is automatically added to your projects every time you create a WCF Data Service.

Even if in most cases you will want to expose EDMs as OData feeds, OData can expose various data formats. For example, you can expose classic .NET objects or late-bound data.

GEOSPATIAL DATA IN WCF DATA SERVICES 5.0

In this new version of the WCF data services, Microsoft has added support for the so-called geospatial primitive types, which are data types for representing geometries and surfaces. This is beyond the scope of this chapter, but in case you are interested in this new addition, you can find further information at: http://www.odata.org/blog/2011/10/14/geospatial-properties

---

In summary, the greatest benefit of using OData is that data can be shared across a plethora of clients. For instance, you can expose a data service that can be used simultaneously by a Windows Phone application, a WPF application, and an application built with Visual Studio LightSwitch 2012. This should make you immediately understand how many business opportunities can be addressed by using OData.

Implementing WCF Data Services

To implement a WCF Data Service, you first create a web application, add your data source, and finally add a service to your project. The goal of the next example is to expose data within a master-detail relationship from the Northwind database via an EDM. Run Visual Studio 2012 and create a new ASP.NET Empty Web application, naming the new project **NorthwindDataService**. Figure 40.1 shows the New project window to explain the selection.

FIGURE 40.1   Creating a new web application for hosting a data service.

When the new project is ready, add a new EDM to the project pointing to the Northwind database, ensuring that `Customers`, `Orders`, and `Order_Details` tables are selected and correctly mapped into the new EDM. If you need a recap on building EDMs, read Chapter 26, "Introducing ADO.NET Entity Framework."

SUPPORT FOR "CODE FIRST"

WCF Data Services 5.0 supports both the `ObjectContext` class, that you use with Entity Data Models, and the `DbContext` class that you use with the Code First approach. This is a new feature that enables you to use data models you created in code. For the sake of simplicity, in this chapter an EDM is used.

When ready, in Solution Explorer right-click the project name and select **Add new item**. In the Add new item dialog box, search for the WCF Data Service template and name the new service **NorthwindService.svc**, as shown in Figure 40.2.

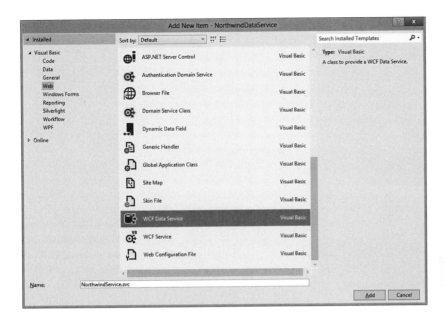

FIGURE 40.2　Adding a data service to the project.

After a few seconds, the WCF service is added to the project. If you double-click the NorthwindService.svc file, the code editor lists the autogenerated code expressed in Listing 40.1.

LISTING 40.1　Starting Code for a Data Service

```vb
Imports System.Data.Services
Imports System.Data.Services.Common
Imports System.Linq
Imports System.ServiceModel.Web


Public Class NorthwindService
    ' TODO: replace [[class name]] with your data class name
    Inherits DataService(Of [[class name]])

    ' This method is called only once to initialize service-wide policies.
    Public Shared Sub InitializeService(ByVal config As DataServiceConfiguration)
        ' TODO: set rules to indicate which entity sets and service operations are
        'visible, updatable, etc.
        ' Examples:

        'config.SetEntitySetAccessRule("MyEntitySet", EntitySetRights.All)
        'config.SetServiceOperationAccessRule("MyServiceOperation",
                                ServiceOperationRights.AllRead)
```

40

```
        config.DataServiceBehavior.MaxProtocolVersion = _
            DataServiceProtocolVersion.V2
    End Sub
End Class
```

This is the point where we need to make some considerations. First, WCF data services are implemented by both the Microsoft.Data.Services.dll and Microsoft.Data.Services.Client.dll assemblies, plus the Microsoft.Data.OData.dll assembly that provides managed support for querying the service via the OData protocol. The most important namespaces exposed by such assemblies are System.Data.Services, System.Data.Services.Common, and System.Data.Services.Client. On the server side, they need to work with the System.ServiceModel namespace that provides support for WCF. The entry point of a data service is the System.Data.Services.DataService(Of T) class that is the base class for each service. If you take a look at the code, you see that the NorthwindService class inherits from DataService(Of T). Comments suggest replacing the standard [[class name]] identifier with the appropriate one, which is NorthwindEntities in our case. With that said, the inheritance declaration becomes the following:

```
Inherits DataService(Of NorthwindEntities)
```

Notice how the InitializeService method (invoked to start the service) receives a config argument of type DataServiceConfiguration; with this class you can configure the service behavior. For example, you can access authorizations for your data source. The SetEntitySetAccessRule enables establishing access authorizations on entities from the EDM. So, if you want clients to gain full access on the Customers entity, you write the following line:

```
config.SetEntitySetAccessRule("Customers", EntitySetRights.All)
```

You need to provide an access rule for each entity. As an alternative, you can use a * character for providing the same access level to all entities. This is not the best approach, but it can be useful for demonstration purposes. Uncomment the line of code for the previously mentioned method and replace the default line with the following one:

```
'Allows clients performing complete C.R.U.D. operations on all entities
config.SetEntitySetAccessRule("*", EntitySetRights.All)
```

The access rule is set via one of the EntitySetRights enumeration's values, which are summarized in Table 40.1.

TABLE 40.1   EntitySetRights Enumeration's Values

Value	Description
All	Provides full access to entities.
AllRead	Provides reading access to both multiple and single entities.
AllWrite	Provides writing access to both multiple and single entities.

Value	Description
None	No authorization is offered.
OverrideEntitySetRights	If entities have explicit access rules, these are overridden with the ones specified here.
ReadMultiple	Provides reading access to multiple entities.
ReadSingle	Provides reading access to a single entity.
WriteAppend	Enables you to add new entities.
WriteDelete	Enables you to delete entities.
WriteMerge	Enables you to merge entities with existing data.
WriteReplace	Enables you to replace entities.

Just remember that if you want to perform classic insert/update/delete operations, you need to provide All access level. You have just completed the most basic steps for getting a data service up and running. If you now press F5 to start the application, your web browser shows the result of the XML serialization of your data, according to the REST model. This result is shown in Figure 40.3.

TURN OFF RSS READING VIEW

If you do not get the result shown in Figure 40.3 and instead see an RSS feeds reading view, you need to turn off this view in your browser. If you run Internet Explorer, you can select **Tools, Internet Options, Content** and then click the Settings button. Then unflag the **Turn On Feed Reading View** check box. You will need to restart Internet Explorer for the change to take effect.

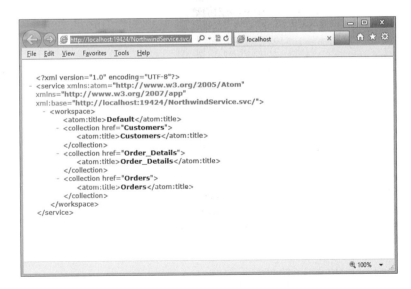

FIGURE 40.3   The data service running shows serialized data in the web browser.

Notice how the `service` tag stores the service address. This is important because you use such an address later when instantiating the service. Also notice how the three entity sets (`Customers`, `Orders`, and `Order_Details`) are serialized. Now type the following URI in the browser addresses bar, replacing the port number with the one you see on your machine:

```
http://localhost:19424/NorthwindService.svc/Customers
```

This line fetches the full customers list, as shown in Figure 40.4.

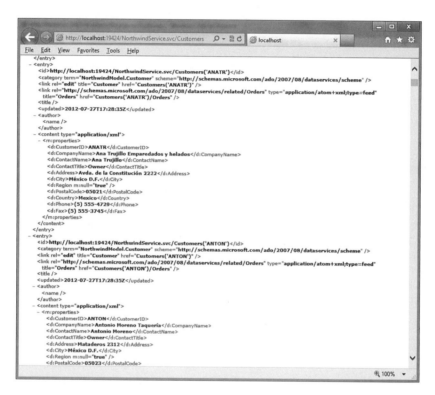

FIGURE 40.4   Fetching the customers list via URI.

You can scroll the page to see how each customer is serialized in the query result. If you look at Figure 40.4, you can easily understand how each customer property is represented. You can also perform some more complex queries. For instance, you might want to retrieve master-details data such as all orders from a specific customer, as in the following URI:

```
http://localhost:19424/NorthwindService.svc/Customers('ANATR')/
➡Orders?orderby=OrderDate
```

This URI will retrieve the result shown in Figure 40.5.

FIGURE 40.5   Retrieving master-details data via URI.

You can perform complex queries via URI, and this is one of the allowed modes for querying data from client applications, so you need to understand how query strings are composed. For this, read the following document from the MSDN Library for a full list of supported operators: http://www.odata.org/documentation/uri-conventions. You do not query your service this way; instead you do it from a client application. This is what the next section begins to show. What has been described up to now is not all about the server side; other interesting features are described later in this chapter, but first you need to know how to reference a data service from the client side.

Deploying WCF Data Services to Internet Information Services

In real-world applications, you will probably host your data services on web servers such as Internet Information Services (IIS). Because they are WCF services, you will deploy them with related techniques described in this page on the MSDN Library: http://msdn.microsoft.com/en-us/library/ms730158(v=vs.110).aspx. For demonstration purposes and for a better focus on services implementation, in this book we deploy data services to the IIS Express development server so that we can take advantage of the Visual Studio environment features.

40

Consuming WCF Data Services

You consume WCF data services the same way you consume pure WCF services. You need to add a service reference from the client and then instantiate the proxy class. Such a class will be generated for you by Visual Studio 2012 and will expose members for accessing data on the server. As mentioned at the beginning of this chapter, WCF data services can be consumed by various kinds of clients such as Windows (Console, Windows Forms, WPF) and web (Silverlight, ASP.NET Ajax) applications. The next example shows you how to consume data services from a Console client application. Such a project template is useful for focusing on concepts that you can apply to other types of applications.

NOTE FOR SILVERLIGHT DEVELOPERS

WCF data services can be consumed from Silverlight applications with the same programming techniques described in this chapter, except that they work asynchronously. If you are interested in this kind of development, I suggest you read this blog post from the Microsoft Visual Studio Data Team Blog: http://blogs.msdn.com/vsdata/archive/2009/10/22/accessing-master-detail-data-through-ado-net-data-service-in-a-silverlight-application-part-1.aspx.

Creating a Client Application

The goal of the next example is to show how you can perform read/insert/update/delete operations against a data service from a client. Follow these steps:

1. Add to the current solution a new Console project and name it **NorthwindClient**.

2. Right-click the project name and select **Add service reference**. This adds a reference to the data service similarly to what happens for WCF services. Because in our example the service is available in the current solution, just click **Discover**. In real applications, you will type the URI of your service. Figure 40.6 shows the **Add service reference** dialog box.

3. Replace the default identifier in the **Namespace** text box with a more appropriate one, such as **NorthwindServiceReference**; then click **OK**.

TIP

If the data service also exposes service operations (see next section for details), these will be listed in the right side of the dialog box.

At this point, Visual Studio 2012 generates what in WCF is defined as a *proxy class*, which is client code. It generates several classes: one class that inherits from `System.Data.Services.Client.DataServiceContext` and that can be considered as the counterpart for the Entity Framework's `ObjectContext` (or for the `DbContext` class if you used Code

First) and a series of counterpart classes for entities in the EDM. This means that, for our example, you have `Customer`, `Order`, and `Order_Detail` classes implemented on the client side. All these classes implement the `INotifyPropertyChanged` interface so that they can notify the user interface (UI) of changes on the original data source. Instead, the `DataServiceContext` class also exposes properties of type `System.Data.Services.Client.DataServiceQuery(Of T)` that are collections of the previously mentioned classes and that represent strongly typed queries against entity sets exposed by a data service. The `DataServiceContext` class in our example (automatically named `NorthwindEntities` for consistency with the related context in the service) exposes the `Customers`, `Orders`, and `Order_Details` properties, respectively, of type `DataServiceQuery(Of Customer)`, `DataServiceQuery(Of Order)`, and `DataServiceQuery(Of Order_Detail)`. Although you should never manually edit autogenerated code, if you are curious, you can inspect previously mentioned classes by expanding the NorthwindServiceReference item in Solution Explorer and clicking the **Reference.vb** file. This is the place where all the client code is implemented. You notice lots of similarities with an entity data model implementation, but do not become confused because WCF data services are a different thing. By the way, such similarities can help you understand how to perform data operations. For example, there are methods for adding objects (`AddToCustomers`, `AddToOrders`) and for removing them (`DeleteObject`). For now, add the following `Imports` directives that enable you to shorten lines of code:

```
Imports NorthwindClient.NorthwindServiceReference
Imports System.Data.Services.Client
```

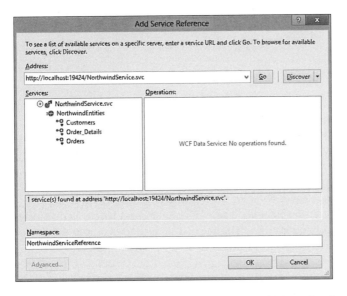

FIGURE 40.6   Adding a reference to the ADO.NET Data Service.

The next step is instantiating the proxy client class. At module level, add the following declaration:

```
Private northwind As New _
        NorthwindEntities(New _
        Uri("http://localhost:1443/NorthwindService.svc"))
```

Notice how the instance requires you to specify the service URI. This is the same that is specified when adding the service reference. The northwind variable represents the instance of the DataServiceContext class that exposes members for working against entities exposed by the data service and that enables you to perform C.R.U.D. operations. The first operation I am going to explain is insertion. Consider the following function:

```
Private Function AddNewOrder(ByVal relatedCustomer As Customer) As Order

    Dim newOrder As New Order
    With newOrder
        .Customer = relatedCustomer
        .OrderDate = Date.Today
        .ShipCountry = "Italy"
        .ShipCity = "Milan"
        .ShipName = "First"
    End With

    northwind.AddToOrders(newOrder)
    northwind.SetLink(newOrder, "Customer", relatedCustomer)
    northwind.SaveChanges()
    Return newOrder
End Function
```

The code first creates an instance of a new order and populates the desired properties. A relationship to the specified customer is also set. This relationship is just set in-memory, but it needs to be explicitly set when sending changes to the actual database. The new order is added to the model via the AddToOrders method, and SetLink explicitly sets the relationship. Such method requires the new object as the first argument, the navigation property in the model as the second argument, and the master object in the master-details relationship. Finally, the code saves the new data to the database by invoking SaveChanges. Later you see how to send to the data source changes in a batch. Performing an update operation is an easy task. You get the instance of the desired object and edit properties. The following snippet demonstrates how to update an existing order:

```
Private Sub UpdateOrder(ByVal OrderID As Integer)
    'Retrieving the one instance of the specified Order with
    'a lambda.
    Dim ord = northwind.Orders.Where(Function(o) o.OrderID = _
            OrderID).First
```

```
    ord.ShipName = "Second"
    ord.ShipCity = "Cremona"
    ord.ShipCountry = "Italy"
End Sub
```

The code shows how you get the instance of your object and replace properties. If you want to save changes at this point, invoke `SaveChanges`. We are not doing this now because we will save changes in the batch later.

EXTENSION METHODS: THE OLD AND THE NEW

WCF data services do not support `First` and `Single` extension methods directly on the data source. This is the reason in the previous code snippet we had to pass through a `Where` method. WCF Data Services 5.0 add support for the `All` and `Any` extension methods so that you can have more granularity when filtering collections. The MSDN Documentation has a specific page about limitations in LINQ when working with data services, available at http://msdn.microsoft.com/en-us/library/ee622463(v=vs.103).

The next step is implementing a deletion method. This is also a simple task, as demonstrated by the following code:

```
Private Sub DeleteOrder(ByVal OrderID As Integer)

    Dim ord = northwind.Orders.Where(Function(o) o.OrderID = _
            OrderID).First
    northwind.DeleteObject(ord)
End Sub
```

Also in this case you get the instance of the object you want to remove and then invoke the `DeleteObject` method. The last step shows how you can save multiple changes to entities in one shot. The following code demonstrates this:

```
Private Sub SaveAllChanges()
    northwind.SaveChanges(Services.Client.SaveChangesOptions.Batch)
End Sub
```

`SaveChanges` receives an argument of type `System.Data.Services.Client.SaveChangesOptions`, which is an enumeration whose most important value is `Batch`. This enables you to save all pending changes with a single HTTP request; thus it is efficient with regard to performances. Now we just need to invoke the various methods from within the `Sub Main`. The following code first creates a new order, updates it, and finally deletes it:

```
Sub Main()

    Dim cust = northwind.Customers.Where(Function(c) c.CustomerID = _
            "ALFKI").First
```

```vb
    Try

        Dim anOrder = AddNewOrder(cust)

        Console.WriteLine("Added new order: {0}", anOrder.OrderID)

        UpdateOrder(anOrder.OrderID)
        Console.WriteLine("Updated order {0}. ShipCity now is {1},
                           ShipName now is {2}",
                           anOrder.OrderID, anOrder.ShipCity,
                           anOrder.ShipName)

        'Replace the order ID with a valid one
        DeleteOrder(anOrder.OrderID)
        Console.WriteLine("Order deleted")

        SaveAllChanges()

        Console.ReadLine()
        northwind = Nothing

    Catch ex As DataServiceQueryException
        Console.WriteLine("The server returned the following error:")
        Console.WriteLine(ex.Response.Error.Message)
        Console.ReadLine()
    Catch ex As Exception

    End Try
End Sub
```

The code also is ready for intercepting a `DataServiceQueryException`—a particular object that provides client information from `DataServiceException` objects thrown on the server side. If you now run the application, you get messages informing you about the data operations progress, as shown in Figure 40.7.

Querying Data

One of the most common requirements of any data framework is the capability of performing queries. WCF data services allow two modes on the client side. The first one uses query strings similar to what you can do with URIs. To accomplish this, you invoke the `Execute(Of T)` method from the `DataServiceContext` class, where `T` is the type you want to retrieve a collection of. For example, the following code returns a collection of orders for the specified customer, sorted by order date:

```vb
Dim myOrders = Northwind.Execute(Of Order)(New _
            Uri("/Customers('ANATR')/Orders?orderby=OrderDate", _
            UriKind.Relative))
```

FIGURE 40.7   The sample application performs all operations.

This way is efficient but avoids the strongly typed approach provided by LINQ. Fortunately, .NET Framework also enables you to use a special LINQ provider known as LINQ to Data Services. The following code snippet demonstrates how you can obtain the same result as previously writing a LINQ query:

```
Dim myOrders = From ord In northwind.Orders
               Where ord.Customer.CustomerID = "ANATR"
               Select ord
```

This is powerful but not necessarily the best choice. For instance, you might want to prevent indiscriminate data access from clients, or you might want better performance implementing queries on the server side and exposing methods returning query results. This is where *service operations* take place.

Implementing Service Operations

Service operations are .NET methods that can perform data operations on the server side. With service operations, developers can preventively establish access rules and customize the business logic, such as data validation or access restrictions. They are WCF extensions for data services and perform operations via HTTP requests, meaning that you can execute service operations within a web browser or from a client application. Service operations can return the following types:

▶ `IQueryable(Of T)` in data-centric scenarios with Entity Framework models or LINQ-to-SQL models

▶ `IEnumerable(Of T)`

▶ .NET primitive types because data services can also expose in-memory collections

▶ No type (`Sub` methods)

40

Service operations can be used for both reading and writing data to the service. In a reading situation, service operations are `Function` methods marked with the `WebGet` attribute, whereas in writing situations they are decorated with the `WebInvoke` attribute. The next example explains how to read order details for the specified order and return fetched data to the client. First, add the following method to the `NorthwindService` class:

```
<WebGet()> Public Function GetOrderDetails(ByVal OrderID As Integer) _
                As IQueryable(Of Order_Detail)

    If OrderID > 0 Then
        Dim query = From det In Me.CurrentDataSource.Order_Details
                    Where det.OrderID = OrderID
                    Select det

        Return query
    Else
        Throw New DataServiceException(400,
                                "OrderID is not valid")
    End If
End Function
```

The method explanation is quite simple. It performs a validation on the `OrderID` argument; if valid, it executes a LINQ to Data Services query for getting related order details returning an `IQueryable(Of Order_Detail)` type. Notice the `CurrentDataSource` object, which represents the instance of the `NorthwindEntities` class on the server side. If the `OrderID` is considered invalid, the method throws a `DataServiceException`, which is specific for throwing errors from the service. You can specify an HTTP error code and an error message. To make a service operation recognizable and executable, you need to set permissions for it. This is accomplished by invoking the `DataServiceConfiguration.SetServiceOperationAccessRule` method; therefore, uncomment the following line of code in the `InitializeService` method:

```
'config.SetServiceOperationAccessRule _
("MyServiceOperation", ServiceOperationRights.AllRead)
```

Then you need to replace the operation name as follows:

```
config.SetServiceOperationAccessRule("GetOrderDetails",
                                ServiceOperationRights.AllRead)
```

In our scenario we just need to read data from the service, so the `AllRead` permission is appropriate. If you now run the service, you can type the following line in the browser address bar to invoke the service operation, being sure to type the appropriate port number of the development server on your machine:

```
http://localhost:19424/NorthwindService.svc/GetOrderDetails?OrderID=10250
```

You invoke the operation by writing its name after the service address. Operations' names and parameters are case-sensitive. You are now ready to call the service operation from the client application. Return to the NorthwindClient project, and add the following method that invokes the service operations for fetching order details:

```
Private Sub ViewDetails(ByVal OrderID As Integer)
    Console.WriteLine("Showing details for Order ID: " _
                    & OrderID.ToString)

    Dim details = northwind.Execute(Of Order_Detail) _
                (New Uri("GetOrderDetails?OrderID=" & _
                OrderID.ToString,
                UriKind.Relative))

    For Each detail In details
        Console.WriteLine("ID: {0}, Unit price: {1}, Quantity: {2}",
                        detail.OrderID,
                        detail.UnitPrice,
                        detail.Quantity)
    Next
    Console.ReadLine()
End Sub
```

The code is still quite simple. It invokes the service operation building a query string concatenating the supplied order ID. The `Execute(Of Order_Detail)` method is invoked because the service operations return a collection of the same type. Such method requires you to specify the URI of the service operation, which in this case is its name followed by the order ID. Before you run the application, you need to update the service reference. This step can be performed later in this case because you do not invoke a managed method, whereas you invoke a service operation via a query string. To update the service reference, in Solution Explorer, just right-click the **NorthwindServiceReference** item and select **Update service reference**. Updating the service reference is something you must do each time you perform changes on the service after a reference has been already added in the client application. If you now run the application, you get details for the specified order, as shown in Figure 40.8.

If you want to perform insertions, updates, or deletions, you can implement web invokes on the server side. This is accomplished by decorating methods with the `WebInvoke` attribute. The MSDN documentation provides examples on `WebInvoke` at this address: http://msdn.microsoft.com/en-us/library/system.servicemodel.web.webinvokeattribute(v=vs.110).aspx.

40

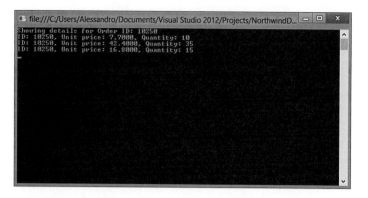

FIGURE 40.8   Getting order details via a service operation.

Implementing Query Interceptors

In the previous section I covered service operations, which act on the server side. But they are not the only server-side feature in data services. Another interesting feature is known as *query interceptors*. Interceptors are .NET methods exposed by the service class and enable developers to intercept HTTP requests to establish how such requests must be handled, both in reading (*query interceptors*) and in writing (*change interceptors*) operations. This section describes both query interceptors and change interceptors.

Understanding Query Interceptors

Query interceptors are public methods intercepting HTTP GET requests and allow developers to handle the reading request. Such methods are decorated with the `QueryInterceptor` attribute that requires specifying the entity set name. For a better understanding, consider the following interceptor (to be implemented within the `NorthwindService` class) that returns only orders from the specified culture:

```
<QueryInterceptor("Orders")> Public Function OnQueryOrders() As    _
                        Expression(Of Func(Of Order, Boolean))
    'Determines the caller's culture
    Dim LocalCulture = WebOperationContext.Current.
                    IncomingRequest.Headers("Accept-Language")

    If LocalCulture = "it-IT" Then
        Return Function(ord) ord.ShipCountry = "Italy"
    Else
        Throw New DataServiceException("You are not authorized")
    End If

End Function
```

`OnQueryOrders` will be invoked on the service each time an HTTP GET request is sent to the service. The code returns only orders where the `ShipCountry` property's value is `Italy`, if the client culture (the caller) is `it-IT`. Differently, the code throws a `DataServiceException`. The most important thing to notice in the code is the returned type, which is an `Expression(Of Func(Of T, Boolean))`. This is an expression tree generated starting from the lambda expression actually returned. You may remember from Chapter 20, "Advanced Language Features," how the `Func` object enables you to generate anonymous methods on-the-fly, receiving two arguments: The first one is the real argument, and the second one is the returned type. The lambda expression is the equivalent of the following LINQ query:

```
Dim query = From ord In Me.CurrentDataSource.Orders
            Where ord.ShipCountry = "Italy"
            Select ord
```

The big difference is that this type of query returns an `IQueryable(Of Order)`, whereas we need to evaluate the result of an expression tree. This is only possible with lambdas. You can easily test this interceptor by running the service and typing the following URI in the browser addresses bar, replacing the port number:

```
http://localhost:19424/NorthwindService.svc/Orders
```

This URI automatically fetches only orders targeting Italy, if your local culture is it-IT. If it is not, the Visual Studio debugger shows an exception. By the way, it is important to provide sufficient information about exceptions from the server side because clients need detailed information for understanding what happened. This is a general rule explained here together with a practical example. WCF data services provide a simple way for providing descriptive error messages other than throwing exceptions. This requires the following line of code in the `InitializeService` method:

```
config.UseVerboseErrors = True
```

On the client side, failures from query interceptors are handled by `DataServiceQueryException` objects. This is why I already implemented such an object in the `Try..Catch` block in the client application's main window. According to the previous example, if your culture is different from `it-IT`, when you run the client application, you should get the error message shown in Figure 40.9.

Notice how, other than the error message you provided via the `DataServiceException`, there is a lot of information that can be useful to help you understand what happened. You thus could implement a log system for redirecting to you, as a developer, all collected information. So far, we have talked about query interceptors, which intercept GET requests. We now cover change interceptors.

40

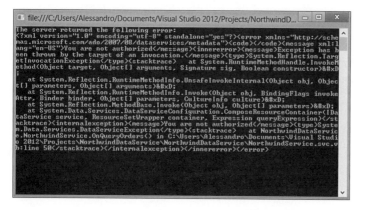

FIGURE 40.9   The detailed information about the error.

Understanding Change Interceptors

Change interceptors are conceptually similar to query interceptors, but they differ in that they can intercept HTTP requests of type POST, PUT, and DELETE (that is, C.R.U.D. operations via URI). They are public methods returning no type; therefore, they are always Sub decorated with the ChangeInterceptor attribute pointing to the entity set name. Each interceptor receives two arguments: the data source (a single entity) and the System. Data.Services.UpdateOperations enumeration, which enables you to understand which request was sent. Take a look at the following interceptor:

```
<ChangeInterceptor("Orders")> _
Public Sub OnOrdersChange(ByVal DataSource As Order,
                          ByVal Action As UpdateOperations)

    If Action = UpdateOperations.Add OrElse _
       Action = UpdateOperations.Change Then

        'If data does not satisfy my condition, throws an exception
        If DataSource.OrderDate Is Nothing Then
            Throw New DataServiceException(400,
                      "Order date cannot be null")
        End If

    ElseIf Action = UpdateOperations.Delete Then
        If DataSource.ShippedDate IsNot Nothing Then
            Throw New DataServiceException(500,
            "You are not authorized to delete orders with full info")
        End If

    End If
End Sub
```

You decide how to handle the request depending on the `UpdateOperations` current value. `Add` corresponds to an insert operation, `Delete` to a delete operation, `Change` to an update operation, and `None` means that no operations were requested for the data source. The preceding code performs the same actions on both `Add` and `Change` operations and throws an exception if the new or existing order has null value in the `OrderDate` property. A different check is instead performed about `Delete` requests; in my example the code prevents you from deleting an order whenever it has value in the `ShippedDate` property. No other code is required for handling situations in which supplied data are valid because the data services framework automatically persists valid data to the underlying source. Change interceptors come in when a client application invokes the `DataServiceContext.SaveChanges` method. On the server side, change interceptors are raised just before sending data to the source and collecting information on the C.R.U.D. operation that sent the request.

Understanding Server-Driven Paging

WCF data services offer an interesting feature known as *server-driven paging*. This feature enables paging data directly on the server and provides developers the ability of specifying how many items a page must return, also offering a URI for browsing the next page. To enable server-driven paging, you invoke the `DataServiceConfiguration.SetEntitySetPageSize` method that requires specifying the entity set name and the number of items per page. The following code demonstrates this:

```
config.SetEntitySetPageSize("Customers", 4)
```

If you now start the service and try to fetch all customers, you get the result shown in Figure 40.10.

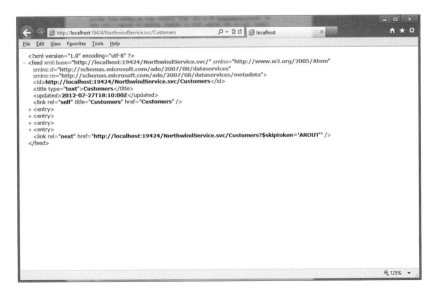

FIGURE 40.10   Server-driven paging demonstration.

For the sake of clarity, all `entry` items within the browser window are collapsed, but you can see how each of them represents a customer. Therefore, the page shows exactly four items for how it was specified within the service. Another thing that is worth mentioning is the `link rel` tag that contains the URI for moving to the next four items as in the following:

```
http://localhost:19424/NorthwindService.svc/Customers?$skiptoken=AROUT
```

Server-driven paging is intended for use within the service; if you instead require to implement paging on client applications, you can still work with client paging. You accomplish this by specifying `$skip` and `$take` clauses within HTTP requests or the corresponding `Skip` and `Take` LINQ clauses.

Summary

WCF data services are REST-enabled WCF services supporting HTTP requests such as `GET`, `POST`, `PUT`, and `DELETE` and constitute a data platform based on the OData protocol for exposing data through networks. In this chapter you got a high-level overview of data services; you first learned about implementing services and how they can be easily created within ASP.NET web applications by adding the WCF Data Service item. Services running within a web browser can then be queried via HTTP requests (URI). Next, you saw how to consume WCF data services from client applications and perform C.R.U.D. operations using the `DataServiceContext` class that exposes appropriate members for such kinds of operations. After this, you learned how to implement service operations and interceptors for best results on the server side. Finally, you took a tour into server-driven paging for better performances on the server side.

CHAPTER 41

Serialization

Most real-world applications need to store, exchange, and transfer data. Due to its special nature, the .NET Framework stores data into objects and can exchange data via objects. If you need to store data only for your application, you have a lot of alternatives. The problem is when you need to exchange and transfer data with other applications. In other words, you need to think of how your objects are represented and decide whether you need to convert them into a different format. This is because another application cannot understand objects in their pure state; therefore, how information is persisted needs to be standardized. Serialization enables you to save your object's state to disk and then re-create the object according to the specified format. With serialization, you store your data and transfer data to other applications that can re-create the information. For example, say you have an application that needs to store and transfer data to another application through a network. With the .NET Framework, you serialize your data (that is, save the result of the serialization process to a stream), transfer your data to the target application, and wait for the target application to deserialize (that is, re-create the object starting from the serialized information) your data and use it. In this chapter, you learn to implement serialization in your applications, understanding what decisions you should make if you need to transfer data to non-.NET and non-Windows applications, too.

Objects Serialization

Serializing .NET objects is the easiest serialization mode. In this particular scenario, you need a file stream where you have to place data and a formatter establishing the serialization mode. When you have the formatter instance, you invoke the `Serialize` method. The `System.Runtime.Serialization.Formatters` namespace provides two sub namespaces, `Binary` and `Soap`. They expose `BinaryFormatter` and `SoapFormatter`, respectively. The first one serializes objects in a binary way. It is efficient, but you should use it only if you are sure that your objects will be deserialized by .NET applications because such binary format is not universal. If you instead want to be sure that your objects can be shared across various applications and platforms, you should use the `SoapFormatter` that produces an XML-based result that is useful when working with SOAP web services.

Binary Serialization

The following example shows how you can serialize a typed collection of strings into a file on disk using the `BinaryFormatter` class:

```
Dim stringSeries As New List(Of String) From
                    {"Serialization", "demo",
                    "with VB"}

Dim targetFile As New _
    FileStream("C:\temp\SerializedData.dat",
              FileMode.Create)
Dim formatter As New BinaryFormatter

formatter.Serialize(targetFile, stringSeries)
targetFile.Close()
formatter = Nothing
```

> **NOTE**
>
> The previous code example requires `Imports System.IO` and `Imports System.Runtime.Serialization.Formatters.Binary` directives.

The code creates a new file named `SerializedData.dat` and puts the result of the binary serialization in the file. If you examine the content of the file with the Windows Notepad, you can obtain a result similar to what is shown in Figure 41.1.

You don't need to know how your objects are serialized, but it is interesting to understand the type of information placed into the target file, such as the serialized type, assembly information, and the actual data. To deserialize a binary file, you invoke the `BinaryFormatter.Deserialize` method, as shown in the following code, which you write immediately after the preceding example:

```
Dim sourceFile As New FileStream("C:\temp\SerializedData.dat",
                                 FileMode.Open)

formatter = New BinaryFormatter
Dim data = CType(formatter.Deserialize(sourceFile),
                 List(Of String))

sourceFile.Close()
formatter = Nothing

'Iterates the result
For Each item In data
    Console.WriteLine(item)
Next
```

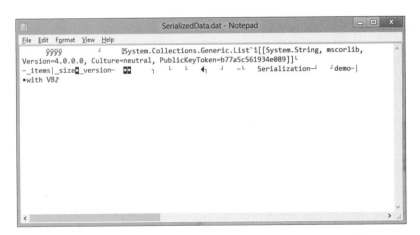

FIGURE 41.1   Examining the result of the serialization process.

Notice that `Deserialize` returns `Object`; therefore, the result needs to be converted into the appropriate type that you expect. If you run the preceding code, you see on your screen how the strings from the collection are correctly listed. This kind of serialization is also straightforward because it enables serializing entire object graphs. Moreover, you can use this technique against user interface controls in Windows Forms and WPF applications to persist the state of your interface objects that can be later re-created.

HANDLING SERIALIZATION EXCEPTIONS

Remember to perform serialization and deserialization operations within a `Try..Catch` block and implement code for handling the `SerializationException` exception that provides information on serialization/deserialization errors.

Creating Objects Deep Copies with Serialization

In Chapter 4, "Data Types and Expressions," I illustrated how to create objects' copies implementing the ICloneable interface and how you can clone an object with the MemberWiseClone method. Such scenarios have a big limitation: They cannot create copies of an entire object graph. Luckily, binary serialization can instead serialize entire object graphs and thus can be used to create complete deep copies of objects. The code in Listing 41.1 shows how to accomplish this by implementing a generic method.

LISTING 41.1   Implementing Deep Copy with Serialization

```
Imports System.Runtime.Serialization
Imports System.Runtime.Serialization.Formatters.Binary
Imports System.IO

Public Class CreateDeepCopy

    Public Shared Function Clone(Of T)(ByVal objectToClone As T) As T

        'If the source object is null, returns the current
        'object (as a default)
        If Object.ReferenceEquals(objectToClone, Nothing) Then
            Return objectToClone
        End If

        'Creates a new formatter whose behavior is for cloning purposes
        Dim formatter As New BinaryFormatter(Nothing,
                                    New StreamingContext(
                                        StreamingContextStates.Clone))
        'Serializes to a memory stream
        Dim ms As New MemoryStream
        Using ms
            formatter.Serialize(ms, objectToClone)

            'Gets back to the first stream byte
            ms.Seek(0, SeekOrigin.Begin)
            'Deserializes the object graph to a new T object
            Return CType(formatter.Deserialize(ms), T)
        End Using
    End Function
End Class
```

Because you are not limited to file streams, taking advantage of a memory stream is good in such a scenario. You invoke the preceding method as follows:

```
Dim result As Object = CreateDeepCopy.Clone(objectToClone)
```

You could also implement extension methods for providing deep copy to all types.

SOAP Serialization

SOAP serialization works similarly to binary serialization. First, you need to add a reference to the `System.Runtime.Serialization.Formatters.Soap.dll` assembly. Then you add an `Imports System.Runtime.Serialization.Formatters.Soap` directive. Then you can serialize and deserialize your objects. To continue the example of the typed collection shown in the previous section, write the following code to accomplish serialization with the SOAP formatter:

```
'Requires an Imports System.Runtime.Serialization.Formatters.Soap directive
Dim stringToSerialize As String = "Serialization demo with VB"

Dim targetFile As New FileStream("C:\temp\SerializedData.xml",
                                 FileMode.Create)

Dim formatter As New SoapFormatter
formatter.Serialize(targetFile, stringToSerialize)
targetFile.Close()
formatter = Nothing
```

There is no difference in the syntax for the SOAP formatter if compared to the binary one.

TIP ON GENERIC COLLECTIONS

The `SoapFormatter` class does not enable you to serialize generic collections. This is why a simpler example against a single string is provided.

You can still examine the result of the serialization process with the Windows Notepad. Figure 41.2 shows how the target file stores information in a XML fashion.

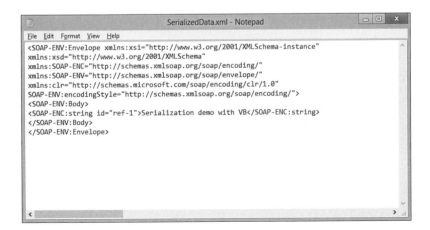

FIGURE 41.2 Examining the result of the SOAP serialization process.

Typically, the SOAP serialization is intended to be used when working with SOAP web services. If you want to serialize objects in a pure XML mode, you can take advantage of XML serialization, which is described in the "XML Serialization" section later in this chapter.

Providing Serialization for Custom Objects

You can make your custom objects serializable so that you can apply the previously described techniques for persisting and re-creating objects' state. To be serializable, a class (or structure) must be decorated with the `Serializable` attribute. This is the most basic scenario and is represented by the following implementation of the `Person` class:

```
Imports System.Runtime.Serialization


<Serializable()>
Public Class Person
    Public Property FirstName As String
    Public Property LastName As String
    Public Property Age As Integer
    Public Property Address As String
End Class
```

If you do not need to get control over the serialization process, this is all you need. By the way, there can be certain situations that you need to handle. For instance, you might want to disable serialization for a member that could become obsolete if too much time passes between serialization and deserialization. Continuing the `Person` class example, we decide to disable serialization for the `Age` member because between serialization and deserialization the represented person might be older than the moment when serialization occurred. To accomplish this, you apply the `NonSerialized` attribute. The big problem here is that this is a field-level attribute; therefore, it cannot be applied to properties. In such situations using auto-implemented properties is not possible, so you must write them the old-fashioned way. The following code shows how you can prevent the `Age` member from being serialized:

```
<NonSerialized()> Private _age As Integer
Public Property Age As Integer
    Get
        Return _age
    End Get
    Set(ByVal value As Integer)
        _age = value
    End Set
End Property
```

The subsequent problem is that you need a way for assigning a valid value to nonserialized members when deserialization occurs. The most common technique is implementing the `IDeserializationCallBack` interface that exposes an `OnDeserialization` method where you can place your initialization code. The following is the revisited code for the `Person` class according to the last edits:

```vb
Imports System.Runtime.Serialization

<Serializable()>
Public Class Person
    Implements IDeserializationCallback


    Public Property FirstName As String
    Public Property LastName As String

    <NonSerialized()> Private _age As Integer
    Public Property Age As Integer
        Get
            Return _age
        End Get
        Set(ByVal value As Integer)
            _age = value
        End Set
    End Property

    Public Sub OnDeserialization(ByVal sender As Object) Implements _
            System.Runtime.Serialization.IDeserializationCallback.
            OnDeserialization
        'Specify the new age
        Me.Age = 32
    End Sub
End Class
```

When the deserialization process invokes the `OnDeserialization` method, members that were not serialized can be correctly initialized anyway. Another consideration that you need to take care of is versioning. When you upgrade your application to a new version, you might also want to apply some changes to your classes, such as by adding new members. This is fine but can result in problems if the previous version of your application attempts to deserialize an object produced by the new version. To solve this problem, you can mark a member as `OptionalField`. In this way, the deserialization process is not affected by new members and both `BinaryFormatter` and `SoapFormatter` will not throw exceptions if they encounter new members during the process. Because the `OptionalField` attribute works at field level, this is another situation in which you cannot take advantage of auto-implemented properties. The following code shows how you can mark the `Address` member in the `Person` class as optional:

```
<OptionalField()> Private _address As String
Public Property Address As String

    Get
        Return _address
    End Get
    Set(ByVal value As String)
        _address = value
    End Set
End Property
```

The member is still involved in the serialization process, but if a previous version of the application attempts to perform deserialization, it will not throw exceptions when it encounters this new member that was not expected.

NonSerialized Events

Visual Basic 2012 offers a feature known as *NonSerialized Events* that was first introduced by its predecessor. You can decorate an event with the NonSerialized attribute in custom serialization. A common scenario for applying this technique is when you work on classes that implement the INotifyPropertyChanged interface because it is more important to serialize data and not an event that just notifies the user interface of changes on data. The following code shows an example about NonSerialized events inside a class that implements INotifyPropertyChanged:

```
<Serializable()>
Public Class Customer
    Implements INotifyPropertyChanged

    <NonSerialized()>
    Public Event PropertyChanged(
            ByVal sender As Object,
            ByVal e As System.ComponentModel.PropertyChangedEventArgs) _
            Implements System.ComponentModel.
                    INotifyPropertyChanged.PropertyChanged

    Protected Sub OnPropertyChanged(ByVal strPropertyName As String)
        If Me.PropertyChangedEvent IsNot Nothing Then
            RaiseEvent PropertyChanged(Me,
                    New PropertyChangedEventArgs(strPropertyName))
        End If
    End Sub
```

XML Serialization

41

> **NOTE**
>
> Code examples shown in this section require `Imports System.IO` and `Imports System.Xml.Serialization` directives.

One of the main goals of serialization is to provide a way for exchanging data with other applications so that such applications can re-create objects' state. If you want to share your objects with non-.NET applications or with applications running on different platforms, a convenient way for serializing objects is provided by the XML serialization. As you know, XML is a standard international file format for data exchange. XML files are text files organized according to a hierarchical structure and thus can be manipulated in whatever platforms and applications you want. XML serialization provides two great benefits: absolute interoperability and background compatibility. If you upgrade or modify your applications, XML format remains the same. Opposite to such benefits, XML serialization has two limitations: It cannot serialize object graphs (therefore single objects) and cannot serialize private members. XML serialization is performed by using objects exposed by the `System.Xml.Serialization` namespace. You can use the `XmlSerializer` class that requires a `System.IO.Stream` object for outputting serialized data and the data itself. The following code shows how you can serialize a typed collection of strings using XML serialization:

```
Dim stringSeries As New List(Of String) From
    {"Serialization", "demo",
     "with VB"}

Dim targetFile As New FileStream("C:\temp\SerializedData.xml",
                                  FileMode.Create)
Dim formatter As New XmlSerializer(GetType(List(Of String)))

formatter.Serialize(targetFile, stringSeries)
targetFile.Close()
formatter = Nothing
```

The `XmlSerializer` constructor requires the specification of the data type you are going to serialize, which is accomplished via the `GetType` operator. To serialize data, you invoke the `XmlSerializer.Serialize` method. As you can see, there are no big differences with other serialization techniques shown in the previous section. To check how your data was serialized, you can open the SerializedData.xml file. You can accomplish this with an XML editor or with a web browser instead of Notepad. Figure 41.3 shows the serialization result within Internet Explorer.

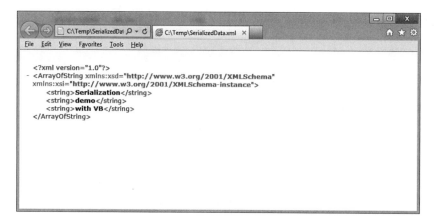

FIGURE 41.3   The XML serialization result shown in Internet Explorer.

Notice how the newly obtained file has a perfect XML structure and therefore can be shared with other applications having the ability to perform XML deserialization. To deserialize your data, you invoke the `XmlSerializer.Deserialize` method, as shown in the following code:

```
Dim sourceFile As New FileStream("C:\temp\SerializedData.xml",
                                 FileMode.Open)

formatter = New XmlSerializer(GetType(List(Of String)))
Dim data = CType(formatter.Deserialize(sourceFile),
                 List(Of String))

sourceFile.Close()
formatter = Nothing

'Iterates the result
For Each item In data
    Console.WriteLine(item)
Next
```

Customizing XML Serialization

Consider the following implementation of the `Person` class:

```
Public Class Person
    Public Property FirstName As String
    Public Property LastName As String
    Public Property Age As Integer
End Class
```

When you serialize an instance of that `Person` class, you would obtain an XML representation similar to the following:

```
<?xml version="1.0" ?>
<Person xmlns:xsi="http://www.w3.org/2001/XMLSchema-instance"
        xmlns:xsd="http://www.w3.org/2001/XMLSchema">
  <FirstName>Alessandro</FirstName>
  <LastName>Del Sole</LastName>
  <Age>35</Age>
</Person>
```

The `System.Xml.Serialization` namespace offers attributes for controlling output of the XML serialization to affect the target file. For example, consider the following code:

```
Imports System.Xml.Serialization

<XmlRoot("Contact")> Public Class Person
    <XmlIgnore()> Public Property FirstName As String
    Public Property LastName As String
    <XmlAttribute()> Public Property Age As Integer
End Class
```

When an instance is serialized, the output looks like the following:

```
<?xml version="1.0" ?>
<Contact xmlns:xsi="http://www.w3.org/2001/XMLSchema-instance"
         xmlns:xsd="http://www.w3.org/2001/XMLSchema"
         Age="35">
  <LastName>Del Sole</LastName>
</Contact>
```

The `XmlRoot` attribute changed the name of the root element from `Person` to `Contact`. The `XmlIgnore` attribute prevented a property from being serialized, and the `XmlAttribute` attribute treated the specified member as an XML attribute instead of an XML element. You can find the complete attributes list in the dedicated page of the MSDN Library at http://msdn.microsoft.com/en-us/library/system.xml.serialization.xmlattributes(v=vs.110). aspx. The reason you should get a reference on the Internet is that XML serialization is a settled concept for most developers, whereas .NET Framework 4.5 provides a more interesting way for XML serialization, known as XAML serialization, which is covered later in this chapter and that is more important to learn.

Custom Serialization

In most cases, the .NET built-in serialization engine is good enough. But if it does not meet your particular needs, you can override the serialization process with custom serialization. This means implementing the `ISerializable` interface that requires the implementation of the `GetObjectData` method. Such a method is important because it is

invoked during serialization. A custom implementation of the class constructor must also
be provided. You have to first reproduce at least what built-in formatters do during serialization. The code in Listing 41.2 shows how to provide custom serialization for the Person
class.

LISTING 41.2   Providing Custom Serialization

```
Imports System.Runtime.Serialization
Imports System.Security.Permissions

<Serializable()>
Public Class Person
    Implements ISerializable

    Public Overridable Property FirstName As String
    Public Overridable Property LastName As String
    Public Overridable Property Age As Integer

    <SecurityPermission(SecurityAction.Demand,
                        SerializationFormatter:=True)>
    Protected Sub GetObjectData(ByVal info As System.Runtime.Serialization.
                                         SerializationInfo,
                        ByVal context As System.Runtime.Serialization.
                                         StreamingContext) _
                        Implements System.Runtime.Serialization.ISerializable.
                                         GetObjectData

        info.AddValue("First name", Me.FirstName)
        info.AddValue("Last name", Me.LastName)
        info.AddValue("Age", Me.Age)
    End Sub

    'At deserialization time
    Protected Sub New(ByVal info As SerializationInfo,
                      ByVal context As StreamingContext)
        MyBase.New()
        Me.FirstName = info.GetString("First name")
        Me.LastName = info.GetString("Last name")
        Me.Age = info.GetInt32("Age")
    End Sub
End Class
```

The GetObjectData method is invoked when you pass an object to the Serialize method
of a formatter and require an information argument of type SerializationInfo. This
class stores all the information needed for serialization. It exposes an AddValue method
that stores data and a value utilized for recognizing data. Notice that the information is

retrieved by the special constructor implementation invoked at deserialization time via `GetXXX` methods, where XXX corresponds to .NET types such as `Int32`, `Boolean`, `Short`, and so on. Also, `GetObjectData` is decorated with the `SecurityPermission` attribute demanding for permissions about the serialization formatter. This is necessary because the permission is allowed only to full-trusted code, thus intranet and Internet zones are not allowed. Both `GetObjectData` and the constructor are `Protected` so that derived classes can still take advantage of them but are prevented from being public. If you are sure that your class will not be inherited, `GetObjectData` can also be Private.

INHERITANCE TIP

When you create a class that inherits from another class where `ISerializable` is implemented, if you add new members, you can also provide a new implementation of both `GetObjectData` and the constructor.

Implementing `ISerializable` is not the only way for controlling serialization. You can control serialization events, too.

Serialization Events

The serialization process raises four events, which are summarized in Table 41.1.

TABLE 41.1   Serialization Events

Event	Description
`OnSerializing`	Occurs just before serialization begins
`OnSerialized`	Occurs just after serialization completes
`OnDeserializing`	Occurs just before deserialization begins
`OnDeserialized`	Occurs just after deserialization completes

Serialization events are handled differently than classic events are. There is an attribute for each event that you can handle as follows:

```
'Invoke this method before
'serialization begins
<OnSerializing()>
Private Sub FirstMethod()

End Sub


'Invoke this method after
'serialization completes
<OnSerialized()>
Private Sub SecondMethod()
```

```
End Sub

'Invoke this method before
'deserialization begins
<OnDeserializing()>
Private Sub ThirdMethod()

End Sub

'Invoke this method after
'deserialization completes
<OnDeserialized()>
Private Sub FourthMethod()

End Sub
```

The runtime takes care of invoking the specified method according to the moment represented by each attribute. In this way, you can provide additional actions based on serialization events.

Serialization with XAML

This book has five chapters dedicated to the Windows Presentation Foundation technology, due to its importance in modern application development. You learned what XAML is and how you use it to define applications' user interface. XAML offers other advantages that can be taken in completely different scenarios; one of these is serialization. The System.Xaml.dll assembly implements the `System.Xaml` namespace. It offers the `XamlServices` class, whose purpose is providing members for reading and writing XAML in serialization scenarios. Because XAML is substantially XML code that adheres to specific schemas, serialization output will be under XML format. The good news is that you are not limited in using XAML serialization only in WPF applications. You need to add a reference to System.Xaml.dll. To understand how it works, create a new console project with Visual Basic and add the required reference. The goal of the code example is to understand how entire objects' graphs can be serialized with this technique. Consider the following implementation of the `Person` class:

```
Public Class Person
    Public Property FirstName As String
    Public Property LastName As String
    Public Property Age As Integer
    Public Property Friends As List(Of Person)
End Class
```

Other than the usual properties, it exposes a `Friends` property of type `List(Of Person)`. This enables you to create a simple object graph. Now consider the following code that creates two instances of the `Person` class that populates the `Friends` property of the main `Person` instance that we serialize:

```
Dim oneFriend As New Person With {.LastName = "White",
                                  .FirstName = "Robert", .Age = 35}
Dim anotherFriend As New Person With {.LastName = "Red",
                                      .FirstName = "Stephen", .Age = 42}

Dim p As New Person With {.LastName = "Del Sole", .FirstName = "Alessandro",
                          .Age = 35,
                          .Friends = New List(Of Person) _
                                     From {oneFriend, anotherFriend}}
```

Using objects and collection initializers makes this operation straightforward. To serialize an object graph, you invoke the `XamlServices.Save` shared method that requires an output stream and the object to be serialized. The following code snippet demonstrates this:

```
Imports System.IO, System.Xaml
'...
Using target As New FileStream("C:\Temp\Person.xaml", FileMode.Create)
    XamlServices.Save(target, p)
End Using
```

SERIALIZING GENERIC COLLECTIONS

When you serialize generic collections, especially custom ones, ensure that they implement the `IList` or `IDictionary` interfaces; otherwise, the serialization process might not work correctly.

The previously described serialization process produces the following output:

```
<Person Age="35"
    FirstName="Alessandro"
    LastName="Del Sole"
    xmlns="clr-namespace:XamlSerialization;assembly=XamlSerialization"
    xmlns:scg="clr-namespace:System.Collections.Generic;
               assembly=mscorlib"
    xmlns:x="http://schemas.microsoft.com/winfx/2006/xaml">

  <Person.Friends>
    <scg:List x:TypeArguments="Person" Capacity="4">
      <Person Friends="{x:Null}" Age="35" FirstName="Robert"
              LastName="White" />
      <Person Friends="{x:Null}" Age="42" FirstName="Stephen"
              LastName="Red" />
    </scg:List>
  </Person.Friends>
</Person>
```

This technique is efficient and makes output readable. As usual in XAML files, the XAML schema is pointed to via the x namespace. The scg namespace points to the System. Collections.Generic .NET namespace, required for deserializing the content as a generic collection. Additionally, the Person.Friends element defines subsequent Person elements storing information on child Person classes being part of the Friends property. Finally, the Friends property for nested Person elements is null. (We did not define child elements for the property.) Deserializing such content is also straightforward. To accomplish this, you invoke the XamlServices.Load shared method by converting its result into the appropriate type. The following code shows how deserialization works, iterating the final result for demonstrating that deserialization was correctly performed:

```
Using source As New FileStream("C:\temp\person.xaml", FileMode.Open)
    Dim result As Person = CType(XamlServices.Load(source), Person)

    'Shows:
    'White
    'Green
    For Each p In result.Friends
        Console.WriteLine(p.LastName)
    Next
    Console.ReadLine()
End Using
```

XAML serialization can be used in different situations, such as persisting the state of WPF controls but also serializing entire .NET objects graphs.

Serialization in Windows Communication Foundation

In some situations serialization is required for persisting state of objects from WCF services. Starting with .NET Framework 3.0, you can serialize objects exposed by WCF services using the DataContractSerializer class (which inherits from XmlObjectSerializer). The usage of such a class is not so different from other serialization classes. The only need is that you must mark your serializable classes either with the Serializable or with the DataContract attribute and, in this case, their members with the DataMember attribute. To see how this works in code, create a new WCF service project within Visual Studio 2012 (refer to Chapter 39, "Creating and Consuming WCF Services," for a recap) and name it **WcfPersonService**. Rename the default IService1 interface to IPersonService; then rename the default Service1 class to PersonService. The new service exposes a special implementation of the Person class. Listing 41.3 shows the complete code for the WCF sample service.

LISTING 41.3   Exposing Serializable Objects from WCF Services

```
<ServiceContract()>
Public Interface IPersonService

    <OperationContract()>
```

```
      Function GetPersonFullName(ByVal onePerson As Person) As String
End Interface

<DataContract()>
Public Class Person

      <DataMember()>
      Public Property FirstName As String

      <DataMember()>
      Public Property LastName As String
End Class
Public Class PersonService
      Implements IPersonService

      Public Function GetPersonFullName(ByVal onePerson As Person) As String _
                  Implements IPersonService.GetPersonFullName

         Dim fullName As New Text.StringBuilder
         fullName.Append(onePerson.FirstName)
         fullName.Append(" ")
         fullName.Append(onePerson.LastName)
         Return fullName.ToString
      End Function
End Class
```

Notice how you decorate the Person class and its members with the DataContract and
DataMember attributes, respectively. Now create a new console project for testing the
WCF service and serialization. Name the new project as **TestWcfSerialization**; then add
a service reference to the WcfPersonService project (refer to Chapter 39 for a recap). This
adds a reference to the WCF service creating a proxy class in Visual Basic. All you need to
do now is to get the instance of the service client and invoke the DataContractSerializer
class that requires a stream for putting serialized data to. The code in Listing 41.4 shows
both serialization and deserialization processes.

LISTING 41.4   Performing WCF Serialization

```
Imports TestWcfSerialization.PersonServiceReference
Imports System.IO
Imports System.Runtime.Serialization

Module Module1

      Sub Main()
```

```
        Dim client As New PersonServiceClient
        Dim p As New Person With {.FirstName = "Alessandro", .LastName = "Del Sole"}

        Dim target As New FileStream("C:\Temp\WcfSerialized.xml", FileMode.Create)
        Dim serializer As New DataContractSerializer(GetType(Person))
        serializer.WriteObject(target, p)
        target.Close()
        serializer = Nothing

        Console.ReadLine()
        Dim source As New FileStream("C:\Temp\WcfSerialized.xml", FileMode.Open)
        serializer = New DataContractSerializer(GetType(Person))

        Dim result As Person = CType(serializer.ReadObject(source), Person)

        Console.WriteLine(result.LastName)
        Console.ReadLine()
    End Sub
End Module
```

In this code, you invoke the `WriteObject` instance method for persisting data. The method requires the file stream instance and the data instance as arguments. `WriteObject` can also serialize an entire object graph, similarly to the binary standard serialization. Data is also serialized to XML format. To deserialize objects, you invoke the `ReadObject` instance method converting the result into the appropriate type. Serialization in WCF can cause special exceptions: `InvalidDataContractException`, which is thrown when the data contract on the service side is badly implemented, and `System.ServiceModel.QuotaExceededException`, which is thrown when serialization attempts to write a number of objects greater than the allowed number. Such a number is represented by the `DataContractSerializer.MaxItemsInObjectsGraph` property, and the default value is `Integer.MaxValue`. The following snippet shows how you catch the previously mentioned exceptions:

```
Try
    serializer.WriteObject(target, p)
Catch ex As InvalidDataContractException
    'Data contract on the service side is wrong
Catch ex As QuotaExceededException
    'Maximum number of serializable object exceeded
Finally
    target.Close()
    serializer = Nothing
End Try
```

If you wonder when you would need WCF serialization, there can be several answers to your question. The most common scenarios are when you have WCF services exposing LINQ to SQL models or Entity Data Models. Data exchange from and to clients is performed via WCF serialization. This requires a little bit of work in LINQ to SQL, whereas Entity Data Models (EDMs) are serialization-enabled, which is covered in the "Serialization in the ADO.NET Entity Framework" section.

JSON Serialization

The .NET languages support the JavaScript Object Notation (JSON) serialization, offered by the `System.Runtime.Serialization.Json` namespace. It is particularly useful when you need to serialize objects as javascript-compliant and is used in WCF and ASP.NET Ajax applications. Conceptually, JSON serialization works like the WCF serialization illustrated previously. The only difference is that you use a `DataContractJSonSerializer` class that works as in the following code snippet:

```
Dim target As New FileStream("C:\Temp\WcfSerialized.xml", FileMode.Create)
Dim jsonSerializer As New DataContractJsonSerializer(GetType(Person))
jsonSerializer.WriteObject(target, p)
```

To deserialize objects, you invoke the `DataContractJSonSerializer.ReadObject` method and convert the result into the appropriate type.

Serialization in the ADO.NET Entity Framework

There are two possible ways to serialize objects when working with the ADO.NET Entity Framework, depending on what code generation strategy you chose. If you generated a data model with the Code First approach or if you generated an EDM with the `None` code generation strategy (which is the default option in Visual Studio 2012), you simply use the `Serializable` attribute and techniques described in the section called "Serialization with Custom Objects." This is because with that code generation strategy, you use Plain Old CLR Objects (POCO) that are platform independent and thus are custom business objects like the ones described previously. When you instead create EDMs with the `Default` code generation strategy (that is, the only way possible before .NET 4.5), entities are automatically decorated with `Serializable` and `DataContract` attributes and their members as `DataMember`. You can easily check this by investigating the code-behind file for EDMs. This enables binary and XML serialization for entities also in WCF scenarios. To understand how this works, create a new console project and add a new EDM wrapping the Northwind database (refer to Chapter 26, "Introducing ADO.NET Entity Framework," for a review), including only the `Customers` and `Orders` tables. You use formatters as you did in the objects serialization with no differences. The code in Listing 41.5 shows how to accomplish this. Notice that the code works the same for both code generation strategies.

LISTING 41.5   Serializing Entities from an Entity Data Model

```vbnet
Imports System.Runtime.Serialization.Formatters.Binary
Imports System.IO

Module Module1
    Sub Main()
        Using northwind As New NorthwindEntities
            'Retrieves the first order, as an example
            Dim anOrder As Order = northwind.Orders.Include("Customer").First

            'Same as classic objects serialization
            Dim formatter As New BinaryFormatter
            Using stream As New FileStream("C:\temp\EFSerialization.dat",
                            FileMode.Create)
                formatter.Serialize(stream, anOrder)
            End Using

            Dim newOrder As Order
            Using source As New FileStream("C:\temp\EFSerialization.dat",
                            FileMode.Open)
                newOrder = CType(formatter.Deserialize(source), Order)
            End Using
        End Using

        Console.ReadLine()
    End Sub
End Module
```

If you need to retrieve data via a WCF service, you use a DataContractSerializer by using serialization in WCF scenarios as described earlier in this chapter. Listing 41.5 shows an example of binary serialization, but you can also take advantage of other techniques described in this chapter as well.

Summary

Serialization is the capability to save objects' state to disk (or memory) and to re-create the states later. The .NET Framework offers several serialization techniques, all provided by the System.Runtime.Serialization namespace. You can perform binary serialization via the BinaryFormatter class or SOAP serialization (XML-based mode for SOAP web services) via the SoapFormatter class. In both cases you need an output stream and then invoke the Serialize method for performing serialization. Deserialize, on the other hand, is for performing deserialization. Another common technique is the XML serialization that creates XML documents starting from your objects, which is useful if you need to exchange your data with non-.NET applications or with non-Windows applications, due to the standard format of this kind of document. If you need deep control over the serialization process, you implement the `ISerializable` interface that requires the implementation of the `GetObjectData`, where you can customize the behavior of the process other than handling serialization events. The .NET Framework 4.5 also offers WCF serialization, which uses the `DataContractSerializer` class or the XAML serialization that is performed via the `XamlServices` class. Finally, you can serialize entities from an Entity Data Model using all the preceding techniques so that you can easily exchange (or save the state of) your data without changing the programming model.

41

CHAPTER 42

Processes and Multithreading

In our everyday lives, we all do a number of things such as go to work, have appointments, and visit with friends or family; we are all very busy, of course. Sometimes we can do two things simultaneously, such as speaking on the phone while writing something on a piece of paper, but in most cases we do just one thing at a time. After all, there is only one of us. It would be great if we could share our things to do with other people so that multiple people could do the same work concurrently. We would be less tired and would have more time for relaxing or being with our families. In the computers' world, a similar problem exists. You can compare a real person to an application. If an application has to complete hard and long work totally alone, it can cause overhead on the system and take more time. Moreover, recent hardware architectures (such as multicore processors) would remain unexploited. So it would be useful to have the ability to split the work of an application among multiple parts that could work concurrently. This is where threading comes in with the .NET Framework development. With *threading*, you can create multiple threads of work to perform multiple tasks concurrently so that your applications can take advantage of optimized performance and resources. But threading is not the only way you request actions. In many circumstances, you need to launch external executables and possibly hold a reference to them in your code, so you also often work with processes. In this chapter, you take a look at how the .NET Framework enables you to manage processes and how you can split operations across multiple threads—both created manually and provided by the .NET thread pool.

Managing Processes

You use the `System.Diagnostics.Process` class to manage processes on your machine.

This class offers both shared and instance members so that you can launch an external process but also get a reference to one or more processes. The following code shows how to launch an external process via the shared implementation of the `Start` method:

```
Process.Start("Notepad.exe")
```

Any call to the `Process.Start` method will return a `Process` object. You can also specify arguments for the process by specifying the second parameter for the method as follows:

```
Process.Start("Notepad.exe", "C:\aFile.txt")
```

One of the most important features of the `Start` method is that you can also supply the username, password, and domain for launching a process:

```
Process.Start("Notepad.exe", "C:\aFile.txt",
              "Alessandro", Password, "\\MYDOMAIN")
```

Notice that the password is necessarily an instance of the `System.Security.SecureString` class, so see the MSDN documentation about this. The `Process` class also has an instance behavior that enables you to get a reference to a process instance. This is useful when you want to programmatically control a process. With regard to this, you first need an instance of the `ProcessStartInfo` class that can store process execution information. The class exposes lots of properties, but the most important are summarized in the following code snippet:

```
Dim procInfo As New ProcessStartInfo
With procInfo
    .FileName = "Notepad.exe"
    .Arguments = "aFile.txt"
    .WorkingDirectory = "C:\"
    .WindowStyle = ProcessWindowStyle.Maximized
    .ErrorDialog = True
End With
```

Particularly, the `ErrorDialog` property makes the `Process` instance display an error dialog box if the process cannot be started regularly. When you have done this, you create an instance of the `Process` class and assign its `StartInfo` property; finally, you invoke `Start` as demonstrated in the following code:

```
Dim proc As New Process
proc.StartInfo = procInfo
proc.Start()

'Alternative syntax:
'Dim proc As Process = Process.Start(procInfo)
```

Approaching processes in this fashion is helpful if you need to programmatically control processes. For example, you can wait until a process exits for the specified number of milliseconds as follows:

```
'Waits for two seconds
proc.WaitForExit(2000)
```

To close a process, you write the following code:

```
proc.Close()
```

Finally, you can kill unresponsive processes by invoking the Kill method as follows:

```
proc.Kill()
```

The Process class also exposes the EnableRaisingEvents Boolean property, which enables you to set whether the runtime should raise the Exited event when the process terminates. Such an event is raised if either the process terminates normally or an invocation to the Kill method occurs. So far, you have learned how to launch processes, but the Process class is also useful when you need to get information on running processes, as discussed in the next subsection.

Querying Existing Processes

You can easily get information on running processes through some methods from the Process class that provide the ability of getting process instances. For example, GetProcesses returns an array of Process objects, each one representing a running process. GetProcessById and GetProcessByName return information on the specified process given the identification number or name, whereas GetCurrentProcess returns an instance of the Process class representing the current process. Then the Process class exposes a lot of useful properties for retrieving information. Each of them should be self-explanatory, such as ProcessName, Id, ExitCode, Handle, and HasExited. However, other advanced information properties are available, such as PageMemorySize or VirtualMemorySize, which return the memory size associated with the process on the page memory and the virtual memory, respectively. The Visual Studio's Object Browser and IntelliSense can help you with the rest of the available properties. At the moment, let's focus on how you can get information on running processes. The coolest way of getting process information is by using LINQ to Objects. The following query, and subsequent For..Each loop, demonstrates how to retrieve a list of names of running processes:

```
Dim processesList = (From p In Process.GetProcesses
                     Select p.ProcessName).AsEnumerable

For Each procName In processesList
    Console.WriteLine(procName)
Next
```

Notice that the query result is converted into IEnumerable(Of String) so that you can eventually bind the list to a user interface control supporting the type.

Introducing Multithreading

A *thread* is a unit of work. The logic of threading-based programming is performing multiple operations concurrently so that a big operation can be split across multiple threads. The .NET Framework 4.5 offers support for multithreading via the System.Threading namespace. But .NET 4.5 also takes from its predecessor an important library, which is discussed in Chapter 43, "Parallel Programming and Parallel LINQ." It provides support for the parallel computing. For this reason, this chapter provides summary information on the multithreading approach so that in the next chapter you get more detailed information on the task-based programming. After reading Chapter 43, approaching the most important new language feature in Visual Basic 2012 will be easier. This is discussed in Chapter 44, "Asynchronous Programming."

Imports DIRECTIVES

The code examples shown in this chapter require an Imports System.Threading directive.

Creating Threads

You create a new thread for performing an operation with an instance of the System. Threading.Thread class. The constructor of this class requires you to also specify an instance of the System.Threading.ThreadStart delegate that points to a method that can actually do the work. Then you invoke the Thread.Start instance method. The following code snippet demonstrates how you can create a new thread:

```
Private Sub simpleThread()
    Dim newThread As New Thread(New ThreadStart(AddressOf _
                                        executeSimpleThread))
    newThread.Start()
End Sub

Private Sub executeSimpleThread()
    Console.WriteLine("Running a separate thread")
End Sub
```

To actually start the new thread, you invoke the method that encapsulates the thread instance, which in this case is simpleThread.

Creating Threads with Lambda Expressions

You might recall from Chapter 20, "Advanced Language Features," that lambda expressions can be used anywhere you need a delegate. This is also true in threading-based programming. The following code snippet demonstrates how you can use statement lambdas instead of providing an explicit delegate:

```
Private Sub lambdaThread()
    Dim newThread As New Thread(New _
                        ThreadStart(Sub()
                                        Console.WriteLine("Thread with lambda")
                                    End Sub))
    newThread.Start()
End Sub
```

Now you can invoke the `lambdaThread` method to run a secondary thread, and with one method you reach the same objective of the previous code where two methods were implemented.

Passing Parameters

In many cases, you might need to pass data to new threads. You can do this by creating an instance of the `ParameterizedThreadStart` delegate, which requires an argument of type `Object` that you can use for sharing your data. The following code demonstrates how you create a thread with parameters:

```
Private Sub threadWithParameters(ByVal parameter As Object)
    Dim newThread As New Thread(New _
                            ParameterizedThreadStart(AddressOf _
                            executeThreadWithParameters))
    newThread.Start(parameter)
End Sub
```

Notice how the `Thread.Start` method has an overload that takes the specified parameter as the data. Because such data is of type `Object`, you need to convert it into the most appropriate format. The following code demonstrates how to implement a method to which the delegate refers and how to convert the data into a hypothetical string:

```
Private Sub executeThreadWithParameters(ByVal anArgument As Object)
    Dim aString = CType(anArgument, String)
    Console.WriteLine(aString)
End Sub
```

You can use lambda expressions if you do not want to provide an explicit delegate in this kind of scenario.

Understanding the .NET Thread Pool

In the previous section, you saw how simple it is to create and run a new thread. When you have one or two threads, things are also easy for performance. But if you decide to split a process or an application across several concurrent threads, the previous approach can cause performance and resources overhead. So, you should manually search for the best configuration to fine-tune system resource consumption with your threads. Your application can run on different configurations in terms of available memory, processors, and general resources, so it is difficult to predict how many threads you can launch concurrently on target machines without affecting performance and causing overhead. Fortunately, the .NET Framework maintains its own set of threads that you can also reuse for your purposes instead of writing code for creating and running new threads, ensuring that only the specified number of threads will be executed concurrently—all controlled by the Framework. The set is named *thread pool*, and you access it via the `System.Threading.ThreadPool` class. This class offers static methods for assigning tasks to threads in the box because the thread pool has a predefined number of available threads. If they are all busy doing something else, the new task is put into a queue and is executed when a thread completes its work. To take advantage of threads in the thread pool, you invoke the `System.Threading.ThreadPool.QueueUserWorkItem` method, as demonstrated in the following code:

```
Sub QueueWork()


    ThreadPool.QueueUserWorkItem(New WaitCallback(AddressOf FirstWorkItem))
    ThreadPool.QueueUserWorkItem(New WaitCallback(AddressOf SecondWorkItem))
    ThreadPool.QueueUserWorkItem(New WaitCallback(Sub()

                                                     Console.
                                                     WriteLine _
                                                     ("Third work item")
                                                 End Sub))


End Sub


Private Sub FirstWorkItem(ByVal state As Object)
    Console.WriteLine("First work item")
End Sub
Private Sub SecondWorkItem(ByVal state As Object)
    Console.WriteLine("Second work item")
End Sub
```

With `QueueUserWorkItem` you ask the runtime to put the specified task in the execution queue so that it will be executed when a thread in the thread pool is available. The `WaitCallBack` delegate allows passing state information and requires referred methods to have an argument of type `Object` in their signatures. Notice how you can still use lambdas to supply the desired action.

THE THREAD POOL AND WINDOWS PHONE

Silverlight for Windows Phone also supports a special version of the thread pool that constitutes the simplest way to create responsive code by splitting tasks over threads. You use `QueueUserWorkItem` in Windows Phone to execute a task outside the user interface (UI) thread, thus preventing your app from freezing.

Getting and Setting Information in the Thread Pool

You can query information on the thread pool by invoking the `ThreadPool.GetMaxThreads`, `ThreadPool.GetMinThreads`, and `ThreadPool.GetAvailableThreads` methods. `GetMaxThreads` return the maximum number of concurrent threads that are held by the thread pool; `GetMinThreads` return the number of idle threads that are maintained waiting for the first new task being requested; and `GetAvailableThreads` returns the number of available threads. Whichever you use, they all return two values: the number of worker threads and the number of completion threads. Worker threads are units of execution, whereas completion threads are asynchronous I/O operations. The following code demonstrates how you get information on available threads:

```
Sub PoolInfo()
    Dim workerThreads As Integer
    Dim completionPortThreads As Integer

    ThreadPool.GetAvailableThreads(workerThreads,
                                   completionPortThreads)
    Console.WriteLine("Available threads: {0}, async I/O: {1}",
                      workerThreads, completionPortThreads)
    Console.ReadLine()
End Sub
```

The `workerThreads` and `completionPortThreads` arguments are passed by reference; this is why you need variables for storing values. Similarly, you can use `SetMaxThreads` and `SetMinThreads` to establish the maximum number of requests held by the thread pool and the minimum number of idle threads. The following line is an example:

```
ThreadPool.SetMaxThreads(2000, 1500)
```

CHANGING DEFAULT VALUES

You should take care when editing the default values for the thread pool. You should do it only when you have a deep knowledge of how many resources will be consumed on the machine and of the system resources so that edits will not be negative for the target system. Default values in the thread pool are high enough, but you can check this out by invoking `GetMaxThreads`.

Threads Synchronization

So far, you have learned how to create and run new threads of execution to split big operations across multiple threads. This is useful, but there is a problem: Imagine you have multiple threads accessing the same data source simultaneously—what happens to the data source, and how are threads handled to avoid errors? This is a problem that is solved with thread synchronization. The idea is that, when a thread accesses a resource, this resource is locked until the required operations are completed to prevent other threads from accessing that resource. Visual Basic and the .NET Framework provide keywords and objects, respectively, to accomplish threads synchronization, as covered in the next subsections.

The `SyncLock..End SyncLock` Statement

The Visual Basic language offers the `SyncLock..End SyncLock` statement, which is the place where you can grant access to the specified resource to only one thread per time. For example, imagine you have a class where you define a list of customers and a method for adding a new customer to the list, as demonstrated by the following code snippet:

```
Private customers As New List(Of String)


Sub AddCustomer(ByVal customerName As String)


    SyncLock Me
        customers.Add(customerName)
    End SyncLock
End Sub
```

The preceding code locks the entire enclosing class, preventing other threads from accessing the instance until the requested operation completes. Locking an entire class is not always the best idea because it can be expensive in terms of resources and performance and other threads cannot also access other members. Unfortunately, you cannot directly lock the resource; the MSDN documentation in fact states that you need to declare a *lock object* that you can use as follows:

```
Private customers As New List(Of String)
Private lockObject As New Object()


Sub AddCustomer(ByVal customerName As String)


    SyncLock lockObject
        customers.Add(customerName)
    End SyncLock
End Sub
```

The lock object is typically a `System.Object`. Using an object like this can ensure that the code block executed within `SyncLock..End SyncLock` will not be accessible by other threads. Another approach is using `GetType` instead of the lock object, pointing to the current type where the synchronization lock is defined. The following code demonstrates this:

```
Class Customers
    Inherits List(Of String)


    Public Sub AddCustomer(ByVal customerName As String)
        SyncLock GetType(Customers)
            Me.Add(customerName)
```

```
        End SyncLock
    End Sub
End Class
```

The `SyncLock..End SyncLock` statement is typical of Visual Basic language grammar. By the way, the statement is translated behind the scenes into invocations to the `System.Threading.Monitor` class, as described in the next section.

Synchronization with the `Monitor` Class

The `System.Threading.Monitor` class is the support object for the `SyncLock..End SyncLock` statement, and the compiler translates `SyncLock` blocks into invocations to the `Monitor` class. You use it as follows:

```
Sub AddCustomer(ByVal customerName As String)
    Dim result As Boolean

    Try
        Monitor.Enter(lockObject, result)
        customers.Add(customerName)
    Catch ex As Exception
    Finally
        Monitor.Exit(lockObject)
    End Try
End Sub
```

> **TIP**
>
> `Monitor.Enter` has an overload that takes a second argument of type `Boolean`, passed by reference, indicating whether the lock was taken.

`Monitor.Enter` locks the object; `Monitor.Exit` unlocks it. It is fundamental to place `Monitor.Exit` in the `Finally` part of the `Try..Catch` block so that resources will be unlocked anyway. At this point, you might wonder why you should use `Monitor` instead of `SyncLock..End SyncLock` because they produce the same result. The difference is that `Monitor` also exposes additional members, such as the `TryEnter` method that supports timeout, as demonstrated here:

```
Monitor.TryEnter(lockObject, 3000, result)
```

This code attempts to obtain the lock on the specified object for three seconds before terminating.

Read/Write Locks

A frequent scenario is when you have a shared resource that multiple reader threads need to access. In a scenario like this, you probably want to grant writing permissions just to a single thread to avoid concurrency problems. The .NET Framework provides the `System. Threading.ReaderWriterLockSlim` class, which provides a lock enabled for multiple threads reading and exclusive access for writing.

Readerwriterlock CLASS

The .NET Framework still provides the `ReaderWriterLock` class, as in its previous versions, but it is complex and used to handle particular multithreading scenarios. Instead, as its name implies, the `ReaderWriterLockSlim` class is a lightweight object for reading and writing locks.

An instance of this class is declared as a shared field and is used to invoke both methods for reading and writing. The following code demonstrates how you enable a writer lock:

```
Private Shared rw As New ReaderWriterLockSlim

Sub AddCustomer(ByVal customerName As String)
    Try

        rw.EnterWriteLock()
        customers.Add(customerName)
    Catch ex As Exception
    Finally
        rw.ExitWriteLock()
    End TrThe
End Sub
```

This ensures that only one thread can write to the customers' collection. The next code snippet shows instead how you can enable a reader lock:

```
Sub GetInformation()
    Try
        rw.EnterReadLock()
        Console.WriteLine(customers.Count.ToString)
    Catch ex As Exception
    Finally
        rw.ExitReadLock()
    End Try
End Sub
```

`ReaderWriterLockSlim` is an object you should use if you expect more readers than writers; in other cases you should consider custom synchronization locks implementations.

Summary

This chapter covered processes management and multithreading with Visual Basic 2012. First, you saw how to utilize the `System.Diagnostics.Process` class for launching and managing external process from your applications, including programmatic access to processes. Next, you got an overview of threads and the `System.Threading.Thread` class, understanding how a thread is a single unit of execution and seeing how you create and run threads both programmatically and inside the .NET's thread pool. In the final part of this chapter, you learned about synchronization locks, which are necessary so that multiple threads access the same resources concurrently. For this, remember the `SyncLock.. End SyncLock` VB statement and the `Monitor` class. Understanding threads is particularly important in the .NET programming—especially to understand how the runtime can handle the application execution. But from the point of view of writing responsive applications, the .NET Framework offers more modern patterns: parallel computing and asynchronous programming. Without a knowledge of threading, it would be difficult to understand how both work. They are discussed in the next chapters.

CHAPTER 43

Parallel Programming and Parallel LINQ

Modern computers ship with multicore architectures, meaning that they have more than one processor. The simplest home computer has at least dual-core architecture, so you surely have a machine with multiple processors. Managed applications do their work using only one processor. This makes things easier, but with this approach you do not unleash all the system resources. The reason is that all elaborations rely on a single processor that is overcharged and will take more time. Having the possibility of scaling the application execution over all available processors instead is a technique that would improve how system resources are consumed and would speed up the application execution. The reason is simple: Instead of having only one processor doing the work, you have all the available processors doing the work concurrently. Scaling applications across multiple processors is known as *parallel computing*, which is not something new in the programming world. The word *parallel* means that multiple tasks are executed concurrently, in parallel. The .NET Framework 4.5 includes a special library dedicated to parallel computing for the Microsoft platform. This library is called Task Parallel Library, and it has been dramatically improved in the new version of .NET, meaning that code can run up to 400% faster than in .NET 4.0. It also includes a specific implementation of Language Integrated Query, known as Parallel LINQ. In this chapter you learn what the library is, how it is structured, and how you can use it for writing parallel code in your applications starting from basic concepts up to writing parallel queries with LINQ and passing through interesting objects such as the concurrent collections.

Introducing Parallel Computing

The .NET Framework 4.5 (as well as its predecessor) provides support for parallel computing through the Task Parallel Library (TPL), which is a set of Application Programming Interfaces (APIs) offered by specific extensions of the System.Threading.dll assembly. The reference to this assembly is included by default when creating new projects, so you do not need to add one manually. The TPL is reachable via the System.Threading and System.Threading.Tasks namespaces that provide objects for scaling work execution over multiple processors. You write small units of work known as *tasks*. Tasks are scheduled for execution by the TPL's Task Scheduler, which is responsible for executing tasks according to available threads. This is possible because the Task Scheduler is integrated with the .NET Thread Pool. The good news is that the .NET Framework can automatically use all available processors on the target machines without the need to recompile code.

> **NOTE**
>
> Parallel computing makes it easier to scale applications over multiple processors, but it remains something complex in terms of concepts. This is because you will face some threading concepts, such as synchronization locks, deadlocks, and so on. Therefore, you should have at least a basic knowledge of threading issues before writing parallel code. Another important consideration is figuring out when you should use parallel computing. The answer is not easy because you are the only one who knows how your applications consume resources. The general rule is that parallel computing gives the best advantage when you have intensive processing scenarios. In simpler elaborations, parallel computing is not necessarily the best choice and can cause performance loss. Use it when your applications require hard CPU loops.

Most of the parallel APIs are available through the System.Threading.Tasks.Task and System.Threading.Tasks.Parallel classes. The first one is described in detail later; now we provide coverage of the most important classes for parallelism.

What's New in .NET 4.5: Custom Task Scheduling

If you already have a good experience with parallel computing in .NET 4.0, you might be interested in knowing that .NET 4.5 introduces the ability to create custom task schedulers. The new version exposes the ConcurrentExclusiveSchedulerPair class, which provides support for coordinating works in various ways. Such a class exposes two instances of the TaskScheduler class via the ConcurrentScheduler and ExclusiveScheduler properties. They provide asynchronous support for reader/writer locks, and the benefit that they provide is that tasks scheduled in this way can run as long as there are no executing exclusive tasks. After an exclusive task is scheduled, no more concurrent tasks are allowed to run. Only when all running concurrent tasks have completed, will the exclusive tasks be allowed to run one at a time. Another useful control you can have over tasks is that the ConcurrentExclusiveSchedulerPair also supports restricting the number of tasks that can run concurrently. You instead use the ExclusiveScheduler class to run queued tasks sequentially. This topic is for readers with an advanced experience with the TPL. You can find further information in the MSDN documentation: http://msdn.microsoft.com/en-us/library/system.threading.tasks.concurrentexclusiveschedulerpair(v=vs.110).aspx

Introducing Parallel Classes

Parallelism in the .NET Framework 4.5 is possible due to a number of classes, some responsible for maintaining the architecture of the TPL and some for performing operations in a concurrent fashion. The following subsection provides a brief coverage of the most important classes, describing their purpose.

The `Parallel` Class

The `System.Threading.Tasks.Parallel` class is one of the most important classes in parallel computing because it provides shared methods for running concurrent tasks and for executing parallel loops. In this chapter, you can find several examples of usage of this class; for now, you just need to know that it provides the `Invoke`, `For`, and `ForEach` shared methods. The first one enables running multiple tasks concurrently, and the other ones enable you to execute loops in parallel.

The `TaskScheduler` Class

The `System.Threading.Tasks.TaskScheduler` class is responsible for the low-level work of sending tasks to the thread queue. This means that when you start a new concurrent task, the task is sent to the scheduler that checks for thread availability in the .NET thread pool. If a thread is available, the task is pushed into the thread and executed. You do not interact with the task scheduler. (The class exposes some members that you can use to understand the task's state.) The first property is `Current`, which retrieves the instance of the running task scheduler. This is required to access information. For example, you can understand the concurrency level by reading the `MaximumConcurrencyLevel` property as follows:

```
Console.WriteLine("The maximum concurrency level is {0}",
              TaskScheduler.Current.MaximumConcurrencyLevel)
```

There are also some protected methods that can be used to force tasks execution (such as `QueueTask` and `TryDequeue`), but these are accessible if you want to create your own custom task scheduler, which is beyond the scope of this chapter.

The `TaskFactory` Class

The `System.Threading.Tasks.TaskFactory` class provides support for generating and running new tasks and is exposed as a shared property of the `Task` class, as explained in the next section. The most important member is the `StartNew` method, which enables creating a new task and automatically starting it.

The `ParallelOptions` Class

The `System.Threading.Tasks.ParallelOptions` class provides a way for setting options on tasks creation. Specifically, it provides properties for setting task cancellation properties (`CancellationToken`), the instance of the scheduler (`TaskScheduler`), and the maximum number of threads that a task is split across (`MaxDegreeOfParallelism`).

Understanding and Using Tasks

The parallel computing in the .NET Framework development relies on the concept of tasks. This section is therefore about the core of the parallel computing, and you learn to use tasks for scaling units of work across multiple threads and processors.

READ THIS SECTION CAREFULLY

This section is particularly important not only with regard to the current chapter, but also because the concept of tasks returns in Chapter 44, "Asynchronous Programming." For this reason it is very important that you carefully read the concepts about tasks; you will reuse them in the next chapter.

What Is a Task?

Chapter 42, "Processes and Multithreading," discusses multithreading and illustrates how a thread is a unit of work that you can use to split a big task across multiple units of work. Different from the pure threading world, in parallel computing the most important concept is the *task*, which is the basic unit of work and can be scaled across all available processors. A task is not a thread; a thread can run multiple tasks, but each task can be also scaled across more than one thread, depending on available resources. The task is therefore the most basic unit of work for operations executed in parallel. In terms of code, a task is nothing but an instance of the `System.Threading.Tasks.Task` class that holds a reference to a delegate, pointing to a method that does some work. The implementation is similar to what you do with `Thread` objects but with the differences previously discussed. You have two alternatives for executing operations with tasks: The first one is calling the `Parallel.Invoke` method; the second one is manually creating and managing instances of the `Task` class. The following subsections cover both scenarios.

Running Tasks with `Parallel.Invoke`

The first way of running tasks in parallel is calling the `Parallel.Invoke` shared method. This method can receive an array of `System.Action` objects as parameters, so each `Action` is translated by the runtime into a task. If possible, tasks are executed in parallel. The following example demonstrates how to perform three calculations concurrently:

```
'Requires an Imports System.Threading.Tasks directive

    Dim angle As Double = 150
    Dim sineResult As Double
    Dim cosineResult As Double
    Dim tangentResult As Double

    Parallel.Invoke(Sub()
                        Console.WriteLine(Thread.CurrentThread.
                            ManagedThreadId)
                        Dim radians As Double = angle * Math.PI / 180
```

```
            sineResult = Math.Sin(radians)
    End Sub,
    Sub()
        Console.WriteLine(Thread.CurrentThread.
                        ManagedThreadId)
        Dim radians As Double = angle * Math.PI / 180
        cosineResult = Math.Cos(radians)
    End Sub,
    Sub()
        Console.WriteLine(Thread.CurrentThread.
                        ManagedThreadId)
        Dim radians As Double = angle * Math.PI / 180
        tangentResult = Math.Tan(radians)
    End Sub)
```

In the example, the code uses statement lambdas; each of them is translated into a task by the runtime that is also responsible for creating and scheduling threads and for scaling tasks across all available processors. If you run the code, you can see how the tasks run within separate threads, automatically created for you by the TPL. As an alternative, you can supply AddressOf clauses pointing to methods performing the required operations, instead of using statement lambdas. Although this approach is useful when you need to run tasks in parallel the fastest way, it does not enable you to take control over tasks themselves. This is something that requires explicit instances of the Task class, as explained in the next subsection.

Creating, Running, and Managing Tasks: The Task Class

The System.Threading.Tasks.Task class represents the unit of work in the parallel computing based on .NET Framework. Differently from calling Parallel.Invoke, when you create an instance of the Task class, you get deep control over the task itself, such as starting, stopping, waiting for completion, and cancelling. The constructor of the class requires you to supply a delegate or a lambda expression to provide a method containing the code to be executed within the task. The following code demonstrates how you create a new task and then start it:

```
Dim simpleTask As New Task(Sub()
                        'Do your work here...
                    End Sub)

simpleTask.Start()
```

You supply the constructor with a lambda expression or with a delegate and then invoke the Start instance method. The Task class also exposes a Factory property of type TaskFactory that offers members for interacting with tasks. For example, you can use this property for creating and starting a new task all in one as follows:

```
Dim factoryTask = Task.Factory.StartNew(Sub()
                                            'Do your work here
                                        End Sub)
```

This has the same result as the first code snippet. The logic is that you can create instances of the `Task` class, each with some code that will be executed in parallel.

GETTING THE THREAD ID

When you launch a new task, the task is executed within a managed thread. If you want to get information on the thread, in the code for the task you can access it via the `System.Threading.Thread.CurrentThread` shared property. For example, the `CurrentThread.ManagedThreadId` property will return the thread ID that is hosting the task.

Creating Tasks That Return Values

The `Task` class also has a generic counterpart that you can use for creating tasks that return a value. Consider the following code snippet that creates a task returning a value of type `Double`, which is the result of calculating the tangent of an angle:

```
Dim taskWithResult = Task(Of Double).
    Factory.StartNew(Function()
                         Dim radians As Double _
                             = 120 * Math.PI / 180
                         Dim tan As Double = _
                             Math.Tan(radians)
                         Return tan
                     End Function)


Console.WriteLine(taskWithResult.Result)
```

You use a `Function`, which represents a `System.Func(Of T)`, so that you can return a value from your operation. The result is accessed via the `Task.Result` property. In the preceding example, the `Result` property contains the result of the tangent calculation. The problem is that the start value on which the calculation is performed is hard-coded. If you want to pass a value as an argument, you need to approach the problem differently. The following code demonstrates how to implement a method that receives an argument that can be reached from within the new task:

```
Private Function CalcTan(ByVal angle As Double) As Double

    Dim t = Task(Of Double).Factory.
        StartNew(Function()
                     Dim radians As Double = angle * Math.PI / 180
                     tangentResult = Math.Tan(radians)
                     Return tangentResult
```

```
            End Function)
    Return t.Result
End Function
```

The result of the calculation is returned from the task. This result is wrapped by the `Task.`
`Result` instance property, which is then returned as the method result.

Waiting for Tasks to Complete

You can explicitly wait for a task to complete by invoking the `Task.Wait` method. The
following code waits until the task completes:

```
Dim simpleTask = Task.Factory.StartNew(Sub()
                                           'Do your work here
                                        End Sub)

simpleTask.Wait()
```

You can alternatively pass a number of milliseconds to the `Wait` method so that you can
also check for a timeout. The following code demonstrates this:

```
simpleTask.Wait(1000)
If simpleTask.IsCompleted Then
    'completed
Else
    'timeout
End If
```

Notice how the `IsCompleted` property enables you to check whether the task is marked
as completed by the runtime. `Wait` has to be enclosed inside a `Try..Catch` block because
the method asks the runtime to complete a task that could raise any exceptions. This is an
example:

```
Try
    simpleTask.Wait(1000)
    If simpleTask.IsCompleted Then
        'completed
    Else
        'timeout
    End If

    'parallel exception
Catch ex As AggregateException

End Try
```

Exception Handling

Handling exceptions is a crucial topic in parallel programming. The problem is that
multiple tasks that run concurrently could raise more than one exception concurrently,

and you need to understand what the actual problem is. The .NET Framework 4.5 offers the System.AggregateException class that wraps all exceptions that occurred concurrently into one instance. Such class then exposes, over classic properties, an InnerExceptions collection that you can iterate for checking which exceptions occurred. The following code demonstrates how you catch an AggregateException and how you iterate the instance:

```
Dim aTask = Task.Factory.StartNew(Sub() Console.
                                       WriteLine("A demo task"))


Try
    aTask.Wait()
Catch ex As AggregateException
    For Each fault In ex.InnerExceptions
        If TypeOf (fault) Is InvalidOperationException Then
            'Handle the exception here..
        ElseIf TypeOf (fault) Is NullReferenceException Then
            'Handle the exception here..
        End If
    Next
Catch ex As Exception

End Try
```

Each item in InnerExceptions is an exception that you can verify with TypeOf. Another problem is when you have tasks that run nested tasks that throw exceptions. In this case you can use the AggregateException.Flatten method, which wraps exceptions thrown by nested tasks into the parent instance. The following code demonstrates how to accomplish this:

```
Dim aTask = Task.Factory.StartNew(Sub() Console.
                                       WriteLine("A demo task"))


Try
    aTask.Wait()
Catch ex As AggregateException
    For Each fault In ex.Flatten.InnerExceptions
        If TypeOf (fault) Is InvalidOperationException Then
            'Handle the exception here..
        ElseIf TypeOf (fault) Is NullReferenceException Then
            'Handle the exception here..
        End If
    Next
Catch ex As Exception

End Try
```

`Flatten` returns an instance of the `AggregateException` storing inner exceptions that included errors coming from nested tasks.

Canceling Tasks

In some situations you want to cancel task execution. To programmatically cancel a task, you need to enable tasks for cancellation, which requires some lines of code. You need an instance of the `System.Threading.CancellationTokenSource` class; this instance tells a `System.Threading.CancellationToken` that it should be canceled. The `CancellationToken` class provides notifications for cancellation. The following lines declare both objects:

```
Dim tokenSource As New CancellationTokenSource()
Dim token As CancellationToken = tokenSource.Token
```

.NET 4.5 IMPROVEMENTS: SETTING TIME FOR CANCELLATION

The .NET Framework 4.5 now enables you to create an instance of the `CancellationTokenSource` class and specify on such an instance how much time will have to pass before a cancellation occurs:

```
Dim tokenSource As New CancellationTokenSource(TimeSpan.FromSeconds(5))
```

You specify a `TimeSpan` value directly in the constructor.

Then you can start a new task using an overload of the `TaskFactory.StartNew` method that takes the cancellation token as an argument. The following line accomplishes this:

```
Dim aTask = Task.Factory.StartNew(Sub() DoSomething(token), token)
```

You still pass a delegate as an argument; in the preceding example the delegate takes an argument of type `CancellationToken` that is useful for checking the state of cancellation during the task execution. The following code snippet provides the implementation of the `DoSomething` method, in a demonstrative way:

```
Sub DoSomething(ByVal cancelToken As CancellationToken)

    'Check if cancellation was requested before
    'the task starts
    If cancelToken.IsCancellationRequested = True Then
        cancelToken.ThrowIfCancellationRequested()
    End If

    For i As Integer = 0 To 1000

        'Simulates some work
        Thread.SpinWait(10000)
        If cancelToken.IsCancellationRequested Then
```

43

```
            'Cancellation was requested
            cancelToken.ThrowIfCancellationRequested()
        End If
    Next

End Sub
```

The `IsCancellationRequested` property returns `True` if cancellation over the current task was requested. The `ThrowIfCancellationRequested` method throws an `OperationCanceledException` to communicate to the caller that the task was canceled. In the preceding code snippet, the `Thread.SpinWait` method simulates some work inside a loop. Notice how checking for cancellation is performed at each iteration so that an exception can be thrown if the task is actually canceled. The next step is to request cancellation in the main code. This is accomplished by invoking the `CancellationTokenSource.Cancel` method, as demonstrated in the following code:

```
tokenSource.Cancel()

Try
    aTask.Wait()
Catch ex As AggregateException
    'Handle concurrent exceptions here...
Catch ex As Exception

End Try
```

DISABLE "JUST MY CODE"

The `OperationCanceledException` is correctly thrown if the Just My Code is disabled (refer to Chapter 5, "Debugging Visual Basic 2012 Applications," for details on Just My Code). If it is enabled, the compiler sends a message saying that an `OperationCanceledException` was unhandled by user code. This is benign, so you can go on running your code by repressing F5.

The `Barrier` Class

The `System.Threading` namespace in .NET 4.5 exposes a class named `Barrier`. The goal of this class is bringing a number of tasks that work concurrently to a common point before taking further steps. Tasks work across multiple phases and signal that they arrived at the barrier, waiting for all other tasks to arrive. The constructor of the class offers several overloads, but all have the number of tasks participating in the concurrent work in common. You can also specify the action to take after they arrive at the common point (that is, they reach the barrier and complete the current phase). Notice that the same instance of the `Barrier` class can be used multiple times, for representing multiple phases. The following code demonstrates how three tasks reach the barrier after their work, signaling the work completion and waiting for other tasks to finish:

```
Sub BarrierDemo()
    ' Create a barrier with three participants
    ' The Sub lambda provides an action that will be taken
    ' at the end of the phase
    Dim myBarrier As New Barrier(3,
                        Sub(b)
                            Console.
                            WriteLine("Barrier has been " & _
                            "reached (phase number: {0})",
                            b.CurrentPhaseNumber)
                        End Sub)

    ' This is the sample work made by all participant tasks
    Dim myaction As Action =
        Sub()
            For i = 1 To 3
                Dim threadId As Integer =
                    Thread.CurrentThread.ManagedThreadId
                Console.WriteLine("Thread {0} before wait.", threadId)

                'Waits for other tasks to arrive at this same point:
                myBarrier.SignalAndWait()
                Console.WriteLine("Thread {0} after wait.", threadId)
            Next
        End Sub

    ' Starts three tasks, representing the three participants
    Parallel.Invoke(myAction, myAction, myAction)

    ' Once done, disposes the Barrier.
    myBarrier.Dispose()
End Sub
```

The code performs these steps:

1. Creates an instance of the `Barrier` class adding three participants and specifying the action to take when the barrier is reached.

2. Declares a common job for the three tasks (the `myAction` object), which perform an iteration against running threads simulating some work. When each task completes the work, the `Barrier.SignalAndWait` method is invoked. This tells the runtime to wait for other tasks to complete their work before going to the next phase.

3. Launches the three concurrent tasks and disposes of the `myBarrier` object at the appropriate time.

The code also reuses the same Barrier instance to work across multiple phases. Such a class also exposes interesting members, such as these:

▶ AddParticipant and AddParticipants—These methods enable you to add one or the specified number of participant tasks to the barrier, respectively.

▶ RemoveParticipant and RemoveParticipants—These methods enable you to remove one or the specified number of participant tasks from the barrier, respectively.

▶ CurrentPhaseNumber property of type Long—This returns the current phase number.

▶ ParticipantCount property of type Integer—This returns the number of tasks involved in the operation.

▶ ParticipantsRemaining property of type Integer—This returns the number of tasks that have not invoked the SignalAndWait method yet.

A Barrier represents a single phase in the process; multiple instances of the same Barrier class, like in the preceding code, represent multiple phases.

Parallel Loops

The Task Parallel Library offers the ability of scaling loops such as For and For Each. This is possible due to the implementation of the shared Parallel.For and Parallel.ForEach methods. Both methods can use a multicore architecture for the parallel execution of loops, as explained in next subsections. Now create a new Console application with Visual Basic. The goal of the next example is to simulate an intensive processing for demonstrating the advantage of parallel loops and demonstrating how the Task Parallel Library is responsible for managing threads for you. With that said, write the following code:

```
'Requires an Imports System.Threading directive

    Private Sub SimulateProcessing()
        Threading.Thread.SpinWait(80000000)
    End Sub

    Private Function GetThreadId() As String
        Return "Thread ID: " + Thread.CurrentThread.
                        ManagedThreadId.ToString
    End Function
```

TIP

The Thread.SpinWait method tells a thread that it has to wait for the specified number of iterations to be completed. You might often find this method in the code samples about parallel computing with the .NET Framework.

The `SimulateProcessing` method just simulates and performs intensive processing against fictitious data. `GetThreadId` can help demonstrate the TPL influence on threads management. Now in the `Sub Main` of the main module, write the following code that takes a `StopWatch` object for measuring elapsed time:

```
Dim sw As New Stopwatch
sw.Start()
'This comment will be replaced by
'the method executing the loop
sw.Stop()
Console.WriteLine("Elapsed: {0}", sw.Elapsed)
Console.ReadLine()
```

This code helps to measure time in both classic and parallel loops as explained soon.

> **NOTE**
>
> Remember that parallel loops get the most out in particular circumstances such as intensive processing. If you need to iterate a collection without heavy CPU business, parallel loops will probably not be helpful, and you should use classic loops. Choose parallel loops only when your processing is intensive enough to require the work of all the processors on your machine.

Parallel.For Loop

Writing a parallel `For` loop is an easy task, although it is important to remember that you can use parallelism against intensive and time-consuming operations. Imagine you want to invoke the code defined at the beginning of this section for a finite number of times to simulate an intensive processing. This is how you would do it with a classic `For` loop:

```
Sub ClassicForTest()
    For i = 0 To 15
        Console.WriteLine(i.ToString + GetThreadId())
        SimulateProcessing()
    Next
End Sub
```

Nothing new here; the code writes the thread identifier at each step and simulates an intensive processing. If you run the code, you get the result shown in Figure 43.1, where you can see how all the work relies on a single thread and how the loop result is ordered.

The next code snippet is how you write a parallel loop that accomplishes the same thing:

```
'Requires an Imports System.Threading.Tasks directive
    Sub ParallelForTest()
        Parallel.For(0, 16, Sub(i)
```

```
                              Console.WriteLine(i.ToString + _
                              GetThreadId())
                              SimulateProcessing()
                         End Sub)
          End Sub
```

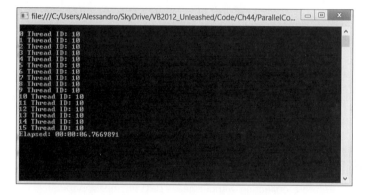

FIGURE 43.1   Running a classic `For` loop to demonstrate single threading.

`Parallel.For` receives three arguments: The first one is the "from" part of the `For` loop, the second one is the "to" part of the `For` loop (and it is exclusive to the loop), and the third is the action to take at each step. Such action is represented by a `System.Action(Of Integer)` that you write under the form of a statement lambda that takes a variable (`i` in the previous example) representing the loop counter. To provide a simpler explanation, the `Sub..End Sub` block in the statement lambda of the parallel loop contains the same code of the `For..Next` block in the classic loop. If you run the code, you can see how things change, as shown in Figure 43.2.

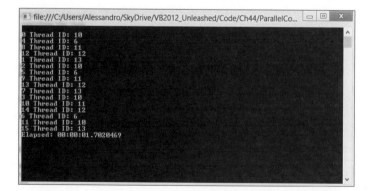

FIGURE 43.2   The parallel loop runs multiple threads and takes less time.

You immediately notice two things: The first one is that `Parallel.For` automatically splits the loop execution across multiple threads, differently from the classic loop in which the execution relied on a single thread. Multiple threads are shared across the multicore architecture of your machine, thus speeding up the loop. The second thing you notice is the speed of execution. Using a parallel loop running the previous example on my machine took about 5 seconds less than the classic loop. Because the loop execution is split across multiple threads, such threads run in parallel. This means that maintaining a sequential execution order is not possible with `Parallel.For` loops. As you can see from Figure 43.2, the iterations are not executed sequentially, and this is appropriate because it means that multiple operations are executed concurrently, which is the purpose of the TPL. Just be aware of this when architecting your code.

`Parallel.ForEach` Loop

Similarly to `For` loops, the `Parallel` class offers an implementation of `For..Each` loops for iterating items within a collection in parallel. Using the methods shown at the beginning of this section for retrieving thread information, simulate intensive processing and the measuring of elapsed time. Imagine you want to retrieve the list of image files in the user-level Pictures folder simulating an intensive processing over each filename. This task can be accomplished via a classic `For..Each` loop as follows:

```
Sub ClassicForEachTest()
    Dim allFiles = IO.Directory.
        EnumerateFiles("C:\users\alessandro\pictures")

    For Each fileName In allFiles
        Console.WriteLine(fileName + GetThreadId())
        SimulateProcessing()
    Next
End Sub
```

The intensive processing simulation still relies on a single thread and on a single processor; thus, it will be expensive in terms of time and system resources. Figure 43.3 shows the result of the loop.

FIGURE 43.3 Iterating items in a collection under intensive processing is expensive with a classic `For..Each` loop.

Fortunately, the Task Parallel Library enables you to iterate items in a collection concurrently. This is accomplished with the `Parallel.ForEach` method, which is demonstrated in the following code:

```
Sub ParallelForEachTest()

    Dim allFiles = IO.Directory.
                    EnumerateFiles("C:\users\alessandro\pictures")
    Parallel.ForEach(Of String)(allFiles, Sub(fileName)
                                    Console.WriteLine( _
                                    fileName + GetThreadId())
                                    SimulateProcessing()
                                End Sub)
End Sub
```

`Parallel.ForEach` is generic and therefore requires specifying the type of items in the collection. In this case the collection is an `IEnumerable(Of String)`, so ForEach takes `(Of String)` as the generic parameter. Talking about arguments, the first one is the collection to iterate, whereas the second one is an `Action(Of T)`. Therefore, it's a reference to a delegate or a statement lambda like in the preceding example, representing the action to take over each item in the collection. If you run the code snippet, you get the result shown in Figure 43.4.

FIGURE 43.4   Performing a `Parallel.ForEach` loop speeds up intensive processing over items in the collection.

The difference is evident. The parallel loop completes processing in almost 10 seconds less than the classic loop on my machine; this is because the parallel loop automatically runs multiple threads for splitting the operation across multiple units of work. Specifically, it takes full advantage of the multicore processor's architecture of the running machine to take the most from system resources.

Partitioning Improvements in .NET 4.5

When a `Parallel.ForEach` loop (and PLINQ queries as well) processes an `IEnumerable`, the runtime uses a default partitioning scheme that involves chunking. This means that every time a thread goes back to the `IEnumerable` to fetch more items, the thread can take multiple items at a time. This provides optimal performances but involves buffering items, which is not always an appropriate approach for some situations. For instance, if you think of data going over networks, you might prefer to process a single data item as soon as it is received rather than waiting for multiple items to be received and processed concurrently. The .NET Framework 4.5 introduces a new enumeration called `System.Collections.Concurrent.EnumerablePartitionerOptions` that enables you to specify whether the runtime should not use the default partitioning scheme and, consequently, avoid the buffering. The following code provides an example with the `Parallel.ForEach` loop that you saw previously:

```
'With no buffering
Parallel.ForEach(Of String)(Partitioner.Create(allFiles,
        EnumerablePartitionerOptions.NoBuffering),
            Sub()
                Console.WriteLine(fileName + GetThreadId())
                SimulateProcessing()
            End Sub)
```

You invoke the `Create` shared method of the `System.Collections.Concurrent.Partitioner` class to specify both the `IEnumerable` source and the partitioning scheme. `PartitionerOptions` has two values: `NoBuffering`, which avoids buffering, and `None` which is the default partitioning scheme (and that you can eventually avoid, using the normal syntax described previously in the "`Parallel.ForEach` Loop" section).

The `ParallelLoopState` Class

The `System.Threading.Tasks.ParallelLoopState` enables you to get information on the state of parallel loops such as `Parallel.For` and `Parallel.ForEach`. For example, you can find out whether a loop has been stopped via the Boolean property `IsStopped` or whether the loop threw an exception via the `IsExceptional` property. Moreover, you can stop a loop with the `Break` and `Stop` methods. The first one requests the runtime to stop the loop execution when possible, but including the current iteration. `Stop` does the same but excludes the current iteration. You need to pass a variable of type `ParallelLoopState` to the delegate invoked for the loop or let the compiler infer the type as in the following example:

```
'The compiler infers ParallelLoopState
'for the loopState identifier
Parallel.For(0, 16, Sub(i, loopState)
                    Console.WriteLine(i.ToString + _
                            GetThreadId())
                    SimulateProcessing()
```

43

```
            If loopState.IsExceptional Then
                'an exception occurred
            End If


            'Breaks the loop at the 10th iteration
            If i = 10 Then
                loopState.Break()
            End If
        End Sub)
```

Debugging Tools for Parallel Tasks

Visual Studio 2012 offers two useful tool windows that you can use for debugging purposes when working on both parallel tasks and loops. To understand how such tooling works, consider the following code that creates and starts three tasks:

```
Sub CreateSomeTaks()
    Dim taskA = Task.Factory.StartNew(Sub() Console.WriteLine("Task A"))
    Dim taskB = Task.Factory.StartNew(Sub() Console.WriteLine("Task B"))
    Dim taskC = Task.Factory.StartNew(Sub() Console.WriteLine("Task C"))
End Sub
```

Place a breakpoint on the End Sub statement and run the code. Because the tasks work in parallel, some of them may be running at this point and others may not be. To understand what is happening, you can open the **Parallel Tasks** tool window (select Debug, Windows, Parallel Tasks if not already visible). This window shows the state of each task, as represented in Figure 43.5.

	ID	Status	Location	Task	Thread Assignment	AppDomain	Process
▼	1	Active		Action<object>	7644 (Worker Thread)	1 (ParallelComputing.vshost.exe)	7016
▼	2	Scheduled		_Lambda$_3		1 (ParallelComputing.vshost.exe)	7016

FIGURE 43.5   The Parallel Tasks tool window.

Among the other information, such a window shows the task ID, the status (that is, if it is running, scheduled, waiting, dead-locked, or completed), the delegate that is making the actual job (in the Task column), and the actual thread that refers to the task. Next, you can use the **Parallel Stacks** tool window (which can be enabled via Debug, Windows, Parallel Stacks) that shows the call stack for threads and their relationships. Figure 43.6 shows an example.

For each thread the window shows information that you can investigate by right-clicking each row.

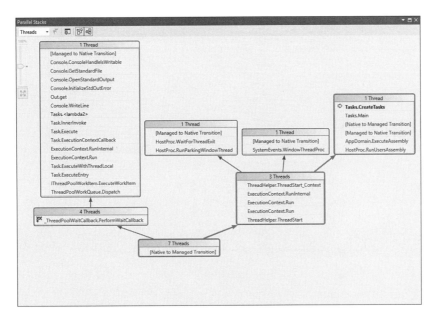

FIGURE 43.6   The Parallel Stacks window.

Concurrent Collections

Parallel computing relies on multithreading, although with some particular specifications for taking advantage of multicore architectures. The real problem is when you need to work with collections because in a multithreaded environment, multiple threads could access a collection attempting to make edits that need to be controlled. The .NET Framework 4.5 retakes from its predecessor a number of *thread-safe* concurrent collections, exposed by the `System.Collections.Concurrent` namespace, which is useful in parallel computing with .NET Framework because they grant concurrent access to their members from threads.

WHAT DOES THREAD-SAFE MEAN?

A collection is *thread-safe* when access to its members is allowed to only one thread per time (or to a few threads in particular cases).

Table 43.1 summarizes concurrent collections in .NET 4.5.

TABLE 43.1   Available Concurrent Collections

Collection	Description
ConcurrentBag(Of T)	Represents an unordered collection of items
ConcurrentQueue(Of T)	Represents a concurrent FIFO collection
ConcurrentStack(Of T)	Represents a concurrent LIFO collection

Collection	Description
ConcurrentDictionary(Of TKey, TValue)	Represents a concurrent Dictionary(Of TKey, TValue)
BlockingCollection(Of T)	A thread-safe collection with bounding and blocking capabilities against threads

The first four listed collections are essentially thread-safe implementations of generic collections you already learned in Chapter 16, "Working with Collections and Iterators." BlockingCollection is a little bit more complex but interesting.

ConcurrentBag(Of T)

The ConcurrentBag(Of T) is the most basic concurrent collection, in that it is just an unordered collection of items. The following code demonstrates how you use it for adding, iterating, counting, and removing items:

```
'Creating an instance
Dim cb As New ConcurrentBag(Of String)

'Adding some items
cb.Add("String one")
cb.Add("String two")
cb.Add("String three")

'Showing items count
Console.WriteLine(cb.Count)

'Listing items in the collection
For Each item In cb
    Console.WriteLine(item)
Next

'Removing an item
Dim anItem As String = String.Empty
cb.TryTake(anItem)
Console.WriteLine(anItem)
```

You add items to the collection by invoking the Add method. The Count property gets the number of items in the collection, and the IsEmpty property tells you whether the collection is empty. To remove an item, you invoke TryTake, which takes the first item, assigns it to the result variable (in this case anItem), and then removes it from the collection. It returns True if removing succeeds; otherwise, it returns False. Keep in mind that this collection offers no order for items; therefore, iteration results are completely random.

ConcurrentQueue(Of T)

The `ConcurrentQueue(Of T)` collection is just a thread-safe implementation of the `Queue(Of T)` collection, so it takes the logic of FIFO (first in, first out), where the first element in the collection is the first to be removed. The following code shows an example:

```
'Creating an instance
Dim cq As New ConcurrentQueue(Of Integer)

'Adding items
cq.Enqueue(1)
cq.Enqueue(2)

'Removing an item from the queue
Dim item As Integer
cq.TryDequeue(item)
Console.WriteLine(item)

'Returns "1":
Console.WriteLine(cq.Count)
```

The main difference with `Queue` is how items are removed from the queue. In this concurrent implementation, you invoke `TryDequeue`, which passes the removed item to a result variable by reference. The method returns `True` in case of success; otherwise, it returns `False`. Still the `Count` property returns the number of items in the queue.

ConcurrentStack(Of T)

`ConcurrentStack(Of T)` is the thread-safe implementation of the `Stack(Of T)` generic collection and works according to the LIFO (last in, first out) logic. The following code shows an example of using this collection:

```
'Creating an instance
Dim cs As New ConcurrentStack(Of Integer)

'Adding an item
cs.Push(1)
'Adding an array
cs.PushRange(New Integer() {10, 5, 10, 20})


Dim items() As Integer = New Integer(3) {}

'Removing an array
cs.TryPopRange(items, 0, 4)
```

```
'Iterating the array
Array.ForEach(Of Integer)(items, Sub(i)
                                      Console.WriteLine(i)
                                  End Sub)
```

```
'Removing an item
Dim anItem As Integer
cs.TryPop(anItem)
Console.WriteLine(anItem)
```

The big difference between this collection and its thread-unsafe counterpart is that you can also add an array of items invoking `PushRange`, but you still invoke `Push` to add a single item. To remove an array from the stack, you invoke `TryPopRange`, which takes three arguments: the target array that will store the removed items, the start index, and the number of items to remove. Both `PushRange` and `TryPopRange` return a Boolean value indicating whether they succeeded. The `Array.ForEach` loop in the preceding code is just an example for demonstrating how the array was actually removed from the collection. Finally, you invoke `TryPop` for removing an item from the stack; this item is then assigned to a result variable, passed by reference.

ConcurrentDictionary(Of TKey, TValue)

The `ConcurrentDictionary` collection has the same purpose as its thread-unsafe counterpart, but it differs in how methods work. All methods for adding, retrieving, and removing items return a Boolean value indicating success or failure, and their names all start with `Try`. The following code shows an example:

```
'Where String is for names and Integer for ages
Dim cd As New ConcurrentDictionary(Of String, Integer)

Dim result As Boolean

'Adding some items
result = cd.TryAdd("Alessandro", 35)
result = cd.TryAdd("Nadia", 31)
result = cd.TryAdd("Robert", 38)

'Removing an item
result = cd.TryRemove("Nadia", 31)

'Getting a value for the specified key
Dim value As Integer
result = cd.TryGetValue("Alessandro", value)

Console.WriteLine(value)
```

The logic of the collection is then the same as `Dictionary`, so refer to this one for details.

BlockingCollection(Of T)

The BlockingCollection(Of T) is a special concurrent collection. At the highest level such a collection has two characteristics. The first is that if a thread attempts to retrieve items from the collection while it is empty, the thread is blocked until some items are added to the collection. The second one is that if a thread attempts to add items to the collection, but this has reached the maximum number of items possible; the thread is blocked until some space is freed in the collection. Another interesting feature is completion. You can mark the collection as complete so that no other items can be added. This is accomplished via the CompleteAdding instance method. After you invoke this method, if a thread attempts to add items, an InvalidOperationException is thrown. The following code shows how to create a BlockingCollection for strings:

```
Dim bc As New BlockingCollection(Of String)

bc.Add("First")
bc.Add("Second")
bc.Add("Third")
bc.Add("Fourth")

'Marks the collection as complete
bc.CompleteAdding()

'Returns an exception
'bc.Add("Fifth")

'Removes an item from the collection (FIFO)
Dim result = bc.Take()
Console.WriteLine(result)
```

You add items invoking the Add method, and you mark the collection complete with CompleteAdding. To remove an item, you invoke Take. This method removes the first item added to the collection, according to the FIFO approach. This is because the BlockingCollection is not actually a storage collection, though it creates a ConcurrentQueue behind the scenes, adding blocking logic to this one. The class also exposes some properties:

- ▶ BoundedCapacity—Returns the bounded capacity for the collection. You can provide the capacity via the constructor. If not, the property returns -1 as the value indicating that it's a growing collection.

- ▶ IsCompleted—Indicates whether the collection has been marked with CompleteAdding, and it is also empty.

- ▶ IsAddingCompleted—Indicates whether the collection has been marked with CompleteAdding.

The class has other interesting characteristics. For example, the beginning of the discussion explained why it is considered blocking. By the way, it also offers methods whose names all begin with `Try`, such as `TryAdd` and `TryTake`, which provides overloads that enable doing their respective work without being blocked. The last feature of the `BlockingCollection` is a number of static methods that you can use for adding and removing items to and from multiple `BlockingCollection` instances simultaneously, both blocking and nonblocking. These methods are `AddToAny`, `TakeFromAny`, `TryAddToAny`, and `TryTakeFromAny`. The following code shows an example of adding a string to multiple instances of the collection:

```
Dim collection1 As New BlockingCollection(Of String)
Dim collection2 As New BlockingCollection(Of String)

Dim colls(1) As BlockingCollection(Of String)
colls(0) = collection1
colls(1) = collection2

BlockingCollection(Of String).AddToAny(colls, "anItem")
```

All the mentioned methods take an array of collections; this is the reason for the code implementation as previously illustrated.

Introducing Parallel LINQ

Parallel LINQ, also known as *PLINQ*, is a special LINQ implementation provided by .NET Framework 4.5 that enables developers to query data using the LINQ syntax but uses multicore and multiprocessor architectures that have support by the Task Parallel Library. Creating "parallel" queries is an easy task, although there are some architectural differences with classic LINQ (or more with classic programming). These are discussed during this chapter. To create a parallel query, you just need to invoke the `AsParallel` extension method onto the data source you are querying. The following code provides an example:

```
Dim range = Enumerable.Range(0, 1000)

'Just add "AsParallel"
Dim query = From num In range.AsParallel
            Where (IsOdd(num))
            Select num
```

You can use Parallel LINQ and the Task Parallel Library only in particular scenarios, such as intensive calculations or large amounts of data. Because of this, to give you an idea of how PLINQ can improve performance, the code presented in this chapter simulates intensive work on easier code so that you can focus on PLINQ instead of other code.

Simulating an Intensive Work

Parallel LINQ provides benefits when you work in extreme situations such as intensive works or large amounts of data. In different situations, PLINQ is not necessarily better than classic LINQ. To understand how PLINQ works, first we need to write code that simulates an intensive work. After creating a new Console project, write the following method that determines whether a number is odd but suspends the current thread for several milliseconds by invoking the `System.Threading.Thread.SpinWait` shared method:

```
'Checks if a number is odd
Private Function IsOdd(ByVal number As Integer) As Boolean
    'Simulate an intensive work
    System.Threading.Thread.SpinWait(1000000)
    Return (number Mod 2) <> 0
End Function
```

Now that we have an intensive work, we can compare both the classic and parallel LINQ queries.

Measuring Performances of a Classic LINQ Query

The goal of this paragraph is to explain how you can execute a classic LINQ query over intensive processing and measure its performance in milliseconds. Consider the following code:

```
Private Sub ClassicLinqQuery()
    Dim range = Enumerable.Range(0, 1000)

    Dim query = From num In range
                Where (IsOdd(num))
                Select num

    'Measuring performance
    Dim sw As Stopwatch = Stopwatch.StartNew

    'Linq query is executed when invoking Count
    Console.WriteLine("Total odd numbers: " + query.Count.ToString)
    sw.Stop()
    Console.WriteLine(sw.ElapsedMilliseconds.ToString)
    Console.ReadLine()
End Sub
```

Given a range of predefined numbers (`Enumerable.Range`), the code looks for odd numbers and collects them into an `IEnumerable(Of Integer)`. To measure performance, we can use the `Stopwatch` class that starts a counter (`Stopwatch.StartNew`). Because, as you already know, LINQ queries are executed when you use them, such a query is executed when the code invokes the `Count` property to show how many odd numbers are stored within the query variable. When done, the counter is stopped so that we can get the number of milliseconds needed to perform the query itself. By the way, measuring time is not enough. The real goal is to understand how the CPU is used and how a LINQ query impacts performance. To accomplish this, on Windows 8 right-click the **Windows Task Bar** and start the **Task Manager**. Then click the **Performance** tab, and then click the **Open Resource Monitor**. This provides a way for looking at the CPU usage while running your code. If you are running Windows 7 or Windows Vista with Service Pack 2, you will not need to open any resource monitor because the Task Manager provides all you need in the main window (just select the Always on Top option for a better view). The previous code, which can be run by invoking the `ClassicLinqQuery` from the `Main` method, produces the following result on my dual-core machine:

```
Total odd numbers: 500
3667
```

This means that executing a query versus the intensive processing took about 3 1/2 seconds. The other interesting thing is about the CPU usage. Figure 43.7 shows that during the processing, the CPU was used for a medium percentage of resources. Obviously, this percentage can vary depending on the machine and on the running processes and applications.

FIGURE 43.7   CPU usage during a classic LINQ query.

That CPU usage was not full is not necessarily good because it means that all the work relies on a single thread and is considered as if it were running on a single processor. Therefore, an overload of work exists for only some resources while other resources are free. To scale the work over multiple threads and multiple processors, a Parallel LINQ query is more efficient.

Measuring Performances of a PLINQ Query

To create a parallel query, you need to invoke the `AsParallel` extension method for the data source you want to query. Copy the method shown in the previous paragraph and rename it as `PLinqQuery`; then change the first line of the query as follows:

```
Dim query = From num In range.AsParallel
```

Different from a LINQ query, `AsParallel` returns a `ParallelQuery(Of T)` that is exposed by the `System.Linq` namespace and that is specific for PLINQ. However, it works as an `IEnumerable(Of T)` but enables you to scale data over multicore processors. Now edit `Sub Main` so that it invokes the `PLinqQuery` method and runs the code again. Figure 43.8 shows what you should see when the application is processing data.

FIGURE 43.8   CPU usage during a Parallel LINQ query.

It is worth noticing how all processors are being used, which is demonstrated by the peaks of CPU usage. Processing was scaled along all available processors. On my dual-core machine, the previous code produces the following result:

```
Total odd numbers: 500
2512
```

The PLINQ query took only 2 1/2 seconds, which is less than the classic LINQ query result. So, PLINQ can dramatically improve your code performance, although there are some other considerations, as discussed in the next paragraphs.

> **CONVERTING TO SEQUENTIAL QUERIES**
>
> PLINQ queries are evaluated in parallel, meaning that they use multicore architectures— also thanks to the `ParallelQuery(Of T)` class. If you want to convert such a result into an `IEnumerable (Of T)` and provide sequential evaluation of the query, you can invoke the `AsSequential` extension method from the query result variable.

Ordering Sequences

One of the most important consequences of Parallel LINQ (and, more generally, of parallel computing) is that processing is not done sequentially as it would happen on single-threaded code. This is because multiple threads run concurrently. To understand this, the following is an excerpt from the iteration on the result of the parallel query:

```
295
315
297
317
299
319
```

You would probably expect something like the following instead, which is produced by the classic LINQ query:

```
295
296
297
298
299
300
```

If you need to work in sequential order but do not want to lose the capabilities of PLINQ query, you can invoke the `AsOrdered` extension method that preserves the sequential order of the result, as demonstrated by the following code snippet:

```
Dim query = From num In range.AsParallel.AsOrdered
```

If you now run the code again, you get an ordered set of odd numbers.

`AsParallel` and Binary Operators

In some situations you use operators that take two data sources; among such operators, there are the following binary operators: `Join`, `GroupJoin`, `Except`, `Concat`, `Intersect`, `Union`, `Zip`, and `SequenceEqual`. To use parallelism with binary operators on two data sources, you need to invoke `AsParallel` on both collections, as demonstrated by the following code:

```
Dim result = firstSource.AsParallel.Except(secondSource.AsParallel)
```

The following code still works, but it won't use parallelism:

```
Dim result = firstSource.AsParallel.Except(secondSource)
```

Using `ParallelEnumerable`

The `System.Linq` namespace for .NET 4.5 provides the `ParallelEnumerable` class, which is the parallel counterpart of `Enumerable` and provides extension methods specific to parallelism, such as `AsParallel`. You can use `ParallelEnumerable` members instead of invoking `AsParallel` because both return a `ParallelQuery(Of T)`. For example, the PLINQ query in the first example could be rewritten as follows:

```
Dim range = ParallelEnumerable.Range(0, 1000)

'Just add "AsParallel"
Dim query = From num In range
            Where (IsOdd(num))
            Select num
```

In this case the range variable is of type `ParallelEnumerable(Of Integer)`, and therefore you do not need to invoke `AsParallel`. Some differences in how data is handled do exist, which can often lead `AsParallel` to be faster. Explaining in detail the `ParallelEnumerable` architecture is beyond the scope in this introductory chapter, but if you are curious you can take a look at this blog post from the Task Parallel Library Team, which is still valid today: http://blogs.msdn.com/pfxteam/archive/2007/12/02/6558579.aspx.

Controlling PLINQ Queries

PLINQ offers additional extension methods and features to provide more control over tasks that run queries, all exposed by the `System.Linq.ParallelEnumerable` class. In this section you get an overview of extension methods and learn how you can control your PLINQ queries.

Setting the Maximum Tasks Number

As explained previously in this chapter, the Task Parallel Library relies on tasks instead of threads, although working with tasks means scaling processing over multiple threads. You can specify the maximum number of tasks that can execute a thread by invoking the `WithDegreeOfParallelism` extension method and passing the number as an argument.

The following code demonstrates how you can get the list of running processes with a PLINQ query that runs a maximum of three concurrent tasks:

```
Dim processes = Process.GetProcesses.
                AsParallel.WithDegreeOfParallelism(3)
```

Forcing Parallelism in Every Query

Not all code can benefit from parallelism and PLINQ. Such technology is intelligent enough to determine whether a query can benefit from PLINQ according to its *shape*. The shape of a query consists of the operator it requires and algorithm or delegates that are involved. PLINQ analyzes the shape and can determine where to apply a parallel algorithm. You can force a query to be completely parallelized, regardless of its shape, by invoking the WithExecutionMode extension methods that receive an argument of type ParallelExecutionMode that is an enumeration exposing two self-explanatory members: ForceParallelism and Default. The following code demonstrates how you can force a query to be completely parallelized:

```
Dim processes = Process.GetProcesses.
                AsParallel.WithExecutionMode( _
                ParallelExecutionMode.ForceParallelism)
```

.NET 4.5 IMPROVEMENTS

Due to some internal implementations, in the first version of PLINQ in .NET 4.0 the compiler determined that some parallel queries would run with better performance if executed sequentially. This was the case of queries involving some particular operators such as OrderBy and Take. In .NET 4.5, a lot of improvements have been brought to Parallel LINQ and now most of the issues have been solved so that most queries can run in parallel.

Merge Options

PLINQ automatically partitions query sources so that it can use multiple threads that can work on each part concurrently. You can control how parts are handled by invoking the WithMergeOptions method that receives an argument of type ParallelMergeOptions. Such enumeration provides the following specifications:

▶ NotBuffered—Returns elements composing the result as soon as they are available

▶ FullyBuffered—Returns the complete result, meaning that query operations are buffered until every one has been completed

▶ AutoBuffered—Leaves to the compiler to choose the best buffering method in that particular situation

You invoke `WithMergeOptions` as follows:

```
Dim processes = Process.GetProcesses.
                AsParallel.WithMergeOptions( _
                ParallelMergeOptions.FullyBuffered)
```

With the exception of the `ForAll` method that is always `NotBuffered` and `OrderBy` that is always `FullyBuffered`, other extension methods/operators can support all merge options. The full list of operators is described in the following page of the MSDN Library: http://msdn.microsoft.com/en-us/library/dd547137(v=vs.110).aspx.

Canceling PLINQ Queries

If you need to provide a way for canceling a PLINQ query, you can invoke the `WithCancellation` method. You first need to implement a method to be invoked when you need to cancel the query. The method receives a `CancellationTokenSource` argument (which sends notices that a query must be canceled) and can be implemented as follows:

```
Dim cs As New CancellationTokenSource

Private Sub DoCancel(ByVal cs As CancellationTokenSource)
    'Ensures that query is cancelled when executing
    Thread.Sleep(500)
    cs.Cancel()
End Sub
```

When you have a method of this kind, you need to start a new task by pointing to this method as follows:

```
Tasks.Task.Factory.StartNew(Sub()
                                DoCancel(cs)
                            End Sub)
```

When a PLINQ query is canceled, an `OperationCanceledException` is thrown so that you can handle cancellation, as demonstrated in the following code snippet:

```
Private Sub CancellationDemo()
    Try

        Dim processes = Process.GetProcesses.
                        AsParallel.WithCancellation(cs.Token)

    Catch ex As OperationCanceledException
        Console.WriteLine(ex.Message)
    Catch ex As Exception

    End Try
End Sub
```

To cancel a query, invoke the `DoCancel` method.

Handling Exceptions

In single-core scenarios, LINQ queries are executed sequentially. This means that if your code encounters an exception, the exception is at a specific point, and the code can handle it normally. In multicore scenarios, multiple exceptions could occur because more threads are running on multiple processors concurrently. Because of this, PLINQ uses the `AggregateException` class, which is specific for exceptions within parallelism and has already been discussed in this chapter. With PLINQ, you might find useful two members: `Flatten` is a method that turns it into a single exception, and `InnerExceptions` is a property storing a collection of `InnerException` objects. Each represents one of the occurred exceptions.

DISABLE "JUST MY CODE"

As you did for Task Parallel Library samples shown previously, to correctly catch an `AggregateException` you need to disable the Just My Code debugging in the debug options; otherwise, the code execution will break on the query and will not enable you to investigate the exception.

Consider the following code, in which an array of strings stores some null values and causes `NullReferenceException` at runtime:

```
Private Sub HandlingExceptions()
    Dim strings() As String = New String() {"Test",
                                            Nothing,
                                            Nothing,
                                            "Test"}

    'Just add "AsParallel"
    Try
        Dim query = strings.AsParallel.
                    Where(Function(s) s.StartsWith("T")).
                    Select(Function(s) s)
        For Each item In query
            Console.WriteLine(item)
        Next

    Catch ex As AggregateException

        For Each problem In ex.InnerExceptions
            Console.WriteLine(problem.ToString)
        Next

    Catch ex As Exception
```

```
    Finally
        Console.ReadLine()
    End Try
End Sub
```

In a single-core scenario, a single `NullReferenceException` is caught and handled the first time the code encounters the error. In multicore scenarios, an `AggregateException` could happen due to multiple threads running on multiple processors; therefore, you cannot control where and how many exceptions can be thrown. Consequently, the `AggregateException` stores information on such exceptions. The previous code shows how you can iterate the `InnerExceptions` property.

Summary

Parallel computing enables you to use multicore architectures for scaling operation execution across all available processors on the machine. In this chapter, you learned how parallel computing in .NET Framework 4.5 relies on the concept of task; for this, you learned how to create and run tasks via the `System.Threading.Tasks.Task` class to generate units of work for running tasks in parallel. You also learned how to handle concurrent exceptions and request tasks cancellation. Another important topic in parallel computing is loops. Here you learned how the `Parallel.For` and `Parallel.ForEach` loops enable multithreaded iterations that are scaled across all available processors. Next, you took a tour inside the concurrent collections in .NET Framework 4.5, a set of thread-safe collections you can use to share information across tasks. Finally, you got information about a specific LINQ implementation known as Parallel LINQ that enables you to scale query executions over multiple threads and processors so that you can get the benefits in improving performances of your code. Specifically, you learned how to invoke the `AsParallel` method for creating parallelized queries and comparing them to classic LINQ queries. You also saw how to control queries forcing parallelism, implementing cancellation, setting the maximum number of tasks, and handling the `AggregateException` exception.

Asynchronous Programming

When you go to the restaurant, there are waiters and waitresses ready to serve your table. A waiter takes your order, brings the order to the kitchen, goes to serve another table, and then comes back to your table to bring you your meals. While waiting for you to finish, the waiter does similar operations for other patrons. So, the waiter does not stand at your table from when you arrive until you finish your meal before going to serve another table; if he did, the restaurant would need to hire one waiter per table to avoid the block of their activity, which is not practical. If you compare this real-world description with computer programming, the waiter is some code in your application. If this code must perform a long-running operation and you write such a code in the user interface (UI) thread or, more generally, in one thread, your code will act like a waiter that waits from the start to the end of the meal on a table and cannot do anything else in the meantime, thereby blocking the application activity. This is what happens when you write code in a synchronous approach; synchronous code performs one task at a time and the next task starts only when the previous one completes. To avoid blocking the application, you can use multithreading and instances of the Thread class, described in Chapter 42, "Processes and Multithreading." With multithreading, you can write code that performs a long-running operation on a separate thread and keep the application responsive. Threading is a way to write asynchronous code that developers have been using for a long time, along with two patterns: the Event-based Asynchronous Pattern and the Asynchronous Programming Model. But actually, asynchrony does not necessarily mean running on a background thread. Instead, it means that a task is executed in different moments. Threading is one way to achieve asynchrony, but it is quite complex and not always the best choice. For this reason, Microsoft introduced new libraries and new keywords to the Visual Basic and Visual C# languages to make asynchronous call easy. In this chapter, you get an overview of both the Event-based Asynchronous Pattern and the Asynchronous Programming Model; then you learn about the new Asynchronous Pattern, which is without a doubt the most important new feature in Visual Basic 2012. You will see how easily you can now write modern and responsive applications via asynchronous code.

Overview of Asynchrony

Modern applications often need to perform complex computations or access resources through a network. Complex computations can become very long, a network resource might not be available, or the application might not scale well on the server. If the code that performs this kind of operation is running in the same thread as the caller, the thread gets blocked until all operations complete. If such a thread is the UI thread, the user interface becomes unresponsive and can no longer accept the user input until all operations have been completed. This type of approach is called *synchronous* because only one operation at a time is executed until all the processes are completed.

Having an unresponsive user interface is not acceptable in modern applications, so this is the place where asynchrony comes in. Asynchrony enables you to execute some pieces of code in a different thread or context, so that the caller thread never blocks. If this is the UI thread, the user interface remains responsive even if other operations are running. The other thread (or context) then tells the caller thread that an operation completed, regardless of the successful or unsuccessful result. The .NET Framework has been offering, for a long time, two thread-based approaches to asynchrony called *Event-based Asynchrony* and *Asynchronous Programming Model* in which you launch operations in a different thread and get notification of their completion via delegates. As you saw in Chapter 43, "Parallel Programming and Parallel LINQ," the .NET Framework 4.0 introduced the Task Parallel Library and the concept of parallelism. TPL makes it easier to create applications capable of scaling long-running operations across all the available processors. TPL also makes applications faster and more responsive while executing complex tasks concurrently, but this all about concurrency, which is not the same as asynchrony. In this chapter, you first learn about the Event-based Asynchrony and the Asynchronous Programming Model to get started with the important concepts; then you start putting your hands on the new possibilities offered by the .NET Framework 4.5. By doing so, it will be easier for you to compare the old way to the new way and understand why you should migrate your exiting code to use the new patterns.

Before .NET 4.5: Event-based Asynchrony

More often than not, applications need to perform multiple tasks at one time, while still remaining responsive to user interaction. One of the possibilities offered by the .NET Framework since the early days is the *Event-based Asynchronous Pattern* (*EAP*). A class that adheres to this pattern implements a number of methods whose names terminate with the

`Async` suffix and that execute some work on a different thread. Such methods mirror their synchronous counterparts, which instead run on the caller thread. Also, for each of these asynchronous methods, there is an event whose name terminates with the `Completed` suffix and that is raised when the asynchronous operation completes. This way, the caller gets notification of the completion. Because the user might want to cancel an asynchronous operation at a certain point, classes adhering to the EAP must also implement methods whose names terminate with `CancelAsync`, each related to one of the asynchronous methods that actually performs the requested work. When such work is completed, a delegate will handle the operation result before control is sent back to the caller; this delegate is also known as *callback*. This pattern also requires classes to support cancellation and progress reporting. To understand how EAP works, let's consider a simple example based on the `System.Net.WebClient` class, which enables you to access networks from client applications. Consider the following code:

```
Sub Main()
    Dim client As New System.Net.WebClient
    AddHandler client.DownloadStringCompleted,
            AddressOf client_DownloadStringCompleted

    client.DownloadStringAsync(New Uri("http://msdn.microsoft.com"))
End Sub
```

A new instance of the `WebClient` class is created. To receive notification of completion, you must subscribe the `DownloadStringCompleted` event (assuming you will download a string, but other methods and related events are available) and supply a delegate that will be invoked when the event is raised. After you have subscribed the event, you can then invoke the desired method; in the current example, it's the `WebClient.DownloadStringAsync` method that downloads contents from the specified URL as a string. If you write other lines of code after the invocation of `DownloadStringAsync`, these are not necessarily executed after the download operation has completed as it would instead happen in synchronous code. So, if you need to manipulate the result of an asynchronous operation, you must do it inside the callback, which is the delegate invoked after the completion event is raised. The following code provides an example:

```
Private Sub client_DownloadStringCompleted(sender As Object,
                                    e As DownloadStringCompletedEventArgs)

    If e.Error Is Nothing Then
        Console.WriteLine(XDocument.Parse(e.Result).ToString)
        Console.WriteLine("Done")
    End If
End Sub
```

As you can see, the `DownloadStringCompletedEventArgs` class contains information about the result of the asynchronous operation. Usually, a specific class inherits from `System.EventArgs` and stores the result of an asynchronous operation, one per asynchronous method. You can check for errors, and if everything is successful, you can then work with the `e.Result` property that contains the actual result of the task. Classes that adhere to

44

the EAP also enable you to report the progress of an asynchronous operation by exposing a `ProgressChanged` event. Continuing the previous example, the `WebClient` class exposes an event called `ProgressChanged` and a class called `DownloadProgressChangedEventArgs` that stores information about the operation progress. To handle such an event, you must first subscribe it like this:

```
AddHandler client.DownloadProgressChanged,
            AddressOf client_DownloadProgressChanged
```

You then handle the `ProgressChanged` event to report progress:

```
Private Sub client_DownloadProgressChanged(sender As Object,
                                            e As DownloadProgressChangedEventArgs)
    Console.WriteLine(e.ProgressPercentage)
    'Use e.BytesReceived for the number of bytes received in progress
    'Use e.TotalBytesToReceive to get the total bytes to be downloaded
End Sub
```

You can eventually use lambda expressions and statement lambdas as anonymous delegates, as demonstrated in the following code:

```
Private Sub Download()
    Dim client As New WebClient
    AddHandler client.DownloadStringCompleted,
            Sub(sender, e)
                If e.Error Is Nothing Then
                    Console.WriteLine(XDocument.
                                        Parse(e.Result).
                                        ToString)
                End If
            End Sub

    client.DownloadStringAsync(New Uri("http://msdn.microsoft.com"))
End Sub
```

The EAP has been very popular among developers for years because the way you write code is similar to how you handle events of the user interface. This certainly makes the asynchronous approach simpler. Later in this chapter, when comparing EAP to the new Async pattern, you will better understand why the old way can lead to confusion and become very complex to handle.

Before .NET 4.5: The Asynchronous Programming Model

The Asynchronous Programming Model (APM) is still based on threading. In this model, an operation is launched on a separated thread via a method whose name starts with `Begin` (e.g. `BeginWrite`). A method like this must accept, among its parameters, an argument of type `IAsyncResult`. This is a special type used to store the result and the state of an asynchronous operation. The most important members of this interface are two properties: `AsyncState` (of type `Object`), which represents the result of the operation under the form of either a primitive or a composite type, and `IsCompleted` (of type `Boolean`), which returns if the operation actually completed. As another parameter, these methods must receive a delegate that will be executed when the asynchronous operation is completing. Within this delegate, you will be able to analyze the result of the asynchronous operation, but you will also need to explicitly end the asynchronous operation by invoking a method whose name starts with `End` (e.g. `EndWrite`). Some classes in the .NET Framework are built to be APM-ready, such as `Stream` and its derived classes. So, to demonstrate how APM works, we can consider an example based on the `FileStream` class. The following code demonstrates how to write some bytes to a stream asynchronously and how the callback receives information from the caller with `IAsyncResult`.

```
Private Sub OpenStreamAsync()
    Dim someBytes(1000) As Byte
    Dim randomGenerator As New Random()
    'Generate a random sequence of bytes
    randomGenerator.NextBytes(someBytes)

    Using fs As New FileStream("Somedata.dat", FileMode.Create, FileAccess.Write)
        Dim result As IAsyncResult =
            fs.BeginWrite(someBytes, 0, someBytes.Length,
                        AddressOf fs_EndWrite, fs)
    End Using

End Sub


Private Sub fs_EndWrite(result As IAsyncResult)
    Dim stream As FileStream = CType(result.AsyncState, FileStream)
    stream.EndWrite(result)
    'Additional work goes here...
End Sub
```

The `IAsyncResult.AsyncState` property contains the actual data sent from the caller and must be explicitly converted into the type that you need to work with; in this case, the stream. The reason is that you also must explicitly invoke the `EndWrite` method that finalizes the asynchronous operation. You can also pass custom objects as the `IAsyncResult` argument for the callback, to pass more complex and detailed information that you might need to elaborate when the task completes.

.NET 4.5: Introducing the Async Pattern

The .NET Framework 4.5 introduces a new pattern that solves some problems related to threading and enables you to write better and cleaner code. It does this by introducing two new keywords: `Async` and `Await`. `Async` is a modifier you use to mark methods that run asynchronous operations. `Await` is an operator that gets a placeholder for the result of an asynchronous operation and waits for the result, which will be sent back at a later time while other operations are executed. This enables you to keep the caller thread responsive. For a first understanding of how this pattern works, let's take a look at the following function that downloads the content of a website as a string, returning the result as an `XDocument` that can be manipulated with LINQ:

```
Function DownloadSite() As XDocument
    Dim client As New System.Net.WebClient
    Dim content As String =
        client.DownloadString("http://www.microsoft.com")

    Dim document As XDocument = XDocument.Parse(content)
    Return document
End Function
```

This code is pretty easy because it creates an instance of the `WebClient` class, then downloads the content of the specified website, and finally returns the XML document converted through `XDocument.Parse`. This code is synchronous, meaning that the caller thread will remain blocked until all the operations in the method body are completed. If the caller thread is the UI thread, the user interface will remain blocked. Figure 44.1 shows a graphical representation of how a synchronous call works.

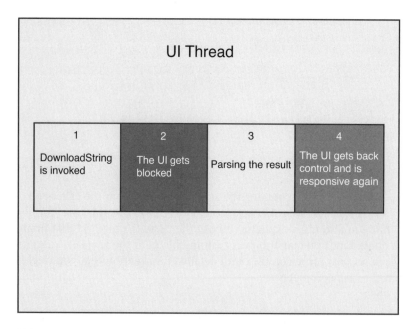

FIGURE 44.1   Representation of a synchronous call.

This is how you can rewrite the previous code using the Async pattern:

```
Async Function DownloadSiteAsync() As Task(Of XDocument)
    Dim client As New System.Net.WebClient
    Dim content As String =
        Await client.DownloadStringTaskAsync("http://www.microsoft.com")

    Dim document As XDocument = XDocument.Parse(content)

    Return document
End Function
```

Await AS A RESERVED KEYWORD

The `Await` keyword is not a reserved word everywhere in the code. It is a reserved word when it appears inside a method or lambda marked with the `Async` modifier and only if it appears after that modifier. In all other cases, it is not a reserved word.

44

This code is asynchronous, so it will never block the caller thread because not all the code is executed at the same time. Figure 44.2 shows a representation of an asynchronous call.

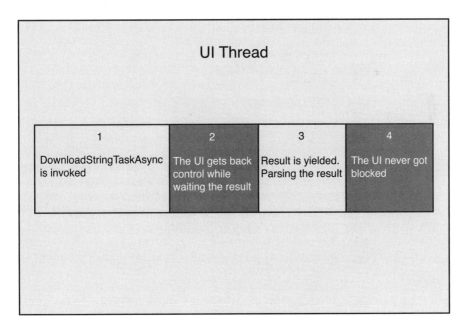

FIGURE 44.2   Representation of an asynchronous call.

THE STORY OF THREADS WITH `Async/Await`

The `Async` pattern relies on the concept of `Task` described in the previous chapter. For this reason, asynchronous code written with `Async/Await` does not necessarily run on a separate thread. In fact, it is represented by an instance of the `Task` class. Because one thread can run multiple `Task` instances, it is normal that asynchronous code can run in the same caller thread, such as the UI thread.

The following is a list of important considerations that will be discussed in the next section:

▶ A method that runs asynchronous code must be marked with the `Async` modifier. When the compiler encounters this modifier, it expects an `Await` expression inside the method body.

▶ Methods marked with `Async` are also referred to as *asynchronous methods.*

▶ By convention, names of asynchronous methods must end with the `Async` suffix.

▶ Asynchronous methods must return a `Task` (if they return no value) or a `Task(Of T)`, where T is the type that you would return with synchronous methods. See the previous `XDocument` example.

▶ Asynchronous methods support the standard access modifiers (such as `Private`, `Public`, and so on), but they cannot be iterator methods at the same time, so the `Iterator` modifier cannot be used along with `Async`.

▶ The `Main` method of an application can never be asynchronous. Notice that if you mark the `Main` method as asynchronous and write asynchronous calls in its body, the background compiler will not throw any warnings or exceptions. It will raise an error when you compile or try to run the code.

▶ Any method that returns a `Task` or `Task(Of T)` can be used along with `Await` ("awaitable").

▶ The `Await` expression puts a placeholder for the result of the invoked task. The result will be returned later at some time, making the application remain responsive. However, the next code will actually run when the result has been returned. This is because the compiler ideally splits the method into two parts; the second part is nothing but a callback that is executed when the awaited task notifies the caller of its completion.

▶ Although you should return a `Task` or `Task(Of T)`, the compiler automatically infers the task-based type even if you return the original type. The second code snippet in the previous example demonstrates how the `Return` statement returns `XDocument` but the compiler automatically infers `Task(Of XDocument)`.

Although these first important considerations might sound confusing, you will soon appreciate the benefits of using the `Async` pattern. It enables you to avoid multithreading and explicit callbacks, enabling you to write much easier and cleaner code. In the next section, you get started with the `Async` pattern with a practical example so that all the concepts described so far will be explained better.

Where Do I Use Async?

The Async libraries are in the .NET Framework 4.5, so you can use the new pattern in whatever technology uses .NET 4.5. WPF, Windows Forms, ASP.NET, Silverlight, or Silverlight for Windows Phone. These are all technologies that can leverage the power of the new libraries. If you want to use Async with ASP.NET, remember to add an `Async="true"` attribute in the XHTML code of the page where you are going to write asynchronous code:

```
<Page Async="True" .... />
```

In other words, you have no limits in using the new pattern and should always use this new way to asynchrony.

> **ASYNC AND WINDOWS 8 STORE APPS**
>
> There is another important reason beyond the availability of the Async pattern in .NET languages now: developing Windows 8 Store Apps. Windows 8 Apps require you to write most of the code asynchronously, and using old techniques would make developing apps really difficult. Instead, with the Async pattern, coding for Windows 8 is much faster, easier, and cleaner. Because the user interface of Windows 8 Apps must always be responsive with no exceptions, using the Async pattern is very common. This is another reason to read this chapter with particular attention.

When and Why to Use `Async/Await` and Comparisons with the TPL

Using the Async pattern enables you to write applications that are more responsive and that perform better, but you will not use it everywhere. In fact, there are specific situations in which Async has benefits. As a general rule, Async's main purpose is to keep the UI responsive while tasks running in the UI thread might become potentially blocking. You use Async in the following scenarios:

▶ Potentially blocking tasks running in the user interface thread

▶ Working with images

▶ I/O operations (disk, networking, web access)

▶ Working with sockets

Using `Async` and `Await` differs from parallel programming because the purpose is not to have pieces of code that run concurrently; instead, the purpose is keeping the user interface responsive. In parallel programming, you have code that is CPU-consuming, so you use `Task` instances to split the execution of your code into multiple units of work. Thus, most of the code is executed at the same time by using a multicore architecture. In Async, instead, you do not have CPU-consuming code. You might have potentially blocking tasks, though, so your goal is to keep the UI thread free. This is possible because the result of an `Await` expression is delayed and control is yielded to the caller while waiting.

Getting Started with `Async/Await`

As usual, the best way to understand how a new technology works is through an example. In this section you see the Async pattern with an example based on retrieving information from the Internet. You will build a WPF application that downloads RSS feeds information from the Web, simulating a long-running process over a network. You first, though, create an application that works synchronously; then you see how to implement the Event-based Asynchronous Pattern described at the beginning of this chapter. Finally, you learn how things change in a third example built using the new `Async` and `Await` keywords.

The Synchronous Approach

Create a new WPF project with Visual Basic 2012 and .NET Framework 4.5. The application will consume the Open Data Protocol (OData) feed exposed by the Microsoft Research website, with particular regard to the list of published videos. Each item in the feed has a large number of properties, but for the sake of simplicity only the most important will be presented in the application's UI. So, the first thing you need to do is create a class that represents a single video described in the feed. Listing 44.1 demonstrates how to implement a class called `Video`.

LISTING 44.1   Representing a Single Video

```
Public Class Video
    Public Property Title As String
    Public Property Url As String
    Public Property Thumbnail As String
    Public Property DateRecorded As String
    Public Property Speaker As String

    Public Shared FeedUrl As String = _
        "http://odata.research.microsoft.com/odata.svc/Videos/"
End Class
```

Notice that all the properties are of type `String` just to represent values as they exactly come from the feed. Also, a shared field contains the feed URL. Because the code will use LINQ to XML to query the feed, you should add an XML schema via XML Schema Inference, which you learned in Chapter 27, "Manipulating XML Documents with LINQ and XML Literals." Select **Project**, **Add New Item** and select the **XML to Schema** item template, as represented in Figure 44.3.

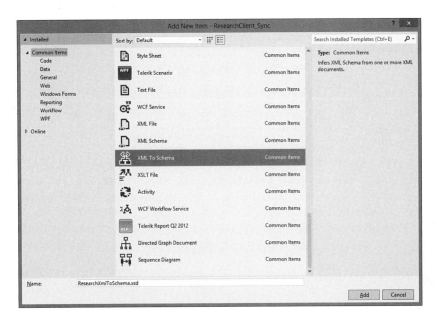

FIGURE 44.3   Adding an XML schema with XML Schema Inference.

Call the new item ResearchXmlToSchema.xsd for consistency with the book. Now open the MainWindow.xaml file, to prepare the application's user interface. The goal is to show the videos' thumbnails and summary information and to provide the ability to click a thumbnail to open the video in its original location. The ListBox control is a good choice to display a collection of items. This will be placed inside the default Grid panel. Each item in the ListBox will be presented via a custom template made of a Border and a StackPanel that contains an Image control (for the video thumbnail) and a number of TextBlock controls that are bound to properties of the Video class. Listing 44.2 shows the full code for the main window.

LISTING 44.2   Implementing the Application's User Interface

```
<Window x:Class="MainWindow"
    xmlns="http://schemas.microsoft.com/winfx/2006/xaml/presentation"
    xmlns:x="http://schemas.microsoft.com/winfx/2006/xaml"
    Title="MainWindow" Height="350" Width="525">
    <Grid>
        <ListBox Name="VideoBox" ItemsSource="{Binding}"
                ScrollViewer.HorizontalScrollBarVisibility="Disabled">
            <ListBox.ItemsPanel>
                <ItemsPanelTemplate>
                    <WrapPanel VirtualizingPanel.IsVirtualizing="True"/>
                </ItemsPanelTemplate>
            </ListBox.ItemsPanel>
            <ListBox.ItemTemplate>
```

```
                  <DataTemplate>
                      <Border BorderBrush="Black" Margin="5"
                              BorderThickness="2" Tag={Binding Url}
                              MouseLeftButtonUp="Border_MouseLeftButtonUp_1"
                              Width="200" Height="220">
                          <StackPanel>
                              <Image Source="{Binding Thumbnail}"
                                     Width="160" Height="120" />
                              <TextBlock Text="{Binding Title}" TextWrapping="Wrap"
                                         Grid.Row="1"/>
                              <TextBlock Text="{Binding DateRecorded}" Grid.Row="2"/>
                              <TextBlock Text="{Binding Speaker}" Grid.Row="3"/>
                          </StackPanel>
                      </Border>
                  </DataTemplate>
              </ListBox.ItemTemplate>
          </ListBox>
      </Grid>
  </Window>
```

It is worth mentioning that the code replaces the default items container (a
VirtualizingStackPanel) with a WrapPanel container so that items are not forced to be
presented on one line horizontally. This requires disabling the horizontal scrollbar on the
ListBox (ScrollViewer.HorizontalScrollBarVisibility="Disabled") and changing the
ListBox.ItemsPanel content with the WrapPanel. Also notice how the Border.Tag property is bound to the Url property of the Video class. This enables you to store the video's
URL and click the Border at runtime to open the video in its original location. Now switch
to the code-behind file. The first thing you must do is add a number of Imports directives,
some for importing XML namespaces needed to map information from the RSS feed and
some for working with additional .NET classes:

```
Imports <xmlns:xa="http://www.w3.org/2005/Atom">
Imports <xmlns:xd="http://schemas.microsoft.com/ado/2007/08/dataservices">
Imports <xmlns:xm="http://schemas.microsoft.com/ado/2007/08/dataservices/metadata">
Imports System.Net
Imports System.Threading
```

The next step is implementing a method that queries the RSS feed returning the list of
videos. In this first implementation, you will use a synchronous approach, which will
block the user interface when the application is running:

```
Private Function QueryVideos() As IEnumerable(Of Video)
    Dim client As New WebClient

    Dim data As String = client.DownloadString(New Uri(Video.FeedUrl))
```

```
        Dim doc As XDocument = XDocument.Parse(data)
        Dim query = From video In doc...<xa:entry>
                Select New Video With {
                        .Title = video.<xa:title>.Value,
                        .Speaker = "Speaker: " + video...<xd:MicrosoftHost>.Value,
                        .Thumbnail = video...<xd:Picture>.Value,
                        .Url = video...<xd:Url>.Value,
                        .DateRecorded = String.Concat("Recorded on ",
                                Date.Parse(video...<xd:DateRecorded>.Value).
                                ToShortDateString)
                }

        Return query
End Function
```

The code is simple. An instance of the `WebClient` class, which provides simplified access to networked resources, is created and the invocation of its `DownloadString` method downloads the entire content of the feed under the form of a `String` object. Notice that this is the point at which the user interface gets blocked. In fact, it will need to wait for `DownloadString` to complete the operation before returning to be responsive. After the feed has been downloaded, it is converted into an object of type `XDocument` and a LINQ query enables you to retrieve all the needed information (refer to Chapter 27 for further information on LINQ to XML). Finally, a method called `LoadVideos` will run the query and assign the result to the Window's `DataContext`; such a method will be invoked at startup. You can change this type of implementation, but it will be more useful later when making comparisons with the asynchronous implementation. The following code demonstrates this, plus the event handler for the `MouseLeftButtonUp` event of the `Border` control, where you launch the video in its original web page:

```
Private Sub LoadVideos()
    Me.DataContext = QueryVideos()
End Sub

Private Sub MainWindow_Loaded(sender As Object,
                            e As RoutedEventArgs) Handles Me.Loaded
    LoadVideos()
End Sub

Private Sub Border_MouseLeftButtonUp_1(sender As Object,
                                    e As MouseButtonEventArgs)
    'Tag is of type Object so an explicit conversion to String is required
    Dim instance = CType(sender, Border)
    Process.Start(CStr(instance.Tag))
End Sub
```

You can now run the application. Figure 44.4 shows the result of the query over the video feed.

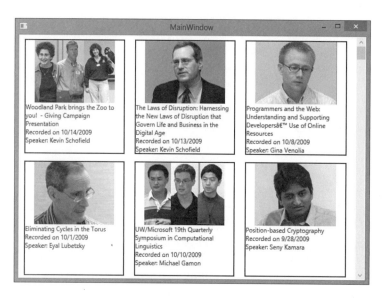

FIGURE 44.4   Loading an RSS feed the synchronous way.

The application works as expected, but the real problem with this approach is that the user cannot interact with the interface while the query is running. The reason is that the query's code is running in the UI thread, so the user interface is busy with the query and does not accept any interaction. This can be easily demonstrated by attempting to move the window while the query is running because you will not be able to move it elsewhere. This has other implications: you cannot refresh controls that display the status of the task because they would be refreshed only when the query completes. Also, you cannot enable users to cancel the operation because you would need a button that the user would never be able to click.

Event-based Asynchrony and Callbacks

A much better approach is moving the long-running operation into a separate thread, so that the UI can remain responsive while the other thread executes the operation. Lots of classes in the .NET Framework—especially those whose job is interacting with the Web and with networks-expose event-based asynchrony through methods that launch and execute an operation on a separate thread and raise an event when it is completed, passing the result to the caller via a callback. The `WebClient` class has an asynchronous counterpart of `DownloadString`, called `DownloadStringAsync`, that you can use to run the query on a separate thread and wait for the query result via a callback. The following code demonstrates how to accomplish this (do not worry if you notice something wrong because an explanation is provided in moments):

```vb
Private Function QueryVideos() As IEnumerable(Of Video)
    Dim client As New WebClient
    Dim query As IEnumerable(Of Video)

    AddHandler client.DownloadStringCompleted, Sub(sender, e)
                                                   If e.Error IsNot Nothing Then
                                                       'Error handling logic here..
                                                   End If

                                                   Dim doc = _
                                                       XDocument.Parse(e.Result)
                                                   query = From video In
                                                           doc...<xa:entry>
                                                           Select New Video With {
                                                           .Title = _
                                                           video.<xa:title>.Value,
                                                           .Speaker = "Speaker: " +_
                                                   video...<xd:MicrosoftHost>.Value,
                                                           .Thumbnail = _
                                                   video...<xd:Picture>.Value,
                                                   .Url = video...<xd:Url>.Value,
                                                   .DateRecorded = _
                                                   String.Concat("Recorded on ",
                                           Date.Parse(video...<xd:DateRecorded>.Value).
                                           ToShortDateString)
                                                                       }

                                               End Sub

    client.DownloadStringAsync(New Uri(Video.FeedUrl))
    Return query
End Function
```

The code specifies a statement lambda as an event handler for the
DownloadStringCompleted event, instead of declaring a separate delegate and pointing to
this via an AddressOf clause. The e object is of type DownloadStringCompletedEventArgs
and contains the result of the operation. The problem in this code is that the Return statement does not work because it is attempting to return a result that has not been yielded
yet. On the other side, you cannot write something like this:

```vb
Private Function QueryVideos() As IEnumerable(Of Video)
    Dim client As New WebClient
    Dim query As IEnumerable(Of Video)

    AddHandler client.DownloadStringCompleted, Sub(sender, e)
                                                   If e.Error IsNot Nothing Then
```

```
                                       'Error handling logic here..
                                 End If

                                 Dim doc = _
                                     XDocument.Parse(e.Result)
                                 query = From ...
                                 Return query


                           End Sub

    client.DownloadStringAsync(New Uri(Video.FeedUrl))
End Function
```

This code does not work because you cannot return a result from a Sub and because it should be returned from the outer method, not the inner. In conclusion, Return statements do not work well with event-based asynchrony. The solution at this point is returning the result via a callback and an Action(Of T) object. So the appropriate implementation of the QueryVideos method in this approach is the following:

```
Private Sub QueryVideos(listOfVideos As Action(Of IEnumerable(Of Video),
                                  Exception))
    Dim client As New WebClient
    AddHandler client.DownloadStringCompleted, Sub(sender, e)
                                 If e.Error IsNot Nothing Then
                                     listOfVideos(Nothing,
                                                  e.Error)
                                     Return
                                 End If

                                 Dim doc = _
                                     XDocument.Parse(e.Result)
                                 query = From video In
                                         doc...<xa:entry>
                                         Select New Video With {
                                         .Title = _
                                         video.<xa:title>.Value,
                                         .Speaker = "Speaker: " +_
                                    video...<xd:MicrosoftHost>.Value,
                                         .Thumbnail = _
                                    video...<xd:Picture>.Value,
                                         .Url = video...<xd:Url>.Value,
                                         .DateRecorded = _
                                         String.Concat("Recorded on ",
                                  Date.Parse(video...<xd:DateRecorded>.Value).
                                  ToShortDateString)
                                                  }
```

```
                                        listOfVideos(query, Nothing)
                                    End Sub

    Try
        client.DownloadStringAsync(New Uri(Video.FeedUrl))
    Catch ex As Exception
        listOfVideos(Nothing, ex)
    End Try
End Sub
```

The previous code does the following:

1. Holds the list of videos from the RSS feed in an `Action(Of IEnumerable(Of Video), Exception)` object. The `Exception` instance here is useful to determine whether an error occurred during the query execution.

2. If the query completes successfully, the query result is passed to the `Action` object (that is, the callback).

3. If an exception occurs during the query execution (see the first `If` block inside the statement lambda), the callback receives `Nothing` as the first parameter because the collection of items was not retrieved successfully and the exception instance as the second parameter.

4. If an exception occurs immediately when the web request is made, the callback still receives `Nothing` and the exception instance. This is at the `Try..Catch` block level.

So using a callback here has been necessary for two reasons: sending the query result back to the caller correctly and handling two exception scenarios. But you are not done yet. In fact, you have to completely rewrite the `LoadVideos` method to hold the result of the callback and determine whether the operation completed successfully before assigning the query result to the Window's `DataContext`. The following code demonstrates this:

```
Private Sub LoadVideos()
    Dim action As Action(Of IEnumerable(Of Video),
                        Exception) = Nothing

    action =
        Sub(videos, ex)
            If ex IsNot Nothing Then
                MessageBox.Show(ex.Message)
                Return
            End If

            If (videos.Any) Then
                Me.DataContext = videos
            Else
                QueryVideos(action)
            End If
```

44

```
        End Sub
    QueryVideos(action)
End Sub
```

As you can see, the code is not easy, unless you are an expert. There is an invocation to the previous implementation of QueryVideos, passing the instance of the callback. When the result is sent back, the statement lambda first checks for exceptions and, if not, takes the query result as the data source. If you now run the application again, you will get the same result shown in Figure 44.4; however, this time the user interface is responsive and the user can interact with it. But reaching this objective had costs. You had to completely rewrite method implementations and write code that is complex and difficult to read and to extend. So, the multithreading in this situation has not been very helpful. This is the point in which the Async/Await pattern comes in to make things simple.

Asynchrony with `Async/Await`

The Async/Await pattern has the goal of simplifying the way developers write asynchronous code. You will learn a lot about the underlying infrastructure, but before digging into that, it is important for you to see how your code can be much cleaner and readable. Let's start by modifying the QueryVideos method to make some important considerations:

```
Private Async Function QueryVideosAsync() As _
        Task(Of IEnumerable(Of Video))
    Dim client As New WebClient

    Dim data = Await client.DownloadStringTaskAsync(New Uri(Video.FeedUrl))

    Dim doc = XDocument.Parse(data)

    Dim query = From video In doc...<xa:entry>
                Select New Video With {
                    .Title = video.<xa:title>.Value,
                    .Speaker = String.Concat("Speaker: ",
                            video...<xd:MicrosoftHost>.Value),
                    .Thumbnail = video...<xd:Picture>.Value,
                    .Url = video...<xd:Url>.Value,
                    .DateRecorded = String.Concat("Recorded on ",
                    Date.Parse(video...<xd:DateRecorded>.Value).
                    ToShortDateString)}

    Return query
End Function
```

Asynchronous methods must be decorated with the Async modifier. When the compiler encounters this modifier, it expects that the method body contains one or more Await statements. If not, it throws a warning saying that the method will be treated as synchronous, suggesting that the Async modifier should be removed. Async methods must return an object of type `Task`. If the method returns a value (`Function`), then it must return a `Task(Of T)` where `T` is the actual result type. Otherwise, if the method returns no value, both following syntaxes are allowed:

```
Async Function TestAsync() As Task
    'You can avoid Return statements, the compiler assumes returning no values
End Function

Async Sub TestAsync()
'...
End Sub
```

The difference between the two implementations is that the first one can be called inside another method with `Await`, but the second one cannot (because it does not need to be awaited). A typical example of the second syntax is about event handlers: they can be asynchronous and can use `Await`, but no other method will wait for their result. By convention, the suffix of async methods is the `Async` literal. This is why `QueryVideos` has been renamed into `QueryVideosAsync`. An exception is represented by asynchronous methods already existing in previous versions of the .NET Framework, based on the EAP, whose name already ends with `Async`. In this case `Async` is replaced with `TaskAsync`. For instance (as you discover in moments), the `DownloadStringAsync` method in the `WebClient` class has a new counterpart called `DownloadStringTaskAsync`. Any method that returns a `Task` or `Task(Of T)` can be used with `Await`. With `Await`, a task is started but the control flow is immediately returned to the caller. The result of the task will not be returned immediately, but later and only when the task completes. But because the control flow immediately returns to the caller, the caller remains responsive. `Await` can be thought as of a placeholder for the task's result, which will be available after the awaited task completes. In the previous `QueryVideosAsync` method, `Await` starts the `WebClient`. `DownloadStringTaskAsync` method and literally waits for its result but, while waiting, the control flow does not move to `DownloadStringAsyncTask`, while it remains in the caller. Because in the current example the code is running in the UI thread, the user interface remains responsive because the requested task is being executed asynchronously.

In other words, what `Await` actually does is sign up the rest of the method as a callback on the task, returning immediately. When the task that is being awaited completes, it will invoke the callback and will resume the execution from the exact point it was left.

After the operation has been completed, the rest of the code can elaborate the result. With this kind of approach, your method looks much simpler, like the first synchronous version, but it is running asynchronously with only three edits (the `Async` modifier, `Task(Of T)` as the return type, and the `Await` operator).

WHY THE `Task` TYPE?

In Chapter 43 you learned a lot about the `Task` class and saw how this can run CPU-intensive work on a separate thread, but it also can represent an I/O operation such as a network request. For this reason, the `Task` class is the natural choice as the result type for asynchronous operations using `Async/Await`.

Continuing considerations on the previous method, take a look at the final Return state-ment. It is returning an IEnumerable(Of Video), but actually the method's signature requires returning a Task(Of IEnumerable(Of Video)). This is possible because the compiler automatically makes Return statements to return a Task-based version of their result even if they do not. As a result, you will not get confused because you will write the same code but the compiler will take care of converting the return type into the appropriate type. This also makes migration of synchronous code to asynchronous easier. Continuing the migration of the code example to the Async/Await pattern, you now need a few edits to the LoadVideos method. The following code demonstrates this:

```
Private Async Function LoadVideosAsync() As Task
    Me.DataContext = Await QueryVideosAsync()
End Sub
```

The method is now called LoadVideoAsync and marked with the Async modifier. The reason is that it contains an Await expression that invokes the QueryVideosAsync method. The result of this invocation is taken as the main window's data source. Finally, you have to edit the MainWindow_Loaded event handler and make it asynchronous like this:

```
Private Async Sub MainWindow_Loaded(sender As Object,
                            e As RoutedEventArgs) Handles Me.Loaded
    Await LoadVideosAsync()
End Sub
```

If you now run the application, you will still get a responsive user interface that you can interact with while the long-running task (the query) is executing, but you have achieved this by modifying existing code with very few edits.

How Async and Await Work Behind the Scenes

Behind the scenes of the ease of the Async pattern, the compiler does incredible work to make the magic possible. When you make an asynchronous call by using Await, that invocation starts a new instance of the Task class. As you know from Chapter 43, one thread can contain multiple Task instances. This means that it is the responsibility of the runtime to decide whether the new task must run in a separate thread or in the same calling thread. So you might have the asynchronous operation running in the same thread but on a new Task. Internally, it's as if the compiler could split an asynchronous method in two parts, a method and its callback. If you consider the QueryVideosAsync shown previously, you could imagine a method defined until the invocation of Await. The next part of the method is moved into a callback that is invoked after the awaited operation is completed. This has two benefits. The first benefit is that it ensures that code that needs to manipulate the result of an awaited operation will work with the actual result, which has been returned after completion of the task (this is in fact the moment in which the callback is invoked). Second, such callback is invoked in the same calling thread, which avoids the need of managing threads manually or using the Dispatcher class in technolo-gies like WPF or Silverlight. Figure 44.5 gives you an ideal representation of how the asynchronous method has been split.

```
Private Async Function QueryVideosAsync() As _
        Task(Of IEnumerable(Of Video))
    Dim client As New WebClient

    Dim data = Await client.DownloadStringTaskAsync(New Uri(Video.FeedUrl))

    Dim doc = XDocument.Parse(data)

    Dim query = From video In doc...<xa:entry>
                Select New Video With {
                        .Title = video.<xa:title>.Value,
                        .Speaker = String.Concat("Speaker: ",
                                video...<xd:MicrosoftHost>.Value),
                        .Thumbnail = video...<xd:Picture>.Value,
                        .Url = video...<xd:Url>.Value,
                        .DateRecorded = String.Concat("Recorded on ",
                        Date.Parse(video...<xd:DateRecorded>.Value).
                        ToShortDateString)
                }

    Return query
End Function
```

FIGURE 44.5   An asynchronous method is split into two ideal parts; the second is a callback.

Beyond considerations like the ones about threading, it is interesting to analyze the code the compiler generated to make asynchrony so efficient in Visual Basic 2012. For this exercise, you need a decompiler tool such as JustDecompile from Telerik, which ships for free and is available at http://www.telerik.com/products/decompiler.aspx. If you open the compiled .exe file with a tool like this, you can see that the implementation of asynchronous methods is completely different from the one you wrote and that the compiler generated several structures that implement a state machine that supports asynchrony. Figure 44.6 shows the `QueryVideosAsync` real implementation.

FIGURE 44.6   Investigating the actual generated code with JustDecompile.

For your convenience, the following is the auto-generated code for `QueryVideosAsync`:

```
<AsyncStateMachine(GetType(VB$StateMachine_0_QueryVideosAsync))> _
<DebuggerStepThrough> _
Private Function QueryVideosAsync() As Task(Of IEnumerable(Of Video))
    Dim asyncTaskMethodBuilder As AsyncTaskMethodBuilder(Of IEnumerable(Of Video)) =
        AsyncTaskMethodBuilder(Of IEnumerable(Of Video)).Create()
    Dim $sm As MainWindow.VB$StateMachine_0_QueryVideosAsync.$State = -1
    $sm.$Builder = AsyncTaskMethodBuilder(Of IEnumerable(Of Video)).Create()
    $sm.$Builder.Start(Of MainWindow.VB$StateMachine_0_QueryVideosAsync)($sm)
    Dim task As Task(Of IEnumerable(Of Video)) = $sm.$Builder.Task
    Return task
End Function
```

You do not need to know the code in detail because this implementation is purely internal; however, the real code relies on the `AsyncTaskMethodBuilder` class, which creates an instance of an asynchronous method and requires specifying a state machine that controls the execution of the asynchronous task (which is returned once completed). For each asynchronous method, the compiler generated a `Structure` object representing the state machine. For instance, the compiler generated a structure called `VB$StateMachine_0_QueryVideosAsync` that represents the state machine that controls the execution of the `QueryVideosAsync` method. Listing 44.3 contains the code of the aforementioned structure.

LISTING 44.3   Internal implementation of a State Machine for Async Methods

```
<CompilerGenerated> _
Private Structure VB$StateMachine_0_QueryVideosAsync
    Implements IAsyncStateMachine
    Friend $awaiter_0 As TaskAwaiter(Of String)

    Friend $Builder As AsyncTaskMethodBuilder(Of IEnumerable(Of Video))

    Friend $Stack As Object

    Friend $State As Integer

    Friend $VB$Me As MainWindow

    Friend $VB$ResumableLocal_client$1 As WebClient

    Friend $VB$ResumableLocal_data$1 As String

    Friend $VB$ResumableLocal_doc$1 As XDocument

    Friend $VB$ResumableLocal_query$1 As IEnumerable(Of Video)
```

```vbnet
<CompilerGenerated> _
Friend Overrides Sub MoveNext()
    Dim $VB$ResumableLocalQuery$1 As IEnumerable(Of Video)
    Dim awaiter As TaskAwaiter(Of String)
    Dim flag As Boolean = False
    Dim flag1 As Boolean = False
    Try
        If (Me.$State = 0) Then
            Me.$State = -1
            flag = True
        End If
        If (Not flag) Then
            Me.$VB$ResumableLocal_client$1 = New WebClient()
            awaiter = Me.$VB$ResumableLocal_client$1.
            DownloadStringTaskAsync(New Uri(Video.FeedUrl)).GetAwaiter()
            If (Not awaiter.IsCompleted) Then
                Me.$State = 0
                Me.$awaiter_0 = awaiter
                Me.$Builder.AwaitUnsafeOnCompleted(Of TaskAwaiter(Of String),
                MainWindow.VB$StateMachine_0_QueryVideosAsync)(awaiter, Me)
                flag1 = True
            End If
        End If
        If (flag OrElse Not flag1) Then
            awaiter = New TaskAwaiter(Of String)()
            Dim result As String = awaiter.GetResult()
            Me.$VB$ResumableLocal_data$1 = result
            Me.$VB$ResumableLocal_doc$1 =
            XDocument.Parse(Me.$VB$ResumableLocal_data$1)
            Me.$VB$ResumableLocal_query$1 = Me.$VB$ResumableLocal_doc$1.
            Descendants(XName.Get("entry", "http://www.w3.org/2005/Atom")).
            Select(Of XElement, Video)(Function(video As XElement)
                Dim value As Video = New Video()
                value.Title = InternalXmlHelper.Value
                value.Speaker = String.Concat("Speaker: ",
➥InternalXmlHelper.Value)
                value.Thumbnail = InternalXmlHelper.Value
                value.Url = InternalXmlHelper.Value
                Dim dateTime As DateTime =
➥DateTime.Parse(InternalXmlHelper.Value)
                value.DateRecorded =
                String.Concat("Recorded on ", dateTime.ToShortDateString())
                Dim video1 As Video = value
            End Function
            )
            $VB$ResumableLocalQuery$1 = Me.$VB$ResumableLocal_query$1
```

```
            End If
        Catch (exception1 As Exception)
            Dim exception As Exception = exception1
            ProjectData.SetProjectError(exception)
            Dim $ex As Exception = exception
            Me.$State = 1
            Me.$Builder.SetException($ex)
            ProjectData.ClearProjectError()
            flag1 = True
        End Try
        If (Not flag1) Then
            Me.$State = 1
            Me.$Builder.SetResult($VB$ResumableLocalQuery$1)
        End If
    End Sub


    <DebuggerNonUserCode> _
    Private Overrides Sub System.Runtime.CompilerServices.IAsyncStateMachine.
➡SetStateMachine(ByVal sm As IAsyncStateMachine)
        Me.$Builder.SetStateMachine(sm)
    End Sub
End Structure
```

The code in Listing 44.3 is certainly complex, and you are not required to know how it works under the hood, but focus for a moment on the MoveNext method. This method is responsible of the asynchronous execution of tasks; depending on the state of the task, it resumes the execution at the appropriate point. You can see how the compiler translates the Await keyword into an instance of the TaskAwaiter structure, which is assigned with the result of the invocation to the Task.GetAwaiter method (both are for compiler-use only). If you compare the result of this analysis with the ease of usage of the Async pattern, it is obvious that the compiler does tremendous work to translate that simplicity into a very efficient asynchronous mechanism.

Documentation and Examples of the Async Pattern

Microsoft offers a lot of useful resources to developers who want to start coding the new way. The following list summarizes several resources that you are strongly encouraged to visit to make your learning of Async complete:

▶ **Visual Studio Asynchronous Programming**: The official developer center for Async. Here you can find documentation, downloads, instructional videos, and more on language specifications. It is available at http://msdn.microsoft.com/en-us/vstudio/async.aspx.

▶ **101 Async Samples**: An online page that contains a huge number of code examples based on Async for both Visual Basic and Visual C#. You can find samples at http://www.wischik.com/lu/AsyncSilverlight/AsyncSamples.html.

▶ **Sample code**: Available on the MSDN Code Gallery (http://code.msdn.microsoft. com).

Do not leave out of your bookmarks the root page of the .NET Framework 4.5 documentation (http://msdn.microsoft.com/en-us/library/w0x726c2).

Exception Handling in Async

Another great benefit of using the Async pattern is that exception handling is done the usual way. In fact, if an awaited method throws an exception, this can be naturally handled within a `Try..Catch..Finally` block. The following code provides an example:

```
Private Async Sub DownloadSomethingAsync()
    Dim client As New System.Net.WebClient
    Try
        Dim result = Await client.
            DownloadStringTaskAsync("http://msdn.com/vbasic")
    Catch ex As Exception
        Console.WriteLine(ex.Message)
    Finally
        Console.WriteLine("Operation completed.")
    End Try
End Sub
```

As you can see, there is no difference in handling exceptions inside asynchronous methods compared to classic synchronous methods. This makes code migration easier.

Implementing Task-based Asynchrony

As you remember from Chapter 43, the `Task` class provides methods and other members that enable you to execute CPU-intensive work, by splitting code across all the available processors so that most of the code is executed concurrently, when possible. Such members of the `Task` class return instances of the `Task` class itself, and therefore can be used along with `Await`. This possibility has some advantages:

▶ You can execute synchronous code on a separate thread more easily.

▶ You can run multiple tasks concurrently and wait for them to complete before making further manipulations.

▶ You can use Await with CPU-consuming code.

This approach is known as Task-based Asynchrony, and in this section you learn how to get the most out of it.

Switching Threads

In Chapter 42 you learned how to write code that can run on a separate thread, how to create new threads manually, and how to use the Thread Pool managed by the .NET Framework. With this approach, you run a portion of synchronous code in a separate thread, thus keeping the caller thread-free from an intensive and potentially blocking work. In the .NET Framework 4.5, you have additional alternatives to reach the same objective but writing simpler code. The `Task.Run` method enables you to run a new task asynchronously, queuing such a task into a thread in the Thread Pool. The result is returned as `Task` handle for the intensive work, so that you can use `Await` to wait for the result. `Task.Run` takes as the first argument a delegate that defines the work that will be executed in the background thread. Such a delegate can be represented either by a method that you point to via the `AddressOf` clause or by lambdas. In the latter case, the delegate can be a `System.Action` represented by a statement lambda or a `System.Func(Of T)` represented by a lambda expression. The following example demonstrates how synchronous code is easily executed in a separate thread by invoking `Task.Run`:

```
Private Async Sub RunIntensiveWorkAsync()
    'This runs on the UI thread
    Console.WriteLine("Starting...")

    'This runs on a Thread Pool thread
    Dim result As Integer = Await Task.Run(Function()
                                               Dim workResult As Integer = _
                                                   SimulateIntensiveWork()
                                               Return workResult
                                           End Function)

    'This runs again on the UI thread
    Console.WriteLine("Finished")
    Console.ReadLine()
End Sub

Private Function SimulateIntensiveWork() As Integer
    Dim delay As Integer = 5000
    Threading.Thread.Sleep(delay)
    Return delay
End Function
```

While the result of `Task.Run` is being awaited, the control is immediately returned to the user interface, which remains responsive in the Console window. All the `Console.WriteLine` and `Console.ReadLine` statements are executed on the UI thread, whereas the simulated CPU-consuming code runs on the separate thread. `Task.Run` schedules a new task exactly as `Task.Factory.StartNew` does; you saw this method in Chapter 43. So, this code has the same effect as using `Task.Run`:

```
Dim result As Integer = Await Task.Factory.StartNew(Function()
                                          Dim workResult As Integer = _
                                              SimulateIntensiveWork()
                                          Return workResult
                                      End Function)
```

In summary, `Task.Run` lets you easily execute intensive computations on a separate thread, taking all the benefits of `Await`.

Using Combinators

The `Task` class has other interesting usages, such as managing concurrent operations. This is possible because of two methods, `Task.WhenAll` and `Task.WhenAny`, also known as *combinators*. `Task.WhenAll` creates a task that will complete when all the supplied tasks complete; `Task.WhenAny` creates a task that will complete when at least one of the supplied tasks completes. For example, imagine you want to download multiple RSS feeds information from a website. Instead of using `Await` against individual tasks to complete, you can use `Task.WhenAll` to continue only after all tasks have completed. The following code provides an example of concurrent download of RSS feeds from the Microsoft Research OData feed used previously:

```
Private Async Sub DownloadAllFeedsAsync()
    Dim feeds As New List(Of Uri) From
        {New Uri("http://odata.research.microsoft.com/odata.svc/Videos/"),
         New Uri("http://odata.research.microsoft.com/odata.svc/Downloads/"),
         New Uri("http://odata.research.microsoft.com/odata.svc/Projects")}

    'This task completes when all of the requests complete
    Dim feedCompleted As IEnumerable(Of String) = _
                                      Await Task.WhenAll(From feed In feeds
                                      Select New System.Net.WebClient().
                                      DownloadStringTaskAsync(feed))

    'Additional work here...
End Sub
```

This code creates a collection of tasks by sending a `DownloadStringTaskAsync` request for each feed address in the list of feeds. The task completes (and thus the result of awaiting `WhenAll` is returned) only when all three feeds have been downloaded, meaning that the complete download result will not be available if only one or two feeds have been downloaded. `WhenAny` works differently because it creates a task that completes when any of the tasks in a collection of tasks completes. The following code demonstrates how to rewrite the previous example using `WhenAny`:

```vbnet
Private Async Sub DownloadFeedsAsync()
    Dim feeds As New List(Of Uri) From
        {New Uri("http://odata.research.microsoft.com/odata.svc/Videos/"),
         New Uri("http://odata.research.microsoft.com/odata.svc/Downloads/"),
         New Uri("http://odata.research.microsoft.com/odata.svc/Projects")}

    'This task completes when any of the requests complete
    Dim feedCompleted As Task(Of String) = Await Task.WhenAny(From feed In feeds
                                        Select New System.Net.WebClient().
                                        DownloadStringTaskAsync(feed))
    'Additional work here...
End Sub
```

In this case a single result will be yielded because the task will be completed when any of the tasks completes. You can also wait for a list of tasks defined as explicit asynchronous methods, like in the following example:

```vbnet
Public Async Sub WhenAnyRedundancyAsync()

    Dim messages As New List(Of Task(Of String)) From
        {
            GetMessage1Async(),
            GetMessage2Async(),
            GetMessage3Async()
        }
    Dim message = Await Task.WhenAny(messages)
    Console.WriteLine(message.Result)
    Console.ReadLine()
End Sub


Public Async Function GetMessage1Async() As Task(Of String)
    Await Task.Delay(700)
    Return "Hi VB guys!"
End Function


Public Async Function GetMessage2Async() As Task(Of String)
    Await Task.Delay(600)
    Return "Hi C# guys!"
End Function


Public Async Function GetMessage3Async() As Task(Of String)
    Await Task.Delay(500)
    Return "Hi F# guys!"
End Function
```

Here you have three asynchronous methods, each returning a string. The code builds a list of tasks including each asynchronous method in the list. `Task.WhenAny` receives the instance of the collection of tasks as an argument and completes when one of the three methods completes. In this example, you are also seeing for the first time the `Task.Delay` method. This is the asynchronous equivalent of `Thread.Sleep`, but while the latter blocks the thread for the specified number of milliseconds, with `Task.Delay` the thread remains responsive.

ADDITIONAL SAMPLES ON Whenany

The 101 Async Samples include a couple of interesting examples of different usages of `WhenAny`, such as interleaving one request at a time and limiting the number of concurrent downloads. You find them under the Combinators node of the samples page mentioned at the beginning of the chapter.

44

Cancellation and Progress

Because the Async pattern relies on the `Task` class, implementing cancellation is something similar to what you have already studied back in Chapter 43, thus the `CancellationTokenSource` and `CancellationToken` classes are used. In this section you see how to implement cancellation both for asynchronous methods and for `Task.Run` operations. Next, you learn how to report the progress of an operation, which is common in asynchronous programming and improves the user experience.

Implementing Cancellation

Let's look at the WPF sample application created in the section called "Getting Started With Async/Await." Imagine you want to give users the ability of cancelling the download of the RSS feed from the Microsoft Research website. First, make a slight modification to the user interface so that the main `Grid` is divided into two rows, and in the first row add a `Button` like this:

```
<Grid.RowDefinitions>
    <RowDefinition Height="40"/>
    <RowDefinition/>
</Grid.RowDefinitions>
<Button Width="120" Height="30" Name="CancelButton"
        Content="Cancel"/>
```

Do not forget to add the `Grid.Row="1"` property assignment for the `ListBox` control. Double-click the new button so that you can quickly access the code editor. Declare a new `CancellationTokenSource` object that will listen for cancellation requests. The event handler for the new button's `Click` event will invoke the `Cancel` method on the instance of the `CancellationTokenSource`:

```
Private cancellationToken As CancellationTokenSource

Private Sub CancelButton_Click(sender As Object, e As RoutedEventArgs) _
    Handles CancelButton.Click
    If Me.cancellationToken IsNot Nothing Then
        Me.cancellationToken.Cancel()
    End If
End Sub
```

The user can now request cancellation by clicking this button. Next, you need to make a couple of edits to the `QueryVideosAsync` method created previously. The first edit is making this method receive a `CancellationToken` object as an argument. This object will handle cancellation requests during the method execution. The second edit requires replacing the `WebClient` class with a new class called `HttpClient`. The reason for this change is that the `WebClient`'s asynchronous methods no longer support cancellation as in the first previews of the Async library, although asynchronous methods in `System.Net.Http.HttpClient` do. Among the others, this class exposes a method called `GetAsync` that retrieves contents from the specified URL and receives the cancellation token as the second argument. The result is returned under the form of a `System.Net.Http.HttpResponseMessage` class. As the name implies, this class represents an HTTP response message including the status of the operation and the retrieved data. The data is represented by a property called `Content`, which exposes methods to convert data into a stream (`ReadAsStreamAsync`), into an array of bytes (`ReadAsByteArrayAsync`), and into a string (`ReadAsStringAsync`). Other than changing the code to use `HttpClient` and to receive the cancellation token, you only need to handle the `OperationCanceledException`, which is raised after the cancellation request is received by the asynchronous method. The following code demonstrates the `QueryVideosAsync` method:

```
'The following implementation with HttpClient supports Cancellation
Private Async Function QueryVideosAsync(token As CancellationToken) As _
        Task(Of IEnumerable(Of Video))
    Try
        Dim client As New HttpClient

        'Get the feed content as an HttpResponseMessage
        Dim data = Await client.GetAsync(New Uri(Video.FeedUrl), token)

        'Parse the content into a String
        Dim actualData = Await data.Content.ReadAsStringAsync

        Dim doc = XDocument.Parse(actualData)

        Dim query = From video In doc...<xa:entry>
                Select New Video With {
                        .Title = video.<xa:title>.Value,
                        .Speaker = String.Concat("Speaker: ",
```

```
                                              video...<xd:MicrosoftHost>.Value),
                        .Thumbnail = video...<xd:Picture>.Value,
                        .Url = video...<xd:Url>.Value,
                        .DateRecorded = String.Concat("Recorded on ",
                        Date.Parse(video...<xd:DateRecorded>.Value).
                        ToShortDateString)
                    }

        Return query
    Catch ex As OperationCanceledException
        MessageBox.Show("Operation was canceled by the user.")
        Return Nothing
    Catch ex As Exception
        MessageBox.Show(ex.Message)
        Return Nothing
    End Try
End Function
```

The very last edit to the application is changing the `LoadVideosAsync` method to launch the query passing a cancellation token:

```
Private Async Function LoadVideosAsync() As Task
    Me.cancellationToken = New CancellationTokenSource

    Me.DataContext = Await QueryVideosAsync(Me.cancellationToken.Token)
End Function
```

If you now run the application, not only will the user interface remain responsive, but you will be also able to click the Cancel button to stop the query execution. Notice that in a synchronous approach, implementing cancellation has no benefits. In fact, if on one side writing code to support cancellation is legal, on the other side the user would never have a chance to click a button because the UI thread would be blocked until the completion of the task. Similarly, you can add cancellation to tasks running in a separate thread and started with `Task.Run`. By continuing the example shown previously about this method, you can first rewrite the `SimulateIntensiveWork` method as follows:

```
Private Function SimulateIntensiveWork(token As CancellationToken) _
        As Integer
    Dim delay As Integer = 5000
    Threading.Thread.Sleep(delay)

    If token.IsCancellationRequested Then
        token.ThrowIfCancellationRequested()
    End If

    Return delay
End Function
```

You should be familiar with this approach because it has been discussed in Chapter 43. The method receives the cancellation token and checks for cancellation requests. If any exist, it throws an `OperationCanceledException`. Next, you add support for cancellation by passing an instance of the `CancellationTokenSource` class to the method invocation inside `Task.Run`:

```vb
Private cancellationToken As CancellationTokenSource

Private Async Sub RunIntensiveWorkAsync()
    cancellationToken = New CancellationTokenSource
    'This runs on the UI thread
    Console.WriteLine("Starting...")

    Try
        'This runs on a Thread Pool thread
        Dim result As Integer = Await Task.Run(Function()
                                                   Dim workResult As Integer = _
                                                   SimulateIntensiveWork( _
                                                   cancellationToken.Token)
                                                   Return workResult
                                               End Function)

        'This runs again on the UI thread
        Console.WriteLine("Finished")
    Catch ex As OperationCanceledException
        Console.WriteLine("Canceled by the user.")
    Catch ex As Exception

    End Try
    Console.ReadLine()
End Sub
```

To request cancellation, you should call the `cancellationToken.Cancel` method. At that point, the request is intercepted and an `OperationCanceledException` is thrown.

Reporting Progress

Reporting the progress of an asynchronous method execution is a common requirement. There is a pattern that you can use and that makes things easier. This pattern relies on the `System.IProgress(Of T)` interface and the `System.Progress(Of T)` class, which expose a `ProgressChanged` event that must be raised when the asynchronous operation is in progress. To provide an example that is easy to understand, imagine you still want to download the content of some feeds from the Microsoft Research website and refresh the progress every time a site has been downloaded completely. The current example is based on a Console application. Consider the following code:

```
Private progress As Progress(Of Integer)
Private counter As Integer = 0

Sub Main()
    Try
        progress = New Progress(Of Integer)
        AddHandler progress.ProgressChanged, Sub(sender, e)
                                                 Console.
                                                 WriteLine("Download progress: " + _
                                                 CStr(e))
                                             End Sub

        DownloadAllFeedsAsync(progress)

    Catch ex As Exception
        Console.WriteLine(ex.Message)
    Finally
        Console.ReadLine()
    End Try
End Sub
```

You first declare an object of type `Progress(Of Integer)` and a counter. The first object will receive the progress value when the `ProgressChanged` event is raised. In this case, the code uses the `Integer` type to pass a simple number, but you can pass more complex information with a different or custom type. Then the code specifies a handler for the `ProgressChanged` event, with type inference for the lambda's parameters. `Sender` is always `Object`, whereas `e` is of the same type as the generic type you assigned to `Progress`. So, in this case it is of type `Integer`. Here you are working in a Console application and are thus displaying the value as a text message. But in real-world applications, this is the value that you could assign to a `ProgressBar` control to report the progress in the user interface. The instance of the `Progress` class must be passed to the asynchronous method that performs the required tasks. The `Progress` class has just one method called `Report`; you invoke it after an `Await` invocation. The following code demonstrates how to report the progress of downloading a number of feeds:

```
Private Async Sub DownloadAllFeedsAsync(currentProgress As IProgress(Of Integer))
    Dim client As New System.Net.WebClient

    Dim feeds As New List(Of Uri) From _
        {New Uri("http://odata.research.microsoft.com/odata.svc/Videos/"),
         New Uri("http://odata.research.microsoft.com/odata.svc/Downloads/"),
         New Uri("http://odata.research.microsoft.com/odata.svc/Projects")}

    For Each URL In feeds
        Await client.DownloadStringTaskAsync(URL)
        counter += 1
```

```
      If currentProgress IsNot Nothing Then _
          currentProgress.Report(counter)
   Next
End Sub
```

`Report` receives as an argument an object of the same type that you assigned as the generic argument of the `Progress` class declaration in this case a counter of type `Integer` that is incremented every time a feed is downloaded. If you run this code, every time a feed is returned, the progress is also shown in the user interface, as demonstrated in Figure 44.7.

FIGURE 44.7   Reporting the progress of an asynchronous method.

This pattern makes reporting the progress of a task and in real-world applications, such as WPF and Windows 8 Apps, easy. It also makes updating controls like the `ProgressBar` incredibly simple by assigning to such controls the value stored in the instance of the `Progress` class.

Asynchronous Lambda Expressions

Methods can be asynchronous, but so can lambda expressions. To be asynchronous, a lambda must have the `Async` modifier and must return `Task` or `Task(Of T)`, but it cannot accept `ByRef` arguments and cannot be an iterator function. A lambda can be asynchronous when its code uses the `Await` operator to wait for a `Task` result. An example of asynchronous lambdas is with event handlers. For instance, you might need to wait for the result of a task when an event is raised, as in the following code snippet that handles a button's `Click`:

```
AddHandler Me.Button1.Click, Async Sub(sender, e)
                        Await DoSomeWorkAsync
                    End Sub
```

You do not need an asynchronous lambda if the work you are going to execute does not return a `Task`. Another typical usage of asynchronous lambdas is with `Task.Run`. The following code shows the same example described when introducing `Task.Run`, but now the lambda that starts the intensive work is marked with `Async` and the method that actually performs intensive computations returns a `Task` so that it can be awaited:

```
Private Async Sub RunIntensiveWorkAsync()
    cancellationToken = New CancellationTokenSource
    'This runs on the UI thread
    Console.WriteLine("Starting...")

    Try
        'This runs on a Thread Pool thread
        Dim result As Integer = Await Task.Run(Async Function()
                                                    Dim workResult As Integer = _
                                                    Await _
                                                    SimulateIntensiveWorkAsync()
                                                    Return workResult
                                               End Function)
        'This runs again on the UI thread
        Console.WriteLine("Finished")
    Catch ex As OperationCanceledException
        Console.WriteLine("Canceled by the user.")
    Catch ex As Exception

    End Try
    Console.ReadLine()
End Sub

Private Async Function SimulateIntensiveWorkAsync() As Task(Of Integer)
    Dim delay As Integer = 1000
    Await Task.Delay(delay)
    Return delay
End Function
```

Asynchronous I/O File Operations in .NET 4.5

In previous versions of the .NET Framework, you could perform asynchronous operations over files and streams by using the Asynchronous Programming Model and methods such as `Stream.BeginRead` and `Stream.EndRead`. This kind of approach can be good, but it has the limitations described in the section called "Getting Started with Async/Await" in this chapter. The .NET Framework 4.5 simplifies asynchronous I/O operations by using the Async pattern and by implementing asynchronous versions of methods that work with files and stream to avoid blocking the main thread. Such methods are exposed by the `Stream`, `FileStream`, `MemoryStream`, `TextReader`, and `TextWriter` classes that you saw in action back in Chapter 18, "Manipulating Files and Streams." Table 44.1 summarizes the available asynchronous methods.

TABLE 44.1   Asynchronous Methods for Stream Classes

Method	Description	Return Type
ReadAsync	Reads a sequence of bytes from a stream and advances the position by the number of bytes read, with an asynchronous approach	Task(Of Integer)
WriteAsync	Writes a sequence of bytes to a stream, with an asynchronous approach	Task
FlushAsync	Clears buffers associated with the stream sending buffered data to the stream, using asynchrony	Task
CopyToAsync	Asynchronously copies a number of bytes from a stream to another	Task
ReadLineAsync	Reads a line of characters using asynchrony and returns a string	Task(Of String)
ReadToEndAsync	Asynchronously reads all characters from the current position to the end of the stream, and returns one string	Task(Of String)

To see some of these methods in action, create a new WPF project. The user interface of this sample application will have to look like Figure 44.8.

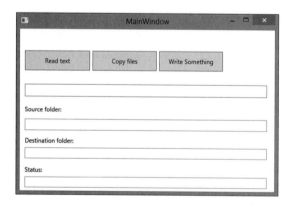

FIGURE 44.8   The user interface of the new sample application.

That said, add the following controls in the designer:

1. Three buttons, named ReadTextButton, CopyButton, and WriteButton. Then, set their Content properties with Read text, Copy files, and Write Something, respectively.

2. Four `TextBox` controls, named `ReadTextBox`, `SourceTextBox`, `DestinationTextBox`, and `StatusTextBox`.

3. Three `TextBlock` controls. You do not need to specify a name, but make sure their `Text` property is set with `Source folder`, `Destination folder`, and `Status`, respectively.

The first example uses the `StreamReader` class to read a text file asynchronously. The event handler for the `ReadTextButton.Click` event looks like this:

```
Private Async Sub ReadTextButton_Click(sender As Object,
                                       e As RoutedEventArgs) _
                                       Handles ReadTextButton.Click
    Using reader As New StreamReader("TextFile1.txt")
        Me.ReadTextBox.Text = Await reader.ReadToEndAsync
    End Using

End Sub
```

You mark the event handler with `Async`, and because this method will not be awaited by any other methods, it does not need to return a `Task`. Therefore, it can be defined as a `Sub`. Notice how you use `Await` together with the `ReadToEndAsync` method, while the rest of the implementation is made the usual way. The next example is about copying streams asynchronously. The following code shows the implementation of the `CopyButton.Click` event handler:

```
Private Async Sub CopyButton_Click(sender As Object,
                                   e As RoutedEventArgs) _
                                   Handles CopyButton.Click
    If Me.SourceTextBox.Text = "" Then
        MessageBox.Show("Please specify the source folder")
        Exit Sub
    End If

    If Me.DestinationTextBox.Text = "" Then
        MessageBox.Show("Please specify the target folder")
        Exit Sub
    End If

    For Each fileName As String In Directory.
        EnumerateFiles(Me.SourceTextBox.Text)

        Using SourceStream As FileStream = File.Open(fileName, FileMode.Open)
            Using DestinationStream As FileStream =
                File.Create(String.Concat(Me.DestinationTextBox.Text,
                                          fileName.
                                          Substring(fileName.LastIndexOf("\"c))))
```

44

```
              Await SourceStream.CopyToAsync(DestinationStream)
              Me.StatusTextBox.Text = "Copied " + DestinationStream.Name
          End Using
      End Using
  Next

End Sub
```

In particular, the code enumerates the content of the source folder and for each file it opens a stream for reading and another one for writing into the target folder. Await enables you to execute asynchronously the operation with the asynchronous method called CopyToAsync. It is worth mentioning that, with this approach, you can refresh the user interface with useful information, like showing the name of the last copied file. In a synchronous approach, this would not be possible because the UI would be blocked until the completion of the operation. The last example demonstrates how to write some text into a file asynchronously. This is the event handler for the WriteButton.Click event:

```
Private Async Sub WriteButton_Click(sender As Object,
                            e As RoutedEventArgs) Handles WriteButton.Click
    Dim uniencoding As UnicodeEncoding = New UnicodeEncoding()
    Dim filename As String =
        "c:\temp\AsyncWriteDemo.txt"

    Dim result As Byte() = uniencoding.GetBytes("Demo for Async I/O")

    Using SourceStream As FileStream = File.Open(filename, FileMode.OpenOrCreate)
        SourceStream.Seek(0, SeekOrigin.End)
        Await SourceStream.WriteAsync(result, 0, result.Length)
    End Using

End Sub
```

In this particular example, the code is written exactly like in the synchronous counterpart, except for the Async modifier and the Await statement that invokes the WriteAsync method (instead of running Write). By using the Async pattern, writing applications that work with streams and remain responsive has become dramatically simpler.

IMPLEMENTING CUSTOM AWAITERS

By using the Task-based asynchrony, you can work with instances of the Task class and use Await when waiting for their results. Using Task.Run and combinators will usually avoid the need to create custom types that can be used along with Await. However, in some situations you might want to define your own awaitable types. Reasons for making this can be various for example, performing some work over a control in the user interface from within a background thread. To accomplish this, you define a Structure that implements the INotifyCompletion interface to expose a method called OnCompleted;

then you need a method called `GetAwaiter`. The MSDN documentation does not provide enough information about building custom types that can be used with Await, but fortunately a blog post by Stephen Toub from Microsoft shows how to create one. You can find it at http://bit.ly/gwQD4S. There is also another blog post from the same author where he discusses how to implement a custom awaitable type to perform asynchronous operations with sockets; you can find it at http://bit.ly/t5hbM6.

Summary

Building applications that remain responsive whatever task they are executing is something that developers must take care of, especially from the user interface perspective. This chapter explained how to use asynchrony to build responsive applications by first discussing old-style programming models such as the Event-based Asynchronous Pattern and the Asynchronous Programming Model. Both provide techniques to write asynchronous code that runs on separate threads. However, both have some limitations, such as code complexity, issues in returning information to caller threads or functions, and managing errors effectively. Visual Basic 2012 introduces a new asynchronous pattern based on the `Async` and `Await` keywords, which enable you to keep the UI thread free and write code that is similar to the synchronous approach and is much easier to read and maintain. You invoke an asynchronous task, and then its result is returned some time later, but the control is immediately returned to the caller. When the result is available, an implicit callback enables you to consume the result of the asynchronous operation effectively. The Async pattern relies on the concept of task and on the `Task` class, which means that asynchrony easily includes support for cancellation, progress, anonymous delegates, and concurrent operations. The .NET Framework 4.5 itself exposes built-in classes that use the new Async pattern for making asynchronous I/O operations much easier with particular regard to streams and network requests. The Async pattern and the new `Async/Await` keywords represent the most important new feature in Visual Basic 2012 and can be used across multiple platforms and presentation technologies.

44

CHAPTER 45

Working with Assemblies

So many times in this book, and of course in many other .NET resources, you find the word *assembly* associating it to managed executable files such as .NET applications and libraries. You need to know some key concepts about assemblies to understand how they actually work, what kind of information they offer, and how you can avoid bad surprises when executing them. In this chapter, you first get an overview of assemblies' structure and base concepts; then you learn about advanced concepts that can help you understand their context of execution.

Assembly Overview

Assemblies can be discussed with two points of view: a physical one and a logical one. From the physical point of view, an assembly is an .exe or .dll file containing executable modules and resources. From a logical point of view, an assembly is the smallest unit for deploying .NET applications that also provides version information and enables code reuse. Chapter 46, "Reflection," discusses how, from the physical perspective, an assembly is a container of Intermediate Language code, metadata, and resources. Now we focus the discussion on the logical perspective so that you can understand some other purposes of this unit of work. In some cases, details of some of the topics have been previously discussed, but for your convenience they are summarized in this chapter.

Information Stored Within Assemblies

An assembly doesn't necessarily coincide with a standalone application. In many cases, assemblies are also compiled class libraries. Independently from what kind of assembly you are working with, it exposes the following information:

▶ **Types**—Through the IL code necessary to the application execution, assemblies can expose reusable types that can be consumed by other assemblies. This is the reason assemblies are considered the smallest unit for code reuse.

▶ **Version**—Assemblies contain version information, and all modules within the assembly have the same version; this is important to the Common Language Runtime (CLR) that can distinguish between assemblies with the same name but with different version numbers without registration.

▶ **Scope**—Assemblies provide the scope of exposed types, establishing whether they can be externally visible. This is accomplished in code by Visual Basic qualifiers such as `Public`, `Friend`, and `Private`.

Assembly Location

To understand where assemblies are located, you must consider that they are generally divided into *private assemblies* and *shared assemblies*. Private assemblies are standalone assemblies or assemblies that reside exclusively in the same folder of the application that holds a reference. This is a common scenario and makes the deployment easier because you just need to distribute the content of the application folder (known as *XCopy deployment*). Every application holding a reference to a private assembly needs to have a copy of the assembly inside its folder. This means that if you have 10 applications referencing the assembly, you will also have 10 copies of the assembly. Shared assemblies are instead files with a digital signature that can be installed to a particular location known as the Global Assembly Cache. It allows having a single shared copy of the assembly only if this comes from a trusted publisher. The Global Assembly Cache (GAC) is an important topic that Chapter 50, "Understanding the Global Assembly Cache," addresses, so read it for further details.

BINDING, CODEBASE, PROBING

When one assembly is referenced by another one, the .NET runtime needs to link them. This process is known as *binding* and is performed based on the assembly version, culture information, and strong name if available. When the runtime resolves binding, it searches for the physical assembly. This search process is known as *probing*. Because a signed assembly also has signature information that is kept when you add a reference, search is first performed in the GAC. If the assembly is not found there, the runtime searches for it looping through the application folder and subfolders until it's found. If you plan to place assemblies to locations different from the GAC and the application folder, you can place a `codeBase` suggestion in the application configuration file to tell the runtime where the required assembly will be found.

Signing Assemblies

To mark your assemblies as trusted, you need to add a digital signature known as a *strong name*. This becomes mandatory if you want to install an assembly to the GAC. Chapter 50 also provides a thorough discussion on signing assemblies with a strong name.

Assembly Information and Attributes

As you saw in various parts of the book, assemblies contain information that can make them recognizable from the external world, such as name, version, author, and copyright information. All these items are part of the assembly metadata and are injected to the assembly by adding some attribute declarations to the AssemblyInfo.vb file through instances of the Assembly attribute. Such attributes are covered in Chapter 3, "The Anatomy of a Visual Basic Project," particularly in Listing 3.3, which shows how to map properties assigned via the My Project Designer. Now that you know more about assemblies' contents and purposes, let's see where the CLR executes these complex units of work.

Understanding Application Domains

An *application domain* is a unit of isolation for executing managed code. For a better understanding, let's make a comparison with the Win32 world. In Win32, you have processes. Each process is isolated from other processes by the system so that a process cannot interfere with other processes or with resources required by such processes. This prevents process corruption and unexpected crashes. In .NET Framework architecture, the idea of isolation is provided by application domains, so an application domain is the place where an assembly runs isolated from other assemblies; when an application is started, the CLR creates one application domain for it. Although a Win32 process can host multiple application domains, when an assembly is executing within an application domain, it cannot interfere with other assemblies within different application domains. However, application domains can communicate with each other. One assembly can create multiple application domains (which are handled by the CLR) and run separate assemblies within such domains, as I will explain in the next section.

Creating Application Domains and Executing Assemblies

You have two ways for executing assemblies inside application domains: getting the instance of the default application domain for the running assembly (that is, your application) and creating a new application domain. The System.AppDomain class provides a shared property named CurrentDomain, of type System.AppDomain, which represents the instance of the current application domain. You get the instance and then execute the assembly as follows:

```
Dim currentDomain As AppDomain = AppDomain.CurrentDomain
currentDomain.ExecuteAssembly("AnotherApp.exe")
```

The `AppDomain` class exposes an instance `ExecuteAssembly` method that enables executing the specified assembly within an application domain. Executing an assembly in the current application domain is not a good idea because you cannot unload the assembly when the execution has completed. Because of this, a better approach is to create a new application domain. For now, let's see how you can get information on application domains:

```
'Shows the AppDomain friendly name
Console.WriteLine(currentDomain.FriendlyName)
'Shows the AppDomain id within the process
Console.WriteLine(currentDomain.Id)
'Shows the working directory for the running
'assembly within the AppDomain
Console.WriteLine(currentDomain.BaseDirectory)
'Returns True if the code is classified as
'fully-trusted
Console.WriteLine(currentDomain.IsFullyTrusted)
```

You can interrogate some properties for retrieving application domain information. The `AppDomain` class offers a number of other advanced properties that are not covered here. A useful resource for finding information related to `AppDomain` properties is the MSDN Library: http://msdn.microsoft.com/en-us/library/system.appdomain(v=vs.110).aspx. Now it's time to understand how you can create new application domains and execute assemblies. You invoke the `AppDomain.CreateDomain` static method and then invoke `ExecuteAssembly`.

Appdomain.Load

The `AppDomain` class exposes a `Load` method that also enables you to load an assembly. According to the official MSDN documentation, usage of this method should always be restricted to COM interoperability scenarios. So always use `ExecuteAssembly` instead.

Also remember to unload the application domain after loaded assemblies have completed their work. The following code provides an example:

```
Dim secondDomain As AppDomain = AppDomain.
    CreateDomain("secondDomain")

Try
    secondDomain.ExecuteAssembly("MyApp.exe")
Catch ex As AppDomainUnloadedException
    Console.WriteLine("The AppDomain was already unloaded")
Catch ex As Exception
Finally
    Try
        AppDomain.Unload(secondDomain)
```

```
        Catch ex As CannotUnloadAppDomainException
            Console.Write("Unable to unload the AppDomain")
        End Try
    End Try
End Try
```

The CLR throws an `AppDomainUnloadedException` if the code attempts to access an already unloaded application domain. As you can see from the code, you unload an application domain by invoking the `AppDomain.Unload` shared method that takes the application domain instance as an argument. If the application domain cannot be unloaded, a `CannotUnloadAppDomainException` is thrown. The `AppDomain.CreateDomain` method offers several overloads. One of them enables you to take an argument of type `AppDomainSetup`. It is a special object that gives you the opportunity to set some application domain properties. The following code provides an example:

```
Dim domainSetup As New AppDomainSetup
With domainSetup
    'Sets the current directory for the AppDomain
    .ApplicationBase = Environment.CurrentDirectory
    'Sets the application name
    .ApplicationName = "App domain demo"
    'Allows assembly binding redirection
    .DisallowBindingRedirects = False
    'Disallows code download from assemblies
    'via http
    .DisallowCodeDownload = True
    'Assigns a config file to the new app domain,
    'in this case the app.config of the current domain
    .ConfigurationFile = AppDomain.CurrentDomain.
                        SetupInformation.ConfigurationFile
End With

Dim thirdDomain As AppDomain = AppDomain.
    CreateDomain("thirdDomain", Nothing, domainSetup)
```

Notice that the second argument is of type `System.Security.Policy.Evidence` and is useful if you want to assign specific security policies to the application domain. In this demonstrative code, this is not accomplished. For this particular topic, application domains are important for security policies that you apply to your code. In the next section, you learn about the managed security model in the .NET Framework 4.5.

CREATING AND EXECUTING DYNAMIC CODE AT RUNTIME

In the next chapter, you learn about Reflection and how you can create assemblies and code at runtime. When you have a dynamically created assembly with custom code, you can execute the assembly within an application domain with the same techniques shown in this section.

Security Model in .NET 4.5

Assemblies contain code that is executed when you run the application. As for the operating system and for any development environment, code is executed according to security rules that prevent the code from unauthorized access to system resources. The .NET Framework 4.5 retakes a new security model introduced by version 4.0, highly simplified if compared to the previous Code Access Security platform. The code will still be classified as fully trusted and partially trusted. Full trust means that the code has elevated permissions for accessing resources, whereas partial trust means that the code is restricted by the permissions it has. The security model provided by the CLR is now easier to understand and to implement, differently from what Code Access Security was in the past.

The following are the major changes in the security model introduced by .NET 4.0 and still available in .NET 4.5:

▶ Code Access Security policies and machine-wide security policies are now turned off by default.

The *transparency model* has been enforced and applied to the .NET Framework and managed applications. The transparency model can separate code that runs as part of the application (transparent code) and code that runs as part of the .NET infrastructure (critical code). As a result, critical code can access privileged resources, such as native code, but transparent code can access only resources allowed by the specified permissions set and cannot invoke or inherit from critical code. With the transparency model, groups of code are isolated based on privileges. Such privileges are divided into full-trust and partial-trust in the sandboxed model. The following is a list of the most important points that you have to care about with the security model in .NET 4.5:

▶ The enforcement of the transparency model is also why the .NET Framework configuration tool is no longer available for setting CAS policies.

▶ The *sandboxed model* enables you to run code in a restricted environment that grants code the only permissions it actually requires, and the natural place for the model is the application domains described in the previous section.

▶ Desktop applications always run as fully trusted. This is also true for applications started from Windows Explorer, a command prompt, and a network share.

▶ Permissions are still a central part in security, but some security actions from the `System.Security.Permission.SecurityAction` class have been deprecated. They are `Deny`, `RequestMinimum`, `RequestOptional`, and `RequestRefuse`.

▶ You can expose partially trusted assemblies via the `AllowPartiallyTrustedCallers` attribute.

▶ To enable constraints on types that can be used as evidence objects, .NET Framework 4.5 has the `System.Security.Policy.EvidenceBase` base class that must be inherited from all objects that want to be candidates as evidence.

45

TRANSPARENCY MODEL

The transparency model is not new in the .NET Framework; it was first introduced with version 2.0 as a mechanism for validating code efficiency. In .NET 4, it has been revisited (this is the reason it is also known as Level 2) and provides an enforcement mechanism for code separation.

The next sections provide explanations and code examples about security features in .NET Framework 4.5 with Visual Basic 2012.

Implementing and Requiring Permissions

With the exceptions described in the previous bulleted list for deprecated security actions, applying permissions in the new security model is similar to the previous versions of the .NET Framework. This means that you can leverage permissions from the `System.Security.Permissions` namespace, such as `FileIOPermission`, `UIPermission`, `IsolatedStoragePermission`, and `EnvironmentPermission`. The following code demonstrates how you use the declarative syntax for implementing a class that requires the caller code having the `FileIOPermission` to execute. Such a class simply implements a method that returns an `XDocument` from a text file:

```
'The caller code will need the FileIOPermission permission
'with unrestricted access otherwise it will fail
<FileIOPermission(Security.Permissions.SecurityAction.Demand,
                  Unrestricted:=True)>
Class XmlParse
```

```
    Shared Function String2Xml(ByVal fileName As String) As XDocument
        'Expects an Xml-formatted string
        Return XDocument.Parse(fileName)
    End Function
End Class
```

You can also use the imperative syntax, which looks like this:

```
Dim fp As New FileIOPermission(PermissionState.Unrestricted)
Try
    fp.Demand()

Catch ex As Security.SecurityException

End Try
```

You create an instance of the required permission and then invoke Demand for checking whether the application has that level of permissions. If not, a System.Security.SecurityException is thrown.

The Transparency Level 2

By default, when you create a new application, it relies on security rules provided by the Transparency Level 2 of .NET Framework 4.5. The level name has this form to allow distinction from the old transparency level of previous .NET versions (known as Transparency Level 1). So the Transparency Level 2 security rules are applied implicitly, but a better idea is applying them explicitly by applying the System.Security.SecurityRules attribute that can be added at the assembly level as follows:

```
<Assembly: SecurityRules(Security.SecurityRuleSet.Level2)>
```

Applying the attribute explicitly is appropriate for code reading and future maintenance and avoids confusion. This level of enforcement brings into the .NET Framework some new ways of thinking about security policies. Most rely on the concept of *host*, where this means an environment is responsible for executing applications; ClickOnce, ASP.NET, and Internet Explorer are host examples. For code trust, applications that are not hosted, such as programs launched from a command prompt, from Windows Explorer, or from a shared network path, now run as full-trust. Instead, hosted or sandboxed applications still run according to host-based policies and run as partial-trust. For hosted and sandboxed applications, they are considered as *transparent* because they run with the limited permissions set granted by the sandbox. This means that you will no longer need to check for permissions when running partially trusted code because transparent applications run with the permissions set granted by the sandbox, so your only preoccupation should be targeting the sandbox permissions set and to not write code requiring the full-trust policy. It is important to mention that the transparency mechanism can separate code that is part of the .NET infrastructure (and that thus requires high privileges such as invoking native code), which is called *critical code*, and code that is part of the application, also known as *transparent code*. The idea behind the scenes is separating groups of code based on privileges. When working with sandboxes, such privileges are of two types: fully trusted, which is the unrestricted level, and partially trusted, which is the level restricted to the permission set established in the sandbox.

DESKTOP APPLICATIONS

With the Transparency Level 2 enabled, desktop applications run as full-trust.

The `System.Security.SecurityRules` attribute is not the only one that you can apply for establishing permissions rules. There are other attributes available, summarized in Table 45.1.

TABLE 45.1   Security Attributes

Attribute	Description
SecurityTransparent	Specifies that the code is transparent, meaning that it can be accessed by partially trusted code, that it cannot allow access to protected resources, and that it cannot cause an elevation of privileges. All types and members are transparent.
SecurityCritical	Code introduced by types exposed from the assembly is considered as security-critical, meaning that it can perform operations that require an elevation of privileges, whereas all other code is transparent. Methods overridden from abstract classes or implemented via an interface must be also explicitly marked with the attribute.
SecuritySafeCritical	Specifies that types expose critical code but allows access from partially trusted assemblies.

If you do not specify any attribute other than `SecurityRules`, for fully trusted assemblies the runtime considers all code as security-critical and thus callable only from fully trusted code, except where this could cause inheritance violations. If the assembly is instead partially trusted, specifying no attribute other than `SecurityRules` will make the runtime consider types and members as transparent by default, but they can be security-critical or security-safe-critical. For further detail on inheritance in the transparency model and on attributes listed in Table 45.1, visit the following page in the MSDN Library: http://msdn.microsoft.com/en-us/library/dd233102(v=vs.110).aspx. This is the reason it is opportune to explicitly provide the most appropriate attribute. The following is an example of applying both the `SecurityRules` and `SecurityTransparent` attributes:

```
<Assembly: SecurityRules(Security.SecurityRuleSet.Level2)>
<Assembly: SecurityTransparent()>
Class Foo
End Class
```

TIPS ON `SecurityTransparent`

Transparency enforcements are handled by the Just-in-Time compiler and not by the CLR infrastructure. This means that if you apply the `SecurityTransparent` attribute to an assembly, the assembly cannot call transparent and security-safe-critical types and members independently from the permissions set (including full-trust). In such a scenario, if the code attempts to access a security-critical type or member, a `MethodAccessException` will be thrown.

Sandboxing

You can execute partially trusted code within a sandbox that runs with the specified permissions set. Code, including assemblies, executed within the sandbox will be also granted to just the specified permissions set. To create and run a sandbox, you need an instance of the `AppDomain` class. The example here creates a sandbox for running an external assembly given the `LocalIntranet` zone's permissions. Before showing the sandbox example, follow these steps:

1. Create a new Console application and name the new project as **ExternalApp**.

2. In the `Main` method, add a `Console.Writeline` statement for showing whatever text message you like.

3. Build the project; then create a new folder named C:\MyApps and copy the newly generated **ExternalApp.exe** into C:\MyApps.

Such steps are required to have a simple external assembly to run inside the security sandbox. Now close the **ExternalApp** project and create a new Console project, naming it **SandBox**. The goal is to create a sandbox with `LocalIntranet` permission and run an external assembly inside the sandbox so that this external application will also be granted the same permissions. When ready, first add the following `Imports` directives:

```
Imports System.Security
Imports System.Security.Policy
Imports System.Reflection
```

Now move inside the `Main` method. The first thing you need is an `Evidence` object that you assign with the required permissions set, as demonstrated by the following code:

```
Dim ev As New Evidence()
ev.AddHostEvidence(New Zone(SecurityZone.Intranet))
```

When you have the `Evidence` instance, you can get a sandbox with the specified permissions as demonstrated by the following line:

```
Dim permSet As PermissionSet = SecurityManager.GetStandardSandbox(ev)
```

The `SecurityManager.GetStandardSandbox` returns a sandbox limited to the specified permissions. This sandbox will be used later when running the external assembly. As an alternative, you can set your own permissions and create your custom permissions set using the `PermissionSet` object as follows:

```
Dim permSet As New PermissionSet(Permissions.PermissionState.None)
permSet.AddPermission( _
        New SecurityPermission(SecurityPermissionFlag.Execution))
permSet.AddPermission(New UIPermission(PermissionState.Unrestricted))
```

At this point, you can put your hands on application domains. The first thing to do is create an instance of the `AppDomainSetup` class for specifying the working directory of the external assembly:

```
Dim ads As New AppDomainSetup()
ads.ApplicationBase = "C:\MyApps"
```

Next, you need to set the host `Evidence` and then create the `AppDomain`, passing the security information; then you'll invoke `AppDomain.ExecuteAssembly` to run the sandboxed assembly:

```
Dim hostEvidence As New Evidence()
Dim sandbox As AppDomain = AppDomain.
    CreateDomain("Sandboxed Domain", hostEvidence, ads, permSet, Nothing)

sandbox.ExecuteAssemblyByName("ExternalApp")
```

The `AppDomain.CreateDomain` method has an overload that enables you to create an application domain with a permissions set. Because the application domain has security permissions, an instance of the `Evidence` class is required to tell the runtime that the assembly will be affected by such permissions. Other arguments are the `AppDomainSetup` instance and the permissions set under which the external assembly is going to be run. The last null argument can be replaced with a reference to the strong name, in case you want to add it to the full trust list. This would first require the current application to be signed with a strong name (covered in Chapter 50) and then by getting a reference to the strong name via the `System.Security.Policy.StrongName` class as shown in the following line:

```
Dim fullTrustAssembly As StrongName = Assembly.
    GetExecutingAssembly.Evidence.GetHostEvidence(Of StrongName)()
```

The `Assembly.Evidence.GetHostEvidence(Of StrongName)` method returns the reference to the strong name. (The `System.Assembly` class is discussed in Chapter 46, "Reflection.") Finally, you pass the strong name reference to `AppDomain.CreateDomain` as follows:

```
Dim sandbox As AppDomain = AppDomain.
    CreateDomain("Sandboxed Domain", hostEvidence, ads,
                permSet, fullTrustAssembly)
```

45

Listing 45.1 shows the complete code example for your convenience.

LISTING 45.1   Running a Sandboxed Assembly

```
Imports System.Security
Imports System.Security.Policy
Imports System.Reflection

Module Module1

    Sub Main()
        Dim ev As New Evidence()
        ev.AddHostEvidence(New Zone(SecurityZone.Intranet))

        Dim permSet As PermissionSet = SecurityManager.GetStandardSandbox(ev)

        Dim ads As New AppDomainSetup()
        ads.ApplicationBase = "C:\MyApps"

        Dim hostEvidence As New Evidence()
        Dim sandbox As AppDomain = AppDomain.
            CreateDomain("Sandboxed Domain", hostEvidence, ads,
                        permSet, Nothing)

        'The assembly runs in a LocalIntranet sandboxed environment
        sandbox.ExecuteAssemblyByName("ExternalApp")
    End Sub
End Module
```

SANDBOXES COMPLEXITY

Working with sandboxes can include complex scenarios. Particularly, you might have the need to execute not-trusted code from an external assembly with customized permissions sets. This also requires advanced application domains concepts. Fortunately, the MSDN Library provides an interesting walk-through covering these scenarios, available at http://msdn.microsoft.com/en-us/library/bb763046(v=vs.110).aspx. This is also useful to get a practical example about implementing the `MarshalByRefObject` for dynamic code execution within application domains.

Conditional APTCA

You can allow an assembly to be called by partially trusted code by applying the `System.Security.AllowPartiallyTrustedCallers` attribute at the assembly level. This can be accomplished as follows:

```
Imports System.Security

<Assembly: AllowPartiallyTrustedCallers()>
```

Without this attribute, only full-trusted code can call the assembly. Different from versions prior to 4.0, in the .NET Framework 4.x this attribute no longer requires an assembly to be signed with a strong name, and its presence involves all the security functions present in the code in the security checks.

Migrating from Old CAS-Based Code

If you move your existing code to .NET Framework 4.x and used Code Access Security policies, you might be advised with a message saying that CAS is obsolete. In these situations, you can add a specific section to the application configuration file, which allows legacy policies that look like this:

```
<configuration>
  <runtime>
    <NetFx40_LegacySecurityPolicy enabled="true"/>
  </runtime>
</configuration>
```

Of course, you always need to check whether legacy policies are appropriate in the particular scenario you are facing. I suggest reading the MSDN documentation about CAS migration, available at http://msdn.microsoft.com/en-us/library/ee191568(v=vs.110).aspx.

Summary

Understanding how assemblies work and how they can be managed is a key topic in .NET development. In this chapter, you first got an overview of assemblies, including their structure; their locations; and the type of information they share, such as code and metadata. Next, the discussion focused on application domains and the System.AppDomain class, which provides units of isolation for executing assemblies. Finally, you got an overview of the security model available in .NET Framework 4.x, starting from discussing the transparency level and the sandboxed model to analyzing specific code examples.

45

Reflection

There are situations in which you need to implement logic for performing some tasks depending on user choices. This kind of a situation is not uncommon. The problem is when you cannot predetermine the code required for executing actions depending on user input. Think of code generators: These tools know how to generate code but cannot predetermine which code has to be generated until the users specify their requirements. Also think of assemblies external from your application. In some cases you might want to use types from an external assembly; in other cases you might just want to get information on types provided by the assembly; and in still other cases you might want to reach members with limited scope visibility that you could not reach by adding a reference. Reflection is a key part in the .NET Framework that enables you to accomplish all these mentioned scenarios. In this chapter, you learn to use Reflection to both inspect assemblies and types and to generate and consume code on-the-fly. Also, in the final part of the chapter you learn about a new feature in Visual Basic 2012 known as Caller Information. It enables you to retrieve information that in the past was available only via advanced Reflection techniques and that is now easier to get.

Introducing Reflection

Reflection is an important part of the .NET Framework and provides the capability for interrogating assemblies' metadata and collecting information on types exposed by assemblies. Reflection also enables you to invoke code from external assemblies and generate code on-the-fly. You can take advantage of Reflection by using objects exposed by the `System.Reflection` namespace. It can be particularly useful when you need to generate code according to some user input or when you are in late bound scenarios where making decisions on which code must be invoked (or generated) is something determined at runtime. Before putting your hands on code, it is necessary to get an overview of how assemblies are structured so that you can have a better understanding of the type of information you can investigate with the Reflection.

Understanding Assemblies' Metadata

As you know, when you build an executable with Visual Basic, you build a .NET assembly. An assembly is a container of metadata and code. Metadata is information that the Common Language Runtime (CLR) uses in correctly loading and running the assembly. Figure 46.1 represents how an assembly is structured.

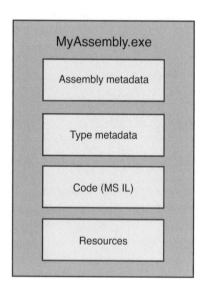

FIGURE 46.1   How an assembly is structured.

The Assembly Metadata, also known as *assembly manifest*, provides assembly information such as the name, version, culture, copyright information, and signature. The Type Metadata contains information on types defined within the assembly, such as class names and names of class members, including their parameters. The Code part is the actual Intermediate Language code that will be executed when the assembly is loaded. The Resources block contains all resources required by the assembly, such as images, icons, and strings. Additionally, types within an assembly can be grouped into multiple modules. A module is a container of types, whereas an assembly is a container of modules. With Reflection, you can inspect metadata and code from an assembly using Visual Basic code, including assembly information.

When talking about assemblies, we usually refer to single file executables. Assemblies can be composed of multiple linked files; keep in mind that assembly metadata needs to reside only in the main assembly. This is a special case and cannot be accomplished with Visual Studio (you should manually use MSBuild), but it is something that it is worth mentioning.

Preparing a Sample Assembly

Before showing Reflection capabilities, a good idea is to prepare an appropriate code example. First, create a new class library project and name it **People**. The goal of the library is to expose a special implementation of the `Person` class, with interfaces and enumeration implementations for a better demonstration on Reflection. When ready, write the code in Listing 46.1, which is quite simple.

LISTING 46.1   Preparing Code for Reflection

```
Imports System.Text

Public Enum Genders
    Male = 0
    Female = 1
End Enum

Public Interface IPerson
    Property FirstName As String
    Property LastName As String
    Property Age As Integer
    Property Gender As Genders
    Event InstanceCreated()
    Function BuildFullName() As String
End Interface

Public Class Person
    Implements IPerson

    Public Property FirstName As String Implements IPerson.FirstName
    Public Property Gender As Genders Implements IPerson.Gender
    Public Property LastName As String Implements IPerson.LastName
    Public Property Age As Integer Implements IPerson.Age
    Public Event InstanceCreated() Implements IPerson.InstanceCreated

    Public Overridable Function BuildFullName() As String _
                    Implements IPerson.BuildFullName
```

46

```
        Dim fullName As New StringBuilder
        fullName.Append(LastName)
        fullName.Append(" ")
        fullName.Append(FirstName)
        fullName.Append(", ")
        fullName.Append(Gender.ToString)
        fullName.Append(", of age ")
        fullName.Append(Age.ToString)
        Return fullName.ToString
    End Function
End Class
```

Build the project; then add a new Console project to the current solution. Finally, add a reference to the People class library so that—just for demo purposes—you can load the assembly for Reflection without specifying the full path.

Getting Assembly Information

You get assembly metadata information by creating an instance of the System.Reflection.Assembly class. This class provides both static and instance members for accessing assembly information. Typically, you use one of the methods summarized in Table 46.1 to load an assembly for getting information.

TABLE 46.1   Methods for Loading an Assembly

Method	Description
GetAssembly	Loads an assembly containing the specified type
GetCallingAssembly	Gets the assembly that stores the code that invoked the current method
GetExecutingAssembly	Returns the instance of the current assembly
GetEntryAssembly	Returns the instance of the assembly that ran the current process
Load	Loads the specified assembly into the current application domain
LoadFile	Loads the specified assembly from the specified path
LoadFrom	Loads the specified assembly into the current application domain, given the specified path
ReflectionOnlyLoad	Like Load, but limits you to only Reflection inspection and not code execution
ReflectionOnlyLoadFrom	Like LoadFrom, but limits you to only Reflection inspection and not code execution

When you get the instance of the assembly you want to inspect, you can access information via some useful properties. The code in Listing 46.2 shows how to accomplish this. (See comments for explanations.)

LISTING 46.2   Inspecting Assembly Information

```
Imports System.Reflection

Module GettingAsmInfo

    Sub Main()
        'Infers System.Reflection.Assembly
        Dim asm = Assembly.ReflectionOnlyLoadFrom("People.dll")

        With asm
            'Gets the full assembly name with
            'version and culture
            Console.WriteLine("Assembly name:")
            Console.WriteLine(.FullName)
            'Gets whether the assembly is fully trusted
            Console.WriteLine("Is full-trust: {0}", .IsFullyTrusted)
            'Gets the assembly entry point. If empty, the
            'constructor is the entry point
            Console.WriteLine("The entry point method is: {0}", .EntryPoint)
            'Gets the .NET version that the
            'assembly was built upon
            Console.WriteLine("Image runtime version: {0}", .ImageRuntimeVersion)
            'Gets whether the assembly was loaded from
            'the GAC
            Console.WriteLine("Loaded from the GAC: {0}", .GlobalAssemblyCache)
            'Gets the assembly location
            Console.WriteLine("Assembly path: {0}", .Location)

            'Gets an array of modules loaded
            'by the assembly
            Console.WriteLine("Loaded modules: ")
            For Each item As System.Reflection.Module _
                In .GetLoadedModules
                Console.WriteLine("   {0}", item.Name)
            Next
        End With
        Console.ReadLine()
    End Sub
End Module
```

Notice how the code uses the `ReflectionOnlyLoadFrom` method to enable only inspection without code execution capabilities. If you run the preceding code, you get the following result:

```
Assembly name:
People, Version=1.0.0.0, Culture=neutral, PublicKeyToken=null
Is full-trust: True
The entry point method is:
Image runtime version: v4.0.30319
Loaded from the GAC: False
Assembly path: C:\Users\Alessandro\documents\visual studio
2012\Projects\Reflection\Reflection\bin\Debug\People.dll
Loaded modules:
     People.dll
```

The `Assembly.GetModules` method returns an array of modules loaded by the instance of the assembly. Other interesting methods are `GetExportedTypes`, which returns an array of publicly visible types, and `GetFiles`, which returns an array of `FileStream` objects, each representing a file in the assembly's resources. Inspecting assembly information is just the first level of Reflection. The next step is inspecting types.

Reflecting Types

Reflection enables retrieving information on programs, including modules, types, and type members defined within an assembly. For example, you might want to enumerate all types and type members defined in the People.dll assembly. Take a look at the following code:

```
Dim asm = Assembly.LoadFrom("People.dll")

Console.WriteLine("Enumerating types:")
For Each t In asm.GetTypes
    Console.WriteLine("Type name: {0}", t.ToString)

    Console.WriteLine(" Constructors:")
    For Each constructor In t.GetConstructors
        Console.WriteLine("      " + constructor.ToString)
    Next

    Console.WriteLine(" Methods:")
    For Each method In t.GetMethods
        Console.WriteLine("      " + method.ToString)
    Next
```

```
    Console.WriteLine(" Properties:")
    For Each [property] In t.GetProperties
        Console.WriteLine("     " + [property].ToString)
    Next

    Console.WriteLine(" Fields:")
    For Each field In t.GetFields
        Console.WriteLine("     " + field.ToString)
    Next

    Console.WriteLine(" Events:")
    For Each [event] In t.GetEvents
        Console.WriteLine("     " + [event].ToString)
    Next
Next
```

You still get the instance of the desired assembly; then you can iterate types (or modules if preferred). The `Assembly.GetTypes` method returns an array of `System.Type` objects defined in the assembly that you can iterate for detailed information. The `System.Type` class exposes several `GetX` methods, in which `x` can stand for `Constructors`, `Properties`, `Methods`, `Fields`, and `Events`. Each of these methods returns an `XInfo` class instance, such as `MethodInfo`, `PropertyInfo`, `FieldInfo`, and so on. Each class exposes interesting properties about the inspected member for further information such as `IsPrivate`, `IsPublic`, or `IsStatic`.

USING `ToString`

Each `XInfo` class also exposes a `Name` property that returns the name of the member. In this case, `ToString` was used instead of the name to return the full member signature.

Also, the `System.Type` class offers some useful properties enabling you to understand what kind of type you are inspecting such as `IsClass`, `IsInterface`, or `IsEnum`. The `Namespace` property enables you to get the namespace exposing the inspected type. Notice that the preceding code inspects all types defined in the specified assembly, including the ones that are usually part of My Project. Also notice that Reflection considers properties' getters and setters such as methods that thus will be listed within this category. For a better understanding, the following is an excerpt of the output produced by the previously illustrated code:

```
Enumerating types:
Type name: People.My.MyApplication
 Constructors:
     Void .ctor()
```

Methods:
    System.String GetEnvironmentVariable(System.String)
    Microsoft.VisualBasic.Logging.Log get_Log()
    Microsoft.VisualBasic.ApplicationServices.AssemblyInfo get_Info()
    System.Globalization.CultureInfo get_Culture()
    System.Globalization.CultureInfo get_UICulture()
    Void ChangeCulture(System.String)
    Void ChangeUICulture(System.String)
    System.String ToString()
    Boolean Equals(System.Object)
    Int32 GetHashCode()
    System.Type GetType()
Properties:
    Microsoft.VisualBasic.Logging.Log Log
    Microsoft.VisualBasic.ApplicationServices.AssemblyInfo Info
    System.Globalization.CultureInfo Culture
    System.Globalization.CultureInfo UICulture
Fields:
Events:
Type name: People.My.MyComputer
Constructors:
    Void .ctor()
Methods:
    Microsoft.VisualBasic.Devices.Audio get_Audio()
    Microsoft.VisualBasic.MyServices.ClipboardProxy get_Clipboard()
    Microsoft.VisualBasic.Devices.Ports get_Ports()
    Microsoft.VisualBasic.Devices.Mouse get_Mouse()
    Microsoft.VisualBasic.Devices.Keyboard get_Keyboard()
    System.Windows.Forms.Screen get_Screen()
    Microsoft.VisualBasic.Devices.Clock get_Clock()
    Microsoft.VisualBasic.MyServices.FileSystemProxy get_FileSystem()
    Microsoft.VisualBasic.Devices.ComputerInfo get_Info()
    Microsoft.VisualBasic.Devices.Network get_Network()
    System.String get_Name()
    Microsoft.VisualBasic.MyServices.RegistryProxy get_Registry()
    System.String ToString()
    Boolean Equals(System.Object)
    Int32 GetHashCode()
    System.Type GetType()
Properties:
    Microsoft.VisualBasic.Devices.Audio Audio
    Microsoft.VisualBasic.MyServices.ClipboardProxy Clipboard
    Microsoft.VisualBasic.Devices.Ports Ports
    Microsoft.VisualBasic.Devices.Mouse Mouse

```
        Microsoft.VisualBasic.Devices.Keyboard Keyboard
        System.Windows.Forms.Screen Screen
        Microsoft.VisualBasic.Devices.Clock Clock
        Microsoft.VisualBasic.MyServices.FileSystemProxy FileSystem
        Microsoft.VisualBasic.Devices.ComputerInfo Info
        Microsoft.VisualBasic.Devices.Network Network
        System.String Name
        Microsoft.VisualBasic.MyServices.RegistryProxy Registry
 Fields:
 Events:
Type name: People.My.MyProject
 Constructors:
 Methods:
        System.String ToString()
        Boolean Equals(System.Object)
        Int32 GetHashCode()
        System.Type GetType()
 Properties:
 Fields:
 Events:
Type name: People.My.MyProject+MyWebServices
 Constructors:
        Void .ctor()
 Methods:
        Boolean Equals(System.Object)
        Int32 GetHashCode()
        System.String ToString()
        System.Type GetType()
 Properties:
 Fields:
 Events:
Type name: People.Genders
 Constructors:
 Methods:
        Boolean Equals(System.Object)
        Int32 GetHashCode()
        System.String ToString()
        System.String ToString(System.String, System.IFormatProvider)
        Int32 CompareTo(System.Object)
        System.String ToString(System.String)
        System.String ToString(System.IFormatProvider)
        Boolean HasFlag(System.Enum)
        System.TypeCode GetTypeCode()
        System.Type GetType()
```

46

```
 Properties:
 Fields:
     Int32 value__
     People.Genders Male
     People.Genders Female
 Events:
Type name: People.IPerson
 Constructors:
 Methods:
     System.String get_FirstName()
     Void set_FirstName(System.String)
     System.String get_LastName()
     Void set_LastName(System.String)
     Int32 get_Age()
     Void set_Age(Int32)
     People.Genders get_Gender()
     Void set_Gender(People.Genders)
     System.String BuildFullName()
     Void add_InstanceCreated(InstanceCreatedEventHandler)
     Void remove_InstanceCreated(InstanceCreatedEventHandler)
 Properties:
     System.String FirstName
     System.String LastName
     Int32 Age
     People.Genders Gender
 Fields:
 Events:
     InstanceCreatedEventHandler InstanceCreated
Type name: People.Person
 Constructors:
     Void .ctor()
 Methods:
     System.String get_FirstName()
     Void set_FirstName(System.String)
     People.Genders get_Gender()
     Void set_Gender(People.Genders)
     System.String get_LastName()
     Void set_LastName(System.String)
     Int32 get_Age()
     Void set_Age(Int32)
     Void add_InstanceCreated(InstanceCreatedEventHandler)
     Void remove_InstanceCreated(InstanceCreatedEventHandler)
     System.String BuildFullName()
     System.String ToString()
```

```
        Boolean Equals(System.Object)
        Int32 GetHashCode()
        System.Type GetType()
    Properties:
        System.String FirstName
        People.Genders Gender
        System.String LastName
        Int32 Age
    Fields:
    Events:
        InstanceCreatedEventHandler InstanceCreated
Type name: People.IPerson+InstanceCreatedEventHandler
    Constructors:
        Void .ctor(System.Object, IntPtr)
    Methods:
        System.IAsyncResult BeginInvoke(System.AsyncCallback, System.Object)
        Void EndInvoke(System.IAsyncResult)
        Void Invoke()
        Void GetObjectData(System.Runtime.Serialization.SerializationInfo,
            System.Runtime.Serialization.StreamingContext)
        Boolean Equals(System.Object)
        System.Delegate[] GetInvocationList()
        Int32 GetHashCode()
        System.Object DynamicInvoke(System.Object[])
        System.Reflection.MethodInfo get_Method()
        System.Object get_Target()
        System.Object Clone()
        System.String ToString()
        System.Type GetType()
    Properties:
        System.Reflection.MethodInfo Method
        System.Object Target
    Fields:
    Events:
```

Notice also how EventHandler types, generated behind the scenes when you implement a simple event, are inspected and illustrated. Also notice how the members' signature recalls the Intermediate Language syntax.

Reflecting a Single Type

Reflecting all types within an assembly can be useful, but in most cases you will probably be interested in reflecting a single type. To accomplish this, you need the instance of a System.Type. Then you need to invoke members described in the previous section. For example, imagine you want to inspect members from the Person class. You first get the type instance, and then you can perform reflection as demonstrated by the following code:

```
Dim myType As Type = (New People.Person).GetType

Console.WriteLine(" Methods:")
For Each method In myType.GetMethods
    Console.WriteLine("      " + method.ToString)
Next

Console.WriteLine(" Properties:")
For Each [property] In myType.GetProperties
    Console.WriteLine("      " + [property].ToString)
Next

Console.WriteLine(" Fields:")
For Each field In myType.GetFields
    Console.WriteLine("      " + field.ToString)
Next

Console.WriteLine(" Events:")
For Each [event] In myType.GetEvents
    Console.WriteLine("      " + [event].ToString)
Next
```

The preceding code produces the following result:

```
Methods:
     System.String get_FirstName()
     Void set_FirstName(System.String)
     People.Genders get_Gender()
     Void set_Gender(People.Genders)
     System.String get_LastName()
     Void set_LastName(System.String)
     Int32 get_Age()
     Void set_Age(Int32)
     Void add_InstanceCreated(InstanceCreatedEventHandler)
     Void remove_InstanceCreated(InstanceCreatedEventHandler)
     System.String BuildFullName()
     System.String ToString()
     Boolean Equals(System.Object)
     Int32 GetHashCode()
     System.Type GetType()
```

```
Properties:
    System.String FirstName
    People.Genders Gender
    System.String LastName
    Int32 Age
Fields:
Events:
    InstanceCreatedEventHandler InstanceCreated
```

For more details, the MSDN documentation on the `System.Reflection` namespace and the `System.Type` class are a good source of information on available members.

REFLECTION SECURITY CONSIDERATIONS

Reflection is both a key topic and a powerful tool in the .NET developer toolbox. By the way, you had the opportunity to understand how fragile your code is in security terms because, with a few lines of code, anyone can see types and members exposed by the assembly. Because preventing Reflection is not possible, if you want to protect your code, you need to use an obfuscation tool such as Dotfuscator (shipped with Visual Studio 2012) that can add more effective protection.

Invoking Code Dynamically

Reflection also enables you to execute dynamic code, meaning that you can pick up types defined within an assembly, creating instances and invoking types from Visual Basic code without having a reference to that assembly. For example, imagine you want to load the People.dll assembly and create and populate an instance of the `Person` class, as shown in Listing 46.3.

LISTING 46.3 Creating and Running Dynamic Code

```
Imports System.Reflection
Module DynamicCode

    Sub DynCode()
        Dim asm = Assembly.LoadFrom("People.dll")

        'Gets the type definition
        Dim personType = asm.GetType("People.Person")

        'Gets the LastName property definition
        Dim lastNameProperty As PropertyInfo = personType.
                                    GetProperty("LastName")
```

```
        'Gets a reference to the property setter
        Dim lastNamePropSet As MethodInfo = lastNameProperty.
                                       GetSetMethod

        Dim firstNameProperty As PropertyInfo = personType.
                                       GetProperty("FirstName")
        Dim firstNamePropSet As MethodInfo = firstNameProperty.
                                       GetSetMethod

        Dim ageProperty As PropertyInfo = personType.GetProperty("Age")
        Dim agePropSet As MethodInfo = ageProperty.GetSetMethod

        'Creates an instance of the Person class
        Dim newPerson As Object = _
            Activator.CreateInstance(personType)

        'Each method is invoked upon the new type instance
        lastNamePropSet.Invoke(newPerson, New Object() {"Del Sole"})
        firstNamePropSet.Invoke(newPerson, New Object() {"Alessandro"})
        agePropSet.Invoke(newPerson, New Object() {35})

        'Gets the BuildFullName method from the Person class
        Dim buildFullNameMethod = personType.GetMethod("BuildFullName")

        'The method returns String but Invoke returns Object, so
        'a conversion is required
        Dim result As String = CStr(buildFullNameMethod.
                            Invoke(newPerson, Nothing))

        Console.WriteLine(result)
        Console.ReadLine()
    End Sub
End Module
```

When you have the type instance, you invoke the GetProperty method to get a reference of the desired property. This returns a PropertyInfo object. To set the property value, you need a reference to the setter method that is obtained via the GetSetMethod and that returns a MethodInfo object. (If you also want the ability to get a property value, you need to instead invoke GetGetMethod the same way.) When you have all the properties, you need an instance of the class. This can be obtained by calling the Activator. CreateInstance method, which takes the type instance as the argument.

The System.Activator class contains members for creating code locally or retrieving code from a remote location. Having an instance of the class is required before you set properties because it is against the instance that property setters will be invoked. To actually run the property setter, you call the MethodInfo.Invoke instance method; the first argument is the type instance, and the second argument is an array of items of type `Object`, each to be used as a property value. In our case, each property in the `Person` class accepts just one value, so each array can store just one item. Similarly, you can get reference to methods by invoking `GetMethod` on the type instance, as it happens in Listing 46.3, to get a reference to the `Person.BuildFullName` method. When you call `Invoke` to run the method, you can pass `Nothing` as the second argument if the original method does not require parameters. The code produces the following result:

```
Del Sole Alessandro, Male of Age: 35
```

After seeing how you can call dynamic code provided by an existing assembly, let's now see how to create code at runtime.

SECURITY NOTE

In many cases, you can also invoke members marked as private or with limited visibility. Although this can seem exciting, be careful. If you invoke a private member but you are not completely sure about its purpose, you expose your code to potentially uncontrollable dangers.

Generating Code at Runtime with `Reflection.Emit`

46

The `System.Reflection.Emit` namespace provides objects for generating assemblies, types, and type members at runtime. You need to perform the following operations sequentially:

1. Create an in-memory assembly within the current application domain with an instance of the `AssemblyBuilder` class.

2. Create a module for containing types via an instance of the `ModuleBuilder` class.

3. Create types with instances of the `TypeBuilder` class.

4. Add members to the `TypeBuilder` via `XBuilder` objects, such as `MethodBuilder`, `FieldBuilder`, and `PropertyBuilder`.

5. Save the assembly to disk if required.

The code in Listing 46.4 demonstrates how to dynamically create a simple implementation of the `Person` class with one property and one method.

LISTING 46.4   Generating Code at Runtime

```
Imports System.Reflection
Imports System.Reflection.Emit

Module CreatingCode
```

```vbnet
Sub CreateAssembly()

    'Creates assembly name and properties
    Dim asmName As New AssemblyName("People")
    asmName.Version = New Version("1.0.0")
    asmName.CultureInfo = New Globalization.CultureInfo("en-US")

    'Gets the current application domain
    Dim currentAppDomain As AppDomain = AppDomain.CurrentDomain

    'Creates a new in-memory assembly in the current application domain
    'providing execution and saving capabilities
    Dim asmBuilder As AssemblyBuilder = currentAppDomain.
                                        DefineDynamicAssembly(asmName,
                                        AssemblyBuilderAccess.RunAndSave)

    'Creates a module for containing types
    Dim modBuilder As ModuleBuilder = _
        asmBuilder.DefineDynamicModule("PersonModule",
                                        "People.dll")

    'Creates a type, specifically a Public Class
    Dim tyBuilder As TypeBuilder = _
        modBuilder.DefineType("Person",
                                TypeAttributes.Public _
                                Or TypeAttributes.Class)
    'Defines a default empty constructor
    Dim ctorBuilder As ConstructorBuilder = _
        tyBuilder.DefineDefaultConstructor(MethodAttributes.Public)

    'Defines a field for storing a property value
    Dim fldBuilder As FieldBuilder = _
        tyBuilder.DefineField("_lastName",
                                GetType(String),
                                FieldAttributes.Private)

    'Defines a property of type String
    Dim propBuilder As PropertyBuilder = _
        tyBuilder.DefineProperty("LastName",
                                PropertyAttributes.None, GetType(String),
                                Type.EmptyTypes)

    'Defines a series of attributes for both getter and setter
    Dim propMethodAttributes As MethodAttributes = _
        MethodAttributes.Public Or
```

```vb
            MethodAttributes.SpecialName Or
            MethodAttributes.HideBySig

        'Defines the getter method for the property
        Dim propGetMethod As MethodBuilder = _
            tyBuilder.DefineMethod("get_LastName",
                                    propMethodAttributes,
                                    GetType(String),
                                    Type.EmptyTypes)

        'Generates IL code for returning the field value
        Dim propGetMethodIL As ILGenerator = propGetMethod.GetILGenerator
        propGetMethodIL.Emit(OpCodes.Ldarg_0)
        propGetMethodIL.Emit(OpCodes.Ldfld, fldBuilder)
        propGetMethodIL.Emit(OpCodes.Ret)

        'Defines the setter method for the property
        Dim propSetMethod As MethodBuilder = _
            tyBuilder.DefineMethod("set_LastName",
                                    propMethodAttributes,
                                    GetType(String),
                                    Type.EmptyTypes)

        'Generates the IL code for setting the field value
        Dim propSetMethodIL As ILGenerator = propSetMethod.GetILGenerator
        propSetMethodIL.Emit(OpCodes.Ldarg_0)
        propSetMethodIL.Emit(OpCodes.Ldarg_1)
        propSetMethodIL.Emit(OpCodes.Stfld, fldBuilder)
        propSetMethodIL.Emit(OpCodes.Ret)

        'Assigns getter and setter to the property
        propBuilder.SetGetMethod(propGetMethod)
        propBuilder.SetSetMethod(propSetMethod)

        'Defines a public method that returns String
        Dim methBuilder As MethodBuilder = _
            tyBuilder.DefineMethod("BuildFullName",
                                    MethodAttributes.Public,
                                    GetType(String),
                                    Type.EmptyTypes)

        'Method body cannot be empty, so just return
        Dim methodILGen As ILGenerator = methBuilder.GetILGenerator
        methodILGen.EmitWriteLine("Method implementation needed")
        methodILGen.Emit(OpCodes.Ret)
```

46

```
        'Creates an instance of the type
        Dim pers As Type = tyBuilder.CreateType

        'Enumerates members for demo purposes
        For Each member In pers.GetMembers
            Console.WriteLine("Member name: {0}", member.Name)
        Next

        'Saves the assembly to disk
        asmBuilder.Save("People.dll")
        Console.ReadLine()
    End Sub
End Module
```

After you create an `AssemblyName` for assigning assembly properties and get the instance of the current application domain, you use the `AppDomain.DefineDynamicAssembly` method to generate an in-memory assembly. The method returns an instance of the `AssemblyBuilder` class and receives the `AssemblyName` instance and a value from the `AssemblyBuilderAccess` enumeration that establishes the access level for Reflection. `RunAndSave` enables you to execute and save the assembly, but you can also limit Reflection with the `ReflectionOnly` value.

The next step is creating an instance of the `ModuleBuilder` class that can act as a container of types. This is accomplished by invoking the `AssemblyBuilder.DefineDynamicModule` method that requires you to specify the module name and the filename. (This one should be the same as for `AssemblyName` if you want metadata to be merged into a single assembly.) When you have a module, you can put your types into it. For each type, you need to create an instance of the `TypeBuilder` class, which you accomplish by invoking the `ModuleBuilder.DefineType` method that receives the type name and qualifiers as arguments. Qualifiers are one or more values from the `TypeAttributes` enumeration; in the current example, `Public` and `Class` values are assigned to the new type to create a new class with public visibility. The `TypeBuilder` class provides lots of methods for adding members, such as constructors, field, properties, and methods. For constructors, the code demonstrates how to add a public, empty, and default constructor by invoking the `TypeBuilder.DefineDefaultConstructor`, but you can supply constructor overloads via the `DefineConstructor` method.

To implement properties, you first need to supply fields. These are implemented via the `TypeBuilder.DefineField` method that requires three arguments: the field name; the type (retrieved via `GetType`); and qualifiers, which are determined with values from the `FieldAttributes` enumeration. Similarly, you implement properties by invoking the `TypeBuilder.DefineProperty` method, but this is not enough because you also need to explicitly generate the getter and setter methods for each property. These are special methods that require providing some properties defined within the `propMethodAttributes` variable that takes values from the `MethodAttributes` enumeration. When you establish method attributes, you create two `MethodBuilder` instances. Such a class generates each kind of method, including special ones. You just supply the method name, the attributes, the return type, and an array of type parameters. The actual problem is how you implement method bodies. As a general rule, methods implemented via Reflection cannot have an empty method body, so you must provide some Intermediate Language code to populate the method body. This is accomplished by invoking methods from the `ILGenerator` class that enable injecting IL code to the method. Consider the following snippet, excerpted from Listing 46.4:

```
'Generates IL code for returning the field value
Dim propGetMethodIL As ILGenerator = propGetMethod.GetILGenerator
propGetMethodIL.Emit(OpCodes.Ldarg_0)
propGetMethodIL.Emit(OpCodes.Ldfld, fldBuilder)
propGetMethodIL.Emit(OpCodes.Ret)
```

The `MethodBuilder.GetILGenerator` method returns an instance of the `ILGenerator` class. Then you invoke the `Emit` method to execute IL code. In the preceding snippet, the IL code returns the value of the `fldBuilder` variable, pushes the value onto the stack, and then returns. Actions to execute via the IL are taken via shared fields from the `OpCodes` class, each related to an IL instruction.

NOTE ON OpCodes

Reflection is powerful, but because you need to know the MS Intermediate Language in detail before implementing dynamic code, and because this would be beyond the scope in this book, you should look at the appropriate MSDN documentation at http://msdn.microsoft.com/en-us/library/8ffc3x75(v=vs.110).aspx.

When you provide the method body for getters and setters, you add them to the related properties via the `PropertyBuilder.SetGetMethod` and `PropertyBuilder.SetSetMethod` methods. Similarly, you implement any other method, and the sample code demonstrates this by providing a simple method body that invokes `EmitWriteLine`. This is a method that sends to the assembly the appropriate IL code for writing a message to the Console window. Finally, you invoke `AssemblyBuilder.Save` to save the assembly to disk. More than running the code, you can ensure that everything works by inspecting the assembly with a Reflection tool such as Microsoft IL Disassembler. Figure 46.2 shows how the assembly looks if opened with ILDasm, demonstrating the correct result of our work.

Typically, you will use code generators instead of Reflection to generate code on-the-fly because in that case you do not need to know about Intermediate Language. After you define your types on-the-fly, you can consume them using the techniques described in the "Invoking Code Dynamically" section.

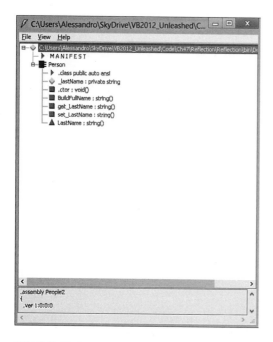

FIGURE 46.2   The assembly created at runtime opened in IL Disassembler.

Late Binding Concepts

Late binding is a particular programming technique that you use to resolve types at runtime and dynamic loading, which is accomplished by assigning objects to variable of type `Object`. For a better understanding, consider its counterpart, the early binding. This happens at compile time where the compiler checks that argument types utilized to invoke methods match their signatures. An example is the background compiler that provides real-time checks for types used in code, thanks to early binding. On the contrary, late binding requires you to specify the function signatures. Moreover, you must ensure that the code uses the correct types. This means that binding requirements, such as binary files to load or methods to invoke, is long delayed—in many cases until before the method is invoked. Reflection frequently uses late binding because in many cases you work with objects of type `Object`, and this requires late resolution for invoking appropriate members. The following example, although not related to Reflection, demonstrates how to invoke members from objects declared as `Object` that are instead of different types, but this is determined late at runtime:

```
' This code creates an instance of Microsoft Excel and adds a new WorkBook.
' Requires Option Strict Off
Sub LateBindingDemo()
    Dim xlsApp As Object
    Dim xlsBook As Object
```

```
    xlsApp = CreateObject("Excel.Application")
    xlsBook = xlsApp.Workbooks.Add
End Sub
```

Option Strict Off BEST PRACTICES

Because in many situations turning Option Strict to Off can be very dangerous, if you need to work with late binding, you should consider moving the code that requires such a technique to a separate code file and just mark this code file with Option Strict Off, instead of setting it Off at the project level.

As you can see, invoking members from Object in late binding is different because the compiler cannot predetermine whether members exist and you don't have IntelliSense support. But if the actual type defines members that you are attempting to invoke, they will be correctly bound at runtime. Just remember that late binding requires an Option Strict Off directive, and that should be used carefully.

Caller Information

Reflection is very powerful and enables you to retrieve every possible bit of information from an assembly and types defined in the assembly, including at runtime. However, you might want to catch some information, typically to log some activities, which would be difficult to retrieve via Reflection, at least with an easy approach. The .NET Framework 4.5 makes this easier by introducing a set of new attributes called *Caller Information*. This is the list of new attributes exposed by the System.Runtime.CompilerServices namespace:

▶ **CallerFilePath**—Returns the name of the file where a specific code block is being executed

▶ **CallerLineNumber**—Returns the line number for the code that has been executed

▶ **CallerMemberName**—Returns the name of a member that has received some changes

In the past, you could retrieve the same information with advanced Reflection techniques, which would also require a full trust context and the inclusion of debug symbol files in the assembly. With Caller Information, you can retrieve such information easily and without the full trust and debug symbol restrictions because they are available through types exposed directly by the .NET Framework. To use Caller Information, you must declare methods that receive optional parameters decorated with the attribute that you need. For a better understanding, let's consider an example. Listing 46.5 demonstrates how to implement a method that writes a log about some information entered by the user.

46

LISTING 46.5   Writing a Log with Caller Information

```
Imports System.Runtime.CompilerServices
Module Module1

    Sub Main()
        'Wait for the user input
        Console.WriteLine("Type something: ")
        Dim input = Console.ReadLine

        'show what the user entered:
        Console.WriteLine("You entered: {0}", input)

        WriteLog()
        Console.ReadLine()
    End Sub

    'Declare optional arguments. These are decorated
    'with CallerFilePath and CallerLineNumber attributes
    Private Sub WriteLog(<CallerFilePath()> Optional ByVal file As String = Nothing,
                        <CallerLineNumber()> Optional ByVal line As Integer = 0)
        Console.WriteLine("File: {0}", file)
        Console.WriteLine("Line number: {0}", line)
    End Sub

End Module
```

In this code, the WriteLog method receives optional arguments, decorated with the CallerFilePath (of type String) and the CallerLineNumber (of type Integer) attributes, respectively. Marking these arguments as optional is mandatory. When you invoke the method, you pass no arguments because the runtime will automatically supply the required information. Figure 46.3 demonstrates how the application shows the name of the file in which the code is executed and the line number.

In this case, line number 12 is the invocation to WriteLog. This means you will invoke a method with Caller Information definition at the exact point in which you want to track the line number. The last attribute, CallerMemberName, is only used together with the INotifyPropertyChanged interface. As you might know, the INotifyPropertyChanged interface is used in WPF and Silverlight to let the runtime know that some change occurred on the value of a property. CallerMemberName makes it easier to understand which property has changed. Consider the special implementation of the Person class shown in Listing 46.6.

FIGURE 46.3   Retrieving the filename and line number for the executed code.

LISTING 46.6   Using `CallerMemberName` to Retrieve Property Changes

```
Imports System.ComponentModel
Imports System.Runtime.CompilerServices

Public Class Person
    Implements INotifyPropertyChanged

    Private _fullName As String
    Public Property FullName As String
        Get
            Return _fullName
        End Get
        Set(value As String)
            Me._fullName = value
            NotifyChange(_fullName, value)
        End Set
    End Property

    Public Event PropertyChanged(sender As Object, e As PropertyChangedEventArgs) _
        Implements INotifyPropertyChanged.PropertyChanged

    Private Sub NotifyChange(Of T As IEquatable(Of T))(
                                        ByRef v1 As T, v2 As T,
                                        <CallerMemberName()>
                                        Optional prop As String =
➥Nothing)
```

46

```
        If v1 IsNot Nothing AndAlso v1.Equals(v2) Then Return
        If v1 Is Nothing AndAlso v2 Is Nothing Then Return
        v1 = v2
        RaiseEvent PropertyChanged(Me, New PropertyChangedEventArgs(prop))
    End Sub
End Class
```

Inside the `Set` method of the `FullName` property definition, the `PropertyChanged` event is not raised directly. Instead, the code invokes a separate method called `NotifyChange` that has an optional argument of type `String`, decorated with the `CallerMemberName` attribute. Such an argument will be populated at runtime with the name of the property that is being changed. To understand how it works, declare an instance of the `Person` class like this:

```
Dim p As New Person With {.FullName = "Alessandro Del Sole"}
```

Next, place a breakpoint on this line by pressing **F9**; then run the code. When the debugger encounters the breakpoint, pass the mouse pointer over the `prop` variable declared as the optional parameter in `NotifyChanges`. You will see how such a variable contains the name of the property (`FullName` in the example) that has been changed when the class has been instantiated.

Summary

In this chapter, we covered one of the most important topics in the .NET development, Reflection. You saw what Reflection is and how assemblies are structured. Talking in code terms, you then saw how to interrogate assembly information and how to reflect types to inspect types and type members exposed by an entire assembly or by a single type. Next, dynamically invoking code from an external assembly without the need of having a reference to that assembly was explained. You then learned how to take advantage of the `System.Reflection.Emit` namespace to create an assembly, types, and members at runtime. Finally, you learned about Caller Information, a new feature in Visual Basic 2012 that enables you to retrieve information such as the name of the file where a code block is executed, the line number, and the name of a property that has been changed, through three new attributes in the .NET Framework 4.5.

Coding Attributes

Executables produced by .NET languages are different from classic (Win32) executables. Other than the Intermediate Language (IL), they store additional information on types defined in the assembly, on members, and on data. The information is referred to as *metadata*. Assemblies' metadata also contains information about *attributes*, which are declarative programming elements that enable annotating types with custom information and that can condition types' behavior according to the information provided. They are pieces of information for types and therefore are part of the application metadata. You can find attributes in a lot of different scenarios in .NET development. For example, you saw attributes in Chapter 26, "Introducing ADO.NET Entity Framework," when discussing how the Entity Framework defines entities. Chapter 41, "Serialization," discussed serialization and the Serializable attribute. In this chapter, you reach two objectives. First, you get information on applying attributes, which is a specific recap of information you should already know. The second objective is to learn to create custom attributes and provide additional information to your applications by using metadata.

Applying Attributes

So far, you have seen a lot of examples about applying attributes, but for the sake of completeness we provide information here. When applying attributes to your own types or members, you enclose the attribute name between angle brackets, as in the following example:

```
<Serializable()>
Public Class Person

End Class
```

In this case, the `Serializable` attribute is parameterless (and in this case you can omit round parentheses).

When you apply an attribute, your object is *decorated* with that attribute. Another common description utilized when applying attributes is that an object is *marked*. Referring to the previous example, you can say that the `Person` class is decorated with the `Serializable` attribute or that it is marked as `Serializable`. Attributes can receive arguments. The following example shows how to pass arguments to the `CLSCompliant` attribute:

```
<CLSCompliant(True)>
Public Class Person

End Class
```

Attributes' arguments are separated by commas according to the number of arguments required. As explained when discussing custom attributes, optional parameters are also allowed. You apply multiple attributes and separate them with commas or write each attribute after the other one. Both the following modes are perfectly legal:

```
<Serializable()>
<CLSCompliant(True)>
Public Class Person

End Class

<Serializable(), CLSCompliant(True)>
Public Class Person

End Class
```

IMPLICIT-LINE CONTINUATION

In the first code snippet, notice how attributes no longer require the underscore character when written on multiple lines. This is one of the allowed scenarios for the implicit-line continuation features in Visual Basic starting from version 2010.

Attributes can be applied to the following programming elements:

- Classes

- Structures

- Methods (including constructors)

- Fields

- Properties

- Interfaces

- Delegates and events

- Parameters and return values

- Enumerations

As mentioned at the beginning of this chapter, attributes are information that is stored in the assembly metadata. Figure 47.1 represents how such information is stored within the assembly, including type information and member information.

FIGURE 47.1   Attribute information stored in the assembly metadata.

Considering the representation shown in Figure 47.1, you might notice the description about assembly metadata. You can apply attributes at the assembly level, in the `AssemblyInformation.vb` file. Assembly-level attributes are set at design time with the My Project window's tabs (refer to Chapter 3, "The Anatomy of a Visual Basic Project," and Chapter 19, "The My Namespace," for details). This means that each application property has a related assembly-level attribute. There is just one attribute named Assembly that requires the specification of nested attributes setting particular properties. For example, the following attributes' specifications set the title, description, and company name properties for the application:

```
<Assembly: AssemblyTitle("CodingAttribute")>
<Assembly: AssemblyDescription("Demo for Chapter 48")>
<Assembly: AssemblyCompany("Alessandro Del Sole")>
```

In the preceding code, `Assembly` is the main attribute, and `AssemblyTitle`, `AssemblyDescription`, and `AssemblyCompany` are other attributes that are nested into the Assembly declaration. Examining AssemblyInfo.vb you can see available assembly-level attributes, and you discover how each attribute is related to an application property settable in My Project. So far, you have seen how to apply existing attributes, but these special objects provide great flexibility over your object development and provide the ability to deeply enhance your types, especially if you create custom attributes, as you will better understand in the next section.

Coding Custom Attributes

A *custom* attribute is a class that inherits, directly or indirectly, from `System.Attribute`. When coding custom attributes, the class name should end with the `Attribute` word. This is not mandatory but—besides being required by Microsoft's Common Language Specification (CLS)—it provides a better way for identifying attributes in code. When applying attributes, you can shorten the attribute names by excluding the `Attribute` word. For example, imagine you have a `Document` class representing a simple text document. You might want to provide further information on the document, such as the author, reviewer, or last edit date. This information can be provided and stored in the assembly metadata using a custom attribute. Code in Listing 47.1 shows the implementation of a custom attribute that exposes document properties, which is explained next.

LISTING 47.1   Writing a Custom Attribute

```
<AttributeUsage(AttributeTargets.Class Or AttributeTargets.Property)>
Public Class DocumentPropertiesAttribute
    Inherits Attribute

    'Attributes can be inherited
    'therefore private fields are Protected
    Protected _author As String
    Protected _reviewer As String

    Public Overridable ReadOnly Property Author As String
        Get
            Return Me._author
        End Get
    End Property
```

```
    Public Overridable ReadOnly Property Reviewer As String
        Get
            Return Me._reviewer
        End Get
    End Property

    Public Overridable Property LastEdit As String

    Public Sub New(ByVal author As String, ByVal reviewer As String)
        Me._author = author
        Me._reviewer = reviewer
        Me._lastEdit = CStr(Date.Today)
    End Sub
End Class
```

In Visual Basic, every custom attribute is a class with `Public` or `Friend` access level and decorated with the `AttributeUsage` attribute that enables you to specify which programming elements can be targeted by the custom attribute. Programming elements are specified via the `System.AttributeTargets` enumeration; the enumeration exposes a number of elements, each of them self-explanatory about the targeted programming element. For example, `AttributeTargets.Class` enables you to apply the attribute to reference types, and `AttributeTargets.Methods` enables you to apply the attribute to methods. IntelliSense shows the full list of the enumeration members, which is straightforward. An available member for each element is described in the previous section for targetable programming elements. `AttributeTargets` members support bitwise operators so that you combine multiple targets using `Or`. Actual metadata is exposed to the external world via properties that can be either read-only or read/write. Attributes can receive arguments, although this is not mandatory. For arguments, it is important to understand how you can ask for required parameters and optional ones. This is not something that you define as you would usually do in other programming elements such as methods. Required parameters are specified in the class constructor. Continuing with the example of Listing 47.1, our custom attribute requires the specification of the author and the reviewer of the document, and the last edit date is optional and is still available via a specific property. Optional parameters initialization is not required; in the mentioned example a default value for the `LastEdit` property is supplied. As explained in the next subsection, optional arguments are invoked with named parameters.

TYPES FOR ATTRIBUTES PARAMETERS

You should have noticed that the `LastEdit` property in the custom attribute is of type `String` instead of type `Date`. There are some limitations in the applicable data types for attributes parameters. For example, `Decimal` and `Date` are not supported (like structured types as well). Supported types are instead numeric types (`Bytes`, `Short`, `Integer`, `Long`, `Single`, and `Double`), string types (`String` and `Char`), enumerations, and the `Boolean` type. Take care of these limitations because they can result in exceptions when passing arguments.

47

There are several other ways to customize attributes, but before discovering them here's how to apply custom attributes to complete the discussion on parameters.

Applying Custom Attributes

The previous subsection discussed the definition of a custom attribute for assigning metadata to a class representing a basic text document. The code in Listing 47.2 implements the related `Document` class that is decorated with the `DocumentPropertiesAttribute`.

LISTING 47.2   Applying Custom Attributes

```
<DocumentProperties("Alessandro Del Sole",
                    "Robert White",
                    LastEdit:="06/05/2012")>
Public Class Document

    Public Property Text As String

    Public ReadOnly Property Length As Integer
        Get
            Return Text.Length
        End Get
    End Property

    <DocumentProperties("Alessandro Del Sole",
                        "Stephen Green")>
    Public Property DocumentName As String

    Public Sub SaveDocument(ByVal fileName As String)
        '...
    End Sub

    Public Sub LoadDocument(ByVal filneName As String)
        '...
    End Sub
End Class
```

When you apply an attribute, you can shorten its name by excluding the `Attribute` word in the identifier. For example, `DocumentPropertiesAttribute` can be shortened to `DocumentProperties`. The Visual Basic compiler correctly recognizes the identifier of an attribute. Then you must provide required arguments, respecting the data type. Such arguments are defined in the constructor of the attribute definition (see the previous subsection). If you want to also specify an optional argument, such as the `LastEdit` one in the previous example, you need to perform it via a named parameter. Named parameters are literals followed by the `:=` symbols and by information of the required type. This is the only way to provide optional arguments. Notice also how the custom attribute is applied at both class and property level; this is allowed by the attribute definition. Attributes are therefore useful for providing additional information that will be stored in the assembly metadata, to custom objects. Attributes are flexible for other reasons that are covered in the next sections.

Applying Attributes Multiple Times

According to the particular nature of your custom attributes, you can decide whether multiple instances can be applied to programming elements. This is accomplished by setting the `AllowMultiple` property as `True` in the `AttributeUsage`. The following is an example:

```
<AttributeUsage(AttributeTargets.Class Or AttributeTargets.Property,
                AllowMultiple:=True)>
Public Class DocumentPropertiesAttribute
    Inherits Attribute
```

`AllowMultiple` is optional and thus is invoked as a named parameter. The following is an example of how you apply multiple instances of an attribute:

```
<DocumentProperties("Alessandro Del Sole",
                    "Stephen Green")>
<DocumentProperties("Alessandro", "Stephen",
                    LastEdit:="07/10/2012")>
Public Property DocumentName As String
```

In the particular example of the `DocumentProperties` attribute, multiple instances probably do not make much sense, but this is the way to apply them.

Defining Inheritance

In some situations you create classes that inherit from other classes that are decorated with attributes. Attribute inheritance is not automatic in that you can establish whether your attributes are inheritable. You establish this behavior by setting the `Inherited` property at `AttributeUsage` level. By default, if you do not explicitly set `Inherited`, it is considered as `True`. The following example shows how you enable attribute inheritance:

```
'Attribute is also inherited
<AttributeUsage(AttributeTargets.Class Or AttributeTargets.Property,
                Inherited:=True)>
Public Class DocumentPropertiesAttribute
```

The following snippet shows instead how to make an attribute not inheritable:

```
'Attribute is not inherited
<AttributeUsage(AttributeTargets.Class Or AttributeTargets.Property,
                Inherited:=False)>
Public Class DocumentPropertiesAttribute
```

47

Inheritance is enabled by default because, if a base class is decorated with attributes, derived classes probably also need them. Because of this, you should be careful when disabling inheritance. The code in Listing 47.3 shows an example of declaring two attributes with inheritance definitions and how a derived type is influenced by attribute inheritance.

LISTING 47.3   Conditioning Attribute Inheritance

```
<AttributeUsage(AttributeTargets.Class Or AttributeTargets.Method,
                Inherited:=False)>
Public Class FirstAttribute
    Inherits Attribute

    'Implement your code here..
End Class


<AttributeUsage(AttributeTargets.Class Or AttributeTargets.Method)>
Public Class SecondAttribute
    Inherits Attribute

    'Implement your code here..
End Class


Public Class Person
    Public Property LastName As String
    Public Property FirstName As String

    'The base class takes both attributes
    <First(), Second()> Public Overridable Function FullName() As String
        Return String.Concat(LastName, " ", FirstName)
    End Function
End Class


Public Class Contact
    Inherits Person

    'This derived class takes only the Second attribute
    'because First is marked as Inherited:=False
    Public Overrides Function FullName() As String
        Return MyBase.FullName()
    End Function
End Class
```

Notice how the FullName method in the Contact class inherits just the Second attribute appliance, but the First attribute is not applied because of inheritance settings.

Reflecting Attributes

Attributes are about applications' metadata. Because of this, you can use Reflection (refer to Chapter 46, "Reflection," for details) to check whether a type recurs to custom attributes and investigate metadata (that is, application information). To accomplish this, you invoke the `System.Reflection.MemberInfo.GetCustomAttributes` and `System.Reflection.Attributes.GetCustomAttributes` shared methods. The first one returns all attributes applied to the specified type; the second one returns an array of custom attributes applied to an assembly, a type or its members, and method parameters. The following is the most basic example for retrieving information about attributes applied to members of the `Document` class:

```
'Requires an Imports System.Reflection directive

    Public Sub GetMyAttributes()
        'About members in the Document class
        Dim info As System.Reflection.MemberInfo = GetType(Document)
        'Retrieves an array of attributes
        Dim attributesList() As Object = info.GetCustomAttributes(True)

        'Enumerates applied attributes
        For i As Integer = 0 To attributesList.Length - 1
            Console.WriteLine(attributesList(i))
        Next (i)
    End Sub
```

The following example is a little bit more complex and shows how you can perform actions on each attribute instance through `Attribute.GetCustomAttributes`:

```
Public Sub GetMyAttributesComplex()
    Dim typeToInvestigate As Type = GetType(Document)

    ' Get the type information for the DocumentName property.
    Dim member_Info As PropertyInfo =
        typeToInvestigate.GetProperty("DocumentName")
    If Not (member_Info Is Nothing) Then

        'Iterate through all the attributes of the property.
        Dim attr As Attribute
        For Each attr In Attribute.GetCustomAttributes(member_Info)
            ' Check for the DocumentPropertiesAttribute attribute.
            If attr.GetType().
                Equals(GetType(DocumentPropertiesAttribute)) Then
                    Console.WriteLine("Author: {0}", CType(attr,
                                 DocumentPropertiesAttribute).Author)
```

```
                'Additional ElseIf conditions here for other attributes..
                End If
            Next attr
        End If
End Sub
```

In this particular scenario, the code is used to iterate applied attributes. Do not forget the simplicity of Caller Information described in the previous chapter, which enables you to retrieve specific information on the current assembly without iterating the assembly's attributes.

Summary

Attributes provide great flexibility in .NET development by giving you the ability to decorate your types and members with custom additional information that is stored in the assembly metadata. All custom attributes are public classes deriving from System. Attribute and can be applied to various programming elements, such as assemblies, classes, modules, methods, properties, and so on. For this, the Visual Basic language requires you to decorate your custom attributes with the AttributeUsage attribute that provides specifications on targeted elements. When defining custom attributes, you can provide both required and optional parameters; the first ones are established in the constructor. All parameters refer to attribute information that is exposed to the external world via properties. Remember that you need to provide a named parameter when invoking optional arguments. You can also decide to make your attributes inheritable (Inherited property) and to make them applicable more than once (AllowMultiple). Finally, you can investigate assemblies' and types' attributes via Reflection.

CHAPTER 48

Platform Invokes and Interoperability with the COM Architecture

The .NET Framework 4.5 Base Class Library offers tons of objects and methods for covering almost everything in modern application development. In most cases, objects and methods are managed wrappers of the Windows Application Programming Interface (API) so you can use them in the managed environment of the Common Language Runtime (CLR). In some situations you might need to access some operating system functionalities that have not been wrapped yet by the .NET Framework, or you might have legacy code exposed by Component Object Model (COM) objects, such as type libraries. Both the .NET Framework and Visual Basic still enable interoperability with the COM architecture, and in this chapter you see how to reach these objectives.

THE WINDOWS 8 STORY

As you know, the Windows Runtime (WinRT) in Windows 8 is based on COM and exposes objects in a way that is known to .NET developers, making such objects appear as if they were managed. WinRT is a wrapper of COM objects, so if you want to build applications that use COM interoperability you might consider interacting with WinRT rather than writing using the old model. You will certainly use techniques described in this chapter if your applications will also run on Windows 7 and Windows Vista, not only Windows 8. If you can't predict the target audience of your application, follow this chapter. If your desktop application will only run on Windows 8, spend a little time getting deeper knowledge of interaction between .NET and WinRT.

Importing and Using COM Objects

The .NET Framework 4.5, like previous versions, offers support for interoperability with the COM architecture via an engine named *Runtime Callable Wrapper*, which is the infrastructure that provides a communication bridge between .NET and COM. It is also responsible for type marshaling and handling events. Because of this engine, you can import COM objects and use them in your managed applications. You can import two kinds of COM components: type libraries and ActiveX components. Importing COM components is accomplished via two command-line tools: **TlbImp.exe**, which is required to import a type library, and **AxImp.exe**, which is required for importing ActiveX controls. This chapter does not discuss how to invoke such tools from the command line, but you do find out how to import COM components from within Visual Studio so that the IDE can do the work for you. The next example shows how to import an ActiveX control into the Visual Studio toolbox and use the control in code.

Importing COM Components into Visual Studio

In this chapter, you learn how to use COM components in a WPF application. The reason you should use WPF is that it is the only technology you should use to create modern desktop applications, even if it requires some more work when compared to Windows Forms. Also, the goal of this chapter is illustrating a very common scenario, which is having the ability of displaying PDF documents. Before going on, make sure you install the Adobe Reader program (www.adobe.com), which includes an ActiveX control to display PDF documents and that will be used in our example. You can replace the Adobe Reader with different software that has an ActiveX control.

At this point, create a new WPF project with Visual Basic. In Windows Forms, you can use COM components directly on `Form` objects, but in WPF you cannot. So the first thing you have to do is add a new Windows Forms user control to the WPF project; this enables you to host COM objects in WPF. To accomplish this, select **Project**, **Add New Item** and select the **User Control** item template in the Windows Forms category. Name the new user control as **PDFControl.vb**. Figure 48.1 demonstrates this.

Ensure the user control is visible in the designer and then open the Visual Studio toolbox. When done, right-click the toolbox and select **Choose Items**. This launches the same-named dialog box that you already know because of adding .NET controls to the toolbox. Select the **COM** tab and search for the **Adobe PDF Reader** item, as shown in Figure 48.2.

When you click **OK**, Visual Studio generates two files for you:

▶ **Interop.AcroPDFLib.dll**—A CLR wrapper for using COM objects exposed by the Adobe Reader type library in a .NET fashion.

▶ **AxInterop.AcroPDFLib.dll**—A Windows Forms proxy that provides the infrastructure required for hosting the control in your forms. You now might better understand why you needed a Windows Forms user control to host a COM component.

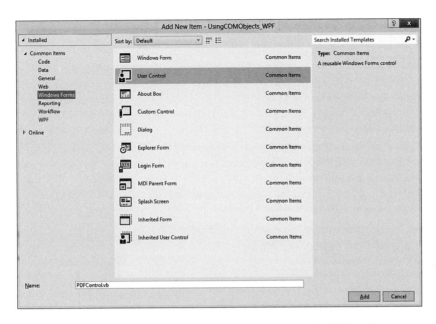

FIGURE 48.1   Adding a Windows Forms user control to the WPF project.

FIGURE 48.2   Choosing a COM component to add to the toolbox.

At this point, the Adobe Reader ActiveX control is available inside the toolbox. Now drag the PDF control over the Windows Forms user control form and resize it as you like. Visual Studio then generates some code for you to declare the control and enables you to use it. If you expand the PDFControl.vb file and double-click the `AxAcroPDF1` item, you find the following initialization code for the ActiveX control:

```
'NOTE: The following procedure is required by the Windows Form Designer
'It can be modified using the Windows Form Designer.
'Do not modify it using the code editor.
<System.Diagnostics.DebuggerStepThrough()> _
Private Sub InitializeComponent()
    Dim resources As System.ComponentModel.ComponentResourceManager = _
        New System.ComponentModel.ComponentResourceManager(GetType(PDFControl))
    Me.AxAcroPDF1 = New AxAcroPDFLib.AxAcroPDF()
    CType(Me.AxAcroPDF1, System.ComponentModel.ISupportInitialize).BeginInit()
    Me.SuspendLayout()
    '
    'AxAcroPDF1
    '
    Me.AxAcroPDF1.Enabled = True
    Me.AxAcroPDF1.Location = New System.Drawing.Point(-15, -15)
    Me.AxAcroPDF1.Name = "AxAcroPDF1"
    Me.AxAcroPDF1.OcxState = CType(resources.GetObject("AxAcroPDF1.OcxState"),
                            System.Windows.Forms.AxHost.State)
    Me.AxAcroPDF1.Size = New System.Drawing.Size(192, 192)
    Me.AxAcroPDF1.TabIndex = 0
    '
    'PDFControl
    '
    Me.AutoScaleDimensions = New System.Drawing.SizeF(6.0!, 13.0!)
    Me.AutoScaleMode = System.Windows.Forms.AutoScaleMode.Font
    Me.Controls.Add(Me.AxAcroPDF1)
    Me.Name = "PDFControl"
    CType(Me.AxAcroPDF1, System.ComponentModel.ISupportInitialize).EndInit()
    Me.ResumeLayout(False)

End Sub
Friend WithEvents AxAcroPDF1 As AxAcroPDFLib.AxAcroPDF
```

AxHost CLASS

ActiveX controls are wrapped by the `System.Windows.Forms.AxHost` class that enables you to treat COM components as you would .NET objects.

Now you can work with the ActiveX control in a managed way, as illustrated in the next subsection.

Using COM Objects in Code

When you have an instance of the ActiveX control, or of a type library, you can access its members like any other .NET object, thus invoking methods, assigning properties, or handling events. The following code loads and shows the specified document in the Adobe's viewer:

```
Private Sub PDFControl_Load(sender As Object, e As EventArgs) Handles Me.Load
    Me.AxAcroPDF1.LoadFile("C:\Users\Alessandro\Documents\TestDoc.pdf")
End Sub
```

You can also handle events if available, as demonstrated by the following code snippet:

```
Private Sub AxAcroPDF1_OnError(sender As Object, e As EventArgs) Handles AxAcroPDF1.
➥OnError
    MessageBox.Show("An error has occurred while loading the document")
End Sub
```

In this particular case, the OnError event is raised when an error occurs while opening the PDF file. At a more general level, wrapping an ActiveX control enables you to import different kinds of members, including events.

Catching Exceptions

When you implement Try..Catch..End Try blocks, you can intercept and handle only CLS-compliant exceptions—that is, exceptions inheriting from System.Exception. Exceptions wrapped by the COM import tools are not CLS-compliant, so a classic Try block would fail. To intercept exceptions coming from wrapped objects, the .NET Framework offers the System.Runtime.CompilerServices.RuntimeWrappedException. It can be used for error handling when working with wrappers. The following code shows an example:

```
Try
    Me.AxAcroPDF1.LoadFile("C:\Users\Alessandro\Documents\TestDoc.pdf")

Catch ex As RuntimeWrappedException

Catch ex As Exception

End Try
```

Other than the usual exception properties, this class exposes a WrappedException property, of type Object, which represents the problem that occurred.

Releasing COM Objects

You should always explicitly release objects that wrap COM components so that the associated resources are also released. You accomplish this by invoking the System.Runtime.InteropServices.Marshal.ReleaseCOMObject method. It is worth noting that calling this method does not explicitly free all resources but decreases the reference count on the COM object, and when the count hits 0, the resources are freed. Continuing with the previous example, you release the AxAcroPDF1 object as follows:

```
System.Runtime.InteropServices.Marshal.ReleaseComObject(AxAcroPDF1)
```

This is important because COM objects treat system resources differently from .NET objects; therefore, an explicit release is required.

Calling COM Objects from WPF

Now that you have completed all the required steps to wrap a COM component into a Windows Forms user control, you need a way to use such a control in WPF. As you learned in Chapter 29, "WPF Common Controls," you use a WindowsFormsHost control to embed Windows Forms contents inside a WPF window or user control. So, double-click the MainWindow.xaml file in Solution Explorer. Then, when the main window of the application is available in the designer, drag the WindowsFormsHost control from the toolbox onto the window. Remove all autogenerated property values and assign a name, so that the WindowsFormsHost definition looks like this:

```
<WindowsFormsHost Name="FormsHost1" />
```

The next step is assigning an instance of the PDFControl user control as the child content of the WindowsFormsHost. This is done in the code-behind file, like in the following code:

```
Public Sub New()

    ' This call is required by the designer.
    InitializeComponent()

    ' Add any initialization after the InitializeComponent() call.
    Dim pdfViewer As New PDFControl
    Me.FormsHost1.Child = pdfViewer
End Sub
```

If you now run the sample application, you will be able to see how the specified PDF document is shown inside the application's main window. You do this by using COM interoperability.

DEPLOYMENT TIPS

When you deploy an application that works with COM interop, you must ensure you also include both the autogenerated AxInterop.XXX.dll and the Interop.XXX.dll files. You should also include the ActiveX control or the type library that your application has a reference to, but in some cases this is not possible for copyright reasons. For instance, the sample discussed in this chapter uses the Adobe Reader's ActiveX control, which is not redistributable. Thus, clients must install the Adobe Reader on their machines and then your application will handle a reference to the ActiveX.

Exposing .NET Objects to the COM World

Although in modern world applications this practice occurs less frequently than in the past, you can expose .NET objects to the COM world. For example, a VB 6 application can consume an object like this. To demonstrate how you accomplish this export, create a new class library and rename Class1.vb to Contact.vb. The first thing you need to do to enable a class to be called from COM is provide COM interoperability support. Now open **My Project** and select the **Compile** tab. Flag the **Register for COM Interop** item at the bottom of the page, as shown in Figure 48.3.

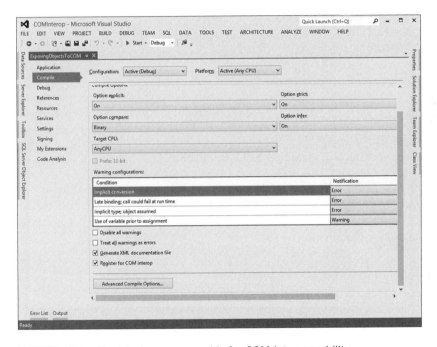

FIGURE 48.3   Registering an assembly for COM Interoperability.

This operation tells Visual Studio that it needs to register the COM component on build and adds the following line of code in AssemblyInfo.vb so that it makes it visible to COM:

```
<Assembly: ComVisible(True)>
```

CLASS REQUIREMENTS FOR COM EXPOSURE

Any class that you want to expose to COM has the following requirements: It must have a public, empty, parameterless constructor; any member, including types, to be exposed must be `Public` (no other modifiers are allowed) and it cannot include abstract classes. (This is just because they cannot be consumed.)

The ComVisible attribute establishes the visibility level and granularity not only at assembly level, but also for classes and class members. The default for this attribute is True, so you need to explicitly set classes and members for False where you do not want them to be exposed. Next, implement the Contact class as follows:

```
Public Class COMContact

    Public Property FirstName As String
    Public Property LastName As String
    Public Property Email As String
    Public Property BirthDay As Date

    Public Sub New()

    End Sub
End Class
```

Now you can decide the visibility level for each member in the class by decorating the class and its members with the System.Runtime.InteropServices.ComVisible attribute. The following code demonstrates how to make COM-visible only some members from the Contact class:

```
Imports System.Runtime.InteropServices

<ComVisible(True)>
Public Class COMContact

    <ComVisible(True)>
    Public Property FirstName As String
    <ComVisible(True)>
    Public Property LastName As String
    <ComVisible(False)>
    Public Property Email As String

    <ComVisible(False)>
    Public Property BirthDay As Date

    Public Sub New()

    End Sub
End Class
```

A public, empty constructor is required for COM-visible objects. You must mark the class as ComVisible(True) to expose it correctly. The only exception is when the class you marked as false gets inherited into a new class marked as true, then the members in the base class will be exposed through the inherited class unless the individual members of the base class were also marked ComVisible(False). The next step should be to register the COM component after the build process. Fortunately, on the development machine, Visual Studio 2012 does the work for you. (This requires the IDE to be launched with elevated privileges.) Therefore, compile the project to have a class library that is consumable from the COM architecture.

WHAT HAPPENS BEHIND THE SCENES?

When you build a class library exposed to COM, Visual Studio first invokes the Visual Basic compiler (vbc.exe) with the /t switch pointing to the executable name; next it launches the type library exporter utility (TlbExp.exe). The conjunction of both tools can build a COM-enabled library.

P/Invokes and Unmanaged Code

One of the biggest benefits of the .NET Framework is that the technology is a bridge between you and the Windows operating system and is responsible for managing a lot of system features (such as memory management). This reduces the risk of bad system resources management that could lead the system to unwanted crashes or problems. This is the reason (as you might recall from Chapter 1, "Introducing the .NET Framework 4.5") that .NET programming is also known as *managed*. The .NET Framework Base Class Library (BCL) exposes managed wrappers for most of the Windows API system so that you do not need to manually handle system resources. It also enables you to reap all the benefits of the CLR. By the way, in some situations you still need to access the Windows API (for example, when there is not a .NET counterpart of an API function), and thus you need to work with *unmanaged code*. Unmanaged code is all code not controlled by the .NET Framework and that requires you to manually handle system resources. When you work with unmanaged code, you commonly invoke Windows API functions; such invocations are also known as *Platform Invokes* or, simpler, *P/Invokes*. In this section I cover both situations, starting with P/Invokes.

48

NOTE ON UNMANAGED CODE

You should always avoid unmanaged code. The .NET Framework 4.5 offers an infinite number of managed objects and methods for performing almost everything. Using unmanaged code means working directly against the operating system and its resources, and if your code does not perfectly handle resources, it can lead to problems. Moreover, when performing unmanaged calls, you need to be certain that they work or exist on all versions of the Windows operating system you plan to support for your application. Always search through the Base Class Library to ensure that a .NET counterpart for the Windows API already exists. It probably does.

Understanding P/Invokes

Calls to Windows API functions are known as Platform Invokes or P/Invokes. The Visual Basic programming language offers two ways of performing platform invokes:

- ▶ `Declare` keyword

- ▶ `System.Runtime.InteropServices.DllImport` attribute

The `Declare` keyword has a behavior similar to what happened in Visual Basic 6, and it has been kept for compatibility; however, you should always use the `DllImport` attribute because this is the one way recognized by the Common Language Specification. Now you can see how to declare a P/Invoke. The next example considers the `PathIsUrl` function, from the Shlwapi.dll system library, which checks whether the specified is a URL and returns a value according to the result. This is with the `Declare` keyword:

```
Declare Function PathIsUrl Lib "shlwapi.dll" Alias _
     "PathIsURLA" (ByVal path As String) As Integer
```

MATCHING NUMERIC TYPES

Keep in mind the difference in numeric types between the Windows API system and the .NET common types system because Windows APIs return `Long`; however, when you perform P/Invokes, you must use the .NET counterpart `Integer`. The same is true for `Integer` in the Windows API, which is mapped by `Short` in .NET. Similarly, remember to use the `IntPtr` structure for declarations that require a handle (or a pointer) of type `Integer`.

As you can see, the API declaration looks similar to what you used to write in VB 6. The following is how you declare the API function via the `DllImport` attribute:

```
'Requires an
'Imports System.Runtime.InteropServices directive
<DllImport("shlwapi.dll", entrypoint:="PathIsURLA")>
Shared Function PathIsURL(ByVal path As String) As System.Int32
End Function
```

Among its many options, the most important in `DllImport` are the library name and the `entrypoint` parameter that indicates the function name. It is important to remember that P/Invokes must be declared as `Shared` because they cannot be exposed as instance methods; the only exception to this rule is when you declare a function within a module. When declared, you can consume P/Invokes like any other method (always remembering that you are not passing through the CLR), as demonstrated here:

```
Dim testUrl As String = "http://www.visual-basic.it"
Dim result As Integer = PathIsURL(testUrl)
```

Both `Declare` and `DllImport` lead to the same result, but from now we use only `DllImport`.

Encapsulating P/Invokes

Encapsulating P/Invokes in classes is a programming best practice and makes your code clearer and more meaningful. Continuing the previous example, you could create a new class and declare inside the class the PathIsUrl function, marking it as Shared so that it can be consumed by other objects. You need to consider one more thing. If you plan to wrap Windows API functions in reusable class libraries, the best approach is to provide CLS-compliant libraries and API calls. For this reason, we now discuss how you can encapsulate P/Invokes following the rules of the Common Language Specification (CLS). The first rule is to create a class that stores only P/Invokes declarations. Such a class must be visible only within the assembly, must implement a private empty constructor, and will expose only shared members. The following is an example related to the PathIsUri function:

```
Friend Class NativeMethods
    <DllImport("shlwapi.dll", entrypoint:="PathIsURLA")>
    Shared Function PathIsURL(ByVal path As String) As System.Int32
    End Function


    Private Sub New()


    End Sub
End Class
```

The class is marked with Friend to make it visible only within the assembly. A CLS-compliant class for exposing P/Invokes declarations can have only one of the following names:

- ▶ **NativeMethods**—Used on the development machine and indicates that the class has no particular security and permissions requirements

- ▶ **SafeNativeMethods**—Used outside the development machine and indicates that the class and methods have no particular security and permissions requirements

- ▶ **UnsafeNativeMethods**—Used to explain to other developers that the caller needs to demand permissions to execute the code (demanding permissions for one of the classes exposed by the System.Security.Permissions namespace)

To expose P/Invokes to the external call, you need a wrapper class. The following class demonstrates how you can expose the NativeMethods.PathIsUrl function in a programmatically correct approach:

```
Public Class UsefulMethods

    Public Shared Function CheckIfPathIsUrl(ByVal path As String) _
        As Integer
      Return NativeMethods.PathIsURL(path)
    End Function

End Class
```

Finally, you can consume the preceding code as follows (for example, adding a reference to the class library):

```
Dim testUrl As String = "http://www.visual-basic.it"
Dim result As Integer = UsefulMethods.CheckIfPathIsUrl(testUrl)
```

Working with unmanaged code is not only performing P/Invokes. There are some other important concepts about error handling and type marshaling, as explained in the next sections.

Converting Types to Unmanaged

When you work with P/Invokes, you might need to pass custom types as function arguments. If such types are .NET types, the most important thing is converting primitives into types that are acceptable by the COM/Win32 architecture. The System.Runtime. InteropServices namespace exposes the MarshalAs attribute that can be applied to fields and method arguments to convert the object into the most appropriate COM counterpart. The following sample implementation of the Person class demonstrates how to apply MarshalAs:

```
Imports System.Runtime.InteropServices

Public Class Person

    <MarshalAs(UnmanagedType.LPStr)>
    Private _firstName As String
    <MarshalAs(UnmanagedType.SysInt)>
    Private _age As Integer

    Public Property FirstName As String
        Get
            Return _firstName
        End Get
        Set(ByVal value As String)
            _firstName = value
        End Set
    End Property

    Public Property Age As Integer
        Get
            Return _age
        End Get
        Set(ByVal value As Integer)
            _age = value
        End Set
    End Property
```

```
    Sub ConvertParameter(<MarshalAs(UnmanagedType.LPStr)> _
                        ByVal name As String)
    End Sub
End Class
```

The attribute receives a value from the `UnmanagedType` enumeration. IntelliSense offers great help about members in this enumeration, showing the full members list and explaining what each member is bound to convert. You can check this out as an exercise.

The `StructLayout` Attribute

An important aspect of unmanaged programming is how you handle types, especially when such types are passed as P/Invoke arguments. Unlike P/Invokes, types representing counterparts from the Windows API pass through the CLR and, as a general rule, you should provide the CLR the best way for handling them to keep performance high. When you write a class or a structure, you give members a particular order that should have a meaning for you. In other words, if the `Person` class exposes `FirstName` and `Age` as properties, keeping this order should have a reason, which is dictated only by some kind of logic. With the `System.Runtime.InteropServices.StructLayout` attribute, you can tell the CLR how it can handle type members; it enables you to decide if it has to respect a particular order or if it can handle type members the best way it can according to performances. The `StructLayout` attribute's constructor offers three alternatives:

▶ `StructLayout.Auto`—The CLR handles type members in its preferred order.

▶ `StructLayout.Sequential`—The CLR handles type members preserving the order provided by the developer in the type implementation.

▶ `StructLayout.Explicit`—The CLR handles type members according to the order established by the developer, using memory offsets.

By default, if `StructLayout` is not specified, the CLR assumes `Auto` for reference types and `Sequential` for structures. For example, consider the `COMRECT` structure from the Windows API, which represents four points. This is how you write it in Visual Basic, making it available to unmanaged code:

```
<StructLayout(LayoutKind.Sequential)>
Public Structure COMRECT

    Public Left As Integer
    Public Top As Integer
    Public Right As Integer
    Public Bottom As Integer

    Shared Sub New()

    End Sub
```

```
    Public Sub New(ByVal left As Integer,
                    ByVal top As Integer,
                    ByVal right As Integer,
                    ByVal bottom As Integer)

        Me.Left = left
        Me.Top = top
        Me.Right = right
        Me.Bottom = bottom
    End Sub
End Structure
```

TIPS ON DEFAULT OPTIONS

StructLayout must be applied explicitly if your assembly needs to be CLS-compliant. This happens because you have two choices, Sequential and Explicit. For classes, though, this is not necessary because they are always considered as Auto. Because of this, in this section we describe only structures.

This is how you can apply StructLayout.Explicit instead, providing memory offsets:

```
<StructLayout(LayoutKind.Explicit)>
Public Structure COMRECT

    <FieldOffset(0)> Public Left As Integer
    <FieldOffset(4)> Public Top As Integer
    <FieldOffset(8)> Public Right As Integer
    <FieldOffset(12)> Public Bottom As Integer

    Shared Sub New()

    End Sub

    Public Sub New(ByVal left As Integer,
                    ByVal top As Integer,
                    ByVal right As Integer,
                    ByVal bottom As Integer)

        Me.Left = left
        Me.Top = top
        Me.Right = right
        Me.Bottom = bottom
    End Sub
End Structure
```

The FieldOffset attribute specifies the memory offset for each field. In this case the structure provides fields of type Integer, so each offset is 4 bytes.

The `VBFixedString` Attribute

The `VBFixedString` attribute can be applied to structure members of type `String`, to delimit the string length because by default string length is variable. Such delimitation is established in bytes instead of characters. This attribute is required in some API calls. The following is an example:

```
Public Structure Contact
'Both fields are limited to 10 bytes size
    <VBFixedString(10)> Public LastName As String
    <VBFixedString(10)> Public Email As String
End Structure
```

Notice that the `VBFixedString` can be applied to fields but is not valid for properties.

Handling Exceptions

Functions from Windows API return a numeric value as their results (called HRESULT), for telling the caller whether the function succeeded or failed. Prior to .NET 2.0, getting information on functions failures was a difficult task. Starting from .NET 2.0 you can handle exceptions coming from the P/Invokes world with a classic `Try..Catch` block. The real improvement is that the .NET Framework can wrap unmanaged errors that have a .NET counterpart into managed exceptions. For instance, if a Windows API invocation causes an out-of-memory error, the .NET Framework maps such error as an `OutOfMemoryException` that you can embrace within a normal `Try..Catch` block. It is reasonable that not all unmanaged errors can have a managed counterpart, due to differences in COM and .NET architectures. To solve this, .NET provides the `System.Runtime.InteropServices.SEHException`, in which SEH stands for *Structured Exception Handling*. It maps all unmanaged exceptions that .NET cannot map. The exception is useful because it exposes an `ErrorCode` property that stores the HRESULT sent from P/Invokes. You use it like this:

```
Try
    'Add your P/Invoke here..
Catch ex As SEHException
    Console.WriteLine(ex.ErrorCode.ToString)
Catch ex As Exception

End Try
```

48

> **TIP**
>
> The `SEHException` does not provide many exception details, unlike managed exceptions, but it is the most appropriate exception for error handling in a `Try..Catch` block within unmanaged code.

There is also an alternative, which requires some explanation. P/Invokes raise Win32 errors calling themselves the `SetLastError` native method that is different from how exceptions are thrown in the CLR. In the earlier days, you could call the `GetLastError` method to retrieve the error code, but this is not the best choice because it can refer to managed exceptions rather than Win32 exceptions. A better, although not the ultimate, approach can be provided by invoking the `System.Runtime.InteropServices.Marshal.GetLastWin32Error` method, which can intercept the last error coming from a Win32 call. To make this work, first you need to set the `SetLastError` property in the `DllImport` attribute as `True`; then you can invoke the method. The following code shows an example of the `Beep` function, which returns a numeric value as the result:

```
<DllImport("kernel32.dll", entrypoint:="Beep", SetLastError:=True)>
Public Shared Function Beep(ByVal frequency As UInteger,
                           ByVal duration As UInteger) As Integer
End Function


    Dim beepResult = NativeMethods.Beep(100, 100)
    If beepResult = 0 Then
        Console.WriteLine(Marshal.GetLastWin32Error())
    End If
```

Here you need to know first which values can return a particular function. `Beep` returns zero if it does not succeed. So, after a check on the result value, the `Marshal.GetLastWin32Error` method is invoked to understand the error code.

References to the Win32 API Calls

Developers can reference the MSDN documentation or the Windows SDK to get detailed information on the Windows API functions and their signatures. The following are resources available on the Internet for your reference:

▶ MSDN reference: http://msdn.microsoft.com/en-us/library/aa383749(VS.85).aspx

▶ Windows SDK: http://msdn.microsoft.com/en-us/windows/desktop/hh852363.aspx

▶ PInvoke.net website: http://www.pinvoke.net

Summary

In this chapter, you learned some concepts on how the .NET technology can interoperate with the COM legacy architecture and components. In the first part of the chapter, you learned how to import COM components into managed applications, understanding how Visual Studio generates .NET wrappers to interact with COM. Next, you learned how to create and expose .NET libraries to COM, utilizing the Visual Studio instrumentation and applying the `ComVisible` attribute to classes and class members to grant visibility granularity. In the last part of the chapter, you saw how to call and run unmanaged code, with particular regard to Platform Invokes and types conversions for working directly against the Windows operating system.

CHAPTER 49

Documenting the Source Code with XML Comments

One of the most common programming rules states that documenting the source code is fundamental. This is the truth, but you have to think about the way source code is commented. Classical comments are useful to explain what code does so that you can easily remember how your code works if you need to reuse it after a long time, or they can help other developers to understand your code. But this is not the only way of documenting code in .NET development. A sophisticated environment such as Visual Studio offers the IntelliSense technology that speeds up the way you write code and shows instructions on how you use objects and members. This is possible because of special kinds of comments that you can add to your code, known as *XML comments*. Such comments enable you to write the source code documentation, explain objects' and members' behavior, and provide descriptions and examples that can be displayed by IntelliSense. But that is not all. Documenting code with XML comments is particularly important if you develop reusable compiled libraries and enables you to automate the process of building compiled documentation files (such as .chm files) in a similar way to the MSDN documentation. In this chapter, you learn to use XML comments to provide simple and complex source code documentation, also learning how to build compiled documentation.

Understanding XML Comments

XML comments are not new in Visual Basic 2012; they were first natively introduced with Visual Basic 2005. (In versions prior to 2005, XML comments were possible only via third-party add-ins.) To understand why XML comments are an essential topic, let's take a look at a method invocation within the code editor. Figure 49.1 shows how IntelliSense appears on an uncommented method.

FIGURE 49.1   Uncommented members make IntelliSense incapable of displaying useful information.

As you can see from Figure 49.1, IntelliSense will correctly display, but it will just show the method name in a tooltip, without providing information on the method usage. This is because the method was not commented with XML comments. Now take a look at Figure 49.2. It shows how IntelliSense can provide information if the method was commented with XML comments.

The difference is evident. Objects and members decorated with XML comments can provide full explanation on their usage. This works in the code editor when IntelliSense displays with both source files and with compiled executables. As mentioned at the beginning of this chapter, providing XML comments is useful not only for IntelliSense, but also when you investigate objects in the Object Browser or for automating the process of building compiled documentation for your libraries. Because of this, adding XML comments to your code is necessary in most cases, especially if you develop reusable assemblies. In the next sections, you learn practical techniques for commenting the source code and getting the most out of XML comments with Visual Basic.

FIGURE 49.2   Commented members are well described when IntelliSense displays in the code editor.

Enabling XML Comments

When Visual Studio builds the project output, it also creates an XML document storing all XML comments. The XML document constitutes the actual code documentation. In Visual Studio 2012, XML comments are enabled by default. Before reading this chapter, ensure that XML comments are enabled in your project. To accomplish this, open **My Project**; select the **Compile** tab and, if it's not checked, check the **Generate XML Documentation file** box. See Figure 49.3 for details.

Behind the scenes, this requires the Visual Basic compiler to be launched by Visual Studio with the /doc option, which makes the compiler also generate the XML documentation. At this point, you are ready to implement XML comments in your Visual Basic code.

49

FIGURE 49.3   Enabling XML comments.

Implementing XML Comments

XML comments have a double purpose. The first one is enabling additional help within IntelliSense when you write code. The second one is generating an XML file storing information that can be built into a compiled documentation file, such as the .chm format that also enables navigation between documented items. In this section, you learn to implement XML comments and learn the various tags and why they are important, although in some cases they might not seem to be. Before implementing comments, create a new Console application and implement a `Person` class as follows:

```
Public Class Person

    Public Overridable Property FirstName As String
    Public Overridable Property LastName As String
    Public Overridable Property Age As Integer

    Public Overridable Function GetFullName() As String
        Dim fn As New Text.StringBuilder
        fn.Append(Me.FirstName)
        fn.Append(" ")
        fn.Append(Me.LastName)
        Return fn.ToString
    End Function
End Class
```

The `Person` class will be the base for our experiments. You implement an XML comment by typing three apostrophes. The Visual Studio code editor adds a comment skeleton to your code that first looks like the following example:

```
''' <summary>
'''
''' </summary>
''' <returns></returns>
''' <remarks></remarks>
Public Overridable Function GetFullName() As String
    Dim fn As New Text.StringBuilder
    fn.Append(Me.FirstName)
    fn.Append(" ")
    fn.Append(Me.LastName)
    Return fn.ToString
End Function
```

As you can see, these comments have typical XML structure according to the `<tag>` `</tag>` syntax. The `summary` XML tag enables describing what an object (or member) does. The description will be also available within IntelliSense. The `remarks` tag enables you to provide additional information on what you already specified in the summary, and the information will also be displayed within the Object Browser (but not within IntelliSense). The `returns` tag specifies the type returned by the member (being a method or a property); if the member is a method that does not return a value, Visual Studio will not add the `returns` tag. For a better understanding, populate comments as follows:

```
''' <summary>
''' Gets the complete person's name
''' </summary>
''' <returns>String</returns>
''' <remarks>This method returns the complete person's name</remarks>
Public Overridable Function GetFullName() As String
    Dim fn As New Text.StringBuilder
    fn.Append(Me.FirstName)
    fn.Append(" ")
    fn.Append(Me.LastName)
    Return fn.ToString
End Function
```

Now go to the Main method in your Console application, and write the following code that instantiates and populates the Person class:

```
Dim p As New Person With {.FirstName = "Alessandro", .LastName = "Del Sole",
                          .Age = 35}

Dim fullName As String = p.GetFullName
```

When typing code, IntelliSense provides information on the GetFullName method according to the XML comment's content. This is represented in Figure 49.4.

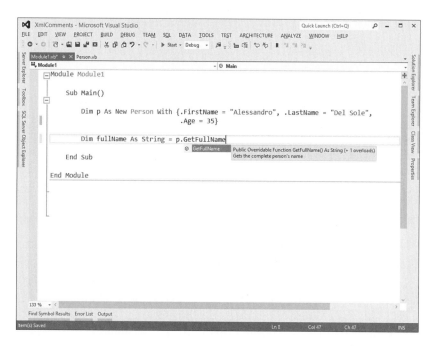

FIGURE 49.4 IntelliSense shows the information provided by the XML comments.

As you can see, IntelliSense shows the content of the summary tag, but it does not show the content of the returns and remarks tags. This makes sense in that IntelliSense's tooltips are the fastest way for getting help. If you instead open the Object Browser on the Person class, you get a result that looks similar to Figure 49.5 (additional information appearing in the window is covered shortly). You obtain the same detailed information if you build a compiled documentation file, as described later in this chapter. The one shown before is the most basic implementation of XML comments. This great Visual Basic feature enables you to define complex documentation over your code, which can be particularly useful due to the integration with the Visual Studio environment.

SCOPE

XML comments can be applied to both public and private objects and members.

Defining Complex Code Documentation

The MSDN documentation says that the Visual Basic compiler can parse any valid XML tag. The MSDN also recommends a series of tags that are specific to the code documentation. Table 49.1 summarizes the recommended tags.

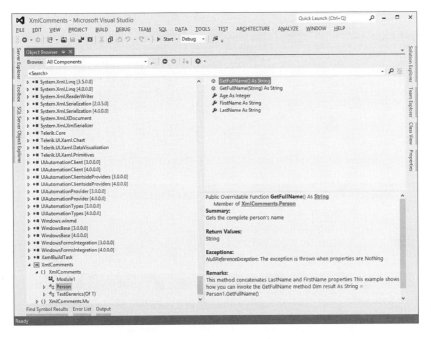

FIGURE 49.5   The Object Browser shows information provided by XML comments.

TABLE 49.1   Recommended Tags for XML Comments

Tag	Description
c	Identifies a code element
cref	Creates a cross reference to another documented object
code	Provides a code snippet about the code usage
example	Provides a description about how code can be used
exception	Enables you to specify the exception that your member could throw
include	Points to an external XML file containing documentation for the code
list	Enables you to generate a bulleted, numbered, or tabled list
para	Enables you to formatting its content as a paragraph
param	Defines a parameter that can be referenced by `paramref`
paramref	Enables you to format a word as a parameter defined via `param`
permission	Specifies the Code Access Security permission required by the commented member
remarks	Provides additional notes on your code
returns	Specifies the .NET type returned by your member

Tag	Description
see	Provides a link to another member
seealso	Adds a member in the See Also section of the compiled documentation
summary	Provides a description about a member; also shown within IntelliSense
typeparam	Provides type parameter name and description when declaring generic types
value	Describes the value of a member (for example, a property)

CASE-SENSITIVENESS

Tags within XML comments are case-sensitive and lowercase. Take note of this to ensure that the Visual Basic compiler correctly recognizes tags.

NOTE ON COMPLEX DOCUMENTATION

You can appreciate complex documentation generated with XML comments only when building compiled help files. This is because within IntelliSense or in the Object Browser, only a few tags' contents will be shown. For example, XML comments enable you to build bulleted lists or specify links to other documentation regarding different code. All this cannot be shown in IntelliSense, but it makes a lot of sense in a help file or a help system built on HTML pages. If you are interested in only building documentation for Visual Studio internal usage, you can theoretically limit XML comments to the basic implementations.

Let's go back to the `Person` class and provide an XML comment for the `FirstName` property. The XML comment must look like this:

```
''' <summary>
''' Contains the person's first name
''' </summary>
''' <value>Person's first name</value>
''' <returns>String</returns>
''' <remarks></remarks>
Public Overridable Property FirstName As String
```

Here there is a new tag, `value`. The `summary` tag describes a property, and `value` describes the property's value. Do the same thing on the `LastName` property, specifying the appropriate description, similarly to `FirstName`. Other tags can be added in a straightforward way, thanks to the always present IntelliSense. Figure 49.6 shows how IntelliSense provides available XML tags, according to the particular context where they have to be added.

FIGURE 49.6   IntelliSense helps you select XML tags according to the particular context.

Referring to Code Elements

XML comments enable references to other code elements with specific tags. The first one is `c` that identifies the element within angle bracket as code. To show an example, rewrite XML comments for the `GetFullName` method as follows:

```vb
''' <summary>
''' Gets the complete person's name
''' </summary>
''' <returns>String</returns>
''' <remarks>This method concatenates <c>LastName</c> and
''' <c>FirstName</c> properties</remarks>
Public Overridable Function GetFullName() As String
    Dim fn As New Text.StringBuilder
    fn.Append(Me.FirstName)
    fn.Append(" ")
    fn.Append(Me.LastName)
    Return fn.ToString
End Function
```

Notice how the `c` tag embraces both the `LastName` and `FirstName` properties, communicating to the compiler that both tags represent a code element. It is enclosed and nested within a remarks tag (IntelliSense can be helpful in choosing the allowed tags). This is not the only way of referring to code; you can provide an entire code example that will be included in your documentation. To accomplish this, you first declare a sample tag, which contains the sample description and then a code tag that contains a code snippet demonstrating the member purpose. Edit the preceding XML comment as follows:

```
''' <summary>
''' Gets the complete person's name
''' </summary>
''' <returns>String</returns>
''' <remarks>This method concatenates <c>LastName</c> and
''' <c>FirstName</c> properties
''' <example>This example shows how you can invoke
''' the <c>GetFullName</c> method
''' <code>
''' Dim result As String = Person1.GetFullName()
''' </code>
''' </example>
''' </remarks>
Public Overridable Function GetFullName() As String
```

This is useful because your documentation also shows examples of your libraries.

WHY DON'T I SEE THEM?

Code, c, and example tags provide documentation that is not available within IntelliSense. It is, however, available within the generated XML file; thus you can appreciate them when building an HTML-based or compiled documentation or within the Object Browser.

XML comments enable you to easily refer to and document members' arguments. For a better understanding, write the following overload of the GetFullName method that accepts a Title argument:

```
Public Overridable Function GetFullName(ByVal Title As String) As String

    If String.IsNullOrEmpty(Title) = True Then Throw New _
                                        ArgumentNullException

    Dim fn As New Text.StringBuilder
    fn.Append(Title)
    fn.Append(" ")
    fn.Append(Me.FirstName)
    fn.Append(" ")
    fn.Append(Me.LastName)
    Return fn.ToString
End Function
```

Now add an XML comment. It looks likes this:

```
''' <summary>
''' Gets the complete person's name
''' </summary>
''' <param name="Title"></param>
''' <returns>String</returns>
''' <remarks></remarks>
Public Overridable Function GetFullName(ByVal Title As String) As String
```

The `param` tag enables you to referr to a member's argument, specified by the name attribute. If you try to type the name on your own, IntelliSense helps you choose the argument. XML comments also enable you to specify an exception that your member could encounter, according to the actions it takes. For example, the `GetFullName` method could throw a `NullReferenceException` if the `Title` argument is an empty or null string. For this, you use an `exception` tag to specify the exception. The tag is used with `cref`. This one is straightforward in that it enables you to point a reference to a .NET object using IntelliSense. The following tag (which must be added before the method definition) specifies which exception can be thrown:

```
''' <exception cref="ArgumentNullException">
''' The exception that is thrown when <paramref name="Title"/> is Nothing
''' </exception>
''' <returns>String</returns>
''' <remarks></remarks>
Public Overridable Function GetFullName(ByVal Title As String) As String
```

When typing `cref`, the IntelliSense window shows all the available objects. You pick the exception you are interested in. This speeds up the way you write your comment, also ensuring that you type a valid object name. You can also specify the description for the exception. The good news about `cref` is that it creates a cross-reference to the documentation related to the pointed object. For instance, when you create a compiled documentation file based on the XML comments, `cref` enables you to redirect to another page showing information on the pointed object. You can also refer to the argument by specifying the `paramref` tag within a descriptive text, which requires a name attribute pointing to the argument. `paramref` also takes advantages of IntelliSense.

Referring to an External Documentation File

The Visual Basic compiler can link documentation to your code from an external XML document. To do this, you use the `include` tag. The tag requires a file attribute that points to the external document and a path attribute that points to the position in the document providing documentation for the given member. The following code sets external documentation for the `Age` property:

```
''' <include file="ExternalDoc.xml" path="Help/Property[@name='Age']"/>
Public Overridable Property Age As Integer
```

49

To understand how the path tag works, here is the XML representation of the external document:

```
<?xml version="1.0" encoding="utf-8" ?>
<Help>
  <Property name="Age">
    <summary>Returns how old a person is</summary>
    <returns>Integer</returns>
  </Property>
  <!-- Other properties...-->
  <Property>

  </Property>
</Help>
```

Creating Lists

Documentation often requires bulleted and numbered lists or tables, as in any other kind of document. Luckily, XML comments enable you to easily build lists. You do this with the `list` tag that requires a `type` attribute specifying whether the list is a bulleted or numbered list or a two-column table. The following example shows how to build a numbered list on the `Person` class documentation:

```
''' <summary>
''' Represents a human being
''' </summary>
''' <remarks>
''' <list type="number">
''' <item><description>Instantiate the class</description></item>
''' <item><description>Populate its properties</description></item>
''' <item><description>Eventually retrieve the full
''' name</description></item>
''' </list>
''' </remarks>
Public Class Person
....
End Class
```

The type attribute can have one of the following values: `bullet` (bulleted list), `number` (numbered list), or `table` (two-column table). Notice how each item in the list is represented by an item tag that requires a nested description tag providing the actual description. If you want to provide a table, each item must contain a term tag and a description tag as in the following example:

```
''' <item><term>Action one</term></item>
''' <item><description>Instantiate the class</description></item>
```

The item's content will be also shown in IntelliSense and the Object Browser, but it will be formatted as a list only in the compiled documentation.

Documenting Permissions Requirements

Sometimes your objects expose members that require special permissions to access system resources. You can provide documentation about required permissions by adding a permission tag with `cref`, pointing to the desired .NET permission. The following example shows how to comment the `GetFullName` method with the `UIPermission` requirement:

```
''' <permission cref="System.Security.Permissions.UIPermission"/>
Public Overridable Function GetFullName() As String
```

Of course, you can specify multiple permissions by adding multiple permission tags.

Specifying Links to Other Resources

When documenting the code, it is not unusual to provide links to other members. XML comments enable you to do this by specifying `see` and `seealso` tags. The `see` tag enables you to specify a link to another member's documentation from within the description text. The `seealso` tag does the same, but it differs in that the link to the other member appears in the *See Also* section of the compiled page. The following example demonstrates this on the `FirstName` property providing a link to `LastName`:

```
''' <remarks>Use the <see cref="LastName"/>
''' property for the person's last name</remarks>
Public Overridable Property FirstName As String
```

If you want the link to be shown in the See Also section, replace `see` with `seealso`.

XML Comments and Generics

When you define your custom generics, you can use XML comments to describe the type parameter. This is accomplished via the `typeparam` tag, as shown in the following code snippet:

```
''' <summary>
''' A test class
''' </summary>
''' <typeparam name="T">
''' A type parameter that must implement IEnumerable
''' </typeparam>
''' <remarks></remarks>
Public Class TestGenerics(Of T As IEnumerable)

End Class
```

The Visual Basic compiler automatically recognizes the generic implementation and thus adds for you the `typeparam` tag when adding the XML comment.

49

Generating Compiled Help Files

When you document your source code with XML comments, you might want to generate compiled help files that you can distribute together with your libraries. Compiled help files are .chm files that can be easily opened with the Windows integrated Help Viewer. The .chm file format is the most appropriate in such situations because it is a standalone and does not require additional applications. Several tools can generate .chm files starting from XML comments. A very popular one is SandCastle, an open source tool from Microsoft that is also used to build documentation. At the moment in which this chapter is being written, SandCastle supports Visual Studio 2010 so our suggestion is to check out the SandCastle website (http://www.codeplex.com/sandcastle) periodically to see if an update is available. Also, a number of third party (paid) tools exist on the market. Popular tools are the following:

▶ Help + Manual from EC Software (http://www.ec-software.com)

▶ HelpNDoc (http://www.helpndoc.com)

These tools are very good in that they enable you to generate multiple output formats, not only .chm files.

Summary

This chapter covered how to use XML comments instead of classic comments. With XML comments, you specify tags that identify an element in the code as a special formatted element in the generated documentation file. Such a file is an XML document that enables IntelliSense documentation for your own code and constitutes the source for automating building compiled help files that accompany your libraries as the documentation. To automate this process, you were informed about the existence of Microsoft SandCastle, a free tool from Microsoft that is available on CodePlex as an open-source application, and of tools produced by other vendors.

CHAPTER 50

Understanding the Global Assembly Cache

The Visual Studio IDE is a great place to create applications, but in most cases, you need to deploy them to your customers. The .NET Framework offers a nice infrastructure for making this possible, but you need to know some concepts about the infrastructure before effectively deploying applications. Often you can create libraries and reference those libraries, or third-party libraries, other than the .NET Framework base libraries in your projects. These libraries need to be deployed together with your application, but the .NET deployment model for assemblies works differently from the COM model. The goal of this chapter is to illustrate how .NET base libraries are organized, why you can be sure to find them on a target machine, and how you deploy your own libraries or third-party libraries that your applications work with. This information is important if you consider deploying an application is not only deploying the executable, but also all libraries required by the application. This is the reason you need to read this chapter before discovering the deploying modes offered by the .NET Framework and Visual Studio 2012.

The Dll Hell Problem

One of the biggest problems of the COM programming model is the *Dll hell*. COM components (such as ActiveX controls or type libraries) need to be registered so the system knows where to find them even if they are not available in the application directory. The problem is when you have different versions of the component installed on the same machine. Registration can be painful, and there are often many problems in making an application recognize the correct version of the component. In many cases, an application will not work correctly. This is the reason the situation is called Dll hell. Since version 1.0, the .NET Framework provides a brilliant way to solve this big problem by introducing assemblies and the *Global Assembly Cache* (GAC). Before discussing the GAC, it is important to understand how assemblies can be deployed and recognized by applications and why they solve the Dll hell problem. To accomplish this, we need to discuss the most basic mode for deploying assemblies—the XCopy deployment.

XCopy Deployment

If you have been an MS-DOS person, you will remember the xcopy command. It enabled you to copy entire directory trees, including files and subdirectories, from one location to another. In honor of this command, the most basic deployment technique in the .NET Framework is XCopy deployment. The reason for this name is that a .NET application can work when the executable and the assemblies referenced by the executable all reside in the same folder. According to this, you can deploy an application by copying its folder. This approach has a huge implication—if an application folder contains a copy of required assemblies, these are isolated from one another and do not require registration anymore. Because they are no longer required to be registered, multiple versions of an assembly can reside on the same machine avoiding the big problem of the Dll hell.

BASE CLASS LIBRARY ASSEMBLIES

The preceding discussion is not valid when talking about the Base Class Library assemblies being part of the .NET Framework and cannot be included in the application folder. They stay in the GAC as covered in next section.

When you compile your project, Visual Studio generates a Bin subfolder within the project folder. Bin contains Debug and Release subfolders (referring to default build configurations). Both folders contain the executable and referenced assemblies. You can perform an XCopy deployment by distributing the content of the Release folder, and your application will work. XCopy deployment is something you have to know to understand how things work. In a business environment, you will deploy your applications with professional installers, such as InstallShield for Windows Installer and ClickOnce, which are discussed in the next two chapters. Another consideration about XCopy deployment is that every application keeps its own copy of referenced assemblies. This means if you have ten applications referring to the same assembly, you will have ten copies of the assembly. This is good in that assemblies will not interfere with each other, especially in the case of different versions. However, it can be annoying if you have ten copies of the same version of your assembly. A solution to this is provided by the Global Assembly Cache, which solves other problems and is the subject of the following section.

The Global Assembly Cache

The .NET Framework consists of hundreds of libraries and tools. Most libraries implement the Base Class Library. The BCL's assemblies are located in GAC. This is the reason you can be sure a .NET application requiring only base assemblies can correctly work on a target machine that has the .NET Framework installed. The GAC can be considered as a repository of shared assemblies. This means that an application can have a reference to an assembly available in the GAC instead of bringing its own copy of the assembly as happens in the XCopy deployment. The GAC is a folder in the system and is located at C:\Windows\Assembly. Because of the particular nature of this folder, its representation within Windows Explorer is a little bit different from other folders. Figure 50.1 shows how the GAC is represented in Windows Explorer.

FIGURE 50.1   The Global Assembly Cache shown in Windows Explorer.

You might notice from Figure 50.1 how the GAC lists installed the assemblies, version number, public key token, and target processor architecture. The public key token is a unique identifier, which identifies the assembly within the .NET infrastructure. If the assembly targets a specific culture, this information is also shown. You can easily notice how different versions of the same assembly can be available in the GAC. (For example, check the `System.Data.SqlServerCe.dll` assembly.) This is important because it means the GAC is responsible for handling different versions of the same assembly, solving the versioning and registration problems.

Installing and Uninstalling Assemblies

A common way for referring to assemblies available in the GAC is saying they are installed into the GAC. (Installing an assembly to the GAC means making the assembly recognizable by the GAC and by the .NET Framework while the physical file stays in its original location.) Suppose you have an assembly named C:\MyAssemblies\MyLibrary.dll and you want to install this assembly into the GAC. The installation procedure adds to the GAC metadata information for the assembly but does not copy the file to the GAC; instead, MyLibrary.Dll remains in C:\MyAssemblies. Installing and uninstalling assemblies to and from the GAC is a step you have to divide in two parts: development time and real deployment time. At development time, you have two opportunities for installing assemblies to the GAC. The first way is invoking the **GacUtil.exe** command-line tool passing the /i option and the assembly name. The following is a command-line example for installing an assembly:

```
GacUtil.exe /i C:\MyAssemblies\MyLibrary.dll
```

You uninstall an assembly from the GAC by passing the /u option to GacUtil, as in the following command line:

```
GacUtil.exe /u C:\MyAssemblies\MyLibrary.dll
```

The second way for installing assemblies is dragging them to Windows Explorer opened to the GAC folder. To uninstall one or more assemblies, right-click the assembly name and select **Uninstall**.

INSTALLING AND UNINSTALLING REQUIRE ELEVATED PRIVILEGES

Administrators using an Access Control List can protect the Global Assembly Cache folder. If this is your situation, remember that installing and uninstalling assemblies to the GAC requires elevated privileges. If you are using Windows Vista, Windows 7, or Windows 8, you will be required to run the command prompt or Windows Explorer with administrator privileges before attempting to install or uninstall assemblies.

Both ways can be useful at development time, but they cannot be absolutely indicated at deployment time for several reasons. The most important reason is that both ways have no reference counting and it is not appropriate to require your user to manually manipulate the GAC with Windows Explorer. Because of this, you should always choose professional installation systems, such as InstallShield for Windows Installer, that install and uninstall assemblies without troubles. The next chapter discusses setup and deployment projects for Windows Installer, covering GAC situations. ClickOnce has some limitations from this point of view because it does not allow installing assemblies to the GAC, which is important to consider when deciding the deployment strategy. In addition, installing assemblies to the Global Assembly Cache has a huge requirement—you can only install assemblies signed with a strong name.

Signing Assemblies with Strong Names

A strong name is a signature added to assemblies to provide uniqueness and represents the assembly's identity. It is composed by the assembly name, version, culture, public key, and digital signature. The public key is generated from the related private key, which is stored in the assembly manifest.

SECURITY ISSUES

To avoid security issues, strong-named assemblies can only use type from other strong-named assemblies (such as the Base Class Library assemblies).

You have two modes for signing an assembly with a strong name. The first is invoking command-line tools such as Sn.exe and Al.exe. But because most of your developer life is spent within Visual Studio, the second mode is offered by the IDE. To add a strong name to your assembly, you first open **My Project** and then select the **Signing** tab where you flag the **Sign the Assembly** check box as shown in Figure 50.2.

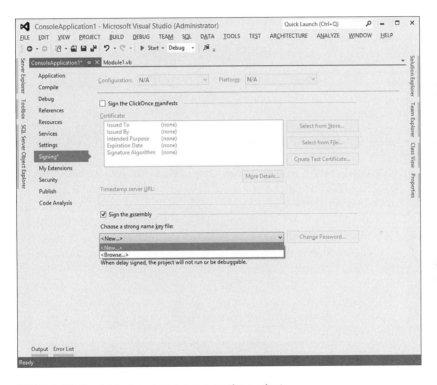

FIGURE 50.2   Adding a strong name to the project.

You can either add a new strong name or import an existing one. To add a new strong name, click the **<New...>** item in the combo box (see Figure 50.2). You will be prompted for specifying the filename and a password. This generates a .pfx file that is added to the project and is visible in Solution Explorer. For instance, in the Create Strong Name Key dialog box, type **MyStrongName** as the filename and **MyStrongName** as the password. Figure 50.3 shows how to accomplish this.

Specifying a password is not mandatory. If you do not provide a password, Visual Studio generates an .snk file instead of a .pfx one. I strongly recommend you provide a password.

50

FIGURE 50.3   Providing name and password for the new strong name.

KEEP YOUR PASSWORD

Take note of the password you assign to strong names. It will be required every time you open the project from another computer different from the one where you first added the strong name.

In Visual Studio 2012, you can specify an encryption algorithm, between **sha256RA** and **sha1RSA**. Both calculate a hash for the input data, which is the signature. The first one produces a 256 bit hash, the second one a 160 bit hash. The default selection is sha256RA and you can leave it unchanged. Choosing an encryption algorithm is a new feature in Visual Studio 2012. Remember that strong names are not the equivalent of certificates (such as Authenticode) that provide security trust, other than uniqueness, according to .NET security requirements. Finally, strong names can be applied to assemblies with the delay signing technique (see the Delay sign option in the MyProject Signing tab). In a few words, this technique writes only the public key in the executable and requires the private key be passed at a later stage, preventing the project from being compiled, debugged, and run from within Visual Studio. Because of this you need to skip the signature verification (e.g. running the Sn.exe tool passing the -Vr option). It is worth noting that you can disable signing enforcement on a machine even at the specific assembly signature level in the event you need to delay sign, but still want to debug. This topic is not covered in more detail because of its particular nature. You can get more information in the official MSDN documentation at http://msdn.microsoft.com/en-us/library/t07a3dye(VS.110).aspx.

CLS-COMPLIANT ASSEMBLIES

Signing assemblies with strong names is mandatory in case you want them to be CLS-compliant.

Top Reasons for Installing (or Not) Assemblies to the GAC

As a rule, installing assemblies to the GAC is something that should be restricted only to particular scenarios. Situations when you want to take advantage of the GAC can be summarized as follows:

▶ **Multiple applications referencing the same assemblies**—In this case, it can be convenient to have a single copy of assemblies in the GAC instead of providing several copies in the application folder.

▶ **Versioning**—The GAC can maintain different versions of the same assembly. This problem is solved by the XCopy deployment, but your company can have a deployment strategy that prefers the GAC.

▶ **Security**—The GAC can be managed by system administrators for controlling permissions using the Access Control List. If you need this control, installing assemblies to the GAC is a good choice.

In all other cases, you should refrain from installing assemblies to the GAC. Remember that this procedure affects the .NET Framework and any mistake can be fatal.

Summary

This chapter discussed important concepts you need to know before deploying .NET applications. You saw how the .NET Framework solves the Dll Hell problem by avoiding the need of component registration and allowing the XCopy deployment. Then you saw what the Global Assembly Cache is and how you can manage it for sharing assemblies among multiple applications. In addition, you got information on strong names and on how to apply them to your assemblies so these can be installed to the GAC. Finally, you understood how to configure Windows Registry for making custom assemblies in the GAC visible from the Add Reference dialog box in Visual Studio. All this information is important to understand how you deploy libraries, controls, and assemblies together with your executables. Now that you know this, you are ready to deploy your applications with Visual Studio tools.

50

Setup and Deployment Projects with InstallShield for Visual Studio

When you deliver your application to your customers, you do not tell them it supports the XCopy deployment and you do not provide technical explanations on how .NET applications work. This is because modern applications require a convenient setup procedure that can install them in a professional fashion, put files in the appropriate places, create shortcuts in the Windows user interface, check for system requirements, and perform components registration. The users are just required to select the target folder and what options in your applications they want to be installed on their machine. Creating a user-friendly setup procedure is something that increases professionalism and gives customers the first good impression of your work. The .NET-based applications, like the ones you create with Visual Basic 2012, can be deployed in several modes. One of these is taking advantage of the Windows Installer engine that provides great flexibility over installation requirements and takes the maximum from integration with the operating system. Visual Studio 2012 breaks with the past, discontinuing the Setup & Deployment projects that were available until version 2010 and replacing these by introducing into the development environment a new tool for creating setup projects based on Windows Installer—InstallShield Limited Edition (LE). This has an important consequence—existing Setup & Deployment projects built with previous editions of Visual Studio are no longer supported and cannot be opened in Visual Studio 2012. Fortunately, InstallShield LE has an option that allows converting old projects into InstallShield projects. In this chapter, you will learn how to create a setup project for Windows Installer using InstallShield and Visual Studio 2012 so you can deploy your Visual Basic applications in the most professional way possible. Even though you now use InstallShield, this still relies on the Windows Installer engine and generates MSI packages. For this reason, an overview of Windows Installer can be useful, especially if you do not have technical experience with an installation engine.

ABOUT WINDOWS 8 STORE APPS

Windows 8 Store Apps have their own specific mechanism for installation, so they cannot be installed with Windows Installer or ClickOnce.

Windows Installer Overview

Windows Installer is the Microsoft technology for deploying applications. This technology has been part of the Windows operating system for many years and can be considered as an engine for installing .msi packages. An .msi package, or installer package, contains all files to be installed with your application and other important information including shortcuts, icons, license agreements, other redistributable packages, and key/values to be written to the Windows Registry.

Windows Installer is the most powerful technology for deploying .NET applications with Visual Studio 2012. This is because Windows Installer has few limitations, whereas it brings many benefits. Windows Installer makes it difficult to provide updates, so if you plan to release frequent updates for your applications, you should consider ClickOnce, which is discussed in the next chapter. You should choose Windows Installer as the deployment system for your application if you meet one or more of the following requirements:

▶ Adding values to the Windows Registry

▶ Customizing installation folders

▶ Installing assemblies to the Global Assembly Cache or installing and registering COM components

▶ Installing Windows services and peripheral drivers

▶ Executing custom actions and specifying launch conditions

▶ Managing ODBC components

▶ Creating custom shortcuts in the Windows user interface

▶ Elevated permissions and deeper interaction with the user

In scenarios different from the ones listed, you might consider ClickOnce. Visual Studio 2012 is the perfect environment for creating projects that can build Windows Installer packages that install your applications on target machines the most appropriate way. In the next section, you can see how to accomplish this.

Introducing InstallShield

InstallShield is software for creating Windows Installer packages. It has been very popular for many years because it has been the first fully-featured environment for building complete MSI packages via a very powerful instrumentation. Other tools existed in the past for creating Windows Installer packages, but InstallShield has always been a step ahead. InstallShield is produced by Flexera (www.flexera.com) and is available both as a standalone environment and as an add-on for Visual Studio 2012. In fact, this is not the first time that InstallShield enters Visual Studio's life. InstallShield LE existed for Visual Studio 2010, but was just an alternative to other deployment technologies. In Visual Studio 2012, however, it is the only way for generating packages for Windows Installer.

Obtaining Your Copy of InstallShield LE

InstallShield is not available by default in Visual Studio 2012, so you need to download it separately. The easiest way to request InstallShield is going in Visual Studio and select **File, New Project**. When the New Project dialog box appears, expand the Other Project Types node and select **Setup and Deployment**. At this point, you will see an item called **Enable InstallShield Limited Edition**, as demonstrated in Figure 51.1.

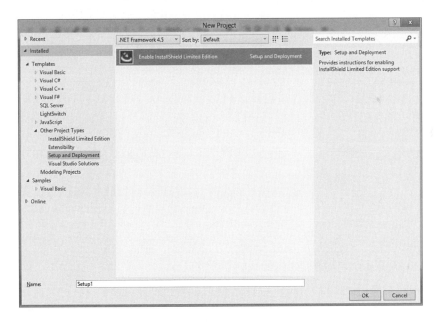

FIGURE 51.1   Enabling InstallShield LE.

At this point, an HTML document already residing on your machine will open. Follow the instructions to download a copy of InstallShield LE and store the activation key that is sent to you via email. This is important for activating InstallShield at the first project. Once you have downloaded your copy, close Visual Studio 2012 and launch the installation of InstallShield. When the installation completes, restart Visual Studio 2012.

Creating a Setup Project

The goal of this chapter is to demonstrate how you create a setup project for a Windows client application. First, create a new WPF project with Visual Basic and name it DeploymentDemo. This project just serves as the demo application to be deployed. When the new project is ready, right-click the solution name in Solution Explorer and select **Add, New Project**. In the New Project dialog box, select the **Other Project Types, Setup and Deployment, InstallShield Limited Edition** templates subfolder and select the **InstalShield Limited Edition Project** template, as shown in Figure 51.2. Name the new project SetupExample and click OK.

FIGURE 51.2   Adding a new setup project to the solution.

When you click OK, Visual Studio generates a new InstallShield project. Notice that during the creation of the very first project you will be prompted to enter the activation code you received via email. When the project is ready, you will see the InstallShield Project Assistant, which is where you start creating your setup package (see Figure 51.3).

AVAILABILITY OF CERTAIN FEATURES

If you look at Solution Explorer, you will see that the InstallShield project offers a number of shortcuts and features. Not all of them are available in the Limited Edition for Visual Studio 2012. So we will explain how to build a setup project by using the Project Assistant instead of selecting features in Solution Explorer because this might lead to confusion.

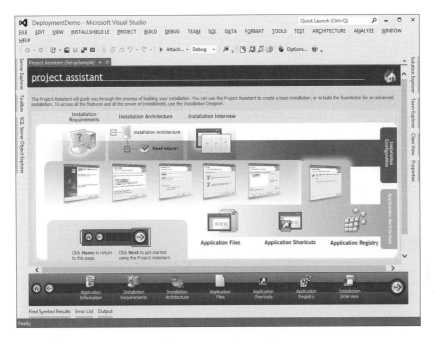

FIGURE 51.3   The InstallShield's Project Assistant.

At the bottom of the Project Assistant you can find a toolbar that provides a number of shortcuts you should follow from the left to the right, so you can start from supplying all the required information and finish with the package generation process. Now you will get an overview of all the available shortcuts to create a sample MSI package for the current project.

Application Information

The Application Information group allows specifying general information for the installation package such as the software's producer name, application version, producer's website. You can specify a custom icon for the installer by clicking the Browse button. Figure 51.4 shows an example.

You can change the target directory for the installed application. The default is set based on the company name and application name under the form of C:\Program Files\ CompanyName\ApplicationName. You can change the target directory by selecting the **Edit the default installation location** hyperlink on the left side of the Project Assistant. InstallShield assigns the target directory value to a variable called INSTALLDIR and is used by the Windows Installer engine to determine the target folder. After setting the Application Information, it is time to set prerequisites.

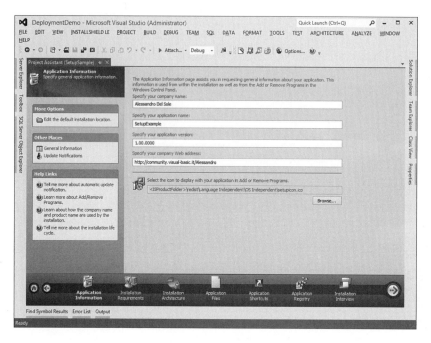

FIGURE 51.4   Specifying general application information for the package.

Installation Requirements

Installation Requirements include the specification of the Windows operating system that the application is going to target and those packages or runtime components that must be installed together with the application so it correctly works. As you can see from Figure 51.5, the Installation Requirement group is divided into two parts. The first part allows specifying the target operating systems, whereas the second part (at the bottom) allows specifying prerequisites like specific versions of the .NET Framework or other components (for example, Adobe Reader, SQL Server, and so on). The .NET Framework 4.5 is included by default and it is not available in the list.

Remember that the .NET Framework 4.5 is not supported on Windows 2000, Windows XP, and Windows Server 2003 so unselect these operating systems if you are deploying applications based on version 4.5 of .NET. Regarding runtime components and prerequisites, you can configure additional options for every single component. You can do this by clicking the Requirements shortcut on the left. This will open the Requirements designer where you can specify hardware requirements and customize installation messages. Figure 51.6 shows the Requirements designer and demonstrates an example about SQL Server 2008 R2. You can click the Edit the Message button to customize the text message that will show if a prerequisite is not found on the target machine.

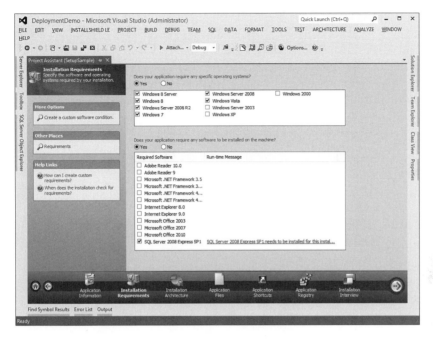

FIGURE 51.5   Configuring Installation Requirements.

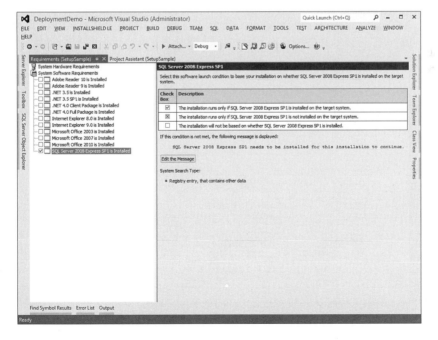

FIGURE 51.6   The Requirements designer.

When you click the Edit the Message button, the Text and Message designer opens. There you will be able to customize predefined values that are stored inside tables of the MSI package. You can finally create a custom software condition, by clicking the same-named shortcut on the left side of the Project Assistant. A custom software condition allows proceeding with the installation only if the specified item is found on the target machine. The installer can search for files, folders, registry keys, and INI file values. Clicking the Custom Software Condition shortcut will launch the System Search Wizard, an easy-to-use tool where you can specify what item will be searched in a convenient step-by-step procedure. This tool is not discussed in further detail because common scenarios are already predetermined in the default settings. We will move to the Application Files group to specify what files of the application will be deployed onto the target machine. You will see the Installation Architecture group first, but this is not available for InstallShield Limited Edition.

Application Files

You can manage files to be installed with your package in the Application Files group. The first thing you have to add is the primary output of the main project, DeploymentDemo in our case. To accomplish this you click **Add Project Outputs** and in the Visual Studio Output Selector dialog box select **Primary Output**, as demonstrated in Figure 51.7.

FIGURE 51.7   Adding the primary output to the installation package.

The primary output represents only the main .exe file, but InstallShield will check for dependencies at build time only in editions higher than the LE so you will have to add referenced assemblies manually with the Limited Edition. After you specify the primary output, this is added to the designer (as shown in Figure 51.8).

You can then click the **Add Files** button, which can be used to include any other kind of required files into your package (including dependencies). You can use the **Add Folder** button to include an entire folder tree. It is worth mentioning that in case your solution contains multiple projects, you can choose the primary output for each project in the Visual Studio Output Selector dialog box. This is useful if you have several assemblies you want to deploy. Finally, you are not limited to the executable file but you can include other items like debug symbols, source code files, documentation, etc. Application files are added by default to the target folder under Program Files. If you select a different folder in the directory tree on the left, then selected files will be installed to the newly selected folder. You can add custom and special folders by right-clicking the root item of the directory tree (Destination Computer) and add a new folder. For instance, if you want to add an assembly that will be installed to the Global Assembly Cache you can follow these steps:

1. Right-click **Destination Computer**.

2. Select Show **Predefined Folder**, then **[GlobalAssemblyCache]**.

3. Select the **GAC** folder in the directory tree and add assemblies to this folder.

FIGURE 51.8   The Application Files group shows target folders and files.

This action is very useful to install files to specific locations, other than application files to the INSTALLDIR directory.

DRAGGING FILES TO THE PACKAGE

If you click the Files and Folders shortcut on the left side of the Project Assistant, Visual Studio will open the Files and Folders designer that shows a view of files and directories on your computer and in the current solution you can easily drag and release onto the application files list.

Assuming you have added all the required application files, or at least the primary output, it is time to specify shortcuts the user will click to launch your application.

Application Shortcuts

Users launch applications via shortcuts. These are normally available on the Desktop or in the Start menu (except for Windows 8 where they are grouped in the applications list). With InstallShield LE you create shortcuts in the Application Shortcuts group. The first thing to do is to click the **New** button. When the Browse for a Destination File dialog box is ready, you have to browse the folders structure and locate the file that will be reachable via the new shortcut, such as the main .exe file. Figure 51.9 shows an example of how to create a shortcut for the DeploymentDemo sample application.

FIGURE 51.9   Creating a new shortcut.

After you click **Open**, a new shortcut called Built is available in the Project Assistant. Click **Rename** to replace the default name with a more meaningful one. You can decide to add a shortcut to the destination Desktop and Start menu (in Windows 8 this will add the shortcut to the applications list). Figure 51.10 shows how the Project Assistant appears at this point, with a renamed shortcut.

Repeat the same operation to add multiple shortcuts in case you have different files you want users to be able to reach easily.

SHORTCUTS HIERARCHY

You can click the **Shortcuts** hyperlink on the left to open the Shortcuts designer where you will be able to get a hierarchical view of shortcuts inside the desktop and the Start menu representations. This is useful to manage shortcuts in a graphical fashion.

You can create a file extension definition so files with the specified extension can be opened or manipulated with your application. Once you have your extension definition, this can be associated to shortcuts. To create an extension definition, follow these steps:

1. Click the **File Extensions** shortcut on the left.

2. When the designer appears, right-click **File Extensions** and select **New Extension**.

3. Specify the extension and then add settings in the properties pane on the right.

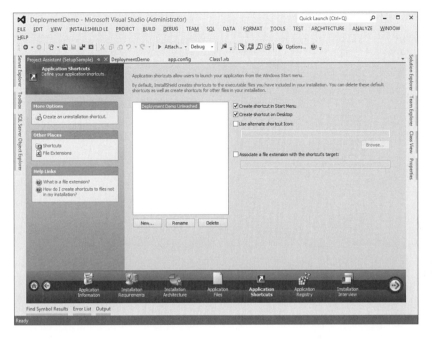

FIGURE 51.10   Specifying shortcut details.

Follow the instructions to specify the **Command** that will be executed by your application when it gets associated to the file extension and in the **File** property specify your application's primary output. If you do not specify any command, Open is assumed by default, which means files with the given extension will be always opened with your application (unless the user changes this setting manually). Figure 51.11 shows an example.

You can specify command line arguments (Arguments) and an icon for the extension (Icon). If you now go back to the Shortcuts group in the Project Assistant, you will see that the new extension has been associated to the selected shortcut. The next step is setting registry keys and values.

Application Registry

One of the biggest benefits in deploying applications with Windows Installer is that you can add keys and values to the Windows Registry on the target machine. You create keys, subkeys, and values by selecting the **Application Registry** in the Project Assistant and then right-click the desired root key. Finally, add the required key or value. Figure 51.12 shows how to accomplish this.

Values are then visible on the right side of the editor. In this way, you have complete control over the Registry so your application can immediately store information onto the target system. The last part of the Project Assistant is all about the user interface of the installer.

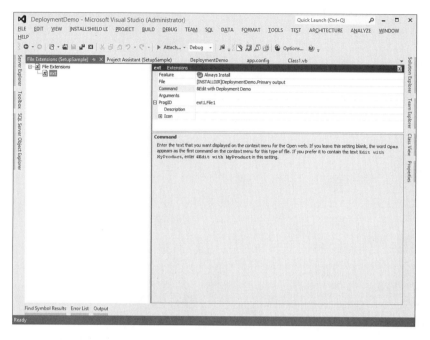

FIGURE 51.11   Creating an extension definition and specifying settings.

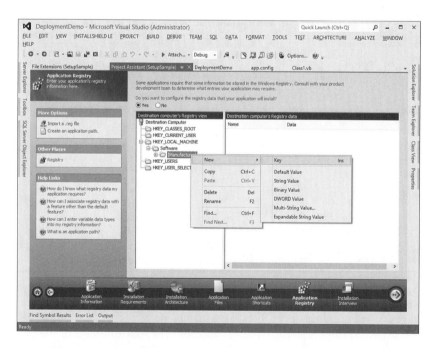

FIGURE 51.12   Adding keys and values to the target Windows registry.

Installation Interview

In the Installation Interview group, you can customize the way users interact with your installation package. Figure 51.13 shows an example.

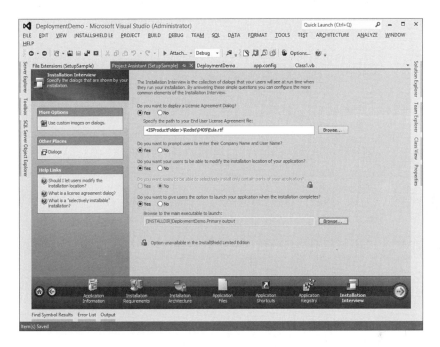

FIGURE 51.13   Customizing the user interface of the installation package.

You can specify an End User License Agreement under the form of a Rich Text Format (RTF) file. You can allow users to change the default installation folder, ask them to launch the application after the installation completes, and provide an opportunity of entering user and company name. Features adorned with a locker are not available in the Limited Edition. Because InstallShield provides default banners and bitmaps for MSI packages, you can replace these with custom ones that will be shown when the installer runs. To accomplish this, click the **Use custom images on dialogs** shortcut and supply the necessary bitmaps. In addition, you can specify a different number of dialogs for your package, each providing a different kind of information. You select dialogs for your package by clicking the **Dialogs** hyperlink. This will launch the Dialogs designer where you can select among the available dialogs and specify properties for each dialog box, as demonstrated in Figure 51.14.

As you can see, you can select a theme and specify banner bitmaps directly from this designer.

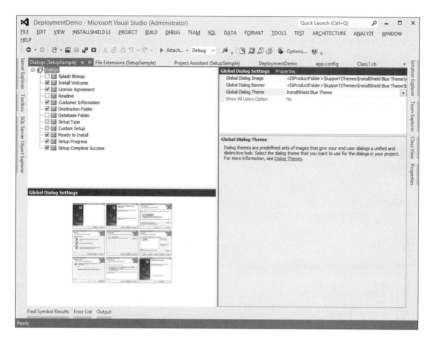

FIGURE 51.14   Specifying dialogs for the installation packages.

Specifying Environment Variables

InstallShield LE allows creating Windows environment variables when the application is installed. To accomplish this, in Solution Explorer double-click the Environment Variables element to open the appropriate designer. When ready, right-click the **Environment Variables** root item and then select **Add Environment Variable**. Enter a name for the variable and then specify the value and other self-explanatory properties on the right. See Figure 51.15.

Environment variables are typically used when applications need special kinds of interaction with the operating system. You will not need this editor if this is not your case.

Configuring the Setup Project

You can supply additional configuration settings for your Windows Installer package by selecting the General Information item in Solution Explorer. This will open the same-named designer and enable you to set a number of package's properties. All the available properties affect layout, messages, and target folders when launching the installer. Figure 51.16 shows an example of how you can set properties.

Properties are self-explanatory, but you can click each of them to get a description at the bottom of the window.

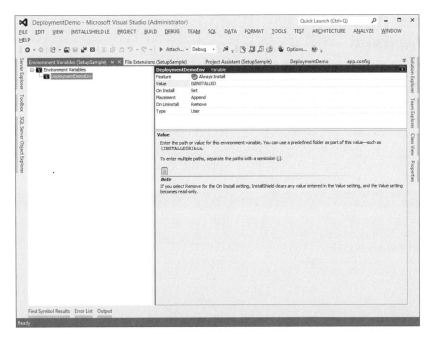

FIGURE 51.15   Adding environment variables.

FIGURE 51.16   Setting additional package properties.

Building and Deploying the Windows Installer Package

To create your Windows Installer distributable package, right-click the setup project name in Solution Explorer and select **Build**. As an alternative, you can choose the appropriate **Build** command from the Build menu. This generates a bootstrapper named Setup.exe and the Windows Installer package with an .msi extension, which in our case is named SetupExample.msi. The output will be available in the Express project subfolder that contains files you need to distribute to your customers for installing your application. They run the Setup.exe bootstrapper that correctly starts the Windows Installer package.

CUSTOMIZING RELEASES

InstallShield can generate different kinds of distribution media, such as a single image, DVD-Rom, CD-Rom. To customize how the installation packages are generated, click the Releases item in Solution Explorer.

Summary

In this chapter, we covered how to create setup projects for Windows Installer in Visual Studio 2012 using InstallShield LE. First, you read about the reasons you should choose a technique. Then you saw how to generate a setup project with InstallShield Limited Edition. Next, the discussion focused on configuring and customizing your project with special integrated editors. Finally, you learned how to build and deploy your Windows Installer package.

CHAPTER 52

Deploying Applications with ClickOnce

Sometimes customers want simple installations for applications they purchase. They do not want to step through complex guided procedures with several dialog boxes and lots of options. They want to make just two or three mouse clicks and nothing more. To accomplish this particular scenario, Microsoft created ClickOnce—the one-click deployment technology for .NET Framework applications. ClickOnce is useful for installations that are just a few steps, but it is the easiest way for bringing automatic updating capabilities to your applications. In this chapter, you will learn about deploying client applications with ClickOnce and discover some new features.

Introducing ClickOnce

ClickOnce is the deployment technology offered by all Visual Studio editions, including the Express versions, which enables you to create distribution procedures for Windows client applications in a simple way, according to *one-click deployment* logic. The idea behind ClickOnce is that the final user will have the ability to install an application with a minimum number of mouse clicks and interactions, even if the user does not have administrative rights on the machine. This technology was first introduced with .NET Framework 2.0 and Visual Studio 2005 and has been improved over the years. Further improvements were introduced in .NET 4.0 and Visual Studio 2010, and Visual Studio 2012 retakes them all. ClickOnce enables you to publish the deployment package to file system folders, FTP servers, and HTTP servers and can make applications available online, offline, or both. Before illustrating how you publish deployment packages with ClickOnce, it is important to understand how it works and when you should use it.

How ClickOnce Handles Applications

Different from the Windows Installer engine, which is integrated in the operating system, ClickOnce is integrated with the .NET Framework. Applications deployed via ClickOnce run in a security sandbox that is fully managed by the .NET Framework. This provides great flexibility because the .NET Framework can apply managed trust rules to ClickOnce-deployed applications and provide the infrastructure for automating application updates. For example, thanks to the .NET integration, developers can write code to programmatically check for updates or to access the deployment system. However, ClickOnce does have some limitations for Windows Installer. The next section explains these limitations and provides information on when you should use ClickOnce for your deployments.

When to Use ClickOnce

ClickOnce is a powerful technology and is useful when you need to deploy applications that require a minimum amount of interaction from the user. ClickOnce is appropriate in the following scenarios:

▶ You want to provide your application with the capability of being frequently updated without writing a single line of code.

▶ Your application makes use of third-party components that are not required to be installed into the Global Assembly Cache.

▶ You want your application to be installed by nonadministrative users.

▶ You want to deploy add-ins for Microsoft Office.

▶ Your installation process does not require you to customize the target system other than creating shortcuts.

ClickOnce does have limitations you must consider when choosing the most appropriate development system:

▶ You cannot install assemblies to the Global Assembly Cache.

▶ ClickOnce does not enable writing values to the Windows Registry.

▶ It does not enable deep installation customization.

▶ It does not let you choose the target folder for the application on the target machine. This is because, as ClickOnce is integrated with the .NET Framework, applications run inside a security sandbox managed by .NET which has its own folders.

If you need to perform just one of these customizations, ClickOnce is not appropriate, and you need to recur to Windows Installer by creating InstallShield projects for Visual Studio 2012 (as explained in the previous chapter). At this point, we can learn to deploy ClickOnce.

52

Deploying Applications with ClickOnce

To deploy an application with ClickOnce, you have three options: the Publish command in the Build menu, right-clicking the project in Solution Explorer, and selecting Publish or the Publish Now button in the ClickOnce configuration page within My Project. For now, we will focus on the first option. (The second option is covered in the next section.)

Create a new WPF project with Visual Basic and name it **ClickOnceDemo**. There is no need to write code for the application because we need only a base for our example. To deploy an application with ClickOnce, follow these steps:

1. Click **Build**, **Publish**, Visual Studio launches the Publish Wizard. Figure 52.1 shows the first dialog box of the wizard, in which you need to specify the location where the application will be published. Notice how the dialog box explains available possibilities, such as disk path, network shared path, ftp server, or website. You can change the target type and location by clicking **Browse**. In this case, publish the application to the local Internet Information Services website, which requires Visual Studio to be running with administrator privileges.

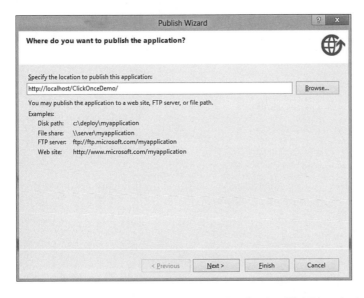

FIGURE 52.1   Choosing the target location for the ClickOnce deployment.

PUBLISHING TO FILE SYSTEM

Publish the application to a local folder on the file system if you want to deploy the application on supported media such as CD-ROM or zipped archives. This option can make the application available only offline.

2. Click **Next**. The second dialog box of the wizard lets you specify if the application will be available offline. In this case, the .NET Framework creates a shortcut in the Start menu for launching the application and another one in the Add/Remove Programs tool for enabling uninstalling the application. Figure 52.2 shows how you set this option. This is all the information Visual Studio needs to create a ClickOnce deployment.

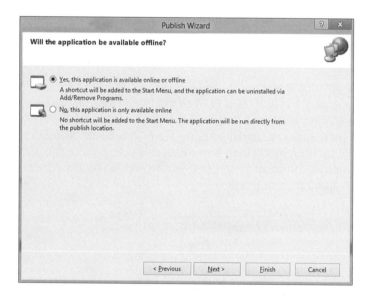

FIGURE 52.2   Specifying how the application will be available.

3. Click **Next**. You will see the last dialog box of the wizard showing the deployment information summary (see Figure 52.3).

4. Click **Finish**. Visual Studio generates all the required files and folders. Because the deployment is currently done for a web server, Visual Studio generates a Publish.htm web page that is the place users can install the application. Figure 52.4 shows the page created for this sample application.

TIPS ON THE PUBLISH.HTM WEB PAGE

Being a simple HTML page, the default Publish.htm can be edited to accomplish your particular needs or just to provide a different appearance. In this case, the web page address points to the local IIS, but if you publish the application onto a real server, you probably publish the application files via an FTP account; users will be able later to install the application from a web address similar to the following: www.something.com/ClickOnceDemo/publish.htm.

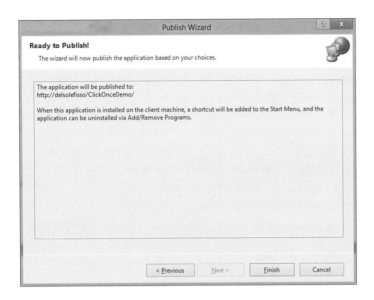

FIGURE 52.3   Collecting summary information for the ClickOnce deployment.

FIGURE 52.4   The web page from which the application will be downloaded.

Now click **Install**. At this point, a security warning informs you the application is downloading from a website with other information about the publisher, as shown in Figure 52.5.

FIGURE 52.5   ClickOnce shows a security warning asking confirmation before installing the application and providing information on the application's publisher and source.

Because you are the publisher and you trust yourself, click **Install**. This installs the application on your system, and a shortcut will be added to the Start menu. To remove the application open the **Control Panel, Programs and Features** tool, and then select the application from the list.

Understanding the Structure of a ClickOnce Deployment

The publish process, whatever target you select, generates a subfolder containing the following elements:

▶ A bootstrapper file named Setup.exe, which launches the installation.

▶ The application manifest, which contains information on how the application has to be run in the ClickOnce context.

▶ The Publish.htm file (only if the application has been published to a Web or FTP space).

▶ A subfolder containing the actual application and related files. This subfolder has a version number that is recognized by the .NET Framework when the application finds updates.

If you publish the application to the file system for deploying to supported media such as a CD-ROM, you just need to copy to the media the content of the publish folder.

> **TIP**
>
> Unless you specify a publish folder, the deployment package is published to Bin\Debug\ Publish or Bin\Release\Publish depending on the selected configuration.

Configuring ClickOnce

52

You can customize your ClickOnce deployment by setting its property page in My Project. Click the **Publish** tab to activate the ClickOnce options designer represented in Figure 52.6.

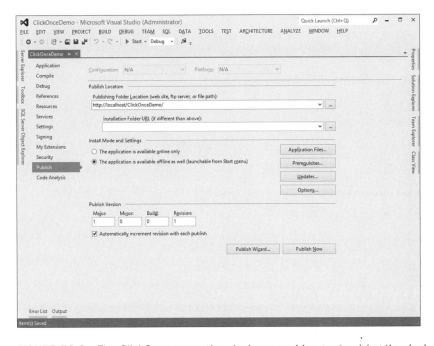

FIGURE 52.6   The ClickOnce properties designer enables customizing the deployment.

The upper part of the designer shows properties you already set with the Publish Wizard. The Publish Version group enables you to specify the deployment version that is important for allowing automatic updates. Automatically incrementing the revision number is a convenient way for allowing installed applications to check for updates. Just remember that the publish version is just a ClickOnce-related version and does not affect the application version. Now let's take a look at the other available options.

Application Files

By clicking the **Application Files** button, you can view or specify files that need to be included in the deployment package. If you want some required files included in the deployment package (such as documents or databases), you need to set their Build Action property as **Content**. Visual Studio can automatically classify files according to their role in the project, so this is something you rarely need to perform manually.

Prerequisites

Prerequisites are those files the application needs to work correctly. An example of this is runtime components such as the .NET Framework or third-party controls, which the installer installs on the target machine before the application is installed. Visual Studio can detect the appropriate prerequisites and select them for you, but there are situations in which you need to perform this manually. An example of this is when you need to install third-party components. Figure 52.7 shows the Prerequisites dialog box.

FIGURE 52.7   Selecting prerequisites for your applications.

If you use third-party components, ensure the producer made available a redistributable package you can include in the deployment prerequisites. The .NET Framework will always be included as a prerequisite because ClickOnce cannot predict if on the target machine the .NET Framework is already available.

Custom Prerequisites

Visual Studio 2012 does not provide a built-in functionality for packaging custom prerequisites. To accomplish this particular need, follow the instructions described in this page of the MSDN Library: http://msdn.microsoft.com/en-us/library/ms165429(v=vs.110).aspx.

Publishing Application Updates

One of the most important features in ClickOnce (and one of the reasons why you should use it) is the capability of updating applications without writing code to accomplish this. The idea is that you publish a new version of the application and when you run the old version, it checks for updates and automatically upgrades to the new version. Automatic updates are not available for applications published to the file system. To enable automatic updates, click the **Updates** button and then in the Application Updates dialog box, check **The Application Should Check for Updates** check box, as shown in Figure 52.8.

FIGURE 52.8   Enabling automatic updates.

You can decide whether the application will be updated before it starts (default option) so users always run the latest updates or if it will be updated after it starts, but in this case changes will be applied only at the next start. You can specify how frequently the application has to check for updates. The default setting is that the application checks for updates each time it runs. Otherwise, you can specify a time interval expressed in days, hours, or minutes. (This option is available only if you decide to update the application after it starts.)

TESTING UPDATES

When you enable updates and you want to ensure this feature works correctly, perform any kind of modification to the application (such as adding a button). Then publish it again. Finally, run the application and check that the new version downloaded and installed.

Options

When you click the **Options** button, you have access to additional features. For instance, you can edit the Description part in the deployment manifest so you can set a full description for your installation. Figure 52.9 shows an example of how you can specify information.

FIGURE 52.9   Setting description options for the deployment package.

Consider that the Publisher name will be used to create a root shortcuts folder in the
Start menu, whereas the Suite name value will be used to create a shortcuts subfolder
for the current application. The Deployment option enables you to set some aspects of
the publish process. Figure 52.10 shows an example for setting these options. You can
decide if the Publish.htm web page has to be created and shown, if the wizard generates an Autorun.inf file for automatic CD start, or if the deployment will use the .deploy
extension. Pay attention to this particular option. Unless you uncheck this check box, the
application files will be deployed with the addition of the .deploy extension, which might
cause errors if your application attempts to access external files. If this is your case, disable
the extension and deploy the application again. The Manifest option lets you establish
how application URLs must be treated, but more particularly, it enables you to set if a
desktop shortcut needs to be created for your application (see Figure 52.11).

FIGURE 52.10   Setting deployment options.

FIGURE 52.11   Setting manifest options.

Another useful option is the File Associations that is the only Registry customization allowed to ClickOnce. This enables you to assign a file extension to your executable.

Security Considerations

Depending on how an application is deployed or what system resources it needs to have access to, it will be considered under the Full Trust or the Partial Trust rules of .NET Framework Code Access Security. For example, an application that needs to access the Registry or other system resources needs to be full-trusted, but this is not a good idea if your application will be deployed via the Internet, which should instead be partial-trusted. You set the trust level for your ClickOnce deployments in the My Project, Security tab (see Figure 52.12).

The ClickOnce manifest can be signed with Full Trust or Partial Trust. This second option is divided into the Internet and intranet zones. You can choose the most appropriate for you or even create a custom configuration by editing the application manifest file (Edit Permissions XML button).

Providing Certificates

To make ClickOnce deployments the most trustable possible, you should use a certificate. If you look at Solution Explorer after you publish the application, you notice that Visual Studio has signed the assembly with a .pfx strong name. This is good in local test scenarios, but the most convenient way (although not mandatory) for providing security information to customers is adding an Authenticode certificate, especially if your application is deployed via the Internet. Visual Studio adds a test certificate, as demonstrated in Figure 52.13, which shows the Signing tab in My Project. The test certificate is intended for local testing purposes only and should never be used in real-life deployment, in which you will prefer an Authenticode certificate you can purchase from the specific authorities. After you add a valid certificate, to sign the ClickOnce manifest, full and trusted information will be shown to your customers when they download and install the application.

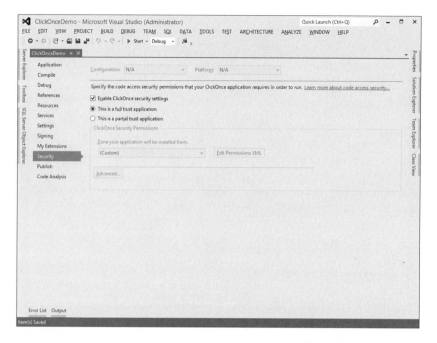

FIGURE 52.12   Specifying security settings for the ClickOnce deployment.

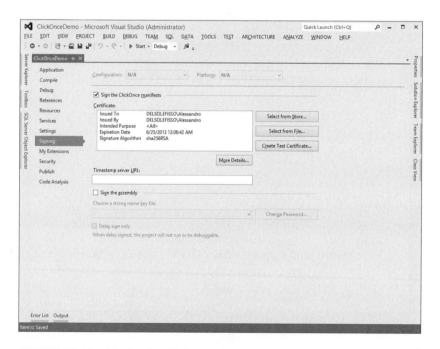

FIGURE 52.13   Signing the ClickOnce manifest.

Programmatically Accessing ClickOnce

As pointed out at the beginning of this chapter, ClickOnce is handled by the .NET Framework, but more precisely it is part of the .NET Framework. This means it can be accessed via managed code. The .NET Framework exposes the `System.Deployment` namespace that offers a managed way for interacting with ClickOnce. The subnamespace `System.Deployment.Application` and the `System.Deployment.Application.ApplicationDeployment` class are the most useful items because they offer objects that enable developers to programmatically access ClickOnce information from an application. The `ApplicationDeployment` class exposes a shared `CurrentDeployment` property that enables access to interesting information on the current application deployment. The following code demonstrates how you can use the property to retrieve information on the current deployment:

```
Private Sub GetClickOnceInformation()
    'Checks if the application has been deployed with ClickOnce
    If ApplicationDeployment.IsNetworkDeployed = True Then

        'Retrieves the data folder for this application
        Dim dataFolder As String = ApplicationDeployment.
                                CurrentDeployment.DataDirectory
        'Retrieves the path where updates will be
        'downloaded from
        Dim updatesPath As Uri = ApplicationDeployment.
                                CurrentDeployment.UpdateLocation
        'Gets the version number for updates
        Dim updateVersion = ApplicationDeployment.
                                CurrentDeployment.UpdatedVersion
        'Determines the last time that updates were checked for
        Dim lastUpdate As Date = ApplicationDeployment.
                                CurrentDeployment.TimeOfLastUpdateCheck

    End If
End Sub
```

You can programmatically check and download updates. This can be useful if you do not want the application to be automatically updated but you still want to provide the user the ability of updating the application manually. The following code demonstrates this:

```
Private Sub ApplicationUpdate()

    Dim isUpdateAvailable As Boolean = _
        ApplicationDeployment.CurrentDeployment.CheckForUpdate

    If isUpdateAvailable = True Then
        ApplicationDeployment.CurrentDeployment.Update()
    End If
End Sub
```

Both methods offer an asynchronous counterpart (`CheckForUpdateAsync` and `UpdateAsync`) that can be used as well.

Registration-Free COM

One of the biggest benefits from ClickOnce is users do not have administrator permissions that can install applications. Note that there are situations in which an application is deployed together with some COM libraries, but this can be a problem because these libraries need to be registered and a non-administrator user does not have the appropriate permissions for this. Fortunately, with ClickOnce you can take advantage of a technique known as Registration-Free COM, which refers to a COM library visible to the application only without the need of registration. You need to right-click the library name in Solution Explorer, References and select Properties. Finally, set the Isolated property as True (see Figure 52.14). When you build the project, Visual Studio generates a manifest file that provides the actual state of isolation of the library. Listing 52.1 shows a sample manifest file.

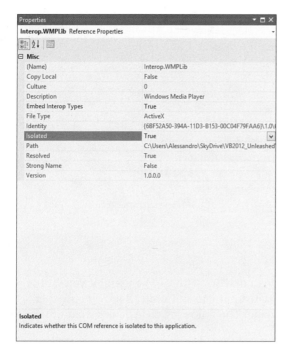

FIGURE 52.14 Isolating the library for Registration-Free COM.

LISTING 52.1   Sample Manifest for Registration-Free COM

```xml
<?xml version="1.0" encoding="utf-8"?>
<assembly xsi:schemaLocation="urn:schemas-microsoft-com:asm.v1 assembly.adaptive.
➥xsd"
          manifestVersion="1.0" xmlns:asmv1="urn:schemas-microsoft-com:asm.v1"
          xmlns:asmv2="urn:schemas-microsoft-com:asm.v2"
          xmlns:asmv3="urn:schemas-microsoft-com:asm.v3"
          xmlns:dsig="http://www.w3.org/2000/09/xmldsig#"
          xmlns:co.v1="urn:schemas-microsoft-com:clickonce.v1"
          xmlns:co.v2="urn:schemas-microsoft-com:clickonce.v2"
          xmlns="urn:schemas-microsoft-com:asm.v1"
          xmlns:xsi="http://www.w3.org/2001/XMLSchema-instance">
  <assemblyIdentity name="Native.MyCOMLibrary" version="1.0.0.0" type="win32" />
  <file name="wmp.dll" asmv2:size="11406336">
    <hash xmlns="urn:schemas-microsoft-com:asm.v2">
      <dsig:Transforms>
        <dsig:Transform
         Algorithm="urn:schemas-microsoft-com:HashTransforms.Identity" />
      </dsig:Transforms>
      <dsig:DigestMethod Algorithm="http://www.w3.org/2000/09/xmldsig#sha256" />
      <dsig:DigestValue> kaMt4lcikbZvNzRrAtbzkM6mAlQQ5fm56Jj8Ed6xm0k=
➥</dsig:DigestValue>
    </hash>
    <typelib tlbid="{6bf52a50-394a-11d3-b153-00c04f79faa6}"
        version="1.0" helpdir="" resourceid="0" flags="HASDISKIMAGE" />
    <comClass clsid="{6bf52a52-394a-11d3-b153-00c04f79faa6}"
              threadingModel="Apartment"
              tlbid="{6bf52a50-394a-11d3-b153-00c04f79faa6}"
              progid="WMPlayer.OCX.7"
              description="Windows Media Player ActiveX Control" />
  </file>
</assembly>
```

The manifest file is part of the setup process, so you need to include it in your ClickOnce deployment (Visual Studio takes care of this for you). If you are interested in understanding how the Registration-Free COM technique works, you can read a specific article in the MSDN Magazine available at http://msdn.microsoft.com/en-us/magazine/cc188708.aspx.

Summary

This chapter described how to build deployment packages with ClickOnce, the one-click deployment technology included in the .NET Framework. You saw how to use the Publish Wizard to create a setup procedure in a few steps. Then you learned how you can configure the deployment options with the Visual Studio designer, including allowing automatic updates and adding publisher information. You then stepped through security considerations required so that you can understand what happens on the target machines. Finally, the discussion focused on how to programmatically interact with ClickOnce by writing Visual Basic code taking advantage of the `System.Deployment.Application.ApplicationDeployment` class.

CHAPTER 53

Advanced IDE Features

The Visual Studio 2012 integrated development environment is a powerful application and is not a simple code editor. In previous chapters, especially in Chapter 2, "Getting Started with the Visual Studio 2012 IDE," you learned about some important features and tools that make your development experience easier. In this chapter, you learn about other interesting features and instrumentations that are not necessarily related with code writing but provide advanced control over the environment and in most cases provide a way for reusing existing work. Last but not least, this chapter guides you through a new feature that allows importing libraries and dependencies with just one-click using the Library Package Manager.

Exporting Templates

Visual Studio 2012, as its predecessors since 2005, lets you export projects and items templates. This feature is useful because you can generate skeletons for applications or single items you can reuse in the future. This section covers both options, starting with project templates.

Exporting Project Templates

Imagine you often create WPF applications that need implementing menus. It would be interesting having a project template that automatically implements basic menus so you don't need to rewrite a lot of code each time. First, create a new WPF project with Visual Basic and name it as **WpfMenuProject**. When ready, open the MainWindow.xaml file and type the following XAML code inside the Grid tags to implement basic menu functionalities:

```
<DockPanel LastChildFill="True" VerticalAlignment="Top">
    <Menu DockPanel.Dock="Top">

        <MenuItem Header="File" IsEnabled="True"
                DockPanel.Dock="Top">

            <MenuItem Header="_Open" Name="Open"/>
            <Separator/>
            <MenuItem IsEnabled="True" Name="Save">
                <MenuItem.Header>_Save</MenuItem.Header>
            </MenuItem>
            <MenuItem IsEnabled="True" Name="Exit">
                <MenuItem.Header>_Exit</MenuItem.Header>
            </MenuItem>
            <Separator />
        </MenuItem>

        <MenuItem Header="Edit"
                DockPanel.Dock="Top">
        </MenuItem>
    </Menu>
</DockPanel>
```

Before going on, save the project. When saved, select the **File, Export template**
command. The first choice is between the project and item template, as shown in
Figure 53.1. Leave unchanged the selection on Project Template and then click **Next**.

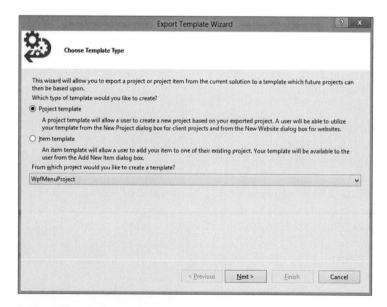

FIGURE 53.1   Exporting a project template.

Visual Studio now asks you to enter some information on the new template, such as the name, description, and optionally an icon image and a preview image. This information will be shown in the New project dialog box. Assign the WpfMenuProject name as the template name and provide a custom description. You can also add images, but this is not mandatory. (Visual Studio will provide a default image for you.) Figure 53.2 shows the dialog box.

FIGURE 53.2   Setting information about the new template.

Projects templates are .zip packages containing the project skeleton and an information file named MyTemplate.vstemplate. By default, custom templates are exported to the %UserProfile%\Documents\Visual Studio 2012\My Exported Templates folder, and by default they are automatically imported into the IDE (although you can decide to remove this option). When you click **Finish**, the new template is available in Visual Studio. You can check this out by selecting the **File, New Project** command. Figure 53.3 shows the new template available in the New Project dialog box.

Now you can create a new project based on the custom template without the need of rewriting code that is already exposed by the template.

Exporting Item Templates

You can export single items, such as classes or controls, to item templates you can later add to other projects. To see an example, add a new class to the current project and name it as **DisposableClass.vb**. The goal of the exercise is to provide a template for classes implementing the IDisposable interface. When ready, implement the IDisposable interface in the new class so Visual Studio will add required members. (You should write custom code for implementing the Disposable pattern, but this is not the goal of the exercise; see Chapter 8, "Managing an Object's Lifetime," for more information.) Now select again **File, Export template**. In the first dialog box of the wizard, select the **Item template** option (as shown in Figure 53.4) and then click **Next**.

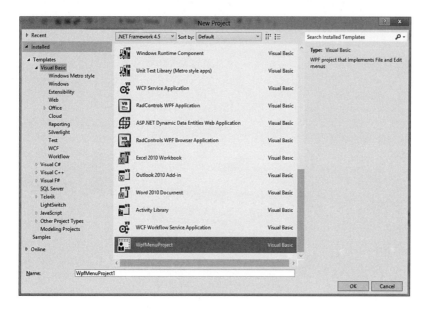

FIGURE 53.3   The New Project dialog box includes the new template.

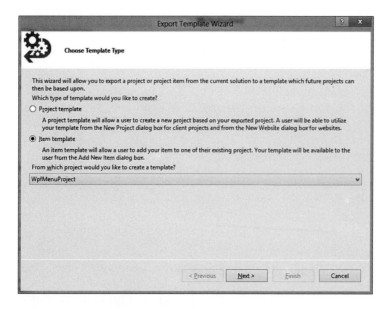

FIGURE 53.4   Setting the Item template option.

The next step is selecting the item you want to be exported as a reusable template. Notice that you can choose multiple items. Select the **DisposableClass.vb** item, as shown in Figure 53.5. Then click **Next**.

FIGURE 53.5   Adding an item to the new template.

The next step is selecting required references so that when you add an item based on the new template Visual Studio will reference the necessary assemblies for you. Figure 53.6 shows how the dialog box appears.

In this case, the template requires nothing but default assemblies, so no references are required. The final step is where you provide information to the custom item template. This information is the same as for project templates. Assign **Template name** with **DisposableClass**, provide a description (see Figure 53.7 for details), and provide icon and preview images if you want. Finally, click **Finish**.

When the export process is completed, the new template is available in Visual Studio. With a project opened, right-click the project name and select **Add New Item**. When the export process is completed, the new item template is available in Visual Studio 2012, as demonstrated in Figure 53.8.

With a few steps, you can produce your custom project and item templates, which can help you save time when you repetitively create the same project types.

FIGURE 53.6   Specifying references for the new item template.

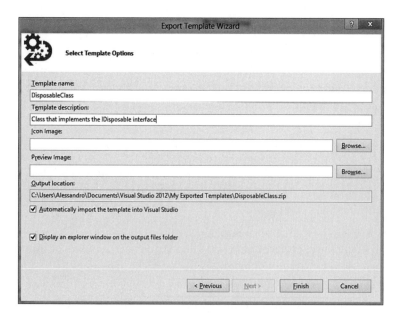

FIGURE 53.7   Providing custom information to the new item template.

FIGURE 53.8   The Add New Item dialog box shows the new item template.

Customizing Visual Studio 2012

Visual Studio 2012 is a customizable environment. In fact, you can personalize existing features such as the Tools menu, menu commands, and toolbars. In this section, you learn how to customize both the Tools built-in menu and toolbars to add functionalities to the environment.

Customizing the Tools Menu

You can customize the Tools menu by providing additional commands pointing to external executables. This is particularly useful if you need to run an external tool against an element within the solution or project. You provide additional commands by selecting **Tools, External tools**. This launches the External tools dialog box where you can specify the executable name and parameters. For example, imagine you want to add a custom command for launching the Microsoft IL Disassembler for the executable generated by the current project. If you already have any tools in the list (such as the Dotfuscator tool), the first step is to click the **Add** button. Then follow these steps:

1. In the Title text box, write IL Disassambler.

2. In the Command text box, write the full path for ILDasm.exe. (It is under the Windows SDK tools directory.)

3. For the Arguments box, click the arrow on the right and select **Target Path** (the related variable is $(TargetPath)). This variable represents the executable generated by the compilation process.

Figure 53.9 shows the result of this editing. Click **OK** so the new command will be added to the Tools menu.

FIGURE 53.9   Setting command properties in the External Tools dialog box.

Now try to open any existing project and build it. Then select the new **Tools, IL Disassembler** command. If no errors occur, you will see IL Disassembler run and analyze the executable produced by the current project.

Customizing Commands and Toolbars

Visual Studio lets you customize other aspects of the IDE such as menus (including context menus) and toolbars. The next subsections cover both scenarios with examples.

Customizing an Existing Toolbar

Imagine you want to add another button to the Standard toolbar, such as the **Close Solution** command. Select **Tools, Customize**. When the **Customize** dialog box displays, select the **Commands** tab. Then select the **Toolbar** item and from the related combo box pick up the **Standard** toolbar. The goal is adding a button, so click **Add command**. This launches the **Add command** dialog box. Here you just select the menu where the command is located (on the left) and the command itself (on the right). Then, select **File** on the left and **Close Solution** on the right. Figure 53.10 shows the result of this step.

When you click **OK**, the command is added to the desired toolbar, as demonstrated in Figure 53.11. In the Customize dialog box, click **Move Up** or **Move Down** to place the command in the preferred position.

Click **Close** to return to the IDE. You see the command appearing on the Standard toolbar.

FIGURE 53.10   Selecting the command to be added to the standard toolbar.

FIGURE 53.11   Arranging the command position in the toolbar.

Creating a New Custom Toolbar

To create a new custom toolbar, follow these steps:

1. Select **Tools, Customize** and be sure the Toolbars tab is selected.

2. Click the **New** button, so the New Toolbar dialog box appears. When ready, type the **CustomBar** name into the dialog box text box and click **OK** (see Figure 53.12).

FIGURE 53.12   Adding a new custom toolbar.

3. Select the **Commands** tab and in the Toolbar combo box, select the **CustomBar** toolbar; Figure 53.13 shows how the Customize dialog box looks at this particular point.

FIGURE 53.13   Preparing the new toolbar for customization.

4. Click **Add command** and follow the instruction explained in the previous subsection to add as many commands as you want to the new toolbar. Figure 53.14 shows an example.

At this point, the new toolbar is available in the IDE. To remove it, right-click one of the existing toolbars and unselect the new one from the pop-up list.

FIGURE 53.14   Configuring the new custom toolbar.

Managing User Settings

When you run Visual Studio for the first time, you are asked to specify a setting that best suits your needs. You can then customize Visual Studio settings and options to make the IDE the best environment for you. Starting from Visual Studio 2005, the IDE provides the ability of exporting settings to disk into a .VsSettings file as a backup for later reuse. This means you have the ability of importing existing settings into the environment. This section explains how you manage Visual Studio settings.

Exporting Settings

You export Visual Studio settings by selecting the **Tools, Import and Export Settings** command. This launches the Import and Export Settings Wizard. The first dialog box is shown in Figure 53.15.

From here, you can decide what you want to do. In this case, select **Export selected environment settings**, which is the default option, and click **Next**. The second dialog box enables deep selections over the available settings to export. Figure 53.16 shows the full list of available settings.

FIGURE 53.15   Starting the Import and Export Settings Wizard.

FIGURE 53.16   Selecting settings to export.

You can export all settings available in the Options dialog box and other settings such as code analysis, database tools, and general development settings. After you select the desired settings, click **Next**. In the next dialog box, you will be asked to specify a filename and the target folder. By default, Visual Studio 2012 proposes a filename based on the current date/time and the user level settings folder as the target folder, as demonstrated in Figure 53.17.

FIGURE 53.17   Providing a target filename and folder for exporting settings.

At this point, click **Finish** to save your settings to disk and return to the IDE. For importing saved settings later, read the next subsection.

Importing Settings

To import existing settings, select **Tools, Import and Export Settings**. When the wizard appears, select **Import Selected Environment Settings** (see Figure 53.15 for your reference). The second dialog box asks your agreement for backing up the current settings before proceeding (see Figure 53.18). This is your choice. When decided, click **Next**.

In the final dialog box, the Wizard asks you to select settings to import from the list of available settings. Notice how in the list there is the .vssettings file saved during the example of the last subsection (see Figure 53.19).

TIP

Notice that you can import only one settings file.

Select the desired settings file and click **Finish**. At this point, selected settings replace existing ones.

FIGURE 53.18   The second dialog box of the Wizard enables backing up current settings.

FIGURE 53.19   Selecting settings to be imported into the IDE.

Customizing the Toolbox

Like its predecessors, Visual Studio 2012 lets you customize the toolbox by adding controls that are not listed by default and are included in the .NET Framework or come from third-party assemblies. To customize the toolbox, select **Tools, Choose toolbox items** or right-click the Toolbox and select Choose Items. This launches the **Choose toolbox items** dialog box, which is represented in Figure 53.20.

FIGURE 53.20   Choosing additional items for the toolbox.

There are some improvements in Visual Studio 2012 because now tabs for selecting Windows 8 controls (Windows XAML Components) and InstallShield controls are available. Select the items you want to add to the toolbox, and then click **OK**.

Using, Creating, and Managing Reusable Code Snippets

Like its predecessors (starting with Visual Studio 2005), Visual Studio 2012 provides support for reusable code snippets. The most important addition to the new version is the support for CSS, JavaScript, and ASP.NET MVC (both versions 3 and 4). The idea is that you can add into the code editor existing code snippets stored in external files with .Snippet extension, reachable from within Visual Studio (and integrated with the IDE) without the need of creating your custom archive. Another huge benefit of code snippets is that they can be shared with other developers allowing you and other friends to increase the code library. Code snippets support is offered in several ways, which are covered in this section.

VISUAL STUDIO CODE SNIPPETS

Visual Studio ships with a large number of code snippets ready for use. To prevent accidental deletions, these code snippets reside in the IDE's own folder and cannot be removed from the Code Snippets Manager. Later in this chapter, you see how to extend and manage (including removing) code snippets by taking advantage of the user level snippets folder.

Consuming Code Snippets

Adding existing code snippets into your code is an easy task. Just for demo purposes, create a new console project with Visual Basic and, when ready, place the cursor within the Sub Main. Right-click and select the **Insert Snippet** command. At this point, the IDE shows a list of available snippets categories, as shown in Figure 53.21.

FIGURE 53.21   The IDE shows a list of available snippets categories.

The first thing to mention is that code snippets files are organized in categories, such as WPF, Code Patterns, Fundamentals, and so on. A category is nothing but a folder containing a number of .snippet files. Double-click the desired category (for example **Code Patterns**). The IDE shows a list of subcategories. Click **Error Handling (Exceptions)**. Now Visual Studio offers the list of available code snippets within the given category, as shown in Figure 53.22.

FIGURE 53.22   A list of code snippets.

Double-click the **Try..Catch..End Try Statement** snippet so that code is added in the code editor. Visual Studio inserts a code snippet for intercepting an exception within a `Try.. Catch` block, as shown in Figure 53.23.

Notice how, in this specific example, the `ArgumentException` has been highlighted. Highlights are also known as *replacements* because they indicate to the developers that they should replace the highlighted code with a more appropriate code block according to their needs. For example, you might want to catch a `FileNotFoundException` instead of an `ArgumentException`; therefore, you should make this replacement, but the rest of the code snippet is still valid.

REPLACEMENT INFORMATION

If you pass with the mouse pointer over replacements, you get information via a tooltip about the replacement.

Code snippets offer lots of information such as the author name, support website, and shortcut. This information is also available in the Code Snippet Manager described in the next subsection.

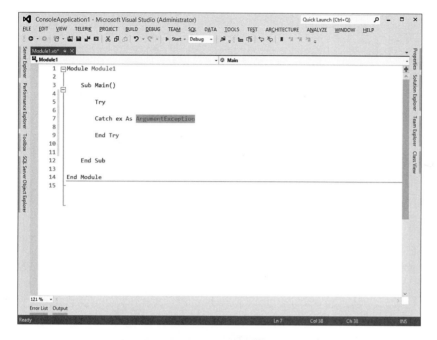

FIGURE 53.23   The code snippet has been added to the current code.

The Code Snippet Manager

The Code Snippet Manager is an integrated tool for adding, removing, and getting information on code snippets. You bring it up by selecting **Tools, Code Snippets Manager**. Figure 53.24 shows how this tool window looks.

FIGURE 53.24   The Code Snippet Manager tool.

You can first select one of the available programming or markup languages from the Language combo box. The tool automatically shows a list of available code snippets related to that specific language. You can browse the snippets tree and select one to get information, such as the **Description**, **Shortcut**, and **Author**. As you can see, code snippets can be organized into subfolders. To create a new subfolder, click **Add** and provide the folder name. If you want to import existing code snippets, click **Import** and select the .snippet files you want to add to the current collection. You can also remove code snippets from the collection, but this is not allowed for snippets shipped with Visual Studio, whereas it is allowed on custom code snippets. Note that the Shortcut property for snippets is useful because in the code editor you can add a code snippet by typing its shortcut and then pressing **Tab**, without the need of performing all steps described in the previous subsection. When you know how to manage snippets, you are ready to learn how to build custom ones.

Creating and Consuming Custom Code Snippets

Code snippets .snippet files are XML files containing the code and information about the snippet. Code snippets have their own XML schema that Visual Studio then uses to correctly identify them within the IDE. To understand how a code snippet is made, consider the following code that is stored in the snippet named Calculate Cosine of an Angle from the Visual Studio snippets library:

```
Dim radians As Double = 120 * Math.PI / 180
Dim cos As Double = Math.Cos(radians)
```

If you open the CalculateCosineOfAngle.snippet file with an XML editor (or just with Windows Notepad), the file content looks like the content of Listing 53.1.

LISTING 53.1   Examining an Existing Code Snippet

```
<?xml version="1.0" encoding="utf-8"?>
<CodeSnippets xmlns="http://schemas.microsoft.com/VisualStudio/2005/CodeSnippet">
  <CodeSnippet Format="1.0.0">
    <Header>
      <Title>Calculate the Cosine of a specified Angle</Title>
      <Author>Microsoft Corporation</Author>
      <Description>Converts an angle from degrees to radians and then calculates
                   cosine of the angle</Description>
      <Shortcut>mathCos</Shortcut>
    </Header>
    <Snippet>
      <Imports>
        <Import>
          <Namespace>System</Namespace>
        </Import>
        <Import>
          <Namespace>Microsoft.VisualBasic</Namespace>
```

```
        </Import>
      </Imports>
      <Declarations>
        <Literal>
          <ID>Degrees</ID>
          <Type>Double</Type>
          <ToolTip>Replace with the measurement in degrees.</ToolTip>
          <Default>120</Default>
        </Literal>
      </Declarations>
      <Code Language="VB" Kind="method body"><![CDATA[Dim radians As Double =
          $Degrees$ * Math.PI / 180
          Dim cos As Double = Math.Cos(radians)]]></Code>
    </Snippet>
  </CodeSnippet>
</CodeSnippets>
```

Code snippets in Visual Studio 2012 still adhere to the first XML schema introduced with
Visual Studio 2005, so there are no changes. A snippet structure is divided into some XML
nodes. The Header node provides information on the snippet, whereas the Snippet node
contains code, required Imports directives, and assembly references. Notice how the real
code is stored inside a CDATA section. As you might know, these kinds of sections can
store any kind of characters, and so it is the most appropriate for storing code. Finally,
the Declarations node stores information on replacement. The ID element specifies
an ID for the replacement, the Type element specifies the data type of the object that
should be replaced, ToolTip provides a descriptive tooltip when the user passes the mouse
over the replacement, and Default provides a default value. Now imagine you want to
create a custom code snippet that will be added to the code snippets library so you can
reuse it inside Visual Studio. First, you need a Visual Basic code snippet. As an example,
consider the following code that implements an extension method for converting an
IEnumerable(Of T) into an ObservableCollection(Of T):

```
<Extension()> Module Extensions
    <Extension()> Function ToObservableCollection(Of T)(ByVal source As  _
                IEnumerable(Of T)) As ObservableCollection(Of T)


        If source IsNot Nothing Then
            Return New ObservableCollection(Of T)(source)
        Else
            Throw New ArgumentNullException("source")
        End If
    End Function
End Module
```

Now the goal is building a custom .snippet file to make the preceding code reusable. Thus,
you must create an XML file according to the snippet schema. Listing 53.2 shows how to

accomplish this. You can use any text editor, such as the Windows Notepad or the Visual Studio's XML editor.

LISTING 53.2   Building a Custom Code Snippet

```xml
<?xml version="1.0" encoding="utf-8"?>
<CodeSnippets xmlns="http://schemas.microsoft.com/VisualStudio/2005/CodeSnippet">
  <CodeSnippet Format="1.0.0">
    <Header>
      <Title>ToObservableCollection</Title>
      <Author>Alessandro Del Sole</Author>
      <Description>Convert an IEnumerable(Of T)
                   into an ObservableCollection(Of T)
      </Description>
      <HelpUrl>http://community.visual-basic.it/Alessandro</HelpUrl>
      <SnippetTypes />
      <Keywords />
      <Shortcut>toObs</Shortcut>
    </Header>
    <Snippet>
      <References />
      <Imports>
        <Import>
          <Namespace>System.Runtime.CompilerServices</Namespace>
        </Import>
        <Import>
          <Namespace>System.Collections.ObjectModel</Namespace>
        </Import>
      </Imports>
      <Declarations>
        <Literal Editable="true">
          <ID>source</ID>
          <Type>IEnumerable(Of T)</Type>
          <ToolTip>Replace with a different identifier if needed</ToolTip>
          <Default>source</Default>
          <Function></Function>
        </Literal>
      </Declarations>
      <Code Language="VB" Kind="" Delimiter="$"><![CDATA[<Extension()> Module
➥Extensions

    <Extension()> Function ToObservableCollection(Of T)(ByVal $source$ As _
                  IEnumerable(Of T)) As ObservableCollection(Of T)

        If $source$ IsNot Nothing Then
            Return New ObservableCollection(Of T)($source$)
        Else
```

```
            Throw New ArgumentNullException("$source$")
        End If
    End Function
End Module]]></Code>
    </Snippet>
  </CodeSnippet>
</CodeSnippets>
```

XML elements are self-explanatory. You need to save the preceding snippet in the C:\Users\UserName\My Documents\Visual Studio 2012\Code Snippets\Visual Basic\My Code Snippets folder. As an example, save it as **ToObservableCollection.snippet**. Now go back to the Visual Basic code editor, and right-click to insert a snippet until you find the new My Code Snippets|ToObservableCollection element. If you add it, you should get a result similar to the one shown in Figure 53.25.

FIGURE 53.25   Adding the new code snippet in Visual Studio.

Notice how you get information on the replacement via the specified tooltip, when the mouse pointer passes over the replacement.

TOOLS FOR PRODUCING CODE SNIPPETS

Writing code snippets manually can be annoying. Fortunately, there are many tools (most of them are open source) for generating code snippets via a graphical user interface to make this task easier. See Appendix A, "Useful Resources and Tools for Visual Basic," for a list of available tools.

Maybe you want to know how to deploy code snippets for sharing with other developers or to create a code snippets database. The most appropriate way for sharing snippets is creating a redistributable .Vsi package based on the Visual Studio Content Installer, a particular engine dedicated to sharing additions for Visual Studio (particularly add-ins and code snippets, the only two additional contents not covered by VSIX packages in Visual Studio 2012). This is appropriate because this engine can install contents into the correct folders so developers will not do this manually. The VSCI is not covered here (read the MSDN documentation at http://msdn.microsoft.com/en-us/library/ms246580(VS.110).aspx). In addition, Appendix A provides tools capable of generating .vsi packages for you. Another way is to create a compressed archive that stores .snippet files you can send to other developers who will just extract the archive content into the snippets folder.

Managing Libraries with NuGet

As a developer, you probably use libraries produced by others in almost all your projects. Often libraries have dependencies, meaning they require other libraries to work correctly. In lots of situations, dependencies are not included with the library you use so you need to perform a manual search and installation and this complicates things if you have to repeat the same steps for multiple projects. To make a developer's life easier, Microsoft developed an extension for Visual Studio called **NuGet** (also known as Library Package Manager). Via a repository of packages, NuGet allows you to find, download, and install a project to the desired library and all of its dependencies with just a couple of clicks. Downloaded libraries and their dependencies are also automatically referenced in your project. This avoids the need of remembering each library's dependencies and of performing a lot of manual steps. In Visual Studio 2010, NuGet was available only as an extension you had to download manually. But in Visual Studio 2012, it is an integrated tool. To understand how it works, create and save a new Console application. Then select Tools, Library Package Manager, Manage NuGet Packages for Solution. This will open the Manage NuGet Packages dialog box, where you can find the libraries you need. Figure 53.26 shows how the dialog box appears.

THE NUGET CONSOLE

NuGet also offers a console where you can type commands to interact directly with the NuGet repository. This chapter does not describe the console because this implies remembering a number of commands that perform actions you can easily accomplish within the Manage NuGet Packages dialog box. In case you want to know more about the NuGet console, visit http://docs.nuget.org/docs/start-here/using-the-package-manager-console.

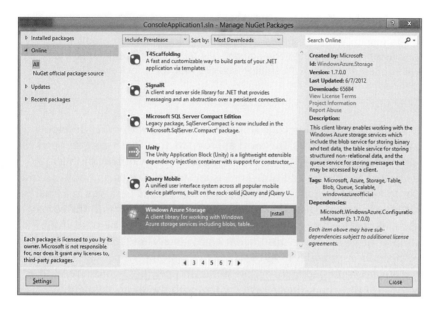

FIGURE 53.26   Searching for NuGet packages.

You can browse the list of available packages or just type a library name in the search box. On the left side of the dialog box you can choose to browse the online gallery (which is the default), the installed packages for the solution (so you can use this tool to remove them), the list of available updates for the currently installed packages, and a list of recently used packages. If you select Include Prerelease in the drop-down box at the top of the dialog box, the tool will include beta versions of products. Just as an example, locate and select the Windows Azure Storage package, which includes libraries for working with the Windows Azure storage in a managed way (see Figure 53.26). After you click Install, Visual Studio 2012 will first ask to specify which projects will receive the library and then it will ask you to accept license agreements. As you can see from Figure 53.27, each library in the package has its own license agreement you have to read before installing.

Click **I Accept** and wait for Visual Studio 2012 to download and install the selected package to your project. After the operation completes, you are ready to use the libraries and the objects they expose exactly as you would do if you manually added references. It is easy to demonstrate that the IDE automatically added a reference to the down-loaded package and, most importantly, Visual Studio downloaded not only the selected component, but also other components required by the selected one. In other words, you selected the Microsoft.WindowsAzure.StorageClient library, but it requires the Microsoft.WindowsAzure.Configuration library that has been provided for you. Enable the Show All Files view in Solution Explorer to see references, as demonstrated in Figure 53.28 (for now see only Solution Explorer). You can get a graphical representation of the package hierarchy, where you can see the selected library and all of its dependencies. To accomplish this, select Tools, Library Package Manager, Package Visualizer. This action will generate a new graphic you can see in Visual Studio, as demonstrated in Figure 53.28.

FIGURE 53.27   Accepting license agreements.

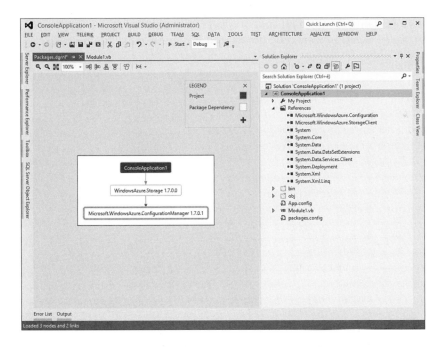

FIGURE 53.28   Showing package references and dependencies.

If you right-click the gray area of the graphic you will be able to access a number of commands related to how the hierarchical representation is shown and you will be able to export the graphic into an XPS file. Without NuGet, repeating the same steps manually in a number of different projects can be difficult and wastes time. With this way, you can automate the download of required libraries with the warranty that also has all the available required dependencies.

SHARING YOUR LIBRARIES WITH NUGET

One of the biggest benefits of NuGet is you can share your own libraries through the Library Package Manager and also keep shared libraries up to date. Publishing a package to the NuGet repository is out of the scope of this chapter, but it is an easy task. You can visit http://nuget.org to find all the necessary information to publish your packages so other developers will be able to install them using NuGet.

Summary

This chapter covered some important features about customizing Visual Studio 2012. We started by explaining how to export both projects and items templates, then moved to customizing the IDE by providing additional commands to the Tools menu and customizing existing toolbars or adding new ones. Then we described how you could export and import Visual Studio settings to keep your environment up-to-date with your preferences. Finally, we took an important tour through code snippets seeing how they can improve the way you write code by creating your code library and using the Visual Studio code snippets library.

CHAPTER 54

Introducing Visual Studio Extensibility

Visual Studio is with no doubt a great application, offering hundreds of integrated tools that cover hundreds of aspects of the development experience. It is also a complex and composite application, made of many components. For example, each tool window is a single component developed separately and then put together with the rest of the environment. Developing Visual Studio components and then putting them together is something made possible because of Visual Studio Extensibility. This means that Visual Studio is an extensible application and that other developers, like you and me, can build their own components to put together within the IDE. Although, Visual Studio offers hundreds of tools that covers many developmental needs, it cannot cover all possible requirements. One of the biggest benefits inside the Visual Studio development environment is your ability to customize it with additional tools, windows, and items that can make your developer life easier. In this chapter, you get started with the Visual Studio 2012 extensibility by building custom components like add-ins and extensions.

Introducing Visual Studio Extensibility

Since previous versions, Visual Studio has always been an extensible environment. This means it can be extended and enhanced with additional tools, windows, add-ins, packages, and macros to increase your productivity with specific instruments you might need for adjusting the environment to your developer needs. Behind the scenes, Visual Studio is a mixed-mode application, which means it is built on both

COM and .NET architectures (although in 2008, 2010, and 2012 versions, the managed architecture plays a bigger role than in the past).

Visual Studio takes advantage of several .NET assemblies whose names begin with Microsoft.VisualStudio.XXX.dll, where XXX stands for a particular environment area, for maintaining its infrastructure. These assemblies expose a lot of namespace whose names begin with `Microsoft.VisualStudio` and play an important role in the IDE extensibility because the developer can build components referencing those assemblies to get access to IDE functionalities and extend these functionalities with custom packages or add-ins. As you can imagine, this opens to interesting development scenarios. Building extensions for Visual Studio can be an important business, and several companies build extensions for Visual Studio. But this is what developers could do with Visual Studio until the 2008 version. With Visual Studio 2010, Microsoft completely revisited the IDE architecture and infrastructure so the environment can be extended in further ways other than classic add-ins. This has been retaken and enhanced in Visual Studio 2012. Let's learn the important concepts about extensibility before showing practical examples.

About Extensibility with Visual Studio 2012

The IDE was completely revisited in Visual Studio 2010, and Visual Studio 2012 retakes most of its infrastructure. Several areas rely on Windows Presentation Foundation, which brought many improvements to the developer experience. The most evident area affected by this infrastructure is the code editor, entirely built upon WPF. Visual Studio 2012 enables extending the code editor with specific WPF objects that can actually enrich the code editor with useful or just attractive extensions. Another key concept is how the IDE infrastructure is built. The extensibility architecture existing until Visual Studio 2008 was replaced in Visual Studio 2010 with the Managed Extensibility Framework (or just MEF), a set of .NET libraries that favors building extensible applications with composition techniques according to a plug-in model. MEF is now an integral part of .NET Framework 4.5 and you can use it to build your own extensible applications. After this brief introduction, we can divide the Visual Studio extensibility into two main areas: packages and add-ins development and code editor extensions development. The next subsection provides more detail on the available projects. For now, focus on the concept of extension. Each component extending the IDE is called extension, independently from its nature (for example, packages or code editor extensions). This concept, together with the WPF-based extensibility features, requires a specific deployment system for extensions. Since Visual Studio 2010, Microsoft introduced the .VSIX file format, specific for deploying extensions and is intended as a replacement for the old .VSI file format (with some exceptions explained later in this chapter). But before going into further discussions, you need some additional tools for developing versus Visual Studio, known as the Visual Studio 2012 SDK.

The Visual Studio 2012 SDK

You create custom extensions for and with Visual Studio taking advantage of specific projects templates. To enable Visual Studio 2012 extensibility projects, you need to download and install the Visual Studio 2012 Software Development Kit, which is available from the

Visual Studio Developer Center at http://msdn.microsoft.com/en-US/vstudio/ff718165. aspx. The SDK setup can install tools, project templates, and documentation so you can build custom extensions for the IDE. In the `Start|Microsoft Visual Studio 2012 SDK`, you can find shortcuts to online tools, samples, and documentation about the extensibility. In addition, in a subfolder named Tools you can find a shortcut for starting Visual Studio under the *experimental instance* and for resetting this environment. The experimental instance is a fully functional instance of Visual Studio used for extension debugging and testing, and in most cases, you do not need to launch it manually because it will launch by the development instance of Visual Studio. The experimental instance keeps track of all extensions you develop and debug, so you can reset the instance when you want it to be clean.

EXTENSIBILITY SAMPLES

The Visual Studio Extensibility team from Microsoft published (and periodically updates) code examples about extending Visual Studio 2012 onto the MSDN Code Gallery. I suggest you visit the dedicated web page at http://code.msdn.microsoft.com/vsx. You can find several interesting examples covering almost every extensibility area.

The SDK installs additional projects templates for the Visual Studio extensibility as summarized in the following list:

▶ Editor extensibility projects. These projects are fully functional code examples you can use for understanding how extensions work.

▶ Add-ins, integration packages, and Visual Studio Shell projects.

▶ Extension deployments projects, including toolbox controls.

All the listed projects templates are available in the New project dialog box. In the next section, you develop your first extension for Visual Studio 2012 taking advantage of the WPF infrastructure.

Building a Visual Studio Package

The goal of this introductory chapter on the Visual Studio extensibility is to show you how to create and deploy a Visual Studio Package. Visual Studio is made of packages. Each package represents a working unit. For example, the toolbox is a package; Solution Explorer is another package, and so on. You can extend Visual Studio by building custom integration packages. There are different kinds of integration packages, such as tool windows, menus, wizards, and languages. The big difference between a package and an add-in is a package can add completely new tools and features to the IDE, whereas add-ins typically extend existing features in the IDE with other features. In the next code example, you learn to build a custom tool window that can provide the ability of compiling code snippets on the fly in both Visual Basic and Visual C#. Open the New project window by selecting **File, New project**. When the New project window appears, select the **Other Project Types, Extensibility** subfolder on the left and then the **Visual Studio Package** project template. Name the new project **SnippetCompilerVSPackage** (see Figure 54.1) and then click **OK**.

FIGURE 54.1   Creating the new extensibility project.

At this point, the Visual Studio Integration Package Wizard starts. Select Visual Basic as the programming language and leave unchanged the new key file option, as shown in Figure 54.2.

FIGURE 54.2   Setting language and key file options.

In the next window, you can set information for the new package, such as author, description, and icon. Figure 54.3 shows an example for these settings.

FIGURE 54.3   Setting package information.

The next step is important and is the place where you can select the package type. Select **Tool window** and then click **Next** (see Figure 54.4). You can select multiple options depending on where you want the tool to be available.

FIGURE 54.4   Package type selection.

Next, you can specify the Window name and Command ID. The Window name is the tool window title, whereas the ID is used internally by Visual Studio for invoking the new package. Figure 54.5 shows an example of setting this information.

FIGURE 54.5   Setting title and ID for the new tool window.

The next step requires you to specify whether you want to add test projects for the new package. For this example, uncheck both projects and go ahead. You can complete the wizard and Visual Studio will generate the new project. When the new project is ready, the first thing you notice is the tool window is nothing but a WPF custom control. Now double-click the MyControl.xaml file in Solution Explorer to enable the designer. Figure 54.6 shows how the IDE appears.

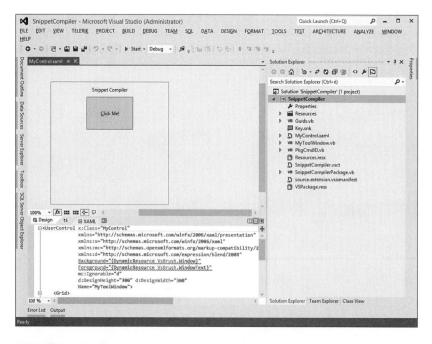

FIGURE 54.6   The IDE is ready on the new extensibility project, showing the WPF custom control.

Visual Studio implements a WPF skeleton for a new tool window you need to customize. But first consider the meaning of files available within Solution Explorer. This is summarized in Table 54.1.

TABLE 54.1   VS Package Code Files

File	Description
Guids.vb	Defines a number of GUIDs that Visual Studio will use to recognize and implement the tool window
MyToolWindow.vb	A class implements the tool window hosting it as a user control
PkgCmdId.vb	Exposes a unique identifier for the package within Visual Studio
Resources.resx	Exposes resources required by the IDE
VSPackage.resx	Exposes resources required by the package
MyControl.Xaml	The WPF custom control implements the tool window content
SnippetCompilerPackage.vb	The class implements the tool window
SnippetCompiler.vsct	An XML file defines the layout of the package, including company information
Source.extension.vsixmanifest	An XML file used for deploying packages as a .Vsix file (see later in this chapter)
Key.snk	Strong name file required for signing the package assembly

In addition, a subfolder named Resources contains the icons used within the package and identifies the new tool in Visual Studio. All code files contain comments that can help you understand what a particular file is for. For instance, look at the SnippetCompilerPackage. vb file. For your convenience, Listing 54.1 shows the content of this file. Notice how comments are detailed and how they provide complete explanations on types and their roles within the user interface.

LISTING 54.1   Understanding Packages Behind the Scenes

```
Imports Microsoft.VisualBasic
Imports System
Imports System.Diagnostics
Imports System.Globalization
Imports System.Runtime.InteropServices
Imports System.ComponentModel.Design
Imports Microsoft.Win32
Imports Microsoft.VisualStudio
Imports Microsoft.VisualStudio.Shell.Interop
Imports Microsoft.VisualStudio.OLE.Interop
Imports Microsoft.VisualStudio.Shell
```

```
''' <summary>
''' This is the class that implements the package exposed by this assembly.
'''
''' The minimum requirement for a class to be considered a valid package for Visual
''' Studio  is to implement the IVsPackage interface and register itself with the
''' shell. This package uses the helper classes defined inside the Managed Package
''' Framework (MPF) to do it: it derives from the Package class that provides the
''' implementation of the IVsPackage interface and uses the registration attributes
''' defined in the framework to register itself and its components with the shell.
''' </summary>
' The PackageRegistration attribute tells the PkgDef creation utility
➥(CreatePkgDef.exe) that this class
' is a package.
'
' The InstalledProductRegistration attribute is used to register the information
➥needed to show this package
' in the Help/About dialog of Visual Studio.
    '
' The ProvideMenuResource attribute is needed to let the shell know that this
➥package exposes some menus.
    '
' The ProvideToolWindow attribute registers a tool window exposed by this package.

    <PackageRegistration(UseManagedResourcesOnly := true), _
    InstalledProductRegistration("#110", "#112", "1.0", IconResourceID := 400), _
    ProvideMenuResource("Menus.ctmenu", 1), _
    ProvideToolWindow(GetType(MyToolWindow)), _
    Guid(GuidList.guidSnippetCompilerPkgString)> _
    Public NotInheritable Class SnippetCompilerPackage
Inherits Package


''' <summary>
''' Default constructor of the package.
''' Inside this method you can place any initialization code that does not require
''' any Visual Studio service because at this point the package object is created
''' but not cited yet inside Visual Studio environment. The place to do all the
''' other initialization is the Initialize method.
''' </summary>
Public Sub New()
    Debug.WriteLine(String.Format(CultureInfo.CurrentCulture, "Entering constructor
➥for: {0}", Me.GetType().Name))
End Sub


        ''' <summary>
''' This function is called when the user clicks the menu item that shows the
''' tool window. See the Initialize method to see how the menu item is associated to
''' this function using the OleMenuCommandService service and the MenuCommand class.
```

```vbnet
''' </summary>
Private Sub ShowToolWindow(ByVal sender As Object, ByVal e As EventArgs)
    ' Get the instance number 0 of this tool window. This window is single instance
➥so this instance
    ' is actually the only one.
    ' The last flag is set to true so that if the tool window does not exists it
➥will be created.
    Dim window As ToolWindowPane = Me.FindToolWindow(GetType(MyToolWindow), 0, True)
    If (window Is Nothing) Or (window.Frame Is Nothing) Then
        Throw New NotSupportedException(Resources.CanNotCreateWindow)
    End If

    Dim windowFrame As IVsWindowFrame = TryCast(window.Frame, IVsWindowFrame)
    Microsoft.VisualStudio.ErrorHandler.ThrowOnFailure(windowFrame.Show())
End Sub


'''''''''''''''''''''''''''''''''''''''''''''''''''''''''''''''''''''''''''''''
' Overridden Package Implementation
#Region "Package Members"

''' <summary>
''' Initialization of the package; this method is called right after the package is
➥cited, so this is the place
''' where you can put all the initialization code that rely on services provided by
➥VisualStudio.
''' </summary>
Protected Overrides Sub Initialize()
    Debug.WriteLine(String.Format(CultureInfo.CurrentCulture, "Entering Initialize()
➥of: {0}", Me.GetType().Name))
    MyBase.Initialize()

            ' Add our command handlers for menu (commands must exist in the .vsct
➥file)
    Dim mcs As OleMenuCommandService = TryCast(GetService(GetType
➥(IMenuCommandService)), OleMenuCommandService)
    If Not mcs Is Nothing Then
                ' Create the command for the tool window
                Dim toolwndCommandID As New CommandID(GuidList.
➥guidSnippetCompilerCmdSet, CInt(PkgCmdIDList.cmdidSnippetCompiler))
        Dim menuToolWin As New MenuCommand(New EventHandler(AddressOf
➥ShowToolWindow), toolwndCommandID)
        mcs.AddCommand(menuToolWin)
            End If
        End Sub
#End Region


End Class
```

54

The class inherits from `Microsoft.VisualStudio.Shell.Package`, the base class exposing the required interface for every functional package. The `ShowToolWindow` method gets an instance of the `Microsoft.VisualStudio.Shell.ToolWindowPane` class pointing to the custom tool window (`Me.FindToolWindow(GetType(MyToolWindow))`). The same exam can be done on the ToolWindow.vb file. After doing this, you can customize the WPF control. The goal of the tool window is enabling on-the-fly compilation for code snippets. With that said, there is the need of implementing the user-interface side. In the XAML editor, type the code shown in Listing 54.2.

LISTING 54.2   Implementing the Tool Window User Interface

```
<UserControl x:Class="MyControl"
            xmlns="http://schemas.microsoft.com/winfx/2006/xaml/presentation"
            xmlns:x="http://schemas.microsoft.com/winfx/2006/xaml"
            xmlns:mc="http://schemas.openxmlformats.org/markup-compatibility/2006"
            xmlns:d="http://schemas.microsoft.com/expression/blend/2008"
            xmlns:vsfx="clr-namespace:Microsoft.VisualStudio.
➥Shell;assembly=Microsoft.VisualStudio.Shell.10.0"
            mc:Ignorable="d"
            d:DesignHeight="300" d:DesignWidth="300"
            Name="MyToolWindow"
            Background="{DynamicResource
            {x:Static vsfx:VsBrushes.ToolWindowBackgroundKey}}">
    <Grid>
        <Grid.RowDefinitions>
            <RowDefinition Height="30" />
            <RowDefinition Height="40" />
            <RowDefinition />
            <RowDefinition Height="50" />
            <RowDefinition Height="40" />
            <RowDefinition />
        </Grid.RowDefinitions>
        <!-- This will allow selecting the compiler -->
        <ComboBox Name="LanguageCombo" Text="VisualBasic" Margin="5">
            <ComboBoxItem Content="VisualBasic" />
            <ComboBoxItem Content="CSharp" />
        </ComboBox>
        <TextBlock Margin="5" Grid.Row="1"
                    Foreground="{DynamicResource
                    VsBrush.ToolWindowTextKey}">
            Write or paste your code here:</TextBlock>
        <TextBox Grid.Row="2"  Name="CodeTextBox" Margin="5"
                    Foreground="{DynamicResource
                    VsBrush.ToolWindowTextKey}"
                    AcceptsReturn="True" AcceptsTab="True"
                    VerticalAlignment="Stretch"
```

```
                    VerticalScrollBarVisibility="Auto"
                    HorizontalScrollBarVisibility="Auto" />
        <Button Grid.Row="3" Content="Compile code" Width="80" Height="40"
                Name="button1"/>
        <TextBlock Grid.Row="4" Margin="10"
                   Foreground="{DynamicResource
                   VsBrush.ToolWindowTextKey}">
            Compilation results:</TextBlock>
        <ListBox Grid.Row="5" ItemsSource="{Binding}"
                 Name="ErrorsListBox" Margin="5"
                 Foreground="{DynamicResource
                 VsBrush.ToolWindowTextKey}"/>
    </Grid>
</UserControl>
```

On the Visual Basic side, enter the **MyControl.xaml.vb** file and write the code shown in Listing 54.3. This adds compile functionalities to the tool window when the button is clicked. The code uses the `System.CodeDom` namespace for getting instances of the .NET compilers, as you will understand through comments in the code.

LISTING 54.3   Code for Compiling On-the-Fly Code Typed Inside the Tool Window

```
Imports System.Security.Permissions
Imports System
Imports System.Reflection
Imports System.Reflection.Emit
Imports System.CodeDom.Compiler
Imports System.Windows.Controls

'''<summary>
'''   Interaction logic for MyControl.xaml
'''</summary>
Partial Public Class MyControl
    Inherits System.Windows.Controls.UserControl

    <System.Diagnostics.CodeAnalysis.SuppressMessage("Microsoft.Globalization",
                   "CA1300:SpecifyMessageBoxOptions")> _
    Private Sub button1_Click(ByVal sender As Object,
                        ByVal e As System.EventArgs) Handles button1.Click
        Try
            If String.IsNullOrEmpty(CodeTextBox.Text) = False Then

                Me.ErrorsListBox.ItemsSource = _
                Compile(CType(Me.LanguageCombo.SelectedItem,
                    ComboBoxItem).Content.ToString)
```

```vb
            End If
        Catch ex As Exception
            'Handle other exceptions here, no compiler errors
        End Try

    End Sub

    Private Function Compile(ByVal language As String) As IEnumerable(Of String)

        'Gets the ComboBox selected language
        Dim languageProvider As String = language

        'Creates an instance of the desired compiler
        Dim CompilerProvider As CodeDomProvider = _
            CodeDomProvider.CreateProvider(languageProvider)

        'Sets compiler parameters
        Dim params As New CompilerParameters()
        Dim results As CompilerResults

        'Configure self-explanatory parameters
        With params
            .GenerateExecutable = False
            .GenerateInMemory = True
            .IncludeDebugInformation = False
            'You can add multiple references here
            .ReferencedAssemblies.Add("System.dll")
        End With

        'Compiles the specified source code
        results = CompilerProvider.
                CompileAssemblyFromSource(params,
                                          CodeTextBox.Text)

        'If no errors, the ListBox is empty
        If results.Errors.Count = 0 Then
            Return Nothing
        Else
            'If any errors, creates a list of errors...
            Dim errorsList As New List(Of String)

            '..iterating the compiler errors
            For Each item As CompilerError In results.Errors
                errorsList.Add(item.ErrorText & " Line " & item.Line.ToString)
            Next
            Return errorsList.AsEnumerable
```

```
        End If

    End Function
End Class
```

You can now test the new tool window. You can do this by pressing **F5** as you would do in any other kind of .NET application. This starts a new instance of Visual Studio known as Experimental Instance. It is a fully functional instance of Visual Studio that is used for debugging custom extensions. If the new tool window is not visible, click the new **View, Other windows, Snippet compiler** command. Figure 54.7 shows how the new tool window appears in the IDE.

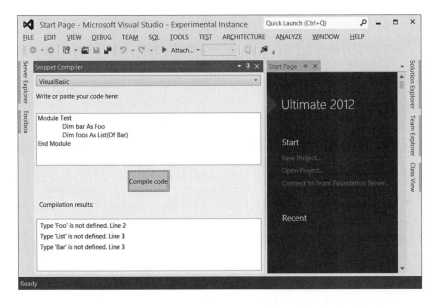

FIGURE 54.7   The new tool window running inside Visual Studio 2012.

The new tool window is a fully functional one, so it can be anchored like any other Visual Studio window. To stop the test environment, close the experimental instance of Visual Studio. Until now, you saw a debugging scenario. When the debugging and testing phase is completed, you need to deploy the extension to other developers. As explained in next section, Visual Studio 2012 offers a specific deployment system for this kind of extensions that is simple to accomplish and has been inherited from the previous versions of the product.

Deploying Visual Studio Extensions

To deploy Visual Studio extensions, you package components inside a file type named VSIX (with .vsix extension). This format is intended as a replacement for the previous .vsi file format first introduced with Visual Studio 2005 (and that actually still survives for the sake of backward compatibility). A VSIX package is nothing but a zip archive that is built with regard of the open packaging convention. This means if you rename the .vsix package into .zip, you can browse its content with any compression tool supporting zips. This kind of package needs to store some other files:

▶ A [Content_Types].xml file that describes the archive content according to the open packaging convention

▶ An extension.vsixmanifest file storing information on the extension and on how it will be deployed

▶ Binary files for the extension (set named product payload)

▶ Support files, such as license, icons, etc.

VSIX packages cannot deploy add-ins, macros, and code snippets, whereas they can deploy any other kind of extensions. You can deploy extensions via Windows Installer packages; this is preferable when you need to accomplish specific requirements such as installing assemblies to the GAC or writing to the Registry. For all other cases, VSIX packages are a good thing.

DEPLOYING ADD-INS AND CODE SNIPPETS

Because you cannot deploy Visual Studio add-ins and code snippets with VSIX packages, you still need to build a .vsi package or recur to Windows Installer projects.

There are some other good reasons for preferring VSIX packages. First, they can check for updates. Second, they can be uploaded to the Visual Studio Gallery so other developers can download your extension directly from the Visual Studio Extension Manager. (The latter will be covered later in this chapter.) Another good reason is that you do not need to edit a VSIX package manually. Visual Studio offers an integrated designer for creating VSIX packages directly into the current project. Continuing from the previous example, double-click the **source.extension.vsixmanifest** file in Solution Explorer. This file is added to each extensibility project at creation time and is the deployment manifest for the extension. Once this is complete, Visual Studio 2012 looks like Figure 54.8.

With the exception of the ID field, which is filled by Visual Studio, you just need to fill blank and self-explanatory fields with custom values, as Figure 54.8 shows. It is worth mentioning that VSIX packages are localizable (check out the Language combo box). Here, you can specify a license agreement (License field) by adding an existing text file or RTF file. If you select the Install Targets tab, you will be able to specify multiple editions of Visual Studio that will be able to receive your extension. Once in the Install Target tab, click the New button to specify another edition of Visual Studio or click Edit or Delete to modify or remove an edition. The Asset tab enables you to specify additional assets that describe your extension and must be installed together with it. The Dependencies tab enables you to specify other extensions that the current one depends on, if any.

You can find further information about the VSIX designer at http://bit.ly/PU9mKf. To build the deployment package, build the project. The VSIX package is now available in the project output folder (Bin\Debug or Bin\Release). With regard to the previous example, the package is named SnippetCompiler.Vsix. If you double-click this file, you will be prompted with some information before installation begins, as seen in Figure 54.9.

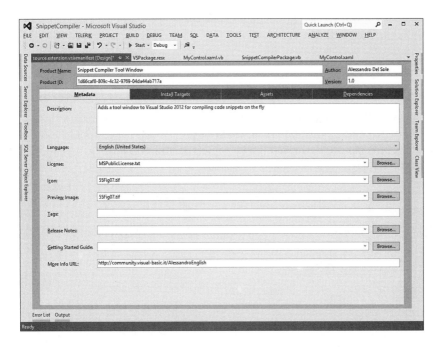

FIGURE 54.8   Customizing properties for the deployment package.

FIGURE 54.9   Installing the new custom extension.

By clicking **Install**, the new custom extension will be available onto the target system. This means you need to deploy the VSIX package and you are done.

Managing Extensions with Extensions and Updates

Visual Studio 2012 has an integrated tool to easily manage installed extensions and to find online extensions that can be installed from the Internet. To enter this tool, select the **Tools, Extensions and Updates** command. Figure 54.10 shows how the **Extension and Updates** dialog box appears.

FIGURE 54.10   The Extensions and Updates tool.

The Extension and Updates tool can be used to find, download, and install extensions to Visual Studio 2012. If you select the **Online**, **Visual Studio Gallery** option on the left, the tool shows all available extensions in the Visual Studio Gallery. This is an online website from Microsoft specific for Visual Studio extensions (http://visualstudiogallery. com). This website will provide a complete overview of extensions and possibly the source code where available. The tool shows the list of available extensions, providing a brief description on the right side of the dialog box. You click **Download** to install the desired extension. Each time you install an extension, Visual Studio might need to be restarted to correctly recognize these additions. Extensions are divided into three categories: Controls, Templates (including project and item templates), and Tools. Each category is divided into subcategories, explaining what the extension is bound to. The Extensions and Updates tool can find only VSIX packages, meaning that add-ins and code snippets are not supported and need to be handled differently. You can search through online additions using the search box in the upper right of the dialog box. A new feature in Visual Studio 2012 that was not available in Visual Studio 2010 is the capability to search for and install code examples from the MSDN Code Gallery. The way examples work was discussed back in Chapter 2, "Getting Started with the Visual Studio 2012 IDE," but with this tool, you can not only download samples but also manage installed samples and search for sample updates. Similarly, you can easily manage installed additions. Click **Installed, All** to get the full list of available extensions on your system. See Figure 54.11, which lists extensions available on my development machine.

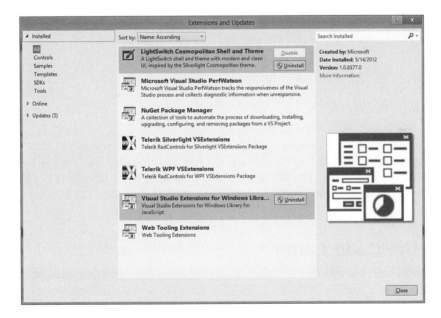

FIGURE 54.11   Managing installed extensions.

Here you can disable an extension, keeping it installed on the machine and available for future reuse, or completely uninstall. As you can see, you can filter the list of extensions by controls, code examples, project and item templates, software development kits, and tools. The dialog box can also find updates for installed extensions. Do this by selecting the **Updates** command on the left side.

Managing Add-Ins with the Add-In Manager

Visual Studio 2012, exactly as its predecessors, lets you enhance the environment with add-ins. As mentioned at the beginning of this chapter, an add-in extends an existing functionality. You can manage installed add-ins via the Add-in Manager tool. You enter the tool by selecting **Tools, Add-In Manager**. Figure 54.12 shows the tool when some add-ins are installed.

FIGURE 54.12   The Add-in Manager.

For each add-in you can specify, it must be loaded at the IDE startup or if it has command-line support. Because building custom add-ins is something that was already available in previous versions of the IDE, this topic is not covered here, so refer to the official MSDN page at http://msdn.microsoft.com/en-us/library/80493a3w(v=vs.110).aspx for more information.

Extending the Code Editor

One of the most important features in the Visual Studio 2012 extensibility is the capability of extending the code editor, which is based on WPF since Visual Studio 2010. Code editor extensions get the instance of the WPF objects keeping the editor itself alive. For a better comprehension, instead of building a particular extension, we explain required objects taking advantage of one of the sample projects added by the Visual Studio 2012 SDK. Create a new project and select the **Visual Basic|Extensibility folder**. Finally, select the **Editor Text Adornment** project template, as shown in Figure 54.13.

The goal of this sample project is simple—adorning each *a* character in the code with a different background color. The most important object in providing editor extension is the `Microsoft.VisualStudio.Text.Editor.IWpfTextView` type that represents the instance of the code editor. For the current example, there is the need of placing an adornment on all occurrences of the specified character. To place adornments, you need an instance of the `IAdornmentLayer` type that represents a space for placing adornments. Listing 54.4 shows the complete code. Be sure to read comments that can help you understand what is under the hood.

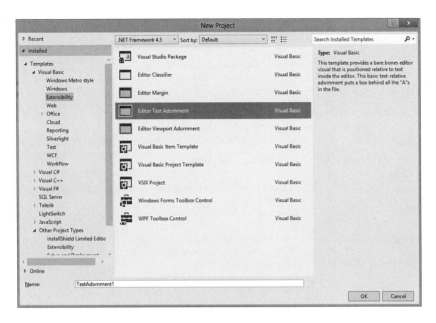

FIGURE 54.13   Selecting the code editor extension template.

LISTING 54.4   Providing a Code Editor Extension with Adornments

```vb
Imports System.Windows
Imports System.Windows.Controls
Imports System.Windows.Media
Imports Microsoft.VisualStudio.Text
Imports Microsoft.VisualStudio.Text.Editor
Imports Microsoft.VisualStudio.Text.Formatting


''' <summary>
''' ScarletCharacter adornment places red boxes behind all
''' the "a"s in the editor window
''' </summary>
Class ScarletCharacter

    Private WithEvents _view As IWpfTextView
    Private ReadOnly _layer As IAdornmentLayer
    Private ReadOnly _brush As Brush
    Private ReadOnly _pen As Pen
```

```vb
'The IWpFTextView object represents the
'instance of the code editor
Public Sub New(ByVal view As IWpfTextView)
    _view = view

    'IAdornmentLayer represents the place where
    'adorners are placed
    _layer = view.GetAdornmentLayer("ScarletCharacter")

    'Create the pen and brush to color the box behind the a's
    Dim brush As New SolidColorBrush(Color.
                    FromArgb(&H20, &H0, &H0, &HFF))
    brush.Freeze()
    Dim penBrush As New SolidColorBrush(Colors.Red)
    penBrush.Freeze()
    Dim pen As New Pen(penBrush, 0.5)
    pen.Freeze()

    _brush = brush
    _pen = pen
End Sub


''' <summary>
''' On layout change add the adornment to any reformatted lines
''' </summary>
Private Sub OnLayoutChanged(ByVal sender As Object,
                    ByVal e As TextViewLayoutChangedEventArgs) _
                    Handles _view.LayoutChanged

    'TextViewLayoutChangedEventArgs provides information when
    'the code editor layout changes
    For Each line In e.NewOrReformattedLines
        Me.CreateVisuals(line)
    Next line
End Sub


''' <summary>
''' Within the given line add the scarlet box behind the a
''' </summary>
Private Sub CreateVisuals(ByVal line As ITextViewLine)
    'grab a reference to the lines in the current TextView
    Dim textViewLines = _view.TextViewLines
    Dim lineStart As Integer = line.Start
    Dim lineEnd As Integer = line.End
```

```
        'Loop through each character, and place a box around any a
    For i = lineStart To lineEnd - 1
        If _view.TextSnapshot(i) = "a"c Then
            Dim charSpan As New SnapshotSpan(_view.TextSnapshot,
                            Span.FromBounds(i, i + 1))
            Dim g As Geometry = textViewLines.GetMarkerGeometry(charSpan)
            If g IsNot Nothing Then
                Dim drawing As New GeometryDrawing(_brush, _pen, g)
                drawing.Freeze()

                Dim drawingImage As New DrawingImage(drawing)
                drawingImage.Freeze()

                Dim image As New Image()
                image.Source = drawingImage

                'Align the image with the top of the bounds of the text geometry
                Canvas.SetLeft(image, g.Bounds.Left)
                Canvas.SetTop(image, g.Bounds.Top)

                'AdornmentPositioningBehavior sets how
                'the adornment is placed
                _layer.AddAdornment(AdornmentPositioningBehavior.
                            TextRelative, charSpan,
                            Nothing, image, Nothing)
            End If
        End If
    Next
    End Sub

End Class
```

Notice how the `Microsoft.VisualStudio.Text` namespace exposes objects and other namespaces for interacting with the code editor. Now run the extension by pressing **F5**. Try to create a new console project and write some text containing the "a" character and you will see how they are surrounded with a different background, as shown in Figure 54.14.

In many scenarios you might need to extend the Visual Studio code editor. You can find more interesting extensions by searching the Visual Studio Gallery with the Extension Manager.

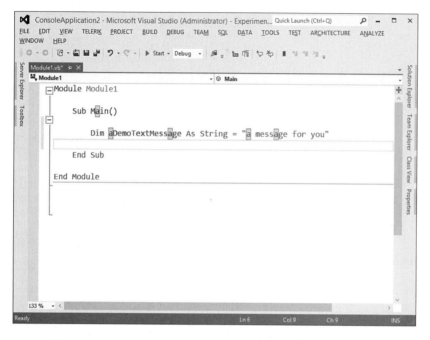

FIGURE 54.14   The WPF editor extension adorning multiple "a"s in a row.

Summary

Visual Studio 2012 is an extensible development environment that can be enhanced with custom extensions such as add-ins, packages, and new code editor extensions due to an efficient architecture based on Windows Presentation Foundation. Instrumentation required for creating extensibility projects is available when installing the Visual Studio 2012 SDK, which provides project templates, tools, and documentation. This chapter explained how to build a custom tool window based on WPF for the Visual Studio development environment. Then you learned how custom extension could be packaged into VSIX files and deployed to other developers. Next, you saw how you could use the new Extension Manager for getting and installing extensions from the Visual Studio Gallery. The last example provided in this chapter was about extending the WPF-based code editor and using Visual Studio's managed assemblies.

CHAPTER 55

Advanced Analysis Tools

Writing code is just one part of the developer life. There are so many other aspects to consider in producing high-quality applications. For example, if you produce reusable class libraries, you must ensure that your code is compliant with Common Language Specification, and this requires deep analysis. Another key aspect is performance. If you produce a great application with the most desired functionalities but with poor performance, perhaps your customer will prefer a faster and less-consuming application even if this has a minor number of features. Continuing from its predecessors, Visual Studio 2012 offers a number of integrated tools for analyzing code and performance to improve your applications' quality. In this chapter, you learn how to use Visual Studio 2012's integrated analysis tools for writing better applications.

VISUAL STUDIO SUPPORTED EDITIONS

Analysis tools are available only in some Visual Studio 2012 editions. To complete tasks explained in this chapter, you need at least Visual Studio 2012 Premium or Visual Studio 2012 Ultimate (which is required for IntelliTrace).

Introducing Analysis Tools

Visual Studio 2012 offers the following analysis tools, which can help you produce high-quality applications:

▶ **Code Analysis**—analyzes code for compliance with Microsoft coding rules.

▶ **Code Metrics**—returns statistic results and analyzes code maintainability according to specific indexes.

▶ **Code Clone Detection**—a new tool that helps you discover code duplicates in certain development scenarios.

▶ **Profiler**—analyzes application performance and suggests solutions for problems.

▶ **IntelliTrace**—formerly known as Historical Debugger, which keeps track of every single event and exceptions that happen during the entire application's lifetime.

In this chapter, you learn to use the listed tools for improving quality in your code.

Performing Code Analysis

Earlier in this book, you learned about Common Language Specification (CLS). These are a set of common rules and guidelines about writing code that can be shared across different .NET languages favoring interoperability and is considered well designed for the .NET Framework. In some cases, it can be hard to ensure all your code is CLS-compliant, especially when you have large projects with tons of lines of code. To help you write better and CLS-compliant code, Microsoft integrated directly inside Visual Studio 2012 a code analysis tool that analyzes compiled assemblies for non-CLS compliant code and reports suggestions and solutions for solving errors. The good news is that in Visual Studio 2012 the code analysis tool is available for Professional, Premium, and Ultimate editions (in Visual Studio 2010 it was available only in the Ultimate edition and for other editions you had to download an external tool called FxCop). You can also customize the code analysis process by setting specific rules. Before examining available rules, it is a good idea to create a simple project for demonstrating how code analysis works by creating a new class library project in Visual Basic 2012. When the code editor is ready, rename the **Class1** file to **HelperClass** and write the code shown in Listing 55.1, which attempts defining a CLS-compliant class, but makes several violations to the Microsoft rules, to which solutions are given later in this section.

LISTING 55.1   Writing a Simple Non-CLS-Compliant Class Library

```
<CLSCompliant(True)>
Public Class HelperClass

    Private CustomField As String

    Public Property customResult As String

    'Just a demo function
    Public Function doubleSum(ByVal FirstValue As Double,
                    ByVal SecondValue As Double) As Double
        Return FirstValue + SecondValue * 2
    End Function
End Class
```

For rules, it is worth mentioning that Microsoft divides guidelines in writing code into the rules summarized in Table 55.1.

TABLE 55.1   Microsoft Code Analysis Rules

Rule Name	Description
Microsoft.Design	Determines if assemblies contain well-designed objects or if the assembly definition is CLS-compliant
Microsoft.Globalization	Determines if globalization techniques are well implemented
Microsoft.Interoperability	Determines if the code makes correct usage of COM interoperability
Microsoft.Maintainability	Checks for code maintainability according to Microsoft rules
Microsoft.Mobility	Checks for timer and processes correct implementation
Microsoft.Naming	Determines if all identifiers match the CLS rules (such as public/private members, method parameters, etc.)
Microsoft.Performance	Checks for unused or inappropriate code for compile time and runtime performances from the CLR perspective
Microsoft.Portability	Determines if the code is portable for invoked API functions
Microsoft.Reliability	Provides rules for a better interaction with the Garbage Collector
Microsoft.Security	Provides security-related rules sending error messages if types and members are not considered secure
Microsoft.Usage	Determines if a code block correctly invokes other code

55

Performing code analysis does not require all the mentioned rules to be checked. You can specify only a subset of preferred rules or specify the complete set. To specify the rules sets involved in the code analysis, follow these steps:

1. Open **My Project** and click the **Code Analysis** tab. Figure 55.1 shows the designer.

2. Expand the **Run this rule set** combo box. You get a list of available rules sets with an accurate description for each set. By default, the offered set of rules is **Microsoft Managed Minimum Rules**. Replace it by selecting **Microsoft All Rules** that includes all sets listed in Table 55.1 and that is the most accurate. To get detailed information on each rule set, click **Open**. Figure 55.2 shows how you can browse rules available in the selected set, getting summary information for each rule, and specifying how you want to get help on violations (for instance, online or offline).

3. Select the **Analyze, Run code analysis** command and wait for a few seconds until the building and code analysis process is completed. When ready, Visual Studio shows a report listing all violations to coding rules encountered in the project. This report is shown in Figure 55.3. Notice that in Visual Studio 2012 the list of violations is shown inside a tool window called Code Analysis. This is different from the past, in which Visual Studio 2010 list was shown in the Error List window.

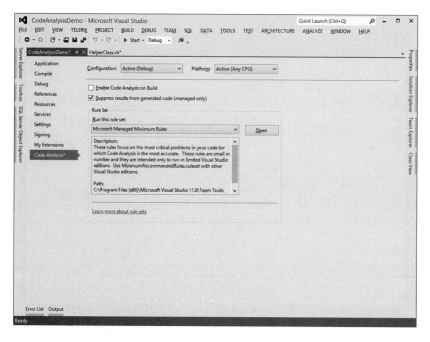

FIGURE 55.1   The Code Analysis designer.

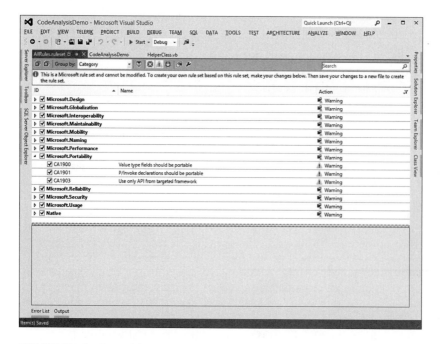

FIGURE 55.2   Browsing rules sets.

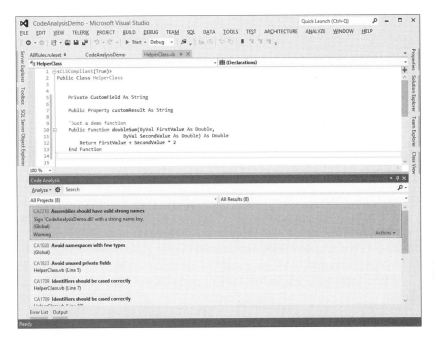

FIGURE 55.3   Report from the code analysis tool.

Each violation message includes the violation ID and a description that can help you fix the error. In most cases, violations are interpreted by the IDE as warnings, but in the code analysis designer you can modify this behavior by setting what violations must be notified as breaking errors. Assembly-level violations do not include the line of code to be fixed, whereas code-level violations do. In this case, you click the error message so the line of code to be fixed will be highlighted.

GETTING ERROR HELP

There are hundreds of Microsoft rules, so summarizing all of them in this book is not possible. You can get detailed information on each violation (and on each solution) by selecting the error message and then by pressing F1.

We can now begin fixing violations. It is worth mentioning there can be situations in which violations cannot be fixed due to particular scenarios. For example, the first violation in our example (CA1020) indicates that we should merge the current type into an existing namespace because a well-formed namespace contains at least five members. Due to our demo scenario, we can ignore this violation that is nonbreaking.

SUPPRESSING ERROR MESSAGES

In situations you know an error is nonbreaking due to a particular context, you can tell the code analysis engine to ignore an error by right-clicking the error message and then selecting Suppress Message. If you choose to suppress the message in the source code file, Visual Studio will decorate the line of code with a `SuppressMessage` attribute whose parameters are an identifier that represents the set of rules in which the error falls and the name of the rule. You can also choose the Suppression File option, which will generate a code file called GlobalSuppressions.vb and is a repository for all suppression messages. Notice that this choice is mandatory in the case of error messages that are not strictly related to fixing code.

The next error message (CA2210) indicates that the assembly must be signed with a strong name. I described strong names and provided instructions to add a strong name file to the library in Chapter 50, "Understanding the Global Assembly Cache." I named the strong name file as TestCode.pfx providing the **TestCode** password. The next violation (CA1014) requires the assembly to be marked as CLS-compliant. To accomplish this, click **the Show all files** button in Solution Explorer, expand **My Project** and add the following line to the AssemblyInfo.vb file:

```
<Assembly: CLSCompliant(True)>
```

The next violation (CA1824) indicates that a neutral-language resource should be supplied to the assembly. Because you have the AssemblyInfo.vb file already open, write the following line:

```
<Assembly: NeutralResourcesLanguageAttribute("en-US")>
```

You could set this property via the Assembly Information dialog box from the Application tab in My Project. With this step, all assembly level violations were fixed. Now it is time to solve code-level violations. The CA1823 violation suggests there is a field named `CustomField` that is never used and because of this, should be removed to improve performance. Now, remove the following line of code:

```
Private CustomField As String
```

The next step is to solve three CA1709 violations, which are all about members naming. We need to replace the first letter of the `doubleSum` method with the uppercase and the first letter of both arguments with lowercase. This is translated in code as follows:

```
Public Function DoubleSum(ByVal firstValue As Double,
                          ByVal secondValue As Double) As Double
```

NAMING CONVENTIONS

Naming conventions were discussed in Chapter 7, "Class Fundamentals." Refer to that chapter for details about methods, method arguments, and properties.

There is another naming convention violation to be fixed on the `customResult` property that must be replaced with `CustomResult`. The last required fix is on performance (CA1822 violation). The code analysis tool determines that the `DoubleSum` method never invokes the class constructor; therefore, it suggest to mark the method as `Shared` or to invoke the constructor. In this particular situation, the method can be marked as `Shared` like this:

```
Public Shared Function DoubleSum(ByVal firstValue As Double,
                    ByVal secondValue As Double) As Double
```

In this particular case, we do not need an instance method. For your convenience, all edits are available in Listing 55.2 (except for assembly level edits).

LISTING 55.2   Fixing Errors Reported by the Code Analysis Tool

```
<CLSCompliant(True)>
Public Class HelperClass

    'Private CustomField As String

    Public Property CustomResult As String

    Public Shared Function Sum(ByVal firstValue As Double,
                    ByVal secondValue As Double) As Double
        Return firstValue + secondValue
    End Function
End Class
```

If you run the code analysis tool again, you can notice that only the CA1020 design rule is still reported (the one on merging types into an existing namespace we decided not to fix due to our particular scenario). The code analysis tool is a helpful instrument, especially if you are a libraries developer. Microsoft has a Code Analysis Team with a blog where you can find more information at http://blogs.msdn.com/fxcop. Remember you can easily retrieve detailed information on violation errors and fixes directly from within Visual Studio.

Calculating Code Metrics

Code metrics is an interesting tool that analyzes a project or a solution and provides results about the ease of maintainability according to specific indexes. To use the tool, go to the Analyze menu by selecting the **Calculate Code Metrics** command or right-clicking the project name in Solution Explorer and then selecting the same-named command. The tool calculates code metrics according to the indexes summarized in Table 55.2.

TABLE 55.2   Code Metrics Analyzed Indexes

Index	Description
Maintainability index	A percentage value indicates ease of maintainability for the selected project or solution. A higher value indicates the project is well structured and easily maintainable.
Cyclomatic complexity	A percentage value indicates complexity of loops, nested loops, and nested conditional blocks, such as nested For..Next loops, Do..Loop loops, or If..End If nested blocks. A higher value indicates you should consider refactoring your code to decrease loop complexity because this leads to difficult maintainability.
Depth of inheritance	Indicates the inheritance level for classes in the project. The result shows the report for the class with the highest inheritance level. A higher value indicates it might be difficult finding problems in a complex inheritance hierarchy.
Class coupling	Calculates how many references to classes there are from method parameters and return values, local variables, and other implementations. A higher value indicates code is difficult to reuse, and you should consider revisiting your code for better maintainability.
Lines of code	Just a statistic value. It returns the number of IL code affected by the analysis.

To understand how it works, in Visual Studio 2012 open the **SnippetCompilerVSPackage** sample project described in the previous chapter. Next, run the Code Metrics tool by selecting the Analyze, Calculate Code Metrics **for solution** command. After a few seconds, you get the report shown in Figure 55.4.

Hierarchy ▲	Maintainability Index	Cyclomatic Complexity	Depth of Inheritance	Class Coupling	Lines of Code
▲ SnippetCompiler (Debug)	83	36	9	58	81
▲ {} AlessandroDelSole.SnippetCompiler	83	36	9	58	81
▷ GuidList	96	2	1	1	2
▷ MyControl	76	27	9	32	59
▷ MyToolWindow	73	1	3	5	5
▷ PkgCmdIDList	100	1	1	0	1
▷ SnippetCompilerPackage	71	5	2	25	14

FIGURE 55.4   Calculating code metrics for the specified project.

As you can see from the report, the project has a maintainability index of 83, which is quite good. Values from 80 to 100 are the best range for maintainability. Visual Studio shows a green symbol if the index is good or a red one if the maintainability index is poor. You can expand the **SnippetCompiler** item to see how the global result is subdivided for each class and for each class member. The global Cyclomatic Complexity index is 36, which is a reasonable number for our kind of project. Depth of Inheritance index is 9, which is also reasonable, meaning one or more class is inheriting from another class that inherits from another one (the third one is `System.Object`). This is an absolutely acceptable value in this particular scenario, especially because it involves a user control that, by its nature, has a deep inheritance hierarchy. The Class Coupling index is a little too high. It is determined by the `SnippetCompilerPackage` class, so this class has a lot of references to other classes. Particularly, if you expand this class you can notice the problem is the `Initialize` method that makes calls to a lot of objects. Obviously, not necessarily a high index indicates problems. In this code example, a high value is acceptable because all invocations are required to make the Visual Studio package work. However, in a reusable class library, a high value should need attention and code refactoring.

EXPORTING TO EXCEL

If you need to elaborate the code metrics results, you can export the analysis report to Microsoft Excel. This can be accomplished with the **Open List in Excel** button on the Code Metrics Result tool window.

55

Code Clone Detection

It is common to have an application that is under development for a long time. In this kind of situation, you might have millions of lines of code and you might forget you had already written a procedure or code snippet to solve a particular problem. So you create a duplicate. Visual Studio 2012 introduces a new tool called Code Clone Detection with the goal of helping developers find code snippets that are equal or very similar. To understand how this new tool works, open the SnippetCompiler project created in the previous chapter. Then enter the MyControl.xaml.vb code file and create a make a copy of the `Compile` method, rename the copy as `CompileCloned`. When ready, select **Analyze, Analyze Solution For Code Clones**. Visual Studio starts searching for cloned code and the result is shown in the Code Clone Analysis Result window, which is represented in Figure 55.5.

Visual Studio will group code clones by their relevance and will show the number of clones for each group, including the line numbers that have been detected as cloned. If you pass with the mouse pointer over an item, a tooltip shows an excerpt of the code. As you can see in this case, Visual Studio shows the Exact Match message because clones are exactly the same. Of course, Visual Studio is powerful enough to identify clones of code snippets too. To demonstrate this, rename some variables in the `CompileCloned` method and rearrange variable declarations. If you run the Code Clone Detection tool again, you will see that Visual Studio still recognizes clones, but this time the message is Strong Match. This means the clones are not exactly the same but are very similar (see Figure 55.6).

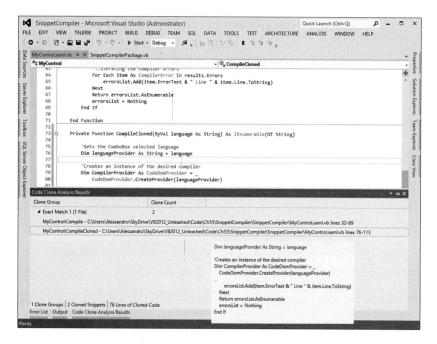

FIGURE 55.5   Finding exact code clones.

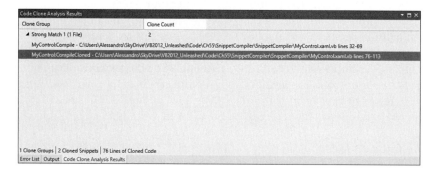

FIGURE 55.6   Finding similar code clones.

If you select two or more clones in the results window and right-click the selection, you can click the Compare command to have a visual comparison of code clones as demonstrated in Figure 55.7.

As you can see, the IDE highlights with different colors the lines of code it has recognized as changed if compared to the original code. Following is a list of useful information about code detection:

▶ Visual Studio can find clones only longer than 10 lines of code.

▶ Type declarations are not analyzed, only methods and properties definitions.

▶ Because code clones often results from copying some code from a location to another one, the tool discovers additions of lines, deletions, and rename actions.

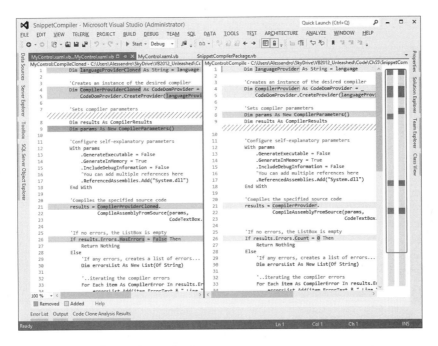

FIGURE 55.7   Comparing code clones.

In this chapter, you saw an example of code clone inside the same code file, but the tool searches throughout the entire solution. This tool is particularly useful for code refactoring and when updating the code due to a long development time.

Profiling Applications

Performances are a fundamental aspect in development. An application with slow performances can discourage customers, even if it has the coolest user interface or features. Visual Studio offers an integrated profiling tool that uses the WPF-based user interface of Visual Studio while also offering great organization for the collected information layout. To understand how the profiler works, we need a test project. Now, create a new console application in Visual Basic. The best way for understanding how the profiler can improve your productivity is to consider the simple example of strings concatenation both using `String` objects and `StringBuilder` ones. In the main module of the console application, write this simple code:

```
Module Module1

    Sub Main()
        ConcatenationDemo()
```

```
        Console.ReadLine()
    End Sub

    Sub ConcatenationDemo()

        Dim testString As String = String.Empty

        For i = 0 To 100000
            testString += "I love VB 2012"
        Next
    End Sub

End Module
```

The preceding code creates a big concatenation of `string` objects. To analyze performance, we now need to start the profiler. Select the **Analyze, Launch Performance Wizard** command. This launches the step-by-step procedure for setting up the profiler running against your project. Figure 55.8 shows the first dialog box in the wizard, where you can select the most appropriate profiling technique according to your needs.

FIGURE 55.8   Selecting the profiling technique.

There are several available profiling modes, which are described in Table 55.3.

TABLE 55.3   Available Profiling Modes

Mode	Description
CPU Sampling	Analyzes performances at predetermined intervals for monitoring CPU usage. This is the recommended mode for applications that use few resources. It collects less information, but it consumes less system resources.
Instrumentation	Collects complete information on the application performances injecting specific testing code. It is suggested for long-running applications and processes and consumes more system resources.
.NET Memory Allocation	Analyzes memory allocation performances.
Resource contention data (concurrency)	Analyzes how multithreaded application consumes resources and their performances.

Leave unchanged the default CPU-sampling option and click **Next**. The second dialog box allows selecting the executable to be analyzed. As you can see from Figure 55.9, you can choose one of the executables resulting from the current solution or an external executable. Select the current executable (the default option) and continue.

FIGURE 55.9   Selecting the executable to be analyzed.

The last dialog box in this wizard is just a summary. Uncheck the one check box available so the Profiler will not be launched when you click **Finish** (see Figure 55.10).

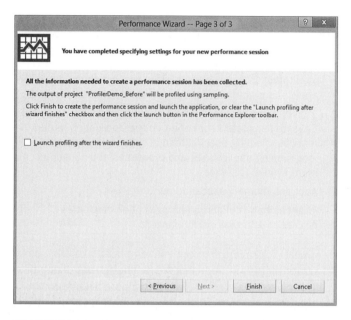

FIGURE 55.10   Setting up the Profiler completed.

You might want to leave the flag on the check box to automatically launch the Profiler if the default settings are okay for you, but in this particular scenario we need to make a couple of manual adjustments. When the wizard shuts down, the Performance Explorer tool window appears in the IDE. Because the sample application does not stress the CPU intensively, we need to set a smaller value for the CPU Sampling intervals. To accomplish this, follow these steps:

1. In the Performance Explorer window, right-click the **ProfilerDemo_Before** item.

2. Select the **Properties** command from the popup menu.

3. In the ProfilerDemo_Before Property Pages dialog box, select the **Sampling** node on the left and then replace the default value in the Sampling Interval text box with **120000**. This will let the profiler collect data at smaller intervals of CPU clock cycles. This small value is appropriate for small pieces of code like the current example, but you could leave unchanged the default value in real-world applications.

4. Click **OK** to close the dialog box and then right-click the **ProfilerDemo_Before** item in Performance Explorer. Finally, click Start Profiling from the pop-up menu. This will launch the Profiler.

If it is the first time you run the Profiler Visual Studio, it requires your permission for upgrading driver credentials to let the Profiler access system resources for monitoring purposes. Give your permission when the appropriate dialog box appears. Visual Studio runs your application with an instance of the Profiler attached. During all the application lifetime, Visual Studio will look like Figure 55.11, showing a work-in-progress message.

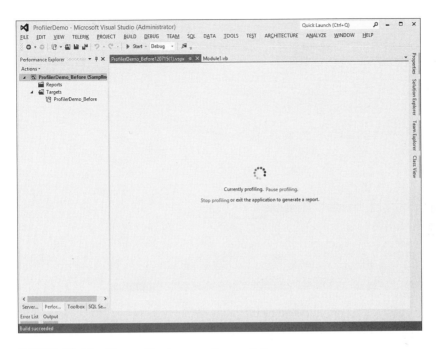

FIGURE 55.11   The profiler is currently running.

The application will be analyzed unless you terminate it. The profiler monitors performances at specific intervals to collect detailed information. When ready, close the application. This detaches the profiler instance. The profiler will now generate a report about the analysis. Figure 55.12 shows the report.

On the top of the report is a graph showing the CPU usage at monitored intervals. In the center of the screen is the **Hot Path** summary, which shows the most resources consuming function calls and their hierarchy. The analyzed executable has a global impact of 100%, which is a high value and can be negative for performances. Notice how the ConcatenationDemo method makes invocations to String.Concat. This is the function doing the most individual work, as evidenced in the Hot Path view and in the Functions Doing Most Individual Work graph. It has a 99.95% impact meaning there is some work to do to improve performances. By default, the profiler report shows results for your code, but not for code invoked at a lower level by and within the CLR. Fortunately, you can also analyze deeper function calls by clicking the **Show all code** link in the upper right. Figure 55.13 shows how behind the scenes the sample code invokes the System.String. wstrcpy system function that also has a high impact.

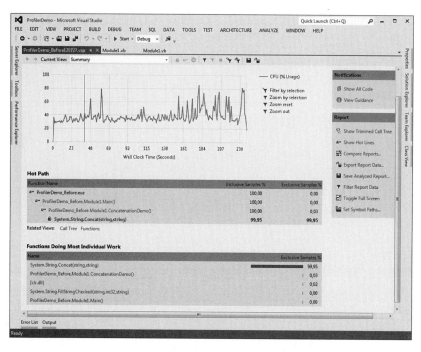

FIGURE 55.12   The analysis report produced by the profiler.

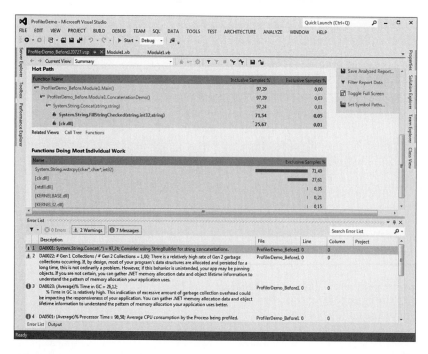

FIGURE 55.13   The Profiler can show system calls and their resource consumption.

The **Current View** combo box enables viewing lots of other useful information, such as processes involved in profiling, function details, lines of code most consuming, and marks. For marks, you can check out intervals and related CPU usage percentage, as shown in Figure 55.14.

FIGURE 55.14   Checking intervals and CPU usage.

The report is saved as a .vsp file, which can be useful for later comparisons. You can export the report to Microsoft Excel or as XML data (**Export Report Data** command). There is other good news. If you check out the Error List window (see Figure 55.13), you notice a warning message saying the invocation to `String.Concat` has a very high impact and you should consider using a `StringBuilder` for string concatenations. Therefore, in several cases Visual Studio can detect the problem and provide the appropriate suggestions to fix it. Following this suggestion, replace the application code as follows:

```
Module Module1

    Sub Main()
        ConcatenationDemo()
        Console.ReadLine()
    End Sub


    Sub ConcatenationDemo()
```

```
    Dim testString As New Text.StringBuilder

    For i = 0 To 100000
        testString.Append("I love VB 2012")
    Next
    End Sub
End Module
```

Now follow the same steps described before about setting the value for the CPU Sampling clock cycles to 120000 for the current project. Then run the Profiler again via the **Analyze, Profiler, Start Profiling** command. You will immediately notice that your edit will dramatically speed up the application execution. And after a few seconds, Visual Studio 2012 generates a new report, represented in Figure 55.15.

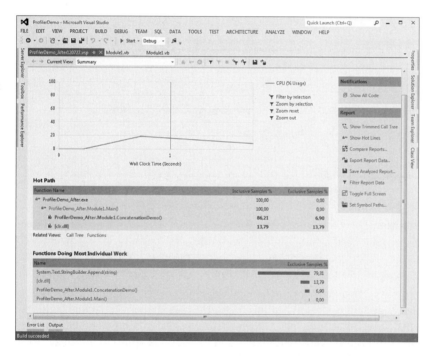

FIGURE 55.15   The new report after code improvements.

The usage of `StringBuilder` reduced the amount of CPU usage from 99.95% to 79.31% for the string concatenation operation. This means our edits improved the application performances, as demonstrated by the Error List window that is now empty. To get a better idea of what happened, you can compare the two generated reports. Right-click one of the available reports in the Performance Explorer tool window and select **Compare Performance Report**. In the appearing dialog box, just browse for the second report and click **OK**. Figure 55.16 shows the result of the comparison.

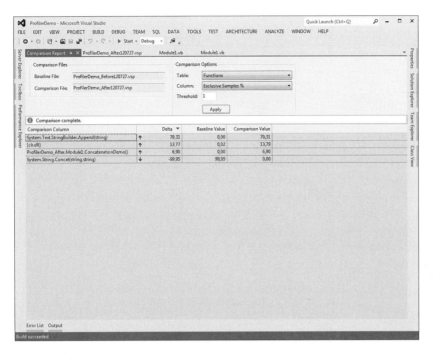

FIGURE 55.16   Comparing two performance reports.

The Delta column indicates the difference between the old value and the new one. The Baseline column indicates the value in the old analysis, whereas Comparison indicates the value in the new analysis. In this specific example, the bad string concatenation operation made by using the `String.Concat` function passed from a bad state to a good one due to the usage of a `StringBuilder` instance. The profiler is a good friend in your developer life and it is suggested to profile applications every time you can. The Visual Studio 2012 profiler offers the opportunity of profiling multithreaded applications, which is useful against parallel programming techniques.

Profiling External Executables

The Visual Studio profiler is not limited to solutions opened in the IDE, but it can be successfully used for profiling standalone executables. With regard to this, the profiler not only allows analyzing .NET applications, it also allows profiling applications built on the Win32 architecture. To demonstrate how this works, close the solution opened in Visual Studio (if any) ensuring nothing is available in Solution Explorer. Now start the Performance Wizard following the steps shown in the previous section until you get the result shown in Figure 55.8. The next step is selecting the **An executable (.EXE file)** option. When this is selected, you need to specify an executable to analyze. Just for demo purposes, select the executable generated in the previous example. Figure 55.17 shows how to accomplish this.

FIGURE 55.17   Selecting a standalone executable.

After completing this wizard, Visual Studio launches the specified executable with an instance of the profiler attached. When completed, Visual Studio generates a report, as shown in the previous section. In this particular case, you get nothing but the same profiling results with it being substantially the same application. In all other cases, you get specific analysis results for the selected executable. The Error List continues to show warning or error messages related to the application performance providing the appropriate suggestions when available. Of course, improving performance requires having the source code for the executable analyzed.

Historical Debugging with IntelliTrace

EDITION NOTE

The IntelliTrace debugger is available only with the Visual Studio 2012 Ultimate edition.

One of the most important tools in Visual Studio 2012 is IntelliTrace, initially known as the historical debugger. This tool was first introduced with Visual Studio 2010 and can improve your debugging experience because it can record and navigate every event occurring during the application lifetime, such as events and failures including information on specific threads. IntelliTrace is fully integrated with the code editor and with the rest of the IDE functionalities, such as Call Stack and Locals tool windows so it can provide a complete debugging environment. The tool is capable of recording (to a file, too) and debugging the following:

▶ Application events, such as user interface events or application exceptions

▶ Playback debugging, which allows deep debugging over specific events occurred before and after a particular code block

▶ Unit test failures

▶ Load test failures and build acceptances test

▶ Manual tests

In this section, you learn how to use IntelliTrace to debug application events, exceptions, and unit test failures. Before showing IntelliTrace in action, it is a good idea to set its options in Visual Studio.

IntelliTrace Options

There are many options for customizing IntelliTrace's behavior. You set its options via the usual **Tools, Options** command and then selecting the IntelliTrace item. Figure 55.18 demonstrates this.

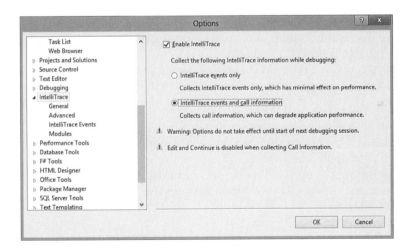

FIGURE 55.18   Setting general options for IntelliTrace.

IntelliTrace is enabled by default. The default behavior is that IntelliTrace will collect events only, but for this discussion select **IntelliTrace Events and Call Information** to get complete information on the code calls, too. This kind of monitoring is the most expensive in terms of system resources and should be used only when necessary. It offers a high-level view of what happens during the application lifetime. You have deep control over application events that IntelliTrace can keep track of. Select the **IntelliTrace Events** item. You see a list of .NET elements, such as ADO.NET, Data Binding, and Threading. For each of them you can specify particular events you want to be traced. For example, the Gesture events collection enables specifying user interface events such as button clicks, shown in Figure 55.19.

FIGURE 55.19   Selecting events to be tracked by IntelliTrace.

The Advanced and Modules items enable you to respectively specify locations and size for logs and which .NET modules must be tracked other than the current application. For this demonstration, leave the default settings unchanged. At this point, we need a sample application to see IntelliTrace in action.

Creating a Sample Application

The goal of this section is to illustrate how IntelliTrace can save you time by tracking events and exceptions with detailed information that can help you to understand what the problem is. According to this, creating a client WPF application can be a good example. To demonstrate both application events and exceptions, we can place a button that invokes a method attempting to open a file that does not exist. After creating a new WPF project named (IntelliTraceDemoApp) with Visual Basic, in the XAML code editor, write the code shown in Listing 55.3.

LISTING 55.3   Setting Up the User Interface for the Sample Application

```
<Window x:Class="MainWindow"
    xmlns="http://schemas.microsoft.com/winfx/2006/xaml/presentation"
    xmlns:x="http://schemas.microsoft.com/winfx/2006/xaml"
    Title="MainWindow" Height="350" Width="525">
    <Grid>
        <Grid.RowDefinitions>
            <RowDefinition />
            <RowDefinition />
        </Grid.RowDefinitions>
        <Button Name="OpenFileButton" Width="100" Height="50"
                Content="Open file" Grid.Row="0"/>
```

```
        <TextBox IsReadOnly="True" Name="FileTextBox"
                Grid.Row="1"/>
    </Grid>
</Window>
```

On the Visual Basic code-behind side, write the code shown in Listing 55.4, which handles the Button.Click event and tries to open a text file.

LISTING 55.4   Writing the Failing Visual Basic Code Before Running IntelliTrace

```
Class MainWindow

    Private Sub OpenFileButton_Click(ByVal sender As System.Object,
                                ByVal e As System.Windows.RoutedEventArgs) _
                                Handles OpenFileButton.Click


        Me.FileTextBox.Text = OpenFile()
    End Sub

    'Just for demo purposes
    'Consider dialogs implementation in real life apps
    Private Function OpenFile() As String

        'Attempting to open a fake file
        Return My.Computer.FileSystem.
                ReadAllText("C:\Alessandro.txt")

    End Function
End Class
```

Now that we have a sample project that will voluntarily fail at runtime, it is time to see how to catch problems using IntelliTrace.

Tracking Application Events and Exceptions with IntelliTrace

Run the demo application and click the button to cause an exception. The application breaks because the specified file is not found. The IntelliTrace tool window appears inside Visual Studio 2012, showing a list of events you can see in Figure 55.20.

FILTERING RESULTS

You can filter information by category and by thread. Use the upper combo box to select which kind of events category you want to check out (for example, Console, ASP.NET, ADO.NET, and so on) and which specific thread you want to get tracking information for, respectively.

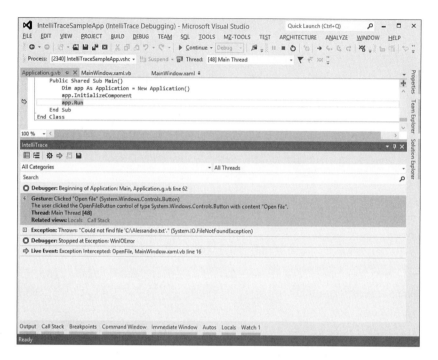

FIGURE 55.20   IntelliTrace in action, showing occurred events.

As you can see, IntelliTrace is not just a debugger showing errors or places where errors occurred. It is a powerful tool capable of tracking every single event occurring during the entire application lifetime—meaning that you could even use IntelliTrace to keep track of events without errors. In the current example, notice how the first tracked event is the application startup. There are other events tracked. Click the **Gesture** event to get information on this kind of event. IntelliTrace informs you the user clicked the `OpenFileButton` control, which is of type `System.Windows.Controls.Button` and whose content is `Open File`, also showing the thread description and ID. This is a predictable event, but as you can imagine you can keep track of all events. For instance, when data-binding is performed on a data-bound control, when the user selects an item from a `ListBox`, or when the application attempts to make a particular action. This can produce a huge amount of information you can analyze later. To get information on the exception thrown, click the exception item. Visual Studio shows the full error message and the line of code that caused the exception. When you click this item, the line of code will automatically highlight in the code editor for your convenience. IntelliTrace offers the capability of checking the entire tree of function calls (just in case you enable call information). In a few words, this feature keeps track of every single function call made by the runtime during the application lifetime. To show this, click the **Show Calls View** button in the IntelliTrace toolbar. Figure 55.21 shows an example, pointing to the place where the user clicked the button.

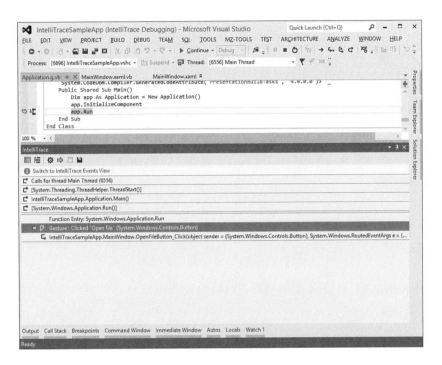

FIGURE 55.21   Showing functions call tree with IntelliTrace.

The sample figure shows the first function call that is a call for starting the main thread. The next functions are calls that the CLR makes to run the application and initialize it. The list is complete, also showing calls made during the rest of the application lifetime until it broke because of the exception. You can easily browse calls using the vertical scroll bar on the right.

Analyzing IntelliTrace Logs

When the application is running with the debugger attached, IntelliTrace records everything happening. (This is the reason you might notice a small performance decrease when you select the events and call recording option.) These recordings are saved to log files available in the `C:\ProgramData\Microsoft Visual Studio\11.0\TraceDebugging` folder and can be analyzed directly from within Visual Studio. To accomplish this, follow these steps:

1. In Windows Explorer, open the `C:\ProgramData\Microsoft Visual Studio\11.0\TraceDebugging` folder.

2. Double-click the last log file related to your application. Notice that log file names all begin with the application name, but you can open the most recent according to the date modified value.

55

Visual Studio opens the log file showing a result similar to what you see in Figure 55.22.

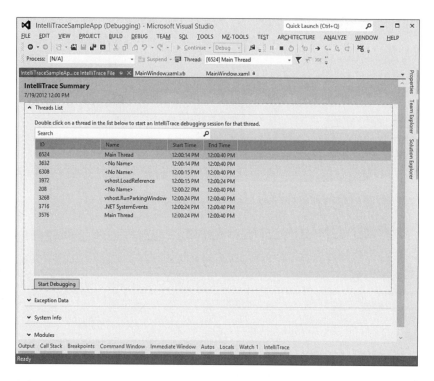

FIGURE 55.22   Analyzing IntelliTrace logs.

Logs contain lots of information. For example, you can understand at what time a specific thread was tracked and can start debugging from a given thread. In addition, information on exceptions will also be shown. You can check about system information and modules involved in the tracking process (this information is placed at the bottom of the page).

Using IntelliTrace for Unit Tests

IntelliTrace is not limited to tracking the application lifetime but can be used for unit tests and understanding what is behind failures. This particular scenario is discussed in Chapter 56, "Testing Code with Unit Tests, Test-Driven Development, and Code Contracts," which provides an overview of unit testing and test-driven development.

Generating Dependency Graphs

Another interesting tool in Visual Studio 2012 is the Dependency Graph generation. This feature enables you to generate a WPF-based, graphical browsable view of dependencies between objects in your projects. Dependency graphs can be generated at assembly level (including all types), namespace level (including only types from a given namespace), or at class level. To demonstrate this feature, create a new console project and add the following items:

- An Entity Data Model mapping the `Customers`, `Orders` and `Order_Details` tables from the Northwind database (see Chapter 26, "Introducing ADO.NET Entity Framework," for a recap).

- A new class named `Helper`, with the purpose of offering a simple method that returns a collection of order details based on the order identifier. The code for this class is shown in Listing 55.5.

LISTING 55.5   Demo Class to Be Mapped into the G Graph

```
Imports System.Data.Objects

Public Class Helper

    Public Shared Function GetOrderDetails(ByRef context As NorthwindEntities,
                            ByVal orderID As Integer) As _
                            ObjectQuery(Of Order_Detail)

        Dim result = From det In context.Order_Details
                Where det.Order.OrderID = orderID
                Select det

        Return CType(result, Global.System.Data.Objects.
                ObjectQuery(Of Global.DependencyGraphDemo.Order_Detail))
    End Function
End Class
```

Now select the **Architecture, Generate dependency graph, For Solution** command. After a few seconds, the new graph will be available inside Visual Studio 2012. You can then expand items and check for their dependencies with other objects, as represented in Figure 55.23.

To understand items mapping, you can check out the legend. To show complete dependencies information, right-click the graph and select the Show Advanced Selection command. This launches the Selection tool window where you can select one or more objects to be investigated and additional objects to be analyzed such as public or private properties. Figure 55.23 shows public properties dependencies from all classes in the project. For example, the `NorthwindEntities` class has dependencies with the `Helper.GetOrderDetails` method because this one receives an argument of type `NorthwindEntities`. The dependency graphs are flexible and can be exported to XPS documents or to images (right-click the graph for additional options).

55

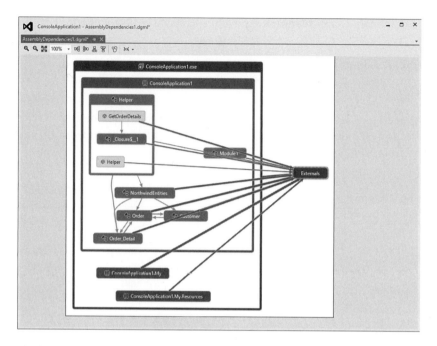

FIGURE 55.23   The newly generated assembly-level dependency graph.

Summary

This chapter covered some important analysis tools available in Visual Studio 2012 Professional, Premium, and Ultimate, which are necessary for improving applications' quality. You discovered how to analyze code for compliance with Microsoft coding rules, required especially when you produce reusable class libraries. Then you saw how to check for code maintainability using the Code Metrics tool. Next, you learned about a new tool called Code Clones Detection that helps you find duplicate code. In the second part of the chapter you were informed about the integrated Profiler that simplifies checking for performance issues and also provides IDE suggestions. You also saw different usages of the Profiler, including standalone executables. The chapter focused on the most interesting addition in Visual Studio 2012—the IntelliTrace debugger. Information was provided on using this tool to understand how to keep track of all application events and exceptions during the entire application lifetime, as well as showing how to analyze summary logs within Visual Studio. Finally, you got an overview of another new addition, the Dependency Graph generation, which provides a graphical view of dependencies at assembly, namespace, and class levels.

CHAPTER 56

Testing Code with Unit Tests, Test-Driven Development, and Code Contracts

When you purchase new software, you expect that such software works. I'm pretty sure you don't like applications you buy to cause unexpected crashes or errors due to apparently unhandled situations. The same is true for users purchasing your software or for colleagues in your company performing their daily work through your applications, so you need to pay particular attention to how your code works. Although implementing error handling routines is fundamental, another important step in application development is testing code. Testing enables you to check for code blocks' correct behavior under different situations, and it should be as deep as possible. In big development teams, testers play an important role, so they need to have good tools for successfully completing their work. In this chapter, you learn about the Visual Studio tools for testing code, starting from unit tests until the new Code Contracts library, passing through the Test Driven Development approach. You also see how such tooling can be successfully used even if you are a single developer.

Testing Code with Unit Tests

Unit tests enable you to test code portions outside the application context to check whether they work correctly so that testing is abstracted from the application. Typically, you create a test project in which classes and methods encapsulate and isolate the original code so that you can test it in a kind of isolated sandbox without editing the source project. Visual Studio 2012 is the ideal environment for performing unit tests, so this section explains how you can accomplish this important task. In this section, you learn how to create unit tests for existing code. This is necessary to give you the basics for learning Test Driven Development in the next section of this chapter, where you instead learn how to start from writing unit tests to moving the code to the actual project.

UNIT TESTS AND WINDOWS 8 DEVELOPMENT

In this chapter we discuss unit testing with desktop applications, but you can use unit testing to test the code you write in developing Windows 8-style apps. For this particular scenario, the MSDN documentation has a specific page available at http://msdn. microsoft.com/en-us/library/windows/apps/hh441482(v=vs.110).aspx

---

Creating Unit Tests

First, you need some code to test. If you already have experience with unit testing in Visual Studio 2010, you will notice some differences in Visual Studio 2012. In particular, you can no longer right-click a method name to create a unit test via the Create unit test command, which has been removed. Now you need some manual work, as you discover soon. Imagine you have a `Rectangle` class that exposes methods for math calculations on rectangles perimeter and area. Thus, create a new class library and name it **UnitTestDemo**; then rename Class1.vb as **Rectangle.vb** and write the following code:

```
Class Rectangle

    Shared Function CalculatePerimeter(ByVal sideA As Double,
                                ByVal sideB As Double) As Double
        Return (sideA * 2) + (sideB * 2)
    End Function

    Shared Function CalculateArea(ByVal sideA As Double,
                                ByVal sideB As Double) As Double
        Return sideA * sideB
    End Function
End Class
```

Imagine you want to test both methods to check if they work correctly but inside an isolated environment, abstracted from the original project. The first thing you need to do is add to the solution a so-called Test Project, which enables the Visual Studio's testing framework. To accomplish this, follow these steps:

1. Select **File, Add, New Project.**

2. In the New Project dialog box, expand the **Visual Basic** node and then select the **Test** element. See Figure 56.1 for a reference.

3. Select the **Unit Test Project** template and then specify a name for the test
project; finally click **OK** (for the current example, you can leave the default name
unchanged).

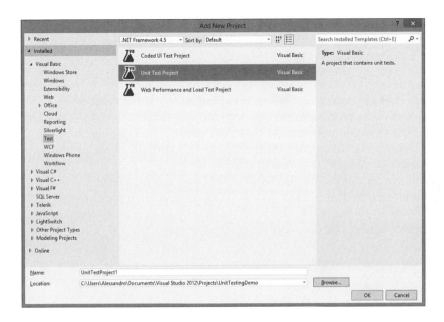

FIGURE 56.1   Creating a new test project.

CODED UI TESTS AND WEB PERFORMANCE AND LOAD TESTS

As you can see from Figure 56.1, Visual Studio 2012 also offers support for Coded UI
tests and the Web performance and Load tests. The first kind of test enables you to test
portions of the user interface to determine whether it behaves correctly and validate user
interface controls. The second kind simulates an environment in which multiple users
concurrently access a web application to determine if this responds correctly to various
levels of usage. Both are related to specific development scenarios so they will not be
covered in this chapter—the goal is providing information on writing unit tests that are
independent from the technology. The MSDN documentation provides detailed information
that you can check out for further studies. The documentation for Coded UI Tests is available at http://msdn.microsoft.com/en-us/library/dd286726.aspx, and the documentation
for web performance and Load tests is available at http://msdn.microsoft.com/en-us/
library/dd293540.aspx.

When Visual Studio finishes generating the new project, you notice a simple test class
called UnitTest1 and that looks like the following code:

```
Imports System.Text
Imports Microsoft.VisualStudio.TestTools.UnitTesting

<TestClass()> Public Class UnitTest1

    <TestMethod()> Public Sub TestMethod1()
    End Sub

End Class
```

The `Microsoft.VisualStudio.TestTools.UnitTesting` imported namespace provides support for the built-in unit test framework. Unit tests are methods contained inside a test class. Such a class must be decorated with the `TestClass` attribute, and all the unit tests contained in the class must be decorated with the `TestMethod` attribute. Both attributes make code recognizable by the IDE as code that must be tested. Now copy the code of the `Rectangle` class into the current code editor window (to avoid adding a reference to the first project), and then rename the `UnitTest1` class `RectangleTest`. You must now write the test logic and create a test method for each original method you want to test. Listing 56.1 shows an example of how you can write a simple test logic.

LISTING 56.1   Writing a Test Class with Test Methods

```
<TestClass()> Public Class RectangleTest

    '''<summary>
    '''A test for CalculateArea
    '''</summary>
    <TestMethod()> _
    Public Sub CalculateAreaTest()
        Dim sideA As Double = 10
        Dim sideB As Double = 20
        Dim expected As Double = 2000
        Dim actual As Double
        actual = Rectangle.CalculateArea(sideA, sideB)
        Assert.AreEqual(expected, actual)

    End Sub

    '''<summary>
    '''A test for CalculatePerimeter
    '''</summary>
    <TestMethod()> _
    Public Sub CalculatePerimeterTest()
        Dim sideA As Double = 10
        Dim sideB As Double = 20
```

```
        Dim expected As Double = 60
        Dim actual As Double
        actual = Rectangle.CalculatePerimeter(sideA, sideB)
        Assert.AreEqual(expected, actual)
    End Sub
End Class
```

Test methods cannot be shared, and they must be public, accept no parameter, and return no value. This is the reason values must be initialized within method bodies. The idea of unit testing is comparing the expected result with the actual result of an action, and this can be done through static methods of the `Microsoft.VisualStudio.TestTools.UnitTesting.Assert` class. Table 56.1 summarizes the most important methods from the `Assert` class (if you examine the class with the Object Browser tool and the IntelliSense, you can get further information, such as about the available overloads and method parameters). Notice that the first method voluntarily causes an error, to demonstrate how unit testing works. The expected value is in fact greater than it should be. You are now ready to run both unit tests.

TABLE 56.1   Methods from the `Assert` Class

Method Name	Description
`AreEqual`	Checks that two objects are equal by using the equality operator. The method throws an exception if objects are not equal.
`AreNotEqual`	Checks that two objects are not equal. The method throws an exception if objects are equal.
`AreSame`	Checks that two object variables refer to the same object and throws an exception if they refer to different objects.
`Fail`	Causes the assertion to fail without checking any conditions.
`Inconclusive`	Used to tell the assertion is not defined yet.
`IsFalse`	Checks that the specified condition is false and throws an error if it is true.
`IsInstanceOfType`	Checks that the specified object is an instance of a given type and throws an error if the type is not found in the object's inheritance hierarchy.
`IsNotInstanceOfType`	Checks that the specified object is not an instance of a given type and throws an error if the type is found in the object's inheritance hierarchy.
`IsNotNull`	Checks that an object is not null and throws an error if it is null.
`IsNull`	Checks that an object is null and throws an error if it is not null.
`IsTrue`	Checks that the specified condition is true and throws an error if it is false.

Running Unit Tests

Visual Studio 2012 introduces the Test Explorer tool window, which is the environment where you run and analyze unit tests' execution. This window is automatically shown if you run unit tests through one of the commands from the Test menu or when you right-click the code editor and select Run tests. It can also be launched manually by selecting Test, Windows, Test Explorer. To see such a tool window in action, right-click the code editor and select **Run tests**. This command runs all unit tests in the project, but you can make a different choice with commands in the Test menu. When all the unit tests are completed, the Test Explorer tool window shows a report about test success or failures. Figure 56.2 shows how such a window looks for the current example.

FIGURE 56.2   Viewing unit test results.

Notice how the `CalculateAreaTest` method failed while `CalculatePerimeterTest` succeeded. You can click the failed method to get details on the error so that you can fix it. In this case, the equality check failed because the method returned a result different from the expected one.

NOTE ON FIXING ERRORS

In a typical real-life scenario, you will not edit the expected result to make a unit test work; you will instead fix errors in the code. The example proposed in this chapter is a demo scenario, and its purpose is explaining how unit tests work. This is why here you are about to fix the expected result, but in real-world applications the expected result will remain unvaried.

In the `CalculateAreaTest` method, replace the expected declaration as follows:

```
Dim expected As Double = 200
```

Now run both unit tests again. At this point, both tests pass because in both cases the expected value and actual value are equal, as demonstrated in Figure 56.3.

FIGURE 56.3   Both unit tests passed.

Enabling Code Coverage

Visual Studio enables you to get information on the amount of code that was subject to the actual test. This can be accomplished by using a feature known as Code Coverage. To see code coverage results, double-click a method name in Test Explorer. The Code Coverage Results window will show information on collected results. Figure 56.4 shows such results.

Hierarchy	Not Covered (Blocks)	Not Covered (% Blocks)	Covered (Blocks)	Covered (% Blocks)
▲ Alessandro_DELSOLEFISSO 2012-08-22 19_55_51.c...	6	40.00 %	9	60.00 %
▲ unittestproject1.dll	6	40.00 %	9	60.00 %
▲ {} UnitTestProject1	1	10.00 %	9	90.00 %
▲ Rectangle	0	0.00 %	4	100.00 %
CalculateArea(Double, Double)	0	0.00 %	2	100.00 %
CalculatePerimeter(Double, Double)	0	0.00 %	2	100.00 %
▷ RectangleTest	1	16.67 %	5	83.33 %
▷ {} UnitTestProject1.My	5	100.00 %	0	0.00 %

FIGURE 56.4   Examining Code Coverage Results.

You can expand the results to get information on the code coverage percentage for single members. For example, both test methods have a 100% coverage against a total 60% for the entire project. If you switch to the test code file, you see that Visual Studio automatically highlights lines of code that were subject to test.

Introducing Test Driven Development

Test Driven Development (TDD, or Test Driven Design) is a programming approach in which developers create applications by first writing unit tests and then writing the actual code after the unit test passes. This particular approach improves code writing because you ensure that it will work via unit tests, but it is also a life philosophy so that you need a change of mind when approaching TDD. TDD is structured into three main moments:

- ▶ **Red**—The developer generates a new unit test from scratch, so that it will typically fail. This is the reason it's called Red.

- ▶ **Green**—The developer focuses on writing code that makes the unit test work and pass. As you saw in the previous section, passing unit tests return a green result.

- ▶ **Refactor**—This is the moment in which the developer reorganizes code, moving it from the unit test to the actual code system in the application project, making the code clearer, and fixing it where necessary.

This chapter is not intended to be a deep discussion on TDD, but it is instead intended to be a guide to Visual Studio 2012 instrumentation for Test Driven Development. Particularly, you see how the Generate from Usage feature discussed in Chapter 17, "Creating Objects: Visual Tools and Portable Libraries," together with unit tests, is the main help you have in TDD with Visual Basic 2012.

Creating a Test Project

The first step in the Test Driven Development approach is creating a Test Project (close any currently opened projects) related to a project you are working on. By remembering the lesson learned in the previous section, follow these steps:

1. Create a new class library named **RectangleLibrary** and remove the Class1.vb default file.

2. Add a new test project to the solution. To accomplish this, select **File, Add, New project**, and then in the Visual Basic, Test folder, select the **Unit Test Project** template.

3. Rename the default class **RectangleTest.vb**. This is the place where you write and run unit tests.

Now imagine you want to test a `Rectangle` class exposing `Width` and `Height` properties and methods for math calculations such as the perimeter. Such class will be exposed by the actual project at the end of the TDD approach. You now need to test class and methods in the test project. As you already know, Visual Studio generates a test class and a test method for you; the code looks like the following:

```
Imports System.Text
Imports Microsoft.VisualStudio.TestTools.UnitTesting

<TestClass()> Public Class RectangleTest

    <TestMethod()> Public Sub TestMethod1()
    End Sub

End Class
```

You can delete the `TestMethod1` method, as unit tests are created from scratch in the next subsection. As a recap, it is worth mentioning that a test class is marked with the `Microsoft.VisualStudio.TestTools.UnitTesting.TestClass` attribute. Now you have a place where you can write your unit tests.

Creating Unit Tests

As you can recap from the "Testing Code with Unit Testing" section, unit tests are methods enabling tests against small, isolated portions of code. To be recognized as unit tests, such methods must be decorated with the `Microsoft.VisualStudio.TestTools.UnitTesting.TestMethod` attribute. Continuing our example and having the requirement of implementing a method for calculating the perimeter for rectangles, this is how the method stub appears:

```
<TestMethod()>
Sub CalculatePerimeter()
End Sub
```

Now go into the method body and write the following line:

```
Dim rect As New Rectangle
```

The `Rectangle` type is not defined yet, so Visual Studio underlines the declaration by throwing an error. Click the error option's pop-up button and click **Generate new type**, as shown in Figure 56.5.

This launches the Generate New Type dialog box, where you can select the Rectangle project in the Location combo box. See Figure 56.6 for details.

FIGURE 56.5   Choosing a correction option.

FIGURE 56.6   Generating a new `Rectangle` type.

WHY GENERATE A TYPE IN THE PRODUCTION PROJECT?

You might ask why the preceding example showed how to add the new type to the actual project instead of the test one. In a demo scenario like this, adding a new type to the test project would be useful, but in real life you might have dozens of new types to add. This can make moving all types from one project to another, including code edits, less productive. The illustrated approach keeps the benefits of TDD and offers a way of implementing types directly in the project that will actually use them.

Next, Visual Studio 2012 automatically imports the `RectangleLibrary` namespace so that you do not need to add it to the instance declaration. Now type the following line of code:

```
rect.Width = 150
```

The `Width` property is not exposed yet by the `Rectangle` class, so Visual Studio underlines it as an error. As for the class generation, click the error correction options and select the **Generate Property Stub for 'Width'** choice, as shown in Figure 56.7.

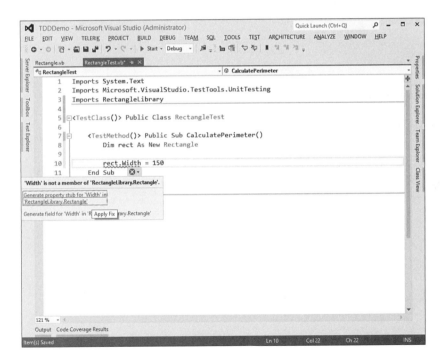

FIGURE 56.7   Generating a property stub.

This adds a property to the `Rectangle` class. Now write the following line of code and repeat the steps previously shown:

```
rect.Height = 100
```

Complete the method body by writing the following lines:

```
Dim expected = 500
Dim result = rect.CalculatePerimeter
Assert.AreEqual(expected, result)
```

You have an expected result (notice I'm using type inference) and an actual result returned by the `CalculatePerimeter` method. This method does not exist yet, so use the **Generate from Usage Feature** to add a new method stub to the `Rectangle` class. Run the unit test and it will fail as expected, being in the Red moment of TDD, as demonstrated in Figure 56.8.

FIGURE 56.8   Running the new unit test fails due to an exception.

The unit test fails because the current method definition for `CalculatePerimeter` is the following:

```
Function CalculatePerimeter() As Object
    Throw New NotImplementedException
End Function
```

So edit the method as follows, to make it return a more appropriate type and perform the required calculation:

```
Function CalculatePerimeter() As Integer
    Return (Width * 2) + (Height * 2)
End Function
```

Now run the unit test again and it will pass. You have thus successfully completed the Green phase of TDD, and you can now move to the final step—Refactor.

Refactoring Code

When your unit tests all pass, it is time to reorganize code. For example, if you take a look at the Rectangle class, you notice that the Generate from Usage Feature generated objects of type Integer. This is also why the CalculatePerimeter method has been forced to return Integer. Although correct, the most appropriate type for math calculations is Double. Moreover, you might want to consider writing a more readable code in the method body. After these considerations, the Rectangle class could be reorganized as follows:

```
Public Class Rectangle

    Public Property Width As Double
    Public Property Height As Double

    Public Function CalculatePerimeter() As Double

        Dim perimeter As Double = (Me.Height + Me.Width) * 2

        Return perimeter
    End Function
End Class
```

In this way you have working code that uses more appropriate types and is more readable. Before you run the unit test again, you need to make a slight modification to the CalculatePerimeter method body in the RectangleTest test class. In fact, because the code uses local type inference with numbers, the following line of code assumes that the return type is Integer:

```
Dim expected = 500
```

Actually, you refactored the code in the Rectangle class to return Double, so you need to explicitly declare this in the test method as follows:

```
Dim expected As Double = 500
```

Now you can run the unit test again and see that it passes. TDD is useful when you have a large number of unit tests, but in the current example you saw how to start from unit test and move code to production, instead of performing unit tests after you already wrote some code.

Understanding Code Contracts

Code Contracts is a library that was first introduced with the .NET Framework 4.0 and is offered by the `System.Diagnostics.Contract` namespace. It enables you to check, both at runtime and compile time, whether the code is respecting specified requirements. This is something that you will often hear about as *Design by contracts*. The idea is that code needs to respect specified contracts to be considered valid. There are different kinds of contracts, known as *preconditions* (what the application expects), *post-conditions* (what the application needs to guarantee), and *object invariants* (what the application needs to maintain). We cover all of them in the next subsections. It is important to understand some other concepts. Code contracts are a useful way for testing code behavior, and this can be accomplished both at runtime (*runtime checking*) and compile time (*static checking*). Runtime checking needs the code to be executed and is useful when you cannot predict some code values; for example, say the application needs the user to enter some values that will be then validated. You can use contracts for implementing validation rules. Static checking can be useful if you have hard-coded variable values and need to check if they are contract-compliant. Both types of checking can be also used together and can be set in the Visual Studio IDE as explained in the next subsections.

Setting Up the Environment

The Code Contracts library is part of the .NET Framework 4.5, so you do not need to install anything more to use it in code. Some components need to be installed separately to access contracts settings in the Visual Studio IDE. So, before continuing to read this chapter, go to the following address: http://msdn.microsoft.com/en-us/devlabs/dd491992. aspx. From the DevLab site, download the Code Contracts tools and proceed with the installation. When installed, you can access design-time settings for code contracts as now explained.

Setting Contracts Properties

You set code contracts properties by first opening My Project and then clicking the **Code Contracts** tab, as shown in Figure 56.9.

Notice how you can enable general settings, such as runtime checking and static checking, and specific settings for both profiles. Particularly, for runtime checking you should leave the default Full selection if you have both preconditions and post-conditions. If you want to enable static checking, too, for compile time contracts checking, by default the Check in background option is also selected. This enables the background compiler to check for contracts violations and send error messages to the Errors tool window. If this option is unselected, eventual error messages will be listed at the end of the build process.

TIP

If you remove the flag on Assert on Contract Failure, instead of an error dialog box showing details about the violation, the control will be returned to the Visual Studio code editor that will break at the line of code that violated the contract.

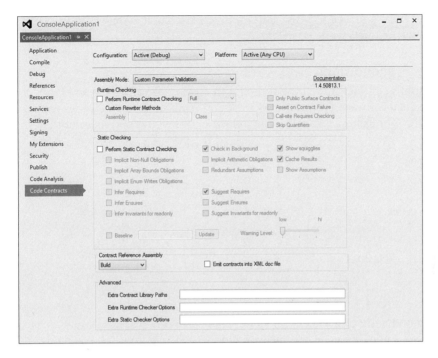

FIGURE 56.9   Accessing code contracts settings.

The next examples show both preconditions and post-conditions, so leave the default settings unchanged. Before getting hands on the code, let's examine the tools that enable Visual Studio to integrate and work with contracts.

Tools for Code Contracts

When you use code contracts, the first requirement is the System.Diagnostics.Contracts namespace, exposed by the Mscorlib.dll assembly. This is not enough to make your code use contracts. Although you never see this, Visual Studio invokes some command-line tools behind the scenes. This subsection provides basic information on these tools and their purpose.

The Binary Rewriter

As you know, when you compile a .NET executable, the file is made of metadata and Intermediate Language. When you use contracts, especially for runtime checking, the Intermediate Language within an executable needs to be modified to recognize contracts. Such edits are performed by the CCrewrite.exe tool that injects the appropriate code for contracts in the appropriate place into your assembly.

The Static Checker

The static checker is represented by the CCCheck.exe tool and provides Visual Studio the capability of performing static analyses and checking for contracts violations without the need of executing code; a typical scenario is the compilation process.

Now that you have basic knowledge of the code contracts system, it is time to write code and understand how contracts work.

Understanding Preconditions

You add preconditions contracts to tell the compiler that the code can be executed only if it respects the specified contract. Preconditions are useful replacements for custom parameters validation rules. For example, consider the following simple method that multiplies two numbers:

```
Function Multiply(ByVal first As Double,
                  ByVal second As Double) As Double

    If first < 0 Or second < 0 Then
        Throw New ArgumentNullException
    Else
        Return first * second
    End If
End Function
```

Inside the method body, the code checks for valid parameters; otherwise, it throws an exception. This is common, but code contracts provide a good way, too. The preceding method could be rewritten with code contracts as follows:

```
Function Multiply(ByVal first As Double,
            ByVal second As Double) As Double

    Contract.Requires(first > 0)
    Contract.Requires(second > 0)
    Return first * second
End Function
```

So, you just invoke the `Contract.Requires` method for evaluating a Boolean condition that will be accepted only when evaluated as `True`. Now consider the following `Rectangle` class:

```
Class Rectangle

    Property Width As Double
    Property Height As Double

    Function CalculatePerimeter() As Double
        Dim result = (Width * 2) + (Height * 2)

        Return result
    End Function
```

```
      Sub New(ByVal width As Double, ByVal height As Double)
          Me.Width = width
          Me.Height = height
      End Sub
End Class
```

The `CalculatePerimeter` instance method takes no arguments and performs calculations on instance properties, but it does not check for valid values. With regard to this, you can use the `Contract.Requires` method that specifies a condition enabling the code to be considered valid if such condition is evaluated as `True`. For example, consider the following reimplementation of the method:

```
Function CalculatePerimeter() As Double
    Contract.Requires(Me.Height > 0)
    Contract.Requires(Of ArgumentOutOfRangeException) _
            (Me.Width > 0)

    Dim result = (Width * 2) + (Height * 2)
    Return result
End Function
```

In this case the contract requires that the `Height` property is greater than zero; otherwise, a runtime error is thrown. You instead use `Contract.Requires(Of T)` when you want to throw a specific exception when the contract is violated. The previous example throws an `ArgumentOutOfRangeException` if the `Width` property is less than zero. Consider the following code that creates an instance of `Rectangle` but violates the contract:

```
Dim r As New Rectangle(0, 80)
Console.WriteLine(r.CalculatePerimeter)
```

When you run this code, the runtime throws an `ArgumentOutOfRageException`, as shown in Figure 56.10, due to an invalid `Width` value.

Preconditions are thus useful when you want to validate code elements before they are invoked or executed. The next subsection discusses post-conditions instead.

Post-Conditions

A post-condition is a contract that is checked after code is executed and is used to check the result of some code execution. Continuing with the previous example, you might want to check that the `CalculatePerimeter` method produces a value greater than zero before returning such result. This kind of post-condition is accomplished via the `Contracts.Ensures` method, as demonstrated in the following snippet:

```
Function CalculatePerimeter() As Double
    Contract.Ensures(Contract.Result(Of Double)() > 0)
    Dim result = (Width * 2) + (Height * 2)

    Return result
End Function
```

FIGURE 56.10 The exception thrown when the code violates a precondition.

Ensures invokes `Contract.Result(Of T)`. This is the representation of the code result, and T is nothing but the expected type, which in this case is `Double`. This line of code must be placed before the code is executed and the compiler can link the actual result with the contract evaluation.

EXCEPTIONAL POST-CONDITIONS

The `Contract` class also provides an `EnsuresOnThrow(Of TException)` method that checks for the condition only when the specified exception is thrown. This approach is discouraged, and you should use it only when you have complete understanding of what kinds of exceptions your method could encounter.

Old Values

You can refer to values as they existed at the beginning of a method by using the `Contract.OldValue(Of T)` method. For example, the following code ensures that a hypothetical value variable has been updated:

```
Contract.Ensures(value) = Contract.OldValue(value) + 1)
```

Invariants

Invariants are special contract that ensure an object is considered valid during all its lifetime. Invariant contracts are provided inside one method decorated with the `ContractInvariantMethod` attribute that affects all members in the enclosing class. Only one invariant method can be declared inside a class, and typically it should be marked as `Protected` to avoid risk of calls from clients. This method is by convention named `ObjectInvariant` (although not mandatory) and is used instead of preconditions and post-conditions. The following code snippet provides an example:

```
<ContractInvariantMethod()>
Protected Sub ObjectInvariant()
    Contract.Invariant(Me.Width > 0)
    Contract.Invariant(Me.Height > 0)
End Sub
```

This code establishes that during the entire lifetime of the `Rectangle` object, both the `Width` and `Height` properties must be greater than zero so that they can be considered in a valid state.

Assertions and Assumptions

The `Contract` class provides an `Assert` method that is used for verifying a condition at a particular point in the program execution. Typically, you use it as follows:

```
Contract.Assert(Width > 0)
```

Another method, named `Assume`, works exactly like `Assert` but is used when static verification is not sufficient to prove the condition you are attempting to check.

Contract Events

The `Contract` class exposes a `ContractFailed` event that is raised when a condition is violated and that you can handle to get detailed information. The following sample event handler shows how to collect violation information:

```
Private Sub Contract_ContractFailed(ByVal sender As Object,
                            ByVal e As ContractFailedEventArgs)
    Console.WriteLine("The following contract failed: {0}, {1}",
                e.Condition, e.FailureKind.ToString)
End Sub
```

The `ContractFailedEventArgs.Condition` property is a string storing the condition, and the `ContractFailedEventArgs.FailureKind` is an enumeration offering the failure kind (for example, `Precondition`, `Invariant`, and so on).

Summary

This chapter illustrated the Visual Studio instrumentation and libraries about testing applications. The first discussion was about unit testing, a technique used for checking whether code blocks work outside the application context, inside a sandbox. For this, you saw how test projects work and how to enable Code Coverage. The second discussion of the chapter was about Test Driven Development, a programming approach in which developers write their software by first writing unit tests. You saw Visual Studio 2012's support for TDD, with special regard of the Generate from usage feature. The final part of this chapter was dedicated to Code Contracts, a library inherited from the .NET Framework 4 that enables writing code in the *design-by-contract* fashion and that is supported by the `System.Diagnostics.Contracts` namespace and the `Contract` class.

APPENDIX A

Useful Resources and Tools for Visual Basic 2012

The Visual Basic 2012 language is an even more powerful version than its predecessors and enables you to access every feature and technology exposed by .NET Framework 4.5. But the Framework is a large technology, and the language has so many features that remembering everything is almost impossible. So, instead of remembering everything, it is important for you to know where to search for information, resources, and learning material. Moreover, Visual Studio 2012 is a powerful development environment that includes a plethora of tools to make your development experience great. There are some situations in which the IDE does not include particular features that are instead provided by third-party tools. This appendix gives you a number of Visual Basic resources inside the MSDN documentation and websites for you to bookmark in your Favorites. Also, this appendix provides a list of useful tools for you as a Visual Basic developer. They are all free tools, so you can enjoy their functionalities.

Visual Basic Resources in MSDN

Following are learning resources for Visual Basic 2012 inside the MSDN Library and websites:

The Visual Studio Developer Center–Visual Basic: The principal website from Microsoft dedicated to Visual Basic: http://msdn.microsoft.com/en-us/vstudio/hh388568.

Visual Basic "How Do I" videos: A portal where you can find a lot of videos illustrating programming techniques and usage of Microsoft technologies with Visual Basic: http://msdn.microsoft.com/en-us/vbasic/bb466226.aspx.

Visual Basic Code Samples: A sub-list of code samples from the MSDN Code Gallery specifically targeting the Visual Basic language: http://bit.ly/ObAnY6.

Asynchronous Programming Developer Center: A specific portal from MSDN where you can find resources about the new asynchronous programming patterns and related language syntax. This is available at: http://msdn.microsoft.com/en-us/vstudio/async.aspx

CodePlex, the famous website hosting open source projects (www.codeplex.com) where you can find complete applications written with Visual Basic, including source code.

Learn Visual Basic, a portal where you can find a list of tutorials covering a great number of Microsoft technologies with VB: http://msdn.microsoft.com/en-US/vstudio/hh388573.

Visual Basic MSDN Library, probably the most important reference for every Visual Basic developer, where you can find documentation, language reference, walkthroughs and examples: http://msdn.microsoft.com/library/dd831853.aspx.

.NET Framework Developer Center, the principal website for information on all .NET-based Microsoft technologies: http://msdn.microsoft.com/en-us/netframework/default.aspx.

Also don't forget to use search engines, which in most cases will be your best friends. Typically they will return the most accurate results if your search is performed by writing English strings.

Useful Developer Tools for Visual Basic

This section provides a list of free useful tools that will enrich your developer toolbox.

Coding Tools

In this section you can find a list of tools to improve your productivity in writing better code.

CodeRush Xpress from DevExpress is a free Visual Studio add-in that enhances the Visual Studio code editor by providing refactoring tools to write better, more-readable, and more-efficient code. If you used Refactor! Express in the past, CodeRush is its more powerful successor. You can find it at http://www.devexpress.com/Products/Visual_Studio_Add-in/CodeRushX/.

Code Snippet Editor is an open source tool written in Visual Basic for creating and exporting reusable code snippets with advanced functionalities in VB, C#, and XML languages via a comfortable graphical user interface. It is available at http://snippeteditor.codeplex.com.

Vsi Builder 2012 is a free extension from the author of this book that enables creating .Vsi packages for deploying code snippets, add-ins, and additional contents for Visual Studio. You can download it from http://VsiBuilder.codeplex.com.

P/Invoke Interop Assistant is an open source tool that lets you write P/Invokes in a better way: http://clrinterop.codeplex.com/.

Networking

One of the most famous tools in networking is **Fiddler**, which is a free Web debugging proxy that can log all http and https traffic between the computer and the Internet. Other than inspecting http traffic, Fiddler can set breakpoints and walk through incoming or outgoing data. You can find it at http://www.fiddler2.com/fiddler2/. Fiddler is particularly useful in debugging WCF services and WCF Data Services, other than requests coming from Web browsers such as Internet Explorer and Firefox.

Data Access

For data access tools, you can find **LINQPad** very useful. This is a free tool that provides advanced instrumentation for querying data sources and that can generate the necessary code using LINQ. Visual Basic is one of the supported languages. You can find it at http://www.linqpad.net. At the moment in which this appendix is being written, LINQPad supports .NET Framework 4.0 and so can be used with no problems against the new release of Visual Basic.

Diagnostics and Performance

This section lists a number of tools for Visual Studio diagnostics and applications performance.

SciTech Memory Profiler is a powerful application which allows investigating the memory usage and allocation of a .NET application. It is particularly useful to search for memory leaks and bad object lifetime management. This is not free, but it is very powerful. You can check it out at: http://memprofiler.com/.

Windows Performance Toolkit is capable of analyzing performances of WPF applications through different kinds of analysis methods. This tool is available with the installation of Visual Studio 2012, shipping as part of the Windows SDK tools.

Miscellaneous

In this section you can find a list of tools not strictly related to a single technology or that cannot be classified in other sections.

Visual Studio Power Tools is a must-have extension that adds a number of useful coding and management tools to the IDE. It is free and is available from Microsoft on the Visual Studio Gallery.

JustDecompile is a free tool from Telerik, capable of exploring .NET assemblies via Reflection. The tool can show the Intermediate Language or offer decompilation results in both Visual Basic and Visual C# of the specified executable. JustDecompile is not only useful for reflecting or decompiling assemblies, but is also particularly useful for inspecting .NET Framework Base Class Libraries and understanding how many things are implemented behind the scenes. You can find it at http://www.telerik.com/justdecompile.aspx.

Windows Azure Management Tool is an open source snap-in for Windows Management Console that provides client-side access to Windows Azure's blob storage and queues, where you can easily upload your contents. It is available at http://wapmmc.codeplex.com/.

Where Do I Find Additional Tools?

If you are interested in enhancing your toolbox with third-party tools, check out the Visual Studio Gallery (http://visualstudiogallery.com) that contains hundreds of useful tools divided into categories. Also visit both the MSDN Code Gallery (http://code.msdn.microsoft.com) and the CodePlex community (http://www.codeplex.com) where you can find hundreds of useful tools, which are free in most cases.

Index

NUMBERS

SYMBOLS

A

B

How can we make this index more useful? Email us at indexes@samspublishing.com

D

F

H

M

MySQL, 541
My.User property, 478, 500-502
My.WebServices property, 478, 502

N

Name method, 500
Name property, 428, 488-490
names
   configuration files, 493-495
   conventions, 8
      CLS, 264-266
      Code Analysis, 1314
      exceptions, 209, 345
      identifiers, 72
      interfaces, 355
      value types, 94
   enumerations, 316-317
   pathnames
      modifying, 453-459
      System.IO.Path class, 454-455
   resources, 80
   strong names, signing GAC assemblies with, 1224-1226
   System.Object class, 91
Namespace..End Namespace blocks, 284, 288
namespaces
   CLS, 295
   compiling, 6
   Global keyword, 295-299
   Imports directives, 292-295
   My namespace. See My namespace
   My.Resources, 478, 506
   nested, implementing, 288-291
   purpose of, 287-288
   root, 34, 291-292
   scope, 291
   System.Collections, 394
   System.Collections.Concurrent, 413
   System.DataSet.DataSetExtensions, 622
   System.Diagnostics, 197

System.Globalization, 842
System.IO, 8, 293
System.Reflection, 1158
System.Reflection.Emit, 1171-1177
System.Runtime.CompilerServices, 1177
System.Runtime.InteropServices, 310
System.Windows.Controls, 6
System.Xml.Linq, 672-674
System.Xml.Serialization, 1043
types
   managing, 283-295
   overview of, 283-284
   Visual Basic 2012 projects, 66-67
   XML, importing, 293, 689
NameValueCollection collection, 401
narrowing conversions, 120-125
Navigated event, 510, 965
Navigate method, 965
NavigateUri property, 806, 910
navigating
   ASP.NET applications, 864-862
   controls, adding, 874
   IDE tabs, 50
   MSDN Library, 56
   My Project, 33-39, 72-75
   Object Browser window, 56-59
   Online Help, 56
   Silverlight Navigation Applications, 908-910
   Solution Explorer windows, 28-30
   Visual Studio 2012, 11
   windows, Error Lists, 30-31
   Windows Phone applications, 963-966
Navigating event, 510, 965
NavigationFailed event, 510, 965
NavigationProcess event, 510
Navigation Properties, EDMs, 640
NavigationService class, 965
NavigationStopped event, 510, 965
NestedClass class, 227
nested classes, 226-227, 348
nested constructor invocations, 256-257
nested namespaces, implementing, 288-291
nested Try..Catch..Finally blocks, 217-218
nested types, 374

O

P

Q

S

U

W

Y–Z

UNLEASHED

Unleashed takes you beyond the basics, providing an exhaustive, technically sophisticated reference for professionals who need to exploit a technology to its fullest potential. It's the best resource for practical advice from the experts, and the most in-depth coverage of the latest technologies.

informit.com/unleashed

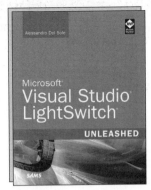

Microsoft Visual Studio LightSwitch Unleashed
ISBN-13: 9780672335532

OTHER UNLEASHED TITLES

Windows Phone 7.5 Unleashed
ISBN-13: 9780672333484

ASP.NET Dynamic Data Unleashed
ISBN-13: 9780672335655

Microsoft System Center 2012 Unleashed
ISBN-13: 9780672336126

System Center 2012 Configuration Manager (SCCM) Unleashed
ISBN-13: 9780672334375

Windows Server 2012 Unleashed
ISBN-13: 9780672336225

Microsoft Exchange Server 2013 Unleashed
ISBN-13: 9780672336119

MVVM Unleashed
ISBN-13: 9780672334382

System Center 2012 Operations Manager Unleashed
ISBN-13: 9780672335914

Microsoft Dynamics CRM 2011 Unleashed
ISBN-13: 9780672335389

SharePoint Designer 2010 Unleashed
ISBN-13: 9780672331053

ASP.NET 4.0 Unleashed
ISBN-13: 9780672331121

Silverlight 4 Unleashed
ISBN-13: 9780672333361

Windows 8 Apps with XAML and C# Unleashed
ISBN-13: 9780672336010

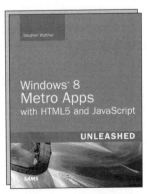

Windows 8 Apps with HTML5 and JavaScript Unleashed
ISBN-13: 9780672336058

SAMS

informit.com/sams

Safari
Books Online

FREE
Online Edition

Your purchase of *Visual Basic® 2012 Unleashed* includes access to a free online edition for 45 days through the **Safari Books Online** subscription service. Nearly every Sams book is available online through **Safari Books Online**, along with thousands of books and videos from publishers such as Addison-Wesley Professional, Cisco Press, Exam Cram, IBM Press, O'Reilly Media, Prentice Hall, Que, and VMware Press.

Safari Books Online is a digital library providing searchable, on-demand access to thousands of technology, digital media, and professional development books and videos from leading publishers. With one monthly or yearly subscription price, you get unlimited access to learning tools and information on topics including mobile app and software development, tips and tricks on using your favorite gadgets, networking, project management, graphic design, and much more.

Activate your FREE Online Edition at
informit.com/safarifree

STEP 1: Enter the coupon code: QEVXOEH.

STEP 2: New Safari users, complete the brief registration form.
Safari subscribers, just log in.

If you have difficulty registering on Safari or accessing the online edition,
please e-mail customer-service@safaribooksonline.com

 Addison Wesley AdobePress ALPHA Cisco Press FT Press FINANCIAL TIMES IBM Press Microsoft Press New Riders O'REILLY

 Peachpit Press PRENTICE HALL Que Redbooks SAMS SAS Publishing vmware PRESS WILEY wrox